THE LSAT TRAINER

THE LSAT TRAINER is written by Mike Kim.

Artisanal Publishing, Irvine 92604

Printed in the United States of America

18 2 3 4 5

ISBN: 9780989081535

THE LSAT TRAINER

A remarkable self-study guide for the self-driven student.

Second Edition

BY MIKE KIM

CONTENTS

Set up a study routine using one of the various schedules available at theLSATtrainer.com.

Facts: This book contains over thirty drills and over two hundred real LSAT questions. Lists of drills and questions can be found in the appendix.

Ideally, you will use this book in conjunction with practice exams put out by the makers of the LSAT. This will be discussed further in lesson one.

Stay organized and keep track of your work by using the notebook organizer tools available on the Trainer website.

May your curse in life be that your hard work is constantly mistaken for talent.

theLSATtrainer.com also has articles and infographics that summarize some of the key points made in this book.

Ready?

1 introduction

The LSAT is the most significant part of the law school admissions process. It is unique among all of the major American standardized exams in that respect. Your SAT score carried far less weight when you applied for college, and if you were to apply to business school, your GMAT score would also be of far less importance. Furthermore, there is a strong correlation between the law school that you attend and your future career success, much more so than in other fields such as medicine or education. All that is to say that your performance on the LSAT can have a significant impact on the future trajectory of your legal career. In particular, a top LSAT score can open doors for you that would be very difficult to open otherwise.

But you already knew all of that. Or, if you didn't, you would have soon enough, whether or not you ever came in contact with the *Trainer*. What you really want from this book is to figure out how to get a top score.

Guess what? I have the answer for you. It's not a trick answer, and it's not a gimmick. In fact, it's an answer that you will likely agree with. I'm going to give it to you right at the end of this first lesson (please, don't peek). By the way, I also guarantee you that this first lesson will be the easiest lesson in the book—all it involves is you reading some words and thinking about some ideas. All of the other lessons will require you to do *work*. So, find yourself a comfortable chair, sit back, relax, and please continue...

> The LSAT is specifically designed to judge your ability to succeed in law school. Keeping in mind what you know about law school classes and being a law student, if it were your job to design the LSAT, how would you design it? More specifically, what are the characteristics of potential law students that you think the LSAT should be designed to test?

LSAT Basics

Before we move further, let's lay out a few basic facts about the exam.

The Test Sections

When you take the official LSAT, you will sit for six sections, only four of which will be relevant to your score. The four scored sections will include two Logical Reasoning sections, a Logic Games section, and a Reading Comprehension section. You will also have one experimental section, which will be an additional Logical Reasoning, Reading Comprehension, or Logic Games section. The experimental section is used to test questions for future administrations of the LSAT, and your performance on that section does not count toward your score. You are given thirty-five minutes for each section, and these five sections can come in any order (historically, the experimental section was consistently one of the first three sections of the exam, but since students figured that out, it has been less consistently true). Your sixth and final section will always be the essay section. The essay is not a part of your 180 score, and carries negligible weight in the admissions process, but it is sent to schools along with your score (so don't write anything immature or offensive). When you sit for the exam, you will be given the first three sections without breaks in between, then a fifteen-minute break, then the remaining three sections.

Logical Reasoning

Two of your four sections will be Logical Reasoning sections, and Logical Reasoning questions will account for roughly half of your overall score. For that reason, Logical Reasoning questions are the most important questions to study for the LSAT. Each Logical Reasoning section will typically contain about twenty-five questions, which averages out to a little more than 1:20 per question. Each Logical Reasoning question consists of a stimulus, which is typically a short two- or three-sentence statement; a question stem, which presents the task at hand; and five answer choices, one of which will be absolutely correct, and four of which will be absolutely incorrect.

Your success on the Logical Reasoning section depends on an equal combination of your reading ability and your reasoning ability. Logical Reasoning also requires a significant amount of mental discipline, in large part because the different question stems often present similar, yet slightly different tasks.

Logic Games

The Logic Games section, more formally known as Analytical Reasoning, consists of four different games. Each game presents a scenario and some rules, then asks five to seven associated questions. The section will typically have twenty-three questions in all.

All games center on organizing elements relative to positions. For the majority of games, these positions relate to one another in some sort of order (for example, five kids stand in positions one through five, numbered from left to right). Your ability to diagram, or visually organize, the situation is crucial for success in this section.

Reading Comprehension

The Reading Comprehension section consists of four different passages. Each passage will have between five and eight associated questions, and the section will typically have about twenty-seven questions total. The four passages will cover four different subject areas: law, history, science, and social science, one passage per general subject. You don't need to have any prior knowledge of the subjects discussed in these passages. Certain questions require a general understanding of the passage, and others require a detailed understanding of specific components, but taken as a whole, Reading Comprehension questions are designed to test your ability to read for reasoning structure.

Sample Logical Reasoning Question

Although the charter of Westside School states that the student body must include some students with special educational needs, no students with learning disabilities have yet enrolled in the school. Therefore, the school is currently in violation of its charter.

The conclusion of the argument follows logically if which one of the following is assumed?

(A) All students with learning disabilities have special educational needs.
(B) The school currently has no student with learning disabilities.
(C) The school should enroll students with special educational needs.
(D) The only students with special educational needs are students with learning disabilities.
(E) The school's charter cannot be modified in order to avoid its being violated.

PT 34, S 2, Q 10

All Logical Reasoning questions involve a stimulus, a question stem, and five answer choices, one of which will be correct. Most stimuli involve arguments—reasons given to justify a point. Depending on how you count them, there are about sixteen common varieties of question stems. They are all related but unique in their own ways. For this question, we are looking for an answer that allows the conclusion to *follow logically*. To *follow logically* is a big deal on the LSAT—we need an answer that, when added to the argument, *guarantees* that the support given leads us to the conclusion reached.

The author's point is that the school is in violation of its charter. The reason he gives? The charter states that the student body must include some students with **special educational needs**, and no students with **learning disabilities** have yet enrolled in the school.

The author has made a flaw of reasoning here—he has assumed that those with learning disabilities are the only ones with special needs. It could be that students have special needs for other reasons. In order for this argument to work, we need to *know* that those with learning disabilities are the only ones with special educational needs, and answer choice (D) gives us that information. (D) is therefore correct. No other answer choice gives us the information we need to *guarantee* the author's conclusion.

This is a question from a previously administered LSAT, and so I've notated where it is from, as I will all official LSAT questions we will use in this book. The notation below the question means that the question is from "**P**ractice **T**est 34, **S**ection 2, and it is **Q**uestion 10."

Sample Logic Games Scenario, Rules, and Question

A bus travels to five cities—G, H, I, J, and K. It will visit each city exactly once. The following conditions apply:

The bus visits H before it visits K.
The bus visits I either first or second.
The bus visits exactly one city in between its visits to I and G.
If the bus visits G third, it must visit H before G.

Each of the following could be true EXCEPT:

(A) The bus visits H first.
(B) The bus visits J second.
(C) The bus visits K fourth.
(D) The bus visits J before G.
(E) The bus visits J last.

All games begin with a scenario and rules, and all games involve placing elements—in this case the five cities—into a set of positions. In this example, we can imagine the positions being defined by the order in which these cities were visited. About two out of every three games place the positions in a similar sort of order. A typical game will have between five and seven associated questions. The right and wrong answers to these questions will generally not be determined directly by the rules as they are written, but rather by the inferences that can be made when the rules are brought together.

For this question, we are told that each of the answers could be true except for one. Our job is therefore to find the one answer that must be false. The answer that must be false is answer choice (B). Looking at the given rules, we know that the bus must visit I first or second. If it visits I first, it must visit G third, and thus H second. If it visits I second, of course it can't visit J second. Therefore, the bus must visit either I or H second, and there is no way J can be second. (B) can't be true.

It is virtually impossible to consistently answer Logic Games questions by doing all of this type of work in your head, and all top scorers that I have worked with depend heavily on diagramming techniques to help make the task of keeping track of all rules easier and to help see how they go together. Developing effective diagramming techniques is *the* key to Logic Games success, and it will be a big focus of our training.

Note that we have not included an example of Reading Comprehension here, but if you would like to take a quick look at an example, you can do so by jumping to page 56.

How Is the LSAT Scored?

The four scored sections will typically contain a total of 100 or 101 questions. The LSAT is scored using a simple system that tallies up the number of questions you got right (your raw score) and compares that with how other people perform on the same exam (or, to be more specific, compares that with a *prediction* of how other people will perform on the same exam, a prediction based on data from experimental sections of previously administered exams). How you do relative to others then determines your overall score on the 120–180 scale. There is no scoring difference between getting questions wrong or leaving them blank, and each question is worth the same amount. The raw score to scaled score conversion rates are slightly different from exam to exam. Over time, however, the scoring scales, and the exam itself, have stayed remarkably consistent. The consistency of the exam is a testament (one of many) to its fine quality.

Misses	2	6	12	19	27	44	60	75
Percentile	99.9	99.5	97.5	92	80	44	13.5	2
Score	180	175	170	165	160	150	140	130

The statistics on this chart represent the average performance to score conversion rate for exams 57–61, reported in terms of the total number of questions missed. The percentile represents how the test taker did relative to other test takers, and the overall score is on a 120–180 scale.

How Effective Are Traditional Study Methods?

Not very.

The numbers speak for themselves: the common study methods have not been particularly effective for most people. Taking a course or using a guide does not, in and of itself, raise scores significantly over the average, even though that average includes a large number of people who choose to do nothing at all to prepare for the exam.

Still, the fact that *most* students do not improve significantly does not mean that there aren't *some* students who do figure out how to improve significantly. These are the students who get the high scores.

The emperor wears no clothes. In order to improve at the LSAT, it's helpful to know that you *shouldn't* study how most other people study.

All statistics in this book are based on information published by LSAC. The numbers on this table represent test takers from the 2010 - 2011 academic year.

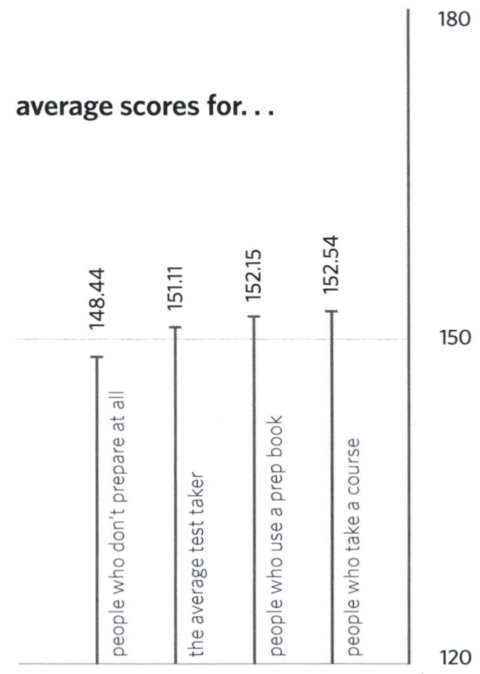

What Is the LSAT Designed to Test?

The LSAT is designed to gauge your ability to succeed as a law student. What do law students have to do?

First of all, law students have to *read* a lot of very dense text—sometimes, they have to read and critically evaluate cases that are hundreds of years old. Typically, the key to correctly reading these passages as a law student is not the ability to absorb every single detail of everything you read (that would be pointless and impossible) but rather to prioritize the important information that is relevant to your purpose.

Secondly, law students have to *think* about what they read. They have to constantly think about how ideas relate to one another (say, for example, how state and federal laws come together), and they have to think about how reasoning leads to a conclusion (for example, whether the evidence provided is enough to convict someone of a crime).

The LSAT is designed to test these types of reading and thinking abilities. But, of course, the LSAT is a multiple-choice, one-hundred question standardized exam, so at its best, it can only test these skills in a very limited and abstract sort of way. The LSAT is thus primarily designed to test four very specific skills, two of which we will think of as reading skills, and two of which we will think of as reasoning skills.

Your Ability to Read for Reasoning Structure

The reading skill that is most consistently tested and rewarded on the LSAT is your ability to read for reasoning structure. Reasoning structure refers to the organization of a passage relative to its purpose; to understand reasoning structure is to understand *why* the author has included the various parts of a passage. Your ability to read for reasoning structure will be relevant to the vast majority of Logical Reasoning questions, and it will also be the *primary* skill that is tested by the Reading Comprehension section.

Your Understanding of Certain Words

Of course, a necessary and integral part of one's reading ability is an expansive and correct vocabulary, and the LSAT does test your ability to understand and use certain words. However, they are not the words you might expect. LSAT writers are not particularly interested in testing the sophistication or depth of your vocabulary. They are much more interested in testing your exact understanding of certain *commonly* used words. The words they care about are the words we all use when we create reasoning relationships, words like "or," "only," "therefore," "must," and "unless." Your specific understanding of these words will be put to the test in both the Logic Games and Logical Reasoning sections.

Your Ability to Bring Two or Three Ideas Together

One of the two ways in which the test writers will test your reasoning ability is by creating situations in which two or three given statements can, when taken together, yield additional inferences. That is, the exam presents situations in which you have to figure new things out by bringing information together. This skill is most important for the Logic Games section, for which these inferences will be what typically differentiate right answers from wrong ones. This skill is also necessary for certain Logical Reasoning questions.

Your Ability to See Why Reasons Don't Justify a Conclusion

The flip side of being able to see when two or three ideas come together to form a valid conclusion is being able to see when two or three ideas *do not* come together to form a particular conclusion. In fact, this ability—the ability to see why reasons given do not justify a conclusion reached—is *the key* reasoning issue that is tested. This will be central to your success in both the Logical Reasoning and Logic Games sections.

Simple Examples to Illustrate Issues

reasoning structure

Why are these two statements different?

A: Jane went to college, so she must be a good student.

B: Since Jane is a good student, she must have gone to college.

word meaning

What does "or" mean, exactly?

A: You can pick a boy puppy or a girl puppy.

B: To check in at the airport, you must have a driver's license or a passport.

inferences

Every day, Sarah eats either eggs or toast for breakfast. When she eats toast, she always eats jam. Sarah did not eat any jam with her breakfast this morning.

What can you infer?

reasoning flaw

Going back to the two examples for reasoning structure, if you wanted to counter both of those statements respectively, what might you say?

The Five Mantras of LSAT Preparation

When we first start to think about the LSAT, and when we begin our studies, there are a lot of reasonable predictions we can make about how it might be designed—it's probably going to reward good reading skills, require attention paid to random details, reward a large vocabulary, require some cleverness or creativity, require mental discipline...all of these predictions are reasonable, but only some of them are actually true. The LSAT is not designed to test all of those issues.

solutions for examples on previous page

Reasoning Structure

In the first argument, the author's point is that Jane must be a good student. Her reasoning is that Jane went to college.

In the second argument, the author's point is that Jane must have gone to college. His reasoning is that Jane is a good student.

Word Meaning

In real life, the meaning of "or" changes based on context.

In the first instance, the "or" implies exclusivity—in real life, this statement likely means that the person can pick a boy puppy or a girl puppy, but not both.

In the second instance, the "or" does not imply exclusivity—in real life, you would likely still be able to check in at the airport if you had both a driver's license and a passport.

The LSAT requires an absolute rather than contextual understanding of words like "or." On the LSAT, the "or" is inclusive, not exclusive, unless otherwise noted.

For most LSAT students, it typically takes a lot of studying—a lot of fumbling around—until they can develop some sort of big-picture macro understanding of exactly what the LSAT tests, and how it is designed. Most students actually do not get a very clear sense of this until they are near the end of their studies, if they ever get it at all.

This puts these students at a huge disadvantage—a disadvantage that virtually guarantees that they will underperform relative to their abilities on test day. For one, it will mean that they invariably waste their study time. If you don't know exactly what you need to improve on and why, it's going to take you longer to improve.

More importantly, what will happen is that, before these students truly understand what type of thinking is rewarded and what type of thinking is not, before they develop proper instincts about the LSAT, they will have already been practicing for the exam for months, and they will have already developed habits—habits based on some vague or perhaps even flawed understanding of the test. This is a fatal issue because habits will, in large part, determine how well you perform on test day, and you cannot change habits simply by learning something new. Most students form their habits before they have the instincts to form good ones.

You can get a huge head start on your competition if you begin your studies with a clearer understanding of the exam and, more importantly, if you begin with a clearer understanding of exactly how you ought to prepare and what you ought to think about as you study. To that end, I want to begin with five short essays that together express what I think is most important for you to consider when you first begin preparing for your exam. These essays discuss what to think about and, more importantly, how to think about these things. The points I make here serve as a summary of much of the wisdom I've gained from working with thousands of students, some of whom drastically improved their scores and some of whom, unfortunately, did not.

Since you've had no exposure to the test yet, some of this will seem like we are jumping the gun a bit, and it's certainly true that the points I make will ring far truer once you have more LSAT experience under your belt.[1] However, I include these points here so that you can start off with as clear an understanding of your task as possible, and so that some of what I mention will serve as a framework that you can use as you organize and prioritize the things we will be learning in future lessons.

1. And you should remember to come back and re-read some of these essays later in your studies.

One: Equate Smart with Simple

We are all used to taking exams based on what we *know*. This is particularly true in elementary school, junior high school, and high school. For whatever reason, the exams we're given at these levels are almost always designed to test our ability to repeat back the things our teachers have taught us, and at their worst, some are even designed to most reward those students who are best at mimicking the way their teachers think.[2]

These experiences shape how we all think about tests, and about preparing for tests. A fundamental aspect of this mindset is that we equate *knowing more* with *being more prepared* for exams. When it comes to the LSAT, this is a dangerous misconception to have.

This mindset tends to have its biggest impact on high achievers, people who are used to succeeding academically by *working harder to know more*. These students are commonly focused on developing as specific an understanding of each type of LSAT question as they possibly can, and these students are commonly drawn to learning systems that are technical and (seemingly) sophisticated.

Let me be clear. You do need to know some things to do well on this exam, of course. And in this book we will discuss everything that you need to know, at great and sufficient depth. However, success on the LSAT depends on the quality, rather than the quantity, of your understanding and your abilities. Success does not favor those who think they will get better by learning a thousand different details about every type of problem that can appear.

The LSAT is designed to be a test of how you think, not what you know. The people who write the problems have little interest in gauging your understanding of advanced logic principles, and they have little interest in testing the expanse of your vocabulary. The test writers actually have an obligation to create an exam that does not (at least on the surface) give an advantage to people of a certain background or life experience, and so they cannot create an exam that rewards, for example, an understanding of formal reasoning that only a philosophy major might have, or the meaning of technical terminology that is unique to a particular scientific field. Like the writers of *Seinfeld*, their *job* is to create a product that is about *nothing in particular*. Their job is to create an exam that determines right and wrong based on the most fundamental elements of public human interaction—our basic ability to understand and organize what we read, and our basic ability to gauge reasoning, that is, our ability to see when the reasoning given justifies a point that is being made, and when it doesn't—what most of us think of on a day-to-day basis as *common sense*.

I am not suggesting that the LSAT is easy. The LSAT is not easy! However, it's important to know that harder questions are generally not more difficult because they test more challenging concepts or require you to know unusual words. Harder questions test exactly the same things easier questions do, but in a more challenging manner. Your job is not to be a master of details, but rather a master of the fundamentals. To that end, I want to encourage you to equate *smart* with *simple* when you think of this exam.

On a practical level, this means that as you learn new concepts and strategies, and as you practice problems and review them, you want to always work toward attaining as simple and clean an understanding as possible, and you want to get in the habit of equating a simple understanding with a complete one. If you truly know what's wrong with an argument, you shouldn't need an official name or formal language to describe it—you should be able to describe it using your everyday language. If you truly feel comfortable with a type of question, you shouldn't have to remind yourself to keep ten things in your mind—you should be able to intuitively focus on just two or three fundamental concerns. Thinking about the LSAT in a simple way has numerous advantages, and will pay off with great effect both in your studies and on test day.

2. Did you ever get points taken off on a math exam for getting the right answer but "not showing your work," or for seeing a different theme in a book than the one your teacher told you to see?

The LSAT is a test of reading ability and common sense

solutions for examples on page 13 (continued)

Inferences

Since Sarah did not eat jam, she must not have eaten toast. Since she didn't eat toast this morning, she must have eaten eggs.

Reasoning Flaw

For the first argument, the author is flawed in assuming that having gone to college ensures that Jane is a good student—maybe she got into college because of connections, never studied, and didn't do so well.

For the second argument, the author is flawed in assuming that because Jane is a good student, she must have gone to college—maybe she chose instead to join a start-up company.

When you understand things simply, it is far easier to organize what you know. You make it easier on your brain to see how this new thing you are learning is related to everything else you've just learned, and by being better able to relate ideas, you can take your thinking ability to greater depths. In the next few months, we are going to be learning a lot of concepts, and developing a lot of strategies. A simple understanding will make it far easier for you to bring together everything you learn.

Thinking simply also makes it far easier to utilize your own natural intelligence and real-life understanding. When you make your studies more complex and formal, it works as a barrier between you and your mental power—instead of using your own good sense to understand a situation, you end up trying to understand a situation in terms of how you understand certain technical terms or abstract concepts. Some LSAT teaching systems even encourage this type of disconnect,[3] but you do not want anything to get in the way of using the talents of your own mind. A simple understanding, as opposed to a technical one, gives you the best chance to utilize your thinking abilities to their fullest. In my experience, when students are able to do this, most have the natural ability to score at a very high level.

3. "Don't trust yourself!" these books tell you. "Think exactly as we tell you to!" These systems aren't particularly effective.

Finally, a simple understanding will be the one that you can apply best on test day. Human beings are only capable of consciously thinking about one thing at a time. *Trying* to think of a hundred things at once does you no good, and an overly complicated understanding will put you in a place where you end up trying to do just that. A simple understanding will help you best apply what you know under pressure.

Two: Focus on What to Think About (Not What to Think)

Imagine riding an elephant.

You can just sit on top of the animal and choose not to do anything. If so, the elephant will do as it chooses, and you will go along for the ride. But if you have the understanding and motivation, you can train this elephant to do what you would like—you can train it to take you where you want to go, for example, or you can train it to lift heavy things for you. This is of great benefit because—and this is very important—you are not capable of doing the work that the elephant does. The rider who is happiest and wisest is the one who understands how to control the elephant, and does not try to do the work himself.

The analogy of a rider and an elephant is commonly used in educational circles to discuss the relationship between our conscious mind and our unconscious mind. If you don't control your unconscious, it can drift. If you train it, it can do amazing things for you.

This analogy is particularly relevant to how we perform during standardized exams. Our conscious mind is the rider. It gets all of the notoriety and attention because it is what we most notice and because it *seems* to be in control. But once that timer starts, your unconscious—your instincts and habits for what to think about and how—takes over.

Let's talk more specifically by discussing just one important skill you are going to have to showcase on test day: your ability to evaluate the reasoning in an argument. Most Logical Reasoning questions require you to evaluate the reasons an author gives in order to justify his or her point, and your success on the entire Logical Reasoning section hinges, in large part, on your ability to do this.

So, you know this is going to be a big part of the LSAT—how do you prepare your rider and your elephant to perform at their best?

The wrong way to go about it would be to place the burden of the work on the rider. We do this when we try to memorize a list of fifty things that could be wrong with arguments, and we do this when we use tips and tricks, "markers," or "keywords," to make our decisions on a technical and conscious level. We do this when we focus on what we need to know rather than what we need to think about. And, of course, we do this when we fail to train our elephant.

The right way to go about doing this is to give your "elephant" everything that it needs to properly prepare—a simple and intuitive *understanding* of the issues that will appear on the exam, logical and usable *strategies* for handling all of these issues, and, most importantly, plenty of *experience* putting this understanding and these strategies to good use (more on understanding, strategies, and experience in just a bit).

Don't spend your time training your rider. Do not think that by hearing about some clever strategy or memorizing some trick, you can do the heavy lifting needed for success on the LSAT. Invest your energy into training the elephant and becoming a good rider. You can do this by focusing on what to think about rather than what to think, by focusing on the decisions to be made rather than the right way to make them, and by making sure you get plenty of experience with the types of situations that you are likely to face on test day.

Three: Utilize the Power of Compound Learning

An understanding of addition and subtraction properties is useful and necessary in life, but an understanding of multiplicative properties, when applied properly, is far more valuable. To explain why, I want to start with a simple fable about twin brothers Wilbur and Wallace.

Both Wilbur and Wallace were taught from an early age to save for their retirements. Wilbur loved addition, and Wallace loved multiplication. For the sixty years that Wilbur worked, he added $1,000 each year to a retirement savings account. At the end of his work years, he retired with $60,000.

Imagine if Wallace, who loved multiplication, put $1,000 into an investment account after his first year of work, and *never put another dime into that account for the rest of his work years.* The account paid him about 10 percent interest per year, which is roughly what the U.S. stock market has paid historically, on average (until the past few years, anyway). Multiplying that $1,000 with 10 percent growth each year, when he retired in sixty years, Wallace would do so with just a tad over $300,000.

Of course, in reality, Wallace had no reason not to keep adding $1,000 to this account each year, and so he did while continuing to earn that 10 percent. And he ended up retiring with a little over *$3,000,000*. Compare that to Wilbur's $60,000. What drove the expansion of Wallace's wealth? The same thing that allows us to calculate the distance to stars—the exponential power of multiplication.

If you'd like, you can use these extra wide margins throughout the book to take notes.

The way in which we build our skills is analogous to the way we build up our wealth, and in both endeavors, multiplication is a far more powerful force than addition. Simply put, when we learn by multiplying what we know, by *connecting* ideas, and by *building upon* the skills we've already developed, we learn far faster and far more effectively than when we learn in pieces—when we try to learn one thing at a time and when we try to simply *add up* the things we learn into some kind of whole. As we make our study plans, and as we think about the path that we are going to be taking toward mastery, one of the best things we can do is recognize the value of compound learning. To that end, let's use the Wilbur and Wallace analogy to think about how we can effectively utilize our study time in order to get the maximum return. How would addition-loving Wilbur and multiplication-loving Wallace think to study for the LSAT?

How to Study Like Wilbur (1.0 & 2.0)

Wilbur 1.0 studies by learning about one question type at a time. He gives himself a certain amount of time to study each type of question, game, or passage to the best of his ability, then moves on to the next. Then, a few weeks before the exam, he reviews everything he's learned. This study situation is a fairly common one, especially among those students who are part of a class and are following some sort of class schedule. Almost all classes are designed around a one-question-type-at-a-time system, and the timing of the classes determines the start and stop of when you study different types of questions.

The consequences of studying like Wilbur 1.0 are mixed. You will definitely get some question-specific learning, and over time you will definitely develop skills that you can apply to a wide range of challenges. On the negative side, you will also have a more difficult time than necessary growing and organizing these skills, and you'll make it more difficult on yourself than it needs to be to create sharp and effective instincts.

To illustrate exactly why, imagine that in your first week of studying Logical Reasoning, you work on "Identify the Conclusion" questions—questions that require you to identify the main point the author is trying to make in an argument—and the next week you study "Find the Assumption" questions—questions that require you to figure out what the author is assuming in thinking his or her point is justified. On a conscious level, it's easy for you to keep the two types of questions apart, so you don't think much about studying them one right after another, and you don't think too much about starting your studying this way. But remember, the goal of your training is not to prepare your rider, it's to prepare your elephant. What does this sort of preparation do for your elephant?

Well, in that first week, your elephant is learning to develop ways to think about and solve Logical Reasoning questions in general, and it's also developing specific systems for Identify the Conclusion questions. Some of what it learns is relevant to all of Logical Reasoning, and some of it is specific to the question type. Some of the processes that it starts to habitualize pertain to all Logical Reasoning questions, and others pertain, again, just to Identify the Conclusion problems. For the most part, your elephant is left to make most of these determinations on its own, for, at the beginning of your studies, even the rider—your conscious mind—doesn't yet really know how to organize everything you are learning.

Now comes the next week and the next type of question, and your elephant has to get used to a similar but slightly different task. It has to learn concepts and strategies that apply to that particular question, while reconciling what it is learning with what it learned in the first week. The process continues week after week, new question type after new question type, until the very end of your process, at which point you take a few practice exams and go into your test. Notice the lack of review, the minimal organization, and, most importantly, the lack of multiplication.

Now you run into an Identify the Conclusion question on the exam. You have about a minute to arrive at an answer. Will you be able to utilize what you learned back in your first week of studying to get the question correct?

Chances are, you very well might. The human mind is simply incredible, and it's very possible that you are able, in that moment, to wade through the months and months of LSAT information you've absorbed in order to find that one particular piece of knowledge that is relevant to the question at hand. But—I think you can agree—you haven't made it easy on yourself to get that question correct, and you certainly haven't given yourself the best chance to correctly utilize what you have learned.

Wilbur 2.0 studies primarily by doing full sections and entire practice exams. Afterwards, he checks his work and carefully reviews the questions he missed.

Wilbur 2.0 gets to a point where each explanation makes one hundred percent complete sense. He understands exactly why he is missing questions. Does this help? Yes, a little bit, but it likely won't lead to significant and fundamental improvement. Even though Wilbur 2.0 knows why he misses questions, every test presents a dozen different issues to study and the list never seems to end, and what he learns never seems to help on the next exam. By not providing himself with any sort of organizational framework, he limits his ability to grow his skill set to its fullest.

How to Study Like Wallace

Wallace is very interested in growing his understanding, and he knows that strong growth always begins with a solid foundation. So he spends some time thinking about what is most important to success for each of the sections, and he develops a learning schedule that allows him to grow his skills out from this foundation.

Of course, I want you to study like Wallace, and to that end I have carefully designed this training guide to be one that helps you multiply your talents as you develop new skills. Here is what that means more specifically...

For Logical Reasoning

Logical Reasoning questions present you with a short—typically two to three sentences—scenario and then ask you to respond to that scenario in some way; perhaps the author will make a point in the scenario and your job will be to select an answer that strengthens that point or weakens it.

We will begin by investing a great amount of time and energy into the one macro skill that is most important for success on the Logical Reasoning section: your ability to critically evaluate **arguments**. A strong majority of LSAT questions hinge on your ability to understand arguments, and, more specifically, almost all such questions hinge on your ability to see the *faults* in arguments. With that in mind, we will start our training by working at becoming expert at finding faults in arguments. We will study every type of argument flaw that can appear on the exam, and we will break down, and practice again and again, the processes necessary for you to recognize and understand them clearly.

An **argument** consists of a point and reasons given to justify that point.

With that foundation built, we will next move on to develop question-specific strategies, starting first with those questions that most directly ask you about the faulty reasoning (Identify the Flaw questions), and gradually panning out to other question types. At each point we will carefully point out and differentiate the characteristics and issues that are generally relevant to many different types of questions, versus those specific to the question type that we are studying.

Finally, we will discuss and practice bringing together all the various skills that you have developed, so that by the time you go into the test, you can be confident you can represent all of your abilities at their best.

For Logic Games

Logic Games are relatively unique to the LSAT. Logic Games present you with a short scenario and a set of rules—this scenario and rules will always involve assigning certain elements into certain positions—and then ask you anywhere from five to seven questions to test your understanding of the given situation.

We will begin by focusing on the one macro skill set that is most important to your Logic Games success: your ability to diagram Logic Games scenarios and rules. The challenge of Logic Games—the thing that makes them so hard—is keeping track of the rules and, more importantly, being able to see very clearly exactly how these rules come together. The questions will gauge your understanding of this again and again.

The complexity of these Logic Games is such that pretty much everyone needs to write the information down in order to track it—it's simply too much to keep in our heads. And this ability to write things down—to diagram—in an effective way is what differentiates top scorers from average scorers from below-average scorers. Your ability to diagram is the key to your Logic Games success.

So, we will spend a great amount of time (think *Karate Kid*) building up your fundamental diagramming skills. We will thoroughly and systematically break down every single significant diagramming challenge you are likely to face on test day and work on developing effective strategies and habits to combat each of those challenges.

Once we are comfortable with our ability to translate scenarios and rules into diagrams, we will dive into full official LSAT games and shift our focus to question-specific strategies. As you'll see, the questions require a different aspect of our diagramming skill—an ability to *utilize* our diagram. We will break down all of the different types of questions that can be asked, and develop optimal strategies for those specific challenges.

Lastly, we will work on bringing all of our skills together on full sections and work to habitualize the processes that will lead to guaranteed success on test day.

multiplication

trumps addition

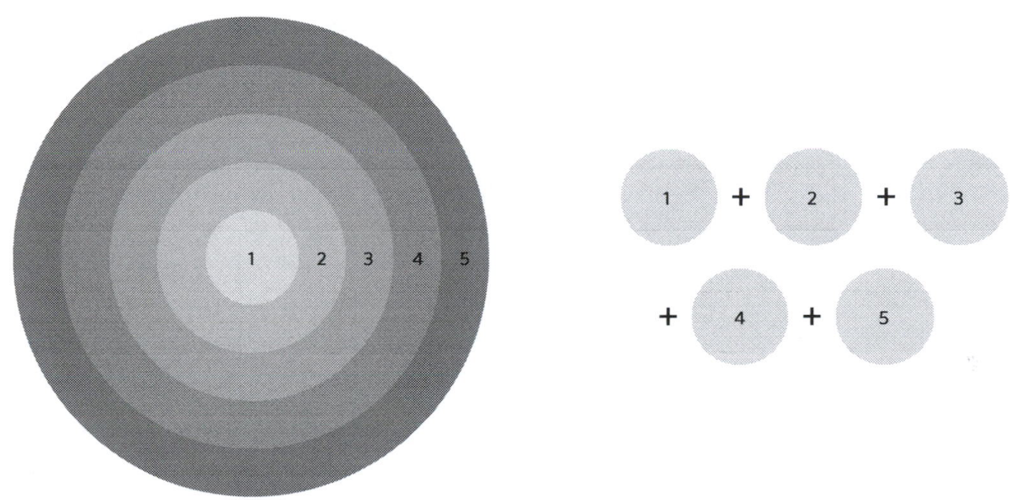

Many students think of their preparation in terms of individual steps. For example, they prepare for the Logic Games section by trying to completely master one "type" of game, and then another type of game, and so on. Or they prepare for Logical Reasoning by trying to master just one question type at a time. Most LSAT preparation systems conform to this learn-by-addition design approach.

While learning by addition can certainly be effective, and has been for thousands of students, learning by multiplication is always *more* effective, and more efficient. For Logical Reasoning, we will start with the one skill that is most important for your success: your ability to critically evaluate the reasoning in an argument. For Logic Games, we will start with diagramming ability. Diagramming ability is the key skill that differentiates top games players from average ones. For Reading Comprehension, we will begin by focusing on understanding and recognizing reasoning structure. As you'll soon see, the vast majority of Reading Comprehension questions will either directly or indirectly test your understanding of reasoning structure, and reading for organization rather than details will put you in the best position to answer questions. Once we have developed these strong core abilities, we will use them to sprout out a deep and varied skill set.

For Reading Comprehension

Reasoning structure refers to the roles that various parts of the passage play relative to one another. Main point, opinion, and background are examples of the types of roles that are relevant to reasoning structure. An effective way to think about reasoning structure is to ask, "Why has the author written this part?" If you can answer that question successfully, you can feel confident that you understand the reasoning structure.

Most of us have some familiarity with Reading Comprehension from previous standardized exams. Most of us have a general sense of what the reading challenges will be, what the questions will ask for, and so on. Of course you might expect, and it's important to know, that LSAT Reading Comprehension test writers *do not* have a *general* sense of how to create questions—they have a very specific sense of exactly what it is they are testing, and they have very specific ways of going about it.

LSAT passages do not test your knowledge of the world or of history, nor do they test the expanse of your vocabulary. The test makers also care very little for your ability to critically evaluate what you read (in this section, at least). What the test writers care most about is your ability to read for structure, specifically **reasoning structure.** The majority of questions hinge on this ability. If you are consistently able to see correctly the reasoning structure of passages, you should have great success in Reading Comprehension.

So, we will begin our Reading Comprehension preparation by building up and strengthening our ability to read for reasoning structure. We will discuss in depth the types of structures you are likely to see on the exam (LSAT passages are very consistent in their structure), and get plenty of practice at seeing those structures accurately.

Once we've gotten ourselves in the habit of reading passages effectively, we will break down the various types of questions that can be asked of us in this section. We'll relate what we understand about structure to what is being asked of us in each of these questions, and we will work on developing effective problem-solving strategies. Lastly, we will work on bringing it all together for full sections.

Four: Understanding, Strategies, and Experience Are Necessary (But Not Enough)

What determines whether someone is a great surgeon?

Is it her *understanding* of surgery? That's certainly a big part of it, but just because someone knows a lot about surgery doesn't mean that she[4] will be a good surgeon. Is it the *strategies* that she chooses to employ? Again, good strategies are certainly necessary, but a good strategy poorly executed won't give the patient the result he hopes for. Is it *experience*? Most surgeons need years of experience to reach a high level of competency, but experience alone doesn't make you a good surgeon—especially if you are consistently bad at surgery.

Fortunately, the LSAT is far less challenging and far less stressful than surgery. Still, there are some similarities and takeaways. What defines a great surgeon? It's not how much she knows, and it's not her strategies nor her experience. What best defines a great surgeon is her ability to *utilize* her understanding, her strategies, and her experience to make decisions and to act correctly *in the moment*. And this is true of the LSAT as well. You need understanding, you need effective strategies, and you need experience, but ultimately your result will be based on how well you are able to use all of this in the moment. There is a better way to think about what makes for a good LSAT test taker: a good LSAT test taker is one who has *skills* and *effective habits*.

4. Here is a riddle that I guarantee will stump almost all of your friends and family:

A father and his son get into a car accident. The man dies instantly, and the son gets taken to the emergency room. The surgeon takes one look down at him and says, "I can't operate on him, he's my son!" How is this possible?

Having read the main body text, hopefully you are in a better position to see the right answer: the surgeon is the boy's mother. However, give this riddle to others, and you are far more likely to hear answers about gay parents and priests than you are about a mother who is a surgeon.

Of course, we all know that in real life there are plenty of female surgeons, but we shouldn't feel ashamed for getting tricked by such riddles. What it does show us is that our brains commonly make incorrect associations (such as surgeon=man). The key to certain difficult LSAT questions is an ability to "disassociate" such false associations.

Five: Use Skills and Habits to Gauge Your Readiness

We can define skill as your ability to *utilize* your understanding, talents, and experience. It's helpful to think of understanding, strategies, and experience as means to an end—they are useful when they combine to form and grow your skill set. As you invest time into preparing for the exam, you want to think about your improvement in terms of skills ("I am now *able* to do X," and "I am now *able* to recognize Y," and so on), and you want to gauge your readiness for the LSAT in terms of your skill set ("I am ready for this Logic Games challenge because I am comfortable *doing* X," or "I am not confident about this Logical Reasoning question because I don't think I am accurate at *doing* Y," and so on).

Thinking about your preparedness in terms of skill set will have numerous benefits for you along your training process, but here are two benefits that you should be aware of from the get-go:

Using Your Skill Set as Your Gauge Will Help You Get Rid of That "Am I Ready?" Uncertainty

For some exams that we take in life, it's very easy for us to tell if we are "ready" for that test. If we go back to high school, if you knew how to spell the words that could show up on a spelling test, then you felt ready. However, let's imagine that you are preparing for a job interview. At what point would you feel "ready?" Do you think you could ever feel "ready" for, say, an IQ test?

If you think of the LSAT as being some sort of undefinable abstract exercise (like an IQ test) then you inevitably come up with arbitrary and indirect ways of gauging your preparedness. You say to yourself that you are ready because you've studied as hard as you can, or because you've done every practice exam, or finished a course, or gotten the best strategies from the most expensive guru. As you get closer and closer to the test, you will find yourself feeling more and more nervous, because those are not objective and honest ways of gauging whether you are truly ready.

U.S.E. (or S.U.E.)

Here is a very general breakdown of the understanding, strategies, and experience that are all necessary for high-level success.

Understanding of...	**S**trategies for...	**E**xperience with...
...the issues that underlie the questions ...the design of the test as a whole	...handling specific challenges ...completing entire sections	...focused study on specific issues ...taking entire sections and full exams

---

The only honest gauge of your preparedness is your skill set and your habits (more on habits in just a bit). If you think about your prep in terms of your skills—I need to be *able* to find the conclusion of an argument, I need to be *able* to identify what's wrong with the author's reasoning, I need to be *able* to diagram ordering rules, etc.—then there will be far less mystery in terms of whether you are truly ready or not. Thinking in terms of a skill set doesn't mean that you'll be perfect at the test, of course, but it will mean that you will have a much clearer sense of what you are good at and what you are not, what you need to skip and where you need to slow down, and it will greatly increase the chances that the exam will go "as you expect." This is a big deal. Most test takers suffer at least a small bit because of nervousness, and it is human nature to be more nervous when we are uncertain. You bring more certainty into the equation when you use your skill set as your gauge, and this will boost your confidence and give you a leg up on your competitors.

Using Your Skill Set as Your Gauge Will Help You Make More Effective Use of Your Study Time

We are far better at learning when there is a goal at the end of our learning process. This is true for all of us, and it's not an issue of willpower. It's an issue of human nature. That is part of the reason that babies are so good at learning—they learn because they want to be able to do things that are critically important, like walking and talking. I'm sure you see the truth of this in your own life. When you are eager to accomplish something, and set off to learn in order to accomplish that thing, you are a far better student than when you learn simply for the sake of learning (a point that our primary schools consistently miss).

Thinking of the LSAT, let's say that you learn how to correctly understand a particular reasoning issue, and you give yourself a pat on the back and stop there. That understanding may or may not translate to better test performance. Same as if you happen to come upon a very effective way to diagram a challenging Logic Games issue—knowing this "system" may or may not translate to better test-day performance. Learning about a

---

connection leads to success

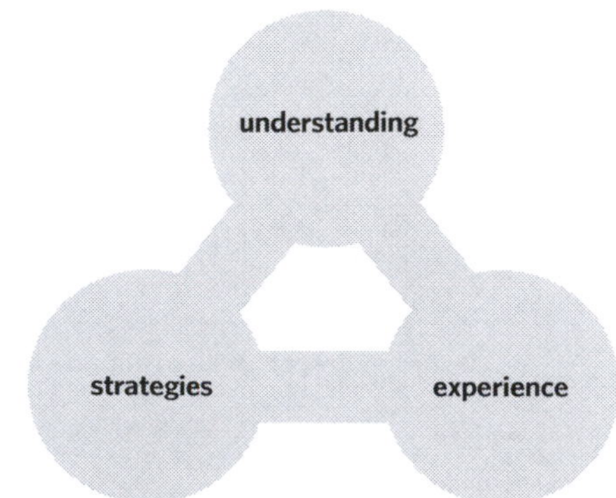

We develop skills and habits when we account for all necessary components of the mastery process and when these critical components come together: when we understand the theory behind strategies and when our strategies help us understand the exam better, when we get experience utilizing our strategies in a variety of contexts and use our experience to shape and define our strategies, and when we get the most out of our experiences because of our understanding, and use our experiences to add to that understanding.

---

particular issue, or learning a particular strategy, and then *using* that understanding or strategy to deal with test-specific challenges—*applying your understanding*—is what will ensure long-lasting improvement.

When you learn concepts for the exam but don't apply them, or learn strategies but don't understand exactly how or why they work and don't practice applying them, you end up a far less efficient learner. The same goes for if you work on problem after problem, but don't think about the underlying structure of them, or fail to figure out the most efficient and effective strategies for solving them correctly. Make the development of a skill set your end goal. Don't learn a concept just for the sake of learning it, or do a problem set just to get it done—keep in mind that the purpose of what you are doing is to develop skills.

Over my years of teaching standardized exams, I've heard over and over again variations of the following statements:

I think I know everything there is to know, but I just don't feel ready.

I know all of the best strategies, but I just don't feel ready.

I've been studying for months and months, but I just don't feel ready.

I thought I was ready because I finally understood everything, but the test felt much harder than I expected.

I thought I was ready because I finally learned all of the best strategies, but the test felt much harder than I expected.

I thought I was ready because I've been studying for months, but the test felt much harder than I expected.

Don't let this happen to you! Using your skill set to gauge your preparation will help you feel more certain about your abilities, and it will make it more likely that the exam will go as you expect it will.

Habits

Your skills have a direct impact on your performance, and you can think of your skill set as representing your *ability* to take the exam. The stronger your skill set, the more potential you have for a higher score.

Now the question becomes "How can you ensure that you reach this potential?"

Strong habits. Simply put, your skills determine how high you can score, and your habits determine whether you will reach that potential or not. You can get better at the exam by carefully developing solid skills, layer after layer, and by working to develop consistent and useful habits. And if you focus on these two things, and if you work diligently, something magical will happen: the test will get easier. I absolutely promise you of that. Questions will start making a lot more sense, you'll be able to predict answers more and more, and you'll find yourself far less reliant on me or any other teacher to tell you what is right or wrong. And this is going to start to happen quickly.

The Key to Success

I started this lesson by promising that I would reveal the key to success on the LSAT, and here it is:

The best way to ensure success is to deserve it

Your skills and your habits will determine how well you perform on test day. These skills and habits do not come cheap—they require a great deal of desire and effort. You cannot beat the LSAT by learning clever tricks, and you cannot make up for months of not studying by cramming for a couple of weeks. This test is simply too well constructed and challenging.

The LSAT is not, as many commonly believe, simply a test of certain natural abilities in the way that an IQ test is arguably meant to be. The LSAT is actually an exam that almost anyone can get much better at; it is a test that rewards those who make the effort to get better at it. I've seen this to be true again and again with the students I've worked with personally. Getting really good at the LSAT is not that different from getting into great shape by working out—some of us naturally start off in better shape than others,

The Five Mantras

1. Equate smart with simple.
2. Focus on what to think about (not what to think).
3. Utilize the power of compound learning.
4. Understanding, strategies, and experience are necessary (but not enough).
5. Skills and habits determine outcome.

but in time, those with better habits and perspective generally not only make up for any lack of natural ability, they commonly end up with just as high a ceiling as those who started out a bit ahead. For the LSAT, you can start off at 140 and get to 170, or you can start off at 160 and end up at 160. You can't determine where you begin, but what you do (or don't do) to prepare *will* determine where your score ends up. There is no magic formula to getting in shape—you have to do the physical work. There is no magic formula to getting better at the LSAT either. The best way to ensure success is to deserve it.

What does it mean to be deserving of success? I'm sure you have a very good idea, and I'm sure it's similar to what's in my head. It involves hard, earnest work and honest self-reflection.

You can master the LSAT. I know you can. But it's not easy, and it requires the right mindset. Work on developing the right skills and the right habits, and be consistent in your study efforts. Ensure that you get the most out of your prep, and that your prep is truly getting you ready for the exam.

This book is unique among the LSAT systems that are available, in that it is built upon the five fundamental tenets that we've just discussed. This book is designed to help you learn concepts simply and correctly, to relate these concepts to the optimum strategies, and, most importantly, to help you turn your understanding and strategies into skills and habits. The *Trainer* will lead you to do the smart, earnest, dedicated work that will leave you far more prepared and far more deserving of success than just about anyone else on test day.

The Road Ahead

Now that we have discussed the five basic tenets that should shape your thinking about how to prepare for the LSAT, let's briefly discuss the road that lies ahead of us.

This book is organized into forty different lessons, each meant to take between an hour and an hour and a half. These lessons are ideally meant to be done in conjunction with the *10 Actual LSATs* books or other practice exams. Using clear, simple instruction, effective drills, and carefully chosen sample questions, we will work to develop a skill set that will leave you feeling confident and in control when you take the LSAT.

We will use the next three lessons to introduce each of the three types of sections that appear on the exam: Logical Reasoning, Logic Games, and Reading Comprehension. Following that, we will focus for a few lessons on just one section type at a time—we'll start by spending five lessons discussing Logical Reasoning. We'll conclude the book with some lessons that will bring together everything that we have learned.

As I just mentioned, this book is designed to be used in conjunction with the *10 Actual LSATs* books, which are published by the LSAC. *The 10 Actuals* each contain ten previously administered LSAT exams—the latest includes Practice Tests 62—71. We will be using these tests to do specific drill work, and we will also use them for our full practice exams.

At the beginning of your studies, your emphasis will be on developing your understanding and your strategies, so you will be spending the bulk of your time in the *Trainer*. Later in your studies, when your emphasis will be on firming up effective habits, the bulk of your study time will be spent practicing and reviewing questions from the *10 Actuals* books. Your study schedule (to be discussed shortly) will detail how to combine the *Trainer* with practice exams.

Let's Get Ready to Study

I hope you enjoyed the relaxing read that this lesson presented. The truth is, the next three introductory lessons will also be mostly reading. After that, however...you better be ready to exercise those mental muscles. The rest of this book is going to be about you doing the work necessary to build up those skills and habits.

Preparing for the LSAT—just getting through this book, in fact—is going to take a whole lot of effort on your part. Let's make sure you are well organized as you begin your study process so you can get off to a good start and stay on track. To that end, here are the two steps for you to take to finish off your work for today.

The LSAT Trainer ♥ 10 Actuals

Why have I designed this book to be used in conjunction with the *10 Actual LSATs* books? It's simple: you need to experience a large volume of practice questions in order to get in LSAT-taking shape, and the *10 Actuals* books represent the most cost-effective way for you, as a student, to get copies of the most recent and relevant published LSAT questions. The LSAC charges licensing fees for books like *The Trainer* to publish official questions, and the fees that they charge publishers are significantly higher than what students pay for questions in the *10 Actuals* books. If I were to include the volume of questions you should be doing as part of your preparation, you would be paying far more for those extra practice questions than you need to (or I would be losing a lot of money). On the other hand, using *The Trainer* in conjunction with the *10 Actuals* books is an extremely cost-effective way to prepare for the exam.

There have been five *10 Actuals* volumes published thus far, and the most recent two include exams 52 -61, and 62 - 71, respectively. More recent exams are slightly more indicative of what you will see on your exam, so you want to give these a higher priority. Still, there is, in general, a great amount of consistency in the LSAT exams that have been administered over the past decade or so, so older exams will also be very useful.

One: Set Up Your Study Schedule

If you go to the *Trainer* website, theLSATtrainer.com, you will see a variety of study schedules available for download. These schedules are set up to account for different study timelines, and they provide specific instructions about how to incorporate your *Trainer* work with the work you do in the *10 Actuals* books.

Go ahead and select a study schedule, and fill in the assignments as per the instructions. Every student is different, but in general, I suggest that you limit yourself to one lesson each time you sit down to study. If you do want to study more than one lesson in one day, I suggest that you plan your study periods for different parts of the day—perhaps one lesson in the morning and one in the evening.

Two: Set Up Your Notebook

You are soon going to be absorbing a lot of information, and you are also, throughout this process, going to be constantly re-evaluating how you think about and solve questions. A notebook is a great tool to have for both organizing the new things that you learn, and keeping a record of the thought processes (say, the way you diagrammed a particular game) you have on various questions.

On theLSATtrainer.com there is a notebook organizer file that you can download. You can, of course, also easily set up your own notebook to your liking. I suggest that in any case you make sure to...

1) Clearly label each page of work, ideally with a date and other information such as question numbers or lesson number, so that you can more easily refer back to previous work if needed.

2) Separate your work into Logical Reasoning, Reading Comprehension, and Logic Games sections, or get separate folders for each.

3) Use a three-ring binder, or some other system that allows you to move around, add, and get rid of pages.

signing up for the exam

- **The LSAT is administered multiple times a year, generally at least once every two to three months.**
- **You are allowed to sit for the exam as many times as you'd like.**
- **Most schools only consider your highest LSAT score (but you should check with the individual schools that you are interested in).**
- **The registration fee is $180, and the standard deadline is about six weeks before each exam.**
- **Find more information and register for the exam at www.lsac.org.**

2 logical reasoning basics

Half of your score will be based on how you perform on the two Logical Reasoning sections. Logical Reasoning questions are the most important types of questions for you to master.

In this lesson, we'll start getting to know Logical Reasoning questions, define our goals and our gauges, and chart a path to success. In just a couple of pages, we'll take a look at four questions that will give you a taste of what various Logical Reasoning questions feel like. Then we'll dig a bit deeper into the underlying design of those questions. We'll do this by discussing the priorities of the test writers, and the specific skills that Logical Reasoning questions require. These skills, and the habits required to apply them successfully, will also help us define the goals of our study process.

Next, we'll start discussing specific ways to *gauge* our progress. Whether or not we get a question correct is the most objective and blunt way to gauge comfort level and ability. However, the reality is that in order to get any one Logical Reasoning question correct, we need to do several things well, and a wrong turn at any one point can steer us toward the wrong answer. To get any one question right, we need *many* skills. Thinking about whether we got questions right or wrong does not give us the type of detailed analysis we need to identify and address specific issues. Maybe we are missing a certain type of question because we don't actually understand exactly what the stem is asking for. Or maybe we misunderstand what we are supposed to be looking for in certain incorrect choices. Maybe there is a reasoning flaw that we consistently have trouble seeing. How, exactly, are we supposed to know?

In this lesson, we'll start getting to know Logical Reasoning questions, define our goals and gauges, and chart a path to success

Hopefully, one of the key benefits of this book will be that it helps you develop a clear, simple, and logical sense of what it is exactly that the exam requires of you at each step along the process. We'll get started on that in this lesson. One way we'll do this is by discussing the specific skills and habits that define top scorers. We'll also, both in this lesson and throughout the book, model the real-time performance of a top scorer, so that you can get a sense of his priorities, and so that you can compare and contrast your experience with his.

Having a clear sense of the end goals, having clear markers that tell you that you are fast on your way, and being able to reliably evaluate your performance on a step-by-step level will help keep you in firm control of your study trajectory. It will not, unfortunately, mean that you will automatically improve at a certain pace; it will mean that you know what you are good at, and what you need to work on, and that you'll have a very good sense of what you need to accomplish in order to get where you want to be.

We will end this lesson by laying out a three-stage plan for conquering the Logical Reasoning section. We'll plan the work to be done at each stage and also discuss how to incorporate these Logical Reasoning lessons with the work you do in the *10 Actuals* books.

details, details

basic facts about logical reasoning

Two of your four scored sections will be Logical Reasoning.

Recently, all Logical Reasoning sections have had twenty-five (most common) or twenty-six (less common) questions.

Twenty-five questions in thirty-five minutes works out to about 1:20 per question. However, keep in mind certain questions should take far less time, and others are designed to take more.

Each question consists of a stimulus (or prompt), a question stem, and five answer choices.

The stimulus will typically be two to three sentences in length.

The question types are clearly defined, and their frequencies are fairly consistent test to test. Question types are listed on page 36.

Each question has one clearly correct right answer and four clearly incorrect wrong answers.

In past years, occasionally there would be two questions related to one stimulus, but this trait has disappeared in recent years.

About two thirds of all questions require a subjective approach from the test taker. All of the stimuli for all subjective questions contain arguments—reasons given to justify a point made. For all questions that require us to think critically, our job will be to evaluate the relationship between the conclusion reached and the support for that conclusion.

About one third of all questions require an objective approach from the test taker. These questions require no evaluation of reasoning and are primarily designed to test reading abilities.

Over the course of a section, the difficulty of questions fluctuates according to somewhat consistent and predictable patterns (to be discussed in later lessons).

The average test taker gets anywhere from ten to twelve wrong per twenty-five-question section.

A 170+ test taker will consistently get anywhere from zero to three wrong per twenty-five-question section.

Sample Questions

Below are four Logical Reasoning questions that have appeared on past LSATs. Set a goal of completing all of them in 6 minutes or less, but take a bit more than that if you need to.

1. Most antidepressant drugs cause weight gain. While dieting can help reduce the amount of weight gained while taking such antidepressants, some weight gain is unlikely to be preventable.

The information above most strongly supports which one of the following?

(A) A physician should not prescribe any antidepressant drug for a patient if that patient is overweight.
(B) People who are trying to lose weight should not ask their doctors for an antidepressant drug.
(C) At least some patients taking antidepressant drugs gain weight as a result of taking them.
(D) The weight gain experienced by patients taking antidepressant drugs should be attributed to lack of dieting.
(E) All patients taking antidepressant drugs should diet to maintain their weight.

2. Some statisticians claim that the surest way to increase the overall correctness of the total set of one's beliefs is: never change that set, except by rejecting a belief when given adequate evidence against it. However, if this were the only rule one followed, then whenever one were presented with any kind of evidence, one would have to either reject some of one's beliefs or else leave one's beliefs unchanged. But then, over time, one could only have fewer and fewer beliefs. Since we need many beliefs in order to survive, the statisticians' claim must be mistaken.

The argument is most vulnerable to criticism on the grounds that it

(A) presumes, without providing any justification, that the surest way of increasing the overall correctness of the total set of one's beliefs must not hinder one's ability to survive
(B) neglects the possibility that even while following the statisticians' rule, one might also accept new beliefs when presented with some kinds of evidence
(C) overlooks the possibility that some large sets of beliefs are more correct overall than are some small sets of beliefs
(D) takes for granted that one should accept some beliefs related to survival even when given adequate evidence against them
(E) takes for granted that the beliefs we need in order to have many beliefs must all be correct beliefs

3. Several critics have claimed that any contemporary poet who writes formal poetry—poetry that is rhymed and metered—is performing a politically conservative act. This is plainly false. Consider Molly Peacock and Marilyn Hacker, two contemporary poets whose poetry is almost exclusively formal and yet who are themselves politically progressive feminists.

The conclusion drawn above follows logically if which one of the following is assumed?

(A) No one who is a feminist is also politically conservative.
(B) No poet who writes unrhymed or unmetered poetry is politically conservative.
(C) No one who is politically progressive is capable of performing a politically conservative act.
(D) Anyone who sometimes writes poetry that is not politically conservative never writes poetry that is politically conservative.
(E) The content of a poet's work, not the work's form, is the most decisive factor in determining what political consequences, if any, the work will have.

4. The higher the altitude, the thinner the air. Since Mexico City's altitude is higher than that of Panama City, the air must be thinner in Mexico City than in Panama City.

Which one of the following arguments is most similar in its reasoning to the argument above?

(A) As one gets older one gets wiser. Since Henrietta is older than her daughter, Henrietta must be wiser than her daughter.
(B) The more egg whites used and the longer they are beaten, the fluffier the meringue. Since Lydia used more egg whites in her meringue than Joseph used in his, Lydia's meringue must be fluffier than Joseph's.
(C) The people who run the fastest marathons these days are faster than the people who ran the fastest marathons ten years ago. Charles is a marathon runner. So Charles must run faster marathons these days than he did ten years ago.
(D) The older a tree, the more rings it has. The tree in Lou's yard is older than the tree in Theresa's yard. Therefore, the tree in Lou's yard must have more rings than does the tree in Theresa's yard.
(E) The bigger the vocabulary a language has, the harder it is to learn. English is harder to learn than Italian. Therefore, English must have a bigger vocabulary than Italian.

1: PT 36, S 1, Q 4; 2: PT 35, S 1, Q 23; 3: PT 35, S 4, Q 19; 4: PT 35, S 4, Q 23

Logical Reasoning Questions Are Hard

Maybe not for you—maybe you found the four questions on the previous page to be a walk in the park. But keep in mind that, in order to get a 170+ score, you need to consistently be able to get about nine out of every ten of these questions correct, and you need to be able to do so in an extremely time-efficient manner.

Before we go further, let's just vent for a bit about why Logical Reasoning questions can be difficult:

(1) The stimulus, or statement, contains a significant volume of information—information that seems connected but is also often disorganized. It can be too much information for us to retain all at once.

(2) This volume of information contains an unusual number of specific details. You can't keep track of them all, but at the same time, it's tough to know which ones are more important, and which ones less so.

(3) The question stems seem simple enough, but the test writers are actually asking you to do very specific things, and it's tough for you to know, at this point, exactly what they are going for.

(4) The answer choices are often written in a way that makes it difficult to understand what they actually mean.

(5) Finally, most of the answer choices are attractive in some way. Most answer choices are such that they could be correct if you thought about the stimulus or your task in a slightly different, slightly incorrect, way.

The worst part of it is that these issues compound one another. If, by the time you get to the answer choices, you have a good but not great understanding of the argument, and a good but not great understanding of the task presented to you in the question stem, it'll be next to impossible for you to anticipate the characteristics of the right and wrong answer choices. Without some sort of compass, your task of selecting the right answer becomes monumentally more difficult. Several answers may look attractive. The question may seem arbitrary, and right and wrong answers somewhat subjective.

How Do Questions Feel for Top Scorers?

They feel hard. However, the difference is that top scorers have the skills and habits necessary to meet the challenges.

Of course, in order to develop these skills and habits, it helps to know exactly what we are up against. Let's take a macro look at exactly what it is that Logical Reasoning questions are designed to test, and discuss how the questions test these issues. We'll return to the questions you've just solved and discuss them in more detail later in this lesson.

Know What Matters

Do you remember first learning how to solve word problems in your elementary school math class? Neither do I, but I do know this: if told a story about adding three dogs to two dogs, some children will naturally think about what types of dogs they are, and others will naturally think about what 3 + 2 is. Guess which ones will have an easier time learning how to solve word problems.

Logical Reasoning questions are very much like mathematical word problems. The math word problem has within it some specific underlying mathematical issue, and the purpose of the word problem is to gauge your mastery over this issue. To the writer of the word problem, the subject matter and the situation are secondary in importance or, at best, a tool to distract students from the math issues that are important.

Logical Reasoning problems have, buried within them, specific reading and reasoning issues, and the purpose of Logical Reasoning problems is to gauge your mastery over these issues. To the writers of these questions, the subject matter is secondary or, at best, a tool used to distract.

It is, of course, to your advantage to be able to see questions in terms of what is important to the test writers—to be able to see the questions with the "covers off." If you are consistently able to do so, you will find that the Logical Reasoning section becomes far more understandable and predictable. With that in mind, let's talk in a basic and fundamental way about the three issues that Logical Reasoning questions are designed to test: your reading ability, your reasoning ability, and your mental discipline.

Logical Reading Questions Test Reading Ability

Reading is fundamental to daily modern human existence—we are all excellent readers, and we all read countless things every day. No standardized exam, certainly not one that only takes a few hours, can gauge something as varied and significant as general reading ability.

The LSAT is designed to gauge two specific reading skills: your ability to read for reasoning structure, and your ability to understand the correct meaning of a few commonly used words

Why do I mention that? Because it leads us to something that is really important to understand, something most test takers do not: the LSAT does not test a broad range of reading skills—no standardized test of its type can. The LSAT is designed to gauge very specific reading skills—two such skills, to be exact: your ability to read for reasoning structure, and your ability to understand the correct meaning of words that are used in common reasoning and discussion.

The *reasoning structure* of a statement is simply the relationship among the parts of that statement. We all naturally read for reasoning structure—always. When we see two sentences next to each other, without telling ourselves to, we think about and, in general, easily understand how they are meant to go together.

The writers of Logical Reasoning questions are very interested in gauging exactly how good you are at being able to see how phrases are meant to go together. Most of the time the pieces will come together in order to service an **argument,** which, for the purposes of the LSAT, we can think of simply as a point made and reasons given for that point. If you are consistently able to see arguments clearly, the test writers will offer up reward after reward; for many questions, just seeing the argument clearly is *the* key to making your work far easier and faster.

An *argument* consists of a point and reasons given to support that point

We will be discussing reasoning structure quite a bit in both the Logical Reasoning and Reading Comprehension sections. This is because I believe almost anyone can become extremely good at recognizing reasoning structure correctly, and I've seen time and time again that the ability to do so serves as a vital characteristic of all top scorers.

The other reading skill you will be tested on is your ability to correctly understand the meaning of certain words commonly used in general reasoning and discussion, words like *must*, *because of*, *most likely*, *some*, and *or*. We will discuss all of these important terms in depth in future lessons.

As we briefly discussed in the initial lesson, the challenge of these words is that they are words we use every day without thinking, and in real life, even if we don't realize it, they are words that *change* in meaning per the context. If a waitress asks, "Would you like soup or salad?" it's generally rude for you to respond, "Both," but if you see a sign that says, "To get in the movie you must be over 17 or with an adult," you understand that in this instance being *both* over 17 *and* with an adult is perfectly fine.

Lawyers have to be very careful about the exact meaning of words. The LSAT, as you might imagine, requires that you utilize a specific and consistent (that is, *not* contextual) understanding of words—such as *or*—that define specific reasoning relationships. The word *or* on the LSAT has just one meaning, and it does not change whether we are talking about soup or movies. For LSAT problems, it is essential that you pay the most attention to the words that define reasoning relationships, and that you have a specific and consistent understanding of what these words mean.

Many Logical Reasoning questions are about random or little-known subjects, and they often include terminology that you will not be totally comfortable with. But your attitude toward this should be as it would be toward the subjects in a tough math word problem—you should see the challenging topics and terminology as a distraction, not as keys to your success. The test writers don't expect you to know anything about these subjects, and even if you did know something, it wouldn't matter. They don't care how expansive your vocabulary is, and they don't care about your ability to guess at the meanings of words you don't know. The fact that an LSAT question is about some strange philosophical stance or some new scientific theory is of little consequence; going back to elementary school, whether the dogs in question were greyhounds or pink puppies, your focus should be on more important issues.

Logical Reasoning Tests Reasoning Ability

When we are asked to critically evaluate reasoning in an argument, our job will always be to see why reasons *don't* justify a point

Logical Reasoning questions are also designed to test your reasoning ability—that is, your ability to judge or form an opinion about the information you are given in the stimulus. By far the most important reasoning relationships for us to judge are those that exist between a point and the support given for that point in an argument.

Let's imagine some different ways they could test our ability to evaluate this relationship within arguments. Perhaps they could sometimes give us arguments that are valid—arguments for which the reasoning does justify the conclusion—and sometimes give us arguments that are not valid, and they could test our ability to decipher which ones are valid and which ones are not. Other questions could be set up much as a case is presented to a jury—we would be given a set of facts, and it would be up to us to determine whether the information proves the conclusion, doesn't prove it, or presents some sort of deadlock.

It's important to know that neither of these scenarios actually represent what will be asked of you on the LSAT.

Logical Reasoning tests reading ability, reasoning ability, and mental discipline

When we are asked to evaluate the reasoning in an argument, it is always in terms of a very specific task: our job is *always* to evaluate and understand why the reasons given *do not* justify the point that is made. For every one of these questions, your understanding of why the support doesn't justify the conclusion will be your primary gauge for evaluating right and wrong answers.

Logical Reasoning problems do not ever require you to differentiate between valid and invalid reasoning within arguments. Instead, they test your ability to see, in a very specific way, why arguments are not valid. If you are good at this, you will be good at solving Logical Reasoning problems.

Logical Reasoning Tests Mental Discipline

We can define mental discipline as the ability to stay focused on the specific task at hand. Success on the LSAT requires extreme mental discipline, and the test is downright cruel to those who don't have it.

We can define mental discipline as the ability to stay focused on the specific task at hand

In terms of developing mental discipline, we give ourselves a huge head start when we have a clear understanding of the job, and of the best way to achieve it. But mental discipline takes far more than knowing. It requires sticking to that task—focusing on the argument, rather than the confusing background information, strengthening or weakening that argument, rather than just the point being made, not jumping to conclusions or forming opinions when the questions specifically ask for you not to judge, and remembering exactly what you are looking for in the right answer as you eliminate the wrong ones.

Your mental discipline is a fairly good representation of the power of your brain, just like the ability to lift a certain amount of weight is a fairly good representation of the power in your arms. Exercising those arm muscles is the best way to develop their strength; working questions correctly, over and over again, is the best way to develop mental discipline.

The Constellation of Questions

Here is a visual representation of the various types of questions that you are likely to see on the Logical Reasoning section of the exam. We'll discuss these using more formal language later. Each type of question is unique, but, as you can see, they are related. The numbers represent the total of that question type that you are likely to see in the two Logical Reasoning sections combined.

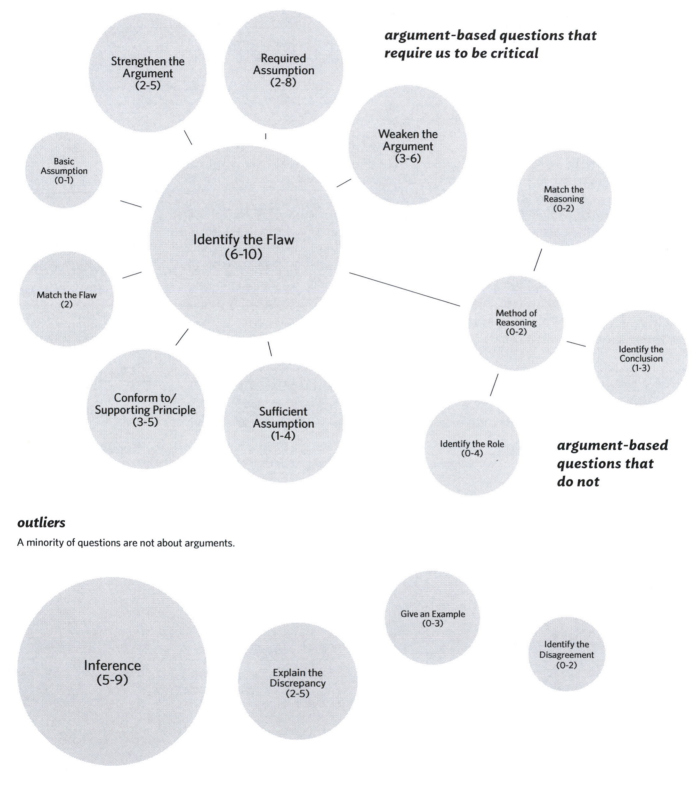

argument-based questions that require us to be critical

Strengthen the Argument (2-5)

Required Assumption (2-8)

Weaken the Argument (3-6)

Basic Assumption (0-1)

Identify the Flaw (6-10)

Match the Flaw (2)

Conform to/ Supporting Principle (3-5)

Sufficient Assumption (1-4)

Match the Reasoning (0-2)

Method of Reasoning (0-2)

Identify the Conclusion (1-3)

Identify the Role (0-4)

argument-based questions that do not

outliers

A minority of questions are not about arguments.

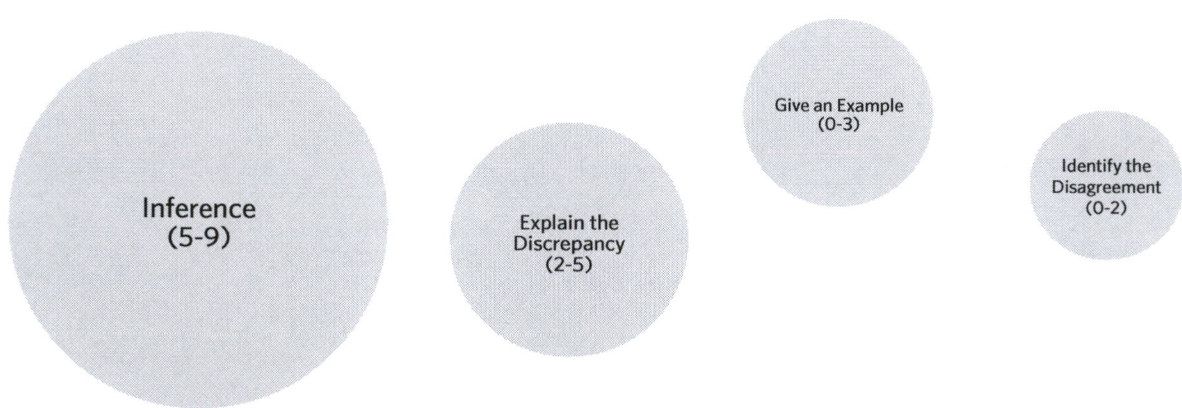

Sample Question Solutions

Next to each of the four questions from before are the hypothetical real-time thoughts of a top-scoring test taker. Keep in mind that many of these thoughts would likely not be as conscious and explicit as I've made them here. In real time, many of these thoughts—for example, how to approach each of the different question types—would be automatic and intuitive, rather than explicitly laid out. Also note that the solutions I write are not meant to be "absolute" ways of thinking. No two test takers will think of every question the same way, and I won't even think of the same question exactly the same way if I happen to look at it on two different days. Take these solutions to be examples of effective problem-solving. You don't have to solve problems the same way they are solved here, but you should be able to use these solutions to reflect on and gauge your own experience.

1. Most antidepressant drugs cause weight gain. While dieting can help reduce the amount of weight gained while taking such antidepressants, some weight gain is unlikely to be preventable.

The information above most strongly supports which one of the following?

(A) A physician should not prescribe any antidepressant drug for a patient if that patient is overweight.
(B) People who are trying to lose weight should not ask their doctors for an antidepressant drug.
(C) At least some patients taking antidepressant drugs gain weight as a result of taking them.
(D) The weight gain experienced by patients taking antidepressant drugs should be attributed to lack of dieting.
(E) All patients taking antidepressant drugs should diet to maintain their weight.

Looking at the question stem: need to use stimulus to justify an answer choice.

Stimulus is about relationship between antidepressant drugs and weight gain. Antidepressant drugs cause weight gain, and you can try to do some stuff to combat the weight gain, but sometimes you can't avoid it. Okay, ready for the answers. Going to look for reasons why four answers are not supported by the text in the stimulus.

The stimulus says nothing about what a physician should or should not do (who says weight is more important than emotional health anyway?), so (A) is obviously not provable. (B) is not provable for pretty much the same reason—we're told of a relationship between antidepressants and weight gain, but the stimulus doesn't say anything about what anyone should do. (C) seems easy to justify—keep. (D) can't be proved by the text—dieting helps reduce weight gain, but it's not the sole contributing factor. (E) is clearly wrong for the same reasons (A) and (B) were—we don't know what people should do. "All" patients taking such drugs? Maybe weight is not their main priority.

I've only got (C)—let's make sure I can justify it. Most drugs cause weight gain, and some of this gain is unlikely to be preventable. So, yes, it does seem that at least some patients taking the drugs gain weight as a result of them. (C) is correct.

2. Some statisticians claim that the surest way to increase the overall correctness of the total set of one's beliefs is: never change that set, except by rejecting a belief when given adequate evidence against it. However, if this were the only rule one followed, then whenever one were presented with any kind of evidence, one would have to either reject some of one's beliefs or else leave one's beliefs unchanged. But then, over time, one could only have fewer and fewer beliefs. Since we need many beliefs in order to survive, the statisticians' claim must be mistaken.

The argument is most vulnerable to criticism on the grounds that it

(A) presumes, without providing any justification, that the surest way of increasing the overall correctness of the total set of one's beliefs must not hinder one's ability to survive
(B) neglects the possibility that even while following the statisticians' rule, one might also accept new beliefs when presented with some kinds of evidence
(C) overlooks the possibility that some large sets of beliefs are more correct overall than are some small sets of beliefs
(D) takes for granted that one should accept some beliefs related to survival even when given adequate evidence against them
(E) takes for granted that the beliefs we need in order to have many beliefs must all be correct beliefs

Looking at the question stem: need to figure out what's wrong with the argument. Start by finding the conclusion.

Point: claim that surest way to increase correctness of beliefs is to cut out wrong ones and not add new ones is mistaken.

Why? Because it would leave us with fewer and fewer beliefs, and we need many beliefs to survive.

What does survival have to do with correctness of beliefs? That's the main problem. The author is using a premise about what we need to survive to try to prove a point about what does or doesn't lead to overall correctness, whatever that is. Okay, ready to eliminate choices.

(A) looks similar to what I thought about—leave it. Confused as to what impact (B) would have, but know that it's not the flaw—has little to do with the point and support. (C) also has very little to do with the point/support. (D) is about "beliefs related to survival"—that's different from needing a lot of beliefs to survive, and it doesn't relate directly to the issue of increasing correctness of beliefs. And (E) is not what is wrong with the argument either—he's not saying the beliefs we need must be correct.

(A) is the only possibility—time to take a careful look. The author is saying something isn't the surest way to increase correctness because it hinders one's ability to survive, and he's wrong for thinking that. (A) is it.

3. Several critics have claimed that any contemporary poet who writes formal poetry—poetry that is rhymed and metered—is performing a politically conservative act. This is plainly false. Consider Molly Peacock and Marilyn Hacker, two contemporary poets whose poetry is almost exclusively formal and yet who are themselves politically progressive feminists.

The conclusion drawn above follows logically if which one of the following is assumed?

(A) No one who is a feminist is also politically conservative.
(B) No poet who writes unrhymed or unmetered poetry is politically conservative.
(C) No one who is politically progressive is capable of performing a politically conservative act.
(D) Anyone who sometimes writes poetry that is not politically conservative never writes poetry that is politically conservative.
(E) The content of a poet's work, not the work's form, is the most decisive factor in determining what political consequences, if any, the work will have.

Need to fix the hole in the argument and make the argument airtight. First, need to find the point.

Point: It's false to think writing any formal poetry is a conservative act.

Why? Two poets who do so are progressive feminists.

So what if they are feminists? Maybe they are feminists, but they happen to write poems about flowers and fairies. I need an answer that specifically shows formal poetry not being a conservative act.

(A) doesn't give us anything about the poetry. (B) is about other types of poets—doesn't matter here. (C) is interesting—would mean these progressive feminists can't write conservative stuff—leave it. (D) is a bit tricky, but we don't need to prove that these feminists would never write politically conservative poetry, just that they could write some that isn't conservative. (E) does not do nearly enough to make our conclusion airtight.

That leaves only (C)—time to take a careful look. If (C) is true, since these two poets are progressive, that means they cannot write conservative poetry. That means the formal poetry they write is not conservative, and that is what I need to prove the point. (C) is correct.

4. The higher the altitude, the thinner the air. Since Mexico City's altitude is higher than that of Panama City, the air must be thinner in Mexico City than in Panama City.

Which one of the following arguments is most similar in its reasoning to the argument above?

(A) As one gets older one gets wiser. Since Henrietta is older than her daughter, Henrietta must be wiser than her daughter.
(B) The more egg whites used and the longer they are beaten, the fluffier the meringue. Since Lydia used more egg whites in her meringue than Joseph used in his, Lydia's meringue must be fluffier than Joseph's.
(C) The people who run the fastest marathons these days are faster than the people who ran the fastest marathons ten years ago. Charles is a marathon runner. So Charles must run faster marathons these days than he did ten years ago.
(D) The older a tree, the more rings it has. The tree in Lou's yard is older than the tree in Theresa's yard. Therefore, the tree in Lou's yard must have more rings than does the tree in Theresa's yard.
(E) The bigger the vocabulary a language has, the harder it is to learn. English is harder to learn than Italian. Therefore, English must have a bigger vocabulary than Italian.

Need to match arguments.

Argument: Higher = thinner. X higher, therefore thinner. Got it. Time to eliminate mismatches.

(A) has a similar structure—leave it. (B)'s got two conditions—more egg whites and longer beaten. That's different from original—cut. (C) doesn't seem right, but can't quite figure out why—leave it. (D) looks good too—leave it. (E) reverses characteristic and consequence—cut.

Have to look carefully at (A), (C), and (D). (C) looked worst, so start there. The part about Charles getting faster is suspicious—original is about comparing two different places, not same place at different moments. Other problems with (C) too, like I don't know if Charles is one of the fastest runners. (A) actually has a similar problem—the premise is about changes within one person, not differences between people. Both (A) and (C) are actually not great matches.

Okay, down to (D)—older = more rings. That matches. X older, therefore, more rings. That's a good match. It's (D).

The Signs of Mastery

Now that you've gotten a little sample of the problem-solving process, let's broaden things out and define, in general, the characteristics of a top scorer in the Logical Reasoning section.

A top scorer...

...has a correct and usable understanding of the task that each type of question presents.
...intuitively prioritizes and correctly orders issues that most directly relate to that task.
...wastes little time on thoughts and decisions that do not directly relate to the task.
...knows when to look for an argument, and when not to.
...knows when to critique the argument, and when not to.
...is always able to identify the main point.
...is always able to identify the support.
...is almost always able to figure out why the support doesn't justify the conclusion.
...knows how much he's supposed to be able to anticipate about the right answer.
...is often able to predict the right answer.
...is always able to predict the characteristics of wrong answers.
...is able to readjust when an answer tips her off that she's missed something.
...has question-type-specific systems for eliminating wrong choices.
...has question-type-specific systems for confirming the right choice.
...expects a high level of certainty before pulling the trigger on an answer. That generally means knowing at least one absolute reason why each wrong answer is wrong, and having a very strong sense of why the right answer is right.

A top scorer does not need...

...the ability to retain a huge volume of information. This is a common misconception, understandable because at first you don't know where to focus your efforts. It seems you have to be accountable for every random bit of information in the stimulus. You don't. There are clues everywhere that help you prioritize the few things you need to focus on.

...familiarity with a wide range of random and technical subject matter. As discussed, the subject matter generally serves as the background for more important issues.

...random bouts of creativity. Logical Reasoning questions reward flexibility, but they do not reward creativity. Questions require a very specific and literal understanding of the text and your task, and they reward organized and disciplined thinking. They do not require you to have moments of brilliance, and they do not require you to come up with unexpected ideas.

The Road Map to Mastery

Do you have it in you to gain Logical Reasoning mastery?

I firmly believe, based on what I know about this exam, and based on what I've experienced with students, that almost anyone who has a fairly strong command of the English language, and a good amount of common sense, can get to a high level of mastery with Logical Reasoning questions. The design of these questions has stayed extremely consistent over time, and they are all simple enough to be learnable. They make clear sense, and with practice you can get good at solving them.

Natural aptitude can affect the pace of improvement, but drive and work ethic are of far more importance to overall outcome

Natural aptitude does play a part in how long the learning process takes—for some of you, the design of the exam will just naturally better align with how you think, and so it will be easier to develop and habitualize skills. For others, the strategies and habits we discuss will butt against other instincts you have (instincts that may serve you well in other parts of your life), and the path to improvement will be steeper and less direct.

However, in my experience, natural aptitude does not have as significant an impact on the overall outcome of the study process as you might think. Of far more importance are drive and work ethic. If you want it badly enough, and if you know how to work, you can get there.

We can think of our path to Logical Reasoning mastery in terms of three major stages:

Stage One

We are going to start our Logical Reasoning preparation by focusing on the reasoning and reading issues and strategies that are most critical to the most questions.

As we just discussed, the primary way in which the Logical Reasoning section tests your reasoning ability is by presenting arguments for which the support given does *not* justify the conclusion reached. The most significant job that your "elephant" must do, again and again, is to figure out exactly why the support given does not justify the conclusion reached. If your elephant is great at doing this, you will have the key skill necessary for Logical Reasoning success.

Getting good at seeing flaws will be the primary goal of our first stage. We will introduce and get experience with all of the different types of flaws that can appear in arguments, and we will work on systems of thought that will help us catch these flaws more consistently and accurately.

And what you will find along the way is that when you are focused on finding the flaw in the argument, you end up naturally *reading* the stimulus the way that you are supposed to—in a way that best matches the design of the questions. Therefore, as we learn more about reasoning flaws and become better at recognizing them, we will also be working on habitualizing the reading strategies that best align with the design of this exam.

Stage Two

The goal of this stage is to round out and solidify our understanding of all important issues, to develop a very clear understanding of the specific tasks that different questions present, and to start to habitualize question-specific approaches.

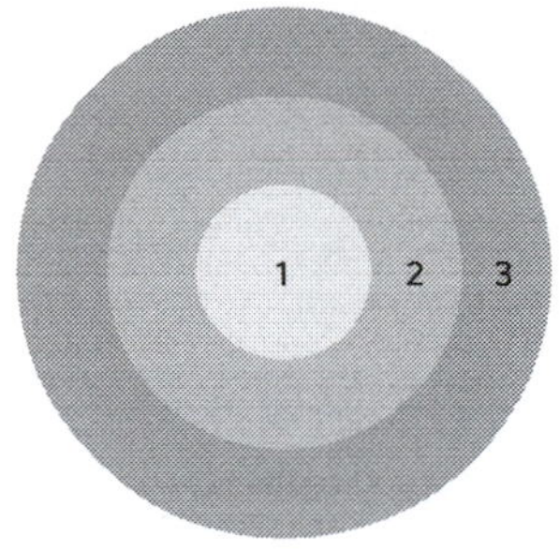

Stages to Mastery

one: get good at reading and critiquing LSAT arguments
two: get good at answering different types of questions
three: habitualize effective processes

Because the LSAT is largely a test of reading ability, it's understandable that the test writers are not casual with the language that they use—the entire exam is worded in a very specific and careful way. Nowhere is their attention to wording detail more evident than in the construction of their question stems. Each type of question presents a unique type of challenge, and the question stem lays out that challenge very specifically. No words are wasted, and every bit of information in that stem is critical to answering the question as efficiently and effectively as possible.

What complicates the challenge is that these various questions require skills and strategies that in some ways overlap, and in other ways don't. The way you solve a "strengthen" question is similar to how you solve a "required assumption" question, and, to put arbitrary numbers on it, 80 percent of the work you do for the two types of questions will be pretty much the same, and 20 percent of the work you do on the questions will be different. In order to develop general mastery, you need to have a very firm sense of that which is common to these questions—the 80 percent. At the same time, in order to reach the upper echelon of scorers, you also need to have a very clear sense of the *specific* challenges that questions present—the other 20 percent—and you need strategies that best align with these unique challenges.

Unfortunately, the vast majority of test takers go into the exam without a very clear sense of what each question requires, and consequently, they go in without strategies that best align with the design of each question. Perhaps, without even being conscious of it, they end up solving a Required Assumption question in pretty much the same way they might a Strengthen question. That can work out most of the time, but that lack of specification will prevent them from getting beyond a certain level of accuracy.

Each type of question presents a unique type of challenge, and the question stem lays out that challenge very specifically

The LSAT is designed to reward a specific understanding of task, and it punishes a fuzzy one. Evidence of this, as always, comes in the differentiation between right and wrong choices. The most attractive wrong answer for a Required Assumption question is commonly something that would strengthen the argument, but isn't an assumption that is required. The right answer might be tough to identify, even though it is required, because it doesn't impact or strengthen the conclusion as significantly as we would like.

In this second stage, we will carefully break down and discuss the specific tasks that the different question types present. We will do so with an eye toward how they are similar and how they are unique. We will also lay out and practice specific strategies that best align with the different types of questions.

Stage Three

The final stage will consist of a significant amount of practice that will help solidify all of the skills that we've been working on, and help form them into effective problem-solving habits. This work will mostly take place in the *10 Actuals* books.

If you develop habits that align with the exam, you can focus on the questions rather than how to solve them

Imagine a top surgeon in the midst of surgery. This surgeon does not have to worry that she understands something correctly, and she doesn't have to consciously remind herself of the strategies she needs to use. Her complete focus is on the needs of that specific patient, and she is naturally able to utilize her understanding and skills to the best of her ability. For us, the goal is that by the time you go into your LSAT, you won't have any concerns about what you know about the exam, and you won't have to consciously remind yourself of how to approach questions. You will be able to put your complete focus into understanding and getting correct the specific question in front of you, and you will naturally be able to use your understanding and skills to the best of your abilities.

U.S.E. (or S.U.E.)

Here is a visual representation of how our priorities evolve at different stages of our Logical Reasoning training. At first we want to pay extra attention to developing our understanding and strategies. As we get deeper in our process, the emphasis will shift toward gaining more and more real test experience.

U = Understanding
S = Strategies
E = Experience

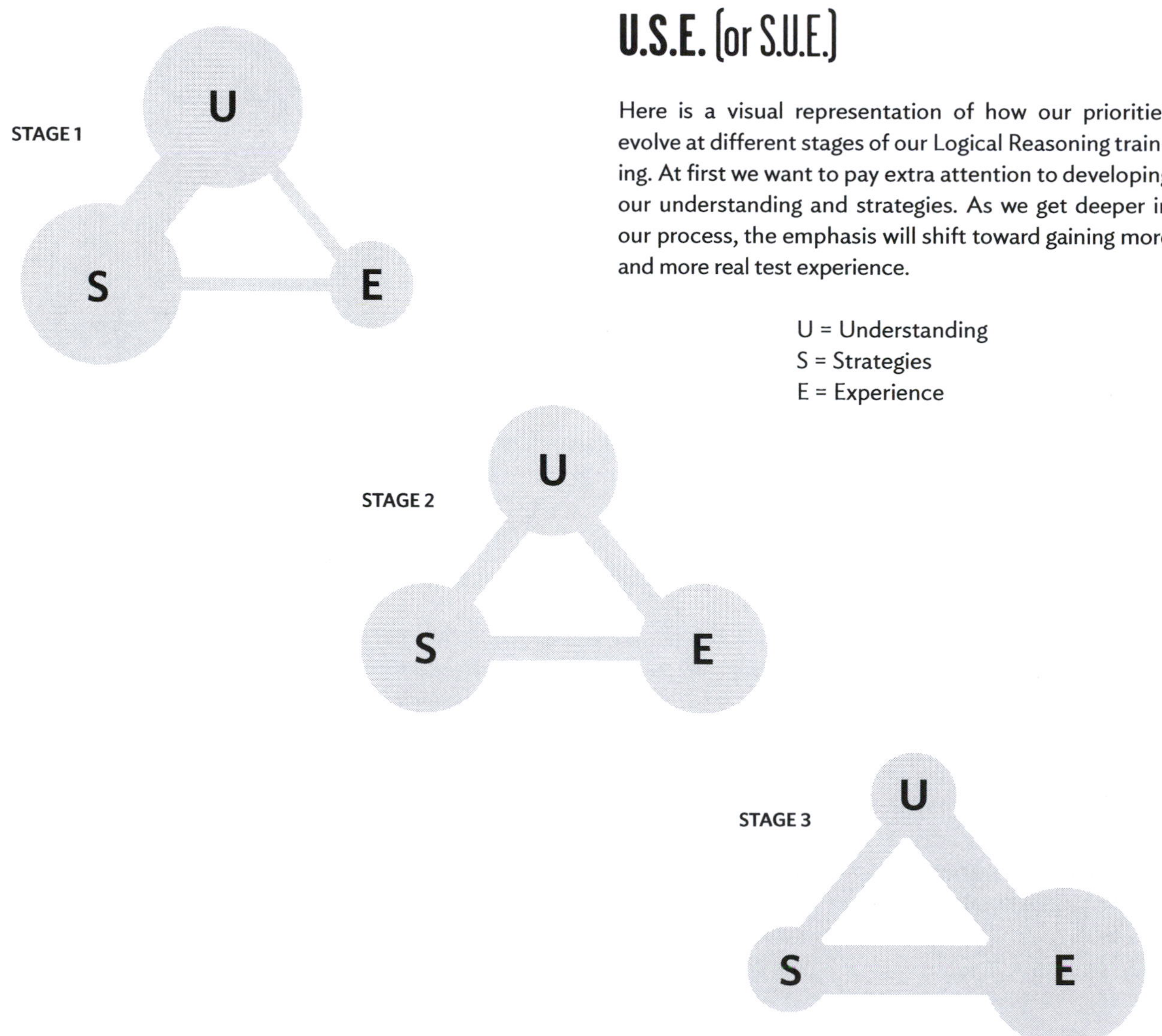

3 logic games basics

When we first begin preparing for the LSAT, we are, in general, far better prepared to tackle the Logical Reasoning or Reading Comprehension sections than we are the Logic Games section. In large part, that is because the things that we have to do and the thoughts we have to have for Logical Reasoning and Reading Comprehension questions don't seem as foreign to us.

Logic games are unique to the LSAT, and they are the most abstract aspect of the exam. They are abstract in that they have very little to do with real life, and playing them well is about handling a series of arbitrary rules. They really are *games*.

The Logic Games section is also commonly the most learnable of all sections. Countless people have started out absolutely lost as to how to solve Logic Games and ended up becoming Logic Games masters. In large part, this is because there is great commonality to all games, and all games questions follow fairly predictable design patterns. The games you see on your exam will be just like the games you see in your practice, if you know what to look for. When you think of most games from real life—Monopoly, Sudoku, poker, and such—you know that you can get better at them by learning and utilizing effective strategies, and by getting experience playing them. That's also absolutely true about Logic Games.

But when you start out, it sure can be tough to believe that you will ever conquer the Logic Games section.

You can do it. This book is going to help.

By the time we are through, there will be nothing about a game that surprises you, and you will have systems to handle every possible situation that can arise.

But we're getting ahead of ourselves. Try your hand at the game that appears on the next page before moving further.

Try This

This is a logic game and full set of questions that appeared on a previously administered LSAT. Do your best to answer the questions per the scenario and the rules given. Try to push the pace, but don't worry about timing for now. If you'd like to try the game again later, make sure to do your work on a separate page.

A messenger will deliver exactly seven packages—L, M, N, O, P, S, and T—one at a time, not necessarily in that order. The seven deliveries must be made according to the following conditions:

P is delivered either first or seventh.
The messenger delivers N at some time after delivering L.
The messenger delivers T at some time after delivering M.
The messenger delivers exactly one package between delivering L and delivering O, whether or not L is delivered before O.
The messenger delivers exactly one package between delivering M and delivering P, whether or not M is delivered before P.

1. Which one of the following is an order in which the messenger could make the deliveries, from first to seventh?

(A) L, N, S, O, M, T, P
(B) M, T, P, S, L, N, O
(C) O, S, L, N, M, T, P
(D) P, N, M, S, O, T, L
(E) P, T, M, S, L, N, O

2. Which one of the following could be true?

(A) N is delivered first.
(B) T is delivered first.
(C) T is delivered second.
(D) M is delivered fourth.
(E) S is delivered seventh.

3. If N is delivered fourth, which one of the following could be true?

(A) L is delivered first.
(B) L is delivered second.
(C) M is delivered third.
(D) O is delivered fifth.
(E) S is delivered first.

4. If T is delivered fourth, the seventh package delivered must be

(A) L
(B) N
(C) O
(D) P
(E) S

5. If the messenger delivers M at some time after delivering O, the fifth package delivered could be any one of the following EXCEPT:

(A) L
(B) M
(C) N
(D) S
(E) T

PT26, S1, G2, Qs 8 - 12

If that game felt easy for you, then fantastic. You've got a head start on just about everyone else. For most people, Logic Games don't feel as comfortable at first.

As we've mentioned before, the good news is that for most test takers, the Logic Games section is the most learnable of all of the sections. If you do the right type of work, you will get better. If you think you can improve at Monopoly or Sudoku with some practice, there is no reason for you to think you can't get better at Logic Games. *But...*

Of course the truth is that a tough Logic Game is harder than your typical Sudoku game, and of course the stakes are higher, and the competition fierce. To get really good—to feel like you have mastery—it takes hard, consistent, careful work.

In this lesson, we'll discuss the basics of the Logic Games section, the common challenges many test takers face, and the skills that top scorers have. Then we'll lay out a road map for how we're going to ensure that you go into the test ready for any Logic Game that can come your way.

In this lesson, we will discuss the common challenges that Logic Games present, the skills that top scorers have, and our plan for mastery

details, details

basic facts about logic games

One of your four scored sections will be a Logic Games section.

Each Logic Games section has four games, and generally twenty-three questions.

Each game will have between five and seven questions associated with it.

Every game that has appeared on the LSAT this decade can be thought of in terms of elements to be assigned, and positions to be filled.

For two or three games in every four-game set, the positions are organized in some sort of order.

For approximately half of all Logic Games, the positions are organized in groups.

Some games have positions organized by group *and* order. Almost no games have positions organized by neither group nor order.

Games are further complicated due to subgroups, or mismatching numbers issues.

For almost all test takers, a diagram is necessary for organizing the information given, and the ability to diagram well is a big key to success.

The purpose of a diagram is to represent what you know about a game in a clear and usable way, and to help facilitate bringing information together.

Of the twenty-three questions, all but two to four of them will come from a small bucket of basic question types. The remaining few will also come from an equally small bucket of minor question types.

For all Logic Games, there is some information that we can uncover, and some that we can't. All questions test your ability to differentiate between what is known, and what remains uncertain. A minority of questions also test your ability to consider a range of possibilities.

all games relate elements to positions

No matter what the specifics are of a particular game, all games are fundamentally about assigning elements to positions. In creating our diagrams, we will always use variables to represent elements and slots to represent positions. In general, we will begin our diagrams by writing out the elements and the slots.

F
G
H
J
K

____ ____ ____ ____ ____

The Challenge of Logic Games

So, why are Logic Games difficult? For people starting out, here are a few common reasons:

One: Logic Games are not, in many ways, what we think they are. As we've discussed, these games present a unique situation for our brains. When you first play, it's very easy to incorrectly associate Logic Games with other types of situations (e.g., other types of games, or other tests of reasoning ability), and it's also very easy to develop misconceptions about how these games work. Considering that these games require extremely careful and correct analysis, these misconceptions can have a big impact on your learning curve.

Two: Logic games require a lot from us. More specifically, Logic Games require us to juggle a lot of information. Some of this information is simple to understand, but some of it is not. Some of it is easy to diagram, and some of it is not. Regardless, when it comes time to answer questions, we have to somehow bring these disparate pieces together to make inference after inference after inference. Sometimes, a question will require that we make four or five inferences before we get to the one that's relevant to the correct answer. It can feel like juggling a bowling ball, a plastic bucket, and a flaming log, all at once.

Three: You don't have Logic Games-specific skills yet. Logic Games are like the long division you did in school, in that in order to work at our best, we have to use tools outside of our brains—we have to be able to write things out to think about them properly. The first few times any of us play games, we don't have any practiced strategies or skills—that means that even if we are writing things down and whatnot, we are not totally able to utilize these "outside of brain" tools. We end up overly dependent on what we can do with no tools, and these games are not designed to be solved that way. Very few of us are any good at long division without our pencil and paper methods for writing things out. The same goes for Logic Games.

The good news is that there is a great similarity to all Logic Games that appear on the exam, and very soon you will have systems that make it much easier for you to think about all of these games correctly. In exactly the same way that learning to do division on paper—as opposed to in your head—increased the range of division issues over which you had mastery, your ability to diagram will have a drastic impact on your level of comfort and mastery here.

How Logic Games Feel for Top Scorers

Top scorers find Logic Games to be challenging, just as everyone else does. Of course, the big difference is that top scorers have the skills to meet these challenges. Here are some characteristics that define Logic Games mastery:

One: Top scorers have the ability to comprehend and lay out a basic setup for any Logic Games scenario.

If you take soy sauce, sugar, sesame oil, and garlic, you can come up with hundreds of different and unique flavors. Something similar happens with Logic Games, but our first experience with them is akin to the person eating the food—what we might first notice is that there seem to be hundreds of different types of Logic Games. Okay, maybe not hundreds, but other strategy guides will divide Logic Games into dozens and dozens of different types for you to master. However, if you look at games from a slightly different perspective, you can see that there is great commonality to all of these games, and actually very little variation from the norm—they are all made of just a few basic ingredients. The simplest, and most effective way to develop a sound ability to "picture" any game is to develop a usable understanding of the fundamental issues that make up the structure of all games. To carry the analogy through, the best way to understand all of the various food dishes quickly and correctly is to develop a simple and usable understanding of the basic ingredients—soy sauce, sugar, sesame oil, and garlic.

Top scorers have a simple and usable understanding of the fundamental issues that underlie all games. This allows them to easily picture the basics of any game situation.

a note of caution

When thinking about improving at Logic Games, it's helpful to have a long-term perspective.

As we've mentioned, it's very natural for people to get better at Logic Games, and it's almost expected that you will make some significant improvement fairly quickly. For a lot of people, just becoming familiar with a few basic tools for diagramming is all it takes to make the first jump. (This is different from Logical Reasoning and Reading Comprehension, where score improvement commonly comes a bit later in the study process.)

However, it's important to note here that the manner in which a person improves and thinks about his or her initial improvement can have a significant, often unseen, impact on how much the person can improve. Simply put, this has to do with the development of habits—you can develop sound fundamental habits that are easier to build upon, or you can develop "pretty good" patchwork habits that serve as a poor foundation for adding further knowledge, and fall apart under the stress of the exam. An analogy can be made here to tennis or golf: You can get "pretty good" while developing bad habits in your form, "trick shots," and "shortcuts," but these bad habits can eventually prevent you from becoming awesome.

What are you meant to get out of this warning? Pay attention to your fundamentals—don't be eager to get to the "hard stuff." I promise that if you understand the fundamentals really well, the hard stuff is actually not going to seem that hard at all. And don't let yourself off the hook when you don't understand something or feel uncomfortable with a strategy, especially in the earlier lessons. You may survive one game not knowing how to do something or not understanding the difference between two very similar rules, but you don't want to go into the test hoping you're going to see the games you feel comfortable with. You want to go into the exam confident that you can handle any game and any issue they can throw your way.

Being able to start a game with a clear, organized understanding of the game situation makes everything else you have to do far easier.

Two: Top scorers have the ability to understand all rules in a specific and usable way.

Imagine that you have a game for which you are splitting eight students into two different teams, A and B. Here are two different rules you could get for this game:

> "Mary and Jon will be assigned to different teams."
> "If Mary is assigned to team A, then Jon will be assigned to team B."

Do you notice the difference in meaning between these two rules? We won't go into too much detail here, but notice that per the first rule, Mary and Jon have to be on separate teams. Per the second rule, they do not.[1]

1. Notice, per the second rule, that if Mary is on team A, Jon will be on Team B. Also, if Jon is on team A, we know Mary can't be, so Mary must be on team B. However, there is nothing preventing both Mary and Jon from being on team B.

Most of the rules that accompany Logic Games are not too difficult to understand. But when we think about the difference between the two rules above, you can see how...

A. It's a challenge to understand each and every rule exactly.

B. It's a challenge to notate the rules in such a way that you don't confuse the meaning with your notation.

C. It's a challenge to bring together your exact and usable understanding of various rules.

Again, the good news is that the same issues show up again and again in the games, and with practice you can develop the skills necessary to handle all subtleties effectively.

Three: Top scorers have the ability to recognize the keys to a game.

For every game, there is certain information, whether it be particular rules or particular inferences, that is most useful for thinking about the game easily and solving questions quickly. Often, prioritizing this information can mean the difference between a game and questions taking six minutes, or a game and questions taking ten minutes.

Even the best game players are not able to come up with this key thought or inference every single time, but many top scorers are able to do so very frequently, and what this means is that they may be able to get through two or three of the games in a section very quickly. This leaves them a lot more time to get through the other games.

Four: Top scorers rarely make diagramming mistakes, and they are able to recover when they do.

As you become more familiar with Logic Games, they will feel less and less like challenges of intelligence or cleverness, and more and more like challenges of consistency and mental discipline.

Most top scorers make very few diagramming errors, and if you are going to invest time in Logic Games training, you should expect that your diagramming process will, in general, be error free.

But games are hard, and errors do happen. There will be moments when you misread a rule, or misunderstand a secondary ramification of a rule, or mis-diagram in some way. Again, you shouldn't expect for this to happen, but you've got to expect that it can.

The good news is that with the right experience and perspective, you should be able to quickly recognize when you've made a mistake, in large part because the process of solving questions won't "flow" in the way that you expect it to, and you should be able to recover in time to still get the questions correct.

Five: Top scorers have specific habits for solving specific types of questions.

The truth is that every single person who takes the LSAT wastes time thinking about issues that are ultimately unrelated to arriving at the correct answers. When you first start out, this is true for pretty much every single LSAT question you try—even when you review a question you got right, you can find things you spent your time thinking about that ultimately didn't matter.

This inefficiency arguably hurts us the most in Logic Games relative to other sections because for most people, Logic Games is the section for which the time pressure is most significant. Top scorers are consistently able to think about the right things at the right time.

Six: Top scorers have confidence.

This is another statement from the "cheesy but true" category. Top scorers have confidence. Confidence is not enough to ensure a top score, but...

A lack of confidence almost always results in underperformance. This is because the games section requires us to make a lot of decisions—a lot of decisions that balance on top of other decisions—and all of us are worse at making decisions when we lack confidence in what we are doing. Students go into the games section lacking confidence if they don't have a simple and clear understanding of what can happen in the section and if they don't trust their skill set. Top scorers have confidence in their skills.

The games section requires us to make lots of decisions, and we are all worse at making decisions when we lack confidence

characteristics of mastery

Let's take a look at how the characteristics we've just discussed relate to the game that you played earlier.

1. The ability to comprehend and lay out a basic setup for any games scenario
All games involve placing elements into positions, and about two thirds of all LSAT games require us to think about these positions in some sort of order. For this game, the seven elements that we must place are L, M, N, O, P, S, and T. The positions represent the order in which these elements are delivered, and we will work under the assumption that order goes from left to right.

2. The ability to understand all rules in a specific and usable way
If each game that appeared on the LSAT was unique, and if you had to consistently come up with ways to notate constraints, diagramming would be a far more difficult endeavor. However, this is not the case. There is great consistency to how games are designed.

Notice that the first rule is about which position a certain element can go in: P can go in first or seventh position. The rest of the rules are all rules that give us more information about the ordering of events. These are all very common types of rules, and we will get plenty of practice with them in the lessons to come. To the side are some effective (though not the only effective) ways to diagram the given rules.

3. The ability to recognize the keys to a game
For an ordering game, the most significant information to know about a game generally has to do with a large grouping of elements. For example, imagine a simpler game with six positions, and you happen to know the relationship between four of the elements that go in those positions. Your understanding of this relationship would certainly be central to your understanding of the game as a whole.

We don't have any such significant rule here, but we do have information about "clusters" of elements, and we can gather this information by bringing various rules together. We'll lay out an effective way to do so on the next page, but before you look, go ahead and think about which rules seem to go together, and think about the significance of the information these clusters give us.

4. The habits necessary to rarely make diagramming mistakes
...And we won't be making any mistakes in this example. We'll discuss ways to recover from such mistakes, if and when they do happen, in later lessons.

5. Specific methods for solving specific types of questions
One of the best ways to combat the significant time pressure that you will face on the exam is to have effective and specific strategies for each type of question. Just like there are no unique rules, there are no unique questions—each question that appears is of a common variety that has appeared on countless exams, and you can habitualize strategies that are most effective for each type of question. On the side are some basic tips on how to handle a sampling of the questions that we saw.

6. Confidence
On the following two pages is a full solution for this game. Note that success does not require brilliance—it does require the consistent execution of a lot of steps. A lack of confidence makes this task much more difficult.

A messenger will deliver exactly seven packages—L, M, N, O, P, S, and T—one at a time, not necessarily in that order. The seven deliveries must be made according to the following conditions:

P is delivered either first or seventh.
The messenger delivers N at some time after delivering L.
The messenger delivers T at some time after delivering M.
The messenger delivers exactly one package between delivering L and delivering O, whether or not L is delivered before O.
The messenger delivers exactly one package between delivering M and delivering P, whether or not M is delivered before P.

1.

We will almost always write out ordering games with left to right order. It matters less how we list the elements.

2.

P/ /P

___ ___ ___ ___ ___ ___ ___

L — N

M — T

L _ O (↑__↑)

M _ P (↑__↑)

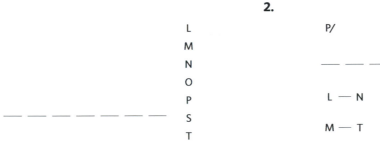

Here are the rules, diagrammed in the order in which they were given. During real games, we will rarely diagram rules in the order given. Rather, we'll diagram them in an order that is best for us.

3.

P is delivered either first or seventh.
The messenger delivers N at some time after delivering L.
The messenger delivers T at some time after delivering M.
The messenger delivers exactly one package between delivering L and delivering O, whether or not L is delivered before O.
The messenger delivers exactly one package between delivering M and delivering P, whether or not M is delivered before P.

Do you notice the overlap of elements in some of the rules? Can you picture how you could draw some of these rules together?

5.

2. Which one of the following could be true?
4. If T is delivered fourth, the seventh package delivered must be

Notice the different approaches that we want to use for these two questions.

If one answer could be true, that means four answers must be false, based on what we should already know about the game. For the first question, we should arrive at the right answer by eliminating the wrong ones.

The second question is conditional, and the expectation is that putting T in fourth determines who must go in seventh. In this case, we should make sure to figure out the right answer before looking at the answer choices.

The Skillful Solution

Let's take a step-by-step look at how a top scorer might solve the game in full. Notice that this solution requires no brilliance or cleverness. It does require a full complement of skills and habits.

A messenger will deliver exactly seven packages—L, M, N, O, P, S, and T—one at a time, not necessarily in that order. The seven deliveries must be made according to the following conditions:

P is delivered either first or seventh.
The messenger delivers N at some time after delivering L.
The messenger delivers T at some time after delivering M.
The messenger delivers exactly one package between delivering L and delivering O, whether or not L is delivered before O.
The messenger delivers exactly one package between delivering M and delivering P, whether or not M is delivered before P.

Step one: Notice that P is limited to one of two fixed positions, the last rule links M to P, and the third relates T to M. We can use this significant cluster of elements to organize the game.

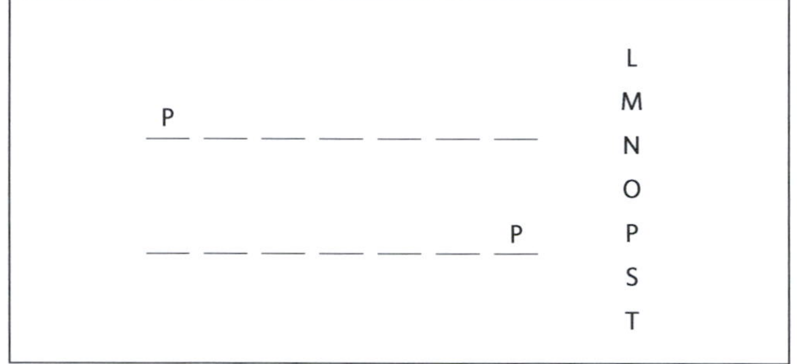

Step two: Instead of using one diagram, we can branch off of the first rule and create two diagrams, one for when P is first, another for when P is seventh. This will help us better organize and keep on top of the information.

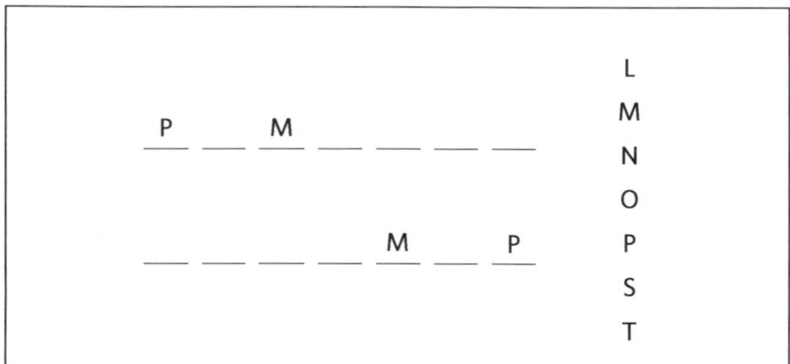

Step three: Since we've drawn P into the diagram, we can also draw in the rule about M being two spaces away from P. Notice how much better we can see the options for P and M than we would be able to if we had used just one diagram.

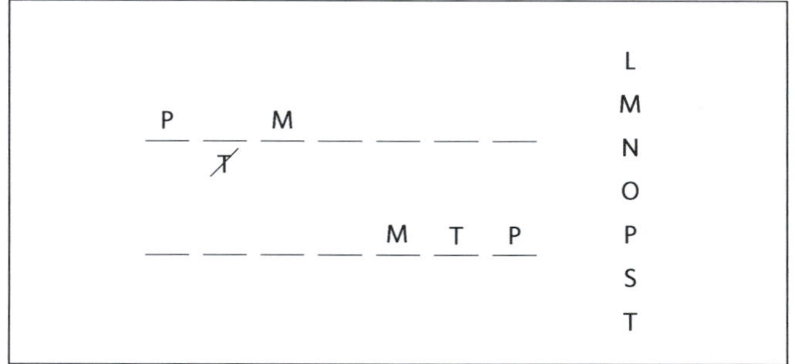

Step four: Now we need to incorporate the rule that T is after M. For the first diagram, that puts T in 4, 5, 6, or 7. That just means T is not in 2, and that's a clean way to notate that rule. For the second diagram, we know that T would have to go sixth.

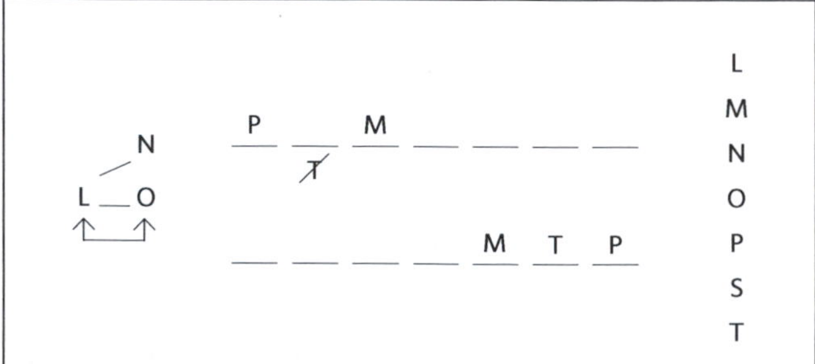

Step five: Now we can diagram the remaining two rules. Notice that these rules also share an element in common, and so we can diagram these two rules together. After diagramming all rules, always check your picture against the rules one last time to make sure you've drawn everything clearly and correctly.

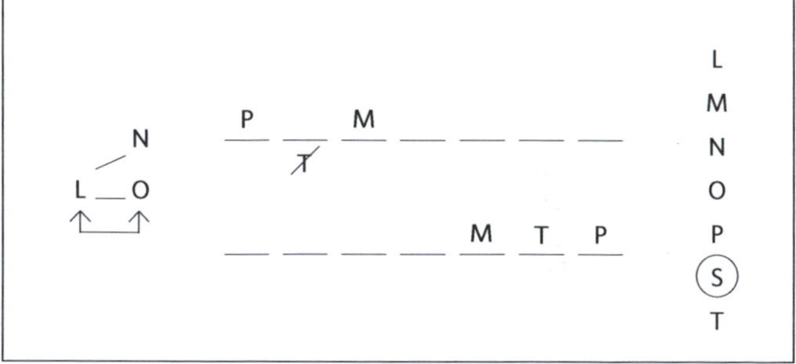

Step six: We want to take note of any elements that didn't get mentioned in the rules. These are "free agents" that can go anywhere. Lastly, we want to take a few more seconds to get very comfortable with our diagram and what it means; we'll need to use it quite a bit to answer the questions.

1. Which one of the following is an order in which the messenger could make the deliveries, from first to seventh?
(A) L, N, S, O, M, T, P
(B) M, T, P, S, L, N, O
(C) O, S, L, N, M, T, P
(D) P, N, M, S, O, T, L
(E) P, T, M, S, L, N, O

Almost all games begin with a question that asks you to identify one possible arrangement of elements. These questions are designed to test your understanding of the rules given, and these questions are very consistent in the way that they are written. Each of the wrong answers must violate at least one rule, and the fastest, most accurate way to arrive at the correct answer is to go down the list of the rules we were given (typically the only time we will use the list of rules instead of our diagram), and to eliminate answers that violate those rules. We can use the first rule (you can see the rules listed on the opposite page) to eliminate (B). We can use the second rule to eliminate (D). We can use the third rule to eliminate (E). We can use the fourth rule to eliminate (A). That leaves us with **(C) as the correct answer.**

2. Which one of the following could be true?
(A) N is delivered first.
(B) T is delivered first.
(C) T is delivered second.
(D) M is delivered fourth.
(E) S is delivered seventh.

We know, per the way the question is asked, that one answer is something that could be true based on what we know of the game, and four answers are ones that must be false. In this situation, it's generally faster and more accurate to eliminate the four answers that must be false than it is to test out all answers to see which one could be true. We can see that in either of our two diagrams, neither (A), (B), (C), nor (D) can be true. Therefore, **(E) is correct.** To confirm, we can come up with a way that works with S seventh: P, L, M, O, N, T, S.

3. If N is delivered fourth, which one of the following could be true?
(A) L is delivered first.
(B) L is delivered second.
(C) M is delivered third.
(D) O is delivered fifth.
(E) S is delivered first.

L/O S L/O N M T P

This question is also asking what could be true, but it also comes with a condition: N is delivered fourth. When we are given a condition, invariably there will be additional information we can figure out from this condition, and this additional information will always be what is key to answering the question. If N is delivered fourth, we know that the first diagram is not an option (no place for L _ O / O _ L). In the second diagram, if N is fourth, L and O can go in 1 and 3 (in either order) and that leaves S for the second spot. In this case, since we've figured out so much, it's easy to jump to the right answer: **(A) is correct.** It's also very easy to eliminate all the wrong ones, and we can do so to confirm our work.

4. If T is delivered fourth, the seventh package delivered must be
(A) L
(B) N
(C) O
(D) P
(E) S

P S M T L N O

We want to start by placing T fourth, and we know that this should eventually tell us which package is in seventh. If T is fourth, we know the second diagram can't work, so we're just left with the first. With T in that fourth position, the only place for L _ O to go is 5 _ 7, and, since L needs to go before N and we need a place for N to go, that means L must be in 5, and O must be in 7. **The correct answer is (C),** and because this was a question for which we identified the answer before looking at the choices, we don't need to worry about eliminating wrong choices.

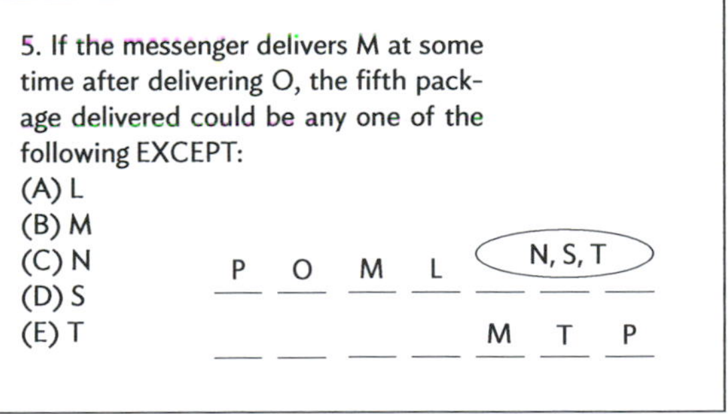
5. If the messenger delivers M at some time after delivering O, the fifth package delivered could be any one of the following EXCEPT:
(A) L
(B) M
(C) N
(D) S
(E) T

M can be delivered after O in either of our diagrams. In the first diagram, M can be delivered after O if O is delivered second. That puts L into the fourth spot. That leaves us with N, S, and T for the remaining three spots, and there are no more rules that restrict where these three elements can now go. So, N, S, and T are all possibilities for the fifth package. In the second of our diagrams, M can be delivered after O in any number of ways, but, of course, in all these different options, M must be the fifth item delivered. That leaves us with N, S, T, and M as the possible options for the fifth delivery. Since we are looking for the one answer that can't be our fifth delivery, **(A) is correct.**

The Road Map to Mastery

Our path to Logic Games mastery is going to take us through three main phases:

One: We will work to develop simple and effective diagramming strategies.

The key to Logic Games success is your ability to comprehend and accurately diagram the situations presented. If you are consistently able to do these two things, your outcome will mostly be a matter of execution.

As we've discussed, all games are constructed according to a few fundamental principles. Become comfortable with these principles, and get practiced at utilizing a simple diagramming system that intuitively ties in to your understanding of the game, and you are going to be well on your way to success.

In this first phase, we will work to develop a simple and usable understanding of all the major issues that can arise in Logic Games. We will also lay out basic diagramming strategies for these various issues and begin to get practice at incorporating these strategies into real-time solutions.

Two: We'll work to develop question-specific strategies.

As mentioned before, there are just a few different types of questions that appear in the games section. However, each type of question requires a somewhat unique thought process. Immersing ourselves more and more into full and actual LSAT games, we'll work to develop a simple and correct understanding of the tasks that each question stem presents, and we'll work through exercises that will further help incorporate our understanding and strategies into how we solve questions in real time.

Three: We'll fine-tune our skills and firm up our habits.

Of course, we'll be playing games throughout the learning process, but in this phase the playing of games will take center stage. We'll use these games to finalize and fine-tune our strategies, and to complete the process of making our strategies as intuitive as possible. We'll also use various systems to analyze and isolate any final weaknesses and work to knead out those final issues.

4 reading comprehension basics

It is very hard—next to impossible—for us to change the way that we walk. You can try it if you'd like. We can do it for five minutes, maybe ten, but soon enough, we'll end up walking the same way we always do. The same thing goes for how we drive, and how we talk. Our conscious efforts are no match for such ingrained and instinctual habits.

All of this also applies to how we read. Reading is one of the most amazing things that human beings can do, and it's something we do by habit, because it takes skills that are well beyond our conscious ability. That's why it's very difficult to change, or even just impact, the way that we read. We can't do it on a purely conscious level (that is, we can't read differently just by telling ourselves to read differently).

We read by habit, and we can't change how we read just by wanting to

But here's the thing: your brain knows how to walk differently in different situations. It is incredible at adapting. When you walk by someone you find attractive, the way that you walk literally changes—whether you know it or not. If a tiger is chasing you, you'll change your walk into a really fast version—a *run*—and you won't need to think about this on a conscious level for it to happen.

Your brain also knows how to adapt to different reading situations. It's amazing at it. Your brain reads a newspaper article differently than it does a recipe, or a work e-mail, or a letter from a friend. It knows that sometimes its job is to be critical, and at other times its purpose is to be empathetic. Again, we adapt almost perfectly, without any conscious effort.

The problem is that your brain does not know how to read LSAT passages. It doesn't yet have the information or experience to have correct instincts. What we need to do is supply it with exactly the right information about how to approach LSAT reading passages. We also need to get plenty of experience, with specific and useful reinforcement, so that we can turn these reading instincts into habits.

Take a look at this next passage, and try your best to answer the accompanying questions. Keep track of your time, but don't prioritize timing for now.

Sample Passage and Questions

On this page and the next are an LSAT passage and all the questions that accompanied that passage when it originally appeared. Time yourself as you read the passage and solve the questions, but do not, at this point, worry about sacrificing accuracy for speed. We will discuss the passage and questions in detail in just a bit.

Experts anticipate that global atmospheric concentrations of carbon dioxide (CO_2) will have doubled by the end of the twenty-first century. It is known that CO_2 can contribute to global warming by trapping solar energy that is being reradiated as heat from the Earth's surface. However, some research has suggested that elevated CO_2 levels could enhance the photosynthetic rates of plants, resulting in a lush world of agricultural abundance, and that this CO_2 fertilization effect might eventually decrease the rate of global warming. The increased vegetation in such an environment could be counted on to draw more CO_2 from the atmosphere. The level of CO_2 would thus increase at a lower rate than many experts have predicted.

However, while a number of recent studies confirm that plant growth would be generally enhanced in an atmosphere rich in CO_2, they also suggest that increased CO_2 would differentially increase the growth rate of different species of plants, which could eventually result in decreased agricultural yields. Certain important crops such as corn and sugarcane that currently have higher photosynthetic efficiencies than other plants may lose that edge in an atmosphere rich in CO_2. Patterson and Flint have shown that these important crops may experience yield reductions because of the increased performance of certain weeds. Such differences in growth rates between plant species could also alter ecosystem stability. Studies have shown that within rangeland regions, for example, a weedy grass grows much better with plentiful CO_2 than do three other grasses. Because this weedy grass predisposes land to burning, its potential increase may lead to greater numbers of and more severe wildfires in future rangeland communities.

It is clear that the CO_2 fertilization effect does not guarantee the lush world of agricultural abundance that once seemed likely, but what about the potential for the increased uptake of CO_2 to decrease the rate of global warming? Some studies suggest that the changes accompanying global warming will not improve the ability of terrestrial ecosystems to absorb CO_2. Billings' simulation of global warming conditions in wet tundra grasslands showed that the level of CO_2 actually increased. Plant growth did increase under these conditions because of warmer temperatures and increased CO_2 levels. But as the permafrost melted, more peat (accumulated dead plant material) began to decompose. This process in turn liberated more CO_2 to the atmosphere. Billings estimated that if summer temperatures rose four degrees Celsius, the tundra would liberate 50 percent more CO_2 than it does currently. In a warmer world, increased plant growth, which could absorb CO_2 from the atmosphere, would not compensate for this rapid increase in decomposition rates. This observation is particularly important because high-latitude habitats such as the tundra are expected to experience the greatest temperature increase.

Practice Test 33, Section 2, Passage 3

15. Which one of the following best states the main point of the passage?

(A) Elevated levels of CO_2 would enhance photosynthetic rates, thus increasing plant growth and agricultural yields.
(B) Recent studies have yielded contradictory findings about the benefits of increased levels of CO_2 on agricultural productivity.
(C) The possible beneficial effects of increased levels of CO_2 on plant growth and global warming have been overstated.
(D) Increased levels of CO_2 would enhance the growth rates of certain plants, but would inhibit the growth rates of other plants.
(E) Increased levels of CO_2 would increase plant growth, but the rate of global warming would ultimately increase.

16. The passage suggests that the hypothesis mentioned in the first paragraph is not entirely accurate because it fails to take into account which one of the following in predicting the effects of increased vegetation on the rate of global warming?

(A) Increased levels of CO_2 will increase the photosynthetic rates of many species of plants.
(B) Increased plant growth cannot compensate for increased rates of decomposition caused by warmer temperatures.
(C) Low-latitude habitats will experience the greatest increases in temperature in an atmosphere high in CO_2.
(D) Increased levels of CO_2 will change patterns of plant growth and thus will alter the distribution of peat.
(E) Increases in vegetation can be counted on to draw more CO_2 from the atmosphere.

17. Which one of the following best describes the function of the last paragraph of the passage?

(A) It presents research that may undermine a hypothesis presented in the first paragraph.
(B) It presents solutions for a problem discussed in the first and second paragraphs.
(C) It provides an additional explanation for a phenomenon described in the first paragraph.
(D) It provides experimental data in support of a theory described in the preceding paragraph.
(E) It raises a question that may cast doubt on information presented in the preceding paragraph.

18. The passage suggests that Patterson and Flint would be most likely to agree with which one of the following statements about increased levels of CO_2 in the Earth's atmosphere?

(A) They will not increase the growth rates of most species of plants.
(B) They will inhibit the growth of most crops, thus causing substantial decreases in agricultural yields.
(C) They are unlikely to increase the growth rates of plants with lower photosynthetic efficiencies.
(D) They will increase the growth rates of certain species of plants more than the growth rates of other species of plants.
(E)They will not affect the photosynthetic rates of plants that currently have the highest photosynthetic efficiencies.

19. The author would be most likely to agree with which one of the following statements about the conclusions drawn on the basis of the research on plant growth mentioned in the first paragraph of the passage?

(A) The conclusions are correct in suggesting that increased levels of CO_2 will increase the photosynthetic rates of certain plants.
(B) The conclusions are correct in suggesting that increased levels of CO_2 will guarantee abundances of certain important crops.
(C) The conclusions are correct in suggesting that increased plant growth will reverse the process of global warming.
(D) The conclusions are incorrect in suggesting that enhanced plant growth could lead to abundances of certain species of plants.
(E) The conclusions are incorrect in suggesting that vegetation can draw CO_2 from the atmosphere.

20. The passage supports which one of the following statements about peat in wet tundra grasslands?

(A) More of it would decompose if temperatures rose four degrees Celsius.
(B) It could help absorb CO_2 from the atmosphere if temperatures rose four degrees Celsius.
(C) It will not decompose unless temperatures rise four degrees Celsius.
(D) It decomposes more quickly than peat found in regions at lower latitudes.
(E) More of it accumulates in regions at lower latitudes.

21. Which one of the following, if true, is LEAST consistent with the hypothesis mentioned in lines 22-25 *(sentence starting "Certain important crops" in paragraph two)** of the passage?

(A) The roots of certain tree species grow more rapidly when the amount of CO_2 in the atmosphere increases, thus permitting the trees to expand into habitats formerly dominated by grasses with high photosynthetic efficiencies.
(B) When grown in an atmosphere high in CO_2 certain weeds with low photosynthetic efficiencies begin to thrive in cultivated farmlands formerly dominated by agricultural crops.
(C) When trees of a species with a high photosynthetic efficiency and grasses of a species with a low photosynthetic efficiency were placed in an atmosphere high in CO_2, the trees grew more quickly than the grasses.
(D) When two different species of grass with equivalent photosynthetic efficiency were placed in an atmosphere high in CO_2, one species grew much more rapidly and crowded the slower-growing species out of the growing area.
(E) The number of leguminous plants decreased in an atmosphere rich in CO_2, thus diminishing soil fertility and limiting the types of plant species that could thrive in certain habitats.

22. According to the passage, Billings' research addresses which one of the following questions?

(A) Which kind of habitat will experience the greatest temperature increase in an atmosphere high in CO_2?
(B) How much will summer temperatures rise if levels of CO_2 double by the end of the twenty-first century?
(C) Will enhanced plant growth necessarily decrease the rate of global warming that has been predicted by experts?
(D) Would plant growth be differentially enhanced if atmospheric concentrations of CO_2 were to double by the end of the twenty-first century?
(E) Does peat decompose more rapidly in wet tundra grasslands than it does in other types of habitats when atmospheric concentrations of CO_2 increase?

* Note that because passages have been reformatted, they are presented here without the original line numbers. Questions that reference line numbers will thus include a brief description, in italics, of where to find the relevant information.

LSAT Reading Comprehension

Imagine that you answer a help wanted ad in your local newspaper, and somehow end up writing Reading Comprehension questions for the makers of the LSAT. They supply you the passage and ask you to come up with some questions. What types of questions would you come up with? I imagine that most of you would be able to come up with some very good ones.

Reading Comprehension questions are carefully constructed, and their design is consistent from passage to passage, and exam to exam

Could the scene above actually play out? The part that's perhaps most suspicious is that the LSAC, the makers of the LSAT, gives you this assignment to write questions without more specific instruction—without far more specific instruction. Keep in mind that the LSAT is a standardized test, a *highly* standardized test, which means that each challenge presented to the test taker has been accounted for and carefully calculated.

LSAT Reading Comprehension questions are not about random reading issues. They are very carefully constructed, and their designs are extremely consistent from passage to passage and exam to exam. LSAT Reading Comprehension passages test us on just a few very specific skills, and they test us in the same ways over and over again.

Therefore, as I mentioned before, the key to Reading Comprehension success is to train yourself so that your reading strategies and priorities perfectly align to the challenges that are typically present on the LSAT—the challenges the test writers are interested in. You want to read an LSAT reading passage in a very different way than you read other things in your life; in fact, the way that you want to read LSAT reading passages is likely very different from how you've read passages on other standardized tests. We want to make this reading method so habitual that you don't have to consciously control it (because you can't anyway). When your reading habits align with the specific challenges of Reading Comprehension, you will find yourself anticipating certain questions, and you will find the challenge of differentiating between right and wrong answers to be far more clear cut.

What Reading Comprehension Tests

Your ability to read for reasoning structure will be the key determinant of your success

In Lesson 1, we broke down all three sections in terms of the two skill sets that they test: reading ability and reasoning ability. Whereas Logical Reasoning tests both skill sets about equally, and the Logic Games section prioritizes your reasoning ability, Reading Comprehension is almost entirely about your reading ability. Two or three questions per section may ask you to use a bit of reasoning—to find an answer to strengthen the author's point, for example—but by and large almost all of the challenges presented in the section are designed to test your reading, rather than reasoning, abilities.

Additionally, there is one particular reading skill that is of the most interest to the test writers: your ability to recognize and correctly understand reasoning structure. We've discussed reasoning structure already in the Logical Reasoning introduction: Reasoning structure is the relationship between the various components of a passage. If you understand what parts are meant to be main points, what parts are meant to support those points, and so on, then you have a clear understanding of reasoning structure.

The Challenges of Reading Comprehension

In light of what we've just discussed, let's consider the general challenges that the Reading Comprehension section presents:

One: Passages can be dense and full of complex or subtle details.

Furthermore, the most difficult questions tend to be associated with those passages that have the most complex or nuanced content. Not only are these complex details necessary for answering certain questions, they impact our ability to read for reasoning structure. Most of us are not as good at using our reading ability when we are faced with unfamiliar subject matter.

Two: Central issues or passage structure can be complex or subtle.

When you think about a great piece of clothing, it can be great because of the materials (the substance of it) or the design (the use of that substance). Reading Comprehension passages can be difficult because of the content (the details involved) or because of the reasoning structure (the relationship between those details).

As you'll see with more experience, most reading passages will present two opposing viewpoints on some sort of issue (one opinion versus another on how a certain law should be interpreted, or an old scientific theory versus the one that replaced it). However, the relationship between these two sides is not always clear cut—in fact, it can be extremely subtle. Furthermore, most passages will inform us of the author's opinion of the content, but often this opinion will be given to us in vague ways, and the opinion can also be somewhat complex. Perhaps a passage will present two sides of an argument, and the author will hint that she somewhat agrees with one side, and feels uncertain about the other.

Three: Questions require us to see the forest *and* the trees.

That is, in order to answer questions successfully, we need to have a strong sense of the general structure of the passage, and, at the same time, we need to have a very clear sense of the details that are directly relevant to specific questions.

We are not very good at reading for the big picture and for small details at the same time, and there is no need for us to try

Many test takers end up trying to focus on both the big picture and the details as they read. In fact, most other preparation books, by giving you a laundry list of thirty specific and general things to notice as you read, indirectly point you toward just that tactic. But here's the thing—we can't do both well at the same time. The key to success is to focus on the big picture as you initially read the passage, and to utilize specific details during the problem-solving process. We'll discuss this strategy quite a bit more in the lessons to come.

Characteristics of Top Scorers

Of course, just as no two people walk in exactly the same way, no two test takers, even top scorers, read in exactly the same way. Still, there is great commonality among those who are able to complete Reading Comprehension sections with few or no misses. Here are some of the key ones:

Top scorers...

...naturally and intuitively read for reasoning structure. It's not just that they know it's important—it's what they think about as they read. That is, as they are reading that super-complicated sentence about a physics experiment, they are less concerned with understanding all of the intricacies of the experiment, and more concerned with figuring out *why*, exactly, the author has chosen to tell us this information.

...are able to recognize when to slow down to carefully absorb important details. As we discussed, trying to absorb every single detail in a passage is an exercise in futility. Effective reading is about prioritizing. Top scorers are able to focus in on details when it is important for them to do so. During the initial read, the details most important to absorb are those that tell us of the main point at issue, and those that hint at the author's opinion. During the process of answering questions, other details will become important when they need to be used to confirm right answers and eliminate wrong ones.

...always know to look out for and are able to recognize subtle hints that point toward author bias or opinion. Most passages give us hints as to what the author feels about the issue at hand. Often these hints are subtle and *seemingly* secondary to the more important parts of a passage, but any hint of author bias is extremely important, for it gets to the heart of understanding reasoning structure—understanding why the author wrote a particular passage and structured it the way he did. Though generally very little text in a passage is dedicated to opinions, the opinions discussed in passages are generally central to the questions, and, in particular, you can expect at least a question or two that hinges on an understanding of the author's opinion. A top scorer understands how important this opinion is and is always able to dig it out.

...have a clear understanding of what each question is asking. LSAT writers do not mince words. Many Reading Comprehension questions sound similar, but subtle differences in wording (such as "according to the passage" versus "the passage suggests") can have a significant impact on what is required of the right answers and what defines wrong answers. We will spend several lessons discussing how to think about and solve specific types of questions. A top scorer, by the time she goes into the exam, will have an exact understanding of all the different types of Reading Comprehension questions that can be asked.

...are able to anticipate characteristics of the right answers for most questions. They are able to do so based on what they are given in the question stem. Now, there are some questions that, per their design, do not have answers that are predictable (such as "The passage mentions which of the following?"). However, most question stems give you a more specific sense of what to look for in a right answer, and top scorers are able to use this understanding to perform the next two steps well.

...are able to consistently and confidently eliminate incorrect answers. There are few characteristics that differentiate top scorers more than the ability to eliminate incorrect answers. If you understand the passage and your task well, the characteristics of incorrect answers become much clearer and more obvious. Furthermore, top scorers recognize that eliminating wrong choices first not only increases overall consistency and accuracy, it also helps make the search for the right answer easier.

Finally, top scorers know when they are certain that an answer is correct, and when they are not. Most top scorers will still have at least a couple of Reading Comprehension questions per section for which they cannot feel certain that they got the correct answer (it's really helpful, in these instances, to have strong elimination skills). However, they will rarely, if ever, have a situation in which they feel certain they got a question right, only to find out they did not. Top scorers know the feeling of matching an answer exactly to the task presented in the question stem, and, more importantly, they have systems for confirming their work. You can feel certain of your answer if it matches what you anticipated, and if you are able to verify it based on the relevant text. Top scorers have these skills.

why do we miss questions?

How do you think you did on the sample passage? If you think you nailed all of the questions, great. If you missed some, even better! Early on in your process, misses are fine—they are better than fine. They are really useful, for they show us exactly what we need to improve on to get the score we want. This test is conquerable, and the best students are the ones who are best at identifying and reacting to challenges (forgive me if I repeat that a few more times throughout the book). We'll talk about assessing our issues in much greater detail in later lessons, but for now, here are a few basic and effective ways to think about your misses. When we miss questions, we do so for one or more of three reasons:

We misunderstand the reasoning structure of the passage

The most significant issues have to do with not recognizing the main points (reading passages very commonly juxtapose two opposing main points about a central issue), and not recognizing the author's opinion about the subject matter. Misunderstanding the reasoning structure of a passage has exactly the same impact that mis-diagramming a Logic Game has: you may just have a small hint that you're doing something wrong as you make your mistake, but the consequences truly reveal themselves at the point of the questions. If you truly understand reasoning structure, most questions will play out as you expect. If you misunderstand it, every question will feel like an uphill battle.

We do not read carefully enough

There is a Catch-22 here. If you try to read the entire passage as carefully as you possibly can, giving each word ample due, chances are you'll do a terrible job of actually understanding what you are reading. Reading is about bringing words together, and you need a certain distance to do that. What you want to do is float like a butterfly and sting like a bee; be a generalist, but zero in on details when it's necessary to do so. One such necessary moment is during the evaluation of answer choices. Their challenge is often in the wording, and often right and wrong answers are differentiated by subtle wording issues.

We approach the question incorrectly

LSAT questions ask very specific things, and require very specific steps from us. Sometimes, we miss questions because we don't think about the answer choices in exactly the right way in relation to the question being asked, and sometimes we miss questions because we don't think about the things we should be thinking about per what we are being asked to do. A question stem is an incredibly useful tool—it generally tells us exactly what we need to look for in an answer, and, if you read carefully enough and know what to look for, it also often tells us how to go about getting that answer. As you become more and more familiar with the exam and the questions, you should expect this last one to become less and less of an issue.

Sample Solution

Here is a solution to the passage and questions you tried earlier. Much of the solution is presented in terms of the real-time thoughts a top scorer might have during an exam.

Real-Time Thoughts

Experts anticipate that global atmospheric concentrations of carbon dioxide (CO_2) will have doubled by the end of the twenty-first century. It is known that CO_2 can contribute to global warming by trapping solar energy that is being reradiated as heat from the Earth's surface. However, some research has suggested that elevated CO_2 levels could enhance the photosynthetic rates of plants, resulting in a lush world of agricultural abundance, and that this CO_2 fertilization effect might eventually decrease the rate of global warming. The increased vegetation in such an environment could be counted on to draw more CO_2 from the atmosphere. The level of CO_2 would thus increase at a lower rate than many experts have predicted.

- background: passage is about consequences of increasing CO_2 levels

- opinion: increased CO_2 could lead to lush green world, which could lead to decreased rate of global warming. This is probably the central issue

However, while a number of recent studies confirm that plant growth would be generally enhanced in an atmosphere rich in CO_2, they also suggest that increased CO_2 would differentially increase the growth rate of different species of plants, which could eventually result in decreased agricultural yields. Certain important crops such as corn and sugarcane that currently have higher photosynthetic efficiencies than other plants may lose that edge in an atmosphere rich in CO_2. Patterson and Flint have shown that these important crops may experience yield reductions because of the increased performance of certain weeds. Such differences in growth rates between plant species could also alter ecosystem stability. Studies have shown that within rangeland regions, for example, a weedy grass grows much better with plentiful CO_2 than do three other grasses. Because this weedy grass predisposes land to burning, its potential increase may lead to greater numbers of and more severe wildfires in future rangeland communities.

- author opinion: CO_2 would impact plants differently, and so wouldn't lead to overall lushness

- support

It is clear that the CO_2 fertilization effect does not guarantee the lush world of agricultural abundance that once seemed likely, but what about the potential for the increased uptake of CO_2 to decrease the rate of global warming? Some studies suggest that the changes accompanying global warming will not improve the ability of terrestrial ecosystems to absorb CO_2. Billings' simulation of global warming conditions in wet tundra grasslands showed that the level of CO_2 actually increased. Plant growth did increase under these conditions because of warmer temperatures and increased CO_2 levels. But as the permafrost melted, more peat (accumulated dead plant material) began to decompose. This process in turn liberated more CO_2 to the atmosphere. Billings estimated that if summer temperatures rose four degrees Celsius, the tundra would liberate 50 percent more CO_2 than it does currently. In a warmer world, increased plant growth, which could absorb CO_2 from the atmosphere, would not compensate for this rapid increase in decomposition rates. This observation is particularly important because high-latitude habitats such as the tundra are expected to experience the greatest temperature increase.

- confirmation of main point from previous paragraph

- CO_2 increase also unlikely to lead to more absorption of CO_2/decrease in global warming

- support

Why Did the Author Write the Passage?

The author wrote this passage to evaluate a specific theory about the consequences of increasing CO_2 levels on global warming: that increased CO_2 could lead to a more lush world, which would lead to more plants that could absorb CO_2, thus lowering the rate of global warming. This theory, and the background necessary to understand it, is presented at the beginning of the passage, and the author spends the rest of the passage presenting points and evidence that are meant to challenge and go against the theory.

How Is the Passage Structured?

In paragraph 1, we are given a general scenario (CO_2 levels are rising, and that is known to cause global warming) and a theory about the scenario (increasing CO_2 will actually lead to lushness, which will lead to a slower rate of global warming).

Paragraph 2 takes issue with one aspect of the theory (lushness), and presents evidence to challenge that idea.

Paragraph 3 takes issue with another aspect of the theory (increased CO_2/decreased rate of global warming) and presents evidence to challenge that idea.

Sample Solution

15. Which one of the following best states the main point of the passage?

(A) Elevated levels of CO_2 would enhance photosynthetic rates, thus increasing plant growth and agricultural yields.
(B) Recent studies have yielded contradictory findings about the benefits of increased levels of CO_2 on agricultural productivity.
(C) The possible beneficial effects of increased levels of CO_2 on plant growth and global warming have been overstated.
(D) Increased levels of CO_2 would enhance the growth rates of certain plants, but would inhibit the growth rates of other plants.
(E) Increased levels of CO_2 would increase plant growth, but the rate of global warming would ultimately increase.

Stem: asking for main point—passage presents theory that increased CO_2 could lead to more lushness, which could lead to slower rate of global warming, then spends majority of text countering that theory.

Answers: You want to always eliminate wrong choices first—(A) is more like the opposite of the main point, so we can cut it. (B) is tempting, but the author does not discuss findings that contradict one another, and (B) does not represent well the *main* point the author is making, so we can cut it. (C) seems like a good answer, so we can leave it. (D) is a part of the passage, but not the main point—cut. (E) goes beyond the text—nowhere does the author state that the rate of global warming is likely to increase. (C) is the only answer remaining—double check it. The theory in the first paragraph is about a possible benefit of increasing CO_2 levels, and the rest of the passage presents information that indicates that the theory may not be correct. (C) is the right answer.

16. The passage suggests that the hypothesis mentioned in the first paragraph is not entirely accurate because it fails to take into account which one of the following in predicting the effects of increased vegetation on the rate of global warming?

(A) Increased levels of CO_2 will increase the photosynthetic rates of many species of plants.
(B) Increased plant growth cannot compensate for increased rates of decomposition caused by warmer temperatures.
(C) Low-latitude habitats will experience the greatest increases in temperature in an atmosphere high in CO_2.
(D) Increased levels of CO_2 will change patterns of plant growth and thus will alter the distribution of peat.
(E) Increases in vegetation can be counted on to draw more CO_2 from the atmosphere.

Stem: asking for a flaw with the theory being challenged—the right answer could be a lot of things, so I should first try to eliminate obvious wrong answers.

Answers: (A) is not something the author states, and we can cut it. (B) looks really good—that's basically what the last paragraph was about. (C) is wrong relative to what the text says, so we can cut that, too. (D) seems attractive—I'll leave it. (E) is what the theory proposes, so it's not something the theory fails to take into account.

Down to (B) and (D). (B) still looks good, but looking at (D) again, it's a bit suspicious—it's not changes in patterns of plant growth that alter "distribution of peat." Rather, the author discusses temperature directly impacting peat. (D) is wrong. The part of the last paragraph starting with "Some studies" and ending with "liberated more CO_2 into the atmosphere" seems to support (B). It's correct.

17. Which one of the following best describes the function of the last paragraph of the passage?

(A) It presents research that may undermine a hypothesis presented in the first paragraph.
(B) It presents solutions for a problem discussed in the first and second paragraphs.
(C) It provides an additional explanation for a phenomenon described in the first paragraph.
(D) It provides experimental data in support of a theory described in the preceding paragraph.
(E) It raises a question that may cast doubt on information presented in the preceding paragraph.

Stem: asking for the function of the last paragraph—we know it's meant to counter the theory in the first paragraph.

Answers: (A) is almost definitely correct. It's what I anticipated—leave it. Take a quick scan though the rest of the choices—(B), (C), (D), and (E) clearly misrepresent the reasoning structure. (A) is correct.

Sample Solution

18. The passage suggests that Patterson and Flint would be most likely to agree with which one of the following statements about increased levels of CO_2 in the Earth's atmosphere?

(A) They will not increase the growth rates of most species of plants.
(B) They will inhibit the growth of most crops, thus causing substantial decreases in agricultural yields.
(C) They are unlikely to increase the growth rates of plants with lower photosynthetic efficiencies.
(D) They will increase the growth rates of certain species of plants more than the growth rates of other species of plants.
(E)They will not affect the photosynthetic rates of plants that currently have the highest photosynthetic efficiencies.

Stem: asking about what Patterson and Flint would agree with (they are mentioned in the second paragraph)—showed that important crops may show reductions because of weeds.

Answers: "Most species of plants" in (A) goes well beyond what they discussed—cut. "Most" in (B) helps us cut that too. (C) doesn't match text (which is about highly photosynthetic plants having trouble) too well—cut. (D) is easy to match with text, and almost definitely correct—leave. (E) clearly goes against the text—cut.

(D) seems to be correct—check it again. Weeds growing faster than corn—yup. They would agree with (D), and it's correct.

19. The author would be most likely to agree with which one of the following statements about the conclusions drawn on the basis of the research on plant growth mentioned in the first paragraph of the passage?

(A) The conclusions are correct in suggesting that increased levels of CO_2 will increase the photosynthetic rates of certain plants.
(B) The conclusions are correct in suggesting that increased levels of CO_2 will guarantee abundances of certain important crops.
(C) The conclusions are correct in suggesting that increased plant growth will reverse the process of global warming.
(D) The conclusions are incorrect in suggesting that enhanced plant growth could lead to abundances of certain species of plants.
(E) The conclusions are incorrect in suggesting that vegetation can draw CO_2 from the atmosphere.

Stem: I know that most of the passage is about why the author *questions* the conclusion reached. Let's see what I can do with these answers.

Answers: (A) is something the author does agree with—it will certainly help rates of certain plants. Leave it. (B) is clearly wrong—"abundance of important crops" goes against the stuff about corn. (C) goes against big point the author is making, so we can cut it. (D) is not correct either—the author does think it will lead to abundance of *certain* plants. Cut. (E) is just silly—of course the author believes the theory is correct in this regard.

(A) is the only decent answer. Let me confirm with the text—yup. Text says that certain crops with higher photosynthetic efficiencies may lose their edge (meaning others plants will increase their photosynthetic rates and catch up). (A) is correct.

20. The passage supports which one of the following statements about peat in wet tundra grasslands?

(A) More of it would decompose if temperatures rose four degrees Celsius.
(B) It could help absorb CO_2 from the atmosphere if temperatures rose four degrees Celsius.
(C) It will not decompose unless temperatures rise four degrees Celsius.
(D) It decomposes more quickly than peat found in regions at lower latitudes.
(E) More of it accumulates in regions at lower latitudes.

Stem: I know that the peat grew at a lot faster rate with higher temperature, and more peat = more CO_2.

Answers: (A) seems to match the text well—leave it. (B) doesn't match what the text says about the peat—cut. (C) also doesn't match text—temperature only impacts *rate* of decomposition. (D) goes beyond text and is too general a blanket statement (*all* regions at lower latitudes?)—cut. (E) doesn't match text at all.

(A) is the only attractive answer—let me confirm. Text says increase in temperature leads to increase in peat, so it definitely supports (A). (A) is correct.

Sample Solution

21. Which one of the following, if true, is LEAST consistent with the hypothesis mentioned in lines 22-25 *(sentence starting "Certain important crops" in paragraph two)* of the passage?

(A) The roots of certain tree species grow more rapidly when the amount of CO_2 in the atmosphere increases, thus permitting the trees to expand into habitats formerly dominated by grasses with high photosynthetic efficiencies.
(B) When grown in an atmosphere high in CO_2 certain weeds with low photosynthetic efficiencies begin to thrive in cultivated farmlands formerly dominated by agricultural crops.
(C) When trees of a species with a high photosynthetic efficiency and grasses of a species with a low photosynthetic efficiency were placed in an atmosphere high in CO_2, the trees grew more quickly than the grasses.
(D) When two different species of grass with equivalent photosynthetic efficiency were placed in an atmosphere high in CO_2, one species grew much more rapidly and crowded the slower-growing species out of the growing area.
(E) The number of leguminous plants decreased in an atmosphere rich in CO_2, thus diminishing soil fertility and limiting the types of plant species that could thrive in certain habitats.

Stem: asking about something that goes against hypothesis that with more CO_2, crops with higher photosynthetic efficiencies will lose edge to those with lower efficiencies.

Answers: (A) is tempting, but not clear if trees also had high photosynthetic properties—cut. (B) also is missing high vs. low factor—cut. (C) definitely goes against the theory—it's probably correct. (D) and (E) are both missing the high vs. low factor. (C) is correct, for it shows high beating low in an environment rich in CO_2.

22. According to the passage, Billings' research addresses which one of the following questions?

(A) Which kind of habitat will experience the greatest temperature increase in an atmosphere high in CO_2?
(B) How much will summer temperatures rise if levels of CO_2 double by the end of the twenty-first century?
(C) Will enhanced plant growth necessarily decrease the rate of global warming that has been predicted by experts?
(D) Would plant growth be differentially enhanced if atmospheric concentrations of CO_2 were to double by the end of the twenty-first century?
(E) Does peat decompose more rapidly in wet tundra grasslands than it does in other types of habitats when atmospheric concentrations of CO_2 increase?

Stem: asking about Billings—looking back, in Billings' study, global warming led to increased plant growth in wet tundra grasslands, but increased CO_2 because of increase in decomposition of peat.

Answers: Billings doesn't compare areas, so (A) is out. (B) is too specific—cut. Not sure if his study addresses (C) exactly, but it's tempting—leave it. (D) is also tempting, I guess—leave it. He doesn't compare areas, so (E) is out.

I don't love any answer, but I'm down to (C) and (D). Checking (C) against the text, it does seem to match it pretty well—the plants are growing more, but there is also more CO_2 (which the text tells us leads to global warming). Looking at (D) again, it's just too specific—doubling seems pretty drastic, and his research is about what happens to plant growth with warmer temperatures, not with increased CO_2. (D) is definitely incorrect, and so (C) is correct.

The Road Map to Mastery

Even if you are in terrific physical shape, if you are used to just doing a few particular activities, you will often find that when you switch activities—learning a new sport for example—you'll end up using certain muscles you've been unknowingly neglecting, or you'll end up using the same muscles you've used before but in a slightly different way. You'll realize you are "in shape" for certain activities but not others, and as a result, you'll wake up feeling sore the next day.

Most of us are in pretty good reading shape. However, LSAT reading requires more from us, and it requires us to exercise our mental muscles in relatively unique ways. None of us, at first, are in optimal "shape" to read the LSAT. Through practice and drilling, you can drastically improve your reading shape as it pertains to this exam.

How are we going to get there? Our Reading Comprehension training plan is going to take us through three main phases:

Phase one: We'll learn how to read LSAT passages.

As we mentioned before, the Reading Comprehension on the LSAT is unique, and if you approach it without much of a strategy, or if you approach it with a general understanding of what it is that they are testing, you simply will not be able to represent your abilities at their best. Reading the passage in the right way is the most important aspect of your Reading Comprehension success.

details, details

basic facts about reading comprehension

One of your four scored sections will be a Reading Comprehension section.

Each Reading Comprehension section contains four passages, along with six to eight questions per passage.

Your Reading Comprehension section will most likely contain 27 questions.

Each full section contains one passage on each of the following subjects: law, science, history, and the humanities.

The subjects are chosen to not give an unfair advantage to any particular group. The subjects will either be arcane (e.g., Willa Cather) or very general (e.g., weather patterns).

Questions will be asked about the passage as a whole and about particular paragraphs, sentences, phrases, or individual words.

Questions will test your understanding of why the author wrote the passage, and they will test your ability to recognize and understand the correct meaning of specific components.

The reading ability most tested and most important is your ability to read for reasoning structure. Questions will test that you understand the structure of the passage as a whole, and they will test whether you correctly understand the roles specific components play.

As with the other sections, our job is never to choose between two viable answers. There is always one absolutely right answer and four absolutely wrong answers.

All questions require careful reading. Wrong answers are often wrong because of subtle wording issues. Most questions require very little extrapolation, and most right answers are directly related to the given text.

In general, the first passage will be the easiest passage, but this will not always be true.

The Reading Comprehension section is very carefully designed to test particular skills in particular ways. It's very clear exactly what they are testing, and what they are not. In this phase, we will focus on developing a clear understanding of exactly how LSAT Reading Comprehension is designed, and we'll work on developing reading strategies that align with LSAT passages and questions. We'll practice all of this while working through real LSAT passages.

Phase two: We'll develop question-specific strategies.

Once you feel comfortable with the basic structure of LSAT passages, and once you have a base of understanding in terms of what this section is designed to test, we will delve into question-specific strategies. We'll discuss each of the different types of questions that you can encounter, work through what you can expect in the right answer and four wrong choices, and of course give you plenty of practice to help facilitate the natural flow between your learning, strategies, and experience.

We will learn how to read passages, develop question-specific approaches, and set effective habits

Phase three: We'll work to set final habits.

In this last phase, we will work to ensure that everything we have learned, and all of the strategies we've derived, can be seamlessly integrated into your performance. Focusing primarily on practicing and reviewing real LSAT passages, we'll make sure you are ready to go into the exam with a specific skill set that aligns with the exam, and that you go into the exam in awesome reading shape.

Recap of Lessons One through Four

Here is a quick summary of some of the main points that we have discussed in these first four lessons:

The LSAT is a test of reading ability and reasoning ability. It is also a test of mental discipline. The Logical Reasoning section tests both reading and reasoning ability, most commonly by testing your ability to understand and critique *arguments*. The Logic Games section primarily tests your ability to reason, and the Reading Comprehension section, as we've been discussing, is primarily designed to test specific aspects of your reading ability.

Success on the LSAT is most directly dependent on two factors: your skills and your habits. Therefore, the primary purpose of your training should be to develop skills and effective habits. We do so by increasing our understanding, by developing effective strategies, and by gaining more experience with the exam. Our skills and habits grow most quickly and effectively when these three components—understanding, strategies, and experience—influence one another. The *Trainer* is designed to help you first develop the skills and habits that are most *fundamentally* important for success on the exam. From there, we will work to carefully grow our skill set and habits until we've addressed every specific aspect of the exam.

The Road Ahead

If you are following one of the suggested study schedules, the next step for you will be to take a full-length diagnostic. This will give you a good sense of what the questions feel like in real time, and it will, of course, also give you a good sense of what your initial strengths and weaknesses are.

Starting from the next lesson, we are going to focus for several lessons at a time on one section type at a time, so that we can get fully immersed. In time, we will gradually cycle through multiple sets of lessons on Logical Reasoning, Logic Games, and Reading Comprehension lessons.

Here's a look ahead at the next few sets:

Lessons 5 through 9 are going to be our first set of Logical Reasoning lessons. We will use these lessons to develop our ability to understand and critique arguments.

Lessons 10 through 15 will get us immersed into Logic Games preparation. We will use these lessons to lay out all the various possibilities for Logic Games and to develop our ability to diagram any and all such scenarios.

Then, for Lessons 16 through 20, we will go back to Logical Reasoning, and we'll start to discuss more specifically how to apply our assessment of the stimulus to the various tasks that different types of questions present. We'll have our first set of in-depth Reading Comprehension lessons after that.

5 LOGICAL REASONING flaws

There are many skills that are necessary for success on the Logical Reasoning sections, but there is one particular skill that is of far more importance than all others: the key to Logical Reasoning success is your ability to see what is wrong with arguments. If you are consistently able to do this, questions will become easier—stimuli that seemed impossibly convoluted before will become far simpler to understand and organize, incorrect answers will seem much more obviously so, and correct answers will be far more predictable across a broad spectrum of question types.

The key to Logical Reasoning success is your ability to see what is wrong with arguments

The majority of questions that appear in the Logical Reasoning section require you to be critical of the reasoning relationship between a conclusion reached and the reasoning given for that conclusion. If, in some of these situations, the reasoning did just happen to justify the conclusion, this would be a far different exam, and many of the strategies that appear in the following lessons would be completely different. However, this is not the case. Every single time a question requires that you evaluate reasoning critically, the support given will not justify the point made. In every single one of these situations, your ability to see as clearly as possible why the support doesn't justify the conclusion will be fundamental to the task the question presents.

Furthermore, it just so happens that developing your ability to evaluate critically will make you better at answering questions that have nothing to do with critically evaluating arguments—that minority of questions that require us to be non-judgemental. Reading for reasoning flaws helps you develop certain habits—such as organizing stimuli in terms of argument structure—that naturally align with many of those other questions.

So, as we said before, the key to Logical Reasoning success is your ability to see what is wrong with arguments. That's what we're going to work on now, and that's what we're going to get really, really good at first. Let's start with some basics.

Know Where to Look for the Flaw

Imagine you saw the following argument on the LSAT: "Ghosts can only be seen by those with kind hearts. Mother Teresa is revered as a person of great kindness. However, she never saw a ghost in her entire life. Therefore, she does not have a kind heart."

Reasoning flaws exist *between* the support and the conclusion

Terrible argument, I know. But why, exactly? If you heard it in real life, you could come up with a lot of reasons why it is flawed, I'm sure. However, it's important for you to know that, in terms of the LSAT, not all flaws are important. The LSAT is only interested in a certain type of flaw—a flaw in the relationship between the conclusion reached and the support used.

Perhaps you disagree with the idea that Mother Teresa has no kindness, and perhaps you know of other examples from her life that justify a different conclusion. However, the flaw that you see in the conclusion has nothing to do with reasoning. It's simply an opinion that you happen to disagree with.

Perhaps you disagree with the idea that ghosts can only be seen by those who have kind hearts. Maybe you don't believe that ghosts are real. But there is no reasoning in this statement. The flaw you see is again simply based on your opinion of the premise.

The LSAT is not a test of opinions. When we encounter an argument on the LSAT, our job is not to evaluate the truth of the conclusion, nor is it to evaluate the truth of the support. Our job is to focus in on one specific arena—the use of that support to justify that conclusion. If we take the support to be true, is it enough, by itself, to absolutely prove the main point?

If we take it to be true that ghosts can only be seen by those with kind hearts, does this absolutely prove that Mother Teresa did not have kindness? No, it doesn't. Why not? Because we only know that ghosts *can* only be seen by those with kindness—this does not tell us that everyone with kindness must have seen at least one ghost. Maybe Mother Teresa does have a kind heart, but she simply never had an opportunity to see a ghost. This is what is wrong with the reasoning of the argument.

---

opinions vs. flaws of reasoning

"Harry Potter is the most popular book series of our time. Therefore, it's the one book series from our era that will most likely be read by future generations."

You may *disagree* with the idea that Harry Potter is the most popular series of our time...
You may *disagree* with the idea that it will be the series most likely read by future generations...

But the *reasoning flaw* has to do with the use of that support to justify the conclusion:

Just because it's popular now doesn't mean that future generations will read it.

Mindset Is *Critical*

We are all experts at evaluating arguments—we hear people (and advertisements) make arguments all day, every day. And whether we are aware of it or not, when we evaluate these arguments, we always do so with a little bit of bias. The word "bias" has many negative connotations, but it's a natural human instinct, and it's a part of our intelligence. When Stephen King makes an argument about how to write a good horror story, you tend to believe it more than you might if your struggling writer neighbor who seems not so bright says exactly the same thing.

In terms of the LSAT, the aspect of our bias that is most important is our natural instinct to either try to go along with an argument, or to be critical of it. It is to your great advantage to think about Logical Reasoning questions from the latter of those perspectives. You don't want to think about arguments in terms of "How could it be that this conclusion is valid?" and you don't think about them in terms of "Does this support validate the conclusion?" In every instance it won't. And in every instance your focus needs to be "Why doesn't the support justify the point?" We'll do a lot of work together in this book to ensure that by test day this is habit. Every time you are asked to be critical of an argument, you want to think to yourself:

We always want to think about why the support *doesn't* validate the conclusion

1) What's the point?

2) How's it supported?

3) What's wrong with that?

Our goal is ambitious: you are going to get to the point where, for nearly all questions that require subjectivity, you will be able to intuitively, without a lot of forceful or conscious action, come up with a clear understanding of exactly what is wrong with the argument. And mindset is going to be a huge part of it.

mindset determines reaction

Receptive

Imagine: You need a new doctor, and so you ask for a suggestion from a friend of yours, who is a nurse who works with lots of different doctors. She suggests Dr. Anderson, and gives reasons to support her choice. The reasons are quoted to the side.

Your reaction: You wouldn't have asked your friend if you didn't trust her advice, and those seem like very good qualifications—exactly the things you were looking for in a doctor. You decide to go with the suggestion.

Critical

Imagine: Dr. Anderson just botched your routine procedure, and now your body is a mess. And, sure, he sat with you afterward to explain what he did wrong, and he seemed sorry about it, but in talking to him you realized he's a total fool. You're up late one night, and you hear this quote on the side in a commercial for Dr. Anderson.

Your reaction: A great doctor is one who helps keep you healthy. None of those characteristics mean that he is a great doctor.

"Dr. Anderson went to a top medical school, and has years of experience. Plus, he genuinely cares about his patients, and will take the time to answer all of your questions. He is a great doctor."

The LSAT rewards a critical mindset.

A True Understanding Is a Conceptual One

I want you to get warm and fuzzy for just a minute. I want you to think about someone you really, really love. Imagine writing down how much you love that person and why.

Do you think you can accurately represent what you feel and why? To the point that the person reading what you wrote could understand exactly how you feel? No, not even if you are the greatest writer in the world. It simply has to do with the fact that words are far more limited and black and white than is our true understanding of things.

If you really know what's wrong with an argument, you should be able to describe the flaw in a variety of ways

When we face tough questions and especially when we feel time pressure, many of us feel the temptation to tell ourselves that we know more than we do—in the case of arguments, that we know the flaw, when in fact we don't. This temptation is understandable—after all, we know deep down that knowing the flaw equals getting correct answers. When we want to fool ourselves, we often do so using words. We'll tell ourselves that a flaw fits a certain catch-phrase, such as "Oh, it's an 'unless' issue" or "That's a sufficient/necessary issue," and think that being able to give a name to a flaw is the same as knowing it. But as we have talked about, knowing something and knowing some phrases to describe it are two different things.

So, don't let yourself off the hook with a catch-phrase for the issue. If you know an issue well, you should be able to describe it in different ways. Furthermore, it's very common for right answers to have the substance you expect, but in a form that is unexpected or difficult to understand. That is, they will represent the flaw that you saw, but from an unexpected angle, or by using unexpected (often unnecessarily complicated) language. A more flexible and conceptual understanding will help you adapt to these types of answers better.

different words / same flaw

"The last two Sundays, I've worn my team's jersey to watch the game, and they have won. It's definitely because I've worn the jersey."

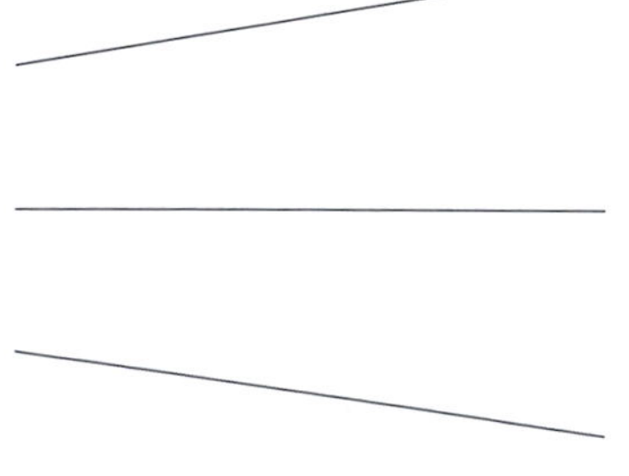

Fails to consider that the connection between the jersey and the wins could just be a coincidence.

Takes for granted that there is a direct relationship between what he chooses to wear and how the team performs.

Falsely assumes that a correlation between wearing the jersey and team victories is sufficient to validate a causal relationship between the two.

Two Mantras for Finding Flaws

Two phrases epitomize the common faults in Logical Reasoning arguments: "The author fails to consider that..." and "The author takes for granted that..."

Nearly every single flaw that appears in an LSAT argument can be thought of in one or both of these ways; in fact, this is the way that the test writers think about flaws. You'll see that a great many answer choices are written using these very words.

Put yourself in the mind of the person making the flawed argument. This person thinks that the reasons she gives are enough to validate the conclusion that she reaches. But they are not. You know for sure that they are not. What is she doing wrong?

We'll talk more specifically about this in the following lessons, but, in general, she's forgetting to think about something she needs to think about (fails to consider) or she's assuming some sort of connection that doesn't actually exist (takes for granted).

You want to get in the habit of having these two phrases run through your head as you read and think about arguments, for they can help you pay attention to, and see better, exactly what the problem is with the way an argument is presented and justified.

Your Logical Reasoning mantras:

"The author fails to consider that..."

&

"The author takes for granted that..."

Instructions for the drill starting on the following page:

On the following pages is a set of drills meant to help you get into a critical mindset. In each case, a scenario is presented and then various arguments are made. There are spaces underneath these arguments, and you are meant to write in what is wrong with the argument. You may prefer just to think about and not write in the flaw, especially when it is obvious, but do keep in mind that these exercises are in large part designed to help you develop habits, and writing down what you think is wrong is really good for you. The phrases "The author fails to consider..." and "The author takes for granted..." have been provided for you underneath the arguments. If you want to practice seeing argument flaws in terms of one phrase or the other, you can go ahead and circle the phrase you would start with, then write in the rest.

Keep in mind that you definitely don't have to think about every flaw in one of these two ways (per the comments on the opposite page), and sometimes it'll make sense for you to word the flaw differently. Check your versions against the solutions after each set. Note that the four sets will increase in difficulty.

Flaw Drill

Scenario one: You are a parent, and the arguments are made by your precocious five-year-old daughter.

Since Billie got a cookie, I should get a cookie.

fails to consider / takes for granted

Candy is healthy because it contains vitamin C, which is good for us.

fails to consider / takes for granted

There is no evidence that the Loch Ness monster is not real. So it probably exists.

fails to consider / takes for granted

Of course *Tangled* is the best movie ever. All of my friends agree.

fails to consider / takes for granted

Last night, I saw a TV show about a Siamese cat that was taught to jump off a diving board. Since our cat Millie is a Siamese cat, I bet we can train her to jump off a diving board.

fails to consider / takes for granted

Did you know Ted is older than Grandma? He must be really old!

fails to consider / takes for granted

Scenario two: You are a teenage girl, and the arguments are made by your very conservative parents.

You should go out with him! He's very smart.

fails to consider / takes for granted

Since it won't help with your homework, you shouldn't watch television.

fails to consider / takes for granted

You can't wear that shirt. It shows your belly button.

fails to consider / takes for granted

This shirt is less formal than my other shirts. So this is my hip shirt.

fails to consider / takes for granted

You can't get a tattoo. Your aunt Barbara got a tattoo, and she is in jail.

fails to consider / takes for granted

You can't stay out after ten. When I was a kid, no one stayed out after ten.

fails to consider / takes for granted

Flaw Drill

Scenario three: You hear the following arguments on the news...

Recent reports that the mayor received illegal campaign contributions seem to be false. It's just been uncovered that a disgruntled former employee has been leaking the stories to the press because of a personal issue with the mayor.

fails to consider / takes for granted

Ironically, in our current general economic state, individuals need to spend more money in order for our general economy to improve. So, go out and spend, spend, spend! It's good for our country.

fails to consider / takes for granted

For the last twenty years, we have consistently enacted systems that have lowered the percentage of income the government collects as tax while also increasing government spending. If we continue to act as we have for the past twenty years, we will continue to increase the amount of debt our nation incurs.

fails to consider / takes for granted

We live under the assumption that the United States is the wealthiest of all nations, but this is not true. Qatar, an Arab country located in Western Asia, has a higher per capita income.

fails to consider / takes for granted

LeBron James is now the most recognized athlete in the world. A recent poll by *Sports Illustrated* showed that he is by far the most recognized athlete amongst its readers.

fails to consider / takes for granted

As everyone knows, consuming a moderate amount of wine can be part of a healthy diet. Wine contains antioxidants, which have been proved to support good health.

fails to consider / takes for granted

Scenario four: Can you disprove the absolute validity of arguments you may agree with in real life?

Objective journalism is a required component of a well-working democracy. However, we live in an age in which the vast majority of our news is delivered with a great deal of bias and affiliation toward one political ideology or another. If we are to have a well-working democracy, government and media corporations must act to restore more objectivity to news media.

fails to consider / takes for granted

Turns out that chimps are not the smartest of all non-human mammals after all. Recently, it was shown that whales are able to compose and communicate with songs that rival and often surpass songs that humans are capable of composing in terms of complexity and aesthetic elegance.

fails to consider / takes for granted

Underlying much of the violence that exists in the world today are differences of opinion about the true nature of God and religion. It is extremely unlikely that we will get proof, in our lifetime, that one religion is definitely correct, or one religion is definitely incorrect, and without such proof, these differences will invariably exist. Therefore, it is to the general benefit of humanity to promote tolerance towards different religious views.

fails to consider / takes for granted

For certain careers, the graduate school that you choose to attend has little impact on future career success. Not so for the legal profession. Lawyers who attend top law programs consistently earn the highest salaries, and all members of the Supreme Court went to either Harvard or Yale.

fails to consider / takes for granted

Creationism is an idea whose leading proponents are politicians and religious figures. Not a single reputable, well-respected scientist has come out in support of Creationism as a valid scientific theory. Therefore, Creationism is not a legitimate scientific theory.

fails to consider / takes for granted

Good intentions line the histories of many of our most environmentally harmful products. For example, plastic was invented, at least in part, to combat the wasting of wood and paper products. This proves that good intentions, coupled with limited foresight, can cause negative consequences for our environment.

fails to consider / takes for granted

Flaw Drill Solutions

Scenario one: You are a parent, and the arguments are made by your precocious five-year-old daughter.

Since Billie got a cookie, I should get a cookie.

Takes for granted that she should get a cookie just because Billie did. It could be that Billie did something special to get the cookie, or it could be that the five-year-old can't eat the cookies in question for health reasons.

Candy is healthy because it contains vitamin C, which is good for us.

Fails to consider that the other components of candy may make it so that candy is, overall, not good for us. It could be that something else in candy, like sugar, makes it not so healthy.

There is no evidence that the Loch Ness monster is not real. So it probably exists.

Takes for granted that since it has not been disproved, it must be real. It could be true that there is also no proof it does exist.

Of course *Tangled* is the best movie ever. All of my friends agree.

Takes for granted that her friends' tastes present an accurate representation of the quality of movies. Perhaps *Tangled* is a movie that appeals a certain way to a certain age group, but is not, overall, the best movie ever.

Last night, I saw a TV show about a Siamese cat that was taught to jump off a diving board. Since our cat Millie is a Siamese cat, I bet we can train her to jump off a diving board.

Fails to consider that other characteristics could differentiate Millie from the cat on the TV. Perhaps the cat on the TV has a world-class trainer and has been working at the skill since birth.

Did you know Ted is older than Grandma? He must be really old!

Takes for granted that being older than Grandma guarantees that one is old. Perhaps Grandma is in her thirties.

Scenario two: You are a teenage girl, and the arguments are made by your very conservative parents.

You should go out with him! He's very smart.

Fails to consider that being smart may not be the characteristic that defines who you should date. Perhaps he's also a jerk. Or maybe you prefer dating dumb people, and you should date who you want to date.

Since it won't help with your homework, you shouldn't watch television.

Takes for granted that one shouldn't do something unless it helps with homework. Perhaps there are other reasons to watch television.

You can't wear that shirt. It shows your belly button.

Takes for granted that you can't wear shirts that show your belly button. Maybe you are wearing the shirt *because* it shows your belly button.

This shirt is less formal than my other shirts. So this is my hip shirt.

Takes for granted that being less formal than other shirts makes one shirt hip. Perhaps none of the shirts are hip, or perhaps it's hip to be formal.

You can't get a tattoo. Your aunt Barbara got a tattoo, and she is in jail.

Takes for granted that getting a tattoo had an impact on Barbara going to jail, and takes for granted that Barbara's case is relevant to yours. Perhaps your aunt Barbara is a violent loon.

You can't stay out after ten. When I was a kid, no one stayed out after ten.

Takes for granted that what applied to the parent when he or she was a kid applies to the teenager now. It could be that what was the norm then isn't the norm now. Also, just because others don't do it doesn't mean you can't.

Flaw Drill Solutions

Scenario three: You hear the following arguments on the news...

Recent reports that the mayor received illegal campaign contributions seem to be false. It's just been uncovered that a disgruntled former employee has been leaking the stories to the press because of a personal issue with the mayor.

Fails to consider that even if a disgruntled employee leaked the stories, the mayor could have received illegal contributions. Whether the employee was disgruntled or not doesn't affect whether the stories are true.

Ironically, in our current general economic state, individuals need to spend more money in order for our general economy to improve. So, go out and spend, spend, spend! It's good for our country.

Takes for granted that what is good for our general economy is what is good for our country. Perhaps there are other, more significant considerations that determine what is good for our country.

For the last twenty years, we have consistently enacted systems that have lowered the percentage of income that government collects as tax while also increasing government spending. If we continue to act as we have for the past twenty years, we will continue to increase the amount of debt our nation incurs.

Takes for granted that a lower percentage tax and increased spending must equate to an increase in debt. Perhaps the economy will grow at a rate that offsets, or more than offsets, such changes.

We live under the assumption that the United States is the wealthiest of all nations, but this is not true. Qatar, an Arab country located in Western Asia, has a higher per-capita income.

Takes for granted that per-capita income is enough to make a determination about the wealth of a nation. Perhaps other factors, such as gross domestic revenue, are more important when considering the wealth of a nation as a whole.

LeBron James is now the most recognized athlete in the world. A recent poll by *Sports Illustrated* showed that he is by far the most recognized athlete amongst its readers.

Takes for granted that a poll of *Sports Illustrated* readers is representative of the entire world population. Perhaps people who don't read *Sports Illustrated* happen to recognize another athlete more.

As everyone knows, consuming a moderate amount of wine can be part of a healthy diet. Wine contains antioxidants, which have been proved to support good health.

Fails to consider that there are other aspects that could make drinking a moderate amount of wine unhealthy overall. Perhaps wine has an ingredient that does far more harm than antioxidants do good.

Scenario four: Can you disprove the absolute validity of arguments you may agree with in real life?

Objective journalism is a required component of a well-working democracy. However, we live in an age in which the vast majority of our news is delivered with a great deal of bias and affiliation toward one political ideology or another. If we are to have a well-working democracy, government and media corporations must act to restore more objectivity to news media.

Takes for granted that government and media corporations must do the work of restoring more objectivity to news media. Perhaps some other entity, such as a blogger, could do the work.

Turns out that chimps are not the smartest of all non-human mammals after all. Recently, it was shown that whales are able to compose and communicate with songs that rival and often surpass songs that humans are capable of composing in terms of complexity and aesthetic elegance.

Takes for granted that the ability to compose and communicate with songs is accurately representative of overall intelligence. Perhaps there are other reasons why chimps are smarter than whales.

Underlying much of the violence that exists in the world today are differences of opinion about the true nature of God and religion. It is extremely unlikely that we will get proof, in our lifetime, that one religion is definitely correct, or one religion is definitely incorrect, and without such proof, these differences will invariably exist. Therefore, it is to the general benefit of humanity to promote tolerance towards different religious views.

Takes for granted that tolerance will lead to a decrease in violence, and that a decrease in violence is for the general benefit of mankind. Perhaps general tolerance inflames certain violent tendencies, or perhaps for some crazy reason, violence is part of a "healthy" humanity.

For certain careers, the graduate school that you choose to attend has little impact on future career success. Not so for the legal profession. Lawyers who attend top law programs consistently earn the highest salaries, and all members of the Supreme Court went to either Harvard or Yale.

Takes for granted that the school has a direct impact on future career success. It could be that they are simply correlated; perhaps some other factor, such as personal drive, causes certain people to get accepted into certain schools and to have success in their careers.

Creationism is an idea whose leading proponents are politicians and religious figures. Not a single reputable, well-respected scientist has come out in support of Creationism as a valid scientific theory. Therefore, Creationism is not a legitimate scientific theory.

Takes for granted that the opinion of the scientific community is accurately representative of what is a legitimate scientific theory. Darwin and Galileo were both initially dismissed by the scientific community at large.

Good intentions line the histories of many of our most environmentally harmful products. For example, plastic was invented, at least in part, to combat the wasting of wood and paper products. This proves that good intentions, coupled with limited foresight, can cause negative consequences for our environment.

Takes for granted that good intentions had a hand in causing these negative consequences. It could be that, even though these items were made with good intentions, what caused them to be harmful was just poor foresight or some other factor.

How Did You Do?

Maybe you found all four sets to be very simple. Maybe you are sitting there wondering why the answers you came up with are totally different from the ones in the solutions. In either case, the most important thing is that you begin to develop certain habits when it comes to thinking about arguments. Namely, that you evaluate them in terms of how the supporting premises are being used to justify the conclusion, and that you do so with a mindset of trying to figure out exactly why the support does not justify the conclusion reached.

In large part, real LSAT arguments will feel harder because the test writers make it difficult for us to recognize the argument and see it clearly

How Does This Work Translate to the LSAT?

LSAT arguments will have flaws that are as clear and significant as the flaws in the simple arguments we discussed in this lesson. However, the hardest LSAT arguments are significantly harder to evaluate than were most of the arguments we practiced here. In large part, LSAT arguments are much harder because the test writers make it a challenge for you to see and understand the argument clearly. They do this in a few different ways:

(1) They will hide the argument within a lot of clutter. Notice that one of the reasons that scenario four was a bit more difficult than one and two was that you simply had more information to process. The LSAT writers will commonly form this clutter by giving us bountiful background information or information that may be used against the argument. This information can be important for understanding context but will not be directly relevant to the reasoning issues in the argument.

(2) They will separate out the conclusion and the support from one another. In addition, also expect that the support will sometimes come split in separate pieces, and that the conclusion will sometimes come split in separate pieces.[1]

(3) They will speak with a tone of authority on subjects about which you are unfamiliar. When we see material written in an "expert" tone, and when we are not ourselves experts in the field, we are often more susceptible to simply accepting the reasoning that we are given.

There is plenty of time to become great at cutting through the extraneous challenges the test writers present, and when you are able to do so, you will see that a majority of questions hinge on your obtaining a simple understanding of why the support given doesn't validate the conclusion reached. Habit and mindset are key. Let's take a look at two full questions that illustrate how the process might play out during the course of the exam. I suggest you try solving the questions on your own before looking at their respective solutions.

1. Consider these two different ways of writing the same main point:

There has been no credible evidence produced by anyone in the world that vampires actually exist. *Therefore, vampires do not exist.*

Shelley thinks vampires exist. However, there has been no credible evidence produced by anyone in the world that actually shows that. *Therefore, she is wrong.*

Note that it's the same point, but the second form just makes it a bit harder for us to identify the point, and a bit harder to retain it in our minds throughout the rest of the problem-solving process.

the process in action

On this page and the next are two examples that illustrate how the ability to recognize the flaw fits into the greater problem-solving process.

Navigation in animals is defined as the animal's ability to find its way from unfamiliar territory to points familiar to the animal but beyond the immediate range of the animal's senses. Some naturalists claim that polar bears can navigate over considerable distances. As evidence, they cite an instance of a polar bear that returned to its home territory after being released over 500 kilometers (300 miles) away.

Which one of the following, if true, casts the most doubt on the validity of the evidence offered in support of the naturalists' claim?

(A) The polar bear stopped and changed course several times as it moved toward its home territory.
(B) The site at which the polar bear was released was on the bear's annual migration route.
(C) The route along which the polar bear traveled consisted primarily of snow and drifting ice.
(D) Polar bears are only one of many species of mammal whose members have been known to find their way home from considerable distances.
(E) Polar bears often rely on their extreme sensitivity to smell in order to scent out familiar territory.

Practice Test 32, Section 1, Question 12

ONE: UNDERSTAND THE JOB

I recommend that you begin every problem by reading the question stem. The question stem will give you a clear sense of what you need to accomplish as you read the stimulus. Here, we need to select an answer that most strongly indicates a problem with the evidence used to justify the point. This answer will invariably exploit the flaw in the relationship between the conclusion and its support, and correctly recognizing that flaw will be the key to our success.

TWO: UNDERSTAND THE ARGUMENT

We need to isolate the main point and its support from the rest of the stimulus, and we need to make sure that we completely and correctly understand the point made, the support being used, and the manner in which the support is meant to justify the point.

The point in question is the naturalists' claim: polar bears can navigate over considerable distances. We are given a very specific definition of navigation in the background information: an animal's ability to find its way from unfamiliar areas to areas it knows, with the areas being outside the animal's sensory range. The evidence used is that of a polar bear that found its way home from 300 miles away.

Argument: A polar bear got home from 300 miles away, so it must be true that polar bears can navigate over considerable distances.

THREE: FIND WHAT'S WRONG

To us, 300 miles seems a long distance to walk, but keep in mind that we've been given a very specific definition of navigation, we have a conclusion about navigation, and **we don't actually know that, for a polar bear, this journey requires navigation.** We don't know that this trip was in territory that was unfamiliar for the bear, and we don't know if 300 miles is beyond a bear's sensory range.

With a clear sense of what is wrong with the conclusion-support relationship, we can head into the answer choices.

FOUR: FINISH THE JOB

Our job is to look for an answer that makes us doubt the use of this evidence to justify this point. The right answer should relate to the fact that the evidence doesn't prove that the bear was in unfamiliar territory or beyond sensory range.

For all Logical Reasoning questions, we want to first work to eliminate answers we know to be incorrect, then confirm the answer we think is best. (A) may be a sign that the navigation skills are not perfect, but it does not play an absolute role in relation to the conclusion-support relationship (perhaps stopping and changing course is part of the bear's strategy). In any case, since it doesn't weaken the idea that the polar bears can navigate, we can eliminate (A). (B) represents a clear problem with the support-conclusion relationship—if the bear was familiar with the route, it did not have to use navigation skills. Let's leave (B). It's unclear how snow and ice relate to the reasoning in the argument, so we can eliminate (C) easily. The fact that polar bears are one of many animals that travel long distances to find home neither helps nor hurts the argument, so we can eliminate (D). (E) relates to an issue we saw in the argument—we weren't sure it hadn't used its senses over the 300 miles—but it does not directly impact the support-conclusion relationship, for it doesn't give us any actual information about whether the polar bear in the example used its senses to find its way home. That leaves only (B), and (B) is the correct answer.

the process in action

Studies have shown that photosynthesis, the process by which plants manufacture life-sustaining proteins from sunlight and carbon, is actually intensified if the level of carbon dioxide in the atmosphere is increased. Since carbon dioxide levels are increased by the burning of fossil fuels and by other human industrial activities, it is obvious that these industrial activities are purely beneficial to agriculture and those of us who depend upon it.

The flawed reasoning in the argument above is most similar to that in which one of the following?

(A) Because a high fiber diet has been shown to be more healthful than a low fiber diet, a diet in which foods with a low fiber content have been entirely replaced by foods with a high fiber content is bound to be even more healthful.
(B) Because exercise has been shown to prevent a number of diseases, injuries, and other human ills, clearly no harm, and a lot of good, can come from exercise.
(C) Consistently consuming more calories than one expends inevitably leads to excessive weight gain, so if one wishes to avoid the health problems associated with this condition, one ought to fast periodically.
(D) It has been shown that one can obtain more vitamins and minerals from fresh fruits and vegetables than from processed fruits and vegetables. One ought, therefore, to completely abandon consumption of the latter in favor of the former.
(E) Excessive use of penicillin tends to increase one's susceptibility to penicillin-resistant infections. The best policy, therefore, is to avoid using penicillin, thereby strengthening the body's innate ability to resist disease.

Practice Test 33, Section 3, Question 18

ONE: UNDERSTAND THE JOB

Our job is to find the reasoning flaw in the original argument, then to find an answer that has a similar reasoning issue. For matching flaw questions, it's imperative that we develop a very strong, clear sense of what is wrong with the original argument, because we will have to be able to retain it in our heads as we evaluate the five new arguments that are presented in the answer choices.

TWO: UNDERSTAND THE ARGUMENT

The author's point comes right at the end, and it's a strong one: "it is obvious that these industrial activities are purely beneficial to agriculture and those of us who depend upon it." What's the support given? These industrial activities increase carbon dioxide, which aids in photosynthesis, which helps plants live.

THREE: FIND WHAT'S WRONG

The support is a bit complicated in that it involves several specific factors and layers (industrial activities related to carbon dioxide related to photosynthesis related to life-sustaining proteins), but the specifics of those links are not necessary for us to see what is wrong with the reasoning here: we're only given one potentially positive benefit of these industrial activities. The author is overreaching in stating such an absolute and general conclusion. **The author fails to consider that there may be other negative consequences that prevent these activities from being "purely beneficial."**

FOUR: FINISH THE JOB

With a clear sense of the flaw in our argument, we can go into the answer choices. As with the previous question, we want to start by focusing on reasons why wrong answers are wrong. The four wrong answers will all have problems, and there will be markers that make this clear—they may reach different types of conclusions (you can't have the same type of flaw if you end up at a different type of conclusion), or use support in a different way. So, when we notice these characteristics, we can use them to knock off answers.

Notice that the argument in (A) reaches a comparative conclusion—one thing will be better than another. This is a different type of conclusion than what was reached in our argument, and so we know that that argument must have had a different sort of reasoning issue. We can eliminate (A) for that reason. The absolute nature of the conclusion in (B)— "clearly no harm, and a lot of good"—is a great match for our original argument, and in looking at the support, it seems that (B) has very similar reasoning issues. Let's leave it. (C) is very different from our original argument—it mentions something in its conclusion (fasting) that is very different than what is discussed in its premises. We can eliminate (C) quickly. (D) reaches a conclusion about choosing one thing over another, and can be eliminated for that reason. (E) is about the best policy—what we *ought* to do, which is a very different type of conclusion than we had in the original argument.

Once we've eliminated wrong choices, there is only one attractive answer remaining: (B). (B) reaches the same type of absolute conclusion, and, like our original argument, fails to consider other, potentially negative considerations (such as that exercise can cause injury) in arriving at that conclusion. (B) is a great match, and (B) is correct.

Matching Double-Dip Drill

Here are some of the arguments that you saw in the earlier drill. Draw lines connecting the pairs of arguments that have the most similar reasoning flaws.

Turns out that chimps are not the smartest of all non-human mammals after all. Recently, it was shown that whales are able to compose and communicate with songs that rival and often surpass songs that humans are capable of composing in terms of complexity and aesthetic elegance.

For certain careers, the graduate school that you choose to attend has little impact on future career success. Not so for the legal profession. Lawyers who attend top law programs consistently earn the highest salaries, and all members of the Supreme Court went to either Harvard or Yale.

Creationism is an idea whose leading proponents are politicians and religious figures. Not a single reputable, well-respected scientist has come out in support of Creationism as a valid scientific theory. Therefore, Creationism is not a legitimate scientific theory.

Good intentions line the histories of many of our most environmentally harmful products. For example, plastic was invented, at least in part, to combat the wasting of wood and paper products. This proves that good intentions, coupled with limited foresight, can cause negative consequences for our environment.

Did you know Ted is older than Grandma? He must be really old!

This shirt is less formal than my other shirts. So this is my hip shirt.

Objective journalism is a required component of a well-working democracy. However, we live in an age in which the vast majority of our news is delivered with a great deal of bias and affiliation toward one political ideology or another. If we are to have a well-working democracy, government and media corporations must act to restore more objectivity to news media.

LeBron James is now the most recognized athlete in the world. A recent poll by *Sports Illustrated* showed that he is by far the most recognized athlete amongst its readers.

As everyone knows, consuming a moderate amount of wine can be part of a healthy diet. Wine contains antioxidants, which have been proved to support good health.

For the last twenty years, we have consistently enacted systems that have lowered the percentage of income the government collects as tax while also increasing government spending. If we continue to act as we have for the past twenty years, we will continue to increase the amount of debt our nation incurs.

Matching Double-Dip Solutions

Turns out that chimps are not the smartest of all non-human mammals after all. Recently, it was shown that whales are able to compose and communicate with songs that rival and often surpass songs that humans are capable of composing in terms of complexity and aesthetic elegance.

As everyone knows, consuming a moderate amount of wine can be part of a healthy diet. Wine contains antioxidants, which have been proved to support good health.

In both of these arguments, a specific characteristic (musical ability/ antioxidants) is used to validate a more general statement (intelligence/healthiness). In both instances, the author fails to consider that other factors could be relevant.

For certain careers, the graduate school that you choose to attend has little impact on future career success. Not so for the legal profession. Lawyers who attend top law programs consistently earn the highest salaries, and all members of the Supreme Court went to either Harvard or Yale.

Good intentions line the histories of many of our most environmentally harmful products. For example, plastic was invented, at least in part, to combat the wasting of wood and paper products. This proves that good intentions, coupled with limited foresight, can cause negative consequences for our environment.

In both of these arguments, a correlation (two things happening at the same time, to the same person, etc.) is used to justify a statement about causation. Correlation never justifies causation. It could be that, though schools and success are linked, the schools are not part of what *causes* success, and the same goes for the good intentions.

Did you know Ted is older than Grandma? He must be really old!

This shirt is less formal than my other shirts. So this is my hip shirt.

In both of these arguments, a comparative statement is used to justify an absolute statement. The second argument has an additional flaw of assuming that formal and hip are in some way opposites.

Objective journalism is a required component of a well-working democracy. However, we live in an age in which the vast majority of our news is delivered with a great deal of bias and affiliation toward one political ideology or another. If we are to have a well-working democracy, government and media corporations must act to restore more objectivity to news media.

For the last twenty years, we have consistently enacted systems that have lowered the percentage of income that government collects as tax while also increasing government spending. If we continue to act as we have for the past twenty years, we will continue to increase the amount of debt our nation incurs.

In both of these arguments, the author is failing to consider some other critical factor that may be relevant to the conclusion. The author of the first argument fails to consider that entities other than government and media corporations have the power to impact society, and the author of the second fails to consider that other factors, such as the amount of income Americans make, play a role in government debt.

LeBron James is now the most recognized athlete in the world. A recent poll by *Sports Illustrated* showed that he is by far the most recognized athlete amongst its readers.

Creationism is an idea whose leading proponents are politicians and religious figures. Not a single reputable, well-respected scientist has come out in support of Creationism as a valid scientific theory. Therefore, Creationism is not a legitimate scientific theory.

In both of these arguments, the author takes the opinions of a group to be representative of the truth.

6 LOGICAL REASONING a piece ≠ the puzzle

Over the course of the next three lessons, we will further break down common argument flaws into three general categories: a piece ≠ the puzzle, apples ≠ oranges, and 1 + 1 ≠ 3. In this lesson, we will focus on a piece ≠ the puzzle issues.

To mistake a piece for the puzzle is to overreach in trying to justify a conclusion, using supporting evidence that may turn out to be just one part of a bigger picture. This is a prominent issue on a significant number of Logical Reasoning questions, and it's pretty easy to see why piece ≠ puzzle issues would be featured on an exam for future lawyers. Here's a small taste of some basic arguments that contain this type of flaw:

"Sally is careful about what she eats, so she must be in great health."
"Ted is strong, so he must be good at football."
"Since the popular girls say I should get a haircut, I should get a haircut."
"Since the house is made of very small bricks, the house itself must be small."
"Since the restaurant is crowded for breakfast, it must be crowded all day."
"Bob has a fancy watch and drives a BMW. He must be rich."

Certainly there are differences among these arguments, and the flaws that they have can be thought of in a variety of ways, but let's focus on one thing that these arguments have in common: in each case, when we think about the conclusion that the author reaches, we can see that it involves far more factors, or considerations, than those discussed in the premises...

Being healthy is about more than just what you eat.
Being good at football is about more than just being strong.
You don't need to get a haircut just because the popular girls say so, and so on...

We want to develop a bloodhound-like sense as to when arguments are flawed in this manner: arguments in which the author falsely overvalues one consideration at the expense of others. Keep in mind that every time an author makes this leap, he or she does so *incorrectly.* Every. Single. Time. And recognizing that he or she is doing so will pay great dividends when it comes time to eliminate wrong answers and select the right ones.

These piece ≠ puzzle flaws can be thought of as generally falling into three broad subsets—overvalues a trait, overvalues an opinion, and overvalues a sample set—and though there is certainly overlap between these various types, each has its defining characteristics. We'll discuss each subset in detail on the pages to come.

Overvalues a Trait

To overvalue a trait is to put too much emphasis on one particular characteristic or one particular "clue" in reaching a conclusion. No matter how compelling that one clue is, if it's not enough to *guarantee* the outcome the author presents, the argument is flawed. And of course it helps to keep in mind that every argument we are asked to critically evaluate *will* be flawed.

In real life, seeing the value in one particular trait, or seeing that one particular trait is the driving force behind someone or something, is very commonly rewarded. In fact, being able to differentiate significant characteristics from secondary ones is one of the primary functions of our intelligence (and something that we have to do for other parts of the LSAT). Think about the following statements, each of which you've probably heard many times before in your life: *Hard work leads to success, Honesty makes for good leaders, Defense wins championships.*

If you are thinking about "primary drivers," then all of the three statements above are very strong ones. Hard work *is* generally a determining factor of success, honesty *is* a very important characteristic for leaders, and in a variety of sports, defense has been proved to be more important than offense.

Remember, the LSAT is testing your ability to understand absolute proof

However, note that determining whether or not a certain characteristic is a "primary driver" is a completely subjective endeavor (how "important" a characteristic is can only, at best, be an *opinion*), and the LSAT is most definitely *not* a test of our opinions. The LSAT is not testing your ability to judge how much, or how little, one trait (such as hard work) impacts a result (success). Never, ever.

What it is testing is your ability to understand absolute proof. Does that characteristic, no matter how important *you* define it to be, guarantee the outcome? Does hard work guarantee success? No. Does honesty definitely make for good leaders? No.

Every single time a primary characteristic (or two) is used to justify a conclusion—every single time—you know that characteristic, while it may be important, is not enough to prove the author's point. Knowing this is a big key to eliminating wrong answers and selecting the right one.

overvalues a trait

"Customers say that picture quality and screen size are the two factors they consider most when deciding on a television to purchase. Since the StarView television has a larger screen than the BlackStar and provides better picture quality, all for the same price, customers will prefer the StarView to the BlackStar."

*The fact that picture quality and screen size are **important** factors does not mean that they are **determining** factors. It could be that the StarView is unreliable, or doesn't have connections that allow you to get cable television. It's not important for you to think of such alternatives, but it is critically important to recognize when an author has overvalued a trait or traits.*

necessary, but not enough

Some of the most difficult arguments to find fault with are those that give us characteristics that are *necessary*, or needed, to reach the conclusion, but are not, by themselves, enough to definitely prove the argument correct. A trait that is enough to justify the conclusion is said to be *sufficient*, and mistaking *necessary* for *sufficient* is one of the most common flaws that appear in LSAT arguments.

Let's think of a fairly basic argument that contains this sort of mistake: "In order to watch the soccer match, one must have a television. Since Ted has a television, he will be able to watch the soccer match."

We are told that one has to have a television in order to watch the match. Having a television is *necessary,* if the conclusion is to be true. Per the premise, though, does having a television guarantee that Ted can watch the game? Is it *sufficient*?

No. We're never told that if he has a television, he will definitely be able to watch the game. Perhaps he doesn't have electricity, or perhaps he doesn't get the channel on which the game is playing because he doesn't have cable or satellite. Note that this author is mistaking something that is *necessary* for the conclusion (Ted needs to have a television if he's going to watch the soccer match) for something that is *sufficient* for the conclusion (the premise would be sufficient if having a television guaranteed that one could watch the match).

Here's another argument where the "necessary" characteristic is much better cloaked as something more important (i.e., "sufficient").

"Company X is required to alert its shareholders with a 'red alert' any time the stock price goes up or down by greater than ten percent in one day. The last red alert occurred in 2008, when the stock price rose by over thirteen percent in one day. Since the company just recently sent out a 'red alert' to shareholders, it must be true that the stock has gone up or down by greater than ten percent."

This one is a bit tougher, but do you see the flaw here? We're told that the company is required to issue a red alert if the price goes up or down by more than ten percent. Does that mean that a red alert guarantees that the price went up or down by more than ten percent? No, not based just on what we are told. The challenge of an argument like this is the "missing information." What if the company also sends out a red alert for other incidents, like when the stock splits, or someone important retires, or it rains! We're not told that "red alerts" are *only* for these price fluctuations, so we can't say that a red alert guarantees the conclusion.

To the side are four arguments. For two of them, the conclusion is actually perfectly valid; the premise we are given does guarantee the conclusion reached. For two of the arguments, the author has mistaken a necessary characteristic for a sufficient one. Make sure you understand which arguments are flawed, and which ones are not.

valid?

Here are four arguments, two of which are valid and two of which are not. Cross out the two arguments in which the author has wrongly mistaken a necessary condition for a sufficient one. (Answers on next page.)

1. Every car at the shop gets washed, and every car that gets washed also gets new floor mats. Since Ted's car was at the shop, it got new floor mats.

2. Anyone who wants to become a pilot has to complete a rigorous training process and must get satisfactory scores on both paper exams and real-time flight exams. Every pilot is given access to private parts of airports. Therefore, if one completes the rigorous training process and gets satisfactory scores on both paper exams and real-time flight exams, he or she will get access to private parts of airports.

3. Tom will never wear his leather jacket on a rainy day because he is concerned that the rain will hurt his leather jacket, and he loves his leather jacket. One issue, though, is that it's the only jacket that he owns. On a recent cold night, Tom went out without his leather jacket on. It must have been raining.

4. Wilbur had six children, and he gave a bit of his vast wealth to each of his children one year as a Christmas present. Each of those children invested that money and in turn got rich themselves. Those that got rich did exactly one of two things: they either gave their money away to charity, or they gave it back to Wilbur. Since Sylvia was a child of Wilbur, she must have gotten rich and given the money either back to Wilbur, or to charity.

Overvalues an Opinion

The truth is never the truth because someone says it is. The truth is only the truth because it's the truth

The truth is never the truth because someone says it is. The truth is only the truth because it's the truth. As simple as that concept is, many an LSAT argument will be faulty because the author makes an assumption that something is true *because someone said so.*

"My financial advisor definitely thinks I ought to be putting more money into mutual funds, so that's the smart move to make."

It's not terribly difficult to see what's wrong with this argument, especially if you read it with the goal of figuring out what's wrong, but notice how this argument plays with what we know, or think of, from real life. People go to financial advisors to be given advice about what to do with money, and in general their advice is useful. And for years many of us have associated mutual funds with "smart and safe investing."

However, when we think about whether the financial advisor's opinion *guarantees* that it's a smart move, we can see what's wrong: no, it doesn't guarantee anything. And again, that's our job on the LSAT—to think of every argument in terms of why the support does not guarantee the conclusion (many financial experts, like John Bogle, would argue that mutual funds are the opposite of "smart and safe investing").

The Flip Side

On a related note, just as an opinion cannot prove that an argument is true, an opinion can't prove that an argument is false.

"Sandra says that the new double bacon avocado hash brown popcorn shrimp burger at Karlle's isn't delicious, but that's only because she's embarrassed to eat at Karlle's with me. Therefore, she's clearly wrong."

Let's take the premise to be true—let's say the only reason Sandra says this *is* because she's embarrassed to eat at Karlle's with the author. Does this *prove* that this concoction actually *is* delicious? Of course not. Sandra can have some bias, and it can still taste really bad. Remember: no opinion can *prove* something as subjective as whether or not a burger is delicious.

overvalues an opinion

"I thought my hair looked bad, but when I went in to get it cut, all of the stylists in the salon thought it looked great and advised me not to cut it. Therefore, I was clearly wrong."

Are stylists professionals who are valued for their opinions? Yes. Are their opinions on style more in tune with culture? Probably. Does that mean that the common ***opinion*** *of the stylists in the salon is the* ***truth****? No. It's still just an opinion.*

Uses a Small Sample Set

This issue is very closely related to the two that we have already discussed. Arguments are flawed when they reach a general consensus based on evidence from a limited portion of whatever group or system that they are discussing. Here is a simple version:

"All my friends love my new sweater vest. I bet everyone at the party will think I am stylish."

In real life, it may be that your friends are lying to you, but again, on the LSAT, our job is not to question whether the reasoning given is in fact true; if we are told that his friends love his sweater vest, well, we're supposed to believe it. However, the fact that his friends love it does not mean that everyone at the party will love it.

Maybe his friends have unique taste.

Additionally, having a sweater vest that people love and having a sweater vest that people find stylish are, sadly enough, not necessarily the same thing.

Here's another one that's a bit more difficult—see if you can figure out what could be wrong with it:

"The new hybrid vehicle from Honda has an engine that weighs fifty percent more than that of a standard automobile. Therefore, it's unlikely that the car will be a lightweight model."

Notice that the characteristic discussed in the premise—weight—is the same characteristic mentioned in the conclusion—we're good there. However, the engine is just one portion of the entire automobile; perhaps having such a heavy engine enables the car to have lower weight overall.

solutions to drill on page 85

1. VALID. We know, since Ted's car was at the shop, that it got washed, and since it got washed, it got new floor mats.

2. NOT VALID. Completing rigorous training and getting satisfactory scores are required to become a pilot, but they don't guarantee that one will become a pilot. Perhaps there are other requirements as well.

3. NOT VALID. We do not know if there are other situations (like snow) in which he will not wear his jacket.

4. VALID. We know Sylvia got rich, and we know there were just two consequences to her getting rich, and they match the options in the conclusion.

uses a small sample set

"I've heard my friends talk about how difficult Logic Games are, but I just tried three of them and found them to be not too bad. I guess some people just have a knack for solving them, and I'm lucky that way."

Maybe he really is a natural at Logic Games, or maybe the three he saw fit into his comfort zone. In any case, three games is not a large enough sample size for him to gauge in any significantly valuable way whether he actually has a "knack" for Logic Games.

The Flip Side: The Puzzle ≠ A Piece

The LSAT does not test a million reasoning issues. It tests just a few, but it likes to test each of them from a variety of perspectives in order to get a rounded-out sense of your fundamental reasoning ability. Therefore, it's very common to see "flip sides" or "reverse images" of many of the issues that appear on the LSAT. Certain questions require critical thinking, so others require that you *not* be critical. Some games have too many elements for the number of spots, so some games have too few elements for the number of spots. Some conclusions are expressed with certainty ("must be true"), so it's important to notice when some are not ("is most likely"). Finally, just as some arguments mistakenly use one clue, one "piece," to conclude something about the whole, some arguments are flawed in that they mistakenly assume that something that is true of the whole is true of each component.

Let's look at an argument similar to one we just discussed:

"The new hybrid Honda weighs in at less than 70 percent the weight of a conventional automobile. It must be true that Honda is using a lighter-than-average-weight engine."

In the earlier argument on the previous page, the engine weight did not determine the weight of the entire car. In this case, the weight of the car does not determine the weight of the engine—perhaps the car is light because of other reasons, and actually has a heavy engine.

In life, there are many times when piece does = puzzle, and puzzle = piece arguments are completely valid.[1] However, it's essential to remember that when you are asked to be critical of reasoning on the LSAT, you are not being asked to determine whether arguments are valid or not. You are being given arguments that you know are not valid and being asked to determine why they are not. So when you recognize that the author is claiming that one characteristic, opinion, or sample set is "enough" to prove something more general or (less commonly) when you notice that the author is using some statement about a group or larger entity to say something about an individual or a part, you know for certain that there is a problem with how the evidence is being used to support the conclusion.

1. Some real-life situations in which piece = puzzle and puzzle = piece arguments are valid:

"Since this bag contains a super-heavy bowling ball, it will be heavy."

"Since the entire cake is made of chocolate, each slice will have chocolate in it."

Flaw Drill

For each argument, write in why you feel the support doesn't prove the conclusion.

1. In order to build a desk, the only materials a person needs are wood, a saw, nails, and a hammer. I have all of those things, so I should be able to build a desk.

2. In a recent online poll about Internet dating, 65 percent of participants said they preferred going on a first date with someone they had met online, rather than a first date set up by an acquaintance at work. This shows that single people, in general, prefer to go on first dates with people they meet online, rather than people they are set up with by coworkers.

3. In order to obtain a driver's license, one must prove that he or she is a resident of that state. Since Terry can prove he is a resident of his state, he will be given a driver's license.

4. Consumer electronics stores make the bulk of their earnings not on the products that they sell, but rather on the insurance that customers often purchase on those products. The stores claim that their service provides a benefit for consumers, but a leading independent consumer magazine recently published statistics showing that a person would earn more income investing his or her money rather than using it for various such insurance plans, and strongly suggested that smart consumers avoid such insurance that is offered. Therefore, the claim that the stores make is false.

5. In a recent poll conducted among readers of a popular surfing magazine, surfing was ranked as the most popular sport and beach volleyball was ranked third. Therefore, it cannot be true that tennis is more popular than both surfing and beach volleyball.

6. Every time I see Janice, she is eating one kind of snack or another. If she doesn't change her behavior, I'm afraid she's going to gain some weight.

7. Most people assume that Neanderthals were creatures far less advanced than humans, and one aspect of that was that they were incapable of verbal communication. However, nearly all scientists who are specialists in the field of Neanderthal research now believe that they did indeed communicate verbally with one another, and this view has been supported by numerous articles and research projects. Therefore, in terms of whether Neanderthals could or could not talk, most people hold an incorrect assumption.

8. More than education level, parents' income, or where one was born, the age at which one starts working is the greatest statistical indicator of one's future earnings. Therefore, if we want to ensure that our daughter will have a successful earnings future, we should make sure to get her a job as soon as possible.

9. Most successful financial advisors have excellent computer skills as well as good people skills. Since Sean has excellent computer skills, and since he's terrific with people, there is a good chance he could be a successful financial advisor.

Flaw Drill

10. Everyone who boards the plane has to show his or her ticket to the attendant. Since Tom has shown his ticket, he will be allowed to board the plane.

11. Prosperous towns almost always have two primary characteristics: jobs for their citizens, and homes that can be purchased for reasonable prices. We've spent the last five years improving our community in terms of these two characteristics. We now find ourselves with ample jobs for our citizens, and more than enough homes that can be purchased for reasonable prices. Therefore, it's reasonable to think that prosperous times are ahead.

12. It is well known that Yatoo Corporation has slashed the amount it pays in salaries by 6 percent this year. Since Jeff works at Yatoo, his salary was reduced by 6 percent.

13. A recently published study claimed that Tat soda contains several chemicals known to sometimes cause unpleasant physical sensations. However, it's important to note that the study was financed by Eager Brands, a direct competitor of the company that produces Tat. Therefore, the study is highly dubious.

14. A successful business must have three characteristics: consistent revenue, low costs, and adequate capital reserves. Since our business has those three characteristics, it must be false that our business is unsuccessful.

15. Of those who tasted our new ice cream flavor just once, 75 percent said that they did not enjoy the taste of it. However, of those who tasted our new ice cream flavor more than five times, 90 percent of people said they liked it. Therefore, it's likely that most people will eventually like the flavor, which seems to be an acquired taste.

16. A recent study on consumer behavior showed that when consumers are deciding on which towels to buy, an evocative name has a far greater impact on buying decisions than does the display design, or the actual quality of the towels. Therefore, if we are able to come up with an evocative name for our new towel collection, it is certain to be a success.

17. You say that Sharon doesn't like soccer, but that can't be true. Sharon is Korean, and Koreans are known to be passionate soccer fans.

18. There are various tests that scientists can perform to determine whether a planet is suitable for life as we know it. Of the over sixty thousand planets that have been carefully analyzed so far—the sixty thousand planets closest to us—none have come close to containing the combination of elements essential for life to exist. Therefore, it's very unlikely that there are other planets in the universe that contain life as we know it.

Flaw Drill Solutions

1. In order to build a desk, the only materials a person needs are wood, a saw, nails, and a hammer. I have all of those things, so I should be able to build a desk.

Fails to consider that there might be other requirements or considerations relevant to the conclusion. Perhaps the person doesn't know how to use a saw, or how to put a desk together.

2. In a recent online poll about Internet dating, 65 percent of participants said they preferred going on a first date with someone they had met online, rather than a first date set up by an acquaintance at work. This shows that single people, in general, prefer to go on first dates with people they meet online, rather than people they are set up with by coworkers.

Takes for granted that online voters are representative of the population in general. Maybe those who are more frequently online, or more into Internet dating, were more inclined to take the survey.

3. In order to obtain a driver's license, one must prove that he or she is a resident of that state. Since Terry can prove he is a resident of his state, he will be given a driver's license.

Mistakes a necessary condition for one that guarantees a result. Maybe there is another reason why he can't get a license, such as that Terry is four years old.

4. Consumer electronics stores make the bulk of their earnings not on the products that they sell, but rather on the insurance that customers often purchase on those products. The stores claim that their service provides a benefit for consumers, but a leading independent consumer magazine recently published statistics showing that a person would earn more income investing his or her money rather than using it for various such insurance plans, and strongly suggested that smart consumers avoid such insurance that is offered. Therefore, the claim that the stores make is false.

Fails to consider that the insurance can benefit customers even if it doesn't give the customer a great financial reward. Perhaps some people are willing to trade in a bit of earnings for some peace of mind.

5. In a recent poll conducted among readers of a popular surfing magazine, surfing was ranked as the most popular sport and beach volleyball was ranked third. Therefore, it cannot be true that tennis is more popular than both surfing and beach volleyball.

Takes for granted that readers of a surfing magazine are representative of the population in general. Maybe a poll of tennis magazine subscribers would have turned out differently.

6. Every time I see Janice, she is eating one kind of snack or another. If she doesn't change her behavior, I'm afraid she's going to gain some weight.

Takes for granted that his experience with Janice is enough to determine her overall behavior. Maybe the only time the author sees Janice is during her lunchtime.

7. Most people assume that Neanderthals were creatures far less advanced than humans, and one aspect of that was that they were incapable of verbal communication. However, nearly all scientists who are specialists in the field of Neanderthal research now believe that they did indeed communicate verbally with one another, and this view has been supported by numerous articles and research projects. Therefore, in terms of whether Neanderthals could or could not talk, most people hold an incorrect assumption.

Fails to consider that these scientists could be wrong. At some point nearly all the scientists in the world agreed that the sun rotated around the earth.

8. More than education level, parents' income, or where one was born, the age at which one starts working is the greatest statistical indicator of one's future earnings. Therefore, if we want to ensure that our daughter will have a successful earnings future, we should make sure to get her a job as soon as possible.

Takes for granted that a characteristic that is important to an outcome will guarantee that outcome. In fact, this correlation between early work and earnings success, which could just be a coincidence, is not even enough to prove that early work has *any* impact on future earnings.

9. Most successful financial advisors have excellent computer skills, as well as good people skills. Since Sean has excellent computer skills, and since he's terrific with people, there is a good chance he could be a successful financial advisor.

Fails to consider that Sean may be lacking some of the other skills that successful financial advisors need to have. Maybe Sean doesn't understand the difference between addition and multiplication (and therefore can't take advantage of the beauty of compound interest).

Flaw Drill Solutions

10. Everyone who boards the plane has to show his or her ticket to the attendant. Since Tom has shown his ticket, he will be allowed to board the plane.

Confuses a necessary condition for a sufficient one. Maybe there is some other reason they won't let Tom board the plane, such as that Tom is very drunk.

11. Prosperous towns almost always have two primary characteristics: jobs for their citizens, and homes that can be purchased for reasonable prices. We've spent the last five years improving our community in terms of these two characteristics. We now find ourselves with ample jobs for our citizens, and more than enough homes that can be purchased for reasonable prices. Therefore, it's reasonable to think that prosperous times are ahead.

Fails to consider that there may be other important factors that will determine whether the town will be prosperous. Perhaps some mysterious bad odor in the town will slow down some of that prosperity.

12. It is well known that Yatoo Corporation has slashed the amount it pays in salaries by 6 percent this year. Since Jeff works at Yatoo, his salary was reduced by 6 percent.

Takes for granted that what is true for a group is true for the individual. We aren't told Yatoo slashed everyone's salary by the same amount.

13. A recently published study claimed that Tat soda contains several chemicals known to sometimes cause unpleasant physical sensations. However, it's important to note that the study was financed by Eager Brands, a direct competitor of the company that produces Tat. Therefore, the study is highly dubious.

Takes for granted that the motivations of those who financed the study impacted the results of the study. Even if the competitor financed the study, that doesn't mean the study must be doubted.

14. A successful business must have three characteristics: consistent revenue, low costs, and adequate capital reserves. Since our business has those three characteristics, it must be false that our business is unsuccessful.

Fails to consider that there may be other determinants of a successful business. Maybe the managers are incompetent.

15. Of those who tasted our new ice cream flavor just once,75 percent said that they did not enjoy the taste of it. However, of those who tasted our new ice cream flavor more than five times, 90 percent of people said they liked it. Therefore, it's likely that most people will eventually like the flavor, which seems to be an acquired taste.

Takes for granted that those who have tried the ice cream multiple times are representative of the population as a whole. Maybe the ice cream has a unique flavor few people like, and it's only the people who liked it to begin with who eat it over and over again.

16. A recent study on consumer behavior showed that when consumers are deciding on which towels to buy, an evocative name has a far greater impact on buying decisions than does the display design, or the actual quality of the towels. Therefore, if we are able to come up with an evocative name for our new towel collection, it is certain to be a success.

Takes for granted that because the name is important to success, it will ensure success. If the towels are of obviously terrible quality, chances are that no clever name will make them a success.

17. You say that Sharon doesn't like soccer, but that can't be true. Sharon is Korean, and Koreans are known to be passionate soccer fans.

Takes for granted that what is true for the whole must be true for individuals of that whole. It could be true that though Koreans in general like soccer, one particular Korean, Sharon, does not.

18. There are various tests that scientists can perform to determine whether a planet is suitable for life as we know it. Of the over sixty thousand planets that have been carefully analyzed so far—the sixty thousand planets closest to us—none have come close to containing the combination of elements essential for life to exist. Therefore, it's very unlikely that there are other planets in the universe that contain life as we know it.

Fails to consider that the sample set of planets is unrepresentative of the whole. Sixty thousand planets seems like a lot of research, until you realize that so far we've discovered the existence of an estimated 400 billion planets. Sixty thousand is much too small a sample size.

Matching Double-Dip Drill

Here are some of the same arguments again. Draw lines connecting the pairs of arguments most similar to one another.

In order to build a desk, the only materials a person needs are wood, a saw, nails, and a hammer. I have all of those things, so I should be able to build a desk.

In a recent online poll about internet dating, 65 percent of participants said they preferred going on a first date with someone they had met online, rather than a first date set up by an acquaintance at work. This shows that single people, in general, prefer to go on first dates with people they meet online, rather than people they are set up with by coworkers.

A successful business must have three characteristics: consistent revenue, low costs, and adequate capital reserves. Since our business has those three characteristics, it must be false that our business is unsuccessful.

Prosperous towns almost always have two primary characteristics: jobs for their citizens, and homes that can be purchased for reasonable prices. We've spent the last five years improving our community in terms of these two characteristics. We now find ourselves with ample jobs for our citizens, and more than enough homes that can be purchased for reasonable prices. Therefore, it's reasonable to think that prosperous times are ahead.

It is well known that Yatoo Corporation has slashed the amount it pays in salaries by 6 percent this year. Since Jeff works at Yatoo, his salary was reduced by 6 percent.

More than education level, parents' income, or where one was born, the age at which one starts working is the greatest statistical indicator of one's future earnings. Therefore, if we want to ensure that our daughter will have a successful earnings future, we should make sure to get her a job as soon as possible.

Of those who tasted our new ice cream flavor just once, 75 percent said that they did not enjoy the taste of it. However, of those who tasted our new ice cream flavor more than five times, 90 percent of people said they liked it. Therefore, it's likely that most people will eventually like the flavor, which seems to be an acquired taste.

You say that Sharon doesn't like soccer, but that can't be true. Sharon is Korean, and Koreans are known to be passionate soccer fans.

Most successful financial advisors have excellent computer skills, as well as good people skills. Since Sean has excellent computer skills, and since he's terrific with people, there is a good chance he could be a successful financial advisor.

A recent study on consumer behavior showed that when consumers are deciding on which towels to buy, an evocative name has a far greater impact on buying decisions than does the display design, or the actual quality of the towels. Therefore, if we are able to come up with an evocative name for our new towel collection, it is certain to be a success.

Matching Double-Dip Solutions

In order to build a desk, the only materials a person needs are wood, a saw, nails, and a hammer. I have all of those things, so I should be able to build a desk.

A successful business must have three characteristics: consistent revenue, low costs, and adequate capital reserves. Since our business has those three characteristics, it must be false that our business is unsuccessful.

It is well known that Yatoo Corporation has slashed the amount it pays in salaries by 6 percent this year. Since Jeff works at Yatoo, his salary was reduced by 6 percent.

You say that Sharon doesn't like soccer, but that can't be true. Sharon is Korean, and Koreans are known to be passionate soccer fans.

Most successful financial advisors have excellent computer skills, as well as good people skills. Since Sean has excellent computer skills, and since he's terrific with people, there is a good chance he could be a successful financial advisor.

Prosperous towns almost always have two primary characteristics: jobs for their citizens, and homes that can be purchased for reasonable prices. We've spent the last five years improving our community in terms of these two characteristics. We now find ourselves with ample jobs for our citizens, and more than enough homes that can be purchased for reasonable prices. Therefore, it's reasonable to think that prosperous times are ahead.

Mistakes necessary characteristics for sufficient ones, and fails to consider other factors necessary or potentially important to the conclusion.

Fails to consider that those mentioned in the premise may be an unrepresentative sample of the general population.

Takes for granted that something true of a group must be true of an individual in that group.

Takes for granted that a characteristic important for an outcome will ensure that outcome.

Takes for granted that having characteristics important for an outcome is enough to reasonably expect that outcome.

Of those who tasted our new ice cream flavor just once, 75 percent said that they did not enjoy the taste of it. However, of those who tasted our new ice cream flavor more than five times, 90 percent of people said they liked it. Therefore, it's likely that most people will eventually like the flavor, which seems to be an acquired taste.

In a recent online poll about internet dating, 65 percent of participants said they preferred going on a first date with someone they had met online, rather than a first date set up by an acquaintance at work. This shows that single people, in general, prefer to go on first dates with people they meet online, rather than people they are set up with by coworkers.

More than education level, parents' income, or where one was born, the age at which one starts working is the greatest statistical indicator of one's future earnings. Therefore, if we want to ensure that our daughter will have a successful earnings future, we should make sure to get her a job as soon as possible.

A recent study on consumer behavior showed that when consumers are deciding on which towels to buy, an evocative name has a far greater impact on buying decisions than does the display design, or the actual quality of the towels. Therefore, if we are able to come up with an evocative name for our new towel collection, it is certain to be a success.

Sample Questions

Here are two LSAT questions that have arguments with piece ≠ puzzle issues. Read the question stem carefully, do your best to identify the flaw in the argument, and select the answer choice you think best addresses that flaw.

24.3.5. Bacteria from food can survive for several days on the surface of plastic cutting boards, but bacteria can penetrate wooden cutting boards almost immediately, leaving the surface free of contamination. Therefore, wooden cutting boards, unlike plastic cutting boards, need not be washed in order to prevent their contaminating food that is cut on them; wiping them off to remove food debris is sufficient.

Which one of the following is an assumption on which the argument depends?

(A) Washing plastic cutting boards does not remove all bacteria from the surface.
(B) Prevention of bacteria contamination is the only respect in which wooden cutting boards are superior to plastic cutting boards.
(C) Food that is not already contaminated with bacteria can be contaminated only by being cut on contaminated cutting boards.
(D) Bacteria that penetrate into wooden cutting boards do not reemerge on the surface after the cutting boards have been used.
(E) Washing wooden cutting boards kills bacteria below the surface of the cutting boards.

24.2.5. Altogether, the students in Ms. Tarnowski's Milton Elementary School class collected more aluminum cans than did the students in any of the school's other classes. Therefore, the Milton student who collected the most aluminum cans was in Ms. Tarnowski's class.

Which one of the following arguments contains flawed reasoning that is most parallel to that in the argument above?

(A) Altogether, more trees were planted by the students in Mr. Kelly's class than were planted by those in Mr. Liang's class and Ms. Jackson's class combined. Therefore, Mr. Kelly's students planted more trees than Ms. Jackson's students planted.
(B) More than half of Milton Elementary School's students play in the band and more than half of the school's students sing in the choir. Therefore, every student at Milton Elementary School either plays in the band or sings in the choir.
(C) Mr. Rowe's Milton Elementary School class raised more money by selling candy bars than Ms. Hunt's class raised by holding a raffle. Therefore, the number of candy bars sold by Mr. Rowe's class was greater than the number of raffle tickets sold by Ms. Hunt's class.
(D) The total number of tickets to the school fair sold by the students in Ms. Ramirez's Milton Elementary School class was greater than the number sold by Milton students from any other class. Therefore, the Milton student who sold the most tickets to the school fair was a student in Ms. Ramirez's class.
(E) Ms. Ventura's Milton Elementary School class assembled more birdhouses than did any of the school's other classes. Since Ms. Ventura's class had fewer students than any other Milton class, her students assembled more birdhouses, on average, than did the students in any other Milton class.

Sample Solutions

Let's think about these two questions in terms of the task the question stem presents (task), the reasoning issue in the argument (flaw), and the process of selecting an answer that best matches the task and the argument (answers).

24.3.5. Bacteria from food can survive for several days on the surface of plastic cutting boards, but bacteria can penetrate wooden cutting boards almost immediately, leaving the surface free of contamination. Therefore, wooden cutting boards, unlike plastic cutting boards, need not be washed in order to prevent their contaminating food that is cut on them; wiping them off to remove food debris is sufficient.

Which one of the following is an assumption on which the argument depends?

(A) Washing plastic cutting boards does not remove all bacteria from the surface.
(B) Prevention of bacteria contamination is the only respect in which wooden cutting boards are superior to plastic cutting boards.
(C) Food that is not already contaminated with bacteria can be contaminated only by being cut on contaminated cutting boards.
(D) Bacteria that penetrate into wooden cutting boards do not reemerge on the surface after the cutting boards have been used.
(E) Washing wooden cutting boards kills bacteria below the surface of the cutting boards.

Task: We need to find an assumption on which the argument **depends.** That means we need an answer that **must be true** for the argument to work. This answer **may or may not be important** to the argument.

Flaw: The author is saying that wooden cutting boards don't need to be washed to prevent contaminating food cut on them—you can just wipe them off. Why? Because the *surface* of wooden boards can be free of contamination. But just because the bacteria can penetrate the wood immediately doesn't mean it must, right? And just the surface being free of contamination is still a problem—surely the contamination right under the surface can impact the food to be cut on the board in some way.

Answers: Let's look for an answer that needs to be true for the argument to work, and we'll first start by eliminating those answers that *don't*. (A) is about the plastic cutting boards, and we can eliminate it quickly. (B) compares plastic and wooden cutting boards—this is not information that is necessary for our argument. We also don't need the information given in (C)—whether food can *only* get contaminated on cutting boards or whether it can also get contaminated elsewhere isn't relevant. **(D) needs to be true** for the argument to work—if the bacteria did re-emerge, then the cutting boards would be contaminated. **(D) is the correct answer.** (E) makes washing cutting boards seem like a good idea, but it doesn't match our task—it doesn't tell us something that needs to be true for us to be able to *not* wash wooden cutting boards.

24.2.5. Altogether, the students in Ms. Tarnowski's Milton Elementary School class collected more aluminum cans than did the students in any of the school's other classes. Therefore, the Milton student who collected the most aluminum cans was in Ms. Tarnowski's class.

Which one of the following arguments contains flawed reasoning that is most parallel to that in the argument above?

(A) Altogether, more trees were planted by the students in Mr. Kelly's class than were planted by those in Mr. Liang's class and Ms. Jackson's class combined. Therefore, Mr. Kelly's students planted more trees than Ms. Jackson's students planted.
(B) More than half of Milton Elementary School's students play in the band and more than half of the school's students sing in the choir. Therefore, every student at Milton Elementary School either plays in the band or sings in the choir.
(C) Mr. Rowe's Milton Elementary School class raised more money by selling candy bars than Ms. Hunt's class raised by holding a raffle. Therefore, the number of candy bars sold by Mr. Rowe's class was greater than the number of raffle tickets sold by Ms. Hunt's class.
(D) The total number of tickets to the school fair sold by the students in Ms. Ramirez's Milton Elementary School class was greater than the number sold by Milton students from any other class. Therefore, the Milton student who sold the most tickets to the school fair was a student in Ms. Ramirez's class.
(E) Ms. Ventura's Milton Elementary School class assembled more birdhouses than did any of the school's other classes. Since Ms. Ventura's class had fewer students than any other Milton class, her students assembled more birdhouses, on average, than did the students in any other Milton class.

Task: We need to find an answer that has the same reasoning flaw as the argument in the stimulus.

Flaw: The author says that the student who collected the most cans is in Ms. T's class. Why? Ms. T's class collected the most cans. But just because the class collected the most cans doesn't mean that the one person who collected the most cans is in the class—perhaps that one person happened to be in another class in which her classmates collected very few cans. This is a puzzle ≠ piece issue: the author is falsely mistaking a characteristic of the group (class) for a characteristic of a part of the group (student).

Answers: We need to find an answer with puzzle ≠ piece issues. A quick look at (A), (B), and (C) makes it clear none of them have the same type of puzzle ≠ piece issues: (A) is about using one mathematical truth to infer another, (B) is about using a percentage to make a (false) inference about *all* of the various individuals in the group, and (C) is about (falsely) equating money made and candy bars sold. (D) is worded in a slightly twisted fashion, but **it has the same type of puzzle ≠ piece problem that the original argument had, and so (D) is correct.** (E) is about an average, and it's not about a puzzle ≠ piece issue.

7 LOGICAL REASONING apples ≠ oranges

In the last lesson, we discussed faulty extrapolation—reasoning issues that arise when the person making the argument places too much significance on one characteristic, one opinion, or an unrepresentative sample set. In each of these cases, the author thought that the one clue was enough to justify his or her conclusion. In each of these cases, it wasn't.

Remember, the LSAT is testing your ability to understand absolute proof

In this lesson, we're going to focus on a different type of faulty argument—not one that falsely extrapolates, but rather, one that falsely transfers, or exchanges. Here are some examples of arguments that are flawed because the author, in his or her thought process, treats two things as if they are the same, or same *enough*, when they clearly are not:

"Since Vivian likes apples, I bet she will like oranges."
"Ted says he loves Janice. Janice must therefore love Ted."
"Sam got fit by working out. Since Ruby also got fit, she too must be working out."
"George makes a lot of money at his job, so we can say he has a successful career."

Note that each of these arguments has faulty reasoning, and, in each case, the problem is not so much that the author is generalizing from what he or she knows, but more so that the answer is *transferring* information or ideas from one situation to the other in some faulty way.[1] We can think of these types of errors as falling into three common categories:

1) The author falsely equates subject matter: The first example, "Since Vivian likes apples, I bet she will like oranges," represents this type of error. The author assumes that what is true about apples is true about oranges—but this assumption is unwarranted.

2) The author falsely equates characteristics: The final example, "George makes a lot of money at his job, so we can say he has a successful career," represents this type of error. The author equates making money with being successful, and as your grandparents would tell you, those two things are not the same.

3) The author falsely equates relationships: The second example, "Ted says he loves Janice. Janice must therefore love Ted," represents this type of error. The third example does so as well, and it contains a special type of flaw that we will highlight in just a bit.

Let's start this lesson by discussing each of these three categories in more depth.

1. Of course, keep in mind that there is great overlap between different types of flaws, and that there are many flaws that fall into multiple categories. These categories of flaws are not meant to be exclusive—they are all simply different vantage points from which we can get a better view of the problem within any particular argument. So, if you can see a flaw as being both one of extrapolation and incorrect equating, then great!

Falsely Equates Subject Matter

In everyday life, sometimes we are rewarded for seeing commonalities, and sometimes for seeing differences. The same is true on the LSAT—at times our job is to look for commonalities, and at times for differences. During your initial read of an argument, when your primary concern is to find fault with what the author is saying, it's best to focus on the *differences* in subject matter between the support and the conclusion. Here are a few basic examples for which the author falsely equates subject matter:

"Cheetahs have developed certain instincts for hunting prey. Household cats, which are related to cheetahs, likely have some of these very same instincts."

Note that underlying this argument is a notion that what is true for the cheetah must be related to what is true for the household cat, just because the two animals are related. However, we know that this does not have to be the case.

"Sitting in and driving a car for long hours has been known to be bad for one's back, so it's likely that flying an airplane for long hours has the same consequences."

When we picture how a pilot sits, perhaps we notice how similar it is to how we sit when we drive our cars. Many of us are also liable to be influenced by some personal bias, having experienced first-hand how uncomfortable airplane seats are. However, without anything else specifically mentioned in the argument, we don't know if the consequences of flying an airplane can be equated to those of driving a car.

Unfamiliar Subjects, Similar Subjects

This issue becomes more difficult when the subjects are very similar to one another, or so foreign to us that we don't have an intuitive way to understand and relate to that topic. Take a look at this example and see if you can figure out what is wrong with the reasoning used to support the conclusion:

"The average salary at the company is currently well over $17,000. Therefore, most of the employees must make over $17,000."

Did you catch the flaw there? If you are rushed in reading this, if you are inappropriately focused on "matching" terms in a mechanical sort of way (*most* with *most*, *over*

falsely equates subject matter

"All of the members of the medical staff at our hospital are required to wear name badges. Since Theron was recently hired to work full time at our hospital, he will be required to wear a medical badge."

Not all of the employees of a hospital are part of the medical staff. Theron could be in janitorial services or accounting, in which case the requirement likely does not apply to him.

$17,000 with *over $17,000*), or if you are trying to see how the premise *does* support the conclusion, this can be a very easy issue to miss on test day.

However, an average salary is not the same thing as what most employees make. In fact, that average could be well over $17,000 if, say, nearly all of the employees make $1 each but the boss pays himself a million bucks. Over and over you will see, in challenging arguments, that subjects in the conclusion and support "seem" the same or almost the same. Know that in these cases you need to be very critical of the differences.

"Old Worlde-style serif fonts are characterized by having slight angles to their serifs. Therefore, if you are reading a serif font from long ago, it is likely to have serifs that have slight angles."

Chances are, you haven't heard of "Old Worlde-style" fonts (because I just made it up), and this can make it more difficult to be critical of how the term is being used. However, what we can see is that it *is* some sort of proper term—a name given to a specific type of font—and we can also see that it would be wrong to assume that *any* "serif font from long ago" would necessarily be exactly the same as other fonts from that age. We don't need to know what Old Worlde serifs are to know what is wrong with the argument.

Falsely Equates Characteristics

In the same way that it's very easy for LSAT arguments to mistakenly relate subject matter, they can also mistakenly relate characteristics about that subject matter.

"Everyone knows Sarah is a friendly person. Therefore, she must be very social."

Friendly and social are somewhat related to one another, but they are not the same, and so, of course, it is wrong to use the fact that she is friendly to try to justify the idea that she is social.

One of the most common ways in which the LSAT will play with this is through the use of assumed, but not actual, opposites. Consider the following statements:

"Since Chris is not tall, he must be short."
"John says he is not a Republican. Therefore, he must be a Democrat."

falsely equates characteristics

"Samantha is obsessed with her work and with rising to the top of her company. It is clear that having a successful career is important to her."

Being driven and wanting a successful career are often related, but they are not the same characteristic. Perhaps Samantha is obsessed with her work because she believes in its purpose, or because she wants to be able to boss people around all day (something quite different than wanting to be successful).

Notice that in each situation, the author is mistakenly equating *not* being something with being some sort of *opposite* of that thing. However, you don't have to be tall or short—you can be somewhere in the middle. Similarly, not being a Republican doesn't make one a Democrat.

solutions for drill on pg. 101

Don't read until after the drill.

1. VALID. Since Charlie attends the convention, we know he must purchase a ticket, and he must use a personal check to do so.

2. NOT VALID. Being an original owner leads to the consequences that Debra experiences, but that doesn't mean she must have been an original owner. Perhaps she bought into the business a few years after it started, but still kept her stake for a long time and ended up very satisfied.

3. VALID. Since Sean is tallest, he was the winner of the jumping contest.

4. NOT VALID. We are told of one characteristic that is sufficient to deny a credit card. There could be other reasons why they would have denied the credit card.

Falsely Equates Relationships

Finally, certain arguments are flawed in that the author falsely assumes that the relationship between elements mentioned in the premise equates to that mentioned in the conclusion. Here are a couple of simple examples:

"Most residents of Hermosa Beach dine at Tom's Diner. Therefore, most of the customers in Tom's Diner must be residents of Hermosa Beach."

"Gerald joined that new exercise class, and it helped him get in incredible shape. That's probably how Jill also got in such great shape."

Notice that in each case, there is a very strong connection between the subjects mentioned in the support and the subjects mentioned in the conclusion. However, the relationship has been altered in some way. In the first example, we go from saying most of X is Y to most of Y is X. That's not valid—it could be that Tom's is hugely popular, and most of the residents of other nearby communities dine there too, making Hermosa Beach residents just a small portion of the overall customer base. The second example is a bit more obvious—since Gerald getting in shape is related to his new exercise, the author assumes that Jill's getting in shape has the same association—however, this assumption is not justified. Jill could have gotten in shape in any number of other ways.

falsely equates relationships

"June says she supports Stacy's decision one hundred percent. That must mean that June agrees with what Stacy is doing."

To support something and to agree with something are not the same thing. Maybe June disagrees with what Stacy is doing but supports her anyway.

enough, but not necessary

In real life, a common way in which people falsely equate characteristics is to assume that one way to do something is the only way to do something. Take the following argument:

"If you finish college, you are certain to be financially successful. Therefore, if you want to be financially successful, you must finish college."

Put yourself in the mind of the person making this argument. What reasoning mistake are you making? Perhaps the most basic way to think of it is that you are mistaking one way for the only way. Perhaps the person to whom you are speaking is the greatest tennis player in the world. If that is the case, chances are that there are other ways that he or she can become financially successful.

A slightly different, more formal way of stating that "one way is the only way" is "mistaking sufficient for necessary." What the latter statement means is that the author uses evidence that one element or characteristic (in this case, graduating college) is *enough* to reach the outcome (financial success) to conclude that *that* element or characteristic *must be* involved in the outcome (one must graduate college to achieve financial success). You may notice that this is a "mirror flaw" of "mistaking necessary for sufficient," which we discussed in the last lesson.

Here are some basic examples of arguments flawed because the author falsely equates *sufficient* with *necessary*:

"Coffee helps one stay awake. Therefore, if one wants to stay awake, one needs to drink coffee."

"Every student in Mrs. Wilber's class went to the museum. Since Sean went to the museum, he must be in Mrs. Wilber's class."

"Having over $10,000 in your account entitles you to free checking. Since you have free checking, you must have over $10,000 in your account."

Even if coffee does help one stay awake, there might be other ways. Even if all of the students in Mrs. Wilber's class went, there might be other students (not in her class) who also went. Even if this one characteristic (having over $10,000) guarantees free checking, it may be that this person got free checking through some other means (maybe as part of a promotion). In each case, sufficient does not mean necessary.

To the side are four arguments. For two of them, the conclusion is actually perfectly valid—the premise we are given does guarantee the conclusion reached. For two of the arguments, the author has mistaken a sufficient condition for a necessary one. Make sure you understand which arguments are flawed and which ones are not. (Answers on page 100.)

valid?

Here are four arguments, two of which are valid and two of which are not. Cross out the two arguments in which the author has wrongly mistaken a sufficient condition for a necessary one.

1. Every convention attendee must purchase a ticket, and every person who purchases a ticket must do so by using a personal check. Since Charlie is a convention attendee, he must have purchased his ticket using a personal check.

2. All of the original owners kept their stake in the business over a long period of time, and anyone who kept their stake in the business ended up very satisfied. Since Debra kept her stake in the business for a long time and ended up very satisfied, it must be that she was an original owner.

3. Sean is the tallest student in the class. What we know about the jumping contest is that the tallest student in the class was the winner. Therefore, Sean was the winner.

4. Terry says that our credit request is going to be denied, but that's not true. A credit request is denied when those who are seeking the credit are shown to have insufficient funds to cover the loan in case of default. However, we have plenty of funds to cover the loan in case of default, and the bank will see that this is indeed the case.

Flaw Drill

Directions: For each argument, write why you think the support doesn't prove the conclusion.

1. Sandy is prone to wild emotional fluctuations, but Charlie is not. In fact, Charlie is the picture of serenity, never getting too up or too down. It is Charlie, not Sandy, who is in a healthier emotional state.

2. You say that most people who own smartphones also own laptops, but that must be incorrect, for fewer than half the people who own laptops own smartphones.

3. You say that Tony is more dangerous than Mary, which can't be true, for Mary is clearly the more aggressive of the two.

4. Ms. Wadkins had dinner at Mr. Crary's house on three occasions last week. The first time, she thought the meal was delicious and told him so. She did not find the next two meals to be delicious, and being that she is not one to lie, she did not tell Mr. Crary that they were so. Mr. Crary concluded that she disliked those meals, and so chose to never make them for her again.

5. In order to join the finance committee, one must have at least six years of accounting experience. Since Tammy has only four years of accounting experience, she is not eligible to become a financial officer.

6. All librarians enjoy spending time organizing books. Since Teri enjoys spending time organizing books, I imagine she is a librarian.

7. Every time you drink, you end up feeling sick the next day. You say you are feeling sick today. You must have gone drinking yesterday.

8. Though individual human beings almost always claim to prefer peace to war, history has shown again and again that societies that wage war rise in power, whereas those they attack generally lose power. Ironically, therefore, societies that wage war have greater capacity to do good for the world.

9. Between 1980 and 1990, the total number of movie theater tickets purchased per year doubled. Therefore, a movie released in 1990 was likely, on average, to have twice the theater viewership of a movie released in 1980.

Flaw Drill

10. You claim that our company is in a better financial situation than it was seven years ago, but this claim is patently false. Not only have company earnings decreased during this time, they've actually decreased each year for seven years in a row.

11. Maxine noticed a particular pattern in her husband: every time he told a lie, he would touch his left ear. On Tuesday she asked him where he had been the night before, and, touching his left ear, he said he was at his mother's house. She concluded he was lying and threw him out of the house.

12. You say that Albert is wiser than Max, but that cannot be true, for Max knows far more than Albert does.

13. The positioning of the fingers on a human hand gives us numerous advantages that we are all aware of—such as being able to hold a pencil and write. The positioning of the toes on our feet is as purposeful as the positioning of our fingers, and though we may not generally be aware of the advantages of our foot and toe design, they must invariably exist to a similar degree.

14. Your claim that our company is becoming less and less profitable is simply not true. Our gross revenue has grown in each of the last six years, and you have stated yourself that you expect this trend to continue.

15. How can you say I got a bad deal on these pants? They were on sale!

16. The Westwood brand of furniture is made using a process that has been handed down generation after generation. Each piece is made by a member of the Westwood family. Therefore, if your furniture was made by a member of the Westwood family, as you claim, then it must be true that it's Westwood brand furniture.

17. Before the teacher returned the essays to the students who had written them, he mentioned the names of the students who received the highest scores. Danielle's name was not called. Therefore, she expected that she did not perform well on the essay.

18. Homes in the area have not been selling for above their asking prices. Sharon is expecting bids greater than her asking price for commercial real estate she owns in the area, but these expectations are clearly unwarranted.

Flaw Drill Solutions

1. Sandy is prone to wild emotional fluctuations, but Charlie is not. In fact, Charlie is the picture of serenity, never getting too up or too down. It is Charlie, not Sandy, who is in a healthier emotional state.

Takes for granted that being less prone to emotional fluctuations equates to being in a healthier emotional state. Perhaps wild emotional fluctuations are signs of a healthy emotional state. Perhaps Charlie is serene because he blocks out his emotions in an unhealthy way.

2. You say that most people who own smartphones also own laptops, but that must be incorrect, for fewer than half the people who own laptops own smartphones.

Takes for granted that if a majority of people with smartphones have laptops, a majority of people with laptops must have smartphones. It could be that one hundred people own smartphones, eighty of whom also own laptops, and one thousand people own laptops, eighty of whom own smartphones.

3. You say that Tony is more dangerous than Mary, which can't be true, for Mary is clearly the more aggressive of the two.

Takes for granted that aggression equates to danger. Perhaps Mary is aggressive but doesn't cause a danger to others, and perhaps Tony is not aggressive, but, because he is extremely clumsy, he poses a danger to all those who are around him.

4. Ms. Wadkins had dinner at Mr. Crary's house on three occasions last week. The first time, she thought the meal was delicious and told him so. She did not find the next two meals to be delicious, and being that she is not one to lie, did not tell Mr. Crary that they were so. Mr. Crary concluded that she disliked those meals, and so chose to never make them for her again.

Takes for granted that because Ms. Wadkins did not find the meal to be delicious, she did not like it. Perhaps she found the taste of it to be just okay, but because it was healthy and made her feel good, she liked eating it.

5. In order to join the finance committee, one must have at least six years of accounting experience. Since Tammy has only four years of accounting experience, she is not eligible to become a financial officer.

Takes for granted that being a member of the finance committee is directly related to becoming a financial officer. It could be that she could become a financial officer without joining the finance committee.

6. All librarians enjoy spending time organizing books. Since Teri enjoys spending time organizing books, I imagine she is a librarian.

Fails to consider that people other than librarians could also enjoy organizing books.

7. Every time you drink, you end up feeling sick the next day. You say you are feeling sick today. You must have gone drinking yesterday.

Takes for granted that because drinking leads to feeling sick, feeling sick was caused by drinking. Fails to consider that other issues—perhaps catching a cold—could cause someone to feel sick.

8. Though individual human beings almost always claim to prefer peace to war, history has shown again and again that societies that wage war rise in power, whereas those they attack generally lose power. Ironically, therefore, societies that wage war have greater capacity to do good for the world.

Takes for granted that having power equates to having a greater capacity to do good. Power is a general term, and perhaps the type of power gained in many of these wars is not of a sort that can be helpful to others.

9. Between 1980 and 1990, the total number of movie theater tickets purchased per year doubled. Therefore, a movie released in 1990 was likely, on average, to have twice the theater viewership of a movie released in 1980.

Takes for granted that the number of films released per year stayed constant, and takes for granted that tickets sold equates to number of viewers. It could be that twice as many movies were released in 1990, so the average per-movie viewership stayed constant. It could be that movie theaters started offering fewer free tickets or fewer buy-one-get-one-free deals.

Flaw Drill Solutions

10. You claim that our company is in a better financial situation than it was seven years ago, but this claim is patently false. Not only have company earnings decreased during this time, they've actually decreased each year for seven years in a row.

Takes for granted that information about earnings is definitely representative of the company's general financial situation. It could be that yearly earnings are down because the company is investing in a massive program that will bring great financial success down the line.

11. Maxine noticed a particular pattern in her husband: every time he told a lie, he would touch his left ear. On Tuesday she asked him where he had been the night before, and, touching his left ear, he said he was at his mother's house. She concluded he was lying and threw him out of the house.

Fails to consider that there are other issues that cause him to touch his left ear. Perhaps every time he thinks of his mother, he touches his left ear. Maybe he had an itch.

12. You say that Albert is wiser than Max, but that cannot be true, for Max knows far more than Albert does.

Takes for granted that knowing more equates to being wiser. As we've all heard all our lives, knowledge and wisdom are not the same thing. We all know people who know a lot but are fools.

13. The positioning of the fingers on a human hand gives us numerous advantages that we are all aware of—such as being able to hold a pencil and write. The positioning of the toes on our feet is as purposeful as the positioning of our fingers, and though we may not generally be aware of the advantages of our foot and toe design, they must invariably exist to a similar degree.

Even if the positioning of the toes is as purpose-driven as the positioning of the fingers, the fingers can still give us greater advantages.

14. Your claim that our company is becoming less and less profitable is simply not true. Our gross revenue has grown in each of the last six years, and you have stated yourself that you expect this trend to continue.

Takes for granted that revenue equates to profit. Perhaps the revenue is increasing, but the costs are increasing at an even higher rate.

15. How can you say I got a bad deal on these pants? They were on sale!

Takes for granted that being on sale equates to being a good deal. Perhaps the pants are a rip-off at any price.

16. The Westwood brand of furniture is made using a process that has been handed down generation after generation. Each piece is made by a member of the Westwood family. Therefore, if your furniture was made by a member of the Westwood family, as you claim, then it must be true that it's Westwood brand furniture.

Takes for granted that because each piece of Westwood furniture is made by a Westwood family member, any furniture made by a Westwood family member must be Westwood brand furniture. Maybe a rogue son unhappy with his spot in the pecking order went to work for a rival company.

17. Before the teacher returned the essays to the students who had written them, he mentioned the names of the students who received the highest scores. Danielle's name was not called. Therefore, she expected that she did not perform well on the essay.

Takes for granted that the only people who did well were those who got the highest scores. Perhaps she got a score that she still considers "performing well" even if it was not one of the highest.

18. Homes in the area have not been selling for above their asking prices. Sharon is expecting bids greater than her asking price for commercial real estate she owns in the area, but these expectations are clearly unwarranted.

Takes for granted that there is a connection between the selling of homes and the selling of commercial real estate. Perhaps homes are selling below asking price, but a shortage of office space, or incorrect pricing, is causing commercial real estate to sell above asking price.

Sample Questions

Here are two LSAT questions that have arguments with piece ≠ puzzle issues. Read the question stem carefully, do your best to identify the flaw in the argument, and select the answer choice you think best addresses that flaw.

24.3.2. Advertisement: Anyone who thinks moisturizers are not important for beautiful skin should consider what happens to the earth, the skin of the world, in time of drought. Without regular infusions of moisture the ground becomes lined and cracked and its lush liveliness fades away. Thus your skin, too, should be protected from the ravages caused by lack of moisture; give it the protection provided by regular infusions of Dewyfresh, the drought-defying moisturizer.

The Dewyfresh advertisement exhibits which one of the following errors of reasoning?

(A) It treats something that is necessary for bringing about a state of affairs as something that is sufficient to bring about that state of affairs.
(B) It treats the fact that two things regularly occur together as proof that there is a single thing that is the cause of them both.
(C) It overlooks the fact that changing what people think is the case does not necessarily change what is the case.
(D) It relies on the ambiguity of the term "infusion," which can designate either a process or the product of that process.
(E) It relies on an analogy between two things that are insufficiently alike in the respects in which they would have to be alike for the conclusion to be supported.

24.2.21. Newspaper editor: Law enforcement experts, as well as most citizens, have finally come to recognize that legal prohibitions against gambling all share a common flaw: no matter how diligent the effort, the laws are impossible to enforce. Ethical qualms notwithstanding, when a law fails to be effective, it should not be a law. That is why there should be no legal prohibition against gambling.

Which one of the following, if assumed, allows the argument's conclusion to be properly drawn?

(A) No effective law is unenforceable.
(B) All enforceable laws are effective.
(C) No legal prohibitions against gambling are enforceable.
(D) Most citizens must agree with a law for the law to be effective.
(E) Most citizens must agree with a law for the law to be enforceable.

24.3.2. Advertisement: Anyone who thinks moisturizers are not important for beautiful skin should consider what happens to the earth, the skin of the world, in time of drought. Without regular infusions of moisture the ground becomes lined and cracked and its lush liveliness fades away. Thus your skin, too, should be protected from the ravages caused by lack of moisture; give it the protection provided by regular infusions of Dewyfresh, the drought-defying moisturizer.

The Dewyfresh advertisement exhibits which one of the following errors of reasoning?

(A) It treats something that is necessary for bringing about a state of affairs as something that is sufficient to bring about that state of affairs.
(B) It treats the fact that two things regularly occur together as proof that there is a single thing that is the cause of them both.
(C) It overlooks the fact that changing what people think is the case does not necessarily change what is the case.
(D) It relies on the ambiguity of the term "infusion," which can designate either a process or the product of that process.
(E) It relies on an analogy between two things that are insufficiently alike in the respects in which they would have to be alike for the conclusion to be supported.

Task: We need to figure out what is wrong with the reasoning.

Flaw: The advertisement says that we should use Dewyfresh to protect our skin from the ravages of drought. As reasoning, it uses the analogy of the earth, which cracks and such when there is a drought. Wait a minute—who says our skin is like the earth?

Answers: The problem with this advertisement is not that it treats something that is needed for good skin as being enough to bring about good skin, so we can eliminate (A) quickly. The advertisement doesn't have a causal flaw, so we can eliminate (B) too. What we think, versus what is, is not the issue, so we can eliminate (C). The term "infusion" is not relevant to the reasoning, so we can eliminate (D). (E) is an unnecessarily complicated way of describing the flaw we saw initially: the argument uses for its reasoning an analogy (between skin and earth) it has no good reason to use. **(E) is correct.**

24.2.21. Newspaper editor: Law enforcement experts, as well as most citizens, have finally come to recognize that legal prohibitions against gambling all share a common flaw: no matter how diligent the effort, the laws are impossible to enforce. Ethical qualms notwithstanding, when a law fails to be effective, it should not be a law. That is why there should be no legal prohibition against gambling.

Which one of the following, if assumed, allows the argument's conclusion to be properly drawn?

(A) No effective law is unenforceable.
(B) All enforceable laws are effective.
(C) No legal prohibitions against gambling are enforceable.
(D) Most citizens must agree with a law for the law to be effective.
(E) Most citizens must agree with a law for the law to be enforceable.

Task: We need an answer that allows the argument to be properly drawn—that means we need an answer that makes the conclusion one hundred percent guaranteed based on the reasoning given.

Flaw: The author says that there should be no prohibition against gambling (yay!). Why? When a law fails to be **effective**, it should not be a law, and gambling laws are impossible to **enforce**. The author is falsely equating here: a law being enforceable is not the same thing as a law being effective. In order to fill this gap, we need to know that if a law is not enforceable, it won't be effective.

Answers: (A) may not be exactly what we expected, but what does it tell us about unenforceable laws? Well, if no effective law is unenforceable, that means that laws that are unenforceable can't be effective. That's what we needed, and **(A) is correct.** (B) tells us something about enforceable laws, but what about unenforceable laws? It doesn't help us with that, and so we can eliminate (B). (C) just restates something we had as support already—it doesn't fix any holes in the argument. We can eliminate (D) and (E) very quickly—what most citizens must agree with doesn't fill the gap we saw between enforcement and effectiveness.

Tips on Review

How did you do on those two questions? If you felt confident solving both of them, and if your thought process matched the one I outlined in the solution, then great. If you felt confident solving both of them, but your thought process was different from mine, that's great too. If you had trouble with either of the questions, hopefully reading the sample solution helped you see where, exactly, things started to go wrong for you, and hopefully it helped you understand the key facets of the questions.

If your aim is to score at a very high level (and there is no reason it shouldn't be), make it your goal to be able to fully understand, after the fact, every question that you review as part of your practice. To that end, here are guidelines for making sure that your understanding is complete:

(1) Read the question stem again carefully. Make sure you recognize exactly what it is that tips you off that you are supposed to be critical of an argument, and make sure you recognize exactly what your task is relative to that argument.

(2) Read the stimulus to correctly identify the argument. Remember, the argument consists of a point made and the reasoning given to support that point.

(3) Once you have the argument separated out, seek out the flaw in reasoning. Every time we are asked to be critical of reasoning, it will be imperfect in some way.

(4) Make sure you understand why the right answer matches the argument and the task. The right answer will address a flaw in the argument, and it will do so in a way that matches the task presented in the question stem.

(5) Make sure you understand why each wrong answer is incorrect. You should be able to clearly articulate at least one absolute reason why each wrong answer is wrong.

At this point in your process, it's expected that you may have trouble understanding certain questions "fully." Take note of such questions, and continue to recycle through them. In time, as your understanding and experience grows, expect the challenges that once felt impossible to feel more and more manageable.

8 LOGICAL REASONING
1 + 1 ≠ 3

In this lesson, we will discuss arguments that are flawed because the author brings together two ideas, or two pieces of information, to conclude something that those components do not warrant.

Here are some examples of arguments with 1 + 1 ≠ 3 flaws. It should be fairly obvious to you why each argument is flawed, but if you do get tripped up (it happens to all of us), make sure that you review the arguments again before you finish this lesson.

"Ted is the tallest in his family, and Sharon is the shortest in hers. Therefore, Ted must be taller than Sharon."

"In 1996, 2001, and 2004, we publicly unveiled plans to radically restructure our company. Those three years happen to be the worst three years in terms of our company stock's price levels. Clearly, the public was unhappy with our restructuring strategies."

If the flaws in the above arguments remind you of the flaws from Lessons 6 and 7, then great. As we've stated before, there is a natural overlap between categories, and it's not something you need to feel rigid about. There is, in particular, a lot of bleed from both Lessons 6 and 7 into this one—the arguments in this lesson will often have the same type of reasoning flaws, but in the context of bringing two premises together.

On the next few pages, we will break down the most common 1 + 1 ≠ 3 arguments and discuss exactly why the reasoning in them is flawed. We'll then wrap up by practicing looking out for such flaws in arguments.

Context Issues

Sometimes, the subjects and characteristics mentioned in the premises will be an almost exact match for those that are in the conclusion, but the argument will still be flawed. Here's an example:

"Seven months ago, Ian's photos took up 6 percent of his computer memory. Today, they take up 4 percent of the memory on his computer. Ian must have deleted some photos, or in some other way lessened the amount of memory they are taking up on his computer."

Note that we haven't shifted subjects—we're talking about photos and computer memory throughout. But can you see how this argument could be wrong? Maybe he upgraded his memory to have more of it, or maybe he is on a different computer.

What this argument fails to take account of is *context*—the situation might be different, but the author assumes it has stayed consistent from six months ago to today. We know that's no good. Here's another one:

"Carla earns the average salary of the people who live in her city, and she lives in a home that is of average value relative to the other homes in her city. Nina lives in a neighboring city and the same can be said for her as well—her income and home value match those of the people in her city. It's likely, therefore, that Carla and Nina earn comparable salaries and live in comparably valued homes."

Again, note that there is a great amount of matching between the support and the conclusion: there are no subject shifts, and the characteristics we are discussing—salaries and home values—stay consistent. The problem is that the author is making an assumption about context—in order for this argument to work, we'd have to know that the two cities are comparable in terms of average salaries and home values. Knowing that the two cities are neighbors is not nearly enough to prove that to us.

Reasoning Issues

In each of the examples we just discussed, if the context had been the same—that is, the computer in question didn't change in any other way, or if the cities that Carla and Nina lived in were indeed similar in terms of average salary and home value—the reasoning in them would actually have been valid. The failure to consider context is the only reason those arguments are wrong.

Far more commonly, $1 + 1 \neq 3$ arguments are flawed, however, for exactly the same types of reasoning issues that plague other arguments—the author jumps to a conclusion, or equates things that shouldn't necessarily be equated (hey, isn't this what context issues are, as well?). A key way to recognize the flaw is to think about changes in subject matter, characteristic, or relationship. Here are three basic examples, one of each:

context issues

"George is the hardest-working employee in his division, but the same cannot be said about Karla and her division. So, if we want to promote a hard worker to the upper management position, George is a stronger candidate than Karla."

Perhaps George happens to be the only person who works moderately hard in a division full of lazy employees, and perhaps Karla actually works far harder than George does.

"Coats and scarves sell better in the winter than in the summer, and T-shirts and shorts sell better in the summer than in the winter. It is expected, then, that jeans sell at a consistent rate year-round."

So, if we try to make the reasoning work, maybe we say to ourselves that jeans are neither a summer item nor a winter item, and so maybe they don't have these cyclical...but wait—that's not our job! We need to find what's wrong here, and what's wrong is that the premises don't tell us anything about jeans! This is a *subject matter issue.*

"Laptops, on average, are more expensive than desktop computers, but tablet systems are cheaper than desktop computers. It's clear that demand for laptops is far greater than that for tablets."

Note that the premises do prove, when taken together, that laptops are more expensive than tablets. However, thinking about what we can prove is a waste of time. What's wrong here is that price does not tell us anything definite about demand. In this case, the author has incorrectly changed the *characteristic*.

"A recent study of our university's graduates reported that students who paid for at least a part of their education themselves ended up earning more, on average, than did students whose parents paid for all of their expenses. This disparity was consistent across all different majors and periods in our school's history. This shows that contributing to the costs of one's own education can have a positive impact on one's future earnings."

This argument is probably the toughest of all to find fault with, but do you see it? Note that the premises give us a correlation, that is, a statistical connection between students paying for school and earning more afterwards, and the author uses this correlation to make a point about causation—paying impacts earnings. This is a reasoning no-no; no amount of correlation can ever prove a causal relationship—perhaps it's the most motivated students who end up paying for a part of their schooling, and it is this motivation, rather than the actual paying itself, that impacts future earnings. We'll discuss causation more on the next page, but this would be an example of a *relationship issue*.

reasoning issues

"Most people who watch television now have methods that allow them to skip commercials, yet most people do not skip commercials. This must mean that people enjoy watching commercials, at least enough to not skip them."

The author adds most people can skip commercials + most people do not to conclude that most people must enjoy the commercials. This does not add up. There could be other reasons people watch commercials even if they don't enjoy them. Maybe people who have these devices don't know how to use them, or perhaps skipping commercials requires one to record shows ahead of time, and people choose not to do that.

Correlation and Causation: The Complicated Relationship

Okay, let's imagine that on Tuesday you drink a Bogo Smoothie and you also get a stomachache. That would be an example of *correlation*—two things that are, through some characteristic (in this case, happening on the same day), related to one another.

Can we say that the smoothie caused your stomachache? We can guess this, but this type of guessing is really not required or rewarded on the LSAT. What we want to focus on is would that be *enough information to be certain*? No.

Okay, how about this? The last five days on which you drank a Bogo Smoothie, you got a stomachache. Is that enough to prove that the Bogos caused the stomachaches? No. It doesn't prove it. It does make the case a bit more interesting, though, right?

How about this! Every day you drink a Bogo Smoothie you get a stomachache, and every day you don't drink a Bogo Smoothie you don't get a stomachache. This is true for your entire life. Is that enough to prove that the smoothie has at least some causal impact on your stomachaches? No.

It could be true that you get Bogo Smoothies whenever you go to see a movie at the mall, and it could be that sitting in a theater and watching a large bright screen gives you a stomachache. In this case, the smoothies and the stomachaches have nothing to do with one another. Or, it could be that nothing helps your stomachache like a Bogo Smoothie, so you run and get one every time you have a stomachache—that is, instead of the smoothie causing the stomachache, the stomachache causes you to get the smoothie.

Are those scenarios more likely than the first? Of course not, but that's far beside the point. The bigger issue is that correlation can never, never, ever, ever(!), prove causation.

Now, if that's all there was to it, it would be simple enough, but let's go back to the smoothie and stomachache example. When the two happen to go together more and more—that is, it just keeps happening that these two events happen together, does it increase the likelihood that they are related, and that one might have a causal impact on the other? Yes, it does. It doesn't absolutely prove it, but hey, if you just happen to be at every bank that gets robbed, your *likelihood* of being involved is greater than that of someone who lives, say, three thousand miles away. So correlation *can* strengthen or weaken.

The flip side is even more convincing. If the correlation proves to not be as strong— let's say the next few days you drank the smoothie you didn't get stomachaches—does that weaken the case that the smoothie causes the stomachaches? Yes, it does.

Hence, the complicated relationship. Evidence of correlation, or lack thereof, can *strengthen* or *weaken* a claim of causation, but it can never, ever *prove* a claim of causation. Only causation proves causation. Let's expand on this and see how this understanding plays out in a variety of potential questions involving a causal argument.

argument & task

Right answers are answers that match the argument and the task. In this first batch of lessons, we have focused primarily on developing our ability to evaluate arguments. In the next batch, we will start discussing how to apply our skills to specific types of questions. Here's a small taste of how our understanding of an argument can relate to the various tasks that question stems can present.

"The last six instances in which our nation has made a public declaration condemning what we felt was an oppressive regime, there was violence in the days that followed that declaration. Therefore, if we want to minimize this type of violence, we should not make such public declarations."

What's wrong: In this case, the causal claim is not directly stated in the conclusion; rather, it serves as the reasoning that underlies the conclusion reached. The author states that not making declarations would minimize the violence, and this would only be true if we were to assume that the declarations have some impact on the violence. The way the evidence is presented makes it seem pretty damaging, but the premise just provides us with a correlation: these two things—our declaration and the violence—happen to happen in the same place at related times. And, as we've discussed, correlation is never enough to justify a claim of causation. Maybe these other countries don't care at all what we declare, and the matching timing is just coincidence. Maybe we make these declarations in areas that are just about to go to war, and we do this in order to minimize the amount of inevitable violence to come. Your job, of course, isn't to necessarily think about these alternatives; rather, your job is to realize that the correlation is not enough to justify the causation (though correlation can strengthen or weaken the claim).

POTENTIAL **QUESTIONS** AND ANSWERS

Which of the following most accurately represents the author's main point? If we want to minimize this type of violence, we should not make these types of public declarations condemning oppressive regimes.

The reasoning in the argument is flawed in that it takes for granted that the declarations have some impact on the violence that follows.

The author assumes that not making such declarations will have a minimizing impact on this type of violence.

Which of the following, if true, would most strengthen the argument? Every country in the world pays significant attention to our nation's declarations, and there is rarely any violence when we do not make such declarations.

Which of the following, if true, most seriously weakens the argument? In each of the six instances, the declarations were made after it became certain that there would be violence in those areas.

What principle could be used to support this point? A correlation between such declarations and such violence is sufficient to show a causal impact.

Which of the following is an assumption the argument requires? Our declarations have at least some impact on the violence that ensues in other countries.

Which one of the following, if assumed, enables the argument's conclusion to be properly drawn? It is true that not making declarations will have a direct consequence of reducing the violence that follows.

The questionable pattern of reasoning in which of the following is most similar to that in the argument above? Over the past few years I've made a conscious effort to floss every night. However, each visit to the dentist reveals more gum decay. Therefore, I should stop flossing if I want to minimize gum decay.

Flaw Drill

Directions: For each argument, write why you feel the support doesn't prove the conclusion.

1. On average, students who have graduated from our university have consistently earned far more than have the graduates of our rival school. It must be that the superior quality of our instruction has some impact on our students' future earnings.

2. Musical geniuses are often poor music teachers, for they are often unable to express in words what it is they do so well. By a similar token, it's expected that those who are geniuses in the art of writing are often poor writing instructors.

3. Ted's father was twenty-three when he got married, his grandfather nineteen, and his great-grandfather twenty-one. Since Ted is twenty-five now and not yet married, it is unlikely he will ever be married.

4. In order to get into the club, it is required that one has a pass, and in order to get a pass, it is required that one is a member of a certain secret society. Therefore, if one is a member of the secret society, he or she will be able to get into the club.

5. In a certain local election, it just so happens that both Republicans and Democrats endorse the same candidate: Candidate X. All members of both parties will vote for him. Therefore, Candidate X will easily win the election.

6. Sarah spends a quarter of her monthly income on clothing, whereas Jonathan spends less than 10 percent of his monthly income on clothing. So, I imagine Sarah spends a lot more on clothing than Jonathan does.

7. When the nurses at a certain hospital were polled on things about the hospital with which they were unhappy, the quality of the cafeteria food came up third on their list. Doctors polled at the same time listed the quality of cafeteria food as their most common complaint. It's clear, therefore, that the doctors are more upset about the quality of the cafeteria food than the nurses are.

8. Thomas says he cares more about the Montecito branch than he does the Thousand Oaks branch, but he spends far less time at the Montecito branch than he does at the Thousand Oaks branch. Therefore, I don't believe him.

9. Most people in the club support the new measure, and most people in the club support the plan to move to new facilities. Therefore, at least one member of the leadership committee supports the new measure and the plan to move to new facilities.

Flaw Drill

10. Sarah is an incredibly creative person, whereas Jeff is not. Therefore, Sarah will be better able to implement the significant changes that our company needs.

11. Most of the congressmen said that they would vote for the bill, but most of those who stated this said that they would do so with some reservations. It stands to reason, thus, that at least one congressman did not vote for the bill.

12. You agree with me that Terry has better leadership qualities than does Francine. Therefore, I'm sure you'll agree that Terry is better qualified for the job than Francine is.

13. When Sharon wears a knee brace while she plays basketball, her knee hurts a lot more than it does when she does not wear a knee brace while playing basketball. She determined that the knee brace was causing her pain and stopped wearing it.

14. Johnny recently broke one of his grandmother's glass jars, but after he explained to her that he was distracted, she did not get upset with him about the jar. Today, he crashed his grandmother's car. He expects, when he explains to her that he was just distracted, that she will not be upset.

15. Every time Val comes and visits, the house becomes a mess. So how can you say that Val is not messy?

16. Greg is the top soccer player in his league, and his league is the top soccer league in the country. It stands to reason that Greg is the best soccer player in the country.

17. Region A and Region B are both equally prone to dangerous tornados. Region A has a sophisticated warning system, whereas Region B does not. Therefore, Region A is better prepared for dangerous tornadoes than Region B is.

18. Everyone in our extended family tried out for the play, and most of the family members who tried out got parts in the play. So, it must be true that most of the parts in the play will be performed by members of my family.

Flaw Drill Solutions

1. On average, students who have graduated from our university have consistently earned far more than have the graduates of our rival school. It must be that the superior quality of our instruction has some impact on our students' future earnings.

Uses a correlation between attending a certain university and future earnings to justify a causal claim about the quality of instruction. It could be that graduating from that university has nothing to do with future earnings, or it could be that something else about the university other than the quality of instruction is responsible for the impact.

2. Musical geniuses are often poor music teachers, for they are often unable to express in words what it is they do so well. By a similar token, it's expected that those who are geniuses in the art of writing are often poor writing instructors.

The argument relates musical and writing genius, and the impact of that genius on teaching, without any warrant to do so. We have no proof that genius in writing has the same impact as genius in music. Perhaps being a genius at writing helps one be able to express ideas in words.

3. Ted's father was twenty-three when he got married, his grandfather nineteen, and his great-grandfather twenty-one. Since Ted is twenty-five now and not yet married, it is unlikely he will ever be married.

The argument falsely relates four generations of a family without a sense of proper context. Perhaps Ted is unmarried because the societal norm is to marry later than people once did.

4. In order to get into the club, it is required that one has a pass, and in order to get a pass, it is required that one is a member of a certain secret society. Therefore, if one is a member of the secret society, he or she will be able to get into the club.

The argument falsely assumes that since membership in a secret society is required to get a pass, all in the secret society can get the pass, and that since a pass is required to get into the club, all who have a pass will get into the club. Perhaps only some society members got passes, and only some of those with passes get into the club.

5. In a certain local election, it just so happens that both Republicans and Democrats endorse the same candidate: Candidate X. All members of both parties will vote for him. Therefore, Candidate X will easily win the election.

The argument falsely assumes that two groups of individuals—Democrats and Republicans—will determine the election results. Perhaps voters from other parties, or independent voters, will determine the election.

6. Sarah spends a quarter of her monthly income on clothing, whereas Jonathan spends less than 10 percent of his monthly income on clothing. So, I imagine Sarah spends a lot more on clothing than Jonathan does.

The argument fails to consider that Sarah and Jonathan may have significantly different incomes. If Sarah makes $4 a month, and Jonathan $1,000,000, it could be true that he spends a lot more on clothing than Sarah does.

7. When the nurses at a certain hospital were polled on things about the hospital with which they were unhappy, the quality of the cafeteria food came up third on their list. Doctors polled at the same time listed the quality of cafeteria food as their most common complaint. It's clear, therefore, that the doctors are more upset about the quality of the cafeteria food than the nurses are.

The argument takes for granted that showing up first on one list is more significant than showing up third on another. Perhaps the nurses have other things they are unhappy about, but still care more about the quality of the cafeteria than the doctors do.

8. Thomas says he cares more about the Montecito branch than he does the Thousand Oaks branch, but he spends far less time at the Montecito branch than he does at the Thousand Oaks branch. Therefore, I don't believe him.

Takes for granted that time spent is equivalent to the amount that Thomas cares about a branch. Perhaps other reasons force him to stay at the Thousand Oaks branch.

9. Most people in the club support the new measure, and most people in the club support the plan to move to new facilities. Therefore, at least one member of the leadership committee supports the new measure and the plan to move to new facilities.

The argument fails to consider that those club members who support the measure or the move to the new facilities may not be members of the leadership committee. Perhaps the majority of the leadership committee happens to hold minority opinions on one or both of those issues.

Flaw Drill Solutions

10. Sarah is an incredibly creative person, whereas Jeff is not. Therefore, Sarah will be better able to implement the significant changes that our company needs.

Takes for granted that creativity is the characteristic that defines whether one will be able to implement the necessary changes. Perhaps Jeff isn't creative himself, but is amazing at getting ideas from others and implementing them successfully. Perhaps Sarah is creative but comes up with terrible ideas.

11. Most of the congressmen said that they would vote for the bill, but most of those who stated this said that they would do so with some reservations. It stands to reason, thus, that at least one congressman did not vote for the bill.

Takes for granted that because most who would vote for the bill have reservations, some will vote against the bill. "Most" does not exclude the possibility of "all," and the fact that they have reservations has no impact on the reasoning issues.

12. You agree with me that Terry has better leadership qualities than does Francine. Therefore, I'm sure you'll agree that Terry is better qualified for the job than Francine is.

The argument takes for granted that leadership qualities define the better candidate for the job. Perhaps Terry has certain undesirable qualities that offset his leadership skills, or perhaps there are other reasons that make Francine better qualified for that particular job.

13. When Sharon wears a knee brace while she plays basketball, her knee hurts a lot more than it does when she does not wear a knee brace while playing basketball. She determined that the knee brace was causing her pain and stopped wearing it.

Uses a correlation to justify a claim of causation. Perhaps, when Sharon wears the brace, she plays much harder, and that's why her knee hurts.

14. Johnny recently broke one of his grandmother's glass jars, but after he explained to her that he was distracted, she did not get upset with him about the jar. Today, he crashed his grandmother's car. He expects, when he explains to her that he was just distracted, that she will not be upset.

Fails to consider differences in context. It's perhaps more understandable for one to be distracted enough to break a glass jar than it is to be distracted enough to crash a car.

15. Every time Val comes and visits, the house becomes a mess. So how can you say that Val is not messy?

Uses a correlation to justify a claim of causation. Perhaps, when Val comes, family members have so much fun with her that they forget to do their own chores, and that's why the house becomes a mess.

16. Greg is the top soccer player in his league, and his league is the top soccer league in the country. It stands to reason that Greg is the best soccer player in the country.

Takes for granted that being the best in his league makes Greg the best in the country. Perhaps there is a better player playing in a lower league.

17. Region A and Region B are both equally prone to dangerous tornados. Region A has a sophisticated warning system, whereas Region B does not. Therefore, Region A is better prepared for dangerous tornadoes than Region B is.

Takes for granted that a sophisticated warning system is what determines which region is better prepared. Perhaps there are other reasons, such as a wiser and more prepared populace, or a simpler but more effective warning system, that make Region B better prepared.

18. Everyone in our extended family tried out for the play, and most of the family members who tried out got parts in the play. So, it must be true that most of the parts in the play will be performed by members of my family.

Takes for granted that since most family members have parts, most parts will be performed by the family members. Perhaps the family members only comprise a small portion of the overall cast.

Sample Questions

Here are two LSAT questions that have arguments with 1 + 1 ≠ 3 issues. Read the question stem carefully, do your best to identify the flaw in the argument, and select the answer choice you think best addresses that flaw.

23.2.8. The caterpillar of the monarch butterfly feeds on milkweed plants, whose toxins make the adult monarch poisonous to many predators. The viceroy butterfly, whose caterpillars do not feed on milkweed plants, is very similar in appearance to the monarch. Therefore, it can be concluded that the viceroy is so seldom preyed on because of its visual resemblance to the monarch.

Which one of the following, if it were discovered to be true, would most seriously undermine the argument?

(A) Some predators do not have a toxic reaction to insects that feed on milkweed plants.
(B) Being toxic to predators will not protect individual butterflies unless most members of the species to which such butterflies belong are similarly toxic.
(C) Some of the predators of the monarch butterfly also prey on viceroys.
(D) The viceroy butterfly is toxic to most predators.
(E) Toxicity to predators is the principal means of protection for only a few butterfly species.

23.2.17. Studies show that the most creative engineers get their best and most useful ideas only after doodling and jotting down what turn out to be outlandish ideas. Now that many engineers do their work with computers instead of on paper, however, doodling is becoming much less common, and some experts fear that the result will be fewer creative and useful engineering ideas. These experts argue that this undesirable consequence would be avoided if computer programs for engineering work included simulated notepads that would allow engineers to suspend their "serious" work on the computer, type up outlandish ideas, and then quickly return to their original work.

Which one of the following is an assumption on which the experts' reasoning depends?

(A) Most creative engineers who work with paper and pencil spend about as much time doodling as they spend on what they consider serious work.
(B) Simulated notepads would not be used by engineers for any purpose other than typing up outlandish ideas.
(C) No engineers who work with computers keep paper and pencils near their computers in order to doodle and jot down ideas.
(D) The physical act of working on paper is not essential in providing engineers with the benefits that can be gained by doodling.
(E) Most of the outlandish ideas engineers jot down while doodling are later incorporated into projects that have practical applications.

23.2.8. The caterpillar of the monarch butterfly feeds on milkweed plants, whose toxins make the adult monarch poisonous to many predators. The viceroy butterfly, whose caterpillars do not feed on milkweed plants, is very similar in appearance to the monarch. Therefore, it can be concluded that the viceroy is so seldom preyed on because of its visual resemblance to the monarch.

Which one of the following, if it were discovered to be true, would most seriously undermine the argument?

(A) Some predators do not have a toxic reaction to insects that feed on milkweed plants.
(B) Being toxic to predators will not protect individual butterflies unless most members of the species to which such butterflies belong are similarly toxic.
(C) Some of the predators of the monarch butterfly also prey on viceroys.
(D) The viceroy butterfly is toxic to most predators.
(E) Toxicity to predators is the principal means of protection for only a few butterfly species.

Task: We need an answer that will hurt the argument by exposing its reasoning flaws in some way.

Flaw: The author's point is that the viceroy isn't preyed on because it looks like the monarch. The reason given? The monarch is poisonous. There are a couple of flaws here (one being that it's unclear whether predators stay away from monarch butterflies because they are poisonous), but the main one has to do with how the author is bringing information together: predators presumably want to stay away from the monarch, and the viceroy looks like the monarch, so predators must want to stay away from the viceroy *because* of this resemblance. Maybe there is some other reason predators want to stay away from the viceroy—like maybe they are ugly or smell really bad.

Answers: (A) has no direct impact on the monarch/viceroy connection and can be eliminated. For the same reason, (B) can be eliminated. It's unclear how (C) would *hurt* the argument, and we can quickly get rid of it as well. (D) finally gives us information that is relevant—if (D) is true, it provides an alternative reason for why predators might stay away from viceroys (and therefore undermines the idea that they stay away *because* viceroys look like monarchs). **(D) is correct.** It's unclear what impact (E) could have on the reasoning, and we can quickly get rid of it as well.

23.2.17. Studies show that the most creative engineers get their best and most useful ideas only after doodling and jotting down what turn out to be outlandish ideas. Now that many engineers do their work with computers instead of on paper, however, doodling is becoming much less common, and some experts fear that the result will be fewer creative and useful engineering ideas. These experts argue that this undesirable consequence would be avoided if computer programs for engineering work included simulated notepads that would allow engineers to suspend their "serious" work on the computer, type up outlandish ideas, and then quickly return to their original work.

Which one of the following is an assumption on which the experts' reasoning depends?

(A) Most creative engineers who work with paper and pencil spend about as much time doodling as they spend on what they consider serious work.
(B) Simulated notepads would not be used by engineers for any purpose other than typing up outlandish ideas.
(C) No engineers who work with computers keep paper and pencils near their computers in order to doodle and jot down ideas.
(D) The physical act of working on paper is not essential in providing engineers with the benefits that can be gained by doodling.
(E) Most of the outlandish ideas engineers jot down while doodling are later incorporated into projects that have practical applications.

Task: We need an answer on which the argument depends; that means we need an answer that must be true if the reasoning in the argument is going to work.

Flaw: The experts' point is that a simulated notepad computer program that allows engineers to doodle would help engineers get useful ideas. Why? Because when engineers doodle on paper it helps them get useful ideas. Wait a minute—I've tried doodling and jotting down ideas on a computer screen—it is not the same thing as doing it on a real paper notepad. The author is smashing together two things (notepad and computer) and making assumptions about the consequences.

Answers: The relative amount of time doodling versus working is not something that is directly relevant to the argument, and so we don't need to know (A) for the argument to work—we can eliminate it quickly. Whether the engineers use the notepads for other things doesn't impact the reasoning either, so we can eliminate (B). (C) might help the argument a little bit, because it gets rid of another obvious way to fix the problem, but it doesn't match the task—(C) does not *need* to be true for the argument to work. (D) does need to be true for the argument to work—if the experts' suggestion is going to pan out, it needs to be not important to the engineer that the doodling be done on paper, and that is exactly what (D) says. **(D) is correct.** Finally (E), which helps show the benefits of doodling, has no impact on the reasoning.

More Tips on Review

At the end of the previous lesson, we discussed the importance of fully understanding each and every question you solve and review as part of your LSAT preparation. For the types of questions we are currently dealing with, that means understanding the task presented in the question stem, correctly identifying the argument, seeing the flaw in the argument reasoning, being able to match the right answer to the argument and the task, and being able to come up with exact reasons for why wrong answers are wrong.

Now let's talk about how to take it a step further.

In order to get the most out of your review, you want to go beyond understanding; you want to think about your outcome in terms of your performance—how you solved the problem in real time. By linking your review with the actions you take during a question, you can most effectively impact and change your problem-solving process and habits. We can think of our misses as being the result of one or more *wrong actions*, and we can think of these wrong actions as falling into three general categories:

1) I read it wrong. Take note of the questions you miss because you misunderstand what you read, or don't see the reasoning structure correctly. Perhaps you didn't see the author's point clearly, you weren't able to isolate the supporting evidence, or you over-prioritized the background information. Maybe you read everything in the stimulus right, but missed the question because you misread, and quickly dismissed, what ultimately turned out to be the right answer.

2) I thought it wrong. Take note of the questions you miss because you don't see what is wrong with the reasoning in the argument. Finding flaws with arguments is what we've been working on most, and hopefully you already see some of the benefits of the work we've done.

3) I solved it wrong. This is most directly related to the process you used to select an answer choice. Perhaps you weren't diligent about eliminating wrong answers, or perhaps you didn't have a clear sense of exactly what the right answer was supposed to do.

For the questions that you miss in your review, or ones you find more challenging than you think you ought to, try to think about why, and try to do so in terms of the three categories mentioned above. Remember, there is plenty of time to gain mastery in all aspects of Logical Reasoning—a big key is to have a very clear sense of what it is exactly that you need to improve on.

9 LOGICAL REASONING flaw review

We've started our Logical Reasoning training with four lessons that have focused on one particular aspect of the problem-solving process: recognizing flaws in arguments.

For a majority of questions that appear in the section, your ability to identify the argument and to recognize the problem that exists between the conclusion and its support will be the *key* determinant of your success. This majority becomes even more pronounced when we isolate the hardest questions in the section—that is, the *vast* majority of the most difficult questions will depend on this skill. Furthermore, the *other* skills that we develop in our quest to identify flaws just happen to be some of the same skills that are required for success on minor question types.

As we'll see in future lessons (and in some examples later in this lesson), some questions do not require us to think about whether or not an argument is valid. In such cases when we are asked *not* to judge, forming an opinion is generally a detriment, for these questions are, in part, specifically testing our ability to stay objective.

However, most questions do require that we use our reasoning skills to evaluate an argument. When we are asked to do so, it is important that we not focus on "whether or not" an argument is valid, for in every such situation we will know that the argument is *not* valid. Our job, then, is to understand as correctly and specifically as we can *why* the argument is not valid. Understand that well, and you will see the matrix behind Logical Reasoning questions. Right answers and wrong answers will be far more obvious and clear cut.

Reading for flawed reasoning is as much habit as it is skill, and hopefully these four lessons have helped start you on the path to the optimal mindset for thinking about arguments critically. In Lesson 5 we discussed two mantras that help put us in this right mindset: "fails to consider" and "takes for granted." These statements accurately generalize the problems with all arguments—the authors of these arguments invariably fail to consider something, or they take for granted something that they should not.

In Lessons 6, 7, and 8, we defined three categories of reasoning flaws—over-extrapolating (piece ≠ puzzle), falsely associating (apples ≠ oranges), and bringing information together incorrectly (1 + 1 ≠ 3). As we discussed, there is great overlap between these categories, and it is not our goal to exclusively assign an issue to one category or another. Rather, we want to use all we know about flaws to help us see the flaws that we encounter in accurate, conceptual, and well-rounded ways. If you see a flaw as an apples ≠ oranges issue *and* a piece ≠ puzzle issue, well then, great! Our goal is not to understand the flaw in one particular way, but rather to understand it the best we can.

Recognizing flaws is the key reasoning skill, and recognizing arguments is the key reading skill

Our understanding of the flaw is the most important tool we have for eliminating wrong choices and identifying the right one. In this lesson, we will start the process of relating the work we've done with flaws to the more general process of solving full questions. We'll do so by talking briefly about the work we need to do in a problem before we start thinking about the flaw (we'll call this "prep work"), the act of finding the flaw in an argument ("the decision"), and finally, the manner in which we want to use this understanding to eliminate wrong answers and select the right choice ("the payoff"). We'll end the lesson by solving and discussing a set of eight Logical Reasoning questions.

Different types of questions will require us to utilize our skills in different ways, and we'll go into great detail about this starting in the next batch of lessons.

Prep Work

Recognizing the flaw in an argument is a *reasoning* skill, and it is the key reasoning skill required for this section. However, it's important to remember that Logical Reasoning is also just as much about your *reading* skills as it is about your reasoning skills. The most significant reading skill is your ability to recognize reasoning structure, that is, your ability to see how various parts of the stimulus are meant to relate to one another.

The reasoning structure with which we need to be most familiar and comfortable is that of an argument. For the sake of the LSAT, we can define an argument simply as a main point, and the reasons given to support that point. Up until now in our studies, I've generally gone ahead and isolated the argument for you, that is, for the drills we've done, almost everything in the stimulus was part of the conclusion or support for that conclusion. Furthermore, for most drill problems, it should have been fairly obvious which component was the conclusion and which parts were meant to be support.

An *argument* consists of a main point, and reasons given to support that point

However, on real LSAT questions arguments are often hidden within stimuli that also contain other types of information—primarily background information and opposing evidence. Furthermore, sometimes the test writers make it a challenge to understand exactly what part is meant to be the conclusion and what part is meant to be the support. This is the key reading challenge that is presented in this section: over and over again, you are going to have to prove that you can correctly identify and focus in on the argument within the stimulus.

In later lessons, we will get plenty of practice in extracting arguments from stimuli. Here's the key tip for now: *do not* try to absorb all parts of the stimulus with equal weight and attention. Rather, as you read through a stimulus, you want to *prioritize*. The main point and the support for it are far more important for you to recognize and understand correctly, and yet to throw you off the scent, the background and opposing points are often written to grab the most attention. For a question that requires us to be critical of argument reasoning, the background and opposing points will not have a direct impact on the differentiation between right and wrong answers. So pay the most attention to the point and the support, and try to push everything else into the background.

Remember: your main job, as you initially read through a stimulus, is to pull out the argument. Do so by first identifying the main point (you can't have an argument without a point). If all you do in your first read through a stimulus is identify the point, that read is a success. Once you have the point, identify the support. Sometimes, the support will be mixed in with background information. That's okay—it's typically not essential for you to draw a clear line of demarcation between the two. Instead, you want to focus on developing a clear conceptual understanding of exactly what reasoning strategy the author is using—just focus on how she's trying to justify the conclusion.

The Decision

Once we've zeroed in on the conclusion and the support, it's time to do our most important "thinking." We have to figure out, in as specific a way as we can, why the support given is not enough to justify the conclusion reached.

Pay the most attention to the point and the support, and try to push everything else into the background

As I've mentioned before, mindset is critical for this task. I've seen many students get "stuck" at a certain level in their training because of their inability to habitualize the correct thought processes. Unfortunately, it becomes harder and harder to change your mindset as you get deeper into your studies. That's why you want to make sure you address your mindset as much as possible at the beginning of your process.

Most of us, especially if we tend to be positive or optimistic people, habitually think about arguments in terms of how they *can* work—that is, we generally read to see how the support given *can* support the conclusion reached. And if something sounds reasonable, well, most of us are not in a mindset to nitpick problems. In life, this is a positive trait, but on the LSAT, this mindset is seriously detrimental.

There is one situation in life in which we don't tend to react to arguments in this way—when the arguments are made by people we strongly mistrust or strongly disagree with. If you know someone who consistently lies to you, and if these lies have a bad consequence on your life, your instinct is to focus on the holes in his or her reasoning. If you're forced to listen to a speech by a political figure with whom you strongly disagree, your instinct will probably be to pick apart his reasoning—to look for reasons why his argument is *not* reasonable. It's tough to go through all of life with this mindset, but this is indeed the optimal mindset for the LSAT. If you can picture arguments as being spoken by the blow-hard radio host you can't stand, or that family member who's always trying to borrow money from you, you'll be in a much better place to think about the issues that affect right and wrong answers.

Lastly, make sure your understanding of the flaw is conceptual and flexible. Challenging right answers will often word flaws in ways we don't expect, or expose these flaws from an unexpected perspective. If you are tied to a particular way of thinking about or wording the argument flaw, these challenges will trip you up far more than they will if you have a generalized understanding of the issue.

The Payoff

Going into the answer choices with a clear understanding of the argument flaw is like going into a knife fight with a gun—you have a clear advantage, and if you are smart about how you use it, you should expect to come out on top.

Each type of question that we see is going to require something different from us, that is, they are going to ask us to utilize, or reach to, our understanding of the argument flaw in different ways. Some may ask that we figure out ways to help fix the issue, or that we find another argument with a similar issue. Many questions will simply ask us

same flaw / different perspectives

Formula X is an effective treatment for disease Y. Since Carmen was recently treated for disease Y, and since her treatment was effective, it must have been Formula X.

-------	Takes for granted that Formula X is the only effective treatment for disease Y that was available to Carmen.
-------	Fails to consider that Carmen could have used another effective treatment for disease Y.
-------	Confuses a condition sufficient for bringing about a certain outcome for one required for that outcome.

to state what the problem is with the argument.

Finally, a minority of questions will not ask us to critique the reasoning at all. We think of these as objective questions. They may ask what the author's point was, or why he or she chose to mention a particular phrase in the stimulus. I've scattered a couple in the upcoming drill set for you to get a taste of these questions.

The quick-change act we need to perform for different types of questions requires us to have a significant amount of mental discipline. You want to consistently remind yourself of your job for that particular question. Many of the most tempting wrong answers are answers that would be correct if the task the question stem presented were to be just a little bit different. Remember that the right answer is one that satisfies two conditions: it matches the argument, and it matches the task presented in the question stem.

One more suggestion is to get in the habit of eliminating wrong choices before beginning to look for the right one. If you have a strong sense of the argument and a strong sense of your task, it will be very tempting to just go seeking the right answer. This will work sometimes, but it is not the optimal strategy for a high scorer. Keep in mind that a strong sense of argument and task are also great tools to use for eliminating wrong choices, and in general, the most difficult Logical Reasoning questions are constructed so that the wrong answers are significantly more obvious than the right answer, that is, at the end of the day, it's easier to see why the four choices were wrong than to see why the right answer is right. Focusing on wrong answers will make the section easier. Going through a two-step process of first eliminating wrongs, then searching for the right choice (as opposed to evaluating in one turn whether answers are right or wrong) will increase your overall accuracy, and in time should also help you actually go *faster* than you would otherwise.

QUESTION STEM
CHEAT SHEET

For each of the questions on the next two pages...

(1) Get in the habit of reading the question stem first. It is an important tool for staying better focused on the task.
(2) Search for the argument in the stimulus. It's best to find the conclusion first, then the support for that conclusion.

...Then focus back on the specific task the question stem presents.

Of the following, which one most accurately expresses the main point of the argument?

For this type of question, we want to simply decide on what we think is the conclusion within the argument, then find the answer that best represents that understanding. The right answer should be predictable, and should require very little inference work on your part. Note that this question does not require us to be critical of the reasoning, so we need not waste time figuring out what's wrong with the argument.

The part about X figures in the argument in which one of the following ways?

We want to decide on the role played by the part in question, then find the answer that best represents that understanding. A component's role is defined by how it relates to the main point. The right answer should be predictable and should require very little inference work on your part. Note that this question type also does not require us to be critical of the argument reasoning in any way.

The argument's reasoning is questionable because the argument...

This question is asking us, in a direct way, what is wrong with the argument. So, we want to make sure that we've thought about the argument critically before moving on to the answers. The right answer should be predictable, but may not be worded as you expect.

Which one of the following, if true, most seriously weakens the argument?

Figure out what is wrong with the argument, then select the answer that exposes that flaw. Tempting wrong answers will relate to the conclusion or the support, but not the problem that exists between them. Remember to treat each answer choice as being true.

Each of the following, if true, would strengthen the argument EXCEPT:

Figure out what's wrong with the argument, then eliminate answers that help fix that issue. Keep in mind that the right answer may or may not weaken the argument—it might actually have no direct impact on the argument. What we do know is that the four wrong answers will strengthen the relationship between support and conclusion, and we want to work to eliminate those answers.

Which one of the following is an assumption on which the psychologist's argument depends?

Start by figuring out what is wrong with the argument. The key term in this question stem is "depends." That does not mean the right answer needs to be *important* in addressing the argument flaw. It simply means that the answer is something that needs to be true in order for the argument to work.

Each of the following describes a flaw in the game show host's reasoning EXCEPT:

Per this question stem, we know that there are going to be a lot of issues between the support and the conclusion. Get as clear a sense as you can of the problems in that relationship before moving on to the answer choices. Eliminate the four answers you think best describe the problems, and select the answer that remains.

Which one of the following arguments contains a flaw in reasoning that is similar to one in the argument above?

This type of question requires a bit more work from us, so give yourself a bit of extra time if need be. Start by figuring out what's wrong with the argument. Then work to eliminate answers that either reach a very different type of conclusion, use different types of support, or seem to have different problems. Confirm the right answer by matching conclusions, support, and reasoning issues.

— work to eliminate incorrect answers before searching for the right answer —

29.1.16. We can learn about the living conditions of a vanished culture by examining its language. Thus, it is likely that the people who spoke Proto-Indo-European, the language from which all Indo-European languages descended, lived in a cold climate, isolated from ocean or sea, because Proto-Indo-European lacks a word for "sea," yet contains words for "winter," "snow," and "wolf."

Which one of the following, if true, most seriously weakens the argument?

(A) A word meaning "fish" was used by the people who spoke Proto-Indo-European.
(B) Some languages lack words for prominent elements of the environments of their speakers.
(C) There are no known languages today that lack a word for "sea."
(D) Proto-Indo-European possesses words for "heat."
(E) The people who spoke Proto-Indo-European were nomadic.

29.1.11. It is well known that many species adapt to their environment, but it is usually assumed that only the most highly evolved species alter their environment in ways that aid their own survival. However, this characteristic is actually quite common. Certain species of plankton, for example, generate a gas that is converted in the atmosphere into particles of sulfate. These particles cause water vapor to condense, thus forming clouds. Indeed, the formation of clouds over the ocean largely depends on the presence of these particles. More cloud cover means more sunlight is reflected, and so the Earth absorbs less heat. Thus plankton cause the surface of the Earth to be cooler and this benefits the plankton.

Of the following, which one most accurately expresses the main point of the argument?

(A) The Earth would be far warmer than it is now if certain species of plankton became extinct.
(B) By altering their environment in ways that improve their chances of survival, certain species of plankton benefit the Earth as a whole.
(C) Improving their own chances of survival by altering the environment is not limited to the most highly evolved species.
(D) The extent of the cloud cover over the oceans is largely determined by the quantity of plankton in those oceans.
(E) Species such as plankton alter the environment in ways that are less detrimental to the well-being of other species than are the alterations to the environment made by more highly evolved species.

28.1.19. The postmodern view involves the rejection of modern assumptions about order and the universality of truth. The grand theories of the modern era are now seen as limited by the social and historical contexts in which they were elaborated. Also, the belief in order has given way to a belief in the importance of irregularity and chaos. It follows that we inhabit a world full of irregular events, and in which there are no universal truths.

The argument's reasoning is questionable because the argument

(A) infers that something is the case because it is believed to be the case
(B) uses the term "universal" ambiguously
(C) relies on the use of emotional terms to bolster its conclusion
(D) uses the term "order" ambiguously
(E) fails to cite examples of modern theories that purport to embody universal truths

27.1.11. A local chemical plant produces pesticides that can cause sterility in small mammals such as otters. Soon after the plant began operating, the incidence of sterility among the otters that swim in a nearby river increased dramatically. Therefore, pesticides are definitely contaminating the river.

Which one of the following arguments contains a flaw in reasoning that is similar to one in the argument above?

(A) The bacteria that cause tetanus live in the digestive tract of horses. Tetanus is a highly infectious disease. Consequently it must be that horses contract tetanus more frequently than do most other animals.
(B) A diet low in calcium can cause a drop in egg production in poultry. When chickens on a local farm were let out in the spring to forage for food, their egg production dropped noticeably. So the food found and eaten by the chickens is undeniably low in calcium.
(C) Animals that are undernourished are very susceptible to infection. Animals in the largest metropolitan zoos are not undernourished, so they surely must not be very susceptible to disease.
(D) Apes are defined by having, among other characteristics, opposable thumbs and no external tail. Recently, fossil remains of a previously unknown animal were found. Because this animal had opposable thumbs, it must have been an ape.
(E) The only animal that could have produced a track similar to this one is a bear. But there are no bears in this area of the country, so this animal track is a fake.

Argument-Based Question Set

28.1.21. Psychologist: Some astrologers claim that our horoscopes completely determine our personalities, but this claim is false. I concede that identical twins—who are, of course, born at practically the same time—often do have similar personalities. However, birth records were examined to find two individuals who were born 40 years ago on the same day and at exactly the same time—one in a hospital in Toronto and one in a hospital in New York. Personality tests revealed that the personalities of these two individuals are in fact different.

Which one of the following is an assumption on which the psychologist's argument depends?

(A) Astrologers have not subjected their claims to rigorous experimentation.
(B) The personality differences between the two individuals cannot be explained by the cultural differences between Toronto and New York.
(C) The geographical difference between Toronto and New York did not result in the two individuals having different horoscopes.
(D) Complete birth records for the past 40 years were kept at both hospitals.
(E) Identical twins have identical genetic structures and usually have similar home environments.

29.4.20. Amphibian populations are declining in numbers worldwide. Not coincidentally, the earth's ozone layer has been continuously depleted throughout the last 50 years. Atmospheric ozone blocks UV-B, a type of ultraviolet radiation that is continuously produced by the sun, and which can damage genes. Because amphibians lack hair, hide, or feathers to shield them, they are particularly vulnerable to UV-B radiation. In addition, their gelatinous eggs lack the protection of leathery or hard shells. Thus, the primary cause of the declining amphibian population is the depletion of the ozone layer.

Each of the following, if true, would strengthen the argument EXCEPT:

(A) Of the various types of radiation blocked by atmospheric ozone, UV-B is the only type that can damage genes.
(B) Amphibian populations are declining far more rapidly than are the populations of nonamphibian species whose tissues and eggs have more natural protection from UV-B.
(C) Atmospheric ozone has been significantly depleted above all the areas of the world in which amphibian populations are declining.
(D) The natural habitat of amphibians has not become smaller over the past century.
(E) Amphibian populations have declined continuously for the last 50 years.

29.4.15. Ambiguity inspires interpretation. The saying, "We are the measure of all things," for instance, has been interpreted by some people to imply that humans are centrally important in the universe, while others have interpreted it to mean simply that, since all knowledge is human knowledge, humans must rely on themselves to find the truth.

The claim that ambiguity inspires interpretation figures in the argument in which one of the following ways?

(A) It is used to support the argument's conclusion.
(B) It is an illustration of the claim that we are the measure of all things.
(C) It is compatible with either accepting or rejecting the argument's conclusion.
(D) It is a view that other statements in the argument are intended to support.
(E) It sets out a difficulty the argument is intended to solve.

28.3.20. Game show host: Humans are no better than apes at investing, that is, they do not attain a better return on their investments than apes do. We gave five stock analysts and one chimpanzee $1,350 each to invest. After one month, the chimp won, having increased its net worth by $210. The net worth of the analyst who came in second increased by only $140.

Each of the following describes a flaw in the game show host's reasoning EXCEPT:

(A) A conclusion is drawn about apes in general on the basis of an experiment involving one chimpanzee.
(B) No evidence is offered that chimpanzees are capable of understanding stock reports and making reasoned investment decisions.
(C) A broad conclusion is drawn about the investment skills of humans on the basis of what is known about five humans.
(D) Too general a conclusion is made about investing on the basis of a single experiment involving short-term investing but not long-term investing.
(E) No evidence is considered about the long-term performance of the chimpanzee's portfolio versus that of the analysts' portfolios.

29.1.16. We can learn about the living conditions of a vanished culture by examining its language. Thus, it is likely that the people who spoke Proto-Indo-European, the language from which all Indo-European languages descended, lived in a cold climate, isolated from ocean or sea, because Proto-Indo-European lacks a word for "sea," yet contains words for "winter," "snow," and "wolf."

Which one of the following, if true, most seriously weakens the argument?

(A) A word meaning "fish" was used by the people who spoke Proto-Indo-European.
(B) Some languages lack words for prominent elements of the environments of their speakers.
(C) There are no known languages today that lack a word for "sea."
(D) Proto-Indo-European possesses words for "heat."
(E) The people who spoke Proto-Indo-European were nomadic.

Prep Work: We're being asked to identify the main point. We know we don't have to figure out what's wrong with the argument for this question; in order to get this question correct, we simply need to identify the argument. Most specifically, we need to identify the point being made.

They've made that task a bit of a challenge, and there are two attractive answers: the general statement that the most highly evolved species are not the only ones to alter their environment for survival, and the more specific point about plankton doing this very such thing.

Only one of those two statements can be the conclusion, and in order to figure out which one it is, we have to think about which statement is meant to support the other—is the general statement made to support the point about plankton, or vice versa? The answer might be different had the argument been phrased differently, but in this case we can see that the plankton is meant to be an example ("for example") of the more general statement.

So we know that the author's main point is that the most highly evolved species are not the only ones to alter their environment for survival. We are ready to go into the answer choices.

No Decision: We are not asked to be critical here, so we want to make sure not to be.

The Payoff: Knowing the conclusion, we want to eliminate the wrong choices. (A), (B), and (D) are specifically about plankton, so we know they cannot be correct. (E) speaks of something ("detrimental") that is not relevant to this discussion. That leaves us with (C). It substantively matches what we expected, and it is the correct answer.

Prep Work: We are asked to weaken the argument, and so we want to focus in on the conclusion and the support for that conclusion. The author's point is clear—these people lived in a cold climate isolated from the sea. The reasoning is also clear—they have words for things that go with cold climates, but they don't have a word for "sea."

The Decision: Does the fact that they don't have a word for sea guarantee they did not live by the sea? No. To give an analogous example, the English language does not have commonly used specific words for "parental love" verses "sibling love," and yet these things exist in the world, and we all know them to be different. The author takes for granted that they were isolated from the sea because they didn't have a word for it. (By the same token, having words for "winter," "snow," etc. doesn't prove they lived by these elements either.)

The Payoff: Knowing what's wrong with the argument, we can look for an answer that exploits this weakness. (A) does not impact the argument, for fish live in rivers, etc., and tells us nothing about proximity to seas. If we take (B) to be true, the reasoning in the argument falls apart. Let's keep it. With (C), it's unclear how the languages of today are relevant, and, besides, information about cultures that know the word for sea tells us little about cultures that don't. We can cut out (C). With (D), "heat," like "fish" from (A), is a universally used word that tells us nothing about proximity to sea. And with (E), whether they were nomadic or not has little impact on whether they lived in a cold climate, and no impact on the problems in the argument. That leaves us with just (B)—again, if it's true, then it directly counters the reasoning the author uses. (B) is correct.

29.1.11. It is well known that many species adapt to their environment, but it is usually assumed that only the most highly evolved species alter their environment in ways that aid their own survival. However, this characteristic is actually quite common. Certain species of plankton, for example, generate a gas that is converted in the atmosphere into particles of sulfate. These particles cause water vapor to condense, thus forming clouds. Indeed, the formation of clouds over the ocean largely depends on the presence of these particles. More cloud cover means more sunlight is reflected, and so the Earth absorbs less heat. Thus plankton cause the surface of the Earth to be cooler and this benefits the plankton.

Of the following, which one most accurately expresses the main point of the argument?

(A) The Earth would be far warmer than it is now if certain species of plankton became extinct.
(B) By altering their environment in ways that improve their chances of survival, certain species of plankton benefit the Earth as a whole.
(C) Improving their own chances of survival by altering the environment is not limited to the most highly evolved species.
(D) The extent of the cloud cover over the oceans is largely determined by the quantity of plankton in those oceans.
(E) Species such as plankton alter the environment in ways that are less detrimental to the well-being of other species than are the alterations to the environment made by more highly evolved species.

28.1.19. The postmodern view involves the rejection of modern assumptions about order and the universality of truth. The grand theories of the modern era are now seen as limited by the social and historical contexts in which they were elaborated. Also, the belief in order has given way to a belief in the importance of irregularity and chaos. It follows that we inhabit a world full of irregular events, and in which there are no universal truths.

The argument's reasoning is questionable because the argument

(A) infers that something is the case because it is believed to be the case
(B) uses the term "universal" ambiguously
(C) relies on the use of emotional terms to bolster its conclusion
(D) uses the term "order" ambiguously
(E) fails to cite examples of modern theories that purport to embody universal truths

Prep Work: Wow, a lot of deep information here. It's virtually impossible to absorb it all at once, and that shouldn't be our goal. We can focus in by first finding the conclusion: we inhabit a world full of irregular events, and in which there are no universal truths. It seems that a whole lot of what comes before is meant to support and lead up to that conclusion, but we can just start by focusing in on the part that seems most closely related: the belief in order has given way to a belief in the importance of irregularity and chaos.

The Decision: It seemed like there was a chain of reasoning that led to the point, and if I don't see the gap between this conclusion and the closest support, I will go "up the reasoning chain" to see where else the gap exists. However, we should expect the flaw to be in the closest link to the conclusion for virtually all arguments, so I really want to scrutinize the relationship I've isolated: does the fact that the belief in order has given way to a belief in the importance of irregularity and chaos definitely prove that we inhabit a world full of irregular events, and in which there are no universal truths? No. Who's to say these beliefs are actually correct, and who's to say that believing in the importance of irregularity means believing that there are no universal truths? Since there are such clear flaws already, we need not look elsewhere for issues.

The Payoff: (A) matches our understanding well, and is the correct answer. (B) would certainly be tempting if we didn't know what we were looking for, but the definition of "universal" is not central to the reasoning issues. (C) would require us to make a very subjective decision about the "level" of emotion in words used, and "regardless" does not describe the problem we saw. (D) gives us much the same feeling that (B) does and can be fairly quickly eliminated. (E) is not required for the argument to work (so what if they don't have examples of this?), and so doesn't represent a flaw.

27.1.11. A local chemical plant produces pesticides that can cause sterility in small mammals such as otters. Soon after the plant began operating, the incidence of sterility among the otters that swim in a nearby river increased dramatically. Therefore, pesticides are definitely contaminating the river.

Which one of the following arguments contains a flaw in reasoning that is similar to one in the argument above?

(A) The bacteria that cause tetanus live in the digestive tract of horses. Tetanus is a highly infectious disease. Consequently it must be that horses contract tetanus more frequently than do most other animals.
(B) A diet low in calcium can cause a drop in egg production in poultry. When chickens on a local farm were let out in the spring to forage for food, their egg production dropped noticeably. So the food found and eaten by the chickens is undeniably low in calcium.
(C) Animals that are undernourished are very susceptible to infection. Animals in the largest metropolitan zoos are not undernourished, so they surely must not be very susceptible to disease.
(D) Apes are defined by having, among other characteristics, opposable thumbs and no external tail. Recently, fossil remains of a previously unknown animal were found. Because this animal had opposable thumbs, it must have been an ape.
(E) The only animal that could have produced a track similar to this one is a bear. But there are no bears in this area of the country, so this animal track is a fake.

Prep Work: We need to match the flaw in the stimulus with a flaw in the answer choice. The first order of business is to get a really good understanding of the flaw in the argument. The point is that pesticides are definitely contaminating the river. Evidence? This is a type of pesticide that can cause sterility in animals like otters, and there has been an increase in sterility among otters.

The Decision: Does the fact that sterility among the otters has increased guarantee that pesticides are contaminating the river? No. Perhaps some other reason—some other contaminant, water levels, change in diet, etc.—is causing the problems for the otters. The flaw is that the author assumes a definite cause for an outcome when the justification isn't definite.

The Payoff: Let's knock off answers that don't have the same problem. Often, they easily give themselves away because they reach a different type of conclusion (imagine, say, a conclusion about likelihood, involving the word "probably," as opposed to the type of "definite" conclusion we had here) or use supporting evidence in a different sort of way. With (A), "more frequently" is a comparative statement that is very different from anything we had in the original argument. We can eliminate it. (B) seems to have a similar type of conclusion as the original argument ("undeniably" has some characteristic) and seems to have the same type of reasoning issues. Let's leave it. (C) uses something about undernourishment to prove something about a lack of undernourishment—a very different reasoning structure from the original, and we can eliminate it quickly. (D) also seems to be very similar to the original argument and reaches an absolute conclusion—let's leave it. (E) uses the characteristics of something to conclude that it is not so—very different from our argument, so we can eliminate (E) quickly.

Down to (B) and (D), let's think more carefully about how they relate to the flaw in the original argument. Comparing (B) to the argument, one thing to notice is the match in terms of "cause." This is actually a defining characteristic of both arguments—they are both falsely attributing a cause. When we look at (D), we see that it doesn't have this causal characteristic. (B) is correct.

28.1.21. Psychologist: Some astrologers claim that our horoscopes completely determine our personalities, but this claim is false. I concede that identical twins—who are, of course, born at practically the same time—often do have similar personalities. However, birth records were examined to find two individuals who were born 40 years ago on the same day and at exactly the same time—one in a hospital in Toronto and one in a hospital in New York. Personality tests revealed that the personalities of these two individuals are in fact different.

Which one of the following is an assumption on which the psychologist's argument depends?

(A) Astrologers have not subjected their claims to rigorous experimentation.
(B) The personality differences between the two individuals cannot be explained by the cultural differences between Toronto and New York.
(C) The geographical difference between Toronto and New York did not result in the two individuals having different horoscopes.
(D) Complete birth records for the past 40 years were kept at both hospitals.
(E) Identical twins have identical genetic structures and usually have similar home environments.

Prep Work: We are asked to find an assumption on which the argument depends. We want to start by figuring out the support and the conclusion. The author's conclusion is that horoscopes do not completely determine our personalities. What's the support? Two individuals born at the same time in different locations had different personalities.

The Decision: Note that just one example could actually be enough to prove that horoscopes don't completely determine personality, so let's think about why it doesn't here. In what instance would the support used not be sufficient to justify the point made?

What are we expected to know about horoscopes? Do we know that two people born at the same time have the same horoscope? I don't. That seems to be a problem with the argument—the author doesn't actually show that these two people that he uses as evidence had the same horoscope.

The Payoff: The word "depends" in the question stem is important. We need to look for an answer that needs to be true if the argument is ever going to work. As always, we'll work by eliminating incorrect choices. Does (A) need to be true for the argument to work? No. Astrologers could have subjected their claims to experimentation, and the argument could still be true. (B) does not have to be true in order to show that our horoscopes don't completely determine our personalities. (C) does have to be true— let's leave that. (D) does not have to be true—if one record was missing, it would likely not impact the argument too much. (E) does not have to be true for the author's argument to work. (C) is the only attractive answer—let's review it carefully. If (C) were not true, it would mean that the two people mentioned in the support would have two different horoscopes. Then it would make no sense for the author to use this support to make this point. (C) needs to be true for the argument to work, and (C) is correct.

29.4.20. Amphibian populations are declining in numbers worldwide. Not coincidentally, the earth's ozone layer has been continuously depleted throughout the last 50 years. Atmospheric ozone blocks UV-B, a type of ultraviolet radiation that is continuously produced by the sun, and which can damage genes. Because amphibians lack hair, hide, or feathers to shield them, they are particularly vulnerable to UV-B radiation. In addition, their gelatinous eggs lack the protection of leathery or hard shells. Thus, the primary cause of the declining amphibian population is the depletion of the ozone layer.

Each of the following, if true, would strengthen the argument EXCEPT:

(A) Of the various types of radiation blocked by atmospheric ozone, UV-B is the only type that can damage genes.
(B) Amphibian populations are declining far more rapidly than are the populations of nonamphibian species whose tissues and eggs have more natural protection from UV-B.
(C) Atmospheric ozone has been significantly depleted above all the areas of the world in which amphibian populations are declining.
(D) The natural habitat of amphibians has not become smaller over the past century.
(E) Amphibian populations have declined continuously for the last 50 years.

Prep Work: When we are asked a strengthen "EXCEPT" or weaken "EXCEPT" question, we know that the argument is going to be heavily flawed, enough so that there are different ways to strengthen or weaken. In this case, the author's point is that the primary cause of the declining population is the depletion of ozone. The evidence? They are more vulnerable to UV-B radiation (which likely has been increasing) and they have eggs that lack the protection of other types of eggs.

The Decision: Do we have proof that the depleting ozone layer actually has any direct impact on the declining amphibian population? No we don't. Amphibians may be vulnerable to UV-B radiation, but perhaps it's not life-threatening. Perhaps their eggs, while not giving as much protection as other types of eggs, give enough protection to be just fine, and perhaps the type of protection being discussed has nothing to do with UV-B. Having said all that, we certainly don't have proof that depletion is the primary cause.

The Payoff: We know that four answers strengthen the argument—that is, we should be able to see in a very direct way that four of the answers help address issues in the argument. The one answer that doesn't, the right answer, may weaken the argument, or it may have nothing to do with the argument—the only thing that will define that answer is that it does not strengthen. With (A), does it matter to the argument that UV-B is the only type that can cause damage? It's tough to see how. Let's leave (A). (B) gives us more proof that their egg type and UV-B are related, and that UV-B could be an issue. (B) helps the argument, so we should eliminate it. (C) also helps prove a link between ozone and decline, so let's eliminate it. (D) eliminates another potential cause of the decreasing population, and in so doing helps the argument—let's eliminate it. (E) is probably the toughest of answers to eliminate, but the fact that the decline is continuous does make it seem a bit more likely that it's connected to the depletion of ozone, which has also been "continuous." (A) is correct.

29.4.15. Ambiguity inspires interpretation. The saying, "We are the measure of all things," for instance, has been interpreted by some people to imply that humans are centrally important in the universe, while others have interpreted it to mean simply that, since all knowledge is human knowledge, humans must rely on themselves to find the truth.

The claim that ambiguity inspires interpretation figures in the argument in which one of the following ways?

(A) It is used to support the argument's conclusion.
(B) It is an illustration of the claim that we are the measure of all things.
(C) It is compatible with either accepting or rejecting the argument's conclusion.
(D) It is a view that other statements in the argument are intended to support.
(E) It sets out a difficulty the argument is intended to solve.

Prep Work: We're being asked to figure out what role a part of the stimulus plays in the argument. This will be easy to do once we recognize the reasoning structure, so we want to start, as always, by identifying the main point. It happens to come right at the beginning (the "for instance" tips us off that it is a point that is going to be supported): ambiguity inspires interpretation. What follows is all support for that idea. Looking again at the question, the part in question happens to be our conclusion.

No Decision: Our job is simply to understand the stimulus—we want to make sure not to distract ourselves by thinking about the reasoning or by bringing ideas together. We know that the part in question is the main point, and that is all we need to know to get the right answer.

The Payoff: (A), (B), and (C) all clearly misrepresent the role and can be eliminated quickly. (E) requires a bit more thought, but there isn't a difficulty to be solved here. (D) is the correct answer.

28.3.20. Game show host: Humans are no better than apes at investing, that is, they do not attain a better return on their investments than apes do. We gave five stock analysts and one chimpanzee $1,350 each to invest. After one month, the chimp won, having increased its net worth by $210. The net worth of the analyst who came in second increased by only $140.

Each of the following describes a flaw in the game show host's reasoning EXCEPT:

(A) A conclusion is drawn about apes in general on the basis of an experiment involving one chimpanzee.
(B) No evidence is offered that chimpanzees are capable of understanding stock reports and making reasoned investment decisions.
(C) A broad conclusion is drawn about the investment skills of humans on the basis of what is known about five humans.
(D) Too general a conclusion is made about investing on the basis of a single experiment involving short-term investing but not long-term investing.
(E) No evidence is considered about the long-term performance of the chimpanzee's portfolio versus that of the analysts' portfolios.

Prep Work: We are asked to find the answer that doesn't represent a flaw in the argument—that means four answers will represent flaws—and that means we must have a very flawed argument. The game show host's main point comes at the beginning: humans are no better than apes at investing. He supports this conclusion with a study involving five stock analysts and one chimpanzee. The chimpanzee performed best.

The Decision: Do not, as I did, get stuck thinking about the exact mechanism by which an ape picks an investment (does he point to a stock in the newspaper?). We are to take as fact the idea that this chimp did indeed invest and that the outcome was what it was.

So what? Does it prove humans aren't better than apes? Of course not. It's one study involving just five people and just one month. This is a terrible argument. Let's look for some descriptions of the flaws.

The Payoff: (A) accurately describes a problem—the argument has extrapolated too much (piece ≠ puzzle). (B) is tempting, because we know this to perhaps be a problem in real life, but is this directly related to the relationship between this premise and this conclusion? Not really. Is (B) something that prevents apes from being just as good at investing? No. They can be just as good without understanding stock reports and by being irrational but somehow correct. Let's leave (B). (C) matches a problem we discussed, and we can eliminate it quickly. (D) also matches a problem we discussed (one month), and we can eliminate it quickly, and (E) is a variation on (D). We can eliminate (A), (C), (D), and (E) easily, so let's go back to (B). Thinking again, understanding stock reports (people make good investment decisions without understanding stock reports all the time) and reasoned decisions (unreasonable decisions are sometimes the best) are not requirements for investing well and more importantly, have nothing to do with the premise-conclusion relationship. (B) is the only answer that doesn't describe a flaw with this argument, and (B) is correct.

How to Review

That was a set of eight fairly challenging questions—more difficult than average (but not murderously so). Hopefully, solving those questions and checking your work against the solutions has confirmed for you the importance of recognizing argument flaws, and opened you up to some areas in which you can improve and thus increase your score. At this step in your study process, missed questions are good for you, for they show you exactly what you need to work on. Of course, the manner in which you review your work plays a large role in determining how quickly you improve. To that end, let's summarize some of the advice we've laid out in these first few lessons.

(1) The primary emphasis of these first few lessons has been on helping you develop your ability to recognize argument flaws in a clear and specific way. For each question that you review, make sure you understand well the reasoning flaw in the argument. You can think about it in terms of what the author is taking for granted, or fails to consider, and you can think about it in terms of the three basic flaw categories: a piece ≠ the puzzle, apples ≠ oranges, and 1 + 1 ≠ 3.

(2) Make sure you understand everything else about the problem that you are meant to understand. We discussed these components at the end of Lesson 7. You want to understand the task presented in the question stem, you want to correctly identify the primary components of the argument, of course you want to specifically understand what is wrong with the argument, you want to see how the right answer addresses the flaw and matches the task presented, and you want to see clear reasons for why each wrong answer is wrong.

(3) Finally, you want to think about the questions that you miss in terms of the process you used to solve them. Misses are caused by challenges in understanding the task, or in reading the stimulus or answer choices, or in evaluating the reasoning. The more specific you can be about the challenges that questions present, the faster and more easily you can adapt your habits.

The Road Ahead

We will take a small rest from working on Logical Reasoning and switch over to discussing the basics of Logic Games. Then, we will return to Logical Reasoning and start to discuss how to attack specific types of questions.

For extra homework, now would be a good time to go back to the questions that you missed from your diagnostic; you can try your hand at reviewing all such questions using the guidelines discussed above.

10 LOGIC GAMES diagramming

As we discussed in the introduction to Logic Games in Lesson 3, all Logic Games are based on the relationship between elements and positions. Each game begins with a short scenario[1]—a sentence or two that lays out the situation at hand—and each game then gives us a few rules about where particular elements can or cannot go. We are then asked five to seven questions that test our understanding of this situation.

1. The *scenario* is the situation given at the beginning of a game. Here are some truncated examples of scenarios: "Eight toys are placed in order, from most expensive to cheapest." "Six students are split into three teams, and each team will have a writer and an editor."

The Key to Logic Games Success

Logic Games require us to keep track of a lot of information, and in order to answer questions successfully, we need to be able to see how this information comes together. This is the primary challenge that Logic Games present. The amount and complexity of the information is such that very few people are able to retain it, with the level of control and understanding that they need, all in their heads. Therefore, in order to be successful at Logic Games, you have to be able to work with a visual representation of the situation—you have to be able to draw out the games. The key to being good at Logic Games is to be good at diagramming Logic Games scenarios. Effective diagramming techniques make it far easier for you to keep a clear understanding of rules and to see how they come together. A lack of diagramming ability makes such tasks nearly impossible.

The ability to diagram is the key to Logic Games success

In these next five lessons, we will work to develop the diagramming skills that will allow you to conquer any and all games. As always, we will start with the fundamentals.

The Three Basic Design Elements

There are three primary characteristics that define the design of the various games that one can expect to see on the LSAT: all games involve relating elements to positions, about two in three games organize these positions in some sort of order, and about half of all games organize these positions into groups. These three characteristics underlie the vast majority of rules, and these are the primary issues behind the inferences[2] that determine right and wrong answers. In this lesson, we will work on developing a rock-solid understanding of these three fundamental issues.

2. When it comes to games, *inferences* are the things we figure out when we bring different rules together. Most questions are designed so that inferences, rather than the given rules, differentiate right answers from wrong ones.

All Games Relate Elements to Positions

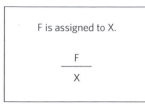

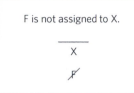

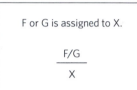

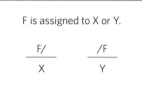

Suggested Notations

F is assigned to X.

F
X

F is not assigned to X.

X
~~F~~

F or G is assigned to X.

F/G
X

F is assigned to X or Y.

F/ /F
X Y

For every game, the scenario will present a list of elements, and your task will be to consider how these elements relate to a set of positions.

When you initially read the scenario and rules for a game, your first job is going to be to write out the elements and to lay out the positions in the form of slots. I recommend that you write out elements vertically—this will help you notate certain rules next to these elements. How you lay out the slots will depend on the game, and it can often be an important decision; you likely won't think twice about it when you lay out the slots correctly, but when you lay them out in an awkward fashion, it'll make the game far more challenging to manage.

Once in a blue moon, the test writers will get creative with the element-to-position relationship. One way they can do this is to make the elements and the positions one and the same. Imagine a game in which five friends make phone calls to one another, and your job is to figure out who called whom. In this case, the friends make the calls and also receive the calls. The test writers can also make it somewhat unclear what we should think of as the elements, and what we should think of as the positions. Imagine a game in which you have pets owned by different children and you have to figure out which child owns which pet. In certain instances it might make sense to list the children as the elements and the pets as the positions, and in other instances the reverse might work better. These types of complications are extremely rare, especially in recent years. As we'll discuss further, the key to dealing with such complications successfully is to think about what sort of setup would make it easiest for you to notate the particular rules you are given.

Below is a sample game and diagram to illustrate some of the issues that we've just discussed.

A Super-Simple Example to Illustrate Elements to Positions

Five students—F, G, H, J, and K—will be assigned to five different tasks—R, S, T, U, and W. One student will be assigned to each task.

J will not be assigned to T.
G will be assigned to U.
Either H or K will be assigned to R.

Notes: Keep in mind this is a simplified example. This game is unrealistic in that a real LSAT game would also involve ordering or grouping considerations. In general, we only want to place elements right into the slots when we know for sure that they occupy those positions. Otherwise, we want to put the rules elsewhere, typically below the position, as we've done with the "not J" rule.

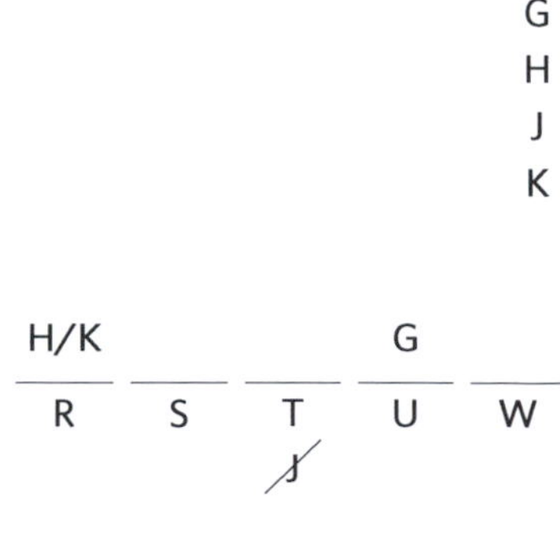

Most Games Involve Ordering

Two or three of the four games that you see on your exam will involve positions placed in some sort of order. Therefore, it is important to get extremely comfortable handling ordering rules and making ordering inferences.

In general, we will arrange positions horizontally for ordering games, with the default order being from left to right. You can see in the example below how to lay out the base for a typical ordering game. This will be fine for almost all ordering games, but keep in mind that there will be situations (imagine a game involving the six vertical floors of a building) for which you may want to adapt this template.

Let's use an example to discuss ordering further: imagine that a DJ will play six different songs, one at a time and each just once. For the sake of convenience, we'll think of these six songs in terms of the first letters of their names: F, G, H, J, K, M.

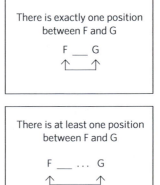

Let's just think about two of these songs: F and G. Imagine F and G appearing at various positions in this order, and think about all of the things you could say about where F and G appear relative to one another. For example, if F is played first and G third, we could say that F is played before G, G is played after F, exactly one song is played between F and G, and so on. Again, imagine F and G appearing at various positions in this order, and see if you can come up with an exhaustive list of the various things that could be said about the ordering relationship between F and G. Afterwards, check your list against the list of suggested notations on this page and on page 138. By the way, page 138 is where we'll pick this discussion back up.

Suggested Notations

F is before G

F — G

G is after F

F is right before G

F G

G is right after F

F is two spots ahead of G*

F ___ G

G is two spots after F

F is at least two spots ahead of G

F ___ . . . G

G is at least two spots after F

F is right before or after G

F G
↑_↑

There is exactly one position between F and G

F ___ G
↑____↑

There is at least one position between F and G

F ___ . . . G
↑________↑

* *This and similar rules can also have two spaces between, three between, etc.*

A Super-Simple Example to Illustrate Ordering

Seth will perform five actions—F, G, H, I, and J—during the course of one day. He will perform these actions one at a time and in order. The following conditions apply:

He will do F immediately before or after H.
He will not perform J third.
He has to do I before he does F.

I — FH
↑↑

F
G
H
I
J

___ ___ ___ ___ ___
1 2 3 4 5
~~J~~ (under 3)

Notes: Again, this is a simplified example, though there are some real LSAT games that are not much more complicated than this one.

Note how two of the ordering rules came together to create a three-element link that will take up a large part of the board and also severely limit where I, F, and H can go. The I, F, H link would be the key factor when dealing with the questions for this particular game.

Making & Using Diagrams

Your ability to diagram is the key to Logic Games success. Using a sample game and questions, let's lay out the basics of how to make a diagram, and how to use it.

1. DRAW OUT A BASE

Start every game by reading the scenario and the rules. Then return to the scenario and use it to set up the base of your diagram. It is essential that you feel very comfortable with the base of your diagram, because you are going to be doing a lot of work in that space. The good news is that there is great commonality to the basic situations that these scenarios present, and you should expect, fairly early in your study process, to be comfortable picturing the base for just about any type of game.

In this particular game, we are asked to figure out some information about the order in which messages were left. We can think of the people leaving the messages as the "elements," and we can think of the messages as positions. Naturally, we want to arrange the positions in a way that represents the ordering aspect of the game, and we can easily do this by ordering the calls one through six from left to right.

2. TAKE CONTROL OF THE RULES

Once you've laid down your base, you need to represent each rule in a way that accurately reflects your understanding. Keep in mind that your diagram needs to serve two general functions: it needs to serve as a clear and simple representation of the rules, and it needs to serve as a system that helps you see how these rules come together. If your diagramming system is unnecessarily complicated, fragmented, or in some other way unintuitive, it won't be as effective in these roles.

For this particular game, we have four rules. Take a look at the various ways in which we noted these rules. Bringing together the rules leads to an inference about the final position: since F, H, and N can't be last, it will be either G or M. You won't catch every inference every time, nor do you need to, but inferences are what the questions are ultimately about, and inferences made during your setup can save you a lot of time and work.

Kendra comes home from work to find six messages left on her answering machine by five people—her father, her grandmother, her half-brother, her mother, and her niece. Her mother left two messages, while everyone else left just one. The following conditions apply:

Her half-brother or grandmother left the first message.
Her niece's message came after one of her mother's messages, but not the other.
Her father left the third message.
Her half-brother did not leave the last message.

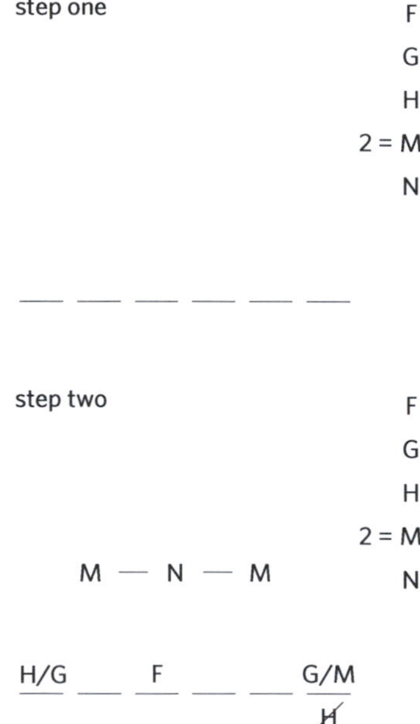

1. If her niece left the fourth message, each of the following could be true EXCEPT:

(A) Her grandmother left the first message.
(B) Her half-brother left the first message.
(C) Her half-brother left the second message.
(D) Her mother left the fifth message.
(E) Her grandmother left the sixth message.

H/G M F N ___ G/M

We can redraw a simple version of our diagram and place N into the fourth slot. The M-N-M rule forces M into the second slot. We don't know much else about positions 5 and 6 (other than that they are very limited at this point), and so we move on to the answers. (A) and (B) both could be true and don't require a lot of thought (we'll come back to them later and look at them more carefully if we can't find the right answer). (C) must be false and so we can select it and stop there.

2. Which of the following could be true?

(A) Her niece left the second message, and her mother the fourth.
(B) Her grandmother left the first message, and her mother the fifth.
(C) Her half-brother left the second message, and her niece the fourth.
(D) Her niece left the fourth message, and her grandmother the fifth.
(E) Her mother left the fourth message, and her grandmother the fifth.

D

We are asked what could be true, so we know that four answers must be false. In this case it's generally easier to see why four answers must be false rather than why one could be true, so we want to arrive at the right answer by eliminating wrong ones.

Looking at our diagram, we can eliminate
(A) because N in 2 leaves no place for M before it
(B) because it leaves no one for the final message
(C) because it leaves no room for M before N
(E) because it either squeezes out N or leaves no one for the final message

That leaves (D) as the correct answer, and to confirm we can come up with one order that works—H, M, F, N, G, M.

You will use your diagram to do the challenging thinking that is required by the questions. Before you step into these questions, check your diagram one final time to make sure you understand your notations and that your notations represent the rules accurately. You want to be in control of a game as you move on to the questions, and your diagram will help you feel this control.

3. UTILIZE THE QUESTION STEM

Test takers commonly underestimate the importance of the question stem, and they do so at their own peril. Question stems tell you how to think about the problem, and with only a minute per question at your disposal, it's critical that you start off on the right path. When a question stem gives us new information, as the stem for number one does, you can expect that the new information will always—*always*—allow us to make new inferences. In this case, the new information forces M into the second position. These inferences will always have a significant impact on right and wrong answers—we know, from the fact that M is in the second position, that C must be false. Note that we redrew a simple version of the diagram next to the question in order to work in the new information. Also note that the question stem helps us predict how the answer choices will be split—in this case, four answers that could be true and one that must be false—and whether we ought to search for the right answer or eliminate wrong ones (much more on this later).

4. KNOW WHAT YOU KNOW

It's a mistake to think that we have to know everything about a game. Logic Games are designed for us to know part of the picture, and the questions then test what is known versus what isn't—what must be versus what could be. Right and wrong answers split among these lines; for question one, the right answer must be false, and the others are all ones that could be true or false. For question two, the right answer could be true, and the wrong answers all must be false. We'll go into great detail about question strategies later in the book, but in general, focus on the answers you know for certain—if a question asks for an answer that must be true or must be false, prioritize finding the right answer over eliminating wrong ones (it's tough to make absolute calls on "could be" wrong answers). If a question asks for an answer that could be true or could be false, work to eliminate all of the incorrect "must be" answers.

F is not before G*

F ~~→~~ G

G is not after F

F is not immediately before G

~~FG~~

G is not immediately after F

F is not two spots ahead of G

F ~~_~~ G

G is not two spots after F

F is not immediately before or immediately after G.

~~FG~~

F and G are not exactly one space apart.

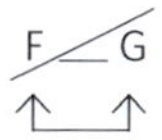

F ~~_~~ G

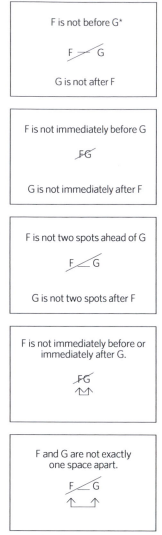

**Note that this will rarely be necessary; unless a game has ties, "F is not before G" can be thought of as "F is after G."*

I want to tell you two things about ordering rules: there are not that many possibilities for what type of rules they can give you, and you have plenty of time to get very comfortable with all of the possibilities. As always, that doesn't mean that ordering rules are going to be easy. When you go into the exam, the challenge will come from the fact that the rules often have subtle differences, and you will need to understand every rule in an exact and usable way.

One final thing to keep in mind is that many ordering rules link together. For example, if we know that F is played before G, and G is played before H, we can infer, and represent in our notation, that F is before H. It's beneficial for you to be mindful of such links, and you should do your best to diagram such rules together whenever possible. We'll discuss this at far greater length in later lessons.

Half of All Games Involve Grouping

...just a tad less than half, actually, and among the games from PT 52 – 61, seventeen of the forty games involve grouping as a significant characteristic of the game.

"Six players are split into three teams," "Five cars will have one or more of four accessories," and "Of eight birds, five are in the forest, and three are out of the forest," would all be examples of grouping situations. In each of these cases, we can expect to see rules about which elements are meant to be grouped together (for example, "L and M are on the same team") and which elements are not meant to go together (for example, "T or S, but not both, is in the forest").

In general, we will want to organize the positions that are meant to be grouped together vertically, as we have done in the example below. We also want to mention that elements are meant to be grouped together, or not grouped together, by lining them up vertically, as we've done in the suggested notations on the opposite page.

Grouping, like assignment, is a bit too simple a task to make an entire game out of, and grouping games will in general also be defined by having other challenges, such as a series of conditional rules, complicated either/or situations, or subgroup issues. In cer-

---

A Super-Simple Example to Illustrate Grouping

Six students—F, G, H, J, K, and L—will be paired up into three teams: the purple team, the red team, and the teal team. The following conditions apply:

F and G cannot be paired together.
J and L will be paired together.
H will be on the red team.

Notes: As mentioned in the body text, this is a simplified example, in that a real LSAT game would likely involve additional challenges. However, keep in mind there are certain grouping games that, though they may have another type of challenge or two, won't necessarily be too much more difficult than this to set up. Also note a new notation—***since K is the only one of the six elements not mentioned in a rule, we want to circle it to remind ourselves it can go anywhere.***

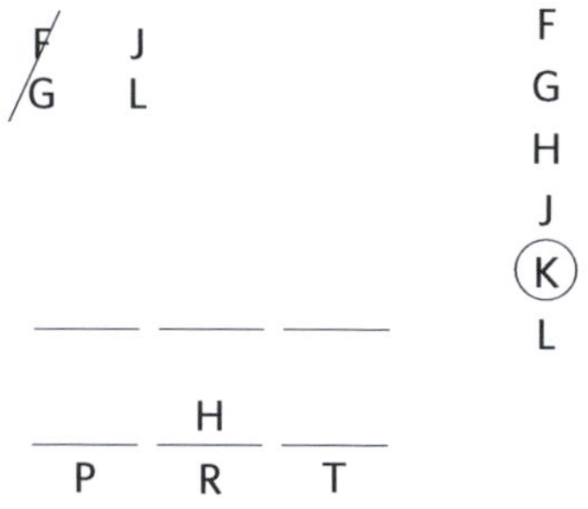

F/G (not together)   J L

F G H J (K) L

P	R	T
___	___	___
___	H	___

---

tain instances, the numbers of elements within each group will be completely defined, and in other instances, figuring out those numbers will be part of the challenge. We will discuss all these issues in specific detail in the next few lessons.

Once in a while, you will run into a game that involves both grouping and ordering; in these instances, the habit of organizing grouping issues vertically and ordering issues horizontally can prove to be especially helpful, for it greatly facilitates keeping track of both issues on the same diagram. We'll see an example of this a bit later in this lesson.

F and G are together

F
G

F and G are not together

F/
/G

All games involve assignment, most games involve ordering, and about half of all games involve grouping

---

Instructions for the Basic Setups Drill Starting on the Following Page

This drill contains three sets of games; your task is to set up diagrams for each game.

For each set of games, the three games on the right side of the page are "twin" versions of the three games on the left: same games, but with different scenarios and wording. Here are suggestions for how to execute the drill:

Diagram the set of three games on the left side of each page. Afterwards, note how long the set took and assess how comfortable you felt diagramming the games.

If you felt confident in your diagrams, go on to the sister set on the right and try to outdo your speed while perhaps diagramming just a bit better. Then review the provided solutions.

If you don't feel confident with your diagrams after doing the set in the left column, review the provided solutions before trying out the sister set. Note that the sets are meant to get progressively more difficult.

It might be a good idea for you to revisit this drill later in your studies, to remind yourself of fundamentals and test how much faster and how much more comfortable you have gotten. If you are interested in doing this, you should do your work in a separate notebook.

Basic Setups Drill Set 1

1. Five children—F, G, H, I, and J—are each given one of five toys—M, N, O, P, and R. Each toy is given to exactly one child. The following conditions apply:

N is given to J.
G gets either P or R.
M is not given to H.

2. Six airplanes—M, N, O, P, R, and S—take off from a runway, one at a time and in order. The following conditions apply:

Exactly one plane departs after N but before R.
Either O or P will depart third.
S departs immediately before or immediately after R.

3. Eight friends—M, N, O, P, Q, R, S, and T—will ride in four cars to a concert, two friends per car. The following conditions apply:

M and N ride together.
O and R do not.
S rides with either P or Q.

4. A chef puts five different types of sauces—T, V, W, X, and Y—on top of five different cuts of steak—filet, hangar, New York, rib eye, and sirloin. Each steak gets one sauce, and each sauce is used once. Additionally...

The hangar steak gets X or Y.
T is not put on the New York.
V is put on the sirloin.

5. Six children—F, G, H, I, J, and K—each take turns whacking at a pinata. Each child gets one turn, and they go one at a time. The following conditions apply:

K takes a turn immediately before or after J.
Exactly one child goes after G but before J.
Either H or I goes third.

6. Eight children—F, G, H, I, J, K, L, and M—will be split into four teams of two. Each child will be on exactly one team. The following rules apply:

F and G are on the same team.
L is teamed with either I or J.
H and K are not on the same team.

Basic Setups Drill Set 2

7. Sarah takes seven swings in a batting cage. On four swings, she makes good contact—on the others she either fouls the ball off or misses it. Additionally, it must be true that...

She does not foul off two consecutive pitches.
She does not miss any of the last four pitches.
She makes good contact on exactly two of the first four pitches.

8. Nine students—F, G, H, I, J, K, L, M, and N—are split evenly into three teams—the purple team, the red team, and the tan team. The following conditions apply:

H is assigned to the red team.
G and I are assigned to the same team.
Either J or M, but not both, is assigned to the purple team.
G and H are not assigned to the same team.
L is not assigned to the tan team.

9. Six workers—F, G, H, J, K, and L—work three shifts as pairs. These shifts occur one at a time and in order. The following conditions apply:

H works a later shift than J.
G does not work the first shift.
J and K work the same shift.

10. Judges see seven auditioners for an upcoming reality show. They say yes to four of them, and give maybes and nos to the rest. The following conditions apply:

None of the last four auditioners get nos.
No two consecutive auditioners get maybes.
Exactly two of the first four auditioners get a yes.

11. Nine pandas—M, O, P, Q, R, S, T, U, and V—live in three different zones of a jungle: the west, the north, and the east. Three pandas live in each zone. The following rules apply:

O and Q live in the same zone.
T is not in the east zone.
P lives in the north.
Either R or U, but not both, lives in the west zone.
O and P do not live in the same zone.

12. Six people—M, O, P, R, S, and T—sit in three rows of an airplane, two people per row. The following conditions apply:

P sits in a later row than R does.
O does not sit in the first row.
R and S sit in the same row.

Basic Setups Drill Set 3

13. Five different companies—M, N, O, P, and Q—each occupy one of five floors in an office building. The following conditions apply:

M is on a higher floor than Q, but not the highest floor.
Exactly one company is between O and N.
P is not on the second floor.

14. Seven dancers—F, G, H, I, J, K, and L—perform in a total of three shows. Two dancers perform in the first and second shows, and three dancers in the third. Each dancer performs just once. The following conditions apply:

G dances in the second performance.
Either H or F, but not both, dances in the first performance.
Either J or L dance with G.
K and I dance in the same performance.

15. Seven trains—F, G, H, I, J, K, and M—depart from a train station, one at a time and in order. The following conditions apply:

At least two trains depart after G but before J.
J departs after H but before M.
F departs immediately before or immediately after G.
K departs neither immediately before nor immediately after I.

16. Five different display pieces—F, G, H, I, and J—are placed on the five shelves of a bookcase, one piece per shelf. Additionally...

There is one shelf in between G and H.
F is placed higher than J, but not on the top shelf.
I is not placed on the second shelf from the bottom.

17. Seven cargo shipments—M, N, O, P, Q, R, and S—are loaded onto three different airplanes that depart from a runway. The airplanes depart one at a time and in order; the first and second planes carry two shipments each, and the third plane carries three. The following rules apply:

R and P are carried on the same plane.
Either Q or S is carried on the same plane as N.
Either M or O, but not both, is carried on the first plane.
N is carried on the second plane.

18. A certain baseball manager uses seven pitchers—N, O, P, Q, R, S, and T—during the course of a game. The pitchers are used one at a time and in order. Additionally...

He uses R after P but before T.
S pitches neither immediately before nor immediately after Q.
He uses at least two pitchers after O but before R.
He uses N either immediately before or immediately after O.

Basic Setups Drill Set 1 Solutions

1/4. Five children—F, G, H, I, and J—are each given one of five toys—M, N, O, P, and R. Each toy is given to exactly one child. The following conditions apply:

N is given to J.
G gets either P or R.
M is not given to H.

You could have made the presents the base and the children the elements, and it wouldn't make much difference. For most LSAT games, the rules will indicate which base will be easiest to work with.

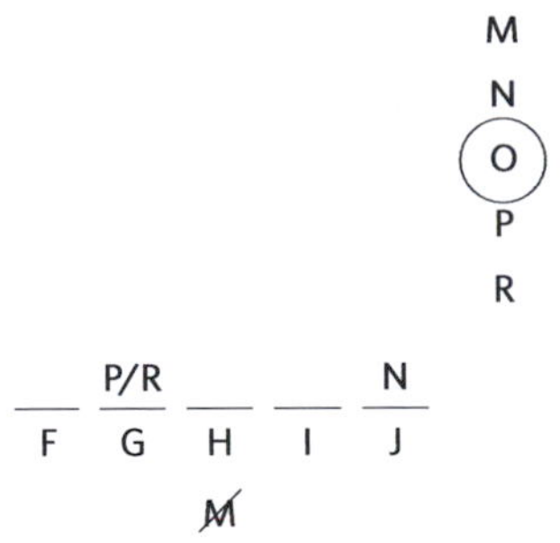

M N (O) P R

F	G	H	I	J
	P/R			N
		~~M~~		

2/5. Six airplanes—M, N, O, P, R, and S—take off from a runway, one at a time and in order. The following conditions apply:

Exactly one plane departs after N but before R.
Either O or P will depart third.
S departs immediately before or immediately after R.

The key to this game is the N, R, S trio. Note that there are only two places it can go, and placing it determines much of the game.

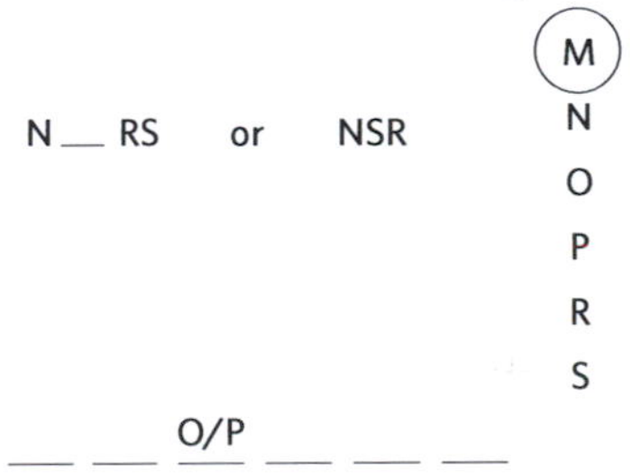

N _ RS or NSR

(M) N O P R S

_ _ O/P _ _ _

3/6. Eight friends—M, N, O, P, Q, R, S, and T—will ride in four cars to a concert, two friends per car. The following conditions apply:

M and N ride together.
O and R do not.
S rides with either P or Q.

You may have notated the rules to the side of the diagram, and that's fine. However, note that since the cars aren't themselves named or defined, we can just go ahead and place groups into any of the 4 "cars" we'd like (this game is not about which car each person goes in, but rather what pair each person is a part of). Placing items into the diagram helps us see some inferences we might not be able to see otherwise—if O and R have to be in different cars, and S has to be with either P or Q, we know at least a little something about each of the four friend pairings.

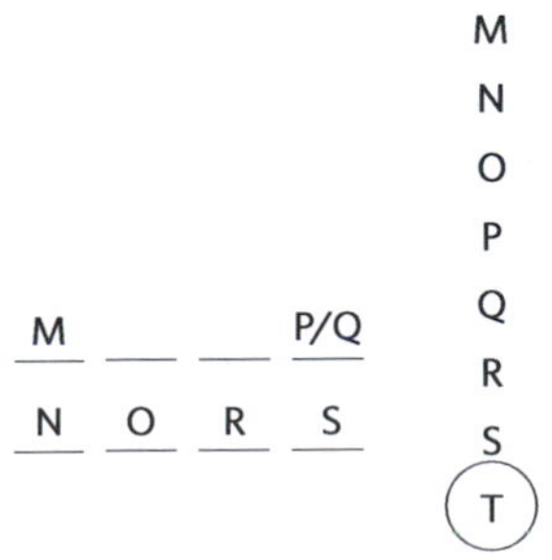

M N O P Q R S (T)

M			P/Q
N	O	R	S

Basic Setups Drill Set 2 Solutions

7/10. Sarah takes seven swings in a batting cage. On four swings, she makes good contact—on the others she either fouls the ball off or misses it. Additionally it must be true that...

She does not foul off two consecutive pitches.
She does not miss any of the last four pitches.
She makes good contact on exactly two of the first four pitches.

There are other ways that we could represent that last rule, but the "cloud" is a very effective tool for showing that you know certain elements go in a general area, but you don't know the exact spots (we'll discuss "the cloud" in more detail in a later lesson). The inference we can make from exactly two Gs in the first four spots is that two of the final three must be Gs.

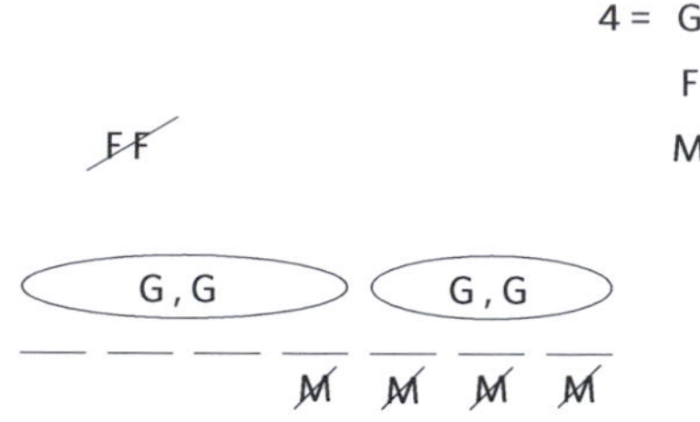

8/11. Nine students—F, G, H, I, J, K, L, M, and N—are split evenly into three teams—the purple team, the red team, and the tan team. The following conditions apply:

H is assigned to the red team.
G and I are assigned to the same team.
Either J or M, but not both, is assigned to the purple team.
G and H are not assigned to the same team.
L is not assigned to the tan team.

There is a slight inference to be made that I cannot be on the red team. During the questions, the placement of the G/I grouping would likely be the key to your process.

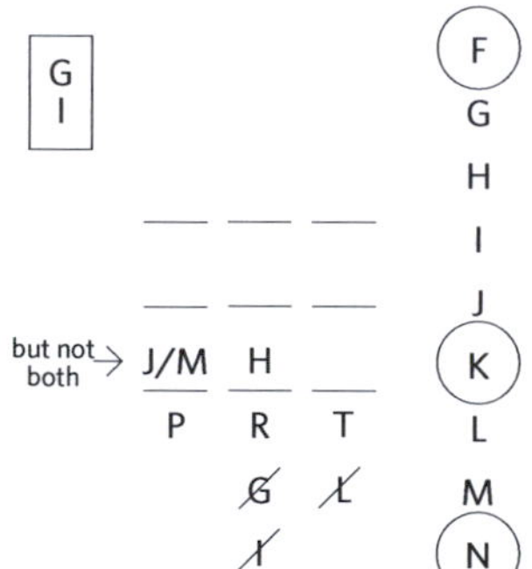

9/12. Six workers—F, G, H, J, K, and L—work three shifts as pairs. These shifts occur one at a time and in order. The following conditions apply:

H works a later shift than J.
G does not work the first shift.
J and K work the same shift.

In this game we've got a combination of ordering and grouping, so we'll use left-to-right order for the shifts (earliest to latest) and up and down for our groups. Thinking about the placement of the K/J/H combo would be the key to this game.

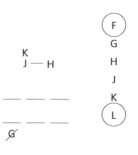

K
J — H

F
G
H
J
K
L

G

Basic Setups Drill Set 3 Solutions

13/16. Five different companies—M, N, O, P, and Q—each occupy one of five floors in an office building. The following conditions apply:

M is on a higher floor than Q, but not the highest floor.
Exactly one company is between O and N.
P is not on the second floor.

This is an ordering game that it makes sense to draw out vertically; after all, we are used to thinking about the floors of a building as going up and down. Make sure you are comfortable with your notation for the second rule.

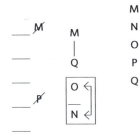

14/17. Seven dancers—F, G, H, I, J, K, and L—perform in a total of three shows. Two dancers perform in the first and second shows, and three dancers in the third. Each dancer performs just once. The following conditions apply:

G dances in the second performance.
Either H or F, but not both, dances in the first performance.
Either J or L dance with G.
K and I dance in the same performance.

Here's another game that involves both ordering and grouping. The K (and consequently I) inference can be made since it can't go in the first performance, and there is no space in the second performance.

15/18. Seven trains—F, G, H, I, J, K, and M—depart from a train station, one at a time and in order. The following conditions apply:

At least two trains depart after G but before J.
J departs after H but before M.
F departs immediately before or immediately after G.
K departs neither immediately before nor immediately after I.

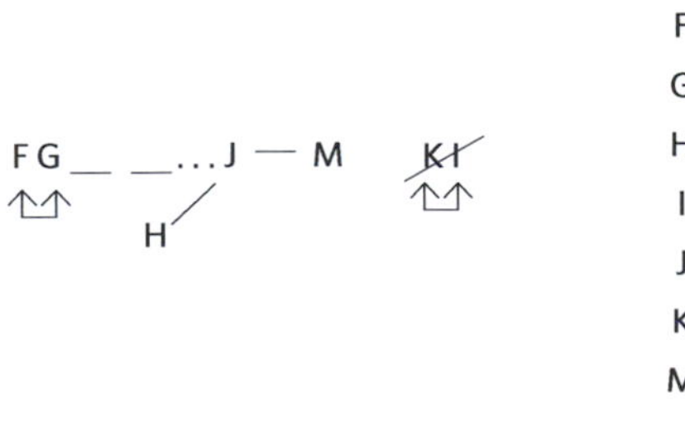

Note how we linked the first, second, and third rules together as we diagrammed them. Bringing rules together whenever possible will serve you well. We'll discuss such moves in greater detail in future lessons, but hopefully this work seems fairly logical to you.

How Did You Do?

Perhaps you feel like you need to do some games with questions before you can really evaluate yourself, and that's certainly fair. We'll get to some questions soon enough. However, keep in mind that your success on the questions is largely determined by the work you do before you even start them, and as I've said before (and as I'll say again), if you feel comfortable diagramming games—if putting a visual representation of the situation down on your paper feels intuitive for you—you are going to be good at answering Logic Games questions.

Strong diagramming skills are best built off of a sound, fundamental understanding of how Logic Games are designed, and we've laid down a lot of foundational keys in this lesson. Hopefully you felt comfortable drawing out the positions for the various scenarios that you were given, and hopefully you see a lot of commonality among these scenarios—not just within the mirror games (obviously) but from drill set to drill set.

Strong diagramming also requires a firm, comfortable handle on all of the rules, and it is this comfort level with the rules, and with the notations for the rules, that commonly separates top scorers from average ones. You should see a lot of commonality within the rules we've discussed in this lesson, and within the various notations we've chosen to use for these rules.

Being great at diagramming doesn't mean you have some slick notation for every unusual rule that you are going to see. It does mean that you have systems that you are very comfortable using for the common rules, and that you know how to slow down and adapt to the less common situations (more on this as we encounter more of these less common situations).

A great way to check on your notational ability is to double back on the written rule once you are done diagramming, that is, you take a look at each notation you've made, think of what it means to you, then read the written rule that it came from—make sure that what you *think* your notation means matches what it is actually supposed to mean. The time you spend doing this is never time wasted. The more comfortable you feel with the rules, the faster and easier the questions will feel, and doubling back is a great way to firm up your understanding before going into the questions.

The Road Ahead

In this lesson we discussed the central issues that form the foundation of all Logic Games. In the next four lessons, we will discuss the common ways in which games are made more unique. The first two issues we'll discuss—subsets, and numbers issues—have to do with the general setup, or design, of the game. The next two issues—conditional constraints and *or* conditions—are issues brought on by particular types of rules. By the time we're done with these five lessons, we will have covered every diagramming issue you are likely to face on test day. Of course, we will carefully layer new discussions over what we have already discussed, and in the lessons to come, you will get plenty of additional practice with the assignment, ordering, and grouping rules that we've introduced in this lesson.

11 LOGIC GAMES subsets

A common way for test writers to **complicate** Logic Game scenarios is to introduce characteristics or categories that split up, or further define, the elements, the positions, or both.

Imagine the difference between a board game for which you use just one color of pieces, versus a board game for which you have some red pieces and some black pieces. Imagine a Scrabble-like game for which each position is worth the same number of points, versus one in which some positions are worth more points. In this lesson, we will discuss how to handle Logic Games that, in the same way, further define the elements or positions.

More **complicated** does not necessarily mean more difficult; some of the most difficult games are ones with the most simple situations, and often a lot of complication results in fewer inferences and inference chains.

Let's say we have a game about a physical education class that has eight students. The teacher ranks the students based on how fast they can run a mile. How can we further define these students? Some can be boys, say, and some can be girls. And we can be told which students are boys and which ones girls, or this can be part of the mystery. How can the positions be further defined? Perhaps the top three students will get medals, and the other five students will not get medals. Then, if we are given a rule such as "Ted received a medal," we know he must have finished in one of the first three positions.

In general, we will notate these characteristics or categories by using lowercase letters. If you are consistent in using lowercase for such subsets, and not for any other situations, it can help you keep organized and at the top of your game. On the following page are some examples of what games with subsets can look like, along with diagramming suggestions and notes. Below are the notations you will use most commonly for diagramming subsets.

*If this were a real game, it would be smarter simply to infer that the position will be occupied by a boy. However, I've included the "not girl" notation here instead, just so you can see it. Games with three or more subsets will often require you to be comfortable with "not" notations.

F is a girl	F is not a girl*	A girl is in position X	A girl is not in position X*
Fg	Fg̸	g over X	g̸ over X

Note that the ordering and grouping rules that we discussed in the previous lesson can be modified to be about subsets. In most instances, replacing the element with the lowercase subset is simple enough, but in some instances it might create confusion. For example, think of how you would notate the rule "F is immediately ahead of a girl." Is it different from how you would notate that F is a girl? What about "F is two spots ahead of a girl"? Any time you worry that a notation might confuse you, it's best to write out what you need to know.

F is immediately ahead of a girl	F is two spots ahead of a girl
F _g	F __ _g

Subset Scenarios

Let's break down the different ways in which subsets appear in Logic Games.

One: The Scenario Tells Us Subset Assignments for All Elements

EXAMPLE

Three managers—P, R, and S—and three interns—V, X, and Y—will take turns testing out the new device. The device will be tested by one person at a time. The following conditions apply:

An intern will test the device first.
An intern will test the device right before and right after R does.
Either S or P will test the device last.

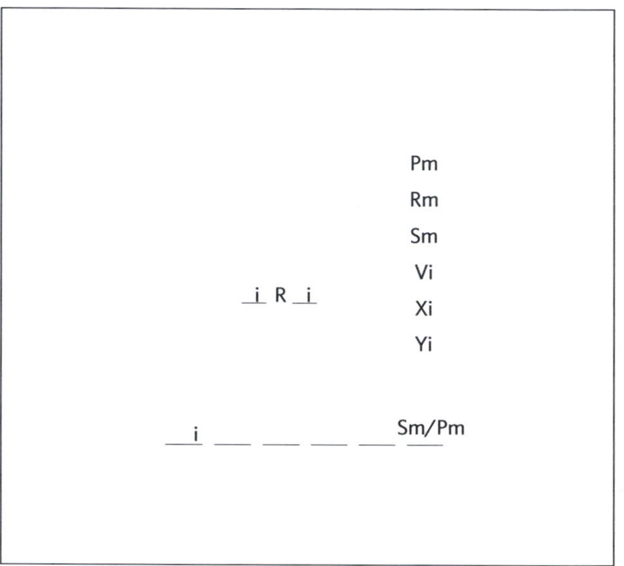

NOTES

Notice that for this game, elements are split up into subgroups—managers and interns—and we are told which elements are in which subgroup. We can notate the subgroup right next to the element (rather than, say, creating a T-chart that separates subgroups), and by doing this we can more easily see how the rules come together (for example, it's easy to visualize the Vi, Xi, Yi notations fitting into spots we know have an "i" at the end).

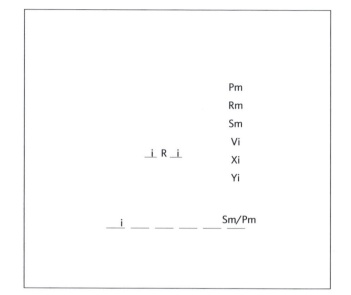

Two: The Scenario Tells Us Subset Assignments for All Positions

EXAMPLE

Six people—F, G, H, I, J, and K—will be split into three teams. Each team will have two different jobs—someone who plans, and someone who reviews. The following rules apply:

G and K will be on the same team.
H and K will have the same job.
F will not be a reviewer.

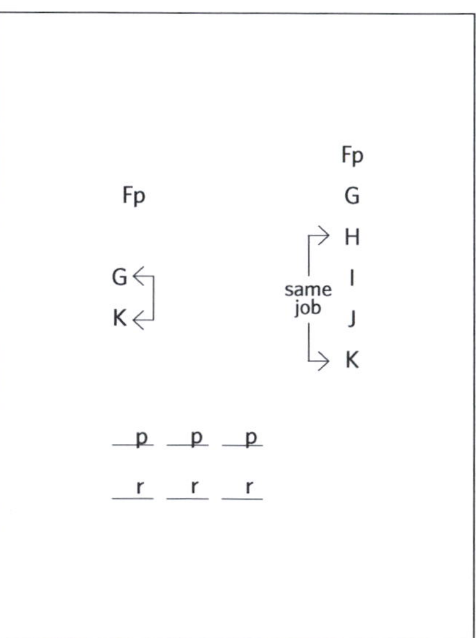

NOTES

We've grouped the three pairs vertically, as we always do. We've simply added the information about the two different jobs. The G/K rule is somewhat dangerous in terms of causing confusion later in your process. If this game didn't have subsets, we could represent it simply by lining G and K up vertically. But deep into this type of game, we don't want to get confused into thinking that our notation means that G has to be a planner and K a reviewer. The double arrow is a nice precaution. You could also have written "same team" next to the G and K notation for the sake of clarification if you felt you needed it.

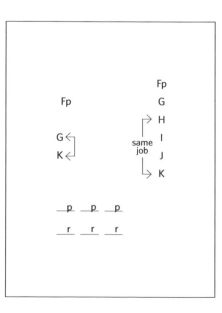

Three: The Scenario Gives Us Subsets, but No Assignments

EXAMPLE

A concert will include five bands—F, G, H, I, and K—which will play one at a time and in order. Each band features a different instrument—the Octaban, Piano, Steel Drum, Tom Tom, and Xylophone. The following conditions apply:

G does not feature the Tom Tom.
The second band that play will feature the Piano.
K, which features the Octaban, will play at some point before G.
The band that features the Tom Tom will play at some point before K.

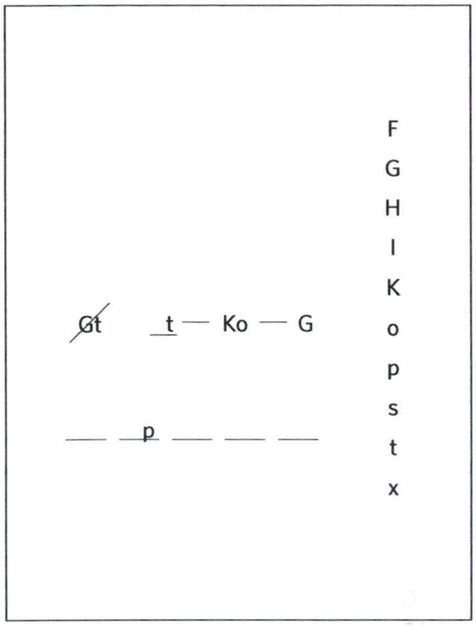

F G H I K
o p s t x

~~Gt~~ t — Ko — G

__ p __ __ __

NOTES

Most games, when they include subsets, include just two or three subsets, but others, like this one, can have as many subsets (in this case, the instrument played) as there are elements and positions. Since there are so many, it makes sense to go ahead and list them out. Take note of how we combined the third and fourth rules—linking rules that go together is a great way to simplify a game. If this were a real game, the t-Ko-G link would most certainly be the key consideration for solving questions.

*Challenge: The Scenario Gives Us Multiple Subsets

EXAMPLE

A steak house will bring out five different types of steaks—a filet, a hanger, a New York, a rib eye, and a sirloin—one at a time and in order. Each steak is either grilled or pan fried, and each steak is served medium rare or well done. The following conditions apply:

The third steak brought out is grilled and well done.
The filet is neither grilled nor medium rare.
The filet is served immediately after the New York steak.
The first steak is either a grilled sirloin or a grilled rib eye.

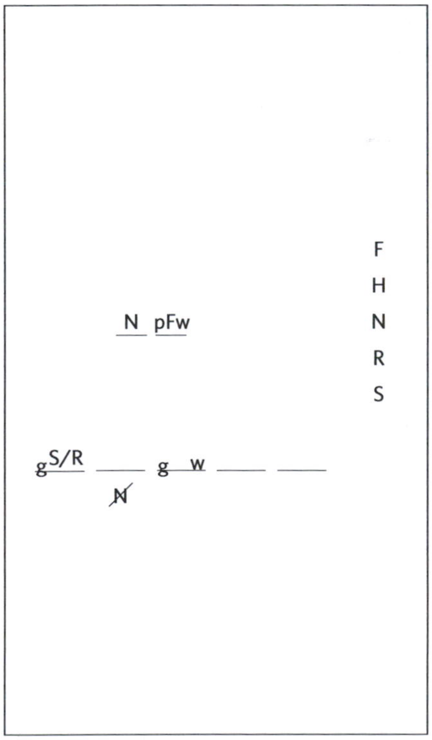

F H N R S

N pFw

gS/R __ g w __ __
~~N~~

NOTES

Once in a while, the test writers will include a game that includes more than one subset differentiation—in this case, the steaks are differentiated by their preparation method and level of doneness. We can deal with these different subsets by notating them on the two different sides of the element. You want to be careful notating N and F together; you want to do what you can, including writing it in if you need to, to make sure it's clear that the p goes with F, and not N.

It may feel a bit intimidating to deal with a game with two or more subset differentiations. Take heart in knowing that for games like this one, for which the scenario itself involves a significant level of complication, the setup tends to be the primary challenge, that is, once you are finally able to get everything organized, the questions will tend to be relatively straightforward and manageable.

Directions for drills starting on the next page...

Simple Setups Drill Set 1 has four basic games for you to set up, each involving characteristics and categories. Simple Setups Drill Set 2 has the same games, but in a different order, and with different scenarios. Keep track of your time for each set. If you feel comfortable with your setups for each game, move on to the next set and try be just a bit faster and more efficient. If you feel uncertain about your setups after Set 1, look through the solutions before trying Set 2. As always, do your work in a notebook if you think you might come back to repeat these exercises later in your studies.

Simple Setups Drill 1

1. Six friends—M, N, O, Q, R, and S—drive in three cars—a Fiat, a Jeep, and a Kia. Each car has a driver and a passenger. The following conditions apply:

M drives the Jeep.
Both S and Q are passengers.
S and N ride in the same car.

2. A band will sing covers of five songs—R, S, T, U, and V—originally sung by one of three bands—Nirvana, Oasis, and Pearl Jam. The order of songs will conform to the following restrictions:

T will be sung immediately after a Nirvana song.
V is a Nirvana song.
A Pearl Jam song will not be first.
They will play exactly one Oasis song.

3. Three parents—F, G, and H—and three children—S, T, and W—will take turns playing miniature golf. They will each take one turn, and they will go in order. The following rules apply:

No two parents go consecutively.
S does not go immediately before or after another child.
G goes third.

4. Four different desks, one each made of metal, oak, pine, and teak, sold for four different prices—$100, $200, $300, and $400—to four different buyers—Mrs. F, Mr. G, Ms. H, and Ms. J. Additionally...

Mrs. F bought the most expensive desk.
The teak desk cost $300.
Ms. H did not buy the cheapest desk.
Mr. G bought the pine desk.

Simple Setups Drill 2

1B. A television station will air three sitcoms—M, N, and O—and three dramas—X, Y, and Z—during the course of a night. The following rules apply:

X does not air immediately before or after another drama.
No two sitcoms air consecutively.
N will air third.

2B. Six workers—F, G, H, J, K, and L—will be assigned to three different stations—S, T, and U. At each station, there will be a maker and an editor. The following conditions apply:

F is the maker at station T.
G and J work at the same station.
Both J and K are editors.

3B. Four suspects—F, G, H, and J—are brought in for a case. One has the mustache, one the nose, one the piercing, and one the round glasses that the witness remembers, and each suspect only has one of these characteristics. The suspects are questioned one at a time. Additionally...

The first suspect questioned wears round glasses.
J has the piercing.
H is the second suspect questioned.
The third suspect questioned has no mustache.

4B. A certain theater will play five movies—M, N, O, P, and Q—made by three different directors—F, G, and H—during the course of a festival. It will play these movies one at a time and in order according to the following:

Q was made by F.
A movie made by H will not play first.
There will be exactly one movie made by G.
O will play immediately after a movie made by F.

Simple Setups Drill 1 & 2 Solutions

1. Six friends—M, N, O, Q, R, and S—drive in three cars—a Fiat, a Jeep, and a Kia. Each car has a driver and a passenger. The following conditions apply:

M drives the Jeep.
Both S and Q are passengers.
S and N ride in the same car.

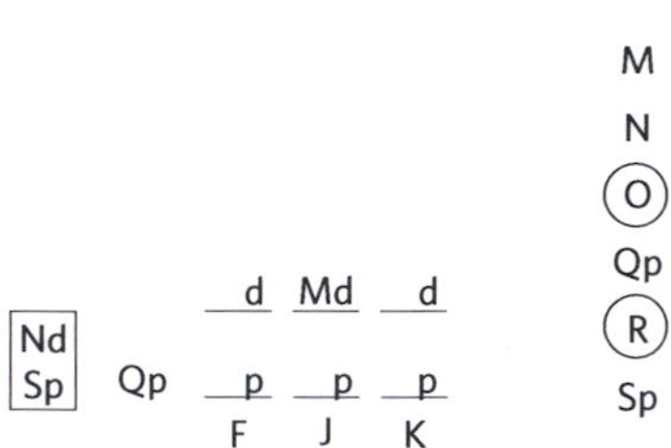

Notes: We noted that Q and S are passengers in two different places to be doubly mindful. We can make a small inference that N drives in the car with S. The N and S grouping, coupled with M driving J, makes this game very easy to manage.

2. A band will sing covers of five songs—R, S, T, U, and V—originally sung by one of three bands—Nirvana, Oasis, and Pearl Jam. The order of songs will conform to the following restrictions:

T will be sung immediately after a Nirvana song.
V is a Nirvana song.
A Pearl Jam song will not be first.
They will play exactly one Oasis song.

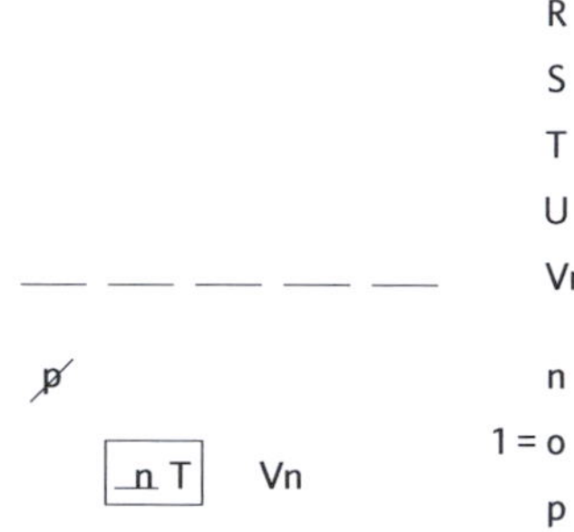

Notes: We can stay a bit more organized by putting information about the bands above the lines, and the songs below the lines. It's easy to over-infer and think that T must be after V, but that is not the case. Since we know very little about where most elements can go, we don't need to circle outliers in the elements list.

3. Three parents—F, G, and H—and three children—S, T, and W—will take turns playing miniature golf. They will each take one turn, and they will go in order. The following rules apply:

No two parents go consecutively.
S does not go immediately before or after another child.
G goes third.

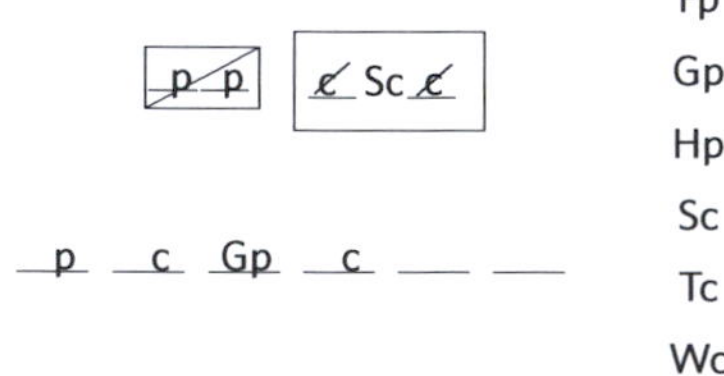

Notes: We can make some inferences about the second and fourth positions once we place G third. Then, because we have two more p's to place and they can't go consecutively in 5 and 6, we know that one of the remaining two parents has to go in the first position.

4. Four different desks, one each made of metal, oak, pine, and teak, sold for four different prices—$100, $200, $300, and $400—to four different buyers—Mrs. F, Mr. G, Ms. H, and Ms. J. Additionally...

Mrs. F bought the most expensive desk.
The teak desk cost $300.
Ms. H did not buy the cheapest desk.
Mr. G bought the pine desk.

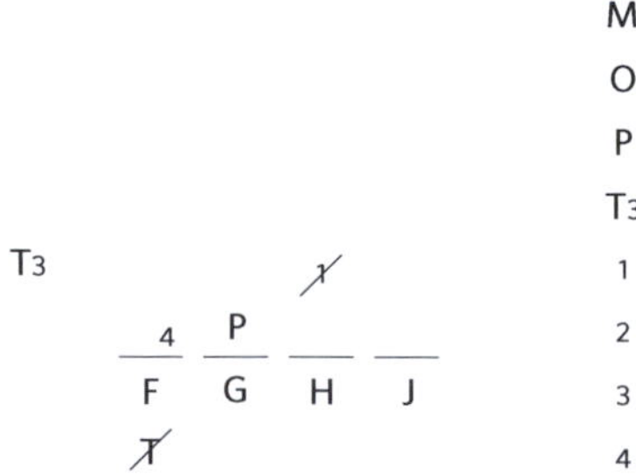

Notes: We could just as easily have thought of the cost as the element and the material as the characteristic, or made the cost the base, and that would have been fine as well.

Full Setups Drill 1

directions below

A recruiter will interview six candidates—M, N, O, P, Q, and R—one at a time and in order. Two of the candidates are experienced, and the rest are not. The following conditions apply:

Neither of the first two candidates interviewed is experienced.
Either M or N, but not both, is experienced.
P interviews before both O and R.
R does not have experience.

Three biologists—R, S, and T—three chemists—U, W, and X—and two doctors—Y and Z—will be split into three teams for a research project. Two teams—F and G—will have two people assigned to them, and team K will have four people assigned to it. The following conditions apply:

No doctors are assigned to team K.
No doctors are assigned to the same team.
R and S are not assigned to the same team.
U and T are assigned to the same team.

An animal show will feature five different animals—S, T, U, V, and X. One is a frog, one a guinea pig, one a hamster, one an iguana, and one is a jack rabbit. The animals will appear one at a time, according to the following conditions:

T will appear at some point after the hamster,
but at some point before the frog.
The iguana will appear either first or last.
S is either a hamster or an iguana.
T is not a guinea pig.

Directions: Here are games that are more representative of the typical level of challenge that you are likely to see on the LSAT. This drill includes three sets of three games each, and the sets get progressively more difficult. Keep track of your time but don't rush.

Full Setups Drill 1 Solutions

A recruiter will interview six candidates—M, N, O, P, Q, and R—one at a time and in order. Two of the candidates are experienced, and the rest are not. The following conditions apply:

Neither of the first two candidates interviewed is experienced.
Either M or N, but not both, is experienced.
P interviews before both O and R.
R does not have experience.

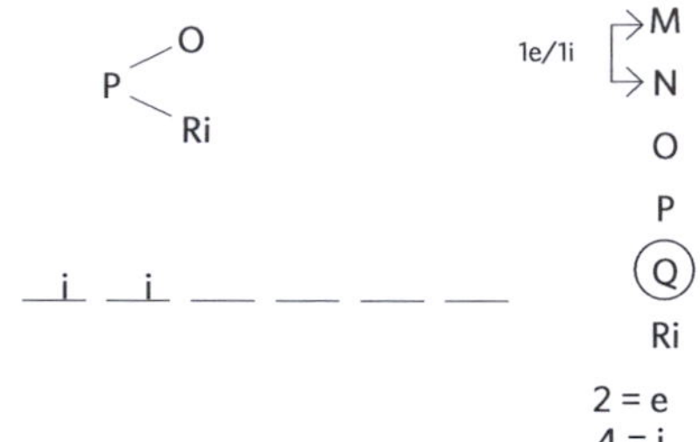

We notated the last rule together with the third and also notated it on the elements list. Note that when there are just two subset groups (which happens fairly often), you want to be in the habit of associating "not X" with "Y," as in "not experienced" with "inexperienced." ***If you didn't mark that Q is not mentioned, that's fine, but keep in mind that "free agents" are particularly useful in games that have two or fewer of them.***

Three biologists—R, S, and T—three chemists—U, W, and X—and two doctors—Y and Z—will be split into three teams for a research project. Two teams—F and G—will have two people assigned to them, and team K will have four people assigned to it. The following conditions apply:

No doctors are assigned to team K.
No doctors are assigned to the same team.
R and S are not assigned to the same team.
U and T are assigned to the same team.

Rb/Sb (crossed out)

Y/Zd Y/Zd Uc
Tb
F G K

Rb
Sb
Tb –
Uc –
Wc
Xc
Yd –
Zd –

In this instance, it really pays off to read all of the rules before you start notating. Namely, the first and second rules together lead to a significant inference (that one doctor has to be on team F and the other on team G) that makes the game much easier to diagram and consider. This also leads to the inference that the U/T pair must be on team K. ***I also wanted to show one extra optional step: you can mark the elements that have already been placed on the elements list.***

An animal show will feature five different animals—S, T, U, V, and X. One is a frog, one a guinea pig, one a hamster, one an iguana, and one is a jack rabbit. The animals will appear one at a time, according to the following conditions:

T will appear at some point after the hamster, but at some point before the frog.
The iguana will appear either first or last.
S is either a hamster or an iguana.
T is not a guinea pig.

Sh or Si Tg (crossed out)

h — T — f

i/ /i
___ ___ ___ ___ ___

S
T
U
V
X
f
g
h
i
j

The key rule in this game is most definitely the first one, considering that it will impact three of the five total positions (with another one of the five, either of the ends, occupied with an i). As you answer questions, whether they specifically refer to h, T, f, or not, that first rule should be your first consideration when you picture your board. One advanced inference you could have made here was that T must be the jack rabbit.

As always, there are many effective ways to diagram games, and if you happened to notate something differently—that's fine—just make sure that your notation is accurate.

Full Setups Drill 2

Six people—M, N, O, P, R, and S—are hired for jobs in three departments—F, G, and H. Two people are hired for each department. Some people are given benefits, while others are not. Additionally...

The two people hired for G are given benefits.
Neither M nor N is given benefits.
S is the only person hired in his department who is given benefits.
M and P are not hired for the same department.

An artist applies six different colors—F, G, H, I, K, and L—to his painting, one color at a time. The first three colors he applies to the sky, and the next three colors he applies to other parts of the painting. It also must be true that:

He applies F to the sky.
He uses K before L but after I.
He uses G fifth.
He uses K or H, but not both, for the sky.

A homeowner receives six different bids from six different contractors—M, N, O, P, R, and S—for a project on her house. Each bid is a different price. Some bids estimate that the job will take two weeks, some that the job will take four weeks, and one bid estimates a six-week job. The following conditions apply:

N's bid price was higher than M's, but lower than R's.
The lowest bid price came with a six-week estimate.
O estimated two more weeks than N did.
R's bid price was the second highest of those that came with a two-week estimate.

Full Setups Drill 2 Solutions

Six people—M, N, O, P, R, and S—are hired for jobs in three departments—F, G, and H. Two people are hired for each department. Some people are given benefits, while others are not. Additionally...

The two people hired for G are given benefits.
Neither M nor N is given benefits.
S is the only person hired in his department
who is given benefits.
M and P are not hired for the same department.

The third rule is a bit tricky to notate, and in any such situation, if you feel stuck on how to notate a rule exactly, it's fine to write the rule out next to the diagram.

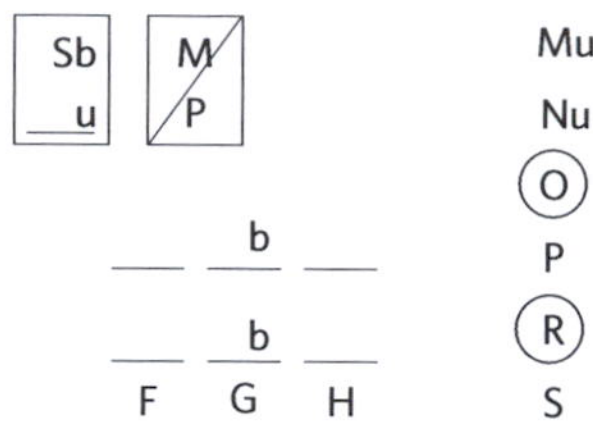

An artist applies six different colors—F, G, H, I, K, and L—to his painting, one color at a time. The first three colors he applies to the sky, and the next three colors he applies to other parts of the painting. It also must be true that:

He applies F to the sky.
He uses K before L but after I.
He uses G fifth.
He uses K or H, but not both, for the sky.

You may have been tempted to draw your diagram to match a visual that you have of a painting—with a sky above and rest below. If so, bravo! The better you can visualize, the better off you will be. One thing you definitely want to make sure of, though, is that any sort of creative design also lets you keep track of order, for order is clearly important in this game. We separated sky and other while keeping the slots in a row for order's sake, but other methods could have been just as effective.

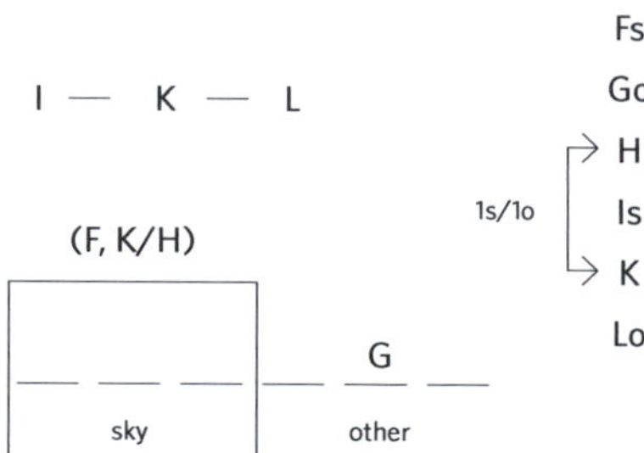

A homeowner receives six different bids from six different contractors—M, N, O, P, R, and S—for a project on her house. Each bid is a different price. Some bids estimate that the job will take two weeks, some that the job will take four weeks, and one bid estimates a six-week job. The following conditions apply:

N's bid price was higher than M's, but lower than R's.
The lowest bid price came with a six-week estimate.
O estimated two more weeks than N did.
R's bid price was the second highest of those that came with a two-week estimate.

It's very important you take the time to carefully evaluate this game before you start laying out your board; the key is to use the prices to set up an order. How should you know to do this? From the rules. Notice that several of the rules reference higher and lower, and we know there can't be any ties. You could have set it up from highest to lowest price, and that would have been great, too. Notice that we didn't have a great way to notate the last rule, and rather than come up with some random notation we'll confuse later on, we just wrote out the rule.

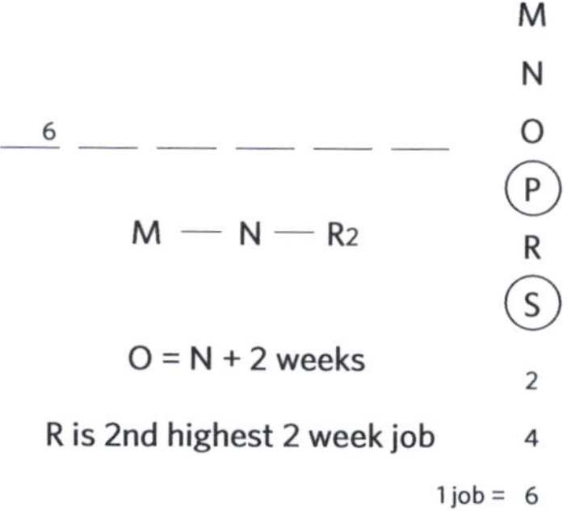

Full Setups Drill 3 Challenge Set*

A certain political campaign has stickers and posters in five different styles—F, G, H, I, and K. They will put these stickers and posters at five hotspots, labeled one through five. They will put one style of sticker and one style of poster at each location, and no style of either will be placed in more than one location. Additionally, the following rules apply:

The G-style sticker will be placed with the F-style poster.
The K-style sticker will be placed with the G-style poster.
No sticker and poster of the same style will be placed
in the same location.
The two H-style items will be used at hotspots 1 and 3.
I cannot be placed with K.

An author has written five novels—M, N, O, P, and R. Three of the novels—M, N, and O—are in Russian, and the other two—P and R—are in French. Two of the novels are best sellers, and three of them are not. The author will read excerpts from all five novels for an audience of fans. Additionally, we know that...

He reads from a best seller second.
Either N or O, but not both, is a best seller.
He reads from exactly two Russian books before his first French book.
He reads from M before O.

Four pairs of mittens are matched up with four pairs of socks for a window display. There is one pair of both in each of four colors—gray, indigo, jade, and khaki. The items are made of either cotton, polyester, or wool only. The following conditions apply:

The gray socks are paired with polyester mittens.
The indigo mittens are paired with wool socks.
The khaki socks are not paired with gray mittens.
Both the gray and jade socks are made of cotton.
Exactly one pair of socks is made of polyester.

** These are not your run-of-the-mill games, and if you saw one of these on the exam, it'd likely be the most difficult of your four games. Don't hesitate to get creative. You can do it!*

Full Setups Drill 3 Challenge Set Solutions

A certain political campaign has stickers and posters in five different styles—F, G, H, I, and K. They will put these stickers and posters at five hotspots, labeled one through five. They will put one style of sticker, and one style of poster, at each location, and no style of either will be placed in more than one location. Additionally, the following rules apply:

The G-style sticker will be placed with the F-style poster.
The K-style sticker will be placed with the G-style poster.
No sticker and poster of the same style will be placed in the same location.
The two H-style items will be used at hotspots 1 and 3.
I cannot be placed with K.

Note the use of two rows of lines for the two different types of items—stickers and posters—used at each locale. Also note that there are probably more elegant ways to notate the third rule, but I've done it in a way that is at least obvious. I wrote out the last rule with a slight inference.

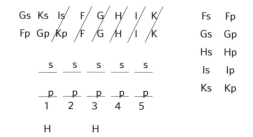

Gs Ks Is/Kp F/F G/G H/H I/I K/K
Fp Gp

s s s s s
p p p p p
1 2 3 4 5
H H

Fs Fp
Gs Gp
Hs Hp
Is Ip
Ks Kp

An author has written five novels—M, N, O, P, and R. Three of the novels—M, N, and O—are in Russian, and the other two—P and R—are in French. Two of the novels are best sellers, and three of them are not. The author will read excerpts from all five novels for an audience of fans. Additionally, we know that...

He reads from a best seller second.
Either N or O, but not both, is a best seller.
He reads from exactly two Russian books before his first French book.
He reads from M before O.

We have two subsets here, but unlike the previous example, that obviously doesn't mean we should have ten positions (he's not going to be reading ten things). We can use lowercase letters placed to the left of where we write in the element to indicate the second layer of subset: whether the book is a best seller or not.

2 b's and 3 u's

M — O

1b/1u → Nr, Or

r b r f _ _

Mr
Nr
Or
Pf
Rf

Four pairs of mittens are matched up with four pairs of socks for a window display. There is one pair of both in each of four colors—gray, indigo, jade, and khaki. The items are made of either cotton, polyester, or wool only. The following conditions apply:

The gray socks are paired with polyester mittens.
The indigo mittens are paired with wool socks.
The khaki socks are not paired with gray mittens.
Both the gray and jade socks are made of cotton.
Exactly one pair of socks is made of polyester.

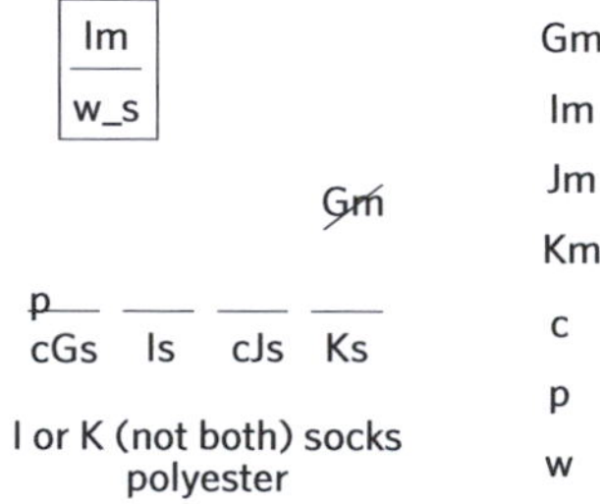

Gm
Im
Jm
Km
c
p
w

In this case, there is overlap between elements and positions—rare, but it has happened in a few games in the past. You could have chosen to make the mittens the base and the socks the elements, as the rules would have worked out just fine that way as well. The key is that you put yourself in a position to match mittens with socks, and we've done that here. Note the slight inference noted at the bottom. Also note that we placed the positions in a horizontal arrangement even though there is no order; that shouldn't confuse us here.

12 LOGIC GAMES numbers issues

About a quarter of all games require us to make inferences regarding numbers—that is, they give us clues about a certain number of elements in a subset or a group, and test our ability to infer something about other numbers based on that information. In most instances, the numbers issues we will have to deal with on the LSAT are similar to one of these two hypothetical scenarios:

• You are at Taco Bell, where they sell four different things that you like. Everything is $1 or $2, and you have $6 in your pocket. You're trying to figure out what combination of food you want for that $6.

• You are trying to figure out how much a co-worker makes. You know that there are four tiers of pay at your company, and you also know that this co-worker makes more than a certain person, less than another person, and so on.

Numbers issues can appear when the elements and positions are not one-to-one or when there are subsets

The numbers issues on the LSAT will be no more complicated than these examples mentioned above. The numbers will always be small and the options very limited. Success won't ever require "hard math." What it will require is a recognition of when you need to think about these issues, as well as an ability to handle these situations with consistency and accuracy.

Numbers issues are not particularly common—the majority of games will not require the skills that we will discuss here. There are just two general situations in which we need to focus on numbers issues: when there is something other than a one-to-one relationship between elements and positions, and when there are subsets.

Up to this point, every game we've looked at has had a natural one-to-one relationship between elements and positions—five elements fill five slots, six elements fill six slots, and so on. However, there are certain games for which there is something other than a one-to-one relationship, either because there are more elements than positions, more positions than elements, or an uncertain number of positions to be filled. In this lesson, we will thoroughly discuss games that have something other than a one-to-one relationship between elements and positions.

We actually dealt with a few basic *subset* numbers issues in the last lesson (by putting "= 2" next to a particular subset and such). We'll look at some more examples of numbers situations that arise because of subsets in this lesson.

Issue One: More Elements than Positions

Just like when you tried out for that high school musical, sometimes there are more people who want spots than there are spots themselves. The natural consequence is that certain roles are assigned to certain individuals, and other individuals don't get positions. In high school, those who didn't make it were quickly forgotten, never to be heard singing in the halls again—but on the LSAT, when there are too many people or elements for positions, it's very important that you keep track of those that *don't* fit in.

We can do this by drawing "out" positions, as we've done below, and by keeping track of which elements are in, and which elements are out. The big vertical line will be our line of demarcation for rules about what is in and what is out. Rules about elements having to be in or out (see side note) can cradle this line of demarcation.

Either F or G, but not both, will be selected.

in	out
F	G

Note that when the number of "out" slots becomes fairly significant, as in the second example, this begins to look very much like a grouping game (with the "in" and "out" being the groups); in fact, there is a lot of natural overlap between the strategies for grouping games, and the strategies for situations with "in" and "out" members. The same strategies are effective in both situations, so this overlap shouldn't cause any problems.

When there are more elements than positions and ordering is not involved, subsets commonly will be involved, and there will often be numbers issues having to do with these subsets. The second example illustrates this sort of situation, and we'll discuss this in greater depth starting on page 164. For now, make sure you understand how we were able to derive the inferences about the numbers for each subset.

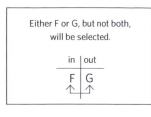

Below are examples of game scenarios and rules that involve more elements than positions.

A coach will pick four of the six swimmers—F, G, H, I, J, and K—on his team to take part in a race. Each of the four selected swimmers will swim one lap, and they will do so in order. The following conditions apply:

Either I or F, but not both, will swim in the race.
Both H and J will swim in the race, and H will go before J.
G will not swim first.

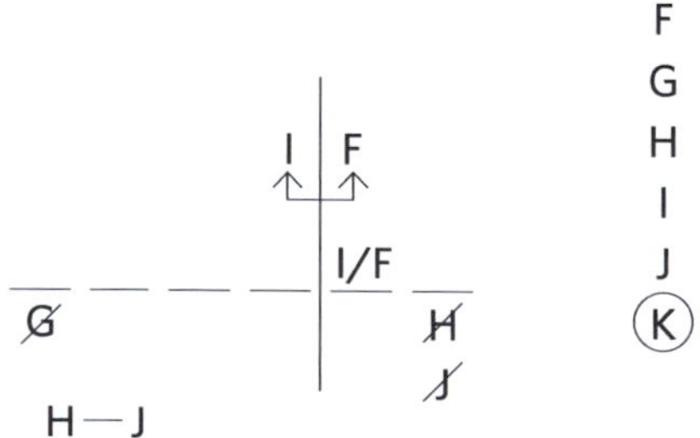

When there are clues in a game about who is selected and who is not, it's just as important to keep track of the "out" positions as it is the "in" positions.

A writer submits three novellas—F, G, H—two poems—L and M— and three short stories—T, U, and V—to be published on a new website. The website chooses exactly five of those items to publish. Additionally, it must be true that:

No more than two short stories were chosen.
Either L or M, but not both, was chosen.
G was chosen.

Gn
Lp/Mp
Lp | Mp
Lp/Mp

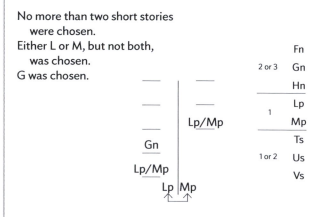

2 or 3	Fn, Gn, Hn
1	Lp, Mp
1 or 2	Ts, Us, Vs

The elements list is a natural place to keep track of subset numbers. Since we know that exactly one poem, and two or fewer short stories were chosen, we know that at least two of the three novels must have been chosen. Even if all three novels were chosen, we're still not at five items, so we know there must be at least one short story.

Issue Two: More Positions than Elements

For certain games, there are fewer elements than there are positions, and a variety of consequences can arise because of this. Let's discuss these types of games here, starting with ordering games that have more positions than elements.

The third position will be filled.

The third position will be empty.

Ordering Games with More Positions than Elements

If an ordering game has more positions than elements, there are two possible consequences—either certain positions will be left blank, or certain elements will be used more than once. Below are examples of these two different ordering scenarios.

When you know that certain spaces are going to be left blank, you want to make sure to keep track of spaces you know must be filled and spaces you know must remain empty. My suggested notations for these situations are to the side.

The same element is in 3 & 4.

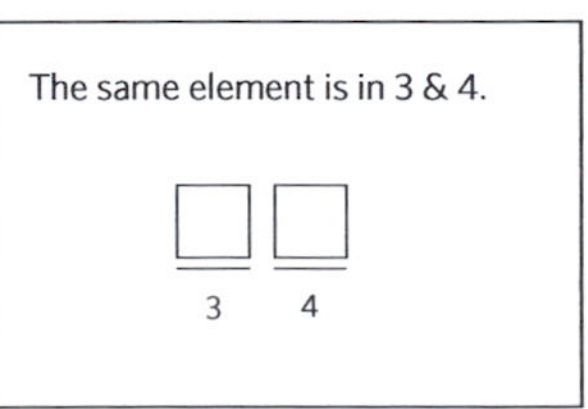

Different elements are in 3 & 4.

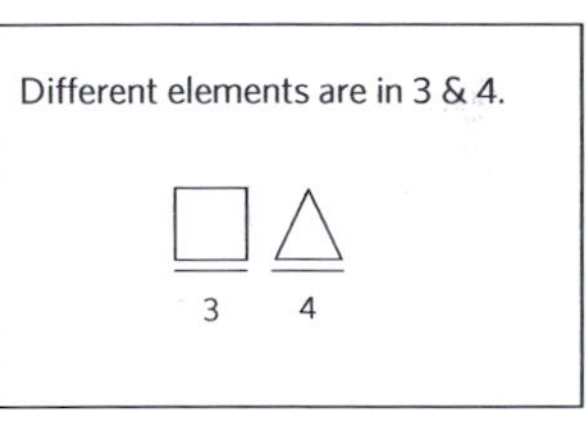

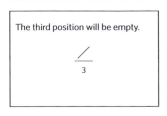

You don't have to use just squares and triangles—use any shape you can draw. The key is consistency or contrast. The shapes may seem childish, but they are great visual tools.

When there are more positions than elements, but all the positions must be filled, then we know that some of the elements will be used more than once. We'll want to remain mindful of this fact throughout the game. If the numbers of each element are a part of the game's mystery, we want to notate clues about this as we get them. If the numbers are made clear from the beginning, I suggest that you write out all the elements (i.e., M, M, N, N, O, O—if you know there are two of each of those elements) to make it easier to see all of the "pieces" you have to place.

Grouping Games with More Positions than Elements

Grouping games with more positions than elements are a bit more common and a bit more interesting than ordering games with more positions than elements.

Below are examples of game scenarios and rules that involve more positions than elements.

Five babies—M, N, O, P, and R—were born over a seven-year span—from 2001 through 2007. No more than one baby was born a year. The following conditions apply:

N was born after both M and P.
No baby was born the year before N was born.
Babies were born in every odd year.

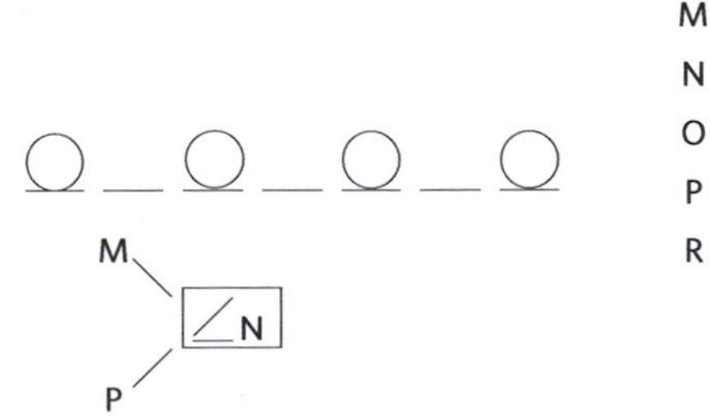

The circles (and triangles and such that we will soon be using) can make you feel like you are ten years old, but they are very visually effective. Remember that you want to try to combine rule notations whenever you can, as we've done with the first and second rule. This will make it easier for us to see how everything comes together.

A jewelry-maker is making a chain of seven beads. She will use at least one bead of each of three colors—magenta, orange, and purple—and beads of no other color. The following rules apply:

The first three beads will be of three different colors.
The second, fourth, and sixth beads will be of the same color.
There are exactly three orange beads used.

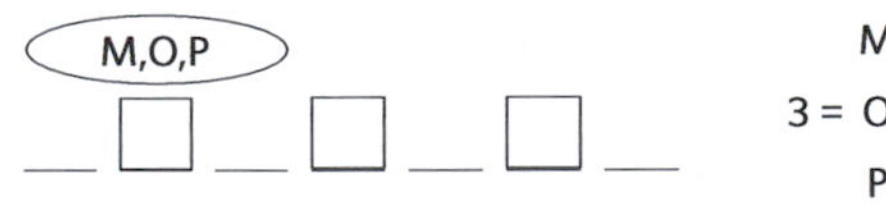

The large oval and commas are very useful when you know that a certain group of elements must go in a certain group of positions, but you don't know any more specifics. Our default understanding would probably be that each bead is used at least once, and so we probably don't need to notate that (though you certainly can if you want). If each bead did not need to be used at least once, that would likely be different from what we'd expect, so in that case it'd be important to make note of it.

Some grouping games are actually not very different from their related ordering games. Imagine the following scenario: four people who work at a company are assigned to three different projects. Two people will be assigned to each project, and each person will be assigned at least once.

In this case, it's fairly easy to see how the skills we've developed so far can be applied, and it's fairly easy to anticipate the key issues for this game; it's likely that we will be given some information about the number of projects each person works on, as well as some rules about how they will be grouped and assigned to specific projects.

Four people—F, G, H, and J—who work together at a company are assigned to three different projects—M, N, and P. Each person is assigned to at least one project, and each project will have two people assigned to it. The following rules apply:

F is assigned to two projects.
G and H are assigned to a project together.
J is assigned to project M or N, but not both.

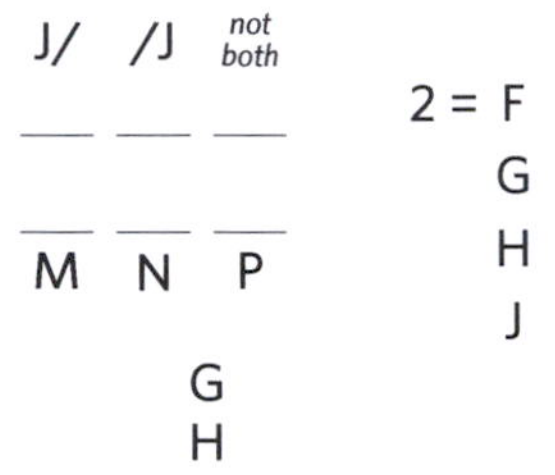

J/ /J not both

__ __ __

__ __ __

M N P

G
H

2 = F
G
H
J

Grouping games with more positions than elements get more interesting when there is *uncertainty* in terms of the number of positions to be filled. Note that this sort of uncertainty is almost non-existent in ordering games (though there will be an example in your practice set) but is fairly common in grouping games.

At the top of the next page is an example of a grouping game that has this sort of issue. Notice that we can use the same circle and slash notation we introduced earlier. No big deal. If you are mindful of the various numeric inferences that can arise, these notations can be very useful for representing your understanding and for making inferences.

what does "or" mean?

In real life, words have a range of meaning, or even a variety of meanings, and all of us naturally adjust our understanding per the situation. When we hear that someone loves hamburgers, we know that this means something different than hearing that the person loves her husband. (Hopefully, it means something different.)

However, when it comes to the words used in reasoning issues, the LSAT requires a very specific understanding of the word's meaning. One of these key words is the word "or."

In real life, "or" has multiple meanings. If you win the lottery and are told that you can get the money in one lump sum, or in monthly payments, the intended meaning is that you can get one or the other, but not both. However, if we say that in order for Debbie to date a guy, he has to either have a job or be in school, chances are we aren't meaning to exclude those that both have a job and go to school.

On the LSAT, the word "or" does not exclude the possibility of both. Thus, a statement like "M or N is selected" means that M, N, or both are selected.

If they do not mean for both to be a possibility, they must state, "but not both."

Also keep in mind that many situations—most situations, actually—just naturally exclude the possibility of both. Let's say we have a race and we are told that people finish one at a time and in order. If we are given the rule, "either R or N finished third," note that the design of the game would prevent us from placing both into the third position.

On the LSAT, the word "or" by itself does not inherently exclude the possibility of both. However, many situations (such as an order without ties) naturally exclude the possibility of "or" meaning "and."

For a certain cooking competition, a chef can use four types of ingredients—F, G, H, and J—to cook five different dishes. Each ingredient must be used at least once, and each dish must contain at least one ingredient. Additionally, the following must be true:

The second dish he cooks has more ingredients than the first, but fewer than the third.
The last dish he cooks has more ingredients than any other.
The second dish and the fourth dish have no ingredients in common.

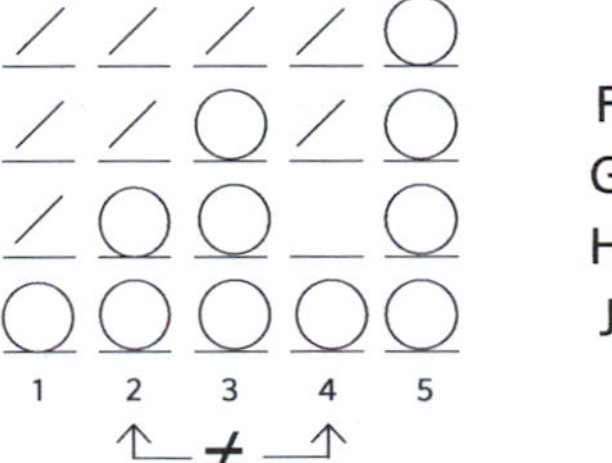

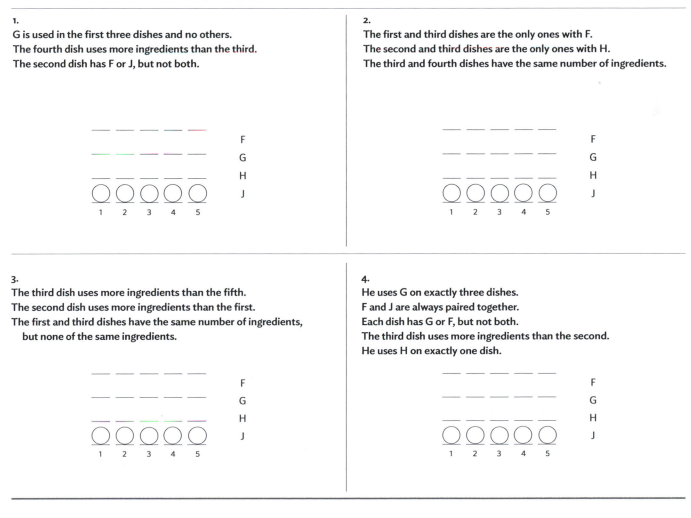

Fun, huh? Remind you of Connect Four? Here's how we figured all of this out: the first rule severely limits how many elements can be in the first, second, and third dishes. One thing it tells us is that since the third dish must have more ingredients than the second dish, which must have more ingredients than the first, the third is either going to have three or four ingredients. Coupling this with the second rule breaks this game wide open; for the second rule to be true, he must use three ingredients in that third dish, and all four ingredients in the fifth. That also determines how many ingredients he uses in the first two dishes. Note that if we knew a bit more about exactly how many ingredients dish four had, we could have used contrasting shapes to represent the final rule.

4-MINUTE UNCERTAIN GROUPS DRILL

Imagine the same scenario as above, but with the different sets of rules written below. Each set of rules allows for significant numeric inferences—do your best to complete each board with accurate inferences, and see if you can do all four in four minutes or less! As always, if you would like to repeat the drill, make sure to do your work on a separate page.

1.
G is used in the first three dishes and no others.
The fourth dish uses more ingredients than the third.
The second dish has F or J, but not both.

F G H J
1 2 3 4 5

2.
The first and third dishes are the only ones with F.
The second and third dishes are the only ones with H.
The third and fourth dishes have the same number of ingredients.

F G H J
1 2 3 4 5

3.
The third dish uses more ingredients than the fifth.
The second dish uses more ingredients than the first.
The first and third dishes have the same number of ingredients, but none of the same ingredients.

F G H J
1 2 3 4 5

4.
He uses G on exactly three dishes.
F and J are always paired together.
Each dish has G or F, but not both.
The third dish uses more ingredients than the second.
He uses H on exactly one dish.

F G H J
1 2 3 4 5

4-MINUTE UNCERTAIN GROUPS DRILL SOLUTIONS

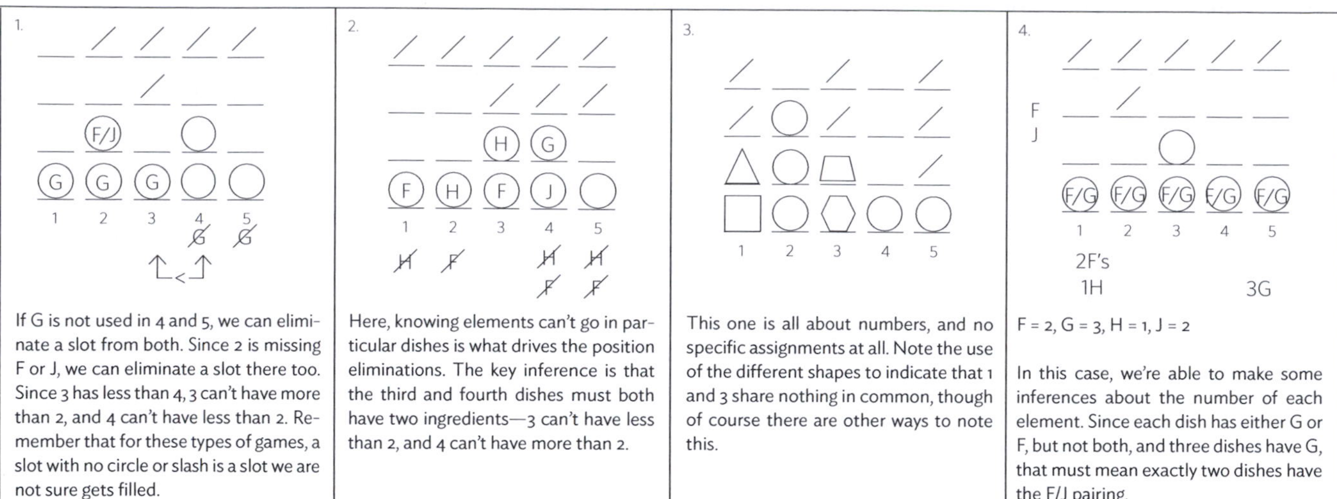

1.
F/J
G G G
1 2 3 4 5
G G
If G is not used in 4 and 5, we can eliminate a slot from both. Since 2 is missing F or J, we can eliminate a slot there too. Since 3 has less than 4, 3 can't have more than 2, and 4 can't have less than 2. Remember that for these types of games, a slot with no circle or slash is a slot we are not sure gets filled.
2.
H G
F H F J
1 2 3 4 5
H F H H
F F
Here, knowing elements can't go in particular dishes is what drives the position eliminations. The key inference is that the third and fourth dishes must both have two ingredients—3 can't have less than 2, and 4 can't have more than 2.
3.
1 2 3 4 5
This one is all about numbers, and no specific assignments at all. Note the use of the different shapes to indicate that 1 and 3 share nothing in common, though of course there are other ways to note this.
4.
F
J
F/G F/G F/G F/G F/G
1 2 3 4 5
2F's
1H
3G
F = 2, G = 3, H = 1, J = 2
In this case, we're able to make some inferences about the number of each element. Since each dish has either G or F, but not both, and three dishes have G, that must mean exactly two dishes have the F/J pairing.

Subset and Group Inferences

When a game has elements that are in subsets, and these elements are then split into two groups, we are commonly required to make deductions about the number of elements from each subset that go in each group.

The zoo game on page 169 is an example of this type of game, and most real LSAT scenarios that involve such deductions have been structured very similarly to this example. It is very common for the LSAT to use three subsets and two groups when it wants us to make these types of deductions. Notice that the rules and situation naturally lead us to think, "How many are selected from each subset?" When a game inspires this type of thinking, chances are that these numerical deductions will be important, especially when it comes to solving questions.

The drills on the next page will help you practice making these types of deductions. Keep in mind that though these deductions are most commonly required for games similar to the zoo game, they have in the past been required for other types of game situations. In short, this is an important skill for you to master.

Math Inferences Drill

Here is an exercise designed to fine-tune your ability to make the type of numerical inferences commonly required by the LSAT. If you feel uncomfortable with your ability to make these inferences, make it a point to revisit these exercises throughout the study process. Solutions are on the next page.

The situation: Five of eight students will be selected to take part in a math competition. The students are from classrooms A, B, and C. The rules of the game have given us some information about the number of students from each class, and that's been added into the chart already. Your job is to fill in the possibilities for the blank spaces. The first line has been filled in for you.

A	B	C	Total
1	*2 or 3*	1 or 2	5
0	<3		5
2		1	5
1	≤2		5
	3	0 or 1	5
	0 or 1	1 or 2	5
	≥2	≥2	5
< 2	1		5
2		0 or 1	5
> 2	< 3		5

Time: Accuracy: /10

A	B	C	Total
1		2 or 3	5
2		1 or 2	5
≤2		≤2	5
1	0 or 1		5
	1	≥2	5
	≥2	0 or 1	5
1		≥2	5
< 2	1		5
2		0 or 1	5
1 or 2		1 or 2	5

Time: Accuracy: /10

A	B	C	Total
≤2		2	5
	<3	0 or 1	5
1		0 or 1	5
2		<3	5
	1 or 2	1 or 2	5
0	≥3		5
	0 or 1	≥2	5
1		≤2	5
≤2		0 or 1	5
0 or 1		2	5

Time: Accuracy: /10

The situation: Joan will pack six accessories in her suitcase. She will pick from four belts, three hats, and three scarves, and **she must take at least one of each type of item.** The rules of the game allow us to fill in some of this information. Your job is to fill in the rest.

B (4)	H (3)	S (3)	Total
3			6
1			6
2 or 3		< 2	6
	3	1 or 2	6
2 or 3		< 3	6
1		> 2	6
	2 or 3	≥2	6
	2	1	6
≥3			6
2		≥2	6

Time: Accuracy: /10

B (4)	H (3)	S (3)	Total
2		1 or 2	6
≤2		2	6
	2 or 3		6
	≤2	1	6
≥3			6
≤2	≤2		6
1 or 2		2	6
	≥2	≥2	6
2		<3	6
1		2 or 3	6

Time: Accuracy: /10

B (4)	H(3)	S(3)	Total
1		> 1	6
1 or 2		≥2	6
	3		6
≤2		≤2	6
2		1 or 2	6
≥3		1	6
≤2		2	6
>2	1		6
1	<3		6
1			6

Time: Accuracy: /10

Math Inferences Drill Solutions

The situation: Five of eight students will be selected to take part in a math competition. The students are from classrooms A, B, and C. The rules of the game have given us some information about the number of students from each class, and your job is to practice filling in the rest. (Note that you could have chosen to write in the missing piece differently, and of course that's fine.)

A	B	C	Total
1	*2 or 3*	**1 or 2**	5
0	**<3**	*3,4, or 5*	5
2	*2*	**1**	5
1	**≤2**	*2,3,or 4*	5
1,2	**3**	**0 or 1**	5
2,3,4	**0 or 1**	**1 or 2**	5
0 or 1	**≥2**	**≥2**	5
< 2	**1**	*3 or 4*	5
2	*2 or 3*	**0 or 1**	5
> 2	**< 3**	*0, 1, or 2*	5

A	B	C	Total
1	*1 or 2*	**2 or 3**	5
2	*1 or 2*	**1 or 2**	5
≤2	*1,2,3,4,5*	**≤2**	5
1	**0 or 1**	*3 or 4*	5
0, 1, or 2	**1**	**≥2**	5
0, 1,2,3	**≥2**	**0 or 1**	5
1	*0, 1, or 2*	**≥2**	5
< 2	**1**	*3 or 4*	5
2	*2 or 3*	**0 or 1**	5
1 or 2	*1, 2, or 3*	**1 or 2**	5

A	B	C	Total
≤2	*1,2, or 3*	**2**	5
2,3,4,5	**<3**	**0 or 1**	5
1	*3 or 4*	**0 or 1**	5
2	*1, 2, or 3*	**< 3**	5
1,2, or 3	**1 or 2**	**1 or 2**	5
0	**≥3**	*0, 1, or 2*	5
0, 1, 2,3	**0 or 1**	**≥2**	5
1	*2, 3, 4*	**≤2**	5
≤2	*2,3,4,5*	**0 or 1**	5
0 or 1	*2 or 3*	**2**	5

The situation: Joan will pack six accessories in her suitcase. She will pick from four belts, three hats, and three scarves, and she must take at least one of each item. The rules of the game allow us to fill in some of this information. Your job is to fill in the rest.

B (4)	H (3)	S (3)	Total
3	*1 or 2*	*1 or 2*	6
1	*2 or 3*	*2 or 3*	6
2 or 3	*2 or 3*	**< 2**	6
1 or 2	**3**	**1 or 2**	6
2 or 3	*1, 2 or 3*	**< 3**	6
1	*2*	**> 2**	6
1 or 2	**2 or 3**	**≥2**	6
3	**2**	**1**	6
≥3	*1 or 2*	*1 or 2*	6
2	*1 or 2*	**≥2**	6

B (4)	H (3)	S (3)	Total
2	*2 or 3*	**1 or 2**	6
≤2	*2 or 3*	**2**	6
1, 2, or 3	**2 or 3**	*1,2, or 3*	6
3 or 4	**≤2**	**1**	6
≥3	*1 or 2*	*1 or 2*	6
≤2	**≤2**	*2 or 3*	6
1 or 2	*2 or 3*	**2**	6
1 or 2	**≥2**	**≥2**	6
2	*2 or 3*	**<3**	6
1	*2 or 3*	**2 or 3**	6

B (4)	H(3)	S(3)	Total
1	*2 or 3*	**> 1**	6
1 or 2	*1, 2, or 3*	**≥2**	6
1 or 2	**3**	*1 or 2*	6
≤2	*2 or 3*	**≤2**	6
2	*2 or 3*	**1 or 2**	6
≥3	*1 or 2*	**1**	6
≤2	*2 or 3*	**2**	6
>2	**1**	*1 or 2*	6
1	**<3**	*3*	6
1	*2 or 3*	*2 or 3*	6

Directions for drill on following page: The following pages contain scenarios and rules for diagramming practice. Don't worry about timing for now—do your best to set up your diagrams as accurately as possible and check against the solutions after each set of games. As always, you shouldn't feel that you need to diagram the rules in exactly the same way that I have; however, when there are differences, you do want to double check that your notations are accurate and effective.

Full Setup Drill 1

Here are two sets of three games each. Choose whether to check the solutions after each game, or after each set.

Fanny, Greg, Harry, and Jane all get chicken burritos. For their burritos, they each get at least one of four toppings—M, N, O, and P. Additionally, the following conditions apply:

Fanny gets fewer toppings than anyone else.
One person gets all four toppings.
Three of the friends get N as a topping.
Greg gets fewer toppings than Jane.
Jane gets O or P, but not both.

Sam has purchased five different models of computers—G, H, I, K, and L. He's never purchased more than one computer in a year. He bought his first computer in 2001 and his last in 2007. Additionally, the following conditions apply:

He bought K after he bought both G and H.
He did not purchase a computer in the year after he purchased G.
He bought a computer in 2002 or 2003, but not both.
He did not purchase L first or last.

A company will choose five employees for a management training program. They will be chosen out of a total of nine employees: F, G, and H from accounting; N, O, and P from marketing; and T, V, and W from sales. The following conditions apply:

Either F or G, but not both, will be chosen.
W will not be chosen.
They will choose fewer people from sales than from marketing.
T or V, but not both, will be chosen.

Full Setup Drill 1 Solutions

Fanny, Greg, Harry, and Jane all get chicken burritos. For their burritos, they each get at least one of four toppings—M, N, O, and P. Additionally, the following conditions apply:

Fanny gets fewer toppings than anyone else.
One person gets all four toppings.
Three of the friends get N as a topping.
Greg gets fewer toppings than Jane.
Jane gets O or P, but not both.

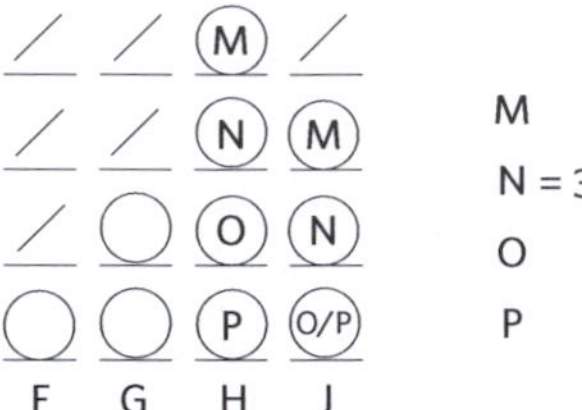

It really pays to handle the rules out of order here. If Jane gets less than four toppings because she will be missing O or P, G gets fewer toppings than Jane, and Fanny gets fewer toppings than anyone else. That must mean that Fanny gets one topping, Greg two, and Jane three. That also means Harry will get all four toppings.

Sam has purchased five different models of computers—G, H, I, K, and L. He's never purchased more than one computer in a year. He bought his first computer in 2001, and his last in 2007. Additionally, the following conditions apply:

He bought K after he bought both G and H.
He did not purchase a computer in the year after he purchased G.
He bought a computer in 2002 or 2003, but not both.
He did not purchase L first or last.

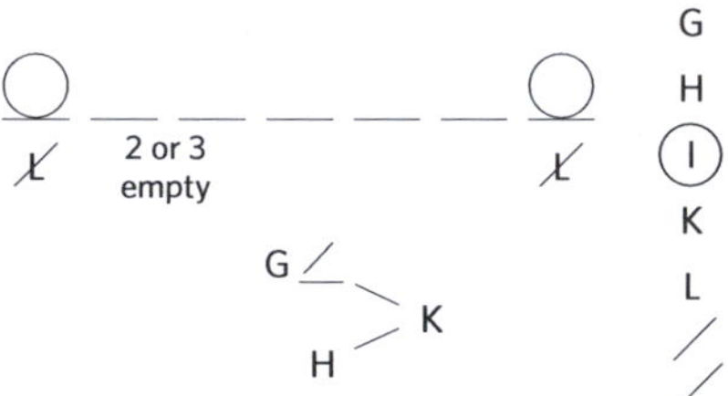

Notice we notated the first and second rules together; we want to combine rules whenever possible. There are other ways to represent the third rule, but don't be hesitant to just write in, rather than symbolize, what you mean, when that seems to be the cleanest option. The two slashes in the list of elements are completely optional, but a good reminder.

A company will choose five employees for a management training program. They will be chosen out of a total of nine employees: F, G, and H from accounting; N, O, and P from marketing; and T, V, and W from sales. The following conditions apply:

Either F or G, but not both, will be chosen.
W will not be chosen.
They will choose fewer people from sales than from marketing.
T or V, but not both, will be chosen.

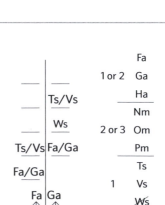

Ts/Vs
Ws
Ts/Vs Fa/Ga
Fa/Ga
Fa Ga
Ts Vs

1 or 2: Fa Ga Ha
2 or 3: Nm Om Pm
1: Ts Vs Ws

The positions on the left of the line are for those who are chosen, and the positions on the right are for those who are not. Note that we can use the third rule to make an inference about the number of elements that must come from marketing.

Full Setup Drill 2

A zoo will feature six of ten animals for its new brochure. Three of the animals—F, G,H—are elephants, three—J, K, L—are monkeys, and four—N, P, Q, and S—are rhinos. The selection of animals will be as follows:

The brochure must feature at least one of each type of animal.
At least two rhinos will be featured.
Either both F and G are featured, or neither of them are.
The brochure will not feature fewer elephants than monkeys.

Ten films—F, G, H, M, N, O, P, R, S, and T—will be shown in four different theaters—W, X, Y, and Z. Each theater will show at least one, but no more than three, of the films, and each film will only be shown in one theater. The following conditions apply:

X will show the same number of films as W.
Y will show the same number of films as Z.
More films are shown at X than at Y.
Both F and N are shown at Z.
O and S are shown in the same theater.

Three friends—Frank, Harry, and Ingrid—leave a total of eight messages on an answering machine. Each friend leaves at least one, but no more than four, messages. The following conditions apply:

The person who left the first message also left the last message.
The person who left the second message also left the seventh message.
Harry left the third message.
No one leaves two consecutive messages.
No one leaves more messages than Frank.

Full Setup Drill 2 Solutions

A zoo will feature six of ten animals for its new brochure. Three of the animals—F, G,H—are elephants, three—J, K, L—are monkeys, and four—N, P, Q, and S—are rhinos. The selection of animals will be as follows:

The brochure must feature at least one of each type of animal.
At least two rhinos will be featured.
Either both F and G are featured, or neither of them are.
The brochure will not feature fewer elephants than monkeys.

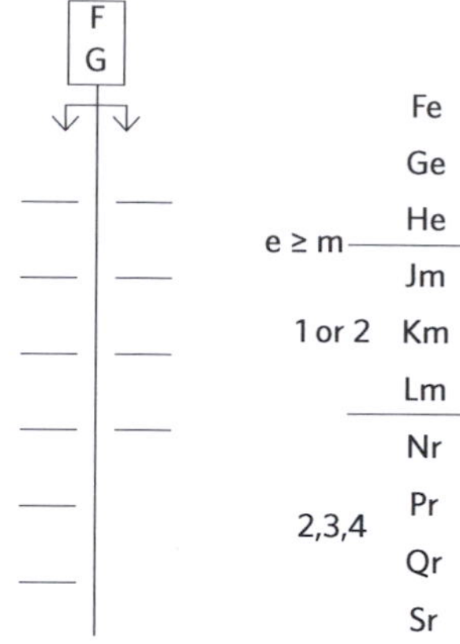

We know at least two rhinos are in—that leaves two to four spaces. If there can't be more monkeys than elephants, that leaves us with one or two monkeys.

Ten films—F, G, H, M, N, O, P, R, S, and T—will be shown in four different theaters—W, X, Y, and Z. Each theater will show at least one, but no more than three, of the films, and each film will only be shown in one theater. The following conditions apply:

X will show the same number of films as W.
Y will show the same number of films as Z.
More films are shown at X than at Y.
Both F and N are shown at Z.
O and S are shown in the same theater.

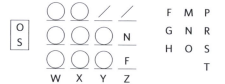

It's helpful to remember here that with ten films to place, and twelve total spots, there will only be two empty positions. The first, second, and third rules, when combined, require us to put three films in W and X, and two each in Y and Z.

Three friends—Frank, Harry, and Ingrid—leave a total of eight messages on an answering machine. Each friend leaves at least one, but no more than four, messages. The following conditions apply:

The person who left the first message also left the last message.
The person who left the second message also left the seventh message.
Harry left the third message.
No one leaves two consecutive messages.
No one leaves more messages than Frank.

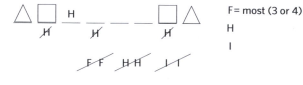

The triangle and square are great tools for reminding yourself that the same element has to go in 1 and 8, and the same one in 2 and 7. Note that we can make an inference that Frank must have left either the first and last, or second and seventh, message (there wouldn't be enough spots for F to appear most otherwise), but that's a fairly subtle inference, and not that useful, so no need to mark it (unless you want to, of course).

13 LOGIC GAMES conditional rules

Up to this point, we've been working with rules that are absolute and always true. If we are told that X is before Y, X will always be before Y, no matter what else happens in the game. If we are told that G is third, G will be third, no matter what. Like your mother's love, we can think of these rules as being *unconditional*.

Now it's time to focus on *conditional* rules. Here are some examples of conditional rules:

"If X is selected, Y will not be."
"If X is before Y, Y will be before Z."
"If X is selected, it will be before Y."

Conditional rules are rules that only apply sometimes

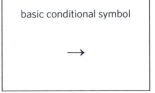

Conditional rules, and conditional reasoning in general, are very important to both Logic Games and Logical Reasoning, and we'll be discussing conditional issues quite a bit in the lessons to come. For now, you can start by thinking about conditional rules as rules that only apply sometimes. They are essentially rules that come into effect when a "trigger," the "if" statement, sets them off.

basic conditional symbol

→

In this lesson, we will work to develop a simple and correct understanding of exactly what conditional statements mean. We will also practice notating conditional statements, and finally, we will discuss how to link conditional rules with other conditional rules. To begin, let's take a look at how some basic unconditional rules and conditional rules impact a sample ordering game and a sample grouping game.

THE ANATOMY OF A CONDITIONAL STATEMENT

"If John is selected, Fanny will not be."

John getting selected is the "trigger" that sets this rule in action. In formal terms, we think of it as being "sufficient," or enough, to guarantee the result.

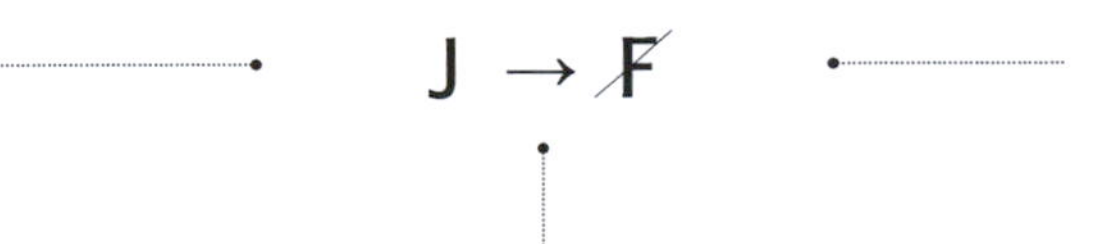

F not getting selected is the "result" of J getting selected. Note that we are using the term "result" a bit loosely. We are not implying causation but rather a resulting inference. If we know J is selected, a result will be that we know F is not selected.

This arrow is the universal symbol for a conditional rule, and it is absolutely iron-clad—if the left side happens, the right side will happen. The most important thing to remember about an arrow is that it points in one direction. Fanny not getting selected will not guarantee that John will be.

Imagine this basic ordering scenario and rules:

Six toys—F, G, H, J, K, and L—are placed into positions 1 through 6 in a display. The following rules apply:

H is put in 3, and J in 5.
If F is put in 2, K will be put in 4.

The first rule is simple to understand and implement, and we can add it to our diagram like this:

The second rule requires a bit more thought. We can't just put F in 2 and K in 4, because we don't know for sure that those things are true.

What this rule does tell us is that once we do know that F is in the second position, then we can place K in the fourth position. We won't write this into the diagram, but rather to the side. We use the arrow symbol to represent conditional understanding:

$$\frac{F}{2} \rightarrow \frac{K}{4}$$

We'll be using this arrow quite a bit, and you always want to think of it as meaning, "If..., then..."

Bonus

Okay, so we know that if F is in 2, K will be in 4. What else do we know from this statement?

What if F is not in 2? Do we know K will not be in 4? No.

What if K is in 4? Must F be in 2? No.

What if K is not in 4? Does that mean that F must not be in 2? Yes, it does! Because we know that if F were in 2, K would be in 4! We can write this inference down as well if we'd like:

$$\frac{\not{K}}{4} \rightarrow \frac{\not{F}}{2}$$

Imagine this basic grouping scenario and rules:

Six pets—F, G, H, J, K, and L—will be assigned to three different groomers—X, Y, and Z. The following rules apply:

H and J are assigned to Y.
If F is assigned to X, K will be assigned to Z.

The first rule is again simple to understand and implement, and we can add it to our diagram like this:

X	Y	Z
___	H	___
___	J	___

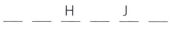

The second rule requires a bit more thought. We can't just put F in X and K in Z, because we don't know for sure that those things are true.

What this rule does tell us is that if we do know that F is assigned to X, then we will know for sure that K will be assigned to Z. We use the arrow symbol to represent conditional understanding:

$$\frac{F}{X} \rightarrow \frac{K}{Z}$$

Bonus

Just as before, let's think: What else do we know from this statement?

What if F is not assigned to X? Do we know K will not be assigned to Z? No.

What if K is assigned to Z? Must F be assigned to X? No.

What if K is not assigned to Z? Does that mean that F must not be assigned to X? Yes, it does! Because we know that if F were assigned to X, K would be assigned to Z. We can write this down as well if we'd like:

$$\frac{\not{K}}{Z} \rightarrow \frac{\not{F}}{X}$$

This additional information we gained for both problems is called the contrapositive, and we will be discussing it in greater detail on the next page.

Understanding Conditional Rules

Does it make sense why we choose to notate conditional rules using arrows? Does it make sense how we were able to make those additional inferences? It's very important that you understand exactly what conditional rules mean and what their implications are, so let's spend a bit of time making sure we start off with a solid foundation.

Here is a basic conditional statement:

"If it rains, John will not go to the park."

This statement is about two things—rain and going to the park. Both of these issues are absolutes; that is, it will either rain or it won't (there is no middle ground) and he'll go to the park or he won't—again, there is no middle ground.

Assuming that this statement is true, and we must assume that all conditional statements are meant to be absolutely true, let's think about exactly what we know based on the information given to us.

First, we know that if it rains, John will not go to the park. That is a *guarantee*, and it's very important you get used to seeing it as such. "If" is a powerful word on the LSAT, and if this statement were in a real LSAT argument or game, John cannot possibly go to the park if it rains.

Per this statement, can we say that if it doesn't rain, the opposite consequence must happen—that is, John must go to the park? No. We cannot say that. If it's 3:00 a.m. and not raining, John does not have to be at the park—and it's clear the statement is not telling us that he does.

***If* is a powerful word on the LSAT**

Note that what I did there was just to take the *opposite* of each part—I switched rain to no rain, and not going to the park to going to the park. Under the pressure of the exam, that sort of move can seem logical enough, but it's absolutely not valid, and it's the type of incorrect reasoning on which wrong answers are commonly built.

Can we say that if John did not go to the park, it was raining? No. The argument didn't say that rain was the only thing that would keep him away from the park.

Notice that in this case, we are *reversing* the elements in the original argument—again, this is not okay, and this type of reasoning also underlies a lot of wrong answers.

Finally, can we say that if John went to the park, it didn't rain?

Yes, we can actually say that. Because we know he wouldn't have gone if it had rained. Let's go ahead and put these issues into symbol form to think about what is going on in a more abstract way. The images are on the top of the next page.

Original	Possible Inferences		
"If it rains, John will not go to the park."	"If it does not rain, John will go to the park."	"If John does not go to the park, it must be raining."	"If John goes to the park, it must not be raining."
$R \rightarrow \not{P}$	$\not{R} \rightarrow P$	$\not{P} \rightarrow R$	$P \rightarrow \not{R}$
	WRONG	WRONG	RIGHT

Notice what happens in the invalid inferences—the elements are either simply negated or reversed. It's always wrong to think this leads to a valid inference.

For the one inference that was valid, notice what happened: the elements were both reversed *and* negated. Turns out, it's *always* going to be *right* to do this.

The **contrapositive** is an inference that can be derived from any and all conditional statements, and in fact should be thought of as a basic part of understanding any conditional statement.

In fact, this is an inference that can be deduced from every conditional statement. Every conditional statement yields this additional inference, and this additional conditional inference is known as the **contrapositive**.

"Contrapositive" is an unfortunately complicated-sounding word, but the concept itself is quite simple to reason through. Let's go back to our original conditional statement:

"If it rains, John will not go to the park."

We can think of the rain as the "trigger" and the not going to the park as a "result," something we know as a consequence of knowing that it rains.

We know that if the trigger happens, it's guaranteed that the result will happen. Therefore, it makes sense that if the result didn't happen, the trigger must not have happened.

This is what the contrapositive will always tell us: if the result isn't true, the trigger isn't true.

Again, remember what we *did* on a more abstract level—we switched what was on the left for what was on the right, and we switched positives and negatives. You can think of this as "reverse and negate," and this system will always work for helping you derive the contrapositive.

reverse & negate

Notice we just switched left and right and positive and negative.

Original	Contrapositive
"If it rains, John will not go to the park."	"Since John went to the park, it must not have rained."
$R \rightarrow \not{P}$	$P \rightarrow \not{R}$
The rain is the trigger that guarantees that we know John will not go to the park.	Since we know that the guaranteed result didn't happen, we know the trigger must not have happened.

Hidden Conditional Rules

There are many ways to write conditional statements, and some of these ways are clearer than others. Most conditional rules that appear in Logic Games are clearly conditional, and the test writers do not often try to challenge us with the way they word these rules (at least not to the degree that they challenge us with the wording of conditional statements in Logical Reasoning questions). However...

Once in a while, the test writers will sneak in a conditional rule that is less obviously a conditional rule, and if you are not careful these "hidden conditional" rules can get you in trouble. In general, these hidden conditionals will appear in games that have subsets or mismatch issues, for these hidden conditionals generally involve elements or characteristics that can appear more or less than once.

Let's imagine that we have a game about an event featuring eight solo artists who perform in an order. We don't know the artists' names; we just know that some of the artists are dancers, some are orators, and the remaining are singers.

And we get the following rule: *"Any time a dancer performs, a singer must immediately follow."* We could, without thinking twice about it, notate it as we have to the side.[1]

1. DS

However, this would be an inaccurate representation of the rule, and this notation would likely cause trouble down the line. Before we explain why, can you see for yourself why this notation is flawed?

Let's imagine that we find out a singer goes fifth. Does that mean a dancer must perform fourth? Absolutely not. To test, just imagine that an orator went fourth, then a singer fifth, and notice that that wouldn't violate our rule in any way.

This is a tricky clue—we know that when a dancer performs, a singer must immediately follow, but that does not mean that a dancer must perform before every singer. Our notation doesn't represent this subtlety well. It is better to notate this rule this way.[2]

2. D → DS

We always read the arrow the same way (that is, as the marker of a conditional rule), and we can read this statement to mean "If there is a dancer, then a singer must immediately follow."

As we mentioned before, these types of rules are fairly rare, and they will generally appear in games that either involve uncertain amounts of elements or members in subgroups. To see why this is the case, let's imagine a situation analogous to the one above, but this time in a game without subgroups and with only one-to-one relationships.

So, let's imagine we've just got eight performers—G, H, I, J, K, L, M, and N—and we get the following rule: *"G performs immediately after M."*

Would it be okay to notate this as "MG"? (After all, that's how we've been doing it up to this point!) Another way to think about it is if we place M, do we know G must immediately follow? If we place G, do we know M must immediately precede? The answer to both questions is yes.

If there is only one G and one M, and we know that G must follow M, then we know M must go before G. With a one-to-one element to position relationship, the situation is naturally more simple.

When in doubt, thinking about a rule as we just did, in "both directions," will generally help you see whether a rule is conditional or not.

To illustrate, let's imagine another situation:

> Thomas is baking pies for five friends—M, N, O, P, and R. Each pie will have at least one of six ingredients: F, G, H, J, K, and L. The following rules apply:
>
> Every pie with F will have H in it.

Let's imagine you see this on the exam, and you are wondering whether or not this is a rule you have to think of conditionally. Let's test it in "both directions."

If we know that the pie has F, do we know that it must have H? Yes, the rule tells us that.

If we know that the pie has H, must the pie have F? No. To test, imagine a pie with just H as an ingredient—notice it wouldn't violate our condition.

Therefore, we know that this is a conditional rule—a rule that applies in certain situations but not others. We want to make sure to notate it conditionally.[3]

3. F → H

What would the contrapositive of such a conditional rule be? In this case, we know that the trigger is having F, and the result is having H. Therefore, we know that if a pie does not have H (i.e., if the result didn't happen) it must not have F (i.e., the trigger did not take effect).[4]

4. ~~H~~ → ~~F~~

Compound Conditional Rules

Perhaps some of the most intimidating rules that appear in Logic Games are the ones that we'll think of as "compound conditionals." Compound conditional rules are conditional rules that discuss more than one element or characteristic in either the trigger or result. Here are some examples of compound conditionals:

"If Tom *and* Sarah are selected, Phil will not be selected."
"If the ice cream has mint, it will also have either nuts *or* caramel."

It's easy to overcomplicate our understanding of these rules, but in reality they are really **paper tigers**; it's likely that you intuitively understand them already. To verify this understanding, let's break down a few compound conditional rules. We can use the same pie-baking scenario from the previous page. Imagine four different compound conditional rules that could appear with that situation (these rules are not meant to go together in the same game):

paper tiger: something that seems scarier than it is

Thomas is baking pies for five friends: M, N, O, P, and R. Each pie will have at least one of six ingredients: F, G, H, J, K, and L. The following rules apply:

Possible rule 1: If a pie has F and G, it must also have J.
Possible rule 2: If a pie has G or H, it will not have K.
Possible rule 3: If a pie has L, it will also have F and G.
Possible rule 4: If a pie does not have H, it will have J or L.

The first rule states, "If a pie has F and G, it must also have J."[5]

In this case, we've got a compound trigger: in order for this rule to take effect, we need to know that two things are true—the pie must have F *and* the pie must have G. Notice that only knowing something about F, or only knowing something about G, does nothing for us—we need to know something about *both* F and G. If both of them are in the pie, then the pie will also have J.

5. F & G → J

Now let's think of the contrapositive, and we can do so in terms of "If the result didn't happen, the trigger must not have happened."

The result not happening is the pie not having J. If the pie does not have J, what must be true? It must not have both F and G—that is, it must be missing F, G, or both F and G.[6]

6. ~~J~~ → ~~F~~ or ~~G~~

To review, let's think about the original rule and the contrapositive one more time. The original rule told us that if the pie has F and G, it must have J. That must mean that if the pie does not have J, it must be missing F or G. The notations for both the original rule and the contrapositive are to the side—keep in mind that as a default, "or" on the LSAT includes the possibility of "both."

The second rule states, "If a pie has G or H, it will not have K."

We can notate this rule as we've done to the side. Now let's reason through the contrapositive. What do we know if the pie has K? It must be missing both G and H. Both the original rule and the contrapositive are notated to the side.[7]

7. G or H → ~~K~~
K → ~~G~~ & ~~H~~

Notice one thing that is different about this statement as opposed to the original one: in this case, we don't actually have to know something about both G and H to know about K—that is, if we just know that G is in the pie, we know for sure that the pie will not have K. We don't need to know anything about H to figure out the consequences for K. In the same way, we can also determine that K is out if we just know that H is in. For the first conditional rule, we had to know something about both elements in the trigger in order to know something about the consequence. For this one, we don't.

Since we know that G in leads to K out, and since we know that H in leads to K out, we can actually just write this compound conditional out as two separate conditional statements, as we've done to the side. Split up this way, it's obviously a bit easier for us to handle the rule, and it's easier to come up with the contrapositives.[8]

8. G → ~~K~~
H → ~~K~~
K → ~~G~~
K → ~~H~~

Okay, that seems simple enough, but maybe you are asking yourself, "How can I know which compound conditionals can be split up, and which ones can't?"

There are certain "mechanical" ways in which you can answer this question, and I've put the information on the side at the top of the next page.

ORIGINAL	If a pie has F and G, it must also have J. F & G → J	If a pie has G or H, it will not have K. G or H → ~~K~~	If a pie has L, it will also have F and G. L → F & G	If a pie does not have H, it will have J or L. ~~H~~ → J or L	ORIGINAL
CONTRAPOSITIVE	~~J~~ → ~~F~~ or ~~G~~ If a pie doesn't have J, it must be missing F or G.	K → ~~G~~ & ~~H~~ If a pie has K, it won't have G and it won't have H.	~~F~~ or ~~G~~ → ~~L~~ If a pie is missing F or G, it does not have L.	~~J~~ & ~~L~~ → H If a pie has neither J nor L, it must have H.	CONTRAPOSITIVE

Here's a "mechanical" explanation of what you can split and what you can't: you can split conditionals that have "or" in the trigger (i.e., either thing can set off the consequence) or "and" in the consequence (i.e., you have two independent results). You cannot split conditionals that have "and" in the trigger, because you need both of those things to happen for the result to happen. You can't split "or" in the result, because it's unclear which of those results happened. Tricky to "memorize," but not too tough to understand, and if you understand you don't need to memorize.

However, by far the easiest way to figure out whether or not compound conditional statements can be split up is to try to split them up. With the first compound conditional rule, it's easy to see that we can't split it up—we need to know something about F and G. With the second compound conditional, it's easy to see that just knowing that G is in, or just that H is in, is enough to know that K is out, that is, we don't need to know something about both G and H to know something about K. That means there is no problem splitting this rule into two simple ones.

Keep in mind that you don't need to split compound conditional statements. You can do just fine not doing so. However, the challenge of knowing which compound conditionals can be split is easy enough and the benefit of doing so is great enough that it warrants you thinking through, with each compound conditional you face, whether or not you can split it. I promise that with just a little practice the decision will become an easy one.

The third rule states, "If a pie has L, it will also have F and G."

In this case, the trigger is simple enough—it's the result that is compounded. We know that if a pie has L, it will have F, and it will also have G. To come up with the contrapositive, let's think, "When will this result not happen?" If the pie is missing either F or G, we know it must not have had L. I've written notations for both the original statement and the contrapositive to the side.[9]

9. L → F & G
~~F~~ or ~~G~~ → ~~L~~

Can we split up this conditional statement? If we know the pie has L, do we know something about just F, or just G? Yes, we do. If the pie has L, we know it must have F, and we don't need to know anything about G to know that this is true. In the same vein, if the pie has L, that means it must have G. This is another compound rule that we can think of as two simpler rules. Again, note that the key decision had to do with the compound component—whether or not we knew something about each component individually. Since we knew independent consequences for F and G, we were able to split up this conditional statement.[10]

10. L → F
L → G
~~F~~ → ~~L~~
~~G~~ → ~~L~~

The final rule states, "If a pie does not have H, it will have J or L."

Again, we've got a simple trigger and a compound result—in this case, if the pie is missing H, it must have either J or L (and remember, "or" includes the possibility of both).

If the pie is missing H, it will include J or L. When will this result not happen? If the pie is missing both J and L, what will this mean? That it has H. I've notated the original statement and the contrapositive to the side.[11]

11. $\not{H} \rightarrow J \text{ or } L$

$\not{J} \,\&\, \not{L} \rightarrow H$

Okay, little quiz: can this compound conditional be split up? If we know that the pie does not have H, do we know something about J, independently, without knowing anything about L?

No, we do not. We only know that at least one of those two, J or L, is in the pie. Since we do not know independent consequences for those elements, this is a compound conditional statement that cannot be split up.

Notice the physical structure of the contrapositives for each of these four statements. In each case we've reversed and negated, as we've always done. The additional step is that we've also switched "and" for "or" and vice versa. If you are comfortable with understanding why the contrapositives work this way, this is a useful "technical" way of thinking about the contrapositives for compound conditionals: you reverse and negate, and switch ands and ors. If your understanding of the original condition was correct, this technique will always yield correct contrapositives.

Again, however, I can't stress enough how dangerous a purely technical understanding is—only use such "systems" when you are completely comfortable with the underlying logic. The LSAT is too well designed to be gamed. To perform well, you absolutely need to understand what you are doing and why.

On the following page is a drill on translating and understanding conditional statements correctly. This is a drill that most people will benefit from trying more than once. Work on accuracy first, then speed.

Conditional Rules Drill

Below are four scenarios, each accompanied by the types of conditional rules that you will see on the exam. Your job is to first translate the statement into conditional form, then derive the contrapositive. As always, use your level of comfort to determine when you should check your work against the answers before moving on to the next set.

Scenario: Eight people—F, G, H, I, J, K, L, and M—are split into two teams: A and B.

If F is on A, M will be on B.	$\frac{F}{A} \rightarrow \frac{M}{B}$	$\frac{M}{A} \rightarrow \frac{F}{B}$
If F is not on A, J will be on A.		
If G is on B, L will be on B.		
H will be on A if J is not.		
If F and G are on A, H won't be.		
If J is on B, H and G will be on A.		
If H or I is on A, K will be on B.		
If L is on B, H or J will be too.		

Scenario: A singer will perform, in order, five of seven songs: L, M, N, O, P, Q, and R.

If L is performed, O will not be.		
If L is third, N will be fifth.		
If L is not third, R will not be fifth.		
O will be performed if L is not.		
If M or O is first, P will be second.		
If M is performed, it will be first.		
If both M and N are performed, Q will not be.		
If N is performed before M, P will be performed before Q.		

Scenario: Three cars will each get at least one of four services—S, T, V, and W—done.

Any car that gets S must get T.		
No car that gets S will get V.		
If a car doesn't get T, it will get S.		
A car won't get S if it gets T.		
Any car that gets S or T will not get V.		
Every car that gets both V and W will also get T.		
No car gets both S and V.		
If a car gets S, it will get V but not W.		

Scenario: Of the eight most common types of pet cats—M, N, O, P, Q, R, S, and T—Kayla owns one each of five types.

If she owns N, she owns P.		
If she doesn't own Q, she owns P.		
She owns M if she owns O.		
If she doesn't own P, she doesn't own Q.		
If she owns M or P, she does not own R.		
If she owns S, she also owns either Q or R.		
If she owns S and Q, she also owns T and P.		
She owns P and N if she owns R.		

Conditional Rules Drill Solutions

As always, you don't have to notate everything exactly the same way I have, but your understanding should be the same.

Scenario: Eight people—F, G, H, I, J, K, L, and M—are split into two teams: A and B.

Rule	Diagram	Contrapositive	Rule	Diagram	Contrapositive
If F is on A, M will be on B.	$\frac{F}{A} \rightarrow \frac{M}{B}$	$\frac{M}{A} \rightarrow \frac{F}{B}$	If F and G are on A, H won't be.	$\frac{F}{A} \& \frac{G}{A} \rightarrow \frac{H}{B}$	$\frac{H}{A} \rightarrow \frac{F}{B} \text{ or } \frac{G}{B}$
If F is not on A, J will be on A.	$\frac{F}{B} \rightarrow \frac{J}{A}$	$\frac{J}{B} \rightarrow \frac{F}{A}$	If J is on B, H and G will be on A.	$\frac{J}{B} \rightarrow \frac{H}{A} \& \frac{G}{A}$	$\frac{H}{B} \text{ or } \frac{G}{B} \rightarrow \frac{J}{A}$
If G is on B, L will be on B.	$\frac{G}{B} \rightarrow \frac{L}{B}$	$\frac{L}{A} \rightarrow \frac{G}{A}$	If H or I is on A, K will be on B.	$\frac{H}{A} \text{ or } \frac{I}{A} \rightarrow \frac{K}{B}$	$\frac{K}{A} \rightarrow \frac{H}{B} \& \frac{I}{B}$
H will be on A if J is not.	$\frac{J}{B} \rightarrow \frac{H}{A}$	$\frac{H}{B} \rightarrow \frac{J}{A}$	If L is on B, H or J will be too.	$\frac{L}{B} \rightarrow \frac{H}{B} \text{ or } \frac{J}{B}$	$\frac{H}{A} \& \frac{J}{A} \rightarrow \frac{L}{A}$

Scenario: A singer will perform, in order, five of seven songs: L, M, N, O, P, Q, and R.

Rule	Diagram	Contrapositive	Rule	Diagram	Contrapositive
If L is performed, O will not be.	$L \rightarrow \cancel{O}$	$O \rightarrow \cancel{L}$	If M or O is first, P will be second.	$\frac{M/O}{1} \rightarrow \frac{P}{2}$	$\frac{\cancel{P}}{2} \rightarrow \frac{\cancel{M/O}}{1}$
If L is third, N will be fifth.	$\frac{L}{3} \rightarrow \frac{N}{5}$	$\frac{\cancel{N}}{5} \rightarrow \frac{\cancel{L}}{3}$	If M is performed, it will be first.	$M \rightarrow \frac{M}{1}$	$\frac{\cancel{M}}{1} \rightarrow \cancel{M}$
If L is not third, R will not be fifth.	$\frac{\cancel{L}}{3} \rightarrow \frac{\cancel{R}}{5}$	$\frac{R}{5} \rightarrow \frac{L}{3}$	If both M and N are performed, Q will not be.	$M \& N \rightarrow \cancel{Q}$	$Q \rightarrow \cancel{M} \text{ or } \cancel{N}$
O will be performed if L is not.	$\cancel{L} \rightarrow O$	$\cancel{O} \rightarrow L$	If N is performed before M, P will be performed before Q.	$N - M \rightarrow P - Q$	$\cancel{P - Q} \rightarrow \cancel{N - M}$

Scenario: Three cars will each get at least one of four services—S, T, V, and W—done.

Rule	Diagram	Contrapositive	Rule	Diagram	Contrapositive
Any car that gets S must get T.	$S \rightarrow T$	$\cancel{T} \rightarrow \cancel{S}$	Any car that gets S or T will not get V.	$S \text{ or } T \rightarrow \cancel{V}$	$V \rightarrow \cancel{S} \& \cancel{T}$
No car that gets S will get V.	$S \rightarrow \cancel{V}$	$V \rightarrow \cancel{S}$	Every car that gets both V and W will also get T.	$V \& W \rightarrow T$	$\cancel{T} \rightarrow \cancel{V} \text{ or } \cancel{W}$
If a car doesn't get T, it will get S.	$\cancel{T} \rightarrow S$	$\cancel{S} \rightarrow T$	No car gets both S and V.	$S \rightarrow \cancel{V}$	$V \rightarrow \cancel{S}$
A car won't get S if it gets T.	$T \rightarrow \cancel{S}$	$S \rightarrow \cancel{T}$	If a car gets S, it will get V but not W.	$S \rightarrow V \& \cancel{W}$	$\cancel{V} \text{ or } W \rightarrow \cancel{S}$

Scenario: Of the eight most common types of pet cats—M, N, O, P, Q, R, S, and T—Kayla owns one each of five types.

Rule	Diagram	Contrapositive	Rule	Diagram	Contrapositive
If she owns N, she owns P.	$N \rightarrow P$	$\cancel{P} \rightarrow \cancel{N}$	If she owns M or P, she does not own R.	$M \text{ or } P \rightarrow \cancel{R}$	$R \rightarrow \cancel{M} \& \cancel{P}$
If she doesn't own Q, she owns P.	$\cancel{Q} \rightarrow P$	$\cancel{P} \rightarrow Q$	If she owns S, she also owns either Q or R.	$S \rightarrow Q \text{ or } R$	$\cancel{Q} \& \cancel{R} \rightarrow \cancel{S}$
She owns M if she owns O.	$O \rightarrow M$	$\cancel{M} \rightarrow \cancel{O}$	If she owns S and Q, she also owns T and P.	$S \& Q \rightarrow T \& P$	$\cancel{T} \text{ or } \cancel{P} \rightarrow \cancel{S} \text{ or } \cancel{Q}$
If she doesn't own P, she doesn't own Q.	$\cancel{P} \rightarrow \cancel{Q}$	$Q \rightarrow P$	She owns P and N if she owns R.	$R \rightarrow P \& N$	$\cancel{P} \text{ or } \cancel{N} \rightarrow \cancel{R}$

Conditional Rules That Link Up

Most of the time when we see conditional rules, there will be one or two of them mixed in with other types of rules, and these conditional rules will play one part, commonly a secondary part, in our thinking process.

Imagine that we see an ordering game similar to the second one in the drill you just did—a singer sings five of seven songs—and you get a rule similar to the second one in that set: "If L is third, N will be fifth."

You should go ahead and notate that condition somewhere near your row of positions, somewhere you are not likely to miss it. If you feel comfortable keeping the contrapositive in your head, you can do so, and if not you can write that down as well.

It is highly unlikely that this conditional rule will play a foundational role in the design of the game, and it's likely you'll only need to think about it in a couple of circumstances—in those moments when you know for sure that L is third, or that N is not fifth.

There are certain games, however, for which conditional constraints play a greater role—they will become the key to playing that particular game. You'll know this to be the case when every rule, or nearly every rule, is conditional. Almost always, this occurs in games that involve elements being split into two groups—games like the first and fourth in the last drill.

When you have a game that is structured around conditional rules, it's likely that these conditional statements will link together, and your ability to see these links will be critical for answering questions.

The concept is simple to understand. Imagine we know that if it rains, John won't go to the park, and we also know that if John doesn't go to the park, he will go to the movies. Now, let's say that it rains—what do we know? We know that John won't go to the park, and so he will go to the movies. Notice how this might look in conditional notation.

$$R \rightarrow \not{P} + \not{P} \rightarrow M = R \rightarrow M$$

They link!

We are able to link the rules because the "result" of one rule matched the trigger for the other. That's the only way to have a link, and that's the only thing we're looking for: the result of one rule matching the trigger for another.

Answers for questions on next page

A: In: JFI, Out: KH
B: In: MFI, Out: H

Now let's imagine a different pair of rules: if it rains, John won't go to the park, and if John goes to the park, he won't go to the movies. Notice how we would notate these two statements. Does a result link up with a trigger? No, it doesn't. We cannot link these two conditional statements to infer anything.

$$R \rightarrow \not{P} + P \rightarrow \not{M} = \text{nothin'!}$$

They don't link!

Now it rains. We know John doesn't go to the park. Does that mean he'll go to the movies? No, absolutely not, and as we've discussed, "assuming" this type of link when it doesn't exist is a common error, one that will surely lead to an incorrect response.

Below is an example of a game that involves linking conditional statements. Notice that once we've written out the rules, we know very little "absolute" information about either group, and that's fine—the game is designed to be that way. Often, questions for these types of games will start the ball rolling by telling us that a certain element is in a certain group, as our different prompts have done.

Starting on the following page are four games that involve linking conditionals. Each game comes with two questions that are representative of the type that you would see when you encounter games heavily dependent on conditional logic on test day.

Imagine the following scenario and rules:

Of seven athletes—F, G, H, I, J, K, and M—some will be selected to attend the Olympics. The following rules apply:

If J or M is selected, F will be selected.
If J is not selected, K will be.
If H is selected, F will not be.
Either H or I, but not both, will be selected.

We can diagram the rules like this:

J or M → F   ~~F~~ → ~~J~~ and ~~M~~

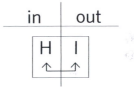

~~J~~ → K   ~~K~~ → J

H → ~~F~~   F → ~~H~~

in	out
H ↑	I ↑

Notice that it feels like we know very little—not even one athlete on the team! That's okay, and that's simply per the design of the game. We've done everything correctly. What we should expect in a game like this is that we'll need to bring rules together to answer questions. Let's take a look at what we can figure out with a little prompting in the question stem.

If J is selected, what must be true?

in	out
J F I	H

If J is selected, F must be selected. If F is selected, H won't be. If H is not selected, I must be.

If H is selected, what must be true?

in	out
H K	F I J M

If H is selected, I will not be. Also, F will not be selected. If F is not, then J and M are not. If J is not selected, K is selected.

Hopefully the inference links make sense, and hopefully you even find the process to be a bit of fun! Try it yourself with the next couple of prompts—answers are written at the bottom of the previous page.

A. If K is not selected, what must be true?

in	out

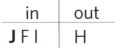

B. If M is selected, what must be true?

in	out

Set 1

Here's a chance to put your work into practice. Here are four games heavily dependent on conditional rules and links. At this point, accuracy is far more important than speed, but do time yourself. Ideally you are able to diagram in three minutes or less, and the questions should take about a minute per.

Joan is donating seven items—J, K, L, M, N, O, and P. The items will go either to charity X, or charity Y, and not both. The following rules apply:

If L is given to charity Y, J will be given to charity X.
If O is given to charity Y, P will be given to charity X.
If M is given to charity X, both N and O will be given to Y.
If L is given to charity X, both K and M will be given to X.

1. If P is given to charity Y, which of the following could be true?
(A) M is given to charity X.
(B) L is given to charity X.
(C) O is given to charity Y.
(D) J is given to charity Y.
(E) K is given to charity X.

2. Which of the following determines where all items are donated?
(A) P is given to charity Y.
(B) L is given to charity Y.
(C) J is given to charity Y.
(D) N is given to charity X.
(E) L is given to charity X.

A certain network has made six pilot shows—Q, R, S, T, V, and W. It will determine which ones to air based on the following:

If it does not air W, it will air Q or V.
It will air T or W, but not both.
If it does not air S, it will not air V.
If it airs R or S, it will not air T.

1. If W is not aired, how many pilots are aired?
(A) 1
(B) 2
(C) 3
(D) 4
(E) It cannot be determined

2. If S is aired, what must be true?
(A) V is aired.
(B) R is aired.
(C) W is aired.
(D) T is aired.
(E) Q is not aired.

Set 2

A young girl will pack some of her seven dolls—F, G, H, I, K, L, and M—to take on a trip. The following rules apply:

She will take K or G, but not both.
She will take H or L, but not both.
If she takes M, she will take F.
If she doesn't take I, she won't take L.
If she takes K, she will not take F.

1. Which of the following could be a complete list of dolls she takes?
(A) F, G, H, I, M
(B) F, G, H, L, M
(C) F, G, H, K, M
(D) G, H, I, M
(E) K, L

2. Which of the following would completely determine which dolls she takes?
(A) She takes F and H.
(B) She takes F, but leaves H.
(C) She takes M, but leaves H.
(D) She takes K and H.
(E) She takes M and H.

Five people are selected from a group of specialists for a medical mission. The specialists consist of three doctors—J, L, M—two medical assistants—N, O—and three physical therapists—R, S, and T. The following conditions apply:

If T is not selected, both O and R will be.
If L is not selected, R will not be selected.
If T is selected, J will not be selected.
Exactly one medical assistant will be selected.

1. If N is selected, what must be true?
(A) L is not selected.
(B) M is selected.
(C) R is selected.
(D) J is not selected.
(E) S is not selected.

2. If all three physical therapists go, who else must go?
(A) J
(B) L
(C) M
(D) N
(E) O

Set 1 Solutions

Joan is donating seven items—J, K, L, M, N, O, and P. The items will either go to charity X, or charity Y, and not both. The following rules apply:

If L is given to charity Y, J will be given to charity X.
If O is given to charity Y, P will be given to charity X.
If M is given to charity X, both N and O will be given to Y.
If L is given to charity X, both K and M will be given to X.

J
K
L
M
N
O
P

Ly → Jx Jy → Lx
Oy → Px Py → Ox
Mx → Ny & Oy Nx or Ox → My
Lx → Kx & Mx Ky or My → Ly

Note that the challenge of diagramming this type of game is different from that of diagramming some of the other types of games we've seen thus far. There is less to do, but each part requires the utmost care—mess up one conditional and you're going to be in trouble. You don't need to spend time looking for additional inferences—once you have translated the conditions and come up with contrapositives you are good to go. For these games, the job of thinking about how rules come together is best saved for the questions.

1. If P is given to charity Y, which of the following could be true?
(A) M is given to charity X.
(B) L is given to charity X.
(C) O is given to charity Y.
(D) J is given to charity Y.
(E) K is given to charity X.

x	y
O J	P M
	L

2. Which of the following determines where all items are donated?
(A) P is given to charity Y.
(B) L is given to charity Y.
(C) J is given to charity Y.
(D) N is given to charity X.
(E) L is given to charity X.

c.

x	y
L K	J N
M P	O

d.

x	y
J N	M L

e.

x	y
K L	N O
P M	

1. Here's where the fun begins: if P is in Y, we can see that O must be in X. That leads to M in Y, which leads to L in Y. We don't know where K and N go.
2. Expect this type of question to generally take a bit more time, because per its design it requires us to spend time evaluating each answer. There are some things you can do to speed up the process. We can use our work from #1 to see that (A) is not a possibility, and we can play out (B) quickly in our minds, without writing things out, and see that it won't lead to nearly enough inferences. (C) works (Jy → Lx → Kx & Mx → Ny & Oy → Px), and if pressed for time, you would just pick it and move on. If you have time, you want to verify that (D) and (E) don't work. (E) is especially tricky, and you must make sure not to over-infer about J.

A certain network has made six pilot shows—Q, R, S, T, V, and W. They will determine which ones to air based on the following:

If it does not air W, it will air Q or V.
It will air T or W, but not both.
If it does not air S, it will not air V.
If it airs R or S it will not air T.

Q
R
S
T
V
W

~W → Q or V ~Q & ~V → W
~S → ~V V → S
R or S → ~T T → ~R & ~S

T	W
↑	↑

1. If W is not aired, how many pilots are aired?
(A) 1
(B) 2
(C) 3
(D) 4
(E) It cannot be determined

T Q	W R
	S V

2. If S is aired, what must be true?
(A) V is aired.
(B) R is aired.
(C) W is aired.
(D) T is aired.
(E) Q is not aired.

W S	T

1. If W is out, Q or V is in. We don't know if it's one, the other, or both, and this can really screw up our counting! Let's put a pin in that for now. If W is out, we also know T is in. If T is in, R and S are out, and if S is out, V is out. That answers our original issue for us: since V must be out, Q must be in. Two of the six shows must be aired, and four will not be.
2. If S is aired, T will not be, and if T is not, W will be. We do not know much else about the other shows, so (A), (B), and (E) are all things that could be true or false. The danger in this problem is in over-inferring about the remaining elements.

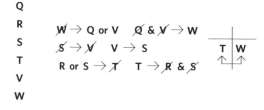

It is very common for test writers to combine conditional rules and *or* rules—makes for fun inferences! The T/W rule can actually be considered a biconditional (a conditional statement that works both ways); we'll discuss biconditionals and their close relationship to *or* statements in the next lesson.

Set 2 Solutions

A young girl will pack some of her seven dolls—F, G, H, I, K, L, and M—to take on a trip. The following rules apply:

She will take K or G, but not both.
She will take H or L, but not both.
If she takes M, she will take F.
If she doesn't take I, she won't take L.
If she takes K, she will not take F.

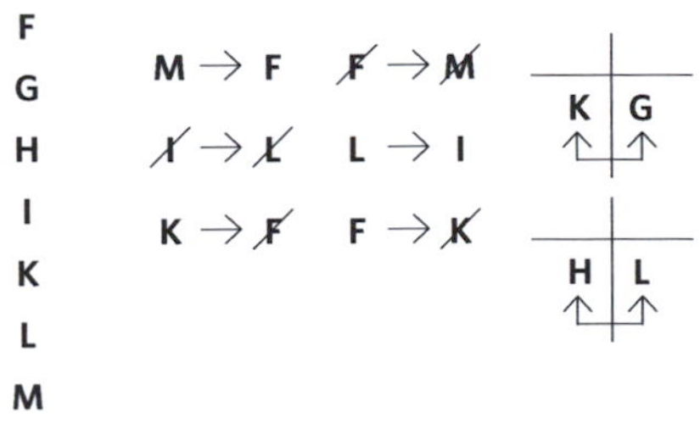

F
G
H
I
K
L
M

M → F ~~F~~ → ~~M~~
~~I~~ → ~~L~~ L → I
K → ~~F~~ F → ~~K~~

K | G
H | L

Here we've got two *or* statements—think for a minute about what they tell us about the number of toys she takes. Without considering any other rules, we know she will take no more than five, and leave no less than two. This setup is fairly straightforward, but the questions are tough.

1. Which of the following could be a complete list of dolls she takes?
(A) F, G, H, I, M
(B) F, G, H, L, M
(C) F, G, H, K, M
(D) G, H, I, M
(E) K, L

2. Which of the following would completely determine which dolls she takes?
(A) She takes F and H.
(B) She takes F, but leaves H.
(C) She takes M, but leaves H.
(D) She takes K and H.
(E) She takes M and H.

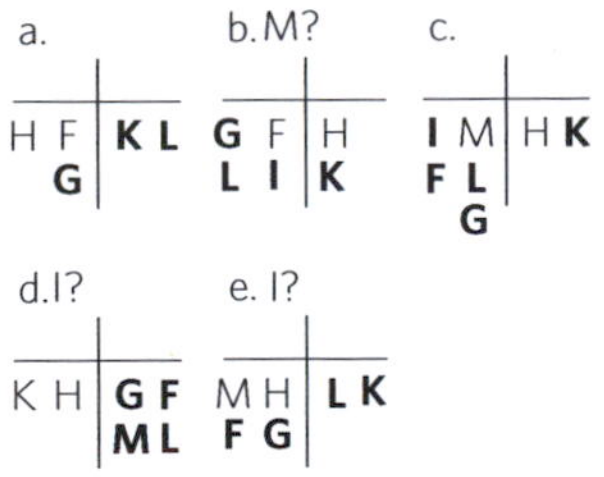

a. H F G | K L
b. M? G F L I | H K
c. I M F L G | H K
d. I? K H | G F M L
e. I? M H F G | L K

1. When a question asks for one possible list or order, there will be problems in the wrong answer choices—problems that are exposed when you compare them against the original rules. If we think about all the elements that are "in" in (A), no element forces any of the others out. (B) <u>M</u>ust <u>B</u>e <u>F</u>alse because H and L can't both be in. (C) MBF b/c G and K can't both be in. (D) MBF because if M is in, F must be in. (E) MBF b/c if L is in, I will be too.
2. Another time-consuming question because all of the answer choices require quite a bit of work. However, note that though this problem is very tough, the challenge is one of executing correctly—you have all the tools to evaluate each answer, but you have to get through all the steps quickly and accurately.

Five people are selected from a group of specialists for a medical mission. The specialists consist of three doctors—J, L, and M—two medical assistants—N, O—and three physical therapists—R, S, and T. The following conditions apply:

If T is not selected, both O and R will be.
If L is not selected, R will not be selected.
If T is selected, J will not be selected.
Exactly one medical assistant will be selected.

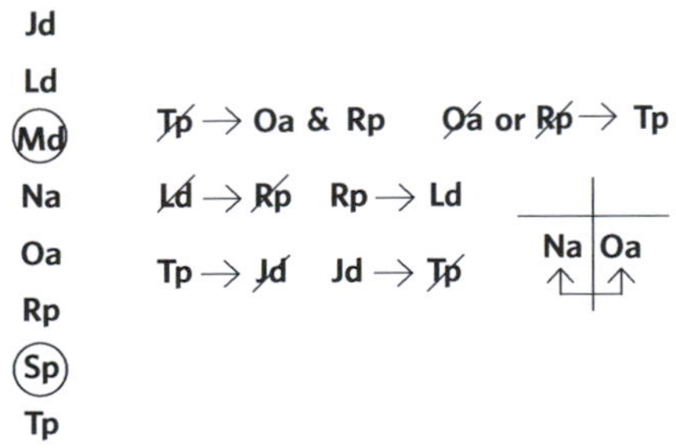

Jd
Ld
(Md)
Na
Oa
Rp
(Sp)
Tp

~~Tp~~ → Oa & Rp ~~Oa~~ or ~~Rp~~ → Tp
~~Ld~~ → ~~Rp~~ Rp → Ld
Tp → ~~Jd~~ Jd → ~~Tp~~

Na | Oa

Here we've got a game that involves subsets and lots of conditional rules. When a game has both of those characteristics, chances are the game will hinge on conditional links, numeric inferences, or a combination of both. If we had a full set of questions, likely they would require us to do more work with the fact that five are in. Notice how we dealt with the last rule—we don't have to deal with that rule this way, but the way we've notated it works well with the other rules.

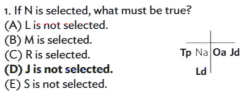

1. If N is selected, what must be true?
(A) L is not selected.
(B) M is selected.
(C) R is selected.
(D) J is not selected.
(E) S is not selected.

Tp Na Ld | Oa Jd

2. If all three physical therapists go, who else must go?
(A) J
(B) L
(C) M
(D) N
(E) O

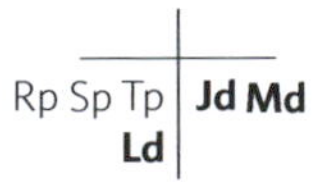

Rp Sp Tp Ld | Jd Md

1. If N is selected, O is not, then T is, and J is not. (We can also infer that L is selected, because otherwise too many elements would fall into the "not selected" category.)
2. If R, S, and T go, L must go and J must not. The M inference is an advanced one. Since we already have four selected, and either N or O must also be selected, there is not enough space for M.

Lesson Review

This was quite a full lesson! Let's highlight the key points we discussed:

• Conditional rules are rules that only apply sometimes.
• You cannot assume the reverse or negation of a conditional statement to be true.
• All conditional statements yield inferences known as contrapositives.
• You can always derive the contrapositive by reversing and negating.
• In games with mismatches or subsets, conditional statements can be hard to spot.
• Compound conditional statements include "and" or "or" in the trigger or the result.
• Conditional statements link together when the result of one condition triggers another condition.

Keep in mind that we'll be expanding on these topics and getting plenty more practice in the lessons to come. Specifically, there are two conditional issues we have yet to discuss:

• Biconditionals: these sound more complicated than they actually are, and we'll be discussing biconditionals in the next lesson.

• Challenging wording: as mentioned before, conditionals that are worded in a challenging fashion are far more common in Logical Reasoning than in Logic Games, so we will revisit the topic in the next batch of Logical Reasoning lessons.

At this point, some of you may already feel completely comfortable with these conditional rules, and of course that's terrific. If you don't yet feel mastery, know that this is normal. This is a lesson that you will likely benefit from revisiting as you continue your studies. As always, a great way to assess where you are, and where you need to be, is in terms of your skill set. When it comes to conditional rules, keep in mind that these are the skills that are required of you:

• You need to be able to recognize and correctly understand.
• You need to be comfortable translating that understanding into notation.
• You need to make valid inferences and recognize invalid inferences.
• You need to be able to see how conditional rules link together.
• You need to be able to apply your understanding to various types of tasks.

As you think about your comfort level with conditional rules, keep it simple and use the above skill set as a gauge. It's expected that you don't feel complete mastery just yet, but you should feel confident that you can master these skills before test day.

14 LOGIC GAMES "or" rules

In the last lesson, we discussed the fact that conditional rules can play either a primary or a secondary role in the design of a game. *Or* rules work in much the same fashion—they can either be just one part of a game, or they can be the key to understanding a game and handling it correctly. In this lesson, we'll start by briefly discussing common and basic *or* rules, then focus the bulk of our energy on more complicated *or* rules, which, as we'll soon discuss, can be some of the most useful rules that we can possibly encounter in a game.[1]

1. In the last lesson, we discussed the fact that conditional constraints are likely to be central to a game's design when there are many of them, and secondary when there are just one or two.

When it comes to *or* rules, there is a different way to tell whether they are central to a game's design: *or* rules are going to be important when they are complicated—when they involve three or more elements. We'll discuss this further as we move forward in the lesson.

Simple *Or* Rules

Most *or* rules are fairly simple to understand, and in fact we've handled a few in our games already, even though we haven't explicitly discussed them. Below are examples of three of the most common types of *or* rules that will appear on the LSAT.

Before we move further, it's important to remember exactly how we should think about the word *or*. Remember that on the LSAT, *or* does not exclude the possibility of *both*; that is, if a statement simply says, "either F *or* G is selected," both F *and* G being selected is a perfectly valid outcome.[2]

2. If you need a refresher on this, you can find the original discussion of *or* on page 162.

At the same time, it's useful to know that most game situations involving the word *or* will in some way naturally exclude the possibility of *both* being a possibility. The first two situations below are examples of this—since two elements can't occupy a position, and since an element can't go in two different positions, *or* does not include *and*. The last situation does not naturally exclude the possibility of *both*, and so the phrase "but not both" was added to the rule.

Jenna has six classes—M, N, O, P, Q, and R—one at a time and in order...

"She has either M or P third."

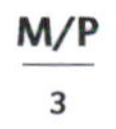

M/P
___
3

"O is either first or fifth."

O/ ... /O
___ ___ ___ ___ ___ ___
1 2 3 4 5 6

M, N, O, P, Q, and R are split into pairs for three games—1, 2, and 3...

"M or P, but not both, play in game 3."

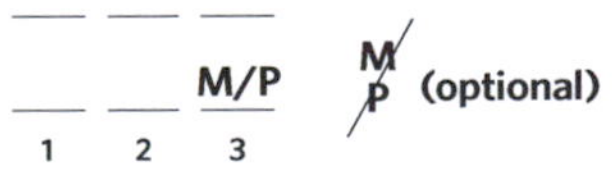

___ ___ ___
___ ___ M/P
1 2 3

M/P crossed out (optional)

simple or rules

Keep in mind that there will be other situations in which *or* will not exclude the possibility of *both*, and because these other situations are less common, they can be easy to mistake. Imagine if the first situation had allowed for a tie, or the second one had allowed elements to go more than once, or if the third did not have the statement "but not both": *both* would definitely be a possibility in all three scenarios, and questions would undoubtedly hinge on a correct understanding of that rule. Any time you might get confused or forgetful—and commonly that will be when both *is* a possibility—it's a good idea to mark your diagram in some clear way (such as simply writing "*both okay*" next to the notation).

What does "only if" mean?

Just two simple words: *only* and *if*. And yet this little phrase causes test takers to lose thousands of points on the exam each and every year. Why? Because it's so easy to mistake the phrase for its more popular, thinner cousin, "if."

The confusion is easy to understand. We use the two phrases interchangeably in real life. If someone says, "I'll kiss you if you brush your teeth," or if the person says, "I'll kiss you only if you brush your teeth," we think of the two statements as essentially meaning the same thing—if we brush our teeth we will get a kiss. The big danger is that on the LSAT, the two phrases mean very different things—in fact, they literally mean opposite things.

Imagine the following situation: you love a certain brand of coffee and you've just found out that your supermarket puts it on sale for half price every Sunday. So, you decide that you will buy coffee "only if" it's Sunday.

Let's think about this situation in terms of conditional logic (i.e., →). Remember that we can think of the left side of a condition as "guaranteeing" the right.

We've got two factors—buying coffee (C) and it being Sunday (S). Per the phrase "I will buy coffee only if it is Sunday," do we know for sure that:

1) If we buy, it must be Sunday? C → S ? Yes.
2) If it's Sunday, we have to buy coffee? S → C? Not at all.

The phrase "I will buy coffee only if it is Sunday" tells us that if we bought coffee, it must be Sunday: C→ S.

Now let's imagine that we work in a cafeteria kitchen and that we make three types of soup: one with beans and tomatoes, one with chicken and tomatoes, and one with chicken, onions, and tomatoes.

Is it true that a soup will have chicken only if it has tomatoes? Yes, it is. We can see that there are two soups with chicken, and they both have tomatoes.

Is it true that a soup will have chicken if it has tomatoes? No. There's a soup that has tomato but no chicken.

The phrase "The soup will have chicken (C) only if it has tomatoes (T)" tells us that if we have chicken, we must have tomatoes: C → T.

It does not tell us that if we have tomatoes, we must have chicken. We cannot infer that T → C.

Not too tough, right? Here's the danger with this. Take a look below at how these two statements compare to their *if* cousins.

We'll return to this topic again later, but for now remember that the statement "A only if B" translates to "A → B." If we know A is true, B must have been as well. This is the reverse of what "A if B" would yield. If you are unsure of your understanding, try playing out the scenario "in both directions" as we've done with our examples, and also remember that "only if" statements will always flow in the reverse direction of "if" statements.

*"I will buy coffee **only if** it's Sunday."* C → S	*"I will buy coffee **if** it's Sunday."* S → C
*"The soup will have chicken **only if** it has tomatoes."* C → T	*"The soup will have chicken **if** it has tomatoes."* T → C

Biconditionals

Biconditionals are conditional statements that work in both directions. Biconditionals can either be thought of as challenging conditional statements or as simple *or* statements. In just a bit, we'll discuss further exactly why this is so. However, before we get there, we need to agree on a definition for the phrase *only if*. So please read the note on *only if* before moving further.

The basic construction of a biconditional statement is designed around the phrase "if and only if." This phrase is actually a combination of two conditional statements: "if" and "only if."

> "Ted will be assigned to a group if and only if Steve is."

Let's break this statement apart:

> "Ted will be assigned if Steve is" gives us S → T.
>
> "Ted will be assigned only if Steve is" gives us T → S.

So, per this statement, we know that if Ted is selected, Steve will be, and if Steve is selected, Ted will be.

Remember that most conditional statements flow in one direction—that is, you will be able to say that A leads to B, but not B leads to A. That is why the biconditional, a conditional statement that flows in "both directions," is a bit of a wrinkle.

A traditional way of notating the biconditional is with a double arrow (S ↔ T), and you'll find that there are instances when we need to use that. However, there is an easier way to think about this rule—it tells us that Ted and Steve will be grouped together. We can simply notate it like we have to the side.[3]

3. S
T

Biconditionals can be tricky when thought of as unusual conditional statements, but they are much simpler when thought of as hidden *or* statements. All biconditionals in the games section can be thought of as *or* situations.

"Fred will be selected if and only if Janice is not" means exactly the same thing as "Fred or Janice, but not both, will be selected," and can be notated as we have to the side.[4]

4. F | J

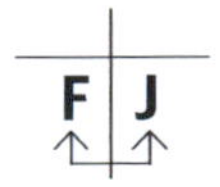

"Sarah will be on Team A if and only if Ryan is" means exactly the same thing as "Either both Sarah and Ryan are on Team A, or they are both not," and can be thus notated.[5]

5. Sa
Ra or Sa̸
R̸a

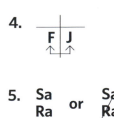

Complex *Or* Rules

We will call *or* rules that involve three or more elements "complex" *or* rules. These rules are some of the most important and useful rules that we will see in the games section.

It's easy to see why. These rules will typically involve half, or nearly half, of all of the elements in a game, and these rules will severely limit where those elements can go. Contrast that with a simple and singular conditional rule, which will typically impact just one or two elements, and will only do so on certain occasions. Few other rules are as likely to have a significant impact on a game as complex *or* rules do.

Here are a few examples of *complex or* rules:

J will arrive before either M or N, but not both.
J will arrive after M or before N, but not both.
J will be on the same team as M or N, but not both.

Note that the first two examples are ordering rules, and the last a grouping rule; *complex or* rules are more likely to appear in ordering games.

Let's take a minute to think about what these rules mean exactly.

"J will arrive before either M or N, but not both."

We'll work under the assumption that this rule comes in a game where no ties are allowed. What possibilities does this rule allow for?

If J arrives before M, we know it can't arrive before N. Therefore, if J arrives before M, the order of arrivals must go N - J - M.[6]

6. N — J — M

If J arrives before N, we know it can't arrive before M. Therefore, if J arrives before N, the order of arrivals must go M - J - N.[7]

7. M — J — N

Are those the only two possibilities? Let's say we find out J arrives after M. What does that tell us? It must arrive before N. Let's say we find out J arrives after N. What does that tell us? It must arrive before M.

Now we know for sure that there are two different ways this rule can play out, and these are the only two ways in which the rule can play out. Either the elements go M-J-N or N-J-M, and we don't have to think about it more beyond that.

If you'd like, go ahead and think about how we might proceed with the other two sample statements before reading further.

"J will arrive after M or before N, but not both."

Again, we are working under the assumption that the game allows for no ties. In what ways can this rule play out?

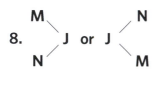

8. M, N — J or J — N, M

If J is after M, it cannot be before N—therefore, it must also be after N. If J is before N, it cannot be after M—therefore, it must also be before M. Here are our two possibilities.[8]

Almost certainly, this would be the most useful rule for the particular game. Just imagine if it happens to be a game with six positions, and you find out at some point that J must be in position 3 or position 4—it's fairly easy to see how significant an impact this *or* rule would have on where all of the other elements could go.

"J will be on the same team as M or N, but not both."

9. J/M or J/N   N/M (crossed out)

This is a simpler rule to understand than the previous two, and can be notated as we have to the side.[9] Notice that this rule yields us an additional inference—since J must be with M or N, but can't be with both, M and N can't be together.

Two Diagrams Instead of One

Sometimes, complex *or* rules are so significant to the design of a game that it makes sense to use them as the basis for creating two separate diagrams for a game. This is either because the *or* rule is built into the basic design of the game, or because the other rules hinge on the outcome of the *or* rule.

Imagine the following scenario:

"Six dancers—F, G, H, J, K, and L—will each perform in the first show or the second show, but not both. Either four dancers will perform in the first show and two in the second, or two dancers will perform in the first show and four in the second."

Note that in this case the *or* situation is built into the basic design of the game—we know we will either have four slots for the first show and two for the second, or vice-versa.

We could create a generic diagram that gives us four possible positions for each show, but then we wouldn't be taking full advantage of what we know. Instead, it makes a lot of sense to create two different diagrams that lay out the two distinct possibilities, as we've done at the top of the next page.

As we answer the questions, we'll make sure to keep both diagrams in mind, and we'll also find that certain questions will allow us to focus on just one set of positions or the other (say, for example, that you infer there must be at least three people in the second show, then you would know to only think about the second set of positions).

It also makes sense to make two diagrams, or two versions of a part of the diagram, when it's clear that the other rules in the game hinge on the outcome of the complex *or* condition.

What impact does the word "either" have?

SHORT ANSWER: On the LSAT, the term "either" has no clear and definable impact on the specific meaning of "or"—that is, the writers of the LSAT will not expect you to think that "either/or" is inherently different from "or."

LONGER ANSWER: Some people who have a background in formal logic or mathematics would argue that "either," by definition, excludes the possibility of both (they would say that "either X or Y attends" means that one must attend, but it can't be that both attend). However, in common everyday language, we use *either* all the time when we don't mean to be exclusive. If someone asks if you prefer steak or chicken and you say "Either is fine," you surely don't mean one of them, but not the other, is fine. How do LSAT writers deal with this dichotomy? By skirting around it. The writers of the LSAT do not choose to test your understanding of a specific definition for "either/or." And, whenever they do use "either" with "or," they typically do so in contexts in which "both" is not actually a possibility. If the situation doesn't naturally exclude both, the authors will make clear their intended meaning by stating, "Either X or Y, but not both, will attend."

two diagrams instead of one

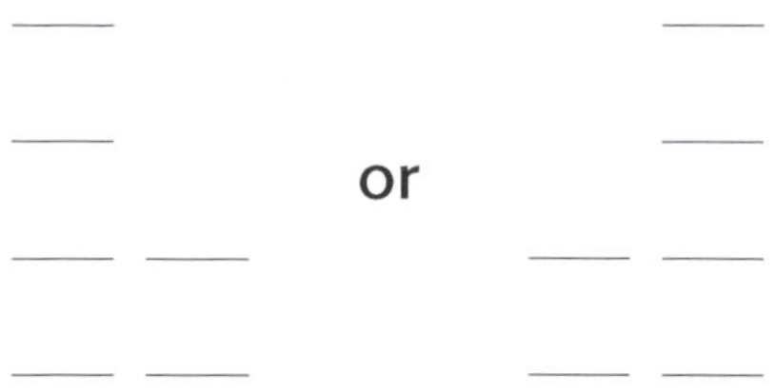

__ __ __ __ __ __ or __ __ __ __ __ __

The game on the opposite page is an example of this type of situation. Notice that I built two "chains" of relationships centered around the two different ways the *or* rule could play out, but just wrote out one set of slots. Keep in mind that there will be plenty more discussion of similar such problem-solving strategies in the lessons to come.

Following the example will be a drill focused on translating complex *or* statements, then five mini-games that will help you practice taking advantage of complex *or* issues.

A way for test writers to write complex "or" rules as conditional statements

"If and only if" is not the only way that test writers will gussy up an "or" situation using conditional statements. A less common, less elegant method is to present a matching pair of conditional statements that, taken together, give us the same information as would a more simple "or" statement. Take a look at how some of the *or* rules that we've already discussed can be converted into matching conditional statements. It should make sense, per the discussion on biconditionals, why this works the way it does. Normally, conditional statements are subtle in that knowing a consequence of, say, J arriving before M tells us nothing about what happens if J arrives after M. However, note that taken together, these conditional statements lose their "direction," that is, you don't have to worry about falsely reversing or negating—you can just think of the pair of conditions as one "or" situation.

J will arrive before either M or N, but not both.	N—J—M or M—J—N	If J arrives before M, it will arrive after N. If J arrives after M, it will arrive before N.
J will arrive after M or before N, but not both.	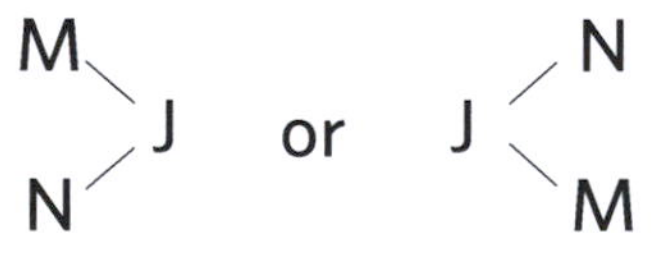 M╲J╱N or J╱N, J╲M	If J arrives after M, it will arrive after N. If J arrives before M, it will arrive before N.
J will be on the same team as M or N, but not both.	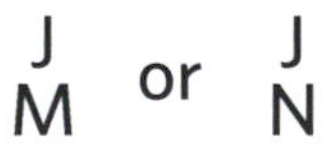 J/M or J/N	If J is with M, it is not with N. If J is not with M, it will be with N.

Directions for drill on page 196: Here is a basic scenario accompanied by four sets of complex *or* rules. All four sets are mirrors of one another, but with the questions reordered and the elements changed. Notate the rules and work to improve on accuracy and timing as you go from set to set.

sometimes two is better than one

Let's take a step-by-step look at how we can use a complex *or* rule to our advantage by using it as a springboard for setting up a pair of diagrams that show us the different possibilities for a game.

SAMPLE GAME

A manager will visit seven different locations—F, G, H, J, K, L, and M—one at a time and in order. The following must be true:

She will visit G before both F and K.
She will visit M immediately after J.
She visits exactly one location after K and before L.
She will visit F before H or J, but not both.

1. Which of the following could be true?
(A) She visits J third and M fourth.
(B) She visits H first and J fourth.
(C) She visits J second and L fourth.
(D) She visits G third and J sixth.
(E) She visits H first and K third.

2. If the manager visits G third, which of the following must be true?
(A) She visits F fifth.
(B) She visits K fourth.
(C) She visits L last.
(D) She visits J first.
(E) She visits H sixth.

STEP 1: NOTICE THE COMPLEX *OR* RULE

You always want to start a game by reading the scenario and rules before setting pen to paper, and this is when you want to make key decisions about how to set up a game. Here, notice that the last rule is a complex *or* rule. Also notice that many of the elements in that rule are repeated in other rules, meaning that this *or* rule impacts other rules. These things tell us that this is a rule off of which we can and probably should build two diagrams (or partial diagrams). After reading the scenario and rules, we begin by laying out this foundation:

J — F — H   H — F — J

__ __ __ __ __ __ __

STEP 2: ADD OTHER RULES

Remember, we noticed that other rules were impacted by the *or* rule; by separating the possibilities the *or* rule presents into two diagrams, we can better represent these other rules as well.

We want to add on what we can to each of the diagrams, and we can add the first and second rules easily. Once those are in place, we can add the third rule. What we end up with is a pair of diagrams that helps us see all of the possibilities in the game more clearly than we would have with just one diagram. We'll get more practice at reading, and using, such diagrams in future lessons, but hopefully this makes a lot of sense to you already.

JM — F — H   H — F — JM
  /   /
G — K_L   G — K_L

__ __ __ __ __ __ __

STEP 3: USE BOTH DIAGRAMS TO ANSWER QUESTIONS

Creating more than one diagram really pays off when it comes time to answer the questions. If you work off of the *or* correctly, and understand how to use your diagrams, they can help you answer questions far faster than you could otherwise. Let's think about how we'd use our diagrams to answer these two questions.

1. This question is asking for one answer that could be true. That means there are four answers that must be false, and it's probably going to be easiest to knock those four wrong answers off. (A) must be false because J can't go third in either the first or second diagram. (B) is very tempting. H can go first in the second diagram. However, with H in first, J in fourth, and M in fifth, there is no place for the K_L group. For (C), she could only visit J second in the first of our diagrams, but in that scenario she cannot visit L fourth. For (D), she can only visit G third in the first diagram, and if that were the case, J would have to go first, so (D) can't be true. That leaves us with (E), the correct answer. She can only visit H first in the second diagram, and in that one we can put K in the third position. The diagram below shows how (E) could work.

H G K F L J M

2. This is a conditional question, and we need to figure out the consequence of G going third. We realize this can only happen in the first diagram, and in that one, JM must go in 1 and 2 if G goes third. Therefore, (D) must be true. F, H, K, and L can go into 4, 5, 6, and 7 in a few different orders, so none of the remaining choices must be true.

Complex "Or" Rules Drill

Scenario: Seven children—F, G, H, J, K, L, and M—will take turns riding a swing. They will ride one at a time, and they will each ride once. The following conditions apply:

Either F or G, but not both, will go before L.	L will go after K or before M, but not both.
J will go after L or M, but not both.	If F goes before J, F will go after K. If F goes after J, F will go before K.
M will go before J or after L, but not both.	H will go before J if and only if H is after M.
Either K or J, but not both, will go after F.	Both H and K go before M, or neither of them does.
M or J, but not both, will go before F does.	L will go before K or J, but not both.

____ / 10 Time:________

L or J, but not both, will go before H does.	L will go before J if and only if L is after G.
F will go after G or before M, but not both.	J will go after H or F, but not both.
Either K or M, but not both, will go before L.	Both H and F go before L, or neither of them does.
H will go before M or J, but not both.	M will go before F or after G, but not both.
Either G or L, but not both, will go after F.	If F goes before L, F will go after H. If F goes after L, F will go before H.

____ / 10 Time:________

Both L and K go before F, or neither of them does.	Either F or H, but not both, will go before M.
J will go after F or H, but not both.	If G goes before F, G will go after K. If G goes after F, G will go before K.
G will go after L or before M, but not both.	H or J, but not both, will go before G does.
F will go before K or after L, but not both.	G will go before J if and only if G is after F.
G will go before K or F, but not both.	Either K or F, but not both, will go after G.

____ / 10 Time:________

Either M or H, but not both, will go after F.	Both G and K go before F, or neither of them does.
H will go before K or after L, but not both.	H will go before G if and only if H is after F.
If G goes before J, G will go after M. If G goes after J, G will go before M.	Either F or L, but not both, will go before M.
G will go after L or F, but not both.	L will go after J or before H, but not both.
L will go before F or G, but not both.	L or J, but not both, will go before G does.

____ / 10 Time:________

Complex "Or" Rules Drill Solutions

Scenario: Seven children—F, G, H, J, K, L, and M—will take turns riding a swing. They will ride one at a time, and they will each ride once. The following conditions apply:

Either F or G, but not both, will go before L. F — L — G or G — L — F	L will go after K or before M, but not both. K, M — L or L — K, M
J will go after L or M, but not both. L — J — M or M — J — L	If F goes before J, F will go after K. If F goes after J, F will go before K. K — F — J or J — F — K
M will go before J or after L, but not both. M — J, L or J, L — M	H will go before J if and only if H is after M. M — H — J or J — H — M
Either K or J, but not both, will go after F. K — F — J or J — F — K	Both H and K go before M, or neither of them does. H, K — M or M — H, K
M or J, but not both, will go before F does. M — F — J or J — F — M	L will go before K or J, but not both. K — L — J or J — L — K

L or J, but not both, will go before H does. L — H — J or J — H — L	L will go before J if and only if L is after G. G — L — J or J — L — G
F will go after G or before M, but not both. G, M — F or F — G, M	J will go after H or F, but not both. H — J — F or F — J — H
Either K or M, but not both, will go before L. K — L — M or M — L — K	Both H and F go before L, or neither of them does. H, F — L or L — H, F
H will go before M or J, but not both. M — H — J or J — H — M	M will go before F or after G, but not both. M — F, G or F, G — M
Either G or L, but not both, will go after F. G — F — L or L — F — G	If F goes before L, F will go after H. If F goes after L, F will go before H. H — F — L or L — F — H

Both L and K go before F, or neither of them does. L, K — F or F — L, K	Either F or H, but not both, will go before M. F — M — H or H — M — F
J will go after F or H, but not both. F — J — H or H — J — F	If G goes before F, G will go after K. If G goes after F, G will go before K. K — G — F or F — G — K
G will go after L or before M, but not both. L, M — G or G — L, M	H or J, but not both, will go before G does. H — G — J or J — G — H
F will go before K or after L, but not both. F — K, L or K, L — F	G will go before J if and only if G is after F. F — G — J or J — G — F
G will go before K or F, but not both. K — G — F or F — G — K	Either K or F, but not both, will go after G. K — G — F or F — G — K

Either M or H, but not both, will go after F. M — F — H or H — F — M	Both G and K go before F, or neither of them does. G, K — F or F — G, K
H will go before K or after L, but not both. H — K, L or K, L — H	H will go before G if and only if H is after F. F — H — G or G — H — F
If G goes before J, G will go after M. If G goes after J, G will go before M. M — G — J or J — G — M	Either F or L, but not both, will go before M. F — M — L or L — M — F
G will go after L or F, but not both. L — G — F or F — G — L	L will go after J or before H, but not both. J, H — L or L — J, H
L will go before F or G, but not both. F — L — G or G — L — F	L or J, but not both, will go before G does. L — G — J or J — G — L

Directions for games starting on next page: Beginning on the next page are five games that hinge on complex *or* rules. At this point, accuracy trumps speed, but do time yourself so you can have a sense of where you are at: three minutes to set up and one minute per question is about ideal. As always, you can decide on when to look at the solutions based on your comfort level, but beware: the solution to the first game is right below it.

Game 1 & Solution

Game one

A food taster will test seven desserts—L, M, N, O, P, Q, and R—one at a time and in order. The following conditions apply:

She tests N after either L or O, but not both.
She tests P immediately after O.
She tests R fourth.
She will not test L first or last.

1. If she tests P immediately before R, each of the following must be true EXCEPT:
(A) She tests M first.
(B) She tests O second.
(C) She tests P third.
(D) She tests N fifth.
(E) She tests L sixth.

2. Which of the following cannot be tested second?
(A) L
(B) N
(C) O
(D) P
(E) Q

Game one

A food taster will test seven desserts—L, M, N, O, P, Q, and R—one at a time and in order. The following conditions apply:

She tests N after either L or O, but not both.
She tests P immediately after O.
She tests R fourth.
She will not test L first or last.

L
(M)
N
O
P
(Q)
R

L̸ (1st) ___ ___ ___ R ___ ___ ___ L̸ (7th)

L — N — OP or OP — N — L

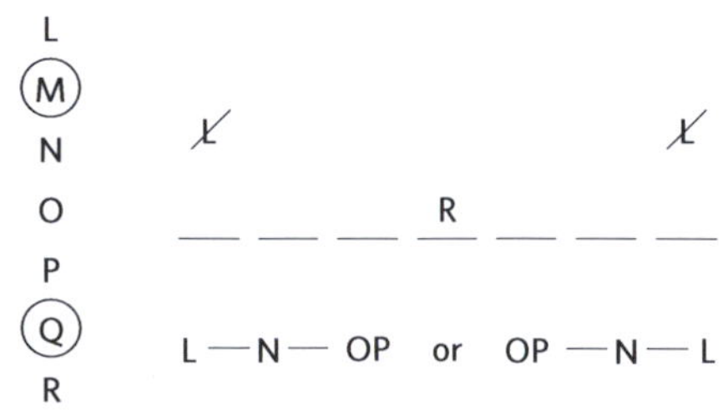

The initial *or* rule is clearly the star in this game. Notice that it utilizes four of seven elements, and the other rules, you could argue, exist in order to impact how you handle these two possible chains—they prevent the ends of the chain (the Ls) from stretching across all seven positions, and the R impacts how the middles of our chains play out.

1. If she tastes P immediately before R, each of the following must be true EXCEPT:
(A) She tests M first.
(B) She tests O second.
(C) She tests P third.
(D) She tests N fifth.
(E) She tests L sixth.

L̸ ___ O P R N L ___ L̸

2. Which of the following cannot be tested second?
(A) L
(B) N
(C) O
(D) P
(E) Q

1. If P is immediately before R, P must be in 3, and O in 2. N and L must come after the R, and since L can't be last, N must be in 5 and L in 6. That leaves M and Q to fill either of the two remaining slots—1 and 7.
2. The chains allow for most of the elements to be tested second; N is the only one that can't in either chain—when L is before N, the earliest N can go is third (because L can't go first), and when OP is before N, the earliest N can go is third.

Games 2 & 3

Game two

Six books—F, G, H, J, K, and L—will be placed on a bookshelf with three shelves—a top shelf, a middle shelf, and a bottom shelf. The following rules apply:

Twice as many books will go on the bottom shelf as on the top shelf.
G and J will go on the same shelf.
If K is on the bottom shelf, L will be on the middle shelf.
F will not go on the top shelf.

1. Which of the following, if true, would determine which books are on which shelves?
(A) H is on the top shelf.
(B) F is on the middle shelf.
(C) L is on the middle shelf.
(D) K is on the bottom shelf.
(E) G is on the bottom shelf.

2. If K is not on the top shelf, which of the following must be false?
(A) G is on the top shelf.
(B) K is on the middle shelf.
(C) J is on the middle shelf.
(D) H is on the middle shelf.
(E) F is on the bottom shelf.

Game three

Six children—R, S, T, V, W, and X—take turns playing with a toy. The following conditions apply:

T plays before R or after V, but not both.
Either T or W will go third.
V plays with the toy after W does.
Neither R nor V plays with the toy last.

1. If W plays first, each of the following must be false EXCEPT:
(A) V plays second.
(B) R plays second.
(C) S plays fourth.
(D) V plays fifth.
(E) X plays fifth.

2. Which of the following must be false?
(A) S plays first.
(B) T plays second.
(C) W plays fourth.
(D) S plays fifth.
(E) T plays last.

Games 2 & 3 Solutions

Game two solutions

Six books—F, G, H, J, K, and L—will be placed on a bookshelf with three shelves—a top shelf, a middle shelf, and a bottom shelf. The following rules apply:

Twice as many books will go on the bottom shelf as go on the top shelf.
G and J will go on the same shelf.
If K is on the bottom shelf, L will be on the middle shelf.
F will not go on the top shelf.

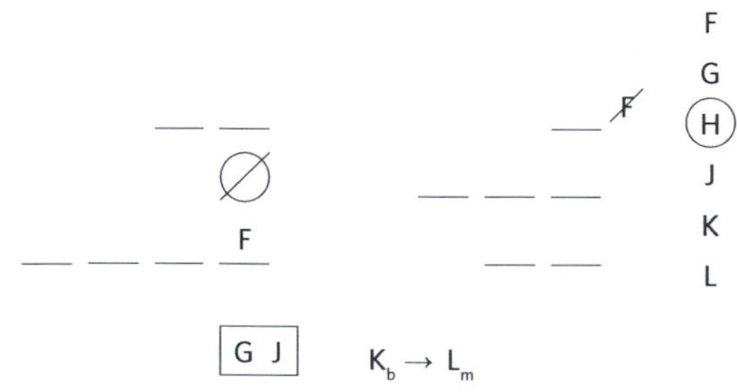

The first rule creates a natural either/or split—either two on top and four on bottom, or one on top and two on bottom.

1. Which of the following, if true, would determine which books are on which shelves?
(A) H is on the top shelf.
(B) F is on the middle shelf.
(C) L is on the middle shelf.
(D) K is on the bottom shelf.
(E) G is on the bottom shelf.

2. If K is not on the top shelf, which of the following must be false?
(A) G is on the top shelf.
(B) K is on the middle shelf.
(C) J is on the middle shelf.
(D) H is on the middle shelf.
(E) F is on the bottom shelf.

1. A big key on these types of questions (which we'll discuss in greater detail in a future lesson) is to not waste time on wrong answers. If you don't see the information given leading to additional inferences, move on. With (D), if K is on the bottom, L must be on the middle—we're dealing with the second diagram. That means G and J must go on the middle shelf, and F on the bottom. That leaves H for the top.

2. If K is not on the top shelf, it must be on the bottom or middle shelf. If it's on the bottom shelf, L is on the middle shelf. So, the diagram on the left can't work. The big inference is that if K is not on the top shelf, it must be the diagram on the right. From that we can conclude that (A) must be false.

Game three solutions

Six children—R, S, T, V, W, and X—take turns playing with a toy. The following conditions apply:

T plays before R or after V, but not both.
Either T or W will go third.
V plays with the toy after W does.
Neither R nor V plays with the toy last.

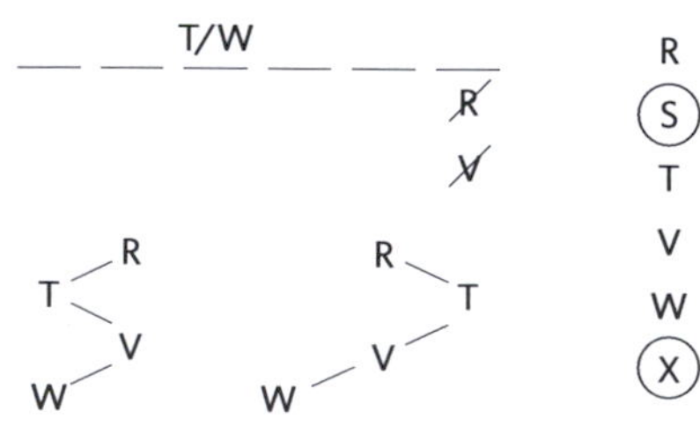

The first rule is challenging to understand correctly, but it is the key to organizing the rules of this game. Notice we end up with two possible "chains" of ordering rules, and we can use these chains to our advantage when it comes time to answer the questions.

1. If W plays first, each of the following must be false EXCEPT:
(A) V plays second.
(B) R plays second.
(C) S plays fourth.
(D) V plays fifth.
(E) X plays fifth.

W __ T R/V R/V __

2. Which of the following must be false?
(A) S plays first.
(B) T plays second.
(C) W plays fourth.
(D) S plays fifth.
(E) T plays last.

1. If W is first, we know we're dealing with the link on the left of our diagram, not the one on the right. Per the links on the left, we know R and V must follow T, but we also know neither can go in 6. Therefore, R and V must go in 4 or 5. If you'd like, you can complete your diagram by placing S/X into the remaining two spots, but in real time that would probably be unnecessary. For a MBF question, you should expect to eliminate four answers to arrive at the correct one—all four wrong answers must be false.

2. Again, a key here is to not waste time on wrong answers. You want to skip over answers that don't seem to lead to clear inferences until you spot an answer that leads to impossible consequences. With (C), if W is fourth, T must be third, forcing us to use the left chain of links. That would require R and V to go in 5 and 6, but since neither can go in 6, we know this answer can't be true.

Games 4 & 5

Game 4 (challenge)
Nine people—F, G, H, I, J, K, L, M, and N—are split into three teams of three. The following conditions apply:

H and K cannot be on the same team.
J and I as a pair will be teamed either with F or with G.
A team will have L if and only if it also has N.

1. Each of the following trios could be teams EXCEPT:
(A) H, L, N
(B) K, L, N
(C) G, H, M
(D) G, L, N
(E) F, K, M

2. Which of the following, if true, would determine all three teams?
(A) G is teamed with J.
(B) L is teamed with H.
(C) M is teamed with H.
(D) N is teamed with K.
(E) F is teamed with K.

Game five (challenge)
Seven models—H, J, K, L, M, O, and P—are placed in positions 1 through 7, from left to right. The following conditions apply:

Exactly one model is placed between K and L.
Exactly three models are placed between O and L.
Either K or J is in the first position.
M is in position 4.

1. Which of the following could be true?
(A) K is placed in the second position.
(B) O is placed in the second position.
(C) L is placed in the second position.
(D) J is placed in the second position.
(E) J is placed in the seventh position.

2. If K is not first, which of the following is a complete list of positions, any one of which can be occupied by H?
(A) 2
(B) 2, 3, 5
(C) 2, 5, 6
(D) 2, 6
(E) 6

Games 4 & 5 Solutions

Game four solutions

Nine people—F, G, H, I, J, K, L, M, and N—are split into three teams of three. The following conditions apply:

H and K cannot be on the same team.
J and I as a pair will be teamed either with F or with G.
A team will have L if and only if it also has N.

L N

F/G __ __
J __ __
I H K

F G H I J K L M N

Note that because the teams aren't differentiated (i.e., given specific names), we can go ahead and put our team rules directly on the slots. If there was, say, a green team, a red team, and a purple team, we'd have to notate all of the rules to the side. In any case, the big inference to be made is that the combination of the first and second rules tells us something about all three teams. We could have made frames off of the second rule, or off the L, N chunk—and if you did so, that's great. We didn't feel the frames were necessary in this instance because the one diagram is simple enough, but they certainly wouldn't hurt either.

1. Each of the following trios could be teams EXCEPT:
(A) H, L, N
(B) K, L, N
(C) G, H, M
(D) G, L, N
(E) F, K, M

2. Which of the following, if true, would determine all three teams?
(A) G is teamed with J.
(B) L is teamed with H.
(C) M is teamed with H.
(D) N is teamed with K.
(E) F is teamed with K.

1. Placing our rules directly onto our diagram really helps us here. Again, it's a danger to spend too much time on wrong answers. If we look at our diagram, it's clear to see we have no place for a G, L, N team.

2. It's easy to spend too much time on the wrong answers for this type of question as well. Move on when the inference trail becomes uncertain. For example, with (A), if G is with J, we know G, J, I is one team. Where can the L, N chunk go? Perhaps there is some unusual and creative reason why it must go with H or K in this context, but don't look for that on your first go around. Instead, once you see that L, N placement doesn't seem restricted, move on to the next answer. With (E), we can see quickly that F with K forces G to be with J and I, and the L, N pair to be with H.

Game five solutions

Seven models—H, J, K, L, M, O, and P—are placed in positions 1 through 7, from left to right. The following conditions apply:

Exactly one model is placed between K and L.
Exactly three models are placed between O and L.
Either K or J is in the first position.
M is in position 4.

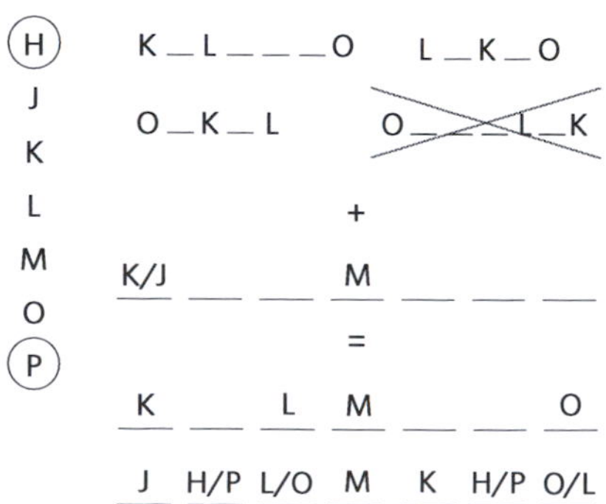

Sometimes, you'll draw out your diagram and note the rules, *then* notice that creating two separate diagrams is advantageous. If you ended up getting to the same two diagrams for this game as the ones listed above, chances are you went through such a two-layer system. In the first layer, the key is thinking through the various ways in which the first and second rules can come together—they give us four (ultimately cut down to three) options for how to organize L, K, and O, and these three sets really tell us a lot about the game. When we couple what we know with the rule that K or J is in the first position, we *really* find out a lot about the game. When K is first, there is only one option for how K, L, and O can be organized, and that will allow us to fill in much of our board. When J is first, we know that we can only fit either O_K_L or L_K_O, and, furthermore, there is only one set of positions (3–5–7) into which that trio can go. That leaves us with just H and P as options for the remaining two positions. Going through two layers of work like that might take just a bit of extra time, and chances are you'd be fine without all that work, but if you were able to come up with it all, it would definitely be time well spent.

1. Which of the following could be true?
(A) K is placed in the second position.
(B) O is placed in the second position.
(C) L is placed in the second position.
(D) J is placed in the second position.
(E) J is placed in the seventh position.

2. If K is not first, which of the following is a complete list of positions, any one of which can be occupied by H?
(A) 2
(B) 2, 3, 5
(C) 2, 5, 6
(D) 2, 6
(E) 6

J __ L M K __ O
J __ O M K __ L

1. We're asked to find one answer that could be true, and so four answers must be false. Our three frames make it much easier to see why the other four answers must be false. (D) works as either K, J, L, M, H, P, O, or K, J, L, M, P, H, O.

2. If K is not first, J must be first. Two frames work with J being first, and it makes sense to draw them both out. Placing the O, K, L chunks around the M in 4 clarifies, quite a bit, where the H can go.

How Did You Do?

Did you feel comfortable handling the complex *or* rules, and were you able to use them as the "centerpiece" of your thinking, both in your diagramming and in your process of solving questions? If so, that's great. As mentioned before, these complex *or* rules are, for most test takers, some of the more intimidating rules to have in a game. At the same time, they are by far some of the most useful rules for setting up diagrams, and they are commonly central to the design of whatever game they are a part of. Any time you take a part of the test that is intimidating and are able to turn it into a key part of your solution process, you are making great progress.

If you feel like you are not quite there yet—maybe the concepts make just 80 percent sense, or maybe they make 100 percent sense but you still make some mistakes, or perhaps you still miss some inferences, or freeze when it's time to answer a question—that's certainly normal for this stage. But I hope you are seeing the benefit of the work you are putting in.

The great news is that we are now done covering every major diagramming issue that can appear in a Logic Game. That's it—you've seen it all. Congratulations! The even greater news is that you are going to have many, many more chances to strengthen the skills we've worked on here.

In the next lesson, we'll do a quick review of what we've learned about diagramming, and then focus the bulk of our attention on a mixed set of practice games. When we come back to Logic Games after a batch of Logical Reasoning lessons, we'll build upon our diagramming basics and develop a simple, brutally effective skill set for attacking a variety of questions.

For your reference, on the following page I've included a visual breakdown of all possible game scenarios and a summary of our key discussions. For a chart of all of the actual notations we've used, please see page 206.

A MACRO VIEW OF GAME DESIGN

Here is a big-picture view of how games are designed. As we've discussed, many of these characteristics can and do overlap. If you can imagine various combinations of these characteristics appearing in any one game, and if you feel comfortable handling any and all such combinations, you are in great shape.

ALL GAMES ARE ABOUT ASSIGNING ELEMENTS TO POSITIONS

ABOUT 2 OUT OF EVERY 3 GAMES INVOLVES ORDERING

ABOUT 1/2 OF ALL GAMES INVOLVE GROUPING

ABOUT 1 IN EVERY 3 OR 4 GAMES INVOLVES SUBSETS

ABOUT 1 IN EVERY 4 GAMES HAS NUMBERS ISSUES

ABOUT 1 IN EVERY 4 GAMES HAS CONDITIONAL RULES INTEGRAL TO THE GAME'S DESIGN

ABOUT 1 IN EVERY 8 GAMES CENTERS ON A COMPLEX "OR" STATEMENT

AN OVERVIEW OF KEY POINTS

Here is a list of the key points that we have discussed in these last five lessons. You can use this checklist to get a sense for which issues you feel comfortable with, and which ones you don't.

BASICS

The ability to diagram is the key to Logic Games success.
All games are about assigning elements to positions.
All game designs involve ordering, grouping, or both.

SUBSETS

We will be asked to figure out subset assignments for elements, positions, or both.
There are commonly just two or three subsets, but the number of subsets can equal the number of elements.
Certain games may present us with more than one set of subsets.

NUMBERS

Numbers issues generally appear when there are more elements than positions, or more positions than elements.
Generally, element/position mismatches appear in ordering games.
Numbers issues can also appear in games involving subsets.
The numbers will generally be simple, but the numeric inferences can be subtle and difficult to notice.

CONDITIONALS

Conditional rules represent guarantees: certain results must happen if certain triggers are set off.
The contrapositive of any condition tells us that if the result didn't happen, the trigger didn't happen.
When a game has multiple conditional rules, our task is to understand correctly how they link together.
Biconditionals (Lesson 14) flow in both directions, and can be thought of as "or" rules.

OR

The term "A or B" can, unless otherwise restricted, allow for A *and* B.
However, most "or" statements are restricted from meaning *and*.
Complex "or" rules are often the key for unlocking games, and may be used to create two diagrams.

15 LOGIC GAMES diagramming review

We've covered a lot of ground in the last five lessons. The examples and drills were carefully designed so that by this point you've been exposed to all of the key diagramming issues that you are likely to see on your exam.

Should you feel *mastery* yet? Of course not (though if you do, and you aren't full of it, of course that's great). We're just partway through the process. You should certainly feel, though, that you are developing a solid foundation, and hopefully you feel confident that you are on the path to greater improvement.

In the introduction to games in Lesson 3, I laid out the skills required for consistent success in Logic Games:

1. You need to be able to see the overall design of the game.
2. You need to understand rules and be able to notate them in an easily usable way.
3. You need to be able to see how rules come together, and how they don't.
4. You need to approach each type of question with a smart plan of attack.

Keep in mind that your skills build on one another; your ability to picture the situation and take control of the rules serves as the foundation. If your foundation is strong, you will get further faster. If your foundation is weak, it will limit how much you can improve.

General Breakdown of Games from *10 New Actual Official LSAT Prep Tests*

Exams	52				53				54				55				56				57				58				59				60				61				t
Game	1	2	3	4	1	2	3	4	1	2	3	4	1	2	3	4	1	2	3	4	1	2	3	4	1	2	3	4	1	2	3	4	1	2	3	4	1	2	3	4	40
Ord	•		•	•		•	•	•		•	•	•		•	•	•	•			•	•	•		•	•		•			•		•	•	•	•			•	•	•	27
Grp		•			•			•	•	•			•					•	•	•			•			•		•	•		•					•	•				16
Sub			•				•		•			•	•		•	•						•	•				•						•			•	•				13
#					•					•				•				•	•			•		•					•						•		•		•		11
Cond		•							•									•					•			•		•			•			•					•		9
Or			•			•						•																										•			4

Here is a chart of how the games from exams 52-61 compare with the issues that we've been covering. Note that this represents about 3 1/2 years' worth of LSATs. Keep in mind that both grouping games (generally about 50% of all games, but at 40% for these games) and games dependent on complex *or* rules (just four in this set, though they are four of the more difficult games) are a bit less common here than they have been historically. Finally, note that for the games marked in each category, that particular issue is a significant rather than secondary issue for that game. For a breakdown of all games from exams 29 - 71, please check out www.thelsattrainer.com.

THE TABLE OF

common notations

F is assigned to X	X will be occupied	X will not be occupied	F or G is assigned to X	F is assigned to X or Y	A boy is assigned to X
F / X	◯ / X	⁄ / X	F/G / X	F/ / X /F / Y	b / X
F is before G F — G G is after F	**F is immediately before G** FG G is immediately after F	**F is at least two spots ahead of G** F__ ...G G is at least two spots after F	**F is after G but before H** G — F — H	**F is exactly two spots ahead of G** F __ G G is exactly two spots after F	**F is immediately before a boy** F _b
There is at least one spot between F and G F__...G	**F is right before or right after G** F G	**F is before both G and H** F < G, H	**F is after both G and H** G, H > F	**There is exactly one spot between F and G** F __ G	**F is exactly two spots ahead of a boy** F__ _b
The same element is assigned to X and Y □ □ X Y	**Different elements are assigned to X and Y** □ △ X Y	**F, G, and H occupy X, Y, and Z** (F, G, H) X Y Z	**F and G are grouped together** F G	**F is grouped with a boy** F _b	**F is a boy** Fb

(+)

not	If...,then...	or	and	free agents	multiple diagrams
⁄	→	or	+	F G H K (L)	— — — — — — — — — — — —
Most of the rules above can be converted into "not" rules by adding a cross-out.	Most of the rules above can be combined into conditional rules.	Most of the rules above can be combined into compound rules through the use of "or" or "and."		If all but one or two of your elements are mentioned in the rules, it can be helpful to track the unrestricted elements.	Once in a while—most commonly in a game defined by a complex *or* rule—it will be helpful to work off of more than one diagram.

WHEN you first start studying Logic Games, it can seem like there are an infinite number of issues that can come up, an endless supply of different types of games that you cannot possibly be prepared for.

However, as you learn more and more about games, you quickly realize that there is great commonality to all games, and that there are just a few basic structural issues—primarily ordering and grouping—that define all games and all rules.

I hope that at this point you feel fairly comfortable with the various possible game scenarios, and the various possible rules that they may throw at you. For review, here are all of the common notations.

Let's do a quick review of the key characteristics that define these rules:

The most basic rules—rules of **assignment**—have to do with how particular positions will be filled. We can be told that a specific element will fill a specific position, that a particular position will not be filled, and so on.

The most common and varied rules, the rules of **order**, relate elements to one another in the context of an ordering game. These rules can be specific, or they can be general. Either two or three of the games you see on your exam will be ordering games, and understanding and utilizing ordering rules well will be the key to your success on those games.

Grouping is a very common game characteristic—appearing in just a little less than half of all games—and though the inferences related to grouping can be just as complicated as those relating to any other issue, methods of notating grouping rules are fairly simple. Unless game scenarios specifically dictate otherwise, we want to represent all grouping issues vertically, and doing so consistently can make visualizing grouping far easier.

The test writers use **subsets** to add an additional layer of complexity to common ordering and grouping games. Subsets can apply to elements, positions, or both. By always using lowercase letters (or numbers) for subset issues, we can easily just adapt our normal notations to accommodate subset rules.

When the number of elements doesn't equal the number of positions, or when games involve subsets, we can run into **numbers issues**. For these games, we have to think about whether elements will be included or not, or whether slots will be filled or not, and simple notations can help us do that.

Finally, the rules of a game can also be defined by the form of the rule itself.

The rule can be **conditional**—that is, it can be a rule that only applies in particular situations. These conditional rules can be some of the most tempting to misunderstand or misuse—accuracy and comfort with your notation systems are essential here.

Or, the rule can give us more complex possibilities through the use of **and** and **or.** These rules can also be more challenging than normal to understand, but the benefit is often great. Because these rules commonly include more than two elements, or because these rules commonly create a clean "divide" between the various possibilities for a particular game, these rules are commonly the most important rules for the games in which they appear.

More on Conditional Rules

Nearly any pair of rules mentioned on the left can be turned into a conditional rule—that is, a rule that is triggered by something else happening. For all conditional rules, the key to success is to understand the rule correctly, and to understand ways in which it can be utilized, and (perhaps more importantly) ways in which it cannot. For every conditional rule, you must account for the contrapositive. You can choose to do so in your head or on paper, based on the game, but you should always put it down on paper if there is a chance it will be forgotten or mistaken. Again, correctly answering questions will likely require a careful understanding of any conditional rules, and many incorrect answers are built off of incorrect understandings of conditional rules.

We use a simple arrow to represent all conditional rules. Here is the basic notation along with the common wordings you will see for the rule. Below that is an example of a biconditional—a rule that is triggered in both directions.

"M → P" contrapositive "- P → - M"

If M, then P
Any with M must have P
All with M have P
No Ms are without Ps
You can't have M unless you have P
M only if P

"M ↔ P" contrapositive "- P ↔ - M"

M if and only if P

More on the Meaning of *Or*

Rules can be brought together through the use of "and" and "or." The meaning of "and" is simple and clear, but the meaning of "or" is a bit more complex.

Keep in mind that unless there are other considerations, the word "or" does not, in and of itself, exclude the possibility of "both." Thus, if a rule states, "F or G will be assigned to the management team," it is entirely possible that both F *and* G can be assigned to the management team.

Also keep in mind that in many instances there are natural restrictions that prevent "or" from including "both." If we are told each person can have one locker, then told F can have "either locker 2 or locker 3," we will know that F getting both is not a possibility.

Basic Logic Games Strategy

Here is the general process that I recommend for solving Logic Games. We will discuss these strategies in greater depth in future lessons.

One: See the Big Picture

Before you set pencil to paper, read the scenario and rules and give yourself a second to take it all in. Keep in mind that your first few decisions are likely your most important.

When we think about a game in terms of the big picture, what we want to consider is...

- How are the positions organized? Are they being grouped or ordered?
- Are there subsets? How much information are we given about them?
- Is it one to one between elements and positions? If not, what type of situation is it?
- What rules seem to be most important?
- What rules seem to go together?
- Are there any rules that make us a bit nervous right off the bat? If so, why?
- Is there anything else unusual about the design of the game?

While this may seem like a lot to think about, you can do it all quite quickly if you have the right skills and habits. This part of the process will end with us writing out the elements and the positions in the way that we think fits the game best.

Two: Understand the Rules and Notate Them

There are certain situations for which accuracy is so important that it makes timing a non-factor, and understanding and notating games rules is just such a situation. No amount of pace can make up for not understanding or notating the rules well.

Take as much time as you need to completely understand all rules and notate them accurately. There are typically just four or five rules to a game, so no matter how careful you are, it won't take too long anyway.

Most rules are written simply and are simple to diagram. However, as we've discussed, certain rules (such as "Any group with T has N," or "The soup will have T only if it has S and O") require a bit more care. Slow down in these moments and make sure you handle these rules properly.

Certain rules are meant to be notated on the actual position slots you've drawn in, and others are meant to be notated off the grid. However, no matter what, you should see cohesion between your diagram and the rules; oftentimes when we find ourselves having a lot of trouble notating the rules, it's because we haven't laid out our diagram correctly.

Make sure you do one final check of your notations before moving on to the questions. A great way to do this is to look at each notation, say to yourself what it means, then check this understanding against how the rule was originally worded.

Three: Bring Rules Together

Or, to be more accurate, make sure you carefully evaluate how the rules come together and how they *do not* come together. This is also a part of your process that is dependent on other parts; during the "picture it" phase, you should have done a quick assessment of which rules might be related, so that by the time you need to notate them, you know to think about them together. Also, the more consistent and transparent your notation of individual rules, the easier it is to see how they come together.

Seeing how rules come together is not a one-time process; rather, you should expect to bring rules together over and over again as you think about the game and answer questions. For now, remind yourself to think about how the rules come together at two critical points—as you are diagramming them and just before you start the questions.

Four: Use Effective Question Strategies

We have not discussed question-specific strategies much at all yet, and they will be a focus of many of our future lessons. For now, here are a few key points to consider:

When a question asks for one answer that must be true, expect to get one answer that must be true, and four answers that could be true or false—that is, four answers about which we don't have enough information to say. If a question asks what must be false, the right answer must be false; the four wrong choices will most likely be ones that we don't know to be true or false. For both of these types of questions, it is generally easier to search for the correct answer than it is to try to eliminate wrong ones.

When new information is presented in the question stem, there will always be additional stuff to infer from that new information, and what you figure out will invariably be what answers the question that you are asked. Take plenty of time to infer all you can from new information in a question stem before you move on to evaluate answer choices.

Finally, make sure to be conscious of how you solve questions, and make sure to compare your process to that mentioned in the solutions. Most test takers don't think twice about specific question-solving strategies, even though they are quite simple to develop, and ultimately play a huge part in answering questions quickly. Just being mindful of the importance of process is half the battle. As mentioned, we'll get into much more depth on this subject in future lessons.

On the next few pages are four pairs of games; each game has two questions. Taken as pairs, the drill sets are meant to be roughly equal in difficulty to one another, and on average, the questions are slightly more difficult than average LSAT questions.

Set a goal of completing each pair of games in a total of ten minutes (roughly three minutes to diagram each game and one minute per question). Note that you should practice creating a full diagram even if you don't think you need it for the two questions. If it takes you longer than suggested, that's fine; make sure you are prioritizing accuracy and completeness over pace at this point. Try to be quick, but it's more important to be careful. After the games will be some tools to help you assess your performance.

Set 1

Seven horses—M, N, O, P, Q, R, and S—will be housed in seven stalls, labeled 1 through 7 from left to right. The following conditions apply:

There will be exactly three stalls between M's stall and Q's stall.
There will be exactly four stalls between R's stall and Q's stall.
Q and O cannot be in adjacent stalls.

1. M can go in each of the following stalls EXCEPT:
(A) 2
(B) 3
(C) 4
(D) 5
(E) 6

2. If O is put in the third stall, which of the following could be true?
(A) R is put in the second stall.
(B) Q is put in the last stall.
(C) M is put in the sixth stall.
(D) Q is put in the first stall.
(E) R is put in the last stall.

Seven coffees—F, G, and H from Brazil, and L, M, N, and O from Colombia—will be showcased on three different displays. One coffee will be displayed by itself on stand 1, and the other six coffees will be evenly split on stands 2 and 3. The following conditions apply:

F is displayed on stand 2.
One of the displays will have exactly two Brazilian coffees.
L and M must be displayed together.
F and H cannot be displayed together.

1. If O is displayed on stand 2, which of the following must be true?
(A) H goes on stand 1.
(B) H goes on stand 3.
(C) G goes on stand 2.
(D) N goes on stand 1.
(E) N goes on stand 2.

2. Which of the following must be false?
(A) A Brazilian coffee is displayed by itself.
(B) A Colombian coffee is displayed by itself.
(C) One stand displays only Colombian coffees.
(D) Two stands each display both Brazilian and Colombian coffees.
(E) No stand displays only Colombian coffees.

Set 2

A professor is scheduling appointments with six students—R, S, T, V, W, and X. She will meet with them one at a time. The following conditions apply:

She will meet with R after she meets with T.
She will meet with S immediately before she meets with V.
X will be one of the first three students she meets with.
She meets with T before either S or W, but not both.

1. Each of the following students either cannot meet with the professor first, or cannot meet with the professor last, EXCEPT:
(A) S
(B) W
(C) R
(D) V
(E) X

2. Which of the following determines the order of all appointments?
(A) S is first and X third.
(B) X is first and T third.
(C) X is immediately after W but immediately before T.
(D) T is immediately before W but immediately after X.
(E) W is immediately after X but immediately before T.

A display designer is dressing four mannequins "named" Fred, Gary, Hwang, and Jack. Each mannequin will wear clothes in at least one of four different colors—navy, orange, purple, and red. The following conditions apply:

Jack wears more colors than any other mannequin.
Gary wears fewer colors than any other mannequin.
Fred and Hwang wear the same number of colors,
but none of the same colors.
Jack must wear every color Fred wears.
Hwang wears red.
Fred wears any color Gary wears.

1. Which of the following could be true?
(A) Three mannequins wear red, and two wear purple.
(B) Three mannequins wear navy, and three wear orange.
(C) G and exactly two other mannequins wear orange.
(D) G and exactly one other mannequin wear navy.
(E) J and H share no colors in common.

2. If exactly two mannequins wear navy, which of the following is a complete list of mannequins that must wear navy?
(A) F
(B) H
(C) J
(D) F and H
(E) F and J

Set 3

Sarah will host five out-of-town friends—M, N, O, P, and Q— at her house over the course of seven months—the first one in March and the last one in September. She will host each friend once, and no more than one friend per month. The following conditions apply:

During this period, she will not go two consecutive months without hosting an out-of-town friend.
She will host P after she hosts both M and Q.
She cannot host M in any odd-numbered month, and she cannot host anyone in the month after she hosts M.
N visits in August or September.

1. If P visits in July, which of the following must be true?
(A) Q visits in March.
(B) Q visits in June.
(C) O visits in March.
(D) O visits in August.
(E) N visits in September.

2. If O stays the month after Q but at some point before M, for how many visitors do we know which month they visited?
(A) 1
(B) 2
(C) 3
(D) 4
(E) 5

Eight people—F, G, H, I, J, K, M, and N—participated in four tennis matches that took place one after another. Each match had a winner and a loser. The matches took place in accordance with the following:

K played in the second match.
H and J played each other.
Both I and K won their matches.
F played before H and after G.

1. Which of the following could be the full list of winners, in order of the matches they won?
(A) G, K, I, H
(B) G, F, K, I
(C) G, K, F, I
(D) F, K, H, I
(E) G, K, F, H

2. If F is a winner, which of the following must be true?
(A) G plays in the first match.
(B) M plays in the second match.
(C) G loses.
(D) H loses.
(E) J loses.

Set 4

A consultant visits five different sites—M, N, O, P, and R—over the course of five days—a different site each day. At some sites she leaves a list of suggestions, and at some sites she doesn't. Additionally, it must be true that:

She leaves suggestions at the second and third sites she visits.
She visits R either first or fourth and leaves a suggestion.
She visits O immediately after she visits a site at which she doesn't leave suggestions.
If she left a suggestion for N, she left a suggestion for M.

1. If she visits O at some point before she visits N, which of the following must be false?
(A) She visited N third.
(B) She visited P third.
(C) She visited M last.
(D) She visited N last.
(E) She visited P last.

2. Which of the following could be true?
(A) P is first and N second.
(B) N is second and R third.
(C) M is third and R fourth.
(D) N is third and O fourth.
(E) O is fourth and N fifth.

A coach will select some of the players trying out for the varsity team, and he will put the rest on the junior varsity team. The eight players trying out are Nick, Otis, Pat, Quinn, Rachel, Sara, Tim, and Wilma. The following conditions apply:

If Nick or Quinn is selected for varsity, Rachel will not be.
Either Sara or Wilma, but not both, will be selected for junior varsity.
Sara and Rachel will be selected for the same team.
If Nick is selected for junior varsity, Otis will be, too.
If Tim is selected for junior varsity, Wilma will be selected for varsity.

1. If Otis is selected for varsity, which of the following could be false?
(A) Nick is selected for varsity.
(B) Wilma is selected for varsity.
(C) Rachel is selected for junior varsity.
(D) Sara is selected for junior varsity.
(E) Tim is selected for junior varsity.

2. Which of the following can be a pair of players, both of whom are selected for varsity?
(A) N and S
(B) O and W
(C) Q and S
(D) O and R
(E) O and S

Set 1 Solutions

Seven horses—M, N, O, P, Q, R, and S—will be housed in seven stalls, labeled 1 through 7 from left to right. The following conditions apply:

There will be exactly three stalls between M's stall and Q's stall.
There will be exactly four stalls between R's stall and Q's stall.
Q and O cannot be in adjacent stalls.

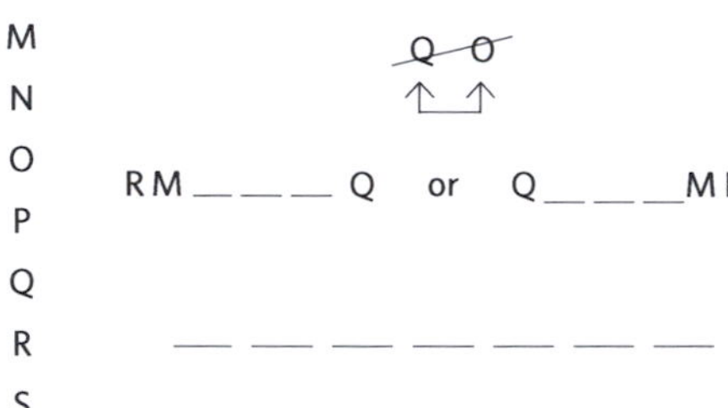

A big key to success for this game is recognizing that there are just a couple of ways in which the first and second rules can go together. The other possible options take up too many spaces. The R, M, Q chains break the game open, since they end up taking up six of the seven possible slots.

1. M can go in each of the following stalls EXCEPT:
(A) 2
(B) 3
(C) 4
(D) 5
(E) 6

2. If O is put in the third stall, which of the following could be true?
(A) R is put in the second stall.
(B) Q is put in the last stall.
(C) M is put in the sixth stall.
(D) Q is put in the first stall.
(E) R is put in the last stall.

R M O _ _ Q _

Q _ O _ M R _

1. We don't want to waste time thinking about where M can go; we want to focus on where it can't. We know that M can't go first or last, but neither of those are answer choices. Notice that M is, in both possibilities, at the "end" of a string—that makes this tough for M to go somewhere in the middle of the chain. Can it go fourth? No—we wouldn't have enough space to place the Q.
2. Putting O into third limits where we can place the R, M, Q link to two options, and we noted them above. After that, our job is to figure out what must be false, and we can see that A, B, C, and E all must be false.

Seven coffees—F, G, and H from Brazil, and L, M, N, and O from Colombia—will be showcased on three different displays. One coffee will be displayed by itself on stand 1, and the other six coffees will be evenly split on stands 2 and 3. The following conditions apply:

F is displayed on stand 2.
One of the displays will have exactly two Brazilian coffees.
L and M must be displayed together.
F and H cannot be displayed together.

Fb Gb Hb Lc Mc (Nc) Oc

_ Fb _ (1 2 3)

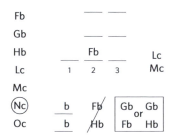

Lc Mc

b b | ~~Fb Hb~~ | Gb Fb or Gb Hb

You could have chosen to create two separate diagrams, and probably the easiest way to do that would be to put L and M into 2 in one diagram, and 3 in another. If you did that, great! The questions were probably much easier to solve.

1. If O is displayed on stand 2, which of the following must be true?
(A) H goes on stand 1.
(B) H goes on stand 3.
(C) G goes on stand 2.
(D) N goes on stand 1.
(E) N goes on stand 2.

1	2	3
	Gb	_
	Oc	Lc
_	Fb	Mc

2. Which of the following must be false?
(A) A Brazilian coffee is displayed by itself.
(B) A Colombian coffee is displayed by itself.
(C) One stand displays only Colombian coffees.
(D) Two stands each display both Brazilian and Colombian coffees.
(E) No stand displays only Colombian coffees.

1. If O is on stand 2, the L/M duo must go on stand 3. That forces G into stand 2.
2. The biggest danger here is wasting time with the wrong answers—it's really hard to see whether each answer could be true or false. It's also very easy to get turned around. For (E) to be true, each stand must have at least one Brazilian coffee. However, this cannot be. Therefore, (E) must be false.

Set 2 Solutions

A professor is scheduling appointments with six students—R, S, T, V, W, and X. She will meet with them one at a time. The following conditions apply:

She will meet with R after she meets with T.
She will meet with S immediately before she meets with V.
X will be one of the first three students she meets with.
She meets with T before either S or W, but not both.

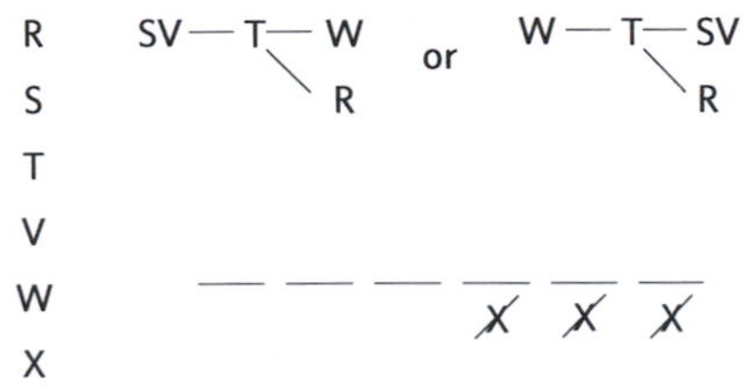

R
S
T
V
W
X

SV — T — W, T — R or W — T — SV, T — R

_ _ _ _ _ _
X̸ X̸ X̸ (under spaces 4, 5, 6)

The either/or rule impacts five of the six elements to be placed, so it makes sense to use that as the focal point of our diagramming. Note that you could have marked that X must go in 1, 2, or 3 with some other notation; however, with such broad information, the "not" notation tends to be a bit easier to think of.

1. Each of the following students either cannot meet with the professor first, or cannot meet with the professor last, EXCEPT:
(A) S
(B) W
(C) R
(D) V
(E) X

2. Which of the following determines the order of all appointments?
(A) S is first and X third.
(B) X is first and T third.
(C) X is immediately after W but immediately before T.
(D) T is immediately before W but immediately after X.
(E) W is immediately after X but immediately before T.

1. The wording of this question is challenging—basically, four of the students have some reason why they can't meet with the professor first or last. R and V can't go first, and S and X can't go last. W is the only one that can go first and can go last.
2. It's easy to waste time on wrong answers; we're hoping for an answer that limits us to one of the either/or's then forces elements into an order, and (D) does that. T can only be before W in the first ordering, and if it immediately follows X, the only possible order is SVXTWR.

A display designer is dressing four mannequins "named" Fred, Gary, Hwang, and Jack. Each mannequin will wear clothes in at least one of four different colors—navy, orange, purple, and red. The following conditions apply:

Jack wears more colors than any other mannequin.
Gary wears fewer colors than any other mannequin.
Fred and Hwang wear the same number of colors, but none of the same colors.
Jack must wear every color Fred wears.
Hwang wears red.
Fred wears any color Gary wears.

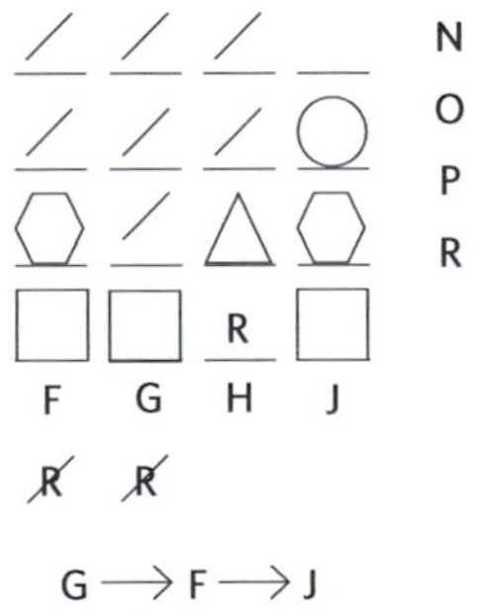

	F	G	H	J
N	/	/	/	_
O	/	/	/	○
P	⬡	/	△	⬡
R	□	□	R	□

Not R: F, G

G → F → J

It's highly unlikely my real-time diagram would look this pretty, but it would have the same information. There are a ton of number inferences to be made here, set off by the relationship between the second and third rules. The different shapes, as long as we are practiced at using them, give us a great visual sense of the fact that what goes in G must also go in F must also go in J, etc. Note that the circle shape should always stay "generic"—that is, we use it when we know a space has to be filled, but have no other association with that space.

1. Which of the following could be true?
(A) Three mannequins wear red, and two wear purple.
(B) Three mannequins wear navy, and three mannequins wear orange.
(C) G and exactly two other mannequins wear orange.
(D) G and exactly one other mannequin wear navy.
(E) J and H share no colors in common.

2. If exactly two mannequins wear navy, which of the following is a complete list of mannequins that must wear navy?
(A) F
(B) H
(C) J
(D) F and H
(E) F and J

1. Generally you will answer a "could be true" by proving four answers must be false. (A) MBF b/c three can't wear red. (B) MBF b/c there isn't enough space to have three of two different colors. (D) MBF b/c whatever G wears, F and J must wear. (E) MBF b/c otherwise there would not be enough colors to fill either H or J's positions.
2. Strangely worded question; we want to think about the ways in which two mannequins wear blue. There are two ways: the pairs are either F and J or H and J. Either way, J must wear blue.

Set 3 Solutions

Sarah will host five out-of-town friends—M, N, O, P, and Q—at her house over the course of seven months—the first one in March and the last one in September. She will host each friend once, and no more than one friend per month. The following conditions apply:

During this period, she will not go two consecutive months without hosting an out-of-town friend.
She will host P after she hosts both M and Q.
She cannot host M in any odd-numbered month, and she cannot host anyone in the month after she hosts M.
N visits in August or September.

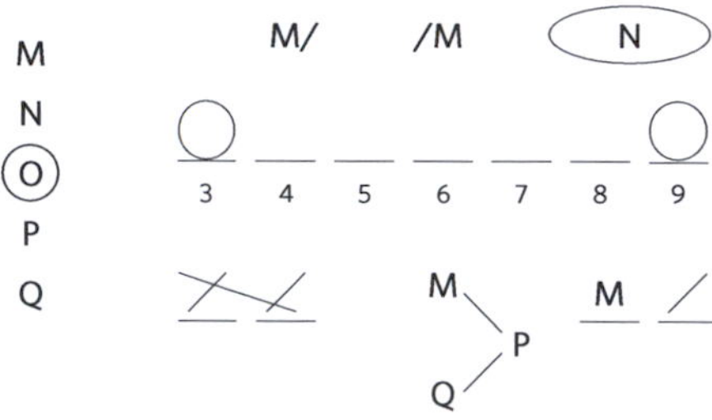

We normally wouldn't mark ordering positions, but since this scenario is somewhat unusual (Mar. to Sept.) it makes sense to do so here. It takes a couple of steps to realize M must go in 4 or 6, so it's likely your paper looks a bit messier. Notice that the empty spots are a big key to this game.

1. If P visits in July, which of the following must be true?
(A) Q visits in March.
(B) Q visits in June.
(C) O visits in March.
(D) O visits in August.
(E) N visits in September.

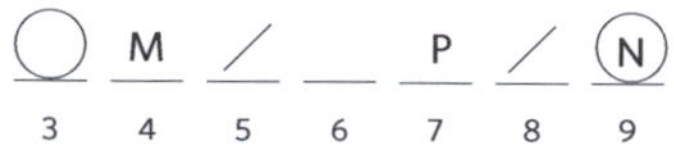

2. If O stays the month after Q but at some point before M, for how many visitors do we know which month they visited?
(A) 1
(B) 2
(C) 3
(D) 4
(E) 5

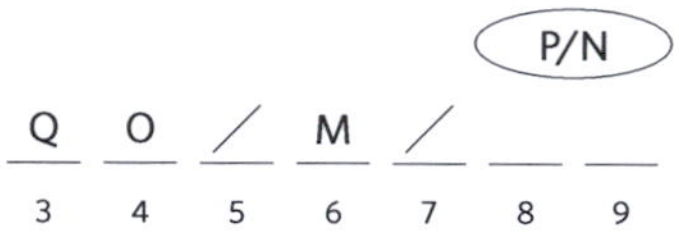

1. If P visits in 7, M must visit in 4. 5 must be empty, so 6 can't be, and the only other place that the other empty spot can be is 8—remember, 3 and 9 must be filled. Therefore, N must be in 9.
2. This condition means M must be in 6, and 7 must be blank. N and P will go in 8 and 9 in either order. The QO chunk must go in 3/4 because 3 can't be left blank.

Eight people—F, G, H, I, J, K, M, and N—participated in four tennis matches that took place one after another. Each match had a winner and a loser. The matches took place in accordance with the following:

K played in the second match.
H and J played each other.
Both I and K won their matches.
F played before H and after G.

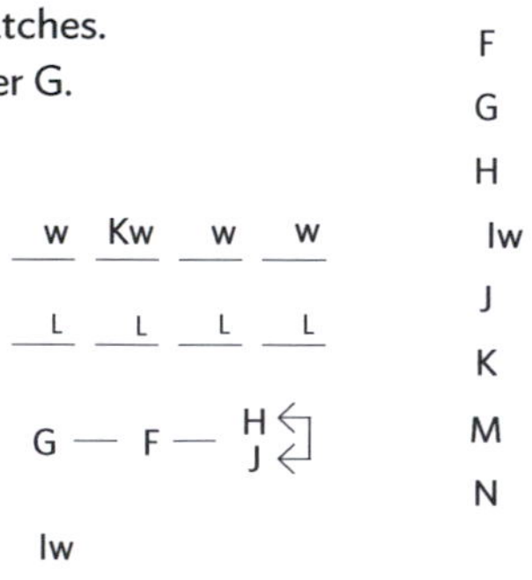

No one aspect of this game is particularly difficult; here the challenge is in keeping track of multiple elements—order, group, and winner versus loser. Laying out a diagram that effectively conveys all of these issues goes a long way toward making these games more manageable.

1. Which of the following could be the full list of winners, in order of the matches they won?
(A) G, K, I, H
(B) G, F, K, I
(C) G, K, F, I
(D) F, K, H, I
(E) G, K, F, H

2. If F is a winner, which of the following must be true?
(A) G plays in the first match.
(B) M plays in the second match.
(C) G loses.
(D) H loses.
(E) J loses.

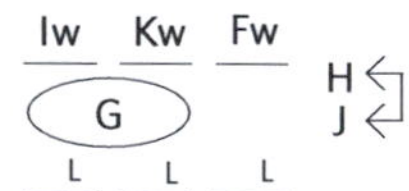

1. If we try out (A), there doesn't seem to be anything wrong with it right off the bat. So we want to prove that the other answers must be false. (B) doesn't have K in position 2. (C) doesn't have a position for H, J. (D) doesn't have a position for G, which we know must go before F. (E) doesn't have I as a winner.
2. F can only go in 2 or 3, and if F is a winner, it must go in 3. That puts H, J in the fourth match, and I into the first as a winner. We know G lost the first or second match.

Set 4 Solutions

A consultant visits five different sites—M, N, O, P, and R—over the course of five days—a different site each day. At some sites she leaves a list of suggestions, and at some sites she doesn't. Additionally, it must be true that:

She leaves suggestions at the second and third sites she visits.
She visits R either first or fourth and leaves a suggestion.
She visits O immediately after she visits a site at which she doesn't leave suggestions.
If she left a suggestion for N, she left a suggestion for M.

M
N Rs/ /Rs
O __ s s __ __ = Rs s s s̸ O
(P) s̸ Os s Rs __
Rs s̸O NⓈ ⟶ MⓈ

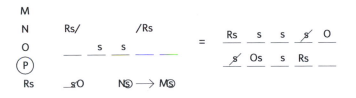

You could have left your diagram as it is on the left, or you could have split it up into two separate diagrams, one with R in the first position, and one with R in the fourth. When R is in 1, we can infer that the only place for O to go is 5, and, when R is in 4, the only place for O to go is 1.

1. If O visits before N, we know we are dealing with the second of the diagrams, which has O in the second position and R in the fourth. In this diagram, N could, per the given condition, go in the third or fifth position. If N is in 3, M, per the last rule, couldn't go in 1 and would have to go in 5, putting P in 1. If N is in 5, either M or P can occupy either 1 or 3. In either case, P cannot be last, and so (E) is the correct answer.

2. Again, with a CBT question, we want to eliminate four answers that must be false. Without two diagrams, (A) is the toughest answer to eliminate, but if P is in 1 and N in 2, that would force R into 4 and O into 5, and that can't be. (B) MBF b/c R can't be in 3. (D) MBF b/c O can't go in 4. (E) MBF b/c O can't go in 4.

1. If she visits O at some point before she visits N, which of the following must be false?
(A) She visited N third.
(B) She visited P third.
(C) She visited M last.
(D) She visited N last.
(E) She visited P last.

2. Which of the following could be true?
(A) P is first and N second.
(B) N is second and R third.
(C) M is third and R fourth.
(D) N is third and O fourth.
(E) O is fourth and N fifth.

A coach will select some of the players trying out for the varsity team, and he will put the rest on the junior varsity team. The eight players trying out are Nick, Otis, Pat, Quinn, Rachel, Sara, Tim, and Wilma. The following conditions apply:

If Nick or Quinn is selected for varsity, Rachel will not be.
Either Sara or Wilma, but not both, will be selected for junior varsity.
Sara and Rachel will be selected for the same team.
If Nick is selected for junior varsity, Otis will be too.
If Tim is selected for junior varsity, Wilma will be selected for varsity.

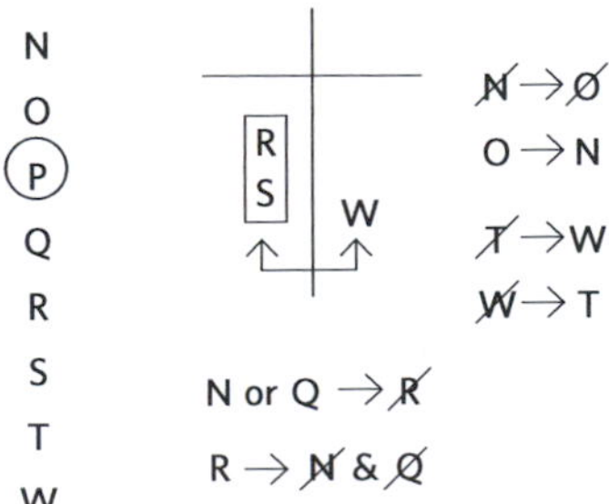

We switched V and JV to yes and no (/) to make the diagram a bit easier to see visually, but that's just an optional step. The link between the second and third rules is probably the most important feature of the game to pay attention to. Note that we don't know of a single person on either team, and that's fine.

1. If Otis is selected for varsity, which of the following could be false?
(A) Nick is selected for varsity.
(B) Wilma is selected for varsity.
(C) Rachel is selected for junior varsity.
(D) Sara is selected for junior varsity.
(E) Tim is selected for junior varsity.

O N W | R S

2. Which of the following can be a pair of players, both of whom are selected for varsity?
(A) N and S
(B) O and W
(C) Q and S
(D) O and R
(E) O and S

1. You can see just how important correct notation and careful work are in a question like this one. O in varsity sets off a chain of inferences illustrated on the T-diagram. O leads to N, which leads to R and S being out, which leads to W being on the team. Notice that (E) could trip you up if you falsely infer from the last rule.

2. Remember that we don't know anyone who is actually selected for either team, so this question is really about how the elements in the answer choices relate to one another. For (A), if N is in, R is out and thus S is out. (A) can't work. With (B) when O is in, R is out, and W is in. So, no problem with O and W being in together. For (C), if Q is in, R is out and S is out. Cut (C). For (D), if O is in, then N is in and R is out. (D) is out. For (E), if O is in, N is in, R is out, and S is out. (E) should be cut, too. This problem really shows the benefit of remembering work done on previous questions—you could have also gotten to (B) much quicker if you happened to remember that situation from question 1.

How Did You Do?

That was a tough set of games, meant to illustrate the benefits of the diagramming systems we've been working on, but also meant to push you and make you think about the next step in your improvement. We started the lesson by discussing the four general parts of the game-solving process; let's revisit them now.

The first step is to see the big picture—many of these games illustrated the advantage of taking a wide view before going into specific rules. On the side of this page are some of the issues I thought were important to notice, right off the bat, for these eight games. If you'd like, you can use the notes to reflect back on your own thought process.

Here are some big-picture issues it would have helped to notice before setting pen to paper.

Set 1
1. The M/Q and R/Q rules are really restrictive and define the game.
2. Not much. Subsets.

Set 2
1. Other rules hinge on last one.
2. Going to be all about #s; G must = 1 and F and H = 2; conditionals link.

Set 3
1. Empty spots and M are keys.
2. Need to organize order, group, and subset. G—F—H link takes up 3 of 4 matches.

Set 4
1. Subsets again! O is very limited.
2. All about linking conditional rules; need to make sure to not confuse rules like the third and fourth for one another. Varsity and junior varsity are easier to think of in terms of yes and no (/).

The next step is to understand the rules and to notate them in such a way that they easily match your understanding and help you see how rules come together. It's not necessary that you notated things the same way that I notated them in the solutions; however, you should take a very careful look at how you notated every rule for every game to pick out moments when your understanding was not quite right, or your notation not as effective as it could have been.

These games also required some key inferences, both in the setup and in the question-solving process—this is consistently true of difficult LSAT games. You don't need to feel you are "perfect" at inferences (I know I'm not). However, you should feel like you are getting better and better.

Finally, it's likely that you solved some questions quickly, and took the longer route for others. Take a minute to reflect on *how* you solved questions. Pay particular attention to how the question stem should have guided your thinking, and also pay attention to the things you spent a lot of time thinking about that ultimately weren't important.

I've left some space below for you to subjectively evaluate your own performance. Be brutally honest, and use this as a gauge of where you are at this point in the study process. Come back to these games and play them again later in your studies to see how you are progressing. It'll be especially satisfying to look back on the challenges you write down once you've mastered these very same games in the near future.

assess & address *Take stock of the things you want to improve on, and the things you want to remind yourself of.*	**I see the big picture**	**I have control over the rules**
	I see inferences	**I use smart approaches to answer questions**

16 LOGICAL REASONING answering questions

Hopefully you found the last six lessons on Logic Games to be useful and perhaps even somewhat fun. Now it's time to get back to Logical Reasoning.

In lessons five through nine, we focused on *the* principal component of your Logical Reasoning skill set: your ability to recognize what is wrong with arguments. In this set of lessons you should see your hard work pay off. But before we go further, let's quickly review some of the big-picture Logical Reasoning issues we've either briefly introduced, or already discussed at length:

- Logical Reasoning questions test both your reading ability and your reasoning ability, in roughly equal parts.
- Two main reading skills are tested: your ability to read for structure, and your ability to understand the meanings of certain words.
- The main reasoning skill tested is your ability to recognize why reasons do not justify a point that is made.
- The final factor that will determine your performance is mental discipline.

In this lesson, we are going to discuss in more depth the specific reading skills required of us, and we will do so as we also discuss general Logical Reasoning strategies. In the lessons to come, we will expand on these strategies and break down specific types of questions.

quick review of lessons five through nine

The skill most important for Logical Reasoning is the ability to recognize what is wrong with an argument. Whenever our job is to be subjective, our primary task is to figure out why the reasons provided are not enough to prove the conclusion reached. Thinking about flaws in terms of these three categories can be extremely helpful for developing effective habits.

a piece ≠ the puzzle overconcludes from limited support	**apples ≠ oranges** falsely equates	**1 + 1 ≠ 3** reaches a conclusion by incorrectly bringing ideas together
Edith has an expensive purse. She must be rich.	**Since Mimi likes Nancy, Nancy must like Mimi.**	**Steve is tall, and he is a good chess player. Therefore, height must somehow help you play chess.**

The Constellation of Questions

Once again, here is a breakdown of the different types of questions that you are likely to see in the Logical Reasoning section, as well as the relationship between them. The numbers represent the total of that question type that you are likely to see in the two Logical Reasoning sections combined.

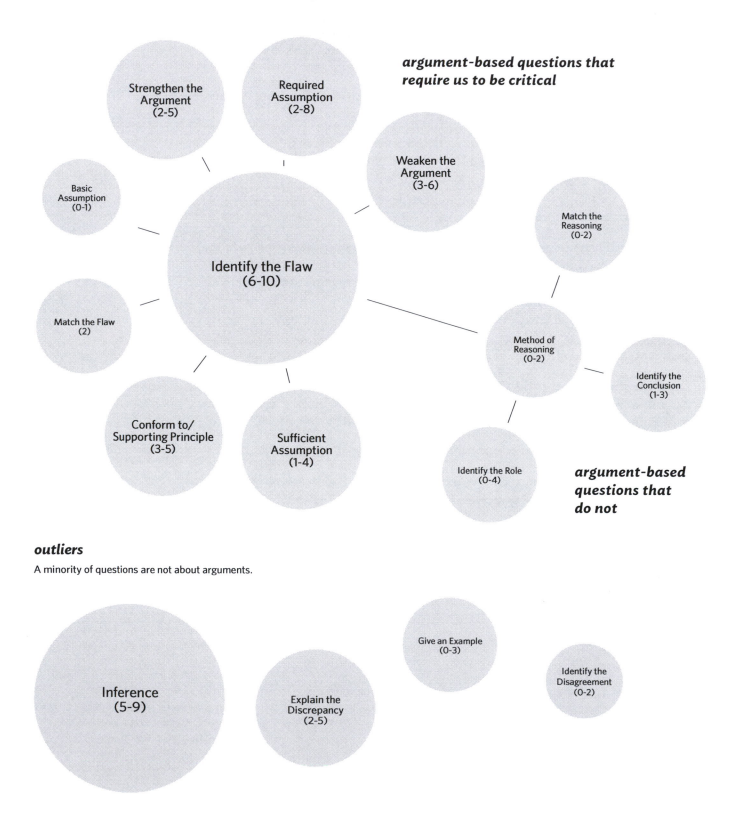

argument-based questions that require us to be critical

Strengthen the Argument (2-5)

Required Assumption (2-8)

Weaken the Argument (3-6)

Basic Assumption (0-1)

Identify the Flaw (6-10)

Match the Flaw (2)

Conform to/ Supporting Principle (3-5)

Sufficient Assumption (1-4)

Match the Reasoning (0-2)

Method of Reasoning (0-2)

Identify the Conclusion (1-3)

Identify the Role (0-4)

argument-based questions that do not

outliers

A minority of questions are not about arguments.

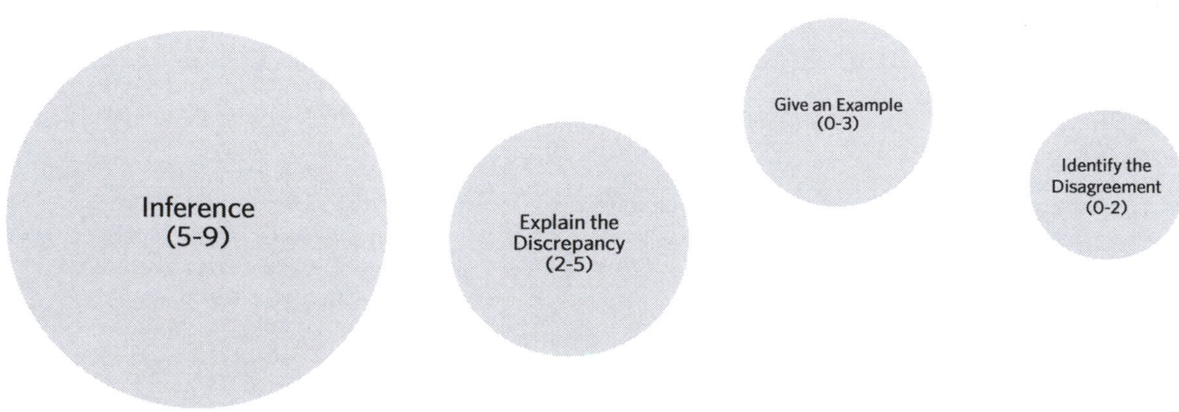

Habits

When we first start studying for the LSAT, it can seem like questions require us to retain a challenging *quantity* of information—so much to keep track of at once, and so disorganized! However, this is a ruse, a **red herring**, and if you don't see it as such, it will block you from becoming truly excellent at Logical Reasoning.

red herring: a false challenge meant to distract you from the real challenge

The test writers don't care about the quantity of information you can retain; they are far more interested in the quality of your understanding. Put simply, your job is to prioritize the important information, and to understand that information very well; trying to keep track of *all* information will hinder you in this effort. In fact, the ability to see the structure of an argument and prioritize certain components is *the* most significant reading skill that is tested. If you are given a long argument, only a few parts of it will be relevant to the question you are being asked. The test writer will give you everything you need to figure out which parts are the important ones, then test you on this understanding, in challenging ways.

An *argument* consists of a main point and reasons given to support that point

You will get better and better at Logical Reasoning as you get better and better at thinking about the right things, at the right times. This will not happen from you wanting it to happen or from you learning something clever. It will happen if you develop the correct habits. Your habits determine what you think about. So let's discuss the critical habits.

Habit 1: Use the Question Stem to Understand Your Task

The first thing we always want to do is to read the question stem to get an understanding of exactly what our job is going to be when we read the argument. We're always going to use the question stem to define our task; during our training, it will help us keep organized the varying approaches that we want to develop for different types of questions.

There are a variety of things a question stem can tell us, and we'll be discussing question stems at length in these upcoming lessons. However, the most important thing that a question stem tells us is whether our job is to read the stimulus objectively or subjectively. Here's why this distinction is so important:

If our job is to be subjective, it's always going to be in the same type of context: our job will be to evaluate arguments—reasons given to justify a point made. In every one of these situations, the reasons given will not justify the point made, and understanding why not is going to be the most important factor in terms of how easy or difficult the question feels for us.

If our job is to be objective, it is absolutely critical that we *not* judge—that we know not to waste time thinking about what is *wrong* with the reasoning, and more importantly we know not to bias ourselves with judgements. When questions ask that we be objective, the "faulty" thinking in the wrong answers is commonly going to prey on our subjectivity.

Subjective versus objective is going to be the critical divide for how we think about and study questions. In this batch of Logical Reasoning lessons, we are going to focus on all the different types of questions that require subjective thinking. These questions are more common and tend to make up a significant majority of the hardest questions in any Logical Reasoning section. In the next batch of Logical Reasoning lessons, we will focus on questions that require an objective read.

Keep in mind that many of the same skills are required for both types of questions. The work you do mastering subjective questions will invariably serve to also make you much stronger at objective questions.

Habit 2: Identify the Conclusion

Once you see that your job is to be critical, the next thing you want to do is figure out exactly what you are supposed to be critical about. And so we always want to look for the point being made.

Expect to read a stimulus multiple times during the course of a question. The first time through the stimulus, of course you want to pay attention to everything, but keep in mind you have one specific job you *must* get done: you have to figure out what the point is. This is not particularly challenging, and this is something you should strive to be able to do accurately, without too much difficulty, for every single question that contains an argument.

When identifying a conclusion, there are two principle criteria:

The conclusion is going to be an opinion of some sort. It may not be worded as such, but if it were a fact, it would not need justification. The conclusion will be something that is debatable and needs to be justified.

The conclusion will have support. You should be able to see that other elements in the argument are meant to compel you to think that a certain statement is true. The statement being supported is the conclusion.[1]

In most instances, the conclusion will be contained within a single clause, or a single sentence. However, for a few questions in each Logical Reasoning section, the test writers will split up the conclusion and challenge you to put the pieces together correctly. They do this in two main ways: by putting a part of the conclusion in some other part of

1. If you are ever unsure about which part of an argument is meant to be the conclusion, and which part the reasoning, the best thing to do is to play out how one part *could* be used to support the other. A great tool for mechanically thinking through this is to stick the word "therefore" in between the two statements. If you try out "A therefore B" and "B therefore A," it can help make it much easier to see which part is meant to be the support, and which part the conclusion.

conclusions in two parts

arguments with split-up conclusions

conclusions with placeholders

Tablets have proved themselves as useful entertainment vehicles, but **they have yet to prove their utility in the workplace**.

Some say **talent** is the key to success; other say it is **hard work**. The truth is, **success requires both of these characteristics**.

rebuttals

Many automotive experts **claim that American car companies will never again develop the best cars in the world**, but they are **wrong.**

The panel concluded that **Mr. Roberts was definitely at fault**, but the **conclusion was unjustified**.

the argument and putting a placeholder—such as a relative pronoun or a statement like "that idea"—in its place, or by having the conclusion be a counter to a different point—an opposing point—presented in the argument.

On the previous page were some examples of conclusions complicated in these ways. In these situations, you want to give yourself some extra time to understand the conclusions correctly. You want to be especially careful to understand "responding" conclusions correctly. In the first of our examples, note that the conclusion is that the original opinion was wrong. In the second, the point is simply that the original conclusion was reached without considering all of the issues. It's left uncertain whether the author actually disagrees with the conclusion, and to over-infer would be a mistake.

Before we move further, let's get in some practice to make sure you feel comfortable identifying conclusions in Logical Reasoning arguments. On the following two pages are twenty arguments—some of them are from official LSAT questions. For each one, your job is simply to identify the conclusion. When the conclusion is presented in multiple parts, mark the multiple parts. When there is an intermediate conclusion, mark that as well.

Here are the conclusions from the opposite page, not split up:

Tablets have yet to prove their utility in the workplace.

Success requires talent and hard work.

American companies will develop the best cars in the world.

The conclusion that Mr. Roberts was at fault is unjustified.

intermediate conclusions

Occasionally—no more frequently than perhaps once per exam—it will be important that you think about an argument in terms of it possibly containing an **intermediate conclusion.** An intermediate conclusion is a conclusion that is used to support another conclusion. Any non-factual support that itself has support is an intermediate conclusion.

Keep in mind, there are plenty of times that we run into intermediate conclusions and don't actually have to think of them as such—in fact, this is the norm.

You typically only have to think about intermediate conclusions in a couple of situations. The first is when there is no, or almost no, gap between the main point and the primary support, coupled with a fairly significant gap between that primary support and the information given that is meant to support it. The second scenario is when you are asked to formally and objectively define the parts of an argument. We'll discuss this second situation further in another lesson. Here are two examples of arguments containing intermediate conclusions, and significant gaps in the reasoning meant to justify those intermediate conclusions.

intermediate conclusion

Ken studies hard SO **he probably does well in school** SO he probably gets good grades.

Josh likes candy SO **he must be overweight** SO he must be out of shape.

Note that in neither case is the intermediate conclusion-to-conclusion relationship ironclad, but in both cases there are more significant jumps from the support to the intermediate conclusion. In general you will only need to look for reasoning issues between support and intermediate conclusion when the gap between intermediate conclusion and conclusion seems small. Also note that this is a surprisingly rare construction for the test writers, and you can go several practice exams without running into an argument with a support-to-intermediate conclusion issue.

Drill: What's the Conclusion?

Directions: Identify and mark the conclusion. When the conclusion is in multiple parts, write it out below.

1. Hospital executive: At a recent conference on nonprofit management, several computer experts maintained that the most significant threat faced by large institutions such as universities and hospitals is unauthorized access to confidential data. In light of this testimony, we should make the protection of our clients' confidentiality our highest priority.

2. When exercising the muscles in one's back, it is important, in order to maintain a healthy back, to exercise the muscles on opposite sides of the spine equally. After all, balanced muscle development is needed to maintain a healthy back, since the muscles on opposite sides of the spine must pull equally in opposing directions to keep the back in proper alignment and protect the spine.

3. You claim that advertising does not play a bigger role in the lives of individuals than it once did. However, twenty years ago the average American was exposed to one thousand advertisements a day. Now that figure is almost ten thousand. Therefore, your claim is false.

4. Gary's wife says he eats too much red meat, but this is simply not true; I eat lunch with him nearly every day, and I never see him eat red meat.

5. The makers of Brand X oatmeal cookies claim that their cookies are healthier than those that are made by our company. They cite the use of natural ingredients and whole grains as two primary factors. However, their cookies have more sugar and salt than do our cookies, and for most Americans both of those ingredients are very unhealthy. Therefore, the makers of Brand X are clearly wrong in their claim.

6. Most societies strive to protect individual freedoms of thought, and most individuals like to think of themselves as independent thinkers. However, nearly everyone is influenced by certain evocative forms of art. Therefore, what people like to think of themselves in this regard is not necessarily correct.

7. Philosopher: An action is morally right if it would be reasonably expected to increase the aggregate well-being of the people affected by it. An action is morally wrong if and only if it would be reasonably expected to reduce the aggregate well-being of the people affected by it. Thus, actions that would be reasonably expected to leave unchanged the aggregate well-being of the people affected by them are also right.

8. Driver: My friends say I will one day have an accident because I drive my sports car recklessly. But I have done some research, and apparently minivans and larger sedans have very low accident rates compared to sports cars. So trading my sports car in for a minivan would lower my risk of having an accident.

9. Serat claims that his new forecasting model is more accurate and useful than that currently used by the majority of the researchers in his field. However, a recent survey of people in his field revealed that fewer than 10 percent of his colleagues agree with him. Therefore, Serat is wrong in his assessment.

10. Commentator: In academic scholarship, sources are always cited and methodology and theoretical assumptions are set out so as to allow critical study, replication, and expansion of scholarship. In open-source software, the code in which the program is written can be viewed and modified by individual users for their purposes without getting permission from the producer or paying a fee. In contrast, the code of proprietary software is kept secret, and modifications can be made only by the producer, for a fee. This shows that open-source software better matches the values embodied in academic scholarship, and since scholarship is central to the mission of universities, universities should use only open-source software.

Drill: What's the Conclusion?

11. We should accept the proposal to demolish the old train station, because the local historical society, which vehemently opposes this, is dominated by people who have no commitment to long-term economic well-being. Preserving old buildings creates an impediment to new development, which is critical to economic health.

12. Of the two hundred students in his class, Thomas is taller than all but three of them. Of the sixty students in Sara's class, all but two are taller than Sara. Since we need someone tall to play the role of "giraffe" in the play, we should call Thomas.

13. All members of Team G have black badges. Only those with black badges are allowed access to the South Wing, which houses the only decompression chamber. Since Teri has access to the wing that houses the decompression chamber, she must be a member of Team G.

14. All Labrador retrievers bark a great deal. All Saint Bernards bark infrequently. Each of Rosa's dogs is a cross between a Labrador retriever and a Saint Bernard. Therefore, Rosa's dogs are moderate barkers.

15. Therapist: Cognitive psychotherapy focuses on changing a patient's conscious beliefs. Thus, cognitive psychotherapy is likely to be more effective at helping patients overcome psychological problems than are forms of psychotherapy that focus on changing unconscious beliefs and desires, since only conscious beliefs are under the patient's direct conscious control.

16. Atrens: An early entomologist observed ants carrying particles to neighboring ant colonies and inferred that the ants were bringing food to their neighbors. Further research, however, revealed that the ants were emptying their own colony's dumping site. Thus, the early entomologist was wrong.

17. When one lives in a rural area, one has an obligation to help others who are in need, if these individuals happen to be stopped on the side of the road. Nina, who lives in a rural area, recently drove past an individual stopped on the side of the road and did nothing to help that individual. Therefore, Nina failed to fulfill this obligation.

18. Senator, you recently stated that national security is your top priority. However, I find this claim to be without merit. Over the past five years, you have steadfastly refused to vote for any bill that increases military spending, and you have stated that your behavior will not change.

19. Although video game sales have increased steadily over the past three years, we can expect a reversal of this trend in the very near future. Historically, over three quarters of video games sold have been purchased by people from thirteen to sixteen years of age, and the number of people in this age group is expected to decline steadily over the next ten years.

20. The government recently made significant emergency loans to certain businesses in order to improve the overall condition of the country's economy. All businesses that received these loans have thus far been successful in improving their economic conditions. Therefore, we can say that the loans have, at least in part, had their desired effect.

What's the Conclusion? Solutions

1. Hospital executive: At a recent conference on nonprofit management, several computer experts maintained that the most significant threat faced by large institutions such as universities and hospitals is unauthorized access to confidential data. In light of this testimony, **we should make the protection of our clients' confidentiality our highest priority**.

2. **When exercising the muscles in one's back, it is important, in order to maintain a healthy back, to exercise the muscles on opposite sides of the spine equally**. After all, balanced muscle development is needed to maintain a healthy back, since the muscles on opposite sides of the spine must pull equally in opposing directions to keep the back in proper alignment and protect the spine.

3. **You claim that advertising does not play a bigger role in the lives of individuals than it once did**. However, twenty years ago the average American was exposed to one thousand advertisements a day. Now that figure is almost ten thousand. Therefore, **your claim is false**.

Advertising does play a bigger role in the lives of individuals than it once did.

4. Gary's wife says **he eats too much red meat,** but **this is simply not true**; I eat lunch with him nearly every day, and I never see him eat red meat.

Gary does not eat too much red meat.

5. The makers of Brand X oatmeal cookies **claim that their cookies are healthier than those that are made by our company**. They cite the use of natural ingredients and whole grains as two primary factors. However, their cookies have more sugar and salt than do our cookies, and for most Americans both of those ingredients are very unhealthy. Therefore, **the makers of Brand X are clearly wrong in their claim**.

Brand X's claim that their cookies are healthier is wrong.

6. Most societies strive to protect individual freedoms of thought, and **most individuals like to think of themselves as independent thinkers**. However, nearly everyone is influenced by certain evocative forms of art. Therefore, **what people like to think of themselves in this regard is not necessarily correct**.

It may not be correct that we are independent thinkers.

7. Philosopher: An action is morally right if it would be reasonably expected to increase the aggregate well-being of the people affected by it. An action is morally wrong if and only if it would be reasonably expected to reduce the aggregate well-being of the people affected by it. Thus, **actions that would be reasonably expected to leave unchanged the aggregate well-being of the people affected by them are also right.**

8. Driver: My friends say I will one day have an accident because I drive my sports car recklessly. But I have done some research, and apparently minivans and larger sedans have very low accident rates compared to sports cars. So **trading my sports car in for a minivan would lower my risk of having an accident.**

9. Serat claims that **his new forecasting model is more accurate and useful than that currently used by the majority of the researchers in his field**. However, a recent survey of people in his field revealed that fewer than 10 percent of his colleagues agree with him. Therefore, **Serat is wrong in his assessment**.

Serat's new forecasting model is not more accurate and useful than that currently used by the majority of researchers in his field. (Note that "not more accurate" ≠ "less accurate.")

10. Commentator: In academic scholarship, sources are always cited and methodology and theoretical assumptions are set out so as to allow critical study, replication, and expansion of scholarship. In open-source software, the code in which the program is written can be viewed and modified by individual users for their purposes without getting permission from the producer or paying a fee. In contrast, the code of proprietary software is kept secret, and modifications can be made only by the producer, for a fee. This shows that open-source software better matches the values embodied in academic scholarship, and since scholarship is central to the mission of universities, **universities should use only open-source software**.

What's the Conclusion? Solutions

11. **We should accept the proposal to demolish the old train station,** because the local historical society, which vehemently opposes this, is dominated by people who have no commitment to long-term economic well-being. Preserving old buildings creates an impediment to new development, which is critical to economic health.

12. Of the two hundred students in his class, Thomas is taller than all but three of them. Of the sixty students in Sara's class, all but two are taller than Sara. Since we need someone tall to play the role of "giraffe" in the play, **we should call Thomas**.

13. All members of Team G have black badges. Only those with black badges are allowed access to the South Wing, which houses the only decompression chamber. Since **Teri** has access to the wing that houses the decompression chamber, **she must be a member of Team G**.

Teri must be a member of Team G.

14. All Labrador retrievers bark a great deal. All Saint Bernards bark infrequently. Each of Rosa's dogs is a cross between a Labrador retriever and a Saint Bernard. Therefore, **Rosa's dogs are moderate barkers**.

15. Therapist: Cognitive psychotherapy focuses on changing a patient's conscious beliefs. Thus, **cognitive psychotherapy is likely to be more effective at helping patients overcome psychological problems than are forms of psychotherapy that focus on changing unconscious beliefs and desires,** since only conscious beliefs are under the patient's direct conscious control.

16. Atrens: An early entomologist observed ants carrying particles to neighboring ant colonies and inferred that the **ants were bringing food to their neighbors**. Further research, however, revealed that the ants were emptying their own colony's dumping site. Thus, **the early entomologist was wrong**.

The ants are not bringing food to their neighbors.

17. When one lives in a rural area, **one has an obligation to help others who are in need**, if these individuals happen to be stopped on the side of the road. Nina, who lives in a rural area, recently drove past an individual stopped on the side of the road and did nothing to help that individual. Therefore, **Nina failed to fulfill this obligation.**

Nina failed to fulfill her obligation to help others in need.

18. Senator, you recently stated that **national security is your top priority**. However, **I find this claim to be without merit**. Over the past five years, you have steadfastly refused to vote for any bill that increases military spending, and you have stated that your behavior will not change.

The senator's claim that national security is his top priority lacks merit.

19. Although **video game sales have increased steadily over the past three years, we can expect a reversal of this trend in the very near future**. Historically, over three quarters of video games sold have been purchased by people from thirteen to sixteen years of age, and the number of people in this age group is expected to decline steadily over the next ten years.

"Reversal" is a bit vague—at the least. The conclusion is that video game sales will stop increasing in the very near future.

20. The government recently made significant emergency loans to certain businesses in order to improve the overall condition of the country's economy. All businesses that received these loans have thus far been successful in improving their economic conditions. Therefore, we can say that **the loans have, at least in part, had their desired effect.**

Habit 3: Find the Support

Once you have the conclusion, your next job is to think about how it is being supported. As we've discussed, LSAT arguments do not, in general, have multi-faceted reasoning issues—the author usually tries to justify his point with just a singular line of reasoning. This reasoning may come to us in one sentence, it may be spread out in a couple of sentences, or it may be all jumbled together with the background information. When the support is spread out, the best way to organize it and bring it together in your head is to think about how the support, as a whole, is meant to justify the point—how the support comes together to form "one" reason for the point. Students run into trouble when they fail to differentiate the support from the other information, and just as commonly, when they choose to, without reason or need, focus on specific portions of the support, rather than thinking about how it works together.

Habit 4: Figure Out What's Wrong

Once you have isolated the support and the reasoning, you can get on with the main task at hand: figuring out what is wrong with how the support justifies the conclusion. We won't spend too much time discussing this here as we've already discussed it in depth elsewhere, but do know that it is expected that by this point you are "naturally," without too much conscious effort, focused on why reasons don't justify a point. It's certainly not expected that you are perfect at figuring out what's wrong, but the habit of looking for the flaw needs to be there for you to get better and better, and it is expected that you've laid this habit down and that it's a foundational part of how you solve questions. If not, you may want to review Lessons 5 – 9 again before moving further.

Habits 5 and 6: Eliminate Wrong Answers and Confirm the Right Answer

We also won't spend much time in this lesson discussing these final two steps, for these are steps that are in certain ways specific to the particular questions that are being asked. We'll discuss these steps as we discuss each type of question, then come back to them and summarize after we get a few question types under our belt.

In general, you want to develop a habit of going through answer choices in two rounds. The first time around, you want to look for reasons to eliminate answers, and the second time around you want to look for reasons to confirm what remains.

On the next few pages are drills that build upon what we've already started. What we're going to do is take the same arguments we used for the conclusion drill and use them to work on identifying the support. Then we'll isolate the support-conclusion relationship (the argument) and practice figuring out what's wrong. Finally, we'll end the lesson by having you solve ten LSAT questions, questions that will then be used as part of the instruction in Lessons 17 – 20.

Use these drills both to refresh yourself on the work we've already done, and to gauge where your focus should be for this batch of lessons. If you feel 80 percent or 90 percent confident about your ability to identify a conclusion or the support, make that a priority as you go through your work, and make it a goal to achieve total mastery of those skills by the time we're done with this set of five Logical Reasoning lessons.

Drill: What's the Support?

Directions: Identify and mark the support. When the support is difficult to notate, write it out below.

1. Hospital executive: At a recent conference on nonprofit management, several computer experts maintained that the most significant threat faced by large institutions such as universities and hospitals is unauthorized access to confidential data. In light of this testimony, **we should make the protection of our clients' confidentiality our highest priority**.

2. **When exercising the muscles in one's back, it is important, in order to maintain a healthy back, to exercise the muscles on opposite sides of the spine equally**. After all, balanced muscle development is needed to maintain a healthy back, since the muscles on opposite sides of the spine must pull equally in opposing directions to keep the back in proper alignment and protect the spine.

3. **You claim that advertising does not play a bigger role in the lives of individuals than it once did**. However, twenty years ago the average American was exposed to one thousand advertisements a day. Now that figure is almost ten thousand. Therefore, **your claim is false**.

4. Gary's wife says **he eats too much red meat,** but **this is simply not true**; I eat lunch with him nearly every day, and I never see him eat red meat.

5. The makers of Brand X oatmeal cookies **claim that their cookies are healthier than those that are made by our company**. They cite the use of natural ingredients and whole grains as two primary factors. However, their cookies have more sugar and salt than do our cookies, and for most Americans both of those ingredients are very unhealthy. Therefore, **the makers of Brand X are clearly wrong in their claim**.

6. Most societies strive to protect individual freedoms of thought, and **most individuals like to think of themselves as independent thinkers**. However, nearly everyone is influenced by certain evocative forms of art. Therefore, **what people like to think of themselves in this regard is not necessarily correct**.

7. Philosopher: An action is morally right if it would be reasonably expected to increase the aggregate well-being of the people affected by it. An action is morally wrong if and only if it would be reasonably expected to reduce the aggregate well-being of the people affected by it. Thus, **actions that would be reasonably expected to leave unchanged the aggregate well-being of the people affected by them are also right.**

8. Driver: My friends say I will one day have an accident because I drive my sports car recklessly. But I have done some research, and apparently minivans and larger sedans have very low accident rates compared to sports cars. So **trading my sports car in for a minivan would lower my risk of having an accident.**

9. Serat claims that **his new forecasting model is more accurate and useful than that currently used by the majority of the researchers in his field**. However, a recent survey of people in his field revealed that fewer than 10 percent of his colleagues agree with him. Therefore, **Serat is wrong in his assessment**.

10. Commentator: In academic scholarship, sources are always cited and methodology and theoretical assumptions are set out so as to allow critical study, replication, and expansion of scholarship. In open-source software, the code in which the program is written can be viewed and modified by individual users for their purposes without getting permission from the producer or paying a fee. In contrast, the code of proprietary software is kept secret, and modifications can be made only by the producer, for a fee. This shows that open-source software better matches the values embodied in academic scholarship, and since scholarship is central to the mission of universities, **universities should use only open-source software**.

Drill: What's the Support?

11. **We should accept the proposal to demolish the old train station,** because the local historical society, which vehemently opposes this, is dominated by people who have no commitment to long-term economic well-being. Preserving old buildings creates an impediment to new development, which is critical to economic health.

12. Of the two hundred students in his class, Thomas is taller than all but three of them. Of the sixty students in Sara's class, all but two are taller than Sara. Since we need someone tall to play the role of "giraffe" in the play, **we should call Thomas**.

13. All members of Team G have black badges. Only those with black badges are allowed access to the South Wing, which houses the only decompression chamber. Since **Teri** has access to the wing that houses the decompression chamber, **she must be a member of Team G**.

14. All Labrador retrievers bark a great deal. All Saint Bernards bark infrequently. Each of Rosa's dogs is a cross between a Labrador retriever and a Saint Bernard. Therefore, **Rosa's dogs are moderate barkers**.

15. Therapist: Cognitive psychotherapy focuses on changing a patient's conscious beliefs. Thus, **cognitive psychotherapy is likely to be more effective at helping patients overcome psychological problems than are forms of psychotherapy that focus on changing unconscious beliefs and desires**, since only conscious beliefs are under the patient's direct conscious control.

16. Atrens: An early entomologist observed ants carrying particles to neighboring ant colonies and inferred that the **ants were bringing food to their neighbors**. Further research, however, revealed that the ants were emptying their own colony's dumping site. Thus, **the early entomologist was wrong**.

17. When one lives in a rural area, **one has an obligation to help others who are in need**, if these individuals happen to be stopped on the side of the road. Nina, who lives in a rural area, recently drove past an individual stopped on the side of the road and did nothing to help that individual. Therefore, **Nina failed to fulfill this obligation.**

18. Senator, you recently stated that **national security is your top priority**. However, **I find this claim to be without merit**. Over the past five years, you have steadfastly refused to vote for any bill that increases military spending, and you have stated that your behavior will not change.

The senator's claim that national security is his top priority lacks merit.

19. Although **video game sales have increased steadily over the past three years, we can expect a reversal of this trend in the very near future**. Historically, over three quarters of video games sold have been purchased by people from thirteen to sixteen years of age, and the number of people in this age group is expected to decline steadily over the next ten years.

20. The government recently made significant emergency loans to certain businesses **in order to improve the overall condition of the country's economy.** All businesses that received these loans have thus far been successful in improving their economic conditions. Therefore, we can say that **the loans have, at least in part, had their desired effect.**

The loans have at least in part improved the overall condition of the country's economy.

What's the Support? Solutions

1. Hospital executive: At a recent conference on nonprofit management, **several computer experts maintained that the most significant threat faced by large institutions such as universities and hospitals is unauthorized access to confidential data**. In light of this testimony, we should make the protection of our clients' confidentiality our highest priority.

2. When exercising the muscles in one's back, it is important, in order to maintain a healthy back, to exercise the muscles on opposite sides of the spine equally. **After all, balanced muscle development is needed to maintain a healthy back**, since the muscles on opposite sides of the spine must pull equally in opposing directions to keep the back in proper alignment and protect the spine.

(Note that you could choose to mark the part that follows "since" as well.)

3. You claim that advertising does not play a bigger role in the lives of individuals than it once did. However, **twenty years ago the average American was exposed to one thousand advertisements a day. Now that figure is almost ten thousand.** Therefore, your claim is false.

4. Gary's wife says he eats too much red meat, but this is simply not true; **I eat lunch with him nearly every day, and I never see him eat red meat.**

5. The makers of Brand X oatmeal cookies claim that their cookies are healthier than those that are made by our company. They cite the use of natural ingredients and whole grains as two primary factors. **However, their cookies have more sugar and salt than do our cookies, and for most Americans both of those ingredients are very unhealthy.** Therefore, the makers of Brand X are clearly wrong in their claim.

6. Most societies strive to protect individual freedoms of thought, and most individuals like to think of themselves as independent thinkers. **However, nearly everyone is influenced by certain evocative forms of art.** Therefore, what people like to think of themselves in this regard is not necessarily correct.

7. Philosopher: An action is morally right if it would be reasonably expected to increase the aggregate well-being of the people affected by it. **An action is morally wrong if and only if it would be reasonably expected to reduce the aggregate well-being of the people affected by it.** Thus, actions that would be reasonably expected to leave unchanged the aggregate well-being of the people affected by them are also right.

(Note that you could choose to mark the part about an action being morally right as well.)

8. Driver: My friends say I will one day have an accident because I drive my sports car recklessly. But I have done some research, and **apparently minivans and larger sedans have very low accident rates compared to sports cars.** So trading my sports car in for a minivan would lower my risk of having an accident.

9. Serat claims that his new forecasting model is more accurate and useful than that currently used by the majority of the researchers in his field. However, **a recent survey of people in his field revealed that fewer than 10 percent of his colleagues agree with him.** Therefore, Serat is wrong in his assessment.

10. Commentator: In academic scholarship, sources are always cited and methodology and theoretical assumptions are set out so as to allow critical study, replication, and expansion of scholarship. In open-source software, the code in which the program is written can be viewed and modified by individual users for their purposes without getting permission from the producer or paying a fee. In contrast, the code of proprietary software is kept secret, and modifications can be made only by the producer, for a fee. **This shows that open-source software better matches the values embodied in academic scholarship, and since scholarship is central to the mission of universities**, universities should use only open-source software.

What's the Support? Solutions

11. We should accept the proposal to demolish the old train station, because **the local historical society, which vehemently opposes this, is dominated by people who have no commitment to long-term economic well-being.** Preserving old buildings creates an impediment to new development, which is critical to economic health.

(Note that "because" is what makes the first part of the support more significant to the reasoning than the last sentence.)

12. **Of the two hundred students in his class, Thomas is taller than all but three of them. Of the sixty students in Sara's class, all but two are taller than Sara. Since we need someone tall to play the role of "giraffe" in the play**, we should call Thomas.

13. **All members of Team G have black badges. Only those with black badges are allowed access to the South Wing, which houses the only decompression chamber. Since Teri has access to the wing that houses the decompression chamber**, she must be a member of Team G.

14. **All Labrador retrievers bark a great deal. All Saint Bernards bark infrequently. Each of Rosa's dogs is a cross between a Labrador retriever and a Saint Bernard.** Therefore, Rosa's dogs are moderate barkers.

15. Therapist: **Cognitive psychotherapy focuses on changing a patient's conscious beliefs**. Thus, cognitive psychotherapy is likely to be more effective at helping patients overcome psychological problems than are forms of psychotherapy that focus on changing unconscious beliefs and desires, since **only conscious beliefs are under the patient's direct conscious control**.

(In this case we need the first bolded part to understand how the second is relevant to the conclusion.)

16. Atrens: An early entomologist observed ants carrying particles to neighboring ant colonies and inferred that the ants were bringing food to their neighbors. **Further research, however, revealed that the ants were emptying their own colony's dumping site.** Thus, the early entomologist was wrong.

17. When one lives in a rural area, one has an obligation to help others who are in need, if these individuals happen to be stopped on the side of the road. **Nina, who lives in a rural area, recently drove past an individual stopped on the side of the road and did nothing to help that individual.** Therefore, Nina failed to fulfill this obligation.

18. Senator, you recently stated that national security is your top priority. However, I find this claim to be without merit. **Over the past five years, you have steadfastly refused to vote for any bill that increases military spending, and you have stated that your behavior will not change.**

19. Although video game sales have increased steadily over the past three years, we can expect a reversal of this trend in the very near future. **Historically, over three quarters of video games sold have been purchased by people from thirteen to sixteen years of age, and the number of people in this age group is expected to decline steadily over the next ten years**.

20. The government recently made significant emergency loans to certain businesses in order to improve the overall condition of the country's economy. **All businesses that received these loans have thus far been successful in improving their economic conditions.** Therefore, we can say that the loans have, at least in part, had their desired effect.

Drill: What's Wrong?

Directions: Each argument has been stripped down. Identify what is wrong, and for extra credit, write down a potential counter-example.

1. Point: We should make protection of our clients' confidentiality our highest priority.
Why?: Computer experts said the most significant threat faced by large institutions like us is unauthorized access to confidential data.
What's Wrong?

2. Point: When exercising back, important to exercise muscles on each side equally.
Why?: Balanced muscle development needed to maintain a healthy back.
What's Wrong?

3. Point: Advertising plays a bigger role in lives than it once did.
Why?: We are exposed to a lot more advertisements than we used to be.
What's Wrong?

4. Point: Gary does not eat too much red meat.
Why? I eat lunch with him nearly every day, and I never see him eat red meat.
What's Wrong?

5. Point: Brand X cookies are not healthier than ours.
Why?: They have more sugar and salt, which are both unhealthy.
What's Wrong?

6. Point: People are not necessarily independent thinkers.
Why?: Nearly all of us are influenced by evocative forms of art.
What's Wrong?

7. Point: Actions that leave unchanged general well-being are right.
Why?: Actions are wrong only if they reduce general well-being.
What's Wrong?

8. Point: Trading in my sports car for a minivan will lower risk of having accident.
Why?: Minivans have lower accident rates.
What's Wrong?

9. Point: Serat's new forecasting model is not more accurate and useful.
Why?: Fewer than 10 percent of people in his field think it is.
What's Wrong?

10. Point: Universities should only use open-source software.
Why?: Open-source software better matches values of academic scholarship, which is central to mission of universities.
What's Wrong?

11. Point: We should accept proposal to demolish the old train station.
Why?: A group opposing it is dominated by people with no commitment to long-term economic well-being.
What's Wrong?

12. Point: We should call Thomas.
Why?: We need someone tall. Thomas is one of the tallest in his class, and Sara is one of the shortest in hers.
What's Wrong?

13. Point: Teri must be a member of Team G.
Why?: Member of Team G → black badge. If allowed access → black badge. Teri is allowed access.
What's Wrong?

14. Point: Rosa's dogs are moderate barkers.
Why?: Dogs are half Lab (barks a lot) half Saint Bernard (barks a little).
What's Wrong?

15. Point: Cognitive psychotherapy likely more effective than forms focused on changing unconscious beliefs and desires.
Why?: Cognitive psychotherapy focuses on changing conscious beliefs, which are the only things under a patient's direct conscious control.
What's Wrong?

16. Point: Ants not bringing food to neighbors.
Why?: Ants emptying their own trash.
What's Wrong?

17. Point: Nina failed in her obligation to help someone in need.
Why?: She drove past someone stopped on the side of the road.
What's Wrong?

18. Point: Senator's claim that national security is his top priority is without merit.
Why?: The senator will not vote for increasing military spending.
What's Wrong?

19. Point: Video game sales will stop increasing in the near future.
Why?: The age demographic that has traditionally bought the most games is shrinking.
What's Wrong?

20. Point: The loans have had some positive impact in improving country's overall economy.
Why?: They have helped the businesses that received the loans.
What's Wrong?

What's Wrong? Solutions

1. Point: We should make protection of our clients' confidentiality our highest priority.
Why?: Computer experts said the most significant threat faced by large institutions like us is unauthorized access to confidential data.
What's Wrong? Takes for granted that we should do what the computer experts say. Perhaps the computer experts are biased and don't have an understanding of other, more important parts of the business.

2. Point: When exercising back, important to exercise muscles on each side equally.
Why?: Balanced muscle development needed to maintain a healthy back.
What's Wrong? Takes for granted exercising each side equally leads to balanced muscle development. Maybe one side (depending on left/right handedness) requires less work to develop.

3. Point: Advertising plays a bigger role in lives than it once did.
Why?: We are exposed to a lot more advertisements than we used to be.
What's Wrong? Takes for granted that more exposure = bigger role. Maybe we've learned to pay less attention.

4. Point: Gary does not eat too much red meat.
Why? I eat lunch with him nearly every day, and I never see him eat red meat.
What's Wrong? Fails to consider that he may be eating the red meat at other parts of the day. Maybe Gary eats a steak every night.

5. Point: Brand X cookies are not healthier than ours.
Why?: They have more sugar and salt, which are both unhealthy.
What's Wrong? Fails to consider other aspects that contribute to overall healthiness. Maybe they are more healthy for a variety of other reasons, such as that our cookies have saturated fats in them.

6. Point: People are not necessarily independent thinkers.
Why?: Nearly all of us are influenced by evocative forms of art.
What's Wrong? Fails to consider that one can be influenced, but also think independently. For example, you can be influenced by the wisdom in your parents' advice but make your own decisions.

7. Point: Actions that leave unchanged general well-being are right.
Why?: Actions are wrong only if they reduce general well-being.
What's Wrong? Fails to consider that there is a middle ground between right and wrong.

8. Point: Trading in my sports car for a minivan will lower risk of having accident.
Why?: Minivans have lower accident rates.
What's Wrong? Mistakes correlation for causation. Perhaps minivans have lower rates because the people who drive them are safer drivers.

9. Point: Serat's new forecasting model is not more accurate and useful.
Why?: Fewer than 10 percent of people in his field think it is.
What's Wrong? Takes for granted that these opinions are correct. Maybe the people in his field are all wrong and reluctant to change.

10. Point: Universities should only use open-source software.
Why?: Open-source software better matches values of academic scholarship, which is central to mission of universities.
What's Wrong? Takes for granted that a product that best matches values is the best selection. Maybe there are more important reasons, such as quality, to pick proprietary software.

11. Point: We should accept proposal to demolish the old train station.
Why?: A group opposing it is dominated by people with no commitment to long-term economic well-being.
What's Wrong? Who cares about the opinions of the opposing group? Maybe there are other reasons not to accept the proposal.

12. Point: We should call Thomas.
Why?: We need someone tall. Thomas is one of the tallest in his class, and Sara is one of the shortest in hers.
What's Wrong? Fails to consider that Thomas and Sara might be coming from different contexts. Maybe Thomas is in first grade, and Sara in twelfth.

13. Point: Teri must be a member of Team G.
Why?: Member of Team G → black badge. If allowed access → black badge. Teri is allowed access.
What's Wrong? Fails to consider that others could have black badges Maybe members of Team H also get black badges.

14. Point: Rosa's dogs are moderate barkers.
Why?: The dogs are half Lab (barks a lot) half Saint Bernard (barks a little).
What's Wrong? Takes for granted that a cross must have an even mix of characteristics. You are not exactly the average of your parents' characteristics.

15. Point: Cognitive psychotherapy likely more effective than forms focused on changing unconscious beliefs and desires.
Why?: Cognitive psychotherapy focuses on changing conscious beliefs, which are the only things under a patient's direct conscious control.
What's Wrong? Takes for granted that what is under the patient's direct conscious control will be more effective.

16. Point: Ants not bringing food to neighbors.
Why?: Ants emptying their own trash.
What's Wrong? Takes for granted that because something is trash, it cannot be food. (Most ants are not as proper as most people are.)

17. Point: Nina failed in her obligation to help someone in need.
Why?: She drove past someone stopped on the side of the road.
What's Wrong? Fails to consider that the person may not have needed help. Perhaps the person was picking flowers.

18. Point: Senator's claim that national security is his top priority is without merit.
Why?: The senator will not vote for increasing military spending.
What's Wrong? Takes for granted that increasing military spending and prioritizing national security are congruent. Maybe building bombs is not the best way to be safe.

19. Point: Video game sales will stop increasing in the near future.
Why?: The age demographic that has traditionally bought the most games is shrinking.
What's Wrong? Takes for granted that the age demographic of users is static. Maybe more people will continue to play games into adulthood than in the past.

20. Point: The loans have had some positive impact in improving country's overall economy.
Why?: They have helped the businesses that received the loans.
What's Wrong? Takes for granted that the improvement of these businesses has improved the overall economic condition. Perhaps these companies have improved at the expense of consumers, who are forced to buy items at an unfair price.

Problem Set

Directions: Go ahead and solve these ten questions to the best of your ability. You will recognize the arguments from our previous exercises. We'll discuss these questions over the next few lessons. All questions are from the June '07 exam.

2.2. All Labrador retrievers bark a great deal. All Saint Bernards bark infrequently. Each of Rosa's dogs is a cross between a Labrador retriever and a Saint Bernard. Therefore, Rosa's dogs are moderate barkers.

Which one of the following uses flawed reasoning that most closely resembles the flawed reasoning used in the argument above?

(A) All students who study diligently make good grades. But some students who do not study diligently also make good grades. Jane studies somewhat diligently. Therefore, Jane makes somewhat good grades.
(B) All type A chemicals are extremely toxic to human beings. All type B chemicals are nontoxic to human beings. This household cleaner is a mixture of a type A chemical and a type B chemical. Therefore, this household cleaner is moderately toxic.
(C) All students at Hanson School live in Green County. All students at Edwards School live in Winn County. Members of the Perry family attend both Hanson and Edwards. Therefore, some members of the Perry family live in Green County and some live in Winn County.
(D) All transcriptionists know shorthand. All engineers know calculus. Bob has worked both as a transcriptionist and as an engineer. Therefore, Bob knows both shorthand and calculus.
(E) All of Kenisha's dresses are very well made. All of Connie's dresses are very badly made. Half of the dresses in this closet are very well made, and half of them are very badly made. Therefore, half of the dresses in this closet are Kenisha's and half of them are Connie's.

2.9. Although video game sales have increased steadily over the past 3 years, we can expect a reversal of this trend in the very near future. Historically, over three quarters of video games sold have been purchased by people from 13 to 16 years of age, and the number of people in this age group is expected to decline steadily over the next 10 years.

Which one of the following, if true, would most seriously weaken the argument?

(A) Most people 17 years old or older have never purchased a video game.
(B) Video game rentals have declined over the past 3 years.
(C) New technology will undoubtedly make entirely new entertainment options available over the next 10 years.
(D) The number of different types of video games available is unlikely to decrease in the near future.
(E) Most of the people who have purchased video games over the past 3 years are over the age of 16.

2.17. Hospital executive: At a recent conference on nonprofit management, several computer experts maintained that the most significant threat faced by large institutions such as universities and hospitals is unauthorized access to confidential data. In light of this testimony, we should make the protection of our clients' confidentiality our highest priority.

The hospital executive's argument is most vulnerable to which one of the following objections?

(A) The argument confuses the causes of a problem with the appropriate solutions to that problem.
(B) The argument relies on the testimony of experts whose expertise is not shown to be sufficiently broad to support their general claim.
(C) The argument assumes that a correlation between two phenomena is evidence that one is the cause of the other.
(D) The argument draws a general conclusion about a group based on data about an unrepresentative sample of that group.
(E) The argument infers that a property belonging to large institutions belongs to all institutions.

2.21. Driver: My friends say I will one day have an accident because I drive my sports car recklessly. But I have done some research, and apparently minivans and larger sedans have very low accident rates compared to sports cars. So trading my sports car in for a minivan would lower my risk of having an accident.

The reasoning in the driver's argument is most vulnerable to criticism on the grounds that this argument

(A) infers a cause from a mere correlation
(B) relies on a sample that is too narrow
(C) misinterprets evidence that a result is likely as evidence that the result is certain
(D) mistakes a condition sufficient for bringing about a result for a condition necessary for doing so
(E) relies on a source that is probably not well-informed

All questions are from the June '07 exam.

2.23. Philosopher: An action is morally right if it would be reasonably expected to increase the aggregate well-being of the people affected by it. An action is morally wrong if and only if it would be reasonably expected to reduce the aggregate well-being of the people affected by it. Thus, actions that would be reasonably expected to leave unchanged the aggregate well-being of the people affected by them are also right.

The philosopher's conclusion follows logically if which one of the following is assumed?

(A) Only wrong actions would be reasonably expected to reduce the aggregate well-being of the people affected by them.
(B) No action is both right and wrong.
(C) Any action that is not morally wrong is morally right.
(D) There are actions that would be reasonably expected to leave unchanged the aggregate well-being of the people affected by them.
(E) Only right actions have good consequences.

3.5. Atrens: An early entomologist observed ants carrying particles to neighboring ant colonies and inferred that the ants were bringing food to their neighbors. Further research, however, revealed that the ants were emptying their own colony's dumping site. Thus, the early entomologist was wrong.

Atrens's conclusion follows logically if which one of the following is assumed?

(A) Ant societies do not interact in all the same ways that human societies interact.
(B) There is only weak evidence for the view that ants have the capacity to make use of objects as gifts.
(C) Ant dumping sites do not contain particles that could be used as food.
(D) The ants to whom the particles were brought never carried the particles into their own colonies.
(E) The entomologist cited retracted his conclusion when it was determined that the particles the ants carried came from their dumping site.

3.13. Therapist: Cognitive psychotherapy focuses on changing a patient's conscious beliefs. Thus, cognitive psychotherapy is likely to be more effective at helping patients overcome psychological problems than are forms of psychotherapy that focus on changing unconscious beliefs and desires, since only conscious beliefs are under the patient's direct conscious control.

Which one of the following, if true, would most strengthen the therapist's argument?

(A) Psychological problems are frequently caused by unconscious beliefs that could be changed with the aid of psychotherapy.
(B) It is difficult for any form of psychotherapy to be effective without focusing on mental states that are under the patient's direct conscious control.
(C) Cognitive psychotherapy is the only form of psychotherapy that focuses primarily on changing the patient's conscious beliefs.
(D) No form of psychotherapy that focuses on changing the patient's unconscious beliefs and desires can be effective unless it also helps change beliefs that are under the patient's direct conscious control.
(E) All of a patient's conscious beliefs are under the patient's conscious control, but other psychological states cannot be controlled effectively without the aid of psychotherapy.

Problem Set (Continued)

All questions are from the June '07 exam.

3.14. Commentator: In academic scholarship, sources are always cited, and methodology and theoretical assumptions are set out, so as to allow critical study, replication, and expansion of scholarship. In open-source software, the code in which the program is written can be viewed and modified by individual users for their purposes without getting permission from the producer or paying a fee. In contrast, the code of proprietary software is kept secret, and modifications can be made only by the producer, for a fee. This shows that open-source software better matches the values embodied in academic scholarship, and since scholarship is central to the mission of universities, universities should use only open-source software.

The commentator's reasoning most closely conforms to which one of the following principles?

(A) Whatever software tools are most advanced and can achieve the goals of academic scholarship are the ones that should alone be used in universities.
(B) Universities should use the type of software technology that is least expensive, as long as that type of software technology is adequate for the purposes of academic scholarship.
(C) Universities should choose the type of software technology that best matches the values embodied in the activities that are central to the mission of universities.
(D) The form of software technology that best matches the values embodied in the activities that are central to the mission of universities is the form of software technology that is most efficient for universities to use.
(E) A university should not pursue any activity that would block the achievement of the goals of academic scholarship at that university.

3.17. When exercising the muscles in one's back, it is important, in order to maintain a healthy back, to exercise the muscles on opposite sides of the spine equally. After all, balanced muscle development is needed to maintain a healthy back, since the muscles on opposite sides of the spine must pull equally in opposing directions to keep the back in proper alignment and protect the spine.

Which one of the following is an assumption required by the argument?

(A) Muscles on opposite sides of the spine that are equally well developed will be enough to keep the back in proper alignment.
(B) Exercising the muscles on opposite sides of the spine unequally tends to lead to unbalanced muscle development.
(C) Provided that one exercises the muscles on opposite sides of the spine equally, one will have a generally healthy back.
(D) If the muscles on opposite sides of the spine are exercised unequally, one's back will be irreparably damaged.
(E) One should exercise daily to ensure that the muscles on opposite sides of the spine keep the back in proper alignment.

Problem Set (Continued)

All questions are from the June '07 exam.

3.20. We should accept the proposal to demolish the old train station, because the local historical society, which vehemently opposes this, is dominated by people who have no commitment to long-term economic well-being. Preserving old buildings creates an impediment to new development, which is critical to economic health.

The flawed reasoning exhibited by the argument above is most similar to that exhibited by which one of the following arguments?

(A) Our country should attempt to safeguard works of art that it deems to possess national cultural significance. These works might not be recognized as such by all taxpayers, or even all critics. Nevertheless, our country ought to expend whatever money is needed to procure all such works as they become available.
(B) Documents of importance to local heritage should be properly preserved and archived for the sake of future generations. For, if even one of these documents is damaged or lost, the integrity of the historical record as a whole will be damaged.
(C) You should have your hair cut no more than once a month. After all, beauticians suggest that their customers have their hair cut twice a month, and they do this as a way of generating more business for themselves.
(D) The committee should endorse the plan to postpone construction of the new expressway. Many residents of the neighborhoods that would be affected are fervently opposed to that construction, and the committee is obligated to avoid alienating those residents.
(E) One should not borrow even small amounts of money unless it is absolutely necessary. Once one borrows a few dollars, the interest starts to accumulate. The longer one takes to repay, the more one ends up owing, and eventually a small debt has become a large one.

Here are the answers. As mentioned, we will not include detailed solutions in this lesson, but rather use these questions for our discussion in the next few lessons. However, if you just can't wait, I've include page numbers for where particular questions are discussed.

	2.2	2.9	2.17	2.21	2.23	3.5	3.13	3.14	3.17	3.20
Correct	B	E	B	A	C	C	B	C	B	C
On page	250	277	242	242	262	262	277	263	270	250

17 LOGICAL REASONING flaw & match the flaw

The third issue.

The LSAT can be thought of as a test of three things: your reading ability, your reasoning ability, and your **mental discipline**. When it comes to developing question-specific strategies, it's important to recognize the significance of the third issue: mental discipline.

As you will see in this lesson and those that follow, the strategies for how to solve questions are fairly obvious and simple—I'm not going to ask you to memorize fifteen steps that you wouldn't think to implement otherwise, and I won't ask you to look at circles and think of them as squares.

The challenge comes from the fact that the optimal strategies for different types of questions sometimes complement one another and sometimes come into dangerous conflict. If you aren't conscious of this fact, and if you haven't trained yourself to retain a specific mental discipline, invariably you will mix up strategies for different types of questions, in ways you may not even be aware of, and this will lead to confusion and fuzziness. Fuzziness is not our friend.

In almost all instances, fuzziness is a consequence of a lack of planning and a misunderstanding of priorities during your study process. Remember that the person who has LSAT mastery isn't any better at thinking about more things but rather is better at thinking about the right things. In the lessons to come, the most important thing for you to do is develop a simple and usable understanding of what each question stem is really asking for, and develop a simple and usable skill set for consistently getting the job done. We are going to practice thinking about exactly the right things. The quote "Smart is simple" is consistently true of the LSAT, but it is particularly true of what we'll be discussing in these lessons.

---

smart → simple

Flaw Questions

"The reasoning in the argument is most vulnerable to criticism on the grounds that it..."
"The reasoning in the argument is flawed in that..."
"Which of the following is an error in the reasoning?"

What's wrong?

We are going to start our breakdown of question types with questions that ask you to identify what is wrong with the reasoning in an argument.

What's most important to remember about reasoning flaws is that they are not contained in the conclusion and they are not contained in the support. What we are interested in is figuring out what is wrong with using that particular support to reach that particular conclusion. Focus on this, and most incorrect answers become far more obviously so. If you critique or find fault with a conclusion without thinking about how it's being supported, you are essentially doing nothing more than giving your opinion on that particular point, and in no way whatsoever is the LSAT ever interested in your opinion about anything. Let's discuss the steps involved in solving a question that asks you to identify what is wrong.

SUPER-SIMPLE EXAMPLE

Carl says he is friends with Frank, but the other day I saw the two of them arguing. Therefore, Carl and Frank are clearly not friends.

The reasoning in the argument is flawed in that

(A) It takes for granted that Frank and Carl do not have other friends in common.
(B) It takes for granted that Carl frequently lies.
(C) It takes for granted that only friends argue.
(D) It takes for granted that only enemies argue.
(E) It fails to consider that Carl and Frank can argue but still be friends.

The correct answer is (E). Certain answers are wrong because they aren't actually related to the argument: (A). Others are wrong because they don't relate to the author's point: (B), and finally others are wrong because they misrepresent the reason/point relationship: (C), (D).

---

step one
understand your job

Begin each question by reading the question stem. Flaw question stems are worded in just a few different ways, and you should have little trouble recognizing that a question is a Flaw question.

We want to use the question stem to set our expectations. Once we see that it's a Flaw question, we know that our job is to find an argument in the stimulus, and to figure out what is wrong with that argument. Our expectation should be to have a very clear understanding of the flaw before moving on to the answer choices. This won't always be possible, but it definitely should be the norm.

two
find the point

You will use your first read of the stimulus to get a handle on the subject matter and the general relationship between the sentences and clauses.

However, your conscious focus should not be set on getting a bunch of different tasks done; rather, during your first read, you want to prioritize identifying the conclusion of the argument.

This conclusion will be the most important thing you think about during the rest of your process, and your understanding of it will play a big part in making easier every other part of the process.

If the conclusion is unclear, do not move on in your process. Figure out the conclusion before moving forward.

three
find the support

It's tough to find the support until you find the conclusion! However, once you know what the main point is, your next job is to dig through the argument to figure out how that point is being supported. Keep in mind that even when the support is spread out in two or three sentences, conclusions are supported either by just one reason or two reasons.

Your understanding of the task really comes into play when you encounter a longer stimulus. Longer stimuli can look intimidating, but in large part they are just testing your ability to wade through secondary information in order to identify a point and its support. Think of a longer stimulus not as an Easter egg hunt with more eggs, but rather the normal amount of eggs spread out over a larger area. When you run into a long stimulus, you should not expect to have to find extra reasoning, or retain more information. Rather, you should see it as more clutter around the typical volume of important information.

figure out what's wrong

four

This is *the* step. Steps one through three serve to put you in a position to perform this step well, and the remaining steps are a reflection of how well you do here.

We've already discussed this step in great detail, and to the side are some simple reminders of what we've discussed. One important point is that you ought to strive for a conceptual, rather than textual, understanding of flaws, that is, you should know what is wrong rather than some wording of what is wrong. Answers will represent flaws in ways you don't expect.

Perhaps most importantly, you should *expect* to have a strong understanding of the flaw for nearly every question you see. Keep in mind that no flaw you see on your exam will be unique; all of them will be ones you've seen numerous times in your prep. There are some ways to survive the few questions for which you don't have a strong sense of the flaw, but it is impossible to consistently perform well unless you are very good at seeing what is wrong with arguments.

get rid of answers

five

The previous step was the most important step, but this is the step that most defines high scorers: in order to do really well (in thirty-five minutes) you need to be awfully good at getting rid of wrong answers. During your first run through the answer choices, leave alone any answers that sound pretty good, and focus on thinking about why answers are wrong. For Flaw questions, you should expect to consistently get rid of at least three (and commonly four) of the answer choices before you seriously consider whether one answer is accurate.

This step is in many ways a reflection of how well you've performed the previous steps, and in particular how well you have prioritized the important information. If you are zeroed in on what is wrong with the relationship between point and support, you will find that most answer choices fall outside that realm. If you are holding the entire stimulus in your head without a sense of priority, many of the wrong choices will seem far more attractive.

Many wrong answers will have nothing to do with the stimulus at all (these answers are commonly about related subjects). Many wrong answers will have something to do with the secondary information in the argument, but no relevance to the point being made. Many wrong answers will relate to the conclusion or premise but not the relationship between the two. And finally, a few wrong answers will misrepresent the relationship between the support and the conclusion in some way. These wrong answers are generally the most attractive ones, and tempting wrong answers are often what defines whether a question is difficult or not.

confirm the right answer

six

Left with just one or two serious contenders, now you should carefully evaluate each answer choice to make sure it matches your understanding of the flaw. Go word for word, and in particular pay attention to modifiers that may create a disconnect between the answer choice and the stimulus.

Keep in mind that it can often seem like you can get away with partially fulfilling steps five or six, but for almost all top scorers, a huge key to success is double-covering the bases—knowing exactly what is wrong and why, and exactly what is right and why. Over the long run, this method of essentially getting to the answer in two ways will be very helpful in ensuring a certain level of accuracy. Finally, keep in mind that all of these strategies are designed to get us to the right answer as quickly as we can (but no quicker).

SIMPLE EXAMPLES OF FLAWS

Piece ≠ Puzzle

All architects must be good at math. Jerry is good with math; it's likely he would be a good architect. (*Maybe Jerry has terrible design sense.*)

Tom says Perry is smart, but Tom is his father and Tom is biased. Therefore, Perry must not be smart. (*Tom can be biased, and Perry can still be smart.*)

Apples ≠ Oranges

Anyone who works at TempKids gets a badge. Since Sara has a badge, she must work at TempKids. (*Other people can get badges too.*)

No one can be all good. Therefore, it must be true that we all have at least some evil. (*Not everything has to be either good or evil.*)

1+1 ≠ 3

Bridget loves Ted, and Ted loves Carol. Therefore, Bridget must love Carol. (*Love does not necessarily transfer.*)

Of those who went on the camping trip, only those who drank my homemade soda got sick. My soda must have made them sick. (*Maybe they all drank the soda while eating bad meat.*)

CONSTELLATION OF WRONG ANSWERS

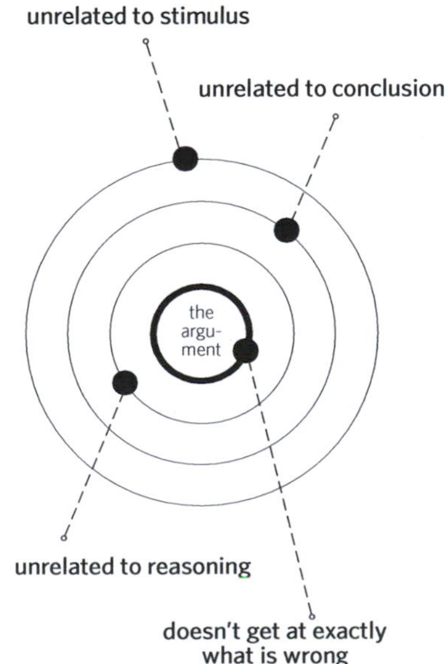

the process in action

Let's model the problem-solving process with two questions you solved at the end of the last lesson.

2.17. Hospital executive: At a recent conference on nonprofit management, several computer experts maintained that the most significant threat faced by large institutions such as universities and hospitals is unauthorized access to confidential data. In light of this testimony, we should make the protection of our clients' confidentiality our highest priority.

The hospital executive's argument is most vulnerable to which one of the following objections?

(A) The argument confuses the causes of a problem with the appropriate solutions to that problem.
(B) The argument relies on the testimony of experts whose expertise is not shown to be sufficiently broad to support their general claim.
(C) The argument assumes that a correlation between two phenomena is evidence that one is the cause of the other.
(D) The argument draws a general conclusion about a group based on data about an unrepresentative sample of that group.
(E) The argument infers that a property belonging to large institutions belongs to all institutions.

Step 1: understand your job: We have to find an argument and figure out what's wrong with it.

Step 2: find the point: His point is that "we should make the protection of our clients' confidentiality our highest priority."

Step 3: find the support: Several computer experts said it ought to be.

Step 4: figure out what's wrong: Of course computer experts would say that! Just because one niche group thinks a certain issue is most important doesn't mean it actually is.

Step 5: get rid of answers: (A) doesn't represent this argument at all. (B) isn't exactly what we expected, but it's tough to say what's wrong. Keep it. (C) is about correlation versus causation, but that's not our problem. (D) sounds good. Keep it. (E) is not directly relevant to this conclusion.

Step 6: confirm the right answer: The "general claim" in (B) is the claim the experts make, and it's true that the issue is that their opinion is just one part of the picture—we haven't been given proof ("is not shown to be sufficiently...") that their opinion is correct. (B) seems good. (D) sounded tempting at first, but looking at it more carefully, we can see that (D) is about "data" from a "sample of that group," and neither of those descriptions fits this argument. (B) is correct.

2.21. Driver: My friends say I will one day have an accident because I drive my sports car recklessly. But I have done some research, and apparently minivans and larger sedans have very low accident rates compared to sports cars. So trading my sports car in for a minivan would lower my risk of having an accident.

The reasoning in the driver's argument is most vulnerable to criticism on the grounds that this argument

(A) infers a cause from a mere correlation
(B) relies on a sample that is too narrow
(C) misinterprets evidence that a result is likely as evidence that the result is certain
(D) mistakes a condition sufficient for bringing about a result for a condition necessary for doing so
(E) relies on a source that is probably not well-informed

Step 1: understand your job: We have to find an argument and figure out what's wrong with it.

Step 2: find the point: His point is that trading in his sports car for a minivan will lower his risk of having an accident.

Step 3: find the support: Minivans have lower accident rates than sports cars.

Step 4: figure out what's wrong: Mistakes the correlation between accident rate and car type for causation—it could be that safer drivers choose minivans, and if he continues to drive recklessly, the type of car won't matter.

Step 5: get rid of answers: (A) seems correct. Keep it. (B) doesn't accurately represent what's wrong. (C) doesn't match the conclusion. We've talked about (D) (in lesson 7), and that's not what is happening in this argument. (E) doesn't match this argument. Who is supposed to be not well informed?

Step 6: confirm the right answer: Here we only have one answer to check. No strange wording in (A), and it does represent what this author is doing—he reaches his conclusion by inferring that there must be some causal connection between the type of car and the accident rate. We don't have information in the argument to say that this is anything more than correlation.

Flaw Questions

Here are three Flaw questions. Use these questions to work on your problem-solving process. Solutions follow.

29.1.14. Prosecutor: Dr. Yuge has testified that, had the robbery occurred after 1:50 A.M., then, the moon having set at 1:45 A.M., it would have been too dark for Klein to recognize the perpetrator. But Yuge acknowledged that the moon was full enough to provide considerable light before it set. And we have conclusively shown that the robbery occurred between 1:15 and 1:30 A.M. So there was enough light for Klein to make a reliable identification.

The prosecutor's reasoning is most vulnerable to criticism because it overlooks which one of the following possibilities?

(A) Klein may be mistaken about the time of the robbery and so it may have taken place after the moon had set.
(B) The perpetrator may closely resemble someone who was not involved in the robbery.
(C) Klein may have been too upset to make a reliable identification even in good light.
(D) Without having been there, Dr. Yuge has no way of knowing whether the light was sufficient.
(E) During the robbery the moon's light may have been interfered with by conditions such as cloud cover.

29.4.18. All actions are motivated by self-interest, since any action that is apparently altruistic can be described in terms of self-interest. For example, helping someone can be described in terms of self-interest: the motivation is hope for a reward or other personal benefit to be bestowed as a result of the helping action.

Which one of the following most accurately describes an error in the argument's reasoning?

(A) The term "self-interest" is allowed to shift in meaning over the course of the argument.
(B) The argument takes evidence showing merely that its conclusion could be true to constitute evidence showing that the conclusion is in fact true.
(C) The argument does not explain what is meant by "reward" and "personal benefit."
(D) The argument ignores the possibility that what is taken to be necessary for a certain interest to be a motivation actually suffices to show that that interest is a motivation.
(E) The argument depends for its appeal only on the emotional content of the example cited.

29.4.25. Formal performance evaluations in the professional world are conducted using realistic situations. Physicians are allowed to consult medical texts freely, attorneys may refer to law books and case records, and physicists and engineers have their manuals at hand for ready reference. Students, then, should likewise have access to their textbooks whenever they take examinations.

The reasoning in the argument is questionable because the argument

(A) cites examples that are insufficient to support the generalization that performance evaluations in the professional world are conducted in realistic situations
(B) fails to consider the possibility that adopting its recommendation will not significantly increase most students' test scores
(C) neglects to take into account the fact that professionals were once students who also did not have access to textbooks during examinations
(D) neglects to take into account the fact that, unlike students, professionals have devoted many years of study to one subject
(E) fails to consider the possibility that the purposes of evaluation in the professional world and in school situations are quite dissimilar

Stick to the steps!
1. understand your job
2. find the point
3. find the support
4. figure out what's wrong
5. get rid of answers
6. confirm the right answer

29.1.14. Prosecutor: Dr. Yuge has testified that, had the robbery occurred after 1:50 A.M., then, the moon having set at 1:45 A.M., it would have been too dark for Klein to recognize the perpetrator. But Yuge acknowledged that the moon was full enough to provide considerable light before it set. And we have conclusively shown that the robbery occurred between 1:15 and 1:30 A.M. So there was enough light for Klein to make a reliable identification.

The prosecutor's reasoning is most vulnerable to criticism because it overlooks which one of the following possibilities?

(A) Klein may be mistaken about the time of the robbery and so it may have taken place after the moon had set.
(B) The perpetrator may closely resemble someone who was not involved in the robbery.
(C) Klein may have been too upset to make a reliable identification even in good light.
(D) Without having been there, Dr. Yuge has no way of knowing whether the light was sufficient.
(E) During the robbery the moon's light may have been interfered with by conditions such as cloud cover.

1. understand your job: We have to find an argument and figure out what's wrong with it (what the prosecutor has overlooked).

2. find the point: The prosecutor's point is that there was enough light for Klein to make a reliable identification.

3. find the support: The moon was giving off light at the time.

4. figure out what's wrong: Maybe the moon was out, but it was dark for some other reason!

5. get rid of answers: (A) questions the support, and doesn't fix the reasoning issue (moon is not the only factor when it comes to brightness). (B) and (C) are both unrelated to the support/conclusion relationship. (D) and (E) both seem like the types of answers we were looking for.

6. confirm the right answer: Did Dr. Yuge have to be there? Is that what is wrong with the argument? No. Yuge is just testifying about when the moon goes down—he didn't have to be at the scene. Plus "no way" is too strong—he could know if he saw an accurate video recording. The "cloud cover" in (E) is fairly specific, but that's just one example, and really what (E) is telling us is that there could have been other lighting factors other than just the amount of moonlight. (E) is correct.

29.4.18. All actions are motivated by self-interest, since any action that is apparently altruistic can be described in terms of self-interest. For example, helping someone can be described in terms of self-interest: the motivation is hope for a reward or other personal benefit to be bestowed as a result of the helping action.

Which one of the following most accurately describes an error in the argument's reasoning?

(A) The term "self-interest" is allowed to shift in meaning over the course of the argument.
(B) The argument takes evidence showing merely that its conclusion could be true to constitute evidence showing that the conclusion is in fact true.
(C) The argument does not explain what is meant by "reward" and "personal benefit."
(D) The argument ignores the possibility that what is taken to be necessary for a certain interest to be a motivation actually suffices to show that that interest is a motivation.
(E) The argument depends for its appeal only on the emotional content of the example cited.

1. understand your job: We have to find an argument and figure out what's wrong with it.

2. find the point: All actions are motivated by self-interest.

3. find the support: Any action that doesn't seem like it was driven by self-interest can be described in terms of self-interest.

4. figure out what's wrong: Just because you can *describe* an action as being motived by self-interest doesn't actually mean that that description is correct.

5. get rid of answers: (A) isn't what is happening in the argument. (B) is somewhat tempting—let's leave it. (C) is about secondary issues. (D) doesn't represent this argument, which has nothing to do with necessary or sufficient. (E) doesn't represent the argument.

6. confirm the right answer: (B) is the only one standing. It didn't look great at first, but let's take another look. It says the argument takes what could be true (actions *could* be motivated by self-interest) to prove that it is true (actions *are* motivated by self-interest). This may not match the way we first thought of the flaw, but it does represent the same issue. (B) is correct.

29.4.25. Formal performance evaluations in the professional world are conducted using realistic situations. Physicians are allowed to consult medical texts freely, attorneys may refer to law books and case records, and physicists and engineers have their manuals at hand for ready reference. Students, then, should likewise have access to their textbooks whenever they take examinations.

The reasoning in the argument is questionable because the argument

(A) cites examples that are insufficient to support the generalization that performance evaluations in the professional world are conducted in realistic situations
(B) fails to consider the possibility that adopting its recommendation will not significantly increase most students' test scores
(C) neglects to take into account the fact that professionals were once students who also did not have access to textbooks during examinations
(D) neglects to take into account the fact that, unlike students, professionals have devoted many years of study to one subject
(E) fails to consider the possibility that the purposes of evaluation in the professional world and in school situations are quite dissimilar

1. understand your job: We have to find an argument and figure out what's wrong with it.

2. find the point: Students should get open textbooks for exams.

3. find the support: Professionals get to consult books in real-life situations.

4. figure out what's wrong: It treats two very different situations as if they are similar.

5. get rid of answers: (A) attacks the support, but isn't directly related to the conclusion. (B) is way off subject. (C) represents the issue incorrectly; what these professionals did as students is irrelevant to the comparison. (D) is tempting, in that it shows a difference between these professionals and the students. Let's keep it. (E) is pretty much what we were looking for. Keep it.

6. confirm the right answer: Yes, (D) does represent a difference, but it's unclear what impact "years of study" have on whether one should get books or not—it doesn't make a ton of sense to say that because professionals have experience and students don't, professionals should get help and students not (seems it should be the other way around). Checking each word of (E), we can confirm it does represent the issue we saw—the author is comparing apples and oranges. (E) is correct.

answer choices with

abstract language

Test writers occasionally write the answer choices for Flaw questions in an abstract fashion, that is, they describe the flaw in general terms—often in terms of formal reasoning issues. These answer choices can be more difficult to understand correctly, and if you have two or three answer choices written in such a way, they can make the question tougher to handle and more time consuming.

Abstract language used to be a more frequent challenge for Flaw questions, but has become less common in the modern era. Today, you can expect this challenge maybe once per every exam or two.

You make your job far easier if you have done two other things well: one, developed a flexible, conceptual understanding of the flaw in your mind, and two, focused on eliminating answers that don't represent that flaw. Go two for two, and it'll commonly leave you with just one answer choice that needs to be evaluated carefully, and you'll be in a better position to evaluate that one choice.

Below is a mini-drill to help you test your own comfort level with abstract answer choices. Listed are "sister" representations of *all* of the more challenging abstract flaw answers that appear in the problems from PT 52-61, along with very obvious examples of each of these flaws. Do your best to match the abstract language with its representative flaw. Solutions are below. If you have trouble with these answers, you should return to review this exercise a few more times later on in your studies.

Match these answers...

1. infers from the fact that a certain factor is sufficient for a result that the absence of that factor is sufficient for the opposite result

2. takes for granted that, if a condition coincided with the emergence of a certain phenomenon, it must have been causally responsible for that phenomenon

3. fails to address adequately the possibility that even if a condition is sufficient to produce an effect, it may not be necessary

4. mistakes a merely relative property for one that is absolute

5. presents as a premise a claim that one would accept as true only if one already accepts the truth of the conclusion

6. bases a generalization on a sample that is likely to be unrepresentative

7. interprets an assertion that certain conditions are necessary as asserting that those conditions are sufficient

...to these faulty arguments.

A. Of course what the mayor is saying is true. He would not be saying it otherwise.

B. In order to become a pop star, one needs to be able to dance well. Since I can dance well, I will become a pop star.

C. Since Jessica has more money than Tara, Jessica must be rich.

D. Since eating sushi makes one healthy, not eating sushi makes one unhealthy.

E. I got sick right after I ate that taco. The taco must have made me sick.

F. I got fit by working out every day. If you want to get fit, you must work out every day.

G. Since the managers at the company state that their employees are thoroughly grateful to be working under them, this must indeed be the case.

Answers: 1D 2E 3F 4C 5A 6G 7B

Basic Assumption Questions

A less common sibling of the Flaw question is the Basic Assumption question. Keep in mind that there are several different types of **assumption** questions, and your task becomes very different when words like "required" or "follow logically" accompany the word "assumption." We will deal with these other types of questions in future lessons. In this lesson, we will just quickly discuss Basic Assumption questions—those that simply ask us what the author is assuming.

For the purposes of the LSAT, we can define an **assumption** as an unstated and unjustified belief.

We don't need to spend a lot of time on these questions, because they are not too common and because you've already prepared for them: Basic Assumption questions are simply Flaw questions in disguise. Any time an author has made a *mistake* in thinking that his evidence is enough to reach his conclusion, he has *assumed* that his evidence is enough to reach his conclusion.

Think of "assuming" as a kinder version of "takes for granted." When you run into an Assumption question, think about the stimulus exactly as you would for a Flaw question. Once you figure out what the flaw is, search for the answer that expresses that flaw as an assumption.

Below are the stimuli for the three Flaw problems you just solved, along with their question stems and correct answers. Right below is the question and answer rewritten as it would be for a Basic Assumption question.

Flaw Questions as Basic Assumption Questions

29.1.14 Prosecutor: Dr. Yuge has testified that, had the robbery occurred after 1:50 A.M., then, the moon having set at 1:45 A.M., it would have been too dark for Klein to recognize the perpetrator. But Yuge acknowledged that the moon was full enough to provide considerable light before it set. And we have conclusively shown that the robbery occurred between 1:15 and 1:30 A.M. So there was enough light for Klein to make a reliable identification.

The prosecutor's reasoning is most vulnerable to criticism because it overlooks which one of the following possibilities?

(E) During the robbery the moon's light may have been interfered with by conditions such as cloud cover.

As a Basic Assumption question...

The prosecutor assumes that...

(E) Other conditions did not interfere with the moon's light during the robbery.

29.4.18 All actions are motivated by self-interest, since any action that is apparently altruistic can be described in terms of self-interest. For example, helping someone can be described in terms of self-interest: the motivation is hope for a reward or other personal benefit to be bestowed as a result of the helping action.

Which one of the following most accurately describes an error in the argument's reasoning?

(B) The argument takes evidence showing merely that its conclusion could be true to constitute evidence showing that the conclusion is in fact true.

As a Basic Assumption question...

The author assumes that...

(B) Because the motivation for all actions can be described in terms of self-interest, all actions are in fact motivated by self-interest.

29.4.25 Formal performance evaluations in the professional world are conducted using realistic situations. Physicians are allowed to consult medical texts freely, attorneys may refer to law books and case records, and physicists and engineers have their manuals at hand for ready reference. Students, then, should likewise have access to their textbooks whenever they take examinations.

The reasoning in the argument is questionable because the argument

(E) fails to consider the possibility that the purposes of evaluation in the professional world and in school situations are quite dissimilar

As a Basic Assumption question...

What does the argument assume?

(E) Purposes of evaluation in the professional world and in school situations are similar.

Match the Flaw

"The pattern of flawed reasoning in which one of the following arguments is most similar to that in the economist's argument?"
"Which one of the following arguments contains flawed reasoning most similar to that in the argument above?"

Common problems.

The two matching questions—Match the Flaw and Match the Reasoning—are on average more labor intensive than other types of questions, so when you run into them, you should give yourself a bit more time (an average of 1:30 to 1:40 per is fine).

On a closely related note, the two types of matching questions are also some of the most dangerous time suckers. If you don't make staying on task a priority, it's very easy to get lost in all of the different arguments. Find out what's wrong with the original and then eliminate mismatches. Get in, get out, and try not to waste time thinking about secondary issues. You can do this if you practice enough to turn efficient strategies into habits.

For whatever reason, these questions tend to most commonly come right at the beginning of a section or right near the end of one. If it is toward the beginning, expect for the flaw to be obvious, and all of the wrong answers to be obviously so. A question that appears later in the section will still have an obvious flaw, but it may have a more complicated support structure, or wrong answers that require a bit more work.

SUPER-SIMPLE EXAMPLE

All of the hats are on sale, and all of the sale items are on the display. Since this item is on the display, it must be a hat.

Which one of the following arguments contains flawed reasoning most similar to that in the argument above?

(A) All of my tools were in the garage, and everything in the garage got packed up. Since this item was packed up, it must be a tool.
(B) All dogs like playing fetch, but few cats do. Therefore, most animals that like playing fetch are dogs.
(C) Every person who went got a stamp. Since Sara did not go, she did not get a stamp.
(D) Some people love television. Some people hate television. Since you do not hate television, you must love it.
(E) Joey says ghosts are real. Since he is not intending to lie, ghosts must be real.

The correct answer is (A). The four wrong answers do not contain the same flaw, and many of them are very different in structure from the original. The original argument has nothing like the dogs versus cats in (B). (C) has a negation from support to conclusion, which our argument didn't have. (D) has "some" issues; our argument doesn't. (E) is about not intending something—we have no match for that in the original.

step one: understand your job

Once we see that it is a Match the Flaw question, we know that our job during the initial read is to find an argument in the stimulus and figure out what is wrong with that argument. Our expectation should be to have a very clear understanding of the flaw before moving on to the answer choices. This won't always be possible, but it definitely should be the norm. We should also expect to spend more time in the answer choices than we normally do.

two: find the point

As you read through a stimulus the first time, you will develop a general sense of the subject matter and argument no matter whether you try or not. The key is to not fragment your primary focus. During your first read, prioritize identifying the main point of the argument.

It is especially important that you have a clear understanding of the conclusion for Match the Flaw questions. These questions require you to wade through a lot of information in the five answer choices, and the conclusion serves as a very clear signal post.

If the conclusion is unclear, do not move on in your process. Figure out that conclusion.

three: find the support

In general (not always), Match the Flaw questions tend to have a bit less secondary information than do other types of questions.

Therefore, most commonly, most of the information in a stimulus other than the conclusion will be support for that conclusion (or background critical for understanding that support).

four
figure out what's wrong

Again, this is *the* step. Steps one through three serve to put you in a position to perform this step well, and the remaining steps are a reflection of how you do here.

The good news is that Match the Flaw questions tend to, on average, have fairly obvious flaws. They are arguments that you know are wrong the first time you read them. The bad news is that Matching questions in general tend to have $1 + 1 \neq 3$ types of flaws. That makes a lot of sense when you think about what these questions are testing (your ability to keep an argument in your mind as you think of other arguments).

Of course, it's not enough to think, "Oh, he's putting two premises together incorrectly," because it's likely that several answers will do that. As always, you want to develop as specific an understanding as possible of exactly what is wrong with the reasoning in that particular argument.

five
get rid of answers

For Match the Flaw questions, this is the step that will make or break you. If you have a great sense of what is wrong with the argument, chances are you will be able to get rid of four of five answers quickly. However, if you run into an argument that you have trouble holding in your head, or if you run into that rare (very rare) Match the Flaw question that has a close-but-no-cigar wrong answer, you can end up wasting a lot of valuable time.

CONSTELLATION OF WRONG ANSWERS

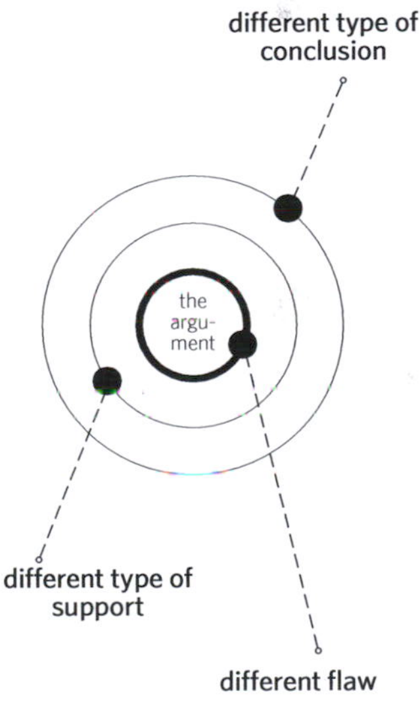

Matching questions work very much like those games you played when you were very little where you look at two almost identical pictures and have to figure out what is different about them. The secret then was to focus on one part of the picture at a time (if you look at both of them as wholes, you won't see the differences as easily).

It's the same key here. You don't have to think about arguments in their entirety to know that they are not good matches. Many answers will be wrong because they clearly reach very different conclusions. Many will be wrong because they use different support (there are qualifiers like "some" when there weren't in the original argument, or the original had an either/or and the answer choice does not). You want to find the quickest and most absolute reason to say that an answer is wrong, and you will know that in general, four of the five answers will have very obvious tells that show you, without you getting too deep into them, that they are different from the original. Do not use physical location (i.e., the support comes before the conclusion or the conclusion comes before the support) to match up arguments. You should only care about the reasoning structure.

Of course, having a great understanding of what is wrong with the original argument is the key to all of this. If that understanding is fuzzy, the elimination process will naturally be more challenging.

six
confirm the right answer

Make sure the conclusion is the same type of conclusion. Make sure you have the same type of support. Make sure there are no stray words that change the meaning of that answer in some way. And of course make sure they have the same flaw.

It is easy, I must admit, to over-think this step. Rely on how confident you feel in your eliminations. If you feel great about them, and you see some slight change in the reasoning issue between the original argument and the correct answer (it happens), let it go. If you didn't feel so confident about eliminating that one last answer, and you're not one hundred percent sure of the match, that could be a sign the question is a bit more difficult than you think.

the process in action

Let's model the problem-solving process with two questions you solved at the end of the last lesson.

2.2. All Labrador retrievers bark a great deal. All Saint Bernards bark infrequently. Each of Rosa's dogs is a cross between a Labrador retriever and a Saint Bernard. Therefore, Rosa's dogs are moderate barkers.

Which one of the following uses flawed reasoning that most closely resembles the flawed reasoning used in the argument above?

(A) All students who study diligently make good grades. But some students who do not study diligently also make good grades. Jane studies somewhat diligently. Therefore, Jane makes somewhat good grades.
(B) All type A chemicals are extremely toxic to human beings. All type B chemicals are nontoxic to human beings. This household cleaner is a mixture of a type A chemical and a type B chemical. Therefore, this household cleaner is moderately toxic.
(C) All students at Hanson School live in Green County. All students at Edwards School live in Winn County. Members of the Perry family attend both Hanson and Edwards. Therefore, some members of the Perry family live in Green County and some live in Winn County.
(D) All transcriptionists know shorthand. All engineers know calculus. Bob has worked both as a transcriptionist and as an engineer. Therefore, Bob knows both shorthand and calculus.
(E) All of Kenisha's dresses are very well made. All of Connie's dresses are very badly made. Half of the dresses in this closet are very well made, and half of them are very badly made. Therefore, half of the dresses in this closet are Kenisha's and half of them are Connie's.

1. understand your job: We have to match flaws. The first part of that is to read for an argument and figure out what's wrong with it.

2. find the point: The point is that Rosa's dogs are moderate barkers.

3. find the support: They are crosses of a dog that barks a lot and a dog that barks a little.

4. figure out what's wrong: Who says her dogs should be an exact mix of the two? We're not all the exact average height of our parents.

5. get rid of answers: (A) has study versus not study—very different from our argument. (B) is almost exactly the same as the original. It's probably correct—keep it. (C) doesn't have the same type of problem. In fact, it's tough to see a problem at all. Different people in a family, living in different areas, is not the same as one dog having a split of characteristics. (D) is pretty close, but the conclusion is about adding together skills rather than mixing them together. (E) has different problems and, like (C), is about a different type of mixture (a closet full of individual dresses, as opposed to one dog).

6. confirm the right answer: Going back to (B), we can see that it's wrong to think the mixture will be somewhere in the middle of the two original items, just as it was wrong to think that way in the original argument. (B) is definitely correct.

3.20. We should accept the proposal to demolish the old train station, because the local historical society, which vehemently opposes this, is dominated by people who have no commitment to long-term economic well-being. Preserving old buildings creates an impediment to new development, which is critical to economic health.

The flawed reasoning exhibited by the argument above is most similar to that exhibited by which one of the following arguments?

(A) Our country should attempt to safeguard works of art that it deems to possess national cultural significance. These works might not be recognized as such by all taxpayers, or even all critics. Nevertheless, our country ought to expend whatever money is needed to procure all such works as they become available.
(B) Documents of importance to local heritage should be properly preserved and archived for the sake of future generations. For, if even one of these documents is damaged or lost, the integrity of the historical record as a whole will be damaged.
(C) You should have your hair cut no more than once a month. After all, beauticians suggest that their customers have their hair cut twice a month, and they do this as a way of generating more business for themselves.
(D) The committee should endorse the plan to postpone construction of the new expressway. Many residents of the neighborhoods that would be affected are fervently opposed to that construction, and the committee is obligated to avoid alienating those residents.
(E) One should not borrow even small amounts of money unless it is absolutely necessary. Once one borrows a few dollars, the interest starts to accumulate. The longer one takes to repay, the more one ends up owing, and eventually a small debt has become a large one.

1. understand your job: We have to match flaws. The first part of that is to read for an argument and figure out what's wrong with it.

2. find the point: We should accept the proposal to demolish the train station.

3. find the support: The people who want to preserve it don't care about economic well-being.

4. figure out what's wrong: Just because the people who want to preserve it aren't thinking about something does not mean the train station should be demolished—it's tough to see how their opinion has any direct impact on the decision at all. It's the common flaw of overvaluing the opinion of one group or person.

5. get rid of answers: (A) doesn't have an argument at all—it just states an opinion twice. (B) is an argument about what happens when you don't preserve—tough to see the relevance to the stimulus. (C) is somewhat tempting—it's recommending doing something based on the motivations of someone who recommends something else. Let's keep it for now. (D) is about heeding a certain opinion—we know that's a different situation than what we have. (E) has a series of premises that add together, and ultimately support a very subjective and general conclusion. This structure is very different from the original. That only leaves (C)!

6. confirm the right answer: (C) is perhaps not what we expected, in part because the scenario is very different, but it has all of the same issues as the original—the opinion of beauticians is simply not significant enough to justify making such a recommendation.

Match the Flaw Questions

Here are two questions that ask us to match reasoning. Use these questions to walk through your problem-solving process. Solutions follow.

29.4.21. All too many weaklings are also cowards, and few cowards fail to be fools. Thus there must be at least one person who is both a weakling and a fool.

The flawed pattern of reasoning in the argument above is most similar to that in which one of the following?

(A) All weasels are carnivores and no carnivores fail to be nonherbivores, so some weasels are nonherbivores.
(B) Few moralists have the courage to act according to the principles they profess, and few saints have the ability to articulate the principles by which they live, so it follows that few people can both act like saints and speak like moralists.
(C) Some painters are dancers, since some painters are musicians, and some musicians are dancers.
(D) If an act is virtuous, then it is autonomous, for acts are not virtuous unless they are free, and acts are not free unless they are autonomous.
(E) A majority of the voting population favors a total ban, but no one who favors a total ban is opposed to stiffer tariffs, so at least one voter is not opposed to stiffer tariffs.

Stick to the steps!
1. understand your job
2. find the point
3. find the support
4. figure out what's wrong
5. get rid of answers
6. confirm the right answer

30.2.6. The student body at this university takes courses in a wide range of disciplines. Miriam is a student at this university, so she takes courses in a wide range of disciplines.

Which one of the following arguments exhibits flawed reasoning most similar to that exhibited by the argument above?

(A) The students at this school take mathematics. Miguel is a student at this school, so he takes mathematics.
(B) The editorial board of this law journal has written on many legal issues. Louise is on the editorial board, so she has written on many legal issues.
(C) The component parts of bulldozers are heavy. This machine is a bulldozer, so it is heavy.
(D) All older automobiles need frequent oil changes. This car is new, so its oil need not be changed as frequently.
(E) The individual cells of the brain are incapable of thinking. Therefore, the brain as a whole is incapable of thinking.

Match the Flaw Solutions

29.4.21. All too many weaklings are also cowards, and few cowards fail to be fools. Thus there must be at least one person who is both a weakling and a fool.

The flawed pattern of reasoning in the argument above is most similar to that in which one of the following?

(A) All weasels are carnivores and no carnivores fail to be nonherbivores, so some weasels are nonherbivores.
(B) Few moralists have the courage to act according to the principles they profess, and few saints have the ability to articulate the principles by which they live, so it follows that few people can both act like saints and speak like moralists.
(C) Some painters are dancers, since some painters are musicians, and some musicians are dancers.
(D) If an act is virtuous, then it is autonomous, for acts are not virtuous unless they are free, and acts are not free unless they are autonomous.
(E) A majority of the voting population favors a total ban, but no one who favors a total ban is opposed to stiffer tariffs, so at least one voter is not opposed to stiffer tariffs.

1. understand your job: We need to find the flaw in the argument, and find an answer that has the same issue.

2. find the point: Miriam takes courses in a wide range of disciplines.

3. find the support: Miriam is a student at this university + students at university take courses in wide range of disciplines.

4. figure out what's wrong: Assumes that what applies to the group applies to the individual. It could be that individual students only take classes in particular disciplines, but when you bring these students together, these disciplines add up to a "wide range."

5. get rid of answers: (A) seems to have exactly the same issue. Let's leave it. Oh no, (B) seems to have the same issue. Let's leave it. (C) doesn't have an issue—that bulldozer will be heavy. (D) has a negation, which is not what's wrong with the original argument. (E) uses information about parts to conclude something about the whole, which is the reverse of the issue we have here.

6. confirm the right answer: Both (A) and (B) were attractive—let's evaluate them more carefully. Does (A) mean that just some students take math, or every student takes math? It's not clear, and reading it carefully again, (A) actually seems to mean that every student takes math. (B) is clearly about a group (board) doing something, in the same way the original argument is about a group (student body) doing something. Then it assumes something about an individual in that group. Looking back at (A), "the students" could mean as a group, but the way it's written the literal meaning is that each student takes math. (B) is correct.

1. understand your job: We need to find the flaw in the argument, and find an answer that has the same issue.

2. find the point: There must be at least one person who is both a weakling and a fool.

3. find the support: All too many weaklings are also cowards, and few cowards fail to be fools.

4. figure out what's wrong: Maybe the weaklings who are cowards are a part of the few who are not fools. Assumes an overlap between weaklings and cowards when we're not certain we have one.

5. get rid of answers: The premises in (A) are absolute (all, no) so we know it can't have the same reasoning issues. (B) is somewhat tempting, but the tone of the conclusion is very different (even though "at least one" and "few" mean similar things, the point the author is making is not consistent), and the structure of the support has a layer the original argument does not (i.e., moralists layered with courage). (C) has a different organizational structure (conclusion first) but the same logical issue—assumes overlap. Let's leave it. (D) is difficult to understand and a classic "time sucker" but is clearly very different from the original argument (conditional links) and should be eliminated quickly. (E) matches a portion (majority) with an absolute (no one) and so has a different reasoning structure from the original (the similar conclusion could certainly be tempting).

6. confirm the right answer: (C) uses different words, but has the same reasoning issue as the original argument. "At least one" and "all too many" are vague terms that can be interpreted in a broad number of ways, just like "some" can. None of those terms guarantee any overlap between groups.

30.2.6. The student body at this university takes courses in a wide range of disciplines. Miriam is a student at this university, so she takes courses in a wide range of disciplines.

Which one of the following arguments exhibits flawed reasoning most similar to that exhibited by the argument above?

(A) The students at this school take mathematics. Miguel is a student at this school, so he takes mathematics.
(B) The editorial board of this law journal has written on many legal issues. Louise is on the editorial board, so she has written on many legal issues.
(C) The component parts of bulldozers are heavy. This machine is a bulldozer, so it is heavy.
(D) All older automobiles need frequent oil changes. This car is new, so its oil need not be changed as frequently.
(E) The individual cells of the brain are incapable of thinking. Therefore, the brain as a whole is incapable of thinking.

18 LOGICAL REASONING sufficient assumption & supporting principle

In this lesson, we are going to discuss two question types: Sufficient Assumption and Supporting Principle. For these two types of questions, what we want to do is figure out what is wrong, and then search for an answer to *completely* fix the issue. That's what Sufficient Assumption and Supporting Principle questions are asking us to do—find the answer that completely fixes the issues in the argument.

You should expect 2 or 3 Sufficient Assumption questions, and 3 or 4 Supporting Principle questions per exam.

You'll note from the information on the side that these two question types are not that common. The reason we're covering just these two question types here is because we are also going to use this lesson to expand our discussion of **conditional logic**. In fact, we'll start with this. Most Sufficient Assumption questions involve conditional logic, and Sufficient Assumption questions most commonly present the most challenging conditional logic issues.

Conditional logic: We discussed conditional logic rules in Lesson 13. We will be expanding on that discussion in this lesson.

Below are a few simple, flawed arguments. Imagine the gap in between the reasoning and the conclusion as a "hole" that needs to be fixed. What is an answer that would completely fill that hole? Can you perhaps come up with *multiple* ways to state what might fill that hole? Finally, for extra credit, can you perhaps come up with an answer that fills the hole, and then goes slightly above and beyond filling the hole? If you're not quite sure what I mean by that, don't worry about it. We'll discuss it shortly.

Sharon must be great at figuring out mysteries. After all, she is the police chief.

All carnivores eat meat. Therefore, all carnivores eat beef.

Bill is a vegetarian. For that reason, he must hate the taste of meat.

Most Texans own hats. Therefore, some Texans own hat racks.

fill the hole

Think about the point, the support, and the hole between the two. Try to come up with answers that will completely fill the hole—answers that leave no gap between the support and the point.

Conditional Logic 101

In Lesson 13, we introduced and discussed conditional reasoning in terms of four major characteristics:

1. Conditional Rules Are Rules That Only Apply Sometimes

To be more specific, they are rules that are set off by a "trigger," more formally known as the *sufficient condition*. Why it is called the sufficient condition? Because it is sufficient, or enough, to guarantee the outcome. Speaking of which, the second characteristic we discussed was...

2. Conditional Statements Represent Guarantees

On the LSAT, "if" is a powerful and absolute word—it represents a guarantee. If the trigger takes effect or, more formally, if the sufficient condition is met, the outcome must result. This idea is fundamental to the make-up of the entire Logical Reasoning section.

It is the "guarantee" part of conditional statements that makes them so important to Logical Reasoning. One way to describe all flawed arguments is to say that they are arguments in which the author *thinks* the support is sufficient, or enough, when in fact it's not.

Notice how we fixed all of the flawed arguments from our "fill the hole" example—we needed to meld the support and premise with some sort of ironclad joint, and that's what a conditional statement provides. Notice that each correct response has a guarantee in it, and that guarantee can be thought of in terms of a trigger and a consequence.

fill the hole answers

Here are a few of the many ways we could represent the gap fillers:

The police chief is required to be good at figuring out mysteries. • (+A bit more) All police chiefs are great at solving mysteries.

Bill is a vegetarian only if he hates the taste of meat. • (+ A bit more) Every vegetarian hates the taste of meat.

All people who eat meat eat beef.

Every person[a] who owns hats owns a hat rack.

[a] *Can you see why "some people" or "most people" wouldn't fill the gap? Neither would ensure that Texans own hat racks.*

3. Conditional Statements Provide Inferences

All conditional statements provide inferences known as contrapositives, and you can think of the original condition and the contrapositive as two different sides of the same coin. For challenging questions, the test writers will commonly give us our gap fillers in terms of their contrapositives. Consider these four answers[1] we could have gotten instead of the four answers we got above. Do you see that they give us the same information—the guarantee we needed?

1. contrapositives

Those who are not good at figuring out mysteries cannot be police officers.

Those who do not hate the taste of meat are never vegetarians.

If you don't eat beef, you don't eat any meat at all.

No one without a hat rack owns a hat.

4. Conditional Statements Link Up

Remember that there were certain games that had a lot of conditional rules, and when this was the case it was often necessary to link these conditions up in order to answer questions. There are certain Logical Reasoning questions that work this way as well. When you see multiple conditional statements in one stimulus, you know that a part of your job will be to see how these statements link up and how they don't.

Conditional Logic Language

What's mentioned on the left represents all of the major "rules" that you need to know for conditional logic, but that's not all that makes conditional logic on the Logical Reasoning section challenging. In fact, many people would argue that a bigger challenge is consistently interpreting conditional statements correctly.

There are various ways in which the test writers can write conditional relationships. Some of these ways make the relationship obvious, while others don't. In fact, there are certain conditional statements that force everyone, even those who have a wealth of formal logic experience, to stop and have to think carefully. In large part, this is because these conditional statements involve words to which, in real life, we give contextual (that is, not universal or absolute) meaning. "Only if" is a statement we use for different meanings in real life, and that's a big reason that it causes us so much trouble. Another word that similarly causes our brains to get fuzzy is the word "unless."

Let's break down the different ways in which conditional statements can be written, and work on developing a system for thinking about them whenever we are uncertain. We'll start by taking a close-up look at just one conditional statement.

"ALL EMPLOYEES MUST WASH THEIR HANDS."

If one is an employee, one must wash his or her hands.

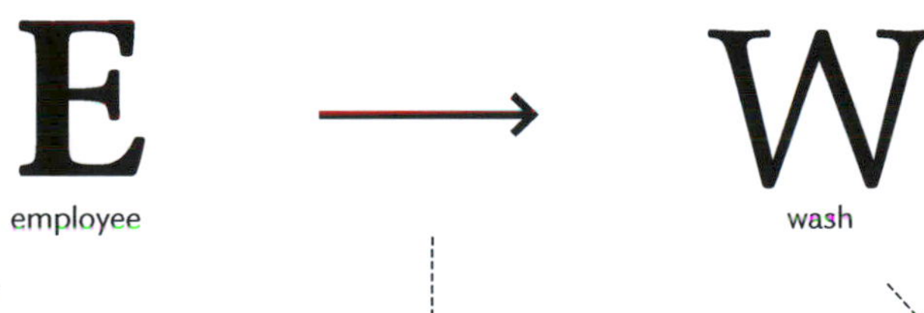

The trigger is known as the "sufficient condition" because it is *enough* to guarantee the outcome. In logic terms, "sufficient" is a powerful word (far more powerful than the word "necessary"). In this case, the word "all" gave us a sense of sufficiency. It tells us that if you have a certain characteristic (are an employee) there is a certain guaranteed result (you have to wash your hands). "If" is the most common word that starts a sufficient condition, but keep in mind that words like "all," "any," and "every," and their negative counterparts "no" and "none," are similar indicators of sufficiency.

Just like certain words inform us of a sufficient condition, certain other words tell us that there is some sort of guarantee. In this case, the word "must" serves this function—it is absolute and gives us the guarantee. The most basic guarantee word is actually "is," and all its other forms (were, was, will be, etc.). "The car is red" can be thought of in conditional terms—if something is the car, then it is red. Keep in mind that just because one *can* think of a statement in conditional terms doesn't mean one *should*. In most instances, you don't want to think of the word "is" in a conditional sort of way.

Finally, certain words indicate that we have the "result" part of a conditional statement, more formally known as the "necessary consequent." Imagine this sentence rewritten as, "If you are an employee, you need to wash your hands." Note that the "need to" indicates what must be the result of being an employee. Another way to say it would be "Employees are required to wash their hands." In this case, "required to" informs us of what must be the consequence of being an employee.

Keep in mind that many conditional statements (such as our example) contain more than one of these conditional markers.

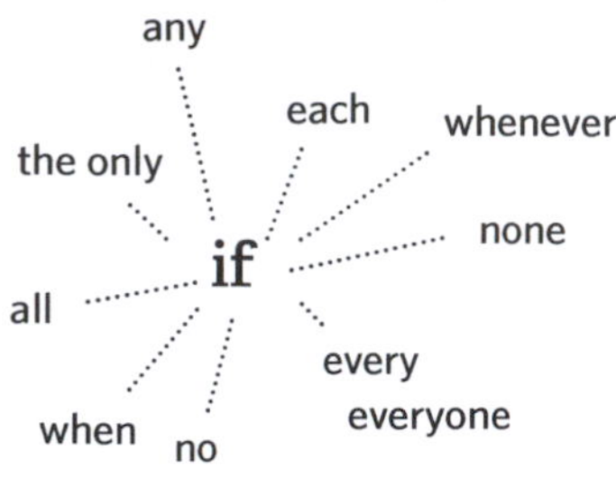

words that indicate sufficiency

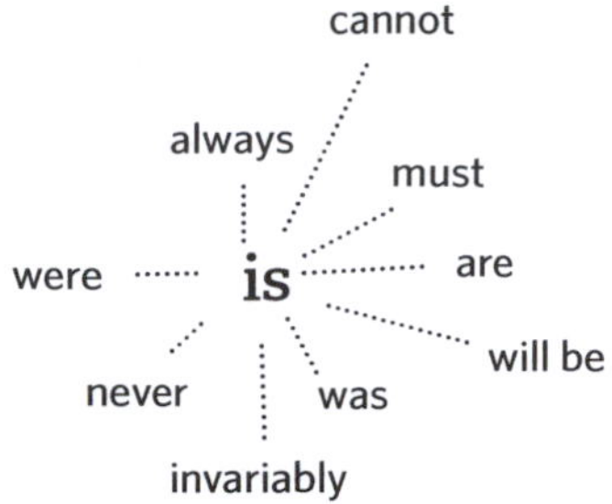

words that indicate guarantees

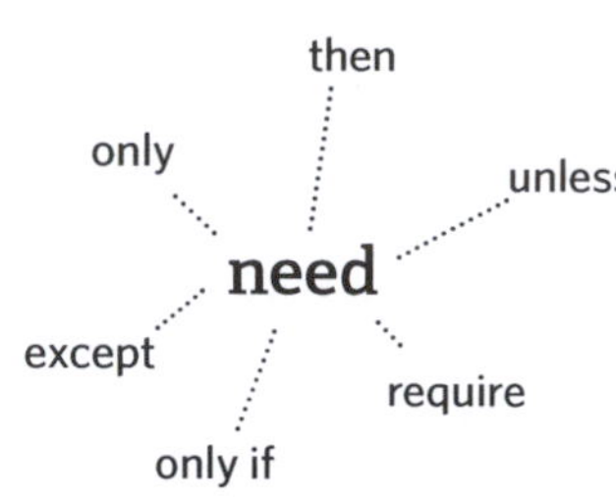

words that indicate a necessary result

translating well

We are going to need to translate conditional statements in the stimuli and in the answer choices. Here's how we want to think through them:

STEP ONE: For the purpose of translating conditional statements, it's best to think of them as **guarantees**. As you read a conditional statement, figure out what the two (or sometimes three) factors at issue are, then think about what the guarantee is in the situation. Does A guarantee B, or does B guarantee A? In most cases, this should help you see clearly the correct way to think about a conditional statement.

STEP TWO: There are two phrases, UNLESS and ONLY IF, that can get us all twisted around no matter how much we practice them. Never fear! A great way to combat these is to memorize a couple of **conditional mantras**. Just fit your difficult phrase into the structure of your mantra, and it should help you see how to translate the statement correctly. The process is modeled in the third example on the side.

conditional mantras

If you have these two phrases memorized, and know how to use them, they can be very helpful in a bind. Of course, you can use any other phrases you want, and come up with mantras for other conditional phrases that you find dizzying. **The key is that the mantras make it clearly obvious to you how you should correctly think about the guarantee.**

"You can't drive **UNLESS** you are at least sixteen" or
"**UNLESS** you are at least sixteen, you can't drive." **Drive → ≥ 16**

These above statements do not mean everyone over sixteen can drive.

"He will eat fish **ONLY IF** it is dead" or
"**ONLY IF** a fish is dead will he eat it." **Eat → Dead**

These statements do not mean that he'll eat any fish as long as it's dead.

EXAMPLES

"Every American likes television."

Does this guarantee that if you like television, you are American? No. Does it guarantee that if you are American, you like television? Yes.

American → like television

"Getting into the house requires a key."

Does this mean that if you have a key you are guaranteed to get into the house? No. (Maybe you had the wrong key.) Does this mean that if you get into the house you are guaranteed to have had a key? Yes.

Get in → have key

"No act can be seen as altruism unless the person seeing it is himself selfless."

Does this mean that if you see an act as altruistic, you are selfless? Hmmm. Does this mean that if you are selfless, you will see an act as altruistic? Hmmm. Does this mean if you are not selfless, you will not see an act as altruistic? Hmmm. Let's stop there. If you feel like you are turned around enough to possibly make a mistake, consider quickly how the statement relates to your conditional mantra.

We know...	*So...*
"You can't drive unless you are at least sixteen."	"No act can be seen as altruism unless the person seeing it is himself selfless."
is	must be
Drive → at least 16	altruism → selfless

Yes! We nailed it! Having a mantra to structure your thinking can help you when the abstract situation makes jelly out of your internal conditional sense.

Drill: Translating Conditional Statements

Directions: Match the statement to the correct interpretation.

D = DUCK **W = LIKE WATER**

D → W, ~~W~~ → ~~D~~ ········ W → D, ~~D~~ → ~~W~~

1. All ducks like water.
2. If you like water, you are a duck.
3. No duck doesn't like water.
4. Every animal that likes water is a duck.
5. No duck likes water.
6. Any animal that likes water is not a duck.
7. Unless an animal is a duck, it will not like water.
8. Ducks need to like water.
9. One does not like water only if one is a duck.
10. In order to like water, you must be a duck.

D → ~~W~~, W → ~~D~~ ········ ~~D~~ → W, ~~W~~ → D

T = TUESDAY **W = GO TO WORK**

T → W, ~~W~~ → ~~T~~ ········ W → T, ~~T~~ → ~~W~~

1. If it's Tuesday, I'll go to work.
2. I never go to work on Tuesday.
3. I'll go to work only if it's Tuesday.
4. Unless it is Tuesday, I will go to work.
5. I go to work every Tuesday.
6. I only work on Tuesdays.
7. Any day that I am not working is not a Tuesday.
8. If it's not Tuesday, I don't work.
9. All Tuesdays are days I go to work.
10. Any day I go to work is a Tuesday.

T → ~~W~~, W → ~~T~~ ········ ~~T~~ → W, ~~W~~ → T

A = AMERICAN **C = LOVES CHEESE**

A → C, ~~C~~ → ~~A~~ ········ C → A, ~~A~~ → ~~C~~

1. Every American loves cheese.
2. Only Americans love cheese.
3. No American loves cheese.
4. Unless you love cheese, you are not American.
5. People love cheese only if they are American.
6. Only those who love cheese are American.
7. Anyone who loves cheese is an American.
8. If you are American, you must love cheese.
9. Loving cheese is required of all Americans.
10. Anyone who is not American loves cheese.

A → ~~C~~, C → ~~A~~ ········ ~~A~~ → C, ~~C~~ → A

Drill: Translating Conditional Statements

Directions: Match the statement to the correct interpretation.

D = DATE F = FUNNY

D → F, ~~F~~ → ~~D~~

F → D, ~~D~~ → ~~F~~

1. Sarah only dates funny guys.
2. If you are funny, Sarah will date you.
3. Sarah will never date a funny guy.
4. Every guy Sarah dates is not funny.
5. Unless you are funny, Sarah will not date you.
6. All guys that Sarah dates are funny.
7. Sarah will go out with a guy only if he is funny.
8. If Sarah won't date you, that means you are funny.
9. Every funny guy has dated Sarah.
10. No funny guy has ever dated Sarah.

D → ~~F~~, F → ~~D~~

~~D~~ → F, ~~F~~ → D

W = WHALE M = LOVES MUSIC

W → M, ~~M~~ → ~~W~~

M → W, ~~W~~ → ~~M~~

1. All whales love music.
2. Only whales truly love music.
3. No whale loves music.
4. One cannot love music unless one is a whale.
5. One cannot be a whale unless one loves music.
6. One can love music only if one is a whale.
7. One can be a whale only if one loves music.
8. Every whale secretly does not love music.
9. All animals other than whales love music.
10. Every music lover is a whale.

W → ~~M~~, M → ~~W~~

~~W~~ → M, ~~M~~ → W

solutions note that you may have thought of some of these in terms of their contrapositives

	1	2	3	4	5	6	7	8	9	10
DUCKS & WATER	D → W	W → D	D → W	W → D	D → ~~W~~	W → ~~D~~	W → D	D → W	~~W~~ → D	W → D
TUESDAYS & WORK	T → W	T → ~~W~~	W → T	~~W~~ → T	T → W	W → T	T → W	W → T	T → W	W → T
AMERICANS & CHEESE	A → C	C → A	A → ~~C~~	A → C	C → A	A → C	C → A	A → C	A → C	~~A~~ → C
DATING & FUNNY GUYS	D → F	F → D	F → ~~D~~	D → ~~F~~	D → F	D → F	D → F	~~D~~ → F	F → D	F → ~~D~~
WHALES & MUSIC	W → M	M → W	W → ~~M~~	M → W	W → M	M → W	W → M	W → ~~M~~	~~W~~ → M	M → W

Conditional-Heavy Stimuli

Just like certain games can be dominated by conditional rules, certain Logical Reasoning stimuli can be over-run by conditional logic statements. In most cases, just as in those types of games, the statements in these types of stimuli will link together.

This is only likely to happen in a few types of questions (Sufficient Assumption, Inference, Match the Flaw, and Match the Reasoning, most commonly) and will not happen more than once or twice per exam. However, these can often be some of the more intimidating questions in any Logical Reasoning section.

When you see a conditional-heavy stimulus for a Sufficient Assumption question ("What exactly is a Sufficient Assumption question?" you say! We'll get to that on the next page), what you can expect is that the supporting premises link together in some way to form the conclusion. Well actually, they almost link together. They are missing one link, and the correct answer will fill that link in.

Keep in mind that just because these stimuli have statements that link up does not mean you *have to* link them up. Oftentimes, hopefully most of the time, you will see the missing link without putting all the different pieces together. Other times you'll just simply see the missing link as a flaw in the argument, and not have to think about it in a conditional sense at all.

However, once in a while, there will be a question that will really require some strong linking skills. You want to be able to whip them out when you need them. You already have the ability to recognize and use links from the Logic Games conditional logic lesson. The extra challenge for Logical Reasoning problems, of course, is that you also need to translate these statements and strip them down before you link them.

Below are examples of a more obvious missing link, and a better hidden one. You want to avoid doing the heavy work when you can, but you also want to make sure you feel you can do it when you need to.

Obvious missing link

If you don't sleep, you will be tired. If you are tired, you will be prone to making mistakes. Therefore, if you don't sleep, you will get fired.

Support: *Don't sleep → tired → prone to mistakes*
Conclusion: *Don't sleep → fired*
Whoa, where did we get fired? We can see the gap here without doing too much linking work.
We need: prone to mistakes → fired

Hidden missing link

All the socks have polyester, and Ted is allergic to anything that has polyester. If something makes Ted feel itchy, he won't buy it. Since Ted never pays attention to things he doesn't buy, he won't pay attention to the sock ad.

Support: *sock → poly → allergic ; itchy → won't buy → won't pay attention to ad*
Conclusion: *sock → won't pay attention to ad*
You don't need to think of the conclusion conditionally, though we did here. We know we need all the support to link up to give us the conclusion. The piece we are missing is that if he's allergic, Ted will be itchy. Notice that if we fit that piece in, all the support can be linked to reach the conclusion.
We need: allergic → itchy

Sufficient Assumption

"The conclusion follows logically if which of the following is assumed?"
"Which of the following, if assumed, allows the conclusion to be properly drawn?"

Fill the hole.

When a conclusion to an LSAT argument "follows logically" or can be defined as "properly drawn," it's a big deal, considering the fact that figuring out why conclusions do not follow logically, or are *not* properly drawn, is our primary task for the Logical Reasoning section.

The biggest key to Sufficient Assumption questions is to have a very clear sense of the flaw. These arguments will have specific, clearly defined gaps in reasoning—you wouldn't be able to make the arguments valid with just one statement in one answer choice otherwise. The second biggest key is to stay on task. Attractive wrong answers might strengthen the argument, or provide the argument with something it needs, without filling the hole to the point that the argument becomes valid. The right answer must leave the reasoning in the argument air-tight.

SUPER-SIMPLE EXAMPLE

Sandy has gotten straight As all through high school. Therefore, she will be a valedictorian.

The conclusion follows logically if which one of the following is assumed?

(A) Sandy has been accepted to every college she applied to.
(B) Sandy did not get any grades lower than an A.
(C) It is exceedingly rare for individuals to get all As through high school.
(D) Some valedictorians do not get all As.
(E) If a student gets all As through high school, that person will be named valedictorian.

The correct answer is (E). Certain answers have no direct relation to the stimulus: (A), (C); some have no connection to the point: (B); and some play a different, or unclear, role relative to the reasoning issue: (D). Note that the right answer leaves NO holes in the argument.

---

step one

understand your job

The question stems for Sufficient Assumption questions are defined by three main characteristics: they have the word "assumption," they almost always phrase that assumption in terms of a condition—"if assumed" (other types of assumption questions almost never have the word "if")—and most importantly, they include some sense that the argument would, with the assumption, be made logical or valid.

It's very important to keep the different Assumption questions clear (which is one of the reasons we are talking about them in different lessons). Basic Assumption, Sufficient Assumption, and Necessary Assumption are asking for different things, and it'll definitely cause you problems if you mix them up in your head.

Once you recognize that it's a Sufficient Assumption question, you should expect two things from the argument: it is more likely than not to have formal reasoning issues (most commonly conditional reasoning), and the argument is going to have one, clearly definable gap in reasoning.

two

find the point

As you go through the argument for the first time, try to get a sense of the overall flow of the reasoning. In particular, pay attention to whether you have a more typical support-to-conclusion relationship (which may be clouded in background and fluff), or a series of supporting premises that are meant to link together. If it's the latter, you know that the gap, or flaw in reasoning, has to do with some sort of missing link in the chain.

All of the above should be done in a fairly cursory way. As always, your primary task during your first read-through is to identify the conclusion. If you notice that it's a complicated argument, you may want to write out the conclusion (perhaps with the → shorthand we've been using in this lesson) in order to have it handy as you break down the support.

three

find the support

As just stated, the support will either be of a more traditional variety (one supporting piece of evidence), or it will come as a series of linking conditions. If it's the former, and it's a difficult question, chances are that there will be a lot of fluff in the argument. It's not unusual to have an argument that takes up seven or eight lines, only to have the last two lines be the only ones that are relevant to the point being made. If it's a series of linking conditions, expect that pretty much everything other than the conclusion will be support. If it's a linking situation, and it's tough to see exactly where the missing link is, you may want to write out the supporting statements.

four
figure out what's wrong

As always, this is *the* step. It's important to remember that the arguments for Sufficient Assumption questions will have one clearly definable hole or flaw. If they didn't—if an argument had multiple holes or a vaguely defined gap in reasoning—they could not create an answer that would be sufficient, or enough, to make the argument logically valid.

Finally, try to keep separate your understanding of what is wrong with the argument—that is, what the hole is in the argument, and how you might go about filling it. For more difficult questions, they may not fill the gap in the way that you might expect—having a sense of the issue, rather than a particular way of fixing it, will help you better adapt in the moment.

five
get rid of answers

The wrong choices are most commonly what determine whether a Sufficient Assumption question is more challenging or less so. Many Sufficient Assumption questions will have four wrong choices that have nothing to do with the argument. If you are diligent about finding the flaw and focusing on why answers are wrong, you can get through some of these questions very quickly. As always, don't try to identify the right answer; carefully evaluate attractive wrong answers. Get rid of answers that are obviously wrong first, then think carefully about the answer choices you are forced to think carefully about.

The hardest Sufficient Assumption questions can have several wrong answer choices that at first glance can seem like they fill the gap. Commonly, these attractive wrong choices match the argument in terms of subject matter, but don't give us the connection that we need in order to validate the conclusion. To illustrate, consider these two sample arguments, and these two sample answers. The first answer validates the first argument because it allows us to use the support to justify the conclusion. The second answer does not validate the second argument because it does not ensure that the conclusion will result (other people could have gotten bonuses too). The most attractive wrong choices for Sufficient Assumption questions commonly tend to work in this way.

Argument 1	Argument 2
Erica earned over $35,000. Therefore, she got a bonus.	**Erica got a bonus. Therefore, she earned over $35,000.**
Sufficient Assumption	*Insufficient* Assumption
Everyone who earned over $35,000 got a bonus.	**Everyone who earned over $35,000 got a bonus.**

Also keep in mind that other attractive wrong answers can help strengthen the argument—sometimes help strengthen it a lot—but that's very different from making the argument valid. The wrong answers can also provide something that needs to be true to reach the conclusion, but doesn't get us all the way to the conclusion (more on this in the next lesson).

six
confirm the right answer

You should be able to see that if you place the answer in between the support and the conclusion, it makes the conclusion one hundred percent justifiable. If it makes the conclusion seem really, really good but somehow not one hundred percent justifiable, there may be something wrong. Keep in mind that the right answer can go above and beyond filling a gap. If, say, we need to know that Manny "makes over $35,000" to get a certain bonus, finding out he makes $50,000 would be more specific than, and above and beyond, what we need to fill the gap, but it would absolutely be the correct answer, because it would be enough (more than enough) to make the conclusion one hundred percent valid.

SAME MEANING/DIFFERENT WORDS

There are many ways of stating the same information, and LSAT writers take advantage of that when they form answer choices. You need to be comfortable understanding statements, particularly conditional statements, in all of their various forms. Consider the following argument, all the ways to fill the gap, and all the ways they could create attractive wrong choices that give us the reverse or negation of what we need.

Argument
Kermit is a frog. Therefore, he loves green.

What will fill the gap?
All frogs love green.
Every frog loves green.
One is a frog only if one loves green.
If you don't love green, you are not a frog.

What won't?
Anything that loves green is a frog.
Everything that loves green is a frog.
One loves green only if one is a frog.
If you are not a frog, you do not love green.

CONSTELLATION OF WRONG ANSWERS

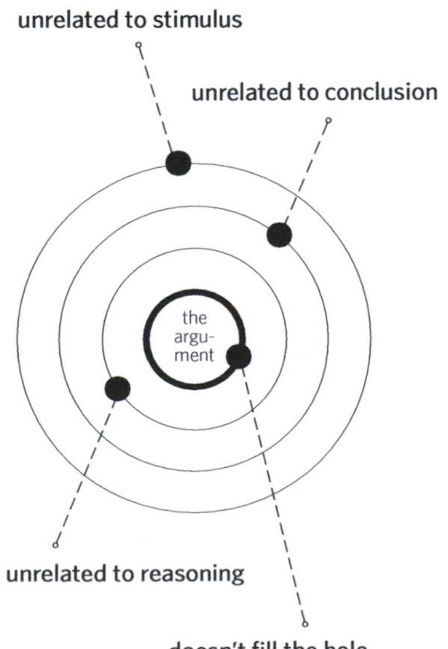

the process in action

Let's model the problem-solving process with two questions you solved at the end of Lesson 16.

2.23. Philosopher: An action is morally right if it would be reasonably expected to increase the aggregate well-being of the people affected by it. An action is morally wrong if and only if it would be reasonably expected to reduce the aggregate well-being of the people affected by it. Thus, actions that would be reasonably expected to leave unchanged the aggregate well-being of the people affected by them are also right.

The philosopher's conclusion follows logically if which one of the following is assumed?

(A) Only wrong actions would be reasonably expected to reduce the aggregate well-being of the people affected by them.
(B) No action is both right and wrong.
(C) Any action that is not morally wrong is morally right.
(D) There are actions that would be reasonably expected to leave unchanged the aggregate well-being of the people affected by them.
(E) Only right actions have good consequences.

1. understand your job: We have to find an argument and figure out what's wrong with it. Then we need to find an answer that plugs that gap.

2. find the point: The point is that actions expected to leave peoples' well-being unchanged are morally right.

3. find the support: There is actually no support for this! If an action increases well-being, it's morally right. If it decreases it, it's morally wrong. Also, if an action is morally wrong, it decreases well-being.

4. figure out what's wrong: We have no information about actions that leave unchanged people's well-being. We need an answer that connects these types of actions to them being morally right.

5. get rid of answers: (A) is a tempting opposite, but if we are thinking about sufficiency, this doesn't help us prove that the actions mentioned in the conclusion are *morally right.* (B) is strange! Let's leave it. (C) looks good. Our action is not yet morally wrong. If we put (C) in there, our action becomes morally right. Let's leave it. (D) simply shows us our conclusion is a possible situation—that's a long way away from proving it must be so. (E) might be tempting if we over-think it, but in no way does it validate the conclusion.

6. confirm the right answer: On the same note, tough to see how (B) impacts our conclusion—it leaves our conclusion neither right or wrong. (C) does impact our conclusion though, and it's the only answer remaining. Let's walk through it carefully. "Any action that is not morally wrong"—we're told only those actions that make people worse off are morally wrong, so we know for sure that an action that has no +/- is not morally wrong. If we add (C) to the conclusion and support, we get that any action that leaves unchanged the aggregate well-being is not morally wrong, and any action that is not morally wrong is morally right. This is enough to justify the conclusion, and (C) is correct.

3.5. Atrens: An early entomologist observed ants carrying particles to neighboring ant colonies and inferred that the ants were bringing food to their neighbors. Further research, however, revealed that the ants were emptying their own colony's dumping site. Thus, the early entomologist was wrong.

Atrens's conclusion follows logically if which one of the following is assumed?

(A) Ant societies do not interact in all the same ways that human societies interact.
(B) There is only weak evidence for the view that ants have the capacity to make use of objects as gifts.
(C) Ant dumping sites do not contain particles that could be used as food.
(D) The ants to whom the particles were brought never carried the particles into their own colonies.
(E) The entomologist cited retracted his conclusion when it was determined that the particles the ants carried came from their dumping site.

1. understand your job: We have to find an argument and figure out what's wrong with it. Then we need an answer that plugs that gap.

2. find the point: Ants do not bring food to their neighbors.

3. find the support: Ants dumping their trash.

4. figure out what's wrong: The issue is tough to see at first, but when you separate out the point and the support, it limits what could be wrong in the argument—the author is taking for granted that the trash does not have food. We need to find an answer that proves this is the case.

5. get rid of answers: (A) is the type of answer a strong sense of task can help you eliminate quickly. (B) too. Neither proves anything about food. (C) is exactly what we need. Let's keep it. (D) is unrelated to the point. (E) does not validate the conclusion, for the entomologist could have been wrong in retracting, and whether he retracted his opinion or not has no bearing on what ants actually do.

6. confirm the right answer: (C) is the only answer standing, and seems like a great hole filler. Let's read through it one more time. If (C) is true, then we know for sure that what the ants are taking to their neighbors has no food in it. (C) is correct.

Supporting Principle Questions

Just as Basic Assumption questions are very close siblings of Flaw questions, Supporting Principle questions are very close siblings of Sufficient Assumption questions. Just like sufficient assumptions, supporting principles serve to bridge the gap between the reasoning given and the conclusion reached.

There are a few secondary differences between Supporting Principle questions and Sufficient Assumption questions. The flaws in the arguments for Supporting Principle questions tend to be less absolute and abstract than those in Sufficient Assumption questions, and by the same token the right answers may not always have the same sense of closure. Furthermore, expect that the right answer will generalize beyond what we need to fill the gap—after all, a principle is just a rule that is generalized.

These are differences that ultimately have very little to do with getting to the right answer. The way you want to think about and solve Supporting Principle questions is no different from how you handle Sufficient Assumption questions—find the problem, and look for the one answer that would plug it up.

A question type that is even less common but still very closely related is the **Conform to a Principle question**. You saw an example of this in Lesson 16, and it's written below. The main difference with these questions is that the gaps will be written less as flaws and more as opinions. Your job is still the same—find the hole and plug it.

supporting principle question stems

Here is how a Supporting Principle question is typically phrased:

Which one of the following principles, if valid, most helps to justify the economist's reasoning?

conform to a principle question stems

Here are some ways in which Conform to a Principle questions can be phrased:

The reasoning above most closely conforms to which of the following principles?

Which one of the following propositions is most precisely exemplified by the situation presented above?

Step 1. Understand Your Job
We have to find an argument and figure out the gap between the support and the point. The right answer will plug that gap.

Step 2. Find the Point
Universities should only use open-source software.

Step 3. Find the Support
Open-source software better matches values embodied in academic scholarship, and academic scholarship is central to the mission of schools.

Step 4. Figure Out What's Wrong
Who says the software you use has to match, in some particular way, your value system? What if proprietary software is far more useful and cheaper? In any case, the author is taking for granted they should do something because it matches the values of the university.

Step 5. Get Rid of Answers
(A) matches our "what's wrong" hypothetical, but doesn't match the author's point. Neither does (B). (C) seems like exactly what we need. (D) is close right to the end, but the author's point is not about efficiency. (E) is not directly related to the stimulus.

Step 6. Confirm the Right Answer
That leaves (C) as the only legitimate contender. Notice how nicely (C) fits in between the support and the conclusion. This is the principle that underlies the author's thinking.

3.14. Commentator: In academic scholarship, sources are always cited, and methodology and theoretical assumptions are set out, so as to allow critical study, replication, and expansion of scholarship. In open-source software, the code in which the program is written can be viewed and modified by individual users for their purposes without getting permission from the producer or paying a fee. In contrast, the code of proprietary software is kept secret, and modifications can be made only by the producer, for a fee. This shows that open-source software better matches the values embodied in academic scholarship, and since scholarship is central to the mission of universities, universities should use only open-source software.

The commentator's reasoning most closely conforms to which one of the following principles?

(A) Whatever software tools are most advanced and can achieve the goals of academic scholarship are the ones that should alone be used in universities.
(B) Universities should use the type of software technology that is least expensive, as long as that type of software technology is adequate for the purposes of academic scholarship.
(C) Universities should choose the type of software technology that best matches the values embodied in the activities that are central to the mission of universities.
(D) The form of software technology that best matches the values embodied in the activities that are central to the mission of universities is the form of software technology that is most efficient for universities to use.
(E) A university should not pursue any activity that would block the achievement of the goals of academic scholarship at that university.

26.3.21. The companies that are the prime purchasers of computer software will not buy a software package if the costs of training staff to use it are high, and we know that it is expensive to teach people a software package that demands the memorization of unfamiliar commands. As a result, to be successful, commercial computer software cannot require users to memorize unfamiliar commands.

The conclusion above follows logically if which one of the following is assumed?

(A) If most prime purchasers of computer software buy a software product, that product will be successful.
(B) Commercial computer software that does not require users to memorize unfamiliar commands is no more expensive than software that does.
(C) Commercial computer software will not be successful unless prime purchasers buy it.
(D) If the initial cost of computer software is high, but the cost of training users is low, prime purchasers will still buy that software.
(E) The more difficult it is to learn how to use a piece of software, the more expensive it is to teach a person to use that software.

29.1.19. Arbitrator: The shipping manager admits that he decided to close the old facility on October 14 and to schedule the new facility's opening for October 17, the following Monday. But he also claims that he is not responsible for the business that was lost due to the new facility's failing to open as scheduled. He blames the contractor for not finishing on time, but he too, is to blame, for he was aware of the contractor's typical delays and should have planned for this contingency.

Which one of the following principles underlies the arbitrator's argument?

(A) A manager should take foreseeable problems into account when making decisions.
(B) A manager should be able to depend on contractors to do their jobs promptly.
(C) A manager should see to it that contractors do their jobs promptly.
(D) A manager should be held responsible for mistakes made by those whom the manager directly supervises.
(E) A manager, and only a manager, should be held responsible for a project's failure.

29.1.20. The price of a full-fare coach ticket from Toronto to Dallas on Breezeway Airlines is the same today as it was a year ago, if inflation is taken into account by calculating prices in constant dollars. However, today 90 percent of the Toronto-to-Dallas coach tickets that Breezeway sells are discount tickets and only 10 percent are full-fare tickets, whereas a year ago half were discount tickets and half were full-fare tickets. Therefore, on average, people pay less today in constant dollars for a Breezeway Toronto-to-Dallas coach ticket than they did a year ago.

Which one of the following, if assumed, would allow the conclusion above to be properly drawn?

(A) A Toronto-to-Dallas full-fare coach ticket on Breezeway Airlines provides ticket-holders with a lower level of service today than such a ticket provided a year ago.
(B) A Toronto-to-Dallas discount coach ticket on Breezeway Airlines costs about the same amount in constant dollars today as it did a year ago.
(C) All full-fare coach tickets on Breezeway Airlines cost the same in constant dollars as they did a year ago.
(D) The average number of coach passengers per flight that Breezeway Airlines carries from Toronto to Dallas today is higher than the average number per flight a year ago.
(E) The criteria that Breezeway Airlines uses for permitting passengers to buy discount coach tickets on the Toronto-to-Dallas route are different today than they were a year ago.

31.2.10. If something would have been justifiably regretted if it had occurred, then it is something that one should not have desired in the first place. It follows that many forgone pleasures should not have been desired in the first place.

The conclusion above follows logically if which one of the following is assumed?

(A) One should never regret one's pleasures.
(B) Forgone pleasures that were not desired would not have been justifiably regretted.
(C) Everything that one desires and then regrets not having is a forgone pleasure.
(D) Many forgone pleasures would have been justifiably regretted.
(E) Nothing that one should not have desired in the first place fails to be a pleasure.

Stick to the steps!
1. understand your job
2. find the point
3. find the support
4. figure out what's wrong
5. get rid of answers
6. confirm the right answer

26.3.21. The companies that are the prime purchasers of computer software will not buy a software package if the costs of training staff to use it are high, and we know that it is expensive to teach people a software package that demands the memorization of unfamiliar commands. As a result, to be successful, commercial computer software cannot require users to memorize unfamiliar commands.

The conclusion above follows logically if which one of the following is assumed?

(A) If most prime purchasers of computer software buy a software product, that product will be successful.
(B) Commercial computer software that does not require users to memorize unfamiliar commands is no more expensive than software that does.
(C) Commercial computer software will not be successful unless prime purchasers buy it.
(D) If the initial cost of computer software is high, but the cost of training users is low, prime purchasers will still buy that software.
(E) The more difficult it is to learn how to use a piece of software, the more expensive it is to teach a person to use that software.

1. understand your job: We have to find an argument and figure out what's wrong with it. Then we need to find an answer that bridges support and conclusion.

2. find the point: The shipping manager is also to blame.

3. find the support: He was aware of the contractor's typical delays and should have planned for this contingency.

4. figure out what's wrong: This argument has a much simpler argument (everything before "he too" is secondary), and a more clearly definable gap (support about being aware and planning, and conclusion is about blame) than the above argument. Note that this isn't as much a flaw (though we can think of it that way) as it is just space between an opinion and reasoning. We need an answer that fills the space—something that connects being aware and needing to plan to being as much to blame.

5. get rid of answers: (A) looks like the type of answer we are looking for—the manager should have "planned for the contingency." Let's leave it. (B) is not the point, and (C) is not a good match for "planned for contingency." (D) gives us "held responsible," which is a great match for blame. Let's leave it. "Only a manager" in (E) makes it clear that this is a not a good match for the arbitrator's point.

6. confirm the right answer: We had two attractive answers—(A) and (D). Let's evaluate them more carefully. (A) talks about what a manager should do, which is a good but not great match for being partly to blame. Looking carefully at (D), it has an even bigger issue—we have no idea if the manager directly supervises the contractor. (D) is definitely wrong, so (A) is close enough and it is correct.

1. understand your job: We have to find an argument and figure out what's wrong with it. Then we need to find an answer that completely fixes the issue.

2. find the point: To be successful, commercial computer software cannot require users to memorize unfamiliar commands.

3. find the support: Expensive to teach people unfamiliar commands, and companies that are prime purchasers won't buy package if costs of training staff to use it are high.

4. figure out what's wrong: This is a very tough issue to spot, and on the real exam this is a situation where you may need to go into the answers without the clear sense of the flaw we normally hope to have. The issue has to do with the modifier "prime"—perhaps the company can be successful even if it doesn't sell to the main purchasers (think Apple computers before they became more mainstream).

5. get rid of answers: (A) is helpful, but doesn't fill any gap in reasoning. (B) is unrelated to the types of expenses being discussed here and so doesn't fill the gap. If you didn't initially recognize the significance of "prime purchasers," maybe you paid more attention to it after you read (C). Let's leave it. (D) hurts the argument. "Difficult to learn" in (E) is irrelevant to our argument.

6. confirm the right answer: (C) is the only attractive answer, and if we fit it into the argument, we can see that it links the support to the conclusion, and connects the two concepts (prime purchases and success) that we needed to connect. The support gave us: need to memorize unfamiliar commands → training expensive → prime purchases won't buy. If we add (C) at the end of that link, it guarantees our conclusion.

29.1.19. Arbitrator: The shipping manager admits that he decided to close the old facility on October 14 and to schedule the new facility's opening for October 17, the following Monday. But he also claims that he is not responsible for the business that was lost due to the new facility's failing to open as scheduled. He blames the contractor for not finishing on time, but he too, is to blame, for he was aware of the contractor's typical delays and should have planned for this contingency.

Which one of the following principles underlies the arbitrator's argument?

(A) A manager should take foreseeable problems into account when making decisions.
(B) A manager should be able to depend on contractors to do their jobs promptly.
(C) A manager should see to it that contractors do their jobs promptly.
(D) A manager should be held responsible for mistakes made by those whom the manager directly supervises.
(E) A manager, and only a manager, should be held responsible for a project's failure.

29.1.20. The price of a full-fare coach ticket from Toronto to Dallas on Breezeway Airlines is the same today as it was a year ago, if inflation is taken into account by calculating prices in constant dollars. However, today 90 percent of the Toronto-to-Dallas coach tickets that Breezeway sells are discount tickets and only 10 percent are full-fare tickets, whereas a year ago half were discount tickets and half were full-fare tickets. Therefore, on average, people pay less today in constant dollars for a Breezeway Toronto-to-Dallas coach ticket than they did a year ago.

Which one of the following, if assumed, would allow the conclusion above to be properly drawn?

(A) A Toronto-to-Dallas full-fare coach ticket on Breezeway Airlines provides ticket-holders with a lower level of service today than such a ticket provided a year ago.
(B) A Toronto-to-Dallas discount coach ticket on Breezeway Airlines costs about the same amount in constant dollars today as it did a year ago.
(C) All full-fare coach tickets on Breezeway Airlines cost the same in constant dollars as they did a year ago.
(D) The average number of coach passengers per flight that Breezeway Airlines carries from Toronto to Dallas today is higher than the average number per flight a year ago.
(E) The criteria that Breezeway Airlines uses for permitting passengers to buy discount coach tickets on the Toronto-to-Dallas route are different today than they were a year ago.

1. understand your job: We have to find an argument and figure out what's wrong with it. Then we need to find an answer that completely fixes the issue.

2. find the point: On average, people pay less for this ticket than they did a year ago.

3. find the support: Full price same + greater percentage sold at a discount.

4. figure out what's wrong: This is a cleverly written problem and a tough flaw to spot—can you see it? It's unclear how much the discounts are for. If most of the discounts this year are for 5 percent, and most last year were for 50 percent, this reasoning won't support the conclusion.

5. get rid of answers: (A) is irrelevant to the argument. (B) fills the gap we saw—let's leave it. (C) gives more detail about a premise we got, but not in a way that fixes any holes or guarantees an outcome. (D) is irrelevant to the argument. (E) explains why a premise may be true, but does not fix a hole.

6. confirm the right answer: (B) is the only attractive answer. If we know that the discounts are the same, the full prices are the same, and a greater percentage of people are getting the discount, that is enough to guarantee that people are on average paying less.

31.2.10. If something would have been justifiably regretted if it had occurred, then it is something that one should not have desired in the first place. It follows that many forgone pleasures should not have been desired in the first place.

The conclusion above follows logically if which one of the following is assumed?

(A) One should never regret one's pleasures.
(B) Forgone pleasures that were not desired would not have been justifiably regretted.
(C) Everything that one desires and then regrets not having is a forgone pleasure.
(D) Many forgone pleasures would have been justifiably regretted.
(E) Nothing that one should not have desired in the first place fails to be a pleasure.

1. understand your job: We have to find an argument and figure out what's wrong with it. Then we need to find an answer that completely fixes the issue.

2. find the point: Many foregone pleasures should not have been desired in the first place.

3. find the support: If something would have been justifiably regretted if it had occurred, then it is something that one should not have desired in the first place.

4. figure out what's wrong: This argument has a very clearly defined gap—we need an answer that tells us that many foregone pleasures would have been justifiably regretted had they occurred.

5. get rid of answers: (A) is about pleasures had, not forgone pleasures. (A) is irrelevant. (B) gives us the reverse of what we need. (C) helps define the premise but not in a way that bridges the gap to the conclusion. (D) seems like what we need—let's leave it. (E) seems tempting at first, but does not match up with "foregone" pleasures.

6. confirm the right answer: Perhaps you were tempted by either (B) or (E) above—if so, this would be the step in which you try to fit them into the space between support and conclusion. Neither does the work that (D) clearly does. (D) is correct.

19 LOGICAL REASONING required assumption, strengthen, & weaken

A Quick Note about Mental Discipline

Questions that ask you to identify a required assumption, strengthen the argument, or weaken the argument require a high level of mental discipline. These three questions test the same skills you've been tested on so far—your ability to read for structure and your ability to be critical of reasoning—but on top of that, they also present additional and specific challenges. These additional challenges are far less significant when you are able to stay on point, and far more dangerous when you are not.

To illustrate exactly why, let's walk through the layers of challenge that a difficult question will present. We'll imagine a question that asks us to Strengthen the Argument, but what we'll discuss is true for all three of these question types. First, it's likely that the stimulus will hold a lot of extraneous information—you'll need discipline not to get bogged down and to quickly identify the point. It's likely that in that sea of clutter that remains, only a phrase or two will be used to support this point—your next job is to dig these out. Then, you need the discipline to isolate this point and support in order to figure out what's wrong. For the toughest questions, it won't always be easy to figure out what's wrong, and the truth is you may be forced to go forward without a complete sense of the problem (though hopefully that won't happen to you too often). As you evaluate the answer choices, some will strengthen the point—but not in any way that relates to the reasoning in the argument. Some answers will prop up questionable supporting premises—but not in a way that impacts the argument. Finally, you'll find that answer that does directly address the argument—but it actually weakens it. You need the discipline to not lose sight of the specific reasoning issue and your specific task.

Phew! If you have weaknesses in one or two of these areas, you can likely survive easier questions. However, you can see how these skills build upon one another: if you are not strong at the individual components, there is no way you will be in control of a beastly question like the one described above. If you have a vague sense of the point, a vague sense of the support, and a vague sense of the reasoning issue, many of the answer choices will surely look good to you.

The great news is that if you can hold a specific understanding of the support-conclusion relationship in your head (even if you can't see exactly what is wrong), and if you can remember that your job is to strengthen the bond between this support and the point, more often than not it should be that only one answer choice remains after eliminating wrong choices. The great news is that if you can stay on point, the wrong answers are far more obviously wrong, and that will determine how quickly and easily you can get these questions correct.

Required Assumption

"Which of the following is an assumption required by the argument?"
"The argument relies on which one of the following assumptions?"
"Which one of the following is an assumption on which the argument depends?"

What *needs* to be true?

Required Assumption questions (a.k.a. Necessary Assumption questions) ask us to think about the problem in an argument in a very specific way. These questions ask that we figure out the gap in reasoning, then find one answer that needs to be true if that gap is going to be filled. Required Assumption questions are very common, and they are the most common of the questions centered on "assumptions."

Compared to the other types of questions we've seen thus far, these questions can more often have less clearly definable flaws. They also commonly have stimuli with an excess of secondary information. A big key to Required Assumption questions is to stick to a specific and narrow understanding of "required"—we are not being asked for answers that strengthen the argument, or perhaps even fix the argument, and many of the most tempting wrong choices will perform these other functions.

SUPER-SIMPLE EXAMPLE

Megan has gotten into great shape recently. She must be going to the gym regularly.

Which of the following is an assumption required by the argument?

(A) Megan goes to the gym the same number of days each week.
(B) Going to the gym is one of the best ways to get in shape.
(C) Everyone who goes to a gym will get in great shape.
(D) Different people have the same sense of what being in great shape means.
(E) Megan did not get into great shape solely by doing yoga in her home.

The author is assuming that going to the gym is the only way to get in great shape. The correct answer is (E). Note that some wrong answers don't relate to the argument (D), some relate (questionably) to the conclusion but not the support (A), and some aid the argument but are not required (B), (C). Note that the right answer is not one we could predict, but is something that must be true if the reasoning in the argument is ever going to work.

---

step one
understand your job

The question stems for Required Assumption questions are defined by two primary characteristics: they almost always have the word "assumption" (though almost never the word "if"), and they *must* have some other word that indicates necessity—such as *required*, *rely*, or *depend*.

two
find the point

Once you recognize the question type, you know that your job is to identify the flaw, and to find the one answer that needs to be true if the support is ever going to actually prove the point. Of course, this starts with understanding the problem in the argument correctly.

three
find the support

Steps one through four are the same for every question that asks you to be critical of the reasoning in an argument. You want to isolate the critical components—the point and the support—then carefully evaluate that relationship. Hopefully you are having to *think* about performing these steps less and less—that is, they are simply becoming habit.

four
figure out what's wrong

Whereas steps two and three are more mechanical, step four is less likely to feel as absolute, at least not until you get very close to the end of your process. Once you get all of your other habits down, knowing what's wrong is ultimately the last thing remaining that makes certain stimuli more difficult than others. For steps one through three, make sure you do not go forward until you are finished with that step. For step four, you may need to occasionally move on without a complete picture of the flaw. That's okay. If you are strong at your other skills, you should be able to compensate. Still, questions are of course always easier when you know what is wrong with the argument, so do always give yourself a fair shot at figuring out what is wrong before moving forward.

five

get rid of answers

Once you have a firm understanding of the argument and flaw, you want to move on to eliminating answers.

One important thing to keep in mind is that, in general, you cannot anticipate the answer for a Required Assumption question. This is very different from, say, a Flaw question, or even a Sufficient Assumption question, both of which will have answer choices that look very much like the exact issue you spotted in the argument.

The reality is, when an argument is flawed, it generally requires many different assumptions; therefore, these questions will tend to have many possible right answers. Knowing this plays an important role in your elimination process. Don't eliminate an answer because it does not match what you were expecting.

Instead, as always, eliminate answers based on your understanding of the argument and your understanding of the task. As always, most wrong choices will have no direct connection to the argument being made, and often you can get rid of all four answer choices with just a strong sense of the argument.

The most attractive wrong choices are ones that seem to support the argument in some way, or perhaps even completely fix the argument. Keep in mind that there are certain assumptions that can fix an entire argument, but are not *needed* or required for that argument to be fixed (more on this on the side and in a couple of pages). A clear sense of task is critical here. There is a difference between helpful and required, and if your focus is on *required*, these wrong choices will be more obviously wrong.

As always, do not think too deeply about right answers in this step. Try to find clear, obvious reasons why answers are wrong, and if you can't find them, leave the answers for your last step.

REQUIRED ≠ IMPORTANT

Remember that required and important are different criteria. A necessary assumption may be important, or it may not be. (More on page 271.)

Megan has gotten into great shape recently. She must be going to the gym regularly.

Required assumptions
(+ negations):
Megan did not get into great shape solely by doing yoga in her home. (*Megan got into great shape solely doing yoga in her home.*)

Megan goes to the gym. (*Megan does not go to the gym.*)

Helpful, but not required:
Going to the gym is one of the best ways to get in shape. (*Going to the gym isn't one of the best ways to get in shape*—so what? It could have still worked for Megan.)

Everyone who goes to a gym will get in great shape. (*Not everyone who goes to the gym gets in great shape*—so what? Ditto as above.)

Note how the negation test can help weed out the truly necessary assumptions from the other answers.

six

confirm the right answer

Left with just one or two serious contenders, now you should carefully evaluate each answer choice to figure out which one is required in order for the argument to work. Again, keep in mind the difference between required and helpful. If one answer needs to be true for the argument to work but hardly helps it, and another answer completely fixes all issues, but not in a way they needed to be fixed, the first answer will be correct.

For Required Assumption questions, a great tool for confirming the correct answer is the negation test (see side for example). If the support is in fact required or necessary in order to reach a conclusion, it stands to reason that if the exact opposite of that support were true, it would severely hurt or even destroy the argument being made. If you negate an answer choice and the negation does not hurt the argument, the answer was not something that was necessary to the argument. The negation test will work on all correct answers to Required Assumption questions, and it's something you should build in to your process for solving all Required Assumption questions.

---

always negate to confirm a required assumption

CONSTELLATION OF WRONG ANSWERS

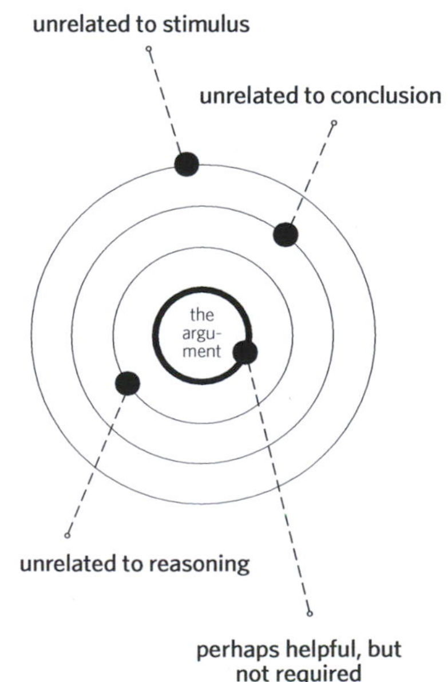

the process in action

Let's model the problem-solving process with a question you solved at the end of Lesson 16.

3.17. When exercising the muscles in one's back, it is important, in order to maintain a healthy back, to exercise the muscles on opposite sides of the spine equally. After all, balanced muscle development is needed to maintain a healthy back, since the muscles on opposite sides of the spine must pull equally in opposing directions to keep the back in proper alignment and protect the spine.

Which one of the following is an assumption required by the argument?

(A) Muscles on opposite sides of the spine that are equally well developed will be enough to keep the back in proper alignment.
(B) Exercising the muscles on opposite sides of the spine unequally tends to lead to unbalanced muscle development.
(C) Provided that one exercises the muscles on opposite sides of the spine equally, one will have a generally healthy back.
(D) If the muscles on opposite sides of the spine are exercised unequally, one's back will be irreparably damaged.
(E) One should exercise daily to ensure that the muscles on opposite sides of the spine keep the back in proper alignment.

1. understand your job
We have to figure out what's wrong with the argument then find an assumption required in order to make the argument work.

2. find the point
When exercising one's back, it's important to exercise muscles on both sides equally.

3. find the support
Balanced muscle development is important for a healthy back.

4. figure out what's wrong
Very tough to see what is wrong here. Both the support and the conclusion are about the same consequence (maintaining a healthy back), and it's tough to see an issue! The argument makes sense—we need balanced development, so we should exercise both sides the same. Maybe there is something to "exercise"...

5. get rid of answers
(A) is more than we need—we don't need to know that this is "enough" for proper alignment. (B) seems really good—it is something we probably need to assume. Let's leave it. (C) is just like (A) —more than we need. (C) does not have to be true for the argument to work—maybe you get a bad back because you sit in a chair all day! (D) is too extreme and not necessary. (E) can be knocked off the second you see "daily." (Why would it be necessary to exercise daily?)

6. confirm the right answer
We weren't one hundred percent sure of the flaw, but with a clear sense of the conclusion and the support, and our task, we were still able to get rid of four answers. Left with just (B), now the gap in the argument makes more sense—maybe we don't need to "exercise" both sides equally for balanced development (perhaps you naturally use one side more depending on whether you are left or right handed, so you need to exercise the other side more in order for your back to balance out). (B) may be easy to overlook because it may seem too obvious, but it does address an assumption in the argument, and it is something we need to assume in order for the argument to work.

The negation of (B) would be "Exercising the muscles on opposite sides of the spine unequally does not tend to lead to unbalanced muscle development." Notice that this would severely hurt how the author is trying to use his reasons to make his point. That's a good sign of a necessary assumption.

required ≠ IMPORTANT

We've now taken a look at all three question types that speak of the *flaw* in an argument as an *assumption* that the author has made. *Basic Assumption* questions simply ask us to state the problem in an argument in terms of an assumption the author has made. *Sufficient Assumption* questions ask us to identify an answer that would completely fix the reasoning issue in an argument. *Required Assumption* questions ask us to identify an assumption that needs to be true for the conclusion to be true.

The three types of questions are very easy to lump together, but they each require something unique from us, and it's important to develop specific habits for each one.

Required Assumption questions are the most common of the three, and also the ones where discipline is most important. Perhaps the most important thing to remember is the specific meaning of the word "required." It's very easy to think of "required" as meaning "important," and while these two characteristics sometimes coincide, they do not define one another. The right answer to a Required Assumption question might be very important to the entire argument—in fact, it may match your exact understanding of the flaw in the argument, or it may be something that is secondary, but nonetheless needs to be true in order for the argument to work.

The reason why this is important to remember is that "importance" is the primary factor the test writers have for creating less attractive right answers, and more attractive wrong ones. Take a look below at two sample arguments, along with potential answer choices. The first two answer choices represent required assumptions—one that goes a long way toward fixing the issues in the argument and one that does not. The last two choices represent potentially attractive wrong answers to Required Assumption questions—one that might make the argument better, and another that might even completely fix it—but neither of which is required. Keep in mind that a required assumption need not fix the argument or even get close to fixing it—it's simply something that needs to be true if the argument is going to work.

We have now discussed three question types that center on the word "assumption." Each of these assumption questions is asking us for a slightly different type of answer. Let's take a quick look at the three different types of assumption questions and the tasks they present.

Basic Assumption
"The argument assumes that..."

Task: Look for an answer that expresses the flaw in reasoning as an assumption.

Sufficient Assumption
"Which of the following, if assumed, allows the argument to be properly drawn?"

Task: Look for an answer that makes the argument air tight.

Necessary Assumption
"Which of the following is an assumption required by the argument?"

Task: Look for an answer that needs to be true if the argument is to work.

required vs **important**

Because we locked the door, no one can break into our house.

Possible Assumptions:
Required and important: There are no other ways to break into the house.
Required and less important: One cannot break into the house going through the chimney.
Helpful but not required: None of the windows to the house can be opened.
Fills the gap but is not required: The door is the only way in and out of the house, and the locked door impenetrable.

My husband says I consume too much caffeine, but that is false. I only drink one cup of coffee a day, and one cup of coffee is not too much caffeine for a person to consume daily.

Possible Assumptions:
Required and important: She does not get her excess of caffeine through other means.
Required and less important: She does not get an excess of caffeine from drinking tea.
Helpful but not required: The coffee she drinks has less caffeine than normal coffee.
Fills the gap but is not required: Coffee is the only substance she consumes that contains caffeine. (Very tempting, but more than we need.)

26.2.7. Speakers of the Caronian language constitute a minority of the population in several large countries. An international body has recommended that the regions where Caronian-speakers live be granted autonomy as an independent nation in which Caronian-speakers would form a majority. But Caronian-speakers live in several, widely scattered areas that cannot be united within a single continuous boundary while at the same time allowing Caronian-speakers to be the majority population. Hence, the recommendation cannot be satisfied.

The argument relies on which one of the following assumptions?

(A) A nation once existed in which Caronian-speakers formed the majority of the population.
(B) Caronian-speakers tend to perceive themselves as constituting a single community.
(C) The recommendation would not be satisfied by the creation of a nation formed of disconnected regions.
(D) The new Caronian nation will not include as citizens anyone who does not speak Caronian.
(E) In most nations several different languages are spoken.

28.3.19. On a certain day, nine scheduled flights on Swift Airlines were canceled. Ordinarily, a cancellation is due to mechanical problems with the airplane scheduled for a certain flight. However, since it is unlikely that Swift would have mechanical problems with more than one or two airplanes on a single day, some of the nine cancellations were probably due to something else.

The argument depends on which one of the following assumptions?

(A) More than one or two airplanes were scheduled for the nine canceled flights.
(B) Swift Airlines has fewer mechanical problems than do other airlines of the same size.
(C) Each of the canceled flights would have been longer than the average flight on Swift Airlines.
(D) Swift Airlines had never before canceled more than one or two scheduled flights on a single day.
(E) All of the airplanes scheduled for the canceled flights are based at the same airport.

28.1.2. If the government increases its funding for civilian scientific research, private patrons and industries will believe that such research has become primarily the government's responsibility. When they believe that research is no longer primarily their responsibility, private patrons and industries will decrease their contributions toward research. Therefore, in order to keep from depressing the overall level of funding for civilian scientific research, the government should not increase its own funding.

Which one of the following is an assumption on which the argument relies?

(A) Governments should bear the majority of the financial burden of funding for civilian scientific research.
(B) Any increase in government funding would displace more private funding for civilian scientific research than it would provide.
(C) Private donations toward research are no longer welcomed by researchers whose work receives government funding.
(D) Civilian scientific research cannot be conducted efficiently with more than one source of funding.
(E) Funding for civilian scientific research is currently at the highest possible level.

29.1.15. Ordinary mountain sickness, a common condition among mountain climbers, and one from which most people can recover, is caused by the characteristic shortage of oxygen in the atmosphere at high altitudes. Cerebral edema, a rarer disruption of blood circulation in the brain that quickly becomes life-threatening if not correctly treated from its onset, can also be caused by a shortage of oxygen. Since the symptoms of cerebral edema resemble those of ordinary mountain sickness, cerebral edema is especially dangerous at high altitudes.

Which one of the following is an assumption on which the argument depends?

(A) The treatment for ordinary mountain sickness differs from the treatment for cerebral edema.
(B) Cerebral edema can cause those who suffer from it to slip into a coma within a few hours.
(C) Unlike cerebral edema, ordinary mountain sickness involves no disruption of blood circulation in the brain.
(D) Shortage of oxygen at extremely high altitudes is likely to affect thinking processes and cause errors of judgment.
(E) Most people who suffer from ordinary mountain sickness recover without any special treatment.

Required Assumption Solutions

26.2.7. Speakers of the Caronian language constitute a minority of the population in several large countries. An international body has recommended that the regions where Caronian-speakers live be granted autonomy as an independent nation in which Caronian-speakers would form a majority. But Caronian-speakers live in several, widely scattered areas that cannot be united within a single continuous boundary while at the same time allowing Caronian-speakers to be the majority population. Hence, the recommendation cannot be satisfied.

The argument relies on which one of the following assumptions?

(A) A nation once existed in which Caronian-speakers formed the majority of the population.
(B) Caronian-speakers tend to perceive themselves as constituting a single community.
(C) The recommendation would not be satisfied by the creation of a nation formed of disconnected regions.
(D) The new Caronian nation will not include as citizens anyone who does not speak Caronian.
(E) In most nations several different languages are spoken.

1. understand your job: Our job is to find what's wrong with the argument, then find an answer that needs to be true for the argument to work.

2. find the point: Cannot form an independent nation with Caronian-speakers as majority.

3. find the support: Caronian-speakers are too spread out to form majority in any one area.

4. figure out what's wrong: The argument seems to make a lot of sense, especially in real-life terms. Still, the fact that they are too spread out does not seem enough to absolutely prove the conclusion—perhaps some of the people can move to form a majority in an area, etc.

5. get rid of answers: (A) is related in subject matter, but if we are thinking about what is required, we can see that (A) is definitely not something that needs to be true for the author's argument to work. Neither is (B)—what they think of themselves has no direct bearing on the point. (C) is not an answer we expected, but it does relate to the premise-conclusion relationship. Let's keep it. (D) is more than needed for the argument, and (E) does not need to be true for the argument to work. That leaves us with only (C).

6. confirm the right answer: We think of a nation as one block of land, so (C) is not an answer most of us will anticipate. However, (C) does need to be true for the argument to work—if a nation could be created by people living in different areas, his support would not justify his conclusion.

28.1.2. If the government increases its funding for civilian scientific research, private patrons and industries will believe that such research has become primarily the government's responsibility. When they believe that research is no longer primarily their responsibility, private patrons and industries will decrease their contributions toward research. Therefore, in order to keep from depressing the overall level of funding for civilian scientific research, the government should not increase its own funding.

Which one of the following is an assumption on which the argument relies?

(A) Governments should bear the majority of the financial burden of funding for civilian scientific research.
(B) Any increase in government funding would displace more private funding for civilian scientific research than it would provide.
(C) Private donations toward research are no longer welcomed by researchers whose work receives government funding.
(D) Civilian scientific research cannot be conducted efficiently with more than one source of funding.
(E) Funding for civilian scientific research is currently at the highest possible level.

1. understand your job: Our job is to find what's wrong with the argument, then find an answer that needs to be true for the argument to work.

2. find the point: Gov't shouldn't increase its own funding.

3. find the support: Gov't increase would result in a decrease in private $, and therefore a decrease in overall funds.

4. figure out what's wrong: In considering a net loss to funding, the author is assuming that the decrease in private $ will be more significant than the increase in gov't money. Who's to say that's the case? Maybe private $ will decrease by $1.00.

5. get rid of answers: (A) does not need to be true for the argument to work and in fact has no direct bearing on the point being made. (B) matches the issue we saw in the argument, so let's leave it. (C) would help the argument, but certainly does not need to be true for the argument to work. Since efficiency is not the point of this argument, we can eliminate (D) quickly. (E) does not need to be true for the argument to work.

6. confirm the right answer: (B) matches our understanding of the gap. To confirm, we can think of the opposite of (B): an increase in gov't funding would not cause a more significant loss of private $.

Required Assumption Solutions

28.3.19. On a certain day, nine scheduled flights on Swift Airlines were canceled. Ordinarily, a cancellation is due to mechanical problems with the airplane scheduled for a certain flight. However, since it is unlikely that Swift would have mechanical problems with more than one or two airplanes on a single day, some of the nine cancellations were probably due to something else.

The argument depends on which one of the following assumptions?

(A) More than one or two airplanes were scheduled for the nine canceled flights.
(B) Swift Airlines has fewer mechanical problems than do other airlines of the same size.
(C) Each of the canceled flights would have been longer than the average flight on Swift Airlines.
(D) Swift Airlines had never before canceled more than one or two scheduled flights on a single day.
(E) All of the airplanes scheduled for the canceled flights are based at the same airport.

1. understand your job: Our job is to find what's wrong with the argument, then find an answer that needs to be true for the argument to work.

2. find the point: Cerebral edema is especially dangerous at high altitudes.

3. find the support: Symptoms of cerebral edema are similar to those of mountain sickness. Cerebral edema is very dangerous, while mountain sickness is not.

It's tough to understand the support here, but essentially the author is saying that because this life-threatening thing is so similar to something common and less life-threatening, it's more dangerous. Ah, maybe because people mistake one for the other.

4. figure out what's wrong: This argument seems strong. While misdiagnosing and being dangerous are two different things, it seems from real life that misdiagnosing a critical condition is dangerous. We're really going to need to rely on task to eliminate answers.

5. get rid of answers: (A) seems attractive—let's leave it. If the treatment were the same, why would the misdiagnosis be dangerous? (B) seems to support the conclusion, but wait—it's not required. (C) explains differences between the two, but is not required. (D) might make it easier to mistake one for the other, but is not required. (E) doesn't impact the conclusion.

6. confirm the right answer: Let's go back to (A)—we can walk through it carefully to see that it is indeed a necessary assumption. If the treatment for both was the same, misdiagnosing one for the other might not be so bad.

1. understand your job: Our job is to find what's wrong with the argument, then find an answer that needs to be true for the argument to work.

2. find the point: Some of the nine cancellations were due to something other than mechanical problems.

3. find the support: Unlikely that mechanical problems would keep more than one or two airplanes on the ground.

4. figure out what's wrong: Hmmm. Tough to see. Maybe there is something with the difference between flights and airplanes.

5. get rid of answers: Not sure how (A) is necessary, but it is about flights and airplanes, and seems relevant. Let's leave it. (B) is nice and all, but it has nothing to do with the support-conclusion relationship. (C) also has nothing to do with the argument. (D) supports the premise, but isn't necessary. (E) provides an alternative explanation for the cancellations (maybe an airport was closed down) but that thought requires a lot of conjecture, and certainly isn't something the argument requires.

6. confirm the right answer: Looking back at (A), the issue with the argument seems obvious now—airplanes make multiple flights a day. Maybe the nine cancellations are just from one or two planes. The negation of (A)—(no more than one or two planes...) hurts the argument and helps prove that (A) is correct.

29.1.15. Ordinary mountain sickness, a common condition among mountain climbers, and one from which most people can recover, is caused by the characteristic shortage of oxygen in the atmosphere at high altitudes. Cerebral edema, a rarer disruption of blood circulation in the brain that quickly becomes life-threatening if not correctly treated from its onset, can also be caused by a shortage of oxygen. Since the symptoms of cerebral edema resemble those of ordinary mountain sickness, cerebral edema is especially dangerous at high altitudes.

Which one of the following is an assumption on which the argument depends?

(A) The treatment for ordinary mountain sickness differs from the treatment for cerebral edema.
(B) Cerebral edema can cause those who suffer from it to slip into a coma within a few hours.
(C) Unlike cerebral edema, ordinary mountain sickness involves no disruption of blood circulation in the brain.
(D) Shortage of oxygen at extremely high altitudes is likely to affect thinking processes and cause errors of judgment.
(E) Most people who suffer from ordinary mountain sickness recover without any special treatment.

Strengthen and Weaken

"Which of the following, if true, most strengthens the argument?"
"Which of the following, if true, most seriously weakens the argument?"
"Which one of the following, if true, most calls into question the author's reasoning?"

Strengthen and Weaken questions are similar to Required Assumption questions in that our job is to identify the flaw in the argument, and then address that flaw in some way. Compared to question types from previous lessons, these questions will more commonly have vague or more difficult to define flaws, and they will often have a lot of secondary "fluff" around the critical components of the argument. Right answers need not make the argument perfect, and generally will not.

Some of the most tempting wrong answers for Strengthen and Weaken questions are ones that strengthen or weaken the author's point, but not in a way that impacts how he made the point originally (i.e., the reasoning). Answers that play an opposite role—strengthen answers for weaken questions and vice-versa—are also often surprisingly tempting. As always, a huge key to success is your ability to focus on the argument and the task.

SUPER-SIMPLE EXAMPLE

Mr. Thomas, the owner of the convenience store, is not friendly to customers. Therefore, it is unlikely that his store will remain open for long.

Which of the following, if true, most strengthens the argument?

(A) It is difficult for businesses to remain open beyond an initial period if their owners are not friendly to their customers.
(B) Mr. Thomas has poor math skills and incorrectly prices many items.
(C) Most owners of convenience stores are naturally outgoing people.
(D) Mr. Thomas is unfriendly because he is trying to be professional.
(E) By working long hours and cutting down on employee costs, Mr. Thomas can offer lower prices than his competitors.

The correct answer is (A). Certain answers are wrong because they don't relate directly to the argument: (C); some give us information about the premise, but not in a way that helps the conclusion: (D); some arguably impact the conclusion but not the support-conclusion relationship: (B); and some arguably weaken the argument: (E).

---

step one
understand your job

Perhaps more so than any other type of question, Strengthen and Weaken questions have somewhat deceptive question stems. What is deceptive about them is that they will invariably ask for the answer that *most* strengthens or *most* weakens but only give you one answer that can possibly strengthen or possibly weaken. This is true every single time. Why do they do this? We could take some educated guesses, but it really doesn't matter.

two
find the point

What does matter is that you approach these questions with the right mindset. A Strengthen or a Weaken question will require you to understand the flaw in the argument and then identify the one answer choice that matches the task.

three
find the support

One other thing to notice is that these questions will always have the statement "if true" contained in the question stem. This tells us not to waste our energy thinking about the validity of the answer choices. Rather, we want to focus on how that answer choice, if true, impacts the relationship between the support given and the conclusion reached.

four
figure out what's wrong

Strengthen and Weaken questions, especially as they get more difficult, can tend to have a lot of secondary information. Just as with Required Assumption questions, when you see a large stimulus, your sense should not be, "Wow, there's going to be a lot to think about" but rather "Wow, there's a lot to dig through to get to what's important."

Once you've isolated the support and the conclusion, your next job is always to figure out what is wrong. Hopefully you feel like you are getting more and more specific in terms of understanding what is wrong with arguments. Strengthen and Weaken questions will test your abilities: the support and conclusion will often be separated by a lot of "fluff," and commonly the issues will be less clear cut than in some other question types. Still, you want to be able to see what is wrong for the vast majority of questions. If you do need to move on to the next step with anything less than a clear picture, there are secondary steps you can take to still get the question correct.

five
get rid of answers

Like all questions, Strengthen and Weaken questions will have answers you can eliminate because they have no direct bearing on the relationship between the support and the conclusion. Even when you can't quite put your finger on exactly what is wrong with an argument, if you can simply isolate the argument from the secondary information, it's not uncommon to see that the four wrong choices have no direct bearing on the argument. By this point, hopefully you feel that you are becoming more and more of an expert at quickly sniffing out and eliminating these incorrect answers.

Of course, answers that have a more direct bearing on the elements within the argument will be far more attractive. Beware of answer choices that strengthen or weaken the conclusion, but not in a way that seems to relate to the reasoning you originally considered. Remember that strengthening or weakening the author's point is not your job. Your job is to strengthen or weaken the bond between the support and the conclusion.

Lastly, do not be swayed by *how much* the answer choice strengthens or weakens. Just like with Required Assumption questions, it's true that certain answers "fix" issues in ways you expect, whereas other correct answers strengthen or weaken the argument *just a little bit*, still leaving it with plenty of flaws. Do not eliminate an answer because it only seems to strengthen or weaken a little—that's fine. Only eliminate answers that you know do not perform the job at all.

six
confirm the right answer

Hopefully the previous step has left you with just one answer, or maybe two (though on occasion there will be one or two questions per section with three or four attractive answer choices). This last step of confirming the right answer is particularly important and useful for Strengthen and Weaken questions.

The key challenges particular to Strengthen and Weaken are that 1) they can have hard-to-pinpoint problems in the argument, 2) attractive wrong choices strengthen or weaken the point but not the reasoning, and 3) attractive wrong choices also often play the opposite role relative to what we need.

All this can lead to mistakes. In this final step, you can confirm that you have selected the right answer. First, take your answer and try to "fit" it in between the support and the conclusion. You should see that it strengthens this bond or weakens it. If you can't see it doing either, it's not the right answer. This step will help you catch yourself when you fall prey to the most tempting wrong choices. Then, as a last step, always make it a habit to double-check the question stem and make sure that your answer performs the task that it is supposed to.

Keys to Strengthen/Weaken

It's important to remember that all strengthen and weaken questions will be asked in terms of an answer that "most" strengthens or weakens, but all strengthen and weaken questions are designed to have just one answer that actually performs that particular task.

This is important for you to remember as you eliminate answer choices (you should expect four not to strengthen or weaken) and as you confirm the right answer (you don't need something that strengthens or weakens a lot, as "most" implies—you just need an answer that actually strengthens or weakens).

It's also important to remember that attractive incorrect choices will strengthen or weaken the conclusion but not the argument (that is, they won't strengthen or weaken the premise-conclusion bond), or they will play an opposite role.

You can avoid many costly mistakes by confirming that the answer you select plays the correct role and by confirming that you can "fit" the answer in between the support and the conclusion.

CONSTELLATION OF WRONG ANSWERS

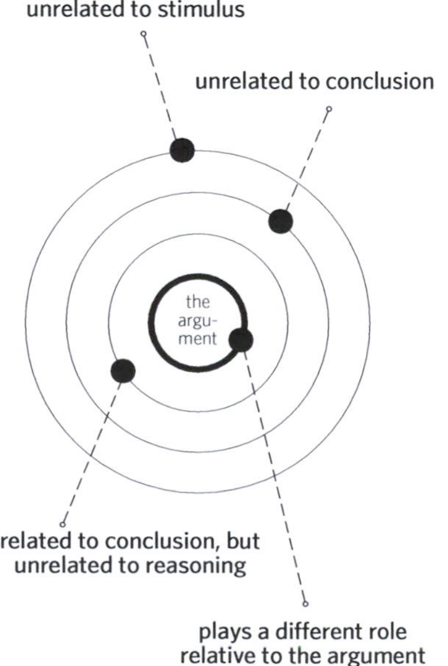

the process in action

Let's model the problem-solving process with two questions you solved at the end of Lesson 16.

2.9. Although video game sales have increased steadily over the past 3 years, we can expect a reversal of this trend in the very near future. Historically, over three quarters of video games sold have been purchased by people from 13 to 16 years of age, and the number of people in this age group is expected to decline steadily over the next 10 years.

Which one of the following, if true, would most seriously weaken the argument?

(A) Most people 17 years old or older have never purchased a video game.
(B) Video game rentals have declined over the past 3 years.
(C) New technology will undoubtedly make entirely new entertainment options available over the next 10 years.
(D) The number of different types of video games available is unlikely to decrease in the near future.
(E) Most of the people who have purchased video games over the past 3 years are over the age of 16.

1: understand your job: We have to find an argument and figure out what's wrong with it. Then we need to find an answer that weakens the support-conclusion relationship.

2: find the point: Video games sales will stop increasing.

3: find the support: Most people who buy games are between 13 and 16, and the number of people in this group is going to shrink.

4: figure out what's wrong: Hmmm. This is a tough one. However, this is a bit of a correlation/causation issue here—just because most past customers were between 13 and 16 doesn't mean that being that age and being a customer are causally related. Maybe some other age group will buy new types of video games in the future.

5: get rid of answers: (A) seems to hurt the argument—let's leave it. (B) is tempting, but actually not related at all (rental). (C) seems to support the conclusion, and has nothing to do with the support-conclusion relationship. Ditto for (D). (E) seems to go against the premise that most people who buy are kids? Hmmm. That can't be. Let's leave it.

6: confirm the right answer: (A) seems correct, but we've got (E) too. (A) is about people over 17 who don't buy games—on second thought, this doesn't have any direct impact on the argument. Who cares if 10 percent or 90 percent of people over 17 have bought a video game—this doesn't tell us anything about the people who actually buy the games. It's a trap. What about (E)? An answer choice cannot contradict the premise, so let's return to the text to figure out what's going on: the premise is about "historically," and (E) is about the last three years—ah, what does that mean? The trend is changing. That weakens the support-conclusion relationship, and now I see what was wrong with the argument to begin with more clearly—maybe the demographic of people who buy games is changing. (E) is correct.

3.13. Therapist: Cognitive psychotherapy focuses on changing a patient's conscious beliefs. Thus, cognitive psychotherapy is likely to be more effective at helping patients overcome psychological problems than are forms of psychotherapy that focus on changing unconscious beliefs and desires, since only conscious beliefs are under the patient's direct conscious control.

Which one of the following, if true, would most strengthen the therapist's argument?

(A) Psychological problems are frequently caused by unconscious beliefs that could be changed with the aid of psychotherapy.
(B) It is difficult for any form of psychotherapy to be effective without focusing on mental states that are under the patient's direct conscious control.
(C) Cognitive psychotherapy is the only form of psychotherapy that focuses primarily on changing the patient's conscious beliefs.
(D) No form of psychotherapy that focuses on changing the patient's unconscious beliefs and desires can be effective unless it also helps change beliefs that are under the patient's direct conscious control.
(E) All of a patient's conscious beliefs are under the patient's conscious control, but other psychological states cannot be controlled effectively without the aid of psychotherapy.

1: understand your job: We have to find an argument and figure out what's wrong with it. Then we need to find an answer that strengthens the argument.

2: find the point: Cognitive psychotherapy is more likely to be effective than therapy that focuses on changing unconscious beliefs and desires.

3: find the support: Cognitive therapy focuses on changing conscious beliefs, and only conscious beliefs are under the patient's direct control.

4: figure out what's wrong: Who says that what we are in better control of is related in any way to what is more effective? There is no reasoning bond between these two ideas, and we need some help here.

5: get rid of answers: (A) hits at the flaw in the argument and would be a great weaken answer, but we are looking to strengthen. (B) gives us the connection we need. Let's leave it. Whether there are other therapies that focus on changing conscious beliefs is not relevant to the comparison in this particular conclusion, so we can knock off (C). (D) uses a lot of the same language as the original argument, but is actually about something else, something more complicated—we don't need to waste time thinking about it. Knowing that it doesn't directly relate to the conclusion is enough to eliminate it. (E) tells us something more about the premise, but doesn't help explain why more control means more help.

6: confirm the right answer: (B) seems to address our gap. Let's check it one more time to make sure it "fits" between support and conclusion—if we take (B) to be true, it makes a lot more sense for the author to use his premise to reach his conclusion. Yes, (B) is definitely correct.

28.1.5. The number of codfish in the North Atlantic has declined substantially as the population of harp seals has increased from two million to more than three million. Some blame the seal for the shrinking cod population, but cod plays a negligible role in the seal's diet. It is therefore unlikely that the increase in the seal population has contributed significantly to the decline in the cod population.

Which one of the following, if true, most seriously weakens the argument?

(A) People who fish for cod commercially are inconvenienced by the presence of large numbers of seals near traditional fishing grounds.
(B) Water pollution poses a more serious threat to cod than to the harp seal.
(C) The harp seal thrives in water that is too cold to support a dense population of cod.
(D) Cod feed almost exclusively on capelin, a fish that is a staple of the harp seal's diet.
(E) The cod population in the North Atlantic began to decline before the harp-seal population began to increase.

28.1.23. Further evidence of a connection between brain physiology and psychological states has recently been uncovered in the form of a correlation between electroencephalograph patterns and characteristic moods. A study showed that participants who suffered from clinical depression exhibited less left frontal lobe activity than right, while, conversely, characteristically good-natured participants exhibited greater left lobe activity. Thus one's general disposition is a result of the activity of one's frontal lobe.

Each of the following, if true, weakens the argument EXCEPT:

(A) Many drugs prescribed to combat clinical depression act by causing increased left lobe activity.
(B) Excessive sleep, a typical consequence of clinical depression, is known to suppress left lobe activity.
(C) Frontal lobe activity is not subject to variation the way general disposition is.
(D) Earlier studies indicated that frontal lobe activity and emotive states are both caused by activity in the brain's limbic system.
(E) Social interaction of the kind not engaged in by most clinically depressed people is known to stimulate left lobe activity.

28.1.15. The town of Springhill frequently must declare a water emergency, making it temporarily unlawful to use water for such nonessential purposes as car washing. These emergencies could be avoided if Springhill would introduce permanent economic incentives for water conservation. Actually, Springhill discourages conservation because each household pays a modest monthly flat fee for any amount of water below a certain usage threshold, and a substantial per-liter rate only after the threshold is reached.

Which one the following, if true, most strengthens the argument?

(A) The Springhill authorities do a poor job of enforcing its water emergency laws and many people break the laws without incurring a penalty.
(B) The town council of Springhill recently refused to raise the threshold.
(C) The threshold is kept at a high enough level to exceed the water requirements of most households in Springhill.
(D) The threshold is not as high in Springhill as it is in neighboring towns.
(E) The threshold remains at the predetermined level specified by law until a change is approved by the Springhill town council.

28.3.25. The interstitial nucleus, a subregion of the brain's hypothalamus, is typically smaller for male cats than for female cats. A neurobiologist performed autopsies on male cats who died from disease X, a disease affecting no more than .05 percent of male cats, and found that these male cats had interstitial nuclei that were as large as those generally found in female cats. Thus, the size of the interstitial nucleus determines whether or not male cats can contract disease X.

Which of the following statements, if true, most seriously weakens the argument?

(A) No female cats have been known to contract disease X, which is a subtype of disease Y.
(B) Many male cats who contract disease X also contract disease Z, the cause of which is unknown.
(C) The interstitial nuclei of female cats who contract disease X are larger than those of female cats who do not contract disease X.
(D) Of 1,000 autopsies on male cats who did not contract disease X, 5 revealed interstitial nuclei larger than those of the average male cat.
(E) The hypothalamus is known not to be causally linked to disease Y, and disease X is a subtype of disease Y.

28.1.5. The number of codfish in the North Atlantic has declined substantially as the population of harp seals has increased from two million to more than three million. Some blame the seal for the shrinking cod population, but cod plays a negligible role in the seal's diet. It is therefore unlikely that the increase in the seal population has contributed significantly to the decline in the cod population.

Which one of the following, if true, most seriously weakens the argument?

(A) People who fish for cod commercially are inconvenienced by the presence of large numbers of seals near traditional fishing grounds.
(B) Water pollution poses a more serious threat to cod than to the harp seal.
(C) The harp seal thrives in water that is too cold to support a dense population of cod.
(D) Cod feed almost exclusively on capelin, a fish that is a staple of the harp seal's diet.
(E) The cod population in the North Atlantic began to decline before the harp-seal population began to increase.

1. understand your job: We have to find an argument and figure out what's wrong with it. Then we need to find an answer that helps fix the issue.

2. find the point: Water emergencies can be avoided if Springhill introduced permanent $ incentives for conserving water.

3. find the support: Springhill discourages saving by charging a flat fee for up to a certain amount, then a high per-liter rate.

4. figure out what's wrong: At first it's tough to see the author's reasoning—the missing piece is that the author is assuming most people don't pass the flat-fee threshold (otherwise, there would be an economic incentive to cut water usage because of the per-liter rate). He has no justification for assuming this is the case.

5. get rid of answers: (A) relates to the background but not the argument. It's tough to see how (B) impacts the argument, but it seems related—let's leave it. (C) is directly related to the argument, and it's exactly what the argument needed. Let's leave it. Who cares about neighbors—let's eliminate (D). (E) gives us technicalities that don't impact our argument.

6. confirm the right answer: With (B), how does not raising the threshold strengthen the argument that the flat fee discourages saving? Tough to see. The issue is about whether the threshold is set to financially encourage, or not encourage, water savings. The author says it's set up to not encourage, and (C) gives him the support he needs to use his premise to support the conclusion. (C) is correct.

1. understand your job: We have to find an argument and figure out what's wrong with it. Then we need to find an answer that weakens the argument.

2. find the point: Unlikely that increase in seal population has contributed to decline in cod population.

3. find the support: Seals don't eat a lot of cod.

4. figure out what's wrong: Perhaps the seals don't eat much cod relative to what else they eat, but they still eat a ton of cod. Or perhaps the seals impact the cod in some other way—maybe seal urine is poisonous to cod (sorry to be gross).

5. get rid of answers: (A) shows how seals can impact the cod population, but if anything, it shows how the seals might improve the cod population. (B) is not directly related—whether other issues pose greater threats isn't directly relevant to whether seals have an impact. (C) might help explain why cod plays a negligible role in the seal's diet, but it doesn't have a clear impact on the conclusion. (D) gives us another way that seals can hurt the cod population—let's leave it. (E) would likely strengthen the author's point that seals aren't related to the decrease.

6. confirm the right answer: (D) is the only attractive answer, and we can see that it weakens the relationship between support and conclusion. (D) shows us how, even if seals don't eat cod, they can impact the cod population. (D) is correct.

28.1.15. The town of Springhill frequently must declare a water emergency, making it temporarily unlawful to use water for such nonessential purposes as car washing. These emergencies could be avoided if Springhill would introduce permanent economic incentives for water conservation. Actually, Springhill discourages conservation because each household pays a modest monthly flat fee for any amount of water below a certain usage threshold, and a substantial per-liter rate only after the threshold is reached.

Which one the following, if true, most strengthens the argument?

(A) The Springhill authorities do a poor job of enforcing its water emergency laws and many people break the laws without incurring a penalty.
(B) The town council of Springhill recently refused to raise the threshold.
(C) The threshold is kept at a high enough level to exceed the water requirements of most households in Springhill.
(D) The threshold is not as high in Springhill as it is in neighboring towns.
(E) The threshold remains at the predetermined level specified by law until a change is approved by the Springhill town council.

28.1.23. Further evidence of a connection between brain physiology and psychological states has recently been uncovered in the form of a correlation between electroencephalograph patterns and characteristic moods. A study showed that participants who suffered from clinical depression exhibited less left frontal lobe activity than right, while, conversely, characteristically good-natured participants exhibited greater left lobe activity. Thus one's general disposition is a result of the activity of one's frontal lobe.

Each of the following, if true, weakens the argument EXCEPT:

(A) Many drugs prescribed to combat clinical depression act by causing increased left lobe activity.
(B) Excessive sleep, a typical consequence of clinical depression, is known to suppress left lobe activity.
(C) Frontal lobe activity is not subject to variation the way general disposition is.
(D) Earlier studies indicated that frontal lobe activity and emotive states are both caused by activity in the brain's limbic system.
(E) Social interaction of the kind not engaged in by most clinically depressed people is known to stimulate left lobe activity.

1. understand your job: An *except* question! We have to find an argument and figure out what's wrong with it. Then we need to eliminate four answers that weaken.

2. find the point: One's mood based on frontal lobe activity.

3. find the support: Correlation between moods and certain frontal lobe activities.

4. figure out what's wrong: They are trying to blind us with science, but correlation does not prove causation! The wrong answers will likely exploit this flaw.

5. get rid of answers: (A) is a consequence that makes sense based on this argument, not something that weakens the argument—let's leave it. (B) shows that mood can influence frontal lobe activity, which is essentially the reverse of the causation proposed in the argument. This definitely weakens the reasoning, so we can eliminate (B). (C) shows a potential lack of correlation between mood and frontal lobe activity—definitely hurts, so let's eliminate. (D) gives us a potential exterior cause—definitely hurts, so let's eliminate. (E) again shows that mood might impact frontal lobe activity, rather than the reverse causal relationship the author is proposing.

6. confirm the right answer: (A) is the only answer remaining. The correct answer for a Weaken EXCEPT question does not need to strengthen the argument (or even have anything to do with the argument at all). It simply needs to not weaken. (A) does not weaken, and (A) is correct.

28.3.25. The interstitial nucleus, a subregion of the brain's hypothalamus, is typically smaller for male cats than for female cats. A neurobiologist performed autopsies on male cats who died from disease X, a disease affecting no more than .05 percent of male cats, and found that these male cats had interstitial nuclei that were as large as those generally found in female cats. Thus, the size of the interstitial nucleus determines whether or not male cats can contract disease X.

Which of the following statements, if true, most seriously weakens the argument?

(A) No female cats have been known to contract disease X, which is a subtype of disease Y.
(B) Many male cats who contract disease X also contract disease Z, the cause of which is unknown.
(C) The interstitial nuclei of female cats who contract disease X are larger than those of female cats who do not contract disease X.
(D) Of 1,000 autopsies on male cats who did not contract disease X, 5 revealed interstitial nuclei larger than those of the average male cat.
(E) The hypothalamus is known not to be causally linked to disease Y, and disease X is a subtype of disease Y.

1. understand your job: We have to find an argument and figure out what's wrong with it. Then we need to find an answer that hurts the argument.

2. find the point: The size of the interstitial nucleus determines whether male cats can get disease X.

3. find the support: Male cats that get disease X have larger than average interstitial nuclei.

4. figure out what's wrong: They are trying to trick us with science again, but we're too strong for that! This is again a classic correlation/causation issue—the correlation between the size of this thing and the chances of getting disease X does not imply causation, as the conclusion claims.

5. get rid of answers: (A) is about female cats—get rid of it. (B) is about another disease—get rid of it. (C) is somewhat tempting, even though it's about female cats...but it's just more correlation! Get rid of it. (D) tells us that it's rare for male cats to have this large thing, but that wouldn't weaken the argument in any way. (E) is about causality, and the only answer left. Let's examine it.

6. confirm the right answer: (E) is not a great answer. So what if X is a subtype of Y? Maybe it's a totally unique subtype. However, a weaken answer does not have to completely destroy the argument—it just needs to hurt the premise-conclusion relationship, and (E) clearly does that. (E) is essentially telling us there is no causal link between this large thing, and the family that includes this disease. Since the problem with the argument was that the author was assuming causation, (E) clearly hurts the author's argument. (E) is correct.

20 LOGICAL REASONING review and assess

Habits.

We started this batch of lessons by discussing the importance of habits. Sound habits help ensure that the work you put in during your study leads to actual and significant improvement, and habits are what we rely on during the pressure of the exam.

Do you feel that you are developing habits that lead to consistent success? By this point, especially if you have been following along with the corresponding work in the *10 Actuals* books, you should be feeling the positive impact of these habits—perhaps the two most significant benefits being that you are naturally zeroing in more and more on the issues that are significant to getting the question correct, and naturally pushing the secondary information more and more into the background.

Do you feel that you are developing habits that lead to consistent success?

If you don't feel that you are developing habits and skills, or if you feel that you are developing less than ideal habits, now is the time to stop and reassess. Remember, LSAT skills build upon one another—if your foundation isn't strong, you will not be able to get too high up the ladder. Let's take this lesson to assess our progress, discuss additional exercises to bolster weaknesses, and also discuss secondary strategies for solving the toughest questions. We'll finish up with a set of problems that will help you assess how far you've progressed, and what you need to focus on as you continue studying.

Habit 1: Understand Your Task

We want to start every question by looking at the question stem. The question stem will help us figure out how to attack the question as efficiently as possible. First, we'll use the question stem to determine whether we are supposed to be critical of the reasoning in the argument or not. Then we will use the question stem to define what to expect in the right and wrong answers.

Many question stems are written like one another, and it's easy if you aren't careful to mistake one question type for another. The good news is that the test writers use exactly the same question stems exam after exam, and there are only a few different phrasings with which you need to get familiar for each type of question.

Think back on the different types of questions that we've discussed and see if you can visualize the different question stems you are likely to encounter. If you have trouble with this, you may want to try the exercise suggested on the right.

To practice recognizing question stems, take any Logical Reasoning section and go through it quickly, looking just at question stems and not at the stimuli themselves. For each question stem, first see if it requires you to be critical, and then determine what type of question it is. Afterwards, walk through the section slowly to see if you got all the question stems correct. Keep a list of stems that trip you up. Repeat until you can recognize every critical question stem without any effort.

Habit 2: Identify the Conclusion

Once you recognize that a question is asking for you to be critical of reasoning, you want to go into the stimulus expecting to find an argument, and the first part of that is figuring out what the conclusion is.

Habit 3: Find the Support

To practice reading for structure, review questions you have already solved. For each question, just focus on the stimulus, and work on zeroing in on the conclusion and the support. Mark what you think the conclusion and support are. After a set of questions, review carefully how the conclusion and support that you marked relate to the correct answer to the question. You should see a connection every single time. Repeat until the process feels automatic, and separate out the process of identifying the conclusion or the supporting premises if you think just that part of your skill set needs more work.

Once you know the point, it generally becomes easier to figure out what the author has given us to help support that point. This support can come in the form of one sentence or one short clause, or it can be the amalgamation of a few different pieces of information and opinion. You want to do your best to understand the support in a conceptual way—what sort of general reasoning strategy is the author using to prove his point?

These two reading habits (2 and 3) should feel fairly automatic, every time. These reading skills are critical for making the question-solving process easier, and if you have trouble with these two steps it's very difficult to consistently get right answers quickly. Try the review exercise to the side if you feel your reading skills need a bit of freshening up.

Habit 4: Figure Out What's Wrong

The money step. In Lessons 5 through 9, we started our Logical Reasoning training process by focusing on the most significant part of a successful Logical Reasoning skill set—your ability to recognize why the reasons provided are not enough to justify the conclusion reached.

To practice recognizing flaws, review questions you have already solved. For each question, just read the stimulus, not the answer choices, and mark down what you think is wrong with the argument. After a set of questions, review carefully how the correct answer relates to this flaw you saw. You should see a connection every single time. If you have a lot of trouble, consider whether your reading skills might be holding you back. Also feel free to repeat the same questions over and over again—this is very good for setting habits, for you will likely see the very same reasoning issues in the arguments on your real exam.

Picture your ability to figure out what is wrong with an argument as a physical shape, maybe as a piece of modern sculpture. The test writers are trying to assess the quality of your understanding—from the front, from the side, from above, and from below—and one could argue that all of the different types of questions we've been dealing with are simply different views, different perspectives, on the same work of modern art—your understanding of what is wrong with the reasoning in an argument.

How do you feel about your piece? Are you proud of it? Do you know that it's solid all the way around? Or do you like how it looks from certain angles but not others?

For all subjective questions, if you know the flaw, you should be able to see how the right answer relates to that flaw, every single time. You should also be able to see, in very clear ways, the many wrong answers that have no direct bearing on the flaw. If you know you have trouble with eliminating wrong answers, it's a sign that you are having trouble seeing the flaw clearly, or integrating the flaw into your process. You will have a chance to assess your skill set at the end of this lesson.

Steps two through four are the same for all subjective questions. Before moving on to step five, you want to re-read the question stem to remind yourself of the task that the particular question presents. The task will play a starring role in helping us determine which answers to eliminate. *(Continued on page 284.)*

Answer Choice Strategies

For all subjective questions, your ability to handle answer choices quickly and with confidence is dependent on how well you understand what's wrong with the argument.

All questions that require you to be critical are prone to having answer choices that have no direct connection to the argument in the stimulus—in fact, it's often true that all four wrong answers can be eliminated for this reason. If you can successfully prioritize the conclusion and support, these answer choices become far less attractive.

All questions are also prone to having answer choices that serve a different function relative to the argument. There will always be just one answer, the correct answer, that functions in the argument the way it's supposed to.

Each question type also has its own subtle tendencies in terms of wrong answers, right answers, and the processes you can use to identify either. Let's summarize some of these nuances here.

Flaw Strategies

The answers for Flaw questions are as directly related to your understanding of the argument as can be. That means that more so than for any other type of question we've discussed thus far, you need to make sure you understand what is wrong with the argument before moving on to the answers. The vast majority of wrong answers will be unrelated to the reasoning in the argument. The right answer will generally hit the issue right on the head. When right answers are difficult to spot, it is commonly because of abstract wording. Make sure you are comfortable with the language you might see, and make it a habit to not eliminate answer choices until you understand them enough to know for certain that something is wrong with them. *(Also applies to Basic Assumption questions.)*

Match the Flaw Strategies

The arguments for Match the Flaw questions also tend to have fairly clearly definable flaws, and very commonly these flaws are of the $1 + 1 \neq 3$ variety. Also, in comparison to other types of questions, the stimuli for these questions tend to have a bit less secondary information, or "fluff." Reasoning structure will allow you to eliminate most wrong answers—they reach different types of conclusions or use a different type of reasoning than what we saw in the original. Left with one answer that you think is correct, make sure to check all of the small words and modifiers to make sure the answer doesn't have a different type of flaw.

Sufficient Assumption Strategies

Sufficient Assumption answers need to completely fix the problem with an argument. You need to have a clear sense of the flaw in order to figure out what will be enough to fix it, and these arguments are designed to have clear and specific problems. You should expect to be able to spot these problems almost every time. Tempting wrong answers might provide a required assumption, or one that is very helpful to the argument but doesn't completely fix it. Right answers need to pass the "sufficiency" threshold—if an answer choice leaves what you feel are definite gaps, that answer choice will not be correct. Finally, keep in mind that right answers can go above and beyond what we need—they can tell us someone has $1,000,000 when we just needed to know that they have more than $100,000. More than enough is fine in an answer. *(Also applies to Supporting Principle questions.)*

Required Assumption Strategies

The arguments for questions that ask for a Required Assumption will sometimes have flaws that are more difficult to determine or define than do arguments for some other question types. Tempting wrong answers commonly support the argument and can even completely fix the issues in an argument, but answer choices will not be correct unless they *need* to be true to reach the conclusion. A great way to confirm that an answer is correct is to use the negation test: consider the opposite of the answer and see if it severely damages how the author is trying to support his point. If it does, it's a good sign that the answer represents something that needed to be true for the argument to work.

Strengthen and Weaken Strategies

The arguments for questions that ask you to strengthen or weaken will sometimes have flaws that are more difficult to determine or define than do arguments for some other question types. Arguments for Strengthen and Weaken questions also commonly have a lot of secondary information that you need to wade through. Tempting wrong answers will often support or weaken the conclusion, but not in a way that impacts the reasoning structure. They can also validate or invalidate the support, but not in a way that impacts the point. A great way to confirm a right answer is to see if it "fits" in between the support and the conclusion. A Strengthen answer should make this bond firmer, while a Weaken answer will weaken it. Even though questions ask for the answer that *most* strengthens or *most* weakens, there will almost always be just one answer choice that strengthens or weakens, and it's possible that the correct answer will strengthen or weaken the argument a lot or just a bit.

Habit 5: Get Rid of Answers

Getting rid of wrong answers is not a luxury, and it's not a time-consuming step—it is a necessary component of a successful skill set

When you first started studying, perhaps you thought, if only for a moment, that all this stuff with eliminating wrong answers was a bunch of fluff. "Oh, I don't have time for that. He can't be serious that I need to do *that* for every question!"

In my years as a trainer of instructors, I worked with and interviewed many, many people who have scored over 172 on the LSAT. Not one of them valued the importance of getting rid of wrong answers much less than I did.

Getting rid of wrong answers is not a luxury, and it is not a time-consuming step—it is a necessary component of a successful skill set, and it is a habit that consistently makes it easier for you to get questions right. To think that just going after the right answer is easier, or saves time, is equivalent to thinking that driving with just one foot pedal, the gas, is somehow easier or faster than driving with the gas and brake.

Okay—that's the last lecture I'll give about eliminating answers, I promise.[1]

1. At least for now.

When it comes to wrong answer characteristics, the question types we've discussed naturally have a lot of overlap, but they also have unique quirks. I've highlighted some of these on the previous page.

Habit 6: Confirm the Right Answer

The correct answer must relate to the reasoning, and it must play the intended role

The final step is to figure out what the correct answer is. If you have done your work correctly, for the vast majority of questions, you will find yourself with just one answer, or perhaps one and a half answers (one answer you feel pretty sure is right, and another you think is wrong but you can't exactly say why) left to evaluate carefully. One caveat is that each test is likely to have one or two questions for which this is not true—challenging questions for which three or four answers may at first seem attractive.

For all subjective questions, there are two factors involved in confirming the right answer—you need to be able to see that the answer choice is directly related to the reasoning relationship between the support and the conclusion, and you need to make sure that the answer choice plays the role it is supposed to relative to the argument. Even when you feel a bit fuzzy headed about the stimulus, or about what is wrong with the argument, if you can remember to think of each answer choice in terms of these two criteria, you can often survive difficult questions and know that you got the right answer, even if you didn't have a great handle on issues during your problem-solving process.

Directions for the drill on the next page: This drill will help you practice evaluating arguments and matching answers to question stems. For each problem, first underline the conclusion and bracket the support. Write in the flaw in the reasoning and follow the question stem prompts. Answers can be used more than once. This is an untimed drill, but do practice being quick.

Drill: One Argument & Ten Answers

underline the conclusion and bracket the support	write in what's wrong	ten answer choices...
A. In recent years, more and more people have been switching to electronic media, such as computers and tablet devices, as their primary means of getting news information. The consequence of this is that the public actually knows less about the news. Studies show that people retain less of what they read when they read on an electronic device, as opposed to when they read on the standard gray paper that newspapers are printed on.		A. Revenue from newspaper advertising has dropped drastically in recent years. B. Prior to this recent trend, most people got their information from magazines, which are printed differently than newspapers. C. Magazines are printed on glossy white paper, which people find less pleasant to read on than the screens of electronic devices. D. The amount that one knows about the news is related to the means by which one gets the news. E. Research has shown a link between the amount of information one retains when taking in news and the amount that one actually knows about the news. F. People who watched television regularly as children are far more likely to get news through electronic media than are people who did not. G. Newspapers were not printed on gray paper until eighty years ago. H. People who get news primarily through electronic media offset the loss in retention by taking in a far greater volume of news. I. A society can prevent a decay of news understanding only if members of that society do not switch to electronic means of obtaining news information. J. A public that knows less about the news is more likely to vote for incompetent leaders.

1. Find at least four answers that have no clear bearing on the reasoning in the argument.
2. Find at least two answers that strengthen the argument.
3. Find at least one answer that weakens the argument.
4. Find one answer that is required by the argument.
5. Find one answer that is sufficient to validate the argument.

B. A study recently published in a leading psychology magazine showed that, surprisingly, those who are in the top 5 percent in terms of the amount of sleep they get daily have, on average, about the same level of anxiety and depression as those who are in the bottom 5 percent. This proves conclusively that the amount of sleep one gets has minimal correlation to the amount of anxiety and depression one feels.		A. People who get the most sleep are actually less likely to take naps than are those who get the least sleep. B. Whether one is anxious or depressed, diet can have a significant impact on sleep patterns. C. The study showed that those who are within 10 percent of the mean for daily sleep were significantly less likely than others to suffer from both anxiety and depression. D. Anxiety and depression are known to exacerbate one another. E. If those who are in the lower or higher 5 percent of a statistical average have minimal differences in terms of a certain trait, then the subject of that statistical average has minimal relation to the certain trait. F. There are other factors besides sleep that impact levels of anxiety. G. It could be true that though there is consistency at the extremes, there is a lack of consistency among people who fall in other parts of the range of average sleep. H. Depression often causes changes in sleeping behavior. I. Anxiety can cause some people to sleep more, and others to sleep less. J. The study also showed that those in the 25th and 75th percentiles also have, on average, about the same level of anxiety and depression as those in the top and bottom 5 percent.

1. Find at least four answers that have no clear bearing on the reasoning in the argument.
2. Find two answers that strengthen the argument.
3. Find one answer that weakens the argument.
4. Find a principle that supports the argument.
5. Find one answer that represents the flaw in the argument.

Drill: One Argument & Ten Answers

underline the conclusion and bracket the support	write in what's wrong	ten answer choices...
C. Joe claims that drinking tea does not cause him any trouble falling asleep. However, before he started drinking tea, he never had trouble falling asleep. In the six months that he's been drinking tea, he's had trouble falling asleep at least one night per week. During this time, there has been no other significant change in what Joe eats or drinks. So, Joe must be wrong in his claim.		A. What one eats and drinks is the primary factor that impacts falling asleep. B. Joe does not drink black tea, which is the tea that contains the greatest amount of caffeine. C. Joe has recently had some stressful life events that he admits he can't stop thinking about at night. D. The tea Joe drinks contains caffeine, which is known to cause people trouble falling asleep. E. People who don't drink tea commonly drink coffee, and coffee is known to cause a great amount of trouble falling asleep. F. Once Joe falls asleep, he rarely has any trouble staying asleep. G. Six months ago Joe got a puppy, and Joe can hear the puppy howling loudly every night the moon is out. H. The tea Joe drinks has natural ingredients that help one sleep more soundly once one is asleep. I. When Joe falls asleep later, he tends to wake up later. J. The tea impacts Joe falling asleep.

1. **Find at least four answers that have no clear bearing on the reasoning in the argument.**
2. **Find at least two answers that strengthen the argument.**
3. **Find two answers that weaken the argument.**
4. **Find one answer that represents the assumption.**

underline the conclusion and bracket the support	write in what's wrong	ten answer choices...
D. Medical Expert: For the past six months, we have been keeping statistics on the surgery time for prostatectomies performed through traditional means, and through a new procedure that uses robotics. The study revealed that surgeries using robotics took an average of forty-three minutes, whereas traditional surgeries took an average of over seventy minutes. The study involved a sufficient enough mix of doctors and hospitals to guarantee that personal surgical skills and access to other types of equipment were not a factor in the study outcome. Therefore, we can conclude that in general it is faster to perform prostatectomies robotically than it is to perform them using traditional means.		A. The differences in relevant characteristics for the patients of both types of surgeries were minimal. B. Traditional surgery, when done well, can result in far less recovery time and medical expense than robotic surgery. C. Surgeons who used robotic surgery were far more likely to stay within five minutes of the mean than were surgeons who performed traditional surgery. D. Robotics are being used in more and more surgeries and at some point will become the most common form of surgery. E. Those who have the surgery done through traditional means are far less likely to have complications days after the surgery than are those who have the surgery done robotically. F. More-complicated prostatectomies cannot be performed as accurately robotically, and so are all performed through traditional means. G. When making decisions about which surgery type is best, how quickly the surgery can be performed should play no part. H. Patients are less likely to feel anxious about robotic surgery than they do about traditional surgery. I. For the most simple prostatectomies, traditional surgeries take, on average, less time than robotic surgeries. J. There may be differences between the typical prostatectomies done robotically and those done through more traditional means.

1. **Find at least four answers that have no clear bearing on the reasoning in the argument.**
2. **Find an answer that strengthens the argument.**
3. **Find at least one answer that weakens the argument.**
4. **Find one answer that represents the flaw in the argument.**

Drill: One Argument & Ten Answers

underline the conclusion and bracket the support	write in what's wrong	ten answer choices...
E. Professor Watkins just received a significant raise, and now Professor Jenson has requested one too. However, Professor Watkins was only eligible to get a raise if she received tenure; she recently was awarded tenure, and was given the raise. Professor Jenson has no desire to get tenure, is not on track to get tenure, and will not get tenure. So, Professor Jenson's request will likely be denied.		A. Professor Watkins has been at the university for three years less than Professor Jenson has. B. Professor Jenson teaches at multiple schools and does not want tenure because he has tenure at a more prestigious university. C. Professor Jenson is well known for the work he does in his field, and the school is known to give raises in order to retain professors who are significant in the areas in which they work. D. Perhaps Professor Watkins and Professor Jenson have different types of agreements with the university about the timing of raises. E. Professor Watkins contributes significantly to campus social life, whereas Professor Jenson does not. F. Professor Watkins works in the English department, and Professor Jenson does not. G. The rules that govern raises are the same for all professors at the university. H. Of those professors who received raises last year, fewer than half had tenure. I. Professor Watkins never requested the raise she was recently given. J. The university is having financial problems and giving out far fewer significant raises than it once did.

1. Find at least four answers that have no clear bearing on the reasoning in the argument.
2. Find one answer that is sufficient to make the argument valid.
3. Find one answer that represents a flaw in reasoning.
4. Find at least two answers that would weaken the argument.

underline the conclusion and bracket the support	write in what's wrong	ten answer choices...
F. Access to information on the internet has enriched our lives in many ways, but in at least one situation it has caused more harm than good. Nowadays people frequently go online to diagnose their own medical issues, in lieu of making a visit to a doctor. These people are almost always incorrect in their own diagnoses, whereas professional doctors rarely are.		A. Doctors are required to spend years studying both in classrooms and in actual situations with patients before they can be professionally licensed. B. Though the information online is generally correct, it is very easy to misunderstand, especially if one does not have a medical background. C. The value of the occasional correct diagnoses outweighs the problems caused by the many incorrect diagnoses. D. All forms of communication that are likely to lead to misunderstanding cause more harm than good. E. Far more people have access to online information now as compared to ten years ago. F. Though people commonly diagnose their own issues, people do not take action based on self-diagnosis until it is confirmed to be true by a professional doctor. G. When people misdiagnose their own medical issues, they commonly alter their daily routine. H. Doctors with more experience are less likely to misdiagnose a medical issue than are doctors with less experience. I. Because of changes in the medical industry, much of the work that was traditionally done by doctors is now done by other medical professionals. J. At least one person who has misdiagnosed his or her own medical issues online has been harmed by this action.

1. Find at least four answers that have no bearing on the reasoning in the argument.
2. Find a required assumption.
3. Find a sufficient assumption or supporting principle.
4. Find two answers that strengthen.
5. Find two answers that weaken.

solutions

A. What's wrong: Just because they retain less of what they read does not mean they know less about the news. Maybe they get a lot more news to make up for the lack of retention. 1. A,C,F,G,J • 2. D,E, I • 3. B, H • 4.D • 5.I

Note that assumptions also work as strengtheners (though the reverse is not always true) and flaws also work as weakeners (though the reverse is not always true). Answer C is not relevant unless we have some sign people used to get news from magazines.

B. What's wrong: Similarities at the extreme ends of the sleep range do not conclusively show there are similarities for all parts of the sleep range. 1. A,B,D,F,H,I • 2. E,J • 3. C • 4. E • 5.G

Answer B is not relevant because whether other things impact sleep or not does not impact our conclusion. Same with F. Though both H and I could be relevant to the discussion, as presented they are too vague to have a decisive impact.

C. What's wrong: Correlation between tea and sleep trouble does not prove causation. 1. B,E,F,H,I • 2. A,D,J • 3. C,G • 4. J

Notice that answer D is relevant to the argument but E is not. Joe drinks tea, and even though it's not guaranteed that caffeine affects him, D certainly gives us more reason to think the argument may be valid. E is based on a characteristic Joe does not have, and requires far more conjecture on our part than D does in order to be relevant.

D. What's wrong: Doesn't take into account that there could have been other differences between the types of surgeries performed robotically and traditionally. 1.B,C,D,E,G,H • 2.A • 3.F,I,J • 4.J

What makes this tough is that in our heads something like "prostatectomy" is one specific type of surgery. However, it could be true that there are a lot of different types of prostatectomies, and if robotics are used for some types and not others, the comparison loses validity.

E. What's wrong: Apples to oranges. The criteria that applied to Watkins may not be the same as that applied to Jenson. 1. A,B,E,F,I,J • 2. G • 3. D • 4. C,D,H

Notice the extra information in C that makes it relevant. E and F give additional reasons for potential raises, but don't tie them into the argument. J hurts the conclusion, but not in a way that relates to the support and reasoning.

F. What's wrong: Assumes that these common incorrect diagnoses cause more harm than good. 1. A,B,E,G,H,I • 2. J • 3. D • 4. D,J • 5. C,F

Our subject-dependent common sense can get us in trouble here, since most of us know that misdiagnosing medical issues generally leads to more harm than good in real life.

These six sets of questions were meant to be challenging. The conclusions were sometimes subtle or hidden, the support sometimes compound or spread out, the reasoning issues unexpected or vague, the wrong answer choices tempting, and the right answers convoluted.

How do you feel about each part of the process? Did you zero in on the right argument, every time? Were you able to see the flaws in reasoning? Were you able to quickly eliminate answers that don't play a clear role relative to the reasoning? Did you use your skills to confirm right answers, and did it work?

In a couple of pages there will be a complete set of all the subjective questions from one section of one exam (fourteen questions total). This set will give you an accurate view of how your skills currently match up with the challenges of the exam. As you work on that set, remind yourself to pay extra attention to those skills that felt weakest for you in this exercise.

tips for
surviving uncertainty

Imagine that you need to find a certain princess who is locked in a castle in the woods, and Dora the Explorer is going to help you do it. If you've ever seen the *Dora the Explorer* show—sorry for the unpleasant experience—you know that she commonly has to go to three different areas to solve whatever problem an episode presents. So, let's imagine that in order to get the princess, you and Dora have to swim across a lake, cross a bridge, then enter a castle. You swim across the lake, but there is a problem—you see two different bridges that you can take. Oh no. But look! If we look beyond the bridge on the left, we can see the castle. The bridge on the right has no such castle behind it. We need to go left!

Gaining LSAT mastery does not mean that every question becomes easy—it does mean that you have the tools to meet the challenges. **When we run into trouble on Logical Reasoning problems, often *the next step* in the process can be a hint for what we should do or how we should think.**

Our first step in understanding an argument is to identify the conclusion. But let's imagine you have trouble here—perhaps there are two statements that seem like they are the conclusion, or it seems like the conclusion can be interpreted in a couple of different ways, and you can't for the life of you determine what is correct. One thing you can do is search for the supporting evidence. Because of the wealth of experience at evaluating argument structure that you now have, the supporting evidence can help you develop a clearer sense of what exactly the conclusion is.

Our next step is to identify all of the support. But maybe the support is spread out and it's tough to pull it together, or maybe it's tough to differentiate the support from the background. If you have a sense of the conclusion, a sense of what would justify that conclusion, and just a partial sense of the support, you can often figure out what could be wrong, and then work backwards to piece that support together.

Did you have trouble seeing what was wrong, exactly, with any of the arguments in the previous exercise? Did you find that when you were unclear of the flaw, or not sure about it, that sometimes the answer choices helped you develop a firmer understanding of what the problem was in the first place? Even incorrect answers, if you pay careful attention to why they are incorrect, can give you clues about the original argument.

Also, under time pressure, sometimes we won't be able to figure out exactly why every wrong answer is wrong. What can we rely on, then? The next step. It's time to figure out why the right answer is right. Finding a right answer can help you see better why other answers were wrong. For the hardest problems, it's often true that the clearest sense you have of the argument will come after you have selected the right answer and are able to see, based on the shape of that right key, exactly what the lock was like.

You don't want to be overly reliant on these "reverse engineering" skills, and being so is an indication of issues in your skill set. Still, the ability to use the next step, in addition to past steps, to figure out what to do in the current step comes in very handy when you are stuck, and using the next step to help when you are uncertain should be a habitual and central part of your problem-solving backup process.

Question Set

Directions: Here are the fourteen subjective questions that together appeared in one LSAT section (section 4 of exam 30). This set of questions will help give you a sense of what your strengths and weaknesses are at this point. Do time yourself, but don't cut yourself off at any point.

1. A government ought to protect and encourage free speech, because free speech is an activity that is conducive to a healthy nation and thus is in the best interest of its people.

The main conclusion above follows logically if which one of the following is assumed?

(A) An activity that is in the best interest of the people ought to be protected and encouraged by a nation's government.
(B) Basic, inalienable rights of the people ought to be protected and encouraged by government.
(C) An activity that helps a government to govern ought to be protected and encouraged by it.
(D) A government ought to protect and encourage an activity that is conducive to the interests of that government.
(E) Universal human rights that are in the best interest of the people ought to be protected and encouraged by a nation's government.

8. Archaeologist: The fact that the ancient Egyptians and the Maya both built pyramids is often taken as evidence of a historical link between Old- and New- World civilizations that is earlier than any yet documented. But while these buildings are similar to each other, there are important differences in both design and function. The Egyptian pyramids were exclusively tombs for rulers, whereas the Mayan pyramids were used as temples. This shows conclusively that there was no such link between Old- and New- World civilizations.

Which one of the following most accurately describes a flaw in the archaeologist's argument?

(A)The argument equivocates with respect to the term "evidence."
(B) The argument appeals to emotion rather than to reason.
(C) The argument assumes the conclusion it is trying to prove.
(D) The argument incorrectly relies on words whose meanings are vague or imprecise.
(E) The argument presumes that no other evidence is relevant to the issue at hand.

6. Commissioner: Budget forecasters project a revenue shortfall of a billion dollars in the coming fiscal year. Since there is no feasible way to increase the available funds, our only choice is to decrease expenditures. The plan before you outlines feasible cuts that would yield savings of a billion dollars over the coming fiscal year. We will be able to solve the problem we face, therefore, only if we adopt this plan.

The reasoning in the commissioner's argument is flawed because this argument

(A) relies on information that is far from certain
(B) confuses being an adequate solution with being a required solution
(C) inappropriately relies on the opinions of experts
(D) inappropriately employs language that is vague
(E) takes for granted that there is no way to increase available funds

11. High school students who feel that they are not succeeding in school often drop out before graduating and go to work. Last year, however, the city's high school dropout rate was significantly lower than the previous year's rate. This is encouraging evidence that the program instituted two years ago to improve the morale of high school students has begun to take effect to reduce dropouts.

Which one of the following, if true about the last year, most seriously weakens the argument?

(A) There was a recession that caused a high level of unemployment in the city.
(B) The morale of students who dropped out of high school had been low even before they reached high school.
(C) As in the preceding year, more high school students remained in school than dropped out.
(D) High schools in the city established placement offices to assist their graduates in obtaining employment.
(E) The anti-dropout program was primarily aimed at improving students' morale in those high schools with the highest dropout rates.

Question Set

12. The television show Henry was not widely watched until it was scheduled for Tuesday evenings immediately after That's Life, the most popular show on television. During the year after the move, Henry was consistently one of the ten most-watched shows on television. Since Henry's recent move to Wednesday evenings, however, it has been watched by far fewer people. We must conclude that Henry was widely watched before the move to Wednesday evenings because it followed That's Life and not because people especially liked it.

Which one of the following, if true, most strengthens the argument?

(A) Henry has been on the air for three years, but That's Life has been on the air for only two years.
(B) The show that replaced Henry on Tuesdays has persistently had a low number of viewers in the Tuesday time slot.
(C) The show that now follows That's Life on Tuesdays has double the number of viewers it had before being moved.
(D) After its recent move to Wednesday, Henry was aired at the same time as the second most popular show on television.
(E) That's Life was not widely watched during the first year it was aired.

15. It is not good for a university to have class sizes that are very large or very small, or to have professors with teaching loads that are very light or very heavy. After all, crowded classes and overworked faculty cripple the institution's ability to recruit and retain both qualified students and faculty.

Which one of the following, if added as a premise to the argument, most helps to justify its conclusion?

(A) Professors who have very light teaching loads tend to focus their remaining time on research.
(B) Classes that have very low numbers of students tend to have a lot of classroom discussion.
(C) Very small class sizes or very light teaching loads indicate incompetence in classroom instruction.
(D) Very small class sizes or very light teaching loads are common in the worst and the best universities.
(E) Professors with very light teaching loads have no more office hours for students than professors with normal teaching loads.

14. Joseph: My encyclopedia says that the mathematician Pierre de Fermat died in 1665 without leaving behind any written proof for a theorem that he claimed nonetheless to have proved. Probably this alleged theorem simply cannot be proved, since—as the article points out—no one else has been able to prove it. Therefore it is likely that Fermat was either lying or else mistaken when he made his claim.

Laura: Your encyclopedia is out of date. Recently someone has in fact proved Fermat's theorem. And since the theorem is provable, your claim—that Fermat was lying or mistaken—clearly is wrong.

Which one of the following most accurately describes a reasoning error in Laura's argument?

(A) It purports to establish its conclusion by making a claim that, if true, would actually contradict that conclusion.
(B) It mistakenly assumes that the quality of a person's character can legitimately be taken to guarantee the accuracy of the claims that person has made.
(C) It mistakes something that is necessary for its conclusion to follow for something that ensures that the conclusion follows.
(D) It uses the term "provable" without defining it.
(E) It fails to distinguish between a true claim that has mistakenly been believed to be false and a false claim that has mistakenly been believed to be true.

17. Researchers have found that people who drink five or more cups of coffee a day have a risk of heart disease 2.5 times the average after corrections are made for age and smoking habits. Members of the research team say that, on the basis of their findings, they now limit their own daily coffee intake to two cups.

Which one of the following, if true, indicates that the researchers' precaution might NOT have the result of decreasing their risk of heart disease?

(A) The study found that for people who drank three or more cups of coffee daily, the additional risk of heart disease increased with each extra daily cup.
(B) Per capita coffee consumption has been declining over the past 20 years because of the increasing popularity of soft drinks and also because of health worries.
(C) The study did not collect information that would show whether variations in level of coffee consumption are directly related to variations in level of stress, a major causal factor in heart disease.
(D) Subsequent studies have consistently shown that heavy smokers consume coffee at about 3 times the rate of nonsmokers.
(E) Subsequent studies have shown that heavy coffee consumption tends to cause an elevated blood-cholesterol level, an immediate indicator of increased risk of heart disease.

Question Set

18. People who have political power tend to see new technologies as a means of extending or protecting their power, whereas they generally see new ethical arguments and ideas as a threat to it. Therefore, technical ingenuity usually brings benefits to those who have this ingenuity, whereas ethical inventiveness brings only pain to those who have this inventiveness.

Which one of the following statements, if true, most strengthens the argument?

(A) Those who offer new ways of justifying current political power often reap the benefits of their own innovations.
(B) Politically powerful people tend to reward those who they believe are useful to them and to punish those who they believe are a threat.
(C) Ethical inventiveness and technical ingenuity are never possessed by the same individuals.
(D) New technologies are often used by people who strive to defeat those who currently have political power.
(E) Many people who possess ethical inventiveness conceal their novel ethical arguments for fear of retribution by the politically powerful.

20. Consumer advocate: The introduction of a new drug into the marketplace should be contingent upon our having a good understanding of its social impact. However, the social impact of the newly marketed antihistamine is far from clear. It is obvious, then, that there should be a general reduction in the pace of bringing to the marketplace new drugs that are now being tested.

Which one of the following, if true, most strengthens the argument?

(A) The social impact of the new antihistamine is much better understood than that of most new drugs being tested.
(B) The social impact of some of the new drugs being tested is poorly understood.
(C) The economic success of some drugs is inversely proportional to how well we understand their social impact.
(D) The new antihistamine is chemically similar to some of the new drugs being tested.
(E) The new antihistamine should be on the market only if most new drugs being tested should be on the market also.

19. Birds need so much food energy to maintain their body temperatures that some of them spend most of their time eating. But a comparison of a bird of a seed-eating species to a bird of a nectar-eating species that has the same overall energy requirement would surely show that the seed-eating bird spends more time eating than does the nectar-eating bird, since a given amount of nectar provides more energy than does the same amount of seeds.

The argument relies on which one of the following questionable assumptions?

(A) Birds of different species do not generally have the same overall energy requirements as each other.
(B) The nectar-eating bird does not sometimes also eat seeds.
(C) The time it takes for the nectar-eating bird to eat a given amount of nectar is not longer than the time it takes the seed-eating bird to eat the same amount of seeds.
(D) The seed-eating bird does not have a lower body temperature than that of the nectar-eating bird.
(E) The overall energy requirements of a given bird do not depend on factors such as the size of the bird, its nest-building habits, and the climate of the region in which it lives.

23. When investigators discovered that the director of a local charity had repeatedly overstated the number of people his charity had helped, the director accepted responsibility for the deception. However, the investigators claimed that journalists were as much to blame as the director was for inflating the charity's reputation, since they had naïvely accepted what the director told them, and simply reported as fact the numbers he gave them.

Which one of the following principles, if valid, most helps to justify the investigators' claim?

(A) Anyone who works for a charitable organization is obliged to be completely honest about the activities of that organization.
(B) Anyone who knowingly aids a liar by trying to conceal the truth from others is also a liar.
(C) Anyone who presents as factual a story that turns out to be untrue without first attempting to verify that story is no less responsible for the consequences of that story than anyone else is.
(D) Anyone who lies in order to advance his or her own career is more deserving of blame than someone who lies in order to promote a good cause.
(E) Anyone who accepts responsibility for a wrongful act that he or she committed is less deserving of blame than someone who tries to conceal his or her own wrongdoing.

Question Set

24. Telephone companies are promoting "voice mail" as an alternative to the answering machine. By recording messages from callers when a subscriber does not have access to his or her telephone, voice mail provides a service similar to that of an answering machine. The companies promoting this service argue that it will soon make answering machines obsolete, since it is much more convenient, more flexible, and less expensive than an answering machine.

Which one of the following, if true, most calls into question the argument made by the companies promoting voice mail?

(A) Unlike calls made to owners of answering machines, all telephone calls made to voice-mail subscribers are completed, even if the line called is in use at the time of the call.
(B) The surge in sales of answering machines occurred shortly after they were first introduced to the electronics market.
(C) Once a telephone customer decides to subscribe to voice mail, that customer can cancel the service at any time.
(D) Answering machines enable the customer to hear who is calling before the customer decides whether to answer the telephone, a service voice mail does not provide.
(E) The number of messages a telephone answering machine can record is limited by the length of the magnetic tape on which calls are recorded.

25. The judgment that an artist is great always rests on assessments of the work the artist has produced. A series of great works is the only indicator of greatness. Therefore, to say that an artist is great is just to summarize the quality of his or her known works, and the artist's greatness can provide no basis for predicting the quality of the artist's unknown or future works.

Which one of the following contains questionable reasoning most similar to that in the argument above?

(A) The only way of knowing whether someone has a cold is to observe symptoms. Thus, when a person is said to have a cold, this means only that he or she has displayed the symptoms of a cold, and no prediction about the patient's future symptoms is justified.
(B) Although colds are very common, there are some people who never or only very rarely catch colds. Clearly these people must be in some way physiologically different from people who catch colds frequently.
(C) Someone who has a cold is infected by a cold virus. No one can be infected by the same cold virus twice, but there are indefinitely many different cold viruses. Therefore, it is not possible to predict from a person's history of infection how susceptible he or she will be in the future.
(D) The viruses that cause colds are not all the same, and they differ in their effects. Therefore, although it may be certain that a person has a cold, it is impossible to predict how the cold will progress.
(E) Unless a person displays cold symptoms, it cannot properly be said that the person has a cold. But each of the symptoms of a cold is also the symptom of some other disease. Therefore, one can never be certain that a person has a cold.

solutions

1. A	6. B	8. E	11. A	12. C	14. C	15. C
17. C	18. B	19. C	20. A	23. C	24. D	25. A

1. A | Point: Gov't ought to protect and encourage free speech. **Support:** Free speech conducive to healthy nation/in best interests of people. **Flaw:** Takes for granted that government ought to protect and encourage what is in best interests of people.
Task: Completely fix issue.
1st Elimination: "Inalienable rights" in (B) not discussed. "Helps a gov't to govern" in (C) not discussed. "Interests of that gov't" in (D) not discussed. "Universal human rights" in (E) not discussed. Leave (A).
Confirm Answer: If you place (A) in between the support and the conclusion, it creates a damn solid bridge.

---

6. B | Point: We can solve the problem only if we adopt this cost-cutting plan. **Support:** Can't increase funds, so must decrease expenditures. **Flaw:** Mistakes one plan for only plan.
Task: Describe the flaw.
1st Elimination: We don't know if information is far from certain, and it's unclear how this impacts the argument, so (A) is out. It's not certain the argument inappropriately relies on the opinion of experts, so (C) is out. No vague language as (D) states. (E) is mentioned as a premise, so it is not taken for granted. Leave (B).
Confirm Answer: "Feasible" means doable or reasonable, which is an okay match with "adequate" in (B). The rest of (B) represents the reasoning flaw exactly, and (B) is correct.

---

8. E | Point: There is no such link (link evidenced by pyramids) between Old- and New- World civilizations. **Support:** Pyramids used for different purposes. **Flaw:** Piece ≠ puzzle. The fact that they were used for different purposes is not enough to definitely prove no link.
Task: Describe the flaw.
1st Elimination: The argument doesn't equivocate (mince words) with "evidence," and even if it did, that would have no bearing on the reasoning, so (A) is out. (B) is not the flaw and is easy to eliminate. (C) is not the problem with the support-conclusion relationship. (D) is also not the reasoning problem here. Leave (E).
Confirm Answer: "This shows conclusively" indicates the high level of (faulty) regard in which the author holds his piece of evidence, and (E) is a fairly accurate representation of the flaw.

11. A (tough!) | Point: Program to improve morale of h.s. students has begun to reduce dropouts. **Support:** Last year's h.s. dropout rate significantly lower than year before. **Flaw:** Correlation does not prove causation. Seems there could be many other reasons for reduction in dropout rate.
Task: Weaken the argument.
1st Elimination: (A) brings in additional information, but it also provides an alternative explanation for why students stayed in school. Leave it. (B) has no direct impact on the reasoning. (C) tells us nothing about what caused a decrease in dropout rate. (D) also gives another reason for dropout rates, so leave it. (E) gives us more information about the support, but not in a way that impacts the conclusion.
Confirm Answer: Both (A) and (D) are attractive answers, so let's break each down carefully. (A) makes a lot of sense—if there are less jobs, then students are likely to stay in school. When we look back at the argument, however, we notice that the students who drop out aren't necessarily ones looking for work ("go to work" is given as a consequence of dropping out, not a cause), but rather ones who feel they are not succeeding in school. So, it's not perfect—maybe jobs have no impact on whether they decide to drop out... If we look at (D), it also gives a reason why students might want to stay in school—now the school is going to give them more help looking for work once they are out. But wait a minute...are these placement offices a part of this "improving morale" plan or not? Shoot, it's not clear at all. This has a big impact on whether this answer weakens or strengthens the argument. Since we don't know, that means (A) must be correct.

---

12. C | Point: Henry was widely watched because it followed That's Life. **Support:** Periods of success correlate to when it followed That's Life. **Flaw:** correlation/causation. Could be, for example, that Henry was just coincidentally only good for that one year it followed That's Life.
Task: Strengthen the argument.
1st Elimination: It's unclear how (A) relates to the argument. (B) would seem to either have no impact (if That's Life is no longer on Tuesdays at same time) or weaken the argument(if That's Life is). (C) shows more correlation between following That's Life and getting more viewers—leave it. (D) provides an alternative explanation for why Henry may have dropped in ratings, so if anything would weaken the argument. (E) has no bearing on the point.
Confirm Answer: (C) is the only viable answer. Of course it does not confirm a causal link, but by giving us more correlation, it makes it more likely.

---

14. C (tough!) | Point: Fermat was not lying or mistaken when he said he could prove theorem. **Support:** The theorem is provable. **Flaw:** Just because the theorem is provable does not mean Fermat must have honestly and correctly proved it.
Task: Describe the flaw.
1st Elimination: (A) doesn't happen in the argument. Quality of a person (B) is not discussed or relevant. (C) is interesting—not a great match for our view of the flaw, but perhaps related. Leave it. (D) does not describe a reasoning flaw (imagine if you had to define every word you ever used to reason something!). (E) is confusing—let's leave it.
Confirm Answer: Could (C) represent the flaw? In order to prove a theorem, it has to be provable—that is the necessary component. However, being provable does not guarantee that he did prove it—so, yes, the author mistakes something necessary for something sufficient. What about (E)? On careful review, it clearly does not represent what is going on in this argument (how is that distinction relevant to this author's point?). (C) is correct.

---

15. C | Point: Not good for university to have classes too big or small, or professors teaching too much or too little. **Support:** Crowded classrooms and overworked teachers hurt school's ability to get qualified students and faculty. **Flaw:** Where's the reason for why small/too little is bad?
Task: Support the point.
1st Elimination: (A) is not directly related to the argument. Unless we assume that classroom discussion is bad, (B) doesn't help the argument. (C) gives us a reason why small/too little is bad—leave it. (D) gives us an anti-reason (weakens the argument, if anything)—cut it. (E) is not directly relevant to the support-conclusion relationship.
Confirm Answer: (C) is the only viable answer, and we knew we needed something about small and light.

17. C | Point: Members limit daily coffee to two cups. **Support:** People who drink five or more cups a day have increased risk of heart disease. **Flaw:** Who's to say five is worse than two? Maybe it's that first cup that's worst of all.
Task: Weaken the argument.
1st Elimination: (A) shows that the more coffee one drinks, the worse it is, so if anything it strengthens the argument. More so, though, it has no direct impact, since it leaves unclear whether that means two is okay or not. (B) is irrelevant to the point. (C) represents the flaw we saw initially, and if (C) is true, it hurts the author's claim—leave it. (D) shows an alternative causal force, but the premise tells us they've already accounted for smoking habits. (E) is tempting, but how do we define heavy consumption? Maybe two cups is heavy consumption?
Confirm Answer: Does (C) destroy the argument? No, and we don't need it to do that. However, if (C) is true, it does make it seem less wise for these members to think the study makes two cups somehow okay.

---

18. B | Point: Tech ingenuity usually brings benefits; ethical inventiveness only brings pain. **Support:** People with political power see tech as means of extending power, and new ethical ideas as threats to it. **Flaw:** Assumes that views of people with political power have some direct impact on those with ingenuity or inventiveness without providing any evidence.
Task: Strengthen this.
1st Elimination: It's unclear how "new ways of justifying power" relates to this particular argument—it does not clearly represent either of the parties (tech/ethical) in this discussion. (B) is what we needed—leave it. Whether (C) is true or not has no impact on the argument (you can have benefit and pain). (D) weakens a premise—cut it. (E) is not directly relevant unless we assume that hiding arguments brings pain.
Confirm Answer: If (B) is true, it makes it much more reasonable to use this support to justify this point.

---

19. C | Point: Seed-eating birds must spend more time eating than nectar-eating birds. **Support:** Same amount of nectar gives more energy. **Flaw:** Presumes a link between volume of food needed and time needed to eat the food. Maybe seeds can be eaten very quickly, whereas eating nectar is for some reason a more tedious process.
Task: Find required assumption.
1st Elimination: We don't need to know that (A) is true for the argument to work. (B) does not have to be true for the argument to work, and without knowing whether it's faster to eat seeds or nectar, it's unclear what the impact of this answer is. (C) matches the flaw we saw—let's leave it. (D) is not relevant to the argument. (E) doesn't match our understanding of the flaw, but seems it is relevant to the support-conclusion relationship—leave it.
Confirm Answer: (C) seems correct. If we negate (C), it tells us eating nectar takes longer, and that does a lot of damage to the reasoning in the argument. Looking back at (E), it no longer looks attractive—we're actually told that this argument is about birds that require the same amount of energy. If we weren't, (E) would be really attractive, but as is we now realize it has no direct bearing on the particular argument being made.

---

20. A (tough!) | Point: Should slow down pace of bringing new drugs now being tested to marketplace. **Support:** New drug should only be introduced if you have a good understanding of social impact. **Flaw:** We've only been given information about one drug. Who says we don't understand social impact of various new drugs?
Task: Strengthen this.
1st Elimination: (A) seems to indicate that the new drugs are not well understood. Leave it. (B) seems to match exactly what we needed. Leave it. (C) has no direct bearing on the reasoning, and the impact of (D) is far from clear (chemically similar does not relate to similar social impact). (E) actually weakens the argument, since the new antihistamine is on market.
Confirm Answer: We are told that the impact of the new antihistamine is far from clear—if this is better than the understanding of most new drugs, that means that the understanding of most new drugs is poor. This strengthens the connection between the support and the conclusion. However, (B) seems to strengthen, too. When we evaluate (B) carefully, though, we notice the word "some"—some can be anything, one drug or all drugs—that does very little to support a "general" (i.e., majority) recommendation. (A) must be correct.

---

23. C | Point: Journalist as much to blame as director. **Support:** They naively accepted what they were told. **Flaw:** Assumes that naively accepting makes one as much to blame as someone who overstated to begin with.
Task: Need to fill the gap.
1st Elimination: (A) has no direct bearing on the conclusion. (B) does not correctly represent the journalists, who were naive rather than being known aids of liars. Leave (C)—looks good. "In order to advance his or her own career" eliminates (D). For (E), accepts responsibility versus conceal is not our issue.
Confirm Answer: (C) creates a solid bridge between support and conclusion.

---

24. D | Point: Voice mail will soon make answering machines obsolete. **Support:** More convenient, flexible, and cheaper. **Flaw:** Maybe there are other reasons people like their answering machines.
Task: Weaken the argument.
1st Elimination: (A) seems to give an advantage for voice mail. It's unclear how (B) impacts the conclusion—cut it. (C) seems to give an advantage (or at least take away a potential disadvantage) for voice mail. (D) gives a reason why people might like answering machines better—leave it. (E) seems to give us a problem with answering machines—cut it.
Confirm Answer: (D) is our only viable choice. It doesn't destroy the argument, but it does give us a reason to question whether the reasons given will actually make it so people prefer voice mail.

---

25. A | Point: Artists' greatness can provide no basis for predicting quality of future work. **Support:** Greatness is only an indication of the past. **Flaw:** Assumes that the past cannot be used to make predictions about the future—seems that past history of creating great art is relevant to future chances of producing great art.
Task: Match the flaw.
1st Elimination: (A) has the same type of flaw—just because symptoms are in the past doesn't mean they can't be used to predict future symptoms. Leave it. (B) is about some unique people and reaches a very different conclusion than our argument. (C) has a similar type of conclusion about not being able to predict the future, but uses a different line of reasoning (infinite number of different colds) that seems far more reasonable than that in the original argument. Not a match. (D) is not about past/future—cut it. (E) is about not being able to properly assess a situation, which is different from being able to predict what will happen in the future. Cut it.
Confirm Answer: (C) was tempting, but (A) is the most attractive answer here. We check to make sure that parts of the answer (conclusion, support) match up to parts in the original argument, and they do. Same parts, same flaw = right answer.

How Did You Do?

If you went -0 or -1, that's incredible. Phenomenal work. Eat a little extra dessert tonight. If you didn't do as well, that is, at this point, to be expected. We still have a lot of work ahead of us. As far as your ultimate score goes, how you react to your performance is far more important than how many you actually got right and wrong.

Taken together, this set of questions nicely represents the range of challenges that you will see on test day, and it also nicely illustrates the variety of skills you will need in order to succeed at a high level.

Start your self-assessment by checking to see if there were any questions you were certain you got right that you ultimately missed. These are the biggest red flags, and generally they indicate that there was a significant mistake made or a significant misunderstanding while solving the problem. By this point in your training, this should be happening very rarely—i.e., you should have a very good sense of when you know you are right, and when you don't. If you are often surprised that you missed a question, it's a sure tell sign that there are problems with your skill set or your understanding of how particular questions are designed.

Next, consider carefully the questions you had difficulty with, and think about where it is exactly that the problems started. Did you not have a clear sense of the argument or the flaw? Did you have a clear sense of wrong answers to avoid? Or did you do everything else right, but make some error in trying to confirm the correct answer?

Finally, consider timing. Timing is most directly a consequence of your thought process—if you are thinking about the right things, timing will be less of an issue. If you are distracted or you don't know exactly what to think about, timing will be a bigger issue. If you had trouble with timing (and at this point, I would generalize that to spending more than twenty-four minutes on the previous set), first and foremost you want to think about all of the extra things you are doing that are not important to answering the question. Go back through each problem, think about what you thought about, and be critical of any time you spent thinking about anything that wasn't ultimately relevant to eliminating wrong answers and identifying the right one. Occasionally, timing issues can also come about even though test takers know what to think about and when, and this is because the test taker is being overly cautious about each decision. Be mindful of over-thinking, and make sure you don't fall prey to decision-making inertia. Still, do know that the vast majority of timing issues are because of time wasted thinking about the wrong things, as opposed to too much time spent thinking about the right things.

We all miss problems once in a while. The biggest issues to take note of are the deepest ones—those having to do with reading the argument, identifying what is wrong, and understanding what our task is. Use these questions to honestly gauge how effective you are at each of these skills, and work from general and fundamental to specific and nuanced as you go about strengthening your skill set.

21 LOGIC GAMES a brief return to games

We will return to games full-time in Lesson 26, but for now here is a small oasis in the game-less desert. Starting in a few pages will be four full games that have appeared on previous LSATs.

Before we get to those games, I want to start out by quickly reviewing diagramming and by discussing some basic games strategies. In addition, I also want to discuss the first of the question types that we will be studying: the Rules question. The Rules question is almost always the first question asked for any game, and there is a simple and effective method for getting any Rules question correct.

The Key to Games Success: Diagramming

In order to answer the questions that are asked in the games section, we need to think about how rules come together with other rules; we need to be able to do so accurately, over and over again, as we think of each answer choice for each question. The tool that allows us to do that is our diagram. When drawn well, our diagram will help us see the rules of a game far more clearly than when those rules are in worded form, and our diagram will aid us as we think about how these rules come together. In Lessons 10 through 15, we focused on developing diagramming strategies. In this lesson and the rest of the Logic Games lessons that follow, we will integrate our diagramming abilities into the bigger task of successfully solving Logic Games questions.

Some Quick Tips on Playing Logic Games

We will be discussing much more specific strategies in later lessons, but here are a few things to keep in mind for now:

For a review of common notations, please return to page 206.

1) Read the scenario and rules and "picture" the general structure of a game before you start your diagram.
2) Diagram first the rule or combination of rules that you think is most significant.
3) Confirm your notations by checking them against the written rules.
4) Always think about how the rules relate to one another.
5) Do as much work at the point of the question stem as possible.
6) Expect to do very little work with each answer. Know that almost all of your work should be done before you consider specific answer choices.

The Rules Question

Over 90 percent of all games begin with a Rules question. A Rules question is a question that asks you to identify, among the answer choices, one assignment of elements that could be true based on what we know about a game. Rules questions always ask about the assignment of all elements to all spots (though, in a few rare instances, they will do so somewhat indirectly), they almost always (over 90 percent of the time) *only* appear as the first question of a game, and they are always asked in terms of what "could be true" based on what we know.

Rules questions are fundamentally different from all other games questions. Every other games question will differentiate between right and wrong answers based on the *inferences* we learn by bringing rules together. For example, if a game tells us that "X is on Team One" and "X and Y are not on the same team," neither of those statements will be helpful in figuring out which answers are right or wrong. What we learn *by bringing two ideas together* (Y is not on Team One) will almost certainly be directly relevant for differentiating between right and wrong answers for at least one of the questions in the set.

Rules questions are unique in that they are not dependent on inferences. They might be if our job was to *come up* with one set of assignments that satisfies the rules, but it's not. Our job is to evaluate the options given to us, and for just these questions, what differentiates right and wrong answers is not the inferences, but rather the given rules themselves (hence the name of the question). Going back to the example about X and Y—each of the two rules given, in their original forms, would likely allow us to eliminate incorrect answers.

This is what makes Rules questions different from other questions—we want to develop methods specific to Rules questions, methods that do not relate to how we approach all other types of questions.

You can probably imagine a few ways to go about solving Rules questions: you can use your diagram, you can check the answers against the rules, or you can use the rules to test the answers. Feel free to try out all options yourself, but I promise you that you will come to a certain conclusion: using the rules to test answers, as I have for the two examples on the side, is the most efficient and accurate way to solve Rules questions. This has to do with the design of the questions themselves —the four wrong choices are consistently written so that individual rules eliminate individual answers. If you are given four rules to a game, it is almost certain that each of those rules will allow you to eliminate exactly one of the four wrong answer choices—the last answer standing—the one that doesn't violate the list of rules—is the one that is correct. If you are given fewer than four rules, you can expect that one of them will eliminate more than one answer, and if you are given more than four rules, you know some won't be useful in eliminating choices. Still, by simply going down the list of given rules[1] and using them to see which answers must be false, you will *always* be able to quickly eliminate the four incorrect choices and identify the right answer.

1. *Tiny caveat: Once in a blue moon, there will be an answer you need to eliminate based on information given* ***in the scenario****. In these cases, this information will typically be more specific (i.e., more rule-like) than the information we typically get in the scenario.*

SUPER-SIMPLE EXAMPLE:

Five people—F, G, H, J,K—take turns using a computer. One person uses it at a time, and they each use it once. The following conditions apply:

F does not use it first.
G uses it before H.
J uses it third.
K does not use it second.

Which of the following could be the order in which people use computers?
(A) G, K, J, F, H
(B) H, F, J, K, G
(C) G, F, K, J, H
(D) F, G, J, K, H
(E) G, F, J, K, H

The first rule tells us (D) must be wrong. The second rule eliminates (B). The third (C). The fourth (A). (E) is correct. With four rules, you can typically expect them to each eliminate one choice.

SUPER-SIMPLE EXAMPLE (B):

Five people—F, G, H, J, and K—take turns using a computer. One person uses it at a time, and they each use it once. The following conditions apply:

F does not use it first.
G uses it before H.
J uses it third.

Which of the following could be the order in which people use computers?
(A) F, G, J, H, K
(B) H, F, J, K, G
(C) G, F, K, J, H
(D) F, G, J, K, H
(E) G, F, J, K, H

Given just three rules, we can expect one to eliminate two answers. If given more than four rules, we would expect some not to eliminate any wrong answers. The first rule eliminates (A) and (D), the second rule eliminates (B), and the third rule eliminates (C). That leaves (E) as our correct answer.

Instructions for next page: Starting on the following page will be four Logic Games, each with their full accompaniment of questions. Taken together, the games are representative of the variety and difficulty present in a typical games section. The one difference is that this set of four has twenty-two total questions, whereas your exam will almost surely have twenty-three. Time yourself for each game. If you are solving the games as a full practice session, don't stop your work at the thirty-five-minute mark, and don't give up on any question because of time constraints. Solutions and discussion will follow. FYI—on the real exam, you will have two pages to do your games work, so feel free to use extra space to diagram and such if you feel you need it.

GAME 1 | PT 27, GAME 1, QUESTIONS 1 – 5

During a period of seven consecutive days—from day 1 through day 7—seven investors—Fennelly, Gupta, Hall, Jones, Knight, López, and Moss—will each view a building site exactly once. Each day exactly one investor will view the site. The investors must view the site in accordance with the following conditions:

Fennelly views the site on day 3 or else day 5.
López views the site on neither day 4 nor day 6.
If Jones views the site on day 1, Hall views the site on day 2.
If Knight views the site on day 4, López views the site on day 5.
Gupta views the site on the day after the day on which Hall views the site.

1. Which one of the following could be the order in which the investors view the site, from day 1 through day 7?

(A) Hall, Gupta, Fennelly, Moss, Knight, López, Jones
(B) Hall, Gupta, López, Fennelly, Moss, Knight, Jones
(C) López, Gupta, Hall, Moss, Fennelly, Jones, Knight
(D) López, Jones, Fennelly, Knight, Hall, Gupta, Moss
(E) López, Jones, Knight, Moss, Fennelly, Hall, Gupta

2. If Jones views the site on day 1, which one of the following investors must view the site on day 4?

(A) Fennelly
(B) Gupta
(C) Knight
(D) López
(E) Moss

3. If Knight views the site on day 4 and Moss views the site on some day after the day on which Jones views the site, which one of the following must be true?

(A) Jones views the site on day 1.
(B) Jones views the site on day 2.
(C) Jones views the site on day 6.
(D) Moss views the site on day 2.
(E) Moss views the site on day 6.

4. If Hall views the site on day 2, which one of the following is a complete and accurate list of investors any one of whom could be the investor who views the site on day 4?

(A) Knight
(B) Moss
(C) Jones, Moss
(D) Knight, Moss
(E) Jones, Knight, Moss

5. If Hall views the site on the day after the day Knight views the site and if Fennelly views the site on the day after the day López views the site, then Jones must view the site on day

(A) 1
(B) 2
(C) 3
(D) 4
(E) 5

GAME 2 | PT 32, GAME 2, QUESTIONS 7 – 11

The organizer of a reading club will select at least five and at most six works from a group of nine works. The group consists of three French novels, three Russian novels, two French plays, and one Russian play. The organizer's selection of works must conform to the following requirements:

No more than four French works are selected.
At least three but no more than four novels are selected.
At least as many French novels as Russian novels are selected.
If both French plays are selected, then the Russian play is not selected.

7. Which one of the following could be the organizer's selection of works?

(A) one French novel, two Russian novels, one French play, one Russian play
(B) two French novels, one Russian novel, two French plays, one Russian play
(C) two French novels, two Russian novels, two French plays
(D) three French novels, one Russian novel, two French plays
(E) three French novels, two Russian novels, one Russian play

8. Which one of the following could be true about the organizer's selection of works?

(A) No Russian novels are selected.
(B) Exactly one French novel is selected.
(C) All three plays are selected.
(D) All three Russian novels are selected.
(E) All five French works are selected.

9. If the works selected include three French novels, which one of the following could be a complete and accurate list of the remaining works selected?

(A) one Russian novel
(B) two French plays
(C) one Russian novel, one Russian play
(D) one Russian novel, two French plays
(E) two Russian novels, one French play

10. The organizer must at least select

(A) one French novel and one French play
(B) one French novel and one Russian play
(C) one Russian novel and one French play
(D) two French novels
(E) two Russian novels

11. Any one of the following could be true about the organizer's selections of works EXCEPT:

(A) No Russian novels and exactly one play are selected.
(B) Exactly one Russian novel and both French plays are selected.
(C) Exactly two French novels and the Russian play are selected.
(D) Exactly two French novels and exactly two plays are selected.
(E) Exactly two Russian novels and exactly one play are selected.

GAME 3 | PT 31, GAME 3, QUESTIONS 14 – 18

During a single week, from Monday through Friday, tours will be conducted of a company's three divisions—Operations, Production, Sales. Exactly five tours will be conducted that week, one each day. The schedule of tours for the week must conform to the following restrictions:
Each division is toured at least once.
The Operations division is not toured on Monday.
The Production division is not toured on Wednesday.
The Sales division is toured on two consecutive days, and on no other days.
If the Operations division is toured on Thursday, then the Production division is toured on Friday.

14. Which one of the following CANNOT be true of the week's tour schedule?

(A) The division that is toured on Monday is also toured on Tuesday.
(B) The division that is toured on Monday is also toured on Friday.
(C) The division that is toured on Tuesday is also toured on Thursday.
(D) The division that is toured on Wednesday is also toured on Friday.
(E) The division that is toured on Thursday is also toured on Friday.

15. If in addition to the Sales division one other division is toured on two consecutive days, then it could be true of the week's tour schedule both that the

(A) Production division is toured on Monday and that the Operations division is toured on Thursday
(B) Production division is toured on Tuesday and that the Sales division is toured on Wednesday
(C) Operations division is toured on Tuesday and that the Production division is toured on Friday
(D) Sales division is toured on Monday and that the Operations division is toured on Friday
(E) Sales division is toured on Wednesday and that the Production division is toured on Friday

16. If in the week's tour schedule the division that is toured on Tuesday is also toured on Friday, then for which one of the following days must a tour of the Production division be scheduled?

(A) Monday
(B) Tuesday
(C) Wednesday
(D) Thursday
(E) Friday

17. If in the week's tour schedule the division that is toured on Monday is not the division that is toured on Tuesday, then which one of the following could be true of the week's schedule?

(A) A tour of the Sales division is scheduled for some day earlier in the week than is any tour of the Production division.
(B) A tour of the Operations division is scheduled for some day earlier in the week than is any tour of the Production division.
(C) The Sales division is toured on Monday.
(D) The Production division is toured on Tuesday.
(E) The Operations division is toured on Wednesday.

18. If in the week's tour schedule the division that is toured on Tuesday is also toured on Wednesday, then which one of the following must be true of the week's tour schedule?

(A) The Production division is toured on Monday.
(B) The Operations division is toured on Tuesday.
(C) The Sales division is toured on Wednesday.
(D) The Sales division is toured on Thursday.
(E) The Production division is toured on Friday.

GAME 4 | PT 33, GAME 2, QUESTIONS 6 – 12

Bird-watchers explore a forest to see which of the following six kinds of birds—grosbeak, harrier, jay, martin, shrike, wren—it contains. The findings are consistent with the following conditions:

If harriers are in the forest, then grosbeaks are not.
If jays, martins, or both are in the forest, then so are harriers.
If wrens are in the forest, then so are grosbeaks.
If jays are not in the forest, then shrikes are.

6. Which one of the following could be a complete and accurate list of the birds NOT in the forest?

(A) jays, shrikes
(B) harriers, grosbeaks
(C) grosbeaks, jays, martins
(D) grosbeaks, martins, shrikes, wrens
(E) martins, shrikes

7. If both martins and harriers are in the forest, then which one of the following must be true?

(A) Shrikes are the only other birds in the forest.
(B) Jays are the only other birds in the forest.
(C) The forest contains neither jays nor shrikes.
(D) There are at least two other kinds of birds in the forest.
(E) There are at most two other kinds of birds in the forest.

8. If jays are not in the forest, then which one of the following must be false?

(A) Martins are in the forest.
(B) Harriers are in the forest.
(C) Neither martins nor harriers are in the forest.
(D) Neither martins nor shrikes are in the forest.
(E) Harriers and shrikes are the only birds in the forest.

9. Which one of the following is the maximum number of the six kinds of birds the forest could contain?

(A) two
(B) three
(C) four
(D) five
(E) six

10. Which one of the following pairs of birds CANNOT be among those birds contained in the forest?

(A) jays, wrens
(B) jays, shrikes
(C) shrikes, wrens
(D) jays, martins
(E) shrikes, martins

11. If grosbeaks are in the forest, then which one of the following must be true?

(A) Shrikes are in the forest.
(B) Wrens are in the forest.
(C) The forest contains both wrens and shrikes.
(D) At most two kinds of birds are in the forest.
(E) At least three kinds of birds are in the forest.

12. Suppose the condition is added that if shrikes are in the forest, then harriers are not. If all other conditions remain in effect, then which one of the following could be true?

(A) The forest contains both jays and shrikes.
(B) The forest contains both wrens and shrikes.
(C) The forest contains both martins and shrikes.
(D) Jays are not in the forest, whereas martins are.
(E) Only two of the six kinds of birds are not in the forest.

How Did You Do?

For many of you, that was your first time handling a full set of games and questions. How did you do? Of course, you'll need to check the answers to be certain, but I'm sure you have a pretty good sense of your general outcome. Logic Games questions are different from Logical Reasoning and Reading Comprehension questions in that there really is no gray area for answer choices—if you've solved a Logic Games question correctly, you'll never have to choose between two attractive answer choices, as you might in a Strengthen Logical Reasoning question. If you've done your work correctly, you should be able to see, for every question, that one answer is definitely right, or four answers are definitely wrong. Thus, even though everyone makes an unexpected mistake here or there, once you get to a high level of mastery, you should not have to check the solutions to see how you've done—you'll have a clear sense of which questions you got right for sure, and which questions you didn't.

Let's think about the four games that you just solved, and let's think about them in terms of the very specific skills that were necessary for success. A list of such skills is provided in the table below. For each game, think carefully about how well you performed at that skill challenge, and give yourself a subjective 1–5 score on your performance. Taking a look at how you perform various tasks across the range of games can help you develop a more accurate sense of your overall abilities. And checking your sense of your own skill set versus the solutions, which will start on the next page, will also help you get a more accurate sense of your abilities.

Go ahead and assess your performance on each game by giving yourself a 1 –5 score on each of the general skill sets that are required of you. You can revisit this chart to reassess after looking at the solutions.

GENERAL SKILL	Game 1	Game 2	Game 3	Game 4	Total
I felt comfortable picturing the general design of the game					/20
I felt comfortable notating rules					/20
I felt good about seeing the inferences that exist					/20
I understood how to approach questions					/20
The work I had to do in the questions went smoothly					/20
TOTAL	/25	/25	/25	/25	

Game One Solution | PT 27, GAME 1, QUESTIONS 1 - 5

Let's take a step-by-step look at how a top scorer might solve this game. There are a variety of solutions that can be effective, and yours is certainly not wrong because it is different from the one below. Still, you can use this diagram and solutions to think about your own process.

During a period of seven consecutive days—from day 1 through day 7—seven investors—Fennelly, Gupta, Hall, Jones, Knight, López, and Moss—will each view a building site exactly once. Each day exactly one investor will view the site. The investors must view the site in accordance with the following conditions:

Fennelly views the site on day 3 or else day 5.
López views the site on neither day 4 nor day 6.
If Jones views the site on day 1, Hall views the site on day 2.
If Knight views the site on day 4, López views the site on day 5.
Gupta views the site on the day after the day on which Hall views the site.

Start by making a general assessment of the game: it's a straightforward ordering game with seven elements for seven positions—there is nothing unusual we have to consider. There also doesn't seem to be any one rule, or combination of rules, that is markedly more significant than the others.

__ __ __ __ __ __ __ F G H J K L M

So, we can just start as we commonly do: by drawing seven positions and listing the seven elements. Looking ahead, we've got a couple of rules about assignment, a couple of conditional rules, and an ordering rule—all fairly typical.

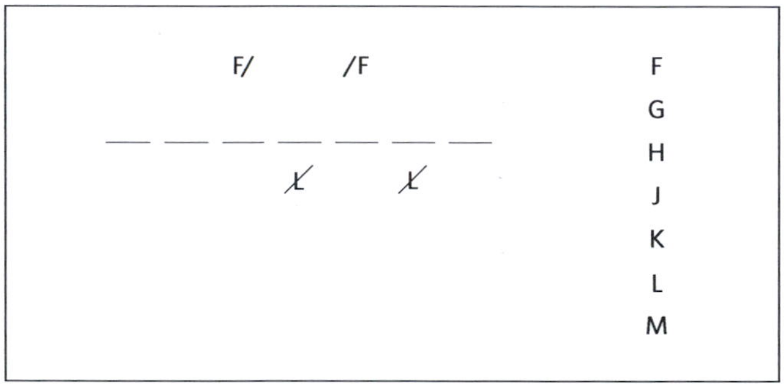

F/ /F
__ __ __ __ __ __ __
~~L~~ ~~L~~
F G H J K L M

We can draw the first two rules above and below our diagram. The notations are close enough so that we won't forget about them when we look at our picture, but we want to keep the positions open so we better imagine various other elements filling them.

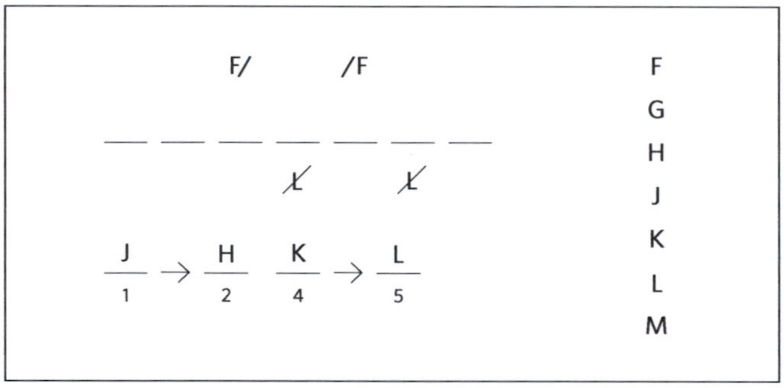

F/ /F
__ __ __ __ __ __ __
~~L~~ ~~L~~
J/1 → H/2   K/4 → L/5
F G H J K L M

We want to notate conditional rules below or beside our diagram. If you'd like, you can write down the contrapositives (if H is not in 2, J is not in 1, and if L is not in 5, K is not in 4) as well. I chose not to because, for me, this conditional felt basic enough that I could easily think about and remind myself of the contrapositive just using my original notation.

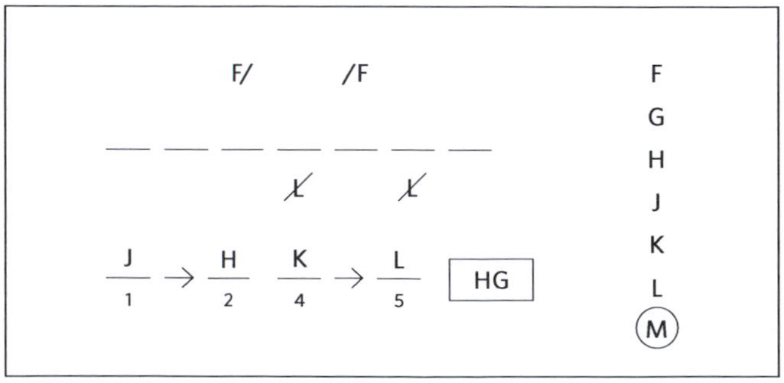

F/ /F
__ __ __ __ __ __ __
~~L~~ ~~L~~
J/1 → H/2   K/4 → L/5   [HG]
F G H J K L (M)

Now we write in the final rule, which, though it only involves two elements, is probably our most useful. I just put a box around it to notice it more, but that's of course optional. We want to notice any elements that didn't get mentioned in the rules, and in this case, since M is not mentioned, we want to circle it to remind ourselves it can go anywhere.

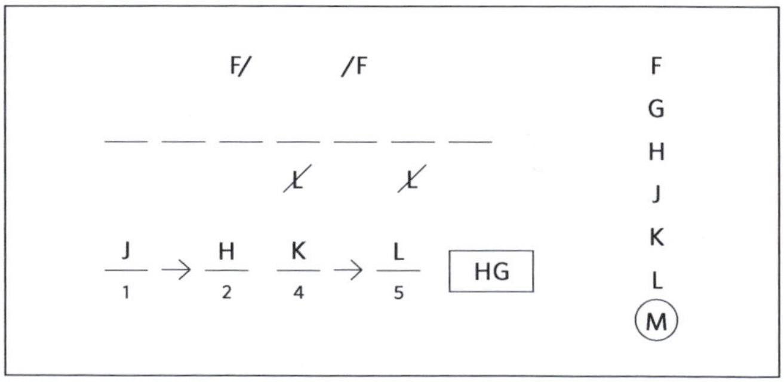

F/ /F
__ __ __ __ __ __ __
~~L~~ ~~L~~
J/1 → H/2   K/4 → L/5   [HG]
F G H J K L (M)

We take one last look at the diagram—no significant inferences to be made, but it's easy enough to see the relationship between rules. Take a second playing with potential inference chains (what happens if J is in 1?) if you'd like. We double-check each notation against the wording, and now let's go into the questions.

1. Which one of the following could be the order in which the investors view the site, from day 1 through day 7?

(A) Hall, Gupta, Fennelly, Moss, Knight, López, Jones
(B) Hall, Gupta, López, Fennelly, Moss, Knight, Jones
(C) López, Gupta, Hall, Moss, Fennelly, Jones, Knight
(D) López, Jones, Fennelly, Knight, Hall, Gupta, Moss
(E) López, Jones, Knight, Moss, Fennelly, Hall, Gupta

This is a standard Rules question—notice it comes first and we are asked for one order that could work. We want to use the rules to eliminate answers. The first rule eliminates (B). The second (A). The fourth rule (D). The fifth rule (C). (E) is therefore the correct answer. If you'd like, you can confirm it by testing each rule against it.

2. If Jones views the site on day 1, which one of the following investors must view the site on day 4?

(A) Fennelly
(B) Gupta
(C) Knight
(D) López
(E) Moss

J H G __ F __ __

K̸
L̸

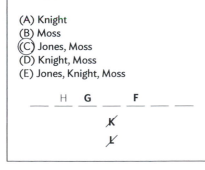

We know, per the way the question is asked, that placing J in 1 will lead us on a chain of inferences that eventually tells us what to place in 4. For this type of question, we should absolutely expect to know the right answer before looking at the answer choices. If J is in 1, H must be in 2, so G must be in 3. That forces F into 5. That means K can't be in 4, and we already know that L can't be in 4. That leaves M as our only option. Notice how helpful it is here to be mindful of M being a free agent. (E) is correct.

3. If Knight views the site on day 4 and Moss views the site on some day after the day on which Jones views the site, which one of the following must be true?

(A) Jones views the site on day 1.
(B) Jones views the site on day 2.
(C) Jones views the site on day 6.
(D) Moss views the site on day 2.
(E) Moss views the site on day 6.

H G F K L J M

J — M

This rule gives us two conditions—the first of which has a more direct impact. If K is in 4, L is in 5, and F must go in 3. That leaves only 1/2 or 6/7 for HG. We know that J must be before M, that HG must go together, and that if J is first, H must be second. Per that last rule, we know J can't be first, and J also can't be second because we wouldn't have enough space for H, G, and M in 6/7. The only configuration that works is putting HG in 1/2 and J and M in 6 and 7. (C) is correct. Note that this is an extremely rare Must Be True question in that we figure out where all elements go.

4. If Hall views the site on day 2, which one of the following is a complete and accurate list of investors any one of whom could be the investor who views the site on day 4?

(A) Knight
(B) Moss
(C) Jones, Moss
(D) Knight, Moss
(E) Jones, Knight, Moss

__ H G __ F __ __

K̸
L̸

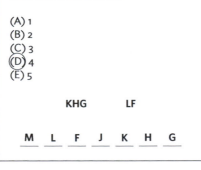

If H is in 2, then G is in 3, and F is in 5. Looking at the rules, that means K can't be in 4, and we also know that L can't be in 4. That leaves just J and M. Since we've already accounted for most of the rules, it's easy enough to mentally picture at least one way that J can work in the fourth position (M, H, G, J, F, K, L) and same with M in the fourth (J, H, G, M, F, K, L). (C) is correct.

5. If Hall views the site on the day after the day Knight views the site and if Fennelly views the site on the day after the day López views the site, then Jones must view the site on day

(A) 1
(B) 2
(C) 3
(D) 4
(E) 5

KHG LF

M L F J K H G

Let's start by notating the new information. If F is right after L, F must go in 3 and L in 2. That means KGH must go somewhere in 4-7, but K can't go in 4 without putting L in 5, so KGH must go 5-6-7. That leaves J and M for 1 and 4. However, if J goes in 1, H must go in 2, and we don't have that. Thus, J must go in 4. (D) is correct.

Game Two Solution | PT 32, GAME 2, QUESTIONS 7 – 11

Let's take a step-by-step look at how a top scorer might solve this game.

The organizer of a reading club will select at least five and at most six works from a group of nine works. The group consists of three French novels, three Russian novels, two French plays, and one Russian play. The organizer's selection of works must conform to the following requirements:

No more than four French works are selected.
At least three but no more than four novels are selected.
At least as many French novels as Russian novels are selected.
If both French plays are selected, then the Russian play is not selected.

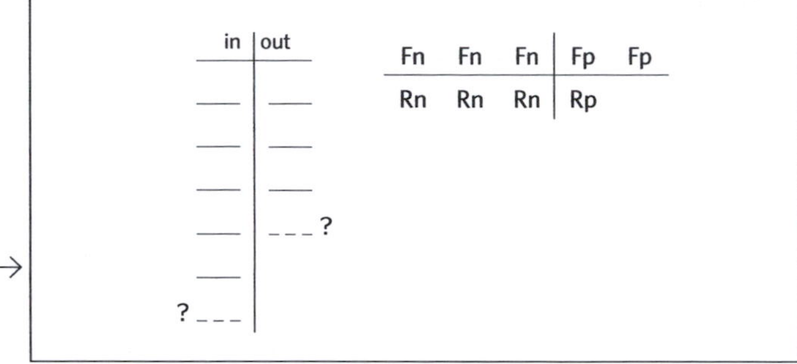

Right away we know this is not a "standard" game. We have an uncertain number of positions in each group, and we don't have individual elements—we have multiples. And we have subsets. Three of the four rules are about numbers—my general sense is that the challenge of the game will be in keeping track of disparate information, and that the game will be heavy on mathematical deductions.

I've taken a little more care than I normally would in notating the elements, because I know that keeping information about the separate groups clear will be important to solving questions. I've used a dashed line with a question mark for the sixth space. You can use whatever notation you'd like here—the key being that you understand the meaning easily.

in | out

Fn Fn Fn | Fp Fp
Rn Rn Rn | Rp

not all 5 F's

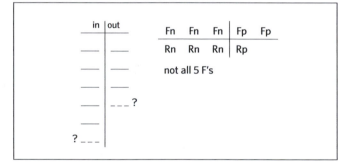

I don't spot any rule or group of rules that stands out, so I just start with the first rule. The way the first rule is written doesn't help me much. It leaves me with 1 F, 2 F's, 3 F's, or 4 F's—too many options. The other way to think about it is that there can't be all five F's, and that's the way I chose to write it.

in	out
n	n
n	n/p
n	p
n/p	p ?
p	
? p	

Fn Fn Fn | Fp Fp
Rn Rn Rn | Rp

not all 5 F's
3 or 4 n, 1-3 p

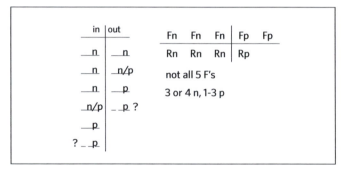

Moving on to the second rule, the math is messy here because it's 3 or 4 out of 5 or 6—if either of those numbers were fixed, the math would be much simpler. Anyway, we can make a small deduction about the number of P's in and out, and, optionally, we can also write this information into our diagram.

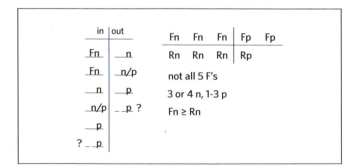

in	out
Fn	n
Fn	n/p
n	p
n/p	p ?
p	
? p	

Fn Fn Fn | Fp Fp
Rn Rn Rn | Rp

not all 5 F's
3 or 4 n, 1-3 p
Fn ≥ Rn

Look at our list of rules: it's a disparate, tough group to work with. That's one of the reasons I've been trying to make small inferences and notations on the board at each point along the way. If there are more French novels than Russian, and a minimum of 3 novels, we know there must be at least 2 French novels.

in	out
Fn	n
Fn	n/p
n	p
n/p	p ?
p	
? p	

Fn Fn Fn | Fp Fp
Rn Rn Rn | Rp

not all 5 F's
3 or 4 n, 1-3 p
Fn ≥ Rn
Fp + Fp → ~~Rp~~
not all 3 plays

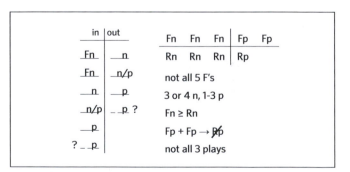

The last rule is a conditional. You choose to write in the contrapositive if you'd like: if Rp is in, at least one of the Fp's is out: (Rp → ~~Fp~~ or ~~Fp~~). An inference we can make here (and I think organizing the elements the way I did, and knowing that number inferences are important, helps us think of this) is that this means not all 3 plays are included.

ALTERNATIVES

This is an unusual game, and there are different ways we could have effectively gone about trying to solve it.

In a typical game, we'd probably be given names for the books, and both French/Russian and novel/play would be subset issues. In this case it's like we have two subsets! There is no reason you have to decide here to make F and R the elements, and n and p the subsets. We could have also just as well written them as Nf, Nf, Nf, and so on. The reason I chose to go with what I did was the same reason I always use in such a situation—I went with what I thought worked best with the rules.

If you haven't already, go ahead and think now about this: if there are either three or four novels chosen, and we can't have more Russian novels than French novels, what are all our options for the different numbers of each novel?

We have four: FnFnFn, FnFnRn, FnFnRnRn, FnFnFnRn. We could have used that, or perhaps some other numeric distribution, to lay out a set of diagrams that would have made answering the questions far simpler. If you thought of this or something else similar, and executed it well, bravo! You are well ahead of pace.

7. Which one of the following could be the organizer's selection of works?

(A) one French novel, two Russian novels, one French play, one Russian play
(B) two French novels, one Russian novel, two French plays one Russian play
(C) two French novels, two Russian novels, two French plays
(D) three French novels, one Russian novel, two French plays
(E) three French novels, two Russian novels, one Russian play

This is a standard Rules question, and we want to use the rules to eliminate incorrect answers. The first rule allows us to eliminate (D), the second (E), the third (A), and the fourth (B). The correct answer is (C).

8. Which one of the following could be true about the organizer's selection of works?

(A) No Russian novels are selected.
(B) Exactly one French novel is selected.
(C) All three plays are selected.
(D) All three Russian novels are selected.
(E) All five French works are selected.

When we are asked about something that could be true, typically the right answer is not something that jumps out at you—we know so little about the game at this point that almost anything could be true! What's more important is that four answers must be false, per what we know of the game. We want to focus on eliminating those. We don't know that (A) must be false, so let's leave it. We can quickly see that (B), (C), and (D) are incorrect per the inferences we made. (E) is incorrect per a rule we were given. (A) is the only answer remaining, and it is correct.

9. If the works selected include three French novels, which one of the following could be a complete and accurate list of the remaining works selected?

(A) one Russian novel
(B) two French plays
(C) one Russian novel, one Russian play
(D) one Russian novel, two French plays
(E) two Russian novels, one French play

We can redraw the diagram if need be, but let's try to take a more direct route and look for inferences—what do we know, per the rules, if all three French novels are selected? We know that either zero or one Russian novel is selected. We also know that the two French plays can't be selected. As with the last "could be" question, we want to knock off answers that can't be. We can easily eliminate (A) because it would leave us with 4 items. We can eliminate (B), (D), and (E) per the simple inferences we made. (C) is the only possible answer, and it is correct.

10. The organizer must at least select

(A) one French novel and one French play
(B) one French novel and one Russian play
(C) one Russian novel and one French play
(D) two French novels
(E) two Russian novels

When a question asks what must be true or false, it's generally a waste of time to focus on eliminating wrong choices (we'll discuss this in more depth in future lessons, but consider that in these cases, the wrong answers represents the "could be's," the information we know less about). We want to look for something that we know has to be true, and in this case we already know that (D) has to be true. We can select it and move on.

11. Any one of the following could be true about the organizer's selections of works EXCEPT:

(A) No Russian novels and exactly one play are selected.
(B) Exactly one Russian novel and both French plays are selected.
(C) Exactly two French novels and the Russian play are selected.
(D) Exactly two French novels and exactly two plays are selected.
(E) Exactly two Russian novels and exactly one play are selected.

We are being asked to identify an answer that must be false. As with the previous question, we don't want to spend a lot of time eliminating wrong choices—we want to search for an answer that looks like it just can't be right. (A) looks like that sort of suspicious answer—how will we fill all the spaces? Let's investigate. If no Russian novels are selected, the most novels that can be selected is 3. 3 + 1 = 4. (A) cannot be true, and (A) is correct. If you are confident in your work, you don't need to check the other answers.

Game Three Solution | PT 31, GAME 3, QUESTIONS 14 – 18

Let's take a step-by-step look at how a top scorer might solve this game.

During a single week, from Monday through Friday, tours will be conducted of a company's three divisions—Operations, Production, Sales. Exactly five tours will be conducted that week, one each day. The schedule of tours for the week must conform to the following restrictions:

Each division is toured at least once.
The Operations division is not toured on Monday.
The Production division is not toured on Wednesday.
The Sales division is toured on two consecutive days, and on no other days.
If the Operations division is toured on Thursday, then the Production division is toured on Friday.

We start by making a general assessment: this seems like a fairly straightforward game. We are ordering three elements into five positions, and some of these elements will be repeated. With that numbers mismatch, we need to be aware of the numeric inferences. The fact that there are only five positions makes me quite happy.

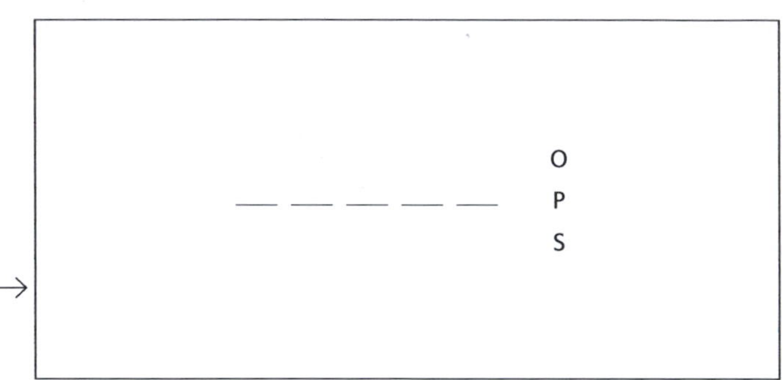

We can start out by drawing positions and listing elements. Again, I'm expecting that we will be given information about the number of each element. The first rule gives us a little information, but I don't write that in—it's not particularly valuable because it's our default expectation and chances are we'll know more about numbers before we're through.

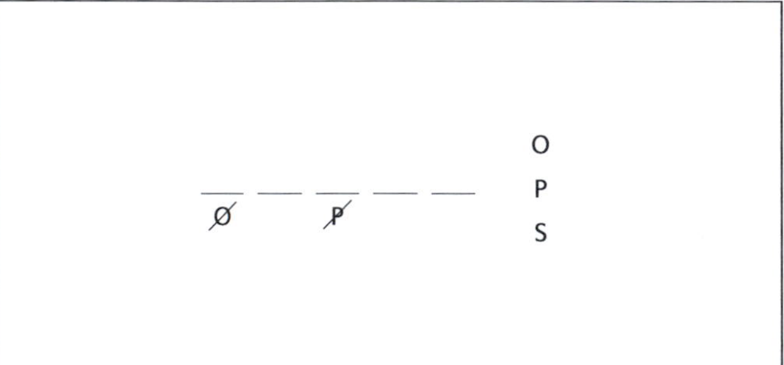

The next two rules are simple enough to notate.

O = 1/2, P = 1/2 — add to 3
S = 2
S S

The fourth rule gives us two important clues: we have a grouping of 2 Ss that have to fit somewhere, and we have 2 Ss total. That means we have 1 of either O or of P, and 2 of the other. You can notate this any way you feel comfortable, even writing it out if you'd like.

O = 1/2, P = 1/2 — add to 3
S = 2
S S $O_{th} \rightarrow P_f$

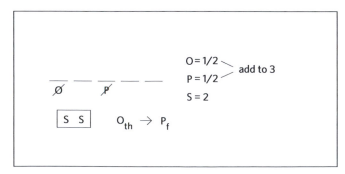

The fourth rule is a conditional, and it's simple enough to understand and notate. I don't feel I need to write in the contrapositive here, because I feel that just looking at the rule, I can infer that if P is not in Friday, O won't be in Thursday. But, it certainly doesn't hurt to write it in if you want. Be careful of using t for either Tuesday or Thursday.

O = 1 or 2, P = 1 or 2 — add to 3
S = 2
S S $O_{th} \rightarrow P_f$

I take one last look at the diagram. The game presents a fairly simple situation, and you should and need to feel solid control over it. Notice that this was the third game when it appeared on the LSAT. Recently, the third game has very commonly been the most difficult in a games section, and it will never be an easy game. So, I can expect that since the setup wasn't challenging, the questions very well might be.

14. Which one of the following CANNOT be true of the week's tour schedule?

(A) The division that is toured on Monday is also toured on Tuesday.
(B) The division that is toured on Monday is also toured on Friday.
(C) The division that is toured on Tuesday is also toured on Thursday.
(D) The division that is toured on Wednesday is also toured on Friday.
(E) The division that is toured on Thursday is also toured on Friday.

Notice that this game does NOT start with a Rules question. This question simply asks about a detail that cannot be true—Rules questions always ask us for a full set of assignments that could be true based on the rules given. It's very unusual for a game to start this way, and it's a sign we can be in for some unique questions. For this one, we are looking for an answer that must be false. We don't want to waste too much time on wrong answers—answers that seem like they could be true or false. Instead, we want to look for that one that we know can't be right. (C) is the correct answer. If Tue = Thurs, there is no place for SS.

15. If in addition to the Sales division one other division is toured on two consecutive days, then it could be true of the week's tour schedule both that the

(A) Production division is toured on Monday and that the Operations division is toured on Thursday
(B) Production division is toured on Tuesday and that the Sales division is toured on Wednesday
(C) Operations division is toured on Tuesday and that the Production division is toured on Friday
(D) Sales division is toured on Monday and that the Operations division is toured on Friday
(E) Sales division is toured on Wednesday and that the Production division is toured on Friday

Per the condition, we know that in addition to an SS, we have to have either an OO or a PP. There are too many different ways that this could play out to make much of a new diagram—instead, let's just work on eliminating wrong choices. (A) can't work because if either the P or O is repeated, there is no space for SS. (B) seems like it can work. Let's leave it. (C) can't work because O can't go in Mon. (D) can't work because the conditional rule would prevent a PP or an OO. (E) can't work for the same reason. That means (B) must be correct. We can confirm the answer by coming up with an option that works: PPSSO.

16. If in the week's tour schedule the division that is toured on Tuesday is also toured on Friday, then for which one of the following days must a tour of the Production division be scheduled?

(A) Monday
(B) Tuesday
(C) Wednesday
(D) Thursday
(E) Friday

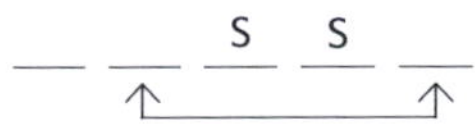

If the same element goes in Tues and Friday, then SS must go in Weds and Thurs. Since O can't go on Mon, that leaves P as the only option. (A) is correct.

17. If in the week's tour schedule the division that is toured on Monday is not the division that is toured on Tuesday, then which one of the following could be true of the week's schedule?

(A) A tour of the Sales division is scheduled for some day earlier in the week than is any tour of the Production division.
(B) A tour of the Operations division is scheduled for some day earlier in the week than is any tour of the Production division.
(C) The Sales division is toured on Monday.
(D) The Production division is toured on Tuesday.
(E) The Operations division is toured on Wednesday.

P ___ ___ ___ ___

Coming off the last question, we can infer that if what goes into Mon is different from what goes into Tues, Mon must be P, and what goes in Tues must not be. This allows us to eliminate (A) - (D) as answers that must be false. (E) is correct.

18. If in the week's tour schedule the division that is toured on Tuesday is also toured on Wednesday, then which one of the following must be true of the week's tour schedule?

(A) The Production division is toured on Monday.
(B) The Operations division is toured on Tuesday.
(C) The Sales division is toured on Wednesday.
(D) The Sales division is toured on Thursday.
(E) The Production division is toured on Friday.

P S S ___ ___

P O O S S

The two ways in which Tues = Weds are if they are occupied by S and S or O and O. Since I can't see the significance of that mentally, I go ahead and try both out (easy enough). In both instances, (P) must go into Mon. We find out little else. (A) is correct.

Game Four Solution | PT 33, GAME 2, QUESTIONS 6 – 12

Let's take a step-by-step look at how a top scorer might solve this game. This game, in particular, lends itself to a variety of effective setups and solution methods. Following this solution will be additional discussion about how you could have set up the game.

> Bird-watchers explore a forest to see which of the following six kinds of birds—grosbeak, harrier, jay, martin, shrike, wren—it contains. The findings are consistent with the following conditions:
>
> If harriers are in the forest, then grosbeaks are not.
> If jays, martins, or both are in the forest, then so are harriers.
> If wrens are in the forest, then so are grosbeaks.
> If jays are not in the forest, then shrikes are.

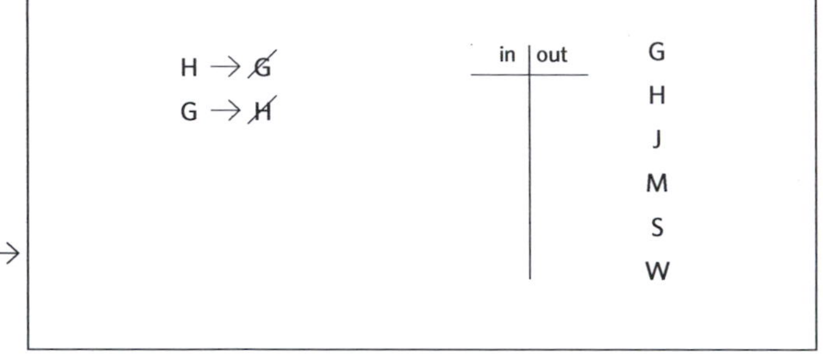

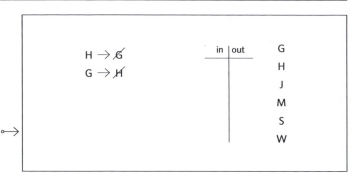

The scenario couldn't be much simpler: there are just six elements to place in or out. The challenge of this game, of course, comes in its rules. None of the rules give us any concrete information. They are all conditional, and in order to successfully solve questions we will need to see how these conditional rules come together. We can do some of the inference work up front (to be discussed), but I prefer to write the rules simply.

This entire game is built upon our understanding of conditional rules; it's imperative we understand each one correctly, and we want to go as slowly and carefully as we need to in order to ensure accuracy. Because we know this game is going to be all about bringing conditional rules together, we want to make sure to write out the contrapositive for each rule.

H → ~~G~~   J → H
G → ~~H~~   ~~H~~ → ~~J~~
M → H
~~H~~ → ~~M~~

in | out: G, H, J, M, S, W

The second rule is the most challenging rule to get right. What is guaranteed if J is in? H must be in. What if M is in? H must be in. Either J or M by itself can ensure that H is in—we can write this as a compound conditional, but I prefer to write it out separately so it's easier to keep track of. If you kept it in compound form, it would read "J or M →H" and the contrapositive would be "~~H~~ →~~J~~ and ~~M~~."

H → ~~G~~   J → H
G → ~~H~~   ~~H~~ → ~~J~~
W → G   M → H
~~G~~ → ~~W~~   ~~H~~ → ~~M~~
~~J~~ → S
~~S~~ → J

in | out: G, H, J, M, S, W

At this point, we've got no part of the diagram filled in, and we have a bunch of intimidating-looking notations. The key to your success has already taken place: if you've written each rule correctly, the work to be done in the questions, though significant, is actually very straightforward. Let's dive into the questions.

H → ~~G~~   J → H
G → ~~H~~   ~~H~~ → ~~J~~
W → G   M → H
~~G~~ → ~~W~~   ~~H~~ → ~~M~~
~~J~~ → S
~~S~~ → J

in | out: G, H, J, M, S, W

The last two rules are simple enough, but do make sure to be as accurate as possible. There is never any need to rush through the rules, and careful work is critical here.

> 6. Which one of the following could be a complete and accurate list of the birds NOT in the forest?
>
> (A) jays, shrikes
> (B) harriers, grosbeaks
> (C) grosbeaks, jays, martins
> (D) grosbeaks, martins, shrikes, wrens
> (E) martins, shrikes

This is an extremely unusual sort of Rules question in that it asks which of the answers could be a list of elements NOT in the forest. Note that each answer also tells us exactly who is in the forest. In any case, we can still use the rules to eliminate choices (though in this case, because we have a lot of conditional language, it's easier to use the rules in notated form than in worded form.) Per the way this question is written, the rules that tell us what happens when elements are *out* are more useful, so let's skip the first rule for now (unless you see a clear way to check it against the answers) and move on to the other rules. The second rule (which allows us to infer that if H is out, J has to be out) eliminates (B). The third (C). The fourth (A). We're down to (D) and (E). Does (E) work with the first rule? No, it doesn't. (D) is correct.

7. If both martins and harriers are in the forest, then which one of the following must be true?

(A) Shrikes are the only other birds in the forest.
(B) Jays are the only other birds in the forest.
(C) The forest contains neither jays nor shrikes.
(D) There are at least two other kinds of birds in the forest.
(E) There are at most two other kinds of birds in the forest.

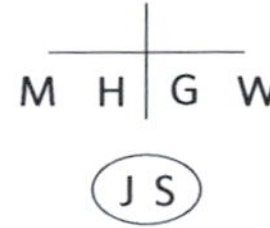

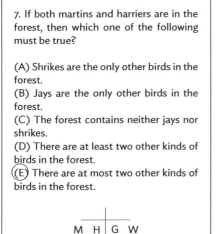

For a conditional question such as this one, we want to use our rules to make inferences, and we can use a T-table to keep the information organized. If M and H are in, we know that G is out, and if G is out, W is out. We don't know about either J or S. Per what we can infer, (E) is correct.

8. If jays are not in the forest, then which one of the following must be false?

(A) Martins are in the forest.
(B) Harriers are in the forest.
(C) Neither martins nor harriers are in the forest.
(D) Neither martins nor shrikes are in the forest.
(E) Harriers and shrikes are the only birds in the forest.

Looking at our conditionals, the only thing we know when J is not in the forest is that S must be in the forest. Fortunately, that's all we need. (D) must be false.

9. Which one of the following is the maximum number of the six kinds of birds the forest could contain?

(A) two
(B) three
(C) four
(D) five
(E) six

J M H S | G W

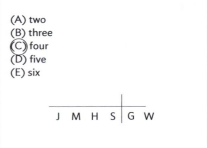

This is probably the most challenging question of the set. From the work we did on #7, we know that we can get 4 birds in. The question then becomes "Can we get 5?" We want to look at the rules that force elements out, and when we do so, they tell us we can't have five. Either H or G has to be out, and when they are, they force others out. H forces out J, and G forces out several elements. There is no way to only have one element out. (C) is correct.

10. Which one of the following pairs of birds CANNOT be among those birds contained in the forest?

(A) jays, wrens
(B) jays, shrikes
(C) shrikes, wrens
(D) jays, martins
(E) shrikes, martins

There is no concrete reason any one bird can't be in the forest. Note that what they are asking is which pair of birds cannot be in the forest at the same time. We need to infer from the elements in the answer choices in order to figure that out. Starting with (A), what do we know if J is in? If J is in, H is in. If H is in, G is out. If G is out, W is out. So, if J is in, W must be out. Jays and wrens can't be in the forest together, so (A) is the correct answer.

11. If grosbeaks are in the forest, then which one of the following must be true?

(A) Shrikes are in the forest.
(B) Wrens are in the forest.
(C) The forest contains both wrens and shrikes.
(D) At most two kinds of birds are in the forest.
(E) At least three kinds of birds are in the forest.

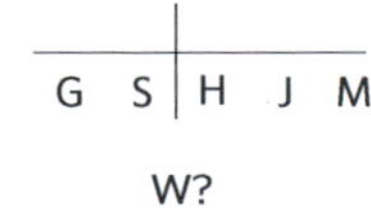

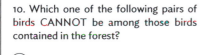

Again, we want to use our conditional rules to make inferences and use our T-table to keep track. If G is in, H is out. If H is out, J and M are out. If J is out, S is in. The only element we don't know about is W. (A) is correct.

12. Suppose the condition is added that if shrikes are in the forest, then harriers are not. If all other conditions remain in effect, then which one of the following could be true?

(A) The forest contains both jays and shrikes.
(B) The forest contains both wrens and shrikes.
(C) The forest contains both martins and shrikes.
(D) Jays are not in the forest, whereas martins are.
(E) Only two of the six kinds of birds are not in the forest.

S → ~~H~~ H → ~~S~~

We want to write the new rule next to the question and combine it with the rules we already know in order to evaluate answers. We know the four wrong answers must be false. For (A), if S is in, H is out, and if H is out, J is out. (A) must be false. For (B), we can't link what we know about W and S—let's leave it. For (C), if S is in, H is out. If H is out, M is out. (C) must be false. (D) is tough to see, and you may want to make a T-table to evaluate it: J not being in forces S in. However, if M is in, H is in, and that forces S out. Since those two things can't be true at once, (D) must be false. We can work off the work we did on #9 to think about (E). We know we could only get the maximum of four birds when H was in. Now that H forces S out, the max we can get would be 3. (E) must be false. (B) is correct.

Game Four Alternative Solution | PT 33, GAME 2, QUESTIONS 6 - 12

Let's take an in-depth look at a different way to think about and set up that last game. Please note that it's not necessary for you to learn these methods, and know that these are methods that are relevant for a small minority of games. It's also true that, for certain games, these strategies can give you a significant advantage, both in terms of how much faster, and how much easier, it makes it to answer questions.

Bird-watchers explore a forest to see which of the following six kinds of birds—grosbeak, harrier, jay, martin, shrike, wren—it contains. The findings are consistent with the following conditions:

If harriers are in the forest, then grosbeaks are not.
If jays, martins, or both are in the forest, then so are harriers.
If wrens are in the forest, then so are grosbeaks.
If jays are not in the forest, then shrikes are.

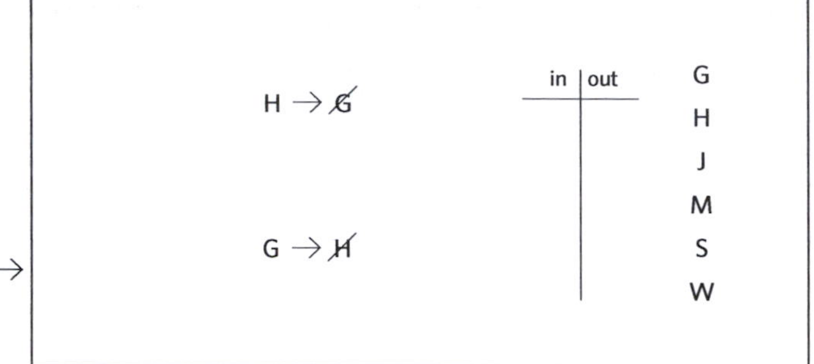

The scenario is simple enough; the most important thing to notice about this game is that all of the rules are conditional. As we've discussed, when games feature lots of conditional rules, it's likely that these rules will link up, and that you will be tested on your ability to link them up. Knowing all of that, we can choose to link the rules during our diagramming process.

We'll start just as we did last time, by writing out the first conditional statement and its contrapositive. The only difference is that we want to leave plenty of space to build on to those conditional statements.

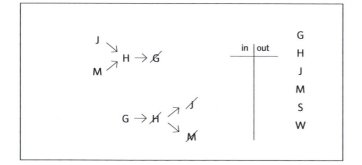

We want to add the second rule to the first one, and we can do so by linking on to the H. Notice how we handle the "or" scenario. We could have kept it as a compound statement, but splitting the rule up makes it easier to work with.

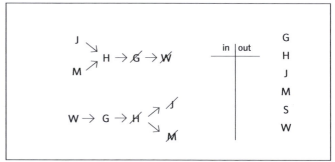

We can add the third rule and its contrapositive to the relevant chains. If the rule didn't link up, we would skip it, then try to link it up later, or otherwise write it off separately.

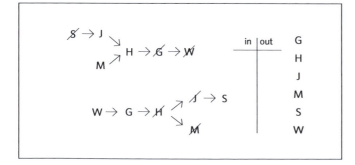

And we'll add the last rule and its contrapositive to the chains. Notice that we now have a clear sense of the relationship between all elements—this will make the process of solving questions much quicker and easier. Not all games featuring conditional rules link up this neatly, but many of them will.

6. Which one of the following could be a complete and accurate list of the birds NOT in the forest?

(A) jays, shrikes
(B) harriers, grosbeaks
(C) grosbeaks, jays, martins
(D) grosbeaks, martins, shrikes, wrens
(E) martins, shrikes

We can use our two chains to see which answers cannot work. When J is out, we know S is in. (A) can't work. When H is out, we can see that J and M have to be out, so we can eliminate (B). When G is out, we can see W must be out, so we can eliminate (C). (D) doesn't violate any rules, so we can keep it for the moment. When S is out, G and W have to be out, so we can eliminate (E). (D) is correct.

7. If both martins and harriers are in the forest, then which one of the following must be true?

(A) Shrikes are the only other birds in the forest.
(B) Jays are the only other birds in the forest.
(C) The forest contains neither jays nor shrikes.
(D) There are at least two other kinds of birds in the forest.
(E) There are at most two other kinds of birds in the forest.

M H | G W

J S

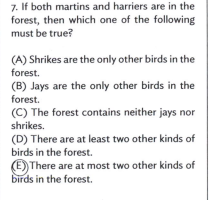

We know, per the condition, that we are dealing with the first of our chains, and it's very easy to see which elements M and H being in tells us more about (G and W) and which elements it doesn't tell us anything about (S and J). With this information, we can see that (E) is the only answer that must be true.

8. If jays are not in the forest, then which one of the following must be false?

(A) Martins are in the forest.
(B) Harriers are in the forest.
(C) Neither martins nor harriers are in the forest.
(D) Neither martins nor shrikes are in the forest.
(E) Harriers and shrikes are the only birds in the forest.

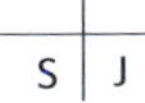

J is not in the forest in the second chain, and the only thing we know from that is that S is in the forest. That gives us (D) as the correct answer.

9. Which one of the following is the maximum number of the six kinds of birds the forest could contain?

(A) two
(B) three
(C) four
(D) five
(E) six

J M H S | G W

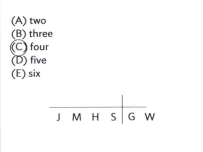

This is still probably the most challenging question of the set, and our diagrams don't help us much here. From the work we did on #7, we know that we can get 4 birds in. The question then becomes "Can we get 5?" We want to look at the rules that force elements out, and when we do so they tell us we can't have five. Either H or G has to be out, and when they are, they force others out. H forces out J, and G forces out several elements. There is no way to only have one element out. (C) is correct.

10. Which one of the following pairs of birds CANNOT be among those birds contained in the forest?

(A) jays, wrens
(B) jays, shrikes
(C) shrikes, wrens
(D) jays, martins
(E) shrikes, martins

We can see in the first chain that when J is in, W is out. (A) is correct.

11. If grosbeaks are in the forest, then which one of the following must be true?

(A) Shrikes are in the forest.
(B) Wrens are in the forest.
(C) The forest contains both wrens and shrikes.
(D) At most two kinds of birds are in the forest.
(E) At least three kinds of birds are in the forest.

G S | H J M

W?

If G is in, we know we're dealing with the second chain, and we can infer everything to the right of the G. This allows us to see that (A) is correct.

12. Suppose the condition is added that if shrikes are in the forest, then harriers are not. If all other conditions remain in effect, then which one of the following could be true?

(A) The forest contains both jays and shrikes.
(B) The forest contains both wrens and shrikes.
(C) The forest contains both martins and shrikes.
(D) Jays are not in the forest, whereas martins are.
(E) Only two of the six kinds of birds are not in the forest.

S → H H → S

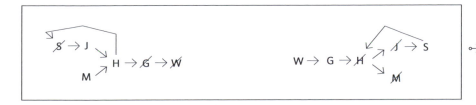

We can add the new information to our chains by drawing an arrow that loops back from H to S in the first chain, and from S to H in the second (see images to side). This makes it easier to evaluate answers. (A) can't work per the second chain. (C) can't work per the first chain. (D) can't work per the second chain. (E) is tougher to evaluate, but both chains do tell us that at least three have to be out. Since (A), (C), (D), and (E) all can't work, (B) is correct.

Timing Basics

Okay, now that you've seen some solutions, how did you do? At this point, you are not expected to be able to answer all questions for four games in thirty-five minutes. What is expected is that you feel you have a solid base of understanding about how games are designed and that you are starting to develop strong diagramming habits. In the next batch of Logic Games lessons, we'll continue to develop our diagramming skills, and turn our primary focus to the task of answering questions.

Let's talk briefly about general timing strategies for Logic Games. We'll discuss these strategies in greater depth in later lessons.

For the past several years, there has been a string of LSATs that have had Logic Games sections with twenty-three questions, and there is no sign that this trend will stop any time soon. Invariably, the trend will stop (as all such LSAT trends must), but when it does, expect to see twenty-two or twenty-four questions (the test does not change much from iteration to iteration). So, it's fairly safe to plan your timing strategies around the idea that you will likely see twenty-three questions (give or take one, in a unique case).

It just so happens that twenty-three questions works very cleanly for a balanced general timing strategy: take an average of 3 minutes to diagram each game (12 minutes total) and an average of 1 minute per question, and 12 + 23 = 35 exactly.

Of course, the reality is that games vary greatly in terms of difficulty, and it's likely that when you go into the exam, one game might take you six minutes, while another will take you eleven. Even when you work well and efficiently, some diagrams might take four minutes while others take less than a minute, and some questions might take two minutes and others twenty seconds. Rigid timing strategies only serve to box you in and limit you unnecessarily—the key is to develop sophisticated strategies that allow you to bend and flow with the section.

For now, think of 3 minutes per setup, and 1 minute per question as very general benchmarks, and use them to think about which sorts of setups and questions take you longer than they should. Don't get overly excited when a setup or question takes you far less time, and don't stress when they take far more.

Think about your timing primarily in terms of process. If you are working on a direct path toward a solution, you are invariably using timing correctly, and if you habitualize a direct path to the answer, timing will be less of an issue—trust that you will get faster and faster at games as you get more of them under your belt. If your path to the answer is indirect, your pace likely won't make up for that.

One thing you definitely do not want to do at this point is panic and look for drastic measures to alter your timing. Focus on not wasting time on unnecessary steps, and trust that you will get much faster. Now is not the time to learn short-cuts or guessing strategies.

22 READING COMPREHENSION reasoning structure

The challenge of mastering Reading Comprehension is very different from the challenge of mastering Logical Reasoning or Logic Games. For those sections, in particular Logic Games, we need to train ourselves to be effective at a new type of mental exercise. We've done things somewhat similar to solving Logical Reasoning problems and Logic Games, but those sections are, generally speaking, relatively unique challenges for our minds to master.

Reading is reading. You are doing it right now, and most of us do it as naturally and intuitively as we breathe, walk, or drive. Though the specific challenges that Reading Comprehension *questions* present are relatively unique to standardized exams, the experience of reading passages is not—we've read passages about things our entire lives.

The challenge of Reading Comprehension is not to develop a new skill but rather to channel a skill that we already have to best match the task at hand

The challenge of Reading Comprehension is therefore not to develop a new skill but rather to channel a skill we already have to best match the task at hand. This is far more difficult to do than it may seem. Because reading is something that happens so naturally for us, it takes a lot of work to actually change how we read—just like it would take a lot of work to change how we walk, or how we drive. In order to achieve success, it's imperative that you have a very clear sense of exactly which reading skills and what type of reading style are rewarded by the LSAT and that you put in the time necessary to develop habits that best align with those characteristics. To that end, we will begin in these first two Reading Comprehension lessons by breaking down exactly what you need to know about the narrow bandwidth of skills that LSAT Reading Comprehension tests, and by discussing general reading strategies that best align with the tasks we need to accomplish.

What Reading Comprehension Tests

For most of us, when we think about our reading ability, it's similar to thinking about our athletic ability, or our ability to make friends—we have a general sense, but we also know that our talents are very situation specific (most of us are better at certain sports than others, for example) and multifaceted. An ability to read well has numerous factors, and it's completely subjective how one prioritizes these factors—that is, it's tough to define what reading ability is as a whole, and it's impossible to rate or rank people based on reading ability as a whole.

All of this is true, but there is another truth that is far more significant to your LSAT performance: LSAT Reading Comprehension is not designed to test general reading abilities, and it is not made easier or more difficult in vague or inexplicable ways. The LSAT Reading Comprehension test writers have very specific jobs to do, in the same way that a test writer of sentence correction questions or algebra questions does. LSAT Reading Comprehension is designed to test very *specific* reading skills, and it is these specific reading skills that form the backbone of all the questions that are asked, and it is these specific skills that are most directly tested when certain passages or questions become too difficult. Furthermore, you could argue that most of the section is designed to test just one specific skill: your ability to read for reasoning structure.

LSAT Reading Comprehension is designed to test very specific reading skills, and it is these specific reading skills that form the backbone of all questions that are asked

Broadly speaking, the reasoning structure of a passage refers to the roles that parts of a passage are meant to play relative to one another. LSAT reading passages are designed to have main points, reasoning given to support and oppose those main points, and background information necessary to understand the situation. If you are consistently able to organize and retain passages in terms of these roles—if you are able to easily understand why an author has written the various things he has written—then you will have a high level of success on LSAT Reading Comprehension.

Questions will test your understanding of the passage as a whole, your understanding of certain paragraphs, and your understanding of sentences or phrases. We will go into great detail about each type of question in future lessons, but keep in mind that there is great commonality among the various question types—the vast majority of them are designed to gauge your ability to read for structure. General questions and those that ask about the author's opinion will test this understanding most directly. Even specific questions—those that ask you to gauge the significance or meaning of a single sentence or phrase—are typically dependent on general structural understanding. The key to understanding specific details is to understand what role they play relative to the passage as a whole, and this understanding will be what commonly allows you to differentiate between right and wrong answers.

In a couple of pages will be an LSAT passage, broken down to illustrate some of the components mentioned above. This passage will have reasoning structure that is very common to the LSAT: we will be given two main points meant to oppose one another, and the reasons that support and oppose these points. It is likely that at least two, and most likely at least three, of the four passages that you see on the LSAT will have this general argument structure. Others passages can have just one main point, or even three or four.

I've also included two of the questions that came with the passage (most passages will come with between five and eight questions). These questions illustrate the significance of understanding reasoning structure.

Make sure the breakdown of the passage and questions makes perfect sense to you before moving on. For some of you, it will match very closely how you might naturally think of a reading assignment. For others, it will be very different from how you thought you'd be thinking about LSAT Reading Comprehension. Nevertheless, structural analysis will form the backbone of everything we discuss when it comes to Reading Comprehension.

What Reading Comprehension Does Not Test

Before we move further, let's lay out a few common misconceptions about Reading Comprehension to help make sure they do not hinder you in developing your own mastery. LSAT Reading Comprehension is **not** designed to test...

One: Your Ability to Retain a Lot of Information

Try to focus on the forest, rather than the trees. Successful reading requires a certain level of comfort with uncertainty (an ability to withhold judgement), as well as an ability to prioritize what is most important. Students who over-retain and want to understand everything, often before they have the context to accurately do so, end up misreading and misunderstanding. Certain questions will ask you about details, but you can focus on those details just when you need to. LSAT Reading Comprehension rewards those who focus on accurately seeing the big picture.

Two: Knowledge of Unusual Subjects and Words

Many of these passages will be about things you know little about, and many of them will involve complicated wording that is unfamiliar to you. Your lack of understanding is not a detriment—it is a function of the design of the test. So when you run into an impossibly complex science topic or some strange, archaic word you don't understand the meaning of, don't see that as a negative and don't try to pretend to know what you don't. Instead, focus on overall reasoning structure, and try to use the reasoning relationships to understand what you can about these unfamiliar subjects and words.

Three: Your Critical Reasoning Ability

Reading Comprehension passages, like Logical Reasoning arguments, are centered around arguments and the reasoning given in relation to those arguments. The way we read and organize Reading Comprehension is very similar to how we read and organize Logical Reasoning, and you can think of your Reading Comprehension strategies as being natural adaptations of Logical Reasoning strategies.

Here's the difference (and it's a big one): for Logical Reasoning, reading for reasoning structure is a means to an end—that is, we need to see the structure in order to perform another, even more important task, which is to be critical of how the reasoning is meant to support a conclusion. For Reading Comprehension, reading for reasoning structure is pretty much the end game—the questions will all hinge on your ability to see structure. Very few questions—two or three per section at most—require critical reasoning, and the vast majority of questions will reward a strongly objective understanding. So, you want to focus on seeing the reasoning structure inherent in the passage, but you want to make sure you don't distract yourself by forming some opinion about it.

Reading for Reasoning Structure

This paragraph gives us background information about the situation at hand. It is unnecessary to attempt to retain all of the details and statistics—the most important thing to note is that dolphins suddenly died. We can anticipate that the passage will likely present a couple of hypotheses about how or why this happened.

Between June 1987 and May 1988, the bodies of at least 740 bottlenose dolphins out of a total coastal population of 3,000 to 5,000 washed ashore on the Atlantic coast of the United States. Since some of the dead animals never washed ashore, the overall disaster was presumably worse; perhaps 50 percent of the population died. A dolphin die-off of this character and magnitude had never before been observed; furthermore, the dolphins exhibited a startling range of symptoms. The research team that examined the die-off noted the presence of both skin lesions and internal lesions in the liver, lung, pancreas, and heart, which suggested a massive opportunistic bacterial infection of already weakened animals.

Again, we also don't need to concern ourselves with trying to master or retain the specifics being discussed. We know the purpose of this paragraph—to act as background for some sort of hypothesis to come, and as long as we understand the reasoning structure we are going to be okay.

Tissues from the stricken dolphins were analyzed for a variety of toxins. Brevetoxin, a toxin produced by the blooming of the alga Ptychodiscus brevis, was present in eight out of seventeen dolphins tested. Tests for synthetic pollutants revealed that polychlorinated biphenyls (PCBs) were present in almost all animals tested.

Here we get our first main point—a hypothesis for what killed the dolphins, which we've bolded. The rest of the paragraph functions to explain and justify this hypothesis.

The research team concluded that brevetoxin poisoning was the most likely cause of the illnesses that killed the dolphins. Although P. brevis is ordinarily not found along the Atlantic coast, an unusual bloom of this organism—such blooms are called "red tides" because of the reddish color imparted by the blooming algae—did occur in the middle of the affected coastline in October 1987. These researchers believe the toxin accumulated in the tissue of fish and then was ingested by dolphins that preyed on them. The emaciated appearance of many dolphins indicated that they were metabolizing their blubber reserves, thereby reducing their buoyancy and insulation (and adding to overall stress) as well as releasing stores of previously accumulated synthetic pollutants, such as PCBs, which further exacerbated their condition. The combined impact made the dolphins vulnerable to opportunistic bacterial infection, the ultimate cause of death.

Now we counter that opinion, and it's clear the author's view is that the first opinion is "not entirely plausible." The next three sentences provide evidence that goes against the first opinion. Then we get our second hypothesis: a sudden influx of pollutants was the cause. The final sentence confirms that the author is clearly on the side of the second opinion.

For several reasons, however, this explanation is not entirely plausible. First, bottlenose dolphins and P. brevis red tides are both common in the Gulf of Mexico, yet no dolphin die-off of a similar magnitude has been noted there. Second, dolphins began dying in June, hundreds of miles north of and some months earlier than the October red tide bloom. Finally, the specific effects of brevetoxin on dolphins are unknown, whereas PCB poisoning is known to impair functioning of the immune system and liver and to cause skin lesions; all of these problems were observed in the diseased animals. **An alternative hypothesis, which accounts for these facts, is that a sudden influx of pollutants, perhaps from offshore dumping, triggered a cascade of disorders in animals whose systems were already heavily laden with pollutants.** Although brevetoxin may have been a contributing factor, the event that actually precipitated the die-off was a sharp increase in the dolphins' exposure to synthetic pollutants.

Practice Test 26, Passage 3

Answering Questions

Questions will ask about the author's purpose, the structure of the passage, or the role that a particular component plays in the passage. Let's take a look at two of the six questions asked about this passage, and discuss the role reasoning structure plays.

14. The passage is primarily concerned with assessing

(A) the effects of a devastating bacterial infection in Atlantic coast bottlenose dolphins
(B) the process by which illnesses in Atlantic coast bottlenose dolphins were correctly diagnosed
(C) the weaknesses in the research methodology used to explore the dolphin die-off
(D) possible alternative explanations for the massive dolphin die-off
(E) relative effects of various marine pollutants on dolphin mortality

Note that all of the answer choices are fairly decent matches for the subject matter discussed—if you were primarily focused on the subjects that were discussed, rather than the reasoning structure, the wrong answers might seem a bit more attractive. However, when we look at the answers in terms of the reasoning structure we discussed, right and wrong become a bit more obvious. (A) is discussed, but it is not the primary reason everything was written. (B) is actually an incorrect representation of the passage—the author does not think the diagnosis was correct, and regardless, (B) does not reflect the overall structure of the passage. (C) doesn't represent the passage correctly—methodology is not discussed. More importantly, however, we know this is not the primary concern of the passage. (D) is the correct answer—the passage is concerned with assessing different explanations for the die-off. (E) is tempting, but not a specific enough match for the scenario being discussed in this argument.

20. The author refers to dolphins in the Gulf of Mexico in the last paragraph in order to

(A) refute the assertion that dolphins tend not to inhabit areas where P. brevis is common
(B) compare the effects of synthetic pollutants on these dolphins and on Atlantic coast dolphins
(C) cast doubt on the belief that P. brevis contributes substantially to dolphin die-offs
(D) illustrate the fact that dolphins in relatively pollution-free waters are healthier than dolphins in polluted waters.
(E) provide evidence for the argument that P. brevis was probably responsible for the dolphins' deaths

This question is about a specific detail in the passage, but note the way the question is being asked—it's requiring us to think about the role the detail plays in a larger context—the context of the passage as a whole. We know that these dolphins in the Gulf of Mexico are mentioned to counter the idea that P. brevis red tides are primarily responsible for the die-off. This allows us to quickly see that such answers as (A), (B), and (D) are not a good match. (E) is tempting, but is actually the exact opposite of the truth. (C), the correct answer, represents the role the component plays relative to the passage as a whole.

THE ELEMENTS OF REASONING STRUCTURE

Author's View

More often than not, the author has a specific opinion about the main points, and every passage will ask questions related to the author's opinion. Though a solid minority of passages are objective, your default mindset as you read should involve thinking to yourself, "Why did the author write this?" If you read every passage with this as a focus, pretty soon, taking note of the author's opinion will become second nature. For many passages, the author's opinion is obvious—it may even be one of the main points, or the main point, of the entire passage. Other times, it'll be far more subtle, and you'll have to glean it based on just a few choice words or phrases. We'll practice and discuss all such varieties in the lessons to come.

Main Points

Main points in Reading Comprehension passages are, in most ways, very similar to what we think of as the "conclusions" of Logical Reasoning arguments. They are *why the passage is written*, and the other parts of a passage can be thought of in terms of their relation to the main points. Here's how they are different from Logical Reasoning conclusions:

1) I'm sure you've noticed the use of the plural—main *points*. Whereas almost all Logical Reasoning problems are designed to have one main point, Reading Comprehension passages are not. They may have one, two, or three. Most commonly, passages will have two somewhat contrasting main points.

2) These main points need not be as subjective as the Logical Reasoning conclusions we've gotten used to. Logical Reasoning questions are designed to test our ability to recognize faults in reasoning, and so they naturally have to get to conclusions that can be viewed as being wrong. Reading Comprehension is not about recognizing fault. Rather, it's simply about seeing the underlying reasoning structure inherent in the passage. Therefore, something like "Cheetahs rely on their speed to capture prey," something most of us understand objectively to be true, could be the one main point of a reading passage, and the rest of the passage can simply contain more information about how and why this is true.

Reasons For and Against

For a majority of passages, the bulk of the text will be information meant to support or oppose these main points, and for these parts of the passage, the most important thing for you to understand is simply the fact that these parts support or oppose particular main points. When you are presented with two main points that contrast one another (coffee is healthy versus coffee is unhealthy, for example), opposition for one point can work as support for the other, and vice versa.

Information and Application

Other parts of a passage can also give additional information about the main points or discuss the application—that is, the result or usage—of one of the main points (imagine a passage that discusses advantages of certain diets, and then discusses what happened to one person after changing to one of the two diets discussed). This form of application very commonly comes at the end of a passage, and it commonly comes after the author has cast her vote with one of two contrasting opinions.

Background

Everything that doesn't play a reasoning role in relation to a main point can be thought of as background information. Background information simply gives us a context for the more important components of the reasoning structure. You certainly want to understand background information to the best of your ability, but it should not be the main focus of your read.

Instructions for the drill starting on the next page: Read each passage two times. The first time through, search only for **main points** and clues as to the **author's views**, and mark the parts where you are certain that you see them. Check against the solutions if you aren't sure of yourself. The second read-through, note the roles that other parts of the passage play. Write **"b.g."** next to background information, and also note what parts of the passage are meant to **support, oppose, apply,** or **give more information** about certain main points. For this exercise, timing and reading strategy are unimportant—take as much time as you need to see the underlying reasoning structure behind each passage. Check the solution to the first passage before moving on to the others.

Recently, a new school of economics called steady-state economics has seriously challenged neoclassical economics, the reigning school in Western economic decision making. According to the neoclassical model, an economy is a closed system involving only the circular flow of exchange value between producers and consumers. Therefore, no noneconomic constraints impinge upon the economy and growth has no limits. Indeed, some neoclassical economists argue that growth itself is crucial, because, they claim, the solutions to problems often associated with growth (income inequities, for example) can be found only in the capital that further growth creates.

Steady-state economists believe the neoclassical model to be unrealistic and hold that the economy is dependent on nature. Resources, they argue, enter the economy as raw material and exit as consumed products or waste; the greater the resources, the greater the size of the economy. According to these economists, nature's limited capacity to regenerate raw material and absorb waste suggests that there is an optimal size for the economy, and that growth beyond this ideal point would increase the cost to the environment at a faster rate than the benefit to producers and consumers, generating cycles that impoverish rather than enrich. Steady-state economists thus believe that the concept of an ever growing economy is dangerous, and that the only alternative is to maintain a state in which the economy remains in equilibrium with nature. Neoclassical economists, on the other hand, consider nature to be just one element of the economy rather than an outside constraint, believing that natural resources, if depleted, can be replaced with other elements—i.e., human-made resources—that will allow the economy to continue with its process of unlimited growth.

Some steady-state economists, pointing to the widening disparity between indices of actual growth (which simply count the total monetary value of goods and services) and the index of environmentally sustainable growth (which is based on personal consumption, factoring in depletion of raw materials and production costs), believe that Western economies have already exceeded their optimal size. In response to the warnings from neoclassical economists that checking economic growth only leads to economic stagnation, they argue that there are alternatives to growth that still accomplish what is required of any economy: the satisfaction of human wants. One of the alternatives is conservation. Conservation—for example, increasing the efficiency of resource use through means such as recycling—differs from growth in that it is qualitative, not quantitative, requiring improvement in resource management rather than an increase in the amount of resources. One measure of the success of a steady-state economy would be the degree to which it could implement alternatives to growth, such as conservation, without sacrificing the ability to satisfy the wants of producers and consumers.

Practice Test 28, Passage 3

Homing pigeons can be taken from their lofts and transported hundreds of kilometers in covered cages to unfamiliar sites and yet, when released, be able to choose fairly accurate homeward bearings within a minute and fly home. Aside from reading the minds of the experimenters (a possibility that has not escaped investigation), there are two basic explanations for the remarkable ability of pigeons to "home": the birds might keep track of their outward displacement (the system of many short-range species such as honeybees); or they might have some sense, known as a "map sense," that would permit them to construct an internal image of their environment and then "place" themselves with respect to home on some internalized coordinate system.

The first alternative seems unlikely. One possible model for such an inertial system might involve an internal magnetic compass to measure the directional leg of each journey. Birds transported to the release site wearing magnets or otherwise subjected to an artificial magnetic field, however, are only occasionally affected. Alternately, if pigeons measure their displacement by consciously keeping track of the direction and degree of acceleration and deceleration of the various turns, and timing the individual legs of the journey, simply transporting them in the dark, with constant rotations, or under complete anesthesia ought to impair or eliminate their ability to orient. These treatments, however, have no effect. Unfortunately, no one has yet performed the crucial experiment of transporting pigeons in total darkness, anesthetized, rotating, and with the magnetic field reversed all at the same time.

The other alternative, that pigeons have a "map sense," seems more promising, yet the nature of this sense remains mysterious. Papi has posited that the map sense is olfactory: that birds come to associate odors borne on the wind with the direction in which the wind is blowing, and so slowly build up an olfactory map of their surroundings. When transported to the release site, then, they only have to sniff the air en route and/or at the site to know the direction of home. Papi conducted a series of experiments showing that pigeons whose nostrils have been plugged are poorly oriented at release and home slowly.

One problem with the hypothesis is that Schmidt-Koenig and Phillips failed to detect any ability in pigeons to distinguish natural air (presumably laden with olfactory map information) from pure, filtered air. Papi's experimental results, moreover, admit of simpler, nonolfactory explanations. It seems likely that the behavior of nostril-plugged birds results from the distracting and traumatic nature of the experiment. When nasal tubes are used to bypass the olfactory chamber but allow for comfortable breathing, no disorientation is evident. Likewise, when the olfactory epithelium is sprayed with anesthetic to block smell-detection but not breathing, orientation is normal.

Practice Test 27, Passage 3

In England before 1660, a husband controlled his wife's property. In the late seventeenth and eighteenth centuries, with the shift from land-based to commercial wealth, marriage began to incorporate certain features of a contract. Historians have traditionally argued that this trend represented a gain for women, one that reflects changing views about democracy and property following the English Restoration in 1660. Susan Staves contests this view; she argues that whatever gains marriage contracts may briefly have represented for women were undermined by judicial decisions about women's contractual rights.

Shifting through the tangled details of court cases, Staves demonstrates that, despite surface changes, a rhetoric of equality, and occasional decisions supporting women's financial power, definitions of men's and women's property remained inconsistent-generally to women's detriment. For example, dower lands (property inherited by wives after their husbands' deaths) could not be sold, but "curtesy" property (inherited by husbands from their wives) could be sold. Furthermore, comparatively new concepts that developed in conjunction with the marriage contract, such as jointure, pin money, and separate maintenance, were compromised by peculiar rules. For instance, if a woman spent her pin money (money paid by the husband according to the marriage contract for the wife's personal items) on possessions other than clothes she could not sell them; in effect they belonged to her husband. In addition, a wife could sue for pin money only up to a year in arrears-which rendered a suit impractical. Similarly, separate maintenance allowances (stated sums of money for the wife's support if husband and wife agreed to live apart) were complicated by the fact that if a couple tried to agree in a marriage contract on an amount, they were admitting that a supposedly indissoluble bond could be dissolved, an assumption courts could not recognize. Eighteenth-century historians underplayed these inconsistencies, calling them "little contrarieties" that would soon vanish. Staves shows, however, that as judges gained power over decisions on marriage contracts, they tended to fall back on pre-1660 assumptions about property.

Staves' work on women's property has general implications for other studies about women in eighteenth-century England. Staves revises her previous claim that separate maintenance allowances proved the weakening of patriarchy; she now finds that an oversimplification. She also challenges the contention by historians Jeanne and Lawrence Stone that in the late eighteenth century wealthy men married widows less often than before because couples began marrying for love rather than for financial reasons. Staves does not completely undermine their contention, but she does counter their assumption that widows had more money than never-married women. She points out that jointure property (a widow's lifetime use of an amount of money specified in the marriage contract) was often lost on remarriage.

Practice Test 26, Passage 4

As one of the most pervasive and influential popular arts, the movies feed into and off of the rest of the culture in various ways. In the United States, the star system of the mid-1920s—in which actors were placed under exclusive contract to particular Hollywood film studios—was a consequence of studios' discovery that the public was interested in actor's private lives, and that information about actors could be used to promote their films. Public relations agents fed the information to gossip columnists, whetting the public's appetite for the films—which, audiences usually discovered, had the additional virtue of being created by talented writers, directors, and producers devoted to the art of storytelling. The important feature of this relationship was not the benefit to Hollywood, but rather to the press; in what amounted to a form of cultural cross-fertilization, the press saw that they could profit from studios' promotion of new films.

Today this arrangement has mushroomed into an intricately interdependent mass-media entertainment industry. The faith by which this industry sustains itself is the belief that there is always something worth promoting. A vast portion of the mass media—television and radio interviews, magazine articles, even product advertisements—now does most of the work for Hollywood studios attempting to promote their movies. It does so not out of altruism but because it makes for good business: If you produce a talk show or edit a newspaper, and other media are generating public curiosity about a studio's forthcoming film, it would be unwise for you not to broadcast or publish something about the film, too, because the audience for your story is already guaranteed.

The problem with this industry is that it has begun to affect the creation of films as well as their promotion. Choices of subject matter and actors are made more and more frequently by studio executives rather than by producers, writers, or directors. This problem is often referred to simply as an obsession with turning a profit, but Hollywood movies have almost always been produced to appeal to the largest possible audience. The new danger is that, increasingly, profit comes only from exciting an audience's curiosity about a movie instead of satisfying its desire to have an engaging experience watching the film. When movies can pull people into theaters instantly on the strength of media publicity rather than relying on the more gradual process of word of mouth among satisfied moviegoers, then the intimate relationship with the audience—on which the vitality of all popular art depends—is lost. But studios are making more money than ever by using this formula, and for this reason it appears that films whose appeal is due not merely to their publicity value but to their ability to affect audiences emotionally will become increasingly rare in the U.S. film industry.

Practice Test 28, Passage 4

Reasoning Structure Drill Solutions

Note that I am not advocating this type of notation process during the exam. The bolding and underlining and such are simply for illustrative purposes.

Recently, a new school of economics called steady-state economics has seriously challenged neoclassical economics, the reigning school in Western economic decision making. According to the neoclassical model, an economy is a closed system involving only the circular flow of exchange value between producers and consumers. Therefore, no noneconomic constraints impinge upon the economy and growth has no limits. Indeed, some neoclassical economists argue that growth itself is crucial, because, they claim, the solutions to problems often associated with growth (income inequities, for example) can be found only in the capital that further growth creates.

more info

This passage makes its intention clear from the get-go: we are going to have a comparison of two economic schools of thought—neoclassical and steady-state.

Neoclassical: economy is a closed system between makers and buyers. No non-economic factors matter, and there is no limit to growth.

Steady-state economists believe the neoclassical model to be unrealistic and hold that the economy is dependent on nature. Resources, they argue, enter the economy as raw material and exit as consumed products or waste; the greater the resources, the greater the size of the economy. According to these economists, nature's limited capacity to regenerate raw material and absorb waste suggests that there is an optimal size for the economy, and that growth beyond this ideal point would increase the cost to the environment at a faster rate than the benefit to producers and consumers, generating cycles that impoverish rather than enrich. Steady-state economists thus believe that the concept of an ever growing economy is dangerous, and that the only alternative is to maintain a state in which the economy remains in equilibrium with nature. Neoclassical economists, on the other hand, consider nature to be just one element of the economy rather than an outside constraint, believing that natural resources, if depleted, can be replaced with other elements—i.e., human-made resources—that will allow the economy to continue with its process of unlimited growth.

Steady-state: economy is based on nature, and ideal use of natural resources.

more info

more info

"Growth" is a point about which there is clear contrast between the two opinions.

Some steady-state economists, pointing to the widening disparity between indices of actual growth (which simply count the total monetary value of goods and services) and the index of environmentally sustainable growth (which is based on personal consumption, factoring in depletion of raw materials and production costs), believe that Western economies have already exceeded their optimal size. In response to the warnings from neoclassical economists that checking economic growth only leads to economic stagnation, they argue that there are alternatives to growth that still accomplish what is required of any economy: the satisfaction of human wants. One of the alternatives is conservation. Conservation—for example, increasing the efficiency of resource use through means such as recycling—differs from growth in that it is qualitative, not quantitative, requiring improvement in resource management rather than an increase in the amount of resources. One measure of the success of a steady-state economy would be the degree to which it could implement alternatives to growth, such as conservation, without sacrificing the ability to satisfy the wants of producers and consumers.

Practice Test 28, Passage 3

more info / application

This last paragraph is a bit different from the previous ones; instead of giving information about one concept or the other, it shows application of one concept (steady-state) to a real situation (Western economies).

background

The passage ends with a way to gauge the success of steady-state strategies. This was the last chance for the author to cast his opinion with one side or the other, and he chose not to do so.

Homing pigeons can be taken from their lofts and transported hundreds of kilometers in covered cages to unfamiliar sites and yet, when released, be able to choose fairly accurate homeward bearings within a minute and fly home. Aside from reading the minds of the experimenters (a possibility that has not escaped investigation), **there are two basic explanations for the remarkable ability of pigeons to "home": the birds might keep track of their outward displacement (the system of many short-range species such as honeybees); or they might have some sense, known as a "map sense," that would permit them to construct an internal image of their environment and then "place" themselves with respect to home on some internalized coordinate system.**

Like the last passage, this one makes clear from the beginning the two primary opinions to be contrasted, which we can call "honeybee" and "map sense."

author opinion/ evidence against honeybee

The first alternative seems unlikely. One possible model for such an inertial system might involve an internal magnetic compass to measure the directional leg of each journey. Birds transported to the release site wearing magnets or otherwise subjected to an artificial magnetic field, however, are only occasionally affected. Alternately, if pigeons measure their displacement by consciously keeping track of the direction and degree of acceleration and deceleration of the various turns, and timing the individual legs of the journey, simply transporting them in the dark, with constant rotations, or under complete anesthesia ought to impair or eliminate their ability to orient. These treatments, however, have no effect. Unfortunately, no one has yet performed the crucial experiment of transporting pigeons in total darkness, anesthetized, rotating, and with the magnetic field reversed all at the same time.

This first line is a clue into what the author thinks of the honeybee argument. The rest of this paragraph serves as evidence against that argument.

The other alternative, that pigeons have a "map sense," seems more promising, yet the nature of this sense remains mysterious. Papi has posited that the map sense is olfactory: that birds come to associate odors borne on the wind with the direction in which the wind is blowing, and so slowly build up an olfactory map of their surroundings. When transported to the release site, then, they only have to sniff the air en route and/or at the site to know the direction of home. Papi conducted a series of experiments showing that pigeons whose nostrils have been plugged are poorly oriented at release and home slowly.

author opinion / evidence for map sense

The first line of this paragraph indicates a more sophisticated author opinion—he finds the second hypothesis more promising, but still not completely understood. The rest of this paragraph presents an experiment in support of one way that map sense might work (through smell).

One problem with the hypothesis is that Schmidt-Koenig and Phillips failed to detect any ability in pigeons to distinguish natural air (presumably laden with olfactory map information) from pure, filtered air. Papi's experimental results, moreover, admit of simpler, nonolfactory explanations. It seems likely that the behavior of nostril-plugged birds results from the distracting and traumatic nature of the experiment. When nasal tubes are used to bypass the olfactory chamber but allow for comfortable breathing, no disorientation is evident. Likewise, when the olfactory epithelium is sprayed with anesthetic to block smell-detection but not breathing, orientation is normal.

Practice Test 27, Passage 3

evidence against smell method of map sense

This final paragraph serves as evidence against the smell idea. Note that it'd be a mistake to overweigh this paragraph—it does not negate the map sense hypothesis (which the author finds promising). Rather, in a more direct sense, it counters one way (smell) that map sense might work, matching the author's opinion that the methods remain "mysterious."

Reasoning Structure Drill Solutions

Another passage for which the argument is clearly laid out at the beginning, but note the slight difference in tone here. There is a slight sense that the historian's view is an out-of-date one and that Staves's view will be the main focus of the passage

In England before 1660, a husband controlled his wife's property. In the late seventeenth and eighteenth centuries, with the shift from land-based to commercial wealth, marriage began to incorporate certain features of a contract. **Historians have traditionally argued that this trend represented a gain for women, one that reflects changing views about democracy and property following the English Restoration in 1660. Susan Staves contests this view; she argues that whatever gains marriage contracts may briefly have represented for women were undermined by judicial decisions about women's contractual rights.**

Historians argue that changes in law represented a gain for women, but Staves says the reality was that the supposed gains were undermined by judicial decisions.

The fact that the author uses the word "demonstrates," rather than, say, "claims," gives a hint as to the author's opinion—he finds the evidence Staves presents to be reasonable. The rest of the paragraph gives supporting reasoning for Staves's view. It's easy to get lost in the details, but as long as you understand reasoning structure you'll be fine for the questions.

support

Shifting through the tangled details of court cases, Staves **demonstrates** that, despite surface changes, a rhetoric of equality, and occasional decisions supporting women's financial power, definitions of men's and women's property remained inconsistent-generally to women's detriment. For example, dower lands (property inherited by wives after their husbands' deaths) could not be sold, but "curtesy" property (inherited by husbands from their wives) could be sold. Furthermore, comparatively new concepts that developed in conjunction with the marriage contract, such as jointure, pin money, and separate maintenance, were compromised by peculiar rules. For instance, if a woman spent her pin money (money paid by the husband according to the marriage contract for the wife's personal items) on possessions other than clothes she could not sell them; in effect they belonged to her husband. In addition, a wife could sue for pin money only up to a year in arrears-which rendered a suit impractical. Similarly, separate maintenance allowances (stated sums of money for the wife's support if husband and wife agreed to live apart) were complicated by the fact that if a couple tried to agree in a marriage contract on an amount, they were admitting that a supposedly indissoluble bond could be dissolved, an assumption courts could not recognize. Eighteenth-century historians underplayed these inconsistencies, calling them "little contrarieties" that would soon vanish. Staves shows, however, that as judges gained power over decisions on marriage contracts, they tended to fall back on pre-1660 assumptions about property.

support

Here the historians get a tiny rebuttal, crowded all around by support for Staves.

support

Staves' work on women's property has general implications for other studies about women in eighteenth-century England. Staves revises her previous claim that separate maintenance allowances proved the weakening of patriarchy; she now finds that an oversimplification. She also challenges the contention by historians Jeanne and Lawrence Stone that in the late eighteenth century wealthy men married widows less often than before because couples began marrying for love rather than for financial reasons. Staves does not completely undermine their contention, but she does counter their assumption that widows had more money than never-married women. She points out that jointure property (a widow's lifetime use of an amount of money specified in the marriage contract) was often lost on remarriage.

This paragraph expands on Staves's ideas by generalizing to other similar contexts.

application

Practice Test 26, Passage 4

Reasoning Structure Drill Solutions

The passage begins with background information about the film studios and the development of the star system. Unlike the previous passages, there is no clear set-up for some type of argument or main opinion.

As one of the most pervasive and influential popular arts, the movies feed into and off of the rest of the culture in various ways. In the United States, the star system of the mid-1920s—in which actors were placed under exclusive contract to particular Hollywood film studios—was a consequence of studios' discovery that the public was interested in actor's private lives, and that information about actors could be used to promote their films. Public relations agents fed the information to gossip columnists, whetting the public's appetite for the films—which, audiences usually discovered, had the additional virtue of being created by talented writers, directors, and producers devoted to the art of storytelling. **The important feature of this relationship was not the benefit to Hollywood, but rather to the press; in what amounted to a form of cultural cross-fertilization, the press saw that they could profit from studios' promotion of new films.**

This looks like the closest thing to an opinion, though it certainly has a more objective, rather than subjective, tone relative to the other arguments we have seen. Perhaps this is a main opinion, or even the author's opinion, but it seems more like a general observation. Let's keep reading...

This paragraph is an expansion of the background information presented in the first paragraph—it discusses the expansion of the star system and its impact on media. It does give us more information about the point made at the end of the final paragraph, but since that wasn't a particularly strong point to begin with, this paragraph seems mostly like background.

Today this arrangement has mushroomed into an intricately interdependent mass-media entertainment industry. The faith by which this industry sustains itself is the belief that there is always something worth promoting. A vast portion of the mass media—television and radio interviews, magazine articles, even product advertisements—now does most of the work for Hollywood studios attempting to promote their movies. It does so not out of altruism but because it makes for good business: If you produce a talk show or edit a newspaper, and other media are generating public curiosity about a studio's forthcoming film, it would be unwise for you not to broadcast or publish something about the film, too, because the audience for your story is already guaranteed.

?

The problem with this industry is that it has begun to affect the creation of films as well as their promotion. Choices of subject matter and actors are made more and more frequently by studio executives rather than by producers, writers, or directors. This problem is often referred to simply as an obsession with turning a profit, but Hollywood movies have almost always been produced to appeal to the largest possible audience. The new danger is that, increasingly, profit comes only from exciting an audience's curiosity about a movie instead of satisfying its desire to have an engaging experience watching the film. When movies can pull people into theaters instantly on the strength of media publicity rather than relying on the more gradual process of word of mouth among satisfied moviegoers, then the intimate relationship with the audience—on which the vitality of all popular art depends—is lost. But studios are making more money than ever by using this formula, and for this reason it appears that films whose appeal is due not merely to their publicity value but to their ability to affect audiences emotionally will become increasingly rare in the U.S. film industry.

Ahhh—we finally get a real opinion, a point, and now what we've been given up to this point all seems like background. His point is that the marketing of films is impacting the creation and promotion of films. The first two paragraphs are meant to set up the situation so that we understand this argument better when it is made.

The rest of this paragraph serves as support for the point that is made. Note that unlike other passages, we do not have a contrasting, or countering, opinion.

Practice Test 28, Passage 4

23 READING COMPREHENSION — reading strategies

We used the last lesson to take an in-depth look into the reasoning structure that underlies all LSAT passages. In this lesson, we'll begin the process of turning that understanding into an effective skill set.

We all know how to read really, really well. We do it every single day, commonly for hours and hours. It's a fundamental part of being human. But (of course there is a but)...

We read very differently in different situations when we have different purposes, and the vast majority of LSAT takers are unclear as to what sort of reading is rewarded by the exam, and commonly they are not as practiced and expert at this type of reading as they are at other types of reading.

Below are a variety of real-life situations that require you to read. Think about your mindset and, most importantly, your sense of purpose during these reading situations. Based on what we discussed in the last lesson, and based on what you know about LSAT Reading Comprehension in general, give a 0-10 score to each scenario based on how well you think these particular situations match the challenges presented by LSAT passages.

At the top of the next page are the scores that I would give. Keep in mind that this is obviously a highly subjective exercise.

---

1. You've just bought some furniture, and now you need to put it together. You realize that there are over two hundred pieces and the manual is five pages of dense prose. You get started reading.

2. It's Sunday morning. You sit down with your coffee, a cat on your lap and a dog at your feet, and you open up the New York Times.

3. After not communicating for months, your deadbeat brother writes you a long email, discussing the virtues of buying a new car. "Why is he telling me all this?" you wonder, until you get to the last few sentences, where he asks you to loan him a few bucks.

4. You are back in high school, and you have a history exam the next day. The exam is going to be multiple choice, and it's going to be about people, events, and dates—you have to match up the people with the dates or events. You've gotten a condensed two-page version of the key events you need to know, and are reading through it.

5. You are a human resources director at Google, and your job is to read through hundreds of cover letters a day. You have two minutes to read each cover letter, and your job is to objectively summarize the most significant points that the candidate attempts to make in the cover letter.

6. You return to your parked car and find that someone has smashed into it. They've left a note—a long explanation of the terrible day they have had and an apology—but no name, phone number, or any other way to get in touch. You read the letter again and again, looking for some clue that might help you find the person.

MY SUBJECTIVE SCORES

1. FURNITURE MANUAL: 0

Unless you are one of those existential types of furniture makers, your thoughts during this process are a poor match for those you would have during the LSAT. For making the furniture, your job is to understand each direction as clearly as possible, and you can't move on until you do so. Thinking that way on the LSAT would typically be disastrous, for it's often impossible to truly understand the significance of certain sentences until far later in your reading process.

2. MORNING PAPER: 0

When you read the paper, you choose what you want to pay attention to, and your level of focus varies based on your level of interest. The things you notice are based on what you want to notice, not necessarily what the author intended for you to focus on, and you don't really care.

3. DEAD-BEAT BROTHER: 9

Note the primary driver of your reading process: "Why is he writing this?" This also happens to be an excellent mindset for the LSAT, as well. As you read the note, you are focused on identifying main points and understanding why each sentence is there—which is pretty much what reading for reasoning structure is all about. The end of the note, like the end of many challenging passages, makes clear the purpose of all that preceded.

4. HISTORY EXAM: 0

Your focus would be to memorize specific details, and this would be an extreme version of "seeing the trees rather than the forest." This type of reading style is a poor match for the LSAT. You will get questions that relate to specific details, but as you'll soon see, the key to such questions is a correct understanding of the passage as a whole.

5. HUMAN RESOURCES: 9

This person's job is to read through passages quickly, searching for main points, not paying as much attention to secondary details. Also note that the purpose of the read is not to interpret, but rather to objectively gauge the author's intentions, which is your goal as well on the LSAT.

6. USELESS NOTE: 1

If some part of you is thinking, "WHY is this person writing this?" then you get a matching score of 1. If not, it goes back to 0. Looking for clues that clearly differ from the intentions of the author—the author has no intention of helping you find him/her—is a strategy that matches the LSAT poorly.

It's likely your scores utilized the range of scores between 1 and 10 better than mine did, and if my intention was a straight-up match/no match (as my scores indicate), certainly I could have given a different set of instructions. The point I want to make clear here is that there is a specific way to read that matches LSAT passages best, rather than some diffuse concept of reading strategy that is somewhat like this, and somewhat like that. If we don't define our reading style clearly, and if we don't actively work to make this reading style a habit by test day, the way that we read in other parts of our lives will creep into our thinking (whether we like it or not), and it will prevent us from performing at our best.

When it comes to reading, mindset and strategy go hand in hand. Let's discuss three tenets that are extremely useful for an effective mindset and for the development of effective reading strategies: focus on why, not what; embrace uncertainty; and use main points to drive your purpose.

One: Focus on Why, Not What

Remember, the LSAT is a test of how you read and how you think. It is not a test of what you know. The test writers are only interested in your ability to understand the words that are on the page. To see why, let's use an extreme example: let's imagine they included a very complex passage about various defensive strategies that NFL teams use. What would be the problem? A percentage of test takers would come in already knowing about these defensive strategies. Not only would this prior knowledge give these test takers an unfair advantage over those that are not interested in football, it would also weaken the validity of the measurements of reading ability.

Subject matter is not important to the test writers, other than for it being obscure enough, or common enough, to create a level playing field. What is far more important to test writers is reasoning structure—the way in which a passage is logically organized.

The subject matter is simply there because, well, you can't test reading skills without subjects. In many ways, the subjects discussed in LSAT passages are akin to the subjects discussed in the word problems you did in high school math. At some point, if you were good at math, you naturally got to a point where you didn't care that you were filling up a pool or a bucket, measuring the height of a box or a building. You were focused on the math concepts being tested, and without much effort you would place the subject matter where it belonged—in the background.

You ought to feel the same way about the subjects discussed on the LSAT. Certain passages, in particular more difficult ones, will try to challenge you by discussing very archaic or confusing subjects—obscure bacteria or ancient Hebrew terms—but these actual subjects are not what matter.[1] You want to be able to push them to the background, and you want to push to the foreground the reasoning relationships *between* subjects, and the structural organization of the passage as a whole. Once you make it a habit to focus on this, you will find yourself unafraid of the subject matter discussed (what does it matter?) and of course your reading will align far better with the tasks that questions present.

1. At least while you read. During the process of solving questions, details will become more important, for you will use them to check answers against the text.

A great way to develop such a reading style into a habit is to continuously ask yourself, as you are reading, *why* the author chose to write what he or she did. When we read something complicated—let's say, for example, a sentence that attempts to conceptualize the theory of relativity—we are often naturally inclined to focus on the *what*. What is actually being said? What does this actually mean? For the LSAT, the *what* does not matter—what matters is the *why*. *Why* has the author written this sentence? Is this the main point he is making? Is this being used to support a main point, or oppose it? If you understand why each part of the passage is there, even if you are not clear on the exact subject matter, you will be prepared for the questions.

Remember, this is not a test of detail retention, even if some questions make it seem that way. Your desire to retain too many details, or to understand intricate details, will prevent you from seeing the big picture. So don't focus too much on the *what*. Work to turn your attention to the *why*, and make sure the *why* drives your thoughts during your read.

Two: Embrace Uncertainty

Imagine yourself in a dream. You are in a room, and someone comes in and gives you a single piece of paper that has on it a few paragraphs about the history of Japanese tea ceremonies. You are told that you have three minutes to read the passage and that you will be asked questions afterwards. You are also told that the outcome of this exam will have some unknown, but drastic, impact on the future of your life.

What do you do? Maybe you first try to recall everything you know about Japanese tea ceremonies, until you woefully realize you know nothing. Then you look down at that piece of paper—it has everything you need! So you grip it in your hands and read each word as carefully as possible, trying to suck as much knowledge into your brain in three minutes as you possibly can...but you can't understand or remember a word of it!

Of course, the dream scenario is a thinly veiled analogy for the LSAT, and a poorly designed one at that. But I wanted to mimic, just for a second, the pressure you will feel during the exam. It is very difficult to read under pressure—in particular, it is very difficult to read complex, convoluted, or unfamiliar material under pressure, and this is precisely what the LSAT is going to require of us.

One of the reasons it is so difficult to read under pressure is the fact that when we are nervous, we have an instinct to seek certainty. We want to completely understand passages, and we also know that we'll be in trouble if we don't. So, you go into a passage and you read the first paragraph and you have no idea what the author is talking about or why he's writing what he's writing, and your brain will start to panic—because you want to know what's going on. Knowing what's going on results in a high score, and not knowing what's going on results in the opposite. So you have all the motivation in the world to make decisions and assign meanings and roles that may or may not be accurate, in order to feel certain.

This desire to want to know more than you do, or to know faster than you can, is a huge problem when it comes to the LSAT. These passages are meant to have complex structures—after all, structure is all that the test writer really cares about—and it's often easiest to see this structure through a wide lens, that is, after you've taken in most, or all, of the passage. However, what happens is that because there is a great desire for certainty, many test takers make decisions about the meaning or purpose of a passage before it's actually been made clear; this tends to have a cascading effect, in that this incorrect perception will color everything else that follows. You misunderstand the first paragraph, and that leads you to misunderstand the second, and so on. A correct and wise understanding requires patience. Pressure often leads us to jump to conclusions—conclusions that are too commonly proved to be incorrect.

Passages are designed like good stories—with twists, turns, and surprises. With stories, it's always easier to see after the fact how everything in the story was meant to fit together, and it's exactly the same with LSAT passages. Know what you know. Just as importantly, know what you don't know, and allow yourself to be okay with uncertainty—the LSAT consistently rewards the ability to withhold judgement. If you don't know exactly why a sentence has been written, the best clue will probably be in the next sentence. If you don't quite understand the significance of a paragraph, the best way to find out is probably to read the next one.

To be clear, I don't mean for you to rush through your read, and your read should have its natural pauses and moments of reflection, as we'll discuss in greater detail in just a bit. The point is to use these reflections to gauge what you know with certainty versus what you don't, and to be okay with not being certain when certainty is not warranted.

Three: Let Main Points Light the Way

When we read in terms of the why, and when we are okay with being uncertain, it makes it much easier for us to organize and gauge our thoughts in terms of the main points being made. These main points give purpose to everything, and can, when used effectively, streamline and drive forward your reading process.

An LSAT reading passage will most commonly have two main ideas or opinions. These viewpoints will commonly be presented in contrast to one another, and in most instances the author makes it known, often subtly, that he or she has an opinion on the matter. Most commonly this opinion will side with one main idea or the other, but it can be more sophisticated than that—perhaps the author finds fault with both ideas, or finds some way to bridge them. The minority of passages—perhaps one or two of the four you will see on your exam—will have one main idea or multiple (usually no more than three) contrasting viewpoints. A minority of passages will present no clear author bias or opinion.

Main points can be presented at different parts of the passage. Sometimes they are all presented up front. Other times, they are spread out. Still other times, commonly in the most difficult passages, they are presented deep into the passage. Also keep in mind that often they will not be as obviously subjective—that is, opinion-like—as the conclusions or main points we've discussed so far in Logical Reasoning questions.[2]

2. This is because the Logical Reasoning arguments we've focused on thus far, and the majority of Logical Reasoning arguments in general, involve reasoning that is purposely designed to be faulty. Other Logical Reasoning arguments, those associated with questions that don't require us to identify reasoning faults, tend to have more objective conclusions, similar to those we will see in Reading Comprehension passages.

No matter the organizational design of the passage, whether the main ideas come at the beginning or the end, you can read each component of the passage with an eye toward what role it does, or could, play relative to the main points. You can read a first paragraph, for example, and see that it's very objective and straightforward, and anticipate that it's background information for some sort of claim that will come in a later paragraph. You can read about a certain type of experiment, or unexpected finding in nature, and predict that it will be used to support some sort of scientific hypothesis.

It is not uncommon for even the best readers to be wrong in predicting this role—in fact, it's natural, for, when you think about it, good writing often involves the build-up of expectation, followed by an unexpected twist or turn. A good reader recognizes that a prediction of a role is simply a prediction (i.e., isn't certain when he shouldn't be), and he recognizes when new clues present a different picture of what he's just read. You want to make it a habit to constantly consider and recalibrate roles as you read, and you should make it a habit to build in moments of reflection—at paragraph breaks and when main points are presented—so that you can keep a tight grip on the passage structure.

And, as mentioned on the previous page, the best time to most easily understand the reasoning structure of a passage is at the end of it. At that point, the uncertainty needs to end. You should be able to clearly see what the main points are, and you should be able to see how each part of the passage relates to these main points. If you cannot, then it's a sign that you don't understand the passage as well as you should, and that you need to go back in to dig out those main points and piece together everything else in relation. Even the best readers are challenged by certain passages, and have to reread certain parts after the fact to completely grasp what they just read. Remember, as I've often said before, the test is difficult for everyone—those who are successful are those who have the skills to conquer adversity. When it comes to difficult reading challenges, a lot of that has to do with a correct mindset ("I need to understand this passage in terms of reading structure"), and plenty of experience reading and organizing actual LSAT passages.

On the next few passages I will break down the reading process in real time, using two passages that we introduced in the last lesson. This will be followed by a summary of what we'd know by the end of the read, as well as a couple of examples of how this type of reading strategy pays off when it comes time to answer questions.

the reading process

Recently, a new school of economics called steady-state economics has seriously challenged neoclassical economics, the reigning school in Western economic decision making. According to the neoclassical model, an economy is a closed system involving only the circular flow of exchange value between producers and consumers. Therefore, no noneconomic constraints impinge upon the economy and growth has no limits. Indeed, some neoclassical economists argue that growth itself is crucial, because, they claim, the solutions to problems often associated with growth (income inequities, for example) can be found only in the capital that further growth creates.

The passage is going to contrast these two ideas

One main point: neoclassical—closed system between sellers and buyers. What is closed?

That's what closed means

More about neoclassical

Steady-state economists believe the neoclassical model to be unrealistic and hold that the economy is dependent on nature. Resources, they argue, enter the economy as raw material and exit as consumed products or waste; the greater the resources, the greater the size of the economy. According to these economists, nature's limited capacity to regenerate raw material and absorb waste suggests that there is an optimal size for the economy, and that growth beyond this ideal point would increase the cost to the environment at a faster rate than the benefit to producers and consumers, generating cycles that impoverish rather than enrich. Steady-state economists thus believe that the concept of an ever growing economy is dangerous, and that the only alternative is to maintain a state in which the economy remains in equilibrium with nature. Neoclassical economists, on the other hand, consider nature to be just one element of the economy rather than an outside constraint, believing that natural resources, if depleted, can be replaced with other elements—i.e., human-made resources—that will allow the economy to continue with its process of unlimited growth.

Other main point: steady-state—economy dependent on nature. Huh?

Okay, I get it—steady-state—economy healthy when it uses natural resources well

More about steady-state—contrasts neoclassical view of growth

More contrast between the two

Some steady-state economists, pointing to the widening disparity between indices of actual growth (which simply count the total monetary value of goods and services) and the index of environmentally sustainable growth (which is based on personal consumption, factoring in depletion of raw materials and production costs), believe that Western economies have already exceeded their optimal size. In response to the warnings from neoclassical economists that checking economic growth only leads to economic stagnation, they argue that there are alternatives to growth that still accomplish what is required of any economy: the satisfaction of human wants. One of the alternatives is conservation. Conservation—for example, increasing the efficiency of resource use through means such as recycling—differs from growth in that it is qualitative, not quantitative, requiring improvement in resource management rather than an increase in the amount of resources. One measure of the success of a steady-state economy would be the degree to which it could implement alternatives to growth, such as conservation, without sacrificing the ability to satisfy the wants of producers and consumers.

Applying steady-state ideas to Western economies—they are not in good shape

Application: steady-state solution to problem is conservation

Way to gauge success of steady-state. Note: no author opinion anywhere

Practice Test 28, Passage 3

15. Based on the passage, neoclassical economists would likely hold that steady-state economists are wrong to believe each of the following EXCEPT:

(A) The environment's ability to yield raw material is limited.
(B) Natural resources are an external constraint on economies.
(C) The concept of unlimited economic growth is dangerous.
(D) Western economies have exceeded their optimal size.
(E) Economies have certain optimal sizes.

In the next batch of Reading Comprehension lessons, we will discuss in depth the language presented in question stems, but for now notice just two things: *would likely* indicates that the answers should, in general, agree with what we've read but that there will not be direct matches for the text, and the EXCEPT tells us, of course, that we're looking for something neoclassicals wouldn't fault steady-state economists for believing.

(A) seems correct—the neoclassicals don't disagree that the world has a limited amount of raw material (they just feel we can deal with it fine if we do run out). Let's see why the other answers are wrong. (B) is something neoclassicals definitely think is wrong, per the end of the second paragraph. (C) is definitely something neoclassicals think is wrong, and growth was set up very early on as one big contrast between the two theories. (D) is also something neoclassicals would think is wrong (since they don't think there can be too much growth). (E) is also definitely something they would disagree with, for the same reason as (D). Since we are able to eliminate all four wrong answers with confidence, we can feel assured that we understood the question correctly, and after checking the wording one more time, we can go ahead and select (A) as the correct answer.

18. Based on the passage, a steady-state economist is most likely to claim that a successful economy is one that satisfies which one of the following principles?

(A) A successful economy uses human-made resources in addition to natural resources.
(B) A successful economy satisfies human wants faster than it creates new ones.
(C) A successful economy maintains an equilibrium with nature while still satisfying human wants.
(D) A successful economy implements every possible means to prevent growth.
(E) A successful economy satisfies the wants of producers and consumers by using resources to spur growth.

Again, the question stem has the phrase *most likely*. Also, we can anticipate a bit about what the right answer will involve—something about a balance between us and nature.

(A) and (B) do not directly relate to steady-state theory and can be quickly eliminated. (C) matches steady-state principles very well and is most likely correct. (D) takes steady-state too far and misunderstands it—the goal is not to prevent growth no matter what. (E) lines up more with the neoclassicals. There are no other attractive answers, so after checking each word in (C) again, we can go ahead and select it as the correct answer.

the reading process

As one of the most pervasive and influential popular arts, the movies feed into and off of the rest of the culture in various ways. In the United States, the star system of the mid-1920s—in which actors were placed under exclusive contract to particular Hollywood film studios—was a consequence of studios' discovery that the public was interested in actor's private lives, and that information about actors could be used to promote their films. Public relations agents fed the information to gossip columnists, whetting the public's appetite for the films—which, audiences usually discovered, had the additional virtue of being created by talented writers, directors, and producers devoted to the art of storytelling. The important feature of this relationship was not the benefit to Hollywood, but rather to the press; in what amounted to a form of cultural cross-fertilization, the press saw that they could profit from studios' promotion of new films.

Background: connection between studio star system and press

Opinion: press got more out of this relationship; is this main point?

Today this arrangement has mushroomed into an intricately interdependent mass-media entertainment industry. The faith by which this industry sustains itself is the belief that there is always something worth promoting. A vast portion of the mass media—television and radio interviews, magazine articles, even product advertisements—now does most of the work for Hollywood studios attempting to promote their movies. It does so not out of altruism but because it makes for good business: If you produce a talk show or edit a newspaper, and other media are generating public curiosity about a studio's forthcoming film, it would be unwise for you not to broadcast or publish something about the film, too, because the audience for your story is already guaranteed.

More on growth of relationship between studio system and press

The problem with this industry is that it has begun to affect the creation of films as well as their promotion. Choices of subject matter and actors are made more and more frequently by studio executives rather than by producers, writers, or directors. This problem is often referred to simply as an obsession with turning a profit, but Hollywood movies have almost always been produced to appeal to the largest possible audience. The new danger is that, increasingly, profit comes only from exciting an audience's curiosity about a movie instead of satisfying its desire to have an engaging experience watching the film. When movies can pull people into theaters instantly on the strength of media publicity rather than relying on the more gradual process of word of mouth among satisfied moviegoers, then the intimate relationship with the audience—on which the vitality of all popular art depends—is lost. But studios are making more money than ever by using this formula, and for this reason it appears that films whose appeal is due not merely to their publicity value but to their ability to affect audiences emotionally will become increasingly rare in the U.S. film industry.

Ahh. This is his main opinion—there is a problem with the relationship

And this is the danger: since anticipation drives sales, film quality going down

Consequence: since system is making money, changes unlikely

Practice Test 28, Passage 4

25. Which one of the following most accurately describes the organization of the passage?

(A) description of the origins of a particular aspect of a popular art; discussion of the present state of this aspect; analysis of a problem associated with this aspect; introduction of a possible solution to the problem
(B) description of the origins of a particular aspect of a popular art; discussion of the present state of this aspect; analysis of a problem associated with this aspect; suggestion of a likely consequence of the problem
(C) description of the origins of a particular aspect of a popular art; analysis of a problem associated with this aspect; introduction of a possible solution to the problem; suggestion of a likely consequence of the solution
(D) summary of the history of a particular aspect of a popular art; discussion of a problem that accompanied the growth of this aspect; suggestion of a likely consequence of the problem; appraisal of the importance of avoiding this consequence
(E) summary of the history of a particular aspect of a popular art; analysis of factors that contributed to the growth of this aspect; discussion of a problem that accompanied the growth of this aspect; appeal for assistance in solving the problem

Most questions, in one way or another, test your understanding of reasoning structure. This question does so in a very general and direct fashion. The attention we gave to the structure during the read is going to pay off with great dividends here.

There is great commonality among these answer choices, and the answer choices themselves require careful reading. Each answer represents the entire passage, separated into components, and in this scenario it's likely that parts of certain answers will match the text, and other parts won't. You want to first focus on trying to identify the faults that make answers incorrect.

(A) is attractive, but we are given no solution to the problem. (B) seems okay—we'll leave it. (C) mentions a solution, which we weren't given. (D) is close, but not quite right—it brings up the problem earlier than the author did, and we haven't been given an appraisal of the importance of avoiding the consequence. (E) discusses an appeal for assistance, which we don't have.

That leaves only (B). If we walk through each component of (B), we see no egregiously false wording, and the answer seems a good match for the structure we saw initially. (B) is correct.

26. The author's position in lines 35-47 (final paragraph) would be most weakened if which one of the following were true?

(A) Many Hollywood studio executives do consider a film's ability to satisfy moviegoers emotionally.
(B) Many Hollywood studio executives achieved their positions as a result of demonstrating talent at writing, producing, or directing films that satisfy audiences emotionally.
(C) Most writers, producers, and directors in Hollywood continue to have a say in decisions about the casting and content of films despite the influence of studio executives.
(D) The decisions made by most Hollywood studio executives to improve a film's chances of earning a profit also add to its ability to satisfy moviegoers emotionally.
(E) Often the U.S. mass media play an indirect role in influencing the content of the films that Hollywood studios make by whetting the public's appetite for certain performers or subjects.

Before we go into the answers, we want to remind ourselves of the author's opinion that is being discussed: the emphasis placed on promotion of films is taking away from the quality of films. From our Logical Reasoning experience, we know that a likely weakener will be an answer that hints at the opposite—the promotion of films may not impact quality.

(A) is tempting, but to what level are they considering it? If they are only considering it a little (and we don't know the degree, per this answer), and if they are considering it less than they used to, then this answer has little impact on our argument. (B) is tempting as well, but requires a lot of inferences to be relevant—who knows if these executives apply this talent to their present jobs? (C) is a very good answer—these are the people, after all, that we're told help improve the quality of films. However, like (A), without a sense of degree, this answer is pretty weak (maybe the writers, producers and directors only have a tiny say, and are overshadowed by the marketing people). (D) is exactly the answer we are looking for—notice it requires little inference on our part to see this answer's relevance—we are being told, directly, that these profit-driven decisions do help the quality of a film. (E) does not contradict or weaken the author's opinion and can be eliminated quickly.

MINDSET & STRATEGIES

FOCUS ON WHY, NOT WHAT

Complex subject matter and the intricate details that are involved in the explanation of complex subject matter are often the most challenging aspects of a passage. They are also the least important things for you to focus on during your read. What is important to you getting questions correct is the relationship *between* these elements. If you understand *why* each part of the passage is there, you hold the key to getting questions right.

EMBRACE UNCERTAINTY

In moments of pressure, we hate to be uncertain. And yet the most challenging parts of the test are often designed to leave you in suspense much of the time, and Reading Comprehension and Logic Games, in particular, reward those who are comfortable lingering in uncertainty when that uncertainty is warranted. Know that it's okay to be uncertain, and know that it's not your job to know everything all of the time. You have until the end of the passage to figure things out, and often it's far easier to see the reasoning structure after you've finished an entire paragraph, or an entire passage.

LET MAIN POINTS LIGHT THE WAY

For the LSAT, reasoning structure is best defined in terms of the relationship various components of a passage have with the main points of the passage. When you read something and don't understand quite why it's there, often it's because that information is given in relation to a main point that hasn't been made yet. When that main point is made, that confusing component of the text will suddenly make more sense. So, prioritize main points and make sure that you understand them as well as you possibly can, for that will impact how easily you understand everything else. Also, when you think of reasoning structure, make sure you are thinking in terms of how various components of a passage relate to the main points being made.

GENERAL READING STRATEGIES

1. The main thing you should be thinking about as you read a piece of text is "Why did the author write this?" Use this to define your level of certainty—when you understand the role each part of the passage plays, you will be ready to answer questions.

2. Do your best to understand the details as well as you can, but do not get bogged down in them. It is very common for people to get bogged down in details (per the desire to understand and be in control of everything) but a successful LSAT test taker must have the mental discipline to overcome this instinct. If you don't understand a sentence, but you know exactly why it's there and you know it's not the main point—then move on. You know it well enough, and you can always come back and review the details if a question happens to ask about them.

3. If you do not get bogged down in details, you can get through a passage fairly quickly—a straight read-through without rushing and without any pauses will take a little less than two minutes for the average passage for the average person. The more experienced you get with LSAT passages, the faster you will get at reading them, for you will naturally be more confident and in control of what to pay attention to and what not to pay attention to, what to make sure you get out of your read and what to not worry about.

4. You should allow yourself to be uncertain, but at the same time you need to stay on top of your uncertainty. If you don't know why the introductory paragraph is there—that's okay—chances are the passage has been purposely designed to make you feel that way. However, you want to remain mindful of this as you read the next paragraph, and the next one, and you want to use your growing bank of knowledge about the passage to go back and reflect on that first paragraph. By the end of your read, you should expect to know exactly why each part of the passage is there.

5. You can let yourself rush a bit through secondary information—background and supporting or opposing details—that is easy to understand and assign a purpose to, for those components of a passage are less important for answering questions. You should also allow yourself moments to pause and reflect on how what you've read comes together. Remember the analogy we made about an LSAT passage being a bit like a movie—with twists and turns that are difficult to predict in the moment, but far easier to understand after the fact; well, imagine that every few minutes, you paused the movie and thought carefully about what you'd seen thus far. You would most certainly have a better sense of the movie's structure than you would if you simply watched it straight through. And, by the time the ending was revealed—even if you couldn't predict it, it would be far easier for you to quickly and accurately see how everything led to that point. The same goes for RC passages. Build in moments of reflection to collect your thoughts and anticipate what might come as you read ahead. Paragraph breaks are terrific moments for pauses, and it should be a habit that you use them to reflect on what you've read and to anticipate what is to come.

6. For some of the most challenging passages, the full structure doesn't reveal itself until the final sentence, when suddenly the author gives that second main point you'd given up waiting for, or gives an opinion that seems unexpected based on what you've read thus far. Leave yourself open for these moments, and as I've stated before, don't rush to understand everything when they haven't given you enough information to do so.

7. Make it a habit to take a few seconds after you are done reading the entire passage to review the passage structure one more time. As per the movie analogy, it is amazing how much clearer the structure can seem after the fact. Furthermore, the more you practice doing this review, the faster you will get at it. If you've understood the passage well, you should be able to skim through and see exactly where the main points are made, where the support is, where the background is, and so on. If you've had a difficult time with the passage, or if the passage has been a particularly challenging one, this review is a great time to finalize any decisions you need to make, and to get rid of all those last uncertainties.

Reading Strategy Drill 1

For each of the next two passages, simply read the passage and answer the two accompanying questions, then read the solution afterwards.

In recent years, a growing belief that the way society decides what to treat as true is controlled through largely unrecognized discursive practices has led legal reformers to examine the complex interconnections between narrative and law. In many legal systems, legal judgments are based on competing stories about events. Without having witnessed these events, judges and juries must validate some stories as true and reject others as false. This procedure is rooted in objectivism, a philosophical approach that has supported most Western legal and intellectual systems for centuries. Objectivism holds that there is a single neutral description of each event that is unskewed by any particular point of view and that has a privileged position over all other accounts. The law's quest for truth, therefore, consists of locating this objective description, the one that tells what really happened, as opposed to what those involved thought happened. The serious flaw in objectivism is that there is no such thing as the neutral, objective observer. As psychologists have demonstrated, all observers bring to a situation a set of expectations, values, and beliefs that determine what the observers are able to see and hear. Two individuals listening to the same story will hear different things, because they emphasize those aspects that accord with their learned experiences and ignore those aspects that are dissonant with their view of the world. Hence there is never any escape in life or in law from selective perception, or from subjective judgments based on prior experiences, values, and beliefs.

The societal harm caused by the assumption of objectivist principles in traditional legal discourse is that, historically, the stories judged to be objectively true are those told by people who are trained in legal discourse, while the stories of those who are not fluent in the language of the law are rejected as false.

Legal scholars such as Patricia Williams, Derrick Bell, and Mari Matsuda have sought empowerment for the latter group of people through the construction of alternative legal narratives. Objectivist legal discourse systematically disallows the language of emotion and experience by focusing on cognition in its narrowest sense. These legal reformers propose replacing such abstract discourse with powerful personal stories. They argue that the absorbing, nonthreatening structure and tone of personal stories may convince legal insiders for the first time to listen to those not fluent in legal language. The compelling force of personal narrative can create a sense of empathy between legal insiders and people traditionally excluded from legal discourse and, hence, from power. Such alternative narratives can shatter the complacency of the legal establishment and disturb its tranquility. Thus, the engaging power of narrative might play a crucial, positive role in the process of legal reconstruction by overcoming differences in background and training and forming a new collectivity based on emotional empathy.

Practice Test 22, Passage 2

9. Which one of the following best states the main idea of the passage?

(A) Some legal scholars have sought to empower people historically excluded from traditional legal discourse by instructing them in the forms of discourse favored by legal insiders.
(B) Some legal scholars have begun to realize the social harm caused by the adversarial atmosphere that has pervaded many legal systems for centuries.
(C) Some legal scholars have proposed alleviating the harm caused by the prominence of objectivist principles within legal discourse by replacing that discourse with alternative forms of legal narrative.
(D) Some legal scholars have contended that those who feel excluded from objectivist legal systems would be empowered by the construction of a new legal language that better reflected objectivist principles.
(E) Some legal scholars have argued that the basic flaw inherent in objectivist theory can be remedied by recognizing that it is not possible to obtain a single neutral description of a particular event.

15. Which one of the following statements about legal discourse in legal systems based on objectivism can be inferred from the passage?

(A) In most Western societies the legal establishment controls access to training in legal discourse.
(B) Expertise in legal discourse affords power in most Western societies.
(C) Legal discourse has become progressively more abstract for some centuries.
(D) Legal discourse has traditionally denied the existence of neutral, objective observers.
(E) Traditional legal discourse seeks to reconcile dissonant world views.

Reading Strategy Solution

In recent years, a growing belief that the way society decides what to treat as true is controlled through largely unrecognized discursive practices has led legal reformers to examine the complex interconnections between narrative and law. In many legal systems, legal judgments are based on competing stories about events. Without having witnessed these events, judges and juries must validate some stories as true and reject others as false. This procedure is rooted in objectivism, a philosophical approach that has supported most Western legal and intellectual systems for centuries. Objectivism holds that there is a single neutral description of each event that is unskewed by any particular point of view and that has a privileged position over all other accounts. The law's quest for truth, therefore, consists of locating this objective description, the one that tells what really happened, as opposed to what those involved thought happened. The serious flaw in objectivism is that there is no such thing as the neutral, objective observer. As psychologists have demonstrated, all observers bring to a situation a set of expectations, values, and beliefs that determine what the observers are able to see and hear. Two individuals listening to the same story will hear different things, because they emphasize those aspects that accord with their learned experiences and ignore those aspects that are dissonant with their view of the world. Hence there is never any escape in life or in law from selective perception, or from subjective judgments based on prior experiences, values, and beliefs.

Background: huh? I have no idea what this means

This makes a bit more sense

Background on objectivism, the idea behind the system (what's the main subject—objectivism or the system?)

Here we go—now the purpose of the passage is clear. Seems objectivism is main subject, and author is not a fan of it

At the end of this paragraph, I go back and reread the beginning sentence. Now it makes a bit more sense—what we think of as objective truth may be biased, and so reformers are now thinking anew about how narrative fits with the law.

The societal harm caused by the assumption of objectivist principles in traditional legal discourse is that, historically, the stories judged to be objectively true are those told by people who are trained in legal discourse, while the stories of those who are not fluent in the language of the law are rejected as false.

Negative impact of objectivism—those who are trained in law better at making their side sound like the more objective one

Legal scholars such as Patricia Williams, Derrick Bell, and Mari Matsuda have sought empowerment for the latter group of people through the construction of alternative legal narratives. Objectivist legal discourse systematically disallows the language of emotion and experience by focusing on cognition in its narrowest sense. These legal reformers propose replacing such abstract discourse with powerful personal stories. They argue that the absorbing, nonthreatening structure and tone of personal stories may convince legal insiders for the first time to listen to those not fluent in legal language. The compelling force of personal narrative can create a sense of empathy between legal insiders and people traditionally excluded from legal discourse and, hence, from power. Such alternative narratives can shatter the complacency of the legal establishment and disturb its tranquility. Thus, the engaging power of narrative might play a crucial, positive role in the process of legal reconstruction by overcoming differences in background and training and forming a new collectivity based on emotional empathy.

Counter to objectivism—replace abstract with personal

Support for use of personal narratives

Practice Test 22, Passage 2

Reading Strategy Solution

COMMENTARY

This passage falls on the high end of the difficulty scale. Like many challenging passages, it presents its biggest challenges at the beginning; the first sentence is probably the most difficult sentence to understand in the entire passage, and the first paragraph is far more challenging and complex than are the ones that follow. In real time, I couldn't understand the first sentence even after a couple of reads, and my understanding of it slowly grew as I read the rest of the paragraph. Also, until we got to the sentence "The serious flaw..." I wasn't sure that objectivism was the main topic of discussion. That one sentence was the key to the entire passage—now I realized that everything that came before was background for a critical analysis of objectivism, and in this light, the first sentence made a lot more sense, as did the rest of the very tough first paragraph.

The second paragraph is very straightforward in function—it gives more support to the author's criticism of objectivism and allows us to see a real-life negative consequence of it. After the second paragraph, I think that there is a very good chance that a contrasting idea will appear in the third, and that is indeed the case. The fact that I understand the structure up to that point, and the fact that I've anticipated the gist of the paragraph, makes this a far smoother and quicker read. One issue I'm looking out for carefully as I read that final paragraph is any sort of subtle inflection on the author's opinion. In this case, there really isn't a lot of subtlety—the author gives only positives of using personal narrative, without qualifying or presenting evidence for the other side.

QUESTIONS

9. Which one of the following best states the main idea of the passage?

(A) Some legal scholars have sought to empower people historically excluded from traditional legal discourse by instructing them in the forms of discourse favored by legal insiders.
(B) Some legal scholars have begun to realize the social harm caused by the adversarial atmosphere that has pervaded many legal systems for centuries.
(C) Some legal scholars have proposed alleviating the harm caused by the prominence of objectivist principles within legal discourse by replacing that discourse with alternative forms of legal narrative.
(D) Some legal scholars have contended that those who feel excluded from objectivist legal systems would be empowered by the construction of a new legal language that better reflected objectivist principles.
(E) Some legal scholars have argued that the basic flaw inherent in objectivist theory can be remedied by recognizing that it is not possible to obtain a single neutral description of a particular event.

We want an answer that represents the passage as a whole, and we want to start off by nit-picking all of the wrong answer choices. (A) is wrong because the passage is not about empowering people by teaching them to talk like lawyers. (B) is wrong because the adversarial atmosphere is not the point of the passage. (C) seems good, so let's leave it. (D) is good right until the end—we don't need a different reflection of objectivist principles. (E) describes some parts of the passage pretty well but does a poor job of summarizing the passage as a whole (where is discussion of the final paragraph?). That leaves us with only (C). We check it carefully, word for word—no objections. (C) is correct.

15. Which one of the following statements about legal discourse in legal systems based on objectivism can be inferred from the passage?

(A) In most Western societies the legal establishment controls access to training in legal discourse.
(B) Expertise in legal discourse affords power in most Western societies.
(C) Legal discourse has become progressively more abstract for some centuries.
(D) Legal discourse has traditionally denied the existence of neutral, objective observers.
(E) Traditional legal discourse seeks to reconcile dissonant world views.

Much of the passage is about legal discourse based on objectivism, so we need to go into the answers with a wide net. Of course, our first job is to eliminate wrong choices. (A) can be eliminated quickly because access to legal training is not discussed. (B) seems well beyond the scope of the passage, but doesn't have something I can find specifically wrong. Let's leave it. (C) can be eliminated because an increase in abstraction is not discussed. (D) can be eliminated because traditional legal discourse did the opposite of denying objective observation. (E) is, like (B), extremely broad. I do a quick scan of the passage—nothing close to world views is mentioned. I can eliminate (E). That leaves only (B). It seems related to the passage but yet so extreme—can I justify it? I know power is mentioned in the last paragraph—looking back, the line does say that those who are excluded from legal discourse are excluded from power. What about "most Western societies"? Ah, there's justification for that in the middle of the first paragraph. (B) is correct.

This is a tough question. The key for me was that I was able to get rid of the four wrong answers quickly and confidently.

Reading Strategy Drill 2

Scientists typically advocate the analytic method of studying complex systems: systems are divided into component parts that are investigated separately. But nineteenth-century critics of this method claimed that when a system's parts are isolated its complexity tends to be lost. To address the perceived weaknesses of the analytic method these critics put forward a concept called organicism, which posited that the whole determines the nature of its parts and that the parts of a whole are interdependent.

Organicism depended upon the theory of internal relations, which states that relations between entities are possible only within some whole that embraces them, and that entities are altered by the relationships into which they enter. If an entity stands in a relationship with another entity, it has some property as a consequence. Without this relationship, and hence without the property, the entity would be different—and so would be another entity. Thus, the property is one of the entity's defining characteristics. Each of an entity's relationships likewise determines a defining characteristic of the entity.

One problem with the theory of internal relations is that not all properties of an entity are defining characteristics: numerous properties are accompanying characteristics—even if they are always present, their presence does not influence the entity's identity. Thus, even if it is admitted that every relationship into which an entity enters determines some characteristic of the entity, it is not necessarily true that such characteristics will define the entity; it is possible for the entity to enter into a relationship yet remain essentially unchanged.

The ultimate difficulty with the theory of internal relations is that it renders the acquisition of knowledge impossible. To truly know an entity, we must know all of its relationships; but because the entity is related to everything in each whole of which it is a part, these wholes must be known completely before the entity can be known. This seems to be a prerequisite impossible to satisfy.

Organicists' criticism of the analytic method arose from their failure to fully comprehend the method. In rejecting the analytic method, organicists overlooked the fact that before the proponents of the method analyzed the component parts of a system, they first determined both the laws applicable to the whole system and the initial conditions of the system; proponents of the method thus did not study parts of a system in full isolation from the system as a whole. Since organicists failed to recognize this, they never advanced any argument to show that laws and initial conditions of complex systems cannot be discovered. Hence, organicists offered no valid reason for rejecting the analytic method or for adopting organicism as a replacement for it.

Practice Test 25, Passage 4

22. Which one of the following most completely and accurately summarizes the argument of the passage?

(A) By calling into question the possibility that complex systems can be studied in their entirety, organicists offered an alternative to the analytic method favored by nineteenth-century scientists.
(B) Organicists did not offer a useful method of studying complex systems because they did not acknowledge that there are relationships into which an entity may enter that do not alter the entity's identity.
(C) Organicism is flawed because it relies on a theory that both ignores the fact that not all characteristics of entities are defining and ultimately makes the acquisition of knowledge impossible.
(D) Organicism does not offer a valid challenge to the analytic method both because it relies on faulty theory and because it is based on a misrepresentation of the analytic method.
(E) In criticizing the analytic method, organicists neglected to disprove that scientists who employ the method are able to discover the laws and initial conditions of the systems they study.

24. The passage offers information to help answer each of the following questions EXCEPT:

(A) Why does the theory of internal relations appear to make the acquisition of knowledge impossible?
(B) Why did the organicists propose replacing the analytic method?
(C) What is the difference between a defining characteristic and an accompanying characteristic?
(D) What did organicists claim are the effects of an entity's entering into a relationship with another entity?
(E) What are some of the advantages of separating out the parts of a system for study?

Reading Strategy Solution

Scientists typically advocate the analytic method of studying complex systems: systems are divided into component parts that are investigated separately. But nineteenth-century critics of this method claimed that when a system's parts are isolated its complexity tends to be lost. To address the perceived weaknesses of the analytic method these critics put forward a concept called organicism, which posited that the whole determines the nature of its parts and that the parts of a whole are interdependent.

Two ideas being contrasted: analytic method (separate parts) and organicism (interdependent parts)

Organicism depended upon the theory of internal relations, which states that relations between entities are possible only within some whole that embraces them, and that entities are altered by the relationships into which they enter. If an entity stands in a relationship with another entity, it has some property as a consequence. Without this relationship, and hence without the property, the entity would be different—and so would be another entity. Thus, the property is one of the entity's defining characteristics. Each of an entity's relationships likewise determines a defining characteristic of the entity.

Expansion of what organicism is

One problem with the theory of internal relations is that not all properties of an entity are defining characteristics: numerous properties are accompanying characteristics—even if they are always present, their presence does not influence the entity's identity. Thus, even if it is admitted that every relationship into which an entity enters determines some characteristic of the entity, it is not necessarily true that such characteristics will define the entity; it is possible for the entity to enter into a relationship yet remain essentially unchanged.

A problem! reason against organicism—some relationships aren't as important as others

The ultimate difficulty with the theory of internal relations is that it renders the acquisition of knowledge impossible. To truly know an entity, we must know all of its relationships; but because the entity is related to everything in each whole of which it is a part, these wholes must be known completely before the entity can be known. This seems to be a prerequisite impossible to satisfy.

Ultimate problem! Renders knowledge impossible

Organicists' criticism of the analytic method arose from their failure to fully comprehend the method. In rejecting the analytic method, organicists overlooked the fact that before the proponents of the method analyzed the component parts of a system, they first determined both the laws applicable to the whole system and the initial conditions of the system; proponents of the method thus did not study parts of a system in full isolation from the system as a whole. Since organicists failed to recognize this, they never advanced any argument to show that laws and initial conditions of complex systems cannot be discovered. Hence, organicists offered no valid reason for rejecting the analytic method or for adopting organicism as a replacement for it.

Explanation of why organicism is wrong—didn't realize analytic method starts with thoughts about whole systems

Succinct explanation of author's (negative) attitude towards organicism

Practice Test 25, Passage 4

Reading Strategy Solution

COMMENTARY

The subject matter of this passage is complex and the discussion abstract, and if you are focused on those aspects this passage can seem quite difficult. The good news is that the reasoning structure is fairly straightforward. Additionally, the author has done us the favor of breaking up the passage into well-organized, compact paragraphs. The paragraph structure helps us see the overall structure:

In the first paragraph, we are given two contrasting ideas—the status quo (the analytic method) and a response by critics (organicism). The next paragraph expands on what organicism is. The next paragraph gives us a problem with organicism, and the fourth an even bigger issue with organicism. By this point the author's opinion is fairly clear. In the final paragraph, the author says the organicists started off on a faulty premise, and he concludes by summarizing the faults with organicism that he has mentioned.

QUESTIONS

22. Which one of the following most completely and accurately summarizes the argument of the passage?

(A) By calling into question the possibility that complex systems can be studied in their entirety, organicists offered an alternative to the analytic method favored by nineteenth-century scientists.
(B) Organicists did not offer a useful method of studying complex systems because they did not acknowledge that there are relationships into which an entity may enter that do not alter the entity's identity.
(C) Organicism is flawed because it relies on a theory that both ignores the fact that not all characteristics of entities are defining and ultimately makes the acquisition of knowledge impossible.
(D) Organicism does not offer a valid challenge to the analytic method both because it relies on faulty theory and because it is based on a misrepresentation of the analytic method.
(E) In criticizing the analytic method, organicists neglected to disprove that scientists who employ the method are able to discover the laws and initial conditions of the systems they study.

We need an answer that represents the passage as a whole, and we'll start by eliminating obvious wrong choices. We want to get rid of answers that are significantly different from the text, or only represent one part of what is being discussed.

(A) represents part of the passage, but not all of it, and can be eliminated quickly. (B) also represents just one part of the argument and can be eliminated. (C) is a bit better, but fails to encompass the final paragraph. Still, let's leave it just in case. (D) seems like exactly what we were looking for—it represents the passage as a whole and informs us of the author's view of the subject. (E) is not the point of the passage and can be quickly eliminated. I do a quick return to (C) and (D)—(D) gives us what (C) gives us (faulty theory) and also represents the other parts of the passage. (D) is correct.

24. The passage offers information to help answer each of the following questions EXCEPT:

(A) Why does the theory of internal relations appear to make the acquisition of knowledge impossible?
(B) Why did the organicists propose replacing the analytic method?
(C) What is the difference between a defining characteristic and an accompanying characteristic?
(D) What did organicists claim are the effects of an entity's entering into a relationship with another entity?
(E) What are some of the advantages of separating out the parts of a system for study?

The format of this question requires that we jump through a few more hoops than we normally need to—we have to think about the information in the text in terms of questions that it might answer, and it's also an EXCEPT question. Thinking about it carefully, it boils down to this—which answer is most removed from what was discussed? Confirming that each wrong answer is actually discussed might be necessary, but it's going to be time consuming. So, before I do that, I want to do a quick scan to see if there are any obviously questionable answers, and (E) jumps out. The entire passage was pretty much about the problems of organicism, and I don't remember reading too much about the advantages of the analytic method. I do one quick scan through the passage to make sure I haven't missed anything, and I haven't. (E) is not related to anything that is discussed, and is therefore the correct answer.

24 READING COMPREHENSION practice set one

In the last two lessons, we've discussed the underlying structure of LSAT Reading Comprehension, as well as the reading strategies that align most effectively with the challenges that the section presents. In this lesson and the next, we'll focus on putting into practice that understanding and the strategies. First, let's do a quick review.

Reading is a fundamental part of all aspects of professional life. Our reading ability comprises numerous facets, and our reading strength is commonly dependent on how well our abilities and mindset align with the specific reading task presented.

LSAT Reading Comprehension is not designed to test all your reading skills, nor is it designed to gauge some vague or general set of reading skills. LSAT Reading Comprehension is primarily designed to gauge a very narrow and specific aspect of your overall reading ability—your ability to read for reasoning structure. We can define this as your ability to see, as you read, what the main priorities of the author are, and how all components of a passage relate to these main points.

Many Reading Comprehension questions are broad by design—of the five to eight questions you see per passage, it's not uncommon to have three or four that you can answer off of a general understanding of the passage as a whole. Certain questions will ask about very specific components of a passage, but commonly these questions will also be about reasoning structure—that is, the questions will be designed to test your understanding of the role this specific component plays in the bigger scheme of things.

Though many of us are used to reading all day long every day, few of us are used to being tested on our reading ability or to reading under pressure. In this unique context, many of us have an instinct to try to focus more, and often this results in paying too much attention to each word. This will be detrimental on the exam, because these instincts will force you to think of the trees instead of the forest. Thinking of the passage as a set of numerous details, and trying to answer questions in terms of these details, makes the section far harder than it needs to be. A solid understanding of the passage as a whole is always the key to making questions easier and more obvious. An understanding of your task, as well as plenty of experience at reading LSAT passages in LSAT-like conditions, will ensure that you represent your reading abilities at their best.

Question Strategy Basics

In the next batch of Reading Comprehension lessons, we will carefully break down the different types of questions you can expect to see in this section. For now, let's just have a very quick and basic discussion about the main things you want to be thinking about as you approach and answer questions.

As with Logical Reasoning and Logic Games, most test takers underestimate the significance of the question stem—that is, they focus on the passage and the answers, but not the question being asked. You want to think of your read, the question stem, and the answer choices as pieces to a jigsaw puzzle; the question stem is the middle of those three pieces—without it, it becomes much more difficult to match your understanding of the passage with the five answer choices.

Make it a habit to think carefully about the question stem, and to use it to **anticipate**[1] what you will see in the answer choices. If you keep practicing this, you will get better and better at recognizing right answers when you see them. More importantly, you will get better and better at predicting the design of the incorrect answer choices; this will allow you to eliminate them with far more accuracy and confidence.

1. Anticipating is an important component of effective reading style, and it's an important part of answering questions. Top test takers predict elements they are likely to see in the right answer, and they use their predictions to increase speed and not get tricked by wrong trains of thought. However, using anticipation goes hand in hand with the ability to remain flexible. Sometimes the right answer will be very different from what you imagined, and you have to have a strong enough sense of the passage and the question stem, and a flexible enough sense about what you've anticipated, in order to recognize this right answer when this turns out to be the case.

Many questions test your general understanding of the passage as a whole. These questions are based on two interrelated issues—the author's reasons for writing the passage, and the structural organization of the passage. Certain questions will be phrased in terms of the former, and some in terms of the latter, but these two things go hand in hand, and most questions require some understanding of both concepts. For general questions, you should expect to have a rough sense of what the right answer should look like before you look at the choices. These questions will, in general, have three or four obviously wrong choices that can be eliminated quickly. It will likely not be necessary for you to return to the text before you review the answers, but you will typically have to go back to the text to confirm the correct answer, or to choose between two attractive answers. Right answers will commonly be a bit broad or vague, or in other ways less than ideal, but nevertheless not false, and the best of the available choices.

Other questions test your understanding of specific parts of the passage, ranging from individual words, to clauses, to sentences, to paragraphs. Some of these specific questions will tell you where the component in question is,[2] others will give you no sense of where the specific information is,[3] and still others will give you *hints* as to where the needed information is.[4] For the first of these situations, you should go back to the text referenced and read it (as well as what is around it) before going into the answer choices. For the second of these situations, you will have to wait until you get down to a couple of attractive choices before going into the text. For the last of these situations, the challenge of identifying the relevant text will typically be the key challenge of that question, so ideally you want to do whatever you can to find that text and understand it before going into the answer choices. As always, you want to eliminate wrong choices before confirming the correct choice. Right answers should always be confirmed, word for word, with the text.

2. Example: "The author uses the word "degree" in line 6 in reference to..."

3. Example: "The passage discusses which of the following?"

4. Example: "According to the passage, proponents of the new era theory would probably agree that..."

Drill Passage One

Directions below

Until the 1980s, most scientists believed that noncatastrophic geological processes caused the extinction of dinosaurs that occurred approximately 66 million years ago, at the end of the Cretaceous period. Geologists argued that a dramatic drop in sea level coincided with the extinction of the dinosaurs and could have caused the climatic changes that resulted in this extinction as well as the extinction of many ocean species.

This view was seriously challenged in the 1980s by the discovery of large amounts of iridium in a layer of clay deposited at the end of the Cretaceous period. Because iridium is extremely rare in rocks on the Earth's surface but common in meteorites, researchers theorized that it was the impact of a large meteorite that dramatically changed the Earth's climate and thus triggered the extinction of the dinosaurs.

Currently available evidence, however, offers more support for a new theory, the volcanic-eruption theory. A vast eruption of lava in India coincided with the extinctions that occurred at the end of the Cretaceous period, and the release of carbon dioxide from this episode of volcanism could have caused the climatic change responsible for the demise of the dinosaurs. Such outpourings of lava are caused by instability in the lowest layer of the Earth's mantle, located just above the Earth's core. As the rock that constitutes this layer is heated by the Earth's core, it becomes less dense and portions of it eventually escape upward as blobs of molten rock, called "diapirs," that can, under certain circumstances, erupt violently through the Earth's crust.

Moreover, the volcanic eruption theory, like the impact theory, accounts for the presence of iridium in sedimentary deposits; it also explains matters that the meteorite-impact theory does not. Although iridium is extremely rare on the Earth's surface, the lower regions of the Earth's mantle have roughly the same composition as meteorites and contain large amounts of iridium, which in the case of a diapir eruption would probably be emitted as iridium hexafluoride, a gas that would disperse more uniformly in the atmosphere than the iridium-containing matter thrown out from a meteorite impact. In addition, the volcanic eruption theory may explain why the end of the Cretaceous period was marked by a gradual change in sea level. Fossil records indicate that for several hundred thousand years prior to the relatively sudden disappearance of the dinosaurs, the level of the sea gradually fell, causing many marine organisms to die out. This change in sea level might well have been the result of a distortion in the Earth's surface that resulted from the movement of diapirs upward toward the Earth's crust, and the more cataclysmic extinction of the dinosaurs could have resulted from the explosive volcanism that occurred as material from the diapirs erupted onto the Earth's surface.

Practice Test 15, Passage 1

4. In the passage, the author is primarily concerned with doing which one of the following?

(A) describing three theories and explaining why the latest of these appears to be the best of the three
(B) attacking the assumptions inherent in theories that until the 1980s had been largely accepted by geologists
(C) outlining the inadequacies of three different explanations of the same phenomenon
(D) providing concrete examples in support of the more general assertion that theories must often be revised in light of new evidence
(E) citing evidence that appears to confirm the skepticism of geologists regarding a view held prior to the 1980s

7. Which one of the following, if true, would cast the most doubt on the theory described in the last paragraph of the passage?

(A) Fragments of meteorites that have struck the Earth are examined and found to have only minuscule amounts of iridium hexafluoride trapped inside of them.
(B) Most diapir eruptions in the geological history of the Earth have been similar in size to the one that occurred in India at the end of the Cretaceous period and have not been succeeded by periods of climatic change.
(C) There have been several periods in the geological history of the Earth, before and after the Cretaceous period, during which large numbers of marine species have perished.
(D) The frequency with which meteorites struck the Earth was higher at the end of the Cretaceous period than at the beginning of the period.
(E) Marine species tend to be much more vulnerable to extinction when exposed to a dramatic and relatively sudden change in sea level than when they are exposed to a gradual change in sea level similar to the one that preceded the extinction of the dinosaurs.

Directions:

On this page and on the pages that follow are four passages that have appeared on past LSATs. Each passage is accompanied by two questions. Read the passages as if you had the full set of questions attached. Then do your best to answer the two questions. Time yourself, and do try to push the pace as much as you feel comfortable pushing it, but at this point worry less about time and more about process and accuracy. Solutions follow each passage.

Passage One Solutions

SUMMARY

P1 - **One main idea (popular until the 1980s)—that non-catastrophic processes caused extinction of dinosaurs.** Then we are given future explanation of this theory—the non-catastrophic process is a dramatic drop in sea level.

P2 - Evidence that challenges that idea—unusual levels of iridium. **Second main idea based on this evidence—meteorite.**

P3 - Current evidence leads to **a third main idea—volcanic eruption theory.** More information about an eruption in India. Explanation of how such an eruption happens.

P4 - More support for third theory—evidence from second paragraph happens to support this idea as well. Explanation of how this happens. Evidence from first paragraph happens to support this idea as well.

COMMENTARY

This is a classic example of the type of passage that can seem far more difficult at the beginning of your studies than it will (hopefully) at the end of your studies. This is a difficult passage to get through, and the reason for that is because the information is scientific and complicated, and because the sentences are dense and oftentimes multifaceted.

However, the reasoning structure of the passage is abundantly clear, and reasoning structure is what we really care about. Therefore, even though many of the sentences are difficult to understand, I would consider this an easier passage, because the reasoning structure is not difficult to understand.

The first sentence gives us, right away, a main idea, and it also gives us a clear sense that this is an opinion that is going to get dismissed—the "until the 1980s" tells us that. It's clear how the next sentence and the one that begins the second paragraph relate to this first main idea, and by the time we get the second hypothesis—the meteorite idea—we should be expecting it.

The third paragraph—and the third theory it presents—is a bit of a twist, but it's certainly easy enough to understand, and it's clear to see that what follows, as complicated as it is, is meant to support and give us more information about this third idea. The author also does a nice job of bringing back information presented in the first and second paragraphs and repurposing it as support for the volcanic eruption theory.

THE QUESTIONS

4. (A) is correct.

The question is about the passage as a whole, and before we go into the answer choices, we should have a very clear sense of what to look for—an answer that discusses various theories for dinosaur extinction, and gives some indication as to the author's preference for the third theory.

(A) seems like the perfect answer, but to be safe we should wait to select it. (B) gives a partial description of the passage (mostly just the second paragraph) but doesn't represent the passage as a whole. (C) does not accurately represent the author's intention. (D) is much broader than the passage itself. (E) represents part of the passage, but does a poor job of describing the passage as a whole. We go back to (A) and double-check each word one last time—it looks good.

7. (B) is correct.

This is a rare type of question in Reading Comprehension—one that requires us to use some of the same critical reasoning skills that many Logical Reasoning questions do. We are asked to weaken the theory presented in the fourth paragraph—that means we are looking for an answer that gives us some reason to doubt the volcanic eruption theory.

(A) would impact the second theory, but doesn't impact the third. (B) is attractive because we know that resultant climate change is indeed an important part of our theory—let's leave it. (C) tells us nothing about this particular situation and can be quickly eliminated. Frequency of meteor strikes is irrelevant to the passage (you may need to do a quick scan to double-check this), and so (D) can be eliminated quickly. Finally, (E) gives us a comparative that doesn't hurt or hinder the idea that gradual change can still cause extinction.

Let's go back to (B), a tough answer choice to understand, to review it one more time, and to compare it to the text. (B) tells us that most volcanic eruptions like the one the author discusses do not cause significant climate change. Why is this important? Because the author proposes in the final paragraph that the dinosaur extinction could have resulted from the volcanic explosion, and in the third paragraph (it's cruel that the question stem only discusses the fourth paragraph when the third paragraph is also relevant to the theory in question) he mentions how the volcanic explosion caused the extinction—by changing climate. If (B) is true, it weakens the idea that this did indeed happen.

Drill Passage Two

In 1964 the United States federal government began attempts to eliminate racial discrimination in employment and wages: the United States Congress enacted Title VII of the Civil Rights Act, prohibiting employers from making employment decisions on the basis of race. In 1965 President Johnson issued Executive Order 11,246, which prohibited discrimination by United States government contractors and emphasized direct monitoring of minority representation in contractors' work forces.

Nonetheless, proponents of the "continuous change" hypothesis believe that United States federal law had a marginal impact on the economic progress made by black people in the United States between 1940 and 1975. Instead they emphasize slowly evolving historical forces, such as longterm trends in education that improved segregated schools for black students during the 1940s and were operative during and after the 1960s. They argue that as the quality of black schools improved relative to that of white schools, the earning potential of those attending black schools increased relative to the earning potential of those attending white schools.

However, there is no direct evidence linking increased quality of underfunded segregated black schools to these improvements in earning potential. In fact, even the evidence on relative schooling quality is ambiguous. Although in the mid-1940s term length at black schools was approaching that in white schools, the rapid growth in another important measure of school quality, school expenditures, may be explained by increases in teachers' salaries, and, historically, such increases have not necessarily increased school quality. Finally, black individuals in all age groups, even those who had been educated at segregated schools before the 1940s, experienced post-1960 increases in their earning potential. If improvements in the quality of schooling were an important determinant of increased returns, only those workers who could have benefited from enhanced school quality should have received higher returns. The relative improvement in the earning potential of educated black people of all age groups in the United States is more consistent with a decline in employment discrimination.

An additional problem for continuity theorists is how to explain the rapid acceleration of black economic progress in the United States after 1964. Education alone cannot account for the rate of change. Rather, the coincidence of increased United States government antidiscrimination pressure in the mid-1960s with the acceleration in the rate of black economic progress beginning in 1965 argues against the continuity theorists' view. True, correlating federal intervention and the acceleration of black economic progress might be incorrect. One could argue that changing attitudes about employment discrimination sparked both the adoption of new federal policies and the rapid acceleration in black economic progress. Indeed, the shift in national attitude that made possible the enactment of Title VII was in part produced by the persistence of racial discrimination in the southern United States. However, the fact that the law had its greatest effect in the South, in spite of the vigorous resistance of many Southern leaders, suggests its importance for black economic progress.

Practice Test 15, Passage 4

22. According to the passage, Title VII of the 1964 Civil Rights Act differs from Executive Order 11,246 in that Title VII

(A) monitors employers to ensure minority representation
(B) assesses the work forces of government contractors
(C) eliminates discriminatory disparities in wages
(D) focuses on determining minority representation in government
(E) governs hiring practices in a wider variety of workplaces

27. The "continuous change" hypothesis, as it is presented in the passage, can best be applied to which one of the following situations?

(A) Homes are found for many low-income families because the government funds a project to build subsidized housing in an economically depressed area.
(B) A depressed economy does not cause the closing of small businesses in a local community because the government provides special grants to aid these businesses.
(C) Unemployed people are able to obtain jobs because private contractors receive tax incentives for constructing office buildings in an area with a high unemployment rate.
(D) A housing shortage is remedied because the changing state of the economy permits private investors to finance construction in a depressed area.
(E) A community's sanitation needs are met because neighborhood organizations lobby aggressively for government assistance.

Passage Two Solutions

SUMMARY

P1 - Background—Government began to enact laws starting in 1964 to eliminate racial discrimination at work.

P2 - Main point—**"continuous change" hypothesis says gradual societal change, such as improving education, is responsible for economic progress of black people**. Expansion of that idea.

P3 - Lots of evidence against that continuous change idea.

P4 - More evidence against continuous change. Same evidence used to support **second main idea—that government laws had impact, author's point**. Possible objections against, then rebuttal.

COMMENTARY

This passage has all of the standard components of a typical passage—background information, two contrasting main points, evidence that supports and opposes those main points, and an author's opinion. The slight twist here is that the order in which the information is presented is a bit unexpected and choppy.

We start with a paragraph of background information, then an opinion that dismisses the significance of that background information, then reasons that oppose that opinion, and then a second opinion—one the author supports—that ties into the original background information. This passage would have been markedly easier had the author not waited until the fourth paragraph to give his opinion.

The unexpected organizational structure lends itself to a bit of a wild ride during the reading process, but the reasoning structure of this passage is quite simple to understand after the fact.

THE QUESTIONS

22. (E) is correct.

This question is simply testing our ability to read information correctly. It helps to know that everything that is relevant to answering the question will be contained in the first two paragraphs, and you certainly want to go back and read them again before looking at the answers.

The wrong choices go beyond what is stated in the text. (A) is tempting, but it's not clear that Title VII includes some monitoring system, and it's also unclear whether the Executive Order required monitoring *by employers*. (B) is tempting but gets the two reversed. (C) is overly broad and relates somewhat to both elements. (D) skews the discussion—prohibiting discrimination is not quite the same thing as "determining," and representation in government is not directly discussed.

(E) is a basic answer that can't be refuted. If it had been presented first (instead of last), chances are this question would have felt much easier. In any case, we know that Title VII related to all employers, and the Executive Order specifically to government contractors.

27. (D) is correct.

What we know about the continuous change folks is that they dismiss the impact of government intervention, and they emphasize the significance of gradual societal change. Questions that test your understanding of one opinion will commonly have many wrong answers that align with the opposite, or contrasting, opinion (because the test writers need to create answers that are provably wrong), and that's the case here.

If you went into the answer choices thinking "right answer—slow change, wrong answers—government intervention," the four wrong answers, (A), (B), (C), and (E), would have all jumped out as being on the wrong side of the fence.

Drill Passage Three

Until recently, it was thought that the Cherokee, a Native American tribe, were compelled to assimilate Euro American culture during the 1820s. During that decade, it was supposed, White missionaries arrived and, together with their part Cherokee intermediaries, imposed the benefits of "civilization" on Cherokee tribes while the United States government actively promoted acculturalization by encouraging the Cherokee to switch from hunting to settled agriculture. This view was based on the assumption that the end of a Native American group's economic and political autonomy would automatically mean the end of its cultural autonomy as well.

William G. McLoughlin has recently argued that not only did Cherokee culture flourish during and after the 1820s, but the Cherokee themselves actively and continually reshaped their culture. Missionaries did have a decisive impact during these years, he argues, but that impact was far from what it was intended to be. The missionaries' tendency to cater to the interests of an acculturating part-Cherokee elite (who comprised the bulk of their converts) at the expense of the more traditionalist full-Cherokee majority created great intratribal tensions. As the elite initiated reforms designed to legitimize their own and the Cherokee Nation's place in the new republic of the United States, antimission Cherokee reacted by fostering revivals of traditional religious beliefs and practices. However, these revivals did not, according to McLoughlin, undermine the elitist reforms, but supplemented them with popular, traditionalist counterparts.

Traditionalist Cherokee did not reject the elitist reforms outright, McLoughlin argues, simply because they recognized that there was more than one way to use the skills the missionaries could provide them. As he quotes one group as saying, "We want our children to learn English so that the White man cannot cheat us." Many traditionalist Cherokee welcomed the missionaries for another reason: they perceived that it would be useful to have White allies. In the end, McLoughlin asserts, most members of the Cherokee council, including traditionalists, supported a move which preserved many of the reforms of the part-Cherokee elite but limited the activities and influence of the missionaries and other White settlers. According to McLoughlin, the identity and culture that resulted were distinctively Cherokee, yet reflected the larger political and social setting in which they flourished.

Because his work concentrates on the nineteenth century, McLoughlin unfortunately overlooks earlier sources of influence, such as eighteenth century White resident traders and neighbors, thus obscuring the relative impact of the missionaries of the 1820s in contributing to both acculturalization and resistance to it among the Cherokee. However, McLoughlin is undoubtedly correct in recognizing that culture is an ongoing process rather than a static entity, and he has made a significant contribution to our understanding of how Cherokee culture changed while retaining its essential identity after confronting the missionaries.

Practice Test 18, Passage 3

17. Which one of the following statements regarding the Cherokee council in the 1820s can be inferred from the passage?

(A) Members of the Cherokee council were elected democratically by the entire Cherokee Nation.
(B) In order for a policy to come into effect for the Cherokee Nation, it had to have been approved by a unanimous vote of the Cherokee council.
(C) Despite the fact that the Cherokee were dominated politically and economically by the United States in the 1820s, the Cherokee council was able to override policies set by the United States government.
(D) Though it did not have complete autonomy in governing the Cherokee Nation, it was able to set some policies affecting the activities of White people living in tribal areas.
(E) The proportions of traditionalist and acculturating Cherokee in the Cherokee council were determined by the proportions of traditionalist and acculturating Cherokee in the Cherokee population.

19. According to the passage, McLoughlin cites which one of the following as a contributing factor in the revival of traditional religious beliefs among the Cherokee in the 1820s?

(A) Missionaries were gaining converts at an increasing rate as the 1820s progressed.
(B) The traditionalist Cherokee majority thought that most of the reforms initiated by the missionaries' converts would corrupt Cherokee culture.
(C) Missionaries unintentionally created conflict among the Cherokee by favoring the interests of the acculturating elite at the expense of the more traditionalist majority.
(D) Traditionalist Cherokee recognized that only some of the reforms instituted by a small Cherokee elite would be beneficial to all Cherokee.
(E) A small group of Cherokee converted by missionaries attempted to institute reforms designed to acquire political supremacy for themselves in the Cherokee council.

Passage Three Solutions

SUMMARY

P1 - First main point—**until recently, thought Cherokee were "compelled" to assimilate to white culture in the 1820s.** More detail about this.

P2 - Contrasting second main point—**McLoughlin counters that Cherokee culture flourished and evolved after 1820s.** More detail about why and how.

P3 - More specific expansion of McLoughlin's points.

P4 - Author's opinion on the debate—he points out a negative of McLoughlin's work (that he overlooks earlier history) then the positive (his emphasis on culture as evolving process, and amount McLoughlin has added to understanding).

COMMENTARY

This passage starts out as we might expect, then takes a somewhat unique turn in the final paragraph. The first paragraph sets up a central opinion, and the paragraph gives us many clues ("Until recently," "it was supposed") that tip us off that this opinion will be countered by a new (probably more correct) one. The second paragraph then gives us the new opinion, and the third paragraph expands on it in ways we would expect.

The fourth paragraph is a bit surprising. It has seemed, up to this point, that the author is likely in agreement with McLoughlin; however, in the final paragraph, the author chooses to point out a significant problem with McLoughlin's work, and only gives a very general endorsement of it.

THE QUESTIONS

17. (D) is correct.

There are a couple of things to note right away about the question stem. For one, it is asking about the Cherokee council, a very specific entity, rather than any other Cherokee group that was discussed in the passage. Secondly, it asks us for an answer that we can infer—we can expect, thus, that the right answer will be one that does not match the text exactly, but rather one we have to be able to validate using the text.

The relevant information comes in the middle of the third paragraph, when we are told that the council supported many changes of the elite, but limited the activities of white settlers. You want to make sure to identify and reread the relevant text before evaluating the answers.

We don't have any relevant information to validate (A), (B), or (E), and those can be eliminated quickly. (C) is tempting, but difficult to justify with the text—we don't have specific proof that the council was able to override policies set by the United States government. We can eliminate (C).

That leaves us with (D), the correct answer. The fact that the council was able to limit activities is enough to allow us to justify the answer.

19. (C) is correct.

This is a different sort of question than #17 was, in that we are asked to find an answer that is true "according to the passage." What that means is that one answer is specifically discussed in the passage, and the other four are not. Before going into the answers, we quickly read through the end of the second paragraph, which talks most specifically about the revival, but because this was a central topic, we want to keep an open mind about which paragraph the relevant information might come from.

(A), (B), (D), and (E) are not specifically discussed by the passage. (C) *is* specifically discussed at the beginning of the second paragraph—we are told that the outcome was far from what it was intended to be, and the impact we are told of is almost word for word what is stated in the text. Therefore (C) is correct.

Drill Passage Four

In the history of nineteenth century landscape painting in the United States, the Luminists are distinguished by their focus on atmosphere and light. The accepted view of Luminist paintings is that they are basically spiritual and imply a tranquil mysticism that contrasts with earlier American artists' concept of nature as dynamic and energetic. According to this view, the Luminist atmosphere, characterized by "pure and constant light," guides the onlooker toward a lucid transcendentalism, an idealized vision of the world.

What this view fails to do is to identify the true significance of this transcendental atmosphere in Luminist paintings. The prosaic factors that are revealed by a closer examination of these works suggest that the glowing appearance of nature in Luminism is actually a sign of nature's domestication, its adaptation to human use. The idealized Luminist atmosphere thus seems to convey, not an intensification of human responses to nature, but rather a muting of those emotions, like awe and fear, which untamed nature elicits.

One critic, in describing the spiritual quality of harbor scenes by Fitz Hugh Lane, an important Luminist, carefully notes that "at the peak of Luminist development in the 1850s and 1860s, spiritualism in America was extremely widespread." It is also true, however, that the 1850s and 1860s were a time of trade expansion. From 1848 until his death in 1865, Lane lived in a house with a view of the harbor of Gloucester, Massachusetts, and he made short trips to Maine, New York, Baltimore, and probably Puerto Rico. In all of these places he painted the harbors with their ships the instruments of expanding trade. Lane usually depicts places like New York Harbor, with ships at anchor, but even when he depicts more remote, less commercially active harbors, nature appears pastoral and domesticated rather than primitive or unexplored. The ships, rather than the surrounding landscapes including the sea are generally the active element in his pictures. For Lane the sea is, in effect, a canal or a trade route for commercial activity, not a free, powerful element, as it is in the early pictures of his predecessor, Cole. For Lane nature is subdued, even when storms are approaching; thus, the sea is always a viable highway for the transport of goods. In sum, I consider Lane's sea simply an environment for human activity nature no longer inviolate. The luminescence that Lane paints symbolizes nature's humbled state, for the light itself is as docile as the Luminist sea, and its tranquillity in a sense signifies no more than good conditions on the highway to progress. Progress, probably even more than transcendence, is the secret message of Luminism. In a sense, Luminist pictures are an ideological justification of the atmosphere necessary for business, if also an exaggerated, idealistic rendering of that atmosphere.

Practice Test 18, Passage 4

22. The passage is primarily concerned with discussing

(A) the importance of religion to the art of a particular period
(B) the way one artist's work illustrates a tradition of painting
(C) the significance of the sea in one artist's work
(D) differences in the treatment of nature as a more active or a less active force
(E) variations in the artistic treatment of light among nineteenth century landscape painters

27. The author's primary purpose is to

(A) refute a new theory
(B) replace an inadequate analysis
(C) summarize current critics' attitudes
(D) support another critic's evaluation
(E) describe the history of a misinterpretation

Passage Four Solutions

SUMMARY

P1 - First main point—**accepted view of Luminist paintings is that they are spiritual and tranquil—guides onlooker toward an idealized vision of the world.**

P2 - Contrasting second main point/author opinion—**look of Luminist paintings actually a sign that man has domesticated nature for our use.**

P3 - Examines one context—harbor scenes by Fitz Hugh Lane—from both perspectives. Mostly focuses on relating paintings to second main point.

COMMENTARY

This is another passage that presents two opposing opinions. In this case, the author makes it quite clear which of the opinions matches his, and spends the majority of the text discussing the subject—Luminist paintings—from his perspective.

Notice that both questions ask us about the passage as a whole, and are, in many ways, quite similar. And yet look at the correct answers—they are, though both in many ways predictable, quite different from one another. You should expect to anticipate characteristics of right answers, but you would be foolish to expect that you can predict exactly what will be in a right answer, for there are many different ways they can go about presenting the relevant information. As we'll discuss in further detail later, this is one of the many reasons why we want to make sure to develop our wrong answer elimination processes. By attacking the question from both directions—eliminating wrong choices and selecting right ones—we give ourselves the best chance to be accurate.

THE QUESTIONS

22. (B) is correct.

We know that the passage spends about half the space discussing the two contrasting views on Luminists, and about half the space discussing how the work of one artist can be interpreted per these two views. With that in mind, let's take a look at the answer choices...

(A) does not reflect any of the main points of the passage and can be eliminated. (B) represents a good deal of the passage, but not all—let's leave it. (C) is even narrower in scope—the sea is not the main purpose of the passage. We can eliminate (C). (D) is tempting in that it touches on the main points the author makes, but it does not inform us specifically about Luminists, or the use of Fitz Hugh Lane as a representative of Luminists. We can eliminate (D). (E) is far too narrow in scope and can be quickly eliminated.

That leaves us with only (B). Thinking about the passage in terms of (B), it works—the first paragraphs serve to give us what we need to understand and think about a tradition in painting, and the last one is about how one artist relates to this tradition. (B) is correct.

27. (B) is correct.

This question is about the passage as a whole, as the last one was, and I'll go into the answers thinking about the same things: the two contrasting views on Luminists, and how the work of one artist can be interpreted per these two views.

The author is not trying to refute a new theory, but rather an accepted one, so we can eliminate (A). (B) sounds good—the "accepted" view is the inadequate analysis that is being replaced, and the author spends the entire passing trying to show why it should be replaced. Let's leave (B). The author's purpose is not to summarize current critical attitudes, and so we can eliminate (C). The author does not support another critic, but rather refutes the only critic mentioned specifically, so we can eliminate (D). Finally, the passage does not give us a history of how Luminist paintings were misinterpreted, and so we can eliminate (E).

(B) is the only attractive answer we saw, the last one standing, and the correct choice. Again, notice how different the two right answers were from one another, and also how they both do accurately describe the passage. Top scorers have a well-rounded understanding of the passage and strong wrong-answer elimination techniques.

25 READING COMPREHENSION practice set two & comparative passages

Now that you've had a chance to get a few passages under your belt, hopefully you feel that you are developing a good sense of the common reasoning structures that underlie all passages, and hopefully you are seeing the direct relationship between this reasoning structure and the design of the questions the test writers choose to ask.

If we take a big-picture look at all the passages that have appeared on the LSAT, strip them of their unique subject matter, and only focus on reasoning structure, the commonality in that reasoning structure becomes clear. We can see that all LSAT passages riff off of a few basic design templates.

A great way to think about LSAT passages as a whole is in terms of defaults and modifications. Most passages present two contrasting main points, so we want to think of that as the default. A minority of passages present maybe just one point, or more than two points. We can think of these as the modifications. Most passages align the author's opinion with one main point or the other—this is our default. A minority will lack an author's opinion, or present a more sophisticated version that doesn't align with either main point. Most passages will present subjective main points that are clearly opinions. A minority will be written in an objective fashion. You want to have a very clear sense of expectations, and you want to be able to recognize when a passage fits right into that sweet spot. You also want to have a clear understanding of the limited ways in which certain passages stray from that norm. Thinking of passages in terms of general tendencies and common twists is a great way to develop your big-picture understanding.

Tendencies and Twists

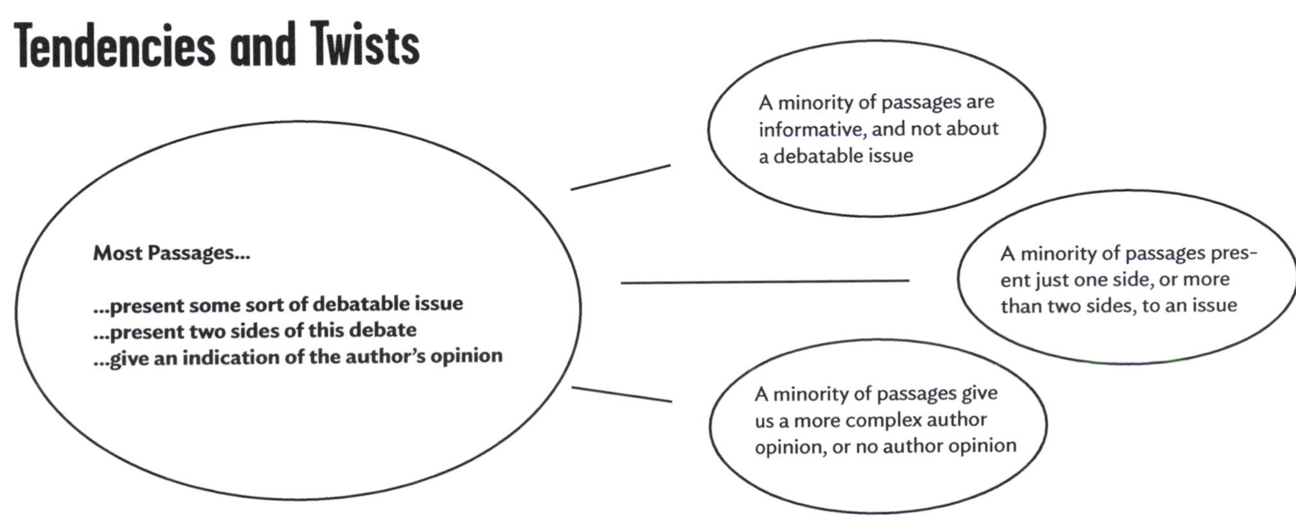

Most Passages...
...present some sort of debatable issue
...present two sides of this debate
...give an indication of the author's opinion
A minority of passages are informative, and not about a debatable issue
A minority of passages present just one side, or more than two sides, to an issue
A minority of passages give us a more complex author opinion, or no author opinion

PASSAGE STRUCTURE: VARIATIONS ON A THEME

Let's imagine that the section is going to include an essay on the health effects of eating popcorn. What kind of passage structures might we expect? Here are six examples of the types of passage structures we could see. Note that if we replace the subject of eating popcorn with another subject, no matter how complex or confusing the new subject might be, it wouldn't affect the ways in which the reasoning of the passage can be structured.

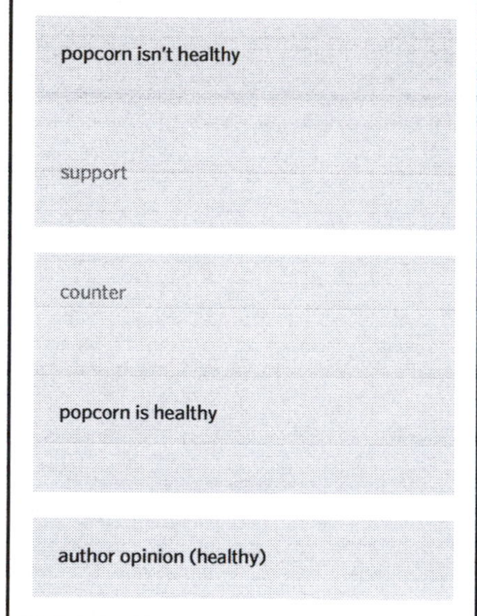

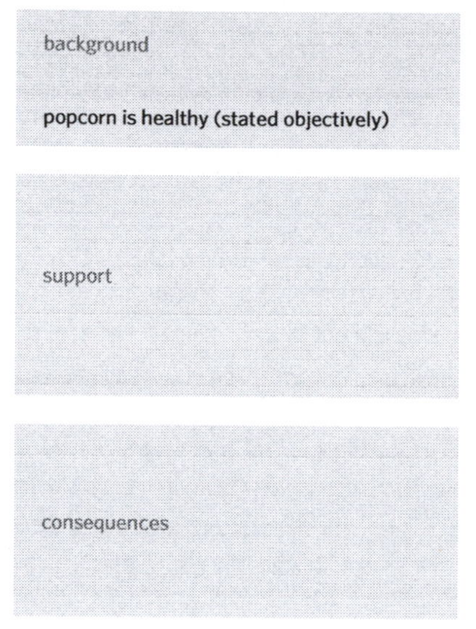

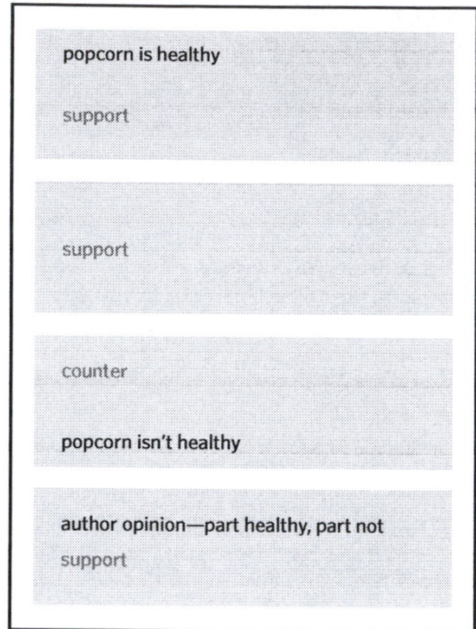

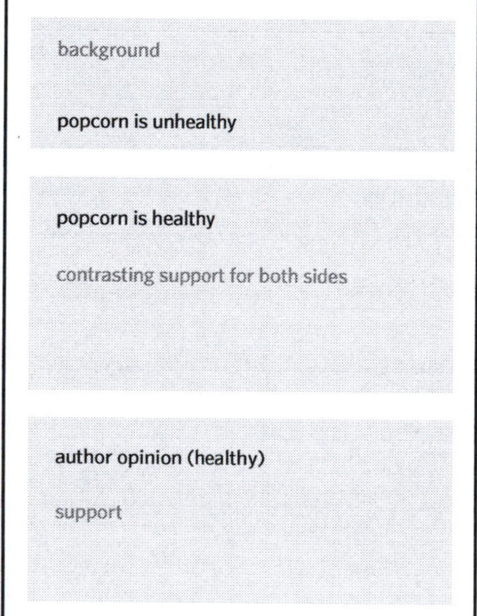

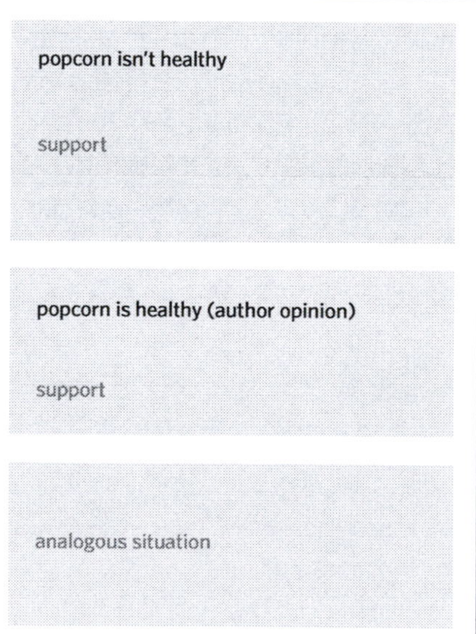

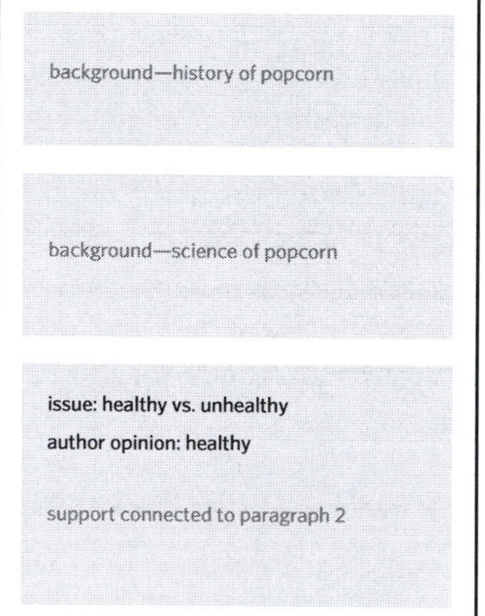

background—history of popcorn
background—science of popcorn
issue: healthy vs. unhealthy
author opinion: healthy
support connected to paragraph 2

Drill Passage One

Directions: Here are two more passages for you to practice with. Try to read and solve both questions for each passage in five minutes or less.

Three kinds of study have been performed on Byron. There is the biographical study—the very valuable examination of Byron's psychology and the events in his life; Escarpit's 1958 work is an example of this kind of study, and biographers to this day continue to speculate about Byron's life. Equally valuable is the study of Byron as a figure important in the history of ideas; Russell and Praz have written studies of this kind. Finally, there are studies that primarily consider Byron's poetry. Such literary studies are valuable, however, only when they avoid concentrating solely on analyzing the verbal shadings of Byron's poetry to the exclusion of any discussion of biographical considerations. A study with such a concentration would be of questionable value because Byron's poetry, for the most part, is simply not a poetry of subtle verbal meanings. Rather, on the whole, Byron's poems record the emotional pressure of certain moments in his life. I believe we cannot often read a poem of Byron's, as we often can one of Shakespeare's, without wondering what events or circumstances in his life prompted him to write it.

No doubt the fact that most of Byron's poems cannot be convincingly read as subtle verbal creations indicates that Byron is not a "great" poet. It must be admitted too that Byron's literary craftsmanship is irregular and often his temperament disrupts even his lax literary method (although the result, an absence of method, has a significant purpose: it functions as a rebuke to a cosmos that Byron feels he cannot understand). If Byron is not a "great" poet, his poetry is nonetheless of extraordinary interest to us because of the pleasure it gives us. Our main pleasure in reading Byron's poetry is the contact with a singular personality. Reading his work gives us illumination—self-understanding—after we have seen our weaknesses and aspirations mirrored in the personality we usually find in the poems. Anyone who thinks that this kind of illumination is not a genuine reason for reading a poet should think carefully about why we read Donne's sonnets.

It is Byron and Byron's idea of himself that hold his work together (and that enthralled early nineteenth-century Europe). Different characters speak in his poems, but finally it is usually he himself who is speaking: a far cry from the impersonal poet Keats. Byron's poetry alludes to Greek and Roman myth in the context of contemporary affairs, but his work remains generally of a piece because of his close presence in the poetry. In sum, the poetry is a shrewd personal performance, and to shut out Byron the man is to fabricate a work of pseudo-criticism.

Practice Test 16, Passage 1

5. The author mentions that "Byron's literary craftsmanship is irregular" (lines 27-28) *(second sentence of second paragraph)* most probably in order to

(A) contrast Byron's poetic skill with that of Shakespeare
(B) dismiss craftsmanship as a standard by which to judge poets
(C) offer another reason why Byron is not a "great" poet
(D) point out a negative consequence of Byron's belief that the cosmos is incomprehensible
(E) indicate the most-often-cited explanation of why Byron's poetry lacks subtle verbal nuances

7. The author indicates which one of the following about biographers' speculation concerning Byron's life?

(A) Such speculation began in earnest with Escarpit's study.
(B) Such speculation continues today.
(C) Such speculation is less important than consideration of Byron's poetry.
(D) Such speculation has not given us a satisfactory sense of Byron's life.
(E) Such speculation has been carried out despite the objections of literary critics.

Passage One Solutions

SUMMARY

P1 - background—three main ways to study Byron. Probable main point has to do with the third way to study Byron: **a study that concentrates on writing style of his poetry but not his life is not valuable.**

P2 - continues on with the point at the end of the first paragraph— he is not a great poet because of his technical skill. Still, his poetry is interesting because of what it shows of his personality.

P3 - finalizes the same train of thought. The author concludes that **because his poetry is so personal, legitimate criticism of Byron's poetry cannot exclude study of "Byron the man."**

COMMENTARY

Both this passage and the next are meant to be examples of somewhat unpredictable (twists and turns!) passage structure. The passage begins as if it might compare and contrast the three different types of studies. However, the first two end up serving as background, then springboard us into the main point about studies that focus just on the techniques in Byron's poetry. The first strong hint we get that this is the main point is the sentence that begins, "Such literary studies are valuable..." This tells us that the author is giving an opinion about that specific type of study, and the author would not give an opinion unless the issue was important.

Still, the second paragraph could have very well returned to discussing the other two types of studies, and the author could have perhaps given his opinions on those. It doesn't. Instead, it continues on to discuss the main point we highlighted, as does the third paragraph.

THE QUESTIONS

5. (C) is correct.

Just before that statement, the author mentioned that he believes Byron is not a "great" poet. The "great" in quotations indicates that he is thinking of a unique meaning for that word, and (C) matches that specific meaning. The sentence involving the part in question also includes the word "too," which helps us validate the statement "another reason."

What makes this question a bit easier is that the wrong answers are all very clearly wrong, and you would have done yourself a great favor if you took the small amount of time necessary to eliminate them all. (A) relates to a different part of the passage, and Shakespeare is not central to the primary themes, so we can quickly eliminate (A). (B) is too general—we're only talking about Byron here. The author hasn't expressed that this characteristic is a negative (quite the opposite), so we can eliminate (D). (E) includes ideas ("most often cited") we can't validate, and can also be easily eliminated.

7. (B) is correct.

Note the wording—"the author indicates"—that tells us that the right answer is something that is specifically mentioned in the text. In this case, the second sentence of the first paragraph gives us justification for (B).

For a detail question such as this one, ideally, you want to be able to read the text in question before evaluating the answer choices in depth. You may have noticed the words "biographer's speculation" in the question stem and gone into the text to find them right away, or maybe you noticed the importance of the word "speculation" in the answer choices. In any case, finding that sentence about speculation first, then evaluating the answers, is much easier than being tempted by each answer and having to check each against the text.

Detail questions are one of the few question types for which it is sometimes not completely necessary to eliminate wrong choices before selecting a right one. Still, it doesn't hurt to take a quick look through all of the wrongs just in case there isn't another attractive choice. (A) is not mentioned, and it's easy to see that in the sentence we just used to prove (B). (C), (D), and (E) do not come too close to matching the substance or themes of the text, and so are not particularly tempting. Knowing the other answers are wrong helps us be one hundred percent sure that (B) is right.

Drill Passage Two

When catastrophe strikes, analysts typically blame some combination of powerful mechanisms. An earthquake is traced to an immense instability along a fault line; a stock market crash is blamed on the destabilizing effect of computer trading. These explanations may well be correct. But systems as large and complicated as the Earth's crust or the stock market can break down not only under the force of a mighty blow but also at the drop of a pin. In a large interactive system, a minor event can start a chain reaction that leads to a catastrophe.

Traditionally, investigators have analyzed large interactive systems in the same way they analyze small orderly systems, mainly because the methods developed for small systems have proved so successful. They believed they could predict the behavior of a large interactive system by studying its elements separately and by analyzing its component mechanisms individually. For lack of a better theory, they assumed that in large interactive systems the response to a disturbance is proportional to that disturbance.

During the past few decades, however, it has become increasingly apparent that many large complicated systems do not yield to traditional analysis. Consequently, theorists have proposed a "theory of self-organized criticality": many large interactive systems evolve naturally to a critical state in which a minor event starts a chain reaction that can affect any number of elements in the system. Although such systems produce more minor events than catastrophes, the mechanism that leads to minor events is the same one that leads to major events.

A deceptively simple system serves as a paradigm for self-organized criticality: a pile of sand. As sand is poured one grain at a time onto a flat disk, the grains at first stay close to the position where they land. Soon they rest on top of one another, creating a pile that has a gentle slope. Now and then, when the slope becomes too steep, the grains slide down, causing a small avalanche. The system reaches its critical state when the amount of sand added is balanced, on average, by the amount falling off the edge of the disk.

Now when a grain of sand is added, it can start an avalanche of any size, including a "catastrophic" event. Most of the time the grain will fall so that no avalanche occurs. By studying a specific area of the pile, one can even predict whether avalanches will occur there in the near future. To such a local observer, however, large avalanches would remain unpredictable because they are a consequence of the total history of the entire pile. No matter what the local dynamics are, catastrophic avalanches would persist at a relative frequency that cannot be altered. Criticality is a global property of the sand-pile.

Practice Test 16, Passage 3

16. The passage provides support for all of the following generalizations about large interactive systems EXCEPT:

(A) They can evolve to a critical state.
(B) They do not always yield to traditional analysis.
(C) They make it impossible for observers to make any predictions about them.
(D) They are subject to the effects of chain reactions.
(E) They are subject to more minor events than major events.

20. Which one of the following is most analogous to the method of analysis employed by the investigators mentioned in the second paragraph?

(A) A pollster gathers a sample of voter preferences and on the basis of this information makes a prediction about the outcome of an election.
(B) A historian examines the surviving documents detailing the history of a movement and from these documents reconstructs a chronology of the events that initiated the movement.
(C) A meteorologist measures the rainfall over a certain period of the year and from this data calculates the total annual rainfall for the region.
(D) A biologist observes the behavior of one species of insect and from these observations generalizes about the behavior of insects as a class.
(E) An engineer analyzes the stability of each structural element of a bridge and from these analyses draws a conclusion about the structural soundness of the bridge.

Passage Two Solutions

SUMMARY

P1 - two slightly contrasting main points are presented, and it's made clear that the latter of the two is the author's view and focus. The two points are that **analysts typically blame some combination of powerful mechanisms when catastrophe strikes, and a minor event can start a chain reaction that leads to catastrophe.**

P2 - as background, discusses old (traditional) methods of analyzing large systems.

P3 - contrasts second paragraph (as expected) to say traditional methods not particularly effective for large systems—leads to a "theory of self-organized criticality," which matches up with the author's original point made in the first paragraph. Expands on the idea.

P4 - a sand pile is used as an analogy for how a small event—the dropping of a bit of sand, which typically leads to no outcome—can sometimes lead to a small avalanche.

P5 - continues on with idea but adds to it some complexity—once in a while, a piece of sand added can start a large avalanche. Author continues on to say that by studying one area, one can predict when avalanches will occur, but not how large the avalanche will be. This is because the size of the avalanche is based on the pile as a whole.

COMMENTARY

This is a fairly straightforward passage to understand until the final paragraph, at which point the difficulty level of the content, as well as the vagueness and challenge of the language, gets ratcheted up.

The first paragraph presents two ways to think about big events (catastrophes); the second paragraph the "traditional" (when you see that word, chances are 9 out of 10 that a "new" method will also be introduced) way to investigate; the third a new way to investigate (relating to main point that minor events can start catastrophes); and the fourth paragraph a simple analogy to help us think about this concept.

The final paragraph takes us on a bit of a side journey—thinking about big events from the small-triggers perspective, the author gives us a bit of an interesting juxtaposition. You have to be close to the avalanches to be able to predict when they will happen, but you need to be far away to be able to see how large the avalanches will be. The author gives us this information in just about as confusing a way as possible. If need be, you can certainly feel free to read the paragraph a few times in order to understand it correctly (I know I did). If you read it two or three times and you still can't get your head around it, move on to the questions. The last paragraph doesn't hinder you from understanding the main point of the passage, and the questions themselves may help you learn more about what the author actually means.

THE QUESTIONS

16. (C) is correct.

We are looking for the one answer that is not connected to what was discussed in the passage. In evaluating the answers, we want to go back into the text to verify any for which we are not sure, but before we get to the ones that we have to carefully evaluate, we want to see if there are any obvious right or wrong choices.

(A) and (B) are both central to the main themes of the passage, so we can easily eliminate them both. (C) is clearly not justifiable based on the text—we know we can make some predictions, and the "impossible" is a tip-off that (C) is too extreme and seems to be the correct answer. Let's keep reading. (D) is mentioned prominently in the passage, and we can eliminate it without checking back. (E) perhaps needs some verification—if need be, the proof can be found in the last sentence of the third paragraph.

We can eliminate (A), (B), (D), and (E) because they all match the text. That leaves us with (C), the correct answer.

20. (E) is correct.

Before evaluating the answers, we want to go back to the second paragraph and remind ourselves of what those investigators were like. In that paragraph, we're given two main characteristics—they think about the whole in terms of individual components, and they think that the size of the disturbance = the size of the response. The meaning of that last characteristic is perhaps a bit unclear, but let's go ahead and see if we can use what we know to differentiate between answers.

(A) is about predicting for a whole based on a small sample—this is very different from what these investigators in the passage are doing (breaking a whole into parts in order to think about it), and (A) can be eliminated quickly. (B) is about piecing together a timeline of events based on documents—again, very different from what we have in our text. (C) and (D) are, like (A), examples in which samples are used to understand larger issues, and that is not what we have in our text.

That leaves us with only (E), and (E) is exactly what we are looking for. In (E), the engineer thinks about the soundness of the structure of the whole by thinking about individual components. He does not take the components to be a sample—it's simply the way he breaks down the whole. This is very similar to how the investigators mentioned in the second paragraph think about large systems, and therefore (E) is correct.

Comparative Passages

In June of 2007, the LSAT test writers instituted a change in the Reading Comprehension section: they replaced one of the four standard passages with a pair of related shorter passages (think of switching out a one-piece for a bikini). One of the four passages that you see on your exam won't be a passage at all but rather a pair of passages that have some sort of relationship to one another. Fortunately, these passage pairs have a lot in common with the passages we have already gotten used to, and test many of the same exact issues, so hopefully the work you've put in thus far will allow you to transition your skills to comparative passages smoothly.

In many of the characteristics of LSAT Reading Comprehension, you can see a strong link to the type of reading you will be doing as a lawyer, and this is especially true for comparative sets.

Please note that because comparative passages are a relatively recent addition to the LSAT, the ones we will be using, unlike the practice questions we use when studying other topics in this book, will be from very recent exams. For a full list of which comparative exams we will be practicing with, please see the appendix. If the comparative passages in this book overlap with those you planned on using for some other part of your preparation, such as practice exams, please adjust accordingly (all *LSAT Trainer* schedules have already been designed to accommodate the use of certain passages for practice in this book).

Let's think for a minute about the type of reading you will be doing as a lawyer. Typically, the underlying context includes two parties who disagree, or disagree in part, about some central issue. Those people will likely be experts in that situation and in their own field, but you will not be, and your task will be to see the underlying reasoning behind the conflict. You will read notes and letters that are meant to directly support one side or the other. You will also read information that wasn't written just for the case but nevertheless proves to be valuable as support for one side or the other, or simply as background that gives you better context to understand the situation that you are dealing with.

Comparative passage sets, in many ways, mimic the types of material you will have to read as a lawyer. The pair of passages will be related in some way to some central argument or issue. The passages may discuss that issue directly, or they may mention the issue in an indirect way. The passages can provide support for one side or the other, or simply provide background.

You have three things you need to accomplish before you go into the questions, and typically, especially for a more challenging comparative set, you will probably have to go deep into the read before you can get these three things done. In order to have success on the questions, you want to go into them with a clear sense of the central issue to which the two passages relate; you want to have a clear understanding of the exact relationship that these passages have toward that central issue; and finally, you want to have a sense of how the two passages relate to one another. The first of those tasks is the big one—normally, by the time you've developed a clear sense of the issue, it's become clear how the passages relate to that issue, and this is the key information that helps us see how the passages relate to one another.

General questions about the passage pair will touch on the three tasks discussed above. Specific questions will typically ask about commonalities and differences between the passages—they will ask about something mentioned in both passages or mentioned in one but not the other, or they will ask about what the authors are likely to agree on or disagree about. As always, a general understanding of the passages is of great help even on specific questions, for it will help you notice the attractive answers and help make the incorrect choices far more obviously so.

COMPARATIVE PASSAGES: THE POSSIBILITIES

The two passages in a comparative set will be related to some central issue, but the way in which they are related can be unpredictable. Figuring out what that central issue is and getting a clear sense of how the passages relate to it will put you in a great position to answer questions. Here are some possible ways the two passages could relate to the popcorn issue discussed earlier.

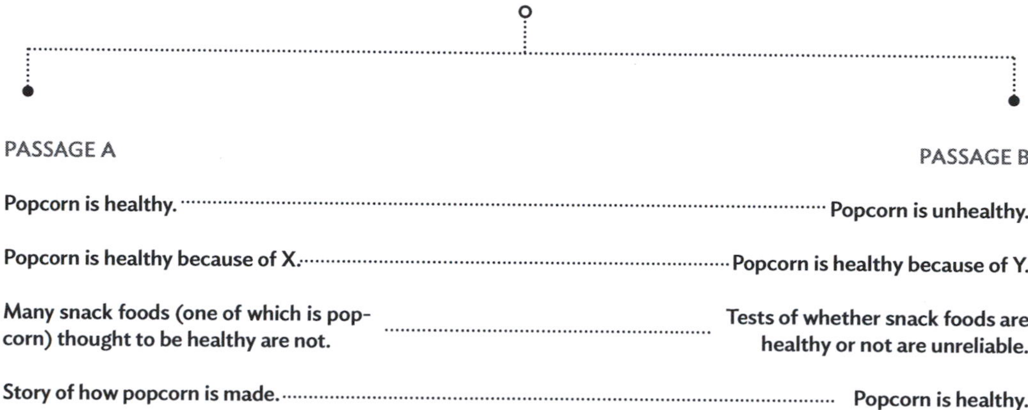

issue: is popcorn healthy?
PASSAGE A
PASSAGE B
Popcorn is healthy.
Popcorn is unhealthy.
Popcorn is healthy because of X.
Popcorn is healthy because of Y.
Many snack foods (one of which is popcorn) thought to be healthy are not.
Tests of whether snack foods are healthy or not are unreliable.
Story of how popcorn is made.
Popcorn is healthy.

YOUR PRIORITIES FOR COMPARATIVE PASSAGES

1. What Is the Central Issue?

The central issue at hand is the thing that relates the passages to one another and gives both passages their purpose—but keep in mind that you don't need to rush in trying to figure out what the central issue is. Be patient. Even figuring it out *after* reading both passages is fine. Still, you do want to consistently be thinking about what the central issue could be; the act of thinking about it will help you correctly organize the passages as you read.

2. How Are These Passages Related to It?

The second issue to consider is how the passages are related to this central issue. A passage may present us with reasons to support one opinion on an issue, or it may provide us with background. It may touch on the debatable issue directly or indirectly—perhaps in just one paragraph of a passage that is meant to be about something else, and so on. As we read and as we think about what the central issue is, we naturally want to think about how the individual passages relate to that central issue...

3. How Do They Relate to One Another?

...And in conjunction with that, we also want to think about how the two passages relate to one another. In the simplest case, the two passages could represent opposing sides of a debate. More likely, however, the relationship will be slightly more complicated. Perhaps the two passages will both support one side but in different ways, or perhaps one passage gives us the general understanding of an industry that is necessary to understand the opinion in the second passage.

Drill: Comparative Passage Set One

Directions: Here are two comparative passage sets for you to practice with. Try to read and solve both questions for each set in five minutes or less, but take more time if you need to.

Passage A

Evolutionary psychology has taught us to examine human behavior from the standpoint of the theory of evolution—to explain a given type of human behavior by examining how it contributes to the reproductive success of individuals exhibiting the behavior, and thereby to the proliferation of the genetic material responsible for causing that behavior. From an evolutionary standpoint, the problem of altruism is a thorny one: what accounts for the evolution of behavior in which an individual expends energy or other valuable resources promoting the welfare of another individual?

The answer probably lies in the psychological experiences of identification and empathy. Such experiences could have initially arisen in response to cues (like physical resemblance) that indicated the presence of shared genetic material in human ancestors. The psychological states provoked by these cues could have increased the chances of related individuals receiving assistance, thereby enhancing the survival and replication of genes influencing the capacity for identification and empathy. This would account, for example, for a mother's rushing to help her injured child; genes promoting their own self-propagation may thus operate through instinctive actions that appear unselfish.

Since human ancestors lived in small, kin-based groups, the application of altruistic mechanisms to the entire group would have promoted the propagation of the genes responsible for those mechanisms. Later, these mechanisms may have come to apply to humans who are not kin when communities grew larger. In this way, apparently altruistic mechanisms may have arisen within a genetically "selfish" system.

Passage B

Evolutionary psychology is a kind of conspiracy theory; that is, it explains behavior by imputing an interest (the proliferation of genes) that the agent of the behavior does not openly acknowledge, or indeed, is not even aware of. Thus, what seemed to be your unsurprising interest in your child's well-being turns out to be your genes' conspiracy to propagate themselves.

Such arguments can appear persuasive on the face of it. According to some evolutionary psychologists, an interest in the proliferation of genes explains monogamous families in animals whose offspring mature slowly. Human offspring mature slowly; and, at least in numerical terms, our species favors monogamous families. Evolutionary psychologists take this as evidence that humans form monogamous families because of our interest in propagating our genes. Are they right?

Maybe yes, maybe no; this kind of inference needs to be handled with great care. There are, most often, all sorts of interests that would explain any given behavior. What is needed to make it decisive that a particular interest explains a particular behavior is that the behavior would be reasonable only if one had that interest. But such cases are vanishingly rare: an interest in Y might explain doing X, but so too would an interest in doing X. A concern to propagate one's genes would explain promoting the welfare of one's children; but so too would an interest in the welfare of one's children. Not all of one's motives can be instrumental, after all; there must be some things that one cares for just for their own sakes.

Practice Test 64, Passage 3

15. According to passage B, which one of the following is an example of a human characteristic for which evolutionary psychologists propose a questionable explanation?

(A) the early human tendency to live in small communities
(B) the slow maturation of human offspring
(C) forming monogamous families
(D) misinterpreting the interests that motivate human actions
(E) caring for some things for their own sakes

17. How does the purpose of passage B relate to the content of passage A?

(A) The author of passage B seeks to support the main claims made in passage A by presenting additional arguments in support of those claims.
(B) The author of passage B criticizes the type of argument made in passage A by attempting to create an analogous argument with a conclusion that is clearly false.
(C) The author of passage B argues that the type of evidence used in passage A is often derived from inaccurate observation.
(D) The author of passage B maintains that the claims made in passage A are vacuous because no possible evidence could confirm or disconfirm them.
(E) The author of passage B seeks to undermine the type of argument made in passage A by suggesting that it relies on questionable reasoning.

Comparative Passage Set One Solutions

SUMMARY

Passage A

P1 - background—presents a way to think about behavior (from the standpoint of evolution) and presents a dilemma (difficulty of justifying altruism from evolutionary standpoint).

P2 - gives an explanation for this dilemma—**identification and empathy—we are empathetic to those most like us (family) to increase family survival.** The way it is presented (in the third person without reference to another individual), it is clear this is the author's opinion.

P3 - continues on with the train of thought to connections beyond family—we learned to practice altruism in order to promote survival of groups, communities, that would, in turn, promote the survival of our own genes.

Passage B

P1 - starts by giving a strong opinion about something the author takes for granted—the legitimacy of evolutionary psychology. It's clear this author doesn't buy it.

P2 - gives an example of a situation the author feels shows a problem with evolutionary psychology—a correlation between monogamous families and slow-maturing offspring is used by these psychologists to justify a causal claim.

P3 - concludes the author's thoughts and gives us his main point **—the correlation *could* show causation, but it doesn't have to, and truly proving such claims takes great care.**

COMMENTARY

The two passages are, in and of themselves, simple enough to understand; what is unusual here is the juxtaposition of them—it's a bit of a challenge to understand correctly exactly how they are related.

After finishing both passages and getting a bit of perspective, the relationship becomes clearer—the first passage uses evolutionary psychology to explain the process of empathy, and the second passage questions the authority of evolutionary psychology.

THE QUESTIONS

15. (C) is correct.

We know we are looking for an answer that is specifically mentioned in the second passage ("according to passage B"). Before going into the text, let's see if we can knock off a few wrong answers and find an attractive one or two. The small communities mentioned in (A) were in the first passage, but not the second, and we can eliminate (A). (B) is tempting—it is discussed in the second passage. Let's leave it. (C) is also mentioned, and (C) is in fact what the psychologists give an explanation for. (C) is likely correct, but let's keep going. (D) describes a characteristic of these psychologists, but not something for which the psychologists give an explanation, and we can eliminate (D). (E) is a topic of the first passage and not the second.

Let's look once again at (B)—slow maturation is mentioned, but that is not what the psychologists are trying to explain. Rather, it's the *reason* they give for trying to explain monogamous families. (C) is the correct answer.

17. (E) is correct.

We discussed in the commentary that we should always be considering the relationship between the two passages as we read, so we should always be ready to answer a question like this one. We know that the first passage uses evolutionary psychology to explain the process of empathy, and the second passage questions the authority of evolutionary psychology.

Based on that understanding, (A), (B), and (D) are all answers that are clearly false and can be quickly eliminated. Both (C) and (E) are attractive answers and need to be evaluated carefully. (C) states that the second passage argues against the "type of evidence" based on "inaccurate observation." This is not really reflective of the second passage, which doesn't argue against the way the evidence was observed, but rather the causal conclusion reached when it's brought together. (E) better reflects the relationship the second passage has to the first, and is therefore correct. The author of the first passage is using evolutionary necessity to spur his reasoning, and the author of the second passage questions that sort of reasoning.

Drill: Comparative Passage Set Two

Passage A

In Canadian and United States common law, blackmail is unique among major crimes: no one has yet adequately explained why it ought to be illegal. The heart of the problem—known as the blackmail paradox—is that two acts, each of which is legally permissible separately, become illegal when combined. If I threaten to expose a criminal act or embarrassing private information unless I am paid money, I have committed blackmail. But the right to free speech protects my right to make such a disclosure, and, in many circumstances, I have a legal right to seek money. So why is it illegal to combine them?

The lack of a successful theory of blackmail has damaging consequences: drawing a clear line between legal and illegal acts has proved impossible without one. Consequently, most blackmail statutes broadly prohibit behavior that no one really believes is criminal and rely on the good judgement of prosecutors not to enforce relevant statutes precisely as written.

It is possible, however, to articulate a coherent theory of blackmail. The key to the wrongness of the blackmail transaction is its triangular structure. The blackmailer obtains what he wants by using a supplementary leverage, leverage that depends upon a third party. The blackmail victim pays to avoid being harmed by persons other than the blackmailer. For example, when a blackmailer threatens to turn in a criminal unless paid money, the blackmailer is bargaining with the state's chip. Thus, blackmail is criminal because it involves the misuse of a third party for the blackmailer's own benefit.

Passage B

Classic Roman law had no special category for blackmail; it was not necessary. Roman jurists began their evaluation of specific categories of actions by considering whether the action caused harm, not by considering the legality or illegality of the action itself.

Their assumption—true enough, it seems—was that a victim of blackmail would be harmed if shameful but private information was revealed to the world. And if the shame would cause harm to the person's status or reputation, then prima facie the threatened act of revelation was unlawful. The burden of proof shifted to the possessor of the information: the party who had or threatened to reveal shameful facts had to show positive cause for the privilege of revealing the information.

In short, assertion of the truth of the shameful fact being revealed was not, in itself, sufficient to constitute a legal privilege. Granted, truth was not wholly irrelevant; false disclosures were granted even less protection than true ones. But even if it were true, the revelation of shameful information was protected only if the revelation had been made for a legitimate purpose and dealt with a matter that the public authorities had an interest in having revealed. Just because something shameful happened to be true did not mean it was lawful to reveal it.

Practice Test 65, Passage 3

14. Which one of the following is the central topic of each passage?

(A) why triangular transactions are illegal
(B) the role of the right to free speech in a given legal system
(C) how blackmail has been handled in a given legal system
(D) the history of blackmail as a legal concept
(E) why no good explanation of the illegality of blackmail exists.

17. Which one of the following is a statement that is true of blackmail under Canadian and U.S. common law, according to passage A, but that would not have been true of blackmail in the Roman legal context, according to passage B?

(A) It combines two acts that are each legal separately.
(B) It is a transaction with a triangular structure.
(C) The laws pertaining to it are meant to be enforced precisely as written.
(D) The blackmail victim pays to avoid being harmed by persons other than the blackmailer.
(E) Canadian and U.S. common law have no special category pertaining to blackmail.

Comparative Passage Set Two Solutions

SUMMARY

Passage A

P1 - presents the primary issue at hand—**blackmail is a difficult crime to define because it is the bringing together of two legal acts.**

P2 - discusses the consequences of not having a clear definition—the author finds the consequences damaging.

P3 - presents the author's main point about the issue—**there is, indeed, a clear way to define blackmail as a crime—blackmail is a crime because it misuses a third party for the blackmailer's benefit.**

Passage B

P1 - gives background on Roman law as it relates to blackmail—**Romans had no special law for blackmail because their concept of legality was based on the consequences of that action.** This turns out to be the central theme of the passage as a whole.

P2 - explains blackmail on these terms—blackmailer got in trouble if blackmail caused harm, and he would need to show just cause.

P3 - concludes the discussion of Roman law—truth was relevant to discussion of blackmail as a crime—but repeats that truth was not the determinant of legality (consequences and harm were).

COMMENTARY

The passages could both be part of a general study on blackmail laws. The first passage presents one way of defining blackmail law per the confines and conventions of current Canadian and United States law. The second passage presents another way of defining blackmail as a crime—one based on consequences for the person being blackmailed.

THE QUESTIONS

14. (C) is correct.

Most questions that accompany comparative passages will require us to compare or contrast the two passages. In this case, we need to look for a central topic for both—that is, we need to look for something they have in common.

Most commonly, wrong answers give us something mentioned in one passage but not the other. Knowing that, let's go in.

(A) is a topic of the first passage, but not the second. (B) is mentioned a bit in the first passage, but is a central topic of neither passage. (C) accurately describes the main topic of each passage—let's leave it for now. (D) is tempting—taken together, the two passages give us parts of the history; however, the question is asking us what each passage is doing by itself, and neither passage gives us a history (as in descriptions at various points in time) of blackmail. (E) is a topic for the first passage but not the second.

That leaves us with only (C)—let's confirm it by checking it against the text. The first passage discusses (primarily in the second paragraph) how blackmail has been handled in the United States and Canada. The second passage discusses how it was handled in Roman law. (C) is correct.

17. (A) is correct.

This question is asking us for something different about the two passages—in particular, for something that is true about Canadian and U.S. common law that isn't true under Roman law.

We know (A) is true for the first passage, but it's not as clear if we can get a clear sense of how these laws related to Roman law from the second passage. Still, it's a pretty good choice—let's leave it for now.

(B) is a general theory about what blackmail is, not what the laws are, and can be quickly eliminated. (C) is not true of the rules for either time, (D) would be true of blackmail throughout history and has nothing to do with specific laws, and we know that the Romans had no special category for blackmail law, so we can eliminate (E).

(B) through (E) are all clear eliminations, and that leaves us with only (A). Is it correct? Let's try to verify. We know for sure that under Canadian and United States law, (A) is true. Can we say that these two acts are not "legal" per Roman law?

Yes, we can. We are told at the end of the first paragraph that the Romans did not consider issues in terms of the legality or the illegality of the act itself. That means that the Romans did not think of the two acts as "legal" (or illegal).

How Did You Do?

It is not expected, at this point, for you to feel completely confident in your ability to get every question correct in the amount of time that you are allotted (though if you do, great). What is expected is that, hopefully, you feel that you now have a much clearer understanding of the design of LSAT passages, and that you have a good sense of what types of reading strategies align well with that design. With a clear sense of things, and an effective plan for improvement, you can and should expect your accuracy and confidence to increase as you gain more experience handling LSAT Reading Comprehension passages.

The Road Ahead

Assuming you are following one of the study schedules, and assuming you are working through this book in conjunction with one or more of the *10 Actuals* books, the next part of your process will be to get some experience, on your own, with some full LSAT passages and questions.

In the last few lessons, we have thoroughly discussed the design of LSAT Reading Comprehension passages, and the intentions of the test writers. We have also had a good deal of experience practicing effective reading strategies that align with the nature of the exam. Hopefully, the work you do on your own reinforces your understanding and helps you along in the process of habitualizing effective reading practices.

On the other hand, other than in the context of discussing specific passages, we have yet to take an in-depth look at the various types of challenges that different types of questions can present. We will do so in the next batch of Reading Comprehension lessons. Just as we have for Logical Reasoning and will for Logic Games, we will break down the specific tasks that particular questions present, and we will discuss strategies that are effective for handling the challenges. However, I expect (and I'm sure you expect) that you will be fine practicing questions before we discuss them, as Reading Comprehension questions tend to be written in a fairly obvious and clear-cut way.

I do want to encourage two habits, habits we will expand upon in later Reading Comprehension lessons.

For one, get in the habit of paying extra careful attention to the question stem, and do your best to read it as literally as you possibly can. Keep in mind that the test writers do not use wording casually in the question stem—questions are worded in very specific ways for very specific reasons. Therefore, if a question begins, "According to the passage..." you know that the answer must be something that is true according to the passage—that is, the right answer needs to be something *specifically mentioned* in the passage. If a question begins, "According to line X, it can be inferred that..." we know two things: the right answer must be connected to those particular lines (tempting wrong answers might be connected to other nearby lines of text), and we know that the right answer is something to be inferred—that is, the right answer will *not* be specifically mentioned.

Additionally, just as in Logical Reasoning, get in the habit of arriving at the right answer by eliminating incorrect choices. By finding reasons why answers are wrong and reasons why an answer is right, you can be far more consistent than someone else who simply seeks a right answer—the tempting wrong answer will have an extra hoop to jump through in order to fool you. Furthermore, though it may seem counter-intuitive, habitually taking the time to eliminate wrong choices, while seemingly adding an extra step, makes you a faster overall test taker. No matter what, you have to look at every answer choice if you want to achieve a high level of accuracy, and it turns out that it's far easier, faster, and more accurate, in general, to think about why these answers are wrong, rather than why they are right. By first focusing on eliminating wrong choices, you will spend less time debating between two or three answers that sound attractive.

Basic Timing Strategies

After this lesson, most of you are going to be spending some time working on a couple of full Reading Comprehension sections. So this is a good time to pause for a minute to discuss general Reading Comprehension timing strategies. We can think about timing from a variety of perspectives. In this lesson, we'll discuss the pace necessary to complete all questions in the allotted time, the primary factors that influence our timing, and also the strategies we can employ if we run short on time and need to make timing decisions. We'll add on to our discussion of timing in the final lessons.

Twenty-Seven Questions in Thirty-Five Minutes

Top scorers in the Reading Comprehension section are consistently able to finish all questions—it's hard enough to get a perfect or near perfect score without leaving possible points on the table. Let's talk about the specific characteristics common to these effective and efficient test takers.

In general, top scorers typically read passages in about two to three minutes, depending on the length and difficulty of the passage. In order to finish a typical passage in this time, most people need to read at a pace that would allow them to get through a passage—if they read it straight through without pausing—in about 1:30 or 2 minutes. You can try the exercise now to see what your natural non-pause pace is. Reading at that pace allows for up to a minute or so to pause at various points and reread when necessary, and to reflect on reasoning structure. Keep in mind that this is an extremely broad guideline, and when it comes to reading pace, there is great variation even among high scorers. I've seen some high scorers take up to 4 or even 4:30 per passage and still have no trouble with time (these folks are able to go through questions very quickly, and seem to have short-term memories that are far more capable than my own). I've also witnessed some exceptional students who are able to finish passages in less than two minutes without sacrificing any retention. Bring together our guidelines, your own reading style, and your experience with actual LSAT passages and work toward developing an ideal that works best for you.

Reading at this pace leaves you with a little bit less than one minute per question, and that's more than enough, in large part because if you read well, there should be a significant number of questions that take very little time. Questions that ask about the passage as a whole, as well as questions that ask about an easily identifiable and understandable detail, are often questions that can go very quickly. Other questions, by their design, are meant to take longer, and you shouldn't hold yourself to a universal timing standard for every question. However, you should develop and habitualize a timing limit—the most time you will spend on any one question. Try setting that limit at 2:00 for now, and try moving it up or down depending on how many questions push you to that limit and how that impacts your overall timing.

How Timing Improves

Generally speaking, by far the most important and significant way to improve your Reading Comprehension timing is to become more effective and more accurate with each of the skills that Reading Comprehension questions require of us. In order to answer a typical question correctly, we need to have correctly understood the main points and the reasoning structure of the passage, we need to have understood the question stem and used it properly to guide our process, we need to be able to anticipate characteristics of the right answer, we need to be able to confidently and accurately eliminate wrong answers, and we need to be able to confirm the right choice. The way this test is designed, the better you get at each of those steps, the faster you will get as well. You want your improving skill set to be the driving force behind your timing improvement, and if you are having significant struggles with your timing, it can be helpful to think about the steps in your process that are holding you back.

In addition to getting faster at the steps necessary to arrive at a right answer, we can also improve our timing by cutting out steps that are unnecessary for arriving at right answers. Typically, the biggest waste of time during the reading of a passage occurs when we get stuck on a part we cannot understand—often one involving a lot of technical details—and even though we understand the role the part plays, we end up reading the section again and again because we *want* to understand. This is commonly time wasted. During the questions, the most wasteful time is that spent on *missed* questions (because that time doesn't result in points). Unless you have time to spare, no question is worth three minutes of your time, and if you are not careful, it's very easy to over-invest in one question. Work on improving your timing by not getting snagged in the passage, and by learning to let go of tough questions after a certain cutoff.[1]

1. We'll discuss this in greater detail later but, for now, one bit of advice is to think about cutoffs in terms of processes, rather than actual time. During the pressure of the actual exam, it's very difficult to keep accurate track of time—it's very difficult to be sure if a minute and a half or two minutes has passed. It's also a waste of energy and a distraction to keep checking your watch during a question. A better way to set a cutoff is to think of it in terms of your problem-solving steps. One way to set a cut-off, perhaps, is "Okay, if I get stuck on a question, I'll give myself one more re-read of the stem, and one more run through the answers. After that, if I don't have a clear choice, I'll pick the best available and move on." Make sure to use your practice time to habitualize such strategies so that by test day you can react to challenges correctly without having to consciously think about which strategies you should employ.

Making Tough Timing Decisions

Even if we learn everything there is to learn about LSAT Reading Comprehension, and even if we do everything we can to habitualize effective problem-solving processes, we may still find ourselves not being able to finish all the questions in the allotted time. In fact, this is true for a majority of test takers. With that in mind, let's talk a bit about how to make tough timing decisions.

If you are okay with missing six or seven questions on the Reading Comprehension section, and find that finishing all four passages in thirty-five minutes is next to impossible, you might be tempted to put all of your energy into just three of the passages, and to skip one passage.[2] I strongly recommend against using such strategies. If you are strong enough to go near perfect on three passages, you should be strong enough to get to four passages. If you are not strong enough to get to four passages, you won't be strong enough to go nearly perfect on the three you do attempt. The best you can hope for with such a strategy is a -9 or -10, and it's very difficult to get a top score with that many misses in any one section.

2. Some preparation systems even endorse such strategies.

One reason the above is such a bad strategy is that questions, rather than passages, most directly determine difficulty. Easier passages commonly have one or two tough questions, and even the toughest passage will have a few questions that can be answered easily. Thus, you don't want to avoid entire passages—instead, if you need to cut time, you want to avoid spending time on the toughest questions. If you find yourself not being able to finish the section in 35 minutes, give yourself a certain number of questions—say four per the section—which you will read, tell yourself, "Okay, this one is too tough," then spend about 15 more seconds taking an educated guess. These four questions are, otherwise, likely ones that you would have spent a significant amount of time on, up to 8 of your 35 minutes perhaps, with the likelihood of very little return for that time invested. Cutting time on these questions is probably the wisest cut you can make, if cuts are necessary.

If you are currently still at the beginning of your Reading Comprehension studying, I strongly encourage you to hold off, for now, on adopting the time-cutting strategy mentioned above. Trust in the fact that improved understanding and skill will naturally result in faster times. If you do end up needing to cut time on some questions, you can work on such strategies later on in your study process.

Where's "the official LSAT Trainer RC notation system"?

There isn't one! Here are the three main reasons why:

1. LSAT Reading Comprehension is not "solved" through notation—unlike with Logic Games, no amount of notation will necessarily make it markedly easier for you to anticipate or answer Reading Comprehension questions.

2. I personally notate very little. I may put a little line next to the main points for a passage, but typically I won't notate anything at all. I would feel disingenuous recommending something I don't do myself.

3. What's most important is not how you notate, but what you notate. All of us have certain notational systems that we have developed and are most comfortable using. Your notations will be most effective if you use what you are used to.

Underlining, marking, or taking small notes on the side as we read can all be very effective ways to enhance our reading experience and our understanding—the act of holding a pencil in our hands and doing something active while reading tends to make almost all of us better readers. So, by all means, please do notate, and don't take this as a vote against notation. But do make sure you have a correct sense of what it is you are meant to get out of your notation. You want to use your marks to emphasize the main points, and the organization of the passage relative to those main points. You can use any notational system that you feel comfortable with to get this done.

I encourage you to try out a few different methods of notation, but make sure you don't let the focus on notation take away from the focus on the passage itself. More specifically, I want to strongly urge you not to try to memorize a very specific and nuanced notational system—for example, one in which you use different types of symbols for main point, opinion, supporting detail, definition, and so on. Any such system will naturally encourage you to focus on the trees, rather than the forest—since our job during the initial read is to see the big picture, these types of systems can be detrimental. As long as you have a strong mental sense of what the main points are and where they are, it's fairly simple to track the organization of any LSAT passage mentally, or by using very simple notations.

26 LOGIC GAMES answering questions

In our first batch of Logic Games lessons, we focused on understanding game scenarios and developing diagramming skills. The first two to three minutes of a game—the time you spend visualizing a situation and representing it—are crucial for your eventual success with a game, and your ability to diagram is ultimately what will determine, for most of you, whether or not you feel control over games.

Still, the majority of the time you spend during a games section will be spent on the process of answering specific questions. And of course, whether you are able to answer questions correctly or not will be, practically speaking, what actually determines your score. In this batch of lessons, we'll focus on integrating your diagram and your diagramming skills into the problem-solving process.

There are three things we need to do to consistently get Logic Games questions right. First, we need to set up a clear, correct, and usable understanding of the situation the game presents. Next, we need to read question stems correctly—that is, we need to be able to figure out from them exactly what our job is. Finally, we need to apply effective strategies in order to perform that job efficiently. We've talked about that first key quite a bit—now we'll focus on the remaining two steps.

For most question stems, there are two main issues to consider: "Is there new information to incorporate?" and "What will the split be between right and wrong answers?"

Reading the Question Stem

Do not dismiss the importance of the question stem. You only have about a minute to answer each question, and that minute goes by very fast when you are under pressure. The question stem presents the instructions for exactly what you should be thinking about during that time. So treat that question stem with utmost care.

For most Logic Games question stems, there are two main issues to consider: "Is there new information to incorporate?" and "What will the split be between right and wrong answers?" For just a few questions per games section—perhaps two or three total—there is a third consideration: "What are the various possibilities for this part of the game being discussed?" We'll focus on the two main issues in this lesson, and cover the third, less common, issue in the next lesson.

New Information

Many questions begin by giving you additional information about a game, and almost all such questions begin, "If..." The common terminology is that these are *conditional* questions, for they give us a new *condition* to deal with. *(Continued on page 372.)*

THE TABLE OF

common notations

F is assigned to X	X will be occupied	X will not be occupied	F or G is assigned to X	F is assigned to X or Y	A boy is assigned to X
F / X	◯ / X	⁄ / X	F/G / X	F/ / X /F / Y	b / X
F is before G F — G G is after F	F is immediately before G FG G is immediately after F	F is at least two spots ahead of G F ___ ...G G is at least two spots after F	F is after G but before H G — F — H	F is exactly two spots ahead of G F ___ G G is exactly two spots after F	F is immediately before a boy F _b
There is at least one spot between F and G F ___ ...G	F is right before or right after G F G	F is before both G and H F < G, H	F is after both G and H G, H > F	There is exactly one spot between F and G F ___ G	F is exactly two spots ahead of a boy F ___ _b
The same element is assigned to X and Y □ □ / X Y	Different elements are assigned to X and Y □ △ / X Y	F, G, and H occupy X, Y, and Z (F, G, H) / X Y Z	F and G are grouped together [F / G]	F is grouped with a boy [F / _b]	F is a boy Fb

(+)

not	If...,then...	or	and	free agents	multiple diagrams
⁄	→	or	+	F G H K (L)	— — — — — — — — — — — —
Most of the rules above can be converted into "not" rules by adding a cross-out.	Most of the rules above can be combined into conditional rules.	Most of the rules above can be combined into compound rules through the use of "or" or "and."		If all but one or two of your elements are mentioned in the rules, it can be helpful to track the unrestricted elements.	Once in a while—most commonly in a game defined by a complex *or* rule—it will be helpful to work off of more than one diagram.

HERE'S a reprint of the table of common notations originally presented in Lesson 15. Let's do a quick review of the key characteristics that define these rules:

The most basic rules—rules of **assignment**—have to do with how particular positions will be filled. We can be told that a specific element will fill a specific position, that a particular position will not be filled, and so on.

The most common and varied rules, the rules of **order**, relate elements to one another in the context of an ordering game. These rules can be specific, or they can be general. Either two or three of the games you see on your exam will be ordering games, and understanding and utilizing ordering rules well will be the key to your success on those games.

Grouping is a very common game characteristic—appearing in just a little less than half of all games—and though the inferences related to grouping can be just as complicated as those relating to any other issue, methods of notating grouping rules are fairly simple. Unless game scenarios specifically dictate otherwise, we want to represent all grouping issues vertically, and doing so consistently can make visualizing grouping far easier.

The test writers use **subsets** to add an additional layer of complexity to common ordering and grouping games. Subsets can apply to elements, positions, or both. By always using lowercase letters (or numbers) for subset issues, we can easily just adapt our normal notations to accommodate subset rules.

When the number of elements doesn't equal the number of positions, or when games involve subsets, we can run into **numbers issues**. For these games, we have to think about whether elements will be included or not, or whether slots will be filled or not, and simple notations can help us do that.

Finally, the rules of a game can also be defined by the form of the rule itself.

The rule can be **conditional**—that is, it can be a rule that only applies in particular situations. These conditional rules can be some of the most tempting to misunderstand or misuse—accuracy and comfort with your notation systems are essential here.

Or, the rule can give us more complex possibilities through the use of **and** and **or.** These rules can also be more challenging than normal to understand, but the benefit is often great. Because these rules commonly include more than two elements, or because these rules commonly create a clean "divide" between the various possibilities for a particular game, these rules are commonly the most important rules for the games in which they appear.

More on Conditional Rules

Nearly any pair of rules mentioned on the left can be turned into a conditional rule—that is, a rule that is triggered by something else happening. For all conditional rules, the key to success is to understand the rule correctly, and to understand ways it can be utilized, and (perhaps more importantly) ways it cannot. For every conditional rule, you must account for the contrapositive. You can choose to do so in your head or on paper, based on the game, but you should always put it down on paper if there is a chance it will be forgotten or mistaken. Again, correctly answering questions will likely require a careful understanding of any conditional rules, and many incorrect answers are built off of incorrect understandings of conditional rules.

We use a simple arrow to represent all conditional rules. Here is the basic notation along with the common wordings you will see for the rule. Below that is an example of a biconditional—a rule that is triggered in both directions.

"M → P" contrapositive "- P → - M"

If M, then P.
Any with M must have P.
All with M have P.
No Ms are without Ps.
You can't have M unless you have P.
M only if P.

"M ↔ P" contrapositive "- P ↔ - M"

M if and only if P.

More on the Meaning of Or

Rules can be brought together through the use of "and" and "or." The meaning of "and" is simple and clear, but the meaning of "or" is a bit more complex.

Keep in mind that unless there are other considerations, the word "or" does not, in and of itself, exclude the possibility of "both." Thus, if a rule states "F or G will be assigned to the management team," it is entirely possible that both F *and* G can be assigned to the management team.

Also keep in mind that in many instances there are natural restrictions that prevent "or" from including "both." If we are told each person can have one locker, then told F can have either "locker 2 or locker 3," we will know that F getting both is not a possibility.

When given new information, it's crucial that you use it as the starting point of your thought process. For all conditional questions, the information presented in the question stem will *always*[1] lead us to figure out more about a game, and—here's the important thing to know—these additional inferences will be what determines the right answer, and, generally, these inferences, or rather mistaken versions of these inferences, are what determines the wrong answers.[2] Put simply, the inferences you make based on the conditional information are what will determine right and wrong.

If you have a strong understanding of a game, it should generally be somewhat routine for you to work off of conditions—they are just an additional rule to fit into your understanding of the game. Often, especially for games that give us few up-front inferences, the information in the condition works as a "trigger" that sets off a chain of consequences, and I'm sure you've experienced that in some of the questions you've already worked on. When you are not able to come up with inferences, or when it seems the information in the condition doesn't mesh correctly with your diagram, it's generally a sign that there is a problem with your initial understanding of that game.[3]

The Split between Right and Wrong Answers

As we've discussed in previous lessons, almost all questions differentiate right answers from wrong ones in terms of that which must be certain versus that which is uncertain or unknown. Let's discuss this idea in a bit more depth.

When we first started talking about games, we talked about the fact that games are, in large part, designed to test your logical reasoning skills—specifically, your ability to see how information comes together (X is before Y and Y is before Z, therefore X is before Z) and your ability to recognize when it doesn't (X is before Z and Y is before Z tells us little about the relationship between X and Y). It makes sense, then, that answer choices would be differentiated in terms of that which is known for sure (that which must be true or must be false) versus what is left uncertain (that which could be true or false).

There are four different ways we will be asked to split up that which *must* be from that which mustn't, and they are presented in the table on the opposite page. Note that the chart represents general tendencies. Occasionally, there is a "must be false" wrong answer to a "must be true" question, or something else similar—this tends to happen when there is not enough uncertainty left in the game to create four viable "could be true or false" wrong answers.

In previous lessons, we've touched on the idea that for certain Logic Games questions, we want to go through the elimination process to arrive at a right answer, and for others, we want to simply search for a right answer. This is a very important strategy, and it's critical that you understand the logic behind it and the consequences of implementing it successfully.

In general, when we think about games, it's best to think about them in terms of what we know for sure—this is easier than trying to simultaneously keep in mind both what we know for sure *and* what we don't. Our diagrams are specifically designed for the purpose of emphasizing that which we know for sure—we only put down what we know for sure, and we leave off the information we don't know about (that's why we don't put conditional rules directly into our diagram). And our diagrams are our key weapon for organizing our thoughts and attacking questions. All that is to say we are much better

1. It doesn't have to be this way. If the test writers wanted to be cruel, they could sometimes include questions that give us new information, but don't actually require it to arrive at the right answer. They do not write questions that work this way. For all conditional questions, the right answer will be something we figure out based on the new condition.

2. Sometimes, a condition will not lead to enough inferences for the test writers to write four quality wrong choices based off of mistaking those inferences. In those cases wrong answers will be wrong based on what we already know about a game before seeing the condition.

3. You should be on the lookout for such markers of trouble—generally you'll know within two or three questions if something is wrong with your initial understanding of the game/diagram. In these cases, stop immediately and go back and check your understanding by re-reading the stimulus, then matching your notations to the written rules. We'll discuss such strategies in greater detail in later lessons.

equipped to think about what *must be* than what *could be*, and prioritizing what *must be* is the best approach for differentiating between answer choices.

Let's imagine a question that asks us which of five answer choices "must be false." What do we know of the right answer? It *must be* false. When we check it against our diagram, it should reveal itself with certainty. What do we know of the wrong answers? They *could be* true (or false)—they will be answers about which we don't know enough to say for sure. When we check them against the diagram, they will leave things uncertain. In this case, we want to focus on identifying the one right answer that must be false, rather than going through an elimination process. Looking out for the one answer we know something about is the most direct way to solve the question.

We are much better equipped to think about what must be than what could be, and prioritizing what must be is the best approach for differentiating between answer choices

The alternative would be to arrive at the right answer by eliminating wrong ones—by confirming that four answers could be true. This would take significantly more time and, because it requires more work, opens you up to errors. If worst comes to worst (that is, you can't find the answer that must be false), you may have to resort to this, but you don't want to do this work unless you have to do.

Now let's imagine a question that asks us which of five answer choices "could be true." What do we know about the right answer? It's something that *could be* true (or false). What do we know about the wrong answers? They *must* all be false. We should be able to see so absolutely with our diagram. In this situation, it will typically be much easier to eliminate answers that must be false, and it will typically take a bit more time and work to see that an answer is correct. So, in this situation, we typically want to arrive at the correct answer by eliminating incorrect answers.

Below are the four different ways test writers can ask us to differentiate between that which must be and that which could be, along with ideal strategies for attacking such questions. Of all the habits for Logic Games, there are none more important than that of correctly searching for the right answer, or choosing to use an elimination process, based on the question stem. If you can develop the correct habits for attacking questions, you will be able to solve questions far more quickly and accurately.

Search for the Right Answer or Eliminate Wrong Ones?

Question Stem	Same As	Wrong Answers	Primary Strategy	Backup Strategy
...must be true?	...could be false EXCEPT:	could be true or false	Search for the right answer	See if answers could be false
...could be true?	...must be false EXCEPT:	must be false	Eliminate wrong choices	See if answer could be true
...could be false? (rare)	...must be true EXCEPT:	must be true	Eliminate wrong choices	See if answer could be false
...must be false?	...could be true EXCEPT:	could be true or false	Search for the right answer	See if answers could be true

Note that for all question stems, the primary strategy is based on what must be, and the secondary strategy is based on what could be. Also note that these are general strategies—in certain situations, it might make more sense to reverse primary and secondary strategies. The most common situation in which this will be true is games that are extremely simple, or games that allow us to "solve" a great deal before evaluating answers. We can test whether answers could be true or could be false by using hypotheticals. Hopefully you won't have to use them too often, but sometimes they are necessary and helpful.

Must be True or False Drill

Directions: On these two pages are scenarios and rules for two fairly straightforward games that appeared on past LSATs. We're going to use these two games to practice two things: working off of conditions in the question stem, and making decisions about what must be true, must be false, or could be either true or false. For each game, first draw out your diagram and check it against the solutions. It's imperative you do so, for working off of an incorrect diagram will significantly dilute the benefit of the exercise. Below the scenario and rules is a set of possibilities that you are meant to evaluate. For each one, write a **"T"** if the possibility is one that **must be true.** Write an **"F"** if it's a possibility that **must be false. If it's something that could be true or false, leave it blank.** The second and third sets begin with conditions—redraw your diagram for these sets, and make sure to check your diagram against the solutions before using your new diagram to evaluate the possibilities.

On a Tuesday, an accountant has exactly seven bills—numbered 1 through 7—to pay by Thursday of the same week. The accountant will pay each bill only once according to the following rules:

Either three or four of the seven bills must be paid on Wednesday, the rest on Thursday.
Bill 1 cannot be paid on the same day as bill 5.
Bill 2 must be paid on Thursday.
Bill 4 must be paid on the same day as bill 7.
If bill 6 is paid on Wednesday, bill 7 must be paid on Thursday.

SET 1

#	Possibility	T/F
1	6 is paid on Thursday	
2	3 is paid on Thursday	
3	Both 6 and 7 are paid on Thursday	
4	Both 3 and 4 are paid on Thursday	
5	Both 4 and 5 are paid on Weds	
6	Both 4 and 6 are paid on Weds	
7	Either 6 or 7 is paid on Weds	
8	Either 3 or 4 is paid on Thursday	
9	2 and 4 are paid on different days	
10	6 and 7 are paid on the same day	

SET 2

condition: If he pays 3 on Thursday...

#	Possibility	T/F
1	4 is paid on Wednesday	
2	5 is paid on Thursday	
3	6 is paid on Thursday	
4	Exactly three bills are paid on Weds	
5	3 and 6 are paid on the same day	
6	1 and 4 are paid on different days	
7	Exactly three bills are paid on Thurs	
8	7 is paid on Thursday	
9	3 and 5 are paid on the same day	
10	5 and 7 are paid on different days	

SET 3

condition: He pays 5 and 7 on the same day...

#	Possibility	T/F
1	3 is paid on Wednesday	
2	4 and 1 are paid on the same day	
3	5 and 2 are paid on the same day	
4	2 and 3 are paid on different days	
5	4 and 5 are paid on different days	
6	4 is paid on Wednesday	
7	Both 3 and 4 are paid on Thursday	
8	6 and 1 are paid on the same day	
9	Both 3 and 5 are paid on Weds	
10	Both 5 and 6 are paid on Weds	

Must be True or False Drill

A college dean will present seven awards for outstanding language research. The awards—one for French, one for German, one for Hebrew, one for Japanese, one for Korean, one for Latin, and one for Swahili—must be presented consecutively, one at a time, in conformity with the following constraints:

The German award is not presented first.
The Hebrew award is presented at some time before the Korean award is presented.
The Latin award is presented at some time before the Japanese award is presented.
The French award is presented either immediately before or immediately after the Hebrew award is presented.
The Korean award is presented either immediately before or immediately after the Latin award is presented.

SET 1

#	Possibility	T/F
1	G is presented before F	
2	F is presented fourth	
3	J is presented fourth	
4	Neither F nor H is presented third	
5	The latest H can go is fourth	
6	Either F or H is presented 2nd or 3rd	
7	G is presented third	
8	L is presented third	
9	G is presented after S but before K	
10	L is presented before F	

SET 2
condition: If F is presented third...

#	Possibility	T/F
1	S is presented before G	
2	L is presented before S	
3	G is presented fifth	
4	G is presented second	
5	K is presented sixth	
6	S is presented second	
7	Earliest J can be presented is sixth	
8	L is presented before G	
9	S is presented first	
10	L is presented fourth	

SET 3
condition: If S is presented last...

#	Possibility	T/F
1	F is presented second	
2	G is presented before J	
3	J is presented before G	
4	Either K or L is presented fourth	
5	G is presented second	
6	K is presented sixth	
7	L is presented third	
8	Either G or J is presented sixth	
9	H is presented third	
10	G is presented after K	

Must be True or False Solutions

On a Tuesday, an accountant has exactly seven bills—numbered 1 through 7—to pay by Thursday of the same week. The accountant will pay each bill only once according to the following rules:

Either three or four of the seven bills must be paid on Wednesday, the rest on Thursday.
Bill 1 cannot be paid on the same day as bill 5.
Bill 2 must be paid on Thursday.
Bill 4 must be paid on the same day as bill 7.
If bill 6 is paid on Wednesday, bill 7 must be paid on Thursday.

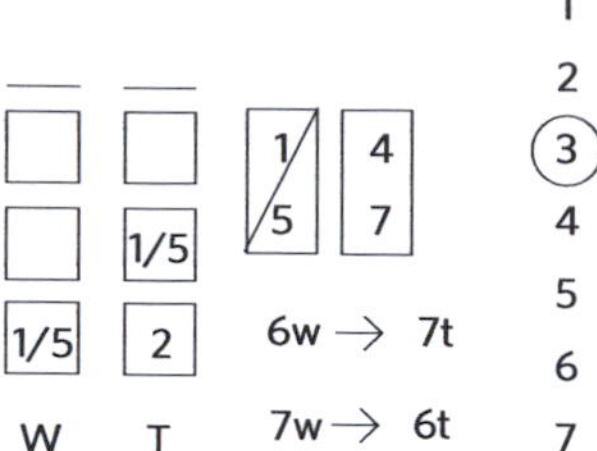

For a more detailed explanation, see page 381. Note that we could have splintered it into two diagrams based on where the 4 and 7 go, and that would certainly make solving the questions a bit easier. However, because the situation is fairly simple to understand, I didn't feel it necessary to do that here.

SET 1

#	Possibility	T/F
1	6 is paid on Thursday	
2	3 is paid on Thursday	
3	Both 6 and 7 are paid on Thursday	F
4	Both 3 and 4 are paid on Thursday	F
5	Both 4 and 5 are paid on Weds	
6	Both 4 and 6 are paid on Weds	F
7	Either 6 or 7 is paid on Weds	T
8	Either 3 or 4 is paid on Thursday	
9	2 and 4 are paid on different days	
10	6 and 7 are paid on the same day	F

SET 2
condition: If he pays 3 on Thursday...

#	Possibility	T/F
1	4 is paid on Wednesday	T
2	5 is paid on Thursday	
3	6 is paid on Thursday	T
4	Exactly three bills are paid on Weds	T
5	3 and 6 are paid on the same day	T
6	1 and 4 are paid on different days	
7	Exactly three bills are paid on Thurs	F
8	7 is paid on Thursday	F
9	3 and 5 are paid on the same day	
10	5 and 7 are paid on different days	

If 3 is paid on Thursday, 4 and 7 must be paid on Wednesday, and that means 6 must be paid on Thursday.

SET 3
condition: He pays 5 and 7 on the same day...

#	Possibility	T/F
1	3 is paid on Wednesday	
2	4 and 1 are paid on the same day	F
3	5 and 2 are paid on the same day	
4	2 and 3 are paid on different days	
5	4 and 5 are paid on different days	F
6	4 is paid on Wednesday	
7	Both 3 and 4 are paid on Thursday	F
8	6 and 1 are paid on the same day	T
9	Both 3 and 5 are paid on Weds	
10	Both 5 and 6 are paid on Weds	F

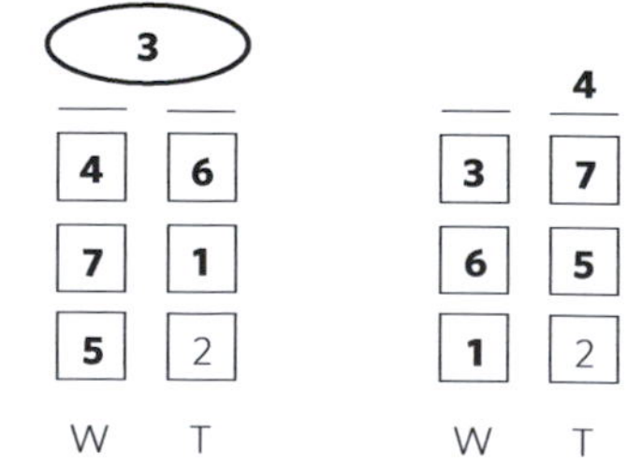

The 5 and 7 can go together either on Wednesday or Thursday, so it makes sense to draw two diagrams for the two possibilities.

If 5 and 7 go on Wednesday, 4 must go on Wednesday, and 1 and 6 on Thursday. If 5 and 7 go on Thursday, 4 must go on Thursday, and the remaining elements Wednesday.

Must be True or False Solutions

A college dean will present seven awards for outstanding language research. The awards—one for French, one for German, one for Hebrew, one for Japanese, one for Korean, one for Latin, and one for Swahili—must be presented consecutively, one at a time, in conformity with the following constraints:

The German award is not presented first.
The Hebrew award is presented at some time before the Korean award is presented.
The Latin award is presented at some time before the Japanese award is presented.
The French award is presented either immediately before or immediately after the Hebrew award is presented.
The Korean award is presented either immediately before or immediately after the Latin award is presented.

_ _ _ _ _ _ _
~~G~~

FH — KL — J

F
G
H
J
K
L
(S)

For a more detailed explanation,
see page 382.

SET 1

#	Possibility	T/F
1	G is presented before F	
2	F is presented fourth	
3	J is presented fourth	F
4	Neither F nor H is presented third	
5	The latest H can go is fourth	T
6	Either F or H is presented 2nd or 3rd	T
7	G is presented third	
8	L is presented third	
9	G is presented after S but before K	
10	L is presented before F	F

SET 2
condition: If F is presented third...

#	Possibility	T/F
1	S is presented before G	T
2	L is presented before S	F
3	G is presented fifth	F
4	G is presented second	
5	K is presented sixth	
6	S is presented second	F
7	Earliest J can be presented is sixth	T
8	L is presented before G	
9	S is presented first	T
10	L is presented fourth	

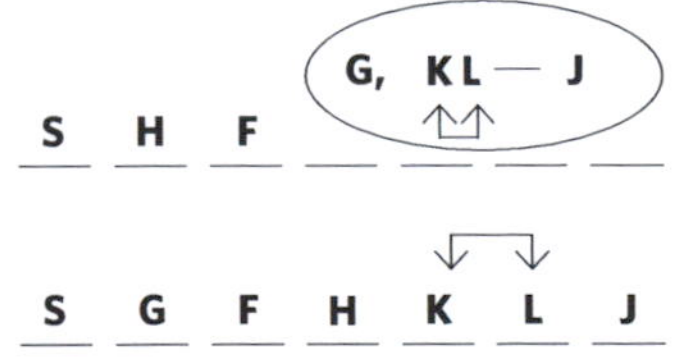

If F is presented third, H can be presented second or fourth, and it makes sense to try out both of these possibilities.

If H is second, K,L—J must go after it. Since G can't go first, that leaves S for first. G, K, L, and J occupy 4-7 with some severe restrictions.

If H is fourth, K,L—J must go after it. That leaves S and G for first and second. Since G can't go first, S must go first and G second. Notice S ends up first in both situations.

SET 3
condition: If S is presented last...

#	Possibility	T/F
1	F is presented second	
2	G is presented before J	
3	J is presented before G	
4	Either K or L is presented fourth	T
5	G is presented second	F
6	K is presented sixth	F
7	L is presented third	
8	Either G or J is presented sixth	T
9	H is presented third	F
10	G is presented after K	

If S is presented seventh, and G can't be presented first, F or H must be presented first. That means F or H must be second. G, and the K,L—J cluster must occupy positions 3-6, with some severe restrictions.

Seating Priorities

Imagine that you are the manager of a tiny, exclusive sushi restaurant. The restaurant seats just eight—most of the seats are clustered together, but some are set apart awkwardly. Each customer spends hundreds of dollars, and your job is to make sure the customers are seated in such a way as to maximize the number of people who can be served throughout the night.

Most customers come as couples, but some come in clusters of three or four. Others come alone. Some customers have requests, such as wanting to sit next to the sushi chef, or wanting to sit away from the bathroom. Others are fine sitting anywhere.

In trying to figure out where to place everyone, what are your priorities? It makes sense to prioritize the large groups (because they fill up a lot of seats and because everyone else has to fit around them) and to prioritize those awkward seats that are set apart. Who would you end up placing last? The customers who come alone and are happy to sit anywhere.

Over and over again, games questions present challenges that are very similar to the one that the restaurant manager faces: just as sushi restaurants tend to have seats in a row at the bar, or in groupings at tables, games present positions in an order, or in groupings. Our job is to figure out how to arrange the elements into these positions.

In Lessons 10-15, we stressed the importance of developing a diagramming system that you feel *comfortable* with—the reason is that, in order to answer questions, you will have to use your diagram over and over again to think about the various ways that the elements can be arranged.

In doing so, it's helpful to have some of the same instincts that the restaurant manager must have: you always want to prioritize the large groups ("clusters") and the positions that are very limited (what we will discuss as "the pinch"). Generally, by dealing with the large group first, you make the rest of the work you have in a question far easier on yourself, and generally, when you recognize a "pinch," that pinch will be directly relevant to the correct answer.

You also want to take note of those customers that come alone and can sit anywhere, or in game terms, the elements that don't have any rules or restrictions. You generally want to place these elements last, and it's always helpful for you to know that they can go anywhere. Below are examples that illustrate clusters and pinches.

Sample Clusters

Imagine we are placing six elements in an order, and we have the following combination of positions and rules:

__ __ __ __ __ __
~~L~~

LM — R

Notice how limited we are in terms of where we can place the LM—R cluster. Also notice that once it gets placed, there will be only three open spaces remaining for you to consider.

Imagine we are splitting eight elements into two different groups:

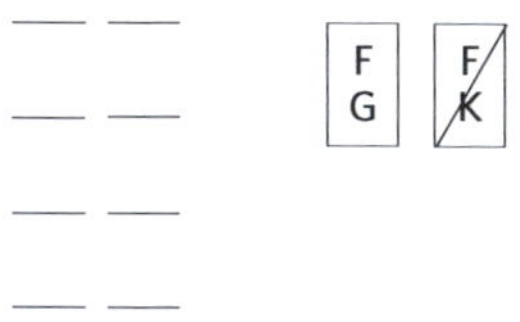

__ __
__ __
__ __
__ __

| F
G | F / K (crossed out) |

Notice how even a two-element cluster can be fairly significant, especially when it is related to other rules. We know that F and G will always be together, and that K must be on the opposite team from them. That is likely to be critical information for the questions.

Sample Pinches

Imagine we are in the middle of playing an ordering game, and have the following board and rules:

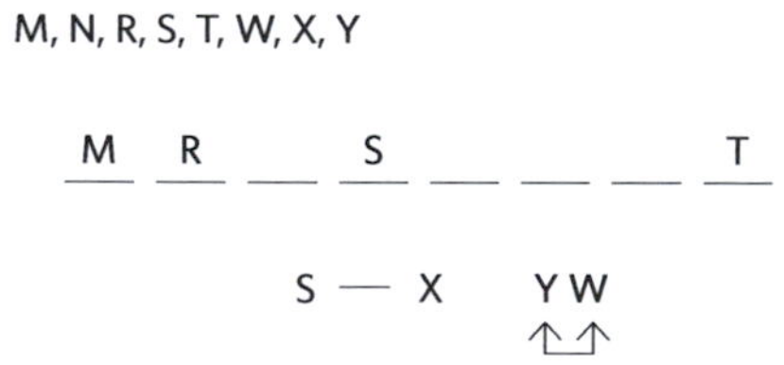

M, N, R, S, T, W, X, Y

M R __ S __ __ __ T

S — X   YW
↑↑

Which element could go third? Notice that it must be N. No rule tells us so, but no other elements can go in that position.

Imagine we are assigning three members from two different groups to three games of chess:

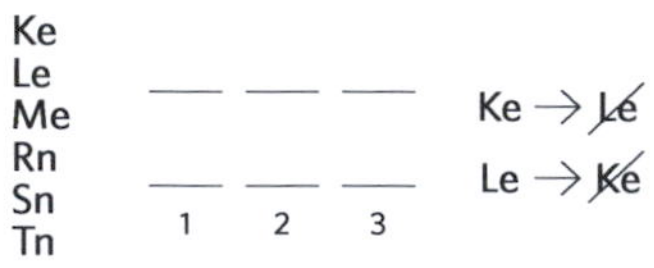

Ke
Le
Me
Rn
Sn
Tn

__ __ __
__ __ __
1 2 3

Ke → ~~Le~~
Le → ~~Ke~~

For a question, we are told that 2 members of team "e" are assigned to the first game. What do we know? Since L and K can't be assigned together, M must be one of the e's assigned.

Full Question Drill

Here are the same games we used for the previous drill, this time with a few of the real questions that accompanied them when these games originally appeared on the LSAT. Use these questions to practice the problem-solving strategies we've discussed. Once you have your diagram laid out, set a goal of three minutes or less for the three questions.

On a Tuesday, an accountant has exactly seven bills—numbered 1 through 7—to pay by Thursday of the same week. The accountant will pay each bill only once according to the following rules:

Either three or four of the seven bills must be paid on Wednesday, the rest on Thursday.
Bill 1 cannot be paid on the same day as bill 5.
Bill 2 must be paid on Thursday.
Bill 4 must be paid on the same day as bill 7.
If bill 6 is paid on Wednesday, bill 7 must be paid on Thursday.

1. If exactly four bills are paid on Wednesday, then those four bills could be

(A) 1, 3, 4, and 6
(B) 1, 3, 5, and 6
(C) 2, 4, 5, and 7
(D) 3, 4, 5, and 7
(E) 3, 4, 6, and 7

4. If bill 6 is paid on Wednesday, which one of the following bills must also be paid on Wednesday?

(A) 1
(B) 3
(C) 4
(D) 5
(E) 7

6. Which one of the following statements must be true?

(A) If bill 2 is paid on Thursday, bill 3 is paid on Wednesday.
(B) If bill 4 is paid on Thursday, bill 1 is paid on Wednesday.
(C) If bill 4 is paid on Thursday, bill 3 is paid on Wednesday.
(D) If bill 6 is paid on Thursday, bill 3 is also paid on Thursday.
(E) If bill 6 is paid on Thursday, bill 4 is also paid on Thursday.

PT 29, S 3, Q's 1, 4, 6

Full Question Drill

A college dean will present seven awards for outstanding language research. The awards—one for French, one for German, one for Hebrew, one for Japanese, one for Korean, one for Latin, and one for Swahili—must be presented consecutively, one at a time, in conformity with the following constraints:

The German award is not presented first.
The Hebrew award is presented at some time before the Korean award is presented.
The Latin award is presented at some time before the Japanese award is presented.
The French award is presented either immediately before or immediately after the Hebrew award is presented.
The Korean award is presented either immediately before or immediately after the Latin award is presented.

14. Which one of the following must be true?

(A) The French award is presented at some time before the Japanese award is presented.
(B) The French award is presented at some time before the Swahili award is presented.
(C) The German award is presented at some time before the Korean award is presented.
(D) The German award is presented at some time before the Swahili award is presented.
(E) The Swahili award is presented at some time before the Hebrew award is presented.

15. If the Hebrew award is presented fourth, which one of the following must be true?

(A) The French award is presented fifth.
(B) The German award is presented third.
(C) The Japanese award is presented sixth.
(D) The Korean award is presented fifth.
(E) The Swahili award is presented first.

16. If the German award is presented third, which one of the following could be true?

(A) The French award is presented fourth.
(B) The Japanese award is presented fifth.
(C) The Japanese award is presented sixth.
(D) The Korean award is presented second.
(E) The Swahili award is presented fifth.

PT 29, S 3, Q's 14, 15, 16

Full Question Solutions

On a Tuesday, an accountant has exactly seven bills—numbered 1 through 7—to pay by Thursday of the same week. The accountant will pay each bill only once according to the following rules:

Either three or four of the seven bills must be paid on Wednesday, the rest on Thursday.
Bill 1 cannot be paid on the same day as bill 5.
Bill 2 must be paid on Thursday.
Bill 4 must be paid on the same day as bill 7.
If bill 6 is paid on Wednesday, bill 7 must be paid on Thursday.

W	T
☐	☐
☐	1/5
1/5	2

1/5 (not together); 4 7 (together)

6w → 7t

7w → 6t

1, 2, (3), 4, 5, 6, 7

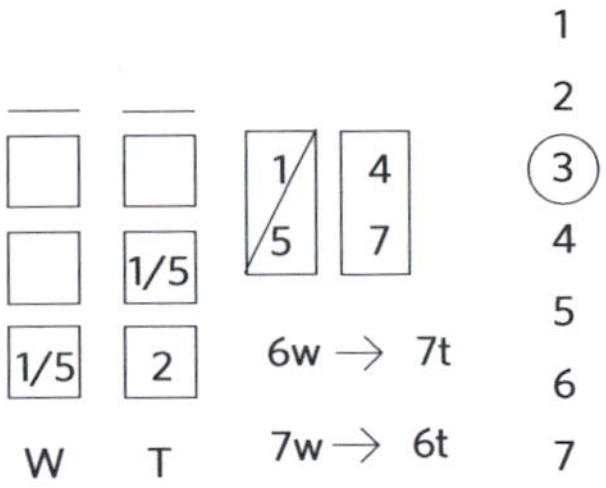

Most of the time we associate numbers with positions, but in this case the numbers represent the elements to be placed. We want to be careful to read the conditional statements in only one direction (knowing that either 6 or 7 is on Thursday, for example, tells us nothing). The only significant up-front inference is that, since 1 and 5 cannot be on the same day, one of them must be on Wednesday, and one of them must be on Thursday. If you missed it initially, you may have picked it up as you solved the first question or two, in which case you'd want to make sure to write it back into your original diagram.

1. If exactly four bills are paid on Wednesday, then those four bills could be

(A) 1, 3, 4, and 6
(B) 1, 3, 5, and 6
(C) 2, 4, 5, and 7
(D) 3, 4, 5, and 7
(E) 3, 4, 6, and 7

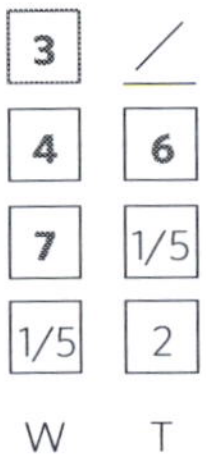

W	T
3	/
4	6
7	1/5
1/5	2

If four bills are paid on Wednesday, three are paid on Thursday. That means the 4 & 7 grouping must go on Wednesday. That means 6 must go on Thursday, and 3 must go in the remaining spot. Since we've figured out so much, this is one rare "could be" where we could simply look for the right answer. However, it'll probably just take less than five seconds for us to also prove the wrong answers wrong, and it'll give us more confidence in our selection, so I would recommend you still use the elimination process here.

4. If bill 6 is paid on Wednesday, which one of the following bills must also be paid on Wednesday?

(A) 1
(B) 3
(C) 4
(D) 5
(E) 7

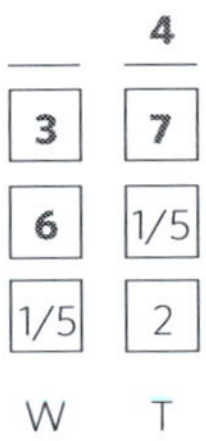

W	T
	4
3	7
6	1/5
1/5	2

If 6 is paid on Wednesday, the 4 & 7 grouping must go on Thursday. That puts 3 into Wednesday.

6. Which one of the following statements must be true?

(A) If bill 2 is paid on Thursday, bill 3 is paid on Wednesday.
(B) If bill 4 is paid on Thursday, bill 1 is paid on Wednesday.
(C) If bill 4 is paid on Thursday, bill 3 is paid on Wednesday.
(D) If bill 6 is paid on Thursday, bill 3 is also paid on Thursday.
(E) If bill 6 is paid on Thursday, bill 4 is also paid on Thursday.

Since this is an unconditional question, we simply want to go down the answer choices looking for one answer that must be true. We can see, looking at the answer choices, that they will each require a bit of work from us.

We already know 2 is paid on Thursday, and that doesn't tell us anything about 3, so we can skip (A). If 4 is paid on Thursday, 7 is on Thursday, and 3 and 6 must go on Wednesday—that tells us nothing about 1, so we can skip (B). If 4 is paid on Thursday, 7 is paid on Thursday. That takes up all the slots for Thursday, so 3 and 6 must go on Wednesday. (C) must be true, and we can stop there and select the answer.

PT 29, S 3, Q's 1, 4, 6

Full Question Solutions

A college dean will present seven awards for outstanding language research. The awards—one for French, one for German, one for Hebrew, one for Japanese, one for Korean, one for Latin, and one for Swahili—must be presented consecutively, one at a time, in conformity with the following constraints:

The German award is not presented first.
The Hebrew award is presented at some time before the Korean award is presented.
The Latin award is presented at some time before the Japanese award is presented.
The French award is presented either immediately before or immediately after the Hebrew award is presented.
The Korean award is presented either immediately before or immediately after the Latin award is presented.

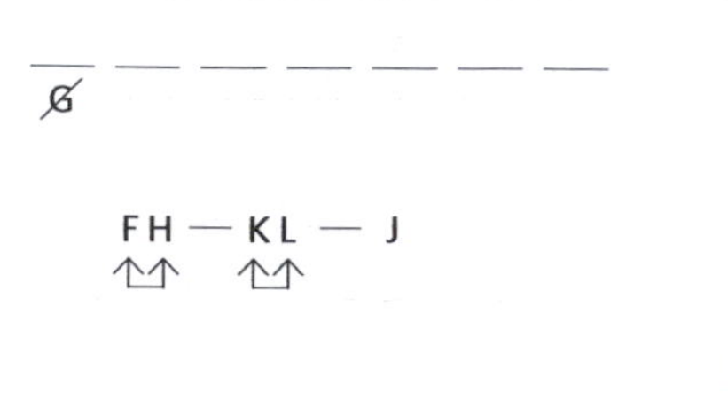

F
G
H
J
K
L
(S)

This is a fairly straightforward game, and a good example of one where we really benefit from taking a "lay of the land" look ahead of time, as recognizing that the second, third, fourth, and fifth rules relate to one another, and notating them together, as we have, can give us a great advantage when it comes to answering questions—the F, H, K, L, J cluster is a significant one that fills up much of the board for us.

14. Which one of the following must be true?

(A) The French award is presented at some time before the Japanese award is presented.
(B) The French award is presented at some time before the Swahili award is presented.
(C) The German award is presented at some time before the Korean award is presented.
(D) The German award is presented at some time before the Swahili award is presented.
(E) The Swahili award is presented at some time before the Hebrew award is presented.

This is an unconditional must-be-true question, so we just want to go down the list to identify one answer we know has to be true. (A) states that F must come at some point before J—since we drew the rules together, it's clear to see that (A) must be true. We can select it and move on.

15. If the Hebrew award is presented fourth, which one of the following must be true?

(A) The French award is presented fifth.
(B) The German award is presented third.
(C) The Japanese award is presented sixth.
(D) The Korean award is presented fifth.
(E) The Swahili award is presented first.

S G F H K/L K/L J

If H is fourth, there are exactly three spots behind it, and since we know that K, L, and J must all follow H, it stands to reason that they must fill in slots 5, 6, and 7. F must go in 3, and since G can't go in 1, it must go in 2. That leaves S to go in 1.

Now we go seeking an answer that must be true, and we find one in (E). Note (though this doesn't impact our process) that because we've figured out so much of the game, a few of our wrong choices are not only ones that *could be* false, but rather *must be* false.

16. If the German award is presented third, which one of the following could be true?

(A) The French award is presented fourth.
(B) The Japanese award is presented fifth.
(C) The Japanese award is presented sixth.
(D) The Korean award is presented second.
(E) The Swahili award is presented fifth.

Once we place G into 3, we are limited in terms of how we fit in our large grouping. We don't have enough space for all five elements in it—F, H, K, L, and J—to go after G, so F and H must go before G. That leaves the remaining elements to follow G. The remaining elements are fairly limited in terms of where they can go, but it's a bit complicated to place elements into specific positions, and so a cloud works nicely here.

Now we're ready to evaluate answers. Since this is a could-be-true question, our hope and expectation is that the work we've done allows us to see that four answers must be false. That is indeed the case—with very little effort we can see that (A), (B), (D), and (E) are all not possible. That leaves (C) as the correct answer.

PT 29, S 3, Q's 14, 15, 16

27 LOGIC GAMES minor question types

In the last lesson, we discussed the standard type of Logic Games question, one that, whether it gives you a new condition to work with or not, requires you to differentiate all answer choices in terms of what is certain versus what is uncertain. A great majority of games questions will play out in this fashion.[1]

In this lesson, we will discuss the other types of questions that can also appear in the section. We already touched on one minor question type—the Rules question—in Lesson 21. You should expect to see a Rules question at the beginning of each of your four games. All of the other minor question types can be thought of as fitting into two general categories:

Several different minor question types ask that you consider a *variety* of possibilities, and we'll call these **Options questions.** For these questions, instead of thinking about what must be true, we want to focus on all of the different ways in which we can satisfy the rules of the game. This is a subtle but significant change in strategy and mindset.

Additionally, typically one question per section will require us to either substitute a rule for a different one or (more commonly) substitute a rule for a matching one. We'll call these **Rule Change questions.** Rule Change questions typically come at the end of a game and can be some of the most intimidating, for they require us to "rethink" what we know about games, and by the time you get to the last question, the last thing you want to do is reorganize that picture you've finally been able to get in your head. The good news is that most of these Rule Change questions are not actually as difficult as they might at first seem. We'll discuss specific strategies that will help you get past them with the least possible difficulty.

Starting on the next page, using two simple games and diagrams as our reference points, we'll break each question type down in depth, and discuss question-specific strategies.

1. In a typical Logic Games section, expect to see 4 Rules questions, 15 - 17 standard questions, and 2 - 4 minor types of questions.

You read that right. Only 2 - 4 questions will require us to change our process.

As we discuss these specific question types starting on the next page, we'll use the terms "common" and "not common" to differentiate them—keep in mind that we are talking about common and not common relative to other minor question types, not relative to the section as a whole.

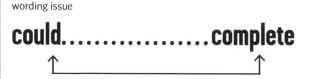

simple sample a

Six kids—M, N, O, P, R, and S—will take turns riding a horse. The following conditions apply:

S will not ride fifth.
P will take a ride after O does.
N will ride second.
M will ride immediately before O does.

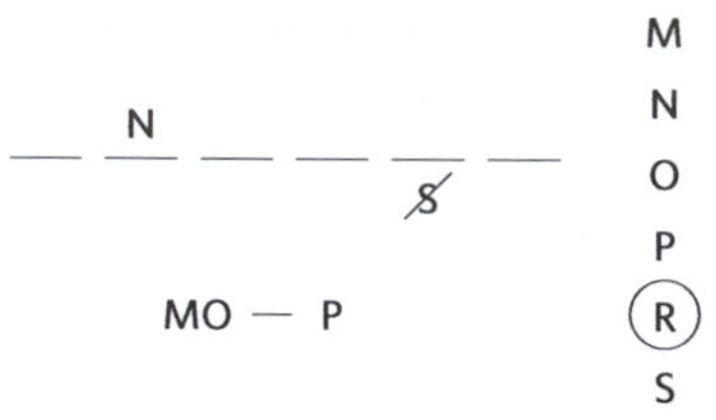

__ N __ __ __ __ (not S in fifth)

MO — P

M N O P (R) S

options question type

tell me one thing...

not common

The earliest that O can ride the horse is
(A) 1st
(B) 2nd
(C) 3rd
(D) 4th
(E) 5th

(from sample a)

This is not a question type that appears often, but it's one that is simple enough to understand and adapt to. "Tell me one thing" questions ask a particular question about a specific element or a position.

These questions, like the ones we discussed in the previous lesson, require you to think about what can and cannot be, but the difference is that these questions also often require you to choose from among a range of possibilities. In this case, our job is to select the earliest out of the range of spots in which O can go.

For these questions, the element or position discussed in the stem is almost always involved in some rule—in this case, the question is about O, and we know that O must immediately follow M. This rule, in turn, almost always interacts with another rule (or two): in this case, the MO group butts against the rule that N is in the second position. Almost always, it is the interaction between the relevant rule and another rule that determines the correct answer. In this case, since O must immediately follow M, and because N occupies the second spot, the earliest MO can go is the third and fourth positions, and so the earliest that O can go is fourth. (D) is correct.

There are two ways to confirm our answer for this type of question. One: make sure that placing O fourth is okay by drawing out one completed hypothetical that satisfies all the rules. Two: eliminate the "better" answers by confirming that O can't go in the third, second, or first spot. If it passes both those tests, you have the right answer.

wording issue

could.................complete

Let's imagine that you win three tickets to a concert from a local radio contest. The stipulation is that you must go with two people you work with. You have four coworkers (whose names conveniently go in alphabetical order)—F, G, H, and J—who are all available to go.

I want to ask you two possible questions about this scenario:

1. Which of the following **could** be a **complete** list of coworkers that you take with you?
(A) F (B) F, G (C) F, G, H, J

2. Which of the following is a **complete** list of coworkers you **could** choose to take with you?
(A)F (B) F, G (C) F, G, H, J

The first is really a modified version of a Could Be True question, and we can simply get to the right answer by eliminating answers that must be false. We can't take one person, and we can't take four; we can only take two. (B) is correct.

The second question is a very common form of the Consider All Possibilities questions discussed on the next page. We need to consider everyone who could be selected, and, since no rule excludes anyone, the correct answer—(C)—must include all four elements.

Both of these forms of wording questions are common on the exam, and they are probably the most frequently misread question stems that appear in the Games section. But if the above makes sense to you, they are easy enough to prepare for. Make sure, in your practice, to slow down to carefully understand the meaning correctly each time you see a question of either type, and take note any time you falter. With a little practice, you should have no trouble correctly understanding your task each time you see either stem.

simple sample b

Six animals—F, G, H, J, K, and L—will each be assigned to one of four cages—one red, one silver, one tan, and one violet. The following rules apply:

Each cage holds at least one, and at most two, animals.
If J is put in the red cage, F will be put in the violet cage.
J and L are not put in the same cage.
F and H are put in the same cage.
Only one animal is put in the tan cage.

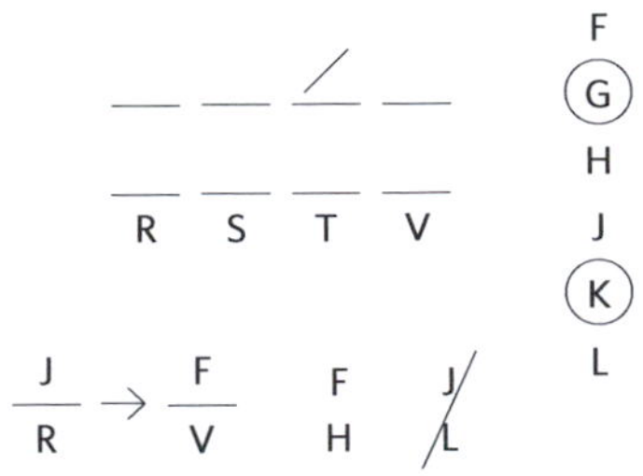

R S T V

F (G) H J (K) L

J/R → F/V   F/H   J/L (crossed out)

options question type

consider all possibilities

common

Which of the following is a complete list of kids who could go third?
(A) S
(B) M, O, R
(C) M, R, S
(D) M, R, S, O
(E) M, R, S, P
(from sample a)

How many different animals could be assigned to share a cage with J?
(A) 0
(B) 1
(C) 2
(D) 3
(E) 4
(from sample b)

This question type is also pretty self-explanatory. "Consider All Possibilities" questions require you to consider all options for the issue at hand—typically, elements that can go in a certain position, positions certain elements can go into, or ways the entire game can be played out. These questions may or may not come with conditions (an example with a condition could be "If M goes third, how many different elements could go first?"). In such a case, we want to just play out the condition as we always do, then answer the question accordingly.

When you think about the positions or elements in question, it's important to consider what could be (for example, maybe you already know from our previous work that M could go third). More importantly, you need to think about what can't work. What can't work is, typically, what defines the question (i.e., the answer includes all elements except those we know can't go in a position). In addition, what we know about what can't work can help us eliminate incorrect answer choices.

Let's talk more specifically about this first question. We are being asked to find an answer that contains all of the elements that could go in the third spot (see opposite page for more about this dangerous question stem).

Again, let's imagine we know, from work done on a previous question, that M is definitely a possibility. Now let's consider—what elements are NOT able to go in the third slot? O can't, because M can't go second. Neither can P, which must follow MO. We know N can't because it's already in position 2.

Let's look to eliminate answers that are missing M, or contain O, P, or N. When we do so, we get rid of (A), (B), (D), and (E), leaving us with (C) as the correct answer. At this point we should move on, but if you are nervous at all, you could certainly come up with some hypotheticals to confirm that R and S can work in the position.

In most instances, once you eliminate based on "can'ts," you will be left with just one or two answers to evaluate critically. If you have more than one choice, focus on differences between the answer choices. For example, imagine we were able to get down to (B) or (C) using our elimination process. At that point, we would focus on testing O and S (rather than M or R), because O and S are what differentiate those answer choices.

The second question doesn't ask about specific elements, but we must do the same type of work as before in order to come up with a total number. We don't have a clear sense of who can go with J, but we know from the other rules that F, H, and L all cannot go with J. That leaves G and K. We know the answer is most likely going to be "2," but if we are wrong, it's going to be an answer smaller than 2 (since we know for sure 2 is the MOST than can work). Considering both G and K are free agents (helpful that we circled them in our diagram), we should be fine pairing either with J, but if you aren't certain, you can create hypotheticals to test them out. Indeed, either can work with J, and (C) is correct.

simple sample a

Six kids—M, N, O, P, R, and S—will take turns riding a horse. The following conditions apply:

S will not ride fifth.
P will take a ride after O does.
N will ride second.
M will ride immediately before O does.

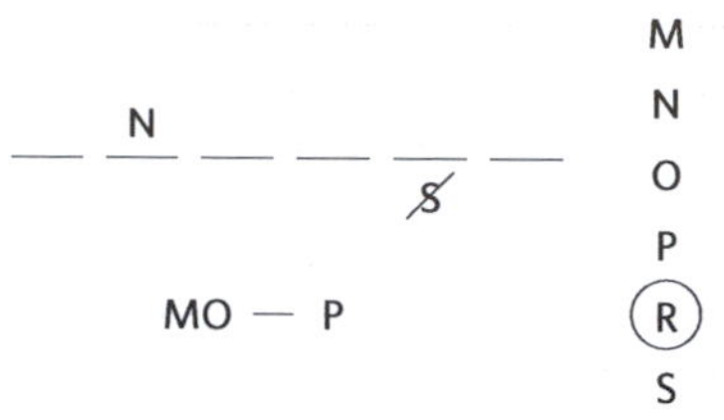

```
    N                      M
__ __ __ __ __ __          N
            S̸              O
                           P
   MO — P                 (R)
                           S
```

options question type

complete the puzzle

not common

Which of the following, if true, determines the order of rides?
(A) M rides third.
(B) M rides fourth.
(C) P rides fifth.
(D) S rides first.
(E) S rides last. (from sample a)

Complete the Puzzle questions are some of the only ones for which you should *expect* to do at least some work with the answer choices themselves (see inset to right). There is no way to know the answer based on the question stem, and it's a mistake to predict the answer before you see which ones you are actually given. The nature of the question requires that we think of each answer individually, by relating the information that answer presents to what we already know about the game.

The question then becomes "How much work should I do for each answer?" and the best performers are those who have the best instincts about this particular issue. In general, if you understand the game well, it will be easier to find a right answer than it will be to eliminate wrong ones. When an answer is correct, and when you understand a game well, there will be a natural progression of inferences, and often, before you know it, the slots will be filled. When an answer is incorrect, you end up at a point where the game could go a few different ways, and though you will be pretty sure that means the answer doesn't determine all positions, the weaker test taker will be concerned he or she is missing some key inferences.

For the question above, (A) - (D) all lead to a few inferences, but none allow us to completely finish the picture. (E), the correct answer, allows us to do so fairly easily—if S goes in six, MO-P must go in 3-4-5, so R must go in 1. Again, the key to success on these questions is typically to move on when you get to a point of uncertainty with answers, and to search out the one answer that leads to a quick string of inferences.

strategy issue

how much work should you expect to do with the answers?

Not much. In general, if you are performing well on the Logic Games section, you should expect that just a few questions—no more than three or four in a section—will cause you to do significant "work" with the answer choices.

In general, most of the important work that leads to the right answer will have been done in your initial setup of the game and in the question stem. When you play games well, selecting the correct answer often feels like the easiest step of all—a reward for all of the great work you've done up to that point: you know a game well, so you can tell what can't be true, or you've worked off the condition correctly, so you know what must be true, and so on. For the questions we discussed on the previous page, you should be able to anticipate the right answer before seeing your choices.

A few questions, per their design, *require* that you do work with each answer choice. Complete the Puzzle questions are like that, as are the Same Effect questions we'll discuss on the next page. For these questions, the only way to get to a right answer is to flesh out each answer choice.

In other instances, we will need to do work with the answer choices because we have not taken advantage of all of our opportunities—that is, we'll need to do work with the answer choices because we missed something earlier. This is going to happen to all of us—we all have to grind it out with games sometimes because we've missed something. However, keep a few things in mind. First, know that this is not the norm, and that if you have to do work with every answer for every question, it's a sign you've misunderstood the game. Second, as you train with more and more games, use the work you have to do with the answer choices as a gauge—having to do less and less work by the time you get to answer choices is one of the key signs of games progress.

simple sample b

Six animals—F, G, H, J, K, and L—will each be assigned to one of four cages—one red, one silver, one tan, and one violet. The following rules apply:

Each cage holds at least one, and at most two, animals.
If J is put in the red cage, F will be put in the violet cage.
J and L are not put in the same cage.
F and H are put in the same cage.
Only one animal is put in the tan cage.

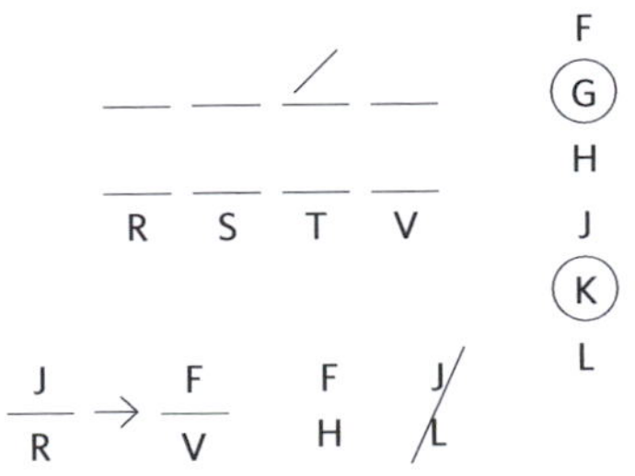

R S T V

F (G) H J (K) L

J/R → F/V

F H

J/L (not together)

---

options question type

minimum/maximum

common

If S is before P, what is the minimum number of children who can ride after S but before P?
(A) 0
(B) 1
(C) 2
(D) 3
(E) 4
(from sample a)

If R is before P, what is the maximum number of children who can go after R and before P?
(A) 0
(B) 1
(C) 2
(D) 3
(E) 4
(from sample a)

The last of our Possibilities questions is the Minimum/Maximum question. Minimum and Maximum questions most frequently appear with ordering games or grouping games for which there is great uncertainty about the number of elements in each group. These questions, like the "Tell me one thing..." question that asks for the "earliest," ask us to identify one possibility out of many as the "*-est*" in the first question above, the small*est* possible space between S and P, and in the second question, the larg*est* possible space between R and P.

For these questions, I recommend a two-step process—try out and confirm. Typically, when you are presented with such a question, you will have some sense, based on what you know of the rules, as to what might be the correct answer. Go ahead and try that out, and make sure that indeed the maximum or minimum you guessed does work. That's the *try* out part.

Once you have the answer, look at the other answer choices and make sure to eliminate the "better" answers. For a Minimum question, better answers would be those that present a smaller number. For a Maximum question, the "better" answers would be the larger numbers.

Let's play this out on our two questions above. The first question asks about the minimum number of children who can go after S but before P. Can it be 0? The only way would be to have M, O, S, P in 3 – 6, but S can't go in 5. S must go first, and the earliest P could go in that situation is fifth (S, N, M, O, P, R). That leaves us with three elements after S but before P.

To confirm our answer, we want to eliminate better choices. Is 2 a possibility? I try it a few different ways, and it actually is—we can put S in the third spot, and have it be R, N, S, M, O, P. That would put two elements between S and P. Could 1 work? I try a few different ways, but nothing works. I already know 0 doesn't work. 2, answer choice (C), is correct.

For the second question, we want to put as many elements between R and P as possible. There doesn't seem to be a reason we can't put R first and P last—let's try it out. We find a combination that works: R, N, S, M, O, P. That gives us four elements in between the two. Since there are no bigger numbers to try, we know we have the correct answer, (E).

INSTRUCTIONS FOR GAME ON NEXT PAGE: On the next page is a game with an example of each of the four question types we've discussed. Keep in mind that no actual game would ever have so many minor questions. Set a goal of completing your setup and answering all questions in seven minutes or less. Warning: solutions will be on the opposite page.

OPTIONS QUESTIONS | Diagram this game and solve the Options questions to the best of your ability.

Four members of the red team—F, G, H, and J—compete against three members of the purple team—K, L, M—in a five-mile race. They finish according to the following conditions:

K finishes after G but before F.
Exactly one person from the purple team finishes in the top three.
L finishes fifth.
J finishes immediately before M, or M finishes immediately before J.

1. If K finished sixth, what is the latest that M could have finished?
(A) first
(B) second
(C) third
(D) fourth
(E) seventh

2. If K finished third, in how many different orders could the racers have finished?
(A) 1
(B) 2
(C) 4
(D) 5
(E) 6

3. Which of the following, if true, determines the order of finish for all racers?
(A) K finishes immediately after G and immediately before L.
(B) K finishes immediately after H and immediately before F.
(C) L finishes immediately after H and immediately before K.
(D) L finishes immediately after F and immediately before M.
(E) L finishes immediately after H and immediately before M.

4. What is the minimum number of racers that finished between K and M?
(A) 0
(B) 1
(C) 2
(D) 3
(E) 4

OPTIONS QUESTIONS SOLUTIONS

Four members of the red team—F, G, H, and J—compete against three members of the purple team—K, L, M—in a five-mile race. They finish according to the following conditions:

K finishes after G but before F.
Exactly one person from the purple team finishes in the top three.
L finishes fifth.
J finishes immediately before M, or M finishes immediately before J.

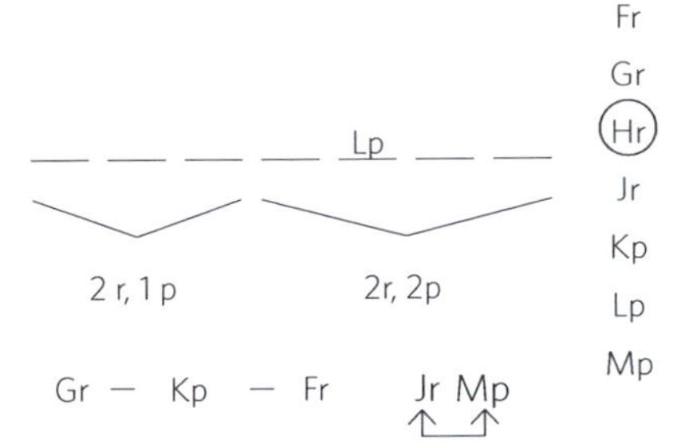

1. If K finished sixth, what is the latest that M could have finished?
(A) first
(B) second
(C) third
(D) fourth
(E) seventh

If K finished sixth, that means F finished seventh. It also means that G must go in one of the first four slots. Most importantly, it means that M must be the purple member who finishes in the top three. The latest M could finish in this case is third. (C) is correct.

2. If K finished third, in how many different orders could the racers have finished?
(A) 1
(B) 2
(C) 4
(D) 5
(E) 6

G,H
M, J
Kp Fr Lp

If K finished third, J and M must finish in 6 and 7 (either as JM or MJ). F must finish fourth. G and H must finish in 1 and 2 (either as GH or HG). Since there are two different options for the first two slots, and two options for the last two, together there are four (2 × 2) different ways the racers could have finished. (C) is correct.

3. Which of the following, if true, determines the order of finish for all racers?
(A) K finishes immediately after G and immediately before L.
(B) K finishes immediately after H and immediately before F.
(C) L finishes immediately after H and immediately before K.
(D) L finishes immediately after F and immediately before M.
(E) L finishes immediately after H and immediately before M.

With (A), the elements in 1, 2, 6, and 7 are unclear. With (B), the elements in 6 and 7 are unclear. With (C), the elements in 1, 2, and 3 are unclear. With (D), the elements in 1, 2, and 3 are unclear. (E) puts H in 4, L in 5, and M in 6. That means G-K-F must go in 1-2-3, and J must go in 7. We have the complete order: G, K, F, H, L, M, J. (E) is correct.

4. What is the minimum number of racers that finished between K and M?
(A) 0
(B) 1
(C) 2
(D) 3
(E) 4

If you place K third, and M sixth, there would be two elements between them. Is there a way to get them closer? Yes, by placing the JM grouping within the G-K-F link. G, J, M, K, L, F, H, gives us 0 spaces between K and M. (A) is correct.

simple sample a

Six kids—M, N, O, P, R, and S—will take turns riding a horse. The following conditions apply:

S will not ride fifth.
P will take a ride after O does.
N will ride second.
M will ride immediately before O does.

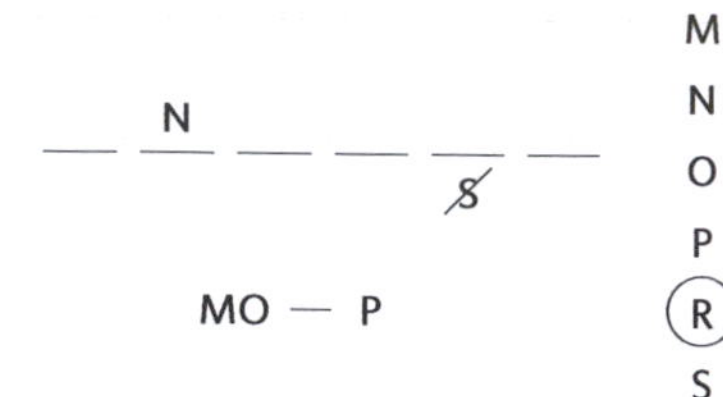

rules change type

same effect

common

Which of the following, if substituted for the rule that P will take a ride after O does, would have the same effect on determining the order in which the children ride?
(A) P rides no earlier than fourth.
(B) O rides no later than fifth.
(C) P rides after N.
(D) M rides after N but before P.
(E) O rides immediately before P.

(from sample a)

Which of the following, if substituted for the rule that if J is put in the red cage, F will be put in the violet cage, would have the same effect on determining the assignment of animals?
(A) If F is put in the violet cage, J will be put in the red cage.
(B) If J is not put in the red cage, H is not put in the violet cage.
(C) If H is put in the silver cage, J is not put in the red cage.
(D) J and F cannot be put in the same cage.
(E) If J is placed with another animal, it must be G or K.

(from sample b)

Whether you have five $20 bills in your pocket, or two $50 bills, it's the same amount of money. Same Effect Rules Change questions work a similar way: they require us to find an answer choice that has the same effect as one of the original rules. This is a fairly new question type, but almost every exam over the last couple of years has contained exactly one Same Effect question (always as the last question of the game in which it appears .

If these questions seem a bit intimidating, they should: if the test writers wanted to, they could make these types of questions particularly cruel, especially by creating clever right answers and close-but-no-cigar tempting wrong answers.

So far, the test writers have chosen not to be as cruel as they can be with these questions, and I expect this trend to continue. The test writers have an obligation to create questions that can be solved in a reasonable amount of time (having a question that takes everyone five minutes to solve would completely screw up their testing algorithm), and, just by their nature, even the easiest of these questions is fairly challenging and time-consuming. All that is to say, there is a ceiling on how tough they can make any one question, and this limits how creative or complex these questions can get. Here is what is most important for you to know about these questions:

1. In general, right answers are fairly closely related to the rules they are meant to replace. In several instances, the right answer has been a rewording (think contrapositive). Otherwise, they typically require just a small, understandable inference.

Let's take a look at the question related to Sample A. We need to find an equivalent for the rule that gives us O - P. We can see that this rule is connected to the MO rule. So we can anticipate that they could replace O - P with M - P and have the same effect.

(D) gives us M - P, but it also tells us M must go after N. Is that addition okay? Sure it is. M must always go after N anyway, so it doesn't change the game in any way. (D) is the correct answer.

That last part was a bit sneaky, huh? Well, you can make your life a lot easier by first getting rid of the wrong choices. Here's the second important thing for you to know about these questions:

2. In general, wrong answers are clearly wrong—that is, if you understand the game and the rule in question well, the differences in effect should be obvious.

This fact becomes clearly evident when we take an aggregate look at all of the same effect questions that have appeared over

simple sample b

Six animals—F, G, H, J, K, and L—will each be assigned to one of four cages—one red, one silver, one tan, and one violet. The following rules apply:

Each cage holds at least one, and at most two, animals.
If J is put in the red cage, F will be put in the violet cage.
J and L are not put in the same cage.
F and H are put in the same cage.
Only one animal is put in the tan cage.

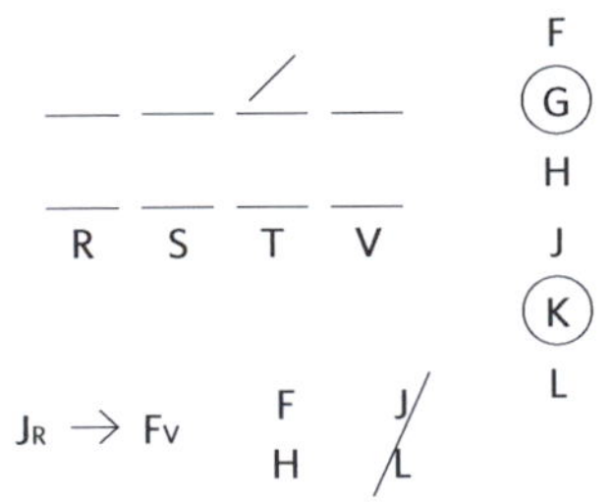

R S T V

F (G) H J (K) L

$J_R \rightarrow F_v$ F H J/L

rule change type

same effect (cont.)

common

time (which I have had the pleasure of doing!). Arguably, only one or two of all the wrong choices that have appeared have been what I would deem "clever" or "sneaky." The rest of them have all been fairly obviously wrong.

Therefore, I strongly recommend that you emphasize the elimination part of your process. I believe it is the key to success on these questions. For the question at hand, (A) could place P before MO, neither (B) nor (C) gets at the O - P relationship, and (E) gives a more specific relationship than our original rule does.

Here are the steps I recommend:
(1) Go back to the original rule and review it carefully.
(2) Look at what other rules it relates to and anticipate simple ways the original rule could be adapted/reworded for the same effect.
(3) Eliminate wrong choices that change the impact, have a greater impact, or don't have as much of an impact as the original rule.
(4) Confirm that the remaining answer does the same, no more or less, as the original rule does. Remember, most right answers are cloaked rewordings, or they work off a slight and direct inference.

Looking at the question for Sample B, we know the rule in question is $J_R \rightarrow F_v$. We know F and H must go together, so we can anticipate that H might be swapped for F. We also know they can write the contrapositive version (so we've got $J_R \rightarrow H_v$, and $\not{H_v} \rightarrow \not{J_R}$ as possibilities).

(A) gives us $F_v \rightarrow J_R$, a reversal we know is incorrect (too easy—do they know who they are messing with?). (B) gives us a negation (with H in for F), which we also know is incorrect. (C) is strange (silver?) but interesting. Let's try the contrapositive: $J_R \rightarrow \not{H_s}$, which means $J_R \rightarrow H_v$, which means $J_R \rightarrow F_v$. Ha! It's what we were looking for (in a form we didn't expect). (D) is far too vague (and we already know it per another rule), and while (E) is true, it clearly doesn't give us the same information as the original rule. The other answers have obvious issues, and (C) is correct.

rules change type

different effect

very rare

Questions for which a rule will change to one with a different impact used to be a bit more frequent, but as Same Effect questions have become more common, Different Effect questions have become far less so—only one has appeared on any exam in the last few years, so we won't spend too much time discussing them here.

The difficulty of the Different Effect question is, in general, dependent on how many connections there are between the rule in question and the other rules of the game. After you read the question stem, quickly go to your diagram to identify the rule in question and to consider the ways in which that rule links with other rules and leads to inferences. If there is just one link there, and only one or two inferences to be made, you may be able to re-envision the scenario in your head with a new rule in place. Whenever this is possible, this will be the quickest path to the answer.

The toughest Rule Change questions involve rules that relate to many other rules and have a lot of "must be" and "could be" consequences on the game. In these situations, it's generally best to redraw a new diagram with the substituted rule before going into the questions. I know what you are thinking ("I don't have time for a new diagram!") but you'll be surprised how quickly you can whip up a new diagram when you are comfortable with the one you already have (the Different Effect question will likely be the last question of that game). Once you have a strong sense of the impact of the rule change, work to eliminate answers. Down to one or two attractive choices, make sure to select your answer after checking that it works with all of the *other* rules of the game.

RULE CHANGE QUESTIONS

| Diagram this game and solve the Rule Change questions to the best of your ability.

A country band will play six of the eight songs—Fight, Get Drunk, Honey I'm Sorry, Just Kidding, Kiss Me, Leave Me Alone, Miss You, and Nevermind—on their new album during a concert. They will play no other songs. The order of the songs played must conform to the following conditions:

Just Kidding will be played after Get Drunk.
Honey I'm Sorry will be played before Miss You.
If Nevermind is played, it will be played third.
If Fight is not played, Leave Me Alone will be.
Honey I'm Sorry will be played right before or right after Just Kidding.

1. Which of the following, if substituted for the rule that Just Kidding will be played after Get Drunk, would have the same effect on the order of songs played?
(A) Get Drunk will be played before Miss You.
(B) Get Drunk will be played before Honey I'm Sorry.
(C) At least two songs will be played after Get Drunk and before Miss You.
(D) At most two songs will be played after Get Drunk and before Miss You.
(E) Get Drunk must be one of the first three songs played.

2. Which of the following, if substituted for the rule that if Fight is not played, Leave Me Alone will be, would have the same effect on the order of songs played?
(A) They will play Leave Me Alone only if they don't play Fight.
(B) They will play Fight only if they don't play Leave Me Alone.
(C) Either Fight or Leave Me Alone is played.
(D) Either Fight or Leave Me Alone is not played.
(E) Either Kiss Me or Nevermind is played.

(Challenge) 3. Which of the following, if substituted for the rule that if Fight is not played, Leave Me Alone will be, would have the same effect on the order of songs played?
(A) They will play Kiss Me or Nevermind, but not both.
(B) If they play Kiss Me, they will not play Nevermind.
(C) If they play Fight, they will not play Leave Me Alone.
(D) If they play Fight, they will play either Kiss Me or Nevermind, but not both.
(E) They cannot play both Fight and Leave Me Alone.

4. Suppose that instead of Just Kidding being played after Get Drunk, we had Get Drunk being played after Just Kidding. If all other restrictions stay the same, which of the following could be the order of songs played?
(A) Just Kidding, Get Drunk, Honey I'm Sorry, Miss You, Leave Me Alone, Kiss Me
(B) Miss You, Honey I'm Sorry, Just Kidding, Get Drunk, Kiss Me, Leave Me Alone
(C) Just Kidding, Honey I'm Sorry, Get Drunk, Nevermind, Leave Me Alone, Miss You
(D) Just Kidding, Honey I'm Sorry, Nevermind, Miss You, Get Drunk, Leave Me Alone
(E) Leave Me Alone, Kiss Me, Nevermind, Just Kidding, Honey I'm Sorry, Get Drunk

RULE CHANGE QUESTIONS SOLUTIONS

A country band will play six of the eight songs—Fight, Get Drunk, Honey I'm Sorry, Just Kidding, Kiss Me, Leave Me Alone, Miss You, and Nevermind—on their new album during a concert. They will play no other songs. The order of the songs played must conform to the following conditions:

Just Kidding will be played after Get Drunk.
Honey I'm Sorry will be played before Miss You.
If Nevermind is played, it will be played third.
If Fight is not played, Leave Me Alone will be.
Honey I'm Sorry will be played right before or right after Just Kidding.

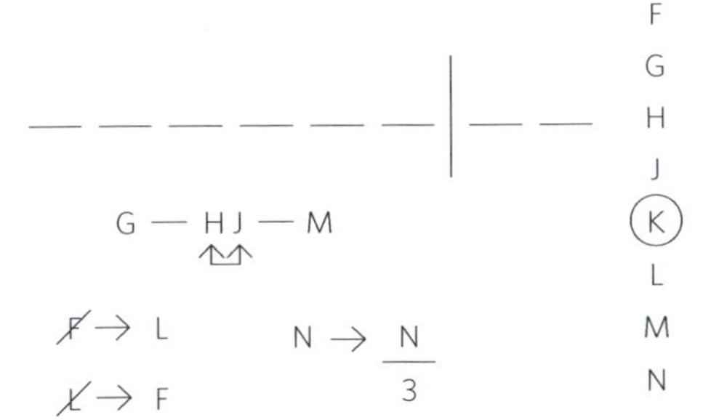

1. Which of the following, if substituted for the rule that Just Kidding will be played after Get Drunk, would have the same effect on the order of songs played?
(A) Get Drunk will be played before Miss You.
(B) Get Drunk will be played before Honey I'm Sorry.
(C) At least two songs will be played after Get Drunk and before Miss You.
(D) At most two songs will be played after Get Drunk and before Miss You.
(E) Get Drunk must be one of the first three songs played.

We want to start by looking at the rule in question in our diagram. G is before J, and we know that's equivalent to being before H. (B) gives us that relationship and is thus correct. (A) doesn't give us the relationship between G and J. (C) and (D) give a more specific relationship than the original rule, and don't relate to G and J directly. (E) allows for J to be before G.

2. Which of the following, if substituted for the rule that if Fight is not played, Leave Me Alone will be, would have the same effect on the order of songs played?
(A) They will play Leave Me Alone only if they don't play Fight.
(B) They will play Fight only if they don't play Leave Me Alone.
(C) Either Fight or Leave Me Alone is played.
(D) Either Fight or Leave Me Alone is not played.
(E) Either Kiss Me or Nevermind is played.

Notice that the rule in question is not directly connected to any other rule. That means that most likely the right answer will be a rephrasing of the original rule. (C) is a fairly simple rephrase of what we know, and it is the correct answer—it tells us that if either F or L is out, the other must be in. "Only if" in (A) gives us the wrong relationship: $L \rightarrow \not F$. Same with (B). (D) doesn't guarantee that F or L is played. (E) does not tell us that either F or L must be played.

A country band will play six of the eight songs—Fight, Get Drunk, Honey I'm Sorry, Just Kidding, Kiss Me, Leave Me Alone, Miss You, and Nevermind—on their new album during a concert. They will play no other songs. The order of the songs played must conform to the following conditions:

Just Kidding will be played after Get Drunk.
Honey I'm Sorry will be played before Miss You.
If Nevermind is played, it will be played third.
If Fight is not played, Leave Me Alone will be.
Honey I'm Sorry will be played right before or right after Just Kidding.

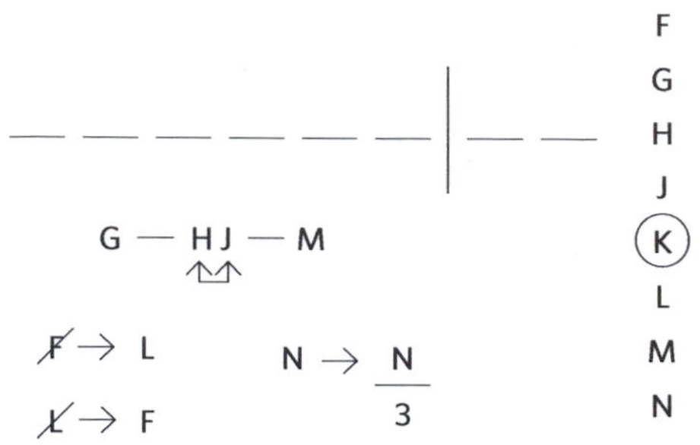

F G H J (K) L M N

G — HJ — M

F̸ → L
L̸ → F
N → N/3

(Challenge) 3. Which of the following, if substituted for the rule that if Fight is not played, Leave Me Alone will be, would have the same effect on the order of songs played?
(A) They will play Kiss Me or Nevermind, but not both.
(B) If they play Kiss Me, they will not play Nevermind.
(C) If they play Fight, they will not play Leave Me Alone.
(D) If they play Fight, they will play either Kiss Me or Nevermind, but not both.
(E) They cannot play both Fight and Leave Me Alone.

Here's the same question, but with more complicated answers to consider. On the real exam, I would look for a quick rephrase answer (like the one for question 2) first, then, realizing we don't have one, look for a creative answer that tells us the same information as the original rule. Remember, what the original rule told us is that either L or F has to be in—if either is out, it will force the other in. It's also helpful to remember that there are six *in* slots and two *out* slots, and we already know of four elements (G, H, J, and M) that must be in. (A) is a very tempting answer, because it would force F or L in. However, (A) makes it so that exactly one of them—either F or L, but not both—is in. That's different from the original rule. (B) tells us that they can't play both K and N at the same time. That means that either F, L, or both need to be played. This is the information we needed, and (B) is correct. Notice that (C), (D), and (E) are all answers that give us consequences for *if* F or L is played—we need to know that F or L is played, not what happens if one of them is played, and if you can see that, you can eliminate (C) - (E) fairly quickly. None of those answers force F or L in.

Note that this question represents an extreme-case situation, and it is extremely unlikely that you will see such a challenging right answer on your real exam.

4. Suppose that instead of Just Kidding being played after Get Drunk, we had Get Drunk being played after Just Kidding. If all other restrictions stay the same, which of the following could be the order of songs played?
(A) Just Kidding, Get Drunk, Honey I'm Sorry, Miss You, Leave Me Alone, Kiss Me
(B) Miss You, Honey I'm Sorry, Just Kidding, Get Drunk, Kiss Me, Leave Me Alone
(C) Just Kidding, Honey I'm Sorry, Get Drunk, Nevermind, Leave Me Alone, Miss You
(D) Just Kidding, Honey I'm Sorry, Nevermind, Miss You, Get Drunk, Leave Me Alone
(E) Leave Me Alone, Kiss Me, Nevermind, Just Kidding, Honey I'm Sorry, Get Drunk

When a question stem changes a rule, you generally want to redraw the game. The act of redrawing will help you think about the implications of the rule change, and having a visual will also help you evaluate answer choices more quickly and easily. Depending on the complexity of the rule, diagram, or game, you may choose to redraw the entire picture, or just the part in question, and reference the original diagram for the positions and other rules as we've done here. Per our new drawing below, (A) can't be true, (B) can't be true, (C) can't be true because N is not in third, and (E) is missing Miss You. (D) is correct.

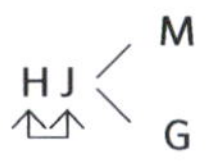

HJ < M, G

THE MINOR QUESTIONS GAME | Here's a full game's worth of minor questions. Solve to the best of your ability.

Eight workers—F, G, H, L, M, N, O, and P—are split into two shifts—the first shift and the second shift. The following conditions apply:

P and N will work the same shift.
P and H will work different shifts.
If L works the first shift, N and O will work the second shift.
If G works the second shift, H will work the first.
F works the second shift.

1. Which of the following could be a complete list of workers for the first shift?
(A) G, M, N, P
(B) G, M, N, O
(C) G, L, M, N, P
(D) F, G, N, P
(E) M, N, O, P

2. Which of the following, if true, determines all members for each shift?
(A) G, N, and P all work the first shift.
(B) G, N, and O all work the first shift.
(C) M, N, and O all work the first shift.
(D) G, H, and M all work the first shift.
(E) G, H, and L all work the first shift.

3. Which two members cannot be on the same shift?
(A) H and N
(B) G and H
(C) L and N
(D) L and O
(E) M and O

4. Which of the following is a complete list of workers any one of whom can work on the first shift with H?
(A) G, L
(B) G, L, M
(C) G, L, M, O
(D) F, G, L, M, O
(E) F, G, L, M, N, O

5. What is the maximum number of people who can work the second shift?
(A) 3
(B) 4
(C) 5
(D) 6
(E) 7

6. Which of the following, if substituted for the rule that P and H will work different shifts, would have the same effect on the assignment of workers?
(A) If N works the first shift, H will work the second.
(B) If N does not work the first shift, H will.
(C) N will work the first shift if, and only if, H works the second.
(D) If P works the first shift, so will G.
(E) P will work the first shift if and only if G works the first shift.

7. If the rule that P and N will work the same shift is replaced by a rule that P and N will work different shifts, which of the following could be a complete list of people who work the first shift?
(A) H, N, L, M, O
(B) G, L, O, P
(C) G, H, M, O
(D) G, M, P
(E) G, L, P, H

THE MINOR QUESTIONS GAME SOLUTIONS

Eight workers—F, G, H, L, M, N, O, and P—are split into two shifts—the first shift and the second shift. The following conditions apply:

P and N will work the same shift.
P and H will work different shifts.
If L works the first shift, N and O will work the second shift.
If G works the second shift, H will work the first.
F works the second shift.

Since we know that P and N must go together, and H must go in the other group, and since there are only two ways this can work per the scenario, it makes sense to draw two diagrams for this situation. We can put P and N in shift one and H in shift two for Diagram 1, and P and N in shift two and H in shift one for Diagram 2. We can note the other conditional rules below, and we're able to make inferences about G and L for Diagram 1.

1	2
G	L
P	F
N	H

1	2
	F
	P
H	N

L1 → N2 & O2   G2 → H1

N1 or O1 → L2   H2 → G1

1. Which of the following could be a complete list of workers for the first shift?
(A) G, M, N, P
(B) G, M, N, O
(C) G, L, M, N, P
(D) F, G, N, P
(E) M, N, O, P

We want to answer this Rules question by using the rules to eliminate incorrect choices. The first rule allows us to get rid of (B). The third (C). The fourth (E). The last (D). That leaves us with (A) as the correct answer.

2. Which of the following, if true, determines all members for each shift?
(A) G, N, and P all work the first shift.
(B) G, N, and O all work the first shift.
(C) M, N, and O all work the first shift.
(D) G, H, and M all work the first shift.
(E) G, H, and L all work the first shift.

The key to a question like this is to not spend too much time on the wrong answers. If an answer leaves you uncertain of where to place elements, don't over-think it—it's likely not correct. (A) doesn't determine where O and M go. (B) doesn't determine where M will go. (C) forces us to use Diagram 1, and if M, N, and O work the first shift, we have M, N, O, G, P in the first, and F, H, and L in the second. (C) is correct. On the test you should choose (C) and move on, but... (D) leaves L and O uncertain, and (E) leaves M uncertain.

3. Which two members cannot be on the same shift?
(A) H and N
(B) G and H
(C) L and N
(D) L and O
(E) M and O

We know that since P and N must be together, and P and H cannot, N and H can't be together. For a question like this, you definitely want to pick and move on, without wasting time on the wrong choices. (A) is correct.

4. Which of the following is a complete list of workers any one of whom can work on the first shift with H?
(A) G, L
(B) G, L, M
(C) G, L, M, O
(D) F, G, L, M, O
(E) F, G, L, M, N, O

If H works the first shift, we know F, P, and N must work the second. That leaves us with G, L, M, and O as options. Looking at the rules, there is nothing that prevents any one of those elements from working the first shift when H does. (C) is correct.

5. What is the maximum number of people who can work the second shift?
(A) 3
(B) 4
(C) 5
(D) 6
(E) 7

Diagram 1 has a minimum of three people already on the first shift, so if we want to maximize the second shift, we want to work with Diagram 2. Diagram 2 starts with H in shift 1, and F, P, and N in shift 2. G, L, M, and O are free to be placed. Is there any reason any one of them cannot be placed in the second shift? Not at all. If it were the first shift, the conditional rules would have an impact, but there is no reason all of those elements can't be in the second shift together. Thus, the most that can work together on the second shift is seven—all workers minus H. (E) is correct.

6. Which of the following, if substituted for the rule that P and H will work different shifts, would have the same effect on the assignment of workers?
(A) If N works the first shift, H will work the second.
(B) If N does not work the first shift, H will.
(C) N will work the first shift if, and only if, H works the second.
(D) If P works the first shift, so will G.
(E) P will work the first shift, if and only if, G works the first shift.

We know that P and N have to work the same shift, and so being told that H and N work different shifts would be the same as being told that P and H work different shifts. So, perhaps we anticipate an answer that tells us that H and N work different shifts, and (C) does that for us. The *if and only if* works as a biconditional that basically tells us that N and H can't work the same shift. (A) doesn't put P and H on opposite shifts if H works the second shift. (B) doesn't put P and H on opposite shifts if H works the first shift. (D) and (E) have an indirect impact on H and can be quickly eliminated. (C) is the correct answer.

7. If the rule that P and N will work the same shift is replaced by a rule that P and N will work different shifts, which of the following could be a complete list of people who work the first shift?
(A) H, N, L, M, O
(B) G, L, O, P
(C) G, H, M, O
(D) G, M, P
(E) G, L, P, H

The P/N rule is so central to our diagram that if we are forced to change it, it makes sense for us to redraw our entire diagram, as we've done to the right. Per this new diagram, (D) is the only possible answer, and (D) is correct.

How Did You Do?

This was a particularly full lesson. Not only did we discuss a large variety of question types, you were also challenged by several difficult games with tough questions attached. Congratulations on getting through it all.

Much of this book has been devoted to discussing the behavior and characteristics of top scorers, but it can also be helpful to think about the challenges that are common to those who don't perform as well as they could. Below is a list of some of the most common characteristics of people who underperform in the games section.

six common characteristics of underperformers

don't let these descriptions fit you!

1. They have trouble seeing the "big picture" for a game. This is often due to inadequate preparation—not being exposed to the different types of issues that can appear in games, and not having a sense of how these issues relate to one another. This can also be due to poor strategy—for example, certain learning systems encourage students to start drawing their diagram as soon as they start reading the scenario, a strategy that is almost certain to lead the test taker to miss the forest for the trees.

2. Their notations do not accurately reflect the rules. This can be due to the fact that the test taker does not understand the rules as specifically as he or she should, or has not practiced enough to be comfortable notating rules in a specific fashion. Underperformers represent some rules perfectly, a few incorrectly, and many "pretty well, but not exactly." This will prevent them from thinking about questions at an advanced level.

3. They cannot think of games intuitively and have trouble making inferences. This is very much related to the two points mentioned above, for in order to have the capacity to think about how rules come together, you have to have a big-picture understanding, and you have to be free from having to consciously think about what your notations actually mean—you have to be able to focus on just using those notations to think about the game itself.

4. They misread. Even though the Logic Games section is mostly a test of your reasoning ability, there are plenty of reading challenges all over the place: think of the difference between *if* and *only if,* and the difference between "complete list of those that could," and "could be a complete list."

5. They misallocate time. This is due to bad timing strategy or lack of timing strategy/lack of self-restraint. Characteristics include wasting time during the setup by creating unnecessary hypotheticals and chasing inferences that aren't there, taking drastic timing measures such as deciding to skip entire games, and wasting a disproportionate amount of time on the hardest questions, only to run out of time for the easier ones.

6. They don't use question-specific approaches. Most commonly, this is simply due to a lack of thought—most test takers do not think about question-specific strategies. To illustrate the consequence of this, let's just think of one common question type: an unconditional Must Be False. The prepared student focuses on finding the one answer that must be false. The misguided student will waste a lot of time trying to confirm that the other answers, which we often won't know a whole lot about, could definitely be true. Students who don't think about their process at all are also liable to waste time thinking about whether answers could be false. It's likely all five answers to a question like this can be false, and knowing that an answer can be false gets us no closer to knowing which one *must* be false.

28 LOGIC GAMES the good and the great

We've covered a lot of ground. And if you feel comfortable with the material you've seen thus far, know that you are in great shape. In fact, I guarantee that, just based on the work we've done thus far, you are far more prepared for the Logic Games section than the vast majority of people who will take the exam. Perhaps you are even thinking to yourself that if everything goes perfectly—if you really nail each of the four games you see—there might be a -0 in your future.

It's not going to happen.

I'm not talking about the -0 part. My hope is that this will be the outcome for a great many of you. I'm talking about the playing each game perfectly part. You are not going to be perfect on all four games.

Perfection is not necessary, and the pursuit of it can sometimes prevent you from just getting on with it and getting the job done

What a jerk I am! How can I say such a thing? For one, I've never been able to do it, and I teach this stuff for a living. I've never done a full section, then looked back at it, and said to myself, "Yup, I set up each diagram perfectly, and I used the most efficient process for every single question." Any time I've reviewed my work, I've noticed better ways to diagram or notate, inferences missed, and time wasted in the problem-solving process. Perfection is not necessary, and the pursuit of it can sometimes prevent you from just getting on with it and getting the job done. Even though I never solve all four games perfectly, I never have trouble with timing, and I can't remember the last time I missed a question. You don't need to be perfect to get a perfect score. Let me say that again: you don't need to be perfect to get a perfect score. What you need to do is always be good, and sometimes be great. Here's how I define that:

Always Good

No matter what, I will never misunderstand the general instructions for a game. Sometimes, it will be difficult for me to see it correctly, and sometimes the process will take me longer than I would like, but I know that I'm setting myself up for failure if I go into the questions having not understood, or having misrepresented, a rule.

I may misunderstand a rule initially (it happens), but I go carefully enough, and I have enough checks built in, that I never go into the questions with a misunderstanding of any rule. I may not always have the perfect notation for every rule, but my notations will always be correct, and I will always know what they mean, even if I have to literally write the rules out in words in order for this to be. Holding myself to an extremely high level of accountability on those two elements really frees me up to think about games on a higher level.

Sometimes Great

And that allows me to sometimes be great. I can put myself in a position to do this by...

...thinking about how the rules relate to one another. A great understanding of this will influence how I notate the rules (and thus how easily I am able to bring them together for the solving of questions), and it will help me in my decisions about which rules are most important. It will also, of course, help me see more easily the inferences that will ultimately lead to right and wrong answers.

...recognizing occasions when I can create multiple diagrams. Often games are designed so that we can splinter all of the various possibilities presented by the scenario and rules into multiple diagrams. We discussed the most common of these situations in the *Or* lesson. For most games that can be organized into multiple diagrams, it's possible to play the game very well whether you stick with one diagram or decide to create multiple ones. However, there are a few games where *not* creating multiple diagrams can lead to excruciating problem solving, and a few games where creative splintering can drastically reduce the amount of time it takes to solve questions.

...seeing why they are asking me a question. I'm sure you've experienced this before—you're playing a game, you read a condition or something else in the question stem, and a key inference immediately comes to you. You're certain it's the right answer, and you look and it's right there. You've solved a question in less than twenty seconds, and you can move on.

Of course this won't happen every question, but if you can get it to happen on just a few, it will give you the time you need for the questions that require more work.

Good and Great Solutions, Then Drill

On the following pages are solutions for all of the games from the June '07 LSAT. For three of the four games, both a good and a great solution have been given. Carefully evaluate these solutions and pay particular attention to the consequences that the different setups have when it comes time to answer questions.

After reading the solutions, you will get a chance to play the games yourself. Certainly—right after you've studied the solutions—it won't feel like a real exam, but you should find that as long as you don't memorize answer choices, it will still be a challenge. Drilling games in this way—by seeing the solutions first—presents a unique learning experience. You'll know exactly what the games are about, and from seeing the good and great solutions, you'll probably know exactly how *you* want to solve all four games. Thus, this exercise is primarily about execution—if you know what to expect, and you know what you want to do, how effective are you at actually getting it done?

THE GOOD SOLUTION

A company employee generates a series of five-digit product codes in accordance with the following rules:

The codes use the digits 0, 1, 2, 3, and 4, and no others.
Each digit occurs exactly once in any code.
The second digit has a value exactly twice that of the first digit.
The value of the third digit is less than the value of the fifth digit.

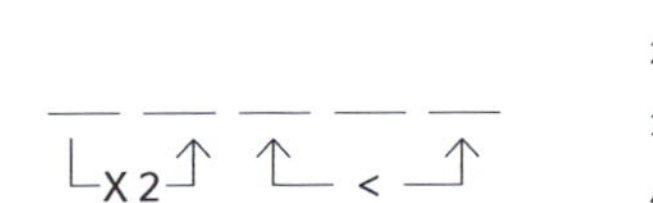

There are actually only two noteworthy rules here—the third and fourth. They are a bit tricky to notate, so I double check that I understand my notations correctly before going into the questions...

1. If the last digit of an acceptable product code is 1, it must be true that the
(A) first digit is 2
(B) second digit is 0
(C) third digit is 3
(D) fourth digit is 4
(E) fourth digit is 0

2 4 0 3 1

If last digit is 1, third must be 0, 1st and 2nd must be 2 and 4, and that leaves 3 for the fourth spot.

2. Which one of the following must be true about any acceptable product code?
(A) The digit 1 appears in some position before the digit 2.
(B) The digit 1 appears in some position before the digit 3.
(C) The digit 2 appears in some position before the digit 3.
(D) The digit 3 appears in some position before the digit 0.
(E) The digit 4 appears in some position before the digit 3.

Can't easily see right answer. Used work from 1 to eliminate (A), (B), and (D). Stuck for a while between (C) and (E) before seeing that first two elements must be 1 and 2 or 2 and 4—either way 2 has to be in there, and so must come before 3.

3. If the third digit of an acceptable product code is not 0, which one of the following must be true?
(A) The second digit of the product code is 2.
(B) The third digit of the product code is 3.
(C) The fourth digit of the product code is 0.
(D) The fifth digit of the product code is 3.
(E) The fifth digit of the product code is 1.

_ _ _ 0 _

Remembered from previous question that 0 can't go in first two spots. Know it can't go fifth. If it doesn't go third, it must go fourth. Can't figure out much else, but fortunately I don't have to.

4. Any of the following pairs could be the third and fourth digits, respectively, of an acceptable product code, EXCEPT:
(A) 0, 1
(B) 0, 3
(C) 1, 0
(D) 3, 0
(E) 3, 4

Didn't even know what to think about (A) - (D) and was nervous I'd have to run hypos to test answers, but fortunately (E) is an obvious MBF. If (E) were true, the fifth number couldn't be higher than the third.

5. Which one of the following must be true about any acceptable product code?
(A) There is exactly one digit between the digit 0 and the digit 1.
(B) There is exactly one digit between the digit 1 and the digit 2.
(C) There are at most two digits between the digit 1 and the digit 3.
(D) There are at most two digits between the digit 2 and the digit 3.
(E) There are at most two digits between the digit 2 and the digit 4.

1 2 _ _ 3
2 4 _ _ 3
2 _ _ _ 4

Fumbled a bit before I figured out the issue. Knew (A) and (B) didn't have to be true from previous questions. Needed to test out (C), (D), and (E) to see if there was some reason one couldn't work. When I got to (E), I could see easily why it wasn't possible to have more than three digits between 2 and 4.

THE GREAT SOLUTION

A company employee generates a series of five-digit product codes in accordance with the following rules:

The codes use the digits 0, 1, 2, 3, and 4, and no others.
Each digit occurs exactly once in any code.
The second digit has a value exactly twice that of the first digit.
The value of the third digit is less than the value of the fifth digit.

1	2	0	3	4
1	2	0	4	3
1	2	3	0	4
2	4	0	1	3
2	4	0	3	1
2	4	1	0	3

In the first read-through, I notice that there are only two ways to satisfy the third rule, and use it to set up two diagrams: one that started 1, 2, and another that started 2, 4. I then realize that in each diagram there are limited ways in which to satisfy the final rule, and so I expand each diagram further by framing out those options. This gives me six total diagrams that completely represent the different ways in which the order of numbers can satisfy all of the given conditions.

1. If the last digit of an acceptable product code is 1, it must be true that the
(A) first digit is 2
(B) second digit is 0
(C) third digit is 3
(D) fourth digit is 4
(E) fourth digit is 0

This only happens in the fifth frame above, and so I used that frame (which is ordered 2, 4, 0, 3, 1) to see that (A) must be true.

2. Which one of the following must be true about any acceptable product code?
(A) The digit 1 appears in some position before the digit 2.
(B) The digit 1 appears in some position before the digit 3.
(C) The digit 2 appears in some position before the digit 3.
(D) The digit 3 appears in some position before the digit 0.
(E) The digit 4 appears in some position before the digit 3.

2 appears before 3 in all six options above, and so (C) is the correct answer.

3. If the third digit of an acceptable product code is not 0, which one of the following must be true?
(A) The second digit of the product code is 2.
(B) The third digit of the product code is 3.
(C) The fourth digit of the product code is 0.
(D) The fifth digit of the product code is 3.
(E) The fifth digit of the product code is 1.

This only happens in the third and sixth frames above, and in both scenarios the fourth digit is 0, so (C) is correct.

4. Any of the following pairs could be the third and fourth digits, respectively, of an acceptable product code, EXCEPT:
(A) 0, 1
(B) 0, 3
(C) 1, 0
(D) 3, 0
(E) 3, 4

(A) - (D) are all options that show up above. 3 and 4 never appear as the third and fourth digits, respectively, so (E) is the correct answer.

5. Which one of the following must be true about any acceptable product code?
(A) There is exactly one digit between the digit 0 and the digit 1.
(B) There is exactly one digit between the digit 1 and the digit 2.
(C) There are at most two digits between the digit 1 and the digit 3.
(D) There are at most two digits between the digit 2 and the digit 3.
(E) There are at most two digits between the digit 2 and the digit 4.

I can find options above that counter answer choices (A) - (D), thereby showing that they do not have to be true. (E) is consistent with all frames, so (E) must be true.

THE GOOD SOLUTION

Exactly three films—Greed, Harvest, and Limelight—are shown during a film club's festival held on Thursday, Friday, and Saturday. Each film is shown at least once during the festival but never more than once on a given day. On each day at least one film is shown. Films are shown one at a time. The following conditions apply:

On Thursday Harvest is shown, and no film is shown after it on that day.
On Friday either Greed or Limelight, but not both, is shown, and no film is shown after it on that day.
On Saturday either Greed or Harvest, but not both, is shown, and no film is shown after it on that day.

		G/L out ↓	G/H out ↓	
1	___	___	___	G
2	___	___	___	H
3	___	/	/	L
	T	F	S	
	H last	G/L last	G/H last	

I know I didn't nail this one, but at least I got all of the information in. Thought of earliest film as "1" and so on. The rules seem simple enough, but without knowing how many films are shown each day, it's tough to know if "H" last means it's the first film shown, the second one, or the third. Same with G/L and G/H. One inference is that neither Friday nor Saturday will show all three films, so we can cross those spots out.

6. Which one of the following could be a complete and accurate description of the order in which the films are shown at the festival?

(A) Thursday: Limelight, then Harvest; Friday: Limelight; Saturday: Harvest
(B) Thursday: Harvest; Friday: Greed, then Limelight; Saturday: Limelight, then Greed
(C) Thursday: Harvest; Friday: Limelight; Saturday: Limelight, then Greed
(D) Thursday: Greed, then Harvest, then Limelight; Friday: Limelight; Saturday: Greed
(E) Thursday: Greed, then Harvest; Friday: Limelight, then Harvest; Saturday: Harvest

Used rules to eliminate answers. (A) was a bit tricky to eliminate—had to go back to scenario to see what was wrong: Greed not listed.

7. Which one of the following CANNOT be true?
(A) Harvest is the last film shown on each day of the festival.
(B) Limelight is shown on each day of the festival.
(C) Greed is shown second on each day of the festival.
(D) A different film is shown first on each day of the festival.
(E) A different film is shown last on each day of the festival.

Easy to see (A) can't be true and can move on quickly.

Exactly three films—Greed, Harvest, and Limelight—are shown during a film club's festival held on Thursday, Friday, and Saturday. Each film is shown at least once during the festival but never more than once on a given day. On each day at least one film is shown. Films are shown one at a time. The following conditions apply:

On Thursday Harvest is shown, and no film is shown after it on that day.
On Friday either Greed or Limelight, but not both, is shown, and no film is shown after it on that day.
On Saturday either Greed or Harvest, but not both, is shown, and no film is shown after it on that day.

		G/L out ↓	G/H out ↓	
1	___	___	___	G
2	___	___	___	H
3	___	/	/	L
	T	F	S	
	H last	G/L last	G/H last	

8. If Limelight is never shown again during the festival once Greed is shown, then which one of the following is the maximum number of film showings that could occur during the festival?
(A) three
(B) four
(C) five
(D) six
(E) seven

1	L	H	L
2	H	L	G
3	___	/	/
	T	F	S

Had to create hypo to see how many I could fit. Tried to place G as late as possible to fit in a lot of Ls. Was also going to try placing G early, but didn't have to after seeing I could get six in. Knew I couldn't get seven in, because that would mean all three elements go in Thursday.

9. If Greed is shown exactly three times, Harvest is shown exactly twice, and Limelight is shown exactly once, then which one of the following must be true?
(A) All three films are shown on Thursday.
(B) Exactly two films are shown on Saturday.
(C) Limelight and Harvest are both shown on Thursday.
(D) Greed is the only film shown on Saturday.
(E) Harvest and Greed are both shown on Friday.

___	H	___
G	G	G
H	/	/
T	F	S

I could see that the order of films wasn't important to the question or answers, so I just focused on which elements could go on which days. Kept in my head that L could go on T or S, but not both.

10. If Limelight is shown exactly three times, Harvest is shown exactly twice, and Greed is shown exactly once, then which one of the following is a complete and accurate list of the films that could be the first film shown on Thursday?
(A) Harvest
(B) Limelight
(C) Greed, Harvest
(D) Greed, Limelight
(E) Greed, Harvest, Limelight

___	___	___
L	L	L
H	/	/
T	F	S
	G (crossed out)	

Similar process as last time. Kept in my head that the other H can go on F or S, and the G can go on T or S. So, L, H, and G can all go on Thursday. Now had to remember that H has to go last. So, L or G could go first.

THE GREAT SOLUTION

Exactly three films—Greed, Harvest, and Limelight—are shown during a film club's festival held on Thursday, Friday, and Saturday. Each film is shown at least once during the festival but never more than once on a given day. On each day at least one film is shown. Films are shown one at a time. The following conditions apply:

On Thursday Harvest is shown, and no film is shown after it on that day.
On Friday either Greed or Limelight, but not both, is shown, and no film is shown after it on that day.
On Saturday either Greed or Harvest, but not both, is shown, and no film is shown after it on that day.

G
H
L

__ __ H | / H/– G/L | / L/– G/H
THU | FRI | SAT

Placing positions horizontally, within their respective days, makes it easier to see order. From the second rule I can infer that at most two films are shown on Friday, and, if more than one film is shown, the earlier film must be H. Similarly, I can infer from the third rule that at most two films can be shown on Saturday, and, if two films are shown, the earlier film must be L.

6. Which one of the following could be a complete and accurate description of the order in which the films are shown at the festival?
(A) Thursday: Limelight, then Harvest; Friday: Limelight; Saturday: Harvest
(B) Thursday: Harvest; Friday: Greed, then Limelight; Saturday: Limelight, then Greed
(C) Thursday: Harvest; Friday: Limelight; Saturday: Limelight, then Greed
(D) Thursday: Greed, then Harvest, then Limelight; Friday: Limelight; Saturday: Greed
(E) Thursday: Greed, then Harvest; Friday: Limelight, then Harvest; Saturday: Harvest

Same process as previous solution.

7. Which one of the following CANNOT be true?
(A) Harvest is the last film shown on each day of the festival.
(B) Limelight is shown on each day of the festival.
(C) Greed is shown second on each day of the festival.
(D) A different film is shown first on each day of the festival.
(E) A different film is shown last on each day of the festival.

Per the second rule H can't be last on Friday, and so (A) can't be true.

8. If Limelight is never shown again during the festival once Greed is shown, then which one of the following is the maximum number of film showings that could occur during the festival?
(A) three
(B) four
(C) five
(D) six
(E) seven

/ L H | / H L | / L G
L G H | / H G | / / G
THU | FRI | SAT

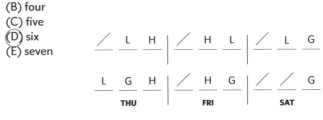

If I'm looking to fit in the maximum number of elements while satisfying the given condition, it makes sense to try a couple of options at the extremes: trying to put G as late as possible, to fit in as many L's as I can, or trying to put G as early as possible, to fit in as many G's as I can. So I try those two options, and the max I can fit in are six elements. I can't find a way to fit in 7 elements, so (D) is correct.

Exactly three films—Greed, Harvest, and Limelight—are shown during a film club's festival held on Thursday, Friday, and Saturday. Each film is shown at least once during the festival but never more than once on a given day. On each day at least one film is shown. Films are shown one at a time. The following conditions apply:

On Thursday Harvest is shown, and no film is shown after it on that day.
On Friday either Greed or Limelight, but not both, is shown, and no film is shown after it on that day.
On Saturday either Greed or Harvest, but not both, is shown, and no film is shown after it on that day.

G
H
L

__ __ H | ⁄ H/– G/L | ⁄ L/– G/H
THU | FRI | SAT

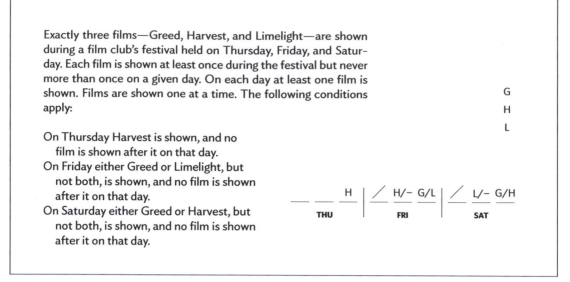

9. If Greed is shown exactly three times, Harvest is shown exactly twice, and Limelight is shown exactly once, then which one of the following must be true?
(A) All three films are shown on Thursday.
(B) Exactly two films are shown on Saturday.
(C) Limelight and Harvest are both shown on Thursday.
(D) Greed is the only film shown on Saturday.
(E) Harvest and Greed are both shown on Friday.

(G) __ __ H | ⁄ H G | ⁄ __ G
THU | FRI | SAT
L/ | | /L

If G is shown three times, it has to be shown as the last film on Saturday, the last film on Friday, and at some point on Thursday. If H is shown twice, it must be shown on Friday because it can't be on Saturday. If L is shown once, it can be shown on either Thursday or Saturday. Based on all this, the only answer that must be true is (E).

10. If Limelight is shown exactly three times, Harvest is shown exactly twice, and Greed is shown exactly once, then which one of the following is a complete and accurate list of the films that could be the first film shown on Thursday?
(A) Harvest
(B) Limelight
(C) Greed, Harvest
(D) Greed, Limelight
(E) Greed, Harvest, Limelight

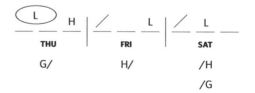

(L) __ __ H | ⁄ __ L | ⁄ L __
THU | FRI | SAT
G/ | H/ | /H
 | | /G

If L is shown three times, it has to be shown as the last film on Friday, the first film on Saturday, and at some point on Thursday. If H is shown twice, it can be shown on Friday or Saturday, but not both, since it is already shown on Thursday. If G is shown once, it can be on Thursday or Saturday, because L is now last on Friday. Based on all this L and G are the options for the first film on Thursday, and so (D) is correct.

JUST THE GOOD SOLUTION

A cruise line is scheduling seven week-long voyages for the ship Freedom. Each voyage will occur in exactly one of the first seven weeks of the season: weeks 1 through 7. Each voyage will be to exactly one of four destinations: Guadeloupe, Jamaica, Martinique, or Trinidad. Each destination will be scheduled for at least one of the weeks. The following conditions apply to Freedom's schedule:

Jamaica will not be its destination in week 4.
Trinidad will be its destination in week 7.
Freedom will make exactly two voyages to Martinique, and at least one voyage to Guadeloupe will occur in some week between those two voyages.
Guadeloupe will be its destination in the week preceding any voyage it makes to Jamaica.
No destination will be scheduled for consecutive weeks.

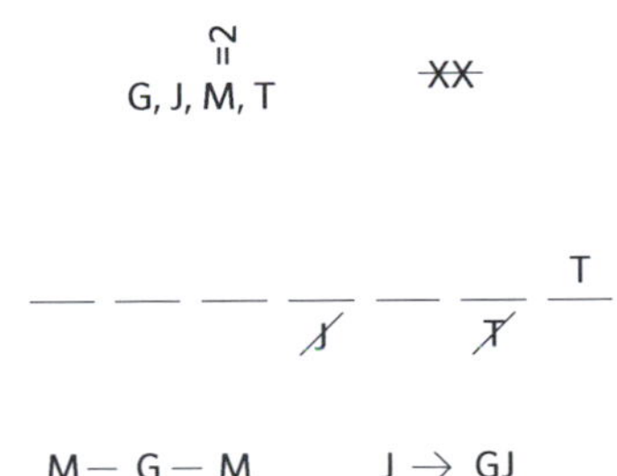

There is no good and great for this game because there is little mystery as to how to set it up or think about it.

It's plenty tough, though—perhaps the toughest game in the set. What it requires from us is spot-on execution. The third and fourth rules (particularly the fourth) are ripe for misreading or mis-notating, and many of the wrong answers are designed to trap those who don't use those rules correctly. The questions are much like the setup—they don't require cleverness, but they do require a lot of correct execution.

11. Which one of the following is an acceptable schedule of destinations for Freedom, in order from week 1 through week 7?
(A) Guadeloupe, Jamaica, Martinique, Trinidad, Guadeloupe, Martinique, Trinidad
(B) Guadeloupe, Martinique, Trinidad, Martinique, Guadeloupe, Jamaica, Trinidad
(C) Jamaica, Martinique, Guadeloupe, Martinique, Guadeloupe, Jamaica, Trinidad
(D) Martinique, Trinidad, Guadeloupe, Jamaica, Martinique, Guadeloupe, Trinidad
(E) Martinique, Trinidad, Guadeloupe, Trinidad, Guadeloupe, Jamaica, Martinique

Used rules to eliminate answers.

12. Which one of the following CANNOT be true about Freedom's schedule of voyages?
(A) Freedom makes a voyage to Trinidad in week 6.
(B) Freedom makes a voyage to Martinique in week 5.
(C) Freedom makes a voyage to Jamaica in week 6.
(D) Freedom makes a voyage to Jamaica in week 3.
(E) Freedom makes a voyage to Guadeloupe in week 3.

Made inference up front.

13. If Freedom makes a voyage to Trinidad in week 5, which one of the following could be true?
(A) Freedom makes a voyage to Trinidad in week 1.
(B) Freedom makes a voyage to Martinique in week 2.
(C) Freedom makes a voyage to Guadeloupe in week 3.
(D) Freedom makes a voyage to Martinique in week 4.
(E) Freedom makes a voyage to Jamaica in week 6.

M G J __ T __ T

G J M G T M T

If Freedom makes a trip to T in week 5, there are only two options for where J can go (since it can't go in four and since it must be preceded by G). Once we've drawn two boards, one with G, J in 2, 3 and the other with G, J in 1, 2, we can use the M-G-M rule to determine that in the first situation, M must go in 1 and either 4 or 6, and in the second, the only place for M-G-M to go would be 3, 4, and 6. We can use these results to confirm that all answers other than (D) must be false.

14. If Freedom makes a voyage to Guadeloupe in week 1 and a voyage to Jamaica in week 5, which one of the following must be true?
(A) Freedom makes a voyage to Jamaica in week 2.
(B) Freedom makes a voyage to Trinidad in week 2.
(C) Freedom makes a voyage to Martinique in week 3.
(D) Freedom makes a voyage to Guadeloupe in week 6.
(E) Freedom makes a voyage to Martinique in week 6.

G __ __ G J M T

Once I placed G and J, I knew M has to go in 6 to fit the M-G-M set in.

A cruise line is scheduling seven week-long voyages for the ship Freedom. Each voyage will occur in exactly one of the first seven weeks of the season: weeks 1 through 7. Each voyage will be to exactly one of four destinations: Guadeloupe, Jamaica, Martinique, or Trinidad. Each destination will be scheduled for at least one of the weeks. The following conditions apply to Freedom's schedule:

Jamaica will not be its destination in week 4.
Trinidad will be its destination in week 7.
Freedom will make exactly two voyages to Martinique, and at least one voyage to Guadeloupe will occur in some week between those two voyages.
Guadeloupe will be its destination in the week preceding any voyage it makes to Jamaica.
No destination will be scheduled for consecutive weeks.

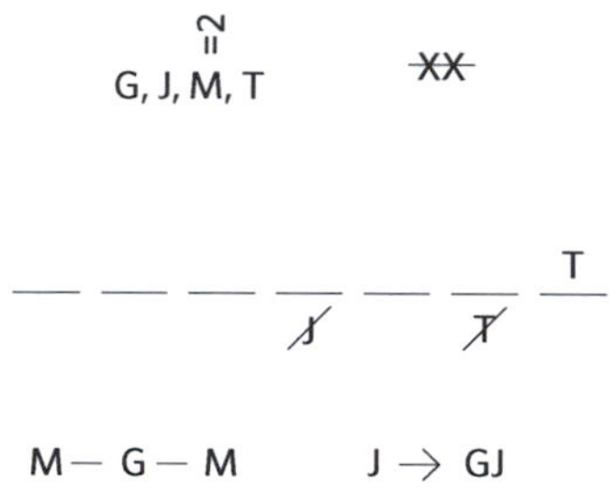

G, J, M, T (=2) ~~XX~~

__ __ __ __ __ __ T
(week 4: not J; week 6: not T)

M — G — M   J → GJ

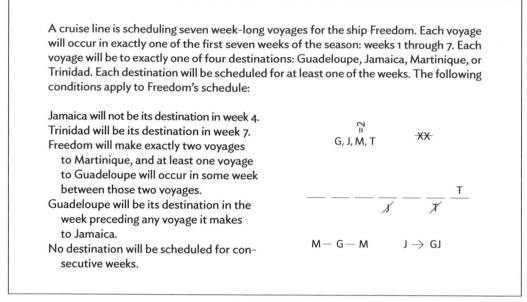

15. If Freedom makes a voyage to Guadeloupe in week 1 and to Trinidad in week 2, which one of the following must be true?
(A) Freedom makes a voyage to Martinique in week 3.
(B) Freedom makes a voyage to Martinique in week 4.
(C) Freedom makes a voyage to Martinique in week 5.
(D) Freedom makes a voyage to Guadeloupe in week 3.
(E) Freedom makes a voyage to Guadeloupe in week 5.

G T M G J M T

We've got to get the M-G-M group and GJ in, and there is only one way to do that.

16. If Freedom makes a voyage to Martinique in week 3, which one of the following could be an accurate list of Freedom's destinations in week 4 and week 5, respectively?
(A) Guadeloupe, Trinidad
(B) Jamaica, Guadeloupe
(C) Martinique, Trinidad
(D) Trinidad, Jamaica
(E) Trinidad, Martinique

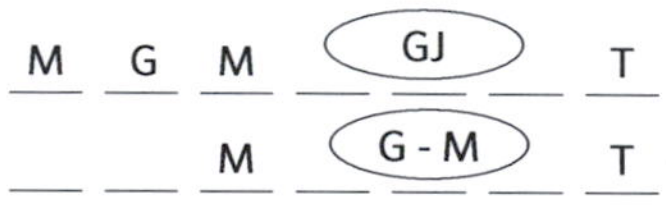

M G M (GJ) __ T
__ __ M (G - M) __ T

I didn't know how to go about solving this problem based on just putting M down in 3, or just adding that to the pile of information, so I decided to play out the different ways in which M could be third, relative to the M-G-M grouping we know of. I was disappointed I couldn't make more inferences, but the diagrams gave me all I needed to eliminate the wrong choices.

17. Which one of the following must be true about Freedom's schedule of voyages?
(A) Freedom makes a voyage to Guadeloupe either in week 1 or else in week 2.
(B) Freedom makes a voyage to Martinique either in week 2 or else in week 3.
(C) Freedom makes at most two voyages to Guadeloupe.
(D) Freedom makes at most two voyages to Jamaica.
(E) Freedom makes at most two voyages to Trinidad.

I was worried I'd have to draw things out for this one too, but once I got to (D) I knew it was correct. If I had 3 Js I'd need 3 Gs, and there isn't enough space for that.

THE GOOD SOLUTION

There are exactly three recycling centers in Rivertown: Center 1, Center 2, and Center 3. Exactly five kinds of material are recycled at these recycling centers: glass, newsprint, plastic, tin, and wood. Each recycling center recycles at least two but no more than three of these kinds of material. The following conditions must hold:

Any recycling center that recycles wood also recycles newsprint.
Every kind of material that Center 2 recycles is also recycled at Center 1.
Only one of the recycling centers recycles plastic, and that recycling center does not recycle glass.

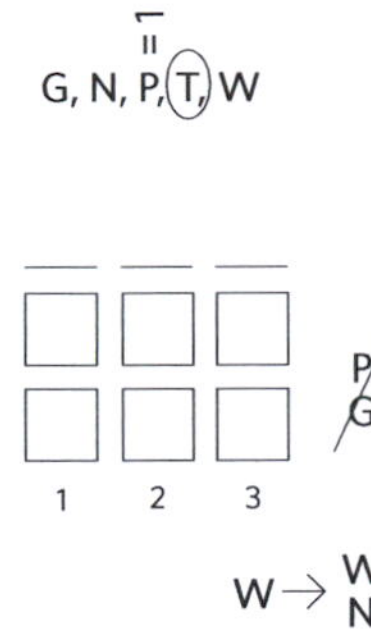

This is a fairly straightforward scenario, but the rules are a bit challenging to notate. In any case, I'm able to get the rules down, and I understand the meaning of my notations. I have a feeling this game is going to be challenging because I haven't been able to make any inferences, and because the rules are all of a different type—that means I have to go through a variety of thought processes as I solve questions.

18. Which one of the following could be an accurate account of all the kinds of material recycled at each recycling center in Rivertown?
(A) Center 1: newsprint, plastic, wood; Center 2: newsprint, wood; Center 3: glass, tin, wood
(B) Center 1: glass, newsprint, tin; Center 2: glass, newsprint, tin; Center 3: newsprint, plastic, wood
(C) Center 1: glass, newsprint, wood; Center 2: glass, newsprint, tin; Center 3: plastic, tin
(D) Center 1: glass, plastic, tin; Center 2: glass, tin; Center 3: newsprint, wood
(E) Center 1: newsprint, plastic, wood; Center 2: newsprint, plastic, wood; Center 3: glass, newsprint, tin

Used rules to eliminate answers. Since there are just three rules here, expect one of them to eliminate two answers, and the third rule does that.

19. Which one of the following is a complete and accurate list of the recycling centers in Rivertown any one of which could recycle plastic?
(A) Center 1 only
(B) Center 3 only
(C) Center 1, Center 2
(D) Center 1, Center 3
(E) Center 1, Center 2, Center 3

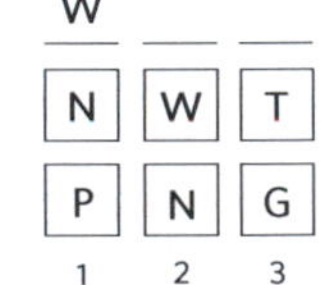

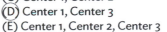

I know that Center 2 can't recycle P, otherwise two centers would have to. That leaves Centers 1 and 3 as options. I know 3 can work per the Rules question. It seems 1 can work, but I want to make sure there isn't some strange reason it can't. I come up with one hypothetical arrangement to make sure it works, and select (D).

20. If Center 2 recycles three kinds of material, then which one of the following kinds of material must Center 3 recycle?
(A) glass
(B) newsprint
(C) plastic
(D) tin
(E) wood

The consequence of Center 2 recycling three types of material is that Center 1 must recycle the same three types of material. That means that P, which can only be recycled in one center, must be recycled in Center 3. That's all I can figure out, and fortunately that's the correct answer, (C).

21. If each recycling center in Rivertown recycles exactly three kinds of material, then which one of the following could be true?
(A) Only Center 2 recycles glass.
(B) Only Center 3 recycles newsprint.
(C) Only Center 1 recycles plastic.
(D) Only Center 3 recycles tin.
(E) Only Center 1 recycles wood.

Per the last question, I've already been thinking about this, and I know that two consequences would be that Centers 1 and 2 recycle the same three materials and that P is recycled in 3. That allows me to get rid of (A), (C), and (E). Looking at (B), if (B) is true, that means that only Center 3 recycles wood. That leaves glass, tin, and plastic as the three elements that must be recycled by 1 and 2, but plastic can't be recycled by both. Thus, (B) can't be true. (D) is the correct answer.

There are exactly three recycling centers in Rivertown: Center 1, Center 2, and Center 3. Exactly five kinds of material are recycled at these recycling centers: glass, newsprint, plastic, tin, and wood. Each recycling center recycles at least two but no more than three of these kinds of material. The following conditions must hold:

Any recycling center that recycles wood also recycles newsprint.
Every kind of material that Center 2 recycles is also recycled at Center 1.
Only one of the recycling centers recycles plastic, and that recycling center does not recycle glass.

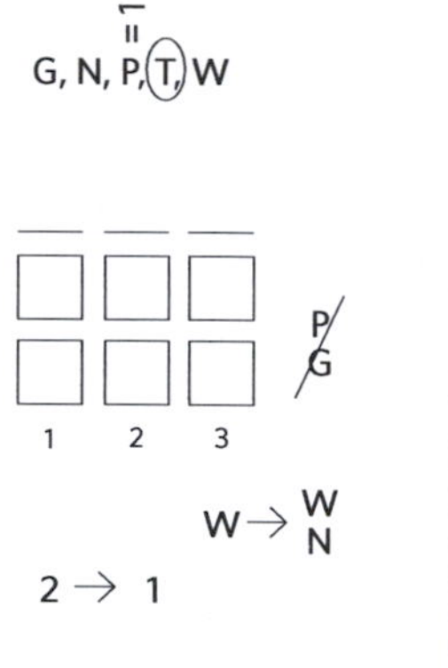

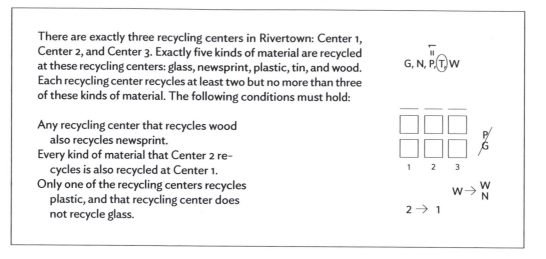

22. If Center 3 recycles glass, then which one of the following kinds of material must Center 2 recycle?
(A) glass
(B) newsprint
(C) plastic
(D) tin
(E) wood

P		G
1	2	3

W, N, or T

If G goes in 3, that means P must go in 1. That leaves W, N, and T as the three possibilities for Center 2. Does W have to be there? No, 2 could just recycle N and T. Does T have to be there? No, it can just recycle W and N. Does N have to be there? Yes, it does, because you can't just have W and T (because of the W → W, N rule). (B) is correct.

23. If Center 1 is the only recycling center that recycles wood, then which one of the following could be a complete and accurate list of the kinds of material that one of the recycling centers recycles?
(A) plastic, tin
(B) newsprint, wood
(C) newsprint, tin
(D) glass, wood
(E) glass, tin

G		
N	G	T
W	N	P
1	2	3

What a strange question. Anyway, I put W into 1, and that means N must also be in 1. That means N must also be in 2. I get stuck at this point and look to my rules. I realize that P must now go in 3, and since G can't go with P, G must go elsewhere, so it must go in 1 and 2. I know I still have T to place, and realize it can only go in 3. All that allows me to eliminate (B) through (E), and it's easy for me to see how (A) can work.

THE GREAT SOLUTION

There are exactly three recycling centers in Rivertown: Center 1, Center 2, and Center 3. Exactly five kinds of material are recycled at these recycling centers: glass, newsprint, plastic, tin, and wood. Each recycling center recycles at least two but no more than three of these kinds of material. The following conditions must hold:

Any recycling center that recycles wood also recycles newsprint.
Every kind of material that Center 2 recycles is also recycled at Center 1.
Only one of the recycling centers recycles plastic, and that recycling center does not recycle glass.

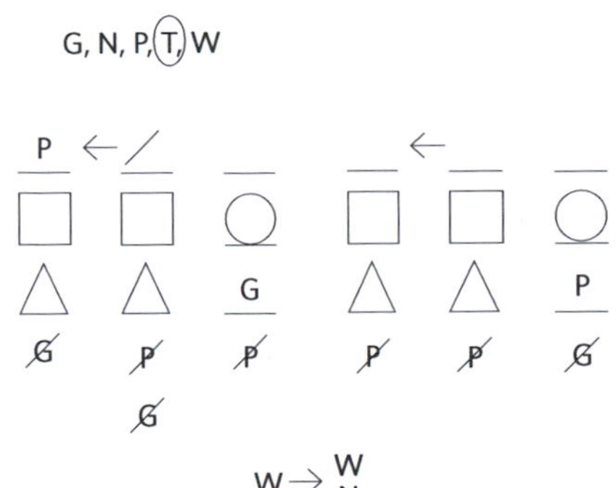

Here I use different shapes to get a clear visual representation of the second rule. (I keep in mind that the circles in Center 3 simply mean that space has to be filled.) Also, I am able to infer that P can't go in 2, and I use the final rule to branch off into two diagrams. One reason I chose to do this is because when P is in Center 1, I know that everything else about Centers 1 and 2 must match. Creating two diagrams also helps me note the part about glass in the last rule in a more visual way.

18. Which one of the following could be an accurate account of all the kinds of material recycled at each recycling center in Rivertown?
(A) Center 1: newsprint, plastic, wood; Center 2: newsprint, wood; Center 3: glass, tin, wood
(B) Center 1: glass, newsprint, tin; Center 2: glass, newsprint, tin; Center 3: newsprint, plastic, wood
(C) Center 1: glass, newsprint, wood; Center 2: glass, newsprint, tin; Center 3: plastic, tin
(D) Center 1: glass, plastic, tin; Center 2: glass, tin; Center 3: newsprint, wood
(E) Center 1: newsprint, plastic, wood; Center 2: newsprint, plastic, wood; Center 3: glass, newsprint, tin

Used rules to eliminate answers. Since there are just three rules here, I expected one of them to eliminate two answers, and the third rule does that.

19. Which one of the following is a complete and accurate list of the recycling centers in Rivertown any one of which could recycle plastic?
(A) Center 1 only
(B) Center 3 only
(C) Center 1, Center 2
(D) Center 1, Center 3
(E) Center 1, Center 2, Center 3

I've made this inference up front. I also know P can go into Center 3 from the previous question. If I need to, I can come up with a hypothetical to check that P can go in Center 1. I can just stick W and N into 1 and 2 and put G and T into 3. I'm comfortable enough with my diagram that I can do this mentally without redrawing.

20. If Center 2 recycles three kinds of material, then which one of the following kinds of material must Center 3 recycle?
(A) glass
(B) newsprint
(C) plastic
(D) tin
(E) wood

Per the condition, we know we're dealing with the second of our diagrams, and we can pick (C) easily.

21. If each recycling center in Rivertown recycles exactly three kinds of material, then which one of the following could be true?
(A) Only Center 2 recycles glass.
(B) Only Center 3 recycles newsprint.
(C) Only Center 1 recycles plastic.
(D) Only Center 3 recycles tin.
(E) Only Center 1 recycles wood.

We know we are dealing with the second diagram, and can eliminate (A), (C), and (E) easily. If 3 is the only center that recycles N, it means it's also the only center that recycles W. That takes N, W, and P away as options for filling the three spaces each for Centers 1 and 2, leaving only G and T. Since G and T can't fill all those spaces, (B) is not possible. (D) is correct.

There are exactly three recycling centers in Rivertown: Center 1, Center 2, and Center 3. Exactly five kinds of material are recycled at these recycling centers: glass, newsprint, plastic, tin, and wood. Each recycling center recycles at least two but no more than three of these kinds of material. The following conditions must hold:

Any recycling center that recycles wood also recycles newsprint.
Every kind of material that Center 2 recycles is also recycled at Center 1.
Only one of the recycling centers recycles plastic, and that recycling center does not recycle glass.

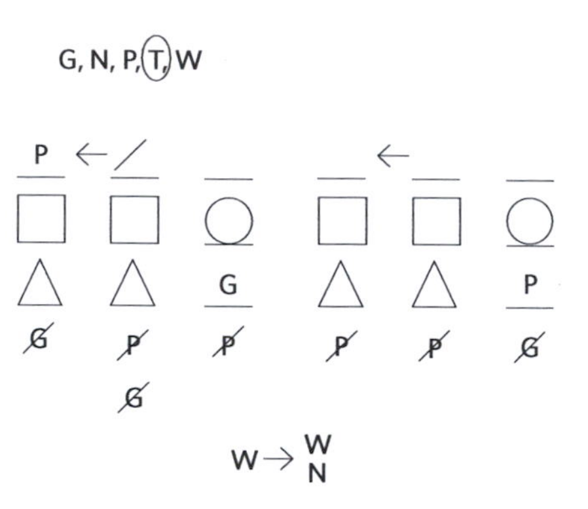

22. If Center 3 recycles glass, then which one of the following kinds of material must Center 2 recycle?
(A) glass
(B) newsprint
(C) plastic
(D) tin
(E) wood

If 3 recycles glass, we know we're dealing with the first of our diagrams. We know that Center 2 can't recycle P and G. That leaves W, N, and T as options, and we know at least 2 of the three must be selected. Leaving W out puts N and T in, which is fine, and leaving T out puts W and N in, which is fine, but putting N out leaves W and T, which is not fine. N must be in Center 2, and (B) is correct.

23. If Center 1 is the only recycling center that recycles wood, then which one of the following could be a complete and accurate list of the kinds of material that one of the recycling centers recycles?
(A) plastic, tin
(B) newsprint, wood
(C) newsprint, tin
(D) glass, wood
(E) glass, tin

W	/	
G	G	T
N	N	P
1	2	3

We know this is only possible in the second diagram. We put W into Center 1. That means N is in Center 1, which means N is also in Center 2. Center 2 can only have 2 elements, because it has to match the remaining two spots for Center 1. G has to go somewhere, and it can't go in 3, so it must go in 1 and 2. That means T has to go in 3. We can eliminate (B) - (E), and (A) is correct.

Directions for opposite page: Here's a chance for you to play the very same games we've been reviewing. Since you've just seen the games, it certainly won't feel like a real exam. It should still be a challenge. See if you can always be good and sometimes great, mark your setup and problem-solving times, and see if you can be as fast (or faster) than me without sacrificing control and accuracy.

GAME 1

A company employee generates a series of five-digit product codes in accordance with the following rules:

The codes use the digits 0, 1, 2, 3, and 4, and no others.
Each digit occurs exactly once in any code.
The second digit has a value exactly twice that of the first digit.
The value of the third digit is less than the value of the fifth digit.

1. If the last digit of an acceptable product code is 1, it must be true that the
(A) first digit is 2
(B) second digit is 0
(C) third digit is 3
(D) fourth digit is 4
(E) fourth digit is 0

2. Which one of the following must be true about any acceptable product code?
(A) The digit 1 appears in some position before the digit 2.
(B) The digit 1 appears in some position before the digit 3.
(C) The digit 2 appears in some position before the digit 3.
(D) The digit 3 appears in some position before the digit 0.
(E) The digit 4 appears in some position before the digit 3.

3. If the third digit of an acceptable product code is not 0, which one of the following must be true?
(A) The second digit of the product code is 2.
(B) The third digit of the product code is 3.
(C) The fourth digit of the product code is 0.
(D) The fifth digit of the product code is 3.
(E) The fifth digit of the product code is 1.

4. Any of the following pairs could be the third and fourth digits, respectively, of an acceptable product code, EXCEPT:
(A) 0, 1
(B) 0, 3
(C) 1, 0
(D) 3, 0
(E) 3, 4

5. Which one of the following must be true about any acceptable product code?
(A) There is exactly one digit between the digit 0 and the digit 1.
(B) There is exactly one digit between the digit 1 and the digit 2.
(C) There are at most two digits between the digit 1 and the digit 3.
(D) There are at most two digits between the digit 2 and the digit 3.
(E) There are at most two digits between the digit 2 and the digit 4.

GAME 2

Exactly three films—Greed, Harvest, and Limelight—are shown during a film club's festival held on Thursday, Friday, and Saturday. Each film is shown at least once during the festival but never more than once on a given day. On each day at least one film is shown. Films are shown one at a time. The following conditions apply:

On Thursday Harvest is shown, and no film is shown after it on that day.
On Friday either Greed or Limelight, but not both, is shown, and no film is shown after it on that day.
On Saturday either Greed or Harvest, but not both, is shown, and no film is shown after it on that day.

6. Which one of the following could be a complete and accurate description of the order in which the films are shown at the festival?
(A) Thursday: Limelight, then Harvest; Friday: Limelight; Saturday: Harvest
(B) Thursday: Harvest; Friday: Greed, then Limelight; Saturday: Limelight, then Greed
(C) Thursday: Harvest; Friday: Limelight; Saturday: Limelight, then Greed
(D) Thursday: Greed, then Harvest, then Limelight; Friday: Limelight; Saturday: Greed
(E) Thursday: Greed, then Harvest; Friday: Limelight, then Harvest; Saturday: Harvest

7. Which one of the following CANNOT be true?
(A) Harvest is the last film shown on each day of the festival.
(B) Limelight is shown on each day of the festival.
(C) Greed is shown second on each day of the festival.
(D) A different film is shown first on each day of the festival.
(E) A different film is shown last on each day of the festival.

8. If Limelight is never shown again during the festival once Greed is shown, then which one of the following is the maximum number of film showings that could occur during the festival?
(A) three
(B) four
(C) five
(D) six
(E) seven

9. If Greed is shown exactly three times, Harvest is shown exactly twice, and Limelight is shown exactly once, then which one of the following must be true?
(A) All three films are shown on Thursday.
(B) Exactly two films are shown on Saturday.
(C) Limelight and Harvest are both shown on Thursday.
(D) Greed is the only film shown on Saturday.
(E) Harvest and Greed are both shown on Friday.

10. If Limelight is shown exactly three times, Harvest is shown exactly twice, and Greed is shown exactly once, then which one of the following is a complete and accurate list of the films that could be the first film shown on Thursday?
(A) Harvest
(B) Limelight
(C) Greed, Harvest
(D) Greed, Limelight
(E) Greed, Harvest, Limelight

GAME 3

A cruise line is scheduling seven week-long voyages for the ship Freedom. Each voyage will occur in exactly one of the first seven weeks of the season: weeks 1 through 7. Each voyage will be to exactly one of four destinations: Guadeloupe, Jamaica, Martinique, or Trinidad. Each destination will be scheduled for at least one of the weeks. The following conditions apply to Freedom's schedule:

Jamaica will not be its destination in week 4.
Trinidad will be its destination in week 7.
Freedom will make exactly two voyages to Martinique, and at least one voyage to Guadeloupe will occur in some week between those two voyages.
Guadeloupe will be its destination in the week preceding any voyage it makes to Jamaica.
No destination will be scheduled for consecutive weeks.

11. Which one of the following is an acceptable schedule of destinations for Freedom, in order from week 1 through week 7?
(A) Guadeloupe, Jamaica, Martinique, Trinidad, Guadeloupe, Martinique, Trinidad
(B) Guadeloupe, Martinique, Trinidad, Martinique, Guadeloupe, Jamaica, Trinidad
(C) Jamaica, Martinique, Guadeloupe, Martinique, Guadeloupe, Jamaica, Trinidad
(D) Martinique, Trinidad, Guadeloupe, Jamaica, Martinique, Guadeloupe, Trinidad
(E) Martinique, Trinidad, Guadeloupe, Trinidad, Guadeloupe, Jamaica, Martinique

12. Which one of the following CANNOT be true about Freedom's schedule of voyages?
(A) Freedom makes a voyage to Trinidad in week 6.
(B) Freedom makes a voyage to Martinique in week 5.
(C) Freedom makes a voyage to Jamaica in week 6.
(D) Freedom makes a voyage to Jamaica in week 3.
(E) Freedom makes a voyage to Guadeloupe in week 3.

13. If Freedom makes a voyage to Trinidad in week 5, which one of the following could be true?
(A) Freedom makes a voyage to Trinidad in week 1.
(B) Freedom makes a voyage to Martinique in week 2.
(C) Freedom makes a voyage to Guadeloupe in week 3.
(D) Freedom makes a voyage to Martinique in week 4.
(E) Freedom makes a voyage to Jamaica in week 6.

14. If Freedom makes a voyage to Guadeloupe in week 1 and a voyage to Jamaica in week 5, which one of the following must be true?
(A) Freedom makes a voyage to Jamaica in week 2.
(B) Freedom makes a voyage to Trinidad in week 2.
(C) Freedom makes a voyage to Martinique in week 3.
(D) Freedom makes a voyage to Guadeloupe in week 6.
(E) Freedom makes a voyage to Martinique in week 6.

15. If Freedom makes a voyage to Guadeloupe in week 1 and to Trinidad in week 2, which one of the following must be true?
(A) Freedom makes a voyage to Martinique in week 3.
(B) Freedom makes a voyage to Martinique in week 4.
(C) Freedom makes a voyage to Martinique in week 5.
(D) Freedom makes a voyage to Guadeloupe in week 3.
(E) Freedom makes a voyage to Guadeloupe in week 5.

16. If Freedom makes a voyage to Martinique in week 3, which one of the following could be an accurate list of Freedom's destinations in week 4 and week 5, respectively?
(A) Guadeloupe, Trinidad
(B) Jamaica, Guadeloupe
(C) Martinique, Trinidad
(D) Trinidad, Jamaica
(E) Trinidad, Martinique

17. Which one of the following must be true about Freedom's schedule of voyages?
(A) Freedom makes a voyage to Guadeloupe either in week 1 or else in week 2.
(B) Freedom makes a voyage to Martinique either in week 2 or else in week 3.
(C) Freedom makes at most two voyages to Guadeloupe.
(D) Freedom makes at most two voyages to Jamaica.
(E) Freedom makes at most two voyages to Trinidad.

GAME 4

There are exactly three recycling centers in Rivertown: Center 1, Center 2, and Center 3. Exactly five kinds of material are recycled at these recycling centers: glass, newsprint, plastic, tin, and wood. Each recycling center recycles at least two but no more than three of these kinds of material. The following conditions must hold:

Any recycling center that recycles wood also recycles newsprint.
Every kind of material that Center 2 recycles is also recycled at Center 1.
Only one of the recycling centers recycles plastic, and that recycling center does not recycle glass.

18. Which one of the following could be an accurate account of all the kinds of material recycled at each recycling center in Rivertown?
(A) Center 1: newsprint, plastic, wood; Center 2: newsprint, wood; Center 3: glass, tin, wood
(B) Center 1: glass, newsprint, tin; Center 2: glass, newsprint, tin; Center 3: newsprint, plastic, wood
(C) Center 1: glass, newsprint, wood; Center 2: glass, newsprint, tin; Center 3: plastic, tin
(D) Center 1: glass, plastic, tin; Center 2: glass, tin; Center 3: newsprint, wood
(E) Center 1: newsprint, plastic, wood; Center 2: newsprint, plastic, wood; Center 3: glass, newsprint, tin

19. Which one of the following is a complete and accurate list of the recycling centers in Rivertown any one of which could recycle plastic?
(A) Center 1 only
(B) Center 3 only
(C) Center 1, Center 2
(D) Center 1, Center 3
(E) Center 1, Center 2, Center 3

20. If Center 2 recycles three kinds of material, then which one of the following kinds of material must Center 3 recycle?
(A) glass
(B) newsprint
(C) plastic
(D) tin
(E) wood

21. If each recycling center in Rivertown recycles exactly three kinds of material, then which one of the following could be true?
(A) Only Center 2 recycles glass.
(B) Only Center 3 recycles newsprint.
(C) Only Center 1 recycles plastic.
(D) Only Center 3 recycles tin.
(E) Only Center 1 recycles wood.

22. If Center 3 recycles glass, then which one of the following kinds of material must Center 2 recycle?
(A) glass
(B) newsprint
(C) plastic
(D) tin
(E) wood

23. If Center 1 is the only recycling center that recycles wood, then which one of the following could be a complete and accurate list of the kinds of material that one of the recycling centers recycles?
(A) plastic, tin
(B) newsprint, wood
(C) newsprint, tin
(D) glass, wood
(E) glass, tin

29 LOGIC GAMES the mastery challenge

I hope you had a good breakfast this morning.

For this lesson, I have handpicked four challenging games that have appeared on past LSATs. Each game was arguably the most difficult game that appeared in its section, and I know each game very well because these are all games students have asked me about over and over again. Each game is challenging in a different and unique way, and each game is presented with its full set of questions. Consider this an extreme assessment of where you are right now with your Logic Games skills.

If you didn't have that good breakfast, you may want to grab a cup of coffee.

In Lesson 3, we laid out a few different characteristics representative of Logic Games mastery. Here they are again:

1) An ability to comprehend and lay out a basic setup for any scenario
2) An ability to understand all rules in a specific and usable way
3) An ability to recognize the most significant aspects of a game
4) An ability to rarely make diagramming mistakes, and to recover when you do
5) An ability to intuitively use the correct strategy for answering questions
6) Confidence

We are going to use these characteristics as the benchmark against which you will assess your performance on these games.

Directions: Solve the next four games as you would if you saw them on the exam, except for two specific differences:

1) Do not think of these games, collectively, as a typical section. A section will have games that take less time, and games that take more, and all of these games are games that take longer than average. Give yourself an extra minute during the setup—it'll likely save you more than a minute in the questions. In addition, keep in mind that there are 26 questions here total, whereas on your exam you will almost certainly have 23 questions total. Work each game at the pace you would during the exam, and we'll discuss ways to assess the outcome afterwards.

2) Keep track of your timing at two points—after you have set up your diagram and after you have finished a game—and do not pause more than a few seconds to write your times. After each game, quickly fill out the assessment form before moving on to the next game. Do not check solutions in the middle of a game or between games.

Game 1 | PT 29, G2

Two mannequins—1 and 2—will be dressed for display in outfits chosen from ten articles of clothing. Each article is in exactly one of three colors: navy, red, or yellow. There are three hats—one in each color; three jackets—one in each color; three skirts—one in each color; and one red tie. Each mannequin wears exactly one of the hats, one of the jackets, and one of the skirts. Furthermore, their outfits must meet the following restrictions:

Neither mannequin wears all three colors.
Each mannequin wears a hat in a different color from the jacket it wears.
Mannequin 2 wears the navy skirt.
Mannequin 1 wears the tie.

Setup time: ______

7. Which one of the following could be complete outfits for the two mannequins?
(A) mannequin 1: navy hat, red jacket, yellow skirt, red tie
mannequin 2: red hat, navy jacket, navy skirt
(B) mannequin 1: red hat, red jacket, yellow skirt, red tie
mannequin 2: yellow hat, navy jacket, navy skirt
(C) mannequin 1: red hat, yellow jacket, red skirt, red tie
mannequin 2: yellow hat, navy jacket, yellow skirt
(D) mannequin 1: yellow hat, red jacket, yellow skirt, red tie
mannequin 2: red hat, navy jacket, navy skirt
(E) mannequin 1: yellow hat, yellow jacket, red skirt
mannequin 2: red hat, navy jacket, navy skirt

8. Which one of the following could be true of the mannequins' outfits?
(A) Mannequin 1 wears the navy jacket and the yellow skirt.
(B) Mannequin 2 wears the red hat and the red jacket.
(C) Mannequin 1 wears exactly one red article of clothing.
(D) Mannequin 1 wears exactly three yellow articles of clothing.
(E) Mannequin 2 wears no red articles of clothing.

9. If mannequin 1 wears the navy jacket, which one of the following could be true?
(A) Mannequin 1 wears the yellow hat.
(B) Mannequin 1 wears the yellow skirt.
(C) Mannequin 2 wears the red hat.
(D) Mannequin 2 wears the yellow hat.
(E) Mannequin 2 wears the yellow jacket.

10. If all four of the red articles of clothing are included in the two mannequins' outfits, which one of the following must be true?
(A) Mannequin 1 wears the red hat.
(B) Mannequin 1 wears the yellow jacket.
(C) Mannequin 2 wears the navy jacket.
(D) Mannequin 1 wears no navy articles of clothing.
(E) Mannequin 2 wears no yellow articles of clothing.

11. If mannequin 2 wears the red jacket, then mannequin 1 must wear the
(A) navy hat
(B) red hat
(C) yellow hat
(D) red skirt
(E) yellow skirt

12. If all three of the yellow articles of clothing are included in the two mannequins' outfits, which one of the following could be true?
(A) Mannequin 1 wears the navy jacket.
(B) Mannequin 1 wears the yellow jacket.
(C) Mannequin 1 wears the red skirt.
(D) Mannequin 2 wears the red hat.
(E) Mannequin 2 wears the red jacket.

13. If mannequin 1 wears the skirt that is the same color as the jacket that mannequin 2 wears, which one of the following must be true?
(A) Mannequin 1 wears the yellow hat.
(B) Mannequin 1 wears the yellow jacket.
(C) Mannequin 2 wears the navy hat.
(D) Mannequin 2 wears the red hat.
(E) Mannequin 2 wears the red jacket.

Total time: ______

Did you feel...	Y	-	N
You understood basic design and laid it out well			
You understood and notated all rules well			
You recognized the most significant aspects			
You didn't make a diagramming mistake			
You used correct question strategies			
You felt confident			

Game 2 | PT 31, G2

A music store carries ten types of CDs—both new and used of each of jazz, opera, pop, rap, and soul. The store is having a sale on some of these types of CDs. The following conditions must apply:
Used pop is on sale; new opera is not.
If both types of pop are on sale, then all soul is.
If both types of jazz are on sale, then no rap is.
If neither type of jazz is on sale, then new pop is.
If either type of rap is on sale, then no soul is.

Setup time: ______

7. Which one of the following could be a complete and accurate list of the types of CDs that are on sale?
(A) new jazz, used jazz, used opera, used pop, new rap
(B) new jazz, used pop, used rap, new soul
(C) used opera, used pop, new rap, used rap
(D) used opera, new pop, used pop, new soul
(E) used jazz, used pop, new soul, used soul

8. If new soul is not on sale, then which one of the following must be true?
(A) New rap is not on sale.
(B) New rap is on sale.
(C) Used opera is not on sale.
(D) At least one type of jazz is not on sale.
(E) At least one type of pop is not on sale.

9. If both types of jazz are on sale, then which one of the following is the minimum number of types of new CDs that could be included in the sale?
(A) one
(B) two
(C) three
(D) four
(E) five

10. Which one of the following CANNOT be true?
(A) Neither type of opera and neither type of rap is on sale.
(B) Neither type of jazz and neither type of opera is on sale.
(C) Neither type of opera and neither type of soul is on sale.
(D) Neither type of jazz and neither type of soul is on sale.
(E) Neither type of jazz and neither type of rap is on sale.

11. If neither type of jazz is on sale, then each of the following must be true EXCEPT:
(A) Used opera is on sale.
(B) New rap is not on sale.
(C) Used rap is not on sale.
(D) New soul is on sale.
(E) Used soul is on sale.

12. If new soul is the only type of new CD on sale, then which one of the following CANNOT be true?
(A) Used jazz is not on sale.
(B) Use opera is not on sale.
(C) Used rap is not on sale.
(D) Used soul is on sale.
(E) Used soul is not on sale.

13. If exactly four of the five types of used CDs are the only CDs on sale, then which one of the following could be true?
(A) Used jazz is not on sale.
(B) Used opera is not on sale.
(C) Used rap is not on sale.
(D) Neither type of jazz is on sale.
(E) Neither type of rap and neither type of soul is on sale.

Total time: ______

Did you feel...	Y	~	N
You understood basic design and laid it out well			
You understood and notated all rules well			
You recognized the most significant aspects			
You didn't make a diagramming mistake			
You used correct question strategies			
You felt confident			

Game 3 | PT 32, G3

At a concert, exactly eight compositions—F, H, L, O, P, R, S, and T—are to be performed exactly once each, consecutively and one composition at a time. The order of their performance must satisfy the following conditions:

T is performed either immediately before F or immediately after R.
At least two compositions are performed either after F and before R, or after R and before F.
O is performed either first or fifth.
The eighth composition performed is either L or H.
P is performed at some time before S.
At least one composition is performed either after O and before S, or after S and before O.

Setup time: ______

12. Which one of the following lists the compositions in an order in which they could be performed during the concert, from first through eighth?
(A) L, P, S, R, O, T, F, H
(B) O, T, P, F, S, H, R, L
(C) P, T, F, S, L, R, O, H
(D) P, T, F, S, O, R, L, H
(E) T, F, P, R, O, L, S, H

13. P CANNOT be performed
(A) second
(B) third
(C) fourth
(D) sixth
(E) seventh

14. If T is performed fifth and F is performed sixth, then S must be performed either
(A) fourth or seventh
(B) third or sixth
(C) third or fourth
(D) second or seventh
(E) first or fourth

15. If O is performed immediately after T, then F must be performed either
(A) first or second
(B) second or third
(C) fourth or sixth
(D) fourth or seventh
(E) sixth or seventh

16. If S is performed fourth, which one of the following could be an accurate list of the compositions performed first, second, and third, respectively?
(A) F, H, P
(B) H, P, L
(C) O, P, R
(D) O, P, T
(E) P, R, T

17. If P is performed third and S is performed sixth, the composition performed fifth must be either
(A) F or H
(B) F or O
(C) F or T
(D) H or L
(E) O or R

18. If exactly two compositions are performed after F but before O, then R must be performed
(A) first
(B) third
(C) fourth
(D) sixth
(E) seventh

Total time: ______

Did you feel...	Y	~	N
You understood basic design and laid it out well			
You understood and notated all rules well			
You recognized the most significant aspects			
You didn't make a diagramming mistake			
You used correct question strategies			
You felt confident			

Game 4 | PT 35, G4

Exactly seven professors—Madison, Nilsson, Orozco, Paton, Robinson, Sarkis, and Togo—were hired in the years 1989 through 1995. Each professor has one or more specialities, and any two professors hired in the same year or in consecutive years do not have a specialty in common. The professors were hired according to the following conditions:

Madison was hired in 1993, Robinson in 1991.
There is at least one specialty that Madison, Orozco, and Togo have in common.
Nilsson shares a specialty with Robinson.
Paton and Sarkis were each hired at least one year before Madison and at least one year after Nilsson.
Orozco, who shares a specialty with Sarkis, was hired in 1990.

Setup time: ______

18. Which one of the following is a complete and accurate list of the professors who could have been hired in the years 1989 through 1991?
(A) Nilsson, Orozco, Robinson
(B) Orozco, Robinson, Sarkis
(C) Nilsson, Orozco, Paton, Robinson
(D) Nilsson, Orozco, Paton, Sarkis
(E) Orozco, Paton, Robinson, Sarkis

19. If exactly one professor was hired in 1991, then which one of the following could be true?
(A) Madison and Paton share a specialty.
(B) Robinson and Sarkis share a specialty.
(C) Paton was hired exactly one year after Orozco.
(D) Exactly one professor was hired in 1994.
(E) Exactly two professors were hired in 1993.

20. Which one of the following must be false?
(A) Nilsson was hired in 1989.
(B) Paton was hired in 1990.
(C) Paton was hired in 1991.
(D) Sarkis was hired in 1992.
(E) Togo was hired in 1994.

21. Which one of the following must be true?
(A) Orozco was hired before Paton.
(B) Paton was hired before Sarkis.
(C) Sarkis was hired before Robinson.
(D) Robinson was hired before Sarkis.
(E) Madison was hired before Sarkis.

22. If exactly two professors were hired in 1992, then which one of the following could be true?
(A) Orozco, Paton, and Togo share a specialty.
(B) Madison, Paton, and Togo share a specialty.
(C) Exactly two professors were hired in 1991.
(D) Exactly two professors were hired in 1993.
(E) Paton was hired in 1991.

23. If Paton and Madison have a specialty in common, then which one of the following must be true?
(A) Nilsson does not share a specialty with Paton.
(B) Exactly one professor was hired in 1990.
(C) Exactly one professor was hired in 1991.
(D) Exactly two professors were hired in each of two years.
(E) Paton was hired at least one year before Sarkis.

Total time: ______

Did you feel...	Y	~	N
You understood basic design and laid it out well			
You understood and notated all rules well			
You recognized the most significant aspects			
You didn't make a diagramming mistake			
You used correct question strategies			
You felt confident			

Game 1 Solutions | PT 29, G 2

Two mannequins—1 and 2—will be dressed for display in outfits chosen from ten articles of clothing. Each article is in exactly one of three colors: navy, red, or yellow. There are three hats—one in each color; three jackets—one in each color; three skirts—one in each color; and one red tie. Each mannequin wears exactly one of the hats, one of the jackets, and one of the skirts. Furthermore, their outfits must meet the following restrictions:

Neither mannequin wears all three colors.
Each mannequin wears a hat in a different color from the jacket it wears.
Mannequin 2 wears the navy skirt.
Mannequin 1 wears the tie.

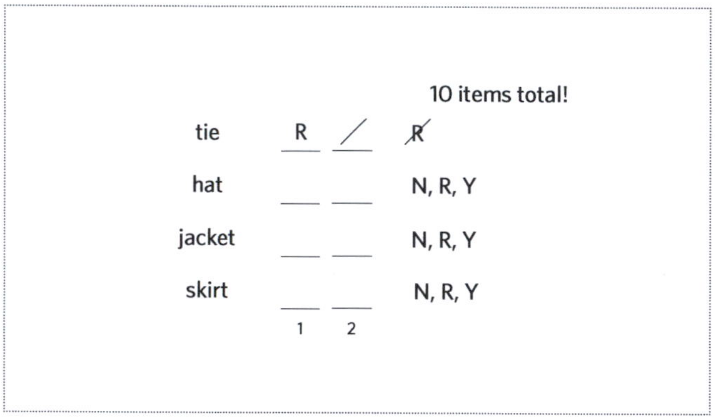

10 items total!

	1	2	
tie	R	/	~~R~~
hat			N, R, Y
jacket			N, R, Y
skirt			N, R, Y

STEP ONE: I draw the diagram like mannequins—hat on top, jacket, then skirt. The last rule eliminated the complication regarding only one mannequin wearing a tie, and I draw that rule in right away. I also write out each possibility (N, R, Y) next to each item line so I can keep track of my very limited options.

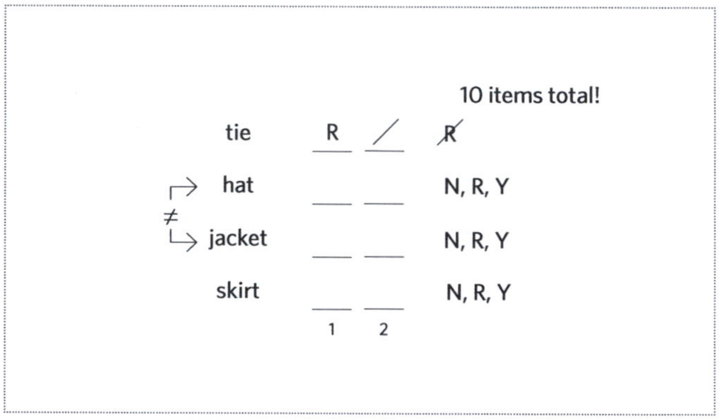

10 items total!

	1	2	
tie	R	/	~~R~~
hat (≠ jacket)			N, R, Y
jacket (≠ hat)			N, R, Y
skirt			N, R, Y

STEP TWO: Not sure exactly how to draw the first rule, so I skip to the second. I have to remember hat and jacket can't be the same for either mannequin. (If you had another method for indicating that more clearly, then great!)

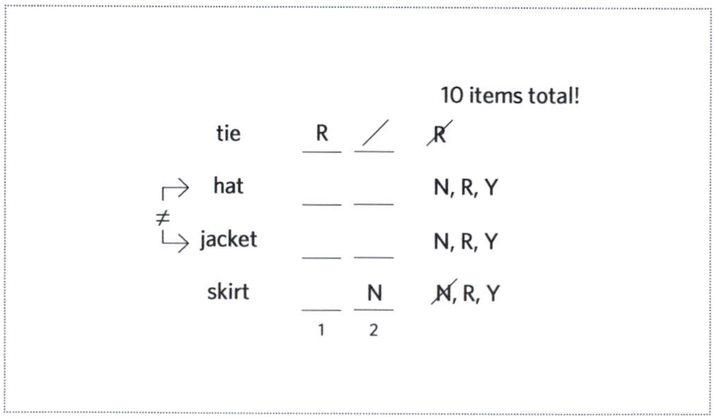

10 items total!

	1	2	
tie	R	/	~~R~~
hat (≠ jacket)			N, R, Y
jacket (≠ hat)			N, R, Y
skirt		N	~~N~~, R, Y

STEP THREE: I draw N into the second diagram. Now I know one color for each of the mannequins, which is kind of a big deal because the mannequins can't wear all three colors...

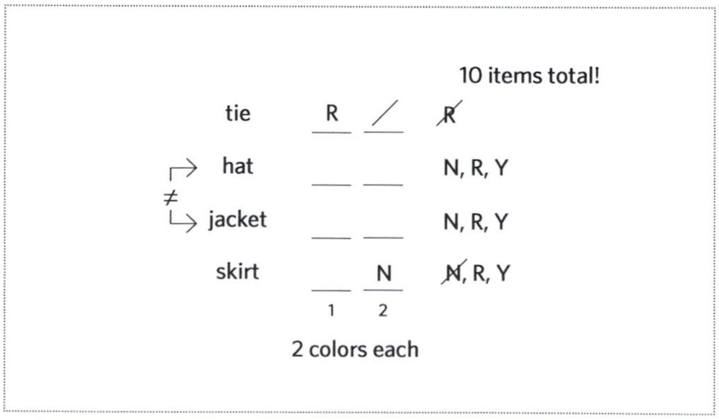

10 items total!

	1	2	
tie	R	/	~~R~~
hat (≠ jacket)			N, R, Y
jacket (≠ hat)			N, R, Y
skirt		N	~~N~~, R, Y

2 colors each

STEP FOUR: Going back to the first rule, if neither mannequin wears all three colors, and if their hats and jackets can't be the same, each mannequin wears exactly two colors. Mannequin 1 wears R and one other color, and Mannequin 2 wears N and one other color. The key inference is that each mannequin can only wear two colors; I know one of the colors for each mannequin, and hat and jacket can't be the same. I'm ready.

comments

The design of this game is not particularly complicated, and it doesn't overwhelm us with the number of rules. It also helps that the hypothetical scenario—the dressing of a mannequin—is something most of us can picture quite easily.

Still, this is a game that can pose significant challenges, especially under time pressure. Though there aren't too many elements or positions, there are three dimensions to consider—the mannequin, the item of clothing, and the color—and it can be a challenge, especially if you rush the beginning of your process, to recognize how you should lay it out.

For this game, it is particularly important to get a careful general understanding of the situation and to make important decisions about how to lay out the base of the diagram before you start putting pencil to paper.

In addition, it's important to understand that there are ten total elements and that there is exactly one navy hat, one red hat, and so on.

The main issue at hand is which color hat, jacket, and skirt each mannequin will wear. The tie is a secondary issue that can be taken care of quickly. Notice we drew that last rule immediately into our diagram because it was easy enough to do so.

The first rule is the most challenging to diagram, and when you find you can't diagram something easily, it makes sense to hold off on it. These problems have a way of fixing themselves (if they don't, and worst comes to worst, we can just write out the rule in words). Combining the first and second rules gives us our one key inference: each mannequin must wear exactly two colors. Considering that we already know of one color for each mannequin, and considering that the hat and jacket have to be different, we can go into the answer choices with an extremely limited range of options for how we occupy each space.

Overall, this is a difficult game to conceptualize, but if you can create a workable diagram, the constraints are quite manageable. If you are able to make the key inference, and if you focus on the limitations of the game, the questions can go quite quickly.

Kudos if you...

Came up with a clever (shapes?) way to mark that the hat ≠ the jacket.

Did you...

Initially think of the colors as subsets and mark your elements Hn, Hr, etc.? If so, did you rush in thinking about the base of your diagram?

Beware...

The danger of forgetting the specific design of the game—namely that there is exactly one each of every color of clothing.

Did you...

Miss the 2 colors each inference or not understand its significance? If so, did you see it after a few questions? If not, you may want to replay the game with it in mind to see the impact it has on the problem-solving process.

Game 1 Solutions | PT 29, G 2

Two mannequins—1 and 2—will be dressed for display in outfits chosen from ten articles of clothing. Each article is in exactly one of three colors: navy, red, or yellow. There are three hats—one in each color; three jackets—one in each color; three skirts—one in each color; and one red tie. Each mannequin wears exactly one of the hats, one of the jackets, and one of the skirts. Furthermore, their outfits must meet the following restrictions:

Neither mannequin wears all three colors.
Each mannequin wears a hat in a different color from the jacket it wears.
Mannequin 2 wears the navy skirt.
Mannequin 1 wears the tie.

10 items total!

	1	2	
tie	R	/	~~R~~
hat (≠ jacket)	__	__	N, R, Y
jacket	__	__	N, R, Y
skirt	__	N	~~N~~, R, Y

2 colors each

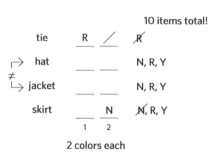

7. Which one of the following could be complete outfits for the two mannequins?

(A) mannequin 1: navy hat, red jacket, yellow skirt, red tie
mannequin 2: red hat, navy jacket, navy skirt
(B) mannequin 1: red hat, red jacket, yellow skirt, red tie
mannequin 2: yellow hat, navy jacket, navy skirt
(C) mannequin 1: red hat, yellow jacket, red skirt, red tie
mannequin 2: yellow hat, navy jacket, yellow skirt
(D) mannequin 1: yellow hat, red jacket, yellow skirt, red tie
mannequin 2: red hat, navy jacket, navy skirt
(E) mannequin 1: yellow hat, yellow jacket, red skirt
mannequin 2: red hat, navy jacket, navy skirt

7. (D): This is your standard Rules question, and we want to employ our usual strategy of using the constraints to eliminate answers. The first rule allows us to get rid of (A). The second rule (B). The third rule (C). The fourth rule (E). That means (D) is correct.

8. Which one of the following could be true of the mannequins' outfits?

(A) Mannequin 1 wears the navy jacket and the yellow skirt.
(B) Mannequin 2 wears the red hat and the red jacket.
(C) Mannequin 1 wears exactly one red article of clothing.
(D) Mannequin 1 wears exactly three yellow articles of clothing.
(E) Mannequin 2 wears no red articles of clothing.

8. (E): This is an unconditional Could Be True question, and this question is a good gauge of our understanding of the game—if we are in control of it, we should be able to see, hopefully without too much effort, that four answers must be false. If we have a lot of trouble seeing that, it's a sign that we are missing key inferences, or that there is something wrong with the diagram.

(A) must be false because that would give Mannequin 1 three colors. (B) must be false because 2's hat and jacket must be different colors. If (C) were true, 1 would have to wear the same color jacket and hat—cut (C). (D) can't be true because hat and jacket can't be the same. (E) seems like it can definitely be true, and it's the only one we haven't eliminated. It just takes a second to make sure it can work: no reason Mannequin 2 can't be navy and yellow.

By the way, if you didn't see initially that each mannequin must wear exactly two colors, the work you did in this problem could have tipped you off on that inference.

9. If mannequin 1 wears the navy jacket, which one of the following could be true?

(A) Mannequin 1 wears the yellow hat.
(B) Mannequin 1 wears the yellow skirt.
(C) Mannequin 2 wears the red hat.
(D) Mannequin 2 wears the yellow hat.
(E) Mannequin 2 wears the yellow jacket.

	1	2
tie	R	/
hat (≠ jacket)	R	N
jacket	N	__
skirt	R	N

9. (E): If Mannequin 1 wears the navy jacket, it must wear the red hat, for its hat and jacket color cannot be the same. It must also wear a red skirt, for it must wear navy or red and the navy skirt is already taken. Mannequin 2 must wear a navy hat or jacket, and since 1 is wearing the navy jacket, 2 must wear the navy hat. The only thing that remains uncertain is the jacket for Mannequin 2.

Since this is a Could Be True, we should expect the work we've done to eliminate the 4 must be false answers, and that is indeed the case. (A), (B), (C), and (D) all must be false. Therefore, (E) is correct.

10. If all four of the red articles of clothing are included in the two mannequins' outfits, which one of the following must be true?

(A) Mannequin 1 wears the red hat.
(B) Mannequin 1 wears the yellow jacket.
(C) Mannequin 2 wears the navy jacket.
(D) Mannequin 1 wears no navy articles of clothing.
(E) Mannequin 2 wears no yellow articles of clothing.

	1	2	
tie	R	/	~~R~~
hat	R/	/R	N, R, Y
jacket	R/	/R	N, R, Y
skirt	R	N	~~N~~, R, Y

hat ≠ jacket

2 colors each

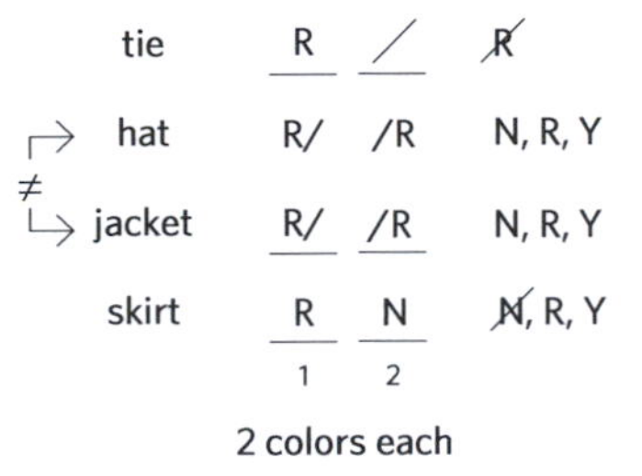

10. (E): If all four red items are included, that must mean Mannequin 1 wears the red skirt, and one mannequin must wear the red hat, and the other the red jacket. We don't know more beyond that, but that's enough to see that (E) must be true.

11. If mannequin 2 wears the red jacket, then mannequin 1 must wear the

(A) navy hat
(B) red hat
(C) yellow hat
(D) red skirt
(E) yellow skirt

11. (B): We know Mannequin 1 must wear the red hat or the red jacket. If Mannequin 2 wears the red jacket, 1 must wear the red hat. No diagram needed here. (B) is correct.

12. If all three of the yellow articles of clothing are included in the two mannequins' outfits, which one of the following could be true?

(A) Mannequin 1 wears the navy jacket.
(B) Mannequin 1 wears the yellow jacket.
(C) Mannequin 1 wears the red skirt.
(D) Mannequin 2 wears the red hat.
(E) Mannequin 2 wears the red jacket.

	1	2	
tie	R	/	~~R~~
hat	R/Y	N/Y	N, R, Y
jacket	R/Y	N/Y	N, R, Y
skirt	Y	N	~~N~~, R, Y

2 colors each

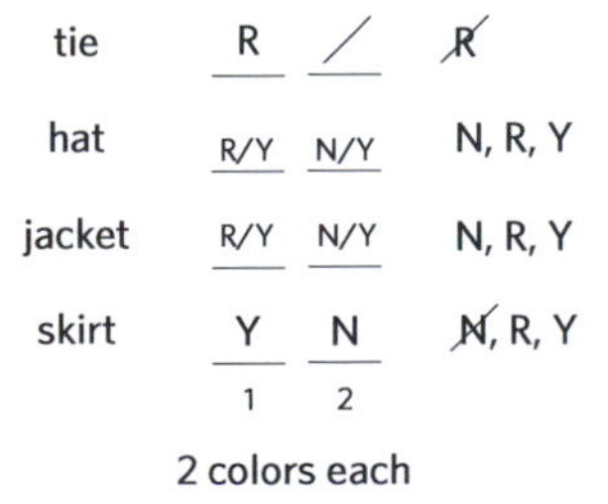

12. (B): If all three yellow items are included, that means that Mannequin 1's colors will be red and yellow, and Mannequin 2's colors will be navy and yellow. 1 must wear the yellow skirt, but we don't know which one wears the yellow hat and the yellow jacket. Now we're ready to evaluate answers. We want to knock off four answers that must be false. (A), (C), (D), and (E) must all be false. Therefore, (B) is correct.

13. If mannequin 1 wears the skirt that is the same color as the jacket that mannequin 2 wears, which one of the following must be true?

(A) Mannequin 1 wears the yellow hat.
(B) Mannequin 1 wears the yellow jacket.
(C) Mannequin 2 wears the navy hat.
(D) Mannequin 2 wears the red hat.
(E) Mannequin 2 wears the red jacket.

	1	2	1	2
tie	R	/	R	/
hat	Y	N	R	N
jacket	R	Y		R
skirt	Y	N	R	N

hat ≠ jacket

2 colors each

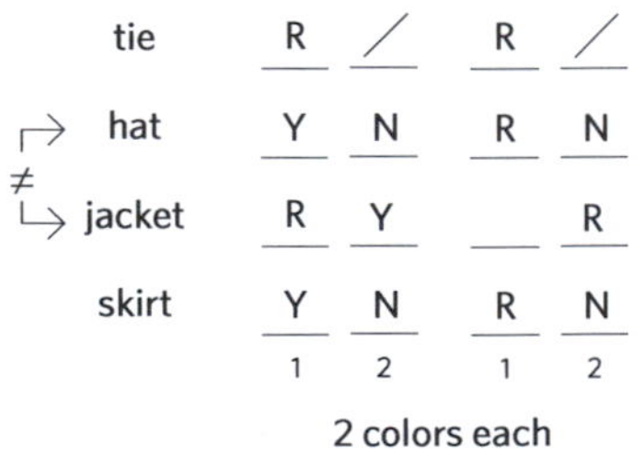

13. (C): The color they share could be yellow or red, so let's play both out. Notice that the only inference true to both scenarios is that 2 must wear a navy hat. Since this is a Must Be True, it's a strong bet that it's going to be the answer, and indeed it's there. (C) is correct.

Game 2 Solutions | PT 31, G 2

A music store carries ten types of CDs—both new and used of each of jazz, opera, pop, rap, and soul. The store is having a sale on some of these types of CDs. The following conditions must apply:

Used pop is on sale; new opera is not.
If both types of pop are on sale, then all soul is.
If both types of jazz are on sale, then no rap is.
If neither type of jazz is on sale, then new pop is.
If either type of rap is on sale, then no soul is.

sale	not

Jn On Pn Rn Sn
Ju Ou Pu Ru Su

STEP ONE: We can start by just drawing a small t-diagram that will help us visualize the situation, and by writing out the different CDs.

sale	not
Pu	On

Jn On Pn Rn Sn
Ju Ou Pu Ru Su

STEP TWO: The first rule is an easy one.

sale	not
Pu	On

Jn On Pn Rn Sn
Ju Ou Pu Ru Su

Pn → Sn + Su
~~Sn~~ or ~~Su~~ → ~~Pn~~

STEP THREE: Now we get to our first conditional. We can make a small inference about this rule because we already know that Pu is on sale. If you wrote Pu + Pn → ..., that's of course fine. Kudos if you split the conditional.

sale	not
Pu	On

Jn On Pn Rn Sn
Ju Ou Pu Ru Su

Pn → Sn + Su
~~Sn~~ or ~~Su~~ → ~~Pn~~

Jn + Ju → ~~Rn~~ + ~~Ru~~
Rn or Ru → ~~Jn~~ or ~~Ju~~

STEP FOUR: The next conditional rule. Of course, we have to be extremely careful about making sure our notations are correct. I go super slow and review my work.

sale	not
Pu	On

Jn On Pn Rn Sn
Ju Ou Pu Ru Su

Pn → Sn + Su
~~Sn~~ or ~~Su~~ → ~~Pn~~
~~Jn~~ + ~~Ju~~ → Pn
~~Pn~~ → Jn or Ju

Jn + Ju → ~~Rn~~ + ~~Ru~~
Rn or Ru → ~~Jn~~ or ~~Ju~~

STEP FIVE: The next conditional rule. By this point it's pretty clear that these rules are intricately related—the P's and J's have all already been mentioned multiple times.

sale	not
Pu	On

Jn On Pn Rn Sn
Ju (Ou) Pu Ru Su

Pn → Sn + Su
~~Sn~~ or ~~Su~~ → ~~Pn~~
~~Jn~~ + ~~Ju~~ → Pn
~~Pn~~ → Jn or Ju

Jn + Ju → ~~Rn~~ + ~~Ru~~
Rn or Ru → ~~Jn~~ or ~~Ju~~
Rn or Ru → ~~Sn~~ + ~~Su~~
Sn or Su → ~~Rn~~ + ~~Ru~~

STEP SIX: And the final conditional. Again, we want to be super careful about making sure our ands and ors and all that are correct. On my actual paper, I had all of the conditionals lined up vertically. That makes it a bit easier to work through them during questions. Ou is the only free agent.

comments

The challenge of this game does not lie in its general design: the idea that some CDs are used and some are not, and we're going to determine which CDs are on sale and which ones are not, is all fairly simple and straightforward.

The challenge of this game comes from the number of rules that we have to keep in mind, and from the complexity of those rules. The simplest constraint we're given, the first one, is actually two rules, and the rest of the constraints are all compound conditionals—that is, conditional statements involving more than two elements. These are difficult to notate correctly, take the contrapositive of correctly, and work with correctly as you solve problems.

What makes it all the more difficult is that many of the questions require you to bring these rules together in complex ways. In order to do so successfully, you need to have complete confidence in your notations.

One subtle but helpful inference has to do with the combining of the first two rules—since we already know that used pop is on sale, the statement "If both types of pop are on sale" can be thought of in terms of "If new pop is on sale." Again, it's a very small inference, and you could have done just fine on the game without it, but when the test writers build in such subtle inferences, they also tend to build in rewards for those who see them—and that is certainly the case here (that is, the rule is more useful using "If new pop is on sale" as the trigger).

It goes without saying that you need to be extremely careful in setting up and diagramming this game—one mistake with a conditional and you will be in trouble. At the same time, since there are few up-front inferences, and little work to be done other than directly translating (and taking the contrapositive of) the rules, the setup should not take you significantly longer than that for other games. The extra burden comes in the process of answering questions—the questions are going to require quite a bit of work from us. Comfort with these diagramming systems is essential for your success.

Did you...

Link certain conditional statements together? It might save you time on the questions if you did, but know that it's not a necessary step. If you are going to do it, make sure you are quick and, most importantly, accurate.

Did you...

Have an easy time understanding why "or" is in the contrapositive of "and" and vice versa? If not, you may want to review Lesson 13 again.

Key considerations:

(1) These are complicated rules—it's worth it to triple check all of your notations to make sure they are correct.
(2) Almost all of the rules are conditional, and there aren't many up-front inferences—we should expect to do a lot of work in the questions themselves.

Game 2 Solutions | PT 31, G 2

A music store carries ten types of CDs—both new and used of each of jazz, opera, pop, rap, and soul. The store is having a sale on some of these types of CDs. The following conditions must apply:

Used pop is on sale; new opera is not.
If both types of pop are on sale, then all soul is.
If both types of jazz are on sale, then no rap is.
If neither type of jazz is on sale, then new pop is.
If either type of rap is on sale, then no soul is.

sale	not
Pu	On

Jn	On	Pn	Rn	Sn
Ju	(Ou)	Pu	Ru	Su

Pn → Sn + Su
~~Sn~~ or ~~Su~~ → ~~Pn~~
~~Jn~~ + ~~Ju~~ → Pn
~~Pn~~ → Jn or Ju

Jn + Ju → ~~Rn~~ + ~~Ru~~
Rn or Ru → ~~Jn~~ or ~~Ju~~
Rn or Ru → ~~Sn~~ + ~~Su~~
Sn or Su → ~~Rn~~ + ~~Ru~~

7. Which one of the following could be a complete and accurate list of the types of CDs that are on sale?

~~(A)~~ new jazz, used jazz, used opera, used pop, new rap
~~(B)~~ new jazz, used pop, used rap, new soul
~~(C)~~ used opera, used pop, new rap, used rap
~~(D)~~ used opera, new pop, used pop, new soul
(E) used jazz, used pop, new soul, used soul

7. (E): This is your standard Rules question, and we want to employ our usual strategy of using the constraints to eliminate answers. The first rule doesn't allow us to get rid of any choices. The second rule allows us to get rid of (D). The third rule (A). The fourth rule (C). The last rule (B). That means (E) is correct.

8. If new soul is not on sale, then which one of the following must be true?

(A) New rap is not on sale.
(B) New rap is on sale.
(C) Used opera is not on sale.
(D) At least one type of jazz is not on sale.
(E) At least one type of pop is not on sale.

sale	not
Pu	On
Jn or Ju	Sn
	Pn

8. (E): We want to start by looking for ~~Sn~~ in the trigger, and see that the only consequence is ~~Pn~~. If Pn is not on sale, Jn or Ju is. That seems to be the last of the inferences. Now we're ready to evaluate answers. We have no information that pertains to (A) - (D), but we know (E) must be true.

9. If both types of jazz are on sale, then which one of the following is the minimum number of types of new CDs that could be included in the sale?

(A) one
(B) two
(C) three
(D) four
(E) five

sale	not
Pu	On
Jn	Rn
Ju	Ru

9. (A): If both Jn and Ju are in, Rn and Ru are out. There are no other obvious inferences to be made. Before we go on to the answers, we want to check if there is some other reason why any of the remaining new CDs must be on sale. If we check Pn, there is no trigger forcing it in or out. If we check Sn, we get the same. Therefore, the minimum number of new CDs on sale is 1, and (A) is correct.

10. Which one of the following CANNOT be true?

(A) Neither type of opera and neither type of rap is on sale.
(B) Neither type of jazz and neither type of opera is on sale.
(C) Neither type of opera and neither type of soul is on sale.
(D) Neither type of jazz and neither type of soul is on sale.
(E) Neither type of jazz and neither type of rap is on sale.

10. (D): This type of question—an unconditional Must Be False question with what appears at first glance to include complex answer choices—is a classic time sucker. What we don't want to do is waste time over-thinking answer choices, wondering if there is something we are not seeing that forces them to be false. The hope is that we can quickly evaluate each answer, see if there are any *simple* reasons that it must be false, and if we don't see any, move on. The hope is that there is an answer that *clearly* must be false, and if you've done your work correctly up to this point, most of the time that will be the case.

For (A), we look for consequences for opera or rap CDs being out—there don't seem to be any. For (B), that neither type of jazz is on sale means Pn must be—while that has a chain of consequences, the consequences have no impact on either of the Os. For (C), opera being out has no consequences; neither type of soul being in does have consequences, but we can't tie them in any way to the Os, so we can't say (C) must be false. For (D), if neither type of jazz is on sale, we see that Pn is, and if Pn is, Sn and Su must be as well. (D) must be false, and (D) is the correct answer. There is no need to check (E), but you can do so if you are uncertain at all about (D).

12. If new soul is the only type of new CD on sale, then which one of the following CANNOT be true?

(A) Used jazz is not on sale.
(B) Use opera is not on sale.
(C) Used rap is not on sale.
(D) Used soul is on sale.
(E) Used soul is not on sale.

sale	not
Pu	On
Sn	Jn
Ju	Pn
	Rn
	Ru

12. (A): We start this question by putting Sn in the *sale* area AND by putting Jn, Pn, and Rn in the *not* area. Then we look for consequences. Ru must be out because Sn is in, and Ju must be in because Pn is out. We can see that (A) must be false, and can pick it and move on. (A) is correct.

11. If neither type of jazz is on sale, then each of the following must be true EXCEPT:

(A) Used opera is on sale.
(B) New rap is not on sale.
(C) Used rap is not on sale.
(D) New soul is on sale.
(E) Used soul is on sale.

sale	not
Pu	On
Pn	Jn
Sn	Ju
Su	Rn
	Ru

11. (A): The condition that both Js are out triggers a long chain of consequences: Pn must be in, so Sn and Su must be in, and so Rn and Ru must be out. Note that every element is accounted for except Ou, which we know is a wildcard anyway. Time to attack these answers: (A) is about Ou, our only uncertainty, and if you really felt confident in your work, you could pull the trigger. However, it also takes very little time to see that (B) - (E) all must be false based on the inferences we made, and I would personally double check those just to feel one hundred percent confident. (A) is correct.

13. If exactly four of the five types of used CDs are the only CDs on sale, then which one of the following could be true?

(A) Used jazz is not on sale.
(B) Used opera is not on sale.
(C) Used rap is not on sale.
(D) Neither type of jazz is on sale.
(E) Neither type of rap and neither type of soul is on sale.

sale	not
Pu	On
Ju	Jn
Ou	Pn
Ru/Su	Rn
	Ru/Su

13. (C): This is probably the most clever of all the questions for this game, and the one that requires the most clarity of thought from us. We're given the condition that exactly four of the five types of used CDs are the only CDs on sale. The immediate thought should be "Do we have clues about which four they could be?" (We must! Otherwise, they would not have designed the question this way.) We're looking for a rule where one used CD forces another used CD out, and the last one does it for us—if either Ru or Su is in, it forces the other one out. That means that either Ru or Su must be out. We can write out what we know, as I did above.

Once we have the elements all laid out, we can check one more time to see if placing elements into *sale* or *not* leads to any more inferences, and it does not. We should expect to eliminate four answer choices. (A) must be false. (B) must be false. (C) could be true. (D) must be false. (E) must be false. (C) is correct.

Game 3 Solutions | PT 32, G 3

At a concert, exactly eight compositions—F, H, L, O, P, R, S, and T—are to be performed exactly once each, consecutively and one composition at a time. The order of their performance must satisfy the following conditions:

T is performed either immediately before F or immediately after R.
At least two compositions are performed either after F and before R, or after R and before F.
O is performed either first or fifth.
The eighth composition performed is either L or H.
P is performed at some time before S.
At least one composition is performed either after O and before S, or after S and before O.

Comments: The overall scenario is a simple and common one: eight elements in an order. The challenge of this game is in the rules—each one is designed to have a certain amount of uncertainty (notice all of the "ors"). The key to this game is to have notations that are easy to understand and easy to work with.

__ __ __ __ __ __ __ __

F P
H R
L S
O T

STEP ONE: We can start by laying out a basic diagram. Note that on my paper I list all of the elements in one column; it's written this way here for the sake of space.

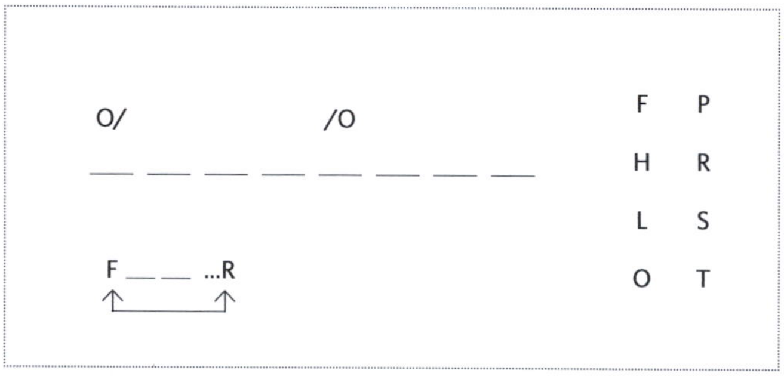

O/ /O
__ __ __ __ __ __ __ __

F __ __ ...R
↑ ↑

F P
H R
L S
O T

STEP TWO: The first rule is not terribly complicated, but it is a bit of a messy rule, and commonly it helps to leave these until later. Let's move on to the second and third rules, and diagram them as I did above.

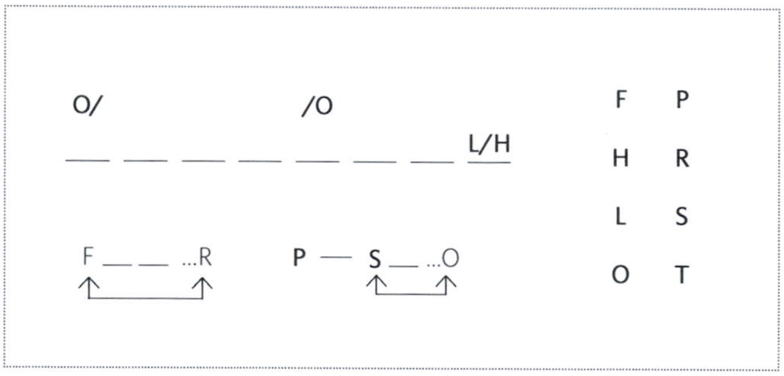

O/ /O
__ __ __ __ __ __ __ L/H

F __ __ ...R   P — S __ ...O
↑ ↑   ↑ ↑

F P
H R
L S
O T

STEP THREE: The fourth, fifth, and sixth rules are all common ones as well, and ones you should be comfortable diagramming. I've drawn the fifth and sixth rules together.

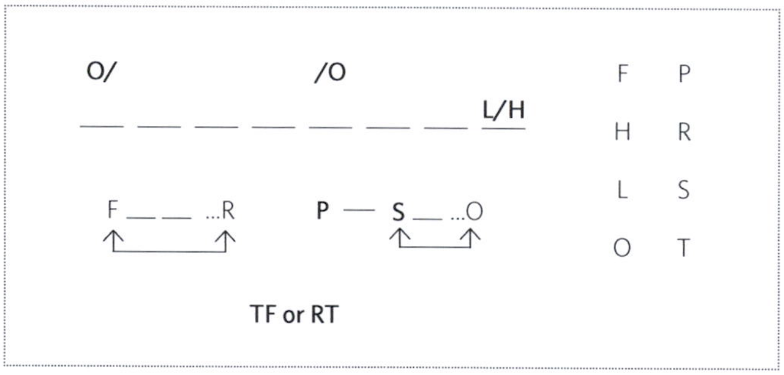

O/ /O
__ __ __ __ __ __ __ L/H

F __ __ ...R   P — S __ ...O
↑ ↑   ↑ ↑

TF or RT

F P
H R
L S
O T

STEP FOUR: Now we need to go back to the first rule. We could try to incorporate it into the notation for the second rule, which involves F and R, and though there are some creative ways we can do this, I can't see any that are going to be intuitive for me (that is, they may be creative, but they won't help me understand the situation in an "easier" way, perhaps because I will forget exactly what my symbol meant). So, I just note it the way I have above. (Notice that the "or" in the first rule could technically mean we have "RTF," but the second rule excludes this possibility.)

Now that we have all of our elements laid out, let's look for some inferences. Unfortunately, there are not a whole lot! This is a complicated game, and there is too much uncertainty for us to see much of anything too clearly up front. We do have the F __ __ ... R (or vice versa) block, and that coupled with the TF or RT rule will likely define much of the game. The O needing to go either first or fifth, and then impacting where the S and P go, will also likely be important. With all that in mind, let's double check all our notations again (look at each notation, say to yourself what it means, and check this understanding against the scenario and rules as written), and move on to the questions.

12. Which one of the following lists the compositions in an order in which they could be performed during the concert, from first through eighth?

(A) L, P, S, R, O, T, F, H
(B) O, T, P, F, S, H, R, L
(C) P, T, F, S, L, R, O, H
(D) P, T, F, S, O, R, L, H
(E) T, F, P, R, O, L, S, H

13. P CANNOT be performed

(A) second
(B) third
(C) fourth
(D) sixth
(E) seventh

12. (A): This is the standard Rules question, so we know that we can use the rules to eliminate answer choices. The first rule eliminates (B). The second (E). The third (C). The fourth rule doesn't eliminate an answer, nor does the fifth. The sixth rule eliminates (D). That leaves us with (A).

13. (E): This is an unconditional question, and we are being asked about something that must be false. Before we look at the answer choices, we want to see for ourselves where P cannot go.

We know that P must go before S, and since S can't go last, the earliest P can go is sixth. There could be some other reason, perhaps involving the placement of the F/R rule, that limits where P can go, but I don't see it and I don't want to waste time digging that out if I don't have to. I go into the answers hoping "seventh" will be there... and it is! We can select (E) and move on.

Note that eighth would NEVER be the right answer in this context. Why? Because the right answer must be something inferred, not something told to us in the rules.

At this point, I realize I did not represent the last rule in the easiest way—it simply means S and O can't be next to each other. I just kept this in mind, but if you want to change your diagram at this point, you could.

14. If T is performed fifth and F is performed sixth, then S must be performed either

(A) fourth or seventh
(B) third or sixth
(C) third or fourth
(D) second or seventh
(E) first or fourth

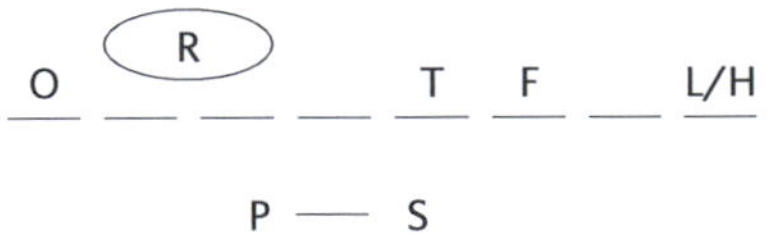

O (R) _ _ _ T F _ L/H

P — S

15. If O is performed immediately after T, then F must be performed either

(A) first or second
(B) second or third
(C) fourth or sixth
(D) fourth or seventh
(E) sixth or seventh

_ _ R T O (F) _ _ L/H

14. (A): This is a conditional question, and so we want to take the conditions and see what else we can figure out. Notice, per the way the question is phrased, that our ultimate goal is to figure out where S can go, and that if we do our work right, we should see that S can only go in two spaces.

If we put T in 5 and F in 6, O must go in 1. We still seem to have a lot of spots where S can go, but we haven't used the F _ _ ...R (and vice versa) rule yet—R must go in 2 or 3. Knowing that, and knowing S must follow P, we know that S must go in 4 or 7.

15. (E): The construction of this question is similar to that of the last one, so we want to play off of the condition, and then try to figure out the two positions where F can be placed.

If O is immediately after T, we know O must be in 5 and T in 4. Since F can't follow T, R must precede T, so R must go in 3. Since L or H must go last, and since F must be at least three spots away from R, F must be in 6 or 7.

Game 3 Solutions | PT 32, G 3

At a concert, exactly eight compositions—F, H, L, O, P, R, S, and T—are to be performed exactly once each, consecutively and one composition at a time. The order of their performance must satisfy the following conditions:

T is performed either immediately before F or immediately after R.
At least two compositions are performed either after F and before R, or after R and before F.
O is performed either first or fifth.
The eighth composition performed is either L or H.
P is performed at some time before S.
At least one composition is performed either after O and before S, or after S and before O.

O/ (1) … /O (5) … L/H (8)
___ ___ ___ ___ ___ ___ ___ L/H

F ___ ___ ...R (↔)   P — S ___ ...O (↔)

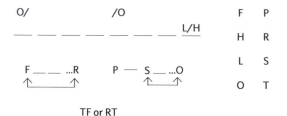

TF or RT

F P
H R
L S
O T

16. If S is performed fourth, which one of the following could be an accurate list of the compositions performed first, second, and third, respectively?

~~(A)~~ F, H, P
~~(B)~~ H, P, L
(C) O, P, R
~~(D)~~ O, P, T
~~(E)~~ P, R, T

O ___ ___ S ___ ___ ___ L/H (P, F/R in 2 and 3)

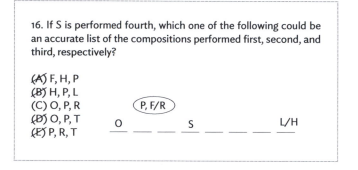

17. If P is performed third and S is performed sixth, the composition performed fifth must be either

(A) F or H
(B) F or O
(C) F or T (circled)
(D) H or L
(E) O or R

O ___ P ___ ___ S ___ L/H

TF or RT

16 (C): We know to work off of the condition, and we know that we will know some things, but not everything, about the placement of elements in 1, 2, and 3.

Since S and O can't be next to one another, if S is in 4, O must be in 1. P must be in 2 or 3 (because it has to be before S). Now we look to the other rules. Because F and R need sufficient space between one another, one of the two must go in one of the first three spots, and unless there is something incredibly clever going on (and if there is, we'll have a chance to double check our work later), that means either F or R (we don't know which one) has to be the final element in the first 3 spots.

Okay, so what do we know? That O is in 1, and that P and F or R need to occupy 2 and 3. Based on O needing to go first, we could eliminate (A), (B), and (E). Per our inferences, (D) is not a possibility. That means (C) is correct.

17. (C): We know, based on the way the question is asked, that once we infer off of the conditions given, we will end up with two possibilities for the fifth spot. If we place P in 3, and S in 6, that means O must be in 1. This still seems to leave a lot of options for F _ _...R (and vice versa). So we draw out what we've got.

The key issue now is that we've got to fit in the TF or RT block, and there is only one place to put it: 4/5. Therefore, the fifth spot must be occupied by F or T. (C) is correct.

18. (D): We know to work off the condition, and we know that at the end of our work we must find an exact position for R. If F is before O, we know O must be in 5, and therefore F must be in 2. Since R must be at least 3 spaces away from F, that puts R in 6 or 7.

18. If exactly two compositions are performed after F but before O, then R must be performed

(A) first
(B) third
(C) fourth
(D) sixth (circled)
(E) seventh

___ F ___ ___ O (R in 6 or 7) ___ L/H

___ F ___ ___ O R T L/H
T F ___ ___ O (R in 6 or 7) ___ L/H

P F S L/H O R T L/H
T F (P, L/H) O R S L/H

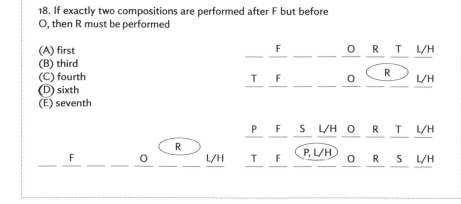

That's a good start, but it's not enough. We've got two rules we haven't used (TF or RT, and P - S), and either can help us more clearly understand the situation. If we try to implement the first, we see that there are two possible locations for T—1 and 7. Let's draw those two out.

At this point, if you were stressed for time, you could just confirm that the first possibility works, then say that R in 6 must be it. However, if you are striving for -0, or just don't think like that, it'll just take a few more seconds to confirm that in both options, R must be in 6. For the lower option, S must follow O, and since S can't immediately follow O, S must go in 7. That places R in 6. (D) is correct.

Game 4 Solutions | PT 35, G 4

Exactly seven professors—Madison, Nilsson, Orozco, Paton, Robinson, Sarkis, and Togo—were hired in the years 1989 through 1995. Each professor has one or more specialities, and any two professors hired in the same year or in consecutive years do not have a specialty in common. The professors were hired according to the following conditions:

Madison was hired in 1993, Robinson in 1991.
There is at least one specialty that Madison, Orozco, and Togo have in common.
Nilsson shares a specialty with Robinson.
Paton and Sarkis were each hired at least one year before Madison and at least one year after Nilsson.
Orozco, who shares a specialty with Sarkis, was hired in 1990.

M N O P R S T

89	90	91	92	93	94	95
		R		M		

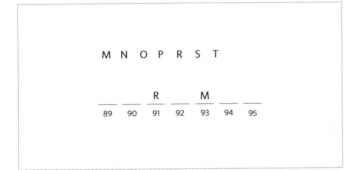

STEP ONE: This is an unusual game, and you probably want to read the comments before walking through the solutions, but in any case, here is the basic layout.

89	90	91	92	93	94	95
		R		M		
			~~O~~	~~O~~	~~O~~	
			~~T~~	~~T~~	~~T~~	

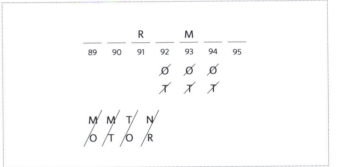

~~M/O~~ ~~M/T~~ ~~T/O~~ ~~N/R~~

STEP TWO: Each rule about specialties is going to be a rule about which elements can't go together. We want to make sure to mark the rules and consequences on the diagram. Here it is after the second and third rules. I'm keeping in mind that my "not" notations below also mean the elements can't be immediately adjacent (writing all that out would be a nightmare).

N — P, S — M

89	90	91	92	93	94	95
		R		M		
			~~O~~	~~O~~	~~O~~	
			~~T~~	~~T~~	~~T~~	

~~M/O~~ ~~M/T~~ ~~T/O~~ ~~N/R~~

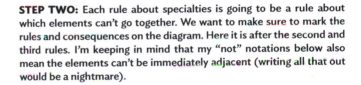

STEP THREE: The fourth rule is a (relatively) standard ordering rule. It's important to remember that multiple elements can go in any one year.

N — P, S — M

89	90	91	92	93	94	95
	O	R		M		
~~S~~	~~N~~	~~N~~	~~O~~	~~O~~	~~O~~	
	~~S~~	~~S~~	~~T~~	~~T~~	~~T~~	
			~~N~~			

~~M/O~~ ~~M/T~~ ~~T/O~~ ~~N/R~~

STEP FOUR: And the final rule gives us a concrete assignment, and another "not" pairing—O and S. Since we know where O is going, we can just cross S out from the relevant years: 89, 90, and 91.

N — P,S — M

N	O	R	S	M		T
89	90	91	92	93	94	95

S N N O O O

S S T T T

N

M/O M/T T/O N/R

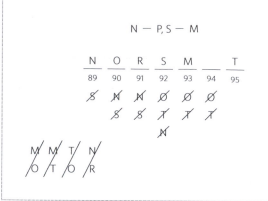

STEP FIVE: We've just input a lot of information—let's think about how it goes together. S must go before M, but can't go in 89, 90, or 91. That means it must go in 92. N needs to go before S, but can't go in 90 or 91, so it must go in 89. Also, T can't be next to O, and so also can't go in 89, 90, or 91. That means T must go in 95. Here's what we've got so far, in its full glory.

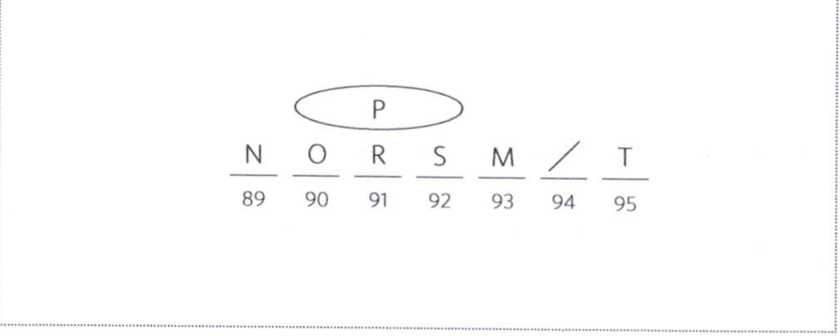

STEP SIX: P is the only remaining element—after double checking, we can see that all we know about it is that it goes in 90, 91, or 92. 94 is blank. At this point, considering that we know so much about the game, and considering that our diagram has gotten so detailed, it's not a bad idea to create a cleaner version to work off of. Note that we no longer need to consider the issues mentioned in the *not* rules and the ordering rule, because they have all already been accounted for in the placing of the elements. We can simply use the above to answer questions.

comments

When this game appeared on the LSAT, it was the fourth game of the section. That was a cruel decision by the test writers because most test takers by the time they get to the fourth game are rushed for time, and this particular game, more so than most, is one that rewards and makes challenging a careful and correct initial understanding.

There are three primary issues that can cause trouble if they are overlooked. The first is that even though the number of elements is equal to the number of positions, there is not a 1-to-1 relationship between elements and positions. There is one strong hint that indicates this in the scenario: "hired in the same year or in consecutive years..." Simple enough, but easy to miss.

The second issue is that of the "specialties." It's easy to assume, at first, that the specialties will just be like other subsets we've gotten used to, and, if you weren't careful, thinking the game is designed this way could lead to a troubled initial diagram. If we don't rush into interpreting specialties, what we notice is that we are never given any information about what these specialties are, and, in fact, the only thing we know about the specialties is that professors who share a specialty cannot be in the same or consecutive years.

The specialty is a red herring—saying two elements share a specialty is a convoluted way of saying two elements are not in the same year, or consecutive years, and that's it. Again, simple enough, but misinterpret it, and the game seems markedly more difficult.

Once you recognize those characteristics of the game for what they are, it's time to get into the rules more specifically. It turns out, if we understand the construction of the game correctly, the rules lend themselves to a long series of inferences. This is both good news and bad news. The good news is that if you are able to execute and uncover those inferences, the game becomes quite limited and the questions simple. The danger is that, with so many inferences out there for you to catch, right answers will surely require significant chains of thought, and if you don't have most or all of those inferences up front, or if you don't capture them during the solving of some of the earlier questions, you can be in for a long game.

All that is to say this is a game that really shows off the importance of a deliberate, careful start.

Kudos if you...

...waited to mark the specialties and saw them for what they truly were (clues about which elements can and cannot go with and next to one another).

Crazy kudos if you...

...ended up finding all of the inferences listed in the above solution. You have mad inference skills!

Exactly seven professors—Madison, Nilsson, Orozco, Paton, Robinson, Sarkis, and Togo—were hired in the years 1989 through 1995. Each professor has one or more specialties, and any two professors hired in the same year or in consecutive years do not have a specialty in common. The professors were hired according to the following conditions:

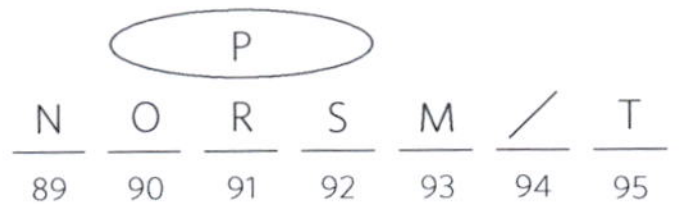

Madison was hired in 1993, Robinson in 1991.
There is at least one specialty that Madison, Orozco, and Togo have in common.
Nilsson shares a specialty with Robinson.
Paton and Sarkis were each hired at least one year before Madison and at least one year after Nilsson.
Orozco, who shares a specialty with Sarkis, was hired in 1990.

		(P)				
N	O	R	S	M	/	T
89	90	91	92	93	94	95

18. Which one of the following is a complete and accurate list of the professors who could have been hired in the years 1989 through 1991?

(A) Nilsson, Orozco, Robinson
(B) Orozco, Robinson, Sarkis
(C) Nilsson, Orozco, Paton, Robinson
(D) Nilsson, Orozco, Paton, Sarkis
(E) Orozco, Paton, Robinson, Sarkis

18. (C): (No Rules Question) As we discussed in Lesson 28, this is a question stem we want to make sure to read carefully ("complete... could"): here, we need to come up with a list of everyone who could have been hired in the years 89 - 91. We know N, O, and R were hired in those years, and we know P could have been hired in 90 or 91. We need an answer that includes all four of those elements and no others. (C) is correct.

19. If exactly one professor was hired in 1991, then which one of the following could be true?

(A) Madison and Paton share a specialty.
(B) Robinson and Sarkis share a specialty.
(C) Paton was hired exactly one year after Orozco.
(D) Exactly one professor was hired in 1994.
(E) Exactly two professors were hired in 1993.

19. (A): (A) could be true. (B) must be false. (C) must be false because P can't go in 91. We know (D) and (E) must be false. (A) is correct.

20. Which one of the following must be false?

(A) Nilsson was hired in 1989.
(B) Paton was hired in 1990.
(C) Paton was hired in 1991.
(D) Sarkis was hired in 1992.
(E) Togo was hired in 1994.

20. (E): We know (E) must be false.

21. Which one of the following must be true?

(A) Orozco was hired before Paton.
(B) Paton was hired before Sarkis.
(C) Sarkis was hired before Robinson.
(D) Robinson was hired before Sarkis.
(E) Madison was hired before Sarkis.

21. (D): We know (D) must be true.

22. If exactly two professors were hired in 1992, then which one of the following could be true?

(A) Orozco, Paton, and Togo share a specialty.
(B) Madison, Paton, and Togo share a specialty.
(C) Exactly two professors were hired in 1991.
(D) Exactly two professors were hired in 1993.
(E) Paton was hired in 1991.

22. (A): (A) could be true. (B) must be false if P is in 92 and M in 93. And our diagram makes it clear that (C) and (D) must be false. Our inference makes (E) false.

23. If Paton and Madison have a specialty in common, then which one of the following must be true?

(A) Nilsson does not share a specialty with Paton.
(B) Exactly one professor was hired in 1990.
(C) Exactly one professor was hired in 1991.
(D) Exactly two professors were hired in each of two years.
(E) Paton was hired at least one year before Sarkis.

23. (E): (E) must be true.

How Did You Do?

You've just faced the best (or worst, depending on your mood) that the Logic Games section can offer. You've taken its hardest punches. How did you hold up?

If you were fairly successful in surviving these four tough games, consider yourself a bit of a games superstar. Make it your goal to not only *feel* that you *can* go -0 in the games section but to be good enough to *know*, going in, that you *will* go -0 in the games section. If you didn't perform as well as you might have hoped, if these games kicked your butt a little bit, know that they were supposed to. These four games were meant to expose you to some of the more extreme challenges that you might face on test day. Each game was tough in its own way, and chances are—depending on your own strengths and weaknesses—you felt some were more difficult than others. Hopefully these games help you reflect on what you need to focus on in the last leg of your preparation.

The first game, the mannequin game, is challenging because it requires us to think about a large variety of information (the two mannequins, the items of clothing, colors of clothing, total number of clothes), and it's very easy to overlook one of those issues; in particular, it's easy to underestimate the importance of knowing there is exactly one item of each color, and ten items total. The key inference is that each mannequin wears exactly two colors. If you had trouble visualizing the game, or missed the key two-color inference, the questions become markedly more difficult.

In contrast to the first game, the second one, the CDs game, does not involve many different types of rules—the entire game hinges on your ability to correctly translate and utilize conditional rules. This game is arguably the most difficult conditional-centered game ever to appear on the LSAT. If you had difficulty, consider whether that difficulty came from having trouble understanding the rules, notating the rules, or using your notations to bring rules together and solve questions.

The situation for the third game, concert compositions, is also simple—just eight elements to be placed in an order. The challenge is the level of uncertainty each rule presents—we're told of spaces in between elements, but not the order of those elements, and nearly every rule is presented as an "or" situation. In order to survive and succeed, you need to be comfortable using notations for these less-than-certain rules, and you need to be very flexible in your thinking.

Finally, the last game, the professors game, was the most sneaky in terms of its setup. It's imperative that you first read all the rules and developed a big-picture understanding (the idea that "specialty" doesn't involve subsets, but rather is a hidden way of giving "not" rules). As long as you did that, chances are you were okay on the questions. However, this is also a game that rewards those who have very strong inference skills. If you were able to make the inferences up front that are included in the solution, the questions go very quickly.

Note that though all these games are unusually challenging, they are not necessarily unique—that is, the challenges they present are simply ratcheted-up versions of challenges that appear in other games. As such, they serve as great barometers of whether you are ready for the toughest challenges of the section. Make sure you use your results to take note of any weaknesses that need to be addressed.

30 LOGICAL REASONING reasoning structure questions

From the beginning of our Logical Reasoning preparation, we've broken up Logical Reasoning questions based on whether they require a subjective understanding or an objective one. The majority of Logical Reasoning questions require a subjective understanding—more specifically, they require us to critically evaluate the use of reasoning to justify a conclusion. Up to this point, these questions have been the focus of our studies. Hopefully, identifying the point, identifying the support, thinking about the flaw in reasoning, and then working off of that understanding, has now become habit.

In this batch of lessons, we will focus on questions that require an objective understanding of the information in the stimulus. These questions are designed to test your ability to understand and apply information. These questions are not designed to test your ability to judge or evaluate that information, and when students have difficulties with objective questions, an inability to quell the part of themselves that wants to interject an opinion or hypothesis is often the culprit. Take that instinct out of the equation, and all objective questions become far more logical and simpler to solve.

We'll be looking at eight different types of objective questions in the next four lessons, and we will divide up our work as follows:

In this lesson, we will discuss objective questions that relate directly to the reasoning structure of arguments: identify the conclusion, identify the role, describe the method of reasoning, and match the reasoning. If you feel comfortable with your ability to solve subjective questions—the questions we've already discussed—then you already have all of the skills necessary to solve argument structure questions, as identifying a conclusion, recognizing the roles that parts of an argument play, and thinking about the reasoning structure of arguments are all fundamental to being able to critically evaluate reasoning. Additionally, these questions consistently reward test takers that have the mental discipline to not judge when judging is not the task at hand, and much of our work will be geared toward developing habits that will help you think about the right things, and no more.

In Lesson 32, we'll move on to Inference questions and Examples of a Principle questions. These will be the first questions we look at that are not dependent on argument reasoning structure—many stimuli for these questions will not contain arguments, and even when they do, your understanding of the argument will often *not* be central to answering the question correctly. These questions are straightforward and simple to understand, but they require a shift in mindset. We'll work on developing skills and habits that align specifically with these tasks.

In Lesson 33, we'll take a look at two final outlier question types—Identify the Disagreement and Explain a Discrepancy. These questions share a lot in common with the other argument-based questions on the exam, but they also present tasks that are somewhat unique.

Reasoning Structure Questions

On each exam, you will encounter several questions that test you on a specific part of the argument-evaluation process: your ability to *recognize* the structure of the argument correctly. These questions will test your understanding of the structure in a few different ways. The most common way is by asking you to correctly identify the main point or conclusion. Other less common questions will ask you what role a particular part of the stimulus plays in the argument as a whole. Other even less common questions will ask more directly—what is the method of reasoning the author uses here? Finally, and fairly commonly, questions will require you to recognize the reasoning structure of an argument and to then identify one argument out of the five that is most similar in its design—these are Match the Reasoning questions.

Once you identify the reasoning structure of the argument, you want to immediately jump back to the task that the question stem presents. You should expect to have a very clear sense of the substance of your right answer before moving on to the answer choices

We'll soon discuss the specifics of each type of question, but it's important to know that there is great commonality to all questions that ask about the intended reasoning structure of the stimulus. You should feel, generally speaking, that you can attack these different types of questions in roughly the same way.

For all such questions, you should read the stimulus in the same way that you have for all of the types of questions we've discussed thus far—that is, you should read first to identify the main point, then the support for that main point. You should always do this, even for questions that ask about parts of the passage that seem to play neither role. Your understanding of the main point and its support is what determines your understanding of the rest of the reasoning structure.

As mentioned before, the one thing you do *not* want to do is evaluate the reasoning in the argument critically—that is, you want to waste no time, and allow yourself no negative influence, thinking about how *well* the reasoning given does or does not support the conclusion. Those thoughts are simply not relevant for right answers, and can very often lead you to be tempted by wrong answers you wouldn't be tempted by otherwise. Once you identify the reasoning structure of the argument, you want to immediately jump back to the task that the question stem presents—whether that be thinking about the structure of the passage as a whole, the role of one component, or (most commonly) the main point. You should expect to have a very clear sense of the substance of your right answer before moving on to the answer choices.

A key strategy that is common to top scorers is that once this pre-phrase is established, they use it not to dig out a right answer but rather to eliminate wrong ones. The right answers for harder versions of these questions are often vague, awkwardly written, and otherwise less than perfect. It can be very hard to say definitively that an answer is correct. However, wrong answers must always be clearly and absolutely incorrect. It is consistently easier and, with practice, faster, to eliminate four wrong answers than it is to identify the right answer. We'll prioritize this elimination process along the way.

Conclusion

"Which of the following best expresses the main conclusion of the argument?"
"Which one of the following most accurately expresses the conclusion of the argument?"

Conclusion, or main point, questions are very common and as straightforward as Logical Reasoning questions get. The key to solving these questions is a strong and singular understanding of task—you make your life much easier by knowing exactly what to think about and, more importantly, what not to think about. Don't overcomplicate these questions—they present a very simple task, and the more basic you consider the task, the better.

step one: understand your job

As always, we want to begin by reading the question stem. Main point questions are easy to identify—just make sure not to confuse them with Inference questions, which we will cover in lesson 32. Main point questions test our ability to understand the argument as the author presented it. They punish test takers who lack a strong understanding of reasoning structure, and they punish those who extrapolate or get influenced by personal bias. Your job is to understand but not judge.

step two: find the point

This is, of course, the key step here. Just as we've always done, we want to make finding the conclusion our primary task for the initial read of the stimulus. As you might expect, these questions will commonly have intermediate or opposing conclusions meant to throw us off the scent. Remember that the main point will always have supporting reasoning, and when deciding between two main points, you should think about which point is being used to support the other. Most commonly, the main point for these questions will be somewhere in the middle of the argument (the most difficult place to find it). It may be split up through the use of a pronoun or some other device (*"but this idea is wrong,"* for example), but it will be one clear, singular idea. You must have a very specific sense of the conclusion before going into the answer choices.

step three: find the support

Once you feel fairly certain you have the main point, you want to look for the reasoning, just as you've always done. If you have the correct conclusion, the reasoning used to support it, and subsequently the parts of the argument meant to oppose or give background, should be fairly clear to see. Finding the support and seeing the rest of the reasoning structure is a great way to confirm that the conclusion you identified is indeed the main point.

step four: get rid of answers

The big difference between how you will solve the questions in this lesson, and how you've solved subjective questions, is that for objective questions you do not want to waste any time (nor do you want to distract yourself) thinking about how well the reasoning supports the conclusion. Instead, confirm your understanding of the main point, keep that in your head, go straight into the answer choices, and actively search for wrong answers to eliminate. Incorrect answers will all have at least one of two characteristics—they will focus on parts of the argument (support, background, etc.) that are not the conclusion, or they will extrapolate from the conclusion, commonly by generalizing, becoming more specific or extreme, or bringing in outside information. If you have a specific sense of the conclusion, these wrong answers should be obvious to see, and your goal should be to quickly eliminate four almost every time.

step five: confirm the right answer

The right answer may use unusual or awkward wording that you may not be able to anticipate, but in its substance the right answer should be a very close match to the conclusion you identified in the text. The most tempting wrong answers will commonly take one extra step beyond what the text gives us, and when choosing between two answers, you want to go with the one that is closest to the actual information in the argument. Keep in mind that right answers will commonly bring up background or opposing points, but if those elements are mentioned, their roles relative to the main point will be made explicitly clear (see notes under super-simple example).

SUPER-SIMPLE EXAMPLE

In a recent interview, the CEO of ABC Tech blamed the current economic climate for the recent decline in sales. However, his response does not take into account several significant issues. For example, other companies are now providing products that are similar to those that ABC makes, and these new products are more durable and far more affordable.

Which of the following best represents the main conclusion of the argument?

(A) The current economic climate has had no impact on the recent decline in sales.
(B) The CEO's statement failed to include issues that are relevant to the recent decline in sales.
(C) Other companies now make products that are better versions of those that ABC makes.
(D) Other companies now make products that are similar to those that ABC makes, but these products cost less and last longer.
(E) The CEO made his statements with the purpose of intentionally misleading the public.

The correct answer is (B). The author's main point comes in the second sentence of the stimulus. The first sentence serves as background, and the last sentence as support for the main point. We want an answer that best matches the second sentence.

(A) is most related to the first sentence, and the "no" takes it far beyond the information in the text. (C) relates more to the support, and overgeneralizes in saying other companies make a better product. (D) matches the text, but unfortunately that text is the support. (E) jumps to conclusions about the CEO's intentions that the text simply cannot support. (B) could have included some more information and would have been easier to pick if it had. However, the key is that any right answer has to have the conclusion that matches, in terms of substance, the point that is made in the actual argument, and (B) matches.

CONSTELLATION OF WRONG ANSWERS

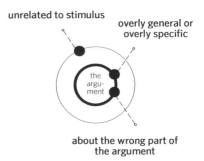

unrelated to stimulus
overly general or overly specific
the argument
about the wrong part of the argument

Identify the Role

"Which one of the following best represents the role played by the claim that...?"
"The reference to ... plays which one of the following roles in the argument?"

Identify the Role questions represent another way of testing our ability to read for reasoning structure. These questions ask us to correctly identify the role that a certain component plays in an argument. Though the wording might be different, the possible roles are conclusion, support, opposing point, background, and intermediate conclusion (remember that an intermediate conclusion is simply a supporting premise that itself has support). The correct answer is, understandably, most commonly related to the roles most critical to reasoning structure—conclusion and support.

Step one: Understand Your Job: These are very straightforward questions. Avoid looking at the part in question in a "vacuum," for context is what gives a part a specific role. Know that your job is to first understand the passage as a whole, *then* to consider the role that the part in question plays.

Step two: Find the Point & Step three: Find the Support: As we've always done, we want to start by identifying the point and the reasoning used to get there. Understanding the point and the support also makes the assigning of other roles—such as opposing points—a snap. You should have a strong prephrase of the right answer, and remember not to judge the validity of the reasoning in any way.

Step four: Get Rid of Answers: This is the step that makes these questions, on average, a bit easier than other question types—the wrong answers for these questions are very obviously wrong. They will all either clearly misrepresent what is stated in the argument (most commonly by changing the conclusion the author reached) or misrepresent the role. If you have a clear understanding of the argument and role, you can typically recognize four wrong answers very quickly.

Step five: Confirm the Right Answer: For a tougher version of this question, the right answer may not be written in a way that you might expect (maybe, instead of saying that a part in question supports the author's point, it says that the part in question goes against the opposing point), but it will represent the information in the argument correctly, and it will not be inaccurate in terms of what role the part in question plays. Keep to these guidelines, and almost all such questions are very straightforward.

CONSTELLATION OF WRONG ANSWERS

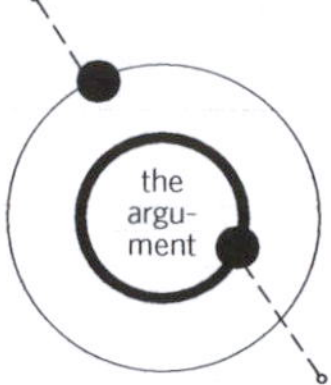

TRUNCATED SUPER-SIMPLE EXAMPLES

My mom says I shouldn't watch television. But the television makes me laugh, so I want to watch it.

1. Which of the following best represents the role that "the television makes me laugh" plays in the argument?

(A)It supports the conclusion that he should be allowed to watch television whenever he wants.
(B) It is used to justify his desire to view it.
(C) It is the point the author is attempting to make.

2. The argument proceeds by

(A) stating a position, and giving reasons why that position will lead to negative consequences
(B) stating a position, then giving reasoning that leads to a second position that may stand in opposition to the first
(C) showing a chain of consequences that leads to an inevitable result

1. (B) is correct. (A) misrepresents the conclusion, and (C) the role.

2. (B) is correct. (A) misrepresents the information in the argument, and (C) the reasoning structure.

**Note that obviously no real LSAT questions will have just three answers, and in recent years, no stimulus has been used for two questions.*

What Is the Reasoning Structure?

"The argument proceeds by"
"X's argument does which of the following?"

Method of Reasoning questions are quite rare, appearing about once every two exams. They ask us most directly about the key issue we've been focusing on—the reasoning structure of the argument.

Step one: Understand Your Job: These are also very straightforward questions. Read the stimulus as you always have, and remember not to judge the validity of what you read.

Step two: Find the Point & Step three: Find the Support: Again, same as we always have. Use your understanding of point and support to consider what other parts act as opposing points or background. Keep the specific relationship between conclusion and support ("The author says X, and his reason is Y") in your head as you go into the answer choices. This is your prephrase.

Step four: Get Rid of Answers: These answers are a bit more challenging to deal with than those that accompany Identify the Role questions, but the criteria for eliminating wrong choices is pretty much the same and just as black and white: get rid of choices that misrepresent the information in the passage or misrepresent the argument structure. Every wrong answer will have a clear issue in at least one of these areas.

Step five: Confirm the Right Answer: Again, for the tougher version of this question, what will happen is that the right answer will represent the argument structure in a circular way, or in a way that you didn't expect. Check to make sure that the information in the answer—i.e., the subjects and actions discussed—is indeed a correct match for the information in the stimulus, and if you can't say that the representation of the reasoning structure is *wrong*, and if you've correctly gotten rid of the wrong choices, it will be the correct answer.

CONSTELLATION OF WRONG ANSWERS

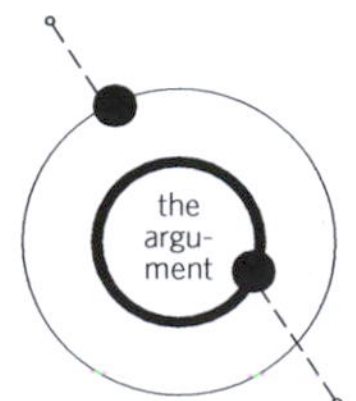

the process in action

Let's model the problem-solving process with four argument structure questions. I recommend you solve the questions first on your own before looking at the steps.

2.10. Double-blind techniques should be used whenever possible in scientific experiments. They help prevent the misinterpretations that often arise due to expectations and opinions that scientists already hold, and clearly scientists should be extremely diligent in trying to avoid such misinterpretations.

Which one of the following most accurately expresses the main conclusion of the argument?

(A) Scientists' objectivity may be impeded by interpreting experimental evidence on the basis of expectations and opinions that they already hold.
(B) It is advisable for scientists to use double-blind techniques in as high a proportion of their experiments as they can.
(C) Scientists sometimes neglect to adequately consider the risk of misinterpreting evidence on the basis of prior expectations and opinions.
(D) Whenever possible, scientists should refrain from interpreting evidence on the basis of previously formed expectations and convictions.
(E) Double-blind experimental techniques are often an effective way of ensuring scientific objectivity.

1. understand your job: Our job is to identify the conclusion that is in the argument. We want to make sure not to judge the argument in any way.

2. find the point: The first sentence is a great candidate to be the main point, and the rest of what follows seems to support it. We want to go into the answers knowing that the right answer should be, in terms of substance, nearly identical to that first sentence.

3. find the support: The support helps confirm the argument structure and thus the conclusion. Here, we see that the first part of the second sentence is meant to help support the main point, and the second part of the second sentence is meant to add significance to that support.

4. get rid of answers: (A) relates to the support, let's leave (B), (C) makes some assumptions and relates closest to the support, (D) relates to the support in the second sentence, and (E) relates closest to the support in the second sentence. None of the incorrect answers relate to the conclusion we found in the argument, and all four can be eliminated quickly.

5. confirm the right answer: (B) is the only answer remaining—if we check each part of it against the conclusion we identified in the argument, it's fairly clear to see that they have just reworded each part ("should" = "advisable," "whenever possible" = "as high a proportion as they can") but that the meaning is very similar.

3.12. Novel X and Novel Y are both semiautobiographical novels and contain many very similar themes and situations, which might lead one to suspect plagiarism on the part of one of the authors. However, it is more likely that the similarity of themes and situations in the two novels is merely coincidental, since both authors are from very similar backgrounds and have led similar lives.

Which one of the following most accurately expresses the conclusion drawn in the argument?

(A) Novel X and Novel Y are both semiautobiographical novels, and the two novels contain many very similar themes and situations.
(B) The fact that Novel X and Novel Y are both semiautobiographical novels and contain many very similar themes and situations might lead one to suspect plagiarism on the part of one of the authors.
(C) The author of Novel X and the author of Novel Y are from very similar backgrounds and have led very similar lives.
(D) It is less likely that one of the authors of Novel X or Novel Y is guilty of plagiarism than that the similarity of themes and situations in the two novels is merely coincidental.
(E) If the authors of Novel X and Novel Y are from very similar backgrounds and have led similar lives, suspicions that either of the authors plagiarized are very likely to be unwarranted.

1. understand your job: Our job is to identify the conclusion that is in the argument.

2. find the point: The "might lead one to suspect" in the first sentence is wording that indicates we're being given an opinion the author will disagree with in his conclusion. The author's point follows "however" in the second sentence. We know to look for an answer that says that similarities are coincidental.

3. find the support: The support follows "since" in the second sentence. The argument is set up with background, opinion, author's contrasting opinion, and support for that opinion.

4. get rid of answers: (A) relates to the background, (B) relates to the opposing point, (C) relates to the support, (D) matches what we expected and we should leave it, and the "if" in (E) does not match the structure of the argument (the argument has no such conditional).

5. confirm the right answer: (D) starts with the opposing opinion, then gives us the main point of the argument. Notice that saying plagiarism is "less likely" than coincidence is akin to saying coincidence is "more likely" than plagiarism.

Note: For this batch of lessons, all questions that are used in "the process in action" pages are, unless otherwise noted, from the June '07 Exam.

the process in action

2.11. It is now a common complaint that the electronic media have corroded the intellectual skills required and fostered by the literary media. But several centuries ago the complaint was that certain intellectual skills, such as the powerful memory and extemporaneous eloquence that were intrinsic to oral culture, were being destroyed by the spread of literacy. So, what awaits us is probably a mere alteration of the human mind rather than its devolution.

The reference to the complaint of several centuries ago that powerful memory and extemporaneous eloquence were being destroyed plays which one of the following roles in the argument?

(A) evidence supporting the claim that the intellectual skills fostered by the literary media are being destroyed by the electronic media
(B) an illustration of the general hypothesis being advanced that intellectual abilities are inseparable from the means by which people communicate
(C) an example of a cultural change that did not necessarily have a detrimental effect on the human mind overall
(D) evidence that the claim that the intellectual skills required and fostered by the literary media are being lost is unwarranted
(E) possible evidence, mentioned and then dismissed, that might be cited by supporters of the hypothesis being criticized

---

1. understand your job: Our job is to understand the reasoning structure of the argument. The most important part of that is the relationship between the support and the point.

2. find the point: The author's point comes in the last sentence—the votes are not a definite representation of the view of the residents. The structure of the passage is a common one—an opinion, evidence against that opinion, and the author's opposing point.

3. find the support: The support comes in the second and third sentences. These sentences are intended to show how unrepresentative the vote actually was. We want to keep this in mind as we go to the next step.

4. get rid of answers: "Questioning a conclusion" in (A) sounds good, but the rest of (A) has little to do with the given argument. (B) is not what is actually stated in the argument ("manipulated to support whatever" has no relation to anything we are given). (C) sounds somewhat tempting, so let's keep it. (D) goes beyond the argument ("impossible to disconfirm"). (E) is a great match for what we saw initially in the argument and expected in the answer. Let's get rid of (A), (B), and (D) and look again at (C) and (E).

5. confirm the right answer: (C) seems fairly close, but the original claim was not about truth in premises "guaranteeing" a truth in the conclusion, but rather the opinions of one group being used as evidence for general opinion. (E) has no such suspicious components, and another careful review of (E) confirms that it is the correct answer. The author is casting doubt on the original opinion, and the purpose of his evidence is to show the limited size of the sample set.

1. understand your job: The question stem sounds complicated, but our task is very simple—we just need to find out what role a part of the argument plays.

2. find the point: The author's point comes in the final sentence, following "so." This argument has a very common structure: an opinion, information that goes against that opinion, then the author's main point.

3. find the support: The support for the conclusion comes in the previous sentence, and that sentence happens to be the one in question. We can go into the answers expecting that the right answer will likely be about the portion in question supporting the main point in the third sentence.

4. get rid of answers: (A) gets the relationships mixed up and has the part in question supporting the wrong point. (B) goes well beyond the scope of the argument, (C) seems a bit general, but let's leave it. (D) isn't what is expected but also seems to be somewhat accurate, so let's leave it. (E), like (A), aligns the support with the wrong conclusion. We can get rid of (A), (B), and (E) quickly.

5. confirm the right answer: Let's take a careful look at (C)—it's not what we expected, and it's not as specific as it can be, but it has no absolute flaws. The second sentence is being used as an example of this point, and "did not necessarily have a detrimental effect" is a good match for "mere alteration...rather than its devolution." A careful look at (D) reveals problems that aren't obvious at first—the author is not necessarily disagreeing in his conclusion with the point that electronic media is having this impact; what he is disagreeing with is the fact that this is something that should be criticized. The second sentence does not serve to show that changes are not happening; it serves to show that the changes are not necessarily bad. (C) is correct.

3.20. Gamba: Muñoz claims that the Southwest Hopeville Neighbors Association overwhelmingly opposes the new water system, citing this as evidence of citywide opposition. The association did pass a resolution opposing the new water system, but only 25 of 350 members voted, with 10 in favor of the system. Furthermore, the 15 opposing votes represent far less than 1 percent of Hopeville's population. One should not assume that so few votes represent the view of the majority of Hopeville's residents.

Of the following, which one most accurately describes Gamba's strategy of argumentation?

(A) questioning a conclusion based on the results of a vote, on the grounds that people with certain views are more likely to vote
(B) questioning a claim supported by statistical data by arguing that statistical data can be manipulated to support whatever view the interpreter wants to support
(C) attempting to refute an argument by showing that, contrary to what has been claimed, the truth of the premises does not guarantee the truth of the conclusion
(D) criticizing a view on the grounds that the view is based on evidence that is in principle impossible to disconfirm
(E) attempting to cast doubt on a conclusion by claiming that the statistical sample on which the conclusion is based is too small to be dependable

31.3.14. Ethicist: Both ASA and TPA are clot-dissolving agents. Recent studies show that the more expensive agent, TPA, would save at most two more lives than would ASA out of every 50 cardiac patients to whom they are postoperatively administered. However, since the relatives of the patients who die simply because they were given the less expensive medicine would be particularly grieved, the financial saving involved in using ASA over TPA must also be weighed against such considerations.

Which one of the following most accurately expresses the conclusion of the ethicist's argument?

(A) ASA should never be given to postoperative cardiac patients in place of TPA.
(B) TPA is a slightly more effective clot-dissolving agent than ASA.
(C) The extra expense of TPA cannot be weighed simply against the few additional lives saved.
(D) ASA is a less expensive clot-dissolving agent than TPA.
(E) Relatives of a patient who has died grieve more if the patient received ASA rather than TPA.

30.4.2. The current theory about earthquakes holds that they are caused by adjoining plates of rock sliding past each other; the plates are pressed together until powerful forces overcome the resistance. As plausible as this may sound, at least one thing remains mysterious on this theory. The overcoming of such resistance should create enormous amounts of heat. But so far no increases in temperature unrelated to weather have been detected following earthquakes.

Which one of the following most accurately expresses the main point of the argument?

(A) No increases in temperature have been detected following earthquakes.
(B) The current theory does not fully explain earthquake data.
(C) No one will ever be sure what the true cause of earthquakes is.
(D) Earthquakes produce enormous amounts of heat that have so far gone undetected.
(E) Contrary to the current theory, earthquakes are not caused by adjoining plates of rock sliding past one another.

Stick to the steps!
1. Understand your job.
2. Find the point.
3. Find the support.
4. Get rid of answers.
5. Confirm the right answer.

30.4.13. Joseph: My encyclopedia says that the mathematician Pierre de Fermat died in 1665 without leaving behind any written proof for a theorem that he claimed nonetheless to have proved. Probably this alleged theorem simply cannot be proved, since—as the article points out—no one else has been able to prove it. Therefore it is likely that Fermat was either lying or else mistaken when he made his claim.

Laura: Your encyclopedia is out of date. Recently someone has in fact proved Fermat's theorem. And since the theorem is provable, your claim—that Fermat was lying or mistaken—clearly is wrong.

13. Joseph's statement that "this alleged theorem simply cannot be proved" plays which one of the following roles in his argument?

(A) an assumption for which no support is offered
(B) a subsidiary conclusion on which his argument's main conclusion is based
(C) a potential objection that his argument anticipates and attempts to answer before it is raised
(D) the principal claim that his argument is structured to refute
(E) background information that neither supports nor undermines his argument's conclusion

29.1.12. It is well known that many species adapt to their environment, but it is usually assumed that only the most highly evolved species alter their environment in ways that aid their own survival. However, this characteristic is actually quite common. Certain species of plankton, for example, generate a gas that is converted in the atmosphere into particles of sulfate. These particles cause water vapor to condense, thus forming clouds. Indeed, the formation of clouds over the ocean largely depends on the presence of these particles. More cloud cover means more sunlight is reflected, and so the Earth absorbs less heat. Thus plankton cause the surface of the Earth to be cooler and this benefits the plankton.

Which one of the following accurately describes the argumentative strategy employed?

(A) A general principle is used to justify a claim made about a particular case to which that principle has been shown to apply.
(B) An explanation of how a controversial phenomenon could have come about is given in order to support the claim that this phenomenon did in fact come about.
(C) A generalization about the conditions under which a certain process can occur is advanced on the basis of an examination of certain cases in which that process did occur.
(D) A counterexample to a position being challenged is presented in order to show that this position is incorrect.
(E) A detailed example is used to illustrate the advantage of one strategy over another.

31.3.14. Ethicist: Both ASA and TPA are clot-dissolving agents. Recent studies show that the more expensive agent, TPA, would save at most two more lives than would ASA out of every 50 cardiac patients to whom they are postoperatively administered. However, since the relatives of the patients who die simply because they were given the less expensive medicine would be particularly grieved, the financial saving involved in using ASA over TPA must also be weighed against such considerations.

Which one of the following most accurately expresses the conclusion of the ethicist's argument?

(A) ASA should never be given to postoperative cardiac patients in place of TPA.
(B) TPA is a slightly more effective clot-dissolving agent than ASA.
(C) The extra expense of TPA cannot be weighed simply against the few additional lives saved.
(D) ASA is a less expensive clot-dissolving agent than TPA.
(E) Relatives of a patient who has died grieve more if the patient received ASA rather than TPA.

1. understand your job: Our job is to find the main point.

2. find the point: The first two sentences are background. The "however," which is a bit awkward and confusing, hints at the argument to come, "since" gives us the support, and then the last point, "the financial savings...must also be weighed..." is the conclusion.

3. find the support: The support comes in the "since" phrase in the same sentence as the conclusion. The reasoning is confusing to understand, let alone judge, but thankfully that's not our job here. Since we know the conclusion with certainty, we can move on to the next step.

4. get rid of answers: (A) goes beyond the intent of the argument—"never" is a clear giveaway. (B) relates to the background. (C) is not the answer we expected, but it is related to the main point—that there is an additional consideration—so let's leave it. (D) is related to the background. (E) relates to the support. We can easily get rid of (A), (B), (D), and (E).

5. confirm the right answer: Here is another instance in which it is far easier to see why wrong answers are wrong than it is to see why the right answer is right. However, to confirm, we can look back through the text, and indeed (C) matches the point well. The first sentence of the argument lays out the situation—one agent is more costly, but more effective. The point is that there is an extra conditional consideration beyond what was in the first sentence. (C) represents that, albeit in a way that we may not have expected.

30.4.2. The current theory about earthquakes holds that they are caused by adjoining plates of rock sliding past each other; the plates are pressed together until powerful forces overcome the resistance. As plausible as this may sound, at least one thing remains mysterious on this theory. The overcoming of such resistance should create enormous amounts of heat. But so far no increases in temperature unrelated to weather have been detected following earthquakes.

Which one of the following most accurately expresses the main point of the argument?

(A) No increases in temperature have been detected following earthquakes.
(B) The current theory does not fully explain earthquake data.
(C) No one will ever be sure what the true cause of earthquakes is.
(D) Earthquakes produce enormous amounts of heat that have so far gone undetected.
(E) Contrary to the current theory, earthquakes are not caused by adjoining plates of rock sliding past one another.

1. understand your job: Our job is to find the main point.

2. find the point: The author's point is that there is a mystery yet to be answered by the theory. Specifically, there should be heat, but there isn't.

3. find the support: This is an unusual argument in that the support is built into the main point—there isn't heat.

4. get rid of answers: (A) discusses the support—the facts behind the point—but doesn't represent the point well. (B) seems to represent the main point in a roundabout way ("at least one thing remains a mystery" = "does not fully explain"), so let's keep it. (C) goes well beyond the scope of the argument. (D) mixes together the background and the point, and adds in some assumptions for good measure. (E) goes too far—the author does not say the theory is wrong.

5. confirm the right answer: Once again, we are left with just one answer after our eliminations. We look at (B) once again, check it against the text, and go ahead and select it.

30.4.13. Joseph: My encyclopedia says that the mathematician Pierre de Fermat died in 1665 without leaving behind any written proof for a theorem that he claimed nonetheless to have proved. Probably this alleged theorem simply cannot be proved, since—as the article points out—no one else has been able to prove it. Therefore it is likely that Fermat was either lying or else mistaken when he made his claim.

Laura: Your encyclopedia is out of date. Recently someone has in fact proved Fermat's theorem. And since the theorem is provable, your claim—that Fermat was lying or mistaken—clearly is wrong.

13. Joseph's statement that "this alleged theorem simply cannot be proved" plays which one of the following roles in his argument?

(A) an assumption for which no support is offered
(B) a subsidiary conclusion on which his argument's main conclusion is based
(C) a potential objection that his argument anticipates and attempts to answer before it is raised
(D) the principal claim that his argument is structured to refute
(E) background information that neither supports nor undermines his argument's conclusion

1. understand your job: Our job is to understand the role that the statement in question plays. We'll do this by understanding the reasoning structure of the argument.

2. find the point: At first, the line in question ("this alleged...") seems like it is the main point, especially considering that what follows it is support. However, the last line gives us an ultimate, or final, main point—Fermat was either lying or else mistaken.

3. find the support: The portion in question is what ultimately leads us to the final point. The portion in question is also, itself, supported (by the statement that begins "since—"). With a clear understanding of the reasoning structure, and a clear understanding of the role the part in question plays, we can easily start eliminating wrong answers.

4. get rid of answers: (A) is incorrect, since it is a statement that does have support. (B) seems correct, so let's leave it for now. (C) misrepresents the role in the argument—the statement is not an objection. (D) also misrepresents the role; he uses the piece to support his conclusion—it is not something he tries to refute. (E) is incorrect—since the final sentence starts "therefore," we know for sure that the part in question is being used as support for the final conclusion.

5. confirm the right answer: Once again we are left with just one attractive answer. We know that the part in question is being used to support the main conclusion, and is itself being supported by other evidence. Remember that a subsidiary, or intermediate, conclusion is simply a supporting premise that itself has support, and the part in question certainly fits the bill. (B) is correct.

29.1.12. It is well known that many species adapt to their environment, but it is usually assumed that only the most highly evolved species alter their environment in ways that aid their own survival. However, this characteristic is actually quite common. Certain species of plankton, for example, generate a gas that is converted in the atmosphere into particles of sulfate. These particles cause water vapor to condense, thus forming clouds. Indeed, the formation of clouds over the ocean largely depends on the presence of these particles. More cloud cover means more sunlight is reflected, and so the Earth absorbs less heat. Thus plankton cause the surface of the Earth to be cooler and this benefits the plankton.

Which one of the following accurately describes the argumentative strategy employed?

(A) A general principle is used to justify a claim made about a particular case to which that principle has been shown to apply.
(B) An explanation of how a controversial phenomenon could have come about is given in order to support the claim that this phenomenon did in fact come about.
(C) A generalization about the conditions under which a certain process can occur is advanced on the basis of an examination of certain cases in which that process did occur.
(D) A counterexample to a position being challenged is presented in order to show that this position is incorrect.
(E) A detailed example is used to illustrate the advantage of one strategy over another.

1. understand your job: Our job is to understand the reasoning structure.

2. find the point: The main point is well hidden in the middle of the text: "however, this characteristic is actually quite common."

3. find the support: It's easy to assume that the main point is about plankton, but the plankton discussion is used as support. If you aren't sure, you can use the "therefore" test: "plankton cause the surface of the earth... and therefore altering environment is a common thing" (yes), "altering environment is a common thing, therefore plankton cause earth's surface..." (no). Thus, the plankton is meant to support the general statement, and not the other way around.

The argument is more complex than most, but the general structure is a common one—a general assumption is stated, a contrasting opinion is presented, and then support is given for that opinion. With that understanding, let's go hunting for wrong answers.

4. get rid of answers: (A) gets the conclusion-support relationship reversed (as we'd expect wrong answers to do here). The "controversial phenomenon" in (B) is not directly related to this argument. (C) seems okay—let's leave it. (D) seems okay too, so let's leave it. "The advantage of one strategy over another" mentioned in (E) has no direct relation to the argument. We can eliminate (A), (B), and (E) quickly.

5. confirm the right answer: Let's look at (C) and (D) more carefully. A lot of (C) matches what we are looking for—"a generalization," "is advanced...on the basis of...certain cases" all sounds good. However, "the conditions under which certain processes occur," does not match our text—our argument is about species, not conditions. We can eliminate (C). (D) is the correct answer. The author's main point challenges a position, and so the support for the author's point acts as a counterexample to the position being challenged.

Match the Reasoning

"Which one of the following arguments is most similar in its reasoning to the argument above?"
"The pattern of reasoning in which of the following is most similar to that in the argument above?"

Whereas the other question types we've discussed in this lesson thus far fall, on average, on the easier end of the difficulty spectrum, Match the Reasoning questions are typically pretty tough. They require us to do a significant amount of work in both the stimulus and the answer choices, so allow yourself a bit of extra time when you see this type of question—20 extra seconds or so—and be happy when you don't need it. Success requires that you consistently recognize basic reasoning structure quickly and accurately, and, perhaps most importantly, that you maintain a high level of mental discipline.

step one: understand your job

Matching questions require you to figure out which two arguments are most alike. The first part of the challenge is to gain as specific an understanding of the fixed target—the initial argument—as possible. Without this, the task of wading through the answers becomes monumentally more difficult. The next part of your job is to find reasons why four answers do not make good matches. If you've done this well, most of the time there will be just one attractive match standing. Your final step is to compare conclusions, support, and reasoning relationships to make sure the match is strong.

step two: find the point

This is the same as for every other question we've dealt with, so I won't say much. Keep in mind that understanding the specific reasoning relationship in the argument is going to be critical to eliminating answers, which, because of the advanced nature of these questions, will commonly have differences that are somewhat subtle—so try to understand the specifics of the conclusion the best you can. Allow yourself to go more slowly than you normally do, or to give yourself an extra read of the conclusion, as needed.

step three: find the support

Once you have the conclusion, you need to relate the support to that conclusion. Understanding this relationship in a specific way will be critical to eliminating wrong choices. Match the Reasoning questions will often have compound reasoning structures—two premises that add to a conclusion, or one point that leads to another that leads to another. Again, take the time to understand this initial relationship carefully and correctly. Quickly take note of any opposing points or background.

step four: get rid of answers

Ultimately, how well you perform in this step will determine whether a question feels easy or difficult, and how well you performed steps two and three will typically determine your success in this step.

As always, keep in mind that wrong answers will have clear markers that tip us off that they are incorrect. For matching questions, we cannot use subject matter to eliminate answers—we must solely rely on our understanding of reasoning structure. Wrong answers will all be wrong for one general reason: they do not have the same reasoning structure as the original argument.

A common way we'll recognize this is that the answer reaches a different type of conclusion (maybe the original reached a causal conclusion, and an answer choice has a conditional conclusion) and the other common way we'll recognize this is that the relationship between support and conclusion will be very different (perhaps in the original argument there is a conditional relationship, and in an answer choice there is a comparative one).

step five: confirm the right answer

If you've performed steps one through four correctly, you should expect, most of the time, to get down to just one, or sometimes two, answers to confirm. Start by making sure that the points made in the conclusions are similar, then check the match between support and conclusion. Lastly, look for any "stray" but limiting or essential components that show up in the argument; or (most commonly) the answer choice that, for whatever reason, changes the reasoning relationship enough to cause a mismatch.

SIMPLE EXAMPLE

Every day, Janice either rides her bike or goes to the gym. When she goes to the gym, she always wears a hat. Since Janice is not going to bike today, she will wear a hat and go to the gym.

Which of the following arguments is most similar to the reasoning in the argument above?

(A) Most people prefer warm weather, but some prefer cold. Since Ted likes cold weather, he is in the minority.
(B) Anyone with a badge can get access, and anyone who can get access can get free sodas. Since John has a badge, he can get a free soda.
(C) Barry can take a job as either an accountant or a project manager. Since he doesn't like being an accountant, he should become a project manager.
(D) Whenever Ted watches television, he drinks soda. Since he either watches television or makes dinner every night, and since he didn't make dinner tonight, he must have drank soda.
(E) The alarm was set off last night. Joe and Stan were the only two who were at the location. So, one of them must have set it off.

The correct answer is (D). The original argument had two premises that link: either she rides her bike or goes to the gym, and if she goes to the gym she wears a hat. The conclusion tells us she did not ride her bike, so therefore she wore a hat. What we have is a conclusion that links an either/or to a conditional in order to say she will definitely do something. We want to knock off answers that have different reasoning structure, and you can often tell that because they reach a different type of conclusion or use different types of premises. (A) and (C) have different types of conclusions from our original (notice the "should" in (C)), (B) lacks the either/or, and (E) lacks both the either/or and the conditional. That leaves (D), which presents information in a different order from the original, but nonetheless matches the structure—support with an either/or connected to a conditional, and a definite conclusion.

WRONG ANSWERS ARE MISMATCHES

mismatching conclusions

mismatching support

mismatching reasoning

the process in action

2.12. Suppose I have promised to keep a confidence and someone asks me a question that I cannot answer truthfully without thereby breaking the promise. Obviously, I cannot both keep and break the same promise. Therefore, one cannot be obliged both to answer all questions truthfully and to keep all promises.

Which one of the following arguments is most similar in its reasoning to the argument above?

(A) It is claimed that we have the unencumbered right to say whatever we want. It is also claimed that we have the obligation to be civil to others. But civility requires that we not always say what we want. So, it cannot be true both that we have the unencumbered right to say whatever we want and that we have the duty to be civil.
(B) Some politicians could attain popularity with voters only by making extravagant promises; this, however, would deceive the people. So, since the only way for some politicians to be popular is to deceive, and any politician needs to be popular, it follows that some politicians must deceive.
(C) If we put a lot of effort into making this report look good, the client might think we did so because we believed our proposal would not stand on its own merits. On the other hand, if we do not try to make the report look good, the client might think we are not serious about her business. So, whatever we do, we risk her criticism.
(D) If creditors have legitimate claims against a business and the business has the resources to pay those debts, then the business is obliged to pay them. Also, if a business has obligations to pay debts, then a court will force it to pay them. But the courts did not force this business to pay its debts, so either the creditors did not have legitimate claims or the business did not have sufficient resources.
(E) If we extend our business hours, we will either have to hire new employees or have existing employees work overtime. But both new employees and additional overtime would dramatically increase our labor costs. We cannot afford to increase labor costs, so we will have to keep our business hours as they stand.

1. understand your job: Since this is a Match the Reasoning question, we want to start by recognizing the reasoning structure of the argument.

2. find the point: The conclusion comes in the last line. One cannot be obliged to do two things at once—honestly answer questions and keep secrets.

3. find the support: The support is the sentence before, which shows that, in a certain situation, it is impossible to do those two things at once.

4. get rid of answers: The original argument had a premise that showed two things can't happen at the same time, and a conclusion that one shouldn't thus be obligated to do both at the same time. We want to eliminate answers with obviously different points or reasoning structures. (A) has two things that can't happen at once, so let's leave it. (B) reaches a conclusion about one action some people *must* take, and so can be eliminated quickly. (C) discusses two possible actions, and a general outcome from both those actions. This is not similar to our original argument. The conclusion of (D) is somewhat similar to the original argument, but note the "chain" of premises in (D)—that's very different from the original. And whereas the original argument is about two things that can't be true at once, this conclusion is about two possible outcomes. That's enough to knock out (D). (E) is about making a decision and can be eliminated quickly.

5. confirm the right answer: Though (D) was somewhat attractive, (A) is the only answer that made it through our elimination process. "Right" and "obligation" are different ideas, but in other ways (A) matches the argument very well—the conclusion is about the challenge of doing two things at once, and the support is an example of a situation in which these two things cannot go together. This is what we were looking for.

30.2.14. It is inaccurate to say that a diet high in refined sugar cannot cause adult-onset diabetes, since a diet high in refined sugar can make a person overweight, and being overweight can predispose a person to adult-onset diabetes.

The argument is most parallel, in its logical structure, to which one of the following?

(A) It is inaccurate to say that being in cold air can cause a person to catch a cold, since colds are caused by viruses, and viruses flourish in warm, crowded places.
(B) It is accurate to say that no airline flies from Halifax to Washington. No airline offers a direct flight, although some airlines have flights from Halifax to Boston and others have flights from Boston to Washington.
(C) It is correct to say that overfertilization is the primary cause of lawn disease, since fertilizer causes lawn grass to grow rapidly and rapidly growing grass has little resistance to disease.
(D) It is incorrect to say that inferior motor oil cannot cause a car to get poorer gasoline mileage, since inferior motor oil can cause engine valve deterioration, and engine valve deterioration can lead to poorer gasoline mileage.
(E) It is inaccurate to say that Alexander the Great was a student of Plato; Alexander was a student of Aristotle and Aristotle was a student of Plato.

1. understand your job: Since we need to match reasoning, we want to start by recognizing the reasoning structure of the argument.

2. find the point: The point comes in the first line—"It is inaccurate to say that a diet high in refined sugar cannot cause adult-onset diabetes."

3. find the support: Everything that follows is support, and this support "chains" together—a sugar diet can make one overweight, and being overweight can increase chances of getting adult-onset diabetes.

4. get rid of answers: We're looking for an answer that proves a statement "inaccurate," and we are looking for support that links up. Let's get rid of answers that obviously don't fit the bill. (A) sounds very good until the very end, when it talks about warm, crowded places—since the conclusion was about cold air, there is a premise-conclusion jump that makes (A) very different from the original argument. (B) reaches a similar conclusion, but by using different support (by showing "exceptions," rather than by linking ideas). (C) reaches a positive, rather than negative conclusion, but otherwise is quite similar (with the linking support). Let's leave it. (D) is pretty much exactly what we were looking for, so let's leave it. (E) also looks good! We've got three to inspect carefully.

5. confirm the right answer: Looking carefully at (C)—"correct" and "primary" allow us to eliminate it, for those words make the conclusion very different from ours. (D) has exactly the same components as our original and seems correct. Looking carefully at (E), the conclusion is that "it is inaccurate to say X is Y," whereas the original was "it is inaccurate to *(continued on next page)*

31.2.23. Town councillor: The only reason for the town to have ordinances restricting where skateboarding can be done would be to protect children from danger. Skateboarding in the town's River Park is undoubtedly dangerous, but we should not pass an ordinance prohibiting it. If children cannot skateboard in the park, they will most certainly skateboard in the streets. And skateboarding in the streets is more dangerous than skateboarding in the park.

The pattern of reasoning in which one of the following is most similar to that in the town councillor's argument?

(A) The reason for requiring environmental reviews is to ensure that projected developments do not harm the natural environment. Currently, environmental concerns are less compelling than economic concerns, but in the long run, the environment must be protected. Therefore, the requirement for environmental reviews should not be waived.
(B) Insecticides are designed to protect crops against insect damage. Aphids damage tomato crops, but using insecticides against aphids kills wasps that prey on insecticide-resistant pests. Since aphids damage tomato crops less than the insecticide-resistant pests do, insecticides should not be used against aphids on tomato crops.
(C) The purpose of compulsory vaccination for schoolchildren was to protect both the children themselves and others in the community against smallpox. Smallpox was indeed a dreadful disease, but it has now been eliminated from the world's population. So children should not be vaccinated against it.
(D) The function of a sealer on wood siding is to retard deterioration caused by weather. However, cedar is a wood that is naturally resistant to weather-related damage and thus does not need additional protection. Sealers, therefore, should not be applied to cedar siding.
(E) Traffic patterns that involve one-way streets are meant to accelerate the flow of traffic in otherwise congested areas. However, it would be detrimental to the South Main Street area to have traffic move faster. So traffic patterns involving one-way streets should not be implemented there.

(*30.2.14 solution continued*) say X cannot be Y." These different conclusions turn out to have different support. The support in (E) is meant to show that Alexander was not (definitive) a student of Plato; the support in the original argument is meant to show that a diet high in refined sugar can (less definitive) cause adult-onset diabetes. (E) is not an ideal match, and (D) is correct.

31.3.18. It is impossible to do science without measuring. It is impossible to measure without having first selected units of measurement. Hence, science is arbitrary, since the selection of a unit of measurement—kilometer, mile, fathom, etc.—is always arbitrary.

The pattern of reasoning in which one of the following is most similar to that in the argument above?

(A) Long hours of practice are necessary for developing musical skill. One must develop one's musical skill in order to perform difficult music. But long hours of practice are tedious. So performing difficult music is tedious.
(B) You have to advertise to run an expanding business, but advertising is expensive. Hence, it is expensive to run a business.
(C) It is permissible to sit on the park benches. To sit on the park benches one must walk to them. One way to walk to them is by walking on the grass. So it is permissible to walk on the grass.
(D) It is impossible to be a manager without evaluating people. The process of evaluation is necessarily subjective. Thus, people resent managers because they resent being evaluated subjectively.
(E) Some farming on the plains requires irrigation. This irrigation now uses water pumped from aquifers. But aquifers have limited capacity and continued pumping will eventually exhaust them. Thus, a new source of water will have to be found in order for such farming to continue indefinitely.

Stick to the steps!
1. Understand your job.
2. Find the point.
3. Find the support.
4. Figure out what's wrong.
5. Get rid of answers.
6. Confirm the right answer.

Match the Reasoning Solutions

For 31.2.23.

1. understand your job: Our job is to match reasoning, so we want to start by understanding the reasoning structure of the argument.

2. find the point: It comes in the middle: we should not pass an ordinance prohibiting skateboarding in the park.

3. find the support: The support comes after the conclusion, but it combines with the background to justify the main point: the only reason for prohibiting it is safety, and it would be more dangerous if children skated elsewhere.

4. get rid of answers: The point is that they shouldn't pass the ordinance because instead of adding to safety, it would add more danger. Let's knock off answers with a very different structure. (A) discusses not getting rid of a law because of the usefulness of a law. This is the opposite of our original argument. (B) is more complicated than the original, but seems somewhat like it—let's leave it. (C) talks about how something used to be necessary, but now no longer is. Very different from our original argument. (D) is about something being unnecessary (rather than making things worse). (E) is about how one action shouldn't be taken, because its intended consequence (accelerating traffic) isn't a consequence that is wanted. We can get rid of (E) quickly.

5. confirm the right answer: (B) didn't look great at first, but it's the only remaining answer. Let's evaluate it more carefully. The conclusion is not to do something. The reasoning: the actual result (doing more harm to crops) would be the opposite of the intended result (preventing more harm to crops). This matches our original argument quite well, and (B) is correct.

For 31.3.18.

1. understand your job: Our job is to match the reasoning , so we want to start by understanding the reasoning structure of the original argument.

2. find the point: It follows "hence"—science is arbitrary.

3. find the support: The main support follows the conclusion—science is arbitrary because the selection of measurements is arbitrary. We learned earlier that it is impossible to do science without measurements. (Note that this is an obviously flawed argument, but it's not our job to focus on that here.)

4. get rid of answers: We want to find an answer that ascribes a characteristic (like arbitrary) to a larger entity (science) because it is a characteristic of something (measurements) necessary to that larger entity. Let's knock off obviously wrong choices. (A) has a different order but somewhat similar argument structure, so let's leave it. (B) is somewhat tempting, but if you notice the difference between "expanding business" and "business" you can quickly knock it off. (C) says since one thing is allowed, another thing should be allowed. This is not the same as our argument. (D) adds "resentment" into the conclusion when resentment isn't related to the background. (E) gives us a very different argument—one way of doing something is no longer going to work, so a new method will need to be found.

5. confirm the right answer: (A) didn't look great initially, but it's our only remaining answer—let's review it carefully. (A) ascribes a characteristic (tedious) to a larger entity (performing difficult music) because it is a characteristic of something (practice) necessary for that larger entity. That's what we were looking for, and (A) is the correct answer.

How Did You Do?

This was a full lesson, and the last question type we discussed was clearly the most difficult—hopefully the work you did in this lesson helps set you on a path to success on structure questions, which typically means being able to get through the easier ones quickly, and being able to use a variety of tools to isolate the correct answers for the tough questions.

Just as we did with Logic Games, let's go ahead and discuss the common characteristics of those test takers who don't perform as well on the Logical Reasoning section as they are capable of performing. Of course *you* probably have none of these characteristics, but if you do, it's no big deal; you have plenty of time to address trouble spots.

five common characteristics of underperformers

don't let these descriptions fit you!

1. They don't pay attention to the right things. In my experience, this is absolutely the most significant difference between scorers at different levels. Top scorers think about the right things in each situation—they think about finding the conclusion when that's their primary task, the flaw when that's their primary task, or finding specific reasons why answers are wrong when that's the primary task, and so on. Lower-level scorers either incorrectly choose to focus on the wrong issues or, more commonly, haven't trained themselves to think about specific issues at all, so they are at the whim of wherever their attention (or "elephant") chooses to wander.

2. They misread or misunderstand and can't recover. The reality is, even top scorers will misread parts of the test. However, top scorers have enough reference points to recognize when they have perhaps misunderstood, and they also have a good sense of when it's really important to understand something specifically (when the information is in the conclusion, for example) and when it's not (when the information is in an answer choice that is wrong for other obvious reasons, for example). Low scorers tend to have fewer checks built in, and they also tend to be more stubborn about sticking to their incorrect understanding, even when the experience of solving the question (none of the answers seem attractive, for example) indicates their understanding might be faulty.

3. They don't fully utilize the question stem. As we've discussed many times, most people go into the exam with a less-than-ideal understanding of the specific tasks that various question stems present—the consequence is that they don't know exactly what to look for in a required assumption question, for example, or exactly what to look out for in incorrect Identify the Conclusion answers. They end up using somewhat unique, somewhat over-generalized strategies for different types of questions, and this limits them from more easily understanding differences between answer choices, particularly for the most difficult questions.

4. They don't use the elimination process. We've also discussed this topic many times, so I won't rehash things too much here. However, it's absolutely true that most average or below-average scorers believe that eliminating wrong answers is some sort of luxury, safety, or secondary strategy. Top scorers understand that it's not only something necessary to maintaining accuracy, it's also something that actually helps make many questions easier and can make the process of solving them much faster.

5. They don't use checks and balances. This is related to many of the points that have already been made. Because underperformers waste time focusing on wrong issues, and because they rely on inefficient strategies, they have to "match" questions really well in order to solve them correctly—that is, they have to be able to come up with somewhat lucky thoughts at exactly the right moments, and the questions have to go as planned, or else they have to scramble. Lucky thoughts won't always come and questions won't always go as planned, so top scorers have a variety of checks and balances naturally integrated into their problem-solving process. For example, if you've been able to absorb and integrate the key strategies discussed in this book, the process of finding supporting evidence reinforces the task of identifying the right conclusion, the task of identifying the correct answer is bolstered by the process of eliminating wrong ones, finding the right answer involves not only matching it against the stimulus, but also against the question stem, and so on. Top scorers have multiple tools they can rely on to recognize when they are having issues and to find their way to the correct answer.

31 LSAT vocabulary

Surprise—this is going to be a very short lesson (though maybe not quite as short as it may first appear). If you've made it this far in the book, you definitely deserve a break. Please, take the rest of the study time you've allotted to do something fun.

As you are by this point most certainly aware, the LSAT is full of complex and unusual words and phrases. However, as we've discussed many times, when it comes time to answer questions, it is the small, common words *between* those unusual ones—the common words that define reasoning relationships—that are most important. We've been highlighting many of these important reasoning words throughout the book. In this lesson, we're going to take a quick break from Logical Reasoning to have a concentrated lesson just on LSAT vocabulary. And, not so coincidentally, I hope you find the work we do in this lesson helpful as you conquer Inference questions in the next one.

When it comes to mastering LSAT vocabulary, there are two different aspects to consider:

Understanding the Words Correctly

Duh. The good news is that nearly all of the important terms are easy and simple to understand. The bad news is that certain terms are very easy to misunderstand no matter how much you prepare. Oftentimes, getting a question correct requires that we translate and utilize many different words in a very short amount of time—your understanding of most key terms needs to be absolute and automatic; furthermore, you need to have a good sense of which words tend to cause you trouble, and you want to make sure you have systems for dealing with these terms.

Prioritizing Key Terms

This second issue is of far more importance than the first. These key terms shape reasoning structure and reasoning relationships—the two things LSAT questions happen to be about. Students who perform poorly, or who spend far more time than they should, invariably waste energy focusing on the wrong parts of an argument or a passage. The main reason I've put this lesson in is not to remind you of what words mean, but rather to remind you of which words to pay attention to.

I've also included a couple of challenging mini-drills at the end, just for fun.

Logic Games

The key terms for Logic Games are the ones that define the various relationships and complications we've already discussed: assignment, ordering, grouping, subsets, mismatches, conditional rules, and "or" rules. Nearly all of the terms used in a typical Logic Games section will be very easy to understand. One key is slowing down and being careful for those few statements (such as "only if") that happen to cause you some trouble. Another key is to keep clear on statements that mean different things but can easily be mistaken for one another ("before" and "no later than," for example, are two statements that often mean the same thing, but don't always mean the same thing—such as in a situation that allows for ties).

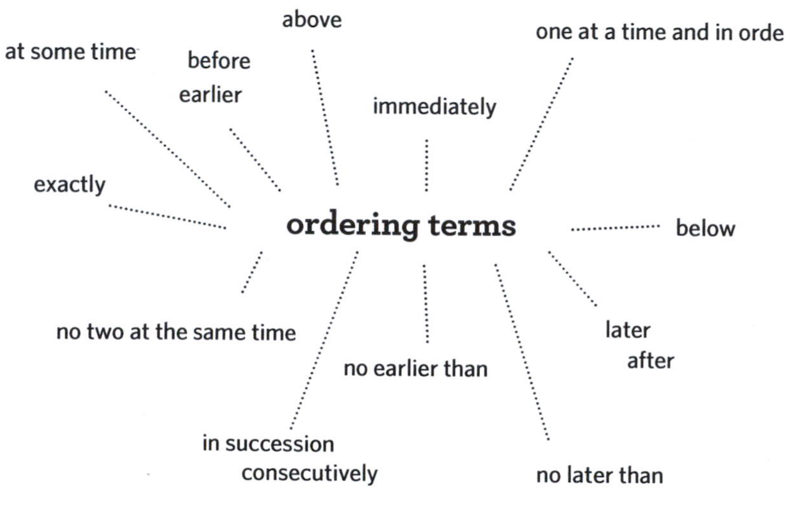

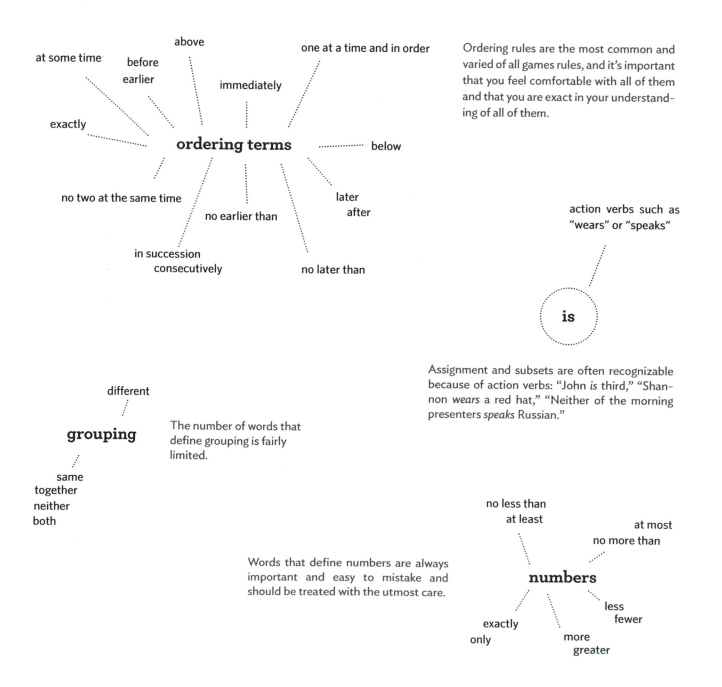

Ordering rules are the most common and varied of all games rules, and it's important that you feel comfortable with all of them and that you are exact in your understanding of all of them.

action verbs such as "wears" or "speaks"

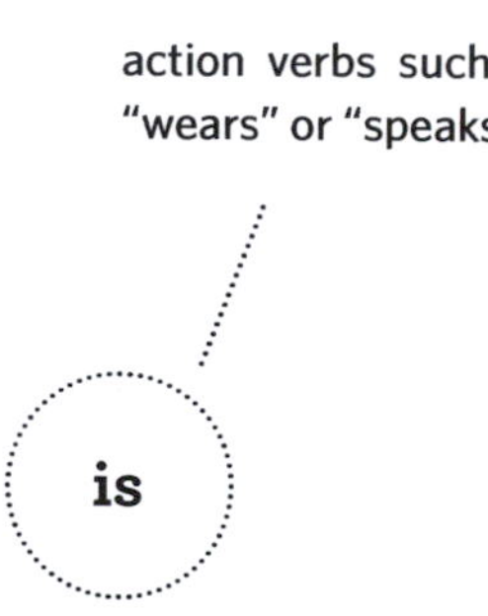

Assignment and subsets are often recognizable because of action verbs: "John *is* third," "Shannon *wears* a red hat," "Neither of the morning presenters *speaks* Russian."

different

grouping

same
together
neither
both

The number of words that define grouping is fairly limited.

Words that define numbers are always important and easy to mistake and should be treated with the utmost care.

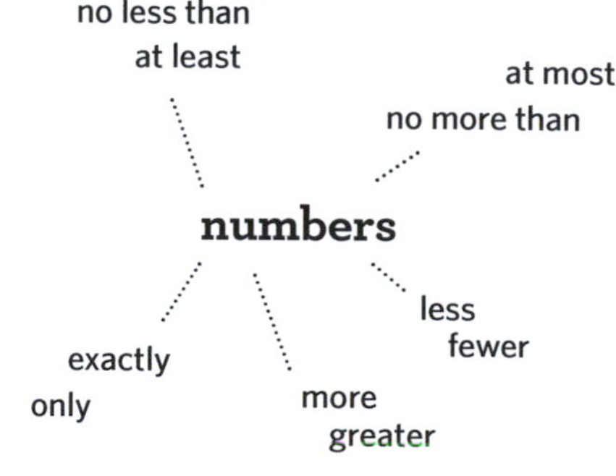

CONDITIONAL TERMS

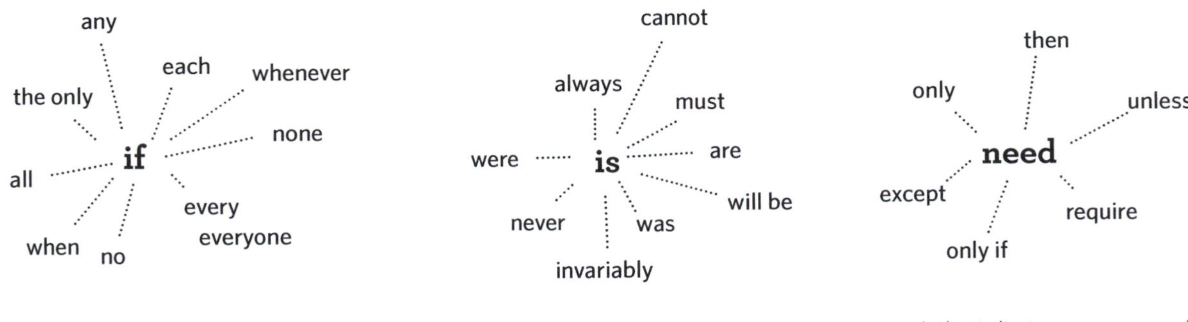

words that indicate sufficiency

words that indicate guarantees

words that indicate a necessary result

And, of course, there are always a variety of ways to express conditional rules. Note that a word like "is" can always be thought of conditionally, but it will only be helpful for us to do so in certain situations.

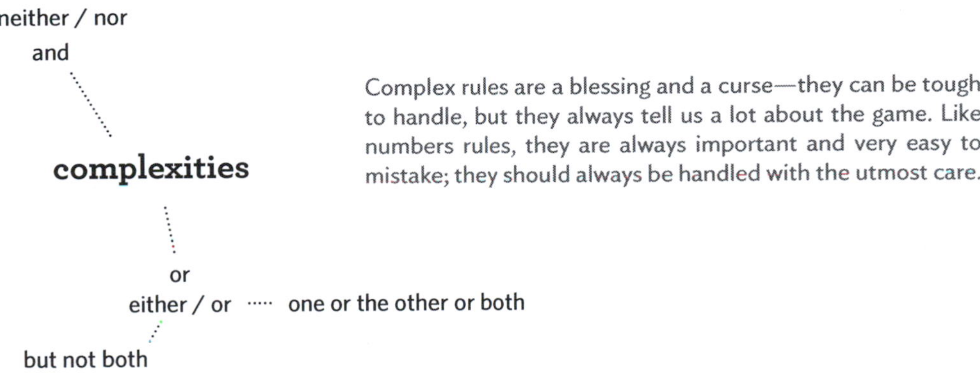

Complex rules are a blessing and a curse—they can be tough to handle, but they always tell us a lot about the game. Like numbers rules, they are always important and very easy to mistake; they should always be handled with the utmost care.

And as we've discussed many times, it's important that we understand the question stem correctly and that we use it to define how we go about solving the question. Expect to spend a bit more time on "if substituted...same effect" questions, and be careful to not confuse "could be a complete list..." with "complete list of those that could..."

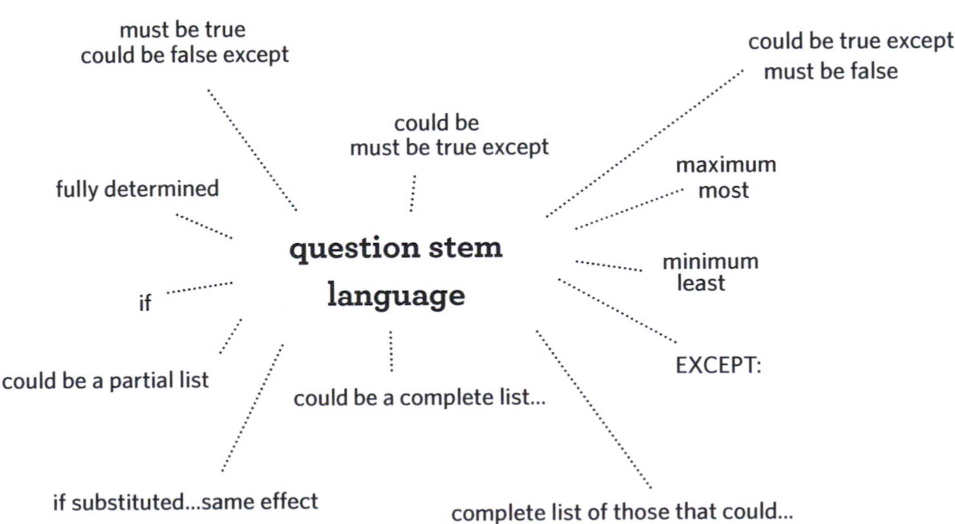

Reading Comprehension

As you might imagine, the Reading Comprehension section is not as dependent on consistent and exact terminology as the Logic Games section is. For example, there are numerous ways for an author to present his or her opinion. For Reading Comprehension, specific terms are less important; the roles these words play are more important. Still, the words listed here are ones used again and again to define reasoning structure, words you will find on every LSAT.

STRUCTURAL TERMS

As we read LSAT Reading Comprehension passages, we want to focus less on subject matter (what is the author discussing?) and more on reasoning structure (why is the author discussing this?). Here are some words that commonly help define this reasoning structure.

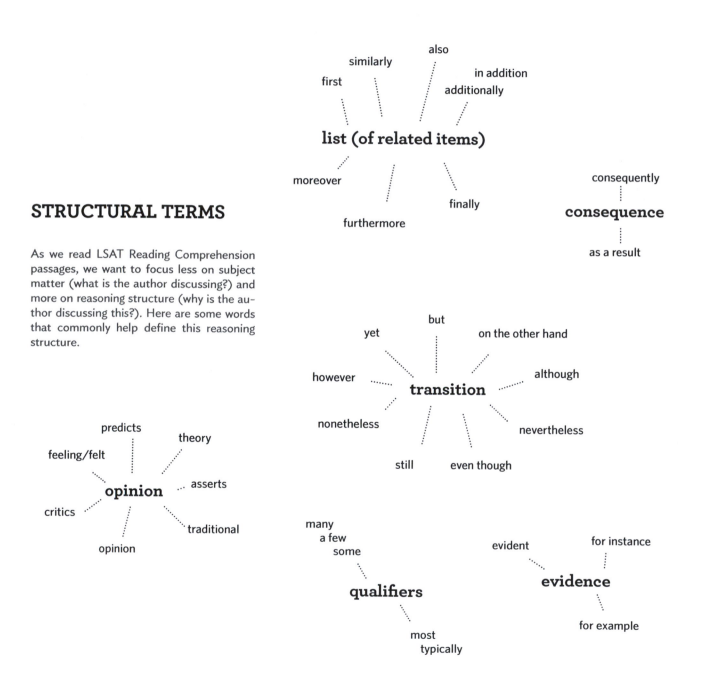

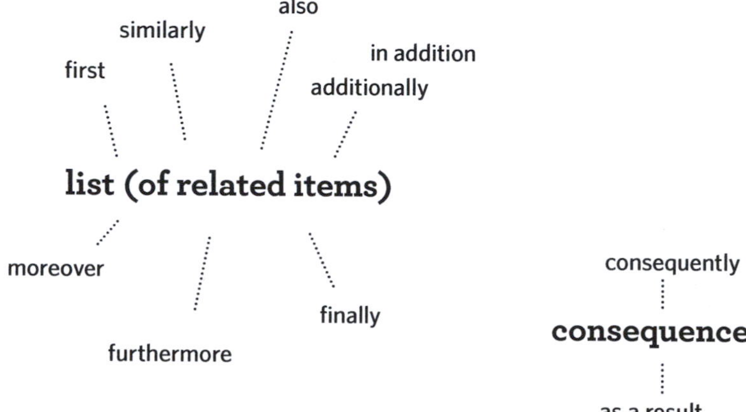

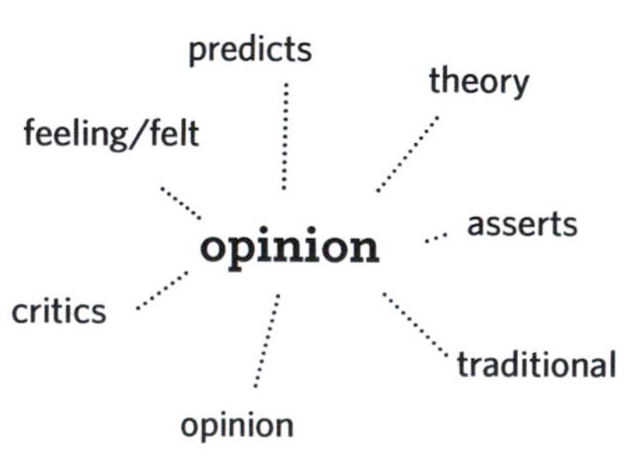

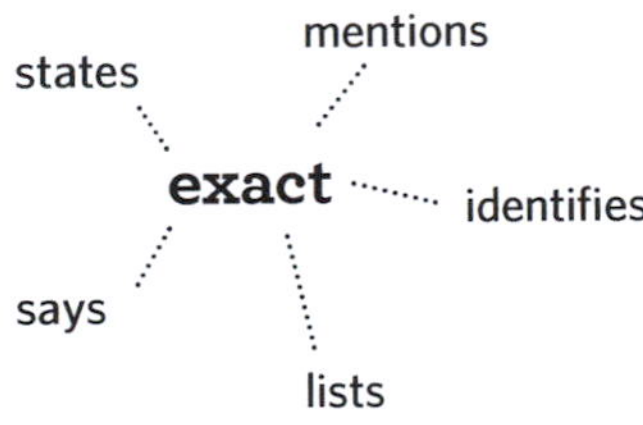

QUESTION STEM TERMS

As we've discussed, LSAT writers are extremely careful about how they write question stems, and they don't throw in superfluous terms. When you see any of these terms (or related ones), they will have a significant impact on the type of answer that you should expect. If a question stem uses the word "states," you should expect to find exact proof for the right answer; if, instead, a question stem uses the word "suggests," you know you will not find exact proof for the right answer—you should expect to have to make a small leap.

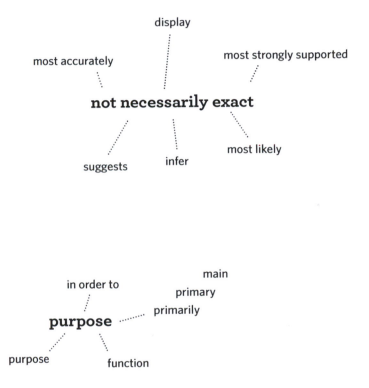

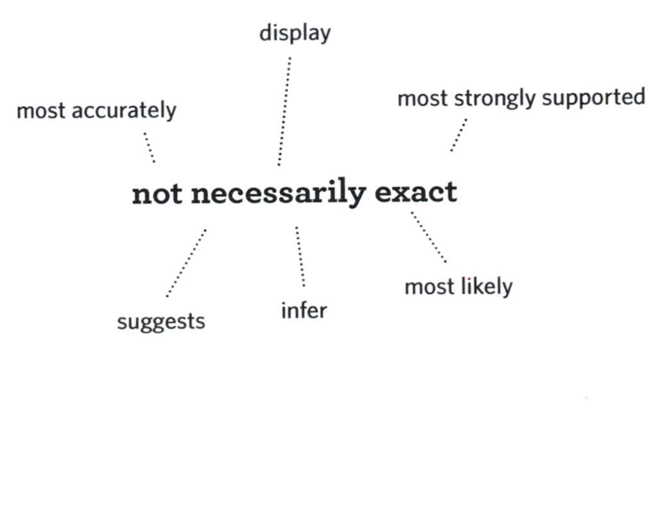

main
in order to
primary
primarily
purpose
purpose
function

Logical Reasoning

Many of the same terms that are important for Logic Games and Reading Comprehension—terms that define reasoning structure and reasoning relationships—are important for Logical Reasoning. Like Reading Comprehension, Logical Reasoning also has many key words that are argument-specific.

or

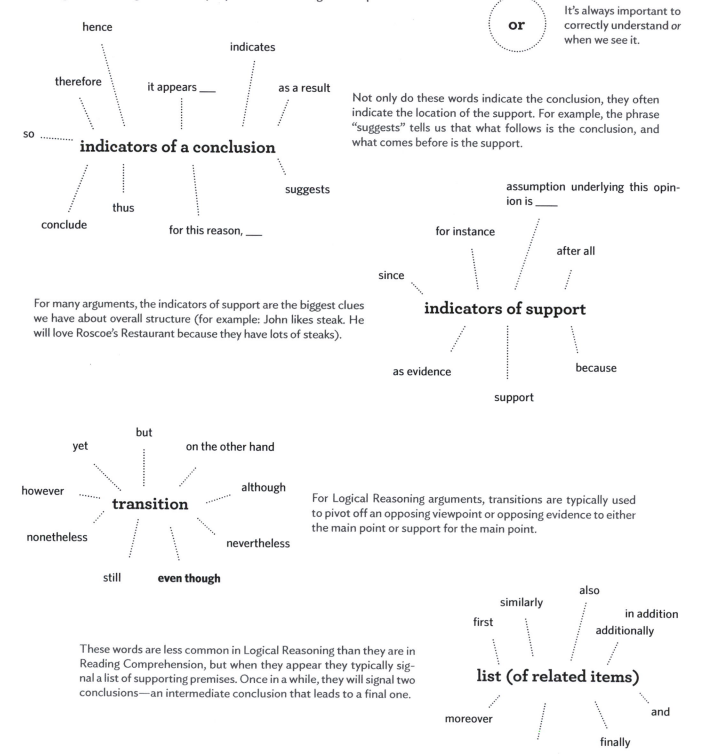

It's always important to correctly understand *or* when we see it.

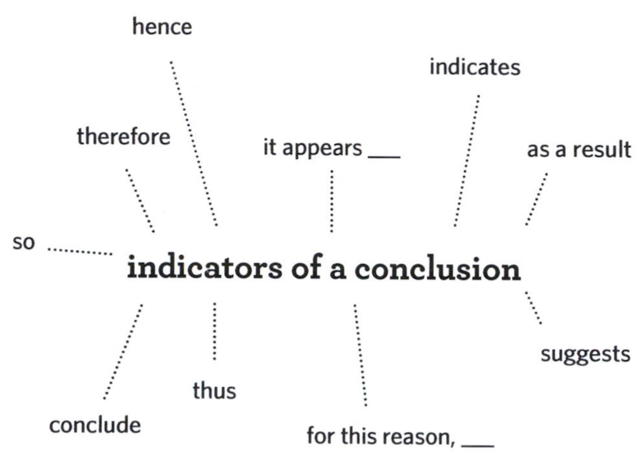

Not only do these words indicate the conclusion, they often indicate the location of the support. For example, the phrase "suggests" tells us that what follows is the conclusion, and what comes before is the support.

For many arguments, the indicators of support are the biggest clues we have about overall structure (for example: John likes steak. He will love Roscoe's Restaurant because they have lots of steaks).

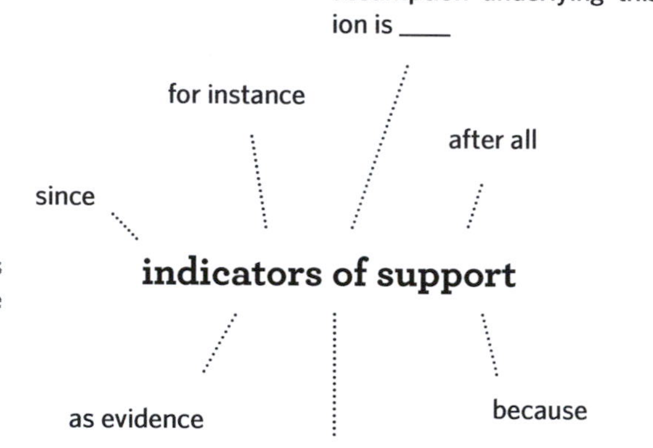

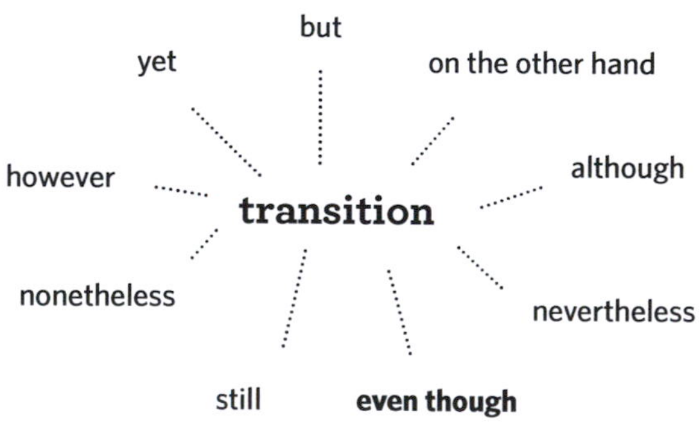

For Logical Reasoning arguments, transitions are typically used to pivot off an opposing viewpoint or opposing evidence to either the main point or support for the main point.

These words are less common in Logical Reasoning than they are in Reading Comprehension, but when they appear they typically signal a list of supporting premises. Once in a while, they will signal two conclusions—an intermediate conclusion that leads to a final one.

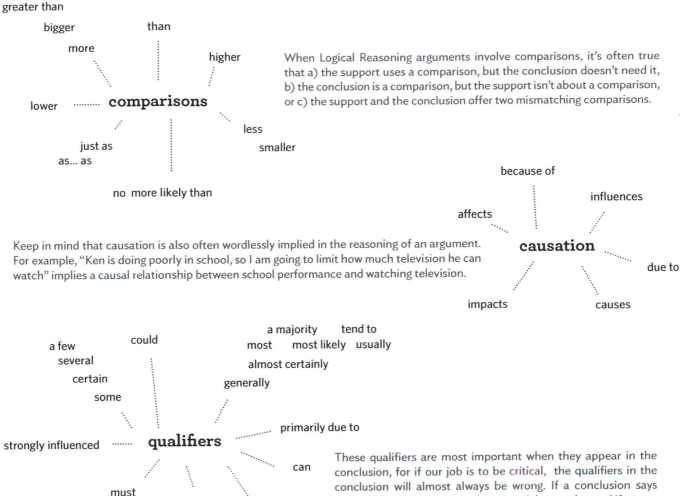

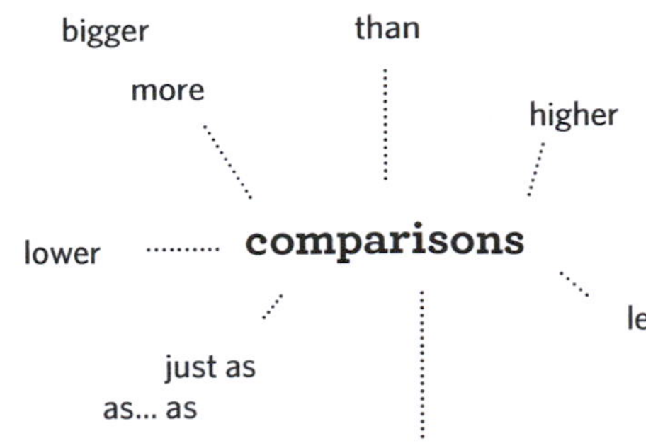

When Logical Reasoning arguments involve comparisons, it's often true that a) the support uses a comparison, but the conclusion doesn't need it, b) the conclusion is a comparison, but the support isn't about a comparison, or c) the support and the conclusion offer two mismatching comparisons.

because of
influences
affects
causation
due to
impacts
causes

Keep in mind that causation is also often wordlessly implied in the reasoning of an argument. For example, "Ken is doing poorly in school, so I am going to limit how much television he can watch" implies a causal relationship between school performance and watching television.

These qualifiers are most important when they appear in the conclusion, for if our job is to be critical, the qualifiers in the conclusion will almost always be wrong. If a conclusion says something must be, expect that it won't have to be, and if a conclusion claims something is most likely, expect that it won't be.

CONDITIONAL TERMS

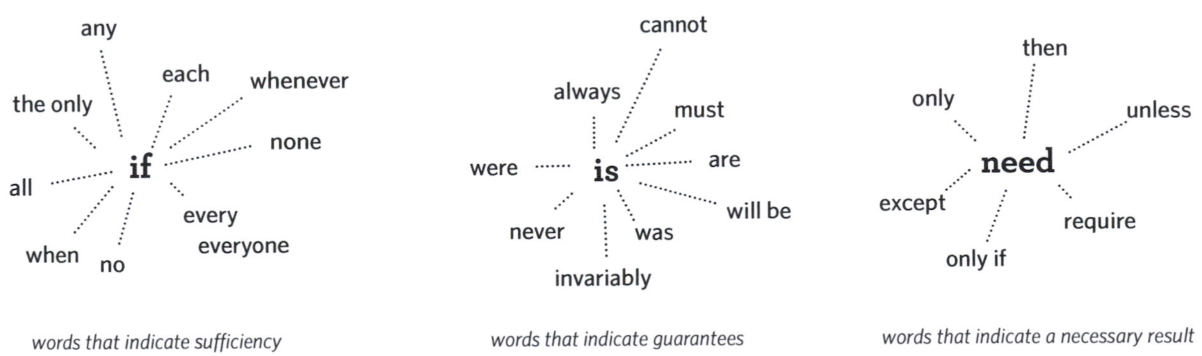

words that indicate sufficiency | *words that indicate guarantees* | *words that indicate a necessary result*

As we've discussed many times, just because statements can be thought of in conditional terms doesn't mean they have to be. If you read an argument, "Jan is Canadian. Therefore, he must love Arcade Fire," hopefully you can see what's wrong with the reasoning without having to think about it in conditional terms. Still, there will certainly be situations for which you need to think about statements in terms of conditional guarantees (typically for Sufficient Assumption, Inference, and Matching questions), and it's certainly important for you to feel confident in your ability to do so.

do you know what some and most mean?

some

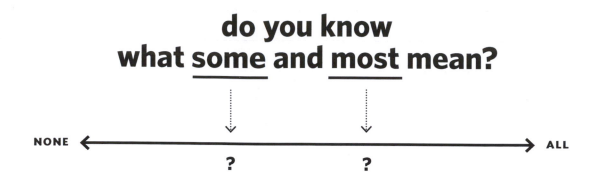

(a.k.a. several, a few, certain)

an unknown amount greater than zero

most

(a.k.a. a majority, usually, generally)

an unknown amount greater than half

Some and *most* are both words that in real life take on a great deal of contextual meaning—these are words that mean different things in different situations. However, as we've discussed, the LSAT requires us to utilize an absolute, non-contextual understanding of words such as *some* and *most*. *Some* does not mean less than half, and it does not exclude the possibility of all. It simply means an unknown amount greater than zero. Thus, knowing that *some* people like jazz does not prove that a majority do not, or even that *any* do not like jazz. *Most* also does not exclude the possibility of all, and thus knowing that *most* of a pie was eaten does not prove that some of it is left. We want to understand these words exactly, and, as always, **we want to be careful not to over-infer.**

qualifier math

What happens when you bring together a statement about *some* elements of a certain group having one characteristic, and *most* in that same group having another characteristic? What, if anything, can be inferred? Occasionally, a challenging Logical Reasoning question will require us to bring together a combination of "qualifier" statements to see what can be inferred, and, more importantly, what cannot. Here are the rules that you need to know.

some + some = no inferences	"**Some** bears dream" **and** "**some** bears swim" **doesn't prove there are any bears that dream and swim.**
some + most = no inferences	"**Some** bears dream" **and** "**most** bears swim" **doesn't prove there are any bears that dream and swim.**
most + most = inferences!	"**Most** bears dream" **and** "**most** bears swim" **combine to mean some bears dream *and* swim.**

The ice cream store

Imagine the following twelve statements, each of which could be made about a certain ice cream store. For five of the statements, the reasoning is perfectly valid—the reasoning provided is enough to prove the conclusion reached. For the remaining seven statements, the reasoning provided does not validate the conclusion reached. Do your best to figure out which statements are valid, and which ones are not.

1. Most customers eat their ice cream in the store. Therefore, some take it to go.

2. Some customers prefer vanilla to chocolate, and no customer has no preference in the matter. Therefore, most customers prefer chocolate.

3. Most people use napkins, and some use a spoon. Thus more people use napkins than use spoons.

4. Some customers use coupons, and most customers pay with cash. So, at least some customers who pay with cash do not use coupons.

5. Most customers prefer a cone to a cup, and most customers ask for toppings. So, most customers who prefer a cone ask for toppings.

6. All of the ice cream is kept in the freezer, and there are chocolate chips in some of the ice cream. So, there are some chocolate chips in the freezer.

7. Most of the customers order ice cream, and most customers come with friends. So, at least some of the customers come with friends and order ice cream.

8. Some customers ask for extra toppings, and no customers refuse extra toppings when offered. So there are fewer customers who are offered free toppings than there are customers who ask for extra toppings.

9. Most customers order chocolate ice cream, and most customers get toppings. All customers who get toppings get a free toy. So, some people who order chocolate ice cream get a free toy.

10. Everyone who orders a sundae gets offered a free extra cherry, and most people say yes to the extra cherry. Some people who order the banana split get offered a free extra cherry, and less than half of those people say yes. Therefore, more customers get a free cherry with a sundae than they do with a banana split.

11. Everyone who orders a sundae gets offered a free extra cherry, and most people say yes to the extra cherry. Some people who order the banana split get offered a free extra cherry, and less than half of these people say yes. Therefore, people who order a sundae are more likely to say yes to a free cherry than are people who order a banana split.

12. Everyone who orders a sundae gets offered a free extra cherry, and most people say yes to the extra cherry. Some people who order the banana split get offered a free extra cherry, and less than half of these people say yes. So, some people who order the banana split do not get an extra cherry.

Solutions
Valid: 6, 7, 9, 11, 12 Not valid: 1, 2, 3, 4, 5, 8, 10

EXTREME LINKS

Certain challenging Logic Games and Logical Reasoning questions require us to evaluate how a complicated set of conditional statements links together. Here's one more drill aimed to help you solidify your linking skills. Note that the last two samples complicate the conditional situation with *some* and *most*. As we've just discussed, this will happen in certain challenging Logical Reasoning questions. I've left space for you to jot down some notations, and you'll probably want to do so. However, also keep in mind that it may be easier in many instances to check the answer directly against the text itself. Finally, keep in mind that these samples are *extreme*—more challenging and complex than what you should expect on test day; if you can nail these, you are in great shape. As always, you should do your work on separate paper if you want to repeat the drill.

Fred won't attend unless Leon does, and Leon will only attend if Sarah does not. If Terrence attends, both Sarah and Rich will attend as well. Either Fred or Jessica, but not both, will attend.

Note which ones are provable and which ones are not.

If Leon attends, Rich will not.
If Sarah attends, Fred will not.
If Fred attends, Sarah will not.
If Rich attends, but Leon does not, Terrence will attend.
If Jessica attends, Leon will not.
If Terrence attends, Leon will not.
If Leon attends, Jessica will not.
If Fred attends, Terrence does not.
Terrence and Leon can't both attend together.
If Sarah does not attend, Jessica will.

Cheaters never win, and winners never brag. And yet all cheaters dream of winning and bragging about it. All winners dream about both of those things too. The public always adores those who win and do not brag about it.

Note which ones are provable and which ones are not.

The public adores all winners.
The public never adores a cheater.
One cannot be adored unless one does not brag.
If one wants public adoration, one must win.
Cheaters do not get to do everything they dream about.
All winners do something they dream about.
Those who never brag always win.
Cheaters get to do at least one thing they dream about.
No one who dreams of bragging is adored.
All winners don't do something they dream about doing.

Every student is required to wear a uniform, and only those wearing uniforms are allowed to ride on the bus. Those who ride on the bus must wear a name tag. Parents are not allowed to wear uniforms, but some nonetheless wear name tags.

Note which ones are provable and which ones are not.

Only students wear uniforms.
Only students ride the bus.
Every student is allowed to ride on the bus.
Parents are not allowed to ride on the bus.
Every student with a name tag is allowed to ride on the bus.
Some people who wear name tags are not allowed to ride on the bus.
No adults are allowed to ride on the bus.
Everyone on the bus wears a uniform and a name tag.
Those without uniforms or name tags cannot ride on the bus.
Those who do not ride on the bus are not students.

If a doll wears a red dress, it will wear the clear glass slippers. If it doesn't wear the red dress, it will wear purple slippers. The doll can only wear one dress at a time, and it can only wear a hat when it wears a purple dress. The doll can't wear a necklace unless it wears a hat.

Note which ones are provable and which ones are not.

If a doll wears clear glass slippers, it wears a red dress.
If a doll does not wear glass slippers, it will wear a purple dress.
If a doll wears a purple dress, it must wear purple slippers.
If the doll wears a necklace, it wears purple slippers.
If a doll does not wear a purple dress, it will wear a red one.
If the doll wears a red dress, it cannot wear a necklace.
Every doll that wears a hat will wear a necklace.
If the doll does not wear purple slippers, it cannot wear a hat.
If a doll doesn't wear a necklace, it must wear the red dress.
If the doll wears a necklace, it also wears a purple dress.

Francine's Lumberyard sells an equal amount of two different categories of wood: lumber and plywood. They sell no other types of wood. Some of the lumber is cut to exact dimensions, some of it is not. All of the plywood is cut to exact dimensions. Most of the wood that is cut to exact dimensions is stored inside; the rest is stored outside. Only wood that is not cut to exact dimensions is currently discounted.

Note which ones are provable and which ones are not.

Most of the lumber is currently discounted.
Most of the wood is inside.
If wood is currently discounted, it is lumber.
At least some plywood is currently discounted.
Less than half of the wood is not cut to exact dimensions.
No plywood is currently discounted.
Most of the wood stored inside is plywood.
Most of the wood stored outside is lumber.
Most of the wood is not currently discounted.
Most of the wood inside is not currently discounted.

Most of the dishes at Oldie's Diner are unhealthy, and most are offered on special during lunchtime. The dishes on special come with the customer's choice of free fries or a free soda. All of the dishes offered on special are written up on the restaurant's chalkboard.

Note which ones are provable and which ones are not.

There are at least some dishes on special that are unhealthy.
One can get free soda with at least one unhealthy dish.
All dishes on the chalkboard come with free fries or a free soda.
There are at least some dishes on the chalkboard that are unhealthy.
All the dishes on the chalkboard are specials.
Most of the dishes on the chalkboard are unhealthy.
Most healthy dishes are not on special.
Most of the dishes are written on the chalkboard.
Most of the dishes on the chalkboard are on special.
There is at least one healthy dish that is not offered on special.

Solutions

	1	2	3	4	5	6	7	8	9	10
Fred	N	Y	Y	N	N	Y	N	Y	Y	N
Cheaters	Y	N	N	N	Y	Y	N	N	N	Y
Student	N	N	N	Y	N	Y	N	Y	Y	N
Dolls	N	N	Y	Y	N	Y	N	Y	N	Y
Lumber	N	N	Y	N	Y	Y	N	N	Y	N
Oldie's	Y	Y	N	Y	N	N	N	Y	Y	N

Lesson Review

That was a pretty challenging drill—I hope you found it useful, and at least somewhat fun. In terms of Logical Reasoning, keep in mind that the scenarios in the drill were more complicated that what you should expect in a real question. Also keep in mind that, even for the most difficult conditional questions, most wrong answers are very obviously wrong, and require very little work to eliminate. Don't get in a habit of overthinking these types of answers. If you have a strong understanding of the stimulus, typically only one or two answers warrant serious consideration.

If the material before that drill made you think about LSAT vocabulary in a somewhat new way, or if you want to reinforce some of the lessons we discussed here, or if you just happened to recognize a few terms that you either need to pay more attention to, or need to understand more clearly, here is a suggested drill for you to do on your own:

Go through past Logical Reasoning questions, Logic Games, and Reading Comprehension passages that you have already worked on. Take the time to systematically circle the key terms mentioned on the previous pages, and take note of how they influence the reasoning relationships in the questions you've solved. Also take note of situations that use unique variations of these terms or that don't use these terms at all (such as a Logical Reasoning argument that doesn't use any specific terminology to point us to the conclusion). This drill will help you see the importance of these key terms, and also help you lock in the intimate connection between these key terms and the tasks you must perform during the exam.

During the real exam, prioritizing these key words should not take much conscious effort (or any conscious effort at all, for that matter). Hopefully, by test day, it's just how you naturally read LSAT passages; these words define reasoning relationships, and if you are focused on reasoning relationships, you will naturally prioritize these words.

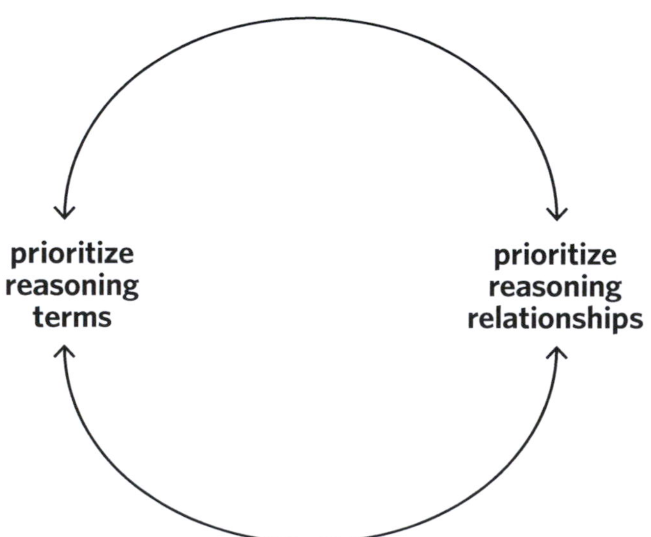

32 LOGICAL REASONING inference & example

In this lesson and the next, we will break down our final Logical Reasoning question types. The question types we will cover—Inference, Give an Example, Find the Disagreement, and Explain a Discrepancy—are outliers. They require unique strategies, and they require a different mindset.

The two types of questions we will focus on in this lesson are Inference and Give an Example. These question types are unique for a variety of reasons. For the first time, your main job is not to understand some sort of argument. In fact, the stimulus may not even contain an argument; the stimulus may just contain a set of related points, with no clear reasoning structure or no clear conclusion. In addition, these questions, like those in the last lesson, require an objective understanding—that is, an understanding not influenced by your judgements or biases. And finally, these questions require you to do most of your critical thinking when you get down to the answer choices; for all other types of questions we've discussed thus far, you have done most of your critical thinking in the stimulus.

For the first time, our job is not to understand some sort of argument

We have much to discuss and work on in this short lesson. Let's get started!

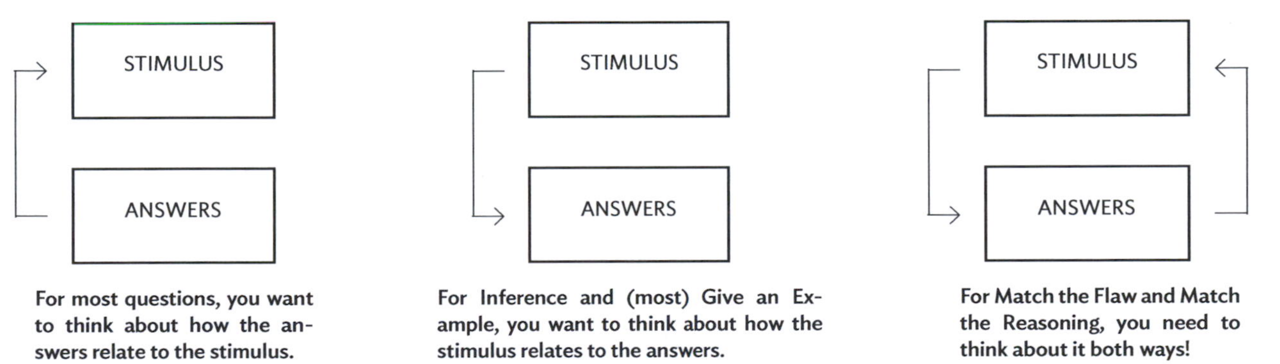

For most questions, you want to think about how the answers relate to the stimulus.

For Inference and (most) Give an Example, you want to think about how the stimulus relates to the answers.

For Match the Flaw and Match the Reasoning, you need to think about it both ways!

Sometimes in life, you have something you want to do and you have to find a friend to do it with, and other times in life, you have a friend you want to spend time with, and you need to find something to do together. Though the results are similar (you end up doing something with a friend), the way that you get to that result will be different. Something similar happens in Logical Reasoning questions. Most of the time, your job is to understand the stimulus well, and then to think about how the answer choices relate to that understanding. In these cases, the stimulus is your focus, and the issue is how well the answers fit the task presented in the question stem relative to the stimulus. Other times, your job is to understand the stimulus well, and then to think about how it relates to the answer choices. In these cases, the answer choices are your focus, and the issue is how well the information in the stimulus helps you justify that choice. Again, the results are similar—you end up with an answer that matches the task, but the ideal path there is understandably quite different. A final minority of questions (Match the Flaw, Match the Reasoning, and a minority of Give an Example) require you to focus equally on both stimulus and answer choices, and for these questions, you should allow yourself a bit of extra time.

Inference

"If the sentences above are true, which of the following must be true?"
"The information above provides the most support for which of the following?"
(following blank space) "Which of the following most logically completes the argument?"

Inference questions are questions that ask us to figure out which of five answers must be true, or is closest to being proved true, based on the information given to us in the stimulus. For all argument-based questions, our job was to figure out which of five answers best played a specific role relative to the stimulus. For Inference questions, we will use the stimulus to see which of five answers is the most provable.

The key to consistent success on Inference questions is the ability to focus your energy and your thoughts on the clear and simple task at hand: figuring out which answer is provable, or closest to provable, based on the stimulus and, more importantly, which four answers are clearly not provable based on the stimulus. It is to your disadvantage if you let habits useful for other questions—namely, the habits associated with trying to deeply understand and critique arguments—waste your time and energies. The test writers are clearly testing your mental discipline here—the wrong answers are often made tempting by including elements or ideas you might consider if you were to stray off the task at hand. So, keep it simple, and work to develop the discipline necessary to switch gears when you run into this type of question.

SUPER-SIMPLE EXAMPLE

All people enjoy listening to music, but that doesn't mean that all people like the same music. Our tastes are influenced by the types of lives we've lived, and the type of people we are. Since no two people are exactly alike, no two people have exactly the same taste in music.

If the sentences above are true, which of the following must be true?

(A) No two people can enjoy the same song at the same time.
(B) Musical tastes are not determined by life experiences alone.
(C) Some people enjoy listening to music that does not fit their own taste in music.
(D) Everybody in the world has a unique favorite song, for a unique reason.
(E) Those who come from very different backgrounds will invariably have very different tastes in music.

The correct answer is (B). (A) and (D) both misinterpret the last line of the stimulus, and give it a more specific meaning than it actually has. (C) goes well beyond the scope of the stimulus (by incorrectly bringing parts together). (E) takes the points in the stimulus too far—very often, people from different backgrounds have similar tastes in music, and the information in this argument doesn't prevent that. (B) is not the main point, but it can be 100% justified—we are told of two factors that contribute to musical taste.

---

step one

understand your job

When we are asked in real life to make inferences, we often instinctively seek answers that represent big insights, main points, or clever ideas. On the LSAT, the first two instincts are useless, and the last one worse than that. The right answer to an Inference question is simply the answer most supported by the text—this answer may or may not be related to the "main point" of the stimulus, and since it must be very close in meaning to the actual text, it will rarely be clever. (It may be *worded* in an unusual, or clever, manner, but the substance of the answer will always be something fairly obvious.) Keep it simple, and just focus on identifying the most provable of five answers.

Note that there are a variety of Inference questions—three main types, actually. They are represented by the three different simple examples on these pages. When a question stem says "must be true," you want to look for an answer that is unequivocally true based on the stimulus. When a question says, "is most supported," you want an answer that is almost completely provable based on the text (and certainly doesn't have any definitive contradictions). Think of it as 90+% true, if that helps. Finally, if asked an Inference question as a fill in the blank, the right answer will have similar characteristics to "most supported," but also commonly represents a main point or the next logical link in a chain of reasoning. Because of this, this last type of Inference question, which happens to be the least common, is the only one where we can make even the most general of predictions about the right answer after reading the stimulus.

SUPER-SIMPLE EXAMPLE

Ted is exactly like his older brother Bob. Bob's favorite sport is tennis, and Ted's favorite sport is tennis. Bob likes watching sitcoms, and Ted ________________.

Which of the following most logically completes the sentence?

(A) enjoys watching situational comedies
(B) likes to watch them with him
(C) prefers to watch dramas
(D) wants to be just like Bob
(E) likes to watch tennis

The correct answer is (A). We know Ted and Bob are alike. That does not mean Bob likes it, nor does it mean they do things in the same location at the same time. (B) is about them doing something together, (C) is about them being different, (D) is about Ted's desires (who knows if he wants to be exactly alike?), and (E) incorrectly connects different parts of the stimulus. (A) follows the train of thought, and is justifiable based on the text.

two

read the stimulus

As I've already mentioned, the stimulus for an Inference question may or may not contain an argument, and, even when it does, there is little assurance that understanding the argument will play a role in answering the question correctly. All that is to say you need not be as focused on identifying argument structure as you read.

Instead, allow yourself a more casual read in which you look for general connections between the ideas mentioned. Note that these stimuli more often than not contain conditional logic, and these statements often link up. It is not necessary to figure out exactly how everything goes together before you go into the answer choices, but if you see a clear connection that you don't want to forget, or you run into a tricky statement you don't want to misread later, feel free to pause and write or notate that in some way next to the stimulus. Note that stimuli are also commonly filled with statements that seem to link up but don't, and these false connections are often related to the most tempting wrong choices.

Do not attempt to predict the correct answer (except for with the rare Complete the Passage, for which it's not a bad idea to come up with a possibility or two). We are looking for an answer provable based on the text, and, for any typical three-sentence stimulus, there are probably six different right answers the test writers could put together. You have no basis for predicting which "truth" will appear.

So, just do your best to understand the stimulus the best you can, take note of any links, and pause to make sure you understand any tricky wording. Go through all of this quickly, because you want to focus most of your time and energy on the answer choices.

SUPER-SIMPLE EXAMPLE

Manager: Our company does everything it can to provide the highest level of customer service. Most customers who purchase our products are extremely satisfied, and customers have also given rave reviews for our return and exchange services.

The information given above provides the most support for which of the following statements?

(A) The manager clearly has a personal bias that prevents him from speaking honestly.
(B) Customer service is the top priority of the company.
(C) At least some customers were either dissatisfied with the product they received, or ended up regretting the decision to purchase the product, enough so to take action.
(D) The return and exchange services are utilized by a majority of customers.
(E) The company sells the finest product in its product category.

The correct answer is (C). The personal bias mentioned in (A) is pure speculation, and we don't know enough about how customer service rates relative to other priorities to justify (B). "Majority" in (D) is far from provable, and (E) goes well beyond the scope of the text. (C) is not 100% ironclad, but we do know that customers definitely returned products, and it's not much of a leap to think they did so because they either found fault with the product or changed their minds.

three

eliminate wrong choices

Keep in mind two things: right answers to Inference questions are not predictable, and right answers to "most supported" questions are impossible to prove definitively. Considering this last point, if the right answer isn't definitely correct, how can you have one answer that must be right and four that must be wrong? By giving the four wrong answers characteristics that make them definitely incorrect.

That last point is the key to becoming an Inference master—though it is commonly difficult to predict or prove a right answer, there are always clear and absolute ways to eliminate wrong answers. Your path to consistent and efficient success is focusing your energy on these wrong answer characteristics.

The elimination process is the key to success

Wrong answers all have some definite reason(s) for not being true. They will give themselves away because they differ from the original text. Either they will mention things not mentioned in the text or they will jump to conclusions that are not justifiable based on the information given (they will commonly do the latter by making connections in the original argument that aren't actually valid).

WRONG ANSWERS CAN'T BE JUSTIFIED

mismatches subject matter

misrepresents relationships

jumps to a conclusion

four

confirm the right answer

For a Must Be True, you should feel that the right answer is definitely true, and for some tougher questions, you may be required to link statements in the stimulus to prove it. For most supported questions, you should feel that the right answer is, in general, consistent with the text (though you may be able to come up with an extreme case in which the two might misalign). The right answer will not contain anything that directly contradicts the stimulus in any way.

When choosing between two answers, look for the one that is "safest," that is, one that requires the smallest leaps from the information in the stimulus. The right answer will always require no leaps, or very small leaps, whereas wrong answers will reveal themselves because they have differences from the text that are more materially significant.

the process in action

2.18. Modern science is built on the process of posing hypotheses and testing them against observations—in essence, attempting to show that the hypotheses are incorrect. Nothing brings more recognition than overthrowing conventional wisdom. It is accordingly unsurprising that some scientists are skeptical of the widely accepted predictions of global warming. What is instead remarkable is that with hundreds of researchers striving to make breakthroughs in climatology, very few find evidence that global warming is unlikely.

The information above provides the most support for which one of the following statements?

(A) Most scientists who are reluctant to accept the global warming hypothesis are not acting in accordance with the accepted standards of scientific debate.
(B) Most researchers in climatology have substantial motive to find evidence that would discredit the global warming hypothesis.
(C) There is evidence that conclusively shows that the global warming hypothesis is true.
(D) Scientists who are skeptical about global warming have not offered any alternative hypotheses to explain climatological data.
(E) Research in global warming is primarily driven by a desire for recognition in the scientific community.

1. understand your job: Our job is to find one answer that is supported by the information in the passage. In addition, because this is a "complete the argument," we will anticipate that the stimulus will lead us to predict a certain inference.

2. read the stimulus: The stimulus has a very familiar structure—an opinion is presented, and then information is given that rebuts that opinion. Proponents say electric cars will result in the stopping of environmental harm from cars. Then evidence is presented that there will be environmental harm from electric cars. This is proof that the proponents' theory is wrong. We should perhaps expect something about that in the correct answer choice.

3. eliminate wrong answers: (A) is what we expected, so let's leave it. (B) is about popularity relative to other cars—we don't have enough information to support this claim. "Purely technical" is a bit suspicious in (C), and, relative to this stimulus, it's very difficult to define how we'd prove that the car will "succeed." (D) goes too far—we're not told that the charge sources will cause more emissions than we have currently. The same problem plagues (E). It makes a comparison for which we don't have enough justification.

4. confirm the right answer: (A) is the only answer remaining—let's check it against the text. Proponents believe it will have zero consequence, and the author shows consequence—thus the inference that it will have worse consequences than the proponents believe is justifiable. (A) it is.

1. understand your job: Our job is to find one answer that is supported by the information in the passage. The best way to achieve this is by understanding the passage as best as possible, and then eliminating those answers that are not supported by the information in the stimulus.

2. read the stimulus: The stimulus starts with a general description of the state of modern science, then applies this to a specific discussion of global warming. It's easy for us to draw our own conclusion from the information—since there is great motivation to disprove global warming, and few scientists are able to do it...it seems that global warming is indeed happening. However, if you went to that step, you went too far! Our job is not to draw our own conclusion. We simply want to understand the information actually presented, and not go beyond that.

3. eliminate wrong answers: (A) states the seeming opposite of what is in the text, for the author shows that the skepticism is a natural component of modern science. (B) is very much supportable—let's leave it. (C) is the trap answer if we draw our own conclusion and overreach. It's simply beyond what is supportable based on what we are told. (D) is tempting, but we are not told that they have "not offered any alternative hypotheses." That goes well beyond the text. (E) is also tempting, but "nothing brings more recognition" is not a good match for "primarily driven by a desire," for we have not been told that recognition is the primary motivator of scientists.

4. confirm the right answer: We only have one answer that has passed through the elimination process. Let's look at (B) again, and carefully check it against the text. "Most" at the beginning of the answer is a bit unsettling, but we're told that "modern science is *built*...," so "most" is not too much of a stretch. (It's like saying, "Most people have significant motive to win the lottery." We don't need to take a poll to prove such a statement, for it's just a statement of general human tendencies.) "Nothing brings more recognition," is a pretty good match for "substantial motive" (though not perfect). The fact that the author follows with "accordingly unsurprising that some scientists are skeptical" gives us further support for the idea that recognition is indeed a motive. (B) is far from ironclad provable, but it is the correct answer.

2.8. Proponents of the electric car maintain that when the technical problems associated with its battery design are solved, such cars will be widely used and, because they are emission-free, will result in an abatement of the environmental degradation caused by auto emissions. But unless we dam more rivers, the electricity to charge these batteries will come from nuclear or coal-fired power plants. Each of these three power sources produces considerable environmental damage. Thus, the electric car ______.

Which one of the following most logically completes the argument?

(A) will have worse environmental consequences than its proponents may believe
(B) will probably remain less popular than other types of cars
(C) requires that purely technical problems be solved before it can succeed
(D) will increase the total level of emissions rather than reduce it
(E) will not produce a net reduction in environmental degradation

LINKING CONDITIONS

mini-drill

We've touched on conditional logic at several points in our study process, and because conditional logic is important to the solving of Inference questions, we should do so again here. Many Inference questions require that you interpret, understand, and infer from conditional statements correctly. The hardest of them, perhaps one question per exam, will require that you link conditional statements together in order to infer the correct answer. A big reason these questions can be more difficult is that they often have very tempting wrong answer choices that match the subject matter in the stimulus, but because they incorrectly link together the conditional relationships, they cannot be proved.

This drill is meant to provide just a little bit of practice with making these difficult determinations. Below are two sample conditional-heavy stimuli. Accompanying each are ten potential inferences—some justified by the information given, some not. Make sure you understand the conditional statements in the stimulus correctly, and use them to evaluate the answer choices.

For questions that require careful analysis of multiple relationships, it can be helpful to notate these relationships in as simple a way as possible (often you can get away with using letters for elements, though when you do so you must be careful to double-check that the right answer is indeed a right match for the exact wording of the original elements in the stimulus). Notating relationships can be especially useful for questions that present attractive wrong answers—wrong answers that you need a very specific understanding of the conditional logic to eliminate.

"A certain group of adults and children went to see a play. All of the adults loved the play, but not all of the children loved the play. All of those who loved the play got posters, and of those who did not love the play, not one went backstage afterwards to meet with the cast."

Which inferences about the group are valid?

1) All adults got posters.
2) No children got posters.
3) Anyone who went backstage was an adult.
4) Anyone who went backstage got a poster.
5) Anyone who did not love the play was not an adult.
6) All adults went backstage.
7) Most viewers loved the play.
8) Anyone who got a poster went backstage.
9) Anyone who did not get a poster is a child.
10) No one went backstage unless they also got a poster.

"At a certain store, none of the items are placed on sale for a discount unless they are not selling well. Brand Y soda has been put on sale for a discount, and Brand X soda is not selling well. All items that are not selling well are advertised in the local paper."

Which inferences about the store are valid?

1) Brand X soda is advertised.
2) Brand Y soda is advertised.
3) Brand X soda is on sale for a discount.
4) Brand Y soda is not selling well.
5) If an item is advertised, it is on sale for a discount.
6) All items on sale for a discount are advertised.
7) If an item is not advertised, it will not be on sale for a discount.
8) Both brands of soda are on sale for a discount.
9) No brands of soda are doing well at the store.
10) If an item is placed on sale for a discount, it is Brand Y.

Solutions

Relationships in stimulus:
A → L (~~L~~ → ~~A~~), L → P (~~P~~ → ~~L~~), B → L (~~L~~ → ~~B~~)
(A = adult, L = love, P = poster, B = backstage)

1) Valid (A → L → P)
2) Not (some children could have loved the play)
3) Not (some children could have loved the play)
4) Valid (B → L → P)
5) Valid (~~L~~ → ~~A~~)
6) Not (loving doesn't guarantee backstage)
7) Not (depends on proportion/views of children)
8) Not (getting a poster doesn't prove much)
9) Valid (~~P~~ → ~~L~~ → ~~A~~)
10) Valid (B → L → P)

Relationships in stimulus:
D → ~~W~~ (W → ~~D~~), Y → D (~~D~~ → ~~Y~~), X → ~~W~~ (W → ~~X~~), ~~W~~ → A (~~A~~ → W)
(D = discount, W = selling well, A = advertised)

1) Valid (X → ~~W~~ → A)
2) Valid (Y → D → ~~W~~ → A)
3) Not (we don't know that not selling well → discounted)
4) Valid (Y → D → ~~W~~)
5) Not (we don't know if they advertise other items as well)
6) Valid (D → ~~W~~ → A)
7) Valid (~~A~~ → W → ~~D~~)
8) Not (we don't know if X is)
9) Not (we don't know of other brands)
10) Not (we don't know if X is)

31.2.20. One of the most vexing problems in historiography is dating an event when the usual sources offer conflicting chronologies of the event. Historians should attempt to minimize the number of competing sources, perhaps by eliminating the less credible ones. Once this is achieved and several sources are left, as often happens, historians may try, though on occasion unsuccessfully, to determine independently of the usual sources which date is more likely to be right.

Which one of the following inferences is most strongly supported by the information above?

(A) We have no plausible chronology of most of the events for which attempts have been made by historians to determine the right date.
(B) Some of the events for which there are conflicting chronologies and for which attempts have been made by historians to determine the right date cannot be dated reliably by historians.
(C) Attaching a reliable date to any event requires determining which of several conflicting chronologies is most likely to be true.
(D) Determining independently of the usual sources which of several conflicting chronologies is more likely to be right is an ineffective way of dating events.
(E) The soundest approach to dating an event for which the usual sources give conflicting chronologies is to undermine the credibility of as many of these sources as possible.

31.2.8. For all species of higher animals, reproduction requires the production of eggs but not necessarily the production of sperm. There are some species whose members are all female; the eggs produced by a rare female-only species of salamander hatch without fertilization. This has the drawback that all offspring have genetic codes nearly identical to that of the single parent, making the species less adaptive than species containing both male and female members.

If the statements above are true, each of the following could be true EXCEPT:

(A) There are some species of salamanders that have both male and female members.
(B) There are some species of higher animals none of whose members produce eggs.
(C) There is a significant number of female-only species of higher animals.
(D) Some species of higher animals containing both female and male members are not very adaptive.
(E) Some offspring of species of higher animals containing both female and male members have genetic codes more similar to one parent than to the other parent.

31.3.10. It is wrong to waste our natural resources, and it is an incredible waste of resources to burn huge amounts of trash in incinerators. When trash is recycled, fewer resources are wasted. Because less trash will be recycled if an incinerator is built, the city should not build an incinerator.

Which one of the following can be properly inferred from the statements above?

(A) All of the city's trash that is not recycled goes into incinerators.
(B) By recycling more trash, the city can stop wasting resources entirely.
(C) The most effective way to conserve resources is to recycle trash.
(D) If the city is to avoid wasting resources, huge amounts of trash cannot be burned in any city incinerator.
(E) If the city does not burn trash, it will not waste resources.

30.2.18. If there are any inspired performances in the concert, the audience will be treated to a good show. But there will not be a good show unless there are sophisticated listeners in the audience, and to be a sophisticated listener one must understand one's musical roots.

If all of the statements above are true, which one of the following must also be true?

(A) If there are no sophisticated listeners in the audience, then there will be no inspired musical performances in the concert.
(B) No people who understand their musical roots will be in the audience if the audience will not be treated to a good show.
(C) If there will be people in the audience who understand their musical roots, then at least one musical performance in the concert will be inspired.
(D) The audience will be treated to a good show unless there are people in the audience who do not understand their musical roots.
(E) If there are sophisticated listeners in the audience, then there will be inspired musical performances in the concert.

31.2.20. One of the most vexing problems in historiography is dating an event when the usual sources offer conflicting chronologies of the event. Historians should attempt to minimize the number of competing sources, perhaps by eliminating the less credible ones. Once this is achieved and several sources are left, as often happens, historians may try, though on occasion unsuccessfully, to determine independently of the usual sources which date is more likely to be right.

Which one of the following inferences is most strongly supported by the information above?

(A) We have no plausible chronology of most of the events for which attempts have been made by historians to determine the right date.
(B) Some of the events for which there are conflicting chronologies and for which attempts have been made by historians to determine the right date cannot be dated reliably by historians.
(C) Attaching a reliable date to any event requires determining which of several conflicting chronologies is most likely to be true.
(D) Determining independently of the usual sources which of several conflicting chronologies is more likely to be right is an ineffective way of dating events.
(E) The soundest approach to dating an event for which the usual sources give conflicting chronologies is to undermine the credibility of as many of these sources as possible.

1. understand your job: Our job is to find one answer that is supported by the information in the passage. We want to understand the information in the stimulus, then spend the bulk of our energy eliminating unsupported answers.

2. read the stimulus: This is a tough stimulus to understand exactly, and almost impossible to keep in one's head. In general, the idea is that when they can't figure out a date for a historical event, they need to narrow down options to those from the most credible sources, then make a decision independent of those sources. Whew! We will definitely need to come back to confirm the right answer.

3. eliminate wrong answers: (A) is too strong—"no plausible" for "most" events goes far beyond the text. (B) does not relate to the main points, but it does relate to a statement made in the text: "though on occasion unsuccessfully." Let's leave it. (C) goes well beyond the text—not every event has conflicting chronologies (you know what day you were born, and there is likely no conflict about that). "Ineffective," in (D) is not supported by the text. "To undermine the credibility" allows us to eliminate (E) quickly.

4. confirm the right answer: (B) is a classic right answer to an inference question. It is not directly relevant to the author's main point, but relates to a secondary issue mentioned, and is justifiable based on the text. Let's review it carefully. We are told in the text that when historians get together to figure out a date, they are occasionally unsuccessful—therefore, it makes sense to say that there are events for which a right date has not been confirmed.

31.2.8. For all species of higher animals, reproduction requires the production of eggs but not necessarily the production of sperm. There are some species whose members are all female; the eggs produced by a rare female-only species of salamander hatch without fertilization. This has the drawback that all offspring have genetic codes nearly identical to that of the single parent, making the species less adaptive than species containing both male and female members.

If the statements above are true, each of the following could be true EXCEPT:

(A) There are some species of salamanders that have both male and female members.
(B) There are some species of higher animals none of whose members produce eggs.
(C) There is a significant number of female-only species of higher animals.
(D) Some species of higher animals containing both female and male members are not very adaptive.
(E) Some offspring of species of higher animals containing both female and male members have genetic codes more similar to one parent than to the other parent.

1. understand your job: This is a slight twist—we are looking for an answer that "must be false." We still want to start off by simply trying to understand the stimulus, and when we get to the answers, the key will be to see which answers directly relate to what the stimulus discusses.

2. read the stimulus: The stimulus is fairly simple to understand—a general statement is made that reproduction for higher species always requires eggs but doesn't always require sperm. Examples of this are given, followed by negative consequences.

3. eliminate wrong answers: Answers that "could be true" are ones that are not directly disproved by the text—so, we want to look for answers that do not directly relate to the subject matter in the stimulus. (A) could be true based on the stimulus, which only discusses one particular "rare" species of salamander. (B) is directly related to the first sentence of the stimulus, and seems to be in opposition to it. Let's leave (B). "Significant number" in (C) is vague, and therefore tough to disprove, especially because the only clue we are working off of is the "some" in the stimulus. Let's eliminate (C). (D) could be true—we've been told nothing about these animals. (E) could be true too—it goes well beyond the scope of our stimulus.

4. confirm the right answer: "None" in (B) is quite strong. When we check it against the text, we see that it's a nice contrast to "all" in the first sentence. (B) is definitely false based on the text, so (B) is correct.

31.3.10. It is wrong to waste our natural resources, and it is an incredible waste of resources to burn huge amounts of trash in incinerators. When trash is recycled, fewer resources are wasted. Because less trash will be recycled if an incinerator is built, the city should not build an incinerator.

Which one of the following can be properly inferred from the statements above?

(A) All of the city's trash that is not recycled goes into incinerators.
(B) By recycling more trash, the city can stop wasting resources entirely.
(C) The most effective way to conserve resources is to recycle trash.
(D) If the city is to avoid wasting resources, huge amounts of trash cannot be burned in any city incinerator.
(E) If the city does not burn trash, it will not waste resources.

1. understand your job: Our job is to find one answer that is supported by the information in the passage. We want to understand the information in the stimulus, then spend the bulk of our energy eliminating unsupported answers. "Properly inferred" means we are looking for an answer that has very strong justification.

2. read the stimulus: The stimulus gives us a lot of linked information related to wasting natural resources, burning trash in incinerators, and recycling. Then it ends with a suggestion that the city should not build an incinerator. The stimulus has classic argument construction, but reasoning structure is not our key focus here. With a general understanding of the stimulus, let's focus on eliminating answers.

3. eliminate wrong answers: "All" in (A) is suspicious, and reading further, (A) is not provable—we don't know of other ways the city deals with trash. (B) goes well beyond the test. "Stop wasting resources entirely" is too strong. "Most effective" makes (C) suspicious, and reading further, (C) is not provable—the stimulus doesn't discuss other ways to conserve resources. (D) seems closely related to the linking information in the stimulus—let's leave it for now. (E) goes beyond the scope of the stimulus. We don't know of other ways the city wastes resources.

4. confirm the right answer: We only have one attractive answer: (D). Let's try to confirm it. We are told that it is a waste of resources to burn huge amounts of trash. Therefore, we know that if they don't want to waste resources, they can't burn huge amounts of trash! (D) is provable based on the text and is correct.

30.2.18. If there are any inspired performances in the concert, the audience will be treated to a good show. But there will not be a good show unless there are sophisticated listeners in the audience, and to be a sophisticated listener one must understand one's musical roots.

If all of the statements above are true, which one of the following must also be true?

(A) If there are no sophisticated listeners in the audience, then there will be no inspired musical performances in the concert.
(B) No people who understand their musical roots will be in the audience if the audience will not be treated to a good show.
(C) If there will be people in the audience who understand their musical roots, then at least one musical performance in the concert will be inspired.
(D) The audience will be treated to a good show unless there are people in the audience who do not understand their musical roots.
(E) If there are sophisticated listeners in the audience, then there will be inspired musical performances in the concert.

1. understand your job: Our job is to find one answer that is supported by the information in the passage. We want to understand the information in the stimulus, then spend the bulk of our energy eliminating unsupported answers. Take note that we are looking for an answer that "must be true."

2. read the stimulus: Wow. There are a lot of statements that do link together, but the links are very confusing to understand. The first sentence gives us a criteria (inspired performances) sufficient to bring about an outcome (a good show). Okay so far. But then it gives us another statement about shows—if there aren't sophisticated listeners, there won't be a good show. It concludes by giving us another conditional to link to sophisticated listeners! It's a challenge to link everything together, and easy to make mistakes doing so. If you see how everything links, great. Otherwise, just know that you've got a series of conditionals that may or may not come together, and that you will need to go into the answer choices looking for ones you can eliminate.

3. eliminate wrong answers: If you went into the answer choices with a fuzzy understanding of the stimulus, you probably quickly realized that there are no answers we can eliminate based on obvious clues—all wrong answers are wrong because they misrepresent the conditional relationships in the stimulus. Therefore, in this case, we want to go back to the stimulus and get a much more specific understanding of the text. Then we will have to evaluate each answer carefully.

The first line gives us a pretty simple conditional: **If any inspired performances → audience will be treated to good show.** The second is a bit tougher to understand, but it says that **if there are no sophisticated listeners → there will not be a good show.** The last conditional is fairly straightforward: **if one is a sophisticated listener → one will understand musical roots.** Okay, let's go through the choices one more time.

4. confirm the right answer: With a clear (likely written out in notation form) understanding, (A) is fairly easy to prove correct. We can link the first two conditions to get the following: if no sophisticated listeners → no good show → no inspired performances.

The only consequence we know of for "if they are not treated to a good show" is that there will not be any inspired performances. We don't have the links to justify (B). We have no conditional triggered by one understanding musical roots, so we can eliminate (C). (D) is tougher to understand, but it means that if the audience is not treated to a good show, there are people in the audience who do not understand roots. This is the same as (B). The only consequence of sophisticated listening is understanding of musical roots, so we can eliminate (E).

(A) is the only answer that is correctly justifiable by linking the conditionals in the stimulus, and so (A) is correct.

Give an Example

"Which of the following best illustrates the principle mentioned above?"

"Which one of the following most closely conforms to the principle that the passage above illustrates?"

In Lesson 18, we discussed questions that asked us to identify a principle among the answer choices that we could use to justify an argument. Give an Example questions work in reverse—the stimulus presents a principle, and our job is to identify an example of that principle among the answer choices. These Give an Example questions are pretty rare—they show up about once every two or three exams. The stimulus will either present the principle directly, or, less commonly, it will illustrate the principle with a (generally simple) example. As always, your key to success is an effective elimination process.

step one: understand your job

For a Give an Example question, you have two primary tasks: understand the principle, and find the answer that best illustrates that principle. Keep it simple.

two: understand the principle

For certain questions, the principle will clearly be stated, and typically it will be stated in such a way so that the meaning is fairly clear. When stimuli present illustrations of a principle, the illustrations are typically simple and clear cut. All that is to say that the challenge of these questions, when they present significant challenges, tends to come in the evaluation of answer choices. The simpler the principle, the more important it is for you to understand it in a very specific manner, for if the question is a hard one, it will be so because the wrong choices vary in slight or subtle ways from that principle.

three: eliminate wrong choices

Again, the challenge of these questions commonly comes in the elimination process. If a question is more difficult, fewer of the wrong answers will have obvious "tells," and it will take some brain power to think through whether an answer is wrong. So, just like other questions, start your answer-choosing process by eliminating wrong choices, but, unlike other questions, give yourself a bit of extra time to evaluate each answer carefully even during the first round of eliminations (as opposed to, say, the first round of eliminations for a Required Assumption question, which should go very quickly). Make it a habit to check specific parts of answer choices against specific parts of the principle. The good news is that you generally won't have to "dig" in the stimulus to find the relevant information.

four: confirm the right answer

If you've carefully walked through an answer looking for reasons to eliminate it but can't find one, chances are you are left with the correct choice. Keep in mind that these answers will commonly not have the absolute, steel-grip sort of connection as do other answers (such as those for "Must Be True" Inference questions) but will rather give you a "Gee, I guess this is in general agreement with the principle" feeling (more akin to "Most Supported" Inference questions). Don't turn the screw so tight that you rip the head—by that I mean don't be so hypercritical that you get rid of the right answer for slight things that don't matter. Trust in your elimination process, focus on that first, and if an answer gets past that, give it a little leeway if need be.

SUPER-SIMPLE EXAMPLE

What makes for a good leader is not charisma, but rather the ability to make others feel important.

Which of the following best illustrates the principle mentioned above?

(A) Since Tara lacks charisma, she is likely a good boss.
(B) Jack is great at making others feel that he is important. Therefore, Jack is a great boss.
(C) Since Rey is charismatic, he cannot be a good boss.
(D) Sean is a good leader. He is not necessarily the most charming boss, but each of his employees feels needed and critical.
(E) Noah is not charismatic, but he also makes his employees feel unimportant. Therefore, he would make for a better employee than boss.

The correct answer is (D). The principle is that making others feel important "makes" for a good leader, and that charisma does not. Note that this does not mean that charisma is bad—it simply means it does not "make" one a good leader. (A) misinterprets the principle—we don't know if she makes others feel important. (B) is tempting if you misread it, but the point isn't for others to feel the boss is important. (C) misinterprets the role of charisma. (E) makes an assumption that he would be better as an employee—maybe he's not good as either.

Note that with (D), the aside "he may not be the most charming boss" is a good match for the aside about "charisma," and note that necessary and critical, while not 100% the same thing as important, are a very good match.

WRONG ANSWERS ARE MISMATCHES

mismatching points

mismatching reasoning

mismatching subject matter

the process in action

2.7. Ethicist: The most advanced kind of moral motivation is based solely on abstract principles. This form of motivation is in contrast with calculated self-interest or the desire to adhere to societal norms and conventions.

The actions of which one of the following individuals exhibit the most advanced kind of moral motivation, as described by the ethicist?

(A) Bobby contributed money to a local charity during a charity drive at work because he worried that not doing so would make him look stingy.
(B) Wes contributed money to a local charity during a charity drive at work because he believed that doing so would improve his employer's opinion of him.
(C) Donna's employers engaged in an illegal but profitable practice that caused serious damage to the environment. Donna did not report this practice to the authorities, out of fear that her employers would retaliate against her.
(D) Jadine's employers engaged in an illegal but profitable practice that caused serious damage to the environment. Jadine reported this practice to the authorities out of a belief that protecting the environment is always more important than monetary profit.
(E) Leigh's employers engaged in an illegal but profitable practice that caused serious damage to the environment. Leigh reported this practice to the authorities only because several colleagues had been pressuring her to do so.

---

1. understand your job: Our job is to clearly understand a principle that is expressed in the stimulus, and then to find the answer choice that best represents that principle.

2. understand the principle: The principle is that the most advanced moral motivation is based solely on abstract principles. It goes on to further explain that this form of motivation is specifically in contrast to two things: calculated self-interest and desire to adhere to societal norms.

3. get rid of wrong answers: From the stimulus, we've gotten a decent sense of what to expect from the right answer (action taken for abstract principles) and a very good sense of what to look for in wrong answers (calculated self-interest and desire to adhere to societal norms). With that in mind, let's eliminate!

(A) has Bobby motivated by societal norms, (B) has Wes motivated by self-interest, (C) has Donna acting out of self-interest, (D) has an action based on a "belief" (let's keep it), and (E) has Leigh motivated by societal pressure.

4. confirm the right answer: (D) is the only attractive answer. Let's review it more carefully—she based her decision on a belief, and it shows no evidence of self-interest or adherence to societal norms. (D) is correct.

35.1.7. Due to wider commercial availability of audio recordings of authors reading their own books, sales of printed books have dropped significantly.

Which one of the following conforms most closely to the principle illustrated above?

(A) Because of the rising cost of farm labor, farmers began to make more extensive use of machines.
(B) Because of the wide variety of new computer games on the market, sales of high-quality computer video screens have improved.
(C) Because a new brand of soft drink entered the market, consumers reduced their consumption of an established brand of soft drink.
(D) Because a child was forbidden to play until homework was completed, that child did much less daydreaming and focused on homework.
(E) Because neither of the two leading word processing programs has all of the features consumers want, neither has been able to dominate the market.

---

1. understand your job: Our job is to clearly understand a principle that is illustrated in the stimulus, and then to find the answer choice that best represents that principle.

2. understand the principle: Because the stimulus is an illustration, we'll have to work a bit harder to understand the principle. Here, it's that the wider availability of a newer type of product has had a negative impact on the sales of another product. Simple enough. With that in mind, let's evaluate answers.

3. get rid of wrong answers: (A) is tempting because it discusses similar concepts, but it's actually discussing how problems with one product cause increases in use of another product—this is the opposite of our principle. (B) is about how the growth of one product has led to the growth of another—again, related, but not exactly a representation of our principle. (C) is what we are looking for—a new item causing decreased sales of an older item. Let's leave it for now. (D) is about how not being allowed to do one thing led to doing more of another thing—close, but not the same. (E) talks about negative characteristics, and negative sales, for two competing products—we can eliminate it.

4. confirm the right answer: (C) is the only attractive answer. The one thing it doesn't have going for it is that with the switch from books to audio recordings, presumably the same key person (the author) gets to keep making money (albeit from a different revenue stream). (C) does not have this type of characteristic. Regardless, it's a fairly strong match for the principle, and we can feel confident picking it, in part because we've eliminated the four wrong choices.

Give an Example Questions

29.4.10. Parents should not necessarily raise their children in the ways experts recommend, even if some of those experts are themselves parents. After all, parents are the ones who directly experience which methods are successful in raising their own children.

Which one of the following most closely conforms to the principle that the passage above illustrates?

(A) Although music theory is intrinsically interesting and may be helpful to certain musicians, it does not distinguish good music from bad: that is a matter of taste and not of theory.
(B) One need not pay much attention to the advice of automotive experts when buying a car if those experts are not interested in the mundane factors that concern the average consumer.
(C) In deciding the best way to proceed, a climber familiar with a mountain might do well to ignore the advice of mountain climbing experts unfamiliar with that mountain.
(D) A typical farmer is less likely to know what types of soil are most productive than is someone with an advanced degree in agricultural science.
(E) Unlike society, one's own conscience speaks with a single voice; it is better to follow the advice of one's own conscience than the advice of society.

28.1.10. It is a principle of economics that a nation can experience economic growth only when consumer confidence is balanced with a small amount of consumer skepticism.

Which one of the following is an application of the economic principle above?

(A) Any nation in which consumer confidence is balanced with a small amount of consumer skepticism will experience economic growth.
(B) Any nation in which the prevailing attitude of consumers is not skepticism will experience economic growth.
(C) Any nation in which the prevailing attitude of consumers is either exclusively confidence or exclusively skepticism will experience economic growth.
(D) Any nation in which the prevailing attitude of consumers is exclusively confidence will not experience economic growth.
(E) Any nation in which consumer skepticism is balanced with a small amount of consumer confidence will experience economic growth.

Stick to the steps!
1. Understand your job.
2. Understand the principle.
3. Get rid of answers.
4. Confirm the right answer.

Give an Example Solutions

29.4.10. Parents should not necessarily raise their children in the ways experts recommend, even if some of those experts are themselves parents. After all, parents are the ones who directly experience which methods are successful in raising their own children.

Which one of the following most closely conforms to the principle that the passage above illustrates?

(A) Although music theory is intrinsically interesting and may be helpful to certain musicians, it does not distinguish good music from bad: that is a matter of taste and not of theory.
(B) One need not pay much attention to the advice of automotive experts when buying a car if those experts are not interested in the mundane factors that concern the average consumer.
(C) In deciding the best way to proceed, a climber familiar with a mountain might do well to ignore the advice of mountain climbing experts unfamiliar with that mountain.
(D) A typical farmer is less likely to know what types of soil are most productive than is someone with an advanced degree in agricultural science.
(E) Unlike society, one's own conscience speaks with a single voice; it is better to follow the advice of one's own conscience than the advice of society.

1. understand your job: Our job is to clearly understand a principle that is illustrated in the stimulus, and then to find the answer choice that best represents that principle.

2. understand the principle: Because the stimulus is an illustration, we'll have to work a bit harder to understand the principle. The stimulus says that parents should not necessarily do what experts say, even if some of the experts are parents themselves, because parents are the ones who see what works and doesn't work with their particular children. To generalize, you shouldn't do what an expert says, because you understand better your specific situation.

3. get rid of wrong answers: With that in mind, let's try to eliminate wrong answers. (A) is about one characteristic not having an impact on another characteristic—that is not a good match. "Need not pay much attention" in (B) is different from the meaning of "not necessarily" in the stimulus, and furthermore (B) represents a disconnect between the person giving advice and the person getting it that the original argument does not. (C) is a good match in that the person "might be well off" to ignore advice, because the person might understand the specific situation better—let's leave it. (D) is not a good match, and we can eliminate it without too much thought. (E) is a general statement about one motivation being better than another—that is significantly different from the principle illustrated.

4. confirm the right answer: (C) is the only attractive answer. "Might do well to ignore" is a good match for "should not necessarily...in ways recommend," and "unfamiliar with that mountain" matches well with the idea that parents have an advantage in having "direct experience" with their children.

28.1.10. It is a principle of economics that a nation can experience economic growth only when consumer confidence is balanced with a small amount of consumer skepticism.

Which one of the following is an application of the economic principle above?

(A) Any nation in which consumer confidence is balanced with a small amount of consumer skepticism will experience economic growth.
(B) Any nation in which the prevailing attitude of consumers is not skepticism will experience economic growth.
(C) Any nation in which the prevailing attitude of consumers is either exclusively confidence or exclusively skepticism will experience economic growth.
(D) Any nation in which the prevailing attitude of consumers is exclusively confidence will not experience economic growth.
(E) Any nation in which consumer skepticism is balanced with a small amount of consumer confidence will experience economic growth.

1. understand your job: Our job is to clearly understand a principle that is mentioned in the stimulus, and then to find the answer choice that best represents that principle.

2. understand the principle: The principle is that a nation can experience economic growth only when consumer confidence is balanced by a small amount of skepticism. So...

3. get rid of wrong answers: We will expect an answer that shows economic growth, based on balancing confidence with a small amount of skepticism, and use that to guide our eliminations. "Any" in (A) is suspicious, and when we check it against the stimulus, we see that it isn't a good fit for "can." Same problem with (B) and (C), which also have some other issues. (D) isn't necessarily what we expected, but it is a representation (a contrapositive representation) of the principle, seemingly. So, let's keep it. (E) is almost exactly like (A) and has the same issues, but it also mixes up skepticism and confidence.

4. confirm the right answer: (D) is the only attractive answer. If we think of it in abstract terms, we get that **confidence only → no economic growth**. The "only when" in the original stimulus gave us the conditional **economic growth → confidence and skepticism**. If we take the contrapositive of the stimulus, we get that **if you don't have either confidence or skepticism → you can't have economic growth**. That's what (D) represents, and (D) is the correct answer.

33 LOGICAL REASONING disagreement & discrepancy

In this lesson, we will discuss the remaining two Logical Reasoning question types: Identify the Disagreement and Explain a Discrepancy. As mentioned in the last lesson, these final two question types can and should be considered outliers.

Identify the Disagreement questions have stimuli that have two components: one person's statement and another person's response. (For example, Coach Willard: "Ted will win the match because he is faster than Fred." Coach Tran's response: "Ted is not faster than Fred.") The response will be related to some issue that was brought up, but it may not be related to the main point the first person made. Your job is to figure out exactly what it is that the second person disagrees with.

The critical work for Identify the Disagreement happens in the reading of the stimulus, and in general, you want to have a clear sense of what the disagreement is before looking at the answer choices. For harder questions, it will often be true that the disagreement is somewhat vague or difficult to see or that the right answer will be phrased in unexpected or challenging ways. We'll discuss strategies that will help overcome these advanced issues.

Explain a Discrepancy questions have stimuli that juxtapose two seemingly conflicting statements (e.g., "My mother says I'm handsome, yet girls won't go out with me"). Our job is to identify one possible explanation for how both things could be true at the same time.

The critical work for these questions also happens in the reading of the stimulus. If you have a very clear sense of exactly what the discrepancy is ("How come his mother says he's handsome, but girls aren't willing to go out with him?"), you will likely be able to see that four answers are not directly related to that discrepancy.

Neither of these question types contains arguments of the support-conclusion variety that we've come to expect. Still, it should be fairly easy for you to see how the skills you've developed for other question types—such as the ability to read objectively and find the gaps between ideas—will be of benefit to you in mastering these final question types.

Identify the Disagreement

"X and Y's statements provide the most support for holding that they disagree about..."
"X and Y disagree over..."

Identify the Disagreement questions are some of the most commonly misunderstood questions in the section, and for good reason. We are used to seeing stimuli that relate to one specific argument, so we have gotten used to thinking about stimuli in terms of components being related to one specific point being made.

But that is not our job in these questions, and, in fact, thinking about our job in terms of one main point is what will get us in trouble. Here's the correct way to think about it: the first person will make a variety of points. The second person will make a statement that either clearly shows disagreement with or strongly hints at disagreement with *one* of the points that the first person made. Your job is to figure out what the point of disagreement is, exactly.

Here's the challenge of these questions: the second person's comment may or may not have anything to do with the first person's main point—more commonly it will not. When it doesn't, trap answers will be designed to punish test takers who assume that the second person must be disagreeing with the main point being made by the first.

---

step one

understand your job

Our job is to identify the point of disagreement. Keep in mind that most of what will be discussed, even if it may seem important, will not be relevant to that point of disagreement. Think of it like a typical television debate where two people with opposing points of view take turns talking but not listening. The points these people make often have very little relation to one another. You want to find that one piece of overlap, the one thing that both people discuss and show some opinion about, and you want as specific a sense of that as possible before going into the answer choices.

DIFFERENT POINTS OF DISAGREEMENT

Note that the disagreement can be about anything that either of the people discuss. Here are four different examples of ways that Bob can disagree with Al:

Al: The incumbent will lose the presidential election. The economy generally determines the election outcome, and the economy is in bad shape.

Bob: I know the economy is an important issue, but the other party simply has no viable candidates. He may win again after all.

The disagreement is about whether the incumbent will win the election.

Al: The incumbent will lose the presidential election. The economy generally determines the election outcome, and the economy is in bad shape.

Bob: It is the general mood of the population, not any other specific issue, that will typically sway the outcome of the election.

The disagreement is about what generally determines an election outcome.

Al: The incumbent will lose the presidential election. The economy generally determines the election outcome, and the economy is in bad shape.

Bob: I disagree. Several economists have recently said that we are overly pessimistic about the state of businesses, and I tend to agree with them.

The disagreement is about the health of the economy.

Al: The incumbent will lose the presidential election. The economy generally determines the election outcome, and the economy is in bad shape.

Bob: I disagree. The GDP is growing at a higher than expected rate, and we are wealthier as a nation than we have ever been.

A less direct disagreement about the health of the economy.

two

read the stimulus to identify the disagreement

Read the first person's statement and try to recognize its underlying reasoning structure. Next, move on to the next statement and try your best to read it with a fresh eye. After you've read both, think carefully about the point of overlap between the two. For easier versions of these questions, the point of overlap will be quite obvious. For more difficult versions, the point of overlap will be more subtle—one person may express an opinion clearly, but the other might just hint at one. In any case, you know that your task is to, by the end of the stimulus, make a decision as to what you think is the point of disagreement.

Again, keep in mind that the main point of the first person may or (more commonly) may not be what the second person responds to. Be super careful about that.

SUPER-SIMPLE EXAMPLE

Al: Smith has been a wonderful CEO. It is because of him that the company is prospering.

Bob: This CEO has had nothing to do with the prospering of the business.

Al and Bob disagree about whether

(A) Smith has been a good CEO
(B) the company is prospering
(C) the office of CEO has never had an impact on economic affairs
(D) Smith is responsible for the company's prosperity
(E) the economics of a company are a way to gauge the efficacy of a CEO

The correct answer is (D). With (A), we don't know if Bob thinks Smith is a good CEO. With (B), there is no proof they disagree about whether the business is prospering, and in fact it seems they may agree on this point. With (C), Al thinks it has, but we only know Bob's opinion about this particular CEO, and that's not enough. We get a sense of Al's opinion about (E), but not Bob's.

Al says directly that it is "because of him" that the company is prospering, and Bob says "this CEO has had nothing to do with the prospering." Those are clear signs they disagree about (D).

three

eliminate wrong choices

This is the key step for this question type. This fact becomes more and more true as questions become more difficult. As disagreements become more subtle, right answers become harder and harder to prove. However, wrong answers will always have clear, defining characteristics that make them wrong.

Look for answers that discuss subjects or relationships that are not discussed in either argument—these are the most common wrong choices. Typically these answers generalize beyond both arguments, get more specific than both arguments, or simply change the subject matter or relationship that is being discussed. Secondly, look for answers that say that the point of disagreement is something that one person discusses, but the other does not. Remember, most commonly, these wrong answers will relate to some main point that one person makes, but the other person doesn't comment on. Finally, it is very rare that you will find some subject or issues for which there is overlapping discussion, but not overlapping opinions. However, this would be the last layer of incorrectness.

CONSTELLATION OF WRONG ANSWERS

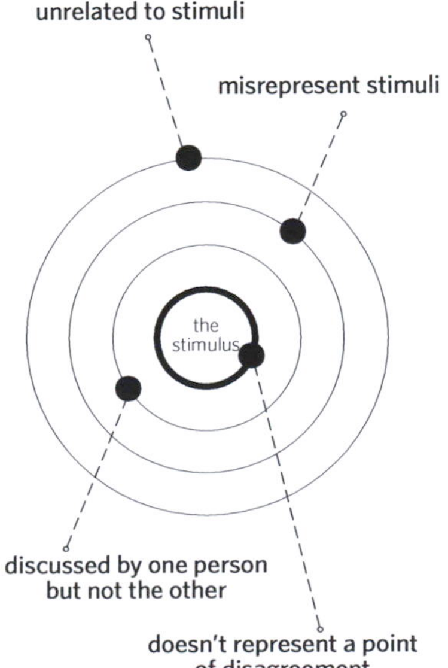

four

confirm the right answer

There is a simple way to confirm a right answer. If you think an answer is correct, check it against what the first person said, to make sure it's clear that person has an opinion about that particular issue. Do the same thing for the second person. Keep in mind that for tougher versions of these questions, you may have to read between the lines slightly (very slightly) to get that second opinion. If you feel confident both people have an opinion about what is being discussed in the answer choice, and if you feel that these opinions contrast, then the answer will be correct.

When stuck between two answers, pick the one that stays closest to the subjects and relationships specifically discussed in the text for both statements. The answer that requires you to make more leaps, assumptions, and generalizations will be incorrect.

the process in action

2.16. Taylor: Researchers at a local university claim that 61 percent of the information transferred during a conversation is communicated through nonverbal signals. But this claim, like all such mathematically precise claims, is suspect, because claims of such exactitude could never be established by science.

Sandra: While precision is unobtainable in many areas of life, it is commonplace in others. Many scientific disciplines obtain extremely precise results, which should not be doubted merely because of their precision.

The statements above provide the most support for holding that Sandra would disagree with Taylor about which one of the following statements?

(A) Research might reveal that 61 percent of the information taken in during a conversation is communicated through nonverbal signals.
(B) It is possible to determine whether 61 percent of the information taken in during a conversation is communicated through nonverbal signals.
(C) The study of verbal and nonverbal communication is an area where one cannot expect great precision in one's research results.
(D) Some sciences can yield mathematically precise results that are not inherently suspect.
(E) If inherently suspect claims are usually false, then the majority of claims made by scientists are false as well.

1. understand your job: Our job is to recognize the point of disagreement. That means we want to read both statements, then figure out the point of overlap before moving on to the answers.

2. identify the disagreement: The non-verbal signals that are the key topic for Taylor are not discussed by Sandra, whose main point about precision being commonplace in areas of life is not directly related to what Taylor discusses. The point of overlap happens to be, for both arguments respectively, a secondary issue—the possible preciseness of scientific claims. Taylor says science cannot get precise results ("claims...established by science"), and Sandra says many scientific disciplines get "extremely precise results." We want an answer that relates to this disagreement...

3. get rid of answers: ...And we want to eliminate answers that don't relate to both of the comments. (A) is about Taylor's specific experiment—we know nothing about Sandra's feelings toward it (maybe there is a reason specific to that experiment that prevents exactness, which Sandra knows about). We can quickly eliminate (A). (B) is very similar to (A)— again, without knowing other things about Sandra's feelings toward this specific experiment, it's tough to say they disagree. (C), though a bit more generalized, has the same issues as (A) and (B). (D) is the answer we expected, so let's leave it. (E) goes beyond the scope of either discussion and can be eliminated quickly.

4. confirm the right answer: Let's check (D) against what both people said. Taylor says all mathematically precise claims are suspect. Sandra says some sciences can obtain extremely precise results, which "should not be doubted." We have strong evidence of disagreement, and (D) is the correct answer.

3.7. Antonio: One can live a life of moderation by never deviating from the middle course. But then one loses the joy of spontaneity and misses the opportunities that come to those who are occasionally willing to take great chances, or to go too far.

Marla: But one who, in the interests of moderation, never risks going too far is actually failing to live a life of moderation: one must be moderate even in one's moderation.

Antonio and Marla disagree over

(A) whether it is desirable for people occasionally to take great chances in life
(B) what a life of moderation requires of a person
(C) whether it is possible for a person to embrace other virtues along with moderation
(D) how often a person ought to deviate from the middle course in life
(E) whether it is desirable for people to be moderately spontaneous

1. understand your job: Our job is to recognize the point of disagreement. That means we want to read both statements, then figure out the point of overlap before moving on to the answers.

2. identify the disagreement: Antonio's main point is that one who lives a life of moderation misses out on opportunities; Marla's point is that one must be moderate in one's moderation. The overlap, again, comes in the supporting information—Antonio says one can live a life of moderation by never deviating, while Marla says that one who does not deviate fails to live a life of moderation. With that in mind, we move on to step three.

3. get rid of answers: "Desirable" is not discussed by either person (though it's somewhat close to "must" mentioned by Marla), and coupled with "great chances," we can quickly eliminate (A). (B) is what we're expecting—let's leave it. The "other virtues" allow us to eliminate (C). "How often" is not a great match, and Antonio does not discuss what one "ought" to do, so we can eliminate (D). "Desirable" makes (E) unattractive. Again, it's similar to "must" in Marla's comments, but Antonio never says one should live an unspontaneous life, and in fact, he says nothing about what one *should* do at all. We can eliminate (E) too.

4. confirm the right answer: That leaves only (B). We check it against what Antonio says—"requires" and "can" are not perfect matches (not on the LSAT, anyway!) but they are pretty close. Marla says a life of moderation requires a bit of non-moderation. (B) is the best representation of what they disagree over, and (B) is correct.

Identify the Disagreement Questions

31.2.1. Moralist: TV talk shows are contributing to the moral decline in our country. By constantly being shown the least moral people in our society, viewers begin to think that such people are the norm, and that there is something wrong with being morally upright.

TV talk show host: Well, if there is such a decline, it's not because of TV talk shows: we simply show people what they want to see. What can be wrong with letting the viewers decide? Furthermore, if restrictions were put on my show, that would amount to censorship, which is wrong.

The moralist's and the TV talk show host's statements provide the most support for holding that they disagree about whether

(A) TV talk shows should be censored
(B) people's moral standards have changed
(C) TV talk shows influence people's conception of what is the norm
(D) TV talk shows, by presenting immoral guests, are causing a moral decline
(E) it is wrong not to let the viewers decide what they want to see

31.3.19. Professor Beckstein: American Sign Language is the native language of many North Americans. Therefore, it is not a foreign language, and for that reason alone, no student should be permitted to satisfy the university's foreign language requirement by learning it.

Professor Sedley: According to your argument, students should not be allowed to satisfy the university's foreign language requirement by learning French or Spanish either, since they too are the native languages of many North Americans. Yet many students currently satisfy the requirement by studying French or Spanish, and it would be ridiculous to begin prohibiting them from doing so.

Their statements commit Professors Beckstein and Sedley to disagreeing about which one of the following:

(A) whether American Sign Language is the native language of a significant number of North Americans
(B) whether any North American whose native language is not English should be allowed to fulfill the university's foreign language requirement by studying his or her own native language
(C) whether the university ought to retain a foreign language requirement
(D) whether any other universities in North America permit their students to fulfill a foreign language requirement by learning American Sign Language
(E) whether the fact that a language is the native language of many North Americans justifies prohibiting its use to fulfill the university's foreign language requirement

30.2.10. Goswami: I support the striking workers at Ergon Foods. They are underpaid. The majority of them make less than $20,000 per year.

Nordecki: If pay is the issue, I must disagree. The average annual salary of the striking workers at Ergon Foods is over $29,000.

Goswami and Nordecki disagree over the truth of which one of the following statements?

(A) The average annual salary at Ergon Foods is over $29,000.
(B) Pay is the primary issue over which the workers are striking at Ergon Foods.
(C) It is reasonable to support striking workers who are underpaid.
(D) The striking workers at Ergon Foods are under paid.
(E) It was unreasonable for the workers at Ergon Foods to go on strike.

Identify the Disagreement Solutions

31.2.1. Moralist: TV talk shows are contributing to the moral decline in our country. By constantly being shown the least moral people in our society, viewers begin to think that such people are the norm, and that there is something wrong with being morally upright.

TV talk show host: Well, if there is such a decline, it's not because of TV talk shows: we simply show people what they want to see. What can be wrong with letting the viewers decide? Furthermore, if restrictions were put on my show, that would amount to censorship, which is wrong.

The moralist's and the TV talk show host's statements provide the most support for holding that they disagree about whether

(A) TV talk shows should be censored
(B) people's moral standards have changed
(C) TV talk shows influence people's conception of what is the norm
(D) TV talk shows, by presenting immoral guests, are causing a moral decline
(E) it is wrong not to let the viewers decide what they want to see

1. understand your job: We have to find the point of disagreement.

2. identify the disagreement: The point of disagreement has to do with the impact of TV talk shows on moral decline. This is the main point for the moralist. We get a hint of the disagreement at the beginning of the TV talk show host's statement: "If there is such a decline" indicates that he's not going to argue with whether there is a moral decline or not. This is followed by "it's not because of TV talk shows," a statement we know directly contradicts the moralist's claim.

3. get rid of answers: Though the talk show host talks about censorship, the moralist does not, and we can quickly eliminate (A). We know they are not debating whether there has been a decline (change), so we can eliminate (B). (C) is tempting, but the talk show host's statements make no clear reference to the "norm." (D) is the answer we expected—let's leave it. (E) is incorrect because the moralist does not make claims about what is right and wrong, and it's unclear what he would think about freedom of viewership.

4. confirm the right answer: We check (D) against the moralist's comments, and there is a great match (immoral guests = least moral people, causing = contributing). We check it against the talk show host, and there is also a great match (causing a decline = such a decline is not due to). (D) is correct.

31.3.19. Professor Beckstein: American Sign Language is the native language of many North Americans. Therefore, it is not a foreign language, and for that reason alone, no student should be permitted to satisfy the university's foreign language requirement by learning it.

Professor Sedley: According to your argument, students should not be allowed to satisfy the university's foreign language requirement by learning French or Spanish either, since they too are the native languages of many North Americans. Yet many students currently satisfy the requirement by studying French or Spanish, and it would be ridiculous to begin prohibiting them from doing so.

Their statements commit Professors Beckstein and Sedley to disagreeing about which one of the following:

(A) whether American Sign Language is the native language of a significant number of North Americans
(B) whether any North American whose native language is not English should be allowed to fulfill the university's foreign language requirement by studying his or her own native language
(C) whether the university ought to retain a foreign language requirement
(D) whether any other universities in North America permit their students to fulfill a foreign language requirement by learning American Sign Language
(E) whether the fact that a language is the native language of many North Americans justifies prohibiting its use to fulfill the university's foreign language requirement

1. understand your job: We have to find the point of disagreement.

2. identify the disagreement: Here the point of disagreement is a bit less clear cut, but Sedley is disagreeing with the idea that because a language is native to certain North Americans, it should not be permitted to fulfill the foreign language requirement. We get a sense this is important from the statement "for that reason alone." Sedley strikes down the reasoning with counterexamples, and says prohibition in the analogous situation would be ridiculous. Note that Sedley does not come out and specifically state that American Sign Language should be permitted.

3. get rid of answers: (A) is not a point of debate and is not related to anything Sedley says. (B) is a bit broad but because we weren't exactly clear on the disagreement, let's leave it. (C) is not discussed by either party. "Other universities" allows us to quickly eliminate (D). (E) is the answer we expected. Let's leave it.

4. confirm the right answer: Having seen (E), (B) looks a lot less attractive. Though the concepts in (B) underlie both arguments, Beckstein is only talking specifically about one language, and Sedley specifically about two others. There is not enough there to support the broad generalizations ("any") in (B). Going back to (E), we know that Beckstein clearly feels that the reason justifies the prohibition. Sedley's opinion is not spelled out as obviously, but we know that the reason behind the evidence Sedley gives is to show that a language being a native language isn't justifiable criteria. (E) is correct.

Identify the Disagreement Solutions

30.2.10. Goswami: I support the striking workers at Ergon Foods. They are underpaid. The majority of them make less than $20,000 per year.

Nordecki: If pay is the issue, I must disagree. The average annual salary of the striking workers at Ergon Foods is over $29,000.

Goswami and Nordecki disagree over the truth of which one of the following statements?

(A) The average annual salary at Ergon Foods is over $29,000.
(B) Pay is the primary issue over which the workers are striking at Ergon Foods.
(C) It is reasonable to support striking workers who are underpaid.
(D) The striking workers at Ergon Foods are underpaid.
(E) It was unreasonable for the workers at Ergon Foods to go on strike.

1. understand your job: We have to find the point of disagreement.

2. identify the disagreement: We're not sure if Nordecki actually supports or doesn't support (or doesn't care about) the striking workers (maybe he supports them for other reasons). The part he disagrees about, he states, is pay. Goswami says they are underpaid. Nordecki states he disagrees about pay, then gives evidence that seems to show that he thinks they are not underpaid. With that in mind...

3. get rid of answers: (A) is a trap answer—it seems that Goswami is perhaps disagreeing with this (especially if your math skills are rusty) but what a majority of people make is different from an average salary, so Goswami never discusses the subject matter of (A). We're unclear if pay is the "primary issue"—neither mentions this, so they can't disagree about it. Get rid of (B). What is "reasonable" or not is not discussed, and (C) goes well beyond the scope of the discussion. (D) is what we expected, so let's leave it. (E) discusses "unreasonable," which the argument does not, and it's unclear what Nordecki feels about the strikers.

4. confirm the right answer: As usual, we are left with one answer that does not have any obvious flaws. Goswami directly states that they are underpaid, and Nordecki says that he disagrees with pay being an issue for striking. (D) is correct.

Explain the Discrepancy

"Which one of the following, if true, most helps to resolve the apparent discrepancy described above?"
"Which one of the following, if true, most helps to explain why...?"

Explain the Discrepancy questions present, within the stimuli, two ideas that could be seen, at least in part, as going against one another. Your job is to identify one answer that could possibly explain how these two ideas could, at the same time, be true.

The key to explaining a discrepancy is understanding it. If you go into the answer choices with a very clear sense of the discrepancy that needs to be explained, the wrong answers will be far more obviously wrong, and the right answer will be far more obviously right.

One helpful tool for thinking about the discrepancy is to start yourself off with "How come," as in "How come my mother says I am handsome but no women find me attractive?" or "How come my family tells me they love my cooking but they never want to have seconds?" Each stimulus that comes with an Explain the Discrepancy question will contain a discrepancy that can be phrased in those terms, and if you get it right, thinking about it that way will make it easier to get through the answer choices.

SUPER-SIMPLE EXAMPLE

Terence says he sent me a fax, but I know he does not own a fax machine.

Which of the following, if true, most helps to resolve the apparent discrepancy described above?

(A) Fax machines were once far more important to businesses than they are now.
(B) Terence has the capacity to send a fax through his computer without the aid of a fax machine.
(C) Terence used to own a fax machine, but he gave it to his sister.
(D) A day earlier, Terence said he left a phone message.
(E) Most faxes are sent through fax machines.

How can he send faxes without a fax machine? The only answer that attempts to answer that question is the correct answer, (B). (A), (C), and (E) shed no light on this particular faxing situation, and (D) has nothing to do with faxing at all. If (B) is true, it explains how he could send a fax even though he doesn't have a fax machine.

---

step one: understand your job

When we recognize that it's an Explain the Discrepancy question, the first thing we often have to do is "de-program" ourselves from looking for an argument—there isn't going to be one here. Instead, there will be one statement made, and then another one that seemingly contradicts it in some way. In the stimulus, our job is to identify these contradicting statements and understand what the contradiction is. In the answer choices, our job is to find one possible explanation for how this discrepancy can be.

two: find the discrepancy

As we read the stimulus, our job is simply to recognize the discrepancy it contains. Note that the discrepancy will often have very obvious and logical explanations, and in general, the discrepancy will not be difficult to locate. The key is to understand it as specifically as you can before going into the answers, and, again, using the phrase "How come..." will help you get in the right mindset.

CONSTELLATION OF WRONG ANSWERS

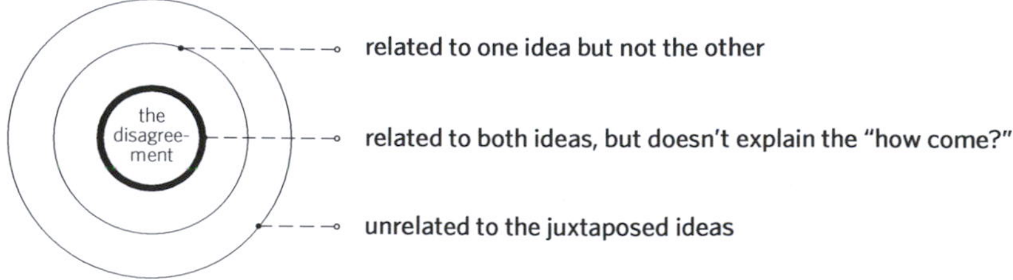

three: eliminate wrong choices

With a clear sense of the discrepancy, you want to go into eliminating answer choices. On a broad level, we can simply say that wrong answers will not explain the discrepancy, and that's generally what you want to look out for. On a more specific level, you will find that wrong answers do not directly relate to the stimulus, or very commonly, wrong answers relate to or explain one of the ideas in question, but not in a way that impacts the discrepancy in any way. The most attractive wrong answers will relate to both subjects or ideas that are being juxtaposed but will do so in a way that doesn't answer the question of "How come..."

four: confirm the right answer

The right answer will provide an answer to the question of "How come..." Keep in mind that the answer does not have to be foolproof (it never will be), nor does it even have to be particularly reasonable or attractive. It simply has to be a *possible* explanation for the discrepancy, and there will always just be one such answer. If you can see how an answer can have a direct impact on the discrepancy, and if you are correct in your thoughts, you have the correct answer.

the process in action

2.25. During the nineteenth century, the French academy of art was a major financial sponsor of painting and sculpture in France; sponsorship by private individuals had decreased dramatically by this time. Because the academy discouraged innovation in the arts, there was little innovation in nineteenth century French sculpture. Yet nineteenth century French painting showed a remarkable degree of innovation.

Which one of the following, if true, most helps to explain the difference between the amount of innovation in French painting and the amount of innovation in French sculpture during the nineteenth century?

(A) In France in the nineteenth century, the French academy gave more of its financial support to painting than it did to sculpture.
(B) The French academy in the nineteenth century financially supported a greater number of sculptors than painters, but individual painters received more support, on average, than individual sculptors.
(C) Because stone was so much more expensive than paint and canvas, far more unsponsored paintings were produced than were unsponsored sculptures in France during the nineteenth century.
(D) Very few of the artists in France in the nineteenth century who produced sculptures also produced paintings.
(E) Although the academy was the primary sponsor of sculpture and painting, the total amount of financial support that French sculptors and painters received from sponsors declined during the nineteenth century.

1. understand your job: Our job is to find a potential explanation for the discrepancy that exists in the stimulus. The first and most important part of that job is to understand exactly what that discrepancy is.

2. find the discrepancy: The first sentence serves as background. In the second sentence, we get the two mismatching facts: the academy, which was the primary sponsor of the arts, discouraged innovation, yet the paintings show a remarkable amount of innovation. Sculpture, on the other hand, showed an expectedly low level of innovation. The question is "How come the painters were able to have so much innovation, even though the primary sponsor discouraged it?" Let's look for an answer that relates to this issue.

3. get rid of answers: (A) mentions something that might be helpful to painters, but remember that it's still the French academy (which discourages innovation) that is giving the money. (B) gives us a complicated mathematical breakdown of the sponsorship money, but it's all a waste of time—it's still money coming from the academy, and it doesn't clearly explain the discrepancy. (C) gives us an explanation for the discrepancy that seems to make sense—let's leave it. It's unclear how (D) relates to the discrepancy. (E) impacts sculptures and paintings in the same way.

4. confirm the right answer: (C) is the only answer that presents a significant difference between sculptors and painters that may help explain the discrepancy—sculptors were dependent on financial support more so than painters. That connects to the wishes of sponsors—sculptors need to pay more heed to their wishes because they are more dependent on them for support. Painting could flourish despite the wishes of sponsors because painting is less dependent on financial help. (C) is probably not an answer you predicted, but (C) is correct.

3.2. After replacing his old gas water heater with a new, pilotless, gas water heater that is rated as highly efficient, Jimmy's gas bills increased.

Each of the following, if true, contributes to an explanation of the increase mentioned above EXCEPT:

(A) The new water heater uses a smaller percentage of the gas used by Jimmy's household than did the old one.
(B) Shortly after the new water heater was installed, Jimmy's uncle came to live with him, doubling the size of the household.
(C) After having done his laundry at a laundromat, Jimmy bought and started using a gas dryer when he replaced his water heater.
(D) Jimmy's utility company raised the rates for gas consumption following installation of the new water heater.
(E) Unusually cold weather following installation of the new water heater resulted in heavy gas usage.

1. understand your job: Our job is to evaluate potential explanations for the discrepancy that exists in the stimulus. The first and most important part of that job is to understand exactly what that discrepancy is.

2. find the discrepancy: Jimmy replaced his water heater with a more efficient one, but his bills went up. The discrepancy is clear: How come his bill went up even though he's using a more efficient water heater?

3. eliminate wrong answers: Since this is an "EXCEPT" question, we know to eliminate answers that actually do explain the increase in costs. In this case, it's fairly simple to anticipate some potential answers—city raised the price of gas, or Jimmy needed to use more of it all of a sudden—and it's a good idea to brainstorm a bit (just a bit) before looking at the choices so you have a better gauge for what is a reasonable explanation. (A) is a tough one to get your head around—you should expect it to use a smaller percentage of total gas because it's more efficient, but maybe this also means that more gas is being used overall in the house? Let's not eliminate it. (B) gives an explanation for increased gas use that makes clear sense. Eliminate (B). (C) does as well, so we can eliminate (C). (D) also helps explain the increase in costs, so we can eliminate that. (E) also helps explain increased use, so we can eliminate that.

4. confirm the right answer: (A) is the only answer remaining. If written differently, perhaps it could serve as proof that Jimmy is using a lot more gas than he did before. However, as written, it's unclear exactly how this impacts the discrepancy or explains the increase in cost. (A) is correct.

31.2.11. Several thousand years ago, people in what is now North America began to grow corn, which grows faster and produces more food per unit of land than do the grains these people had grown previously. Corn is less nutritious than those other grains, however, and soon after these people established corn as their staple grain crop, they began having nutrition-related health problems. Yet the people continued to grow corn as their staple grain, although they could have returned to growing the more nutritious grains.

Which one of the following, if true, most helps to explain why the people mentioned continued to grow corn as their staple grain crop?

(A) The variety of corn that the people relied on as their staple grain produced more food than did the ancestors of that variety.
(B) Modern varieties of corn are more nutritious than were the varieties grown by people in North America several thousand years ago.
(C) The people did not domesticate large animals for meat or milk, either of which could supply nutrients not provided by corn.
(D) Some grain crops that could have been planted instead of corn required less fertile soil in order to flourish than corn required.
(E) The people discovered some years after adopting corn as their staple grain that a diet that supplemented corn with certain readily available nongrain foods significantly improved their health.

31.2.13. Studies have shown that, contrary to popular belief, middle-aged people have more fear of dying than do elderly people.

Each of the following, if true, contributes to an explanation of the phenomenon shown by the studies EXCEPT:

(A) The longer one lives, the more likely it is that one has come to terms with dying.
(B) Middle-aged people have more people dependent upon them than people of any other age group.
(C) Many people who suffer from depression first become depressed in middle age.
(D) The longer one lives, the more imperturbable one becomes.
(E) Middle-aged people have a more acute sense of their own mortality than do people of any other age group.

31.3.2. One way kidney stones can form is when urine produced in the kidneys is overly concentrated with calcium or oxalate. Reducing dietary calcium has been thought, therefore, to decrease the likelihood that calcium will concentrate and form additional stones. Oddly enough, for many people the chances of recurrence are decreased by increasing calcium intake.

Which one of the following, if true, most helps to resolve the apparent discrepancy described above?

(A) Laboratory studies on animals with kidney stones reveal that they rarely get additional stones once calcium supplements are added to the diet.
(B) Increasing dietary oxalate while reducing dietary calcium does not reduce the chances of kidney stone recurrence.
(C) Kidney stone development is sometimes the result of an inherited disorder that can result in excessive production of calcium and oxalate.
(D) Increasing calcium intake increases the amount of calcium eliminated through the intestines, which decreases the amount to be filtered by the kidneys.
(E) Some kidney stones are composed of uric acid rather than a combination of calcium and oxalate.

Explain the Discrepancy Solutions

31.2.11. Several thousand years ago, people in what is now North America began to grow corn, which grows faster and produces more food per unit of land than do the grains these people had grown previously. Corn is less nutritious than those other grains, however, and soon after these people established corn as their staple grain crop, they began having nutrition-related health problems. Yet the people continued to grow corn as their staple grain, although they could have returned to growing the more nutritious grains.

Which one of the following, if true, most helps to explain why the people mentioned continued to grow corn as their staple grain crop?

(A) The variety of corn that the people relied on as their staple grain produced more food than did the ancestors of that variety.
(B) Modern varieties of corn are more nutritious than were the varieties grown by people in North America several thousand years ago.
(C) The people did not domesticate large animals for meat or milk, either of which could supply nutrients not provided by corn.
(D) Some grain crops that could have been planted instead of corn required less fertile soil in order to flourish than corn required.
(E) The people discovered some years after adopting corn as their staple grain that a diet that supplemented corn with certain readily available nongrain foods significantly improved their health.

1. understand your job: We have to find a potential explanation for the discrepancy. The first step is to get a clear sense of exactly what the discrepancy is.

2. find the discrepancy: The word "yet" in the last sentence tips us off to the discrepancy: Why did people continue to grow corn, when it caused them health issues?

3. get rid of answers: There are many answers that could work here, but we want to first focus on eliminating the four that don't effectively help answer the question we posed above. (A) states that the corn those people grew produced more edible parts than that grown before. Comparing corn of one era to another doesn't help us answer the question. By the same token, we can eliminate (B). (C) explains partly why they were getting ill, but not why they continued to grow corn. (D) doesn't explain why they stuck with corn. That leaves us with only (E).

4. confirm the right answer: If (E) is true, it explains why they continued to grow corn, even though it caused some health issues: they would be able to find ways to overcome these health issues. (E) is correct.

31.2.13. Studies have shown that, contrary to popular belief, middle-aged people have more fear of dying than do elderly people.

Each of the following, if true, contributes to an explanation of the phenomenon shown by the studies EXCEPT:

(A) The longer one lives, the more likely it is that one has come to terms with dying.
(B) Middle-aged people have more people dependent upon them than people of any other age group.
(C) Many people who suffer from depression first become depressed in middle age.
(D) The longer one lives, the more imperturbable one becomes.
(E) Middle-aged people have a more acute sense of their own mortality than do people of any other age group.

1. understand your job: We have to find a potential explanation for the discrepancy. The first step is to get a clear sense of exactly what the discrepancy is.

2. find the discrepancy: The words "contrary to popular belief" tip us off as to the discrepancy, and we can ask ourselves, why do middle-aged people fear death more than do the elderly?

3. get rid of answers: Since this is an EXCEPT question, we want to get rid of the four answers that do indeed help to answer the question we posed above. (A) helps explain why the elderly have less fear, so it can be eliminated. (B) explains why middle-aged people would worry (have fear) about dying, so it can be eliminated. (C) is about depression, and it's unclear what the link is to fear of dying—let's leave it. (D) helps explain why the elderly have less fear, and (E) helps explain why the middle-aged have more.

4. confirm the right answer: (C) is the only answer that didn't seem to directly impact the discrepancy. Check it one more time against the stimulus—there is no link given between depression and fear of death. We need not think of the reasoning any further. (C) is correct.

Explain the Discrepancy Solutions

31.3.2. One way kidney stones can form is when urine produced in the kidneys is overly concentrated with calcium or oxalate. Reducing dietary calcium has been thought, therefore, to decrease the likelihood that calcium will concentrate and form additional stones. Oddly enough, for many people the chances of recurrence are decreased by increasing calcium intake.

Which one of the following, if true, most helps to resolve the apparent discrepancy described above?

(A) Laboratory studies on animals with kidney stones reveal that they rarely get additional stones once calcium supplements are added to the diet.
(B) Increasing dietary oxalate while reducing dietary calcium does not reduce the chances of kidney stone recurrence.
(C) Kidney stone development is sometimes the result of an inherited disorder that can result in excessive production of calcium and oxalate.
(D) Increasing calcium intake increases the amount of calcium eliminated through the intestines, which decreases the amount to be filtered by the kidneys.
(E) Some kidney stones are composed of uric acid rather than a combination of calcium and oxalate.

1. understand your job: We have to find a potential explanation for the discrepancy. The first step is to get a clear sense of exactly what the discrepancy is.

2. find the discrepancy: The words "oddly enough" in the last sentence tip us off to the discrepancy: if *reducing* calcium decreases the likelihood of calcium forming into additional stones, why, for many people, does *increasing* calcium decrease chance of kidney stone recurrence?

3. get rid of answers: We want to get rid of the answer choices that don't help resolve the question we posed above. (A) does not provide us with a "why" answer and can be quickly eliminated. (B) is very tough to understand, especially in the context of the stimulus, but we don't really need to, for it's clear to see that it doesn't help explain the strange consequences of *increasing* calcium intake. (C) also doesn't explain why people's chances decrease when they increase calcium intake. (D) may explain it—at least it shows one way that increasing intake has a positive effect on stones. Let's leave it. It's unclear how (E) can help explain why an increase of calcium can lead to a decrease in kidney stone incidence.

4. confirm the right answer: (D) is the only answer we did not eliminate. If we take (D) to be true, it tells us that increasing calcium intake decreases the amount of calcium the kidney must filter. Since we are talking about problems in the kidney caused by calcium, it makes sense that this is a possible explanation for the discrepancy. (D) is correct.

Question Stem
Quick Quiz

We've now taken a careful look at every type of Logical Reasoning question that will appear on your LSAT. Each type of question we've discussed requires something unique from us, and we can use the question stem to define our focus and our priorities. The question stem tells us what our job is in reading the stimulus, and, of course, it tells us what our job is in evaluating the answer choices.

The trouble is that there is great overlap in terms of the tasks the different questions present. And while certain strategies may be effective for two different questions, others won't be, and unless you are careful, you will suffer from carrying over or melding strategies for different types of questions, especially if you are seeing them all mixed together in a section. For example, both ID the Conclusion and Flaw require us to understand argument structure, but ID the Conclusion doesn't require us to be critical of the argument, whereas Flaw questions do. If we aren't careful, we will waste time looking for flaws during ID the Conclusion questions or, on a more subtle level, allow our bias about flawed reasoning to influence which answers we find attractive or not.

There are five main factors when it comes to how we define how to think about question tasks. There are the four general overlapping ways to define the tasks presented in the question:

1) Whether we are meant to search for an argument
2) Whether we are meant to be critical of an argument
3) To what degree we should expect to predict the main answer
4) Whether we are meant to apply the answers to the stimulus, or the stimulus to the answers

Then there is the specific task (find the required assumption, the most supported answer, etc.) that the question presents most directly.

The mini-quiz on the left requires that you think about each type of question in terms of the four overlapping characteristics. I expect that most of you will have very little trouble with most of the answers (though you may disagree with me on an answer or two, which is fine). What's actually more important is whether the answer is instinctual or whether you have to think about it for a while. If you have to go back and forth before making a decision, then you know you are not performing that task intuitively when you solve those types of questions. For example, if you aren't sure for a Flaw question whether you should be able to predict the answer or not (you should), then you probably aren't consistently trying to predict the flaw.

So use this little quiz to get a sense of where your instincts are now. Abbreviations for each type of question have been provided—for each task characteristic, put the question types into the categories in which they fit best. Answers and further discussion are on the next page.

question type abbreviations

A (assumption)	**MF** (match flaw)
AS (argument structure)	**MR** (match reasoning)
C (ID the conclusion)	**R** (find role)
E (give an example)	**RA** (required assumption)
ED (explain the discrepancy)	**S** (strengthen)
F (flaw)	**SA** (sufficient assumption)
I (inference)	**SP** (supporting principle)
ID (ID the disagreement)	**W** (weaken)

Should I look for an argument?

yes	no

Should I be critical of the reasoning?

yes	no

Should I always expect to predict the answer?

yes	no

Should I apply the answers to the stimulus, or vice versa?

answers to stimulus	both	stimulus to answers

Solutions

question type abbreviations

A (assumption)	**MF** (match flaw)
AS (argument structure)	**MR** (match reasoning)
C (ID the conclusion)	**R** (find role)
E (give an example)	**RA** (required assumption)
ED (explain the discrepancy)	**S** (strengthen)
F (flaw)	**SA** (sufficient assumption)
I (inference)	**SP** (supporting principle)
ID (ID the disagreement)	**W** (weaken)

Should I look for an argument?

yes	no
F, A, MF, SA, SP, RA, S, W, C, R, AS, MR	I, E, ID, ED

Notes:

The vast majority of question types will require that you look for an argument. Inference, Give an Example, and ID the Disagreement questions may have points and arguments within the stimulus, but in those situations your understanding of the argument will not necessarily be related to or important to your primary tasks.

Should I be critical of the reasoning?

yes	no
F, A, MF, SA, SP, RA, S, W	C, R, AS, MR, I, E, ID, ED

When you are meant to be critical, your critical evaluation of the stimulus will always be important to answering the question. When you are not asked to be critical, being so can often be a detriment, for these questions are often designed to test your ability to stay objective.

Should I always expect to predict the answer?

yes	no
F, A, C, R, AS, ID	MF, SA, SP, RA, S, W, MR, I, E, ED

The questions listed under "yes" are all ones that ask directly about something in the stimulus—something you should be able to figure out without needing the answers. The ones under "no" all require you to think about the relationship between answer and stimulus—that is, you need to think about whether a particular answer strengthens an argument or a certain assumption is required. For all of the questions on the right, there will generally be many, many potential right answers. For the ones on the left, there will be only one, though it may be worded differently than you might expect.

Should I apply the answers to the stimulus, or vice versa?

answers to stimulus	both	stimulus to answers
F, A, MF, SA, SP, RA, S, W, C, R, AS, ID, ED	MF, MR	I, E

For most questions, we apply the answers to the stimulus—for example, we find an answer that weakens the stimulus or a principle to prop up the stimulus. For a few questions, we have to change gears and think about what the stimulus tells us about the answer choices—which answer choice is true based on the stimulus, or what is an example representative of the stimulus. You should expect to spend a bit more time on the two types of questions (MF, MR) that require careful analysis of arguments in both the stimulus and the answer choices.

34 LOGICAL REASONING strategy review

Back to basics.

Find the Flaw. Find the Assumption. Match the Flaw. Sufficient Assumption. Supporting Principle. Required Assumption. Strengthen. Weaken. Identify the Conclusion. Identify the Role. Identify the Argument Structure. Match the Reasoning. Inference. Give an Example. Identify the Disagreement. Explain a Discrepancy.

We've done it. We've taken a detailed look at every nook and cranny that the Logical Reasoning section presents, and we've discussed every nuance of strategy and thought process that could possibly be of relevance on test day. If you feel a bit of information overload at this point, take it as a sign of how much we've learned.[1]

In these final stages, we're going to focus on bringing together everything we've worked on, with the goal of getting you ready to present all of your skills at their sharpest and most optimal point on test day.

Starting in the first lesson, I presented the LSAT as a test of three fundamental issues: *your reading ability, your reasoning ability,* and *your mental discipline.* These are extremely general terms, so it's understandable and expected that you began with a broad and general sense of what to expect from the exam. If I've done a decent job as an instructor, my hope is that throughout your studies, these terms have taken on more and more specific meaning, and I hope that by this point, you are able to see, in a clear fashion, how every single challenge presented on the LSAT can be defined in terms of those three issues.

In Lesson 5, when we really started to dig deep into Logical Reasoning, I prioritized one skill as the key skill necessary for mastering the section—your ability to recognize what is wrong with the relationship between a point being made and the support for that point. My hope is that you see very clearly why this ability to find flaws is central to how you solve a majority of questions, and I hope it's clear how the micro-skills necessary for finding fault—those having to do with an ability to recognize reasoning structure—are also, commonly, the keys to your success for the minority of questions that do not require you to figure out what is wrong with arguments.

Let's take a bit of time to organize all that we have learned about specific types of questions in terms of the three fundamental issues: your ability to read, reason, and retain mental discipline.

1. Here's another way to think about how far we've come: can you imagine what would have happened if you'd gone into the test without learning all of this stuff?

Logical Reasoning Tests Your Ability to Read

No one-day, hundred-question, multiple-choice standardized exam can do an adequate job of accurately gauging something as complex and difficult (if not impossible) to define as general reading ability—for our ability to read, write, and use words goes to the core of how we think. Yet the LSAT by its nature needs to be *standardized*—that is, it is an exam that must be built upon absolute principles of right and wrong, "correct" reading and "incorrect" reading.

The way in which the test writers standardize it is by limiting what they test to a very, very narrow range of specific and clearly definable reading skills: your ability to read for reasoning structure and understand the exact meaning of certain words that are important for defining reasoning relationships.

Understanding reasoning structure is essential for success on all Logical Reasoning questions. The reasoning relationship most important, of course, is that between a point that is made and the support for that point. Find the Flaw, Find the Assumption, Match the Flaw, Sufficient Assumption, Supporting Principle, Required Assumption, Strengthen, Weaken, Identify the Conclusion, Identify the Role, Identify the Argument Structure, and Match the Reasoning are all questions that require you to see this relationship clearly. Inference, Give an Example, Identify the Disagreement, and Explain a Discrepancy also require an understanding of reasoning structure, but for these questions it is more important that you are able to see which statements link together, and which do not.

Understanding the meaning of words is, of course, also essential for good reading, and will be in any context. LSAT questions are often about abstract or unique subjects, and they often discuss things or use words that are unfamiliar to us. It's essential to understand that they are not testing our understanding of these strange words. The words they care about are the words that are fundamental to reasoning structure—the words, like *some, since, but,* and *require*, that appear in every question and define the narrow range of logical issues that underlie the exam. Your understanding of these words is essential to your understanding of the stimulus, and it's also critical to your ability to relate answer choices to that stimulus.

Logical Reasoning Tests Your Ability to Reason

The ability to recognize reasoning structure, and the ability to reason, are two very different skills. The first is an objective skill—the author has intended something in the text, and your job is to understand correctly what that intention was. The second is a subjective skill—your job is to give your personal opinion as to whether the points made by that author do in fact align in the manner in which he says they do.

Because reasoning ability is once again for the test writers an impossibly difficult issue to define, let alone evaluate, they are forced to limit what they test to a very narrow scope. By and large, they limit the testing arena to one specific issue—the faulty relationship between a point that is made and the support for that point. Find the Flaw, Find the Assumption, Match the Flaw, Sufficient Assumption, Supporting Principle, Required Assumption, Strengthen, and Weaken all test this specific ability.

Logical Reasoning Tests Your Mental Discipline

Lastly, Logical Reasoning questions and the Logical Reasoning section as a whole are designed to test your mental discipline—which we can loosely define as your ability to control your thought process and align it with the specific task at hand.

The test writers do this by juxtaposing questions that alternatively reward or punish certain actions on your part. We just discussed questions that require and reward your reasoning abilities—on the flip side of that, there are questions that specifically test your ability to turn off those reasoning abilities, that reward your ability to not judge. Many wrong answers to questions such as Identify the Conclusion and Inference are designed specifically to match up with and tempt those who cannot show the discipline to know when to not inject personal judgment.

On a more subtle level, they do this by using questions that are very closely related to one another but not exactly alike. Certain wrong answers to Required Assumption questions are designed to be tempting because they seem sufficient to fix the argument's issue; certain wrong answers to Sufficient Assumption questions are designed to be tempting because they seem to include information the argument requires.

General Strategies for All Questions

With these three central issues in mind, let's bring together all of the question-specific strategies we've discussed.

Step one: understand your task

The first step is to read the question stem and use it as a trigger for how you will be thinking about the question. The plans and expectations considered in those first few seconds are absolutely critical to consistent and efficient success.

The question stem will help you define your task at various parts of your process, but initially what's most important to get out of that question stem is a sense of how you should approach the reading of the stimulus.

There are two primary decisions to be made. The first is "Do I read for an argument (yes, the vast majority of the time), or do I read for something else (such as a general understanding or a clear sense of a discrepancy)?" For the majority of instances in which your job is to recognize the argument, the second decision is "Is my job to critically evaluate and find fault with the reasoning in the argument (yes, most of the time), or is my job to understand but not evaluate?"

There are also expectations to be set. If it is a question that requires you to critically evaluate an argument, you should expect to go through a certain thought pattern (identifying the conclusion *then* the support) to arrive at a particular point (figuring out why the support does not justify the point). For these types of questions, you should expect to have a clear sense of the flaw in the argument before going into the answer choices. On the flip side, if you don't have a clear sense of the flaw, you should expect that it will be more difficult for you to evaluate answers and that you will likely have to "grind it out" if you are to get to a right answer. Other question types come with their own expectations of what you need to extract from your read: Match the Reasoning questions, for example, require a clear understanding of reasoning structure, and Explain a Discrepancy questions require a clear understanding of the discrepancy to be explained.

There are also expectations to be set about your experience with the answer choices. For some questions, such as Find the Flaw, you should have a very strong sense of the right answer before going into the answers. For others, such as Inference, you should expect to have very little sense of what will be in the right answer before going into the answer choices. Most other types of questions will fall somewhere in between those two extremes. A Give an Example question, for example, will allow you to have some expectations because you know exactly what type of example you are looking for, but there will be aspects of the answer choice—such as the subject matter—that you will not be able to predict.

To sum up, use the question stem to define your task and to set your expectations. You will come back to it throughout the question to refocus yourself at various points, but at first, use it to determine how you should attack and what you should get out of the stimulus.

Step two: evaluate the stimulus

With a clear sense of your job, the next step is to evaluate the stimulus. Even before you read the first word, you should have a very clear sense of the goals you want to accomplish: I want to find the main point, I need to eventually figure out the flaw, etc. These goals will coincide for certain questions—what you need to get out of the stimulus for a Required Assumption question and a Weaken question, for example, are virtually identical, but will be very different for others (what you need to get out of the stimulus for Match the Reasoning, Sufficient Assumption, and Inference are very different).

The most significant distinction comes between those questions that require objectivity and those that require subjectivity. For those that require you to critically evaluate arguments, you need to do everything you can to understand the problems in reasoning before you go into the answers. Keep in mind that all flaws can be thought of as fitting into three main categories—the author mistakes a piece for the puzzle, mistakes apples for oranges, or adds 1 + 1 and gets 3. When you feel lost or uncertain, use these three basic guides to center yourself and understand the argument as simply as you can.

Step three: eliminate wrong choices

For all Logical Reasoning questions, I strongly suggest that you focus on eliminating wrong answers before selecting the correct one. For certain questions, such as Find the Flaw, you will be less dependent on the elimination process because you will have a much stronger sense of what the right answer will be. For others, you will be more dependent on the elimination process because the right answer can be somewhat subjective and can often be in many ways unpredictable. Regardless, it is to your benefit to focus on this step in this process, and this is especially true for those seeking top scores. To have one final discussion of why, let's return one more time to thinking from the perspective of the test writers. These test writers have a specific burden that is relevant to this particular discussion: they need to create questions that have a definite correct answer. Even if they, say, create a question that asks which of five answers "most strengthens" a point that is made, they cannot actually have two answers that strengthen, one just a bit more than the other, because determining which of those two answers strengthens more would be a subjective exercise—that is, one based on debatable opinion, and they can't have that. They must have one right answer and four wrong answers.

How can they accomplish this? They can do so by having a definite right answer. However, the majority of Logical Reasoning questions are too complex to have a definite right answer. So, the only way for the test writers to create a clear distinction is to have four definitely wrong answers. This is why, once you've become skilled at recognizing answer characteristics, it's generally clearer to see why answers are wrong than it is to see why answers are right. This is especially true for the hardest questions.

Answers are wrong for at least one of three main reasons: they discuss subjects or actions or ideas that are different from those discussed in the text, they misrepresent that information in the text, or they don't fulfill the specific task the question stem requires—they represent weaknesses in the reading skills, reasoning skills, and skills of mental discipline that the section is designed to test. Every single wrong answer in Logical Reasoning can be defined in those terms, and hopefully by this point these issues define the way you naturally think about, and attack, wrong answer choices. If you are at a level of mastery with this skill, you should be able to consistently eliminate three or four answers before you have to really dig in deep for the careful comparisons. This is a hugely valuable skill for making questions easier and getting higher scores. If you don't yet feel this level of aptitude, but still feel you have a significant amount of studying left to do, definitely make sure to make elimination skills a top priority in your training.

Step four: confirm the right answer

Once you are down to a few, or (hopefully) one attractive answer, it is finally time to see if it truly is the one. Students new to the LSAT commonly rush to this step, or incorrectly see it as a cause, rather than a consequence, of their troubles. Students experienced at the LSAT recognize that selecting the right answer is the last step in a multi-step process, and it's always true that the better you perform steps one through three, the easier step four will be.

Do not select the right answer by thinking about it in a vacuum, and do not select the best of two answers by comparing them against one another.[2] What makes an answer correct is how it relates to the stimulus, so the best way to confirm that an answer is correct is by checking it against that stimulus. Make sure the answer does not reach beyond the text, and make sure the answer does not disagree with the text. If it passes on those two points, and if it fulfills the task presented in the question stem, it will be the correct answer.

2. Note that a comparison of answer choices can be useful for recognizing what you should be looking out for when you compare the answer choices to the text in the stimulus.

The Factors That Determine Test-Day Performance

People have good days and bad, some people perform better under pressure and others worse, and so on, but there are two main characteristics that differentiate top scorers from average scorers from below-average scorers: skills and habits. Your skills and your habits will determine how well you perform on test day.

Remember, we defined a skill, at least in terms of how it relates to the LSAT, as the ability to apply understanding and strategies to the solving of problems. The requirements for skill are correct understanding, effective approaches, and experience at applying that understanding and those approaches.

Your habits are defined by the way in which you utilize your skill set. In real life, we all know people who make the most of limited talents and people who make little of significant talents—the same applies to the LSAT, and the habits you've developed will, in large part, determine whether you test up to your potential.

Habits are like muscles—the key to getting them is putting in the work. You can't get good habits by wanting them or knowing about them. You have to get them by practicing them. In addition, good habits always require a healthy amount of self-reflection—you need to be able and willing to think carefully and honestly *about how you think*. Figure out what it is you think about during a question that ends up being useful, and more importantly, figure out what you think about during a question that ends up being not useful, or not relevant to getting the correct answer. Wanting to get every question right is like wanting to make every basket during a game—it's a nice thought to have, but it's not particularly noble or useful. What is far more important and effective is knowing that you did everything you could to put yourself in the best position to succeed on each question, and the development of sound habits, habits that always push you toward the right answers, is the key representation of this commitment.

Starting on the next page is a set of fifteen questions—they are all questions you have seen before in the question-specific lessons. Use this set to reflect carefully on your skills and habits. Worry less about right and wrong (since you've seen and reviewed these before, right and wrong is not going to be so reflective of your abilities anyway), and rather focus on the process you use to solve the questions. Work, as dancers and other performers do, to have *perfect form*—that is, work to solve questions as directly, efficiently, and correctly as possible. Following the question set are assessment tools meant to help you reflect on your process. You can look at them after each problem, or after the set of problems, but do make sure to look at them while your solution process is still fresh in your mind. Take note of the steps where you went sideways, or steps you found to be particularly difficult, and look for patterns. Finally, use these questions to think about the similar but different tasks that the different types of questions present, and to gauge how specific your skills and habits have become, relative to those tasks. Worry less about timing for this drill, but, as always, do try to solve questions at a real-time pace.

Process Practice

Problem Redo

30.2.6. The student body at this university takes courses in a wide range of disciplines. Miriam is a student at this university, so she takes courses in a wide range of disciplines.

Which one of the following arguments exhibits flawed reasoning most similar to that exhibited by the argument above?

(A) The students at this school take mathematics. Miguel is a student at this school, so he takes mathematics.
(B) The editorial board of this law journal has written on many legal issues. Louise is on the editorial board, so she has written on many legal issues.
(C) The component parts of bulldozers are heavy. This machine is a bulldozer, so it is heavy.
(D) All older automobiles need frequent oil changes. This car is new, so its oil need not be changed as frequently.
(E) The individual cells of the brain are incapable of thinking. Therefore, the brain as a whole is incapable of thinking.

29.1.12. It is well known that many species adapt to their environment, but it is usually assumed that only the most highly evolved species alter their environment in ways that aid their own survival. However, this characteristic is actually quite common. Certain species of plankton, for example, generate a gas that is converted in the atmosphere into particles of sulfate. These particles cause water vapor to condense, thus forming clouds. Indeed, the formation of clouds over the ocean largely depends on the presence of these particles. More cloud cover means more sunlight is reflected, and so the Earth absorbs less heat. Thus plankton cause the surface of the Earth to be cooler and this benefits the plankton.

Which one of the following accurately describes the argumentative strategy employed?

(A) A general principle is used to justify a claim made about a particular case to which that principle has been shown to apply.
(B) An explanation of how a controversial phenomenon could have come about is given in order to support the claim that this phenomenon did in fact come about.
(C) A generalization about the conditions under which a certain process can occur is advanced on the basis of an examination of certain cases in which that process did occur.
(D) A counterexample to a position being challenged is presented in order to show that this position is incorrect.
(E) A detailed example is used to illustrate the advantage of one strategy over another.

28.1.5. The number of codfish in the North Atlantic has declined substantially as the population of harp seals has increased from two million to more than three million. Some blame the seal for the shrinking cod population, but cod plays a negligible role in the seal's diet. It is therefore unlikely that the increase in the seal population has contributed significantly to the decline in the cod population.

Which one of the following, if true, most seriously weakens the argument?

(A) People who fish for cod commercially are inconvenienced by the presence of large numbers of seals near traditional fishing grounds.
(B) Water pollution poses a more serious threat to cod than to the harp seal.
(C) The harp seal thrives in water that is too cold to support a dense population of cod.
(D) Cod feed almost exclusively on capelin, a fish that is a staple of the harp seal's diet.
(E) The cod population in the North Atlantic began to decline before the harp-seal population began to increase.

28.1.10. It is a principle of economics that a nation can experience economic growth only when consumer confidence is balanced with a small amount of consumer skepticism.

Which one of the following is an application of the economic principle above?

(A) Any nation in which consumer confidence is balanced with a small amount of consumer skepticism will experience economic growth.
(B) Any nation in which the prevailing attitude of consumers is not skepticism will experience economic growth.
(C) Any nation in which the prevailing attitude of consumers is either exclusively confidence or exclusively skepticism will experience economic growth.
(D) Any nation in which the prevailing attitude of consumers is exclusively confidence will not experience economic growth.
(E) Any nation in which consumer skepticism is balanced with a small amount of consumer confidence will experience economic growth.

28.3.19. On a certain day, nine scheduled flights on Swift Airlines were canceled. Ordinarily, a cancellation is due to mechanical problems with the airplane scheduled for a certain flight. However, since it is unlikely that Swift would have mechanical problems with more than one or two airplanes on a single day, some of the nine cancellations were probably due to something else.

The argument depends on which one of the following assumptions?

(A) More than one or two airplanes were scheduled for the nine canceled flights.
(B) Swift Airlines has fewer mechanical problems than do other airlines of the same size.
(C) Each of the canceled flights would have been longer than the average flight on Swift Airlines.
(D) Swift Airlines had never before canceled more than one or two scheduled flights on a single day.
(E) All of the airplanes scheduled for the canceled flights are based at the same airport.

30.4.2. The current theory about earthquakes holds that they are caused by adjoining plates of rock sliding past each other; the plates are pressed together until powerful forces overcome the resistance. As plausible as this may sound, at least one thing remains mysterious on this theory. The overcoming of such resistance should create enormous amounts of heat. But so far no increases in temperature unrelated to weather have been detected following earthquakes.

Which one of the following most accurately expresses the main point of the argument?

(A) No increases in temperature have been detected following earthquakes.
(B) The current theory does not fully explain earthquake data.
(C) No one will ever be sure what the true cause of earthquakes is.
(D) Earthquakes produce enormous amounts of heat that have so far gone undetected.
(E) Contrary to the current theory, earthquakes are not caused by adjoining plates of rock sliding past one another.

31.3.2. One way kidney stones can form is when urine produced in the kidneys is overly concentrated with calcium or oxalate. Reducing dietary calcium has been thought, therefore, to decrease the likelihood that calcium will concentrate and form additional stones. Oddly enough, for many people the chances of recurrence are decreased by increasing calcium intake.

Which one of the following, if true, most helps to resolve the apparent discrepancy described above?

(A) Laboratory studies on animals with kidney stones reveal that they rarely get additional stones once calcium supplements are added to the diet.
(B) Increasing dietary oxalate while reducing dietary calcium does not reduce the chances of kidney stone recurrence.
(C) Kidney stone development is sometimes the result of an inherited disorder that can result in excessive production of calcium and oxalate.
(D) Increasing calcium intake increases the amount of calcium eliminated through the intestines, which decreases the amount to be filtered by the kidneys.
(E) Some kidney stones are composed of uric acid rather than a combination of calcium and oxalate.

28.1.15. The town of Springhill frequently must declare a water emergency, making it temporarily unlawful to use water for such nonessential purposes as car washing. These emergencies could be avoided if Springhill would introduce permanent economic incentives for water conservation. Actually, Springhill discourages conservation because each household pays a modest monthly flat fee for any amount of water below a certain usage threshold, and a substantial per-liter rate only after the threshold is reached.

Which one the following, if true, most strengthens the argument?

(A) The Springhill authorities do a poor job of enforcing its water emergency laws and many people break the laws without incurring a penalty.
(B) The town council of Springhill recently refused to raise the threshold.
(C) The threshold is kept at a high enough level to exceed the water requirements of most households in Springhill.
(D) The threshold is not as high in Springhill as it is in neighboring towns.
(E) The threshold remains at the predetermined level specified by law until a change is approved by the Springhill town council.

29.4.18. All actions are motivated by self-interest, since any action that is apparently altruistic can be described in terms of self-interest. For example, helping someone can be described in terms of self-interest: the motivation is hope for a reward or other personal benefit to be bestowed as a result of the helping action.

Which one of the following most accurately describes an error in the argument's reasoning?

(A) The term "self-interest" is allowed to shift in meaning over the course of the argument.
(B) The argument takes evidence showing merely that its conclusion could be true to constitute evidence showing that the conclusion is in fact true.
(C) The argument does not explain what is meant by "reward" and "personal benefit."
(D) The argument ignores the possibility that what is taken to be necessary for a certain interest to be a motivation actually suffices to show that that interest is a motivation.
(E) The argument depends for its appeal only on the emotional content of the example cited.

29.1.19. Arbitrator: The shipping manager admits that he decided to close the old facility on October 14 and to schedule the new facility's opening for October 17, the following Monday. But he also claims that he is not responsible for the business that was lost due to the new facility's failing to open as scheduled. He blames the contractor for not finishing on time, but he too, is to blame, for he was aware of the contractor's typical delays and should have planned for this contingency.

Which one of the following principles underlies the arbitrator's argument?

(A) A manager should take foreseeable problems into account when making decisions.
(B) A manager should be able to depend on contractors to do their jobs promptly.
(C) A manager should see to it that contractors do their jobs promptly.
(D) A manager should be held responsible for mistakes made by those whom the manager directly supervises.
(E) A manager, and only a manager, should be held responsible for a project's failure.

31.3.10. It is wrong to waste our natural resources, and it is an incredible waste of resources to burn huge amounts of trash in incinerators. When trash is recycled, fewer resources are wasted. Because less trash will be recycled if an incinerator is built, the city should not build an incinerator.

Which one of the following can be properly inferred from the statements above?

(A) All of the city's trash that is not recycled goes into incinerators.
(B) By recycling more trash, the city can stop wasting resources entirely.
(C) The most effective way to conserve resources is to recycle trash.
(D) If the city is to avoid wasting resources, huge amounts of trash cannot be burned in any city incinerator.
(E) If the city does not burn trash, it will not waste resources.

30.2.10. Goswami: I support the striking workers at Ergon Foods. They are underpaid. The majority of them make less than $20,000 per year.

Nordecki: If pay is the issue, I must disagree. The average annual salary of the striking workers at Ergon Foods is over $29,000.

Goswami and Nordecki disagree over the truth of which one of the following statements?

(A) The average annual salary at Ergon Foods is over $29,000.
(B) Pay is the primary issue over which the workers are striking at Ergon Foods.
(C) It is reasonable to support striking workers who are underpaid.
(D) The striking workers at Ergon Foods are under paid.
(E) It was unreasonable for the workers at Ergon Foods to go on strike.

30.4.13. Joseph: My encyclopedia says that the mathematician Pierre de Fermat died in 1665 without leaving behind any written proof for a theorem that he claimed nonetheless to have proved. Probably this alleged theorem simply cannot be proved, since—as the article points out—no one else has been able to prove it. Therefore it is likely that Fermat was either lying or else mistaken when he made his claim.

Laura: Your encyclopedia is out of date. Recently someone has in fact proved Fermat's theorem. And since the theorem is provable, your claim—that Fermat was lying or mistaken—clearly is wrong.

13. Joseph's statement that "this alleged theorem simply cannot be proved" plays which one of the following roles in his argument?

(A) an assumption for which no support is offered
(B) a subsidiary conclusion on which his argument's main conclusion is based
(C) a potential objection that his argument anticipates and attempts to answer before it is raised
(D) the principal claim that his argument is structured to refute
(E) background information that neither supports nor undermines his argument's conclusion

29.1.20. The price of a full-fare coach ticket from Toronto to Dallas on Breezeway Airlines is the same today as it was a year ago, if inflation is taken into account by calculating prices in constant dollars. However, today 90 percent of the Toronto-to-Dallas coach tickets that Breezeway sells are discount tickets and only 10 percent are full-fare tickets, whereas a year ago half were discount tickets and half were full-fare tickets. Therefore, on average, people pay less today in constant dollars for a Breezeway Toronto-to-Dallas coach ticket than they did a year ago.

Which one of the following, if assumed, would allow the conclusion above to be properly drawn?

(A) A Toronto-to-Dallas full-fare coach ticket on Breezeway Airlines provides ticket-holders with a lower level of service today than such a ticket provided a year ago.
(B) A Toronto-to-Dallas discount coach ticket on Breezeway Airlines costs about the same amount in constant dollars today as it did a year ago.
(C) All full-fare coach tickets on Breezeway Airlines cost the same in constant dollars as they did a year ago.
(D) The average number of coach passengers per flight that Breezeway Airlines carries from Toronto to Dallas today is higher than the average number per flight a year ago.
(E) The criteria that Breezeway Airlines uses for permitting passengers to buy discount coach tickets on the Toronto-to-Dallas route are different today than they were a year ago.

31.2.23. Town councillor: The only reason for the town to have ordinances restricting where skateboarding can be done would be to protect children from danger. Skateboarding in the town's River Park is undoubtedly dangerous, but we should not pass an ordinance prohibiting it. If children cannot skateboard in the park, they will most certainly skateboard in the streets. And skateboarding in the streets is more dangerous than skateboarding in the park.

The pattern of reasoning in which one of the following is most similar to that in the town councillor's argument?

(A) The reason for requiring environmental reviews is to ensure that projected developments do not harm the natural environment. Currently, environmental concerns are less compelling than economic concerns, but in the long run, the environment must be protected. Therefore, the requirement for environmental reviews should not be waived.
(B) Insecticides are designed to protect crops against insect damage. Aphids damage tomato crops, but using insecticides against aphids kills wasps that prey on insecticide-resistant pests. Since aphids damage tomato crops less than the insecticide-resistant pests do, insecticides should not be used against aphids on tomato crops.
(C) The purpose of compulsory vaccination for schoolchildren was to protect both the children themselves and others in the community against smallpox. Smallpox was indeed a dreadful disease, but it has now been eliminated from the world's population. So children should not be vaccinated against it.
(D) The function of a sealer on wood siding is to retard deterioration caused by weather. However, cedar is a wood that is naturally resistant to weather-related damage and thus does not need additional protection. Sealers, therefore, should not be applied to cedar siding.
(E) Traffic patterns that involve one-way streets are meant to accelerate the flow of traffic in otherwise congested areas. However, it would be detrimental to the South Main Street area to have traffic move faster. So traffic patterns involving one-way streets should not be implemented there.

Self-Assessment Tools

key priorities and rhetorical questions

Priorities: *(C) = conclusion, (S) = support, (F) = flaw* (C): M takes courses in wide range (S): Student body takes courses in wide range (F): What's true about entire student body may not be right for M	**30.2.6 (B)** **Questions:** Did you understand the conclusion correctly? Did you understand the support? Did you clearly see what was wrong with the reasoning? Did you eliminate (C), (D), and (E) easily? Did you see why (A) is not correct? Did you see why (B) is correct?
Priorities: (C): Adapting environment for benefit common (S): Plankton example Strategy: specific example given to justify point	**29.1.12 (D)** **Questions:** Did you identify the correct conclusion? Did you see the general relationship between support and conclusion? Do you see why (A) is tempting if you identify the wrong conclusion? Were you able to get rid of (B) and (E) easily? Do you see what's wrong with (C)? Do you see why (D) is correct?
Priorities: (C): Seals aren't causing cod decline (S): Seals don't eat a lot of cod (F): Maybe seals impact cod population in another way	**28.1.5 (D)** **Questions:** Did you understand the conclusion correctly? Did you understand the support? Did you clearly see what was wrong with the reasoning? Did you eliminate (A), (B), (C), and (E) easily? If not, did you get mixed up about your task during the question (most wrong answers seem to strengthen the argument)? Was it easy for you to see that (D) was correct?
Priorities: Principle: Nation can experience economic growth only when confidence balanced with bit of skepticism Notice: Stimulus about possibilities—something needed if growth is to happen. Answers are all absolutes. What is the absolute aspect of the principle? If a nation doesn't have confidence balanced with skepticism, it won't experience growth	**28.1.10 (D)** **Questions:** Did you understand the principle correctly? Did you get rid of (A), (B), (C), and (E) easily? Did you see how your understanding of the principle could be adapted to the nature of the answer choices? Did you easily see why (D) is correct?

Full solutions on the following pages: 252, 445, 279, 474.

Priorities:	**28.3.19 (A)**
(C): Unlikely cancellations due to something other than mechanical problems (S): 9 cancellations, unlikely mechanical problems with more than 1 or 2 planes (F): Planes fly multiple times a day—maybe all the cancellations were due to those planes	**Questions:** Did you understand the conclusion correctly? Did you understand the support? Did you clearly see what was wrong with the reasoning? Did you eliminate (B), (C), and (D) easily? If you were tempted by (E), did you see that it is not required for the argument to work? Do you see why (A) needs to be true for the argument to work? Can you negate (A) to see that it is necessary?

Priorities:	**31.3.2 (D)**
Discrepancy: why does increase in calcium lead to decrease in recurrence of kidney stones?	**Questions:** Did you focus in on the right discrepancy? Did you get rid of (A), (B), (C), and (E) because they don't explain the discrepancy? Do you see why (D) does?

Priorities:	**30.4.2 (B)**
(C): At least one thing about current theory remains unexplained/unproved	**Questions:** Did you identify the correct conclusion? Did you move on to the answers without thinking about unnecessary issues? Were you able to get rid of (A), (C), (D), and (E) easily? Do you see why (B) is correct?

Priorities:	**28.1.15 (C)**
(C): S discourages water conservation (S): Each house pays modest flat fee to a threshold and only pays substantial per-use fee above threshold (F): Assumes threshold is high enough so that most people don't go over it into the expensive cost zone	**Questions:** Did you understand the conclusion correctly? Did you understand the support? Did you clearly see what was wrong with the reasoning? Did you see that (A) doesn't relate to support/conclusion relationship? Did you see that (B), (D), and (E) don't directly impact conclusion? Do you see why (C) is correct?

Full solutions on the following pages: 274, 486, 444, 279.

Priorities:
(C): All actions are motivated by self-interest
(S): Any action that seems altruistic can be described in terms of self-interest
(F): Just because actions *can be described* in terms of self-interest doesn't mean all actions *are* motivated by self-interest

29.4.18 (B)

Questions:
Did you understand the conclusion correctly?
Did you understand the support?
Did you clearly see what was wrong with the reasoning?
Did you eliminate (A), (C), and (E) easily?
If (D) initially challenged you, do you see that no necessary/sufficient issues are important here?
Did you see why (B) is correct?

Priorities:
Initial read: stimulus is argument about wasting natural resources, incinerators, and recycling
(A) cannot be proved
(B) doesn't match text/cannot be proved
(C) cannot be proved
(E) doesn't match text/cannot be proved

31.3.10 (D)

Questions:
Did you understand the information in the stimulus correctly?
Did you focus the bulk of your energy on evaluating the answer choices?
Did you clearly understand why (A), (B), (C), and (E) cannot be proved?
Did you see that (D) was attractive enough to investigate carefully?
Did you see the proof for (D) in the first sentence of the stimulus?

Priorities:
(C): Manager is also to blame
(S): Aware of contractor's typical delays and should have planned for this contingency
Principle: since manager was aware and should have prepared, he is also to blame

29.1.19 (A)

Questions:
Did you understand the conclusion correctly?
Did you understand the support?
Did you clearly see the relationship between support and conclusion?
Do you see how (B), (C), and (D) don't relate to support/conclusion relationship?
Do you see that (E) misrepresents the conclusion?
Do you see why (A) is correct?

Priorities:
Find overlap/disagreement: pay

30.2.10 (D)

Questions:
Did you see the correct overlap/disagreement?
Did you eliminate (A), (B), (C), and (E) with confidence?
Do you see why (D) is correct?

Full solutions on the following pages: 244, 470, 265, 481.

Priorities:
(C): Likely Fermat either lying or mistaken when he said he proved certain theorem
(S): Probably alleged theorem can't be proved
Role: used to support the conclusion

30.4.13 (B)

Questions:
Did you understand the conclusion correctly?
Did you understand the support?
Did you clearly see the role correctly?
Were you able to get rid of (A), (C), (D), and (E) easily?
Did you see how (B) was correct and represents a more specific version of the role noted in the priorities?

Priorities:
(C): On average, people pay less today for tickets than they did a year ago
(S): 90% of sales now are discounted/only 50% discounted a year ago/full fare has remained constant
(F): Doesn't factor in the amount of discount for tickets that are discounted

29.1.20 (B)

Questions:
Did you identify the correct conclusion?
Did you understand the support?
Did you clearly see what was wrong with the reasoning?
Did you know you need an answer that makes the conclusion completely valid?
Were you able to get rid of (A), (C), and (E) easily?
If tempted by (D), could you reason through why it wasn't relevant?
Do you see how if (B) is true the argument would be valid?

Priorities:
(C): Shouldn't prevent skateboarding at River park
(S): Only reason to prevent is to protect children from danger, and if they can't skate there, the children will skate somewhere else
Pattern of reasoning: should pick less-than-ideal solution because it is better than alternative

31.2.23 (B)

Questions:
Did you understand the conclusion correctly?
Did you understand the support?
Did you see clearly the relationship between support and conclusion?
Did you see that (A) compares one issue with another, and eliminate it?
Did you see that (C) has a different reasoning structure and eliminate it?
Did you see that (D) has a different reasoning structure and eliminate it?
Did you see that (E) has a different reasoning structure and eliminate it?
Do you see how (B) offers up one option as less bad than another?

Notes:

Full solutions on the following pages: 445, 266, 449.

35 READING COMPREHENSION question strategies

In the first batch of Reading Comprehension lessons, we focused on the underlying design of LSAT passages and the reading habits that best aligned with that design. In this batch of lessons, we'll close the loop by discussing how to align effective reading habits with an effective problem-solving process.

A master locksmith needs to know about two things really, really well in order to be good at his job: keys and locks. His success consistently depends on his ability to bring these two things together. A Reading Comprehension master needs to know two things really, really well: the reasoning structure of passages, and the tasks that specific questions present. On test day, your success will be a consequence of how well you bring these two skills together.

Answers are correct when they are consistent with the text and match the task that questions present. Wrong answers are wrong because they either misrepresent the given text or don't match the given task

Answers are correct when they are consistent with the text and match the task that questions present. Wrong answers are wrong because they either misrepresent the given text or don't match the given task. Text and task are the two fundamental priorities of Reading Comprehension. Having a clear sense of both makes it far easier to anticipate and confirm right answers. And perhaps even more importantly, having a clear sense of both makes it far easier to anticipate and eliminate wrong answers.

Hopefully, you feel that it's getting easier and easier for you to recognize and prioritize reasoning structure as you read a passage. In this batch of lessons, we will continue working on our reading skills, but we will also work on developing a simple, clear, and intuitive understanding of the specific tasks that the various questions present, and we'll work on developing problem-solving habits that best align with those tasks.

Most of this lesson is devoted to specific instructions for each type of question that appears in the Reading Comprehension section. You'll see that there is great overlap among the question types, but I think an easy way to think about them, as a whole, is that they represent different possible combinations of just a few characteristics.

Imagine a wardrobe of just five shirts and four pairs of pants. How many different shirt-pants "outfits" could you put together? Twenty—almost enough for a full month of work days. Reading Comprehension questions work in a similar way—there are maybe about fifteen or so question types that we will discuss, but when you think about them as a whole you see that they are all just different combinations of a few characteristics.

As you read through the question descriptions to come, and as you focus on refining your problem-solving process in the Reading Comprehension work to come, there are two simple questions you can ask yourself in order to understand the task that a specific test question presents: what is the genre of the question, and what is the scope? Let's discuss genre and scope in further detail.

One: What Is the Genre of the Question?

All questions are designed to test your understanding of three primary issues: the reasoning structure of the passage, the opinions presented in the passage, or the information presented in the passage. We will discuss these three issues as the "genres" of questions. All question stems can be defined in these terms, and if you know what to read for, the question stem will always tell you exactly what the genre is.

The question stem will specifically ask about the structure of the passage or the purpose of a component of a passage (reasoning structure); or it will make direct mention that it is about an opinion, either the author's or someone else's; or it will state directly that it is testing your ability to correctly identify a specific piece of information in the text and correctly understand it ("according to the text" is an example of a common marker of this). When you first read a question and you think about what type it is, and what type of task it is presenting to you, the "genre" of the question should be your primary consideration.

The most common questions are those that ask you directly about your understanding of the reasoning structure of the passage. These questions test whether you can identify the main points, describe the organization of the passage, or recognize the roles that certain parts of the passage—whether they be individual phrases or entire paragraphs—play. These questions are most directly tied to the type of reading experience we've encouraged in this book. Typically, if you understand the overall structure of the passage well, these will be some of the easiest questions you'll face. If you have a lot of difficulty understanding or recognizing the overall structure of the passage, these can feel like the most difficult questions.

Questions that ask about opinions are very much related to questions that ask about structure. This relationship is natural and unavoidable, for often the opinion that an author has, or the opinions that an author presents, drives the purpose of the passage, and for any good writer (and most passages you will read on the LSAT are written by good writers), purpose drives structure—that is, the design of the passages is intended to serve its purpose.

The most common opinion questions are those that relate to the author's opinion. The reading strategies we've practiced thus far are an ideal match for the design of these questions. For certain passages, the author's opinions are obvious, and for others they're far more subtle. Regardless, when it comes time to answer questions, a correct understanding of author opinion will be absolutely necessary.

Questions that ask about other opinions mentioned in the passage (that is, any opinion other than that of the author) are also common. These opinions are often those of "critics" or "supporters" and are typically directly related to the main points of the passage. When we get the rare Reading Comprehension question that requires us to use our critical reasoning skills—questions that ask us to think about what might strengthen or weaken a point that is being made—these questions are typically linked to the non-author opinions presented in the passage.

The last class of questions is designed to test your ability to understand the information presented in the text. For some of these questions, you will be asked to identify information in the text and find the answer that best matches that information. For others of these questions, you will be asked to identify information in the text and make an inference off of that information.

Even these "detail" questions are designed to reward those who have a strong understanding of overall reasoning structure. Often, the key challenge of some of these questions is identifying the relevant information—the clues to help you do this will always be based on reasoning structure. Furthermore, an understanding of the main points of the passage will make obvious certain wrong choices that would not be obvious otherwise.

Two: What Is the Scope of the Question?

The other defining characteristic of a question is its scope: is it a question about the passage as a whole, or is it a question about just one sentence, phrase, or word in the passage? Many answer choices are incorrect, at least in part, because they do not match the scope of the question. More importantly, the strategies you want to use for thinking about right and wrong answers for a question that asks about the entire passage are very different from what you would use for thinking about right and wrong answers for a question about the definition of, say, just one word. You want to work on developing thinking habits that align best with the specific tasks that questions present.

Certain question stems are designed to leave the scope uncertain. Imagine a question stem that states, "The author would most likely agree that..." The right answer could relate to the passage as a whole, or it could relate to a very specific opinion about a secondary issue. In this case, as in many others presented on the LSAT, the best way to deal with the uncertainty is to remain uncertain—whether the question is about specifics or generalities will be revealed once you go into the answer choices. We'll discuss specific strategies for such questions in just a bit.

Starting on the next page, we will discuss each specific type of question that can appear in the section. We'll do so in terms of actionable steps—what you ought to think about and do before you go into the answers, what you ought to look for in eliminating wrong choices, and how you should define your expectations for the answers you select. If I've done my job as a teacher well, the suggestions should seem logical and in line with the mindset for this section that I've encouraged thus far. Keep in mind that your goal, at the end of the day, is to have an effective process for each question type that is completely intuitive, that is, a strategy you implement without conscious effort, a strategy you implement because that's how it makes natural sense to think about the task at hand.

Strategies for Structure Questions

Main Point / Main Purpose (most common)

Which one of the following most accurately expresses the main idea of the passage? The primary purpose of the passage is to...

Technically speaking, main idea and primary purpose are not the same thing. When it comes to LSAT questions, however, the commonalities between these two are far greater than the differences, so much so that you can think of both types of questions as essentially requiring the same thought process. In both instances, we are looking for the answer that best represents the passage as a whole and best indicates why it was written.

Main point questions are the most common questions in the section, and also the questions for which your initial read should best prepare you. If you've understood the passage well, you should be able to go into the answer choices with a fairly clear set of expectations about the right answer. If you have any fuzziness about the passage, make sure you do a quick paragraph-by-paragraph scan of the text before going into the answer choices.

RIGHT ANSWERS are answers that best represent the entirety of the passage. For many questions, the right answer will be written in much the same way that you might think about the passage yourself. For certain, more challenging questions, right answers will commonly fall short of your ideal. They may slightly overemphasize one part of the passage over another, or they may leave as secondary something you felt was prominent. The right answer may also present what is, in your view, an overly vague or simplified version of the text. What the right answer will never, ever do is contain incorrect information. It will not switch around a detail that is in the text, and it will not assign an opinion that is inaccurate. If you know you are dealing with a tough main point question and you have an answer that isn't close to the ideal you have in your head but does represent most of the passage and doesn't have any clear, egregious issues, it could very well be the right answer.

WRONG ANSWERS are the key to your success on main point questions. Right answers for tough questions are tough to spot; wrong answers are consistently easier to see as being incorrect. Wrong answers for main point questions commonly have one of two issues. The first is that the answer will take a particularly narrow component of the passage—say, the point of a supporting paragraph—and hold that up as the main point. The second is that the answer will have an error—a detail that doesn't match, or goes beyond, the information in the text. Often these distortions are quite obvious. So, for main point questions, make sure you are lenient on "just okay" answers at first, and really focus on finding reasons why wrong choices are wrong.

General Organization (very uncommon)

Which one of the following most accurately describes the organization of the passage?

Of course, thinking about the general organization of the passage is critical for answering many questions, but historically very few questions have asked about the overall structure directly. Typically, the answers to these questions will break up a passage in terms of its paragraphs, and so you will want to review the purpose of each paragraph quickly before going into the answers.

RIGHT ANSWERS will represent each part of the passage accurately. They are usually written as a sequence of elements, typically meant to roughly mimic the organization of the passage, and you want to be able to go through that list without feeling uncertain about any one of the elements on it.

WRONG ANSWERS are what define this question, just like they did the main point questions. Wrong answers will clearly state the wrong purpose for at least one component of the passage. Your first time through the answer choices, you should focus all of your energy on finding these inconsistencies and eliminating answers based on them. Right answers often won't feel perfect, and the key to always getting this type of question right is being able to spot the defining characteristics of wrong choices, which tend to be far more obvious.

Purpose of a Paragraph (common)

What is the main purpose of the fourth paragraph? The main purpose of the third paragraph is to...

These questions are very similar to other structure questions in that the quality of your initial read will, in large part, determine whether or not the question feels difficult. Thus, if you have a strong initial read, you should, to a large degree, be able to anticipate the substance of the right answer.

When asked this type of question, think about how the paragraph relates to the passage as a whole and to the paragraphs before and after it. Make sure you have a clear sense of what you expect in the right answer before moving forward.

RIGHT ANSWERS will match, in substance if not in wording, your understanding of how the paragraph fits into the reasoning structure of the passage. The answer may discuss this role from a slightly different vantage point than you might expect, or it may use challenging wording, so be open, at first, to "just okay" answers.

WRONG ANSWERS are again the key to answering this type of question quickly and confidently. All wrong answers will be absolutely wrong—they will represent the role in a clearly incorrect way or discuss something that isn't in the passage. Focus most of your energy on finding reasons why answers are wrong.

Purpose of Word or Phrase (very common)

The author most likely describes the theory as "X" in order to... The primary function of the reference to "X" is to... Which one of the following most accurately expresses the primary purpose of the sentence in lines X - X ?

These word, clause, or sentence purpose questions, like general and paragraph purpose questions, are direct tests of your ability to see reasoning structure. For almost all such questions, the challenge will not be in identifying the relevant information—the question stem will either give it to you, or it will be obvious where the important information is. The key work to be done has to do with thinking about the purpose of that component relative to the passage as a whole.

As with other structure questions, you should be able, to a large degree, to anticipate the substance, if not the wording, of the correct answer. However, don't take this understanding and simply look for matches in the answers. A far more consistently effective method is to first use this understanding to eliminate incorrect choices. If you develop the correct habits, eliminating incorrect choices becomes far faster and more accurate than simply trying to identify correct choices.

RIGHT ANSWERS should almost always match the substance of what you anticipated if you read the passage correctly and understood the purpose of the word or phrase correctly. However, keep in mind that, especially as questions get more difficult, right answers are likely to approach that explanation of the role from a more obscure angle. Imagine a text that presents two contrasting theories—information that clearly seems to support one theory could also correctly be said, often, to oppose the other theory, and the answer may very well represent this relationship from the less obvious perspective. The most common roles that answers play are those that relate to the main points—supporting, opposing, showing an application, and so on. Right answers that actually represent main opinions are less common, and right answers that relate to background information—because background information has little relevance to reasoning structure—are almost unseen.

WRONG ANSWERS are all clearly going to be wrong for at least one of two reasons: they will clearly misrepresent the role that the information plays, or they will misrepresent the actual passage in some way (i.e., change the subject matter). The most attractive wrong choices will take a correct stance and embellish it so that if, say, the author uses an experiment to weaken a theory, an answer might take it further and say the experiment makes the theory "obsolete." Down to two attractive choices, choose the one that, even if a bit more vague or awkward, has less such embellishment.

Contextual Definition (very common)

The phrase "X" as used in line Y most nearly means... In using the term "X," the author suggests that "Y" is considered to be...

At first it may seem that this question doesn't quite belong in the "structure" section. The reason it belongs here is because the thought process required for this type of question is very much in line with the thought process required for other structure questions, in particular the purpose questions just described.

When questions ask that you define a word or phrase as it is being used in the passage, the manner in which it is used is almost always, in some way, related to the general reasoning structure of the passage. When you formulate your own thoughts about the meaning of the word or phrase, it is far easier to do so when you understand why the author has placed the sentence where he or she has.

The challenge of these questions will not be in the hunt for information, since the question stem will give you the element in question as well as the location. Your primary task is to develop as clear a sense of the definition as you can before going into the answers, again, using your understanding of reasoning structure as your main guide. Relative to other structural questions, the right answer is a bit more obvious, and the wrongs a bit less so, so you need not feel as reliant on your elimination process as you should for the other types of structure questions we've discussed on these two pages.

RIGHT ANSWERS will hopefully match, fairly closely, the thoughts you had, and in any case—this is especially helpful to know if you have trouble pre-phrasing an answer—the right answer should make sense in terms of the role that phrase or sentence plays relative to the passage as a whole. For example, imagine that you just can't figure out the meaning of a particular word, but you do know that it's in a group of sentences meant to go against a certain theory. Look for the answer that, once you plug that definition in, allows that phrase or sentence to function in the role you expect it to.

WRONG ANSWERS for these questions are created a few different ways. Authors put in answers that would match correct meanings in different contexts, and they put in answers that match the substance of other parts of the passage (but not the part in question). Many answers are wrong because they would clearly give the sentence a purpose different from what the author intended. As always, a strong sense of author intention and overall structure is extremely helpful here.

Strategies for Author Opinion Questions

Author Opinion (very common)

The author of the passage would be most likely to agree with which of the following statements? The author's feelings toward X (main subject) can best be described as...

The author's view of the subject matter is always intrinsically tied in to the reasoning structure of the passage, and a strong understanding of the author's views is a necessary component of a strong read. If you've read the passage well, you should be well prepared to answer most author's opinion questions quickly and with confidence.

Keep in mind that vague question stems can refer to the author's general opinion (more common) or a more specific opinion that the author holds (less common). You won't know until you evaluate the answer choices.

RIGHT ANSWERS will be broad and safe, and in general should match fairly closely the thoughts you have in your own head. The "language" of opinions—that is, the way in which answer choices describe various opinions—is a bit less complex than the "language" of reasoning structure, so the challenge of matching your thought process to their wording should be less difficult.

Keep in mind that for a minority of passages, the author stays objective and has no opinion—it's important to note when passages are written in this manner (you will still get opinion questions). When the author does have an opinion, it will tend to be subtle and mitigated. An answer that is more vague or more "politically correct" than you would write is typically okay. An answer that goes beyond what the author said is typically not going to be okay.

WRONG ANSWERS are very often on the complete opposite side of the fence—that is, wrong answers, even attractive ones, often state that the author has the exact opposite opinion of the one he does. Other wrong answers will embellish and make more extreme the author's views, or discuss issues that are not discussed in the passage.

Specific Author Opinion (common)

Based on the passage, with which one of the following statements regarding X would the author agree? Which one of the following best describes the author's attitude toward X?

When you are asked general opinion questions, "no opinion" is sometimes a legitimate answer. However, when you are asked about the author's opinion toward a specific component, "no opinion" is not going to be a common part of your thought process. These questions concern things about which the author definitely has an opinion. For the hardest of these questions, the author's opinion will be extremely subtle—perhaps only evident from just one modifier, placed somewhere you didn't expect it (that's part of the reason why you want to pay careful attention to any clue of any author opinion as you read the passage). The challenge is to dig that opinion out, and understand it as clearly as you can before going into the answers.

RIGHT ANSWERS will typically involve ideas or issues that the author has. If the author's opinion is clear and absolute, expect the answer to represent that, and if the author's opinion is subtle and mitigated, the answer should represent that as well.

WRONG ANSWERS will often clearly misrepresent the author's opinion, and a strong understanding will often help you get rid of three or four of these answers quickly. More attractive wrong choices will misrepresent the degree of the author's opinion or, in very sly ways, introduce information that is a bit different from the information presented in the passage. Look for extreme signs of wrong answers first—down to two choices, look to eliminate one that goes too far or contains a detail not in the passage.

Strategies for Other Opinion Questions

Other Opinions (somewhat common)

The critic mentioned in the second paragraph would be most likely to agree with which of the following statements?... X's view differs from Y's in that...

Almost always, the other opinions in question are related to the central issue of the passage. Therefore, these are questions for which, most of the time, you should have a very good sense of what to expect in a right answer. Still, unless you are absolutely certain of your understanding of the opinion, it's always a good idea to go back into the text to reread the information. If you have a pretty good sense of the opinion already, the reread should go very quickly. The reread may save you some time eliminating wrong choices and selecting the right one.

As always, pay particular attention to the wording of the question, for it will give you insight into what to look for in right and wrong answers. If, for example, the question involves the phrase "would most likely agree," we know that we won't get "slam dunk" evidence to connect the text and right answer. Utilizing those types of nuances is critical for success on difficult questions.

RIGHT ANSWERS should be ones that you can do a fairly good job of anticipating—again, because the opinions in question will generally be related to the main points of the passage, they should be fresh in your mind. Even if you reread the relevant text before going into the answers, it's still a good idea to confirm the right answer with the text in the passage—this should be a quick step, and it's good for your accuracy.

WRONG ANSWERS will commonly have one of two characteristics—they will either represent the opposite of the opinion in question (as you can imagine, these answers generally align with the *other* opinions in a passage) or they'll go beyond the information in the text. To think of it another way, wrong answers punish those who confuse the opinions in a passage, and they confuse those who don't pay attention to specific details. Use your general understanding of how the opinion relates to the passage to get rid of obvious wrong choices (there will always be a few), then use specific necessary details to eliminate attractive wrong choices that just miss the mark in terms of subject matter or meaning.

Strengthen / Weaken (somewhat common)

Which of the following, if true, would weaken the author's argument against X? Each of the following could be used as support for X's view EXCEPT:

Strengthen and weaken questions are unique among Reading Comprehension questions in that they require you to use your reasoning ability. In order to see if an answer strengthens or weakens an argument or an opinion, you need to first evaluate that argument or opinion critically, just as we have for Logical Reasoning strengthen and weaken questions. Other Reading Comprehension questions do not require us to think critically, and, in fact, other questions are sometimes specifically designed to reward an objective, rather than judgemental, read of the material. Make sure you have a very clear sense of the argument or conclusion before going into the answers, otherwise you will not have a good gauge for differentiating between right and wrong choices.

RIGHT ANSWERS will clearly support or weaken an opinion presented in the text (keep in mind the difference between impacting an opinion and impacting an argument, the latter of which involves the use of the specifically mentioned evidence to reach the given conclusion).

WRONG ANSWERS will either play an incorrect role (commonly the opposite, such as strengthen when we are looking for a weaken answer, and so on) or an unclear role relative to the opinion.

Illustrate (not common)

Which of the following is an example of X? Which of the following scenarios best illustrates the dangers mentioned by the critics?

These questions are also unique among Reading Comprehension questions, not because they require you to be critical (they don't) but rather because they require you to relate your understanding to the answer choices. Before you evaluate the answers, say to yourself in your own words what exactly the opinion in question is.

RIGHT ANSWERS will illustrate the opinion or issue. They may not be slam-dunk illustrations, and they may not match the subject matter of the text, but they will illustrate nonetheless. The one thing a right answer definitely will not do is go out on a limb and present an idea more strongly or more specifically than was presented in the text.

WRONG ANSWERS will represent a misunderstanding of the original opinion. Commonly, wrong answers will illustrate the opposite of the original opinion. On a more subtle level, attractive wrong choices will just be different because of a small difference in degree or a small but significant difference in detail. As always, work from wrong to right to give yourself the best chance to get the question correct.

Strategies for Detail Questions

Identify the Detail (very common)

Which of the following statements about X is made in the passage?... According to the passage, X is a factor in Y because... Which of the following is mentioned in the passage? The passage contains information to answer which of the following questions?

These questions are designed to test two things—your ability to identify information, and your ability to understand it. Certain questions give you a hint about information that is located in the question stem—the first and second examples mentioned above are examples of these types of questions. If you are given any such hint, you want to make sure you read the relevant text (and the parts immediately adjacent) before evaluating the answers. For these questions, working from wrong to right is a bit less important—if you find a great match and you are certain of the right answer, you can quickly scan the other choices, then make your selection. If the question stem gives no clues as to the position of the information (such as the last example), you should go back to leaning on your elimination skills. You want to run through the answer choices first and eliminate the obviously wrong choices (there will always be obviously wrong choices) then go back into the text to try to match the one or two most attractive choices to the information in the text.

RIGHT ANSWERS will very closely match the text. Notice the wording of all of these types of questions—"according to," "directly mentioned." This is no accident. These questions are testing your ability to correctly understand without embellishing. The right answer will always require no significant assumptions or inferences.

WRONG ANSWERS will often stray from the text, and the most attractive wrong choices will stray in very reasonable ways. For questions that give you a hint of location, wrong answers may bring up things mentioned in incorrect parts of the passage.

Infer from a Detail (somewhat common)

The passage suggests which of the following is true about the relationship between X and Y? In the second paragraph, the author implies that X is...

These questions are very similar to identification questions, but the differences between the two are quite significant. Like identification questions, questions that require you to infer from a detail commonly require that you find the detail and understand it contextually and correctly. However, for identification questions, the right answer should require little inference. For inference questions, the right answer, by nature, will require an inference.

RIGHT ANSWERS will not be directly stated in the text—otherwise, no inference would be required. However, for many questions, just as in Logical Reasoning, the inference required is a very small one. However, keep in mind that right answers often do not have the stringent burden of proof that Logical Reasoning answers do. Basically, you want an answer that is very reasonable to infer based on the given text, and commonly one that nearly matches the given text, but isn't exactly the same as the given text (there won't actually be an answer that is, but many wrong choices are written to appear that way).

WRONG ANSWERS are commonly easy to recognize because, even for these detail questions, they misrepresent in some way the main thrust of the passage or the author's opinion. All wrong answers are ones that, obviously, are not inferable, and you want to use the question "Does that part of the text prove this or not?" as your primary gauge. As with many identification questions, often the right answer will jump out at you faster than the wrong ones will—if that's the case, don't fight it. Confirm that right answer, then quickly scan for wrongs.

Infer from...? (not common)

The passage suggests that... Which of the following could we infer? The information in the passage is sufficient to infer which of the following?

These inference questions are uncertain in terms of scope—based on the question stem, it's unclear whether the inference is related to the passage as a whole or to one or two lines. For these questions, you want to do a quick scan of answer choices to eliminate obvious wrongs (there will always be a few) before you think about what can actually be inferred from the text. During this initial phase, you should get a good sense of whether the question is asking for a specific type of inference (more common) or a more general passage-as-a-whole type inference (less common). If it's the former, work to identify the relevant specific text and do a careful word-by-word check to ensure that no great leaps have been taken. If it's the latter, treat it much like a main point question and look for an answer that best represents the author's main points and general opinion. Check each component of the most attractive choice or two against the text to make sure that various parts of the passage can be used to support the answer.

RIGHT ANSWERS will require very little inference—and typically the more specific the text in question, the less inference required. Unlike in Logical Reasoning, right answers are very rarely "creative," unexpected truths one can pull from the text. Rather, right answers are far more typically inferences that fall in line with the thought processes most relevant to the text.

WRONG ANSWERS will require too much inference (duh), or they will often give themselves away by misrepresenting the text. Use your understanding of passage structure and detail to get rid of obvious wrong choices before you do the more subtle work of thinking about inferences that are or are not reasonably supported.

Find an Analogy (not common)

The relationship between X and Y described in the passage is most like... As described in the passage, X is most similar to which one of the following?

Questions that ask you to find an analogous situation or relationship can either refer back to a secondary detail in the original passage, or to the main subject matter of the original passage. The reason we categorize it here is because the key to success is to have a correct understanding of the original material.

RIGHT ANSWERS will not always be perfect, and sometimes you will have to pick an analogous situation that doesn't have all of the exact nuances that you felt the original component had. For the answer to be somewhat vague or incomplete is acceptable for more difficult questions, though you shouldn't expect it to be the norm.

WRONG ANSWERS are what really define these answer choices. Each wrong answer will have something that is definitively flawed with it. They will either not match the situation or include some extraneous modifier or modification. Down to two answers, follow the Price Is Right "closest price but not over" model—look for an answer that matches best the original situation, but it's better to "undermatch" than it is to "overmatch." Avoid answers that go too far.

The General Problem-Solving Process

As your teacher, my goal for this lesson was to impress upon you two seemingly incongruous truths. For one, each type of question is unique, and it's important that you pay attention to the specific task that each question presents. But at the same time there is great commonality to these questions, and you don't need to (and shouldn't) go into the section thinking you have fifteen different problem-solving strategies to employ. You should see all questions as different combinations of just a few basic characteristics.

Read each question stem carefully. That's a given. As you do so, you should be thinking about two general issues: is this question about the passage as a whole, or one specific component, and is this question testing my understanding of reasoning structure, opinions, or details? These two thoughts need not take place on a very "conscious" level—hopefully, by the time you go into the exam, it will simply be habit that you define the challenges presented in the question stem according to these two characteristics.

Your question stem should tell you one more thing: at which points you should expect to go back into the text. For certain questions, we should expect to go into the text and find an "answer" before looking at the answer choices. For other questions, there is very little to do until we see what the answers themselves are.

For all questions, your ideal problem-solving process should involve eliminating the four wrong answers before selecting the right one. For all types of questions, wrong answers are commonly wrong because they misrepresent the substance or purpose of the text. Some of the more attractive wrong choices are attractive because they match the text well, but don't match the task presented in the question stem well.

The key to strong elimination skills is a clear sense of passage structure *and* task. If you know the passage and you can keep in mind the genre and scope of the question, most of the time at least three wrong choices should be clearly incorrect.

The right answer is right if it matches what you know of the text, and if it fits the task presented in the question stem. For most questions, I suggest you take the time to find specific information in the original passage to confirm the right choice.

Time constraints prevent most test takers from using the "ideal" process to solve every question. When timing is a concern, you may need to select an answer you think is right without getting a chance to eliminate wrong choices—that's okay, but do keep in mind that more time spent eliminating will increase your accuracy. A big key to not having timing issues is not getting "stuck" on any one question. If, after the elimination and selection process, you can't whittle it down to just one answer, do not allow yourself to spin your wheels. Either restart the entire question (if you have the time) or do your best to find something wrong or something right, force yourself to pick an answer, and move on.

Instructions for the drill starting on the following page:

Starting on the next page are two passages, each with its full complement of questions. The questions, however, have been organized for you by genre, so you will first handle all reasoning structure questions, then all opinion questions, then all detail questions, in order to get a better sense of how these genres are different from one another. Solutions follow each passage and question set.

For this exercise, pay the most careful attention to the question stems—make sure you work to develop a habitual sense of their scope and genre. Practice utilizing the task presented in conjunction with your understanding of the passage to eliminate wrong choices. My suggestion is to time yourself, but worry less about time for this drill. However, as I advise in the column to the left, do always practice not getting stuck on any one particular question.

Drill: Questions in Categories

For some years before the outbreak of World War I, a number of painters in different European countries developed works of art that some have described as prophetic: paintings that by challenging viewers' habitual ways of perceiving the world of the present are thus said to anticipate a future world that would be very different. The artistic styles that they brought into being varied widely, but all these styles had in common a very important break with traditions of representational art that stretched back to the Renaissance.

So fundamental is this break with tradition that it is not surprising to discover that these artists—among them Picasso and Braque in France, Kandinsky in Germany, and Malevich in Russia—are often credited with having anticipated not just subsequent developments in the arts, but also the political and social disruptions and upheavals of the modern world that came into being during and after the war. One art critic even goes so far as to claim that it is the very prophetic power of these artworks, and not their break with traditional artistic techniques, that constitutes their chief interest and value.

No one will deny that an artist may, just as much as a writer or a politician, speculate about the future and then try to express a vision of that future through making use of a particular style or choice of imagery; speculation about the possibility of war in Europe was certainly widespread during the early years of the twentieth century. But the forward-looking quality attributed to these artists should instead be credited to their exceptional aesthetic innovations rather than to any power to make clever guesses about political or social trends. For example, the clear impression we get of Picasso and Braque, the joint founders of cubism, from their contemporaries as well as from later statements made by the artists themselves, is that they were primarily concerned with problems of representation and form and with efforts to create a far more "real" reality than the one that was accessible only to the eye. The reformation of society was of no interest to them as artists.

It is also important to remember that not all decisive changes in art are quickly followed by dramatic events in the world outside art. The case of Delacroix, the nineteenth-century French painter, is revealing. His stylistic innovations startled his contemporaries—and still retain that power over modern viewers—but most art historians have decided that Delacroix adjusted himself to new social conditions that were already coming into being as a result of political upheavals that had occurred in 1830, as opposed to other artists who supposedly told of changes still to come.

Practice Test 29, Passage 1

STRUCTURE

1. Which one of the following most accurately states the main idea of the passage?

(A) Although they flourished independently, the pre-World War I European painters who developed new ways of looking at the world shared a common desire to break with the traditions of representational art.
(B) The work of the pre-World War I European painters who developed new ways of looking at the world cannot be said to have intentionally predicted social changes but only to have anticipated new directions in artistic perception and expression.
(C) The work of the pre-World War I European painters who developed new ways of looking at the world was important for its ability to predict social changes and its anticipation of new directions in artistic expression.
(D) Art critics who believe that the work of some pre-World War I European painters foretold imminent social changes are mistaken because art is incapable of expressing a vision of the future.
(E) Art critics who believe that the work of some pre-World War I European painters foretold imminent social changes are mistaken because the social upheavals that followed World War I were impossible to predict.

4. The author presents the example of Delacroix in order to illustrate which one of the following claims?

(A) Social or political changes usually lead to important artistic innovations.
(B) Artistic innovations do not necessarily anticipate social or political upheavals.
(C) Some European painters have used art to predict social or political changes.
(D) Important stylistic innovations are best achieved by abandoning past traditions.
(E) Innovative artists can adapt themselves to social or political changes.

5. Which one of the following most accurately describes the contents of the passage?

(A) The author describes an artistic phenomenon; introduces one interpretation of this phenomenon; proposes an alternative interpretation and then supports this alternative by criticizing the original interpretation.
(B) The author describes an artistic phenomenon; identifies the causes of that phenomenon; illustrates some of the consequences of the phenomenon and then speculates about the significance of these consequences.
(C) The author describes an artistic phenomenon; articulates the traditional interpretation of this phenomenon; identifies two common criticisms of this view and then dismisses each of these criticisms by appeal to an example.
(D) The author describes an artistic phenomenon; presents two competing interpretations of the phenomenon; dismisses both interpretations by appeal to an example and then introduces an alternative interpretation.
(E) The author describes an artistic phenomenon; identifies the causes of the phenomenon; presents an argument for the importance of the phenomenon and then advocates an attempt to recreate the phenomenon.

OPINIONS

2. The art critic mentioned in lines 19-20 *(end of second paragraph)* would be most likely to agree with which one of the following statements?

(A) The supposed innovations of Picasso, Braque, Kandinsky, and Malevich were based on stylistic discoveries that had been made in the Renaissance but went unexplored for centuries.
(B) The work of Picasso, Braque, Kandinsky, and Malevich possessed prophetic power because these artists employed the traditional techniques of representational art with unusual skill.
(C) The importance of the work of Picasso, Braque, Kandinsky, and Malevich is due largely to the fact that the work was stylistically ahead of its time.
(D) The prophecies embodied in the work of Picasso, Braque, Kandinsky, and Malevich were shrewd predictions based on insights into the European political situation.
(E) The artistic styles brought into being by Picasso, Braque, Kandinsky, and Malevich, while stylistically innovative, were of little significance to the history of post-World War I art.

DETAILS

3. According to the passage, the statements of Picasso and Braque indicate that

(A) they had a long-standing interest in politics
(B) they worked actively to bring about social change
(C) their formal innovations were actually the result of chance
(D) their work was a deliberate attempt to transcend visual reality
(E) the formal aspects of their work were of little interest to them

6. According to the author, the work of the pre-World War I painters described in the passage contains an example of each of the following EXCEPT:

(A) an interest in issues of representation and form
(B) a stylistic break with traditional art
(C) the introduction of new artistic techniques
(D) the ability to anticipate later artists
(E) the power to predict social changes

Solution

SUMMARY

P1 - Main point: painters developed art some have described as prophetic. Styles were varied but were all different from old styles.

P2 - Support for/expansion of main point: styles so novel that these painters are said to have predicted the future. Claim that this is what gives paintings their value.

P3 - Background: artists dream of future, as many others do. Second main point/author's opinion: artists are forward thinking in their style, not in their view of the world. Support/expansion: Picasso and Braque concerned with issues of representation, not commentary on the world.

P4 - Information that goes against the first main point: not all changes in art are followed by changes in life. Example to support: the painter Delacroix, who was rather influenced by changes in life that had already happened.

COMMENTS

We're given a main point right away, albeit with a bit of background around it to distract us, and with a bit of vagueness in the term "some." Then the paragraph goes on to discuss something that feels, perhaps, somewhat indirectly related to the idea that the artists were prophetic—that their styles were a break from tradition.

The second paragraph brings these concepts together more clearly—the novelty of the styles is part of what makes them (perhaps) prophetic. And the paragraph ends with more support for the point the passage began with.

Still, at this point, many readers might anticipate a counterpoint coming. Language such as "some have described," and "even goes so far as to claim," while certainly not definite signs of an opinion, hint that there is a flip side to things. When the author starts the third paragraph with "No one will deny," a lot of experienced readers will feel a "but..." coming on, and indeed the next sentence gives us a counterpoint, which is clearly the author's point of view. The forward thinking was about art, not political or social trends. The rest of the third paragraph gives us more support for that point (and you can't get more authoritative, in the art world, than Picasso).

The final paragraph gives us information that is meant to serve as a final bit of evidence against the idea that the artists were prophetic. In Delacroix's case, his art was influenced by changes that were already occurring.

1. There were two contrasting main points presented: that this art was prophetic in terms of social change, or that it was simply innovative in terms of actual artistic technique. The author is in agreement with the latter view, and we want an answer that represents this general understanding best.

Elimination: (A) relates to some of the components in the passage, but doesn't match the main points in any way—a shared common desire to break apart from tradition is not the main thrust of the passage. (A) can be quickly eliminated. (B) sounds complicated, but similar to what we are expecting. Let's leave it. (C) puts the author on the opposite side of the issue and can be quickly eliminated. The latter part of (D) is very general and goes well beyond the scope of this passage, so (D) can be quickly eliminated. The latter part of (E) does not match the text, so (E) can be quickly eliminated.

Selection: Let's return to the only remaining answer, (B), and check it word for word. The wording in (B) is a bit more absolute, perhaps, than that in the text ("cannot" versus "should"), but otherwise it's a pretty good match for what we expected. Since we've confidently eliminated the other four answers, we can pick (B) and move on. **(B) is correct.**

4. We know that his story is meant to serve as evidence against the "prophetic" opinion. We can go into the answers with that in mind.

Elimination: The "usually" in (A) is too strong, and this does not match what we saw as the role it plays relative to the passage as a whole. (B) is exactly what we anticipated—let's leave it. (C) is not what Delacroix is meant to represent, but rather the opposite. Both (D) and (E) have nothing to do with the main purposes of the passage.

Selection: That leaves us with (B). We go back and check it word for word—that is what the example is being used to show, so we pick it and move on. **(B) is correct.**

5. The question stem is fairly general, but if you were uncertain at all, a quick scan of the answer choices shows us that it's an organization question. If we quickly think about the organization of the passage, we have: one main theory, explanation/reasons, another main theory/author opinion, explanation/reasons, and reasons against first main theory. We want an answer that best represents this.

Elimination: (A) is a fairly good match for what we expected, so let's keep it. (B) does not mention the competing theories and does not match the structure we discussed and can be quickly eliminated. (C) does not match the second half of the passage at all and can be quickly eliminated. (D) misrepresents the fact that the second main opinion is the one the author agrees with and can be quickly eliminated. (E) describes a passage very different from this one (an attempt to recreate?) and can be eliminated quickly.

That leaves us with just (A). Let's take a closer look. If we go part by part, it's easy to match up each part of the answer choice with parts of the text. (A) is a great answer, and **(A) is correct.**

2. Note that passages on the real exam will have line numbers, whereas our copies do not.

What we know of this art critic is that he finds the prophetic nature of the art to be hugely significant to its value. Let's think of this as we eliminate answers.

Elimination: (A) is unrelated to the opinion discussed. The first part of (B) sounds good, but the second part is not related to the opinion. (C) matches the author's opinion but not that of the critic. (D) isn't a great match for what we predicted, but it's the only answer that even somewhat relates to the text. Let's leave it. (E) does not relate to the opinion discussed.

Selection: We've quickly eliminated four obviously wrong answers, and are left with one answer, (D), that we don't love. However, checking (D) against the text, we see that it's a pretty good match, especially when considering that it's a "most likely" question (i.e., inference rather than exact match) and, also considering that the information came before the opinion and is related to it, is a fairly good match for some of the information in the answer. (D) is the best available choice. **(D) is correct.**

3. The statements of Picasso and Braque are mentioned in the second half of the third paragraph, and we should return there and read it again before looking at the answers. They are concerned with issues of representation (i.e., the visual, not the political).

Elimination: (A) and (B) are completely opposite of the text and can quickly be eliminated. (C) is not right—chance is not discussed—and can quickly be eliminated. (D) sounds good. Leave it. (E) is wrong. We have been given no sense that formal aspects of their work weren't important to them and a lot of clues that they were likely very important.

Selection: That leaves only (D)—"transcend reality" is a great match for "a far more 'real.'" **(D) is correct.**

6. This is a broad question that requires us to take information from a large stretch of text—let's see if we can form a better idea of the answer choices before we go back into the text.

(A), (B), and (C) are central to the passage, and we can know that they are discussed without having to go back. Did the author say they had the power to anticipate later artists? Yes, in the second paragraph. We can eliminate (D).

Selection: That leaves only (E), the obvious right answer. The author, we know, is on the other side of the fence when it comes to the artist's ability to predict future change. **(E) is correct.**

Drill: Questions in Categories

Some of the philosophers find the traditional, subjective approach to studying the mind outdated and ineffectual. For them, the attempt to describe the sensation of pain or anger, for example, or the awareness that one is aware, has been surpassed by advances in fields such as psychology, neuroscience, and cognitive science. Scientists, they claim, do not concern themselves with how a phenomenon feels from the inside; instead of investigating private evidence perceivable only to a particular individual, scientists pursue hard data—such as the study of how nerves transmit impulses to the brain—which is externally observable and can be described without reference to any particular point of view. With respect to features of the universe such as those investigated by chemistry, biology, and physics, this objective approach has been remarkably successful in yielding knowledge. Why, these philosophers ask, should we suppose the mind to be any different?

But philosophers loyal to subjectivity are not persuaded by appeals to science when such appeals conflict with the data gathered by introspection. Knowledge, they argue, relies on the data of experience, which includes subjective experience. Why should philosophy ally itself with scientists who would reduce the sources of knowledge to only those data that can be discerned objectively?

On the face of it, it seems unlikely that these two approaches to studying the mind could be reconciled. Because philosophy, unlike science, does not progress inexorably toward a single truth, disputes concerning the nature of the mind are bound to continue. But what is particularly distressing about the present debate is that genuine communication between the two sides is virtually impossible. For reasoned discourse to occur, there must be shared assumptions or beliefs. Starting from radically divergent perspectives, subjectivists and objectivists lack a common context in which to consider evidence presented from each other's perspectives.

The situation may be likened to a debate between adherents of different religions about the creation of the universe. While each religion may be confident that its cosmology is firmly grounded in its respective sacred text, there is little hope that conflicts between their competing cosmologies could be resolved by recourse to the texts alone. Only further investigation into the authority of the texts themselves would be sufficient.

What would be required to resolve the debate between the philosophers of mind, then, is an investigation into the authority of their differing perspectives. How rational is it to take scientific description as the ideal way to understand the nature of consciousness? Conversely, how useful is it to rely solely on introspection for one's knowledge about the workings of the mind? Are there alternative ways of gaining such knowledge? In this debate, epistemology—the study of knowledge—may itself lead to the discovery of new forms of knowledge about how the mind works.

Practice Test 31, Passage 4

STRUCTURE

21. Which one of the following most accurately summarizes the main point of the passage?

(A) In order to gain new knowledge of the workings of the mind, subjectivists must take into consideration not only the private evidence of introspection but also the more objective evidence obtainable from disciplines such as psychology, neuroscience, and cognitive science.
(B) In rejecting the traditional, subjective approach to studying the mind, objectivists have made further progress virtually impossible because their approach rests on a conception of evidence that is fundamentally incompatible with that employed by subjectivists.
(C) Because the subjectivist and objectivist approaches rest on diametrically opposed assumptions about the kinds of evidence to be used when studying the mind, the only way to resolve the dispute is to compare the two approaches' success in obtaining knowledge.
(D) Although subjectivists and objectivists appear to employ fundamentally irreconcilable approaches to the study of the mind, a common ground for debate may be found if both sides are willing to examine the authority of the evidence on which their competing theories depend.
(E) While the success of disciplines such as chemistry, biology, and physics appears to support the objectivist approach to studying the mind, the objectivist approach has failed to show that the data of introspection should not qualify as evidence.

26. The author characterizes certain philosophers as "loyal to subjectivity" (line 20) *(start of second paragraph)* for each of the following reasons EXCEPT:

(A) These philosophers believe scientists should adopt the subjective approach when studying phenomena such as how nerves transmit impulses to the brain.
(B) These philosophers favor subjective evidence about the mind over objective evidence about the mind when the two conflict.
(C) These philosophers maintain that subjective experience is essential to the study of the mind.
(D) These philosophers hold that objective evidence is only a part of the full range of experience.
(E) These philosophers employ evidence that is available only to a particular individual.

OPINIONS

22. Which one of the following most likely reflects the author's belief about the current impasse between subjectivists and objectivists?

(A) It cannot be overcome because of the radically different conceptions of evidence favored by each of the two sides.
(B) It is resolvable only if the two sides can find common ground from which to assess their competing conceptions of evidence.
(C) It is unavoidable unless both sides recognize that an accurate understanding of the mind requires both types of evidence.
(D) It is based on an easily correctable misunderstanding between the two sides about the nature of evidence.
(E) It will prevent further progress until alternate ways of gaining knowledge about the mind are discovered.

27. Based on the passage, which one of the following is most clearly an instance of the objectivist approach to studying the mind?

(A) collecting accounts of dreams given by subjects upon waking in order to better understand the nature of the subconscious
(B) interviewing subjects during extremes of hot and cold weather in order to investigate a connection between weather and mood
(C) recording subjects' evaluation of the stress they experienced while lecturing in order to determine how stress affects facility at public speaking
(D) analyzing the amount of a certain chemical in subjects' bloodstreams in order to investigate a proposed link between the chemical and aggressive behavior
(E) asking subjects to speak their thoughts aloud as they attempt to learn a new skill in order to test the relationship between mental understanding and physical performance

DETAILS

24. According to the passage, subjectivists advance which one of the following claims to support their charge that objectivism is faulty?

(A) Objectivism rests on evidence that conflicts with the data of introspection.
(B) Objectivism restricts the kinds of experience from which philosophers may draw knowledge.
(C) Objectivism relies on data that can be described and interpreted only by scientific specialists.
(D) Objectivism provides no context in which to view scientific data as relevant to philosophical questions.
(E) Objectivism concerns itself with questions that have not traditionally been part of philosophical inquiry.

28. Which one of the following is most closely analogous to the debate described in the hypothetical example given by the author in the fourth paragraph?

(A) a debate among investigators attempting to determine a criminal's identity when conflicting physical evidence is found at the crime scene
(B) a debate among jurors attempting to determine which of two conflicting eyewitness accounts of an event is to be believed
(C) a debate between two archaeologists about the meaning of certain written symbols when no evidence exists to verify either's claim
(D) a debate between two museum curators about the value of a painting that shows clear signs of both genuineness and forgery
(E) a debate between two historians who draw conflicting conclusions about the same event based on different types of historical data

Solution

SUMMARY

P1 - (initial) Main point: some philosophers find the subjective approach to studying the mind ineffectual. Explanations and reasoning.

P2 - (initial) Main point: philosophers loyal to subjectivity disagree. Explanations and reasoning.

P3 - Relates the two opinions—difficult to reconcile them because they lack common context. This is the secondary, but more significant, main point.

P4 - Analogy to conflict between views—like that of those with different religions. Solution is further investigation concerning true authority of those religious texts.

P5 - Relates analogy to this conflict: what is required to resolve the conflict between opinions is a look into the authority of the different perspectives. Explanation of what such a look would look like, as well as a description of the possible positive outcome—new forms of knowledge about how the mind works.

COMMENTS

The first two paragraphs are set up very much like a traditional, more basic, LSAT passage. One opinion is given and then explained, then a second opinion is given and then explained. The passage defines itself as being somewhat unique in the third paragraph, which focuses on reconciling the two contrasting viewpoints (many passages present contrasting viewpoints, but few discuss reconciling them). As we read on to the fourth and fifth paragraphs or perhaps after we've read through them, it becomes clear that the initial debate between subjective versus not almost serves as a type of "backdrop," and the challenge of reconciling the two views is the primary subject of the passage. The fourth paragraph gives us an analogy meant to further explain exactly what the conflict is, and ends with a potential solution, one "sufficient" to resolve the issue. It makes sense, then, that the final paragraph would begin with a potential application of this solution to our situation.

21. We know the passage had a complex structure—two contrasting opinions then a main point about the challenge of reconciling those contrasting opinions. We can expect that incorrect answers will misrepresent this point, and probably give us just parts of the puzzle.

Elimination: (A) is only about subjectivists, and in that way it is way too narrow. It also gives us more information about the subjectivists than we got in the text and is thus too extended (wrong all around). (B) is just about objectivists and can be eliminated quickly. (C) sounds somewhat attractive, as does (D), so let's leave both. (E) is too narrow and can be quickly eliminated.

Selection: Returning to (C) and (D)—(C) ends with success at obtaining knowledge. That seems unfamiliar, and when we check back against the text, success at obtaining knowledge, while surely relevant in real life, is simply not discussed. The authority of evidence discussed in (D) is very much in line with the main themes of the passage. **(D) is correct.**

26. Those who are loyal to subjectivity are an important group in the passage, and we know a lot about them—so it makes sense they could create an "EXCEPT" question in this context. In these cases, the one "EXCEPT" situation (the right answer) will jump out at you more obviously than the wrong answers, and that's the case here. (A) is simply not in line with what we know of the subjectivists. In fact, it's the opposite. Still, we want to eliminate wrong choices just to be sure:

Elimination: (B) is pretty much mentioned directly in the first line of the second paragraph. (C) and (D) are also discussed in that same paragraph, and (E) is discussed indirectly in the first paragraph. **(A) is correct.**

22. We have a fairly good sense of the author's opinion about the impasse, since it is central to the point of the passage, so we can go ahead right into the answer choices.

Elimination: "Cannot" is much too strong, and we can eliminate (A). (B) seems good—let's leave it. (C) is about requiring both—this is not a match for the passage, and we can eliminate (C). "Easily correctable" it is not, and we can eliminate (D). (E) makes alternative forms far more significant than the passage did.

Selection: For this problem, we only have one attractive answer. Still, "common ground" is a bit fishy—let's try to confirm it. We can find justification for it in this line: "For reasoned discourse to occur, there must be shared assumptions or beliefs." **(B) is correct.**

27. What we know of the objectionist view is that they are looking for evidence that is absolute and not subjective—that is, not subject to personal opinion or bias. With that in mind, let's take a look at the answers.

Elimination: A clear sense of the objectionist view makes the incorrect answers very obvious here. (A), (B), (C), and (E) are all clearly designed to involve subjective and personal experience and so can be eliminated quickly.

Selection: That leaves only (D). Though such an experiment is not directly mentioned in the passage, the lack of subjectivity it represents is in line with what we know of the objectionists. **(D) is correct.**

24. We know that the bulk of the information about subjectivists is in the second paragraph, so it's a good idea to go back to it and read it again before looking at the answers. Since we know the information we are looking for, we can go ahead and search for the right answer as we eliminate wrong ones.

Elimination/Selection: For this type of problem, especially if you are focused in on one paragraph, you want to be a bit careful with your eliminations—perhaps the right answer will be a detail mentioned in passing in another paragraph. Eliminate an answer if you are absolutely certain it is wrong, but otherwise, focus on finding the right choice. (A) seems unfamiliar, but let's leave it. (B) is a direct match for the text in the second paragraph, in particular the last sentence. Let's select (B) but look at the other choices quickly. "Scientific specialists" eliminates (C), "no context" eliminates (D), and we have no information to support (E). With all the time in the world, maybe we double check before eliminating (A) and (E), but otherwise, since we know (B) is correct, we can select it and move on. **(B) is correct.**

28. What we know about this debate in the fourth paragraph is that each side sees itself as being legitimate based on its own evidence. We're given this analogy in the context of conflicts with no common ground.

Elimination: Conflicting evidence is not a great match for our situation, so we can eliminate (A). (B) is about a debate within those who are witness to two contrasting viewpoints, rather than between those two contrasting viewpoints, so we can eliminate (B). (C) is about "no evidence," and that's not what the situation in paragraph four was about, so we can eliminate (C). (D) is about one element—a painting—with conflicting characteristics. This does not match our situation, and we can eliminate (D). (E) is the type of answer we are looking for.

Selection: Religions, by definition, give theories on the creation of the world and the meaning of life, and per the passage, different religions draw on different texts for evidence. (E), which is about different theories on the same event drawn on different types of data, is a very good match for the paragraph. **(E) is correct.**

Tips on Practicing, and Reviewing Your Work

Each of the *10 Actuals* books gives you exposure to forty recent Reading Comprehension passages. My feeling is that, coupled with the ample practice available in this book, that is enough preparation for the typical student. Some of you may feel that you need more practice than that, and of course you know yourself best. If that is the case, you may want to purchase some additional Reading Comprehension sections to practice with. Unless you are consistently getting -0 on all Reading Comprehension sections, I do not recommend you practice fewer passages than what is prescribed on your practice schedule. Each passage that you practice can be very valuable on multiple levels. Here are a few tips to help make sure you are maximizing all of your study opportunities.

Each passage that you practice, both in this book and in the *10 Actuals*, should be used to **develop positive habits.** To that end, make sure to read the exact passage, and to answer each set of questions, exactly as you plan to on the exam. Remember that a big part of your practice involves training that powerful elephant of yours. If you practice passages with half your focus elsewhere, or with half the effort you ought to, your elephant will develop less effective habits. If you are consistent in how you approach each passage, you will develop skills at a far quicker pace.

Each passage that you practice should **increase your understanding** of the LSAT passages in general. A simple and effective way to quickly build up understanding is in terms of tendencies and twists. That is, as you review a passage and think about how it relates to other passages that appear on the LSAT, do so in terms of "Oh, this aspect of the passage is very typical" versus "This final paragraph was really unexpected." Use the same process in reviewing questions—now that you have a clear "baseline" for all question types, review questions in terms of whether they went as you expected or, if not, why not. And of course, it goes without saying that you should review passages until you have both a complete understanding of the reasoning structure of the passage and the reason why one answer is correct and four answers incorrect for each problem you solve.

Each passage you practice should help you **fine-tune your strategies**. One way to think about this is in terms of how you chose to invest your time during the read and the questions. If you spent too long on the read, which parts did you slow down at that were ultimately not that important in terms of understanding the reasoning structure or answering questions? If you got through the read quickly but struggled with the questions, what was it that you missed in that initial read? What were the places where you should have invested more time? Did you approach question stems as you should have? Did you go back to the passage when you should have? Did you reflect on the big-picture issues you should have? Were you quickly able to eliminate wrong answers? If not, what was the characteristic, in retrospect, that could have allowed you to quickly eliminate those tempting but wrong answer choices? Did you pull the trigger on the right answer when you should have? Too rushed? Too nervous?

Use each passage to work on your habits, increase your understanding, and fine-tune your strategies. This type of review can be tedious and boring, but it is like steroids for your brain. Feed your head!

36 READING COMPREHENSION more practice & comparative passages

Hopefully, the work we did in the previous lesson once again impressed upon you the importance of two key understandings: your understanding of the reasoning structure of the passage and your understanding of the specific task each question presents.

If you clearly understand the reasoning structure of a passage and clearly understand the task the question stem presents, it becomes much easier to differentiate between the right answer and the four wrong ones. Furthermore, if you solve each problem by first eliminating four wrong choices, then by confirming the correct choice, you will have a far greater chance at being more accurate and consistent. This book has been designed to specifically aid you in developing these skills and habits, and as you continue on in your studies outside of this book, it is these skills and habits that you want to continue to grow.

Let's start this lesson by continuing to work on our problem-solving processes. On the next few pages are two practice passages, each with three actual questions attached. These passages also each have ten hypothetical questions. These questions have no answer choices, and as such there won't be a written solution for them. The purpose of these hypothetical questions is simply for you to practice handling different types of question stems and to reflect on how you might go about thinking about the answer choices.

Why Are Wrong Answers Wrong?

Being able to eliminate wrong answers is a skill critical for success. It can be helpful to keep in mind that all wrong answers either misrepresent the text or do not match the task.

Misrepresent the text by

...incorrectly identifying or translating main points
...misorganizing opinions or evidence relative to main points
...swapping out key details with information that doesn't match what the text discusses

Do not match the task in that they

...do not align with the genre of the question
...do not align with the scope of the question

Passage One

Tragic dramas written in Greece during the fifth century B.C. engender considerable scholarly debate over the relative influence of individual autonomy and the power of the gods on the drama's action. One early scholar, B. Snell, argues that Aeschylus, for example, develops in his tragedies a concept of the autonomy of the individual. In these dramas, the protagonists invariably confront a situation that paralyzes them, so that their prior notions about how to behave or think are dissolved. Faced with a decision on which their fate depends, they must reexamine their deepest motives, and then act with determination. They are given only two alternatives, each with grave consequences, and they make their decision only after a tortured internal debate. According to Snell, this decision is "free" and "personal" and such personal autonomy constitutes the central theme in Aeschylean drama, as if the plays were devised to isolate an abstract model of human action. Drawing psychological conclusions from this interpretation, another scholar, Z. Barbu, suggests that "[Aeschylean] drama is proof of the emergence within ancient Greek civilization of the individual as a free agent."

To A. Rivier, Snell's emphasis on the decision made by the protagonist, with its implicit notions of autonomy and responsibility, misrepresents the role of the superhuman forces at work, forces that give the dramas their truly tragic dimension. These forces are not only external to the protagonist; they are also experienced by the protagonist as an internal compulsion, subjecting him or her to constraint even in what are claimed to be his or her "choices." Hence all that the deliberation does is to make the protagonist aware of the impasse, rather than motivating one choice over another. It is finally a necessity imposed by the deities that generates the decision, so that at a particular moment in the drama necessity dictates a path. Thus, the protagonist does not so much "choose" between two possibilities as "recognize" that there is only one real option.

A. Lesky, in his discussion of Aeschylus' play Agamemnon, disputes both views. Agamemnon, ruler of Argos, must decide whether to brutally sacrifice his own daughter. A message from the deity Artemis has told him that only the sacrifice will bring a wind to blow his ships to an important battle. Agamemnon is indeed constrained by a divine necessity. But he also deeply desires a victorious battle: "If this sacrifice will loose the winds, it is permitted to desire it fervently," he says. The violence of his passion suggests that Agamemnon chooses a path—chosen by the gods for their own reasons—on the basis of desires that must be condemned by us, because they are his own. In Lesky's view, tragic action is bound by the constant tension between a self and superhuman forces.

Practice Test 30, Passage 2

HYPOTHETICAL QUESTIONS

A. Which of the following best describes the author's main purpose?

B. Lesky uses the example of Agamemnon in order to

C. Which of the following best describes the function of the third paragraph?

D. Each of the following is discussed in relation to Rivier's viewpoint EXCEPT

E. Snell would most likely agree that

Passage One

F. The passage best answers which of the following questions?

G. Each of the following is discussed in the passage EXCEPT

H. Which of the following, if true, would strengthen Lesky's theory?

I. Which of the following best describes the organization of the passage?

J. According to the passage, Snell's opinion is that...

ACTUAL QUESTIONS

7. Based on the information presented in the passage, which one of the following statements best represents Lesky's view of Agamemnon?

(A) Agamemnon's motivations are identical to those of the gods.
(B) The nature of Agamemnon's character solely determines the course of the tragedy.
(C) Agamemnon's decision-making is influenced by his military ambitions.
(D) Agamemnon is concerned only with pleasing the deity Artemis.
(E) Agamemnon is especially tragic because of his political position.

9. Which one of the following statements best expresses Rivier's view, as presented in the passage, of what makes a drama tragic?

(A) The tragic protagonist is deluded by the gods into thinking he or she is free.
(B) The tragic protagonist struggles for a heroism that belongs to the gods.
(C) The tragic protagonist wrongly seeks to take responsibility for his or her actions.
(D) The tragic protagonist cannot make a decision that is free of divine compulsion.
(E) The tragic protagonist is punished for evading his or her responsibilities.

14. The primary purpose of the passage is to

(A) argue against one particular interpretation of Greek tragedy
(B) establish that there are a variety of themes in Greek tragedy
(C) present aspects of an ongoing scholarly debate about Greek tragedy
(D) point out the relative merits of different scholarly interpretations of Greek tragedy
(E) suggest the relevance of Greek tragedy to the philosophical debate over human motivation

Passage One Solutions

Tragic dramas written in Greece during the fifth century B.C. engender considerable scholarly debate over the relative influence of individual autonomy and the power of the gods on the drama's action. One early scholar, B. Snell, argues that Aeschylus, for example, develops in his tragedies a concept of the autonomy of the individual. In these dramas, the protagonists invariably confront a situation that paralyzes them, so that their prior notions about how to behave or think are dissolved. Faced with a decision on which their fate depends, they must reexamine their deepest motives, and then act with determination. They are given only two alternatives, each with grave consequences, and they make their decision only after a tortured internal debate. According to Snell, this decision is "free" and "personal" and such personal autonomy constitutes the central theme in Aeschylean drama, as if the plays were devised to isolate an abstract model of human action. Drawing psychological conclusions from this interpretation, another scholar, Z. Barbu, suggests that "[Aeschylean] drama is proof of the emergence within ancient Greek civilization of the individual as a free agent."

Central issue: role of individual versus role of gods in Greek drama.

First opinion (Snell): Greek tragedies emphasize power of individual.

To A. Rivier, Snell's emphasis on the decision made by the protagonist, with its implicit notions of autonomy and responsibility, misrepresents the role of the superhuman forces at work, forces that give the dramas their truly tragic dimension. These forces are not only external to the protagonist; they are also experienced by the protagonist as an internal compulsion, subjecting him or her to constraint even in what are claimed to be his or her "choices." Hence all that the deliberation does is to make the protagonist aware of the impasse, rather than motivating one choice over another. It is finally a necessity imposed by the deities that generates the decision, so that at a particular moment in the drama necessity dictates a path. Thus, the protagonist does not so much "choose" between two possibilities as "recognize" that there is only one real option.

Second opinion (Rivier): gods choose fate and individual simply recognizes what it is.

A. Lesky, in his discussion of Aeschylus' play Agamemnon, disputes both views. Agamemnon, ruler of Argos, must decide whether to brutally sacrifice his own daughter. A message from the deity Artemis has told him that only the sacrifice will bring a wind to blow his ships to an important battle. Agamemnon is indeed constrained by a divine necessity. But he also deeply desires a victorious battle: "If this sacrifice will loose the winds, it is permitted to desire it fervently," he says. The violence of his passion suggests that Agamemnon chooses a path—chosen by the gods for their own reasons—on the basis of desires that must be condemned by us, because they are his own. In Lesky's view, tragic action is bound by the constant tension between a self and superhuman forces.

Third opinion (Lesky): tragic action is based on tension between individual and superhuman forces.

Practice Test 30, Passage 2

Passage One Solutions

7. Based on the information presented in the passage, which one of the following statements best represents Lesky's view of Agamemnon?

(A) Agamemnon's motivations are identical to those of the gods.
(B) The nature of Agamemnon's character solely determines the course of the tragedy.
(C) Agamemnon's decision-making is influenced by his military ambitions.
(D) Agamemnon is concerned only with pleasing the deity Artemis.
(E) Agamemnon is especially tragic because of his political position.

Stem: We know that Lesky sees Agamemnon as dealing with conflict between individual and superhuman forces.

Elimination: (A) misrepresents that conflict, as does (B). (C) isn't what I expected, but I do remember reading he wanted to win—leave it. (D) misrepresents the text, and (E) doesn't match what the text discusses.

Confirmation: (C) is the only viable answer—can I prove it? Yes—in the final paragraph, it says Lesky believes Agamemnon deeply desires victory in battle. (C) doesn't represent Lesky's complete view, but it does accurately represent one part of Lesky's view. (C) is correct.

9. Which one of the following statements best expresses Rivier's view, as presented in the passage, of what makes a drama tragic?

(A) The tragic protagonist is deluded by the gods into thinking he or she is free.
(B) The tragic protagonist struggles for a heroism that belongs to the gods.
(C) The tragic protagonist wrongly seeks to take responsibility for his or her actions.
(D) The tragic protagonist cannot make a decision that is free of divine compulsion.
(E) The tragic protagonist is punished for evading his or her responsibilities.

Stem: I know Rivier feels gods choose fate, and we are simply forced to eventually recognize it. Reading the paragraph again, the "tragedy" specifically refers to the role the gods play.

Elimination: (A) is mentioned in the Rivier section, though it's not the main issue—leave it. (B) is not accurate. Rivier's work isn't about protagonist gaining the heroism of the gods. (C) is tempting, like (A) is, but doesn't seem quite perfect. Let's leave it. Oh no—(D) is also tempting. (E) is definitely wrong.

Confirmation: (A), (C), and (D) all match up with elements mentioned in that paragraph—which one is correct? Looking back at (A), we don't know if the gods are actually deluded. It's not correct. (C) has "wrongly seeks to take responsibility"—that's a little different from being free, and I'm not sure if it's wrong to "seek" taking responsibility. (D) is basically saying humans can't act without divine influence—thinking again, that's similar to what I anticipated initially (gods play role). (D) is correct.

14. The primary purpose of the passage is to

(A) argue against one particular interpretation of Greek tragedy
(B) establish that there are a variety of themes in Greek tragedy
(C) present aspects of an ongoing scholarly debate about Greek tragedy
(D) point out the relative merits of different scholarly interpretations of Greek tragedy
(E) suggest the relevance of Greek tragedy to the philosophical debate over human motivation

Stem: The passage presents three different views on role of individual versus role of gods in Greek drama—imagine the answer will be something related to that.

Elimination: (A) misrepresents the text. One interpretation is not singled out as being wrong. (B) misrepresents the text—the passage is about different ways to think about Greek tragedy, not the different themes in Greek tragedy. (C) is okay—this is a debate, and we've been given three different "aspects," or views, I guess. I'll leave it. (D) seems like a much better answer—I think it's correct. (E) doesn't represent the main substance of the passage. It's not correct.

Confirmation: I didn't love (C), but looking back at it I can't find much wrong with it. The passage does present aspects of an ongoing debate—the answer is terribly broad, but not wrong. Looking at (D) again, I see the word "merits," which has a positive connotation. Has the author talked positively about these various interpretations? No—he's just given information, not "the positives." I realize (C) is right, not (D).

Passage Two

While historians once propagated the myth that Africans who were brought to the New World as slaves contributed little of value but their labor, a recent study by Amelia Wallace Vernon helps to dispel this notion by showing that Africans introduced rice and the methods of cultivating it into what is now the United States in the early eighteenth century. She uncovered, for example, an 1876 document that details that in 1718 starving French settlers instructed the captain of a slave ship bound for Africa to trade for 400 Africans including some "who know how to cultivate rice." This discovery is especially compelling because the introduction of rice into what is now the United States had previously been attributed to French Acadians, who did not arrive until the 1760s.

Vernon interviewed elderly African Americans who helped her discover the locations where until about 1920 their forebears had cultivated rice. At the heart of Vernon's research is the question of why, in an economy dedicated to maximizing cotton production, African Americans grew rice. She proposes two intriguing answers, depending on whether the time is before or after the end of slavery. During the period of slavery, plantation owners also ate rice and therefore tolerated or demanded its "after-hours" cultivation on patches of land not suited to cotton. In addition, growing the rice gave the slaves some relief from a system of regimented labor under a field supervisor, in that they were left alone to work independently.

After the abolition of slavery, however, rice cultivation is more difficult to explain: African Americans had acquired a preference for eating corn, there was no market for the small amounts of rice they produced, and under the tenant system—in which farmers surrendered a portion of their crops to the owners of the land they farmed—owners wanted only cotton as payment. The labor required to transform unused land to productive ground would thus seem completely out of proportion to the reward—except that, according to Vernon, the transforming of the land itself was the point.

Vernon suggests that these African Americans did not transform the land as a means to an end, but rather as an end in itself. In other words, they did not transform the land in order to grow rice—for the resulting rice was scarcely worth the effort required to clear the land—but instead transformed the land because they viewed land as an extension of self and home and so wished to nurture it and make it their own. In addition to this cultural explanation, Vernon speculates that rice cultivation might also have been a political act, a next step after the emancipation of the slaves: the symbolic claiming of plantation land that the U.S. government had promised but failed to parcel off and deed to newly freed African Americans.

Practice Test 30, Passage 4

HYPOTHETICAL QUESTIONS

A. The purpose of the fourth paragraph is to

B. The author's purpose is primarily to

C. The 1876 document is mentioned in the first paragraph to

D. In stating that rice cultivation was a "political act," the author most nearly means that

E. Which of the following could be inferred about the "after hours" cultivation of rice?

Passage Two

F. The author would likely agree that

G. Each of the following is discussed in the first paragraph EXCEPT

H. Which of the following, if true, would weaken Vernon's theories about continued rice cultivation after the war?

I. African Americans' changing preference for corn is mentioned in order to

J. Each of the following opinions is attributed to Vernon EXCEPT

ACTUAL QUESTIONS

23. Which one of the following most completely and accurately describes the author's attitude toward Vernon's study?

(A) respectful of its author and skeptical toward its theories
(B) admiring of its accomplishments and generally receptive to its theories
(C) appreciative of the effort it required and neutral toward its theories
(D) enthusiastic about its goals but skeptical of its theories
(E) accepting of its author's motives but overtly dismissive of its theories

24. As described in the last paragraph of the passage, rice cultivation after slavery is most analogous to which one of the following?

(A) A group of neighbors plants flower gardens on common land adjoining their properties in order to beautify their neighborhood and to create more of a natural boundary between properties.
(B) A group of neighbors plants a vegetable garden for their common use and to compete with the local market's high-priced produce by selling vegetables to other citizens who live outside the neighborhood.
(C) A group of neighbors initiates an effort to neuter all the domestic animals in their neighborhood out of a sense of civic duty and to forestall the city taking action of its own to remedy the overpopulation.
(D) A group of neighbors regularly cleans up the litter on a vacant lot in their neighborhood out of a sense of ownership over the lot and to protest the city's neglect of their neighborhood.
(E) A group of neighbors renovates an abandoned building so they can start a program to watch each other's children out of a sense of communal responsibility and to offset the closing of a day care center in their neighborhood.

25. Which one of the following most completely and accurately describes the organization of the passage?

(A) A historical phenomenon is presented, several competing theories about the phenomenon are described, and one theory having the most support is settled upon.
(B) A historical discovery is presented, the method leading to the discovery is provided, and two questions left unanswered by the discovery are identified.
(C) A historical fact is presented, a question raised by the fact is described, and two answers to the question are given.
(D) A historical question is raised, possible answers to the question are speculated upon, and two reasons for difficulty in answering the question are given.
(E) A historical question is raised, a study is described that answers the question, and a number of issues surrounding the study are discussed.

Passage Two Solutions

While historians once propagated the myth that Africans who were brought to the New World as slaves contributed little of value but their labor, a recent study by Amelia Wallace Vernon helps to dispel this notion by showing that Africans introduced rice and the methods of cultivating it into what is now the United States in the early eighteenth century. She uncovered, for example, an 1876 document that details that in 1718 starving French settlers instructed the captain of a slave ship bound for Africa to trade for 400 Africans including some "who know how to cultivate rice." This discovery is especially compelling because the introduction of rice into what is now the United States had previously been attributed to French Acadians, who did not arrive until the 1760s.

Central issue: (old idea) African slaves contributed little beyond labor / main idea (author opinion). This is not true.

Support—evidence African slaves developed cultivation of rice.

Vernon interviewed elderly African Americans who helped her discover the locations where until about 1920 their forebears had cultivated rice. At the heart of Vernon's research is the question of why, in an economy dedicated to maximizing cotton production, African Americans grew rice. She proposes two intriguing answers, depending on whether the time is before or after the end of slavery. During the period of slavery, plantation owners also ate rice and therefore tolerated or demanded its "after-hours" cultivation on patches of land not suited to cotton. In addition, growing the rice gave the slaves some relief from a system of regimented labor under a field supervisor, in that they were left alone to work independently.

Never mind—this is the main issue (previous paragraph was background): why did they keep growing rice?

Two possible reasons—slave owners permitted/required it, allowed them to work on their own.

After the abolition of slavery, however, rice cultivation is more difficult to explain: African Americans had acquired a preference for eating corn, there was no market for the small amounts of rice they produced, and under the tenant system—in which farmers surrendered a portion of their crops to the owners of the land they farmed—owners wanted only cotton as payment. The labor required to transform unused land to productive ground would thus seem completely out of proportion to the reward—except that, according to Vernon, the transforming of the land itself was the point.

More on main issue—after slavery, more difficult to explain.

Vernon suggests that these African Americans did not transform the land as a means to an end, but rather as an end in itself. In other words, they did not transform the land in order to grow rice—for the resulting rice was scarcely worth the effort required to clear the land—but instead transformed the land because they viewed land as an extension of self and home and so wished to nurture it and make it their own. In addition to this cultural explanation, Vernon speculates that rice cultivation might also have been a political act, a next step after the emancipation of the slaves: the symbolic claiming of plantation land that the U.S. government had promised but failed to parcel off and deed to newly freed African Americans.

Explanation (Vernon)—did it not for rice, but for action. Liked to "remake" ground. Might also be political act—taking control of land.

Comment: the point of this final paragraph is a bit theoretical and difficult to understand exactly. If you struggle to do so, that's okay—make sure you understand the overall gist of it (did it for some emotional/personal reason rather than for rice), and most importantly, make sure you understand the purpose of the information (explains why they continued to cultivate rice after slavery).

Practice Test 30, Passage 4

Passage Two Solutions

23. Which one of the following most completely and accurately describes the author's attitude toward Vernon's study?

(A) respectful of its author and skeptical toward its theories
(B) admiring of its accomplishments and generally receptive to its theories
(C) appreciative of the effort it required and neutral toward its theories
(D) enthusiastic about its goals but skeptical of its theories
(E) accepting of its author's motives but overtly dismissive of its theories

Stem: Only time author really gives any hint of opinion is at beginning—"helps dispel"—otherwise fairly objective, I think, but definitely doesn't seem opposed in any way to Vernon's ideas.

Elimination: (A) clearly misrepresents the opinion. (B) seems good, though stronger than I expected. The tone of (C) is right, but I don't really like it—"appreciative of effort" doesn't match what I remember, but I'll leave it just in case. The author doesn't express any skepticism, so (D) is out. The author doesn't dismiss the theories, so (E) is out.

Confirmation: (B) seemed good, thought a bit stronger than what I would say. (C) seemed wrong. I'll double check (C) again—no specific mention of effort. (C) is wrong. Looking at (B) again, I guess it's not too strong—"generally receptive" is how I'd put things, and "helps dispel" and "especially compelling" help support "admiring." (B) is correct.

24. As described in the last paragraph of the passage, rice cultivation after slavery is most analogous to which one of the following?

(A) A group of neighbors plants flower gardens on common land adjoining their properties in order to beautify their neighborhood and to create more of a natural boundary between properties.
(B) A group of neighbors plants a vegetable garden for their common use and to compete with the local market's high-priced produce by selling vegetables to other citizens who live outside the neighborhood.
(C) A group of neighbors initiates an effort to neuter all the domestic animals in their neighborhood out of a sense of civic duty and to forestall the city taking action of its own to remedy the overpopulation.
(D) A group of neighbors regularly cleans up the litter on a vacant lot in their neighborhood out of a sense of ownership over the lot and to protest the city's neglect of their neighborhood.
(E) A group of neighbors renovates an abandoned building so they can start a program to watch each other's children out of a sense of communal responsibility and to offset the closing of a day care center in their neighborhood.

Stem: Okay, I remember that paragraph said that rice wasn't cultivated for sake of eating but for the act itself—could be seen as political act. Will wait to return to passage until after eliminating some obvious mismatches.

Elimination: I don't think (A) fits—I don't remember anything about a group, and they don't plant the rice for an express purpose. (A) is out. (B) is out—it's about growing for the purpose of eating. I don't see a match for "civic duty" and "forestalling" from (C), so that's out. I don't really like (D), but it's the best so far—at least it's somewhat political. I'll leave it. I don't think "communal" was an issue, so I think I can knock off (E).

Confirmation: Shoot, no great answers—is (D) really correct? Read answer again, text again—(D) is definitely correct. It doesn't match what I thought about, but that last paragraph discusses ownership and political protest.

25. Which one of the following most completely and accurately describes the organization of the passage?

(A) A historical phenomenon is presented, several competing theories about the phenomenon are described, and one theory having the most support is settled upon.
(B) A historical discovery is presented, the method leading to the discovery is provided, and two questions left unanswered by the discovery are identified.
(C) A historical fact is presented, a question raised by the fact is described, and two answers to the question are given.
(D) A historical question is raised, possible answers to the question are speculated upon, and two reasons for difficulty in answering the question are given.
(E) A historical question is raised, a study is described that answers the question, and a number of issues surrounding the study are discussed.

Stem: Quick review: general issue (slaves did/didn't contribute beyond labor) presented, then more specific issue (why did African Americans cultivate rice after slavery?) becomes main issue—gives explanation. Time to eliminate.

Elimination: (A) doesn't match structure at all. (B) is a little tempting (two questions) but has too many mismatches—I'll leave it just in case. I like (C)—leave it. (D) doesn't match latter part of the passage. (E) also doesn't match latter part of the passage (it doesn't discuss issues with the study itself).

Confirmation: Looking at (B) again, it explains the first part of the passage pretty well, actually (discovery: slaves cultivated rice from early on; method: papers; two questions: why did they cultivate rice during, then after slavery?). However, (B) doesn't represent the second half of the text. (C) better matches the entire passage—the historical fact (slaves producing rice) is mentioned early, a question (why?) is discussed, and two answers (for during slavery, then after) are given. (C) is correct.

Strategies for Comparative Passage Questions

When we first discussed comparative passage sets, one point of emphasis was that they require the same reading skills and strategies traditional passages require, but in a slightly different context. The same can be said about the *questions* that accompany these comparative sets. They require you to think about the same considerations—whether questions are general or specific, or directly asking about structure, opinions, or details—but in a slightly different context. Instead of thinking of these issues in relation to one passage, now you must think of these issues in relation to a set of related passages.

As with standard passages, the key to your success on comparative sets will be your understanding of reasoning structure. If you have a clear sense of the central issue or debate that both passages relate to, and if you have a clear sense of how both passages relate to that central issue or debate, you will be in top shape to answer all types of questions that may appear.

Some questions that accompany these passages will be pretty much exactly the same as those that accompany traditional passages—they will ask about one author's opinion, or the main point of one passage, or details mentioned in one passage. However, these questions will be in the minority.

The majority of the questions that you will see will require you to think about both passages and compare them against one another. As expected, some of these questions will ask about differences between the passages—differing opinions the authors have, or perhaps details mentioned in one passage but not the other. These questions naturally align with the differences between passages, and these questions are plentiful.

Interestingly, even more plentiful are questions that ask about similarities between passages—ideas that both authors may agree with or details that are mentioned in both passages. Even though the passages are commonly designed to fall at least somewhat on opposite sides of some sort of debate, for whatever reason the test writers choose to put in more questions about commonality than they do about differences.

Another unique characteristic of comparative question sets is that they tend to lean more toward specifics rather than big-picture issues. Questions that ask about details are far more common than in other types of passages, and broad general questions are far less common. This should not impact your reading strategies. A strong understanding of reasoning structure is the key to identifying details quickly and answering detail questions correctly. Now let's discuss the general categories of questions that appear with comparative passage sets.

General Comparative Questions (common)

These questions can ask about things on which the authors agree or disagree. Both of these types of questions are very common. The two authors may, in general, agree, but questions may ask about points on which they disagree. Similarly, the two authors may be in general disagreement, but our job will be to focus on something they agree on.

A strong sense of the central argument and the role that each passage plays relative to that central argument (and thus one another) can help make these questions fairly straightforward, in large part because it can help us recognize more easily the incorrect answers. Wrong answers really are our best friends here; if we understand the passages well, most of the wrong choices will be very obviously wrong.

Non-Comparative Questions (uncommon)

A minority of the questions that accompany a comparative set will have nothing to do with the fact that they are a comparative set—they will ask about one passage or the other.

You want to treat these questions just as you would any others—reflect on that particular passage as a whole, look for certain details, or dive into the answer choices—just as you would with any other question.

The one arena in which it's important to remember that these questions are part of a comparative set is the answer choices. Many of the answers will be wrong for the same reasons they've always been wrong, but you will also have certain answer choices that are wrong because they actually describe the other passage. Be mindful of keeping the passages separate and you'll be fine.

Specific Comparative Questions (most common)

For comparative passage sets, expect to field a lot of questions about what was mentioned in one passage, the other, both, or neither. These questions are extremely common, and they can also be time consuming. It's important that you are good at solving these questions.

If asked about something mentioned in both passages, you can expect that some answers will likely be mentioned in neither, and some in one or the other. If asked about a detail mentioned in one but not the other, of course you should expect answers that give you the reverse of what you need.

These questions generally require you to think about both passages, but you don't really have time to check each answer against both passages. The key is to have a strong enough sense of the passages that you can whittle down the answer choices, hopefully to just a couple, before you have to do much serious digging. Even then, it's very likely that you'll be able to remember seeing one thing in one passage (and be able to confirm quickly) and so will only have to "dig" in the other. These detail questions tend to be subtle and sneaky, and you want to do everything you need to in order to confirm your answer. At the same time, you have to control the amount of time you spend. The key is to have a strong understanding of the passages and the ability to get rid of some more obviously wrong answers.

Comparative Passage One

Directions below

Passage A

Because dental caries (decay) is strongly linked to consumption of the sticky, carbohydrate-rich staples of agricultural diets, prehistoric human teeth can provide clues about when a population made the transition from a hunter-gatherer diet to an agricultural one. Caries formation is influenced by several factors, including tooth structure, bacteria in the mouth, and diet. In particular, caries formation is affected by carbohydrates' texture and composition, since carbohydrates more readily stick to teeth.

Many researchers have demonstrated the link between carbohydrate consumption and caries. In North America, Leigh studied caries in archaeologically derived teeth, noting that caries rates differed between indigenous populations that primarily consumed meat (a Sious sample showed almost no caries) and those heavily dependent on cultivated maize (a Zuni sample had 75 percent carious teeth). Leigh's findings have been frequently confirmed by other researchers, who have shown that, in general, the greater a population's dependence on agriculture is, the higher its rate of caries formation will be.

Under some circumstances, however, nonagricultural populations may exhibit relatively high caries rates. For example, early nonagricultural populations in western North America who consumed large amounts of highly processed stone-ground flour made from gathered acorns show relatively high caries frequency. And wild plants collected by the Hopi included several species with high cariogenic potential, notably pinyon nuts and wild tubers.

Passage B

Archaeologists recovered human skeletal remains interred over a 2,000-year period in prehistoric Ban Chiang, Thailand. The site's early inhabitants appear to have had a hunter-gatherer-cultivator economy. Evidence indicates that, over time, the population became increasingly dependent on agriculture.

Research suggests that agricultural intensification results in declining human health, including dental health. Studies show that dental caries is uncommon in pre-agricultural populations. Increased caries frequency may result from increased consumption of starchy-sticky foodstuffs or from alterations in tooth wear. The wearing down of tooth crown surfaces reduces caries formation by removing fissures that can trap food particles. A reduction of fiber or grit in a diet may diminish tooth wear, thus increasing caries frequency. However, severe wear that exposes a tooth's pulp cavity may also result in caries.

The diet of Ban Chiang's inhabitants included some cultivated rice and yams from the beginning of the period represented by the recovered remains. These were part of a varied diet that also included wild plant and animal foods. Since both rice and yams are carbohydrates, increased reliance on either or both should theoretically result in increased caries frequency.

Yet comparisons of caries frequency in the Early and Late Ban Chiang Groups indicate that overall caries frequency is slightly greater in the Early Group. Tooth wear patterns do not indicate tooth wear changes between Early and Late Groups that would explain this unexpected finding. It is more likely that, although dependence on agriculture increased, the diet in the Late period remained varied enough that no single food dominated. Furthermore, there may have been a shift from sweeter carbohydrates (yams) towards rice, a less cariogenic carbohydrate.

Practice Test 62, Passage 3

Directions: Go ahead and read the comparative sets and solve questions to the best of your ability. Please note that these comparative sets were taken from recent exams (because there are no comparative sets from older exams), so if these recent exams are part of your practice schedule, please adjust accordingly.

Comparative Passage One

16. Which one of the following distinguishes the Ban Chiang populations discussed in passage B from the populations discussed in the last paragraph of passage A?

(A) While the Ban Chiang populations consumed several highly cariogenic foods, the populations discussed in the last paragraph of passage A did not.
(B) While the Ban Chiang populations ate cultivated foods, the populations discussed in the last paragraph of passage A did not.
(C) While the Ban Chiang populations consumed a diet consisting primarily of carbohydrates, the populations discussed in the last paragraph of passage A did not.
(D) While the Ban Chiang populations exhibited very high levels of tooth wear, the populations discussed in the last paragraph of passage A did not.
(E) While the Ban Chiang populations ate certain highly processed foods, the populations discussed in the last paragraph of passage A did not.

18. Which one of the following is mentioned in both passages as evidence tending to support the prevailing view regarding the relationship between dental caries and carbohydrate consumption?

(A) the effect of consuming highly processed foods on caries formation
(B) the relatively low incidence of caries among nonagricultural people
(C) the effect of fiber and grit in the diet on caries formation
(D) the effect of the consumption of wild foods on tooth wear
(E) the effect of agricultural intensification on overall human health

19. It is most likely that both authors would agree with which one of the following statements about dental caries?

(A) The incidence of dental caries increases predictably in populations over time.
(B) Dental caries is often difficult to detect in teeth recovered from archaeological sites.
(C) Dental caries tends to be more prevalent in populations with a hunter-gatherer diet than in populations with an agricultural diet.
(D) The frequency of dental caries in a population does not necessarily correspond directly to the population's degree of dependence on agriculture.
(E) The formation of dental caries tends to be more strongly linked to tooth wear than to the consumption of a particular kind of food.

Comparative Passage One Solutions

Passage A

Because dental caries (decay) is strongly linked to consumption of the sticky, carbohydrate-rich staples of agricultural diets, prehistoric human teeth can provide clues about when a population made the transition from a hunter-gatherer diet to an agricultural one. Caries formation is influenced by several factors, including tooth structure, bacteria in the mouth, and diet. In particular, caries formation is affected by carbohydrates' texture and composition, since carbohydrates more readily stick to teeth.

Background (?): dental caries linked to agriculture; can use caries to figure out when a culture became agricultural.

Many researchers have demonstrated the link between carbohydrate consumption and caries. In North America, Leigh studied caries in archaeologically derived teeth, noting that caries rates differed between indigenous populations that primarily consumed meat (a Sious sample showed almost no caries) and those heavily dependent on cultivated maize (a Zuni sample had 75 percent carious teeth). Leigh's findings have been frequently confirmed by other researchers, who have shown that, in general, the greater a population's dependence on agriculture is, the higher its rate of caries formation will be.

Never mind—that there is a link between caries and agriculture is the main point of this passage. More support here for that.

Under some circumstances, however, nonagricultural populations may exhibit relatively high caries rates. For example, early nonagricultural populations in western North America who consumed large amounts of highly processed stone-ground flour made from gathered acorns show relatively high caries frequencies. And wild plants collected by the Hopi included several species with high cariogenic potential, notably pinyon nuts and wild tubers.

Exceptions—nonagricultural but high-caries cultures/explanations.

Passage B

Archaeologists recovered human skeletal remains interred over a 2,000-year period in prehistoric Ban Chiang, Thailand. The site's early inhabitants appear to have had a hunter-gatherer-cultivator economy. Evidence indicates that, over time, the population became increasingly dependent on agriculture.

Background—about switch to agricultural society.

Research suggests that agricultural intensification results in declining human health, including dental health. Studies show that dental caries is uncommon in pre-agricultural populations. Increased caries frequency may result from increased consumption of starchy-sticky foodstuffs or from alterations in tooth wear. The wearing down of tooth crown surfaces reduces caries formation by removing fissures that can trap food particles. A reduction of fiber or grit in a diet may diminish tooth wear, thus increasing caries frequency. However, severe wear that exposes a tooth's pulp cavity may also result in caries.

Explanation of how agriculture leads to caries—same point as first passage.

The diet of Ban Chiang's inhabitants included some cultivated rice and yams from the beginning of the period represented by the recovered remains. These were part of a varied diet that also included wild plant and animal foods. Since both rice and yams are carbohydrates, increased reliance on either or both should theoretically result in increased caries frequency.

Background: setting us up to get a "twist" in the final paragraph. Based on what we know, Ban Chiang should have higher caries, but...

Yet comparisons of caries frequency in the Early and Late Ban Chiang Groups indicate that overall caries frequency is slightly greater in the Early Group. Tooth wear patterns do not indicate tooth wear changes between Early and Late Groups that would explain this unexpected finding. It is more likely that, although dependence on agriculture increased, the diet in the Late period remained varied enough that no single food dominated. Furthermore, there may have been a shift from sweeter carbohydrates (yams) towards rice, a less cariogenic carbohydrate.

Explanation—variety in diet, switch to less cariogenic agriculture could be reasons why they don't.

Practice Test 62, Passage 3

Comparative Passage One Solutions

16. Which one of the following distinguishes the Ban Chiang populations discussed in passage B from the populations discussed in the last paragraph of passage A?

(A) While the Ban Chiang populations consumed several highly cariogenic foods, the populations discussed in the last paragraph of passage A did not.
(B) While the Ban Chiang populations ate cultivated foods, the populations discussed in the last paragraph of passage A did not.
(C) While the Ban Chiang populations consumed a diet consisting primarily of carbohydrates, the populations discussed in the last paragraph of passage A did not.
(D) While the Ban Chiang populations exhibited very high levels of tooth wear, the populations discussed in the last paragraph of passage A did not.
(E) While the Ban Chiang populations ate certain highly processed foods, the populations discussed in the last paragraph of passage A did not.

Stem: The populations at end of previous paragraph were non-agricultural, whereas the Ban Chiang were agricultural. Could be something else too. Time to eliminate.

Elimination: (A) is not true—both consumed cariogenic foods. Cut. (B) looks like my answer—leave. Not sure about "primary" regarding Ban Chiang or other populations—cut (C). (D) is incorrect relative to the passage—cut. (E) sounds like the right answer too—leave.

Confirmation: Both (B) and (E) look good—time to look more carefully. What's the difference between cultivation and processing? Cultivation is growing stuff—agriculture. Processing doesn't have to be agriculture, and populations in passage A do process their food (though they don't grow it). (B) is correct.

18. Which one of the following is mentioned in both passages as evidence tending to support the prevailing view regarding the relationship between dental caries and carbohydrate consumption?

(A) the effect of consuming highly processed foods on caries formation
(B) the relatively low incidence of caries among nonagricultural people
(C) the effect of fiber and grit in the diet on caries formation
(D) the effect of the consumption of wild foods on tooth wear
(E) the effect of agricultural intensification on overall human health

Stem: Both discuss research involving pre-agricultural/agricultural societies, I think. Could be something else though—time to eliminate.

Elimination: "Processed" doesn't directly impact the relationship between caries and carbs (as I just thought about on #16)—can cut (A). I think (B) is right—leave. I see fiber and grit in passage B—quickly look in passage A, not there. Eliminate (C). What are "wild" foods? Nothing like that discussed in second passage—cut (D). (E) is only discussed in second passage, I think. Double check—yup.

Confirmation: Double check that (B) is discussed by both passages—it is. (B) is correct.

19. It is most likely that both authors would agree with which one of the following statements about dental caries?

(A) The incidence of dental caries increases predictably in populations over time.
(B) Dental caries is often difficult to detect in teeth recovered from archaeological sites.
(C) Dental caries tends to be more prevalent in populations with a hunter-gatherer diet than in populations with an agricultural diet.
(D) The frequency of dental caries in a population does not necessarily correspond directly to the population's degree of dependence on agriculture.
(E) The formation of dental caries tends to be more strongly linked to tooth wear than to the consumption of a particular kind of food.

Stem: Both give main points that caries and carbs linked, while also discussing exceptions.

Elimination: (A) is tempting—they do give reasons why increases happen. Leave. "Difficult to detect" in (B) not discussed by passages. (C) goes against what passages say. (D) is correct, I think—leave. (E) doesn't match passage, which is about food's impact on caries.

Confirmation: Looking at (A) again—is it saying caries increases in all populations? Also, who says it's predictable? Not sure what I was thinking, but (A) is not inferable. Both authors give examples in which dependence on agriculture doesn't match up with the amount of caries, so they would definitely agree with (D). (D) is right.

Comparative Passage Two

Passage A

Central to the historian's profession and scholarship has been the ideal of objectivity. The assumptions upon which this ideal rests include a commitment to the reality of the past, a sharp separation between fact and value, and above all, a distinction between history and fiction.

According to this ideal, historical facts are prior to and independent of interpretation: the value of an interpretation should be judged by how well it accounts for the facts; if an interpretation is contradicted by facts, it should be abandoned. The fact that successive generations of historians have ascribed different meanings to past events does not mean, as relativist historians claim, that the events themselves lack fixed or absolute meanings.

Objective historians see their role as that of a neutral judge, one who must never become an advocate or, worse, propagandist. Their conclusions should display the judicial qualities of balance and evenhandedness. As with the judiciary, these qualities require insulation from political considerations, and avoidance of partisanship or bias. Thus objective historians must purge themselves of external loyalties; their primary allegiance is to objective historical truth and to colleagues who share a commitment to its discovery.

Passage B

The very possibility of historical scholarship as an enterprise distinct from propaganda requires of its practitioners that self-discipline that enables them to do such things as abandon wishful thinking, assimilate bad news, and discard pleasing interpretations that fail elementary tests of evidence and logic.

Yet objectivity, for the historian, should not be confused with neutrality. Objectivity is perfectly compatible with strong political commitment. The objective thinker does not value detachment as an end in itself but only as an indispensable means of achieving deeper understanding. In historical scholarship, the ideal of objectivity is most compellingly embodied in the powerful argument—one that reveals by its every twist and turn its respectful appreciation of the alternative arguments it rejects. Such a text attains power precisely because its author has managed to suspend momentarily his or her own perceptions so as to anticipate and take into account objections and alternative constructions—not those of straw men, but those that truly issue from the rival's position, understood as sensitively and stated as eloquently as the rival could desire. To mount a telling attack on a position, one must first inhabit it. Those so habituated to their customary intellectual abode that they cannot even explore others can never be persuasive to anyone but fellow habitues.

Practice Test 63, Passage 4

24. The author of passage B and the kind of objective historian described in passage A would be most likely to disagree over whether

(A) detachment aids the historian in achieving an objective view of past events
(B) an objective historical account can include a strong political commitment
(C) historians today are less objective than they were previously
(D) propaganda is an essential tool of historical scholarship
(E) historians of different eras have arrived at differing interpretations of the same historical events

25. Which one of the following most accurately describes an attitude toward objectivity present in each passage?

(A) Objectivity is a goal that few historians can claim to achieve.
(B) Objectivity is essential to the practice of historical scholarship.
(C) Objectivity cannot be achieved unless historians set aside political allegiances.
(D) Historians are not good judges of their own objectivity.
(E) Historians who value objectivity are becoming less common.

27. The argument described in passage A and the argument made by the author of passage B are both advanced by

(A) citing historical scholarship that fails to achieve objectivity
(B) showing how certain recent developments in historical scholarship have undermined the credibility of the profession
(C) summarizing opposing arguments in order to point out their flaws
(D) suggesting that historians should adopt standards used by professionals in certain other fields
(E) identifying what are seen as obstacles to achieving objectivity

Comparative Passage Two Solutions

Passage A

Central to the historian's profession and scholarship has been the ideal of objectivity. The assumptions upon which this ideal rests include a commitment to the reality of the past, a sharp separation between fact and value, and above all, a distinction between history and fiction.

(Likely) background: objectivity central to job of being historian—description of what objectivity requires.

According to this ideal, historical facts are prior to and independent of interpretation: the value of an interpretation should be judged by how well it accounts for the facts; if an interpretation is contradicted by facts, it should be abandoned. The fact that successive generations of historians have ascribed different meanings to past events does not mean, as relativist historians claim, that the events themselves lack fixed or absolute meanings.

More about objectivity and historians—this is the author's main point: objectivity is important to historians. More on this—says that historical facts are independent and true, even if this meaning changes over time.

Objective historians see their role as that of a neutral judge, one who must never become an advocate or, worse, propagandist. Their conclusions should display the judicial qualities of balance and evenhandedness. As with the judiciary, these qualities require insulation from political considerations, and avoidance of partisanship or bias. Thus objective historians must purge themselves of external loyalties; their primary allegiance is to objective historical truth and to colleagues who share a commitment to its discovery.

More on what is required to be an objective historian.

Passage B

The very possibility of historical scholarship as an enterprise distinct from propaganda requires of its practitioners that self-discipline that enables them to do such things as abandon wishful thinking, assimilate bad news, and discard pleasing interpretations that fail elementary tests of evidence and logic.

Similar to end of previous passage—seems like characteristics required of objective historian.

Yet objectivity, for the historian, should not be confused with neutrality. Objectivity is perfectly compatible with strong political commitment. The objective thinker does not value detachment as an end in itself but only as an indispensable means of achieving deeper understanding. In historical scholarship, the ideal of objectivity is most compellingly embodied in the powerful argument—one that reveals by its every twist and turn its respectful appreciation of the alternative arguments it rejects. Such a text attains power precisely because its author has managed to suspend momentarily his or her own perceptions so as to anticipate and take into account objections and alternative constructions—not those of straw men, but those that truly issue from the rival's position, understood as sensitively and stated as eloquently as the rival could desire. To mount a telling attack on a position, one must first inhabit it. Those so habituated to their customary intellectual abode that they cannot even explore others can never be persuasive to anyone but fellow habitues.

Twist—this passage is about something a little different, objectivity versus neutrality. "Political commitment" part contradicts what it says about objectivity in first passage. (Author of first passage sees neutrality as part of objectivity; author of second passage doesn't, I think.)

Another change of issue—says non-neutrality important to making a good argument.

(Comment: can see both being related to central issue of what is required to be an objective historian. Author of first passage sees neutrality as requirement of objectivity, but second doesn't. The second also discusses value of not having neutrality.)

Practice Test 63, Passage 4

Comparative Passage Two Solutions

24. The author of passage B and the kind of objective historian described in passage A would be most likely to disagree over whether

(A) detachment aids the historian in achieving an objective view of past events
(B) an objective historical account can include a strong political commitment
(C) historians today are less objective than they were previously
(D) propaganda is an essential tool of historical scholarship
(E) historians of different eras have arrived at differing interpretations of the same historical events

Stem: I know they disagree about political commitments (specifically) and seem to disagree about neutrality (generally) but it can be something else too. Time to eliminate.

Elimination: I think both authors see value of (A). (B) is the right answer—leave. (C) is not discussed by either passage, nor is (D). The second passage doesn't speak of (E), and I think both authors would agree on it anyway.

Confirmation: Double check—passage A says objective historian needs to isolate self from political commitments, and passage B says objectivity is perfectly compatible with strong political commitment. (B) is correct.

25. Which one of the following most accurately describes an attitude toward objectivity present in each passage?

(A) Objectivity is a goal that few historians can claim to achieve.
(B) Objectivity is essential to the practice of historical scholarship.
(C) Objectivity cannot be achieved unless historians set aside political allegiances.
(D) Historians are not good judges of their own objectivity.
(E) Historians who value objectivity are becoming less common.

Stem: I know that both passages present objectivity as useful and characteristic of historians, but let's see what the answers are about.

Elimination: I don't think either discussed (A). (B) is the right answer, I think. (C) is not something passage B agrees with. (D) is not specifically discussed in either passage, nor is (E).

Confirmation: Don't even need to double check this—both passages are *about* (B).

27. The argument described in passage A and the argument made by the author of passage B are both advanced by

(A) citing historical scholarship that fails to achieve objectivity
(B) showing how certain recent developments in historical scholarship have undermined the credibility of the profession
(C) summarizing opposing arguments in order to point out their flaws
(D) suggesting that historians should adopt standards used by professionals in certain other fields
(E) identifying what are seen as obstacles to achieving objectivity

Stem: "Advanced by"—the question is asking about structure. Let's see—passage A sets up objectivity as being important to historian, then expands. Passage B discusses importance of objectivity, then switches gears to discuss neutrality relative to objectivity, then expands on that. They seem pretty different...

Elimination: Neither cites failed scholarship, I think, so (A) is out. (B) is not relevant to either passage. Neither cites opposing arguments, so (C) is out. Other professionals? Quick scan—nope, not discussed. (D) is out. (E) seems okay—not great, but it's the only one left.

Confirmation: Does each passage specifically mention "obstacles"? I guess the first passage does at the end—the political considerations, allegiances, and such could be seen as obstacles. Second passage definitely presents obstacles in the first paragraph. (E) is correct.

37 READING COMPREHENSION — review, timing strategies, and final thoughts

We have two Reading Comprehension lessons left. In this lesson, we will review the main points we have discussed in other Reading Comprehension lessons, walk through timing strategies, and talk about the work you'll be doing after this book. In the next lesson, we'll work on our final practice set of passages.

A Review of Lessons

Here is a snapshot review of the key points made in the various Reading Comprehension lessons. The lesson number has been listed after the point. You can use this list to reflect on what we've discussed and also to note areas in which it might help to do a bit of review.

The Reading Comprehension section tests your reading ability—primarily your ability to recognize reasoning structure (22).

The reasoning structure of a passage is the relationship between various parts of a passage; typically, the relationships in LSAT passages are structured around (often opposing) main points (22).

Reading Comprehension passages are not designed to test, in a significant way, your ability to retain a lot of information, your understanding of unusual subjects and words, or your critical reasoning ability (22).

You are never required to be critical of reasoning as you read a passage, but one or two questions may ask for you to evaluate one of the opinions critically.

It's helpful to think about all parts of a passage in terms of the following roles, all of which are defined by the main points made in the passage: main points, author's view of those points, reasons for and against those points, more information about those points as well as potential applications, and, finally, background on the subject matter related to those points (22).

Getting good at LSAT Reading Comprehension is less about developing new skills and more about correctly utilizing tools you already have (23).

As we read, we want to focus on reasoning structure more than subject matter, we want to embrace uncertainty when uncertainty is warranted, and we want to use main points to organize our thoughts (23).

The best time to most easily understand a passage is at the end of it, and for certain difficult passages, it will be nearly impossible to completely understand the passage before that point (23).

The question stem is the third piece of the jigsaw puzzle; it brings together the passage and the correct answer. In general, it will tell you whether the answer relates to the passage as a whole or to a specific component (24).

There is great commonality to the reasoning structures for different passages, and it can be helpful to think about the reasoning structure of passages in terms of tendencies and twists (25).

Comparative passage sets present two passages related to some central issue. Your primary tasks are to figure out what that central issue is, how the passages relate to it, and how the passages relate to one another (25).

General comparative passage set questions will ask about these primary tasks mentioned above. A strong majority of specific questions will be about commonalities and differences between the two passages (25).

You can encounter a large variety of questions in the Reading Comprehension section, but they are all just different combinations of a few specific characteristics (35).

The two fundamental considerations for any question are the genre (is it asking about reasoning structure, an opinion, or information?) and the scope (general or specific?) (35).

Use specific strategies for different types of structure, opinion, and detail questions (35).

Strengthen and Weaken questions are unique in that they require critical reasoning skills (35).

Read each question stem carefully. Use it to decide scope and genre and to decide how much you are expected to anticipate about the right answer (35).

Wrong answers are typically easier to spot than right ones, especially for more challenging questions, and in most instances you should aim to eliminate four wrong choices before selecting an answer (35).

Wrong answers are wrong because they misrepresent the text or because they don't match the task presented in the question stem (36).

The majority of questions for comparative passage sets will require you to compare the passages against one another (36).

Comparative passage sets tend to have more specific questions and less general questions than other types of passages (36).

Timing

We discussed some basic Reading Comprehension timing strategies back in Lesson 25. Let's revisit some of the key points we made and discuss timing in more depth.

In recent years, every Reading Comprehension section has contained twenty-seven questions. This might change any minute, but it won't change drastically. In general, you want to spend about 2:30 to 3 minutes reading each passage and about 0:45 to a minute per question. Different questions will require varying amounts of time; however, most passages are of similar length, and once you settle into your practice exams, you should be able to set a fairly consistent reading pace.

Different test takers take different amounts of time initially reading a passage; people have been successful with a variety of strategies. In general, if you average more time (say, 4:00 or so) per read, you should expect to retain a bit more of the passage than what I typically suggest in the solutions, and you should expect that questions will go faster for you than I suggest. If you read faster than 2:30 or 3:00 per passage, you'll certainly have a bit more time for questions, but if you are reading at that fast of a pace, you want to make sure it's not putting you at risk for misunderstanding the main points or the reasoning structure.

In Lesson 25, we also discussed the fact that pace typically matches process—if your skills and habits are strong, timing becomes less of an issue. Timing is a more significant issue when your path to the right answer is less direct. Finally, we also discussed the fact that, when we have to make difficult decisions in terms of time, it's best to cut out individual questions rather than entire passages. We'll expand on both of those points in this lesson.

Basic Timing Instincts

Answering any LSAT question correctly involves a series of correct steps. These steps can overlap, and sometimes you can get away with not being "perfect" at one of them, but for every Reading Comprehension question, you will be required to

1) Understand the relevant information about the passage
2) Understand what the question stem is asking of you
3) See why the wrong answers are wrong
4) See why the right answer is right

The best way to think about the efficient use of time is to think about what you are doing relative to these necessary steps. Here's what I mean, in a bit more detail:

It is an ***efficient*** use of time to stop during your read to think, when necessary, about the reasoning structure of the passage. If you are certain that the second paragraph plays one role, but then, in reading the third paragraph, you are not so sure you understand the point of the passage at all, quickly go back and think about the second paragraph again. If you feel pretty certain about the two sides of an issue, but then something you read makes you feel like your priorities are out of whack, take the time to stop, reassess, and reread as necessary. Of course, you can't spend an inordinate about of time (to be discussed further in just a bit) doing this, but in general this will be time well spent. The reason? Reasoning structure is always relevant to several of the questions you will see, and, as I'm sure many of you have experienced, it's next to impossible to get through the questions in an efficient manner if you don't have a good sense of reasoning structure.

It is commonly an ***inefficient*** use of time to stop during your read to think about the meaning of complex phrases or sentences. This is not true if that complex phrase or sentence is necessary for you to understand the central issue or a key opinion. However, in just about every other instance, you don't have to concern yourself with being perfectly in tune with every detail mentioned. Those random details are, mathematically speaking, unlikely to factor into any questions, and even if they do turn out to be relevant to a question, you can always come back to reread them as needed. If you find yourself rereading and rereading a sentence, ask yourself, do I understand why it is here? If you are not so clear on the what, but clear on the why, then move on and keep reading forward.

It is always an ***efficient*** use of time to stop and carefully think about the question stem. The question stem tells us a lot of things: it tells us what to expect from right answers and, less directly, what to expect from wrong answers. It also tells us what we should do—whether we should go back into the text to look at certain relevant information before looking at the answer choices, or whether we should move right into eliminating wrong choices.

It is an ***inefficient*** use of time (and an unnecessary distraction) to try to predict questions as you read, and it is an extremely inefficient use of your time to read the questions before you read the passage. Frankly, these strategies are so bad that I don't even want to bring them up, but I need to do so because they somehow exist in the general stratosphere of commonly used LSAT strategies. Do not read questions ahead of the passage, and do not try to anticipate questions as you read. These are both ineffective strategies for test takers at all score levels.

You use time ***efficiently*** when you eliminate incorrect answers quickly and for concrete reasons. You use your time ***inefficiently*** when you eliminate when you are less than certain and commonly have to go back to answers you've already eliminated. There are definite reasons that answers are wrong, and the elimination process is about using these definite reasons to get rid of answers with confidence. Do not linger during the elimination process. If an answer seems wrong but you just can't put your finger on why, it may just be the right answer in disguise—leave it for after the elimination round. Your eliminations should be certain and quick, and you should never (or very, very rarely) expect to go back to an answer you have crossed off. Make sure to use your practice to improve your ability to eliminate more and more of the wrong answers with accuracy and pace.

You use time ***efficiently*** when you confirm right answers and eliminate wrong answers by comparing them against the passage and against the task in the question stem. You use time ***inefficiently*** when you compare answers against one another and think about which one is "more right." Hopefully, at the end of your first-round elimination process, there is an answer that stands out as being either certainly, or most likely, correct. However, when there isn't an answer that looks great, or when there are two or more answers that seem correct, focus on trying to find what is right or wrong with these answers relative to text and task. Do not get stuck comparing the answers to one another, for you will surely get biased by their relative "attractiveness," and test writers are great at making right answers seem less attractive and wrong ones more so. Always keep your eye on the ball—work to match the text of one answer at a time against the passage and the question, and look for concrete reasons to like an answer or be suspicious of it.

Finally, you use time ***inefficiently*** when you get stuck on a question and spin your wheels. In general, the time that is most commonly wasted by all students is the time spent in indecision on questions that the student finds most difficult. I'll discuss this more on the next page.

Essential Timing Habits

In just a few lessons, you will officially enter the final phase of your preparation (woo-hoo!). As we have discussed, the primary purpose of the final phase of your training is to develop the habits that will help you apply your skills at your best. When it comes to Reading Comprehension, there are three key habits I really want you to keep in mind.

One: Habitualize a Reading Pace

And make sure it's a brisk one. You want to read slowly enough that you can eventually understand why each part of the passage is there, but fast enough that you do not get bogged down in details.

For most of us, the pressure of the exam (even the pressure of a timed practice test) wreaks havoc on our sense of time. We suddenly become terrible at estimating how long we are taking at reading a passage or answering a question. We can't help it—when we get to a certain point of focus or stress, our sense of time begins to wobble.

That's why it's imperative that you habitualize a certain reading pace. Get used to reading all LSAT passages at a certain pace, and try to stay as consistent as possible throughout your practice while making your practice as realistic as possible. And get comfortable pushing that pace whenever you can.

Two: Go Fast on Questions That Go Fast

It's important to use perfect form, and it's important to get the questions we find easier right, but I also want to encourage you to push the pace during a question whenever you feel that your confidence is high and warranted. By this point, you know this test well, and there should be a lot of questions that go exactly as you expect—sometimes you can get through these questions in twenty seconds or less. Being able to go very fast on certain questions is a secret to the success of many top test takers—this leaves them plenty of time to carefully think through the situations that require more thought. Make sure you use your practice to work on getting through easier questions quickly while maintaining your accuracy.

Three: Don't Spin Your Wheels

If you were to take a sample section and time each question you solved, it is very likely that you'd discover at least four questions for which you spent two or more minutes. Of these four, it's very unlikely that you would get more than two correct—these questions take a long time because you don't understand them.

Those four problems likely took you about 8 - 9 minutes, which is 25% of the time you have for the section. Getting two correct answers in eight to nine minutes represents a terrible rate of return (if you were to extrapolate, it'd be equivalent to getting 32 questions correct for the entire exam). You can get an advantage over most test takers if you can lessen the impact of these time-sucking questions—if you can develop a strong habit of spending no more than 1:30 on all but the most challenging questions, and no more 2:00 on any one question, no matter how challenging that question is (that is, unless you have that time to spare, as we'll discuss in just a bit). Remember, harder questions aren't worth more points, and your goal is to answer as many questions right as possible. Invest your time in making sure you get right the ones you can, and make time for this by cutting your time on the toughest questions.

Timing Patterns for Top Scorers

When it comes to timing, top scorers in the Reading Comprehension section—those who are consistently able to miss two or fewer questions per section—typically share two common characteristics:

Top Scorers Have Time to Get through Every Step of the Process

In order to consistently answer questions correctly, we need to understand the reasoning structure of the passage, the task presented in the question stem, the reasons wrong answers are wrong, and the reason why the right answer is right—generally in that order. When you first started studying, you may have felt that it would be impossible to successfully satisfy these steps for each and every question; hopefully, you see more and more as you study that thinking about your process in terms of these steps not only makes you more accurate but faster, because it helps you use your time more efficiently.

When we are rushed for time, sometimes we need to move on from the passage to the questions without completely understanding the reasoning structure, and commonly we are forced to pick an answer without getting a chance to confirm with certainty that it is indeed correct or that the others are indeed incorrect. It is very hard to consistently score at a very high level if you are consistently facing these challenges.

Top scorers are fast enough that their scores are not limited by these types of constraints. They are fast enough to slow down when they need to as they read in order to understand reasoning structure, and they are fast enough to thoroughly vet the right answer, and every wrong answer, for almost all questions.

Top Scorers Can Finish the Section in Less Than Thirty-Five Minutes

Notice I said "can"—that doesn't mean a top scorer won't end up using all thirty-five minutes. The point I want to make is that top scorers are capable of going at a pace that would allow them to, if they choose not to spend a significant amount of extra time on any particular question, finish the section in well less than thirty-five minutes.

A typical Reading Comprehension section will have a few (anywhere from two to four, depending on the exam and how you tend to judge these things) questions that are extremely difficult to solve, even for top scorers. It's a huge advantage to have extra time for these questions. If, for example, you are able to consistently get through reading passages and answering all but the hardest two or three questions in a section in twenty-five minutes or less, then you know you have ten minutes or so for those two or three killer questions—in other words, as much time as you need. If your goal is to keep improving your score, and if you struggle at all with finishing in thirty-five minutes, your goal should be to limit the time you spend on the toughest questions. However, if you have improved to the point where you are trying to go -0 or -1 in a section, these toughest questions are your most important. Extra time for just these questions can be a huge advantage, and generally it's very hard to get a top score without it.

How to Get There

Just tap your heels three times and...

It's obviously easier to describe a top scorer than it is to become a top scorer. However, keep in mind that for every administration of the exam there are plenty of people who do rise up to get those top scores, and there is no reason to think that you shouldn't be one of them. Here are some suggestions for how to get there.

One: Work to Be Able to Finish the Section in Thirty-Five Minutes

The first step in the process is to be able to finish a section in thirty-five minutes while feeling reasonably comfortable with your reading pace and your problem-solving process. There is a difference between getting faster at solving questions and just going faster through each of your steps. The first is generally a consequence of understanding and focus, and the second is akin to rushing. The key to getting to this thirty-five-minute pace is to get strong at using your time effectively. In particular, if you are finding yourself challenged, keep working on eliminating inefficient uses of time.

Two: Push the Pace with Each New Practice Test

Obviously, if it seems you need about thirty-seven or thirty-eight minutes to satisfactorily finish a practice section, you want to push the pace to get to the thirty-five-minute mark. However, even when you get to a point at which you can finish a practice test in thirty-five minutes, keep pushing the pace—try to finish the next one in thirty-three or thirty-four, the next one in thirty-one, and so on. Try to cut your time in two primary ways—by getting rid of the instances in which you "spin your wheels" and by working to get faster at the questions with which you are most comfortable. Of course, do not sacrifice accuracy for pace. However, as you get better and better at this exam, you should find yourself more capable of going faster and faster. It's okay to push yourself to see how fast you can go without sacrificing accuracy, and in fact, that should be something that is embedded into your mindset from this point forward as you get ready for your exam.

Three: Practice Using That Extra Time

Imagine that you get to a point at which you feel confident that you can consistently get through a Reading Comprehension section in about thirty minutes. That leaves you a full five extra minutes to spend as you like. That's a big deal, for if you play your cards right, that means you will have plenty of time to think through the most challenging aspects of the section.

One effective way to spend this extra time is to give yourself an extra minute or two when you recognize that you are dealing with a particularly challenging reading passage. An extra minute or two, as I'm sure you know by now, can be extremely useful on the most difficult of passages. Even just knowing that you have an extra minute or two, and being able to slow down and relax, can do a world of good. Or, if you catch on later in a passage that you've missed the point somewhat, two minutes is even enough to read the entire passage over again if need be. Keep in mind that if you are at this level, it's highly unlikely that more than one passage per section, or two passages in the rarest of circumstances, will make you feel like you really need to slow down and reassess.

Another effective use of extra time is to give yourself an extra minute, ideally from as early a point as possible, when you notice that you've run into a particularly difficult question. This should give you plenty of time to carefully try to understand the relevant text and confirm that answers are right or wrong.

Some students like to have time left over at the end of the section to serve as a buffer in case the last passage is unexpectedly difficult, or in order to return to the challenging questions. The first reason is perfectly legitimate, and it is very comforting to go into the final passage with ten or more minutes remaining. The second use of time, in my experience, has been of questionable value to students. In general, it's better to use that time when you are initially focused on the passage and the question, if possible. Of course, when you take the exam, you do want to mark a question or two to return to in case you happen to find yourself with extra time at the end of a section.

Mitigating Strategies

We've just laid out the ideal timing strategies for top scorers and some suggestions for how to get there. But of course, not everyone can or needs to be a top scorer in the Reading Comprehension section. Maybe your strong suit is Logic Games or Logical Reasoning, and getting -4, or -6, or -8 on the Reading Comprehension is going to ensure your overall goals. Let's discuss more specifically some timing strategies that can help you get the best score possible on test day. Keep in mind that all these strategies we will discuss are based on two basic tenets—we want to spend the time necessary to get the questions right that we have the best chance of getting right, and we want to avoid spending extra time on questions we are most likely to get wrong.

If you find near the end of your studies that you are not able to comfortably finish the section in thirty-five minutes, you will need to make some difficult time-allocation decisions, specifically decisions about when to cut your work short or spend less time than you would like to. There are two ways to cut your time: spend less time reading passages or spend less time answering questions.

Less Time Reading Passages

If you are spending an average of more than three minutes reading each passage, and if you are struggling to finish questions on time, you should try to improve the pace at which you read. One way to try to do this is by pushing the pace on passages that feel easy or comfortable. Of course, don't ever rush.

More importantly, save time by really limiting yourself on the most difficult passages. It's very easy to get lost in those more difficult passages and to spend four or five minutes reading those passages. This is never a good idea. Set a firm cut-off—say, 3:30 maximum on any one passage, with the goal of a 2:45 average for the set of four.

Stick to that 3:30 maximum by simplifying and streamlining your goals when you find that a passage is particularly difficult for you to understand and organize. If need be, strip down the goal of your read to just two simple tasks and nothing else: you will spend the 3:30 just trying to figure out the main points and the author's opinion. If the main points are convoluted or subtle, do your best to come up with simplified and accurate versions and move on (later, you may be able to use the answers for general questions to verify and fine-tune your understanding). Practice sticking to these limits so that you don't accidently over invest time in any one passage on test day.

Less Time Answering Questions

The other way in which we can cut our time, of course, is by spending less time answering questions. Just as with the passages, part of this has to do with going faster on questions you feel comfortable with. However, for those who are having significant timing issues, typically the bigger problem is that the hardest questions are taking too much time.

Set a maximum time limit for any one question (1:45 or 2:00 are nice numbers) and allow yourself to "max out" your time just a few times (I'd suggest 3 or 4) per section. Now, keep in mind that during the pressure of the exam, it's tough to keep track of and stick to those numbers, and it can certainly be an unnecessary distraction. The better way to track time is through processes—have set processes for how you handle difficult questions, and stick to them no matter what. For example, sometimes a problem is difficult because it's very hard to find the relevant information—maybe you give yourself 30 seconds to go as slowly as you can through the text to find it, then select the best available answer no matter what. Sometimes a problem will go just as you expect until the very end (when you realize the answer you expected isn't there)—sometimes the best thing to do is just try to solve it again from the beginning. For most test takers, 2:00 is about how long it takes to try solving a question twice—if you are going to go this route, give yourself that second shot, but force yourself to pick an answer at the end of it **no matter what**. If you can think of your question "maximums" in terms of steps rather than just time spent, it's much easier to be consistent and in control.

Cutting time on the hardest questions will be much better for your overall score than trying to rush through every question more quickly, and it's certainly much better than not getting to certain questions because you run out of time. Make sure you habitualize the processes that will stop you from spending too much time on any one question on test day.

It's easier to keep track of processes than it is to keep track of time

Your Next Steps

If you are following one of the recommended study schedules, your final Reading Comprehension preparation will center on the sections you do as part of your final practice exams. You want to use this final work to polish and round out your skill set and, most importantly, to solidify effective habits. Here are some recommendations to help ensure that you get the most out of this final work.

One: Before Each Exam, Remind Yourself of Key Considerations

Don't spend an hour (or even five minutes) thinking through these key considerations, but do remind yourself of a few important things: your general timing strategies and goals, other strategies that you know are important to your success, and issues that may have come up for you in the past. A good idea is to jot this down on a three-by-five note card (you can make a note card for each of the sections) and review the note card before beginning your exam.

Two: During the Exam, Keep Track of Certain Markers

As per the instructions in your study schedule, it can be very helpful to keep track of certain issues as you are taking your practice exams. These things will help you review and assess your progress afterward and should be simple enough so as not to significantly impact your overall performance.

For Reading Comprehension, the key things to keep track of are
(A) The amount of time each passage takes you to read
(B) The amount of time each question set takes
(C) The questions for which you were not certain of your answer
(D) (Optional) the questions on which you felt you spent a lot of time

You can keep track of (A) and (B) by marking the time at which you finish reading each passage and the time at which you finish each set of questions. You can keep track of (C) by circling those questions. And you can choose to notate (D) in some other way (such as stars).

Some people feel comfortable keeping track of the amount of time each question takes. They often use electronic tools that allow them to just click something after each question. The information you get from this would be extremely useful, so if you can do it and if you don't think it'll be a distraction, give it a shot. It can show you things such as what happens when you go through a question very quickly (do I ever make silly mistakes when I answer questions in thirty seconds or less?) or when you spend a lot of time on questions (oh my goodness, did I really spend four minutes on that one problem!?). For a lot of people, keeping track of the time for each question is too much of a distraction, and if that's the case, don't worry about it. Just remember to review two main issues: whether you are accurate when you go through questions quickly, and whether you end up spinning your wheels and spending too much time on particular problems. It should be fairly easy for you to assess this even without using some sort of timing mechanism.

Three: Review Your Work Carefully

The time you spend reviewing your work is arguably just as important as the time you spend solving problems. You're going to want to review these final five practice exams carefully—they will be the final barometer of your skills and habits.

Make sure, as per our discussions, that you carefully review timing—the pace of your reads and the pace at which you answered questions. Look for questions that took more time than they should, and think carefully about why those questions took so long. Did you not see the right answer, or did you have problems eliminating a tempting wrong one? Did you have trouble finding the relevant text in the passage? Also think about whether the question was general or specific and look for patterns in the types of questions that cause you to spend too much time.

Also make sure you review the content of every practice section, in particular the questions you missed. Break down each miss carefully, and try to completely understand exactly why the right answer is right on your own (then look up the solution online if need be). At the end of Lesson 38, I've listed some resources for finding solutions.

Lastly, make sure you think about your process. What actions did you take or not take that led to you selecting the wrong answer? What was it about your read that ended up causing you trouble, and what could you have noticed in your read that would have helped you get through questions faster?

If the questions for a passage cause you particular trouble, do that passage again, fresh, a few days later. If it still causes you trouble, do it a few days after that.

Finally, set specific goals for each practice exam—try to get a bit faster and a bit more accurate with each one. It's unlikely that your path of improvement will be smooth—you may make a huge leap from one test to the next only to regress on the following one. However, you should expect overall improvement, and you should set goals for yourself with each practice exam. We all want to go faster and do better, and writing down specific goals about timing and score can help turn those goals into real actions.

Final Thoughts

A lot of test takers are understandably nervous about the potential impact of the pressure they will feel while taking the real exam. Most people I've talked with express a hope/desire/plan to perform just as well under pressure as they do otherwise...

But is it possible that pressure can actually help one perform *better*? Absolutely.

Pressure helps us focus, and it helps us get the best out of ourselves. It goes back to our cavemen days—we are programmed to run a little faster, jump a little higher, and think a little faster and better when the pressure is on. In the modern world, we can see this manifested in world-class athletes, who often perform at their best when the pressure is at its highest.

Of course, pressure can also have the opposite effect—it can make us perform worse than we would otherwise. I've personally experienced this an unfortunate number of times in my own life.

What determines the impact of pressure? I don't pretend to be a psychologist, and I'm sure the real answer is far too complex for me to understand...

However, I have worked with thousands and thousands of students in my life, and I've gotten very good at predicting which ones will perform better because of pressure and which ones will perform worse. If I could place bets on this in Vegas, I'd be a millionaire.

In my experience, and with the LSAT students I've worked with, the key difference has been the test taker's trust in his or her own instincts. Whether these instincts are correct or not is one thing—and it determines the ceiling for the score. Trust in these instincts is another, and the student who trusts in his or her instincts is far more likely to match or surpass practice performance. The student who does not trust in his or her own instincts, no matter the ability level, is very often likely to underperform on the real exam. This is a big reason why I have designed *The LSAT Trainer* exactly the way I have—to help you develop sound instincts that you can and should have confidence in on test day.

Do you feel that you can trust your gut when it comes to how to read a passage or answer questions? Don't go into the exam thinking that you're going to do something different from what you've done in your practice, and don't go into the exam with a list of one hundred things you want to make sure you stay on top of—it's not going to happen. Any sort of overly conscious approach—any approach that makes the rider do the work of the elephant—is likely to be less effective under pressure.

Make sure you use these final practice sections to firm up your habits. The goal is to have to think less and less about how to read passages and solve questions. The more right actions and right habits, the better chance you have to utilize your abilities at their best when you need them most.

38 READING COMPREHENSION sample section

Instructions

Starting on the next page is the full set of passages and questions that appeared in the Reading Comprehension section of the June '07 administration of the exam. Please go ahead and take this section as realistically as possible.

Practice Section Passage One

For decades, there has been a deep rift between poetry and fiction in the United States, especially in academic settings; graduate writing programs in universities, for example, train students as poets or as writers of fiction, but almost never as both. Both poets and writers of fiction have tended to support this separation, in large part because the current conventional wisdom holds that poetry should be elliptical and lyrical, reflecting inner states and processes of thought or feeling, whereas character and narrative events are the stock-in-trade of fiction.

Certainly it is true that poetry and fiction are distinct genres, but why have specialized education and literary territoriality resulted from this distinction? The answer lies perhaps in a widespread attitude in U.S. culture, which often casts a suspicious eye on the generalist. Those with knowledge and expertise in multiple areas risk charges of dilettantism, as if ability in one field is diluted or compromised by accomplishment in another.

Fortunately, there are signs that the bias against writers who cross generic boundaries is diminishing; several recent writers are known and respected for their work in both genres. One important example of this trend is Rita Dove, an African American writer highly acclaimed for both her poetry and her fiction. A few years ago, speaking at a conference entitled "Poets Who Write Fiction," Dove expressed gentle incredulity about the habit of segregating the genres. She had grown up reading and loving both fiction and poetry, she said, unaware of any purported danger lurking in attempts to mix the two. She also studied for some time in Germany, where, she observes, "Poets write plays, novelists compose libretti, playwrights write novels—they would not understand our restrictiveness."

It makes little sense, Dove believes, to persist in the restrictive approach to poetry and fiction prevalent in the U.S., because each genre shares in the nature of the other. Indeed, her poetry offers example after example of what can only be properly regarded as lyric narrative. Her use of language in these poems is undeniably lyrical—that is, it evokes emotion and inner states without requiring the reader to organize ideas or events in a particular linear structure. Yet this lyric expression simultaneously presents the elements of a plot in such a way that the reader is led repeatedly to take account of clusters of narrative details within the lyric flow. Thus while the language is lyrical, it often comes to constitute, cumulatively, a work of narrative fiction. Similarly, many passages in her fiction, though undeniably prose, achieve the status of lyric narrative through the use of poetic rhythms and elliptical expression. In short, Dove bridges the gap between poetry and fiction not only by writing in both genres, but also by fusing the two genres within individual works.

June 2007 Exam, Passage 1

1. Which one of the following most accurately expresses the main point of the passage?

(A) Rita Dove's work has been widely acclaimed primarily because of the lyrical elements she has introduced into her fiction.
(B) Rita Dove's lyric narratives present clusters of narrative detail in order to create a cumulative narrative without requiring the reader to interpret it in a linear manner.
(C) Working against a bias that has long been dominant in the U.S., recent writers like Rita Dove have shown that the lyrical use of language can effectively enhance narrative fiction.
(D) Unlike many of her U.S. contemporaries, Rita Dove writes without relying on the traditional techniques associated with poetry and fiction.
(E) Rita Dove's successful blending of poetry and fiction exemplifies the recent trend away from the rigid separation of the two genres that has long been prevalent in the U.S.

2. Which one of the following is most analogous to the literary achievements that the author attributes to Dove?

(A) A chef combines nontraditional cooking methods and traditional ingredients from disparate world cuisines to devise new recipes.
(B) A professor of film studies becomes a film director and succeeds, partly due to a wealth of theoretical knowledge of filmmaking.
(C) An actor who is also a theatrical director teams up with a public health agency to use street theater to inform the public about health matters.
(D) A choreographer defies convention and choreographs dances that combine elements of both ballet and jazz dance.
(E) A rock musician records several songs from previous decades but introduces extended guitar solos into each one.

3. According to the passage, in the U.S. there is a widely held view that

(A) poetry should not involve characters or narratives
(B) unlike the writing of poetry, the writing of fiction is rarely an academically serious endeavor
(C) graduate writing programs focus on poetry to the exclusion of fiction
(D) fiction is most aesthetically effective when it incorporates lyrical elements
(E) European literary cultures are suspicious of generalists

4. The author's attitude toward the deep rift between poetry and fiction in the U.S. can be most accurately described as one of

(A) perplexity as to what could have led to the development of such a rift
(B) astonishment that academics have overlooked the existence of the rift
(C) ambivalence toward the effect the rift has had on U.S. literature
(D) pessimism regarding the possibility that the rift can be overcome
(E) disapproval of attitudes and presuppositions underlying the rift

5. In the passage the author conjectures that a cause of the deep rift between fiction and poetry in the United States may be that

(A) poets and fiction writers each tend to see their craft as superior to the others' craft
(B) the methods used in training graduate students in poetry are different from those used in training graduate students in other literary fields
(C) publishers often pressure writers to concentrate on what they do best
(D) a suspicion of generalism deters writers from dividing their energies between the two genres
(E) fiction is more widely read and respected than poetry

6. In the context of the passage, the author's primary purpose in mentioning Dove's experience in Germany (lines 32–36) *(last sentence of third paragraph)* is to

(A) suggest that the habit of treating poetry and fiction as non-overlapping domains is characteristic of English-speaking societies but not others
(B) point to an experience that reinforced Dove's conviction that poetry and fiction should not be rigidly separated
(C) indicate that Dove's strengths as a writer derive in large part from the international character of her academic background
(D) present an illuminating biographical detail about Dove in an effort to enhance the human interest appeal of the passage
(E) indicate what Dove believes to be the origin of her opposition to the separation of fiction and poetry in the U.S.

7. It can be inferred from the passage that the author would be most likely to believe which one of the following?

(A) Each of Dove's works can be classified as either primarily poetry or primarily fiction, even though it may contain elements of both.
(B) The aesthetic value of lyric narrative resides in its representation of a sequence of events, rather than in its ability to evoke inner states.
(C) The way in which Dove blends genres in her writing is without precedent in U.S. writing.
(D) Narrative that uses lyrical language is generally aesthetically superior to pure lyric poetry.
(E) Writers who successfully cross the generic boundary between poetry and fiction often try their hand at genres such as drama as well.

8. If this passage had been excerpted from a longer text, which one of the following predictions about the near future of U.S. literature would be most likely to appear in that text?

(A) The number of writers who write both poetry and fiction will probably continue to grow.
(B) Because of the increased interest in mixed genres, the small market for pure lyric poetry will likely shrink even further.
(C) Narrative poetry will probably come to be regarded as a subgenre of fiction.
(D) There will probably be a rise in specialization among writers in university writing programs.
(E) Writers who continue to work exclusively in poetry or fiction will likely lose their audiences.

Practice Section Passage Two

The two passages discuss recent scientific research on music. They are adapted from two different papers presented at a scholarly conference.

Passage A

Did music and human language originate separately or together? Both systems use intonation and rhythm to communicate emotions. Both can be produced vocally or with tools, and people can produce both music and language silently to themselves. Brain imaging studies suggest that music and language are part of one large, vastly complicated, neurological system for processing sound. In fact, fewer differences than similarities exist between the neurological processing of the two. One could think of the two activities as different radio programs that can be broadcast over the same hardware. One noteworthy difference, though, is that, generally speaking, people are better at language than music. In music, anyone can listen easily enough, but most people do not perform well, and in many cultures composition is left to specialists. In language, by contrast, nearly everyone actively performs and composes. Given their shared neurological basis, it appears that music and language evolved together as brain size increased over the course of hominid evolution. But the primacy of language over music that we can observe today suggests that language, not music, was the primary function natural selection operated on. Music, it would seem, had little adaptive value of its own, and most likely developed on the coattails of language.

Passage B

Darwin claimed that since "neither the enjoyment nor the capacity of producing musical notes are faculties of the least [practical] use to man they must be ranked amongst the most mysterious with which he is endowed." I suggest that the enjoyment of and the capacity to produce musical notes are faculties of indispensable use to mothers and their infants and that it is in the emotional bonds created by the interaction of mother and child that we can discover the evolutionary origins of human music. Even excluding lullabies, which parents sing to infants, human mothers and infants under six months of age engage in ritualized, sequential behaviors, involving vocal, facial, and bodily interactions. Using face-to-face mother-infant interactions filmed at 24 frames per second, researchers have shown that mothers and infants jointly construct mutually improvised interactions in which each partner tracks the actions of the other. Such episodes last from one-half second to three seconds and are composed of musical elements—variations in pitch, rhythm, timbre, volume, and tempo. What evolutionary advantage would such behavior have? In the course of hominid evolution, brain size increased rapidly. Contemporaneously, the increase in bipedality caused the birth canal to narrow. This resulted in hominid infants being born ever-more prematurely, leaving them much more helpless at birth. This helplessness necessitated longer, better maternal care. Under such conditions, the emotional bonds created in the premusical mother-infant interactions we observe in Homo sapiens today—behavior whose neurological basis essentially constitutes the capacity to make and enjoy music—would have conferred considerable evolutionary advantage.

June 2007 Exam, Passage 2

9. Both passages were written primarily in order to answer which one of the following questions?

(A) What evolutionary advantage did larger brain size confer on early hominids?
(B) Why do human mothers and infants engage in bonding behavior that is composed of musical elements?
(C) What are the evolutionary origins of the human ability to make music?
(D) Do the human abilities to make music and to use language depend on the same neurological systems?
(E) Why are most people more adept at using language than they are at making music?

10. Each of the two passages mentions the relation of music to

(A) bonding between humans
(B) human emotion
(C) neurological research
(D) the increasing helplessness of hominid infants
(E) the use of tools to produce sounds

11. It can be inferred that the authors of the two passages would be most likely to disagree over whether

(A) the increase in hominid brain size necessitated earlier births
(B) fewer differences than similarities exist between the neurological processing of music and human language
(C) brain size increased rapidly over the course of human evolution
(D) the capacity to produce music has great adaptive value to humans
(E) mother-infant bonding involves temporally patterned vocal interactions

Practice Section Passage Two

12. The authors would be most likely to agree on the answer to which one of the following questions regarding musical capacity in humans?

(A) Does it manifest itself in some form in early infancy?
(B) Does it affect the strength of mother-infant bonds?
(C) Is it at least partly a result of evolutionary increases in brain size?
(D) Did its evolution spur the development of new neurological systems?
(E) Why does it vary so greatly among different individuals?

13. Which one of the following principles underlies the arguments in both passages?

(A) Investigations of the evolutionary origins of human behaviors must take into account the behavior of nonhuman animals.
(B) All human capacities can be explained in terms of the evolutionary advantages they offer.
(C) The fact that a single neurological system underlies two different capacities is evidence that those capacities evolved concurrently.
(D) The discovery of the neurological basis of a human behavior constitutes the discovery of the essence of that behavior.
(E) The behavior of modern-day humans can provide legitimate evidence concerning the evolutionary origins of human abilities.

14. Which one of the following most accurately characterizes a relationship between the two passages?

(A) Passage A and passage B use different evidence to draw divergent conclusions.
(B) Passage A poses the question that passage B attempts to answer.
(C) Passage A proposes a hypothesis that passage B attempts to substantiate with new evidence.
(D) Passage A expresses a stronger commitment to its hypothesis than does passage B.
(E) Passage A and passage B use different evidence to support the same conclusion.

Practice Section Passage Three

The World Wide Web, a network of electronically produced and interconnected (or "linked") sites, called pages, that are accessible via personal computer, raises legal issues about the rights of owners of intellectual property, notably those who create documents for inclusion on Web pages. Some of these owners of intellectual property claim that unless copyright law is strengthened, intellectual property on the Web will not be protected from copyright infringement. Web users, however, claim that if their ability to access information on Web pages is reduced, the Web cannot live up to its potential as an open, interactive medium of communication.

The debate arises from the Web's ability to link one document to another. Links between sites are analogous to the inclusion in a printed text of references to other works, but with one difference: the cited document is instantly retrievable by a user who activates the link. This immediate accessibility creates a problem, since current copyright laws give owners of intellectual property the right to sue a distributor of unauthorized copies of their material even if that distributor did not personally make the copies. If person A, the author of a document, puts the document on a Web page, and person B, the creator of another Web page, creates a link to A's document, is B committing copyright infringement?

To answer this question, it must first be determined who controls distribution of a document on the Web. When A places a document on a Web page, this is comparable to recording an outgoing message on one's telephone answering machine for others to hear. When B creates a link to A's document, this is akin to B's giving out A's telephone number, thereby allowing third parties to hear the outgoing message for themselves. Anyone who calls can listen to the message; that is its purpose. While B's link may indeed facilitate access to A's document, the crucial point is that A, simply by placing that document on the Web, is thereby offering it for distribution. Therefore, even if B leads others to the document, it is A who actually controls access to it. Hence creating a link to a document is not the same as making or distributing a copy of that document. Moreover, techniques are already available by which A can restrict access to a document. For example, A may require a password to gain entry to A's Web page, just as a telephone owner can request an unlisted number and disclose it only to selected parties. Such a solution would compromise the openness of the Web somewhat, but not as much as the threat of copyright infringement litigation. Changing copyright law to benefit owners of intellectual property is thus ill-advised because it would impede the development of the Web as a public forum dedicated to the free exchange of ideas.

June 2007 Exam, Passage 3

15. Which one of the following most accurately expresses the main point of the passage?

(A) Since distribution of a document placed on a Web page is controlled by the author of that page rather than by the person who creates a link to the page, creating such a link should not be considered copyright infringement.
(B) Changes in copyright law in response to the development of Web pages and links are ill-advised unless such changes amplify rather than restrict the free exchange of ideas necessary in a democracy.
(C) People who are concerned about the access others may have to the Web documents they create can easily prevent such access without inhibiting the rights of others to exchange ideas freely.
(D) Problems concerning intellectual property rights created by new forms of electronic media are not insuperably difficult to resolve if one applies basic commonsense principles to these problems.
(E) Maintaining a free exchange of ideas on the Web offers benefits that far outweigh those that might be gained by a small number of individuals if a radical alteration of copyright laws aimed at restricting the Web's growth were allowed.

16. Which one of the following is closest in meaning to the term "strengthened" as that term is used in line 8 *(middle of first paragraph)* of the passage?

(A) made more restrictive
(B) made uniform worldwide
(C) made to impose harsher penalties
(D) dutifully enforced
(E) more fully recognized as legitimate

17. With which one of the following claims about documents placed on Web pages would the author be most likely to agree?

(A) Such documents cannot receive adequate protection unless current copyright laws are strengthened.
(B) Such documents cannot be protected from unauthorized distribution without significantly diminishing the potential of the Web to be a widely used form of communication.
(C) The nearly instantaneous access afforded by the Web makes it impossible in practice to limit access to such documents.
(D) Such documents can be protected from copyright infringement with the least damage to the public interest only by altering existing legal codes.
(E) Such documents cannot fully contribute to the Web's free exchange of ideas unless their authors allow them to be freely accessed by those who wish to do so.

18. Based on the passage, the relationship between strengthening current copyright laws and relying on passwords to restrict access to a Web document is most analogous to the relationship between

(A) allowing everyone use of a public facility and restricting its use to members of the community
(B) outlawing the use of a drug and outlawing its sale
(C) prohibiting a sport and relying on participants to employ proper safety gear
(D) passing a new law and enforcing that law
(E) allowing unrestricted entry to a building and restricting entry to those who have been issued a badge

19. The passage most strongly implies which one of the following?

(A) There are no creators of links to Web pages who are also owners of intellectual property on Web pages.
(B) The person who controls access to a Web page document should be considered the distributor of that document.
(C) Rights of privacy should not be extended to owners of intellectual property placed on the Web.
(D) Those who create links to Web pages have primary control over who reads the documents on those pages.
(E) A document on a Web page must be converted to a physical document via printing before copyright infringement takes place.

20. According to the passage, which one of the following features of outgoing messages left on telephone answering machines is most relevant to the debate concerning copyright infringement?

(A) Such messages are carried by an electronic medium of communication.
(B) Such messages are not legally protected against unauthorized distribution.
(C) Transmission of such messages is virtually instantaneous.
(D) People do not usually care whether or not others might record such messages.
(E) Such messages have purposely been made available to anyone who calls that telephone number.

21. The author's discussion of telephone answering machines serves primarily to

(A) compare and contrast the legal problems created by two different sorts of electronic media
(B) provide an analogy to illustrate the positions taken by each of the two sides in the copyright debate
(C) show that the legal problems produced by new communication technology are not themselves new
(D) illustrate the basic principle the author believes should help determine the outcome of the copyright debate
(E) show that telephone use also raises concerns about copyright infringement

22. According to the passage, present copyright laws

(A) allow completely unrestricted use of any document placed by its author on a Web page
(B) allow those who establish links to a document on a Web page to control its distribution to others
(C) prohibit anyone but the author of a document from making a profit from the document's distribution
(D) allow the author of a document to sue anyone who distributes the document without permission
(E) should be altered to allow more complete freedom in the exchange of ideas

Practice Section Passage Four

In tracing the changing face of the Irish landscape, scholars have traditionally relied primarily on evidence from historical documents. However, such documentary sources provide a fragmentary record at best. Reliable accounts are very scarce for many parts of Ireland prior to the seventeenth century, and many of the relevant documents from the sixteenth and seventeenth centuries focus selectively on matters relating to military or commercial interests.

Studies of fossilized pollen grains preserved in peats and lake muds provide an additional means of investigating vegetative landscape change. Details of changes in vegetation resulting from both human activities and natural events are reflected in the kinds and quantities of minute pollen grains that become trapped in sediments. Analysis of samples can identify which kinds of plants produced the preserved pollen grains and when they were deposited, and in many cases the findings can serve to supplement or correct the documentary record.

For example, analyses of samples from Long Lough in County Down have revealed significant patterns of cereal-grain pollen beginning by about 400 A.D. The substantial clay content of the soil in this part of Down makes cultivation by primitive tools difficult. Historians thought that such soils were not tilled to any significant extent until the introduction of the moldboard plough to Ireland in the seventh century A.D. Because cereal cultivation would have required tilling of the soil, the pollen evidence indicates that these soils must indeed have been successfully tilled before the introduction of the new plough.

Another example concerns flax cultivation in County Down, one of the great linen-producing areas of Ireland during the eighteenth century. Some aspects of linen production in Down are well documented, but the documentary record tells little about the cultivation of flax, the plant from which linen is made, in that area. The record of eighteenth-century linen production in Down, together with the knowledge that flax cultivation had been established in Ireland centuries before that time, led some historians to surmise that this plant was being cultivated in Down before the eighteenth century. But pollen analyses indicate that this is not the case; flax pollen was found only in deposits laid down since the eighteenth century.

It must be stressed, though, that there are limits to the ability of the pollen record to reflect the vegetative history of the landscape. For example, pollen analyses cannot identify the species, but only the genus or family, of some plants. Among these is madder, a cultivated dye plant of historical importance in Ireland. Madder belongs to a plant family that also comprises various native weeds, including goosegrass. If madder pollen were present in a deposit it would be indistinguishable from that of uncultivated native species.

June 2007 Exam, Passage 4

23. Which one of the following most accurately expresses the main point of the passage?

(A) Analysis of fossilized pollen is a useful means of supplementing and in some cases correcting other sources of information regarding changes in the Irish landscape.
(B) Analyses of historical documents, together with pollen evidence, have led to the revision of some previously accepted hypotheses regarding changes in the Irish landscape.
(C) Analysis of fossilized pollen has proven to be a valuable tool in the identification of ancient plant species.
(D) Analysis of fossilized pollen has provided new evidence that the cultivation of such crops as cereal grains, flax, and madder had a significant impact on the landscape of Ireland.
(E) While pollen evidence can sometimes supplement other sources of historical information, its applicability is severely limited, since it cannot be used to identify plant species.

24. The passage indicates that pollen analyses have provided evidence against which one of the following views?

(A) The moldboard plough was introduced into Ireland in the seventh century.
(B) In certain parts of County Down, cereal grains were not cultivated to any significant extent before the seventh century.
(C) In certain parts of Ireland, cereal grains have been cultivated continuously since the introduction of the moldboard plough.
(D) Cereal grain cultivation requires successful tilling of the soil.
(E) Cereal grain cultivation began in County Down around 400 A.D.

Practice Section Passage Four

25. The phrase "documentary record" (lines 20 and 37) *(very end of second paragraph and second sentence of fourth paragraph)* primarily refers to

(A) documented results of analyses of fossilized pollen
(B) the kinds and quantities of fossilized pollen grains preserved in peats and lake muds
(C) written and pictorial descriptions by current historians of the events and landscapes of past centuries
(D) government and commercial records, maps, and similar documents produced in the past that recorded conditions and events of that time
(E) articles, books, and other documents by current historians listing and analyzing all the available evidence regarding a particular historical period

26. The passage indicates that prior to the use of pollen analysis in the study of the history of the Irish landscape, at least some historians believed which one of the following?

(A) The Irish landscape had experienced significant flooding during the seventeenth century.
(B) Cereal grain was not cultivated anywhere in Ireland until at least the seventh century.
(C) The history of the Irish landscape during the sixteenth and seventeenth centuries was well documented.
(D) Madder was not used as a dye plant in Ireland until after the eighteenth century.
(E) The beginning of flax cultivation in County Down may well have occurred before the eighteenth century.

27. Which one of the following most accurately describes the relationship between the second paragraph and the final paragraph?

(A) The second paragraph proposes a hypothesis for which the final paragraph offers a supporting example.
(B) The final paragraph describes a problem that must be solved before the method advocated in the second paragraph can be considered viable.
(C) The final paragraph qualifies the claim made in the second paragraph.
(D) The second paragraph describes a view against which the author intends to argue, and the final paragraph states the author's argument against that view.
(E) The final paragraph offers procedures to supplement the method described in the second paragraph.

Sample Solution Passage One

Here are real-time solutions for the section that you just tried. The thoughts represent those that a high scorer might have during the exam.

For decades, there has been a deep rift between poetry and fiction in the United States, especially in academic settings; graduate writing programs in universities, for example, train students as poets or as writers of fiction, but almost never as both. Both poets and writers of fiction have tended to support this separation, in large part because the current conventional wisdom holds that poetry should be elliptical and lyrical, reflecting inner states and processes of thought or feeling, whereas character and narrative events are the stock-in-trade of fiction.

This is likely background, and the issue is going to be about some difference between poetry and fiction.

Certainly it is true that poetry and fiction are distinct genres, but why have specialized education and literary territoriality resulted from this distinction? The answer lies perhaps in a widespread attitude in U.S. culture, which often casts a suspicious eye on the generalist. Those with knowledge and expertise in multiple areas risk charges of dilettantism, as if ability in one field is diluted or compromised by accomplishment in another.

Nope. The issue is treating poetry and fiction as distinct versus teaching them together. Attributes separation to widespread prejudice against generalists; author seems to support bringing together.

Fortunately, there are signs that the bias against writers who cross generic boundaries is diminishing; several recent writers are known and respected for their work in both genres. One important example of this trend is Rita Dove, an African American writer highly acclaimed for both her poetry and her fiction. A few years ago, speaking at a conference entitled "Poets Who Write Fiction," Dove expressed gentle incredulity about the habit of segregating the genres. She had grown up reading and loving both fiction and poetry, she said, unaware of any purported danger lurking in attempts to mix the two. She also studied for some time in Germany, where, she observes, "Poets write plays, novelists compose libretti, playwrights write novels—they would not understand our restrictiveness."

This line confirms author's opinion on matter: she clearly thinks separation isn't good.

Rita Dove example supports teaching poetry and fiction together.

It makes little sense, Dove believes, to persist in the restrictive approach to poetry and fiction prevalent in the U.S., because each genre shares in the nature of the other. Indeed, her poetry offers example after example of what can only be properly regarded as lyric narrative. Her use of language in these poems is undeniably lyrical—that is, it evokes emotion and inner states without requiring the reader to organize ideas or events in a particular linear structure. Yet this lyric expression simultaneously presents the elements of a plot in such a way that the reader is led repeatedly to take account of clusters of narrative details within the lyric flow. Thus while the language is lyrical, it often comes to constitute, cumulatively, a work of narrative fiction. Similarly, many passages in her fiction, though undeniably prose, achieve the status of lyric narrative through the use of poetic rhythms and elliptical expression. In short, Dove bridges the gap between poetry and fiction not only by writing in both genres, but also by fusing the two genres within individual works.

A lot more about Rita Dove—not only is she support for idea, she's also herself a main subject of passage.

June 2007 Exam, Passage 1

Sample Solution Passage One

1. Which one of the following most accurately expresses the main point of the passage?

(A) Rita Dove's work has been widely acclaimed primarily because of the lyrical elements she has introduced into her fiction.
(B) Rita Dove's lyric narratives present clusters of narrative detail in order to create a cumulative narrative without requiring the reader to interpret it in a linear manner.
(C) Working against a bias that has long been dominant in the U.S., recent writers like Rita Dove have shown that the lyrical use of language can effectively enhance narrative fiction.
(D) Unlike many of her U.S. contemporaries, Rita Dove writes without relying on the traditional techniques associated with poetry and fiction.
(E) Rita Dove's successful blending of poetry and fiction exemplifies the recent trend away from the rigid separation of the two genres that has long been prevalent in the U.S.

Stem: Looking for answer that discusses fiction and poetry being together versus apart and/or Rita Dove's melding of fiction and poetry.

Elimination: (A) overemphasizes a secondary detail. Same with (B). (C) is a little too specific, but better than (A) and (B)—keep it. (D) doesn't match the text. (E) is a good match for the text.

Confirmation: (C) is definitely too specific. (E) matches text (fortunate recent trend/Rita Dove blends) and is correct.

2. Which one of the following is most analogous to the literary achievements that the author attributes to Dove?

(A) A chef combines nontraditional cooking methods and traditional ingredients from disparate world cuisines to devise new recipes.
(B) A professor of film studies becomes a film director and succeeds, partly due to a wealth of theoretical knowledge of filmmaking.
(C) An actor who is also a theatrical director teams up with a public health agency to use street theater to inform the public about health matters.
(D) A choreographer defies convention and choreographs dances that combine elements of both ballet and jazz dance.
(E) A rock musician records several songs from previous decades but introduces extended guitar solos into each one.

Stem: We know she works in two genres and brings aspects of fiction into poetry and poetry into fiction.

Elimination: (A) isn't a great match because she doesn't create a new "genre" or style of writing, and she doesn't combine traditional and untraditional. (B) is not like Rita Dove at all. Neither is (C). (D) is a great match—blending of two genres. Keep it. Not sure how (E) relates to Dove.

Confirmation: (D) is the only attractive answer—does Dove defy convention? Yes, and she blends elements. (D) is correct.

3. According to the passage, in the U.S. there is a widely held view that

(A) poetry should not involve characters or narratives
(B) unlike the writing of poetry, the writing of fiction is rarely an academically serious endeavor
(C) graduate writing programs focus on poetry to the exclusion of fiction
(D) fiction is most aesthetically effective when it incorporates lyrical elements
(E) European literary cultures are suspicious of generalists

Stem: General American views are discussed mostly in the first and second paragraphs (poetry and fiction should be separate, suspicion of generalists) and just a little bit at beginning of fourth (restrictions).

Elimination: (A) seems a bit too strong, but characters and narrative were discussed in terms of fiction—keep it. (B) doesn't match text and doesn't make reasonable sense. (C) doesn't match what the text states. (D) goes too far beyond text. (E) does not match text (it's Americans who are suspicious).

Confirmation: (A) is the only viable answer—can I confirm it? Yes—character and narrative are elements of fiction, and there is a widely held view that fiction and poetry shouldn't have mingling of characteristics. (A) is correct.

Sample Solution Passage One

4. The author's attitude toward the deep rift between poetry and fiction in the U.S. can be most accurately described as one of

(A) perplexity as to what could have led to the development of such a rift
(B) astonishment that academics have overlooked the existence of the rift
(C) ambivalence toward the effect the rift has had on U.S. literature
(D) pessimism regarding the possibility that the rift can be overcome
(E) disapproval of attitudes and presuppositions underlying the rift

Stem: I know the author thinks the rift is unnecessary.

Elimination: I can eliminate (A)—she's not confused at why it exists. (B) also clearly misrepresents. "Ambivalence" in (C) doesn't match her tone, nor does "pessimism" in (D). (E) is more negative than her tone was, but it's the only viable answer.

Confirmation: She doesn't believe there should be a rift, and she doesn't buy the reasons for there being one—(E) states as much, and (E) is correct.

5. In the passage the author conjectures that a cause of the deep rift between fiction and poetry in the United States may be that
(A) poets and fiction writers each tend to see their craft as superior to the others' craft
(B) the methods used in training graduate students in poetry are different from those used in training graduate students in other literary fields
(C) publishers often pressure writers to concentrate on what they do best
(D) a suspicion of generalism deters writers from dividing their energies between the two genres
(E) fiction is more widely read and respected than poetry

Stem: Not sure what the answer will be, but one place author did discuss potential cause is second paragraph—suspicion toward generalists.

Elimination: Author didn't discuss feelings of superiority—can eliminate (A). Training? Not sure—maybe leave (B). (C) is not discussed by the passage. (D) matches the second paragraph—it's probably correct. (E) does not match text.

Confirmation: Training is discussed, but the methods of training and specifically methods of training poets relative to all other literary fields are not. (B) doesn't match the text. (D) matches the text nicely, and the beginning of the third paragraph helps confirm that the suspicion of generalism is something that the author thinks "deters writers."

6. In the context of the passage, the author's primary purpose in mentioning Dove's experience in Germany (lines 32–36) *(last sentence of third paragraph)* is to

(A) suggest that the habit of treating poetry and fiction as nonoverlapping domains is characteristic of English-speaking societies but not others
(B) point to an experience that reinforced Dove's conviction that poetry and fiction should not be rigidly separated
(C) indicate that Dove's strengths as a writer derive in large part from the international character of her academic background
(D) present an illuminating biographical detail about Dove in an effort to enhance the human interest appeal of the passage
(E) indicate what Dove believes to be the origin of her opposition to the separation of fiction and poetry in the U.S.

Stem: The description puts Germany in sharp contrast to the U.S.—could be to support author's views or help explain Dove's development.

Elimination: (A) is tempting, but the "English-speaking but not others" part goes too far beyond what I know (which is just U.S. versus Germany). (B) looks really good—keep it. (C) misrepresents the text a bit—her "strengths" and such are not really discussed. (D) is silly—"enhance human interest" is not really a reasoning structure issue. (E) is far removed from the text.

Confirmation: (B) is the only attractive answer. Looking back through, the text seems to match up with (B).

Sample Solution Passage One

7. It can be inferred from the passage that the author would be most likely to believe which one of the following?

(A) Each of Dove's works can be classified as either primarily poetry or primarily fiction, even though it may contain elements of both.
(B) The aesthetic value of lyric narrative resides in its representation of a sequence of events, rather than in its ability to evoke inner states.
(C) The way in which Dove blends genres in her writing is without precedent in U.S. writing.
(D) Narrative that uses lyrical language is generally aesthetically superior to pure lyric poetry.
(E) Writers who successfully cross the generic boundary between poetry and fiction often try their hand at genres such as drama as well.

Stem: Pretty open-ended question. Let's see where the answers go.

Elimination: (A) is an "ugly-looking" right answer, I think—after all, it's not like she's created some genre in between poetry and fiction. The author doesn't discuss the opinion referred to in (B). Who knows if Dove is without precedent? Certainly the author doesn't say that. The author doesn't offer a comparative opinion that matches (D). (E) goes well beyond text.

Confirmation: (A) is the only surviving answer. Does it match text? Sure. Author discusses Dove writing poetry and fiction, with influences, but not some middle genre between the two.

8. If this passage had been excerpted from a longer text, which one of the following predictions about the near future of U.S. literature would be most likely to appear in that text?

(A) The number of writers who write both poetry and fiction will probably continue to grow.
(B) Because of the increased interest in mixed genres, the small market for pure lyric poetry will likely shrink even further.
(C) Narrative poetry will probably come to be regarded as a subgenre of fiction.
(D) There will probably be a rise in specialization among writers in university writing programs.
(E) Writers who continue to work exclusively in poetry or fiction will likely lose their audiences.

Stem: Predictions about near future? What? Only "change" discussed is greater acceptance for bridging of poetry and fiction.

Elimination: (A) seems reasonable, I guess. (B) goes beyond the text and doesn't really make sense. (C) goes well beyond what the text says. (D) is the opposite of bridging. (E) goes well beyond the text—just because some authors bridge doesn't mean others that don't will be impacted.

Confirmation: (A) is the only surviving answer. It's not a slam-dunk, but considering there wasn't much cross-over before, the bias against the cross-over is diminishing, and some successful writers today are cross-over writers. (A) is the only good answer.

Sample Solution Passage Two

The two passages discuss recent scientific research on music. They are adapted from two different papers presented at a scholarly conference.

Passage A

Did music and human language originate separately or together? Both systems use intonation and rhythm to communicate emotions. Both can be produced vocally or with tools, and people can produce both music and language silently to themselves. Brain imaging studies suggest that music and language are part of one large, vastly complicated, neurological system for processing sound. In fact, fewer differences than similarities exist between the neurological processing of the two. One could think of the two activities as different radio programs that can be broadcast over the same hardware. One noteworthy difference, though, is that, generally speaking, people are better at language than music. In music, anyone can listen easily enough, but most people do not perform well, and in many cultures composition is left to specialists. In language, by contrast, nearly everyone actively performs and composes. Given their shared neurological basis, it appears that music and language evolved together as brain size increased over the course of hominid evolution. But the primacy of language over music that we can observe today suggests that language, not music, was the primary function natural selection operated on. Music, it would seem, had little adaptive value of its own, and most likely developed on the coattails of language.

Likely the main issue for both passages: did musical and linguistic abilities originate together or separately?

Two abilities linked, but people better at language than music.

Author's main point: both evolved together, but music was secondary consequence of language.

Passage B

Darwin claimed that since "neither the enjoyment nor the capacity of producing musical notes are faculties of the least [practical] use to man they must be ranked amongst the most mysterious with which he is endowed." I suggest that the enjoyment of and the capacity to produce musical notes are faculties of indispensable use to mothers and their infants and that it is in the emotional bonds created by the interaction of mother and child that we can discover the evolutionary origins of human music. Even excluding lullabies, which parents sing to infants, human mothers and infants under six months of age engage in ritualized, sequential behaviors, involving vocal, facial, and bodily interactions. Using face-to-face mother-infant interactions filmed at 24 frames per second, researchers have shown that mothers and infants jointly construct mutually improvised interactions in which each partner tracks the actions of the other. Such episodes last from one-half second to three seconds and are composed of musical elements—variations in pitch, rhythm, timbre, volume, and tempo. What evolutionary advantage would such behavior have? In the course of hominid evolution, brain size increased rapidly. Contemporaneously, the increase in bipedality caused the birth canal to narrow. This resulted in hominid infants being born ever-more prematurely, leaving them much more helpless at birth. This helplessness necessitated longer, better maternal care. Under such conditions, the emotional bonds created in the premusical mother-infant interactions we observe in Homo sapiens today—behavior whose neurological basis essentially constitutes the capacity to make and enjoy music—would have conferred considerable evolutionary advantage.

Suggests another explanation for evolution of music: for mother and child relationship.

All support for that hypothesis.

This passage is not about language at all. Central issue for both passages is instead, perhaps, what are the evolutionary origins of musical ability?

June 2007 Exam, Passage 2

Sample Solution Passage Two

9. Both passages were written primarily in order to answer which one of the following questions?

(A) What evolutionary advantage did larger brain size confer on early hominids?
(B) Why do human mothers and infants engage in bonding behavior that is composed of musical elements?
(C) What are the evolutionary origins of the human ability to make music?
(D) Do the human abilities to make music and to use language depend on the same neurological systems?
(E) Why are most people more adept at using language than they are at making music?

Stem: Just thought about this—evolutionary origins of musical ability.

Elimination: (A) isn't central focus of either, and (B) isn't related to first passage. (C) is definitely correct. (D) is not relevant to second passage, nor is (E).

Confirmation: (C) matches prediction, and (C) is correct.

10. Each of the two passages mentions the relation of music to

(A) bonding between humans
(B) human emotion
(C) neurological research
(D) the increasing helplessness of hominid infants
(E) the use of tools to produce sounds

Stem: Not sure—could be a lot of things.

Elimination: Shoot—(E) is the only one that is clearly not right. Time to go digging.

Confirmation: Bonding between humans (A) is key to passage B, mentioned slightly, maybe (communicate emotion) in passage A. Leave. Wait—(B) is actually a better match for the text. Emotion is mentioned specifically in both passages. I don't think neurological research is mentioned in the second passage—nope, it's not. And (D) is not actually discussed in the second passage. (B) is correct.

11. It can be inferred that the authors of the two passages would be most likely to disagree over whether

(A) the increase in hominid brain size necessitated earlier births
(B) fewer differences than similarities exist between the neurological processing of music and human language
(C) brain size increased rapidly over the course of human evolution
(D) the capacity to produce music has great adaptive value to humans
(E) mother-infant bonding involves temporally patterned vocal interactions

Stem: One thing I know—disagree about evolutionary development of musical ability. Could be something else, though.

Elimination: Passage B discusses this. A doesn't—cut (A). They don't disagree about similarities versus differences—cut (B). Both actually mention (C), and it's not a very debatable point—cut. (D) is an answer I expected—leave it. I know there is nothing in passage A related to (E), so I can cut that answer too.

Confirmation: The writer of A thinks musical ability is a secondary consequence of speaking ability; the writer of B gives a critically important reason for musical ability—mother and child bonding. Do I have proof for "adaptive value?" Yes, last paragraph—"What evolutionary value..." Author talks of bonding in terms of adaptive value, and (D) is correct.

Sample Solution Passage Two

12. The authors would be most likely to agree on the answer to which one of the following questions regarding musical capacity in humans?

(A) Does it manifest itself in some form in early infancy?
(B) Does it affect the strength of mother-infant bonds?
(C) Is it at least partly a result of evolutionary increases in brain size?
(D) Did its evolution spur the development of new neurological systems?
(E) Why does it vary so greatly among different individuals?

Stem: What do they agree about? Not sure—time to eliminate.

Elimination: (A) is discussed in the second passage but not the first. Same with (B). Like the language (at least partly) in (C). I know I saw this in the second passage, think I saw in first—keep it. Don't think (D) is discussed in either passage. Neither is (E)—the "why" gives it away immediately as being wrong.

Confirmation: (C) is the only remaining answer—author of passage A discusses it toward the bottom, and the second passage has it about two thirds of the way down. (C) is correct.

13. Which one of the following principles underlies the arguments in both passages?

(A) Investigations of the evolutionary origins of human behaviors must take into account the behavior of nonhuman animals.
(B) All human capacities can be explained in terms of the evolutionary advantages they offer.
(C) The fact that a single neurological system underlies two different capacities is evidence that those capacities evolved concurrently.
(D) The discovery of the neurological basis of a human behavior constitutes the discovery of the essence of that behavior.
(E) The behavior of modern-day humans can provide legitimate evidence concerning the evolutionary origins of human abilities.

Stem: Again, something the passages have in common. Not sure—time to eliminate.

Elimination: Don't think (A) is a principle of either argument. (B) is a good answer—they both try to explain in terms of evolution because they work under assumption that evolutionary purpose is what explains change. I think that's right. (C) is not relevant to the second passage. (D) over emphasizes neurology. (E) isn't an answer I expected, but it does underlie the argumentative structure for both arguments—they both use the behavior of modern-day humans as evidence for their points about evolution. Leave (E).

Confirmation: Looking back at (B), "all" is simply too strong, especially relative to *both* arguments. If (E) didn't underlie both of them, they couldn't use the reasoning they both use. (E) is right.

14. Which one of the following most accurately characterizes a relationship between the two passages?

(A) Passage A and passage B use different evidence to draw divergent conclusions.
(B) Passage A poses the question that passage B attempts to answer.
(C) Passage A proposes a hypothesis that passage B attempts to substantiate with new evidence.
(D) Passage A expresses a stronger commitment to its hypothesis than does passage B.
(E) Passage A and passage B use different evidence to support the same conclusion.

Stem: Relationship—we know they offer different explanations of evolution.

Elimination: (A) seems to represent the relationship well—leave it. (B) and (C) misrepresent the relationship. (D) represents an unsupported opinion, and (E) misrepresents the relationship.

Confirmation: (A) is the only attractive answer, and I know (A) is right.

Sample Solution Passage Three

The World Wide Web, a network of electronically produced and interconnected (or "linked") sites, called pages, that are accessible via personal computer, raises legal issues about the rights of owners of intellectual property, notably those who create documents for inclusion on Web pages. Some of these owners of intellectual property claim that unless copyright law is strengthened, intellectual property on the Web will not be protected from copyright infringement. Web users, however, claim that if their ability to access information on Web pages is reduced, the Web cannot live up to its potential as an open, interactive medium of communication.

This is most likely the main issue—should web pages get more copyright protection or not? Owners of intellectual property on one side, users on other.

The debate arises from the Web's ability to link one document to another. Links between sites are analogous to the inclusion in a printed text of references to other works, but with one difference: the cited document is instantly retrievable by a user who activates the link. This immediate accessibility creates a problem, since current copyright laws give owners of intellectual property the right to sue a distributor of unauthorized copies of their material even if that distributor did not personally make the copies. If person A, the author of a document, puts the document on a Web page, and person B, the creator of another Web page, creates a link to A's document, is B committing copyright infringement?

More specifics about issue—is linking illegal?

To answer this question, it must first be determined who controls distribution of a document on the Web. When A places a document on a Web page, this is comparable to recording an outgoing message on one's telephone answering machine for others to hear. When B creates a link to A's document, this is akin to B's giving out A's telephone number, thereby allowing third parties to hear the outgoing message for themselves. Anyone who calls can listen to the message; that is its purpose. While B's link may indeed facilitate access to A's document, the crucial point is that A, simply by placing that document on the Web, is thereby offering it for distribution. Therefore, even if B leads others to the document, it is A who actually controls access to it. Hence creating a link to a document is not the same as making or distributing a copy of that document. Moreover, techniques are already available by which A can restrict access to a document. For example, A may require a password to gain entry to A's Web page, just as a telephone owner can request an unlisted number and disclose it only to selected parties. Such a solution would compromise the openness of the Web somewhat, but not as much as the threat of copyright infringement litigation. Changing copyright law to benefit owners of intellectual property is thus ill-advised because it would impede the development of the Web as a public forum dedicated to the free exchange of ideas.

Author's opinion (given indirectly): person chooses to put document up for free use on Internet, and that person can restrict access, so person who links is not responsible.

Author clearly against strengthening copyright laws as they relate to web.

June 2007 Exam, Passage 3

Sample Solution Passage Three

15. Which one of the following most accurately expresses the main point of the passage?

(A) Since distribution of a document placed on a Web page is controlled by the author of that page rather than by the person who creates a link to the page, creating such a link should not be considered copyright infringement.
(B) Changes in copyright law in response to the development of Web pages and links are ill-advised unless such changes amplify rather than restrict the free exchange of ideas necessary in a democracy.
(C) People who are concerned about the access others may have to the Web documents they create can easily prevent such access without inhibiting the rights of others to exchange ideas freely.
(D) Problems concerning intellectual property rights created by new forms of electronic media are not insuperably difficult to resolve if one applies basic commonsense principles to these problems.
(E) Maintaining a free exchange of ideas on the Web offers benefits that far outweigh those that might be gained by a small number of individuals if a radical alteration of copyright laws aimed at restricting the Web's growth were allowed.

Stem: Central issue is whether copyright laws should be strengthened, and author thinks no.

Elimination: (A) is pretty good, but a bit narrow—leave it. (B) goes too far beyond text (changes amplify/necessary to democracy). (C) is much too narrow to be main point. (D) is not the author's main point at all. (E) is somewhat attractive, though I don't like "radical."

Confirmation: I don't love any answer and am down to (A) and (E). (A) places a strong emphasis on person who created versus person who links. Is that justified? I guess so—both the second and third paragraphs relate to that. Okay, (A) looks pretty good. What about "radical" in (E)? Looking back at the text, nothing matches up to that. And now that I look at it again closely, (E) is about restricting web growth. Yikes—that's not what the laws are directly meant to do. (E) is definitely wrong, and (A) is correct.

16. Which one of the following is closest in meaning to the term "strengthened" as that term is used in line 8 *(middle of first paragraph)* of the passage?

(A) made more restrictive
(B) made uniform worldwide
(C) made to impose harsher penalties
(D) dutifully enforced
(E) more fully recognized as legitimate

Stem: I know that "strengthened" has to do with making it harder to gain access to the online files.

Elimination: (A) seems pretty good. (B) does not. Could (C) or (D) be right? Don't think so—checking quickly. Neither of those things is discussed or hinted at. (E) is not relevant.

Confirmation: (C) and (D) were somewhat tempting, but (A) was what I expected, and it's correct.

17. With which one of the following claims about documents placed on Web pages would the author be most likely to agree?

(A) Such documents cannot receive adequate protection unless current copyright laws are strengthened.
(B) Such documents cannot be protected from unauthorized distribution without significantly diminishing the potential of the Web to be a widely used form of communication.
(C) The nearly instantaneous access afforded by the Web makes it impossible in practice to limit access to such documents.
(D) Such documents can be protected from copyright infringement with the least damage to the public interest only by altering existing legal codes.
(E) Such documents cannot fully contribute to the Web's free exchange of ideas unless their authors allow them to be freely accessed by those who wish to do so.

Stem: Need something that pretty closely matches what author expressed. Could be a lot of things. Time to eliminate.

Elimination: (A) doesn't match author's points. (B) seems a little strong, but it's decent—keep it. (C) isn't true according to what the author says. (D) disagrees with author's points. (E) seems a bit strong but does seem related to some of the negatives of limiting access in last paragraph. Leave it.

Confirmation: Both (B) and (E) relate to the last portion of the passage, so I go back, read it again, and read both answers again. (B) now seems wrong—"cannot be protected" goes against fact that author says some things can be done, and, even worse, there is not nearly enough support for "significantly" diminishing. (E) seemed too strong at first, but the passage tells us limitations would "compromise the openness of the Web somewhat," so we can infer they would be able to *fully* contribute. Sneaky inference, but (E) is correct.

Sample Solution Passage Three

18. Based on the passage, the relationship between strengthening current copyright laws and relying on passwords to restrict access to a Web document is most analogous to the relationship between

(A) allowing everyone use of a public facility and restricting its use to members of the community
(B) outlawing the use of a drug and outlawing its sale
(C) prohibiting a sport and relying on participants to employ proper safety gear
(D) passing a new law and enforcing that law
(E) allowing unrestricted entry to a building and restricting entry to those who have been issued a badge

Stem: Strengthening current copyright laws is a blanket solution that would have a negative impact on web users, and instead he suggests more individual responsibility—passwords. Let's eliminate.

Elimination: (A) is somewhat tempting because of the restrictive element, but strengthening currently laws isn't like letting everyone use the facility. We can eliminate (A). (B) is about making one thing illegal verses another—not what we have here. (C) is attractive. Prohibiting is like restricting web access, and relying on players to use proper gear is like people using passwords. I think (C) is right—leave it. (D) isn't a good match—passing and enforcing are two aspects of the same law. (E) is a great analogy for using passwords, but allowing unrestricted entry doesn't match strengthening copyright laws.

Confirmation: (C) was the only attractive answer. We double check it, and there is nothing extreme or egregious about it. (C) is correct.

19. The passage most strongly implies which one of the following?

(A) There are no creators of links to Web pages who are also owners of intellectual property on Web pages.
(B) The person who controls access to a Web page document should be considered the distributor of that document.
(C) Rights of privacy should not be extended to owners of intellectual property placed on the Web.
(D) Those who create links to Web pages have primary control over who reads the documents on those pages.
(E) A document on a Web page must be converted to a physical document via printing before copyright infringement takes place.

Stem: Looking for something that matches text pretty closely.

Elimination: Nothing in the passage implies (A). I think (B) matches the text—leave it. (C) isn't right. They can control it as they like (by restricting access and such). (D) doesn't match text and doesn't make sense. People who make links can't control what viewers do when they get on the Internet. (E) doesn't match anything in text at all.

Confirmation: (B) was the only attractive answer. Can I confirm it? Yep—passage says person who puts it on web (who happens to be the same person who restricts access, etc.—i.e., controls it) is offering it for distribution. (B) is correct.

20. According to the passage, which one of the following features of outgoing messages left on telephone answering machines is most relevant to the debate concerning copyright infringement?

(A) Such messages are carried by an electronic medium of communication.
(B) Such messages are not legally protected against unauthorized distribution.
(C) Transmission of such messages is virtually instantaneous.
(D) People do not usually care whether or not others might record such messages.
(E) Such messages have purposely been made available to anyone who calls that telephone number.

Stem: A big characteristic of the outgoing message was that it was purposely made for others to hear, in same way lots of web pages are, but answer could be anything...

Elimination: Author doesn't care that they are both electronic. (B) is somewhat tempting—keep it. (C) has nothing to do with author's points, nor does (D). (E) matches what I expected.

Confirmation: (E) is what I was hoping for, but (B) is also good—can I confirm (B)? No, not sure if websites have no legal protection, and not sure about that for phone messages either. (E) is correct—"anyone who calls can listen to the message; that is its purpose."

Sample Solution Passage Three

21. The author's discussion of telephone answering machines serves primarily to

(A) compare and contrast the legal problems created by two different sorts of electronic media
(B) provide an analogy to illustrate the positions taken by each of the two sides in the copyright debate
(C) show that the legal problems produced by new communication technology are not themselves new
(D) illustrate the basic principle the author believes should help determine the outcome of the copyright debate
(E) show that telephone use also raises concerns about copyright infringement

Stem: The author uses the telephone analogy to show that those who link to websites shouldn't be punished for copyright violation and that those who put up websites can control the situation by limiting access, etc.

Elimination: (A) doesn't match text. (B) is a little tempting, but the analogy doesn't show other side of debate—cut. (C) is not the point of the analogy. (D) is, I think, correct—that's why he's using it. Leave. (E) doesn't match at all.

Confirmation: (D) is the only decently attractive answer. He uses the telephone analogy to show who should be responsible for information distributed on a website, so he uses it to illustrate a principle to help determine the outcome of that debate. (D) is correct.

22. According to the passage, present copyright laws

(A) allow completely unrestricted use of any document placed by its author on a Web page
(B) allow those who establish links to a document on a Web page to control its distribution to others
(C) prohibit anyone but the author of a document from making a profit from the document's distribution
(D) allow the author of a document to sue anyone who distributes the document without permission
(E) should be altered to allow more complete freedom in the exchange of ideas

Stem: Hmmm. I'm not sure what the author thinks specifically of present copyright laws—I just know he doesn't think they ought to become more restrictive.

Elimination: (A) is not true—the author talks about passwords, etc. (B) is not true. The author thinks the person who puts up the page controls distribution. (C) goes beyond the scope of the passage (and seems too extreme). I don't remember reading about (D) at all. Cut it. (E) is tempting, but I don't think he says that—shoot.

Confirmation: Oh man, let's look at (E) again and check it against text—yep, he never says they need to be altered to allow more freedom. It's one of the other answers I crossed out, but I have no idea which one. The question says "according to the passage," so the answer has to be in the text. Scan text for "current copyright laws"—ah, there's the specific information, right in the middle of the second paragraph! (D) is right.

Sample Solution Passage Four

In tracing the changing face of the Irish landscape, scholars have traditionally relied primarily on evidence from historical documents. However, such documentary sources provide a fragmentary record at best. Reliable accounts are very scarce for many parts of Ireland prior to the seventeenth century, and many of the relevant documents from the sixteenth and seventeenth centuries focus selectively on matters relating to military or commercial interests.

Likely just background—it's been difficult to trace changes in Irish landscape.

Studies of fossilized pollen grains preserved in peats and lake muds provide an additional means of investigating vegetative landscape change. Details of changes in vegetation resulting from both human activities and natural events are reflected in the kinds and quantities of minute pollen grains that become trapped in sediments. Analysis of samples can identify which kinds of plants produced the preserved pollen grains and when they were deposited, and in many cases the findings can serve to supplement or correct the documentary record.

Seems to be main subject. Pollen grains can be used as clue to trace changes.

For example, analyses of samples from Long Lough in County Down have revealed significant patterns of cereal-grain pollen beginning by about 400 A.D. The substantial clay content of the soil in this part of Down makes cultivation by primitive tools difficult. Historians thought that such soils were not tilled to any significant extent until the introduction of the moldboard plough to Ireland in the seventh century A.D. Because cereal cultivation would have required tilling of the soil, the pollen evidence indicates that these soils must indeed have been successfully tilled before the introduction of the new plough.

Example of how pollen grains help correct understanding of history. Three paragraphs in, "pollen as clue" definitely seems to be main subject of passage.

Another example concerns flax cultivation in County Down, one of the great linen-producing areas of Ireland during the eighteenth century. Some aspects of linen production in Down are well documented, but the documentary record tells little about the cultivation of flax, the plant from which linen is made, in that area. The record of eighteenth-century linen production in Down, together with the knowledge that flax cultivation had been established in Ireland centuries before that time, led some historians to surmise that this plant was being cultivated in Down before the eighteenth century. But pollen analyses indicate that this is not the case; flax pollen was found only in deposits laid down since the eighteenth century.

Another example to illustrate same thing.

It must be stressed, though, that there are limits to the ability of the pollen record to reflect the vegetative history of the landscape. For example, pollen analyses cannot identify the species, but only the genus or family, of some plants. Among these is madder, a cultivated dye plant of historical importance in Ireland. Madder belongs to a plant family that also comprises various native weeds, including goosegrass. If madder pollen were present in a deposit it would be indistinguishable from that of uncultivated native species.

Modifies main point—though pollen is effective clue, it does have its limitations.

June 2007 Exam, Passage 4

Sample Solution Passage Four

23. Which one of the following most accurately expresses the main point of the passage?

(A) Analysis of fossilized pollen is a useful means of supplementing and in some cases correcting other sources of information regarding changes in the Irish landscape.
(B) Analyses of historical documents, together with pollen evidence, have led to the revision of some previously accepted hypotheses regarding changes in the Irish landscape.
(C) Analysis of fossilized pollen has proven to be a valuable tool in the identification of ancient plant species.
(D) Analysis of fossilized pollen has provided new evidence that the cultivation of such crops as cereal grains, flax, and madder had a significant impact on the landscape of Ireland.
(E) While pollen evidence can sometimes supplement other sources of historical information, its applicability is severely limited, since it cannot be used to identify plant species.

Stem: Pollen is a useful clue, but it has some limitations. Time to eliminate.

Elimination: (A) looks good—keep. (B) shifts the main point from pollen to historical documents + pollen—eliminate. The "identification of ancient plant species" part of (C) doesn't match the text, so we can eliminate it. (D) misrepresents the text a bit—the pollen evidence isn't about increasing sense of significance but rather accuracy. (E) overemphasizes the point in the last paragraph and plays down the points everywhere else in the passage. It can be eliminated too.

Confirmation: (A) is the only remaining choice, and it represents the text well. It doesn't discuss the mitigation mentioned in the last paragraph, but overall it does a nice job of expressing the main point of the passage.

24. The passage indicates that pollen analyses have provided evidence against which one of the following views?

(A) The moldboard plough was introduced into Ireland in the seventh century.
(B) In certain parts of County Down, cereal grains were not cultivated to any significant extent before the seventh century.
(C) In certain parts of Ireland, cereal grains have been cultivated continuously since the introduction of the moldboard plough.
(D) Cereal grain cultivation requires successful tilling of the soil.
(E) Cereal grain cultivation began in County Down around 400 A.D.

Stem: Both the third and fourth paragraphs give us examples of what the pollen record was used to disprove, so it's likely our answer will come from that area. It's a bit too much to read again—going to eliminate choices first.

Elimination: Pollen record doesn't help inform of when plough was introduced—can eliminate (A). (B) seems like the right answer. That entire third paragraph was about pollen for cereal grain appearing earlier than expected. Pollen didn't prove anything about equipment, so we can cut (C), and it doesn't tell us directly about tilling required—cut (D). (E) is a possibility. Not sure if I remember reading that.

Confirmation: Going back into text, definitely have proof that was the assumption, and that pollen record goes against that assumption, in paragraph 3. Looking again carefully, can find no information to confirm (E). (B) is correct.

25. The phrase "documentary record" (lines 20 and 37) *(very end of second paragraph and second sentence of fourth paragraph)* primarily refers to

(A) documented results of analyses of fossilized pollen
(B) the kinds and quantities of fossilized pollen grains preserved in peats and lake muds
(C) written and pictorial descriptions by current historians of the events and landscapes of past centuries
(D) government and commercial records, maps, and similar documents produced in the past that recorded conditions and events of that time
(E) articles, books, and other documents by current historians listing and analyzing all the available evidence regarding a particular historical period

Stem: Documentary record—record from documents from past that give clues about history of landscape. Time to eliminate.

Elimination: Documents not about pollen—eliminate (A) and (B). (C) is about "current" historians—not right. (D) seems good. (E) is also about "current" historians.

Confirmation: Does document record have to be old records? Seems like it—paragraph one introduces document record in terms of old documents. (D) is correct.

Sample Solution Passage Four

26. The passage indicates that prior to the use of pollen analysis in the study of the history of the Irish landscape, at least some historians believed which one of the following?

(A) The Irish landscape had experienced significant flooding during the seventeenth century.
(B) Cereal grain was not cultivated anywhere in Ireland until at least the seventh century.
(C) The history of the Irish landscape during the sixteenth and seventeenth centuries was well documented.
(D) Madder was not used as a dye plant in Ireland until after the eighteenth century.
(E) The beginning of flax cultivation in County Down may well have occurred before the eighteenth century.

Stem: Previously held assumptions mentioned in paragraphs 3 & 4—cereal before plough, and flax before 18th century. Answer likely related to one of those.

Elimination: (A) isn't discussed. (B) is definitely correct—I think. (C) is not specifically discussed, nor is (D), and (E) is what was mentioned and contradicted by pollen evidence, I think. (E) seems good too.

Confirmation: Looking again at (B)—it's about "anywhere" in Ireland. Do I have evidence of that? No, I don't. (B) is not right. Looking in fourth paragraph, I have direct proof for (E): some historians surmise that this plant was being cultivated in Down before the eighteenth century. (E) is correct.

27. Which one of the following most accurately describes the relationship between the second paragraph and the final paragraph?

(A) The second paragraph proposes a hypothesis for which the final paragraph offers a supporting example.
(B) The final paragraph describes a problem that must be solved before the method advocated in the second paragraph can be considered viable.
(C) The final paragraph qualifies the claim made in the second paragraph.
(D) The second paragraph describes a view against which the author intends to argue, and the final paragraph states the author's argument against that view.
(E) The final paragraph offers procedures to supplement the method described in the second paragraph.

Stem: Thinking back—the second paragraph introduced the main point—pollen is useful clue, and the last paragraph modified the point just a tad—pollen evidence has limitations.

Elimination: (A) doesn't accurately state that relationship. Nor does (B)—it's not a problem that needs to be solved before pollen evidence is useful. (C) accurately reflects the relationship—qualifies is exactly what the last paragraph does. Leave (C). (D) grossly misrepresents the structure of the text—eliminate. (E) is not true. The final paragraph doesn't offer procedures at all.

Confirmation: (C) is what we expected, and (C) is correct. The claim is that pollen is useful for understanding history, and the final paragraph qualifies this statement by saying pollen record has its limits.

The Road Ahead

How do you feel about your performance on the practice section? At this point, it's not necessary to feel like you are an absolute Reading Comprehension master. In particular, it's very likely that your processes are not as intuitive or automatic as you'd like. That's to be expected, and of course that's fine. However, it is also expected that by this point you feel like you have a comfortable understanding of the design of LSAT Reading Comprehension and that you feel you have strategies for handling any and all situations—you have the tools, you can see the finish line, and you know exactly what you need to do in order to have a great Reading Comprehension section. At this point, it's just a matter of getting better—faster, more accurate, and more confident. Hopefully you feel that this final set of practice tests is the last bit of preparation you need to ensure that you go into the exam in top form.

In the next lesson, we will do a final review of Logic Games and discuss Logic Games timing strategies. In the final lesson, we'll do the same for Logical Reasoning. If you are following one of the recommended study schedules, the final leg of your preparation will mostly consist of full practice exams and individual review sessions. Below is a list of tools that you may find helpful for this last stage.

auxiliary study tools

here are some additional tools you may find useful in the final stage of your preparation.

LSAT TRAINER TOOLS

Notes: If you've been keeping tidy notes on your progress, now is the time they will really pay off. Use your notes to review what you have learned, and to corral all issues to study again.

Appendix: The appendix provides lists of the drills in the book and the questions used in the book. You can use the appendix to consider which drills to return to and which questions to review again.

theLSATtrainer.com: Offers study schedules, notebook organizers, and a breakdown of all Logical Reasoning questions and Logic Games from exams 29 - 71. Also offers instructional articles, videos, and infographics.

NON-LSAT TRAINER TOOLS

Additional Questions and Practice Tests: If you feel you need additional practice, you can purchase additional exams from LSAC (through Amazon), and you can also purchase additional exams and question packets from third-party vendors such as Cambridge LSAT.

Problem Solutions: There are several sites online that provide free solutions, and these are valuable resources for checking the work you do on practice exams. The **Manhattan LSAT** site has a free forum that includes solutions, written by instructors, for almost all official guide questions. If a solution is not available, or if a solution isn't satisfactory, you can post on the forum yourself and solicit further dialog. Additionally, **7Sage** offers quality video solutions for Logic Games for free. Finally, you can always go on **top-law-schools.com** to talk with other high-scoring students and get any peer help that you need (just remember that you can't actually post official questions online—you can reference them by practice test if need be just as we have in this book).

39 LOGIC GAMES

review, timing strategies, and final thoughts

How do you feel about your Logic Games abilities right now? How do your abilities compare with a month ago, or two months ago, or when you first started studying? Do you feel that you are at the top of the mountain, or do you feel you still have a ways to go?

At this point, you should be feeling confident about your skill set, but it's understandable if you don't feel you've had quite enough practice to solidify your habits. If you are at a point where you feel your final practice exams are enough to make sure your skill set is solid and that your habits are firm, then you are in great shape.

If you don't feel that you are quite there yet, it may be worth it for you to take a bit of time to reassess and review what you've learned. If you've considered getting extra help from a tutor or a friend, this would be a good time to use that ace card. Ideally, you want to be able to use your last set of practice tests in the manner described in the previous paragraph, but it's fine if you don't feel you are there yet—just hit the pause button and do a bit more work.

What do you fear about the Logic Games section?

How do you know if you are there yet or not? Not to be cheesy, but it's in your gut. Here's the key question I want you to consider: what do you fear about the section? Do you fear that you'll see something you aren't prepared for? Do you hope that any one particular type of game or rule or question won't appear on the exam? If you have these fears, they could be signs of holes in your understanding, strategies, or experience—signs of problems with your skill set. It's fine to have these fears, but be honest about them and use them to figure out what you need to work on in order to get to the top of the mountain.

Here is a checklist of the key issues we've discussed in the book. If you are having problems, you may want to use this to mark which lessons you want to review. If you feel confident that you are ready for the next step in the process, you can use this list to double check your strength in every key aspect of the Logic Games section.

The ability to diagram is the key to Logic Games success (10).

All games assign elements to positions. About two thirds of all games involve ordering, and about half of all games involve grouping. Assignment, ordering, and grouping are the three basic design elements of LSAT Logic Games (10).

Games can further be complicated by subsets. Subsets can appear in the elements or the positions. We can be told the subset assignments or not (11).

Numbers issues can appear when there is something other than a one-to-one relationship between elements and positions or when there are subsets (12).

Non-one-to-one relationships involve more elements than positions or more positions than elements (12).

Certain rules are conditional, meaning that they are only relevant to particular situations (13).

Every conditional rule yields at least one inference: the contrapositive (13).

When games have multiple conditional rules, typically your primary task will be to see how these rules link together (13).

Biconditionals can be thought of as *or* rules in disguise (14).

Complex *or* rules can be very difficult to understand, but they can also be extremely useful for organizing your diagram or for setting up multiple diagrams (14).

Sometimes setting up two (or more) diagrams can help you understand the scenario and notate rules more clearly (14).

An effective Logic Games process includes seeing the big picture, understanding and notating rules correctly, bringing rules together correctly, and using effective question strategies (15).

Nearly every game begins with a Rules question. The fastest way to get Rules questions correct is to use the written rules to eliminate incorrect answers (21).

For most questions, there are two issues to consider in the stem: "Is there new information to incorporate?" and "How will the answer choices split up?" (26).

When given new information in the question stem, we will always be able to infer additional facts from that information, and these inferences will differentiate the right answer from the wrong ones (26).

In evaluating answers, we want to rely on what we know must be. So we want to search for right answers when asked what must be true or must be false, and we want to eliminate wrong answers when asked what could be true or what could be false (26).

A less common family of questions, options questions, require us to think of could be's, the variety of possibilities that a game presents. These questions require a subtle but significant change in mindset (27).

An even less common type of question, the Rule Change question, will require us to consider the significance of replacing one rule in the game with another in the answer choices. These questions require clear understanding and specific strategy (27).

You don't have to be perfect to have great success on the Logic Games section. You do have to be very good, and you have to avoid making mistakes (28).

Timing Strategies

I talked briefly about Logic Games timing back in Lesson 21: the typical Logic Games section has twenty-three questions, and this works out neatly for you to average 3 minutes per game setup and 1 minute per question.

We also discussed that it's virtually impossible (and unnecessary) to stick to a consistent setup timing and problem-solving timing strategy game after game. Whereas most Reading Comprehension passages take about the same amount of time to read, different types of Logic Games take significantly different amounts of time to properly set up. Furthermore, certain games are designed to have question sets that require a lot more work, and thus require more time, and others less so. All that is to say that different games can take drastically different amounts of time.

There are two general tendencies that can be helpful to keep in mind. The first is that, typically speaking, games that take longer to set up often have questions that require less time to solve, and games that are full of questions that require a lot of your time typically have setups that don't. Sometimes you will run into a game with a very short setup and questions that fly by (yay!), and sometimes you will run into games that require, even when you play them well, a significant amount of time to set up and a significant amount of time to get through questions (boo). However, most of the time this won't be the case.

It makes sense why long setups often equate to quick questions, and vice versa. Games that require a lot of setup often involve a great many inferences, and by making these inferences up front, you end up "solving" much of the game. The questions then become more of a test of what you've already figured out. For other games, the scenario and rules take very little time to set up because there aren't many inferences—a great amount of uncertainty is left lingering in the air. That often means that questions will take longer. You'll have to make the inferences and "solve" the games as you solve each individual problem.

The other general tendency to keep in mind is that even though individual games can vary greatly, entire game sections cannot—in fact, the difficulty of entire games sections is extremely consistent administration to administration. If your first two games are easier than normal, your next two will be harder. If your first three games are killer, your fourth will be easier than normal. Games sections even out, and you want to make sure you use this understanding to stay calm and keep to your timing strategies.

Timing Instincts

Keeping in mind the topsy-turvy nature of the section, it makes little sense to try to keep to a rigid timing strategy. You will want to have some benchmarks, and you'll want to keep track of time (to be discussed shortly), but since different games and questions are meant to take different amounts of time, it's imperative that you work to develop correct instincts about whether or not you are using time well. As with Reading Comprehension, it's really an issue of whether or not you are using your time efficiently. Are you taking more time because the situation requires it or because you are wasting time? Let's talk about effective versus ineffective uses of time during the setup and during the questions.

Tendencies and Twists

Typically, games that require lots of setup have questions that go quickly, and vice versa. However, the section is very inconsistent, and there are certain games that are just naturally meant to take much less time (short setup and short questions) and others that are meant to take more time (long setup and questions that require a lot of work and time). A big key to success is being able to tell the difference between a game that warrants extra time and a game that you are having problems with.

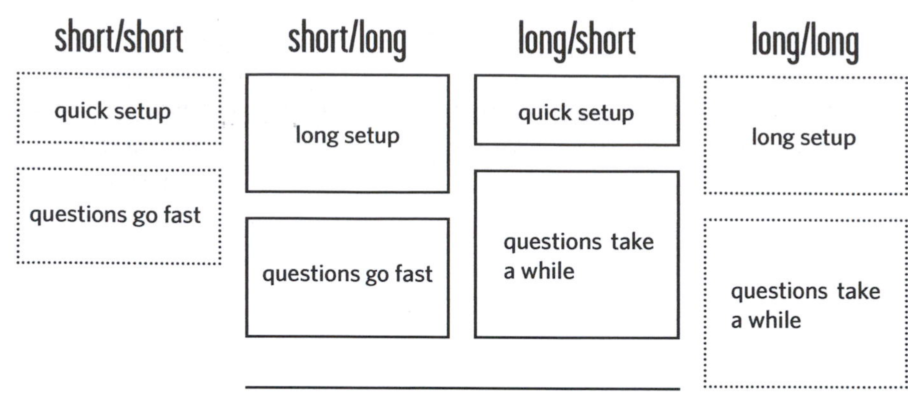

Using Setup Time Efficiently

Put simply, you use setup time efficiently when you are actively working toward one of three specific goals: seeing the big picture, understanding and correctly notating rules, or making absolute inferences. If you need to spend time on any of these three goals, it'll generally be time well spent.

By this point, seeing the big picture for most games should be fairly automatic. However, as I'm sure you are well aware, the LSAT is definitely capable of throwing some curveballs that force you to stop and think.[1] If a game requires an unusual setup, don't panic—understand that the setup likely feels unusual for everyone taking the exam, and give yourself the time you need to lay out a game correctly and wisely.

By this point, notating most rules should be fairly automatic as well. However, time and time again, we've seen both the danger of making small notational errors, and the benefit of making wise notational decisions (such as picking which rule to diagram first, or which rules to diagram together). And some rules are just tough—they require time to understand correctly and notate correctly.

Time spent carefully understanding rules and notating them is always time well spent. Unless you are doing something unnecessarily complicated, this part of the process will never end up taking up much of your thirty-five total minutes. A strong, usable understanding of the rules is always rewarded, and a shaky understanding of the rules is always exposed. Make sure your notations are easy to understand—write out notes next to them if need be.

Finally, time spent making significant and absolute inferences is always time well spent. In general, you want to think about inferences before you notate rules, as you notate rules, and after you notate rules. There are certain inferences game makers expect you to make, and in these cases, games can be very difficult if you don't make these inferences.

1. How might you handle the following types of scenarios?

"Eight children sit at a round table. J sits to the right of M. F, and L cannot sit directly opposite one another..."

"Stores line the north and south sides of a boardwalk. The stores either have canopies or they don't, and they either open on the weekends or they don't. Three of the stores on the north side of the street have canopies. No two adjacent stores on the south side open on the weekends..."

"Four people—F, G, H, and J—start the morning on island A, and two people, S and T, start the morning on island B. By the end of the day, two of the people are on island A, and four are on island B. Either F or H went to island B, but not both. If J went to island B, S went to island A..."

There are other inferences (such as those that allow us to create two diagrams instead of one for a game) that aren't necessarily expected or required, but are instead clever and, when discovered, can break open a game and make it much easier to answer questions. Spending time making and exploring these inferences is also time well spent.

However, unlike with picturing the game or notating rules, with inferences there is no clear stopping point, and it's easy to spend too much time looking for them. It's also easy to make mistakes over-inferring. It requires some practice to get good at knowing when to stop making inferences and move on to the questions. As long as you have a strong sense that there are more to be found, keep looking. If you find yourself spinning your wheels for more than a few seconds, move on.

Using Setup Time Inefficiently

As I just mentioned, you can use setup time inefficiently looking for inferences that aren't there or that are just too confusing (say you figure out that one element can only go in one of three spots if another one goes in one of three spots) to notate. Remember that you can keep finding out more about a game as you solve questions, and, even if you miss an inference up front, you may be able to pick it up as you solve the first few questions. It helps to set some limits for yourself ("I'll jump into questions if I can't find another inference in the next ten seconds" is a good one) and practice keeping to them so that you keep your inference time in check.

Traditionally speaking, test takers have often wasted a lot of time up front setting up hypotheticals. There are certain companies that endorse these strategies, and I'm sure some students have had some success with them. However, creating a bunch of hypotheticals up front is a strategy that matches up very poorly with the rest of the strategies in this book, and in my experience, it's a crude and unnecessarily complicated way of thinking about games.

Spend time up front figuring out what *must* be, and if what must be is limited to a couple of interesting scenarios (imagine that an order of elements must either be built around X - Y - Z or Z - Y - X), you may want to explore those multiple scenarios. However, don't spend a lot of time thinking about what *could* be—mapping out where every element *could* go, what elements *could* be grouped together, and so on. Don't waste time exploring unnecessary hypotheticals. This type of thinking will lead to errors and limit your ability to use your diagram to differentiate between what must be and what could be.

Finally, the last way to waste time during the setup is to rush through it. Rushing through the setup will invariably lead to you having to spend more time in the questions. At the least, for every game, you should have a very clear understanding of the scenario and every rule, and hopefully you'll also have the insight of a few inferences. Make sure you give yourself enough time to go into the questions prepared.

Using Problem-Solving Time Efficiently

We use time efficiently during questions when we are heading directly toward an answer. We use time efficiently when we make inferences off of the question stem and when we either search for the right answer or eliminate wrong ones based on the situation the question stem presents.

In general, time spent in the question stem is time well spent. Whenever a question stem leads to a chain of inferences, follow it through. If the information in a question stem limits a situation to just two options, write them out. Make sure you spend the time to understand the stem, make full use of it, and prepare yourself for how to think about the answer choices.

Finally, time spent confirming a right answer is generally time well spent. If you've eliminated four choices but feel somewhat suspicious about the answer that remains, do play it out just to make sure. Chances are the confirmation process will just take a few seconds.

Using Problem-Solving Time Inefficiently

Keep in mind that extra time spent in the questions is commonly the result of a bad set-up. If you think your question-specific strategies are fine but you keep having to spend too much time on the questions, chances are you aren't setting up the games efficiently or you aren't as comfortable with your notations as you should be.

However, even when we do understand games well, and even when we do use effective notations, we can often end up spending too much time on questions simply because of the way we solve them. Furthermore, this time suck often happens "silently" without us even knowing about it or being aware of it—when we use inefficient systems, even when we get questions right, we end up spending a bit more time than we needed to, and over the course of a section, those differences add up.

The most inefficient use of time during the Games section is the time spent having to create hypotheticals to evaluate answer choices. Certain questions require this of us, and we are all forced to make such hypotheticals when questions don't go the way we want, but you shouldn't have to make such hypotheticals often (I would say on average it should happen to a top test taker less than three or four times per section).

If you find yourself commonly having to make hypotheticals to evaluate answers, it's a sign that you are not diagramming well, not inferring correctly off the question stem, or not approaching the answers correctly. Carefully evaluate your mistakes on those terms.

For many students, hypotheticals go hand in hand with not fully utilizing the question stem. They have to go to hypotheticals to test answers when they don't make all of the inferences they should or when they go searching for a right answer when they should be eliminating wrong ones and vice versa.

In particular, looking to eliminate wrong answers when the person should be looking for the right answer is a very common time sucker. It can take a lot of time to prove that four wrong answers could be true or could be false. If you are playing a game well, it's typically much faster to see which answer must be false or must be true. Don't waste time eliminating wrong answers if you don't need to.

Top performers...

- Understand scenarios easily and use notations well
- Use effective approaches to questions
- Know when to try something new, and when to move on
- Only need to use hypotheticals occasionally

Those who struggle with games...

- Can't picture the scenarios and can't trust their notations
- Solve questions inefficiently, often using lots of hypotheticals
- Are afraid to restart or give up on questions and waste time spinning their wheels

Tracking Your Time During a Test

Okay, having discussed all of the challenges of using time well in Logic Games, and having discussed efficient and inefficient uses of time, let's lay out a basic strategy for thinking about and keeping track of your time during an exam.

Note that the strategies I suggest are extremely simple, and that's out of necessity. You don't want to waste precious time or energy trying to use some complex timing strategy during the exam. Here's what I suggest:

One: Memorize Some Basic Benchmarks

35 minutes / 4 games = 8:45 per game. On average, games get slightly more difficult as the section goes on. So try to keep the following markers in mind as you go through a section.

Goal after first game: under 7-minute mark
Goal after second game: under 16-minute mark
Goal after third game: under 25-minute mark

You can play around with the numbers if you'd like to fit your own needs and preferences, but for most people the above will serve as an effective general benchmark. Don't keep these numbers in your head and try to remember them as you are working through a section. Instead, write them down in the front of your booklet before the timer starts. This will give you peace of mind and help free you up to focus on the games themselves.

Two: Evaluate Your Experience Relative to Those Benchmarks

Remember that games vary greatly in terms of how long they take, and also remember that sections, as a whole, even out.

As you finish playing games, trust your instincts about whether those games felt harder than usual or easier than usual, and use these instincts to get a deeper understanding of where you are relative to your benchmarks.

For example, imagine that you've just finished playing the first two games, and they were brutal. In particular, the second game was one of the hardest you've seen, and you barely clawed and fought your way through it. You check your watch after that second game and find that you are 18 minutes into the section.

Should you panic? Should you try to rush through the next game? No. Chances are, if your instincts are right (and after all this work, they certainly should be!) the third and fourth games should be a bit easier than normal, and you should still be able to finish on time.

On the other hand, imagine you run into a very easy first game, and you take the time to make sure your form is picture perfect. You know you got every question right, and afterwards you check your watch and you are at the nine-minute mark.

This is a much more significant cause for alarm. A very easy first game is likely a sign that there are going to be some significant challenges ahead. If it truly was an easy game, you should have tried to speed through it in less than seven minutes. In this situation, you want to use this as a sign that your pace is too slow, and you want to be very conscious of trying to go faster on the next game.

Three: Check Your Timing after Your First Setup and after Each Complete Game

As I just mentioned, a somewhat common timing concern has to do with pace; it's easy to get started at the wrong pace, especially if we are trying to be too careful, and this can come back to haunt us later in the section.

For this reason, it's best to check your pace early in the section. I recommend you first check your time after you set up your first game. You should be able to gauge whether the timing is right relative to the difficulty of the scenario and rules, and then either keep your pace, slow it down, or speed it up.

what if you just can't finish in thirty-five minutes?

Okay, so you've pretty much done all of the prep you are going to do for the LSAT, you are just a few weeks out, and you are still having significant timing issues with the Logic Games section. You're not alone. How do you best handle the situation to maximize your score?

As I've mentioned before, I do not recommend skipping entire games. This puts too much pressure on you to perform well on the games that you solve, and you miss the chance to potentially pick up a few easy points. My recommendation is not based on some theoretical or philosophical belief—it's born out of personal experience. I've worked with many students who did not perform as well as they could in large part because of this strategy, and I've yet to meet the student who performed better than he or she would have otherwise by skipping a game.

If you must skip, skip questions. If, twenty seconds into a question, you have no clear sense of what the right answer might be, and you have no clear sense of how to go about answering the question (you often get this sinking feeling after your first go around with the answers, when you either can't eliminate as many answers as you'd hoped or can't find the one answer you thought you might find), take a good guess and move on. If you can take these four or five questions that you likely would have missed, save yourself the ten or so minutes that you would have likely spent on these questions, and instead use thirty seconds per question to solve them, you can drastically cut your overall timing without sacrificing full games. Work to recognize when questions are challenging for you, and practice cutting bait and taking educated guesses on a certain number of the hardest questions per section.

After that, as long as games are going fine and you don't run into any unusual trouble, you should be fine checking your time after every complete game. It's not necessary to time every setup or every question during the real exam, and trying to do so will only be a distraction.

If a game is going particularly badly, of course you'll want to check your time throughout it to make sure your timing doesn't get out of hand. Don't let one game ruin your entire section. Try to answer the questions you can (per the article on the previous page), and don't waste time on the ones you can't.

How to Improve Timing

Most of you have at least five more prep tests and many more weeks of studying before the exam; you want to make sure you use this period to improve on your timing. Here are some general thoughts on what you want to focus on:

One: Getting More Comfortable with Your Diagram

As we've discussed from the beginning, your ability to diagram is the key to Logic Games success, and of course, your ability to diagram has a huge impact on timing. It not only impacts the amount of time you spend up front, but more importantly, it impacts the time you spend in the questions. If you don't set up games as efficiently as you can, and if your notations are not intuitive for you, you'll have to do a lot more work, and a lot harder work, when it comes to answering questions. If you are able to represent games easily, and if you readily understand what your notations mean, the work you need to do for answering questions becomes markedly easier and goes much faster. If you have any weaknesses in your diagramming ability, make sure to focus on this in your prep and your review.

Two: Approaching Questions More Efficiently

Most test takers waste a ton of their valuable time thinking about things they do not have to think about. Each question type presents an optimal path to the correct answer, and if you are able to follow this path, questions will go much faster.

Three: Knowing When to Let Go

Especially if you are having trouble finishing the section in thirty-five minutes, this is the issue you really want to focus on. Think about the time you have in a section as a limited amount that you have to invest, with the goal of getting as many right answers as possible. Where do you want to invest that time? You want to invest it in the questions you are most likely to get right. After all, harder questions aren't worth any more. However, many test takers get in a lot of trouble, and score worse than they should, because they focus all their energy and time in the hardest questions. In general, making tough timing decisions has to do with being able to let go of questions. You want to work on getting better and better at letting go during your practice so that by test day, it's far less of a stress.

Your Next Steps

If you are following one of the recommended study schedules, your final Logic Games preparation will center on the sections you do as part of your final practice exams. Just as with Reading Comprehension, you'll want to use this final work to polish and round out your skill set and, most importantly, solidify effective habits. Here are some recommendations:

One: Before Each Practice Exam, Remind Yourself of Key Considerations

Again, a three-by-five note card with maybe two to five points on it is all you need. Remind yourself of the things you need to focus on in the section: personal reminders, such as going slower during the setup, or timing strategies.

For Logic Games, I challenge you to set specific goals for improvement with each game section you try. More on this in just a bit.

Two: During Each Practice Exam, Keep Track of Certain Markers

In general, it can be helpful for you to keep track of the following as you take your exam:

(A) The amount of time each setup takes
(B) The amount of time each set of questions takes
(C) The questions for which you were not certain of your answer
(D) (Optional) the questions on which you felt you spent a lot of time

You can keep track of (A) and (B) by marking the time at which you finish each passage and set of questions. You can keep track of (C) by circling those questions. And you can choose to notate (D) in some other way (such as stars).

As with Reading Comprehension, if you'd like to track the timing for each question, have an easy means to do so, and don't think it will be a distraction, absolutely go ahead—you will certainly find the information useful. If you think tracking time with every question will be any sort of distraction, don't worry about it. Your main focus should be on taking the section just as (or 99% the same) you would during the real exam.

Three: Review Your Work Carefully

This step is critically important, especially for studying Logic Games. You are going to use these final games to triple check your skill set and make sure it's rock solid. And you'll use these final games to evaluate and confirm habits.

If you can bear one more sports analogy, reviewing your games sections is akin to athletes reviewing game tape. Many of the top winners have reputations for spending a lot of time in the video room for a reason.

After every section, walk through each game carefully. Think about the optimal way that you could have set up the game and compare that with how you really set it up. Think about the perfect way to diagram each rule, and compare this to how you actually did it. Take time to carefully dig out every inference, and compare these inferences with what you got initially.

While the section is still fresh in your mind, review each question whether you got it right or not. Look at the work you did, think about the processes you used, and try to look for as many areas for improvement as you can. Additionally, for games that caused you trouble, use your "perfect" diagram, and take as much time as you need to walk through a "perfect" process for each problem.

For games that make you nervous about your abilities, take the following two steps:

(1) Play the game again the next day. And the next one. Keep replaying it until the game seems easy.

(2) Think about the defining characteristics of the game (subsets? conditionals?), review the relevant lessons, replay similar games you've played before (you can use the appendix for reference), and, finally, play other games from past exams that have similar characteristics (more on this below).

Set specific goals for each practice exam—push yourself to keep getting faster and more accurate with each experience. You'll find certain game sections harder than others, and your performance will likely go up and down, but you should expect to continue to see overall improvement.

Final Thoughts

I believe that 10 to 16 exams is more than enough practice for you to experience everything you need to experience for Logical Reasoning and Reading Comprehension. Because so many different things can happen in a Logic Game, and because there are only four Logic Games per exam, some of you may benefit from getting some additional Logic Games to practice with. You can purchase games on Amazon by buying books and exams put out by LSAC or private companies such as Cambridge LSAT.

If you still feel shaky about your skill set, focus on drill sets—that is, concentrate on games that have subset issues, or conditional rules, or whatever else it is that causes you trouble (again, you can use the appendix for reference). If you feel good about your skills but just can't seem to bring them together well, work on full games sections.

At this moment, take a second to think about where you are in terms of Logic Games, and give yourself an honest grade. See how your situation relates to the three listed below:

1. Skills: D, Habits: D: If you feel really shaky with your skills and habits, reread the games lessons in this book and take notes. Don't underline, highlight, or copy and paste—write down notes using your own hands and a pen or pencil and paper. Consider tutoring if you can afford it, or consider other ways to get outside help (such as forums) if you can't. Do a ton of drill work in specific types of games, and don't worry about full sections until you feel more confident about your skills.

2. Skills: B, Habits: D: Expect that practice will naturally bring both grades up, but keep on top of your progress. Pay particular attention to what challenging games expose in your skill set, and focus on your methodology—how you solved games and problems—during your review. Set goals for improvement with each game, and focus more on drill sets than sections.

3. Skills: A, Habits: B: If you are here, you are in really great shape. My guess is that you are missing questions once every few games, and sometimes you are able to comfortably finish in thirty-five minutes, while other times it's a struggle.

Trust that this final practice will get you where you need to be. It's just a matter of muscle memory at this point, and you're naturally going to get a little faster and more accurate with a bit more practice. If you want additional practice beyond your assigned practice exams, you should focus on taking full games sections. Focus on the games and questions that lie at the extremes in terms of timing—those that should take very little time and those that are designed to take a lot of time, and review these games and questions more carefully.

I think games are fun. I know I'm a nerd, but I also know I'm not the only one who feels this way. If you agree that they are fun, buy yourself a bunch of games, and play them as a hobby between now and the exam. The more practice you can get, the better. If you are not a nerd like me, hopefully this book has at least made the games far more understandable and manageable. Make sure you have practiced enough that you can rely on your habits and instincts on test day.

40 LOGICAL REASONING review, timing strategies, and *final* final thoughts

Our final lesson. I hope you've enjoyed the ride. And, of course, more importantly, I hope you feel that you are much better at the LSAT than you were at the start of this book. Let's finish by talking about the most important section: Logical Reasoning.

Here is a quick rundown of the key Logical Reasoning issues we have discussed:

There are many skills necessary for Logical Reasoning success, but the key skill required for success is the ability to see what is wrong with arguments (5).

Reasoning flaws exist between the support and the conclusion (5).

Mindset impacts what we think about, and we want to read all arguments with a critical mindset (5).

You can describe any flaw using the phrases "The author fails to consider..." or "The author takes for granted..." (5).

Many arguments are flawed because the author overestimates the importance of one piece of support. In these cases, the author often overvalues a trait, overvalues an opinion, or uses a small sample set (6).

The type of support that is often easiest to overvalue is that which is necessary for the conclusion but is not enough to prove that the conclusion is definitely true (6).

Many arguments are flawed because the author equates two things that are not necessarily the same. In these cases, the author often falsely equates subject matter, characteristics, or relationships (7).

Fairly frequently, arguments are flawed because the author equates one way of arriving at an outcome with the only way of arriving at an outcome (7).

Many arguments are flawed because the author brings together two supporting premises to conclude something that the combination of premises doesn't warrant. These arguments often have context issues, and they often have the same issues mentioned in Lessons 6 and 7 (8).

Correlation can be used to strengthen a point about causation, and more commonly, a lack of correlation can weaken a point about causation. However, correlation is not causation, and correlation can never prove causation (8).

Each type of question presents a unique task, but the question types are all related. It helps to read the question stem first so that you can go into the stimulus with a clear understanding of your task (16).

The main point of an argument will be subjective, and it will have support (16).

Intermediate conclusions are supporting premises that are themselves subjective and have support (16).

For all Logical Reasoning questions, you want to look to eliminate wrong answers before you look to confirm the right one (16).

For Flaw questions, you should expect that you can anticipate the substance of the correct answer. For harder questions, prepare for the answers to be written in an abstract or complex way (17).

Basic Assumption questions are Flaw questions, but with the flaws described as assumptions made by the author (17).

An assumption is an unstated and unjustified belief (17).

For Match the Flaw questions, make sure you have a clear understanding of the flaw before moving on to the answers, and give yourself extra time to get through your process (17).

A sufficient assumption is one that fills all holes between support and conclusion and makes the conclusion 100% valid (18).

Understanding the language of conditional logic can be as challenging as understanding the relationships. The key is to be comfortable and automatic with the most common and simple terms and to have systems for handling the more challenging ones (18).

Supporting Principle and Conform to a Principle questions are very similar to Sufficient Assumption, and the same strategies can be used. However, these questions tend to talk more in generalities, and they tend to be less exact than Sufficient Assumption questions (18).

Required Assumption questions ask us to identify one answer that needs to be true if the conclusion is to be valid. The right answer need not prove the conclusion to be true or even play a big role in proving the answer true (19).

A great way to confirm whether an answer is necessary to the conclusion or not is the negation test (19).

Strengthen and Weaken questions ask us to strengthen or weaken not just the conclusion but the bond between support and conclusion. Though questions ask which answer would most strengthen or most weaken, typically there will be just one answer that weakens or strengthens, respectively (19).

The importance of developing the correct problem-solving habits cannot be understated. The same six-step process can be used for all argument-based questions. When you are not certain about your performance on a step, often the next step in the process is the best tool for regaining control of a question (20).

Objective questions require you to understand the author's meaning and purpose, but they do not require critical evaluation of reasoning (30).

For almost all Reasoning Structure questions, you should be able to predict the substance of the correct answer before looking at the answer choices, but you should still go through the process of eliminating wrong answers before selecting the right one (30).

Inference questions require us to use the stimulus to evaluate the answer choices, and the best way to arrive at an answer is to eliminate the four choices that are not justified by the text (32).

Certain Sufficient Assumption and Inference questions require us to handle a lot of conditional statements. In these cases, our job is to be able to recognize valid links and invalid links (32).

Give an Example questions are the mirrored twins of Supporting Principle questions, and the key is to retain as simple an understanding of the principle as possible as you eliminate incorrect answer choices (32).

For Identify the Disagreement questions, person two disagrees with one part of person one's statement, but it may or may not be person one's main point (33).

For Explain the Discrepancy questions, the key is to have a clear sense of the discrepancy before going into the answer choices. You can make this easier by asking yourself "How come...?" (33).

Logical Reasoning tests your ability to read and to reason, and it tests your mental discipline (34).

Your skills and habits will determine test-day performance (34).

Timing Strategies

A typical Logical Reasoning section has twenty-five questions, and that works out to about 1:24 per question. However, just as with Logic Games, you should expect that the amount of time required will vary drastically from question to question. You may find that, over the course of five problems, you spend 1:30, 0:40, 1:50, 1:15, and 0:25. Such inconsistency is fine and healthy; the key is to have an average rate that allows you to work at a comfortable pace.

The variations in how long a question takes are based off of two factors: the design of the question and the difficulty of the question. To give an analogy, in thinking about how long it will take to do a bathroom remodel, one has to consider the different things that need to get done (a bathroom with two sinks, a shower, and a bathtub will likely take longer than a half bath with just a sink) and the difficulty of the work (it's one thing to install IKEA cabinets; it's another to custom-make and install your own cabinets). Down below and to the side you will see some additional notes about questions that you should expect to take less time or more time.

These general guidelines should help give you a sense of when you are using time efficiently and when you are not. In particular, if you find that you spend more time on certain types of questions than you perhaps should, it may be an indication that you should review your process for those questions.

Pattern of Difficulty for a Typical Section

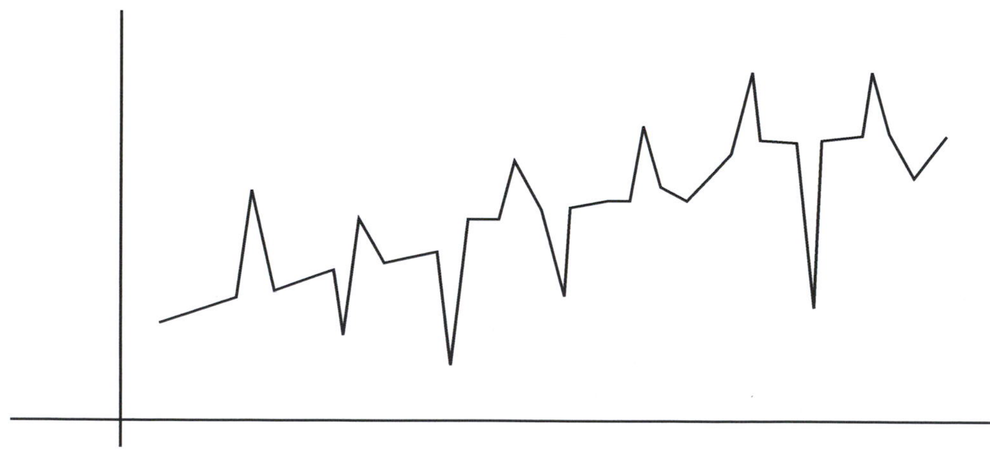

In general, and on average, questions get more difficult as a Logical Reasoning section progresses. And typically the sections will rise in difficulty, plateau (that is, the difficulty will even out), rise in difficulty, and, around question 18 or so, plateau a final time. Keep in mind that the difficulty of individual questions can be quite unpredictable. The test writers love to sneak in an unassumingly difficult question or two in the first ten, and there are sometimes questions beyond #20 that are no more difficult than the first few questions in a section.

Question types that typically take a little less time...	Question types that typically take a little more time...
What's the flaw?	Match the flaw
What's the assumption?	Match the reasoning
Find the conclusion	Sufficient assumption
Identify the role	Supporting principle
Explain this	Inference
	Give an example

Tracking Time During a Test

As we've discussed, the pressure of the exam wreaks havoc on our internal sense of timing. That's a big reason why it's particularly dangerous not to track time during an exam. Even if your normal pace is fast enough that you never have timing issues during practice, you may find that the pressure of the exam causes you to slow down (or speed up), and of course you don't want to find that you've either finished the section way early, while guessing on many questions you should have spent more time on, or that you were too deliberate on the earlier questions and so didn't leave yourself enough time to handle the later ones.

Therefore, of course it's imperative that you go into the exam with some sort of system for tracking your time. It's also important that you practice using this system a lot before test day so you're able to implement it without much thought or effort during the real exam.

Thinking about your timing after every question would be a huge distraction and is not recommended. Thinking about your timing just once or twice during a section is not enough to catch issues and stay on top of things. Somewhere in between those extremes lies the sweet spot.

In my experience, checking your time once every five questions is an effective strategy. Five questions is enough to even out the question-to-question fluctuations, and every five questions is frequent enough so that you can keep on top of your timing and adjust it as needed.

Per the graph on the previous page, it makes sense to allocate more time to questions that appear later in the section—these are more difficult and will on average take you more time. If we think of a twenty-five question section in terms of five five-question sections, you can use a simple escalating scale to allocate time to each section: 5 minutes for the first 5 questions, 6 minutes for the next five, 7 minutes for the next five, 8 minutes for the next five, and 9 minutes for the final five.

Of course, you don't want to waste precious time and mental energy doing arithmetic in your head, so it's easier to use benchmarks to think of your timing. Here are the benchmarks you can use for the timing strategy we just laid out:

After question 5: 5-minute mark
After question 10: 11-minute mark
After question 15: 18-minute mark
After question 20: 26-minute mark

Just as with Reading Comprehension and Logic Games, don't try to keep these benchmarks in your head—instead, write them on the front cover of your workbook before the section officially begins. If at all possible, try to stay a minute or two in front of your benchmarks—you'll find that this gives you a great boost of confidence. And don't fret if you fall a minute or two behind. Maybe you've encountered an unusual set of challenging early questions, and the ones in the middle of the section will be easier than normal—you can make up that time just through the normal course of events. Practice using these benchmarks on every practice exam. This will help you develop a strong natural pace, and it will make it so you need to spend less time and energy thinking about your pace and your timing on test day.

Finally, don't be afraid to personalize the benchmarks listed above. If your goal is to survive the section with four or five misses, you may want to devote extra time to the earlier questions and spend less time on certain questions that appear later in the section. If your goal is 180, and you can't afford to miss any questions, you may want to work on going even faster through the first ten or fifteen questions so that you have plenty of time for the hardest ones. These two sample adjustments are broken down in greater detail below.

Frank Goal: -5

Issues: Makes mistakes on easy questions and gets stuck on some of the hardest ones.

Sample modified strategy:

After question 5: 6-minute mark
After question 10: 13-minute mark
After question 15: 21-minute mark
After question 20: 28-minute mark

What this accomplishes:

It allows Frank extra time on the questions he needs to get right—he needs to get the great majority of those between 1 and 15 correct. It also forces him to make tough timing decisions on the later questions, which are likely to be the hardest (that is, the ones that provide the least chance of points returned on time invested).

Franny Goal: -0

Issues: Gets stuck every once in a while on the hardest questions.

Sample modified strategy:

After question 5: 5-minute mark
After question 10: 10-minute mark
After question 15: 15-minute mark
After question 20: 25-minute mark

What this accomplishes:

Franny is at a level where she is seeking perfection—this likely means that two other things are also true about her: one, she doesn't find the easier questions to be challenging and doesn't make mistakes on them, and two, she's probably very fast at these easier questions.

For Franny, the later questions will likely determine her score, and she needs as much time as possible to deal with those tough questions. Therefore, it makes sense to practice pushing the pace as much as possible on all the others.

How to Improve Timing

Let's first think about two different types of timing issues:

(1) You've spent most of your prep time focusing on individual question types, and during the course of a section, having to jump from one type of question to another throws you off your game and forces you to waste time.

This is certainly understandable, and we all experience this to a certain extent. Get thrown only fastballs for a while, or only curveballs, and when you have to go up to bat not knowing which one to expect, it's understandable you might not perform as well.

For most people, working on full sections is the best way to combat this, and the best way to get used to jumping from one question type to another. If the ten sections in your final five exams are not enough for you, re-solve full sections of questions from 52-56, or purchase additional sections to practice on.

If you want to try to accelerate the process of getting used to jumping from question type to question type, I have one extra exercise that you might find useful: write down basic strategies (no more than a few steps and maybe one reminder for yourself) for each question type on three-by-five note cards, and have these note cards spread out in front of you as you take a practice exam. For each question, read the stem, quickly look at the corresponding note card, then go back to solving the question.

A second reason you can have trouble with timing in the section is...

(2) You are not as fast at certain types of questions as you should be.

As we've discussed many times, timing is most directly a by-product of process. If you use an efficient process, even if you are not a fast reader or a fast thinker, you can easily finish all the questions on time. When people spend too long on questions, it's typically not because they can't read or think fast enough. It's because they spend a lot of time thinking about things that don't help them get to the right answer or don't help them get to the right answer as efficiently as they could.

If, at the end of your preparation, you are still having some trouble finishing the section in 35 minutes...

Even if you are having trouble finishing a section 35 minutes, you want to give yourself a fair shot with every single question. That means, at the least, reading the question stem, reading the stimulus, and reading enough of the answer choices to select one.

If you are having trouble finishing the section, and you are nearing your exam, the best way to cut your time is to spend less time on the most difficult questions. Depending on your specific timing issues, pick a certain number of questions (say, 3 or 5 questions) for which you know, going in, that you are going to spend 20 to 30 seconds tops, then select the answer you think is best. By short-changing these questions, hopefully you can give yourself a fair shot at all of the rest.

Of course, you will be most successful implementing this strategy if you are good at knowing which questions to cut bait on. The charts on pages 588 and 589 should give you some indication, and I'm sure that by this point you've developed a strong internal sense for which questions happen to give you the least return for time invested. Again, do what you can to not waste time on the questions you are most likely to miss anyway, and make sure to give yourself enough time to get the questions right that you need to get right.

If your timing issues arise from having difficulty with certain problem types, it's best to continue doing focused work on those question types—that means reviewing lessons related to those questions and doing drill sets of just that question type. You can use the question breakdown on the Trainer website to make them yourself, or purchase questions that are already separated by type.

One final thing you may find useful is to go through this book and try solving all of the questions from the *process in action* examples. Solve the questions, read my solutions, and compare your process to mine. One thing to keep in mind is that the thoughts represented in the solution are not some distilled version of my thought process—they accurately represent what I think about during a problem (presented with a bit more clarity, of course). Think about all the extra things you may have focused on during your process, and think about why those thought processes weren't necessary. Additionally, I expect you'll find that there are times you are more efficient than I am—maybe you have a faster way to eliminate a certain wrong answer or confirm a right one. Take note of these situations, as well.

Your Next Steps

If you are following one of the recommended study schedules, your final Logical Reasoning preparation will center on the sections you do as part of your final practice exams. Just as with Reading Comprehension and Logic Games, you'll want to use this final work to polish and round out your skill set and, most importantly, to solidify effective habits. Here are some recommendations:

One: Before Each Exam, Remind Yourself of Key Factors

Notes might include "focus on the argument," "be critical," "only eliminate when I'm certain," and so on. Think of a few things you need to remind yourself of, put them on a note card, and review the note card before the practice exam.

Two: During the Exam, Keep Track of Certain Markers

The instructions in your study schedule have more specific details, but in general it can be helpful for you to keep track of the following as you take your exam:

(A) The amount of time each set of five takes
(B) The questions for which you were not certain of your answer
(C) The questions on which you felt you spent a lot of time

You can keep track of (A) by marking the time at which you finish every fifth question. You can keep track of (B) by circling those questions. And you can choose to notate (C) in some other way (such as stars).

As with the other sections, if you'd like to track your timing for each question, have an easy means to do so, and don't think it will be a distraction, absolutely go ahead—you will certainly find the information useful. If you think tracking time with every question will be any sort of distraction, don't worry about it.

One thing you definitely do want to keep track of are questions where you realize you've spent a lot of time. Even if that time results in a correct answer, you want to carefully review the processes you used for such questions. Speaking of which...

Three: Review Your Work Carefully

At this point in your process, it's probably not necessary for you to carefully review every single problem you do in each exam. Rather, you want to focus on the questions on which you clearly could have done better. These include

- The easier question that took longer than it should have
- The question you thought was tough and either got right or missed
- The hard question you got right that took way too long
- The question you thought you got right but missed

Each of these can be useful in helping you figure out which skills and habits need some final tweaking. The easy question that should take thirty seconds but actually takes you a minute and a half can hint at issues in your process that might make it so that the next time you see a harder version of that question, not only do you spend more time than you should, you end up missing it.

The questions to which you want to pay the most attention are those that you thought you got right but missed. Think of these as the ones you missed the most. Review the reasoning underlying the questions, review your process, and make sure you know exactly why you got duped. At the end of Lessons 7 and 8, I discussed reviewing your work in greater detail—if you've forgotten some of those suggestions, you may want to take another look at them now.

Additionally, remember to think about your misses as a whole and to look for patterns in them. Are your misses due more to the type of question or the difficulty of the question? Is there a relationship between the types of questions you miss most often? Why are you great at Flaw questions but have trouble with Match the Flaw questions? Or how come you are great at Match the Flaw but struggle with Match the Reasoning? At this point, I trust that you have the wisdom necessary to spot these patterns and to evaluate what they mean about your strengths and weaknesses.

As always, set goals for each exam. Don't expect a straight slope up the score ladder, but do expect significant progress over time, and push yourself to go a bit faster and to miss fewer questions with each new section or test that you try.

Final Final Thoughts

You've reached the end of the book.

Can you believe it? You are finally DONE with this thing!

First of all, congratulations. I know that it takes a lot of effort to get through this book, and I have no doubt that you are in much better shape to conquer the LSAT because of the hard work you've put in.

All the way back in Lesson 1, I laid out my very cheesy secret for success: the best way to ensure success is to deserve it.

It's a statement I absolutely believe in. Not just because I want to believe in it but because I've seen it to be true again and again and again. The best doctors tend to be the people who are most passionate about helping others and perfecting their craft, and the best hardware store owners are the ones who are most passionate about tools and serving their customers to the best of their abilities. The top LSAT scorers are the ones who are most passionate about reaching their goals, and perhaps even more importantly, they are the ones who have the greatest capacity to work toward those goals.

By doing all of the work in this book, and all of the listed work on your schedule outside of this book, and by finishing your final practice exams, which *I am certain you will do*, you've proved yourself most deserving of success.

Now it's time to go get it.

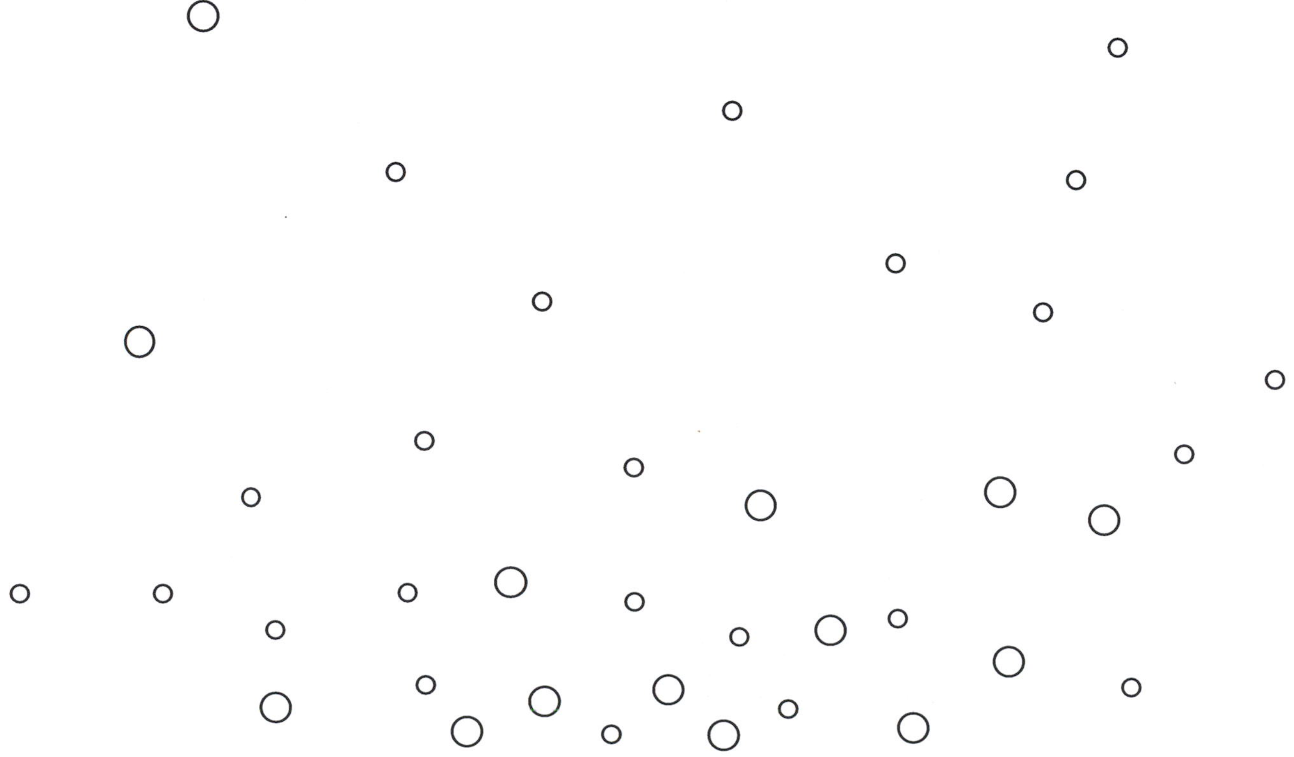

APPENDIX

LIST OF DRILLS

lesson	pages	name	subject
5	76 - 77	Flaw Drill	Logical Reasoning
5	83	Flaw Drill Matching Double Dip	Logical Reasoning
6	91 - 92	Piece Puzzle Flaw Drill	Logical Reasoning
6	95	Piece Puzzle Flaw Drill Double Dip	Logical Reasoning
7	104 - 105	Apples Oranges Flaw Drill	Logical Reasoning
8	116 - 117	$1 + 1 \neq 3$ Flaw Drill	Logical Reasoning
10	142 - 144	Basic Setups Drill	Logic Games
11	152 - 153	Subsets Simple Setups Drill	Logic Games
11	155-159	Subsets Setups Drill	Logic Games
12	165	Uncertain Groups Drills	Logic Games
12	167	Math Inferences Drill	Logic Games
12	169 - 171	Numbers Setups Drill	Logic Games
13	182	Conditional Rules Drill	Logic Games / Logical Reasoning
13	186-187	Conditional Setups Drill	Logic Games
14	198	Complex *Or* Rules Drill	Logic Games
14	200 - 203	*Or* Setups Drill	Logic Games
15	212-215	Full Setups Drill	Logic Games
16	226 - 227	What's the Conclusion? Drill	Logical Reasoning
16	231-232	What's the Support? Drill	Logical Reasoning
16	235-236	What's Wrong with the Argument? Drill	Logical Reasoning
18	259-260	Translating Conditional Statements Drill	Logical Reasoning / Logic Games
20	287 -288	One Argument & Ten Answers Drill	Logical Reasoning
22	325 - 326	Reasoning Structure Drill	Reading Comprehension
26	378 - 379	Must Be True or False Drill	Logic Games
27	392	Possibilities Questions (Trainer-Made Game)	Logic Games
27	396	Rules Questions (Trainer-Made Game)	Logic Games
27	399	Minor Questions Game (Trainer-Made Game)	Logic Games
31	462 - 463	Extreme Links Drill	Logical Reasoning / Logic Games
33	489	Question Stem Quick Quiz	Logical Reasoning
36	522 - 527	Hypothetical Questions Drill	Reading Comprehension

Note that mini-drills and quizzes have not been listed.

LOGICAL REASONING QUESTIONS DISCUSSED

COLUMNS = LESSONS | ROWS = PRACTICE TESTS

	1	2	5	6	7	8	9	16	17	18	19	20	30	32	33
23						2.8 2.17									
24				3.5 2.5	2.21										
25					3.2										
26										3.21	2.7				
27							1.11								
28							1.21 3.20 1.19				1.2 3.19 1.5 1.15 1.23 3.25			1.10	
29							4.20 4.15 1.11 1.16		1.14 4.18 4.21 4.25	1.19 1.20	1.15		1.12	4.10	
30									2.6			†	4.2 2.14		2.10
31										2.10			3.14 2.23 3.18		2.21 3.19 2.11 2.13 3.2
32			1.12 3.18												
33															
34	2.10														
35		1.23 4.19 4.23												1.7	
36		1.4													
JUNE '07								*					2.10 3.12 2.11 3.20 2.12	2.18 2.8 2.7	2.16 3.7 2.25 3.2

*** This lesson included the following questions from the June '07 exam: 2.2, 9, 17, 21, and 23; 3.5, 13, 14, 17, and 20. These questions were used for discussion in subsequent lessons.**

† This lesson included a series of questions from Practice Test 30, Section 4: 1, 6, 8, 11, 12, 14, 15, 17, 18, 19, 20, 23, 24, and 25.

LOGIC GAMES & READING COMPREHENSION QUESTIONS DISCUSSED

LEFT = LOGIC GAMES | RIGHT = READING COMPREHENSION

	3	21	26	28	29
26	1.8 1.9 1.10 1.11 1.12				
27		2.1 2.2 2.3 2.4 2.5			
29			3.1 3.4 3.6 3.14 3.15 3.16		3.8 3.9 3.10 3.11 3.12 3.13
31					2.8 2.9 2.10 2.11 2.12 2.13
JUNE '07				*	

* This lesson included all game questions from the June '07 exam.

	4	23	24	25	35	36	38
15			1.4 1.7 1.22 1.27				
16				4.5 4.7 4.16 4.20			
18			3.17 3.19 3.22 3.27				
22		1.9 1.15					
25		1.22 1.24					
28		3.15 3.18 4.25 4.26					
29					2.1 2.4 2.5 2.2 2.3		
30						3.7 3.9 3.14 3.23 3.24 3.25	
31					4.21 4.26 4.22 4.27 4.24 4.28		
33	2.15 2.16 2.17 2.18 2.19 2.20 2.21 2.22						
JUNE '07							†
RE-CENT				64.15* 64.17 65.14 65.17		62.16 62.18 62.19 63.24 63.25 63.27	

† This lesson included all Reading Comprehension questions from the June '07 exam.

* Questions from recent exams listed by PT and question number.

Why Older Questions?

You may notice that most of the questions used in this book come from exams that are a few years old. These questions were selected for two main reasons:

1. Older questions cost just a bit less to license. That means I can fit more questions in and charge less for the book without sacrificing any quality.

2. More importantly, I used older questions to ensure that you have more recent questions for your drilling and practice exams.

Please do keep in mind that I did have to use some recent exams to discuss comparative passages (which did not appear until the June '07 exam).

For additional resources,
please check out

thelsattrainer.com

Made in the USA
San Bernardino, CA
27 March 2020

66417060R00332